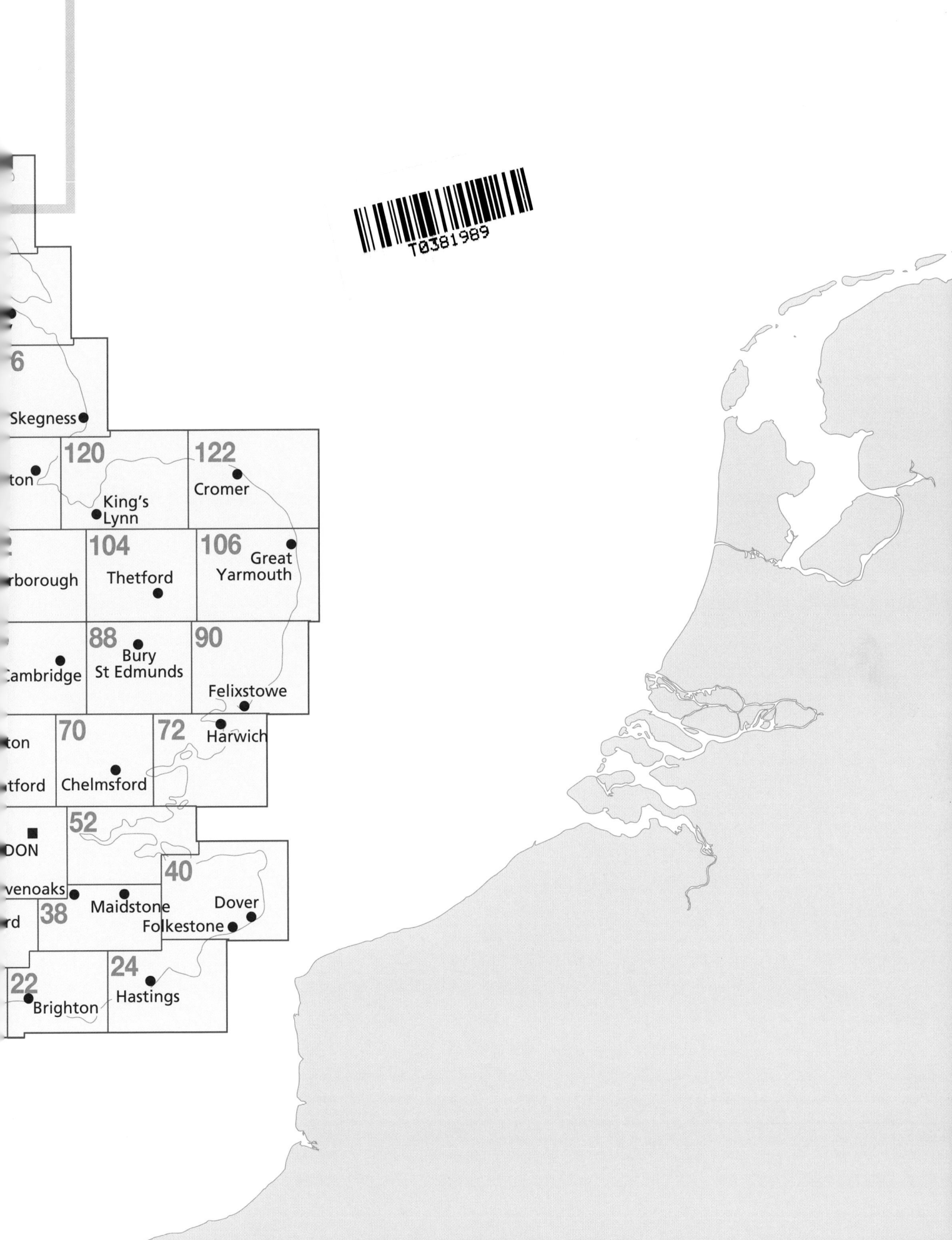

6

Skegness

120

122

Cromer

ton

King's
Lynn

104

106

rborough

Thetford

Great
Yarmouth

88

90

Cambridge

Bury
St Edmunds

Felixstowe

70

72

Harwich

ton

tford

Chelmsford

52

DON

40

venoaks

Dover

38

Maidstone

rd

Folkestone

22

24

Brighton

Hastings

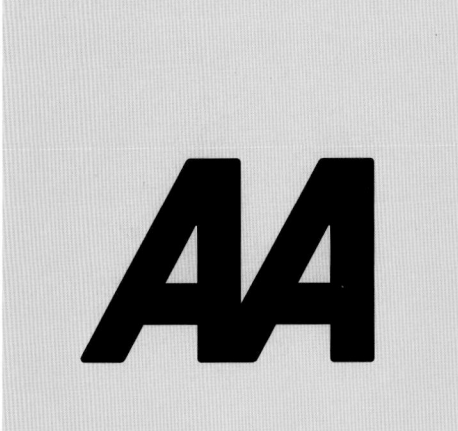

2025
EASY READ
BRITAIN

Scale 1:148,000
or 2.34 miles to 1 inch

24th edition May 2024 © AA Media Limited 2024
Original edition printed 2000.

All cartography in this atlas edited, designed and produced by the Mapping Services Department of AA Media Limited (A05868).

This atlas contains Ordnance Survey data © Crown copyright and database right 2024. Contains public sector information licensed under the Open Government Licence v3.0

Published by AA Media Limited, whose registered office is Grove House, Lutyens Close, Basingstoke, Hampshire RG24 8AG, UK. Registered number 06112600.

ISBN: 978 0 7495 8396 5

A CIP catalogue record for this book is available from The British Library.

Acknowledgements: AA Media Limited would like to thank the following for information used in the creation of this atlas: Cadw, English Heritage, Forestry Commission, Historic Scotland, National Trust and National Trust for Scotland, RSPB, The Wildlife Trust, Scottish Natural Heritage, Natural England, The Countryside Council for Wales. Award winning beaches from 'Blue Flag' and 'Keep Scotland Beautiful' (summer 2023 data): for latest information visit *www.blueflag.org* and *www.keepscotlandbeautiful.org*
Printed by 1010 Printing International Ltd, China

* Nielsen BookScan Total Consumer Market (UK Standard scale atlases) 1–39 weeks to 2 October 2023.

Contents

Map pages south	inside front cover
Route planner	II–VII
Atlas symbols	VIII–1
Road maps 1:148,000 scale	2–283
Channel Islands 1:100,000 scale	9
Isle of Man 1:200,000 scale	154
Isles of Scilly 1:148,000 scale	10
Orkney Islands 1:450,000 scale	275
Shetland Islands 1:450,000 scale	281
Western Isles 1:480,000 scale	282–283
Restricted junctions	284–285
Index to place names	286–368
County, administrative area map	286–287
Place name index	288–368
Map pages north	inside back cover

DUBLIN

(Mar–Oct)

REPUBLIC
OF
IRELAND

Rosslare

WALES

Cardigan Bay

Holyhead
Anglesey
Llandudno
Colwyn Bay
Rhyl
Holywell
Bangor
Conwy
Abergele
Bethesda
Caernarfon
Denbigh
Mold
Queensferry
Ellesmere Port
Northwich

Pwllheli
Porthmadog
Betws-y-Coed
Bala
Ruthin
Wrexham
Whitchurch
Llangollen
Oswestry

Abersoch
Barmouth
Dolgellau
Welshpool
Shrewsbury
Machynlleth
Newtown
Bridgnorth

WOLVERHAMPTON
Church Stretton
Telford
Dudley
Stourbridge
Halesow
Kidderminster

Aberystwyth
Llangurig
Rhayader
Knighton
Ludlow
Bromsgrov
Leominster

Aberaeron
New Quay
Tregaron
Llandrindod Wells
Kington
Worcester
Malvern

Cardigan
Lampeter
Builth Wells
Hay-on-Wye
Hereford
Ledbury
Tewkest

Fishguard
Newcastle Emlyn
Llandovery
Brecon
Ross-on-Wye

St Davids
Carmarthen
Llandeilo
Bannau Brycheiniog (BRECON BEACONS)
Abergavenny
Gloucester

PEMBROKESHIRE COAST
Haverfordwest
St Clears
Monmouth
Stroud

Milford Haven
Pembroke Dock
Pembroke
Tenby
Llanelli
Swansea
Neath
Merthyr Tydfil
Cwmbran
Chepstow

Port Talbot
Pontypridd
Newport
Avonmouth

Bridgend
CARDIFF
Cardiff
Clevedon
BRISTOL

Bristol Channel
Weston-super-Mare
Bristol
Bath
Cheddar
Frome
Trow

Lundy
Wells
Shepton Mallet
Wa

Ilfracombe
Lynton
Minehead
Glastonbury

EXMOOR
Bridgwater
Wincanton

Barnstaple
Taunton
A303

Bideford
Great Torrington
South Molton
Ilminster
Yeovil
Sherborne
Shaftesbury

Bude
Tiverton
Chard
Crewkerne
Blandford Forum

Holsworthy
Hatherleigh
Crediton
Axminster
Bridport

Launceston
Okehampton
Exeter
Honiton
Lyme Regis
Dorchester

DARTMOOR
Exmouth
Dawlish
Weymouth
Fortuneswell

Wadebridge
Tavistock
Teignmouth
Newton Abbot

Cornwall Newquay
Bodmin
Buckfastleigh
Torquay

Newquay
Liskeard
PLYMOUTH
Totnes
Paignton

Lostwithiel
Saltash
Dartmouth

St Austell
Fowey
Torpoint
Kingsbridge

Redruth
Truro
Guernsey
Jersey
St-Malo

Camborne
Penzance
Land's End
Helston
Falmouth
Lizard

Roscoff
Santander (Apr–Oct)

Legend

═══	Motorway
━━━	Toll motorway
═══	Primary route dual carriageway
───	Primary route single carriageway
───	Other A road
⛴ or Ⓥ	Vehicle ferry
⛴	Fast vehicle ferry or catamaran
▭	National Park
◼	City with clean air or low/zero emission zone

ENGLISH

LIVERPOOL
Birkenhead
Widnes
Runcorn
Knutsford
Chester
Crewe
Nantwich
Newcastle-under-Lyme
Market Drayton
Newport
Cann

EMERGENCY DIVERSION ROUTES

In an emergency it may be necessary to close a section of motorway or other main road to traffic, so a temporary sign may advise drivers to follow a diversion route. To help drivers navigate the route, black symbols on yellow patches may be permanently displayed on existing direction signs, including motorway signs. Symbols may also be used on separate signs with yellow backgrounds.

Legend:

- Motorway
- Toll motorway
- Primary route dual carriageway
- Primary route single carriageway
- Other A road
- or Ⓥ Vehicle ferry
- Fast vehicle ferry or catamaran
- National Park
- City with clean air or low/zero emission zone

0   10   20   30 miles
0 10 20 30 40 kilometres

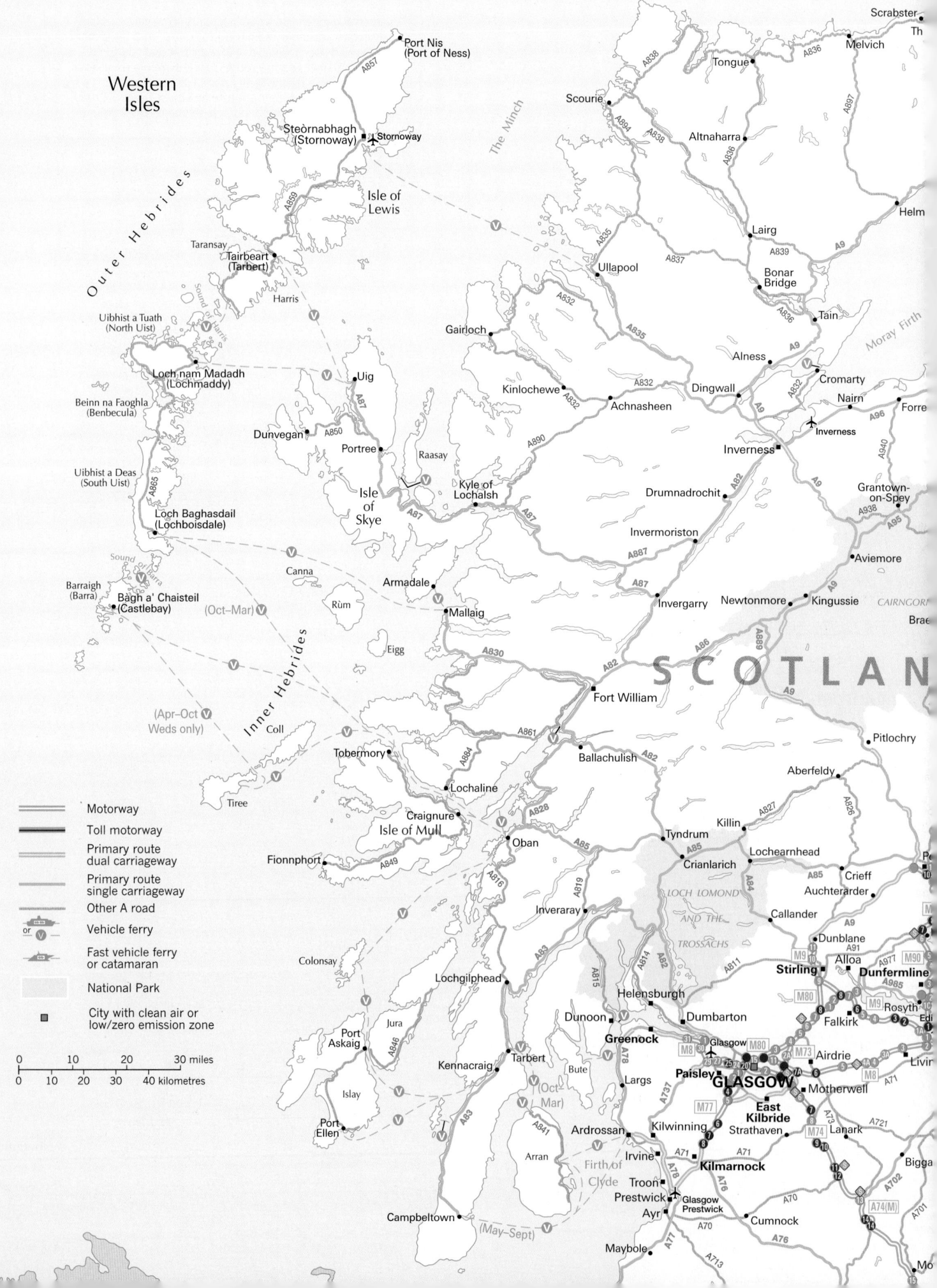

Western
Isles

Port Nis
(Port of Ness)

Steòrnabhagh
(Stornoway)
Stornoway

Isle of
Lewis

The Minch

Scrabster
Th

Melvich

Tongue

Scourie

Altnaharra

Helm

Lairg

Bonar
Bridge

Taransay

Tairbeart
(Tarbert)

Ullapool

Harris

Tain

Moray Firth

Uibhist a Tuath
(North Uist)

Sound of Harris

Gairloch

Alness

Cromarty

Nairn

Forre

Loch nam Madadh
(Lochmaddy)

Uig

Kinlochewe

Achnasheen

Dingwall

Inverness

Inverness

A96

Beinn na Faoghla
(Benbecula)

Dunvegan

Portree

Raasay

Drumnadrochit

Grantown-
on-Spey

Uibhist a Deas
(South Uist)

Isle
of
Skye

Kyle of
Lochalsh

Invermoriston

Aviemore

Loch Baghasdail
(Lochboisdale)

Canna

Armadale

Mallaig

Invergarry

Newtonmore

Kingussie

CAIRNGORM

Brae

Barraigh
(Barra)

Bàgh a' Chaisteil
(Castlebay)

(Oct–Mar)

Rùm

Eigg

SCOTLAN

Sound of Barra

Inner Hebrides

(Apr–Oct
Weds only)

Coll

Tobermory

Lochaline

Fort William

Ballachulish

Pitlochry

Aberfeldy

Fionnphort

Isle of Mull

Craignure

Oban

Killin

Tyndrum

Crianlarich

Lochearnhead

Crieff

Auchterarder

Tiree

Inveraray

LOCH LOMOND

AND THE

TROSSACHS

Callander

Pe

Colonsay

Lochgilphead

Helensburgh

Dunoon

Dumbarton

Dunblane

Stirling

Alloa

Dunfermline

Rosyth

Edi

Falkirk

Livin

Jura

Port
Askaig

Tarbert

Bute

Largs

Greenock

Glasgow

Paisley

GLASGOW

Airdrie

Motherwell

East
Kilbride

Lanark

Islay

Ardrossan

Kilwinning

Strathaven

Bigga

Port
Ellen

(Oct–
Mar)

Irvine

Kilmarnock

Arran

Troon

Prestwick

Glasgow Prestwick

Firth of
Clyde

Ayr

Cumnock

Campbeltown

(May–Sept)

Maybole

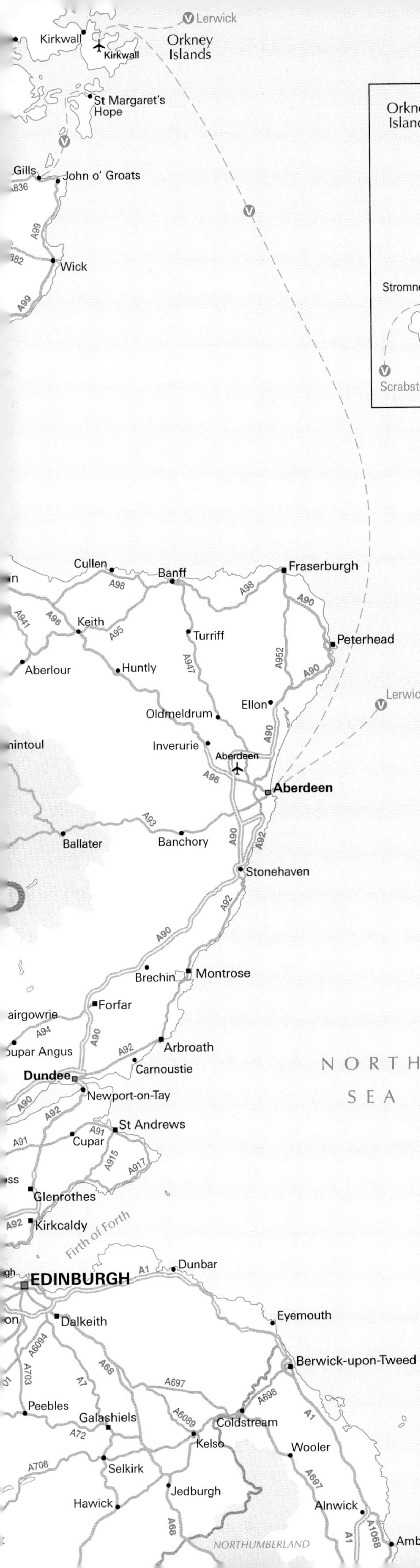

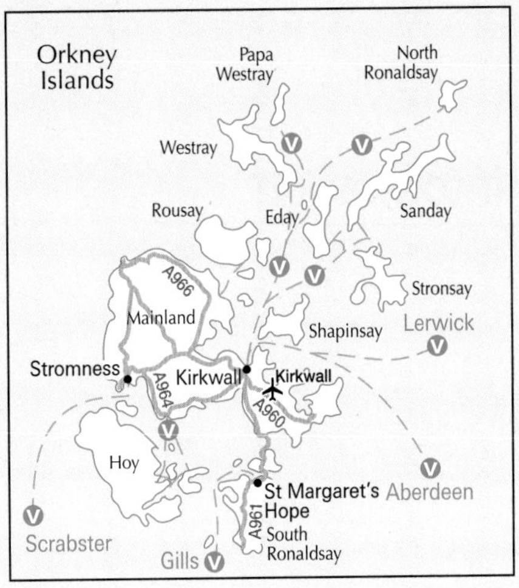

Kirkwall
Orkney
Islands
Lerwick

St Margaret's
Hope

Gills
John o' Groats
Wick

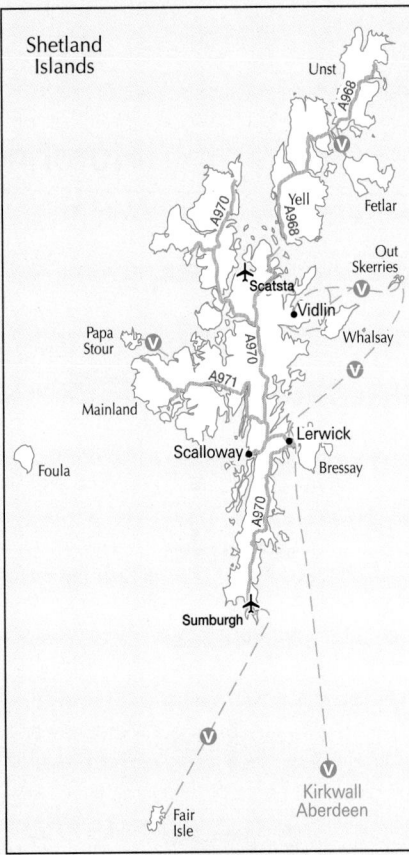

Orkney Islands

Papa
Westray
North
Ronaldsay
Westray
Rousay
Eday
Sanday
Mainland
Stronsay
Stromness
Shapinsay
Lerwick
Kirkwall
Kirkwall
Hoy
St Margaret's
Hope
Aberdeen
South
Ronaldsay
Scrabster
Gills

Shetland Islands

Unst
Yell
Fetlar
Out
Skerries
Scatsta
Vidlin
Papa
Stour
Whalsay
Mainland
Lerwick
Scalloway
Bressay
Foula
Sumburgh
Fair
Isle
Kirkwall
Aberdeen

Cullen
Banff
Fraserburgh
Keith
Turriff
Peterhead
Aberlour
Huntly
Ellon
Lerwick
Oldmeldrum
Inverurie
Aberdeen
Aberdeen
Ballater
Banchory
Stonehaven

NORTH
SEA

Brechin
Montrose
Forfar
airgowrie
Arbroath
upar Angus
Carnoustie
Dundee
Newport-on-Tay
St Andrews
Cupar
Glenrothes
Kirkcaldy
Firth of Forth
EDINBURGH
Dunbar
Dalkeith
Eyemouth
Berwick-upon-Tweed
Peebles
Galashiels
Coldstream
Kelso
Wooler
Selkirk
Jedburgh
Hawick
Alnwick
Amble
NORTHUMBERLAND

FERRY OPERATORS

Hebrides and west coast Scotland
calmac.co.uk
skyeferry.co.uk
western-ferries.co.uk

Orkney and Shetland
northlinkferries.co.uk
pentlandferries.co.uk
orkneyferries.co.uk
shetland.gov.uk/ferries

Isle of Man
steam-packet.com

Ireland
irishferries.com
poferries.com
stenaline.co.uk

North Sea (Scandinavia and Benelux)
dfdsseaways.co.uk
poferries.com

Isle of Wight
wightlink.co.uk
redfunnel.co.uk

Channel Islands
condorferries.co.uk

France and Belgium
brittany-ferries.co.uk
condorferries.co.uk
eurotunnel.com
dfdsseaways.co.uk
poferries.com

Northern Spain
brittany-ferries.co.uk

Atlas symbols

Motoring information

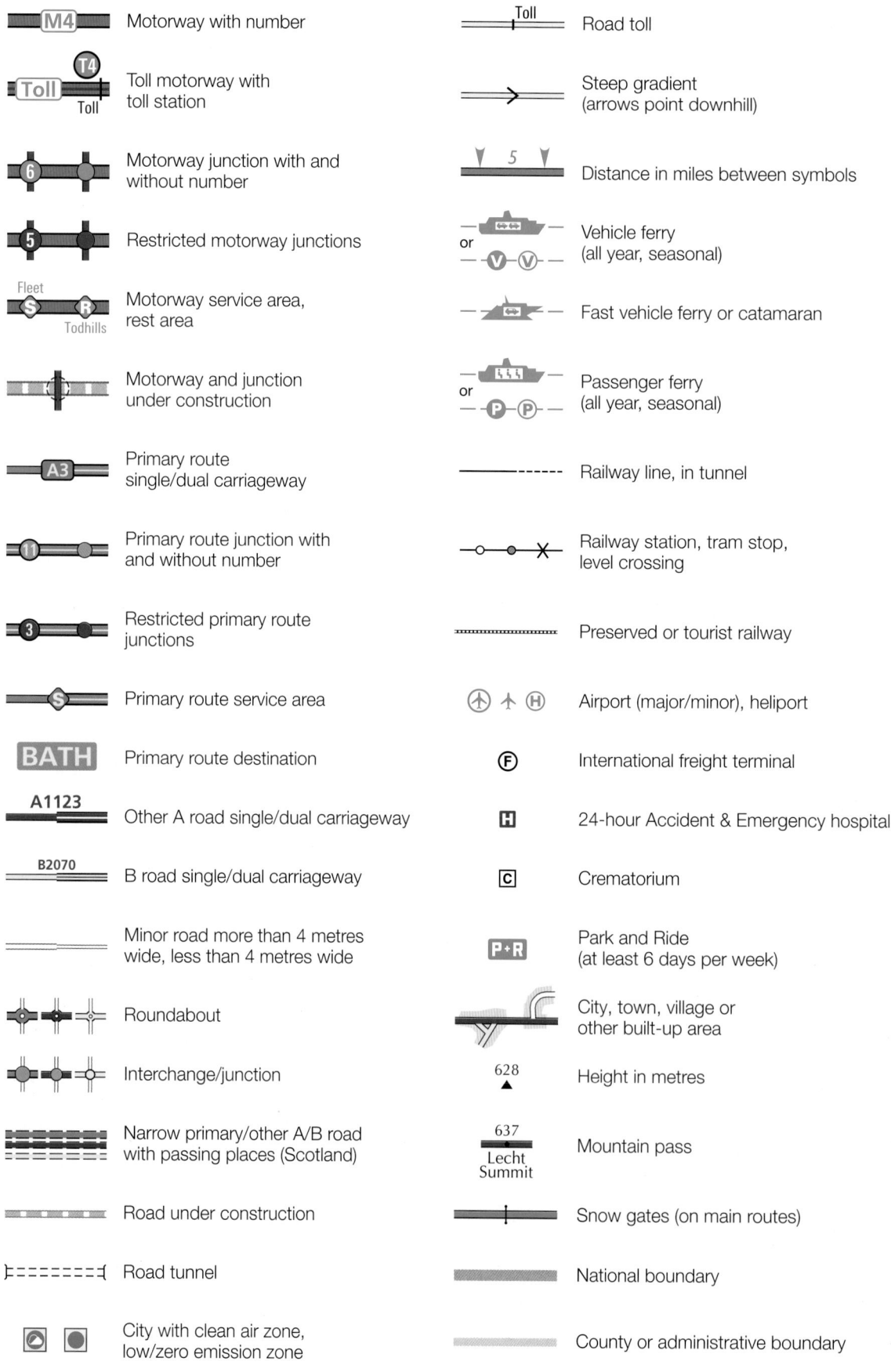

Motorway with number

Toll motorway with toll station

Motorway junction with and without number

Restricted motorway junctions

Fleet
Todhills
Motorway service area, rest area

Motorway and junction under construction

Primary route single/dual carriageway

Primary route junction with and without number

Restricted primary route junctions

Primary route service area

BATH — Primary route destination

A1123 — Other A road single/dual carriageway

B2070 — B road single/dual carriageway

Minor road more than 4 metres wide, less than 4 metres wide

Roundabout

Interchange/junction

Narrow primary/other A/B road with passing places (Scotland)

Road under construction

Road tunnel

City with clean air zone, low/zero emission zone

Toll — Road toll

Steep gradient (arrows point downhill)

5 — Distance in miles between symbols

Vehicle ferry (all year, seasonal)

Fast vehicle ferry or catamaran

Passenger ferry (all year, seasonal)

Railway line, in tunnel

Railway station, tram stop, level crossing

Preserved or tourist railway

Airport (major/minor), heliport

Ⓕ — International freight terminal

Ⓗ — 24-hour Accident & Emergency hospital

Ⓒ — Crematorium

P+R — Park and Ride (at least 6 days per week)

City, town, village or other built-up area

628 ▲ — Height in metres

637
Lecht
Summit
— Mountain pass

Snow gates (on main routes)

National boundary

County or administrative boundary

Touring information

To avoid disappointment, check opening times before visiting

▬▬▬	Scenic route
i	Tourist Information Centre
i	Tourist Information Centre (seasonal)
V	Visitor or heritage centre
⚲	Picnic site
🚐	Caravan site (AA inspected)
▲	Camping site (AA inspected)
▲🚐	Caravan & camping site (AA inspected)
⛪	Abbey, cathedral or priory
⛪	Ruined abbey, cathedral or priory
🏰	Castle
🏛	Historic house or building
Ⓜ	Museum or art gallery
🏭	Industrial interest
⌗	Aqueduct, viaduct
❀ 🌲	Garden, Arboretum
🍇	Vineyard
🛢	Brewery or distillery
🌳	Country park
🐂	Showground
🎢	Theme park
🛒	Farm or animal centre

🦌	Zoological or wildlife collection
🐦 🐟	Bird collection, aquarium
RSPB	RSPB site
◪ ⬇	National Nature Reserve (England, Scotland, Wales)
🦆	Local nature reserve
🗺	Wildlife Trust reserve
·········	Forest drive
- - - -	National trail
☀	Viewpoint
♨	Waterfall
⚘	Hill-fort
🗿	Roman antiquity
🗿	Prehistoric monument
✕ 1066	Battle site with year
🚂	Preserved or tourist railway
◉	Cave or cavern
🗼	Windmill
⬇	Monument or memorial
🏖	Beach (award winning)
🗼	Lighthouse
⚑	Golf course
⚽	Football stadium

🏏	County cricket ground
🏉	Rugby Union national stadium
⬭	International athletics stadium
🏇	Horse racing
🏇	Show jumping/equestrian circuit
🏁	Motor-racing circuit
✈	Air show venue
⛷	Ski slope (natural)
⛷	Ski slope (artificial)
⬛	National Trust site
⬛	National Trust for Scotland site
⌗	English Heritage site
⬛	Historic Scotland site
✚	Cadw (Welsh heritage) site
★	Other place of interest
☐	Boxed symbols indicate attractions within urban area
◉	World Heritage Site (UNESCO)
	National Park and National Scenic Area (Scotland)
	Forest Park
⌣	Sandy beach
⋯	Heritage coast
🏬	Major shopping centre

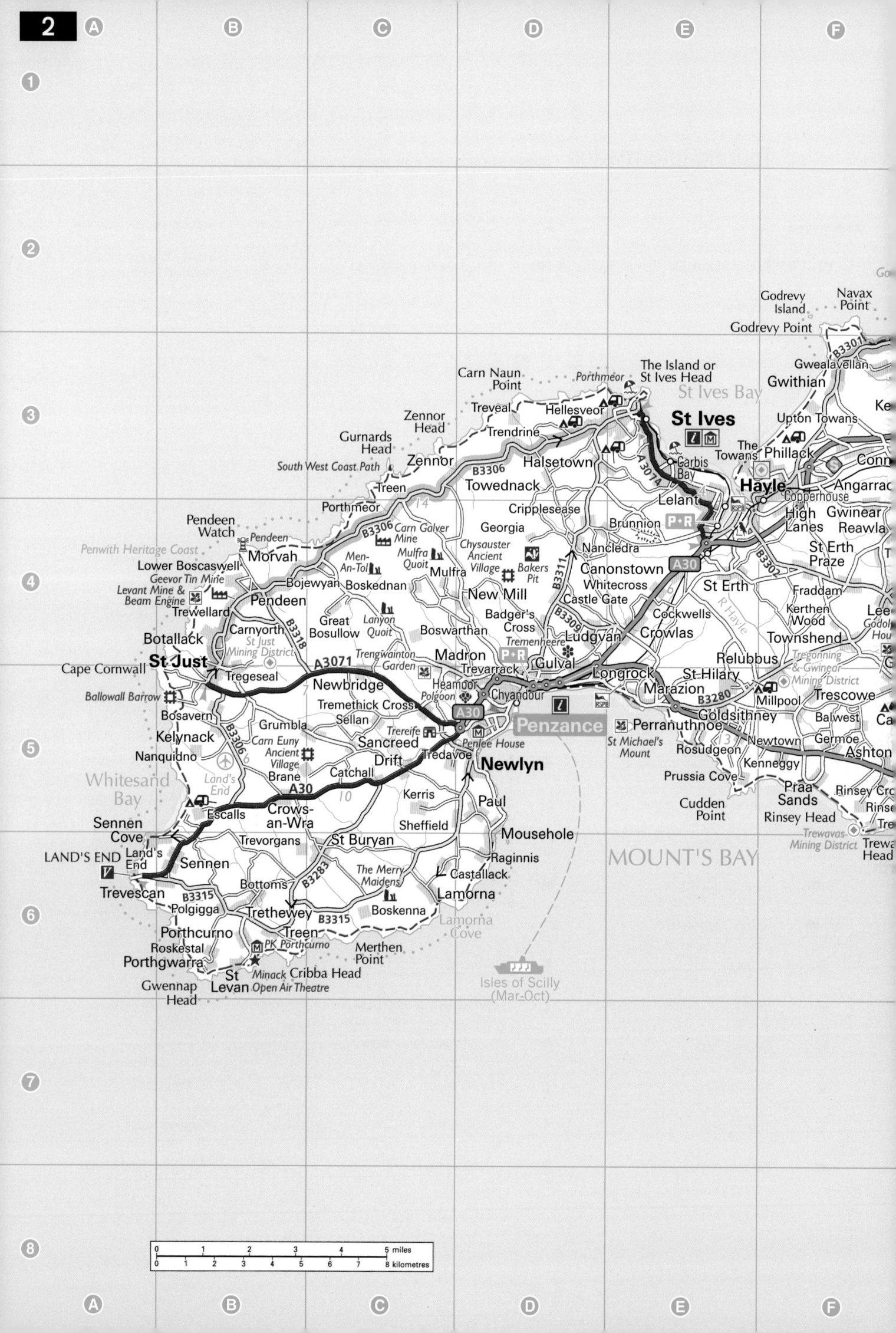

Cligga Point
Trevellas Downs
St Agnes Heritage Coast
ST AGNES HEAD
St Agnes
Cross Coombe
Wheal Coates
Goonvrea
St Agnes Mining District
Porthtowan
Mount Hawke
Chiverton Cross
Mawla
Menagissey
Wheal Peevor
Wheal Rose
North Country
Chacewater
Scorrier
Blackwater
Mount Ambrose
St Day
Twelveheads

Bolingey
Cocks
Perranwell
Carnkief
Perranzabuloe
Penhallow
Marazanvose
Callestick
Mithian
Barkla Shop
Goonbell
Coldharbour
Silverwell

Carnhave
Zelah
Trelassick
Trewarthen
St Allen
Trispen
Treworgan
St Erme
Treverbyn
Allet
Idless
Kenwyn
Higher Town
Truro
St Clement
Calenick
Malpas
St Michael Penkevil
Merther
Tregenna
Tresawle
Probus
Ladock
New Mills

Portreath
Illogan
Tehidy
Park Bottom
South Tehidy
Tuckingmill
Pool
Camborne
Penponds
Carn Brea
Carharrack
Carnkie
Lanner
Four Lanes
Troon
Praze-an-Beeble
Blackrock
Croft Mitchell
Burras Farm Common
Porkellis
Lezerea
Crowan
Releath
Nancegollan
Trenwheal
Wendron Mining District
Trenear
Prospidnick
Wendron
Crowntown
Sithney Green
Lower Town
Sithney
Helston
Sithney Common
Coverack Bridges
Trewennack

Redruth
Carn Brea
Trevarth
Frogpool
Gwennap
Bissoe
Perranwell
Perranarworthal
Ponsanooth
Burnthouse
Stithians
Tregolls
Carnkie
Longdowns
Mabe Burnthouse
Rame
Edgcumbe
Trenoweth
Argal & College Reservoirs
Seworgan
Treverva
Manhay
Brill
High Cross
Constantine
Porth Navas
Gweek
Mellangoose
Mawgan
Gear
Helford

Cross Lanes
Killiow
Chyeowling
Carnon Downs
Devoran
Penelewey
Playing Place Coombe
Old Kea
Trelissick Garden
Trelissick
Philleigh
Treworga
Treworthal
Trelonk
Ruan Lanihorne
Lamorran
Ruan High Lanes
Veryan Green

Kea
Baldhu
Newbridge
Greenbottom
Threemilestone
Penpol
Feock
Mylor Bridge
Angarrick
Perran Wharf
Lower Treluswell
Trelew
St Gluvia's
Penryn
Budock Water
Lamanva
Penjerrick
Barreppa
Carlidnack
Trebah
Glendurgan Garden
Durgan
Mawnan
Helford Passage
Helford River
Trevilla
Restronguet
St Just-in-Roseland
Mylor
Tregew
Flushing
Roseland Castle
St Mawes
Bohortha
South West Coast Path
St Anthony Head
ZONE POINT
Falmouth Bay
Carrick Roads
Pendennis Castle
Pendennis Point
Falmouth
Treluggan
Trewithian
Cargurrel
Gerrans Bay
Rosevine
Portscatho
Gerrans
Greeb Point
Nare Head

Mawnan Smith
Maenporth
ROSEMULLION HEAD
St Anthony-in-Meneage
Gillan
Nare Point
Lestowder
Manaccan
Carne
Roskorwell
St Martin
Tregidden
Tregarne
Porthallow
Newtown-in-St Martin
Treleague
Trenance
Porthoustock
Manacle Point
St Keverne
Rosenithon
Traboe
Zoar
Roskilly's Farm
Lowland Point
North Corner
Coverack
Black Head

Trelowarren
Halliggye Fogou
Garras
Cross Lanes
White Cross
Cury
Trewoon
GOONHILLY DOWNS
Trelan
Ponsongath
Gwenter
Kuggar
Trewillis
Treleaver
Poltescoe
Ruan Minor
Cadgwith
Devil's Frying Pan
Church Cove
Bass Point

Porthleven
Higher Pentire
Penrose
Flambards
Country Life
Chyvarloe
Gunwalloe
Chyanvounder
Berepper
Angrouse
Poldhu Point
Marconi Memorial
Mullion Cove
Mullion Island
Mullion
Penhale
Ruan Major
Predannack Head
Predannack Wollas
Mount Hermon
St Ruan
Grade
Vellan Head
The Lizard Heritage Coast
Lizard Head
Kynance Cove
Lizard
LIZARD POINT
Lizard Lighthouse & Heritage Centre
The Lizard

Seal Sanctuary
Trebah

Poldark Mine
Kennall Vale
Devoran & Perran
Roseworthy
Kadinnick
South West Coast Path

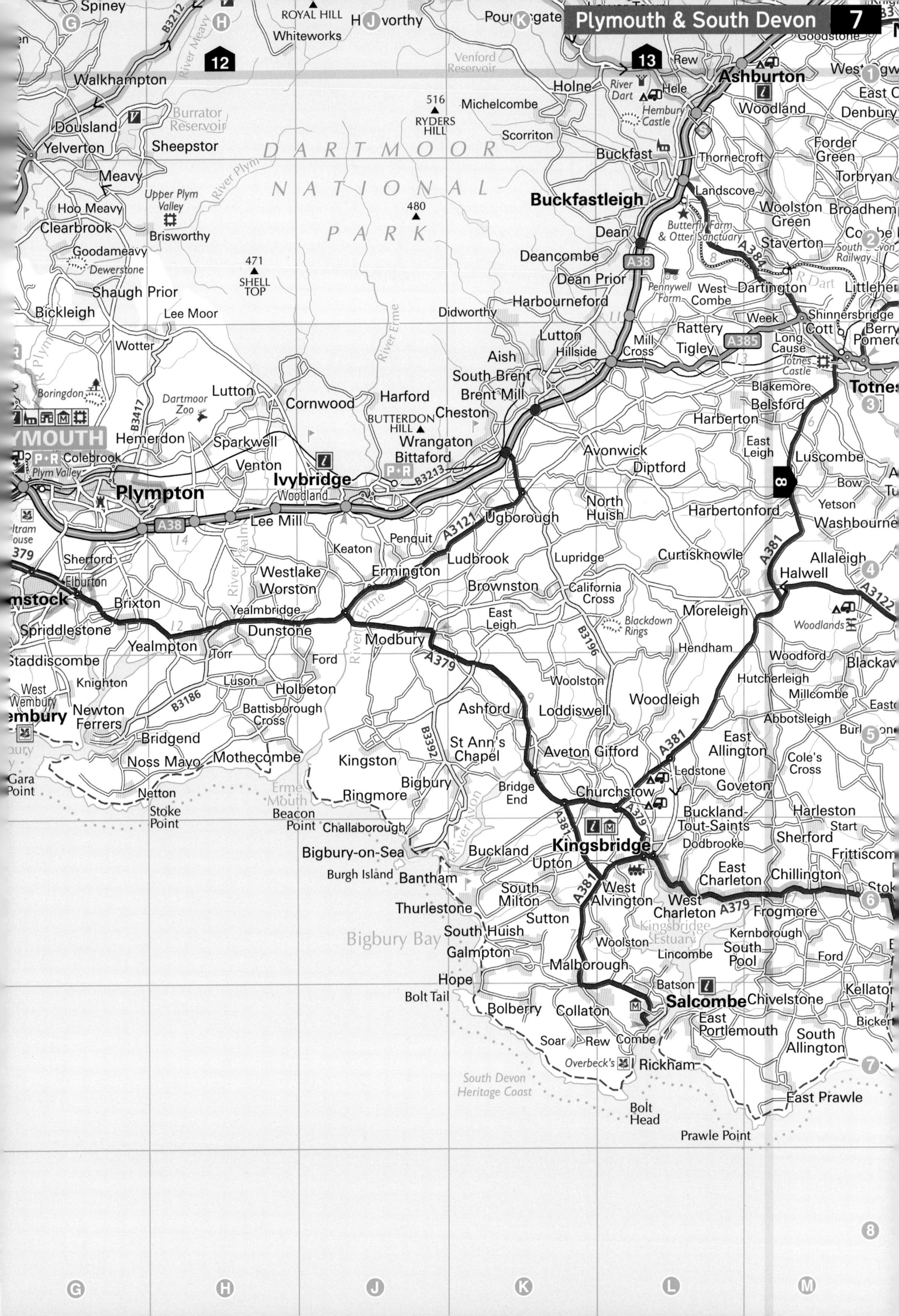

Spiney
ROYAL HILL
H Jvorthy
Pou K gate
Goodstone
West gw
G
H
Walkhampton
Whiteworks
Venford Reservoir
13
Rew
Ashburton
East C
12
Holne
River Dart
Hele
Woodland
Denbury
Dousland
V
Burrator Reservoir
Michelcombe
Hembury Castle
Forder Green
Yelverton
Sheepstor
516
RYDERS HILL
Scorriton
Buckfast
Thornecroft
Torbryan
Meavy
River Plym
Michelcombe
Buckfastleigh
Landscove
Woolston Broadhem
Hoo Meavy
DARTMOOR
Butterfly Farm & Otter Sanctuary
Green
Clearbrook
Upper Plym Valley
480
Dean
Staverton
Combe
Brisworthy
NATIONAL
Deancombe
Pennywell Farm
West Combe
Dartington
Littleher
Goodameavy
Dewerstone
471
SHELL TOP
PARK
Dean Prior
A38
Week
Shinnersbridge
Shaugh Prior
Didworthy
Harbourneford
Rattery
Tigley
A385
Long Cause
Cott
Berry Pomero
Bickleigh
Lee Moor
Lutton
Mill Cross
Totnes Castle
Wotter
Aish
Hillside
Totnes
Boringdon
Lutton
Cornwood
Harford
Cheston
South Brent
Brent Mill
Avonwick
Blakemore
Belsford
3
YMOUTH
Dartmoor Zoo
BUTTERDON HILL
Wrangaton Bittaford
Diptford
Harberton
East Leigh
Luscombe
Hemerdon
Sparkwell
P+R
B3213
North Huish
Harbertonford
Bow
Colebrook
Venton
Ivybridge
Woodland
Ugborough
A38
Yetson
Washbourne
Plympton
A38
Lee Mill
Penquit
Ludbrook
Lupridge
Curtisknowle
A381
Allaleigh
Halwell
Sherford
Keaton
Ermington
Brownston
California Cross
Moreleigh
A3122
Elburton
Westlake Worston
Woodlands
mstock
Yealmbridge
East Leigh
B3196
Hendham
Woodford
Blackav
Spriddlestone
Brixton
Dunstone
Modbury
Woolston
Hutcherleigh
Millcombe
Blacka
Staddiscombe
Yealmpton
Torr
Ford
A379
Woodleigh
Abbotsleigh
Burl
Knighton
Luson
Holbeton
Ashford
Loddiswell
East Allington
Cole's Cross
West Wembury
Newton Ferrers
Battisborough Cross
St Ann's Chapel
Aveton Gifford
A381
Goveton
embury
Bridgend
Mothecombe
Kingston
Bigbury
Ledstone
Buckland-Tout-Saints
Harleston
Gara Point
Noss Mayo
Netton
Ringmore
Bridge End
Churchstow
A379
Dodbrooke
Start Sherford
Stoke Point
Beacon Point
Challaborough
Buckland
Kingsbridge
East Charleton
Chillington
Bigbury-on-Sea
Upton
West Alvington
West Charleton
A379
Frogmore
Sto
Burgh Island
Bantham
South Milton
A381
Kingsbridge Estuary
Kernborough
6
Thurlestone
Sutton
Woolston
Lincombe
South Pool
South Huish
Bigbury Bay
Galmpton
Malborough
Batson
Ford
Hope
Bolt Tail
Bolberry
Collaton
Salcombe
Chivelstone
Kellato
Soar
Rew
Combe
East Portlemouth
South Allington
Bicker
Overbeck's
Rickham
7
South Devon Heritage Coast
East Prawle
Bolt Head
Prawle Point
8
G
H
J
K
L
M

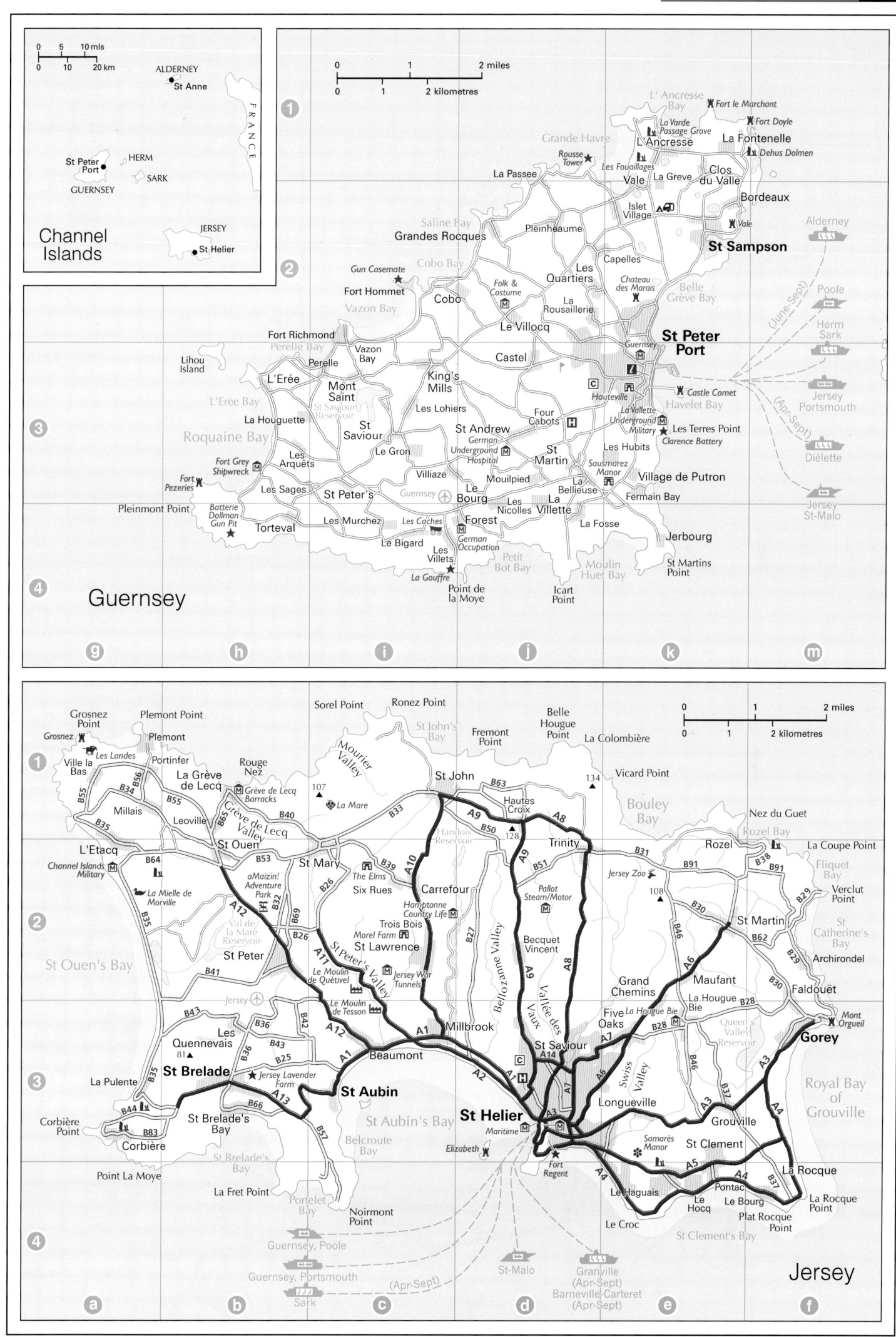

Channel Islands

ALDERNEY
• St Anne

FRANCE

St Peter Port • HERM
SARK
GUERNSEY

JERSEY
• St Helier

Guernsey

L' Ancresse Bay
Fort le Marchant
La Varde Passage Grave
Fort Doyle
Grande Havre
L'Ancresse
La Fontenelle
Rousse Tower
Les Fouaillages
Dehus Dolmen
La Passee
Vale
La Greve
Clos du Valle
Islet Village
Vale
Bordeaux
Saline Bay
Pleinheaume
Grandes Rocques
Les Quartiers
Capelles
St Sampson
Cobo Bay
Gun Casemate
Folk & Costume
Chateau des Marais
Belle Grève Bay
Fort Hommet
Cobo
La Rousaillerie
Vazon Bay
Le Villocq
Guernsey
St Peter Port
Fort Richmond
Perelle Bay
Vazon Bay
Castel
Perelle
Lihou Island
King's Mills
Hauteville
L'Erée
Mont Saint
Les Lohiers
Four Cabots
La Vallette Underground Military
Castle Cornet
Havelet Bay
L'Eree Bay
St Saviour Reservoir
Les Terres Point
Clarence Battery
La Houguette
St Saviour
St Andrew
German Underground Hospital
St Martin
Les Hubits
Roquaine Bay
Le Gron
Sausmarez Manor
Village de Putron
Fort Grey Shipwreck
Les Arquêts
Villiaze
Mouilpied
La Bellieuse
Fermain Bay
Fort Pezeries
Les Sages
St Peter's
Le Bourg
Les Nicolles
La Villette
Pleinmont Point
Les Murchez
Les Caches
La Fosse
Batterie Dollman Gun Pit
Forest
Torteval
Le Bigard
German Occupation
Jerbourg
Les Villets
St Martins Point
La Gouffre
Petit Bot Bay
Point de la Moye
Icart Point
Moulin Huet Bay

Alderney (June–Sept)
Poole
Herm Sark
Jersey Portsmouth (Apr–Sept)
Diélette
Jersey St-Malo

Jersey

Grosnez Point
Plemont Point
Sorel Point
Ronez Point
Belle Hougue Point
La Colombière
Grosnez
Les Landes
Plemont
Ville la Bas
Portinfer
Rouge Nez
Mourier Valley
St John's Bay
Fremont Point
Vicard Point
Nez du Guet
La Grève de Lecq
Grève de Lecq Barracks
107
La Mare
St John
Hautes Croix
Bouley Bay
Rozel Bay
Millais
Leoville
Grève de Lecq Valley
128
Trinity
Rozel
La Coupe Point
L'Etacq
St Ouen
St Mary
Carrefour
Jersey Zoo
108
Fliquet Bay
Channel Islands Military
La Mielle de Morville
The Elms
Six Rues
Pallot Steam/Motor
Verclut Point
aMaizin! Adventure Park
Hamptonne Country Life
Becquet Vincent
St Martin
St Catherine's Bay
Val de la Mare Reservoir
Morel Farm
Trois Bois
St Lawrence
Grand Chemins
Maufant
Archirondel
St Peter
Jersey War Tunnels
Vallée des Vaux
La Hougue Bie
Faldouët
Le Moulin de Quétivel
Five Oaks
La Hougue Bie
81
Le Moulin de Tesson
Millbrook
St Saviour
Mont Orgueil
Les Quennevais
Beaumont
St Aubin's Bay
Longueville
Gorey
St Brelade
Jersey Lavender Farm
St Aubin
St Helier
Swiss Valley
Queen's Valley Reservoir
La Pulente
Grouville
Royal Bay of Grouville
Maritime
Samarès Manor
St Clement
Corbière Point
St Brelade's Bay
Elizabeth
Fort Regent
Le Haguais
La Rocque
Corbière
Belcroute Bay
St Brelade's Bay
Le Hocq
Le Bourg
Pontac
La Rocque Point
Point La Moye
Portelet Bay
Noirmont Point
Le Croc
Plat Rocque Point
La Fret Point
Le Croc
St Clement's Bay

Guernsey, Poole
Guernsey, Portsmouth (Apr–Sept)
Sark
St-Malo
Granville (Apr–Sept)
Barneville-Carteret (Apr–Sept)

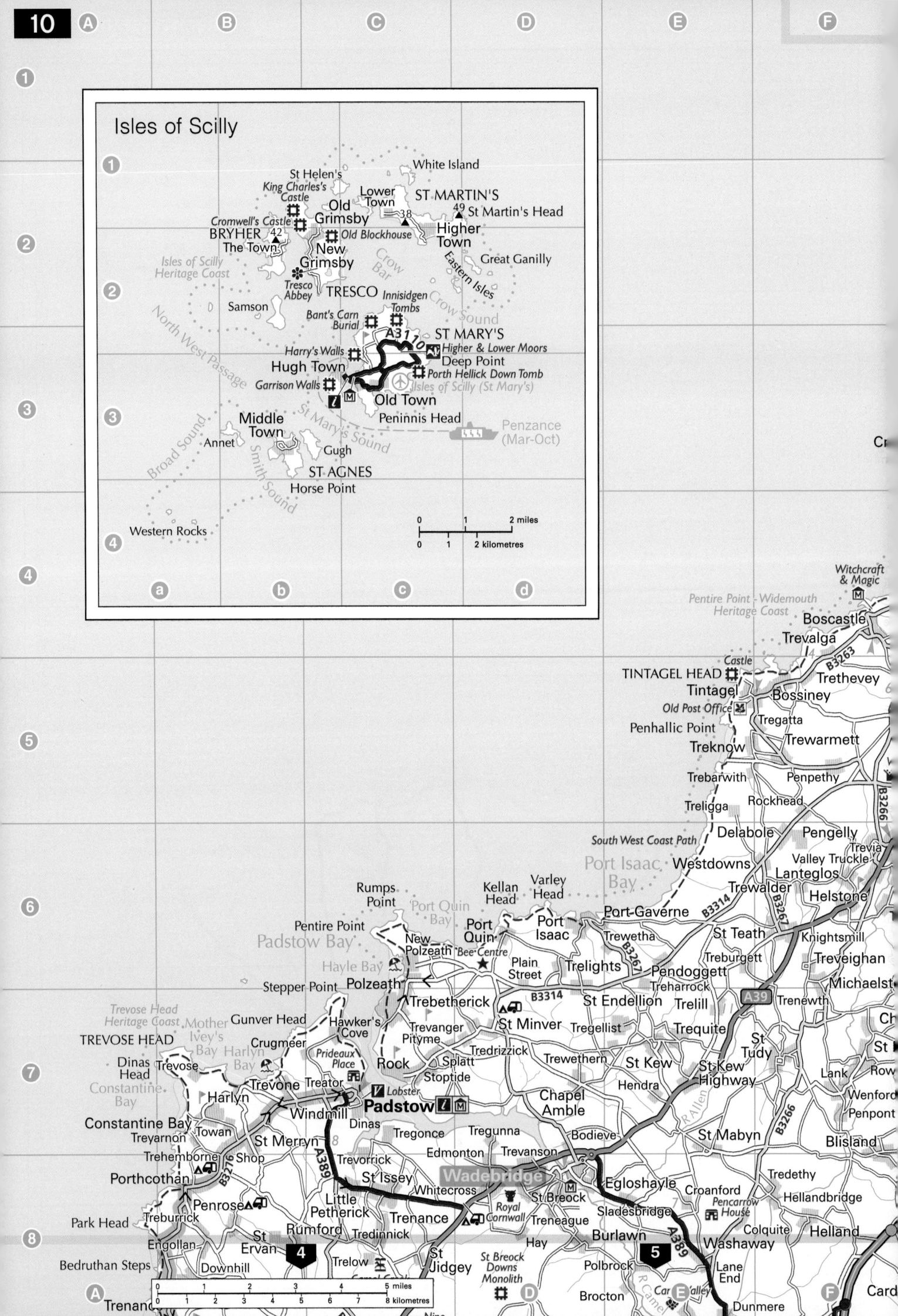

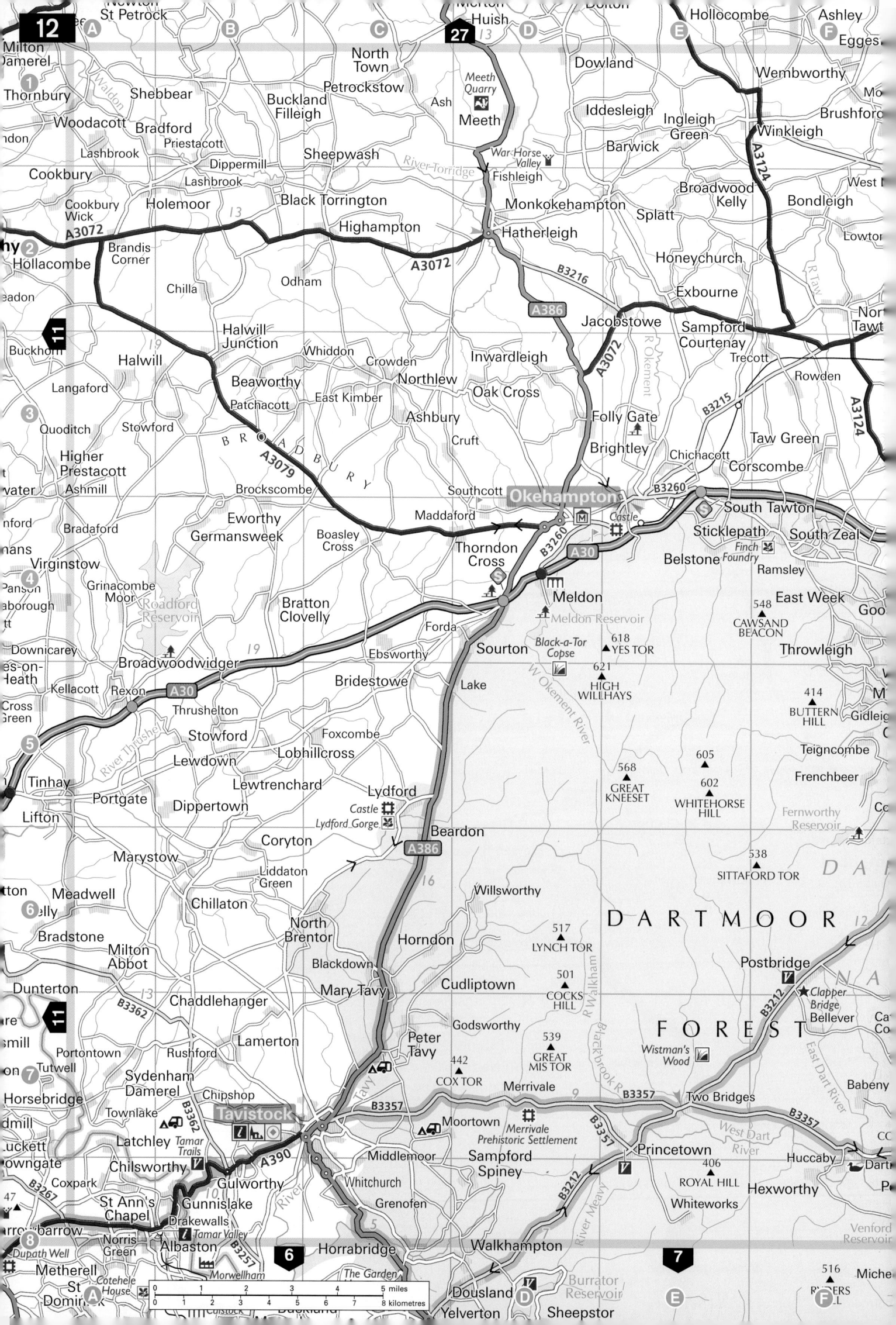

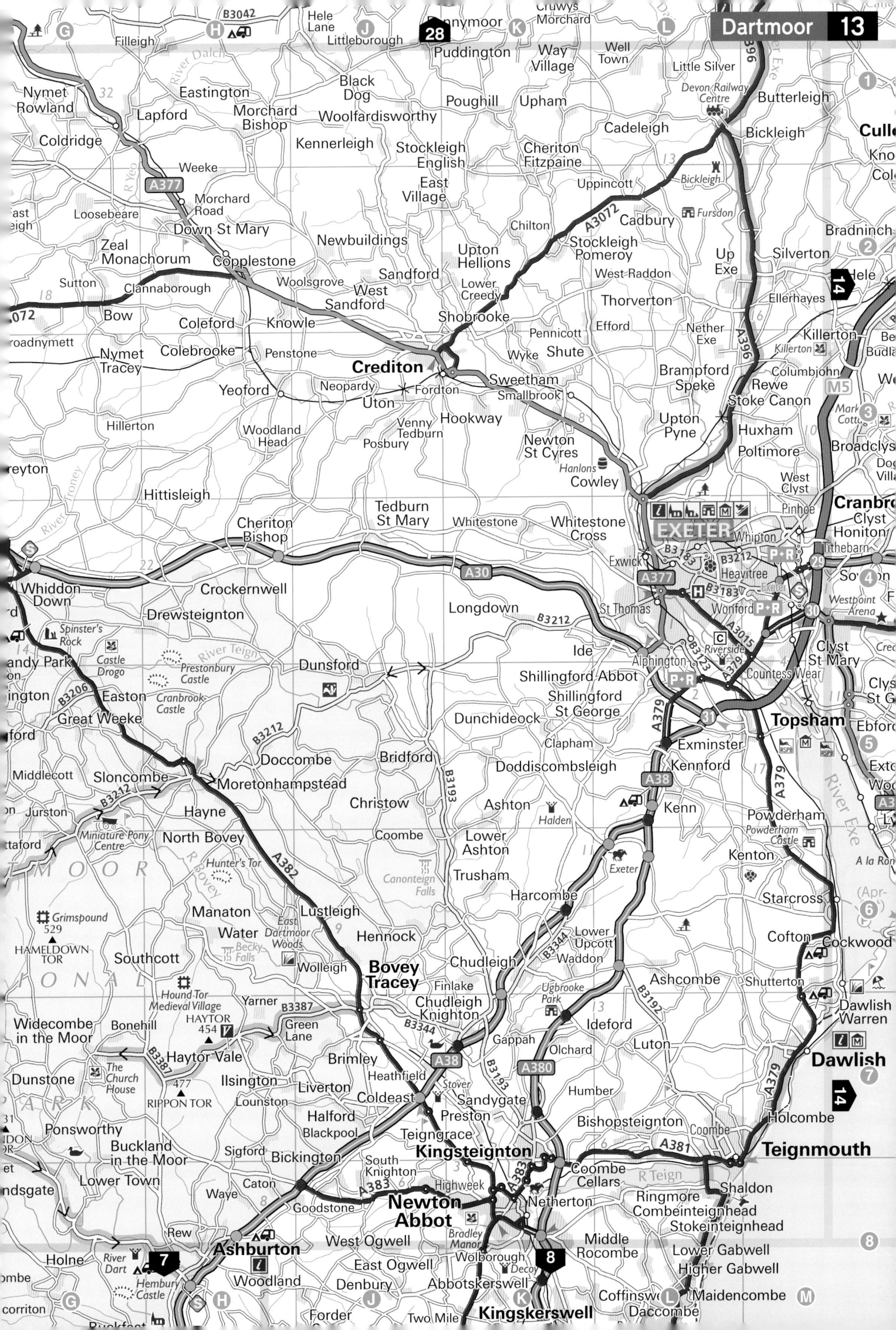

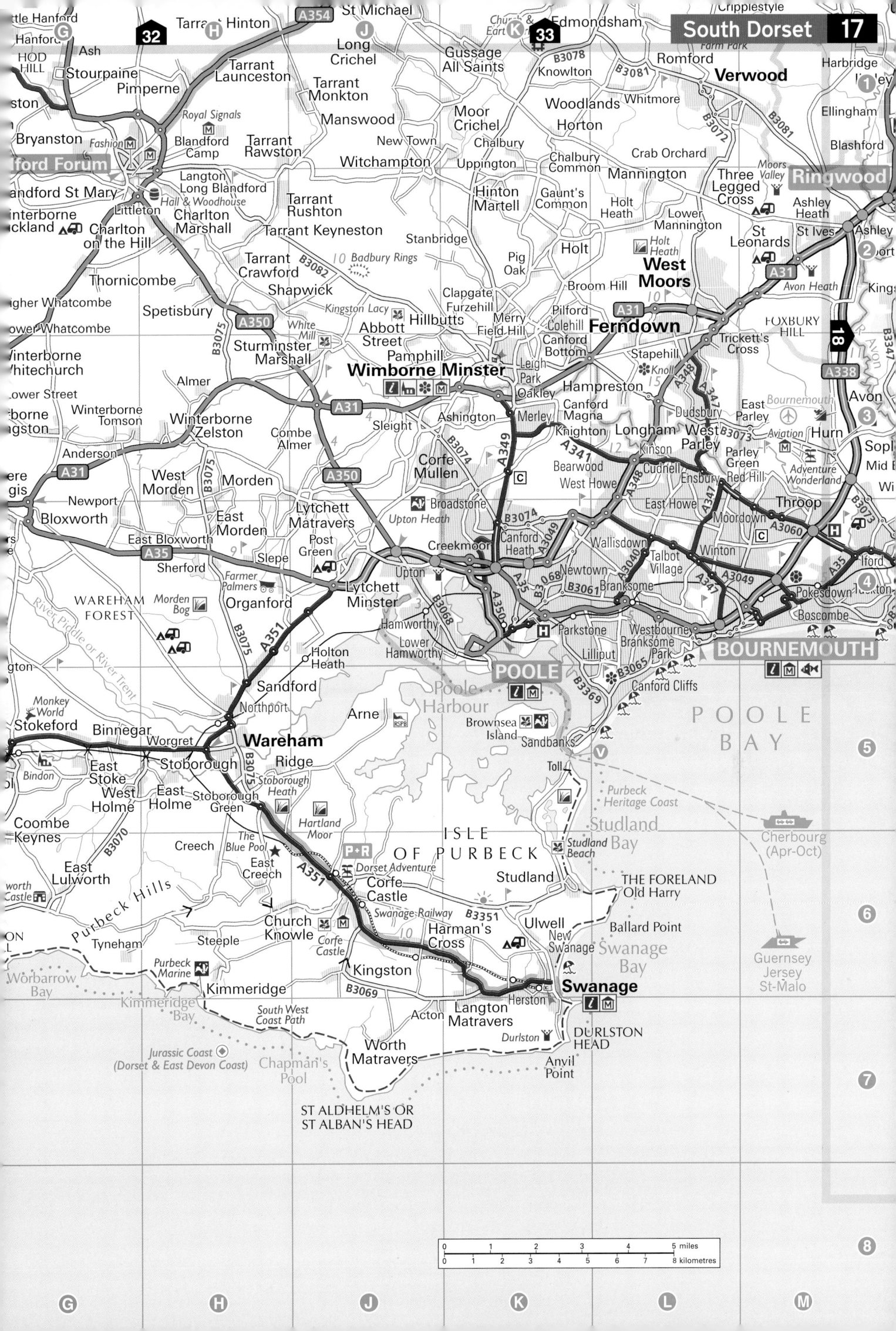

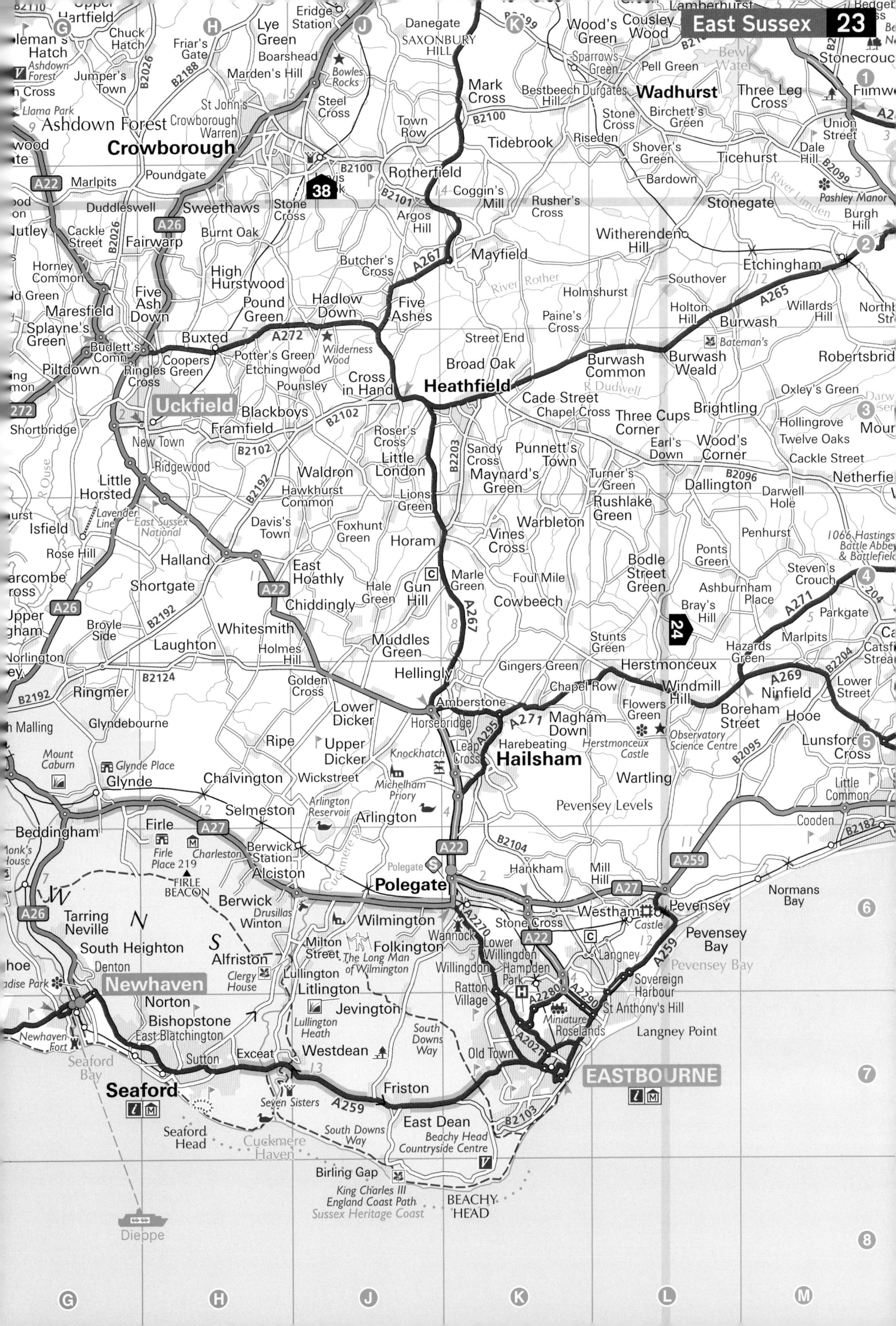

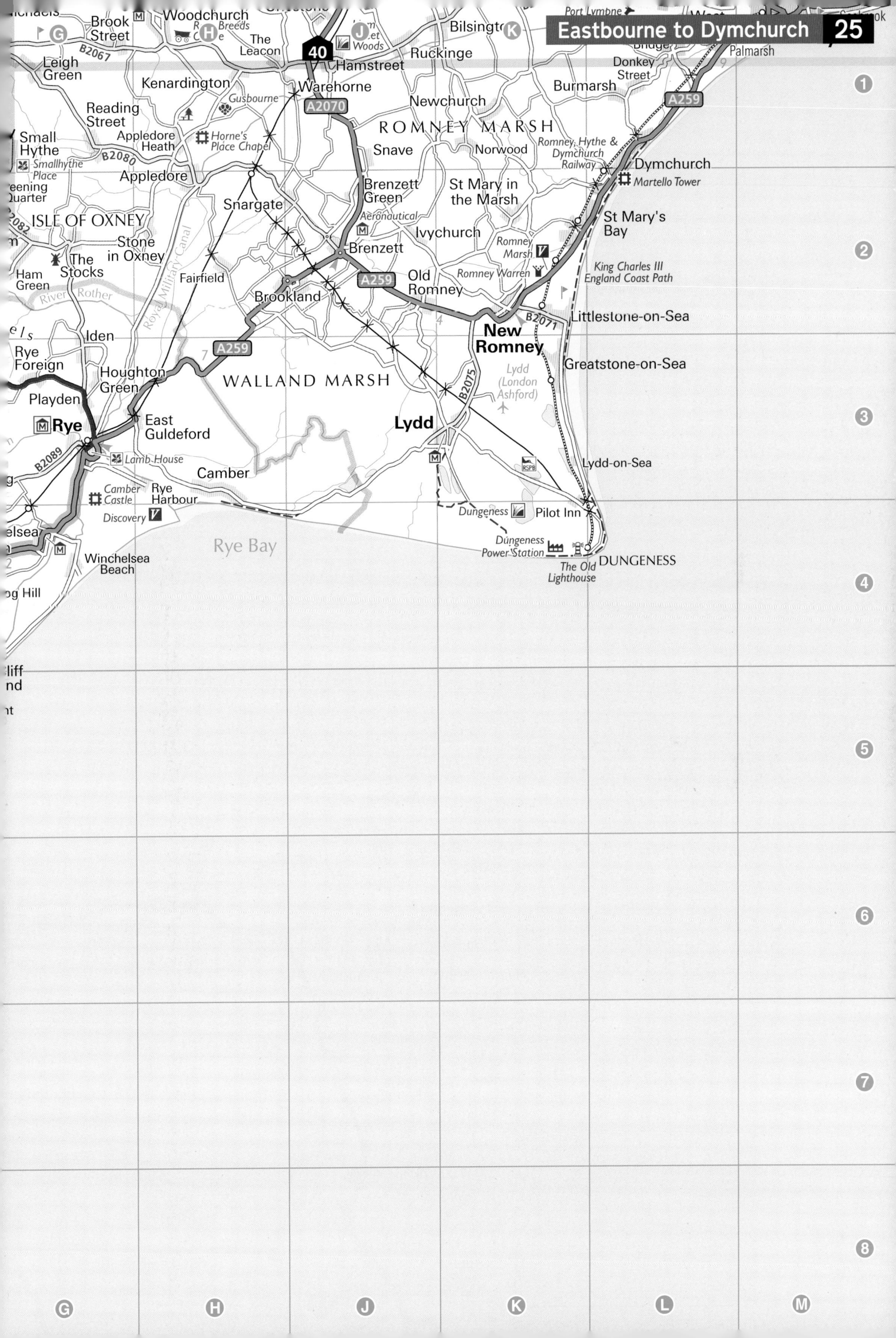

A B C D E F

1

2

North West
Point

*Lundy
Heritage Coast*

 LUNDY

▲ 142

*Marine
Reserve*

Shutter Point

Surf Point

(P) (Apr-Oct)

3

(Apr-Oct) (P)

4

B A R N S T A P L E

O R

5

B I D E F O R D   B A Y

HARTLAND POINT

Shipload
Bay

Titchberry

Brownsham

*Hartland
Heritage C*

Damehole
Point

*Hartland Abbey
& Gardens*

Velly

V

Clovelly

Buck's
Mills

Stoke

B3248

4

B3237

Higher
Clovelly

Hartland Quay

*Speke's Mill
Mouth*

Hartland

*Docton
Mill*

Philham

Milky Way

Buck's
Cross

A39

6

Milford

Edistone

Woolfardisworthy

Parkh

Elmscott

Tosberry

Cranford

Parkham
Ash

Hardisworthy

South
Hole

Welcombe

Meddon

Ashmansworthy

East
Putford

Mead

Darracott

*Gooseham
Mill*

Woolley

East
Youlstone

Dinworthy

*Gnome
Reserve* ★

West
Putfor

7

Gooseham

Eastcott

Colscott

Ha

Morwenstow

West Youlstone

Bradworthy

Higher Sharpnose Point

*South West
Coast Path*

Shop

A39

*Tamar
Lakes*

Kimworthy

Sutcombe

Woodford

Bic

Lower Sharpnose Point

Kilkhampton

Alfardisworthy

Sutcombemill

Steeple Point

Stibb

Thurdon

Soldon

Mil
Dan

8

River

A B

0   1   2   3   4   5 miles
0   1   2   3   4   5   6   7   8 kilometres

D **11** E F

B325

Soldon
Cross

Mouth

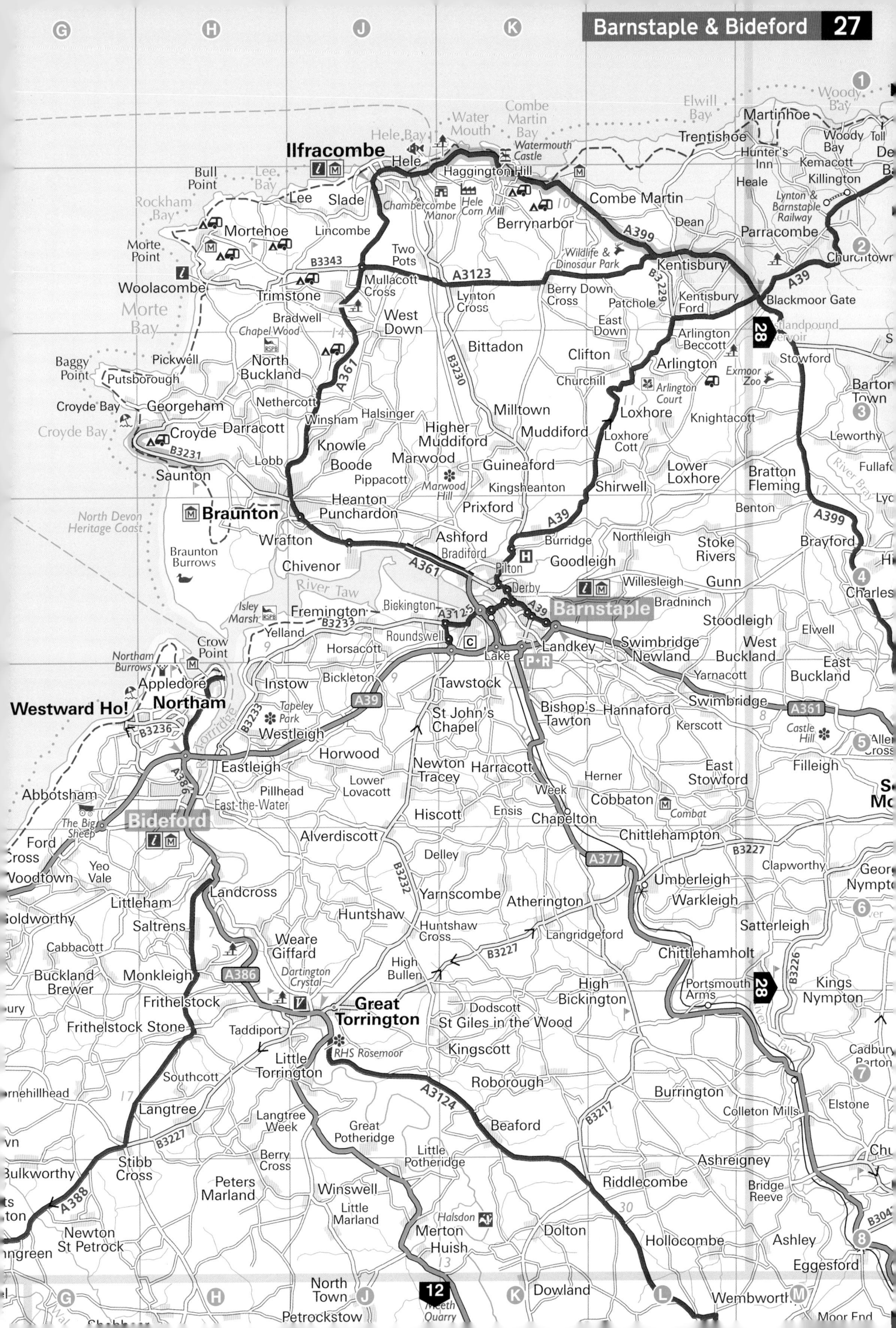

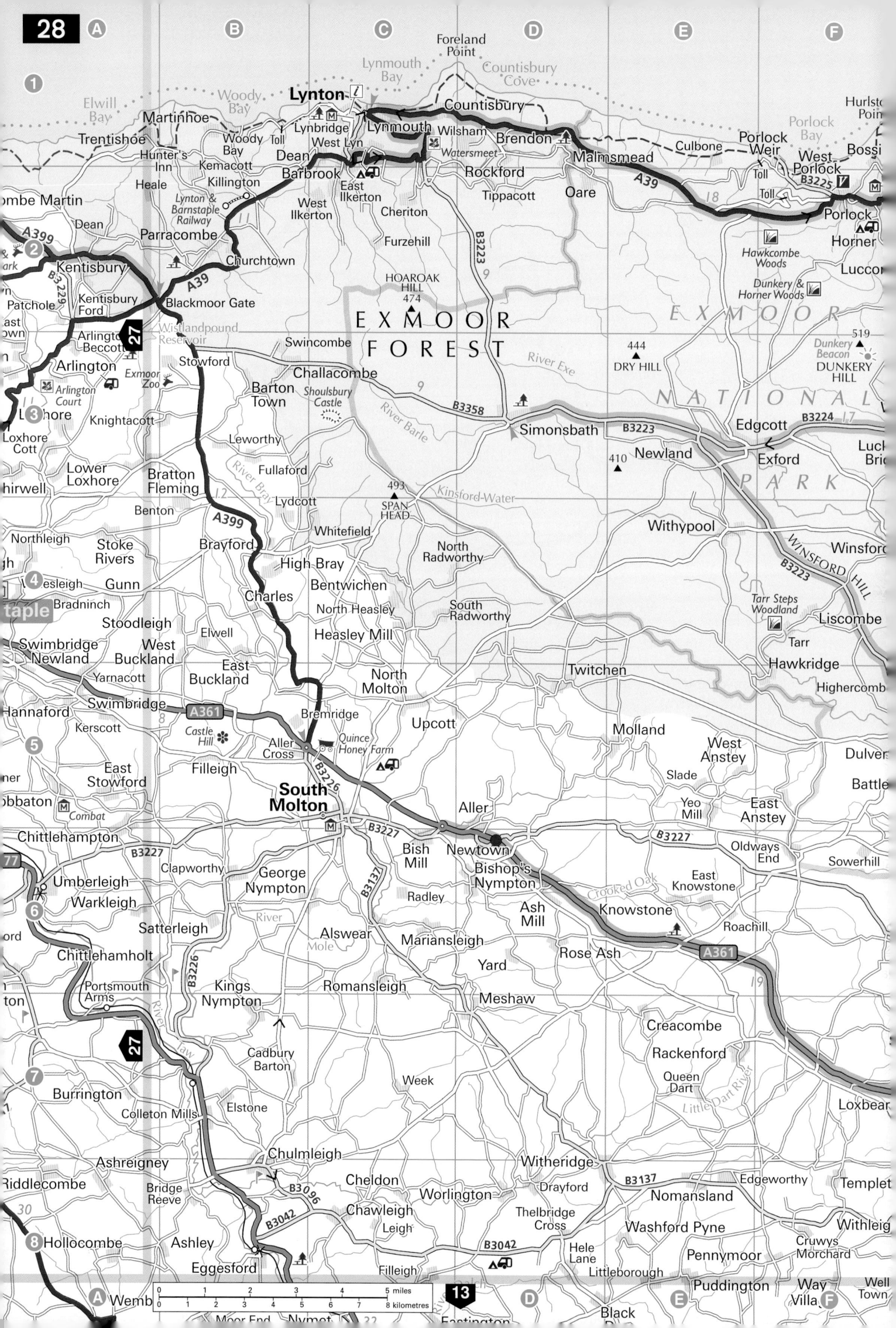

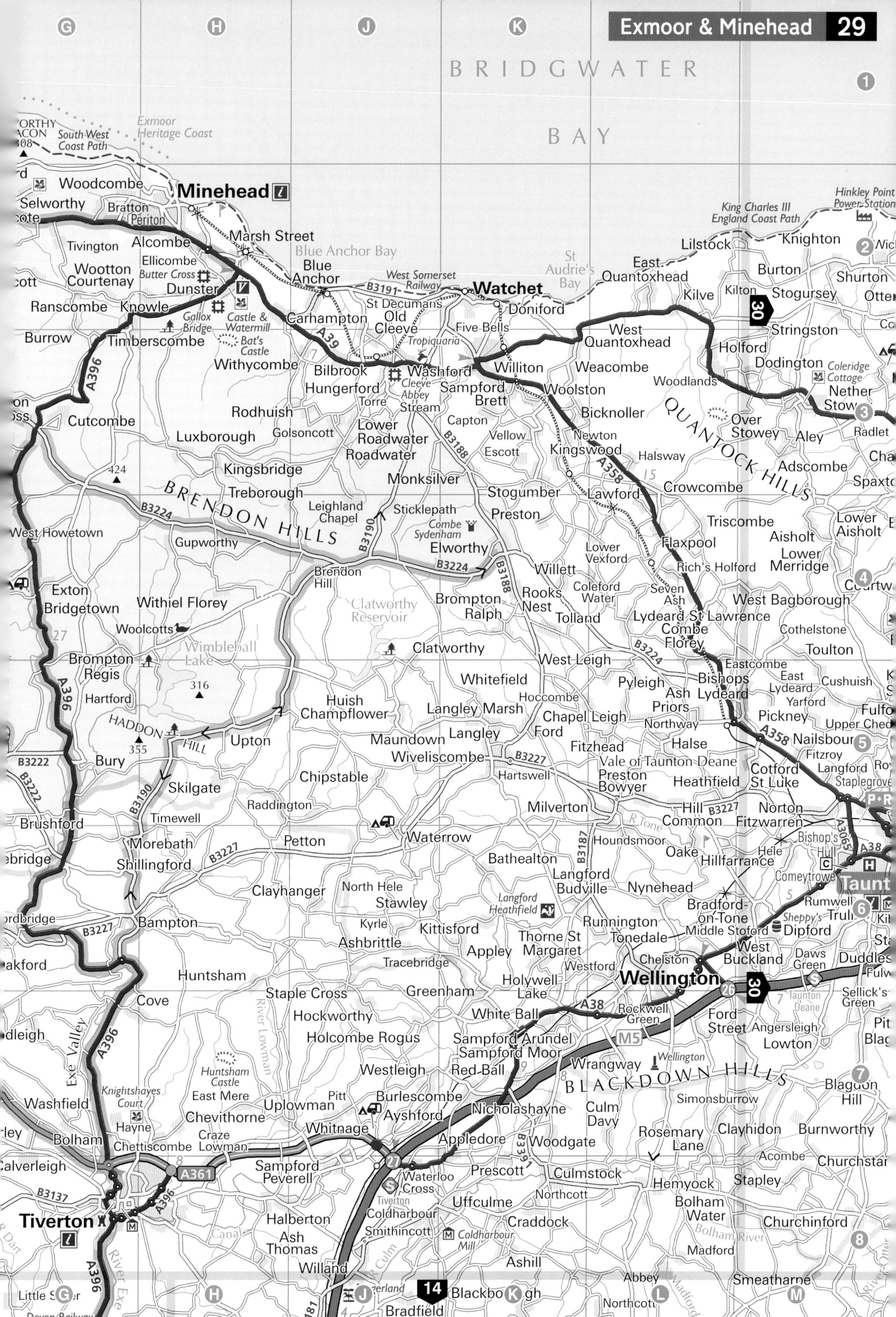

BRIDGWATER

BAY

G H J K 1

South West Coast Path
Exmoor Heritage Coast

WORTHY
BEACON
808

Woodcombe

Selworthy
cote

Minehead *i*

Tivington

Alcombe

Marsh Street

Bratton
Periton

Blue Anchor Bay

Hinkley Point
Power Station

King Charles III
England Coast Path

Lilstock
Knighton

East
Quantoxhead
Burton
Shurton

Kilve
Kilton
Stogursey
Otter

Ellicombe
Butter Cross

Wootton
Courtenay

Blue
Anchor

B3191

West Somerset
Railway

Watchet

St Audrie's
Bay

Doniford

West
Quantoxhead

Holford

Stringston

Ranscombe

Knowle

Dunster

Carhampton

Old
Cleeve

Five Bells

Williton

Woolston

Weacombe

Woodlands

Dodington
Coleridge
Cottage

Nether
Stowey

Burrow

Timberscombe

Gallox
Bridge

Castle &
Watermill

Bat's
Castle

A39

St Decumans

Tropiquaria

Sampford
Brett

Bicknoller

Newton

Kingswood

Halsway

Over
Stowey

Aley
Radlet

Withycombe

Bilbrook

Washford

Cutcombe

Hungerford

Torre

Cleeve
Abbey
Stream

Capton

Vellow
Escott

Halsway

Crowcombe

Adscombe

Spaxto

Rodhuish

Lower
Roadwater

Roadwater

Stogumber

Preston

Lawford

QUANTOCK HILLS

A396

Luxborough

Golsoncott

B3188

Triscombe

Aisholt

Lower
Aisholt

Kingsbridge

Treborough

Monksilver

Lower
Vexford

Flaxpool

West Howetown

BRENDON HILLS

Gupworthy

Leighland
Chapel

B3190

Sticklepath

Combe
Sydenham

Elworthy

B3224

Willett

Rich's Holford

Seven
Ash

West Bagborough

Courtw

Cothelstone

B3224

Brendon
Hill

Clatworthy
Reservoir

Brompton
Ralph

Rooks
Nest

Tolland

Coleford
Water

Lydeard St Lawrence

Combe
Florey

Toulton

Exton
Bridgetown

Withiel Florey

Woolcotts

Wimbleball
Lake

424

316

Clatworthy

West Leigh

Whitefield

Hoccombe

Pyleigh
Priors

Ash
Priors

Northway

Bishops
Lydeard

Eastcombe

East
Lydeard

Cushuish

Yarford

Pickney

Fulfo
Upper Ched

Brompton
Regis

Hartford

HADDON HILL

355

Bury

Upton

Huish
Champflower

Langley Marsh

Langley

Maundown

Wiveliscombe

Chapel Leigh

Fitzhead

Halse

A358

Nailsbour

Fitzroy

Langford
Staplegrove

5

B3222

Skilgate

Chipstable

B3227

Hartswell

Vale of Taunton Deane

Preston
Bowyer

Heathfield

Cotford
St Luke

Norton
Fitzwarren

P+R

Timewell

Raddington

Milverton

R Tone

Hill
Common

B3227

A303

A38

B3222

Brushford

Morebath

Petton

Waterrow

Houndsmoor

Oake

Hillfarrance

Hele

Bishop's
Hull

Comeytrowe

Taunt

C

H

Shillingford

B3227

Clayhanger

North Hele
Stawley

Bathealton

Langford
Budville

Nynehead

Bradford-
on-Tone

Rumwell

Truli

6

ebridge

ordbridge
akford

Bampton

Huntsham

Cove

Kyrle

Ashbrittle

Tracebridge

Kittisford

Appley

Thorne St
Margaret

Runnington

Tonedale

Middle Stoford

Sheppy's

Chelston

Dipford

West
Buckland

Daws
Green

Duddles

Langford
Heathfield

Holywell
Lake

Westford

Wellington

5

Sta

Staple Cross

Greenham

White Ball

A38

Rockwell
Green

Ford
Street

Taunton
Deane

Sellick's
Green

Hockworthy

A396

Huntsham
Castle

Knightshayes
Court

East Mere

Chevithorne

Holcombe Rogus

Sampford Arundel

Sampford Moor

Wrangway

Simonsburrow

Angersleigh

Lowton

Pit
Blag

7

Washfield

Hayne

Craze
Lowman

Westleigh

Red Ball

9

8

Wellington

BLACKDOWN HILLS

Blagdon
Hill

ley

Bolham

Chettiscombe

Uplowman

Pitt

Burlescombe

Ayshford

Nicholashayne

Culm
Davy

Rosemary
Lane

Clayhidon

Burnworthy

calverleigh

A361

Whitnage

Appledore

Woodgate

Acombe

Churchstar

Tiverton *i*

A396

B3137

Sampford
Peverell

Waterloo
Cross

Whitage

Tiverton
Coldharbour

Halberton

Ash
Thomas

Smithincott

Coldharbour
Mill

Willand

Uffculme

Prescott

Culmstock

Craddock

Ashill

Hemyock

Northcott

Bolham
Water

Stapley

Churchinford

Little S

Devon Railway

Canal

R Culm

R Culm

Madford

Abbey

Smeatharne

Northcott

Bradfield

Blackbo gh

14

8

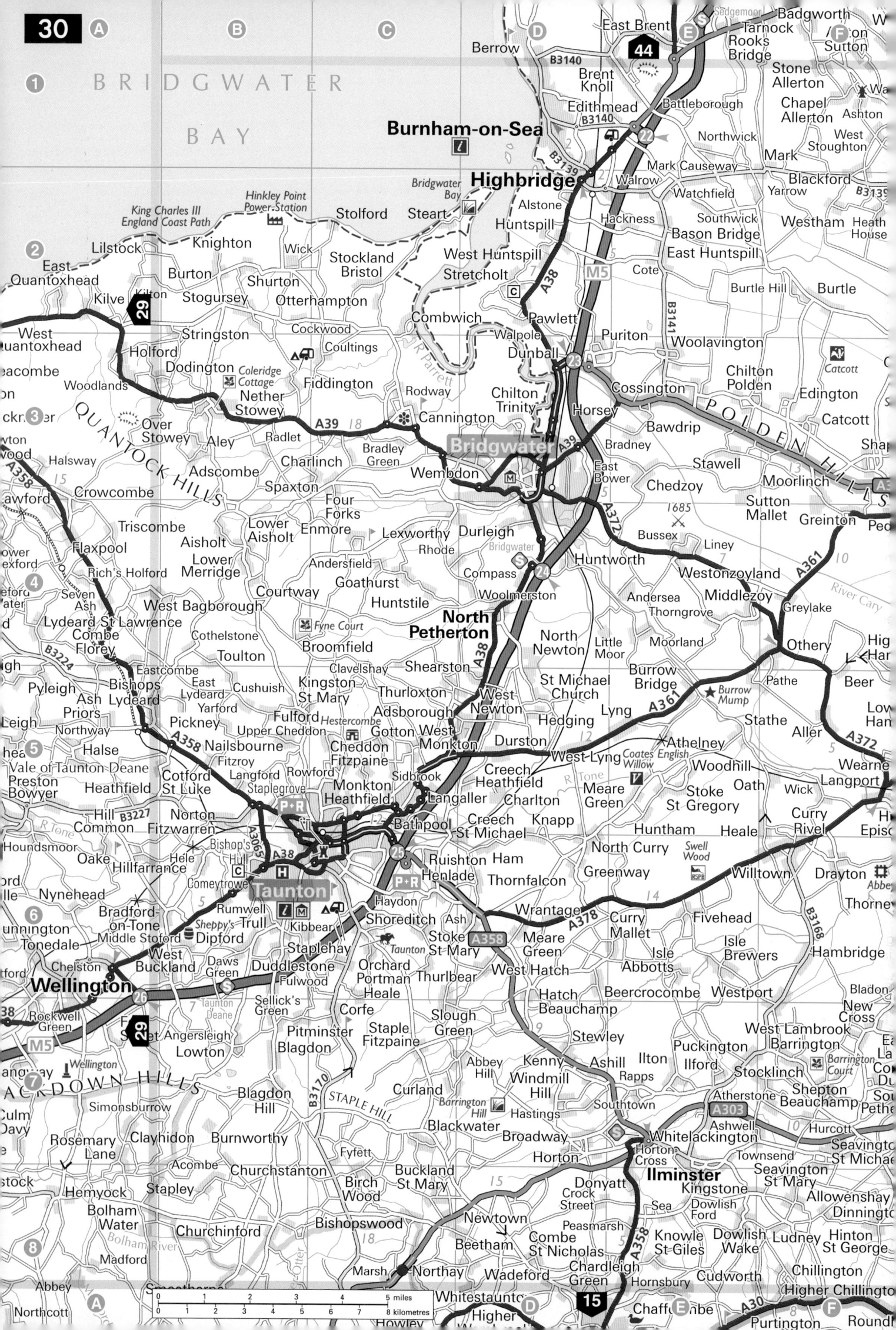

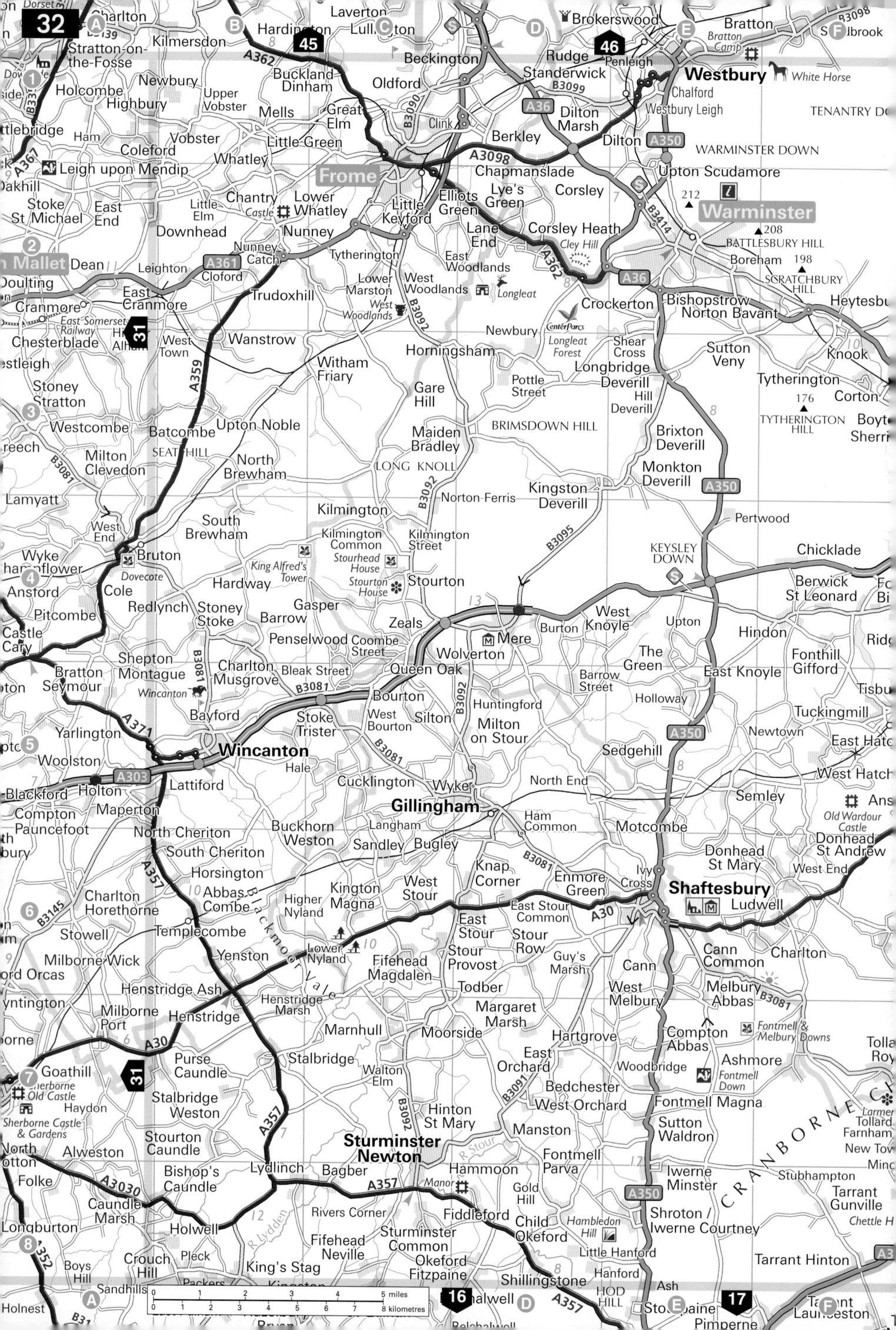

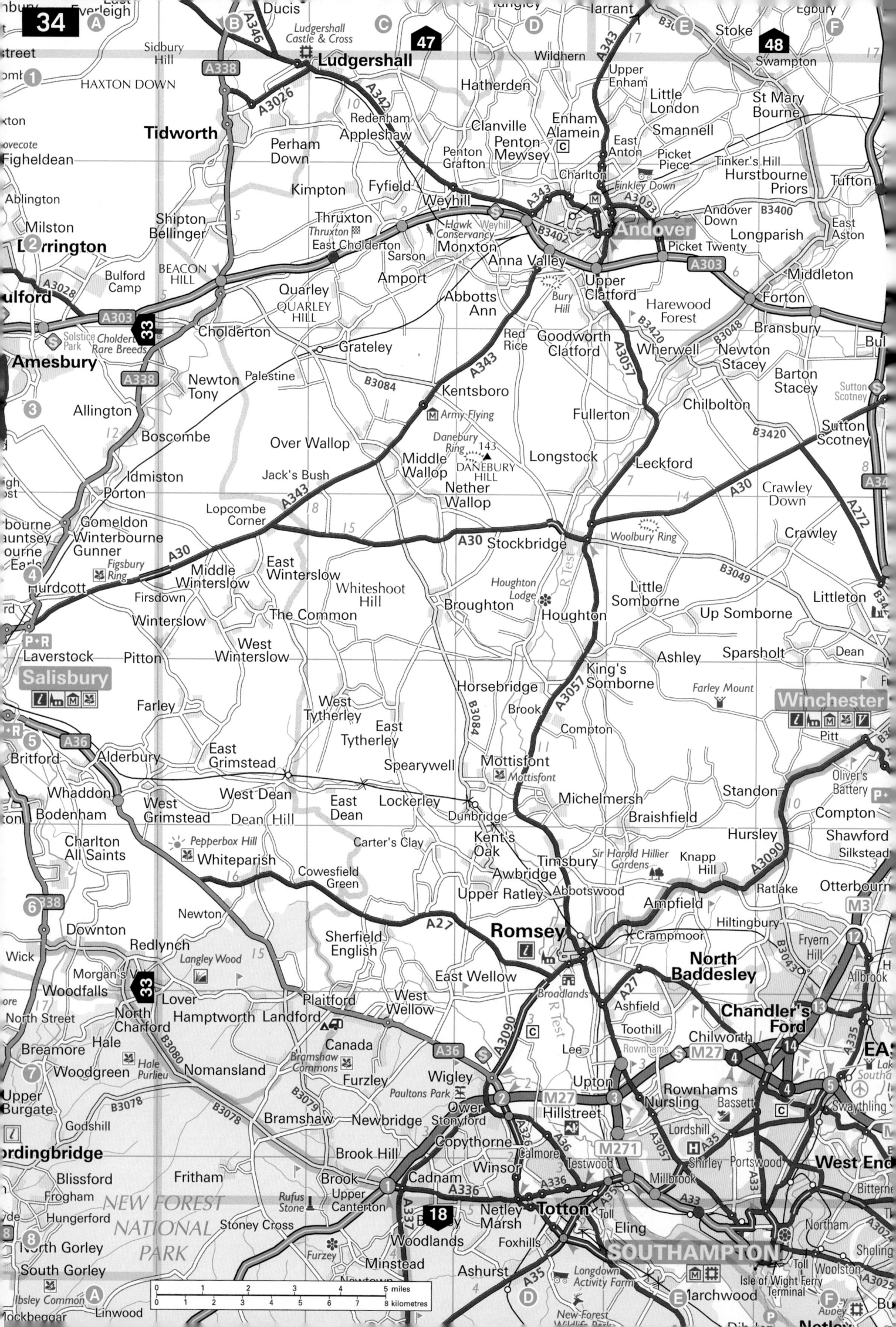

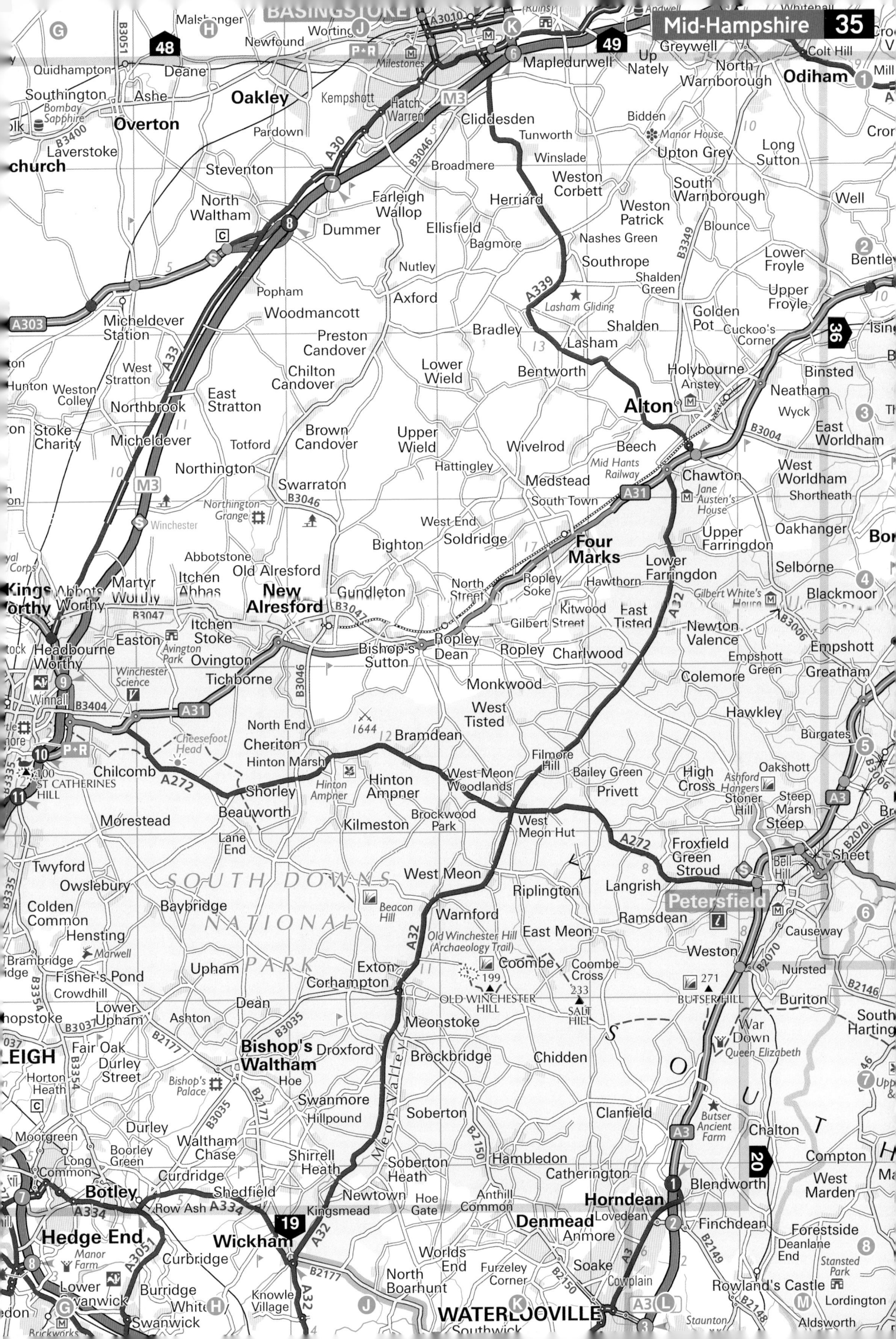

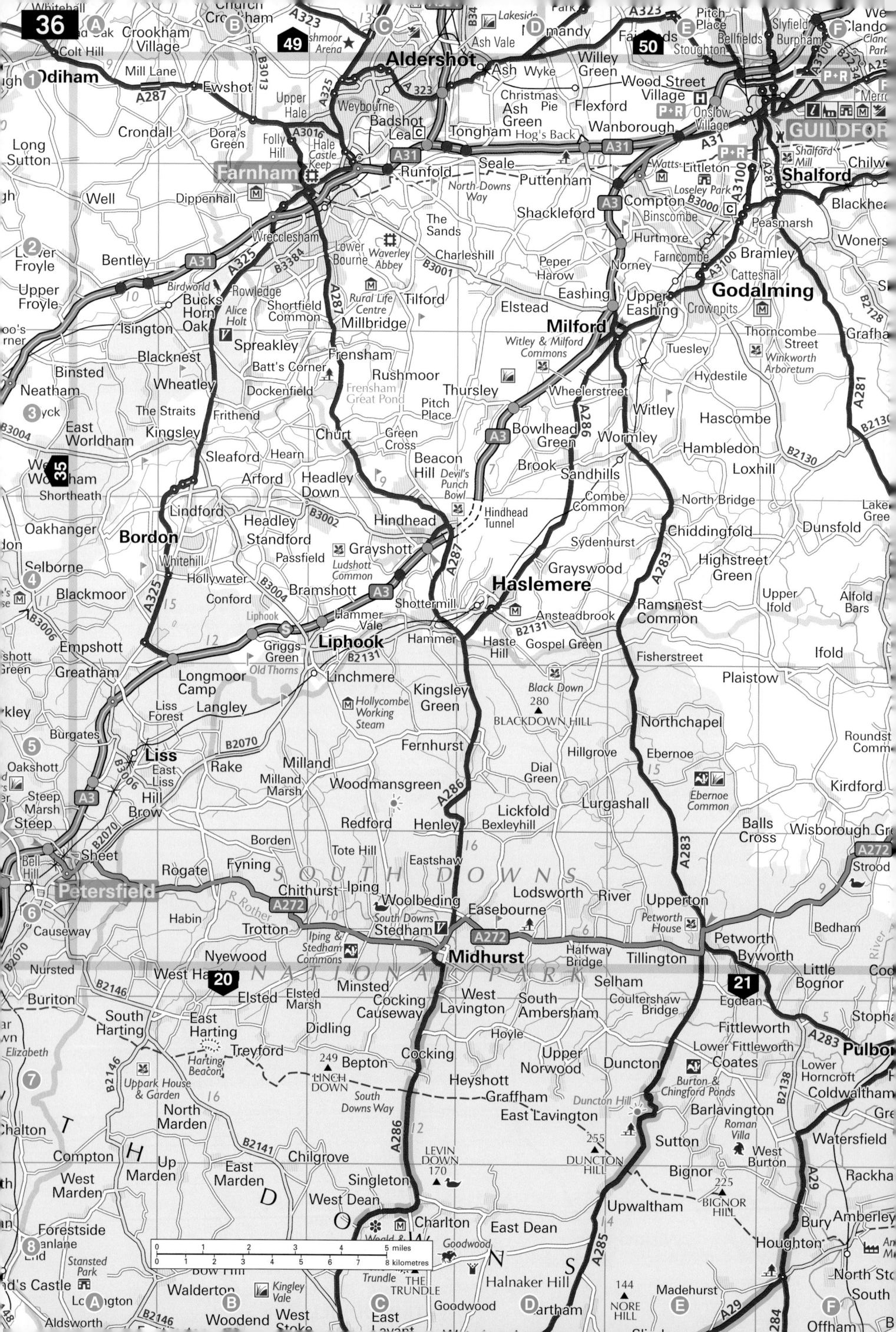

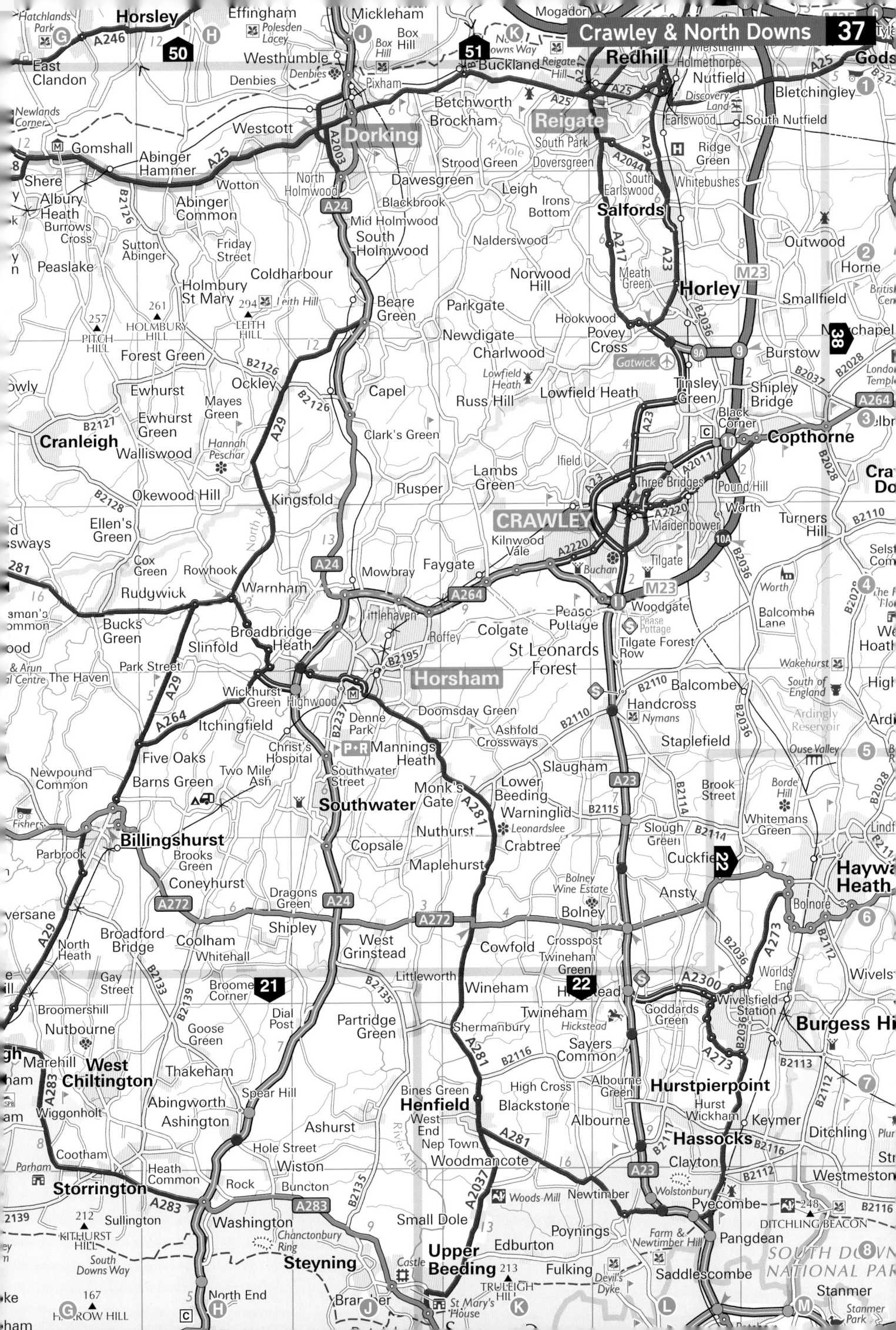

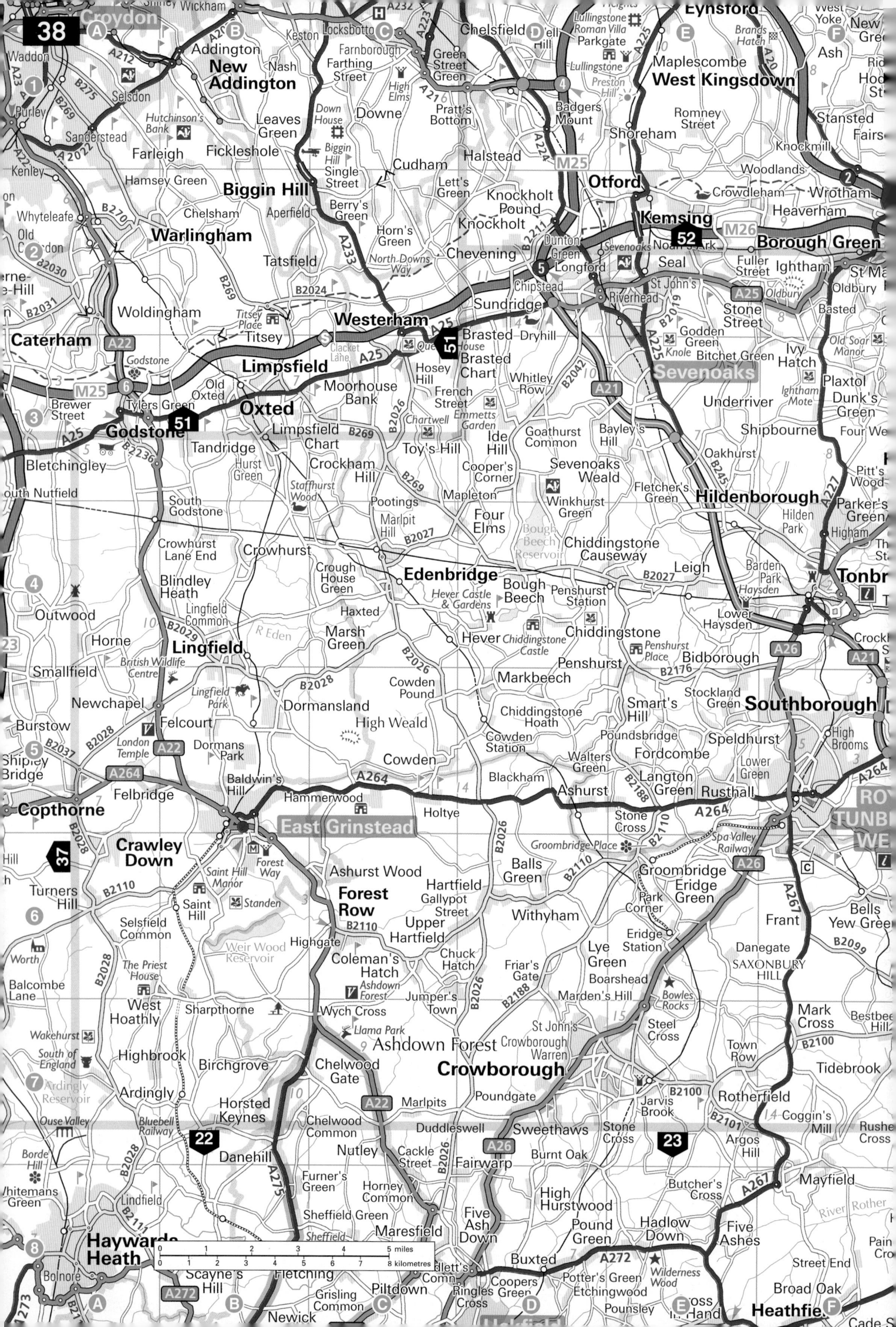

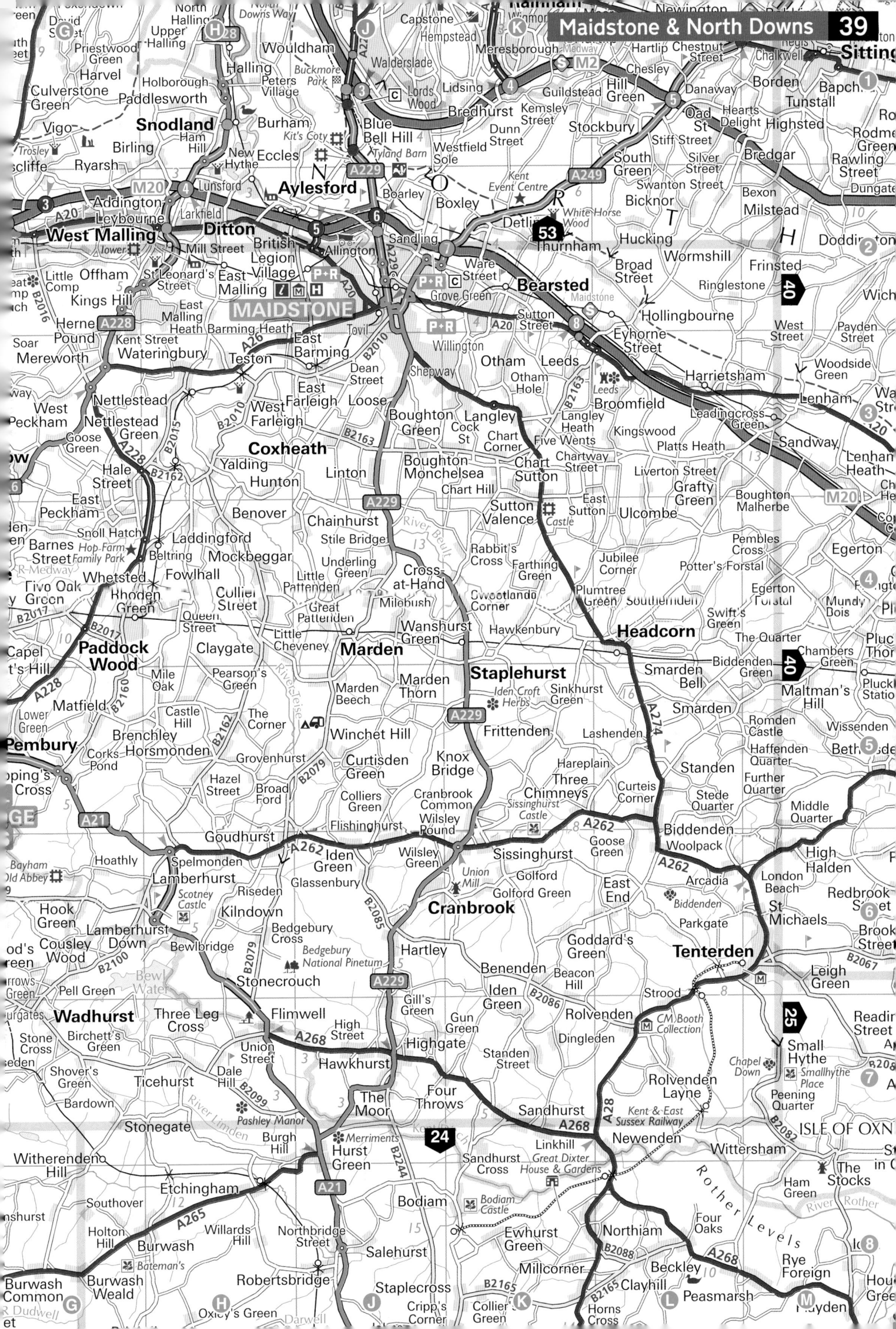

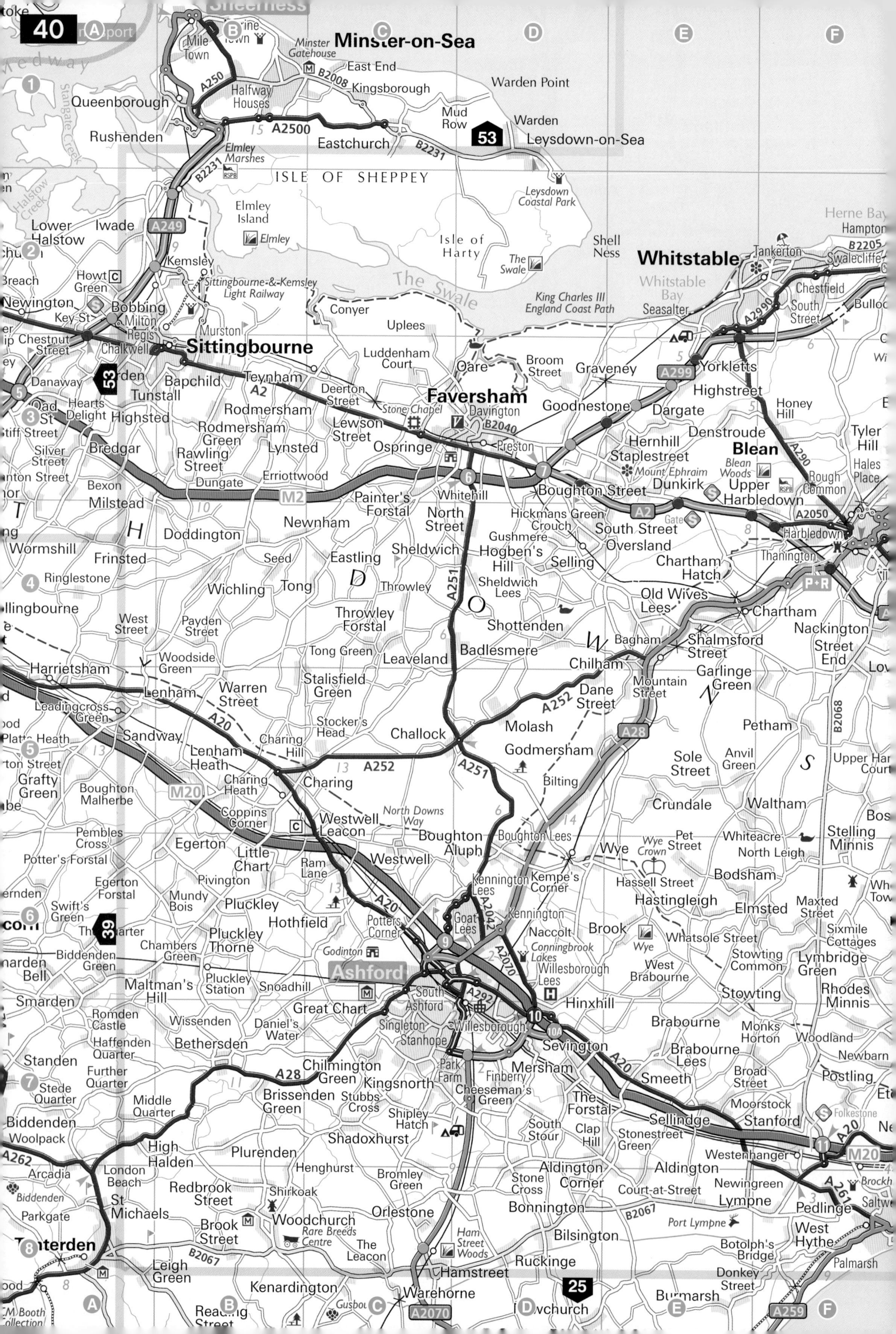

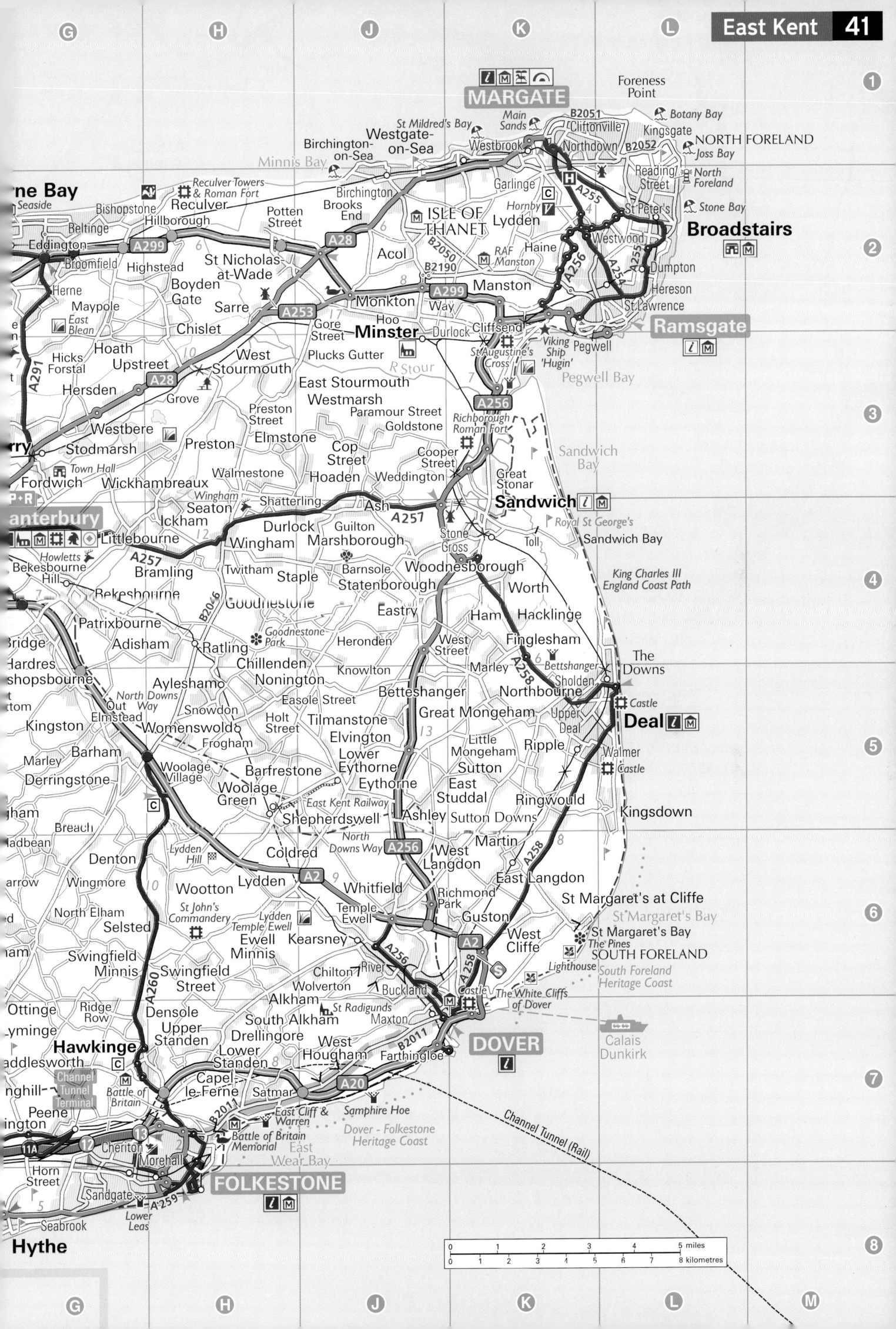

G H J K L

Foreness
Point

MARGATE

St Mildred's Bay Main Botany Bay
Westgate-on-Sea Sands B2051 Kingsgate
Birchington- Westbrook Cliftonville NORTH FORELAND
on-Sea Northdown B2052 Joss Bay
Minnis Bay Garlinge North
Foreland
ne Bay Birchington Reading
Seaside Brooks Hornby C Street
Bishopstone Reculver Towers End Lydden A255 St Peter's Stone Bay
Reculver & Roman Fort ISLE OF 4 Westwood Broadstairs
Hillborough THANET St Peter's
Beltinge Potten Acol A256 A254 A255 Dumpton
Eddington Highstead Street B2050 Haine A255
Broomfield A299 St Nicholas- A28 Manston RAF Hereson
Herne at-Wade B2190 Manston St Lawrence
Maypole Boyden Sarre Manston Ramsgate
East Gate A253 Way Durlock Cliffsend
Blean Chislet Monkton A299 St Augustine's Viking Pegwell
Hoath Hicks Gore Hoo Cross Ship i M
Forstal Upstreet Street Minster 'Hugin'
Hersden A28 West Plucks Gutter Pegwell Bay
Grove Stourmouth R Stour
Westbere Preston East Stourmouth Richborough Sandwich
Stodmarsh Street Westmarsh Roman Fort Bay
Fordwich Elmstone Paramour Street Cooper Great
rry Town Hall Preston Goldstone Street Stonar
P+R Wickhambreaux Cop Hoaden Weddington Sandwich i M
anterbury Walmestone Street Ash Royal St George's
i M Seaton Shatterling A257 Stone Sandwich Bay
Howletts Ickham Durlock Guilton Cross Toll
Bekesbourne Littlebourne Wingham Marshborough Woodnesborough King Charles III
Hill A257 Twitham Barnsole England Coast Path
Bramling Staple Statenborough Worth
Bridge Patrixbourne Goodnestone Eastry Ham Hacklinge
Hardres Adisham Ratling Goodnestone Heronden West Finglesham
shopsbourne Park Street Bettshanger The
ttom Chillenden Knowlton Marley Sholden Downs
Kingston Aylesham Nonington Betteshanger Northbourne Deal i M
Elmstead Snowdon Easole Street Great Mongeham Upper Castle
Marley Barham Womenswold Holt Tilmanstone Deal
Derringstone Frogham Street Ripple Walmer
ham Woolage Barfrestone Elvington Sutton Castle
Village Lower East Little
Breach C Woolage Eythorne Studdal Mongeham Kingsdown
adbean Green Eythorne Ashley Sutton Downs Ringwould
Denton East Kent Railway Shepherdswell Martin
arrow Lydden North A256 West A258
Wingmore Hill Downs Way Langdon
North Elham Coldred West East Langdon
Selsted Wootton A2 Whitfield Langdon
Lydden 9 Richmond St Margaret's at Cliffe
Swingfield Temple Park St Margaret's Bay
Minnis St John's Ewell Guston The Pines SOUTH FORELAND
Commandery Lydden A256 St Margaret's Bay
Swingfield Temple Ewell West Lighthouse South Foreland
Densole Street Ewell Kearsney Cliffe Heritage Coast
Ottinge Upper Minnis Chilton A258
yminge Standen Alkham River Castle The White Cliffs
Hawkinge Lower Wolverton A256 Buckland of Dover
addlesworth Standen South Alkham Maxton A2 Calais
nghill C West St Radigunds Dunkirk
Peene Channel Capel Hougham Farthingloe DOVER
ington Tunnel le-Ferne Satmar A20 i
Terminal Battle of East Cliff &
11A Britain Warren Samphire Hoe Channel Tunnel (Rail)
12 Cheriton Battle of Britain Dover - Folkestone
Morehall 2 Memorial East Heritage Coast
Horn 13 Wear Bay
Street Sandgate FOLKESTONE i M
Seabrook A259
Lower
Hythe Leas

1
2
3
4
5
6
7
8

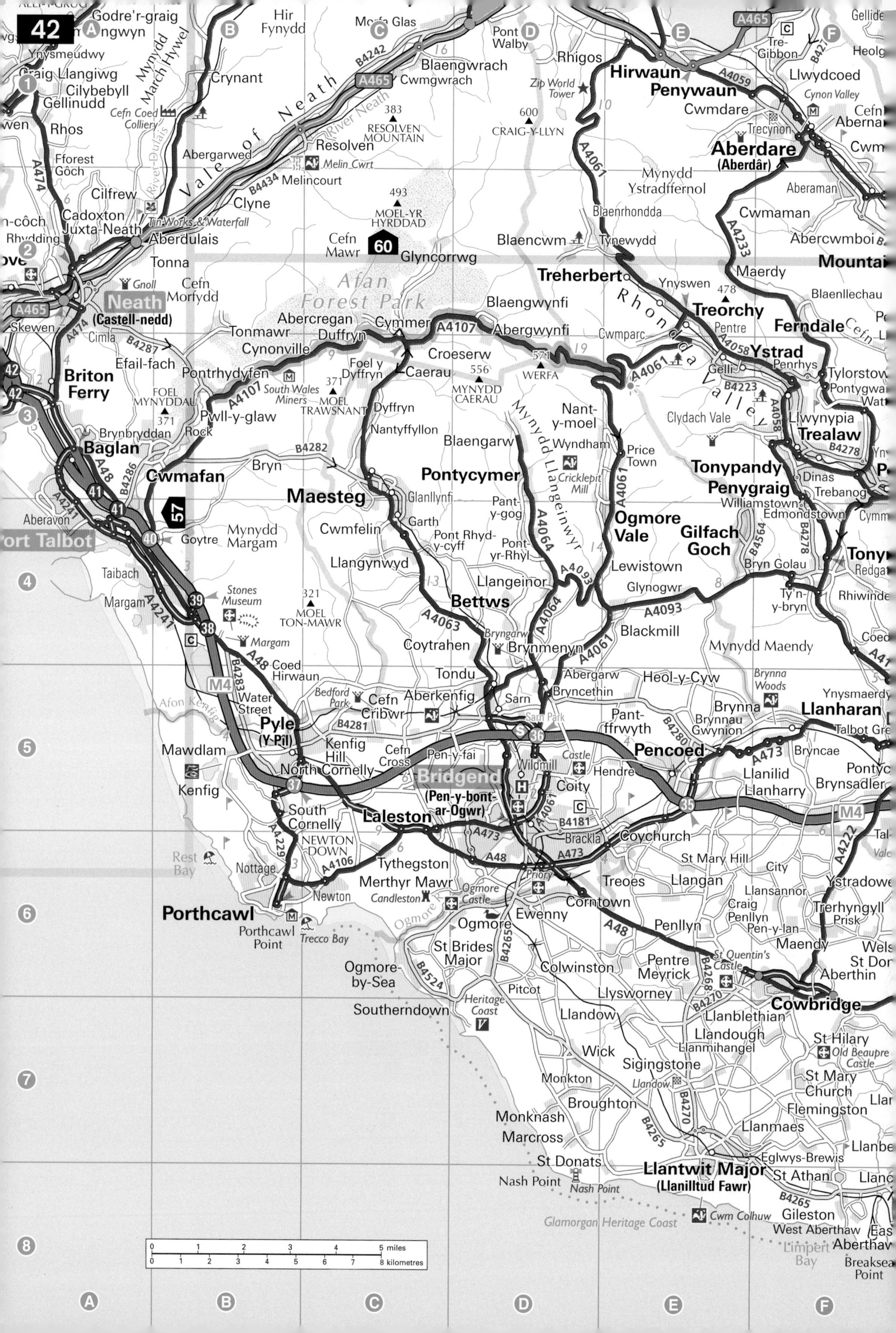

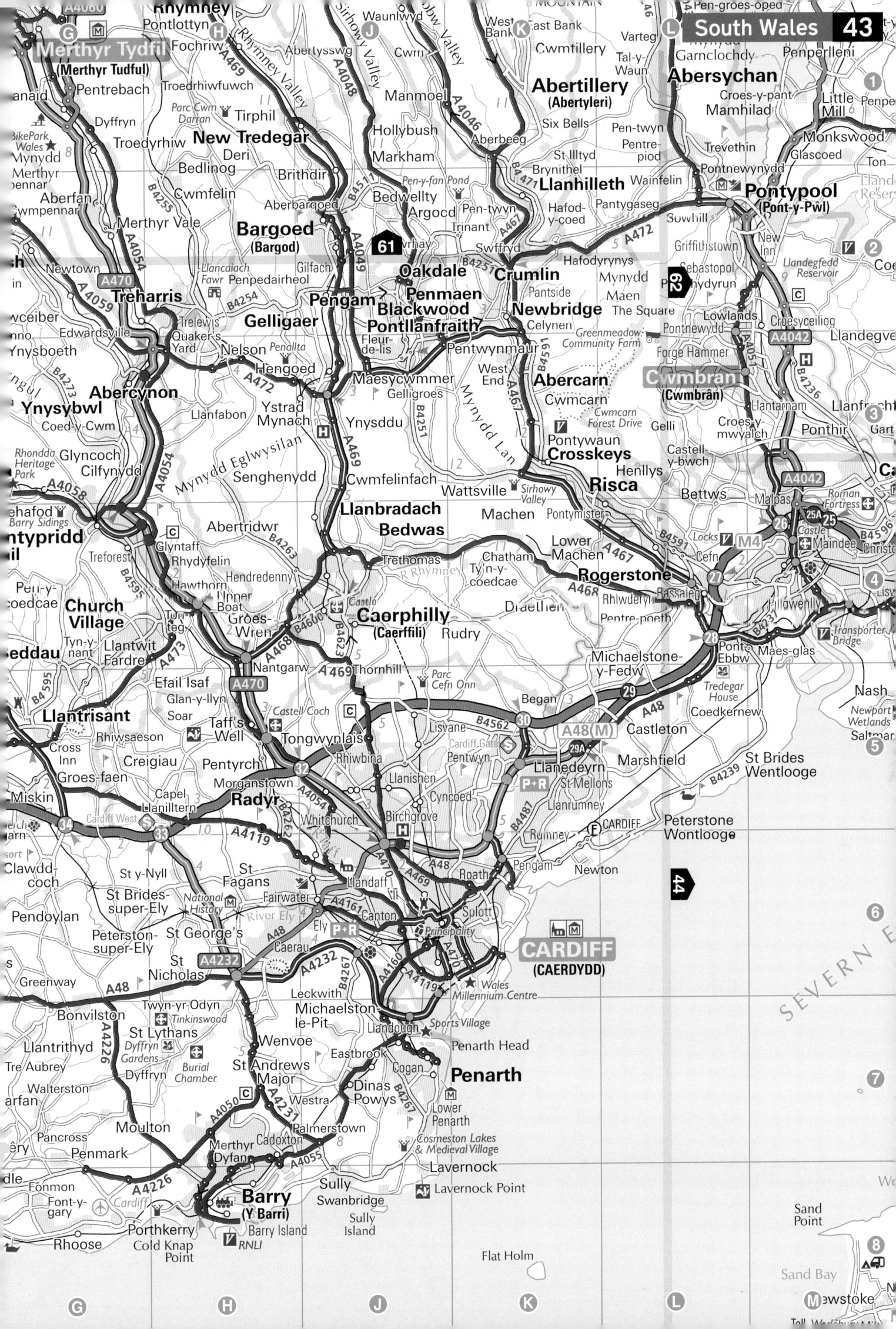

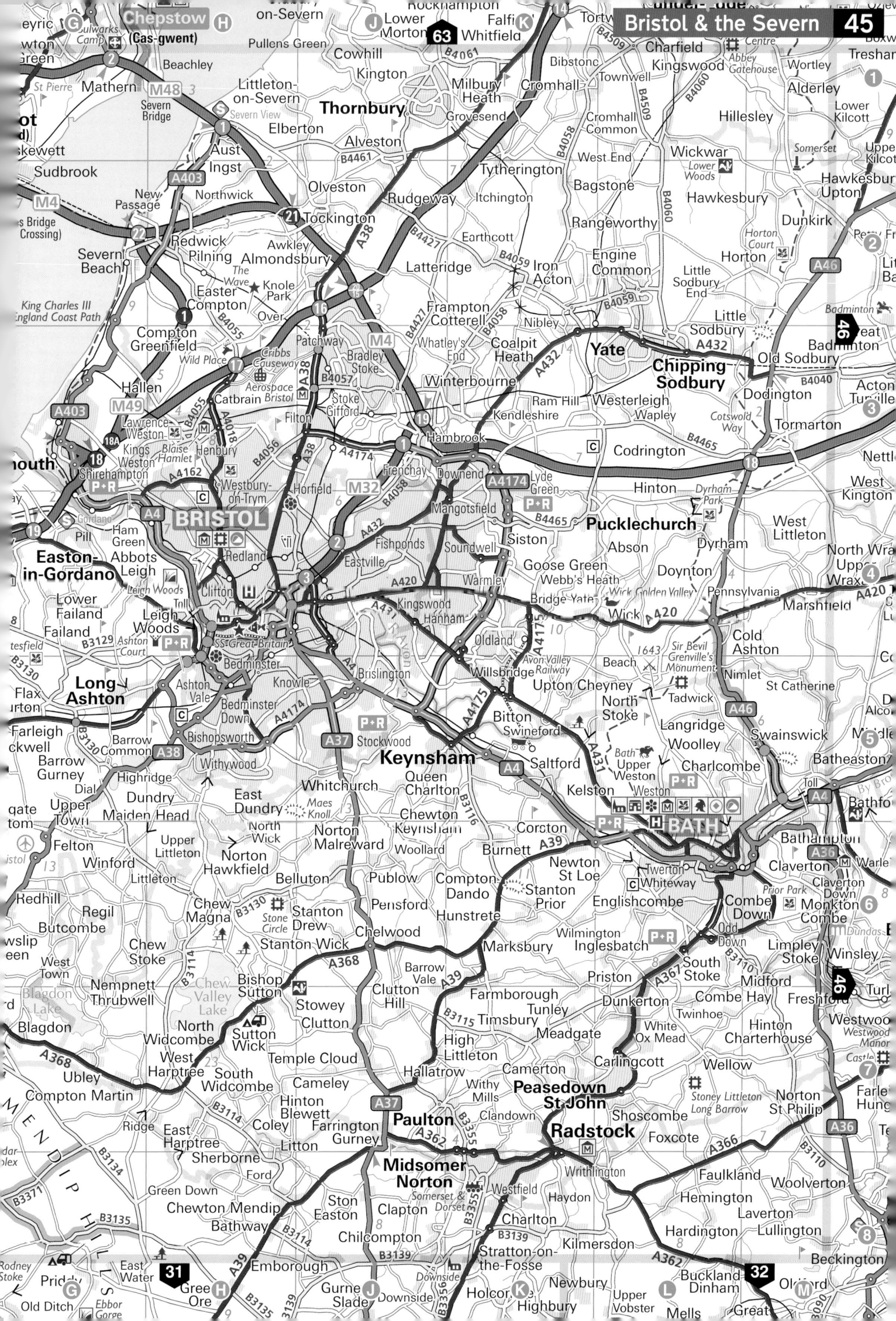

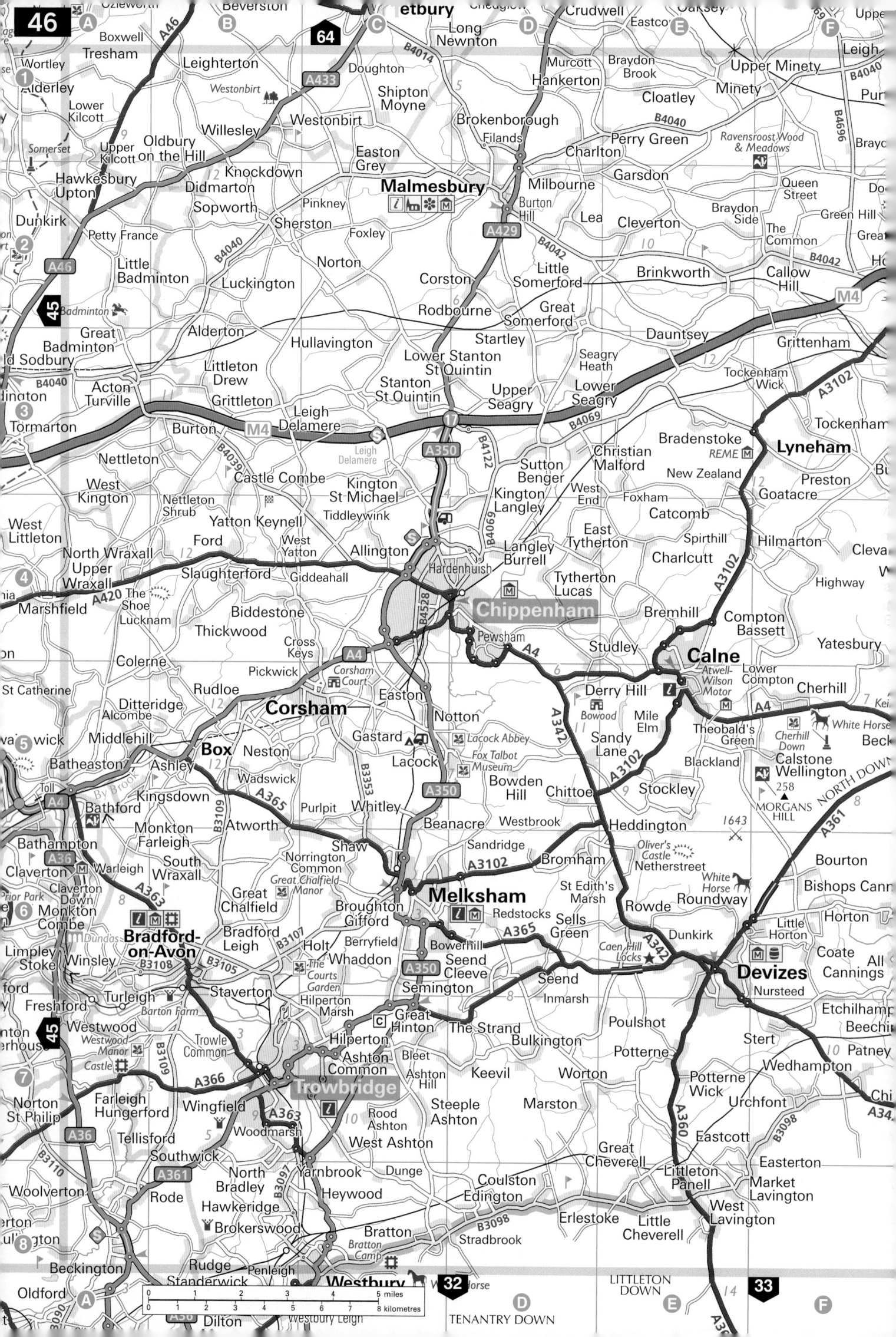

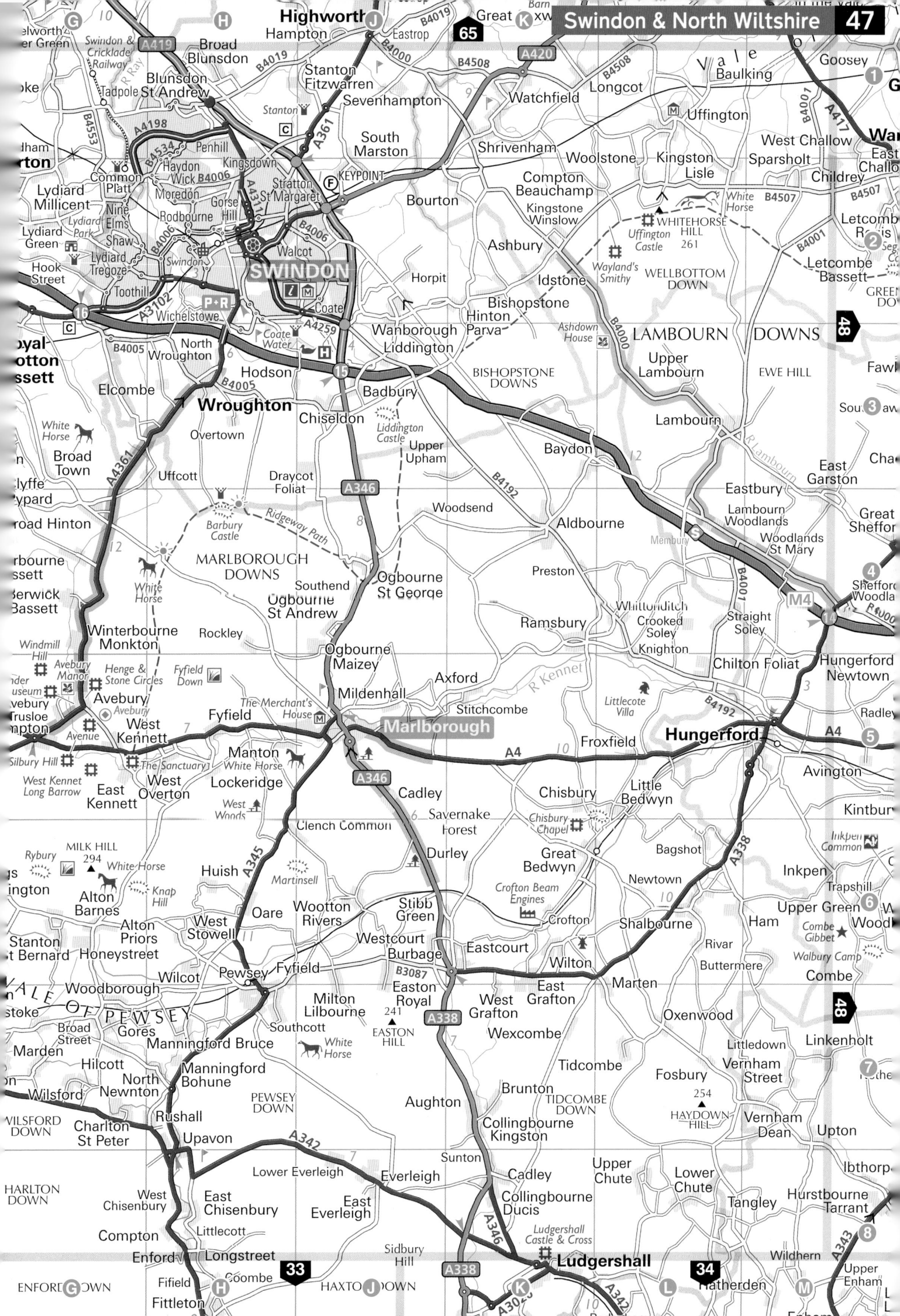

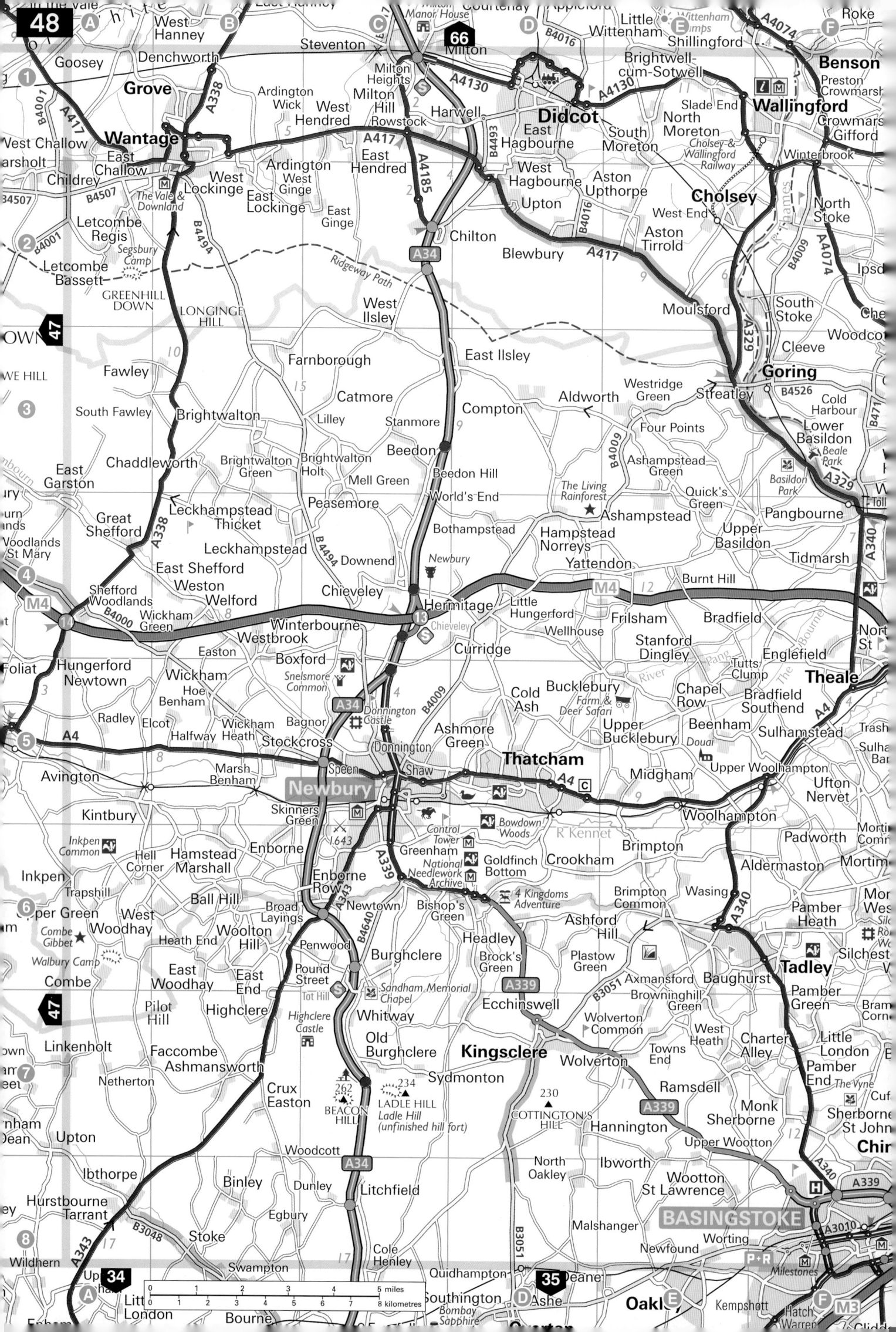

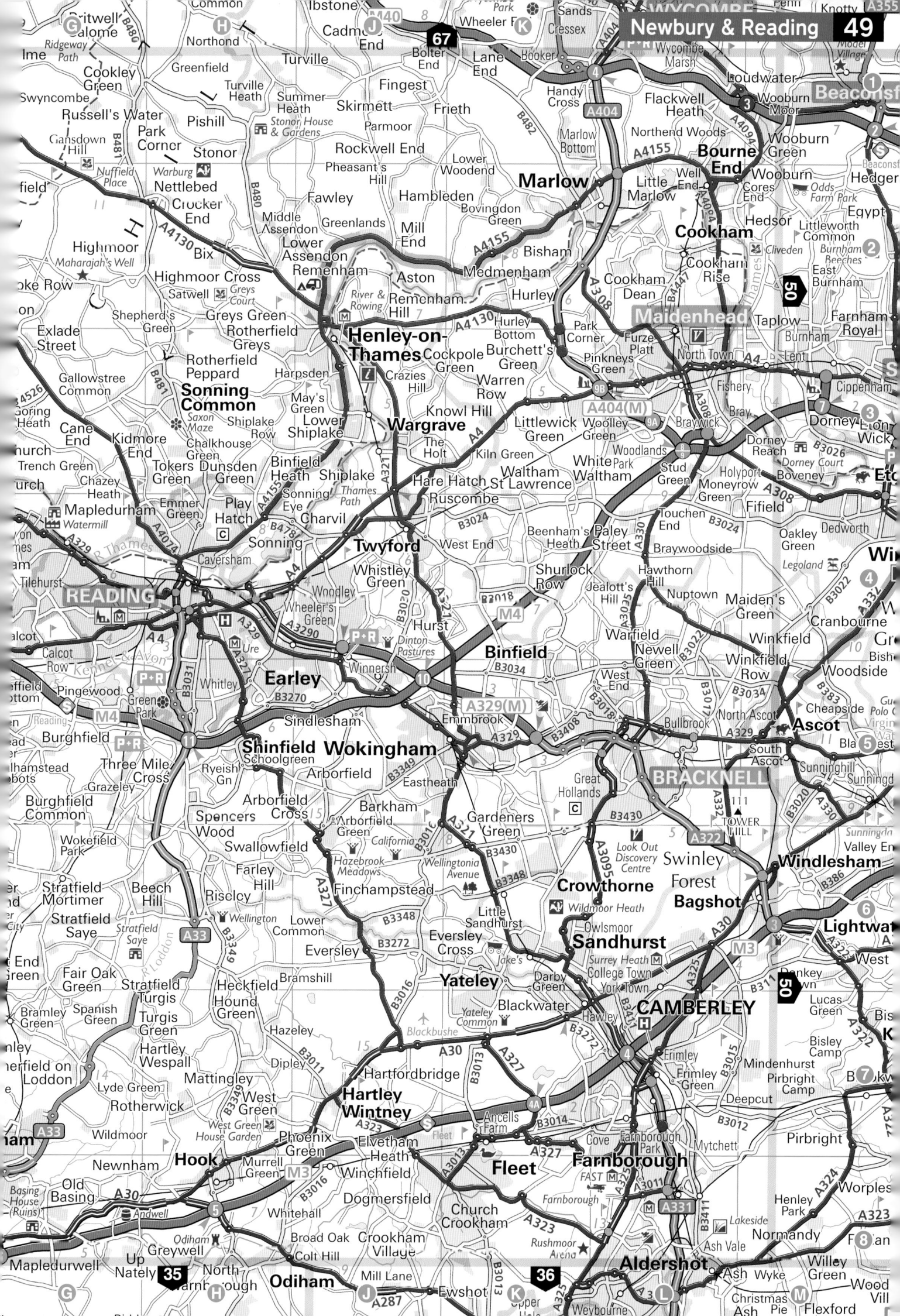

FOULNESS ISLAND

Potton Island

Ashingdon
Halesville
J
72

Hawkwell
G
71
A1245
gate
Wick
evendon
A129
H
Hockley
B1013
Hawkwell
Rayleigh
Stroud Green
Rochford
R. Roach
Barling
Great Stambridge
Ballan gore
RSPB

New Thundersley
A127
A130
A1015
Eastwood
Southend
Little Wakering
Great Wakering
B1017

Thundersley
A129
Daws Heath
A1159
Bournes Green
North Shoebury

Benfleet
A13
Belfairs Woodland
Prittlewell
H
C
Southchurch
Shoeburyness

Hadleigh
Leigh-on-Sea
Westcliff-on-Sea
A13
Thorpe Bay
East Beach

South nfleet
B1006
Hadleigh Castle
Leigh
B1016
Shoebury Ness

B1014
SOUTHEND-ON-SEA

Leigh Beck
Canvey Heights
Canvey Point

A130
Canvey Island

THAMES ESTUARY

3

PENINSULA
King Charles III
England Coast Path
Allhallows-on-Sea

St Mary's Hoo
Allhallows

Northward Hill
RSPB
Fenn Street
Lower Stoke
Isle of Grain
Grain
B2001

High Halstow
North Street
Middle Stoke
Stoke
Wallend
Sheerness
Marine Town
Minster Gatehouse
Minster-on-Sea

A228
Sharnal Street
Thamesport
Mile Town
East End
B2008
Kingsborough
Warden Point

Hoo St Werburgh
River Medway
Stangate Creek
A250
Halfway Houses
Mud Row
Warden

Broad Street
Lower Upnor
Upnor Castle
Nor Marsh
RSPB
Queenborough
Leysdown-on-Sea

Upper Upnor
Motney Hill
Rushenden
A2500
Eastchurch
B2231

The Historic Dockyard, Chatham
Riverside
RSPB
Ham Green
B2231
40
RSPB
Elmley Marshes
ISLE OF SHEPPEY
Leysdown Coastal Par

M
A289
Lower Rainham
Wetham Green
Halstow Creek
Elmley Island
Isle of Harty
The Swale

Fort Amherst
Grange
East Rainham
Lower Halstow
Iwade
A249
Elmley

GILLINGHAM
B2004
Upchurch
Kemsley
Sittingbourne-&-Kemsley Light Railway

HAM
A230
A2
Luton
Darland
Otterham Quay
Breach
Howt Green
C
Murston
The Swale
King Charles III
England Coast Pa

Capstone
Hempstead
Wigmore
Rainham
Moor Street
Hartlip
Newington
Key St
Bobbing
Milton Regis
Conyer
Uplees

Meresborough
Medway
Lower Hartlip
Chestnut Street
Chalkwell
Sittingbourne
Luddenham Court
Oare
Broom Street

Walderslade
S
M2
Hempstead
Breach
Borden
Bapchild
Teynham
A2
Deerton Street
Lewson Street
Faversham

Lords Wood
C
Lidsing
4
Guildstead
Hill Green
Danaway
Tunstall
Rodmersham
Stone Chapel
Davington
Goodnest

Bredhurst
Kemsley Street
Stockbury
Oad St
Hearts Delight
Higsted
40
Rodmersham Green
Rawling Street
Lynsted
Ospringe
Preston
2
7

Blue Bell Hill
Dunn Street
South Green
Silver Street
Bredgar
Bexon
Dungate
Erriottwood
M2
Painter's Forstal
Whitehill
6
Boughton

Westfield Sole
Tyland Barn
Swanton Street
Bicknor
Milstead
10
Newnham
North Street
Selling
7

Boarley
Boxley
Kent Event Centre
R
White Horse Wood
T
Doddington
Seed
Eastling
D
Sheldwich
Hogben's Hill
Gushmere
Crouch

Sandling
6
A249
Detling
Thurnham
Hucking
Wormshill
Frinsted
Ringlestone
Wichling
Tong
Throwley
Sheldwich Lees
Hickmans Green

39
Ware Street
Broad Street
West Street
Payden Street
Throwley Forstal
Leaveland
Badlesmere
Chilh

P+R
C
Grove Green
Bearsted
Hollingbourne
Woodside Green
Stalisfield Green
Shottenden

P+R
A20
Sutton Street
Eyhorne Street
Lenham
A20
Warren Street
A251
O

Willington
Otham
Leeds
Harrietsham
Lenham Heath
Stockbro Head
Challock
Molash
dre

Shepway
Otham Hole
B2163
Leeds
Broomfield
Leadingcross Green
Kingswood
Platts Heath
Sandway
Charing Hill
L
A252
Bilting

Boughton Green
Langley
Cock St
Langley Heath
Five Wents
Liverton Street
K
Charing
Charing Heath
M
dmersham

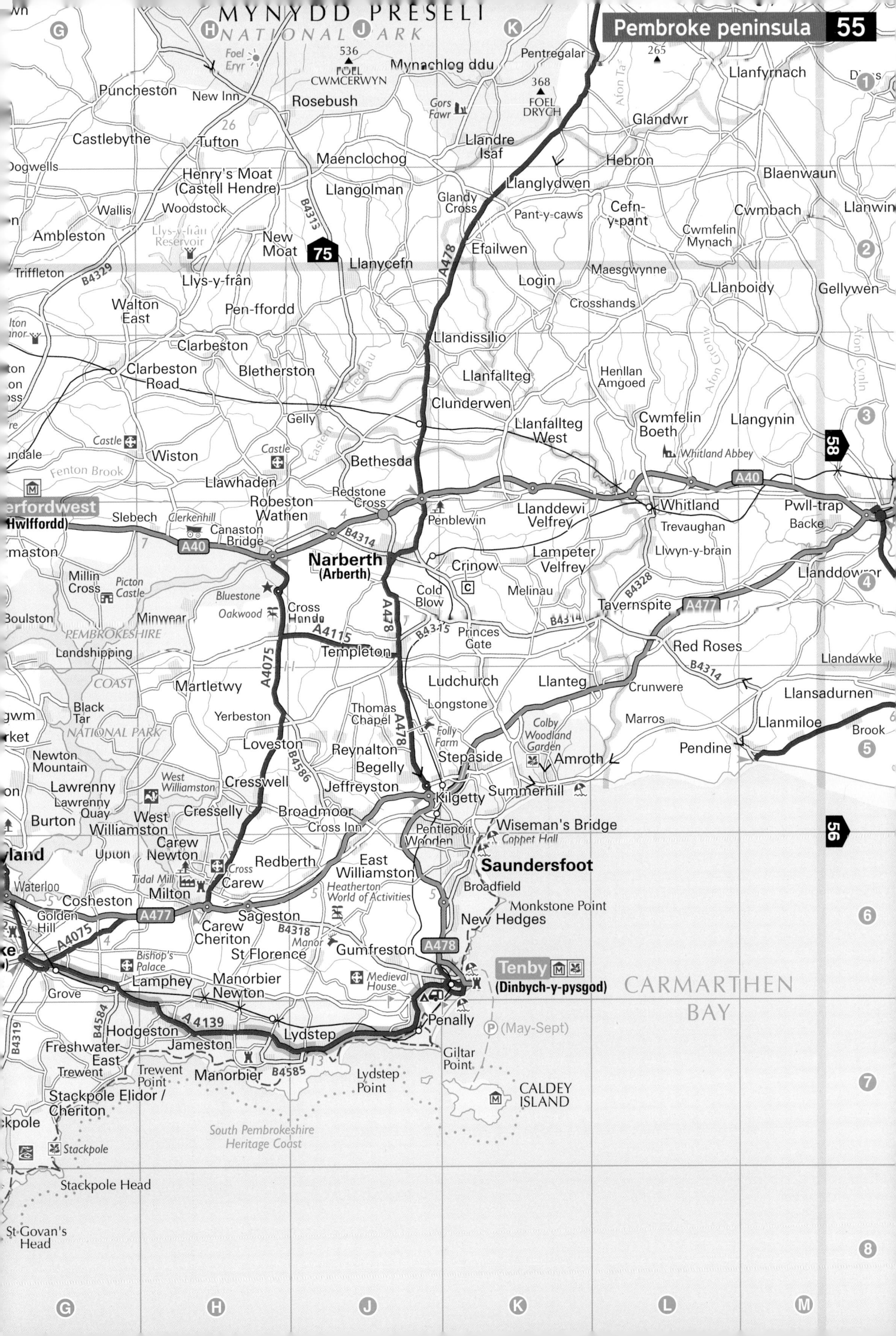

MYNYDD PRESELI
NATIONAL PARK

G   H   J   K

Foel
Eryr

Puncheston   New Inn   536   Mynachlog ddu   Pentregalar   265   Llanfyrnach
FOEL
CWMCERWYN

Castlebythe   Tufton   Rosebush   Gors   368   Glandwr
Fawr   FOEL
DRYCH

Dogwells   Henry's Moat   Maenclochog   Llandre   Hebron   Blaenwaun
(Castell Hendre)   Isaf

Wallis   Woodstock   Llangolman   Glandy   Cefn-   Cwmbach   Llanwin
Cross   Pant-y-caws   y-pant

Ambleston   Llanglydwen   Cwmfelin
Mynach

B4313   New   Efailwen   Maesgwynne   Llanboidy
Moat   A478   Login
Trifleton   B4329   75   Llanycefn   Crosshands   Gellywen

Llys-y-frân   Llandissilio
Reservoir

Walton   Pen-ffordd   Llanfallteg   Henllan   Llangynin
East   Llys-y-frân   Amgoed   58

Clarbeston   Bletherston   Clunderwen   Cwmfelin   A40
Boeth
Castle   Gelly   Llanfallteg   Whitland Abbey
Clarbeston   West
Road   Castle   Bethesda   Pwll-trap
Wiston   Whitland   A40
Fenton Brook   Llawhaden   Redstone   Backe
Cross   Llanddewi
Haverfordwest   Slebech   Clerkenhill   Canaston   Penblewin   Velfrey   Trevaughan   Llanddowror
(Hwlffordd)   Bridge   A40   Crinow   Lampeter   Llwyn-y-brain   A477
Narberth   Velfrey
Millin   Picton   (Arberth)   Cold   C   Melinau   B4328   Tavernspite   A477
Cross   Castle   Blow   Princes   B4314   Red Roses   Llandawke
Boulston   Minwear   Cross   B4315   Gate   Llanteg   Crunwere   Llansadurnen
Oakwood   Hands   A4115   Ludchurch   Marros   Llanmiloe
PEMBROKESHIRE   Templeton   Longstone   Colby   Pendine   Brook
Landshipping   A4075   Woodland
Garden
COAST   Martletwy   Thomas   Folly   Amroth
Black   Yerbeston   Chapel   Farm   Stepaside
Tar   A478   Summerhill
NATIONAL PARK   Reynalton   Wiseman's Bridge
Newton   Loveston   Begelly   Kilgetty   Coppet Hall
Mountain   B4586   Jeffreyston   Pentlepoir
Lawrenny   Cresswell   Broadmoor   Wooden   Saundersfoot
Lawrenny   Cresselly   Cross Inn   East   Broadfield
Quay   West   Williamston   Heatherton   Monkstone Point
Burton   Williamston   Carew   Redberth   World of Activities   New Hedges
Newton   Cross
Waterloo   Tidal Mill   Carew   Sageston   A478   CARMARTHEN
Cosheston   Milton   B4318   Tenby   BAY
A477   Manor   Gumfreston   (Dinbych-y-pysgod)
Golden   Carew   St Florence   Medieval
Hill   A4075   Cheriton   House
Lamphey   Bishop's   Manorbier   Penally
Grove   Palace   Newton   P (May-Sept)
A4139   Giltar
Hodgeston   Lydstep   Point
B4584   Jameston   B4318
Freshwater   Manorbier   B4585   Lydstep   CALDEY
East   Point   ISLAND
Trewent
Stackpole Elidor /   Trewent   Lydstep
Cheriton   Point   Manorbier   Point

Stackpole   South Pembrokeshire
Heritage Coast
Stackpole

Stackpole Head

St Govan's
Head

G   H   J   K   L   M

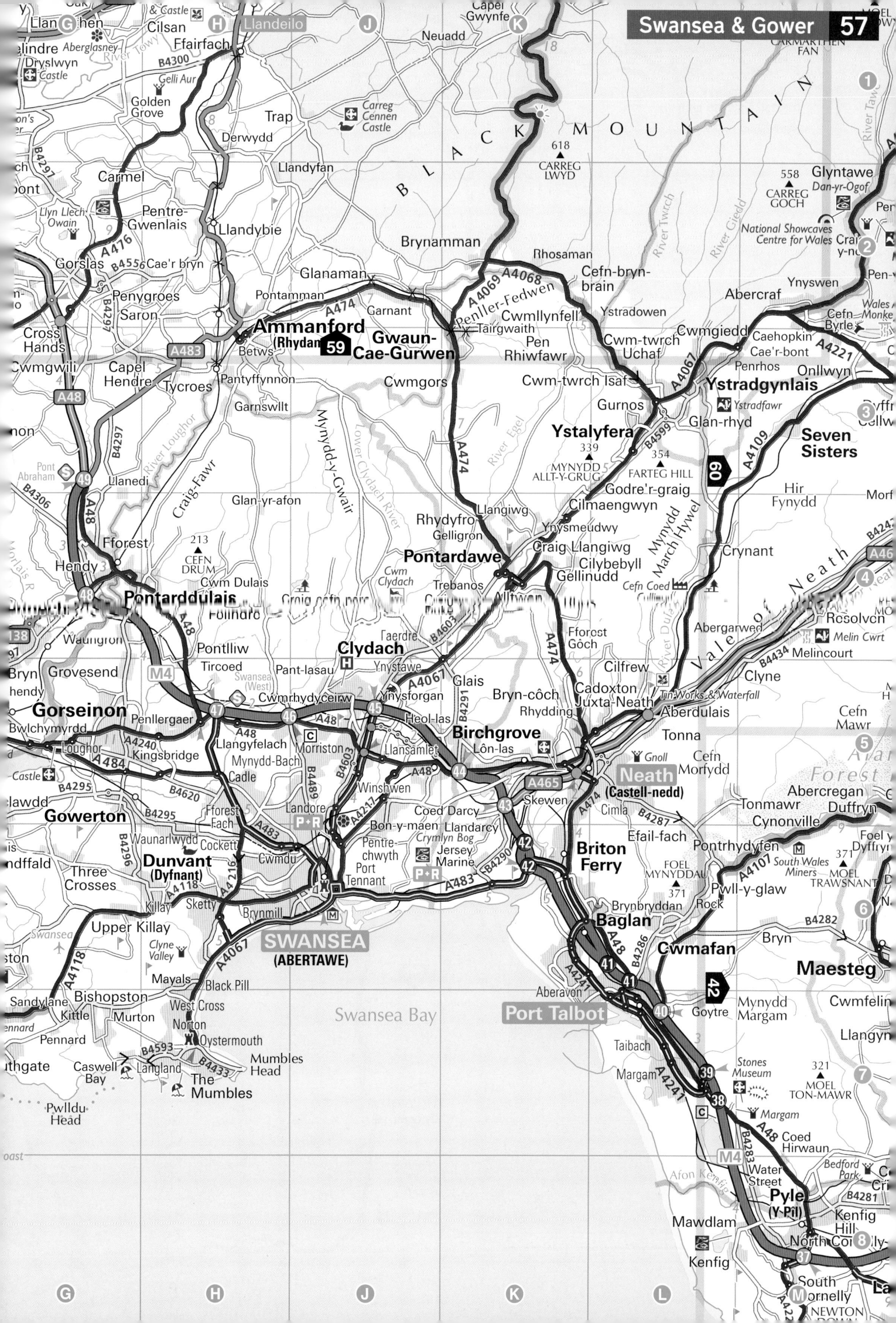

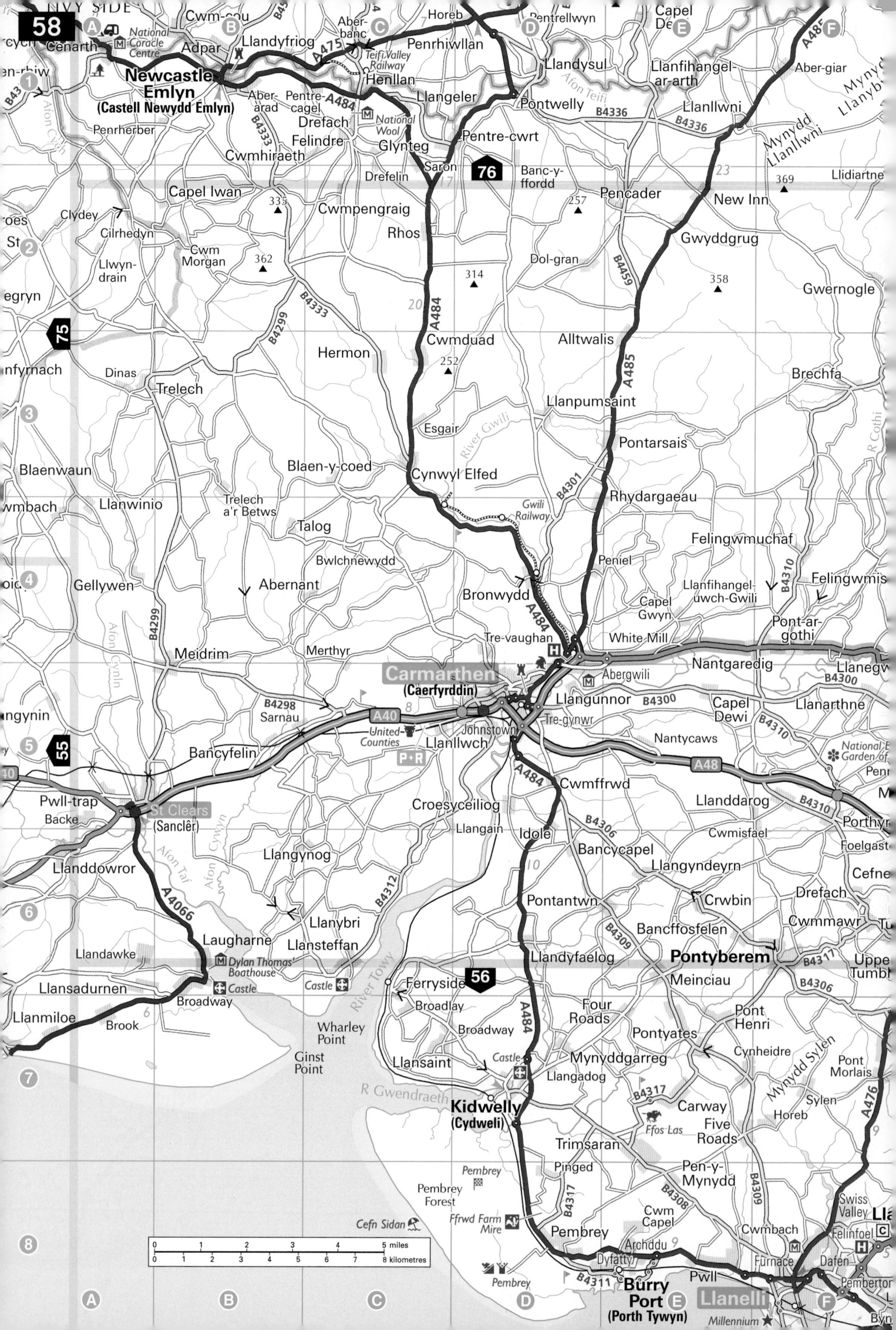

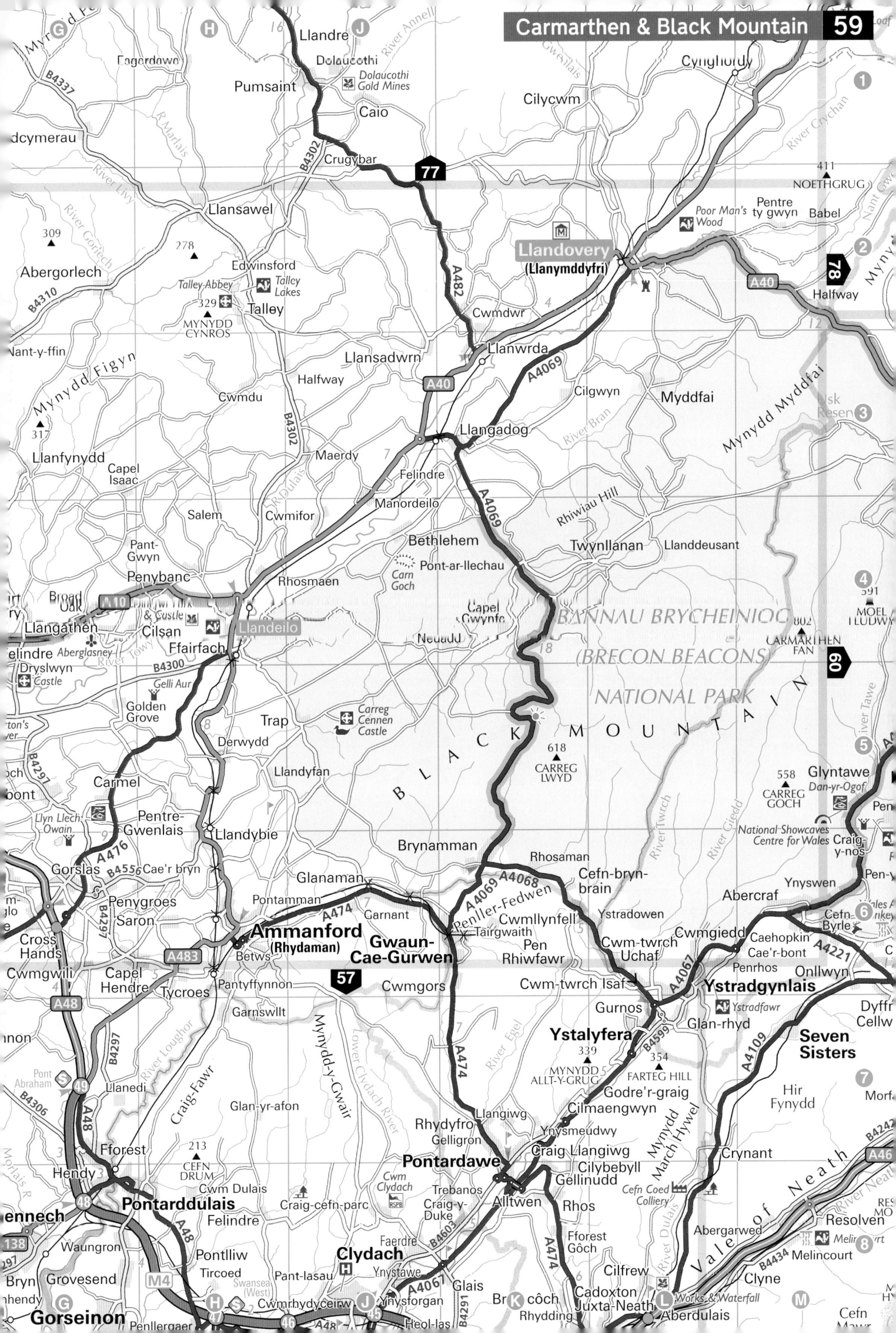

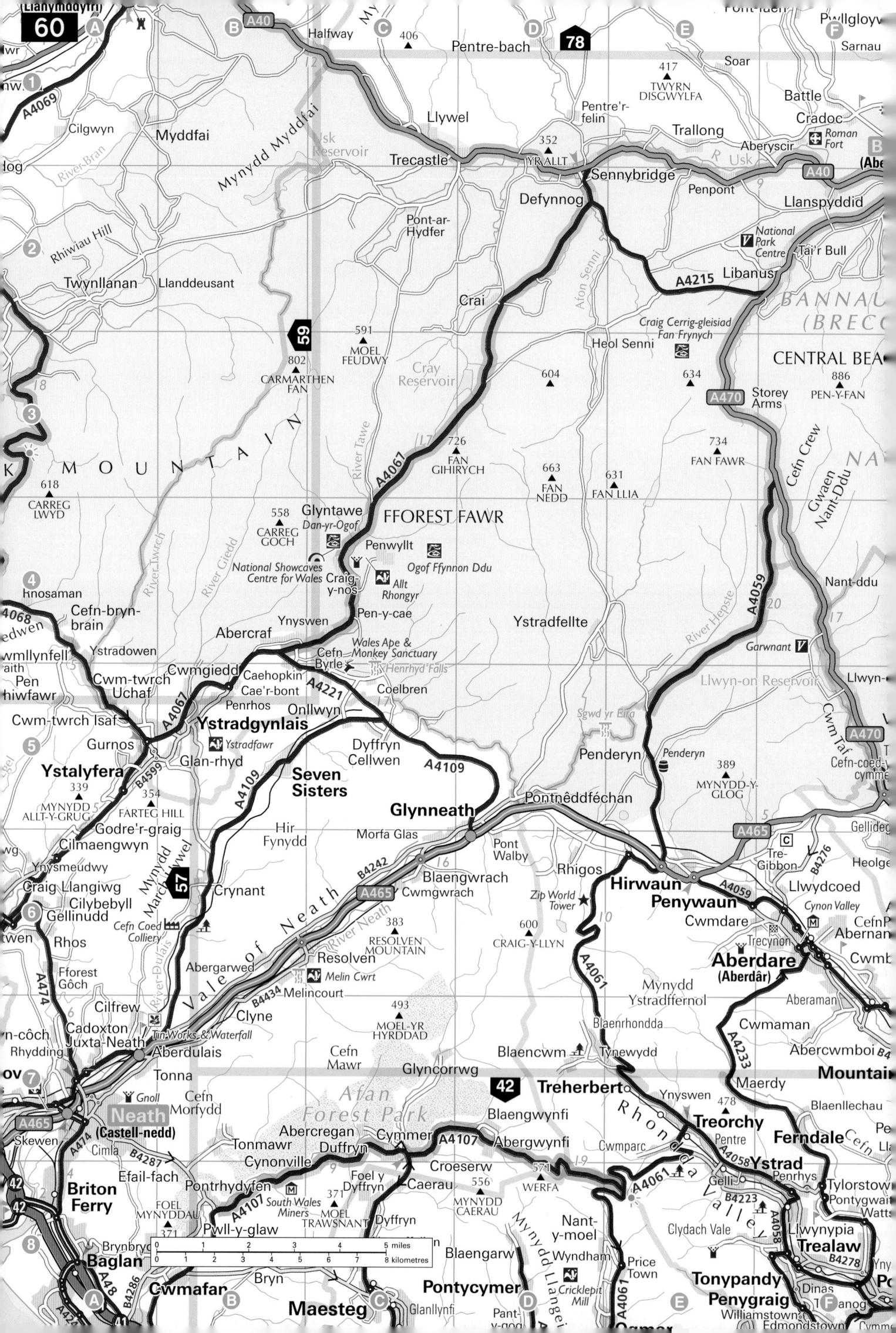

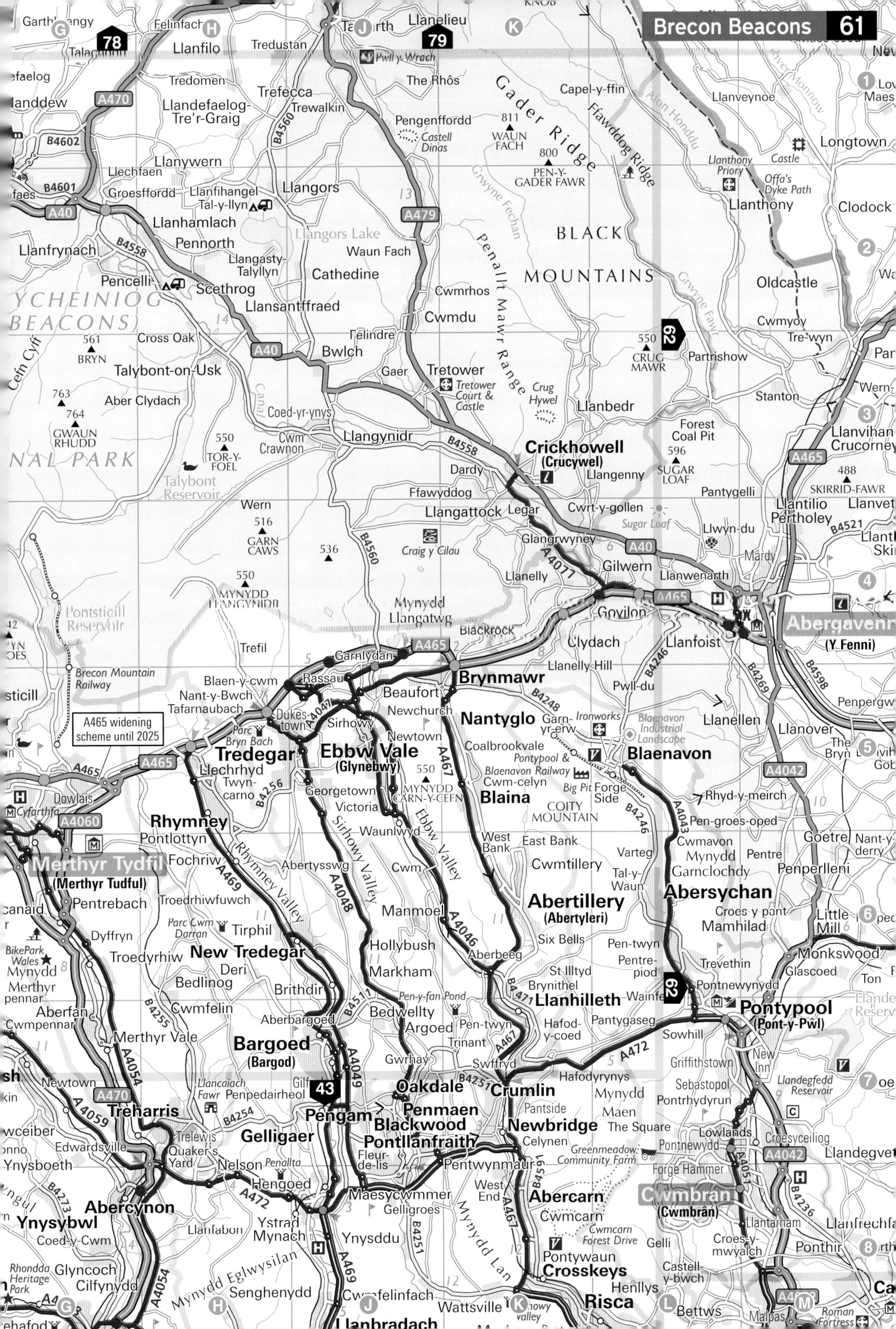

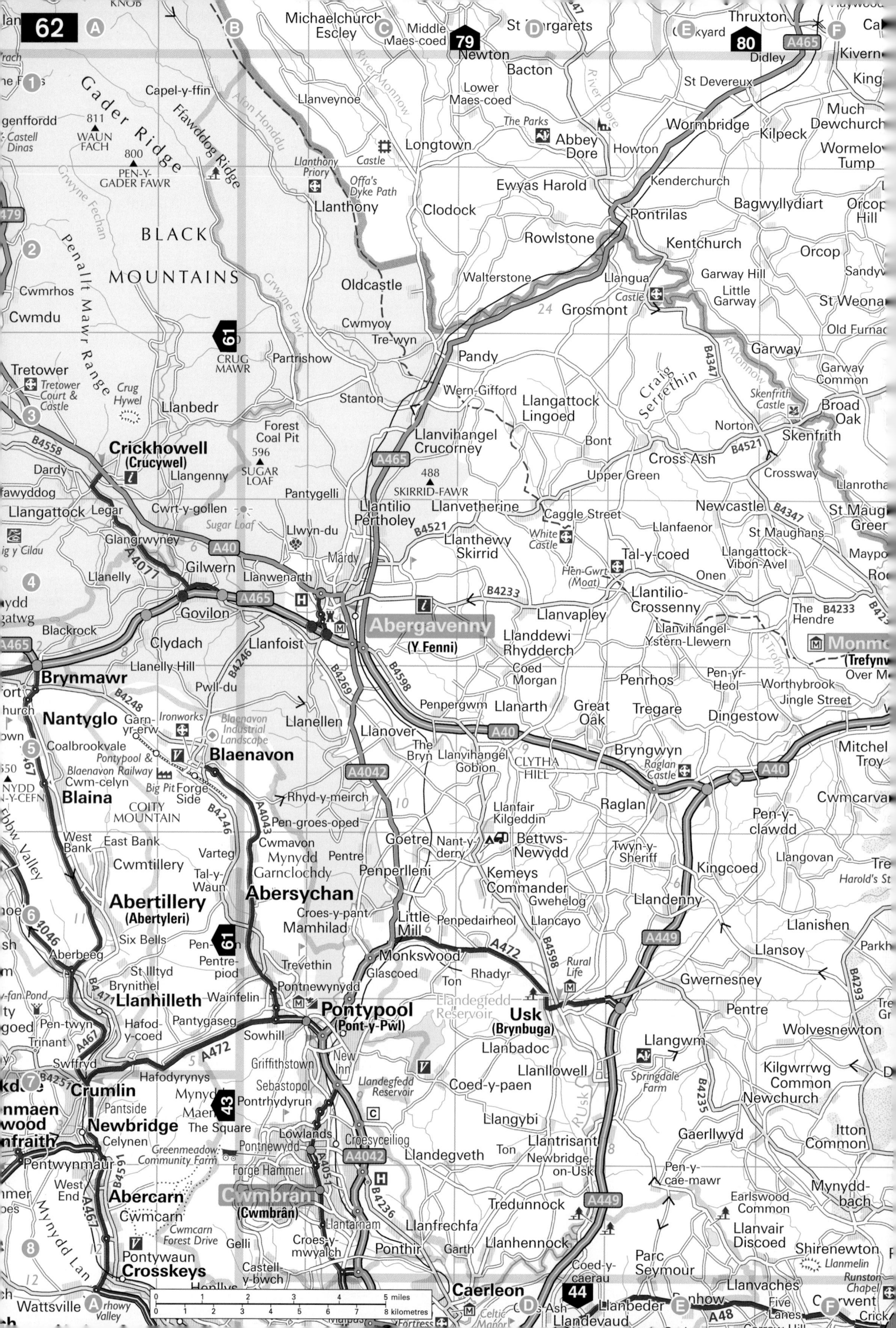

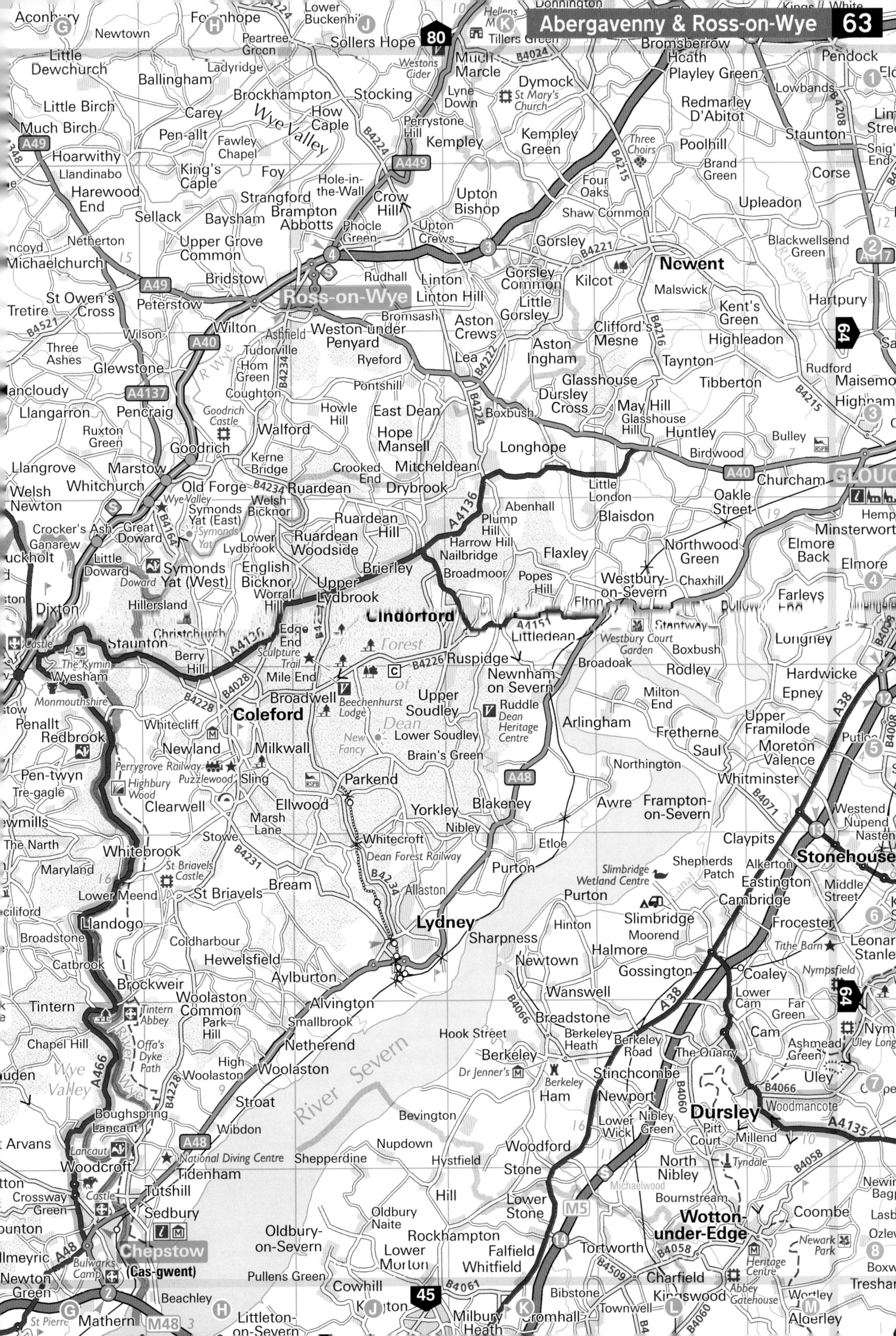

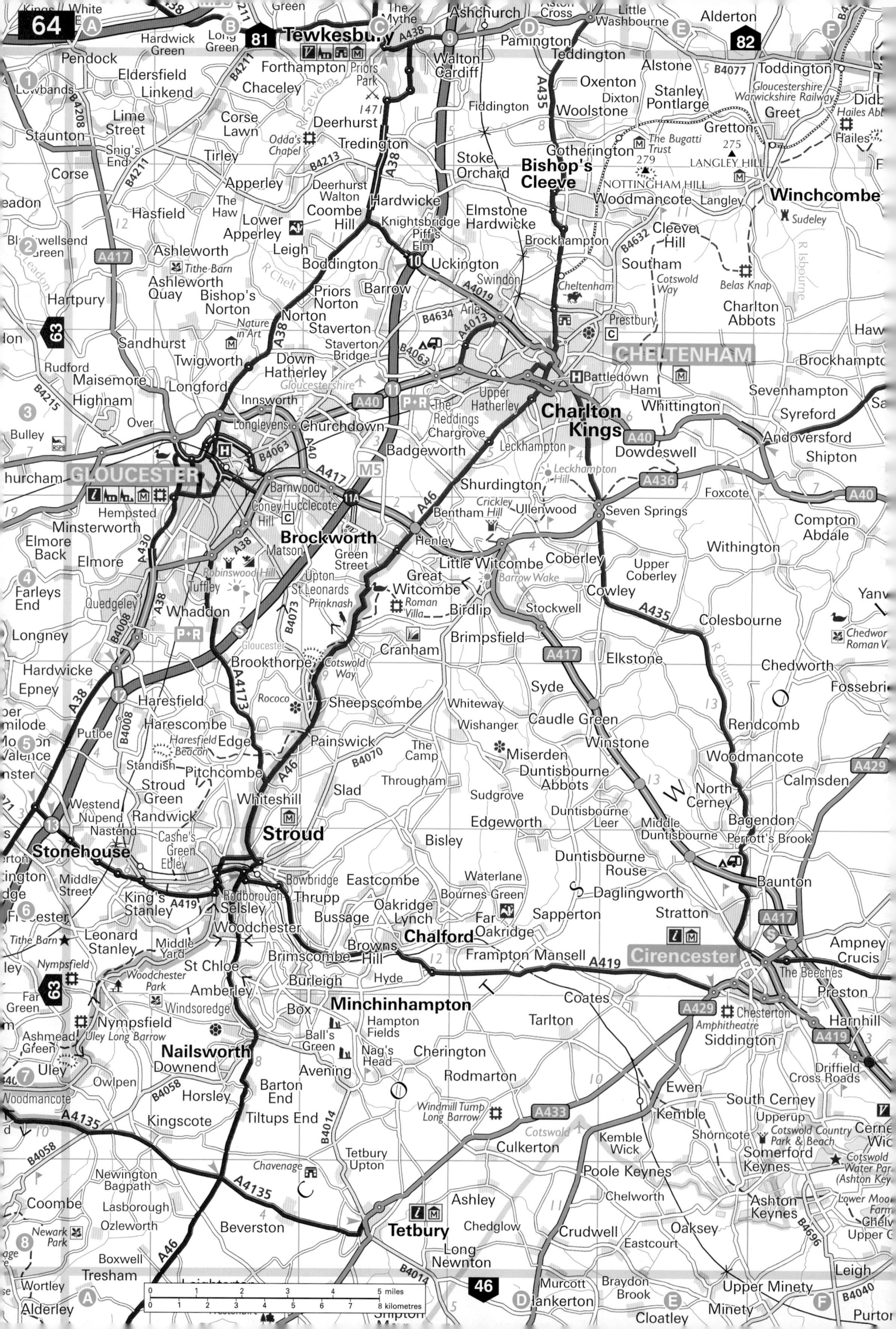

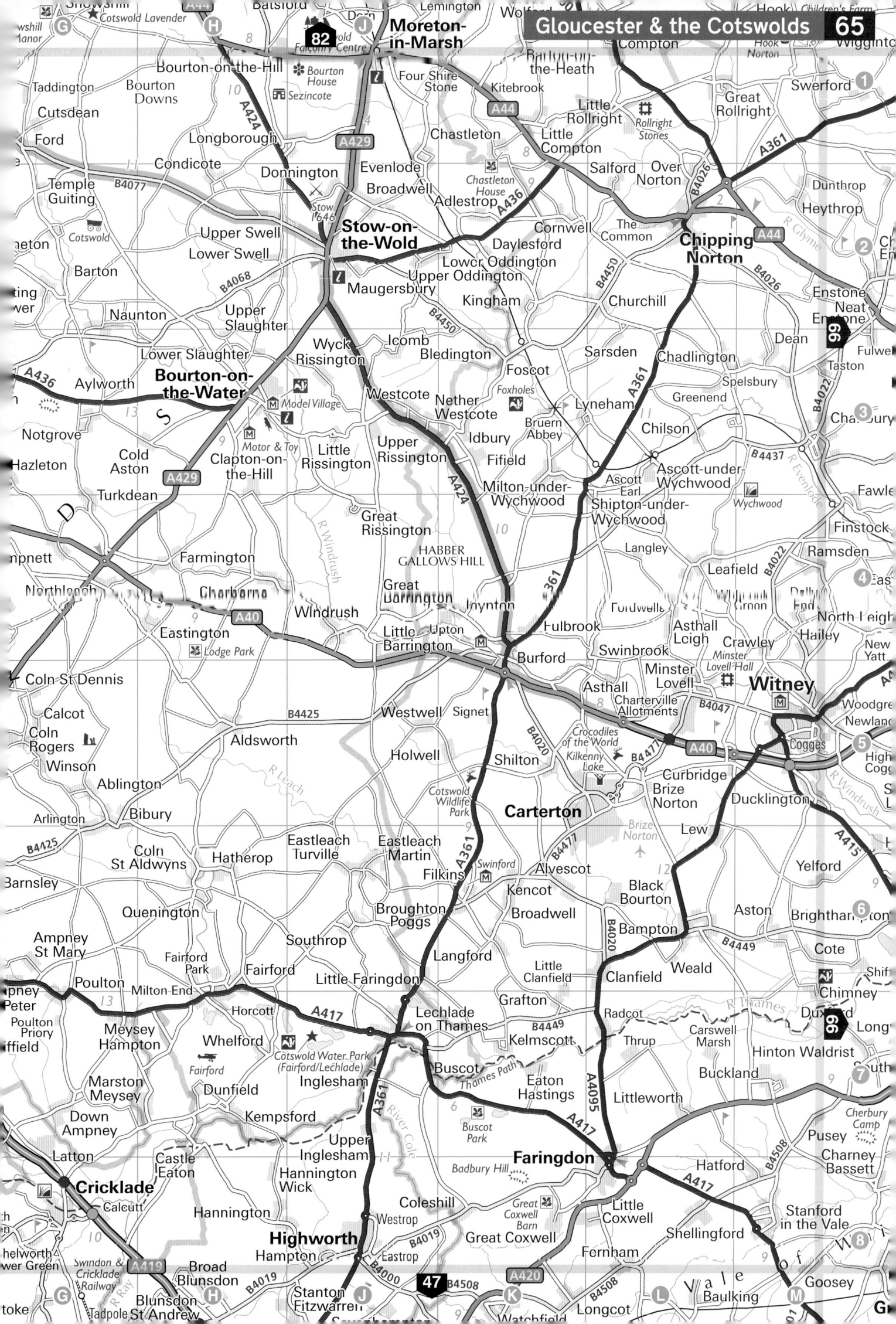

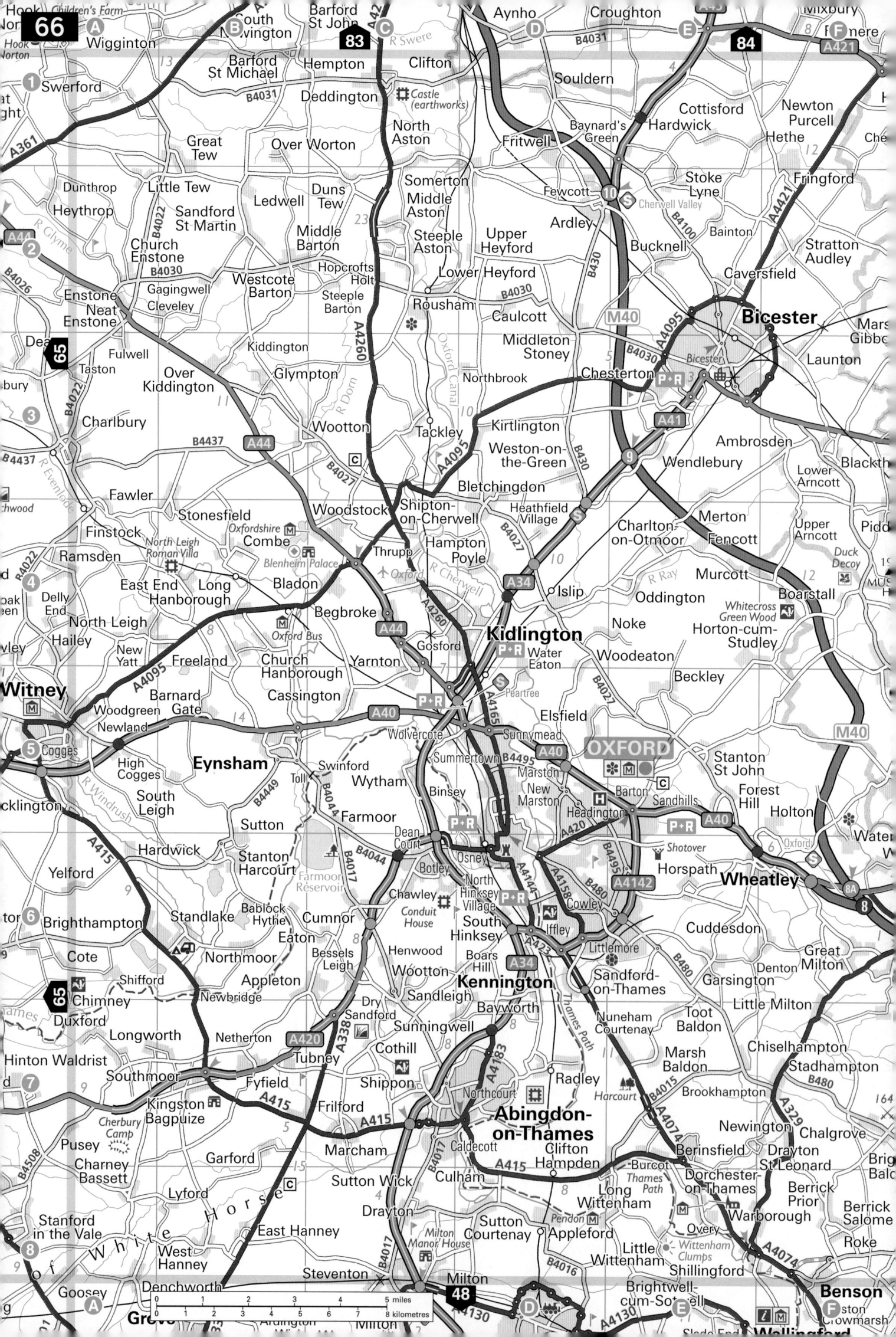

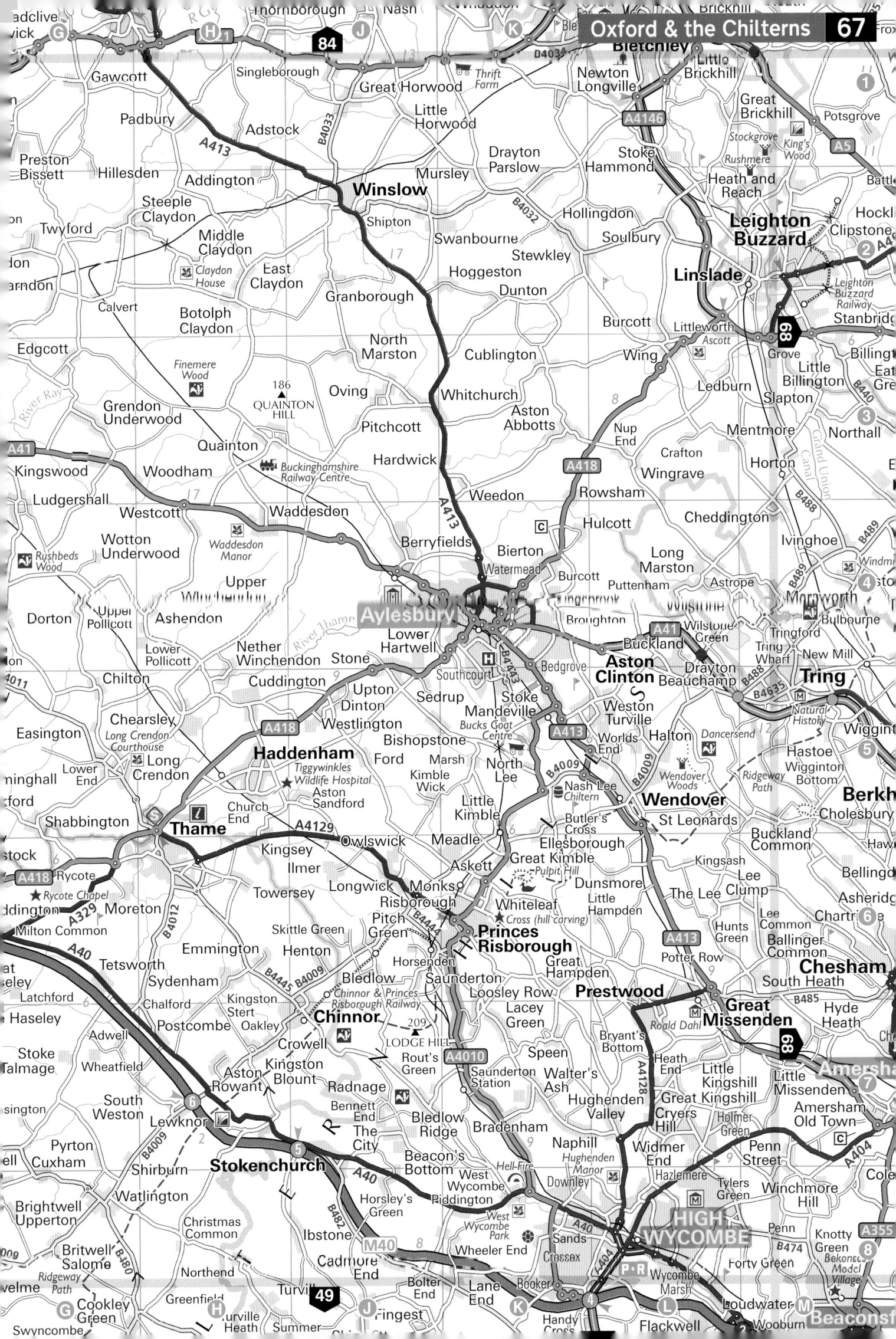

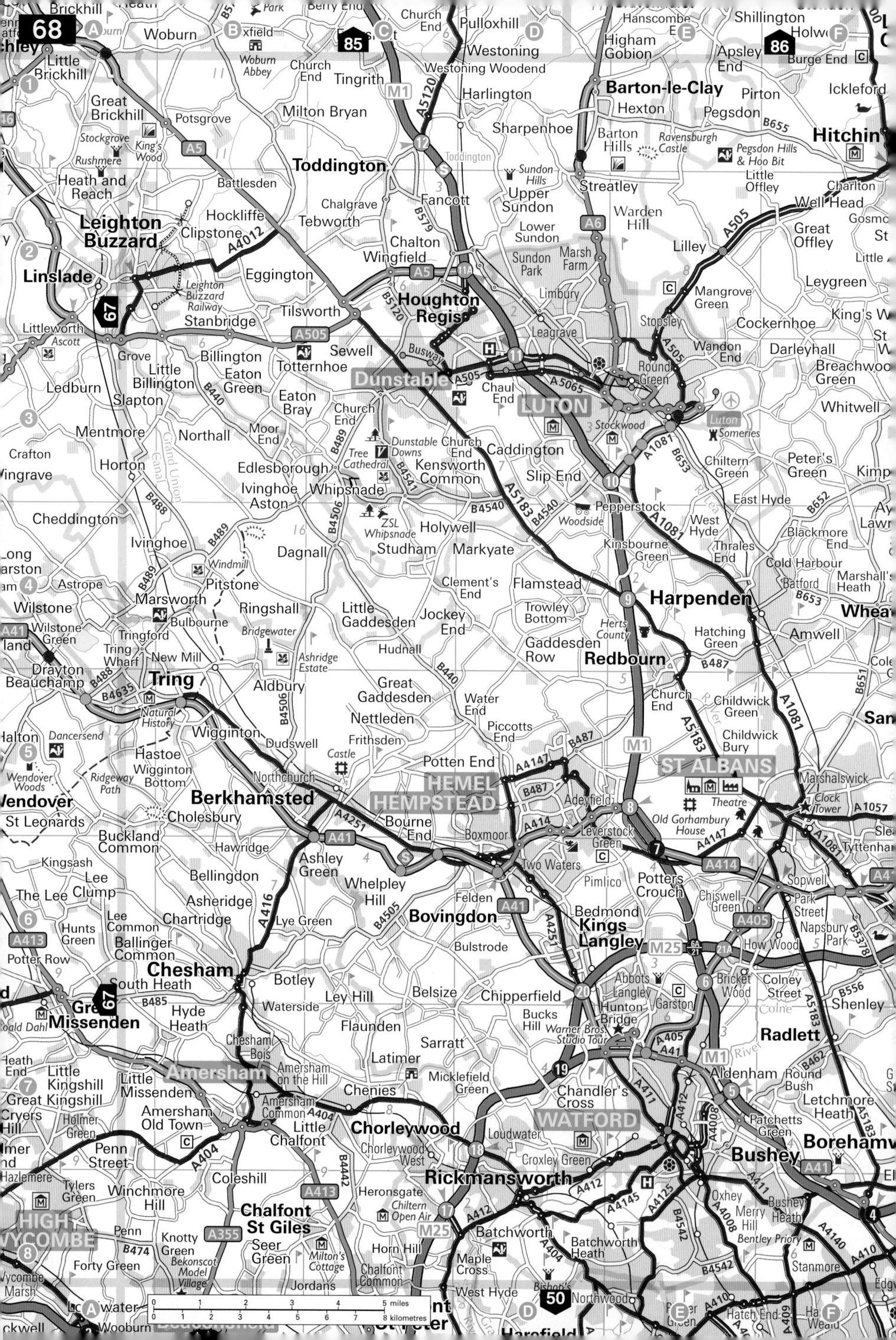

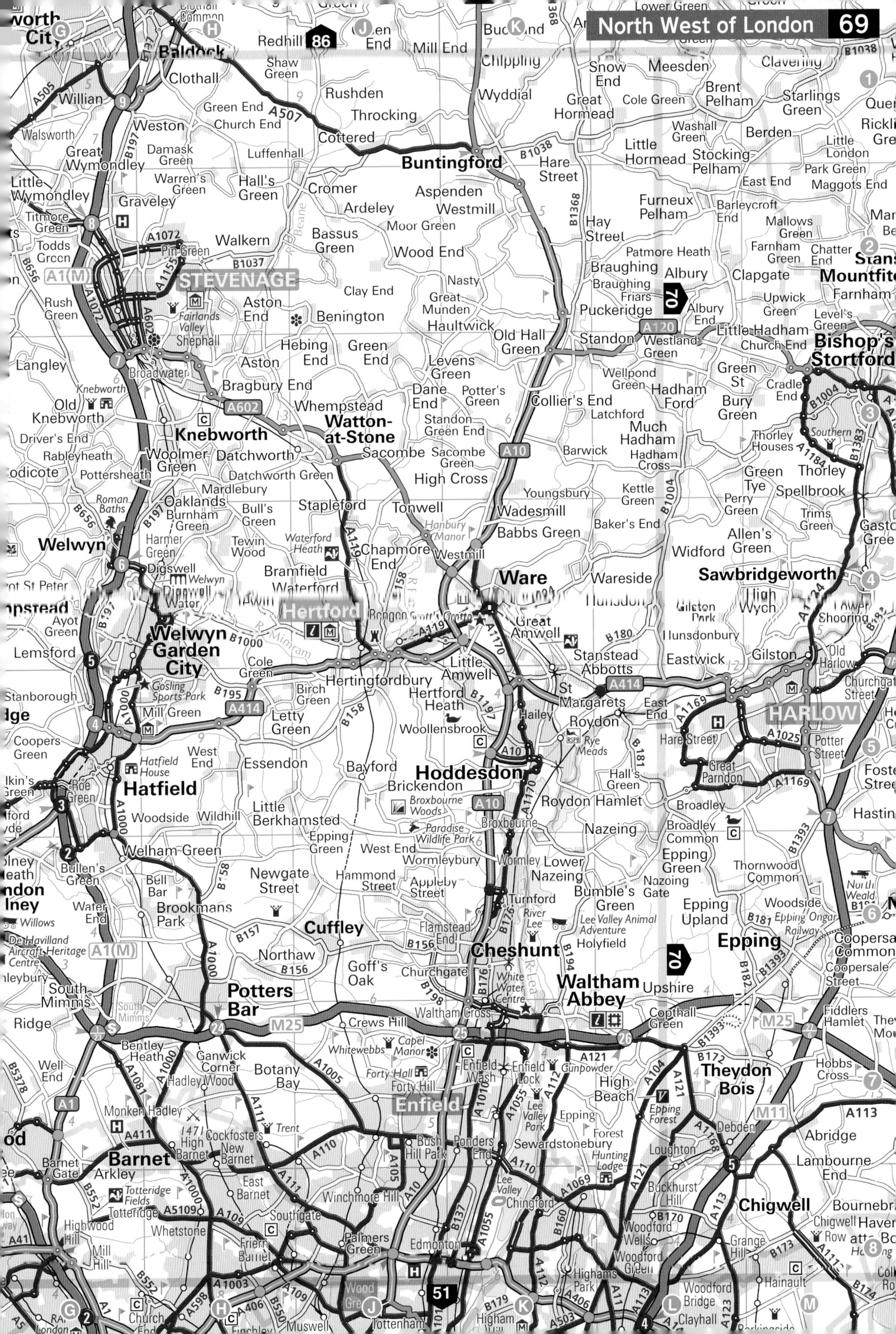

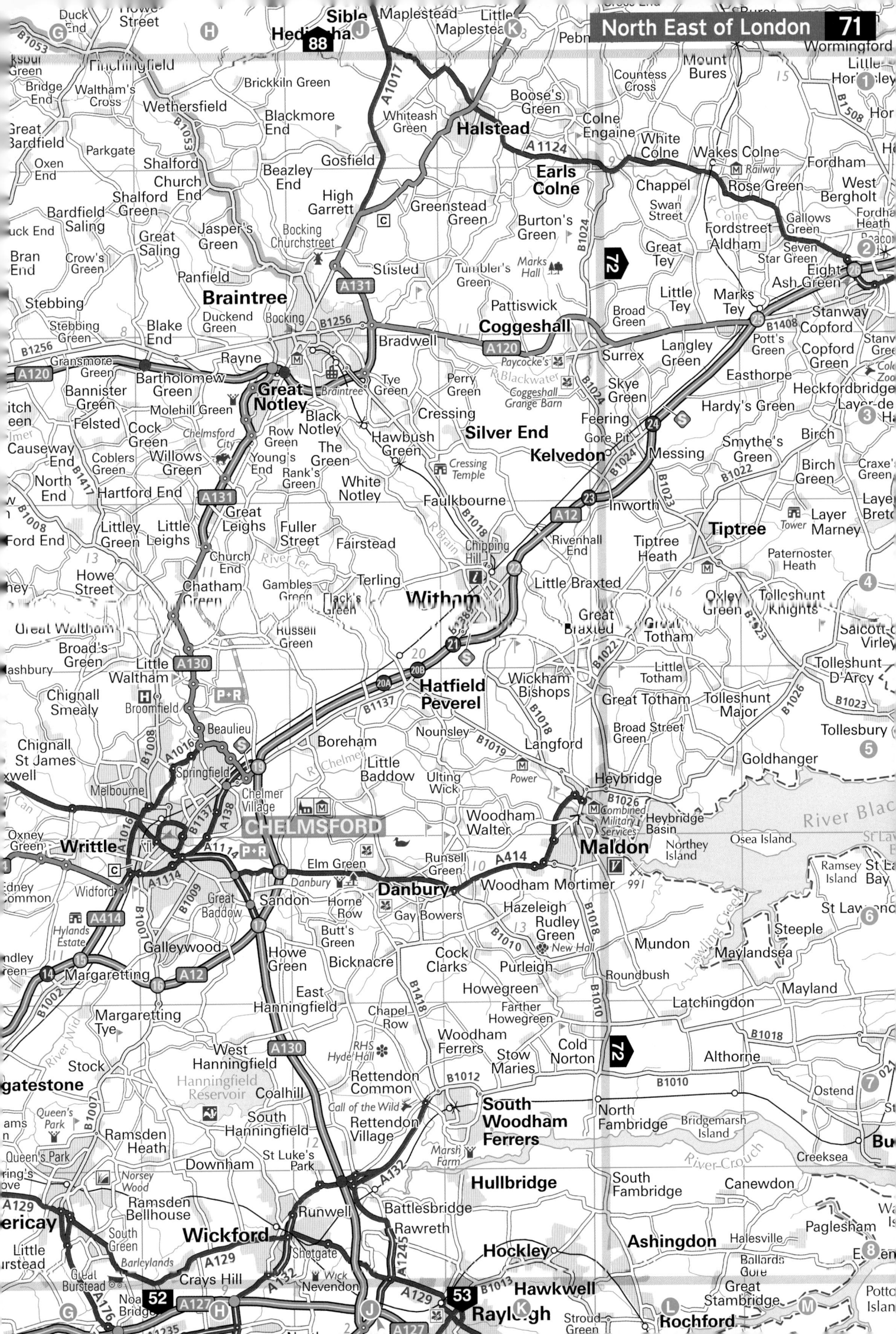

Brantham
Cattawade
Holbrook
International Ferry Terminal
Gate
The Redoubt
Felixstowe

River Stour
Wrabness
Parkeston Quay
Parkeston

Mistley Towers
Mistley
New Mistley
Stour Estuary
RSPB
Upper Dovercourt
Bath Side
Harwich Harbour
Landguard Fort

ingtree
Bradfield
Mistley Heath
Ramsey
Dovercourt
Landguard Point

awford
Little Bromley
Bradfield Heath
A120
Little Oakley
Harwich

B1035
Horsleycross Street
Wix

Horsley Cross
Wix Green
Stones Green
Great Oakley

Tendring Heath
Great Bromley
Little Bentley

Pennyhole Bay

Hook of Holland

Tendring Green
Goose Green
B1414

Hare Green
A133
Beaumont
Horsey Island
Hamford Water

B1035

Frating Green

Tendring
Thorpe Green
Thorpe-le-Soken
The Naze & Tower
The Naze

Frating
Great Bentley
C
Weeley
Kirby-le-Soken
B1034

stead Row
S
B1033
Kirby Cross
Walton-on-the-Naze

ford
B1441
Weeley Heath
B1033

Aingers Green
B1414
Frinton-on-Sea

Thorrington
A133
Cook's Green
B1032

Little Clacton
Great Holland

Samson's Corner
B1442
Great Clacton
Holland Haven

Hurst Green

B1027
Holland-on-Sea

sea
St Osyth
Rush Green

CLACTON-ON-SEA

Point Clear
Jaywick
B1032

Colne Point

Colne Point

G   H   J   K   L   M

G   H   J   K

1

2

3

Ceredigion Heritage Coast

Cardigan Island

Mwnt Beach   Parcllyn

Pe

Tresa
Aberporth

B4333

Cardigan Island Coastal Farm   Y Ferwig   Blaenannerch

A487

Gwbert on Sea   Penparc   Tremain   Blaenpor

Poppit Sands   **76**

B4546   B4548   Beula

Pembrokeshire Coast Path   Abbey & Coach House   **Cardigan**   B4570

St Dogmaels   **(Aberteifi)**   Ponthirv

Llangoedmor

St Dogmaels Moylegrove Heritage Coast   Bridgend   Welsh Wildlife Centre   Llechryd   Llandygwydd

Ceibwr Bay   A484

Pen-y-bryn   Teifi Marshes   *Afon Teifi*   **TIVY SIDE**

Moylegrove   Castle

Monington   Cilgerran   Abercych   Nat Cor Cen

Trwyn y bwa   Llantood   Genarth

Glanrhyd   Bridell   Pen-rhiw   Ve

Dinas Head Heritage Coast   B4582   Rhoshill   A332   **(Castell**

DINAS HEAD   Gethsemane   Nevern   Pontgarreg   Pengelli Forest   Nowchapel   Ponrhorbo

Newport Bay   Berry Hill   Felindre   A487   Cylwyswrw   Blaenffos   Boncath

Dinas Henllan   Parrog   Newport   Farchog   Castell Henllys   B4332   Whitechurch

A487   Dinas Cross   Carreg Coetan   Pontygynon   Llanfair-Nant-Gwyn   Bwlch-y-groes   Clydey

guard   Mynydd Melyn   Pentre Ifan   Crosswell   Pontyglasier   Star   Cilrhedy

rgwaun)   311   MYNYDD CAREGOG   Llwyndrain

Llanychaer   Penlan Uchaf   Brynberian   Crymych   Tegryn

Cwm Gwaun   Tafarn-y-bwlch   Foel Drygarn   Hermon

Pontfaen   **PEMBROKESHIRE COAST**   A478

cwn   B4329   *NATIONAL PARK*   Pentregalar   265   Llanfyrnach   **58**   Dinas

MYNYDD PRESELI   Foel Eryr   536   Mynachlog ddu

Puncheston   FOEL CWMCERWYN   368   Glandwr   6

New Inn   Rosebush   Gors Fawr   FOEL DRYCH

Castlebythe   Tufton   Llandre Isaf   Hebron   Blaenwaun

t Dogwells   Maenclochog   Llanglydwen   Cefn-y-pant   Cwmbach   Llanwir

Henry's Moat (Castell Hendre)   Llangolman   Glandy Cross   Pant-y-caws   Cwmfelin Mynach

Wallis   Woodstock   B4313   Efailwen   Maesgwynne   Llanboidy   Gellyw

Ambleston   Llys-y-frân Reservoir   New Moat   **55**   Login   7

Trifleton   B4329   Llanycefn   Crosshands

colton Manor   Llys-y-frân   A478

xton   Walton East   Pen-ffordd   Llandissilio

ston   Clarbeston Road   Bletherston   Llanfallteg   Henllan Amgoed   Llangynin

Cross   Gelly   Clunderwen   Llanfallteg West   Cwmfelin Boeth

shire   Castle   Castle   Dethesda   Whitland Abbey   8

Castle   Wiston   Redstone   A40

Fenton Brook   Llawhaden   Penblewin   hitland   P M-trap

rundale   Llanglydwen   Robeston Wathen   Racke

verford Gest   Slebech   Clerkenhil   Klanddewi Velfrey   Truy

(Hwlffordd)   J   ss   K   L   M

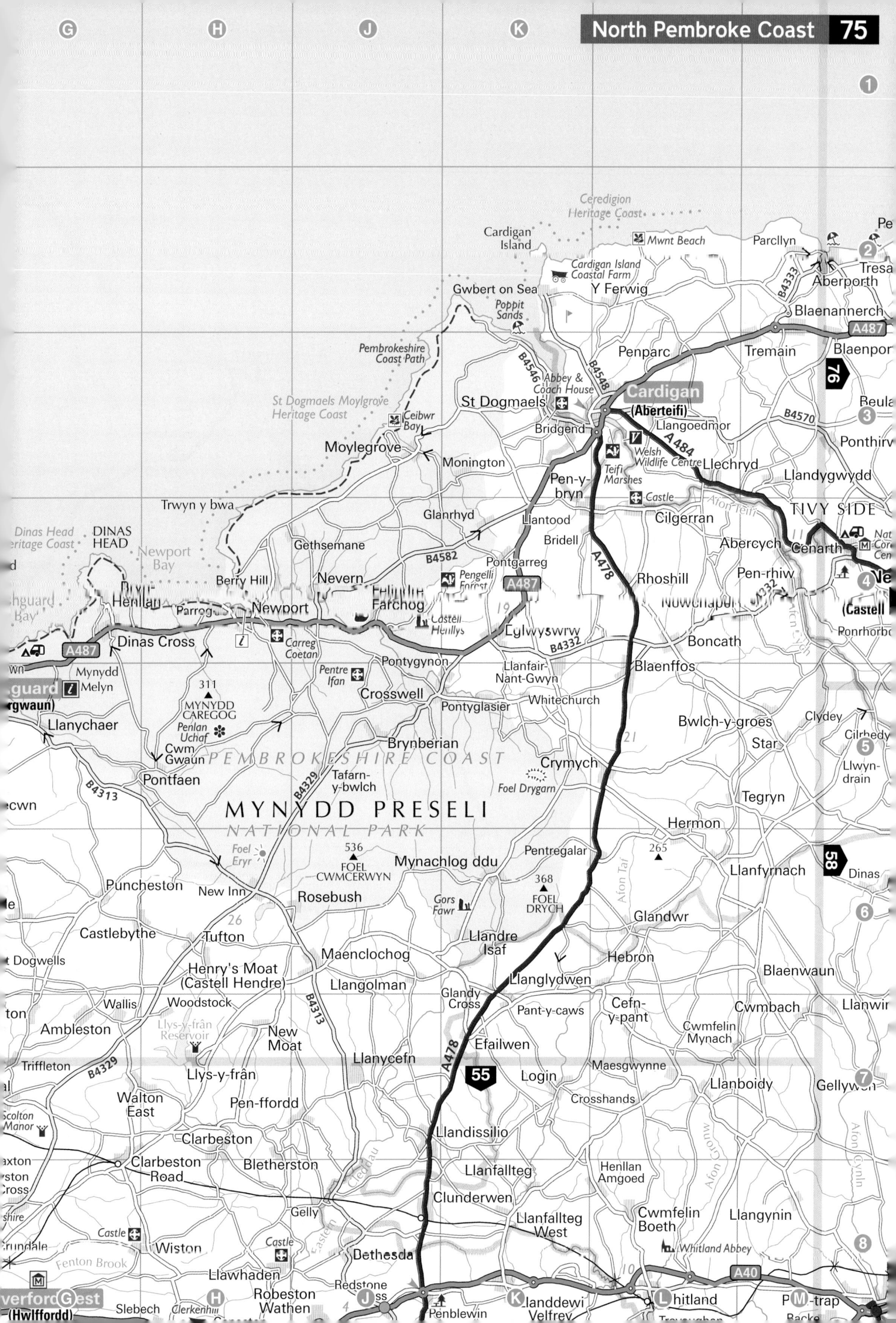

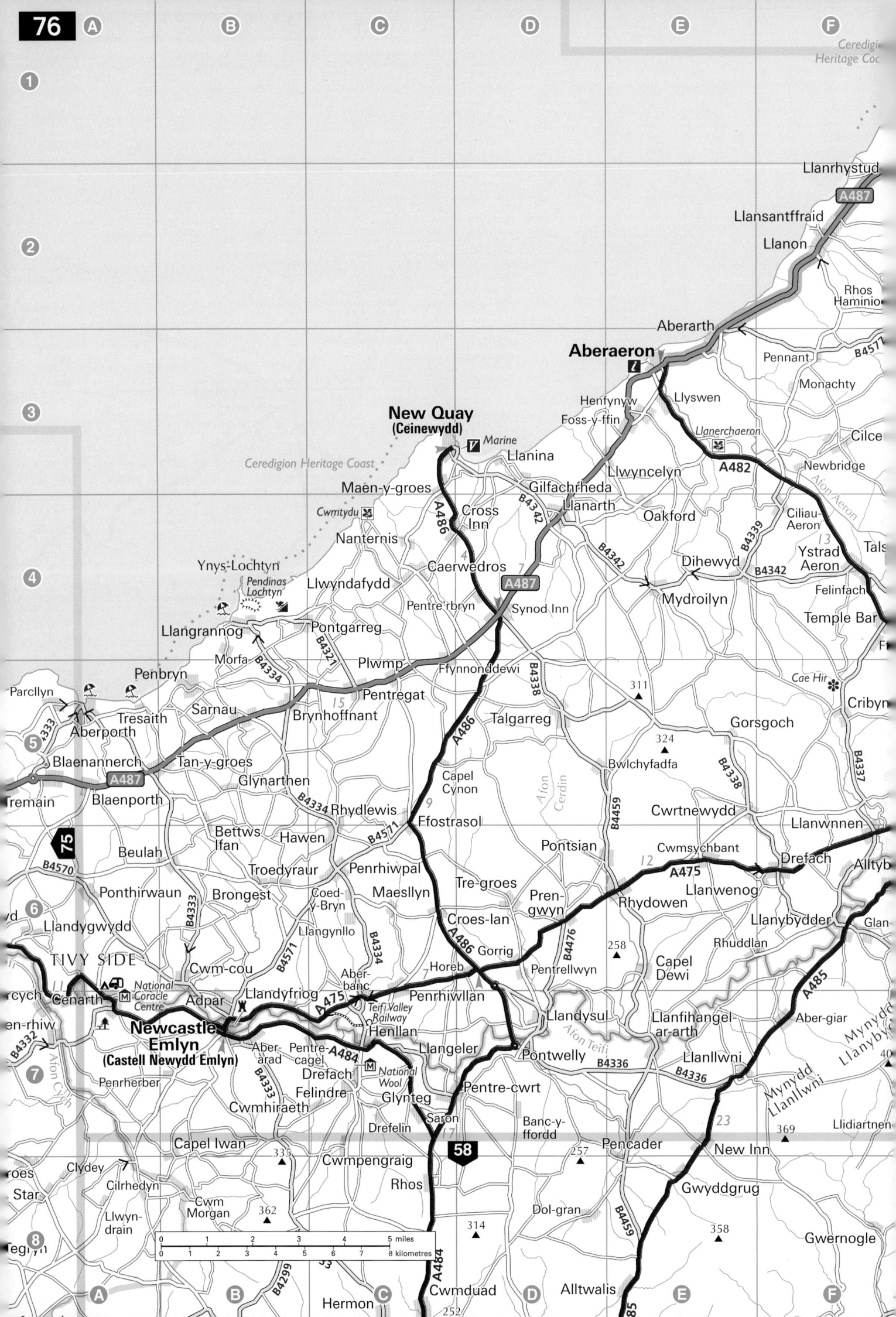

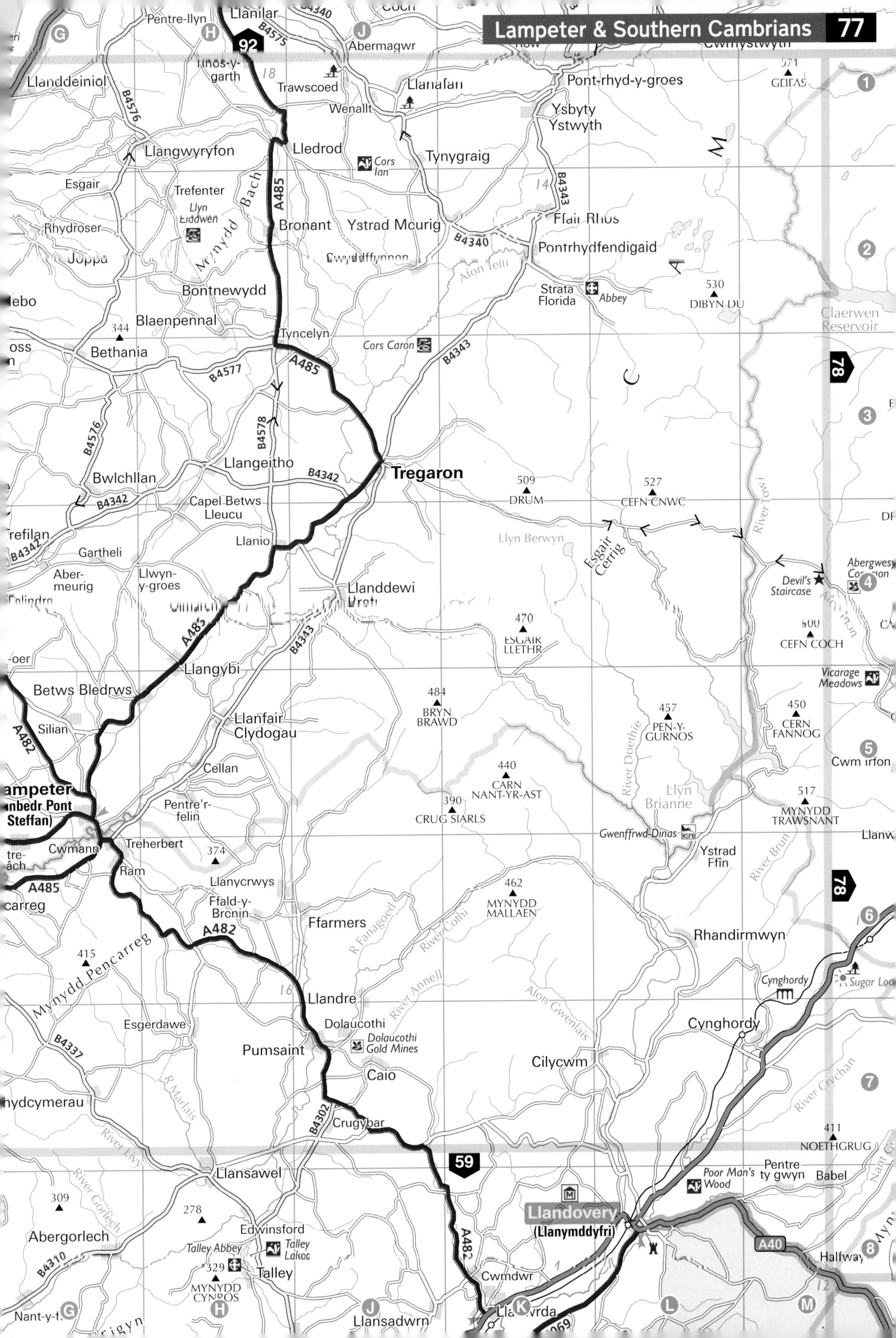

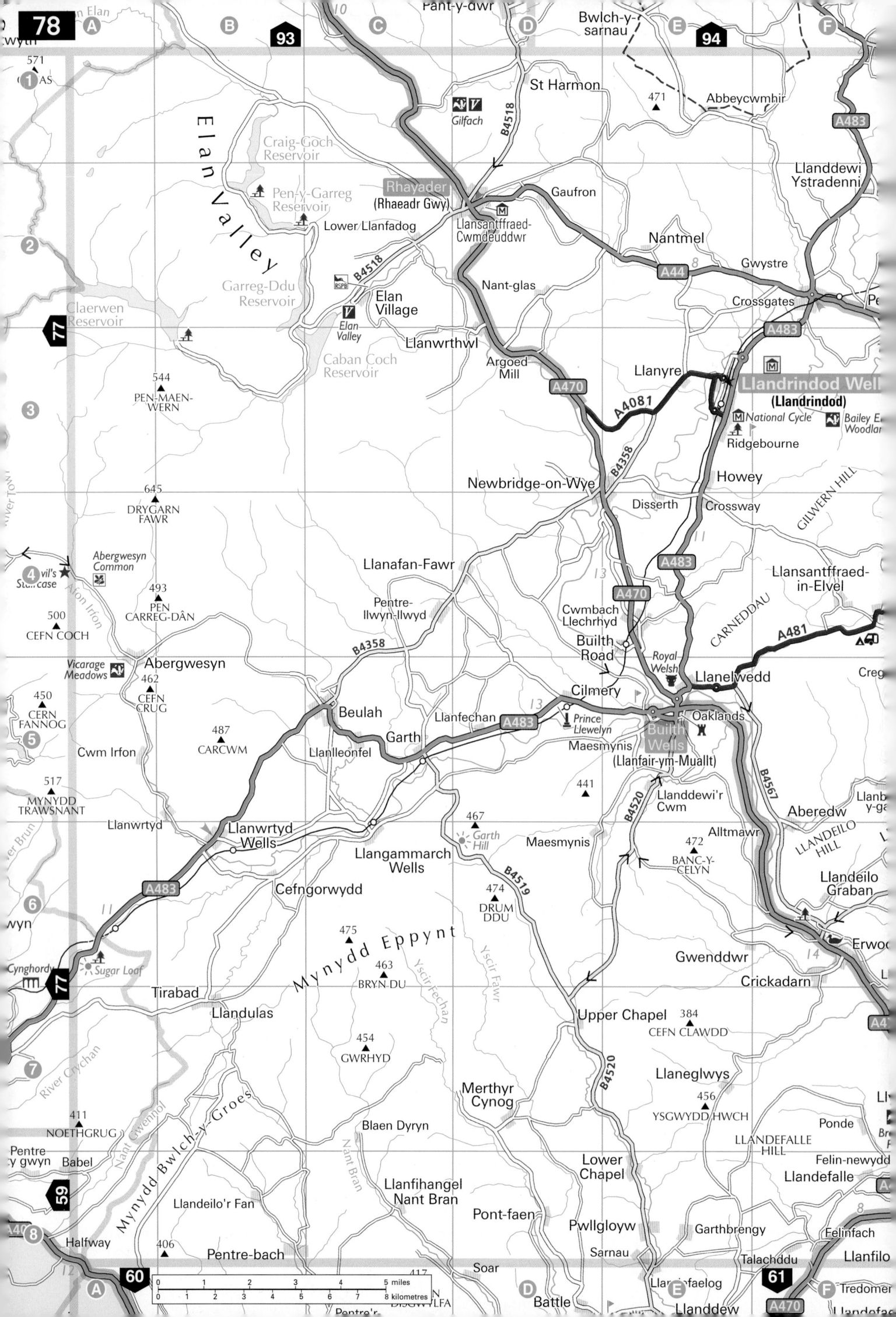

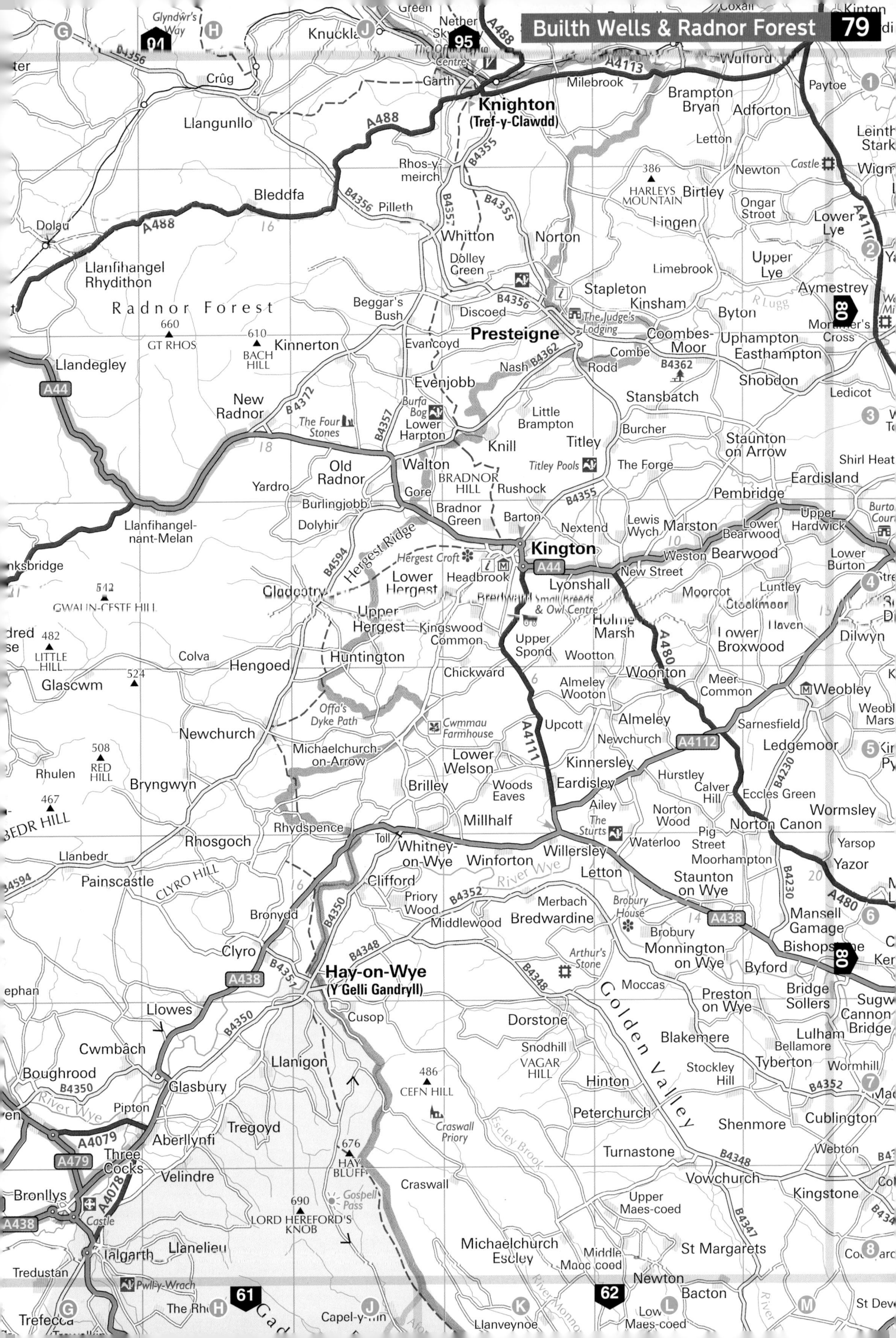

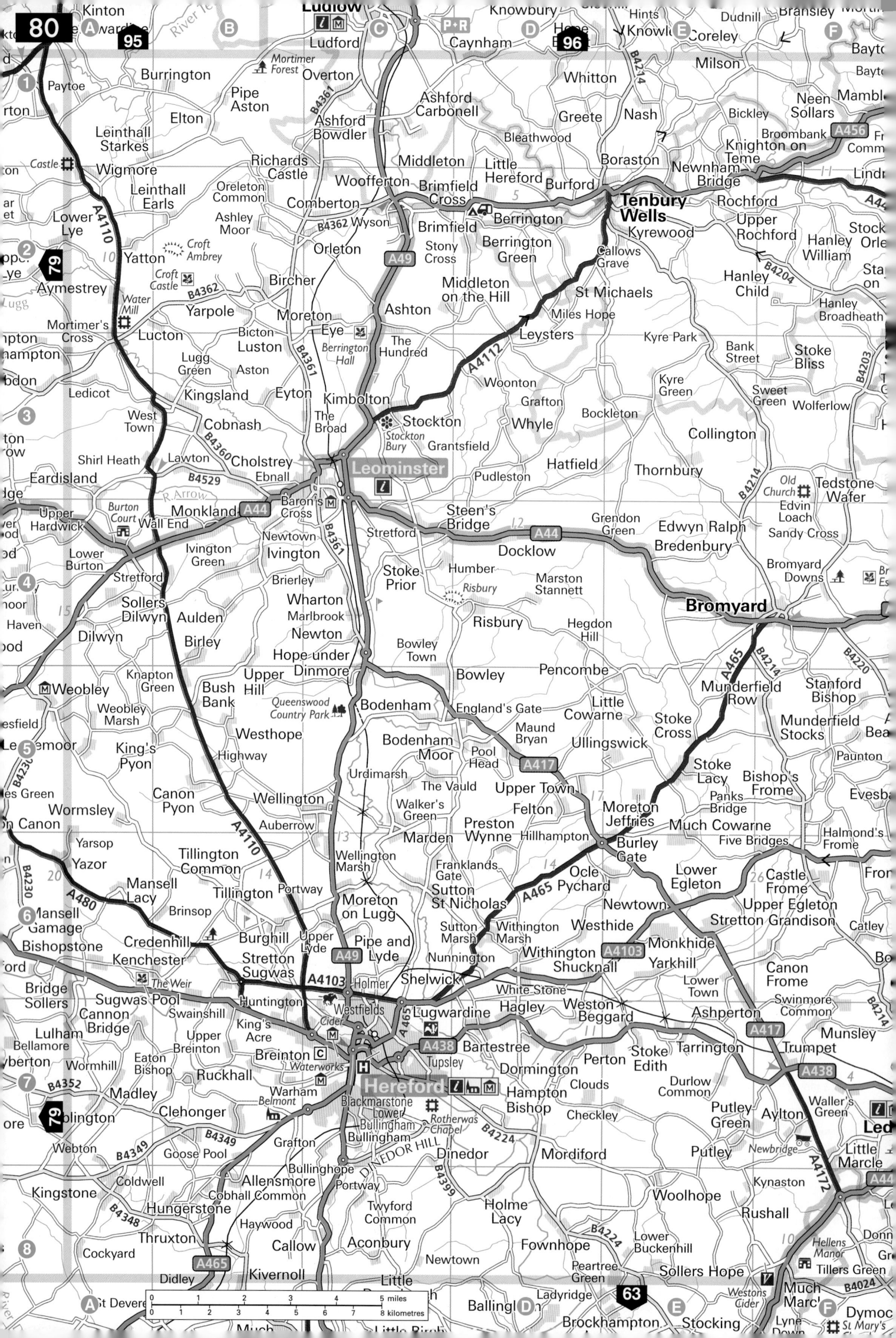

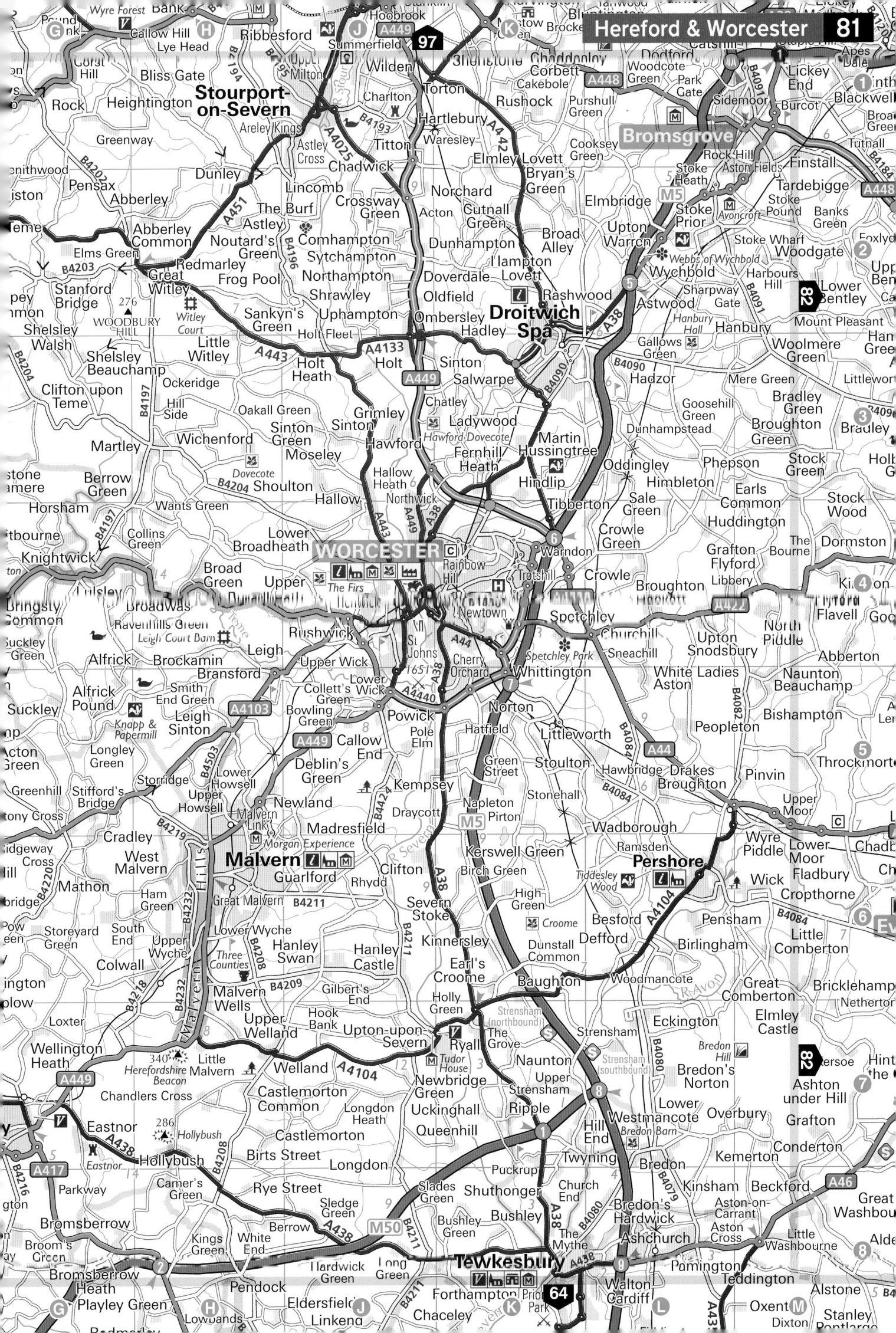

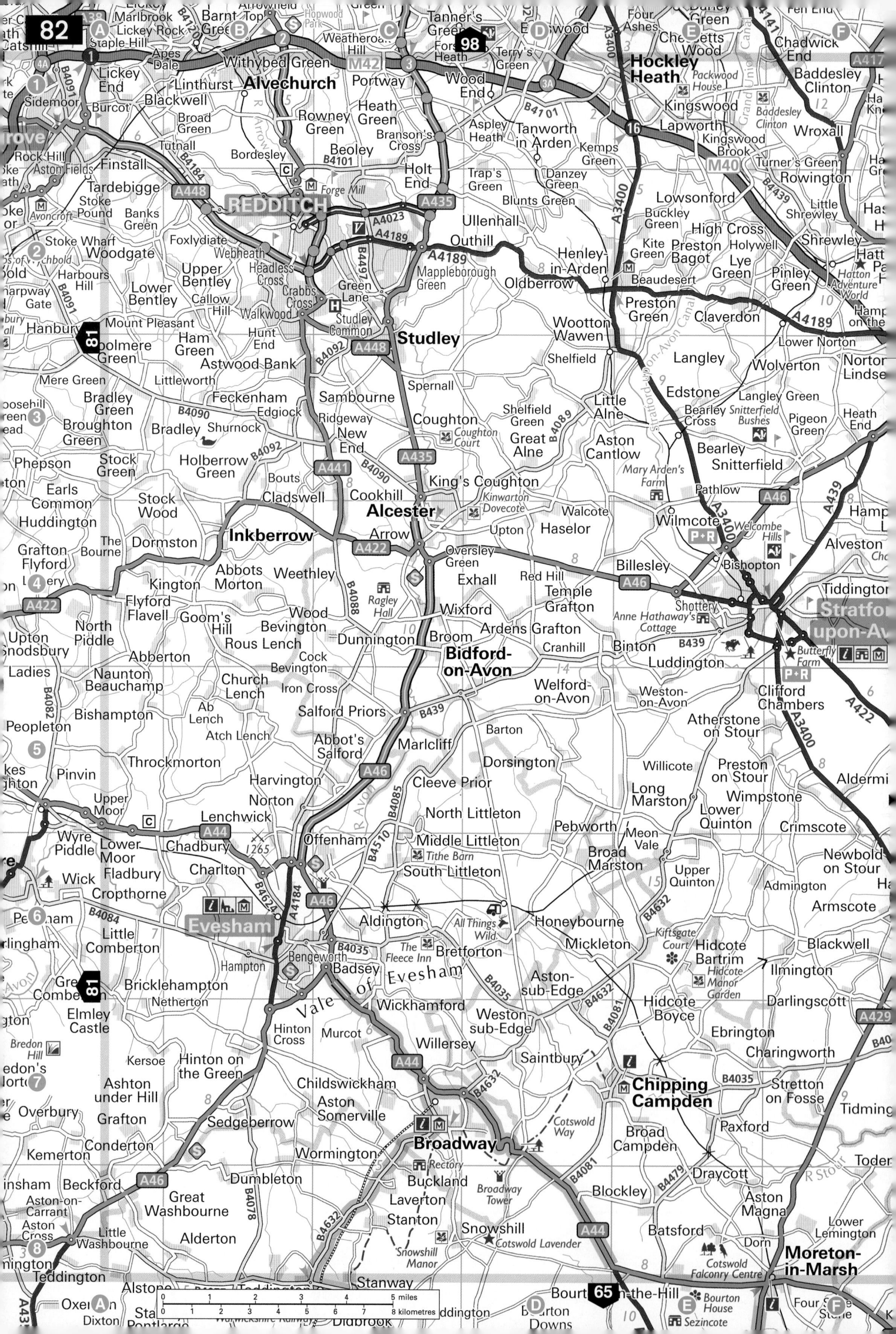

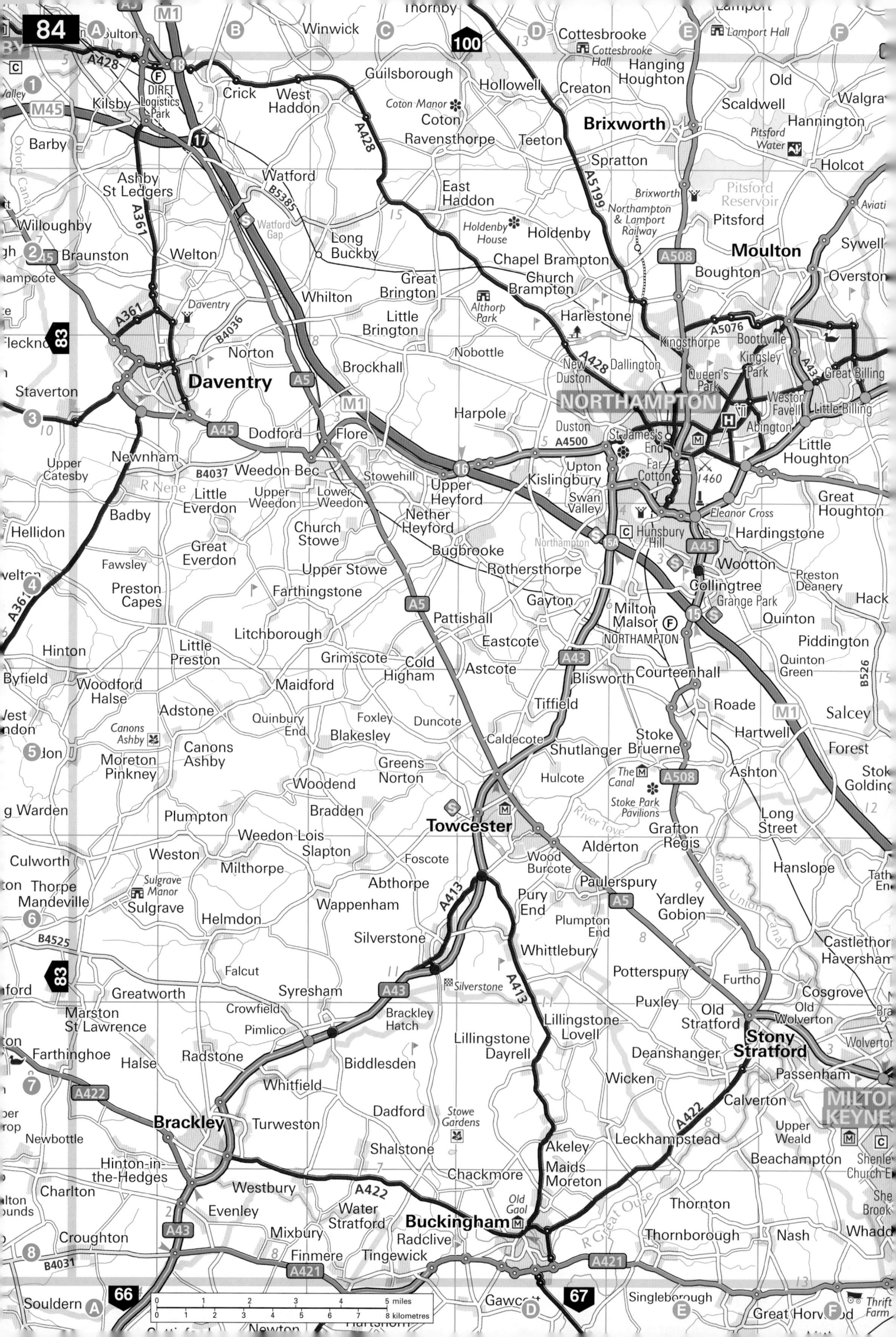

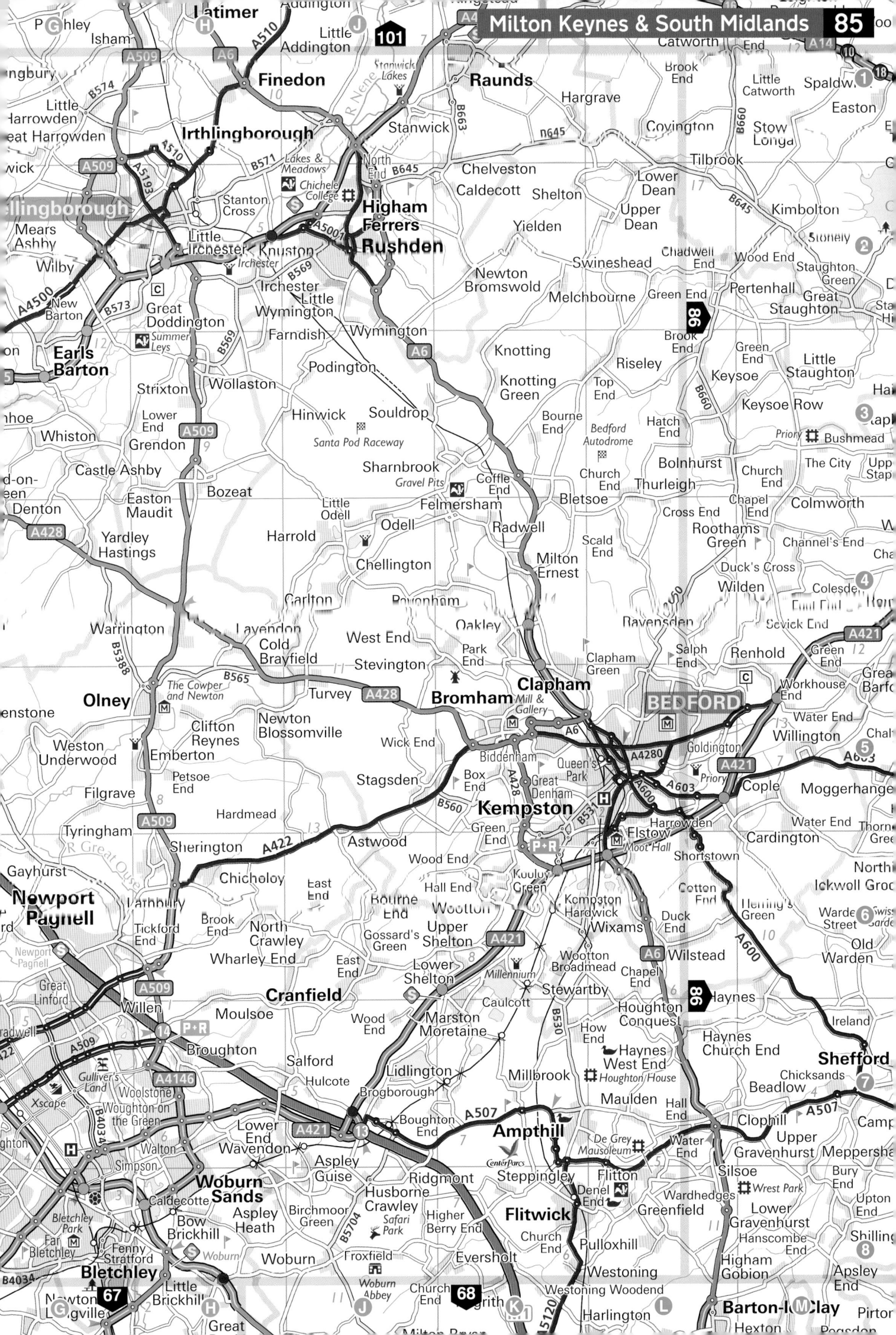

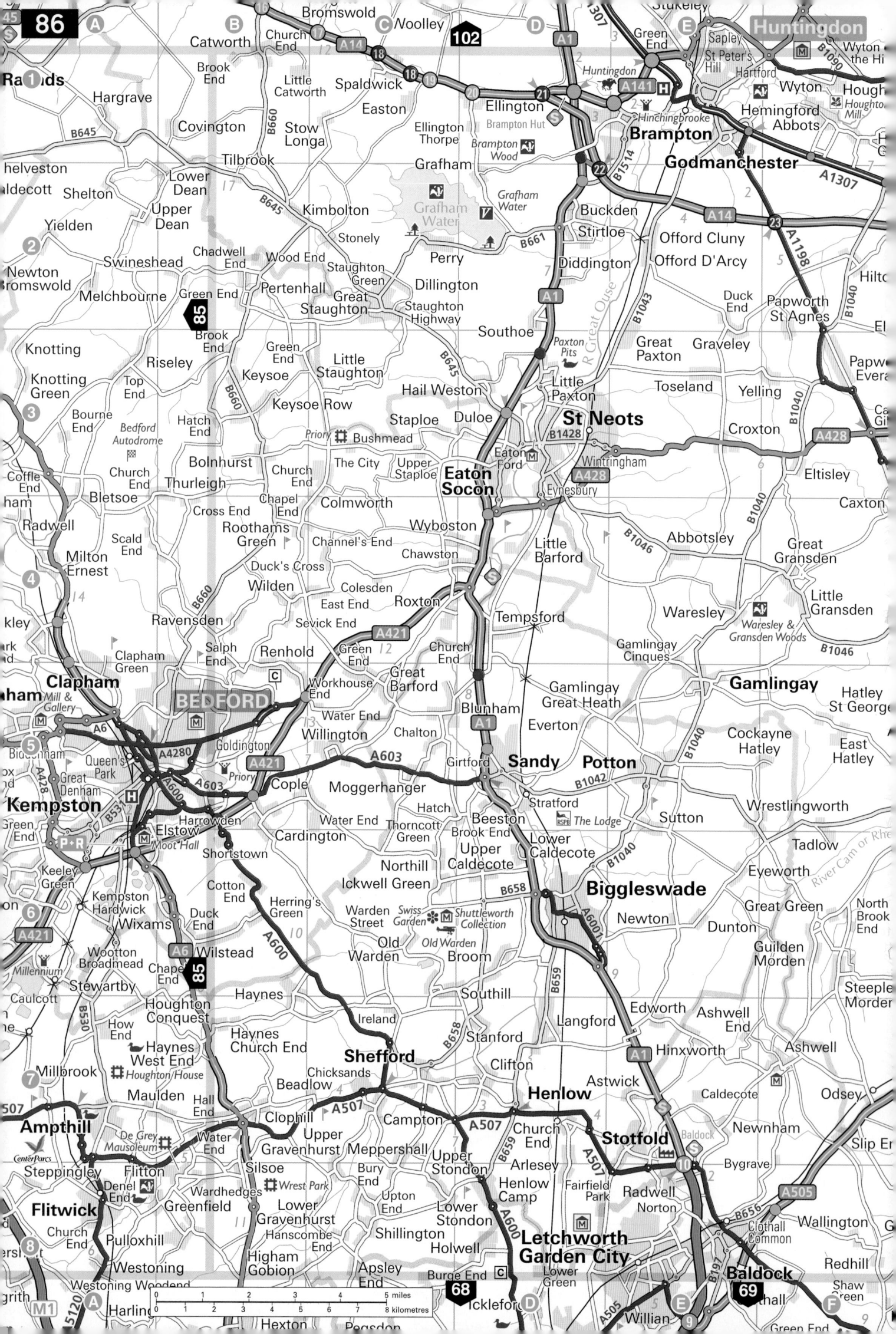

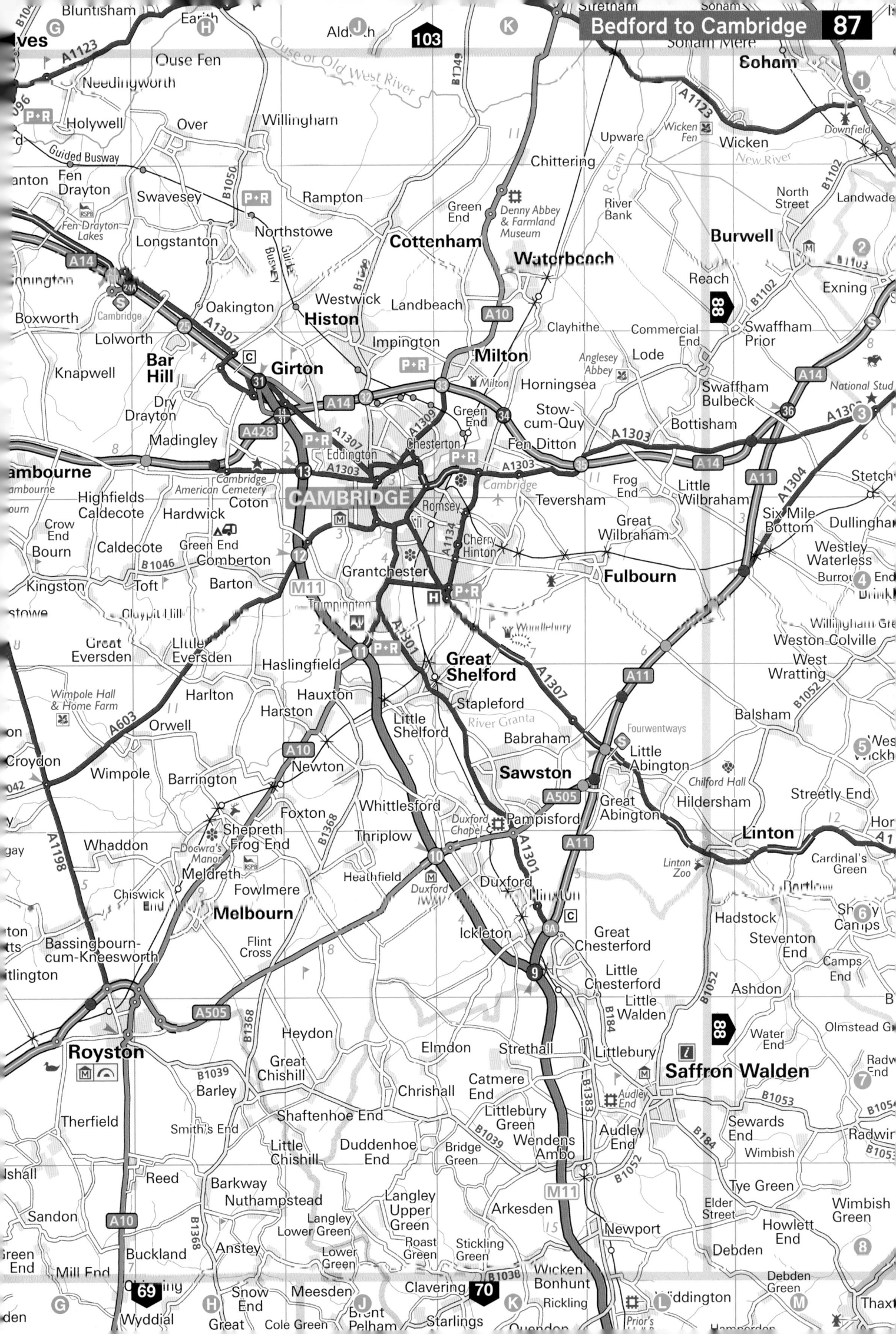

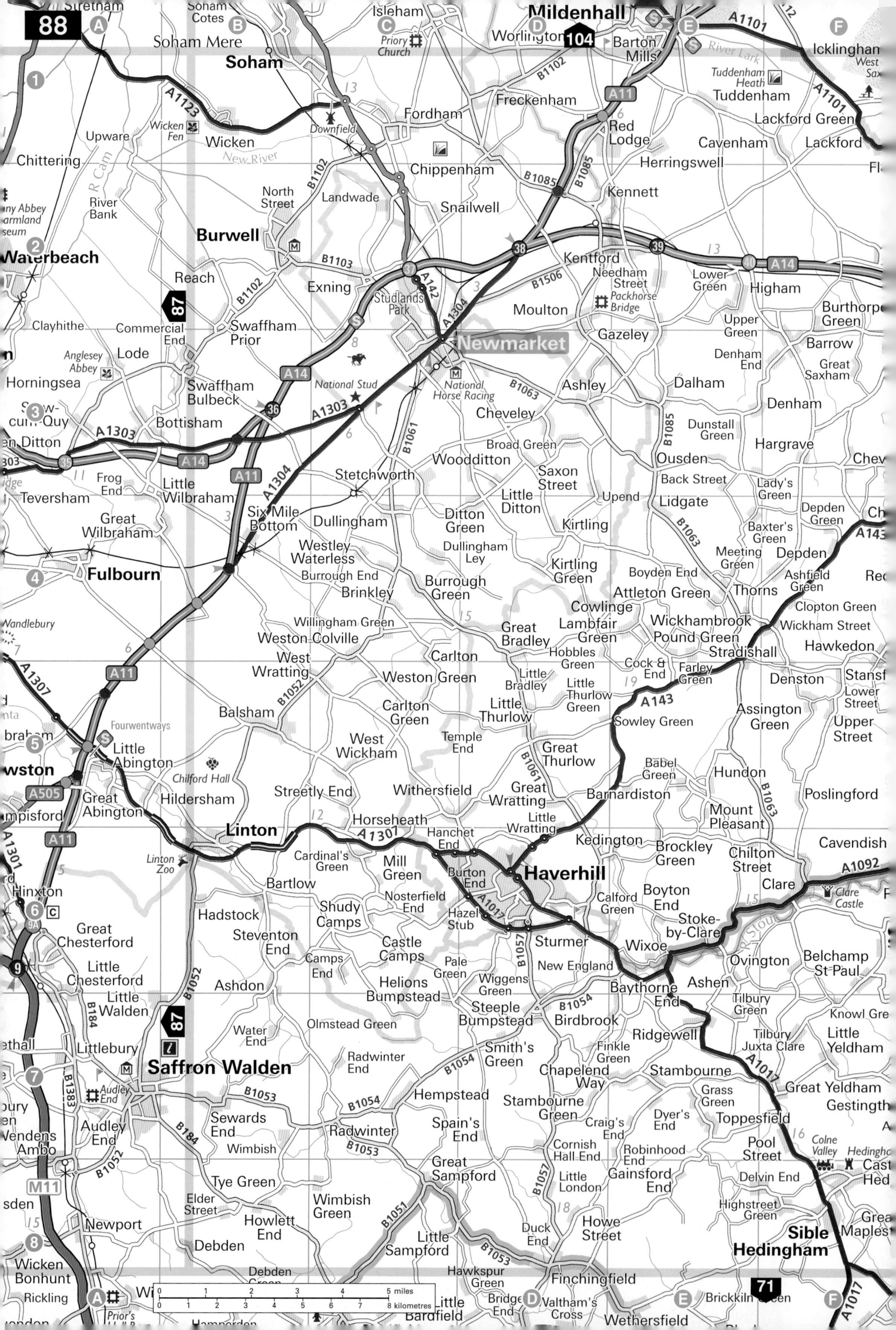

G   H   J   105   K

Bardwell
Ixworth Thorpe
Bangrove
Stanton   Wattisfield
Wyken
Upthorpe   Walsham le Willows   Cranmer Green   Allwood Green   Mill Street   Thornham Parva
West Street   Thornham Magna
Troston   Great Livermere   Gislingham   Wickham Street   Wickham Skeith
Ampton   Ixworth   Langham   Crowland   Finningham   Wickham Green
Brockley
Culford   Timworth   Hunston   Four Ashes   Badwell Green   Westhorpe   Cotton   Brockford Street
Ingham   Grimstone End   Badwell Ash   Long Thurlow   Wyverstone Street   Wyverstone   Bacton
Timworth Green   Conyer's Green   Stowlangtoft   Great Ashfield   Canhams Green   Mendlesham
Fornham St Genevieve   Upper Town   Stanton Street   Hunston Green   Cow Green   Lord's Green   Mendlesham Green
Fornham St Martin   Pakenham   Norton Little Green   Bacton Green   Haughley Green   Brown Street   Middlewood Green
Thurston   Great Green   Norton   Earl's Green   Base Green   Wetherden   Gipping   Old Newton   Saxham Street
Bury St Edmunds   Cattishall   Thurston Planche   Tostock   Elmswell   Haughley   Dagworth   Stowupland   Little Stonham
Moreton Hall   Battlies Green   Beyton Green   Broadgrass Gn   Harleston   Stowmarket   Forward Green   Creeting St Peter   Earl Stonham
Blackthorpe   Beyton   Woolpit   Borley Green   Onehouse   Great Finborough   Combs   Needham Market   Creeting St Mary
Horringer   Kingshall Street   Hessett   Woolpit Green   Clopton Green   Buxhall   Combs Ford
Nowton Park   Rushbrooke   Drinkstone   Buxhall Fen Street   Mill Green   Great Finborough
High Green   Rougham   Drinkstone Green   Rattlesden   Gedding   Hightown Green   Battisford   Moats Tye   Barking   Lower Street
Pinford End   Sicklesmere   Bradfield St George   Maypole Green   Felsham   Brettenham   Battisford Tye   Ringshall   Barking Tye   Baylham
Hawstead   Little Welnetham   Bradfield St Clare   Bush Green   Great Green   Cross Green   Charles Tye   Ringshall Stocks   Upper Street
Mickley Green   Great Welnetham   Bradfield Woods   Cooks Green   Bird Street   Wattisham   Nedging Tye   Great Bricett   Offton   Somersham
Melon Green   Bradfield Combust   Oldhall Green   Hitcham Causeway   Hitcham   Greenstreet Green   Naughton
Harrow Green   Stanningfield   Cross Green   Thorpe Morieux   Hitcham Street   Nedging   Ash Street   Flowton
Lawshall   Windsor Green   Cockfield   Preston St Mary   Kettlebaston   Bildeston   Somer   Whatfield   Aldham   Elmsett
Lawshall Green   Shimpling Street   Lavenham   Little Hall   Brent Eleigh   Monks Eleigh   Lindsey Tye   Stone Street
Audley End   Alpheton   Guildhall   Swingleton Green   Chelsworth   Lindsey   Wolves Wood
Shimpling   Bridge Street   Milden   Rose Green   St James's Chapel   Kersey   Burstall   Hintlesham
Boxted   Stanstead   Kentwell Hall & Gardens   Little Waldingfield   Kersey Tye   Hadleigh   Duke Street
Glemsford   Melford Hall   Acton   Great Waldingfield   Kersey Upland   Coram Street   Chattisham   Washbrook
Long Melford   Liston   Newman's Green   Mill Green   Wicker Street Green   Hadleigh Heath   Upper Layham   Coles Green
Foxearth   Chilton   Edwardstone   Horners Green   Bower House Tye   Layham   Copdock
Borley   Cornard Tye   Groton   Calais Street   Polstead Heath   Great Wenham   Little Wenham
Sudbury   Great Cornard   Boxford   Stone Street   Whitestreet Green   Raydon   Capel St Mary
Ballingdon   Newton   Hagmore Green   Polstead   Shelley   Bentley
Bulmer   Little Cornard   Leavenheath   Stoke-by-Nayland   Lower Raydon   Holton St Mary   East Bergholt
Middleton   Assington   Workhouse Green   Rose Green   Stratford St Mary
Bulmer Tye   Great Henny   Dorking Tye   Honey Tye   Thorington Street   Higham   East End
Wickham St Paul   Henny Street   Nayland   Old Boxted   Dodham
Alphamstone   Twinstead   Lamarsh   Boxted Cross   Flatford Mill & Bridge Cottage   Mistley
Cross End   Bures   Wissington   Wormingford   Langham   Manningtree   Dedham Heath
Pebmarsh   Mount Bures   Little Horkesley   72   Boxted

A143   A1088   A14   A1308   B1113   B1115   B1078   B1071   B1115   A134   A1071   B1070   B1068   B1087   A12   A131

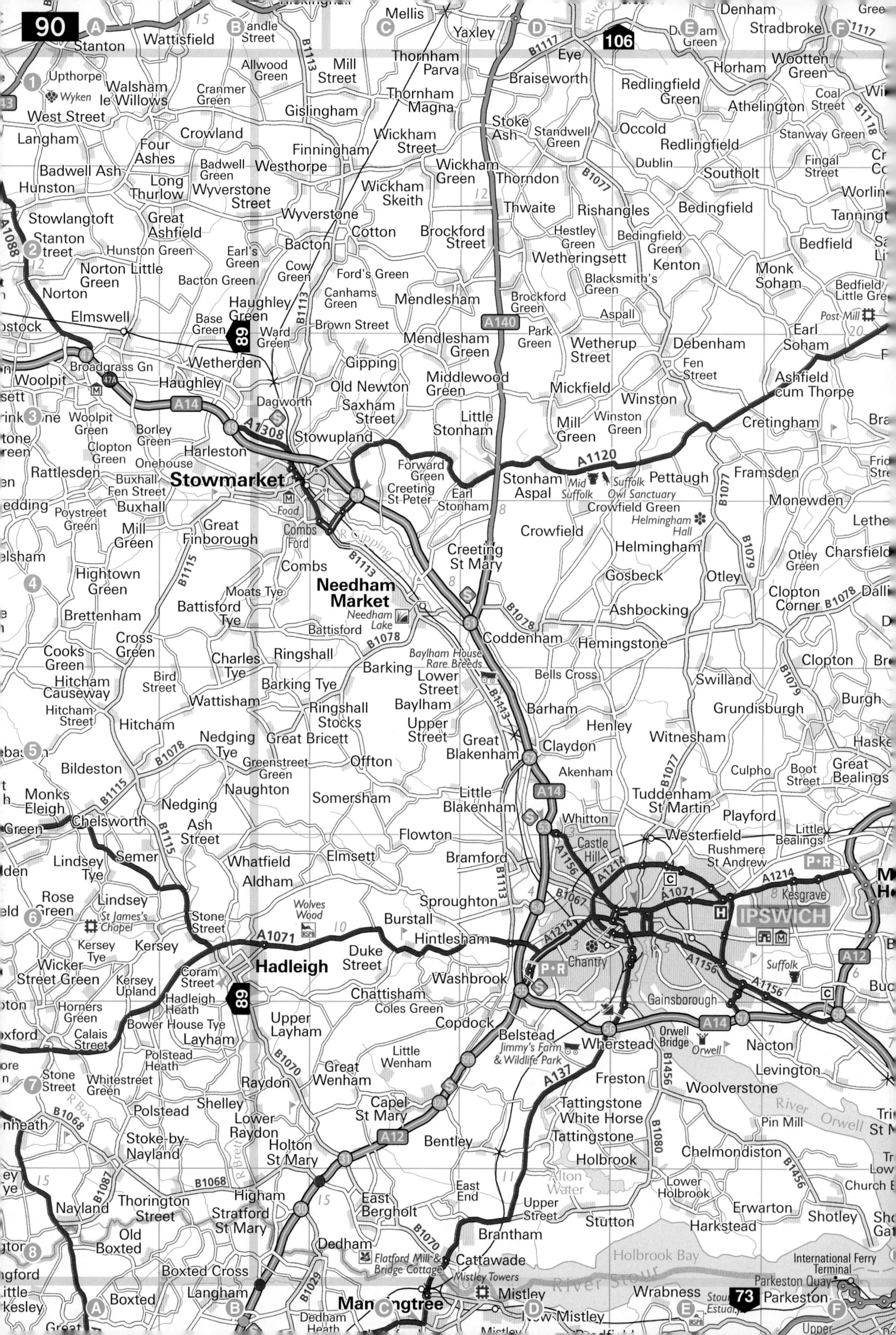

G   H   B1117   Walpole   J   107   ington   K   B1387   1

Huntingfield
Bramfield

Laxfield   Heveningham   Dunwich   Suffolk Coast
Ubbeston   Forest
Green   Pouy   Suffolk Coast
ndish Street   Street   High Street   Darsham   Westleton   Dunwich
dish   Owl's   Heath
Green   Peasenhall   Sibton   Yoxford   Grey Friars
Goddard's Corner   A1120   B1122   Middleton   Westleton   Minsmere   Dunwich
Capon's   Badingham   Middleton Moor   RSPB   Heath
Green
Dennington   Druisyard   North Green   Theberton   Lastbridge
stead   Brulsyard   A12   East   Poplar Street
Shawsgate   Street   Green   Leiston
Cransford   Carlton Meres   Kelsale   Abbey   Power
Castle   Rendham   Carlton   Station
Brabling   B1119   Saxmundham   Sizewell
Green   Swefling   Benhall   B1119   Knodishall   Leiston
North Green   Great   Benhall   Green   Sternfield   Coldfair   Aldringham   Thorpe
Mill   Glemham   Street   Green   Ness
Green   Stratford   Knodishall
Parham   St Andrew   Friday   Common   Thorpeness
Silverlace   Street   B1121   Friston   A1094   B1122
Easton   Green   Farnham   Snape   North
Marlesford   Hacheston   Little   Gromford   Snape   A1094   Warren   RSPB
Lower   Glemham   Street   Snape
Hacheston   Blaxhall   Maltings   Aldeburgh
Wickham   B1069   RSPB   Snape   Iken
Market   Campsea   Tunstall   High   Aldeburgh
Ash   Tunstall   Forest   Street   Bay
Upper   Rendlesham   B1078   River Alde
Ufford   A1152   Sudbourne
A12   Ufford   Chillesford
B1438   Lower Ufford   Friday
Melton   Eyke   Street   Butley   B1084
Bromeswell   B1084   12   Orford
Woodbridge   Rendlesham   Butley High   Castle   Orford Ness
Forest   Corner
Sutton   Capel   Capel   Orford Ness
Hoo   Heath   Green   St Andrew   RSPB   Ness
Woodbridge
Tide Mill   B1083   Boyton   Orfordness-
sham   Sutton   Havergate
ham   Waldringfield   North Weir Point   Suffolk Heritage Coast
Newbourne   Hollesley
well   Hemley   B1083   Shottisham   Hollesley
Ramsholt   Shingle   Bay
River Deben   Alderton   Street
Kirton   Bawdsey
Falkenham
Trimley   Felixstowe
St Mary   Ferry
Old
Walton   Felixstowe
Felixstowe
A154
Side   Landguard Fort
arwich   Landguard
arbour   Point

0   1   2   3   4   5 miles
0   1   2   3   4   5   6   7   0 kilometres

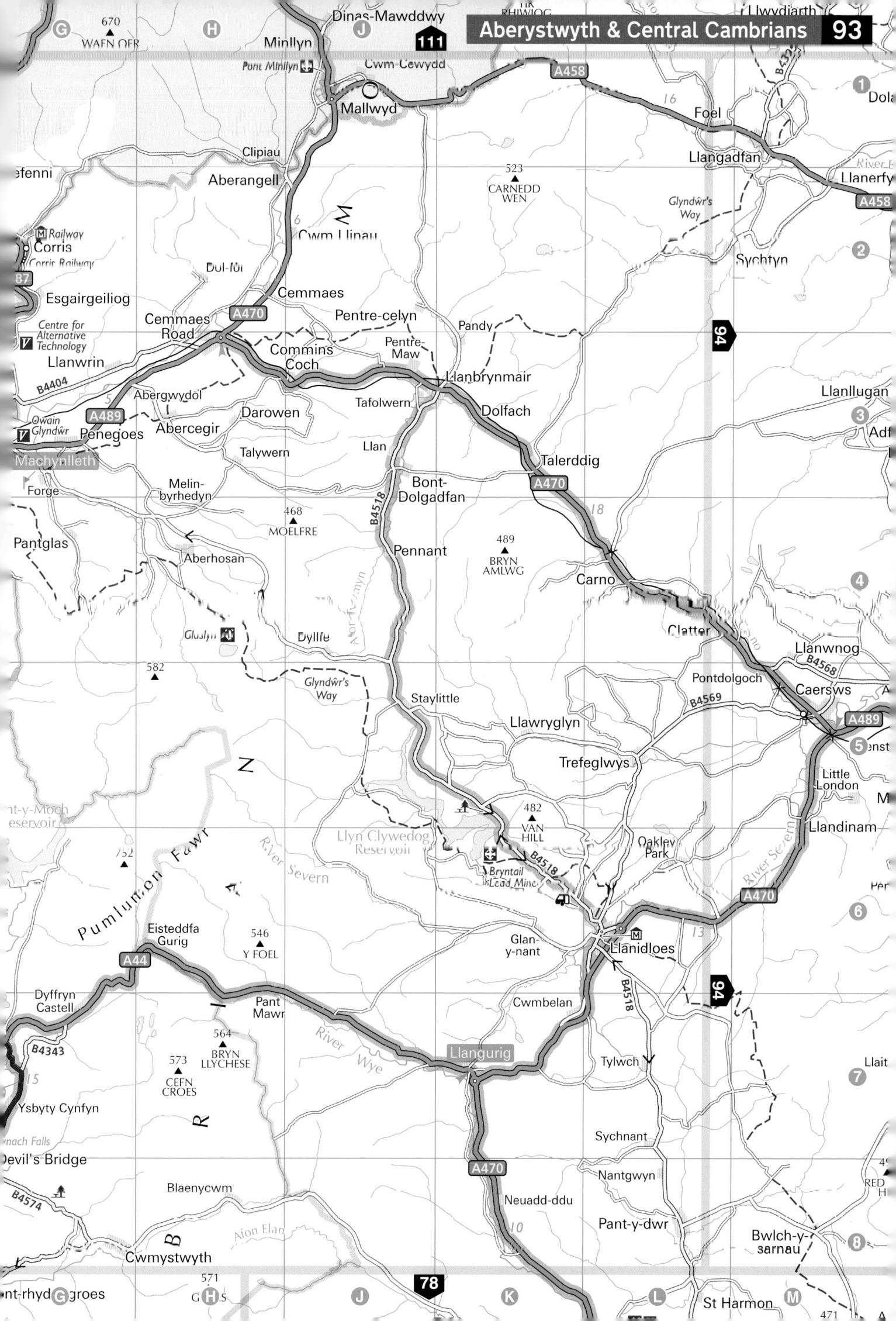

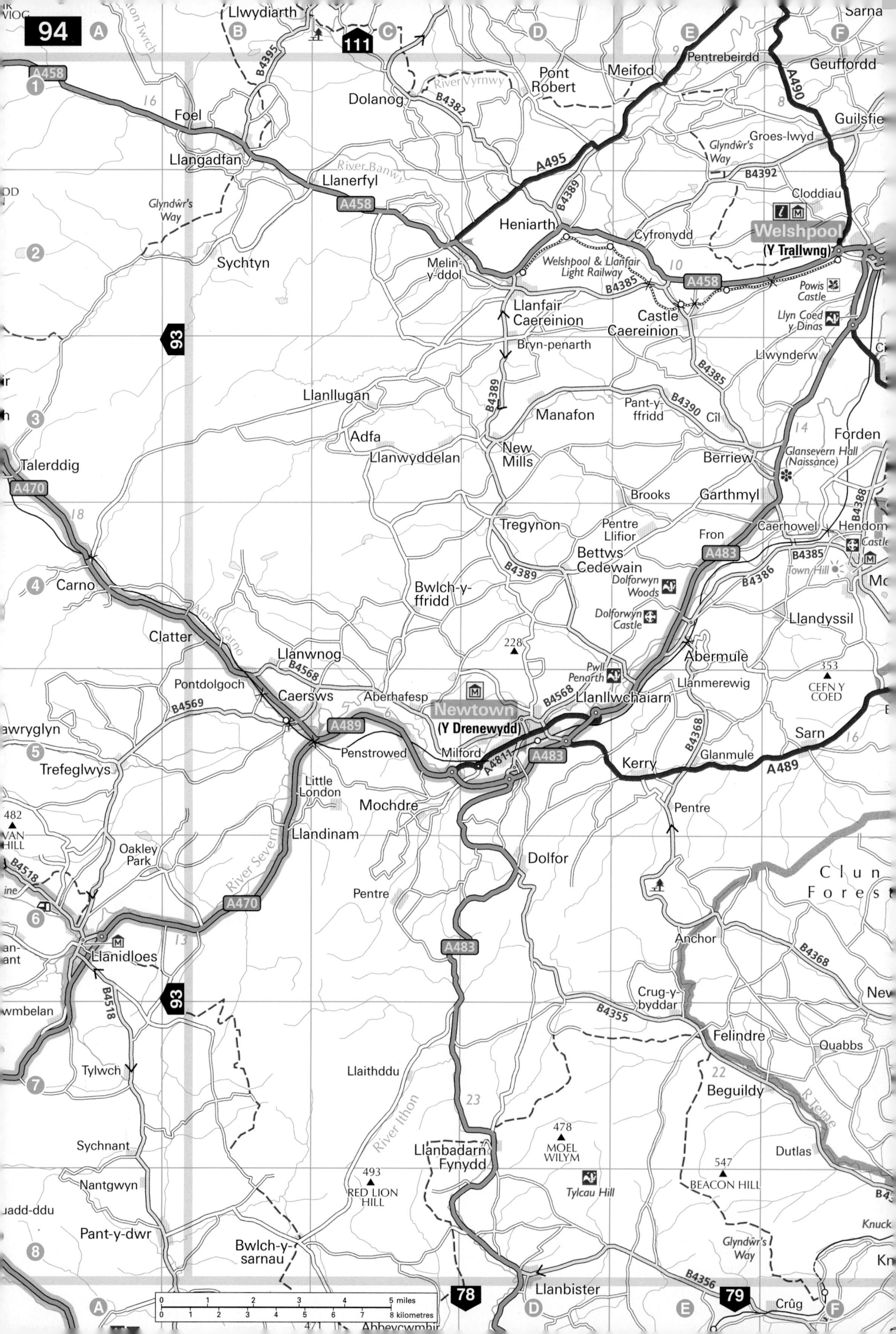

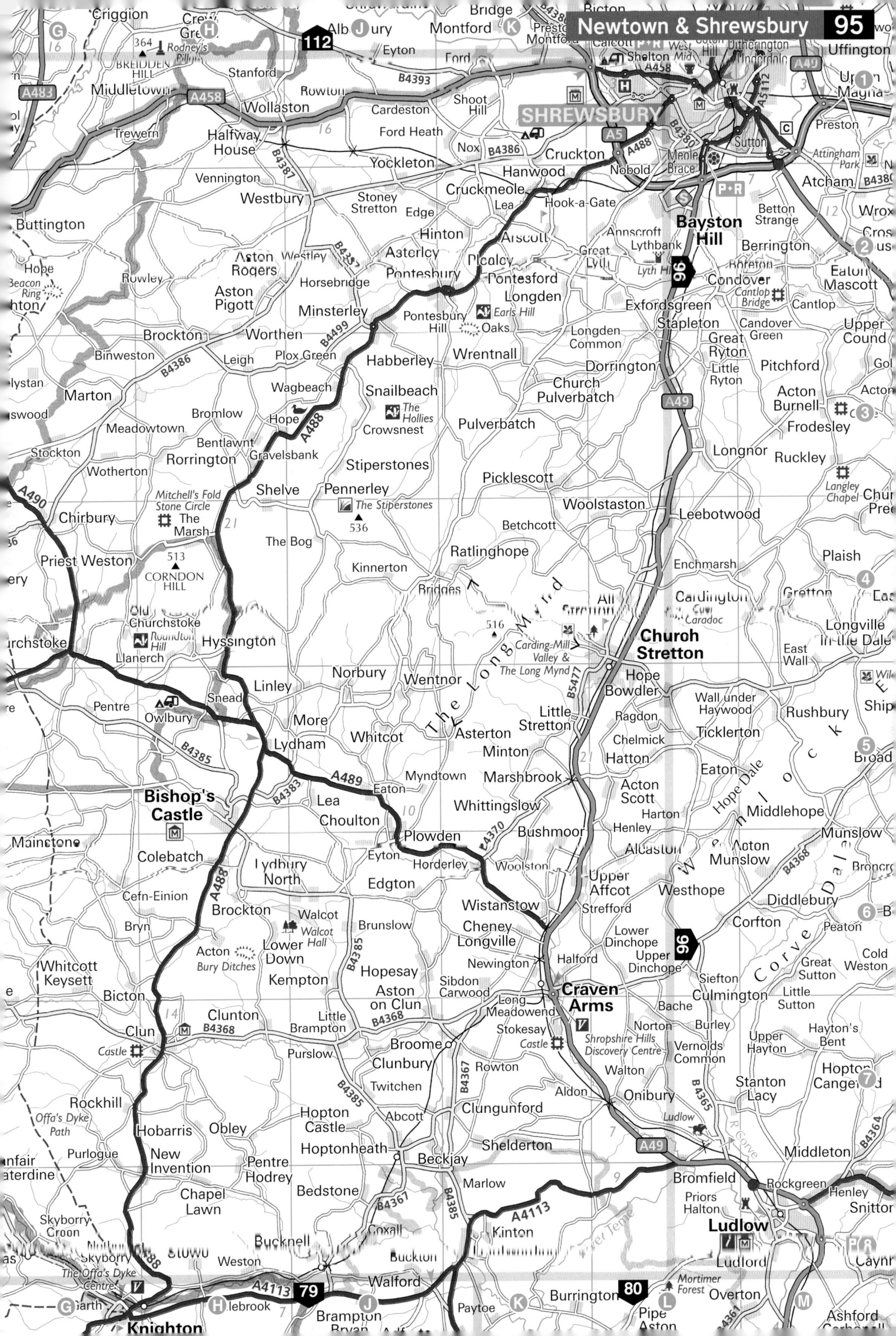

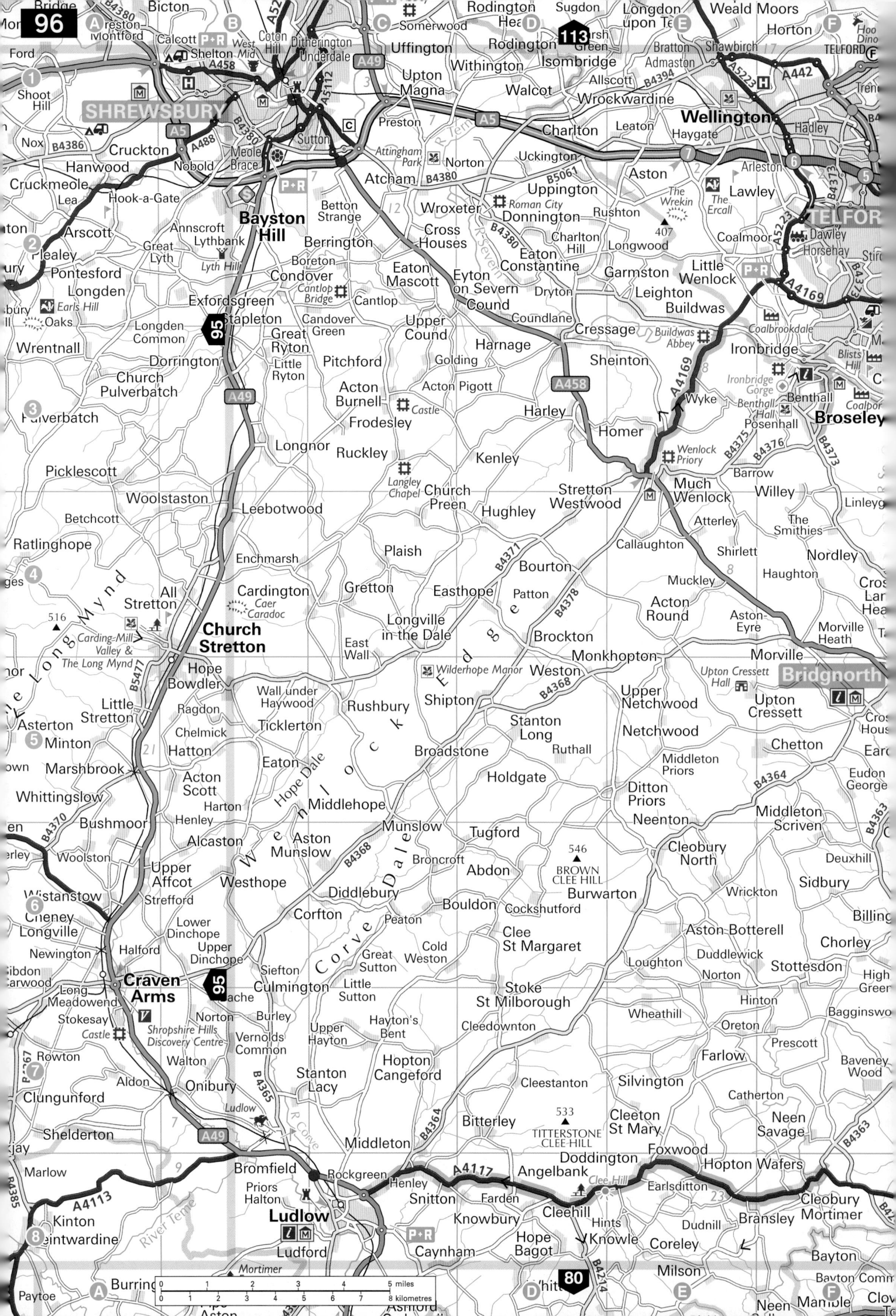

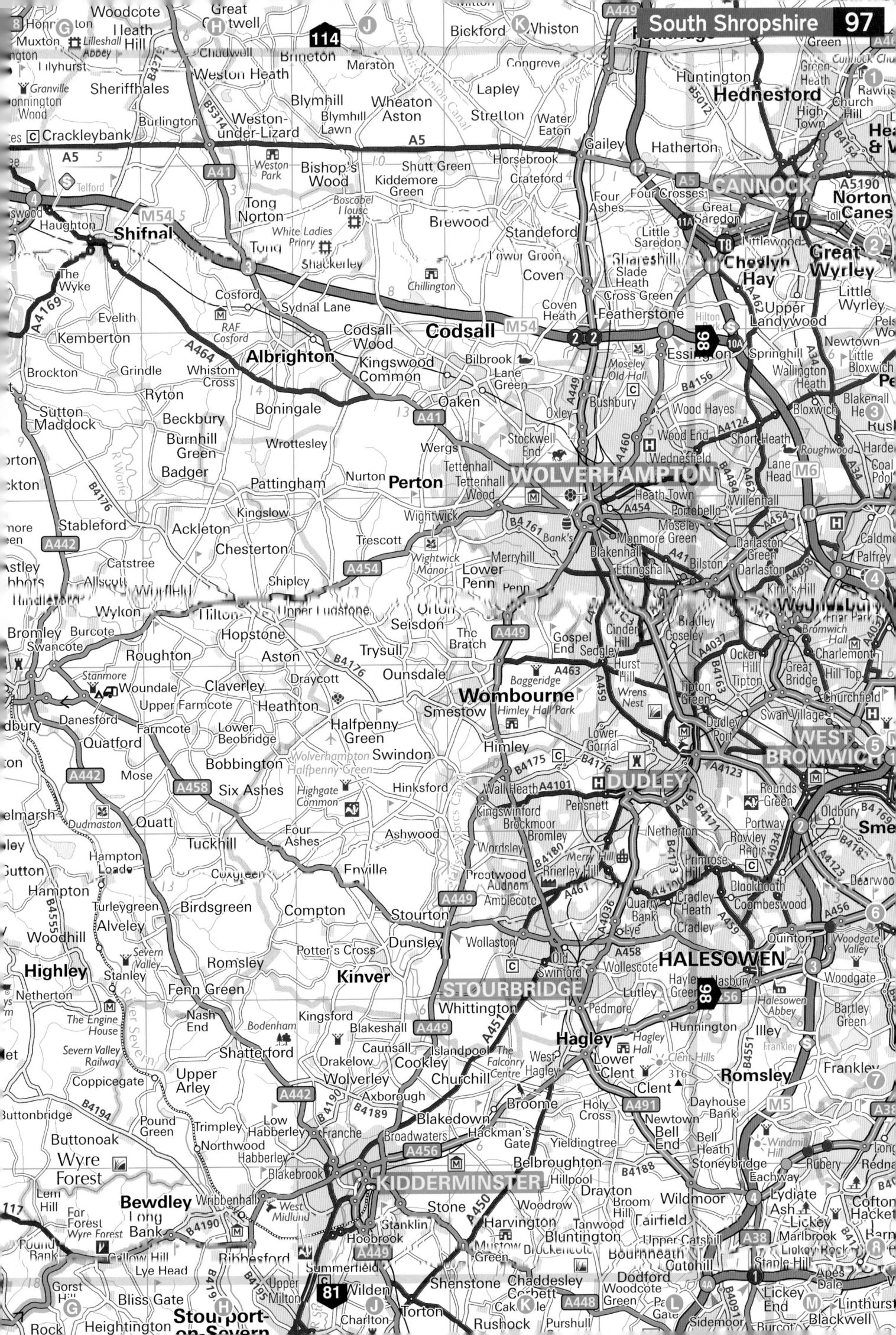

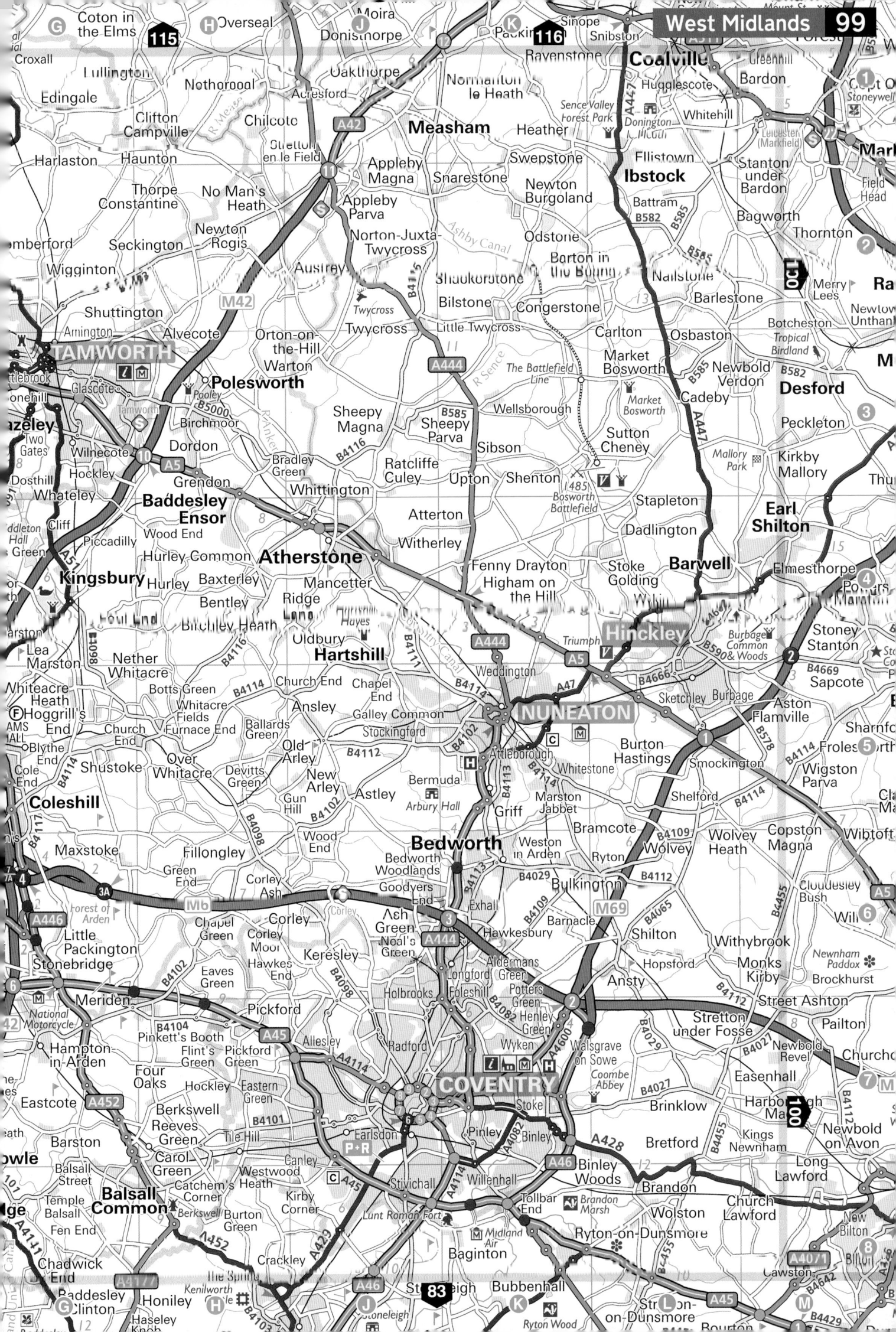

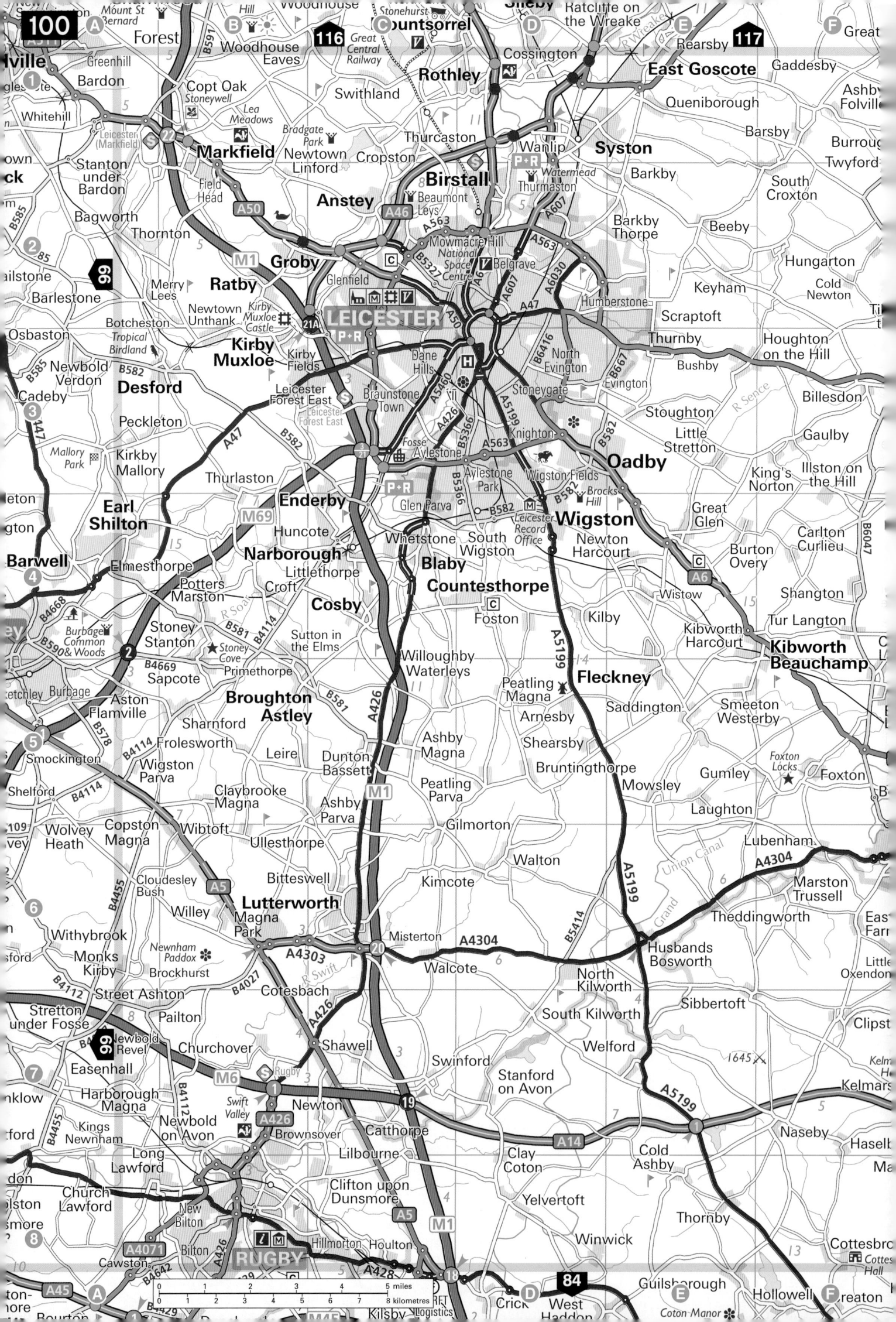

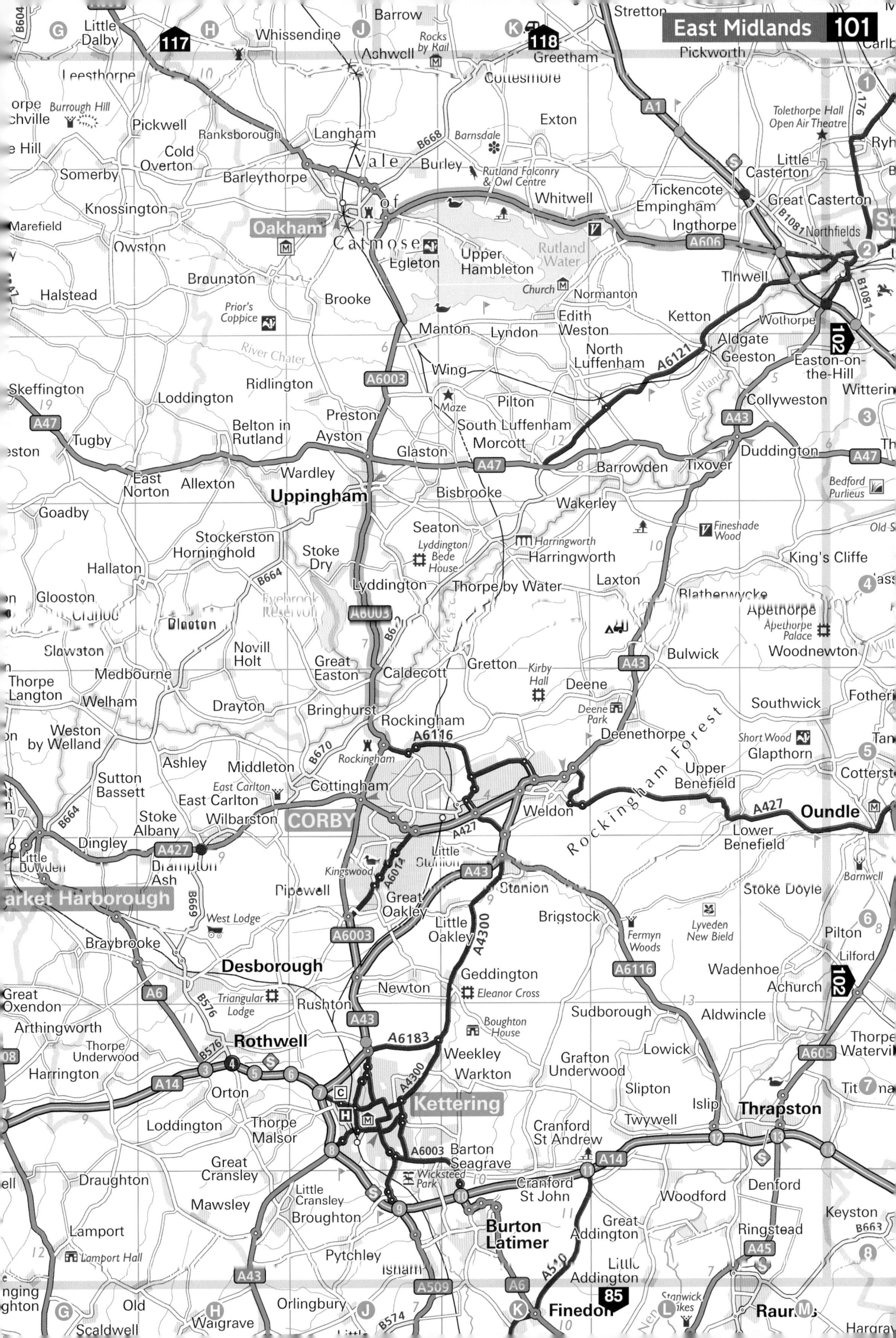

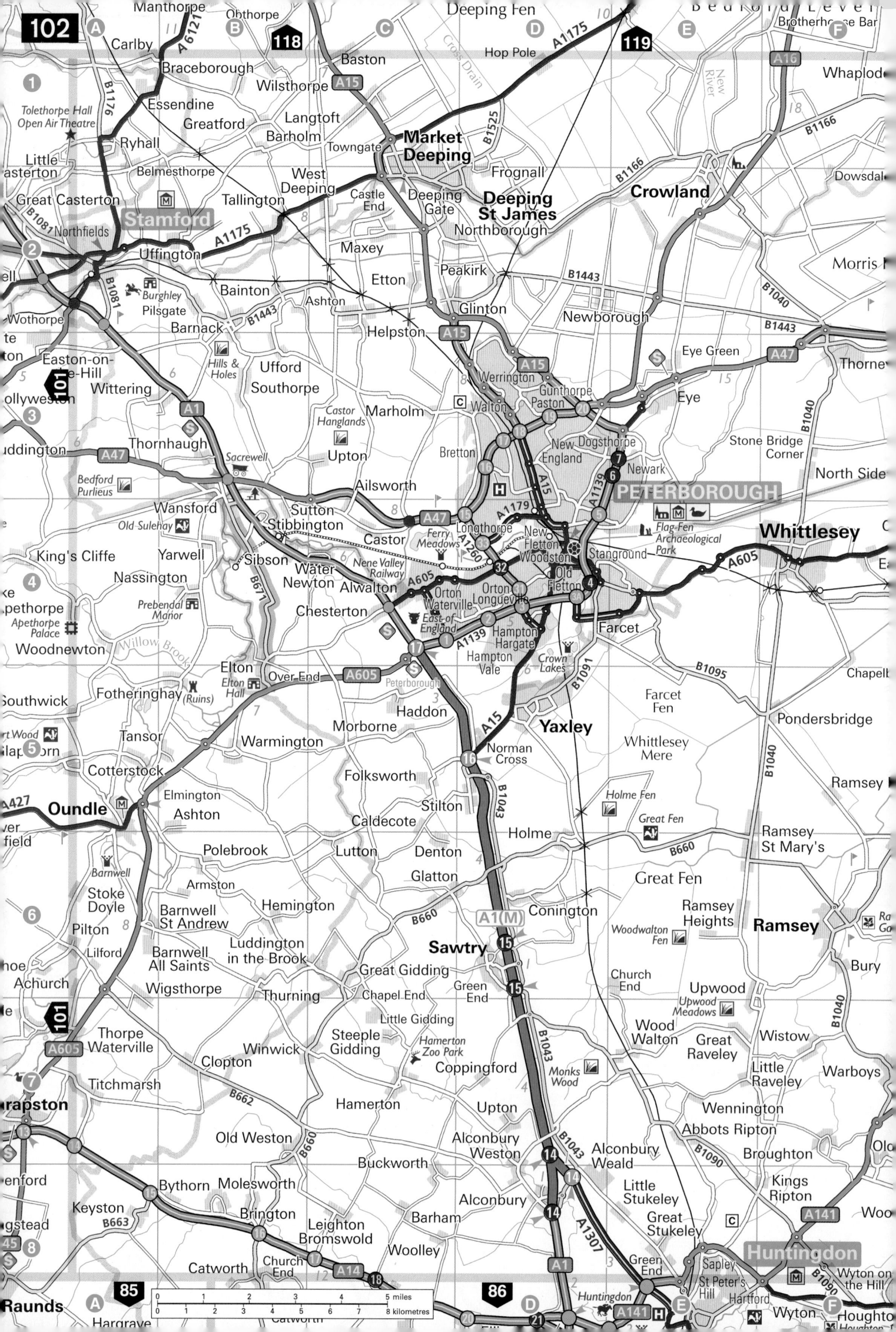

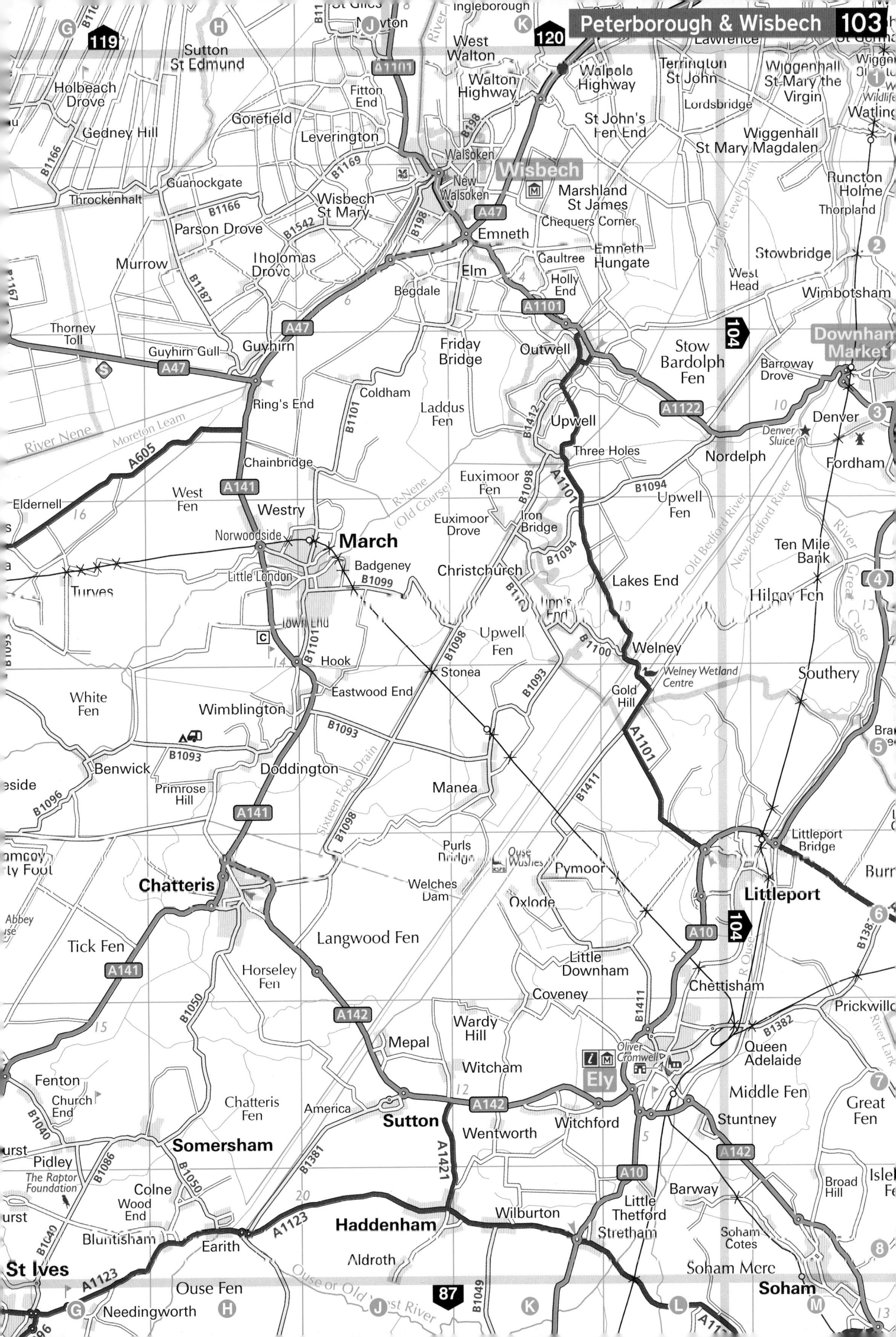

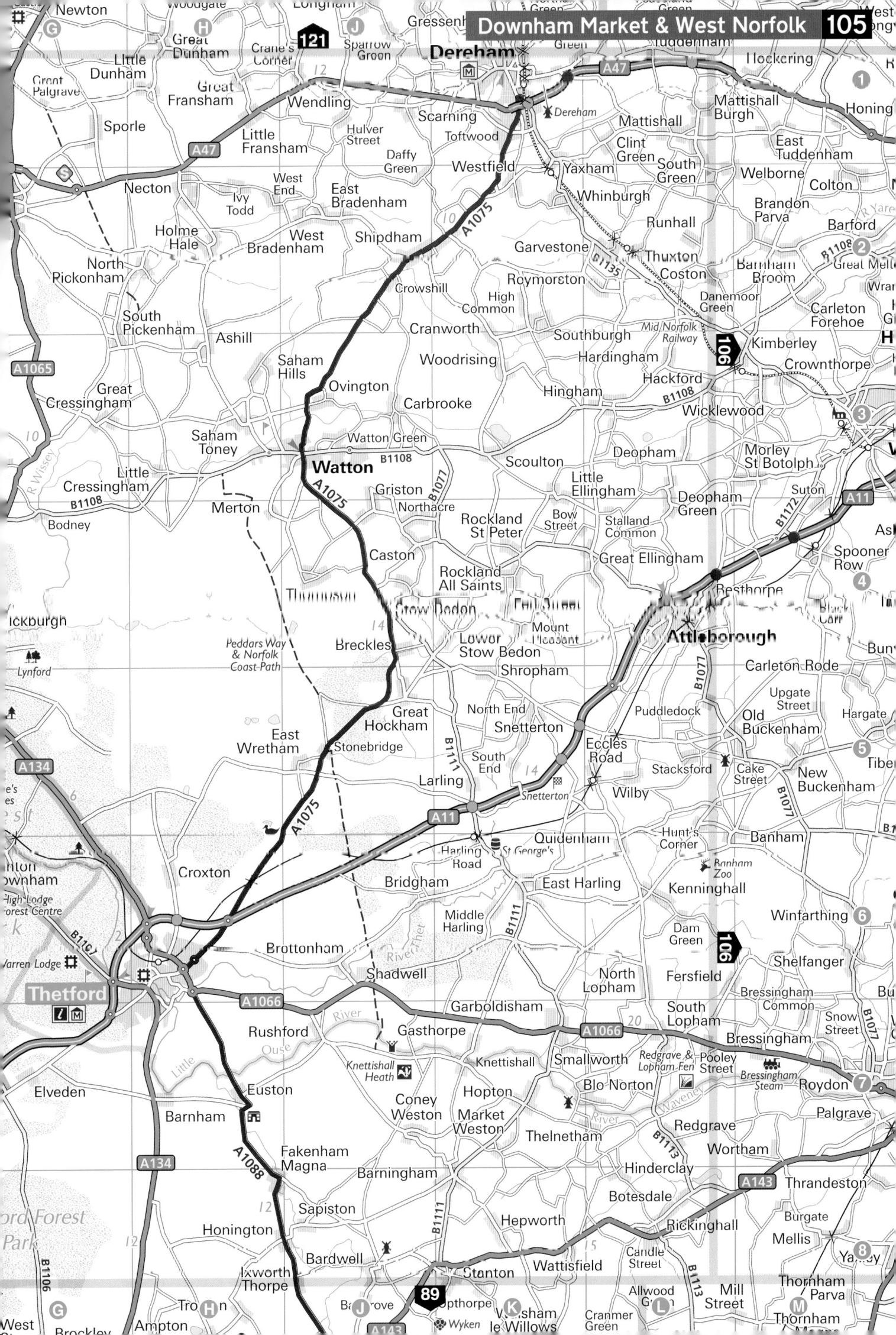

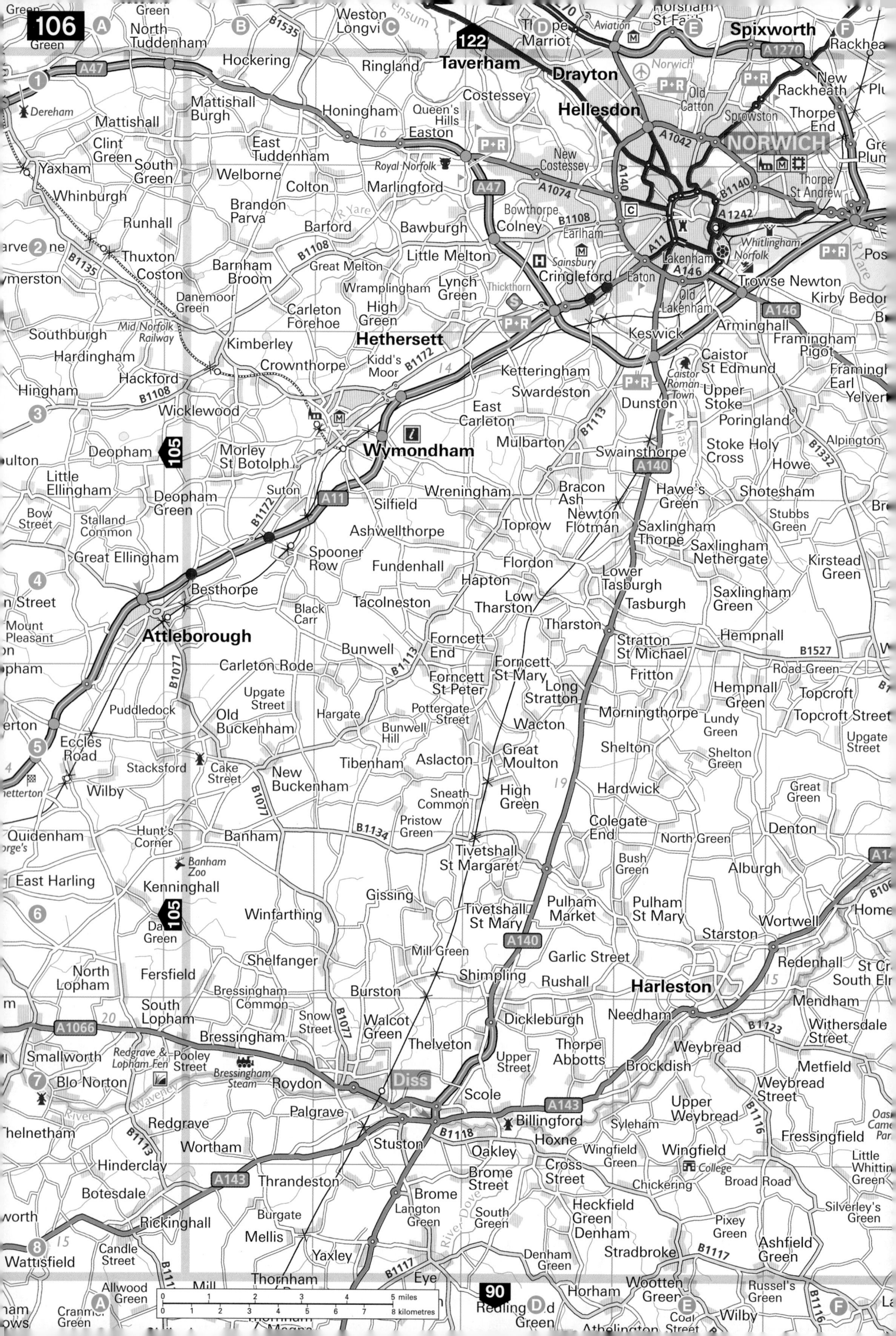

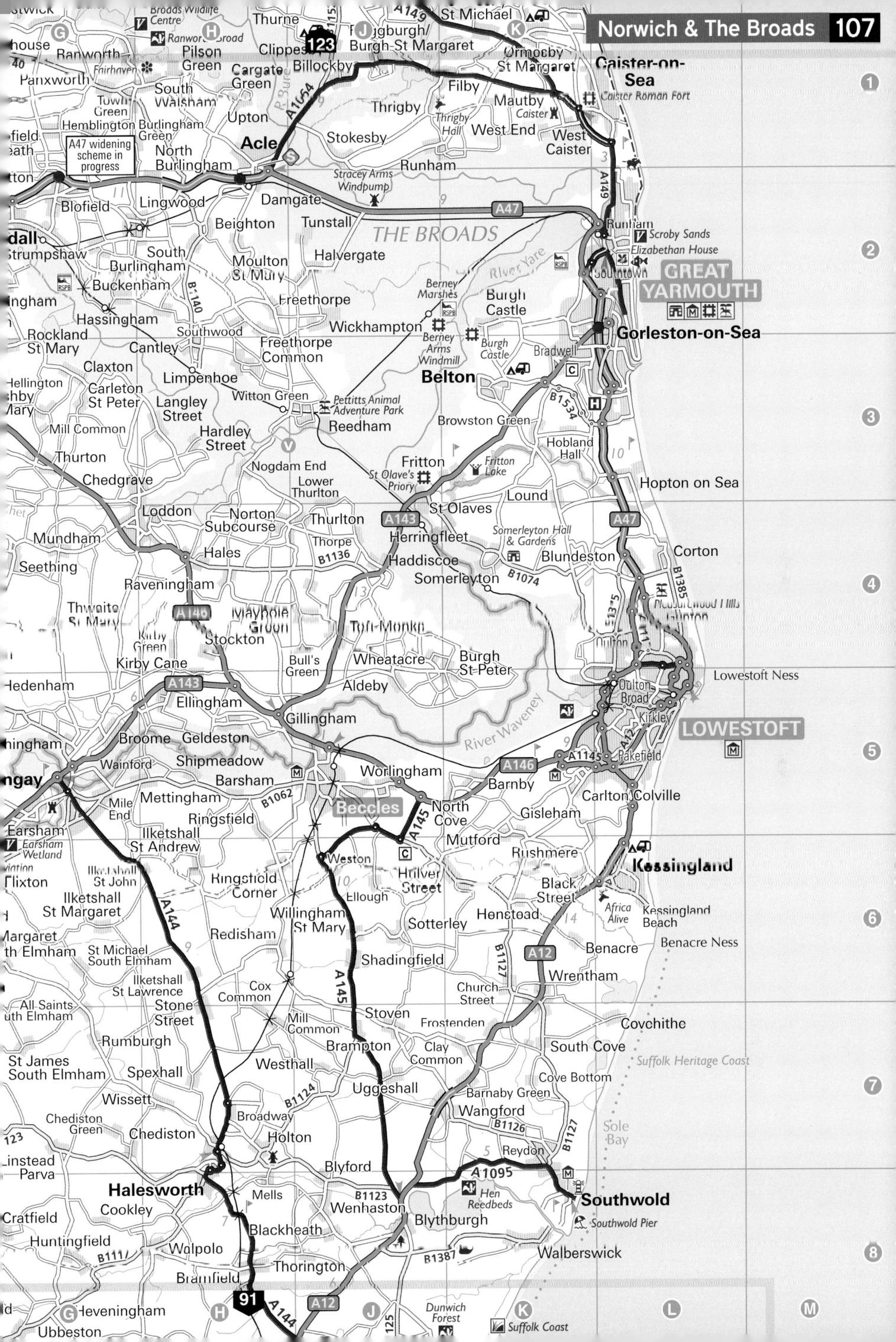

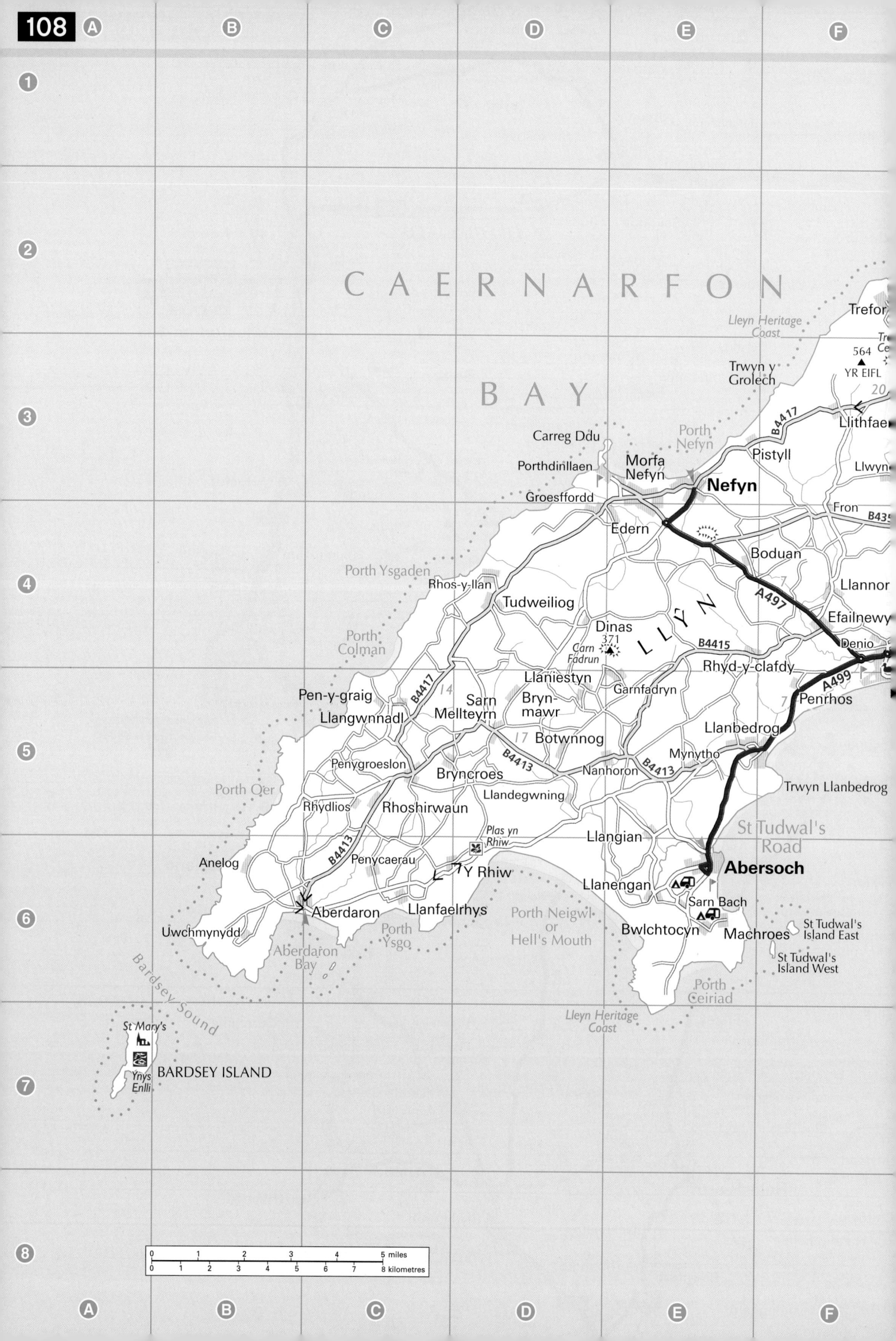

CAERNARFON

BAY

Lleyn Heritage Coast

Trefor

564 ▲ YR EIFL

Trwyn y Grolech

Carreg Ddu

Porthdinllaen

Groesffordd

Morfa Nefyn

Porth Nefyn

Pistyll

B4417

Llithfae

Llwyn

Edern

Nefyn

Porth Ysgaden

Rhos-y-llan

Tudweiliog

Boduan

Fron

B435

LLYN

Llannor

Dinas

371 Carn Fadrun

B4415

Efailnewy

Denio

Porth Colman

Llaniestyn

Garnfadryn

Rhyd-y-clafdy

A497

Pen-y-graig

B4417

14

Sarn Mellteyrn

Bryn-mawr

A499

Penrhos

Llangwnnadl

7

Llanbedrog

Botwnnog

Mynytho

Penygroeslon

B4413

17

Bryncroes

Nanhoron

B4413

Trwyn Llanbedrog

Porth Oer

Llandegwning

St Tudwal's Road

Rhydlios

Rhoshirwaun

Plas yn Rhiw

Llangian

Abersoch

Anelog

B4413

Penycaerau

Y Rhiw

Llanengan

Sarn Bach

Uwchmynydd

Aberdaron

Llanfaelrhys

Porth Ysgo

Porth Neigwl or Hell's Mouth

Bwlchtocyn

Machroes

St Tudwal's Island East

St Tudwal's Island West

Aberdaron Bay

Porth Ceiriad

Bardsey Sound

Lleyn Heritage Coast

St Mary's

Ynys Enlli

BARDSEY ISLAND

0   1   2   3   4   5 miles
0   1   2   3   4   5   6   7   8 kilometres

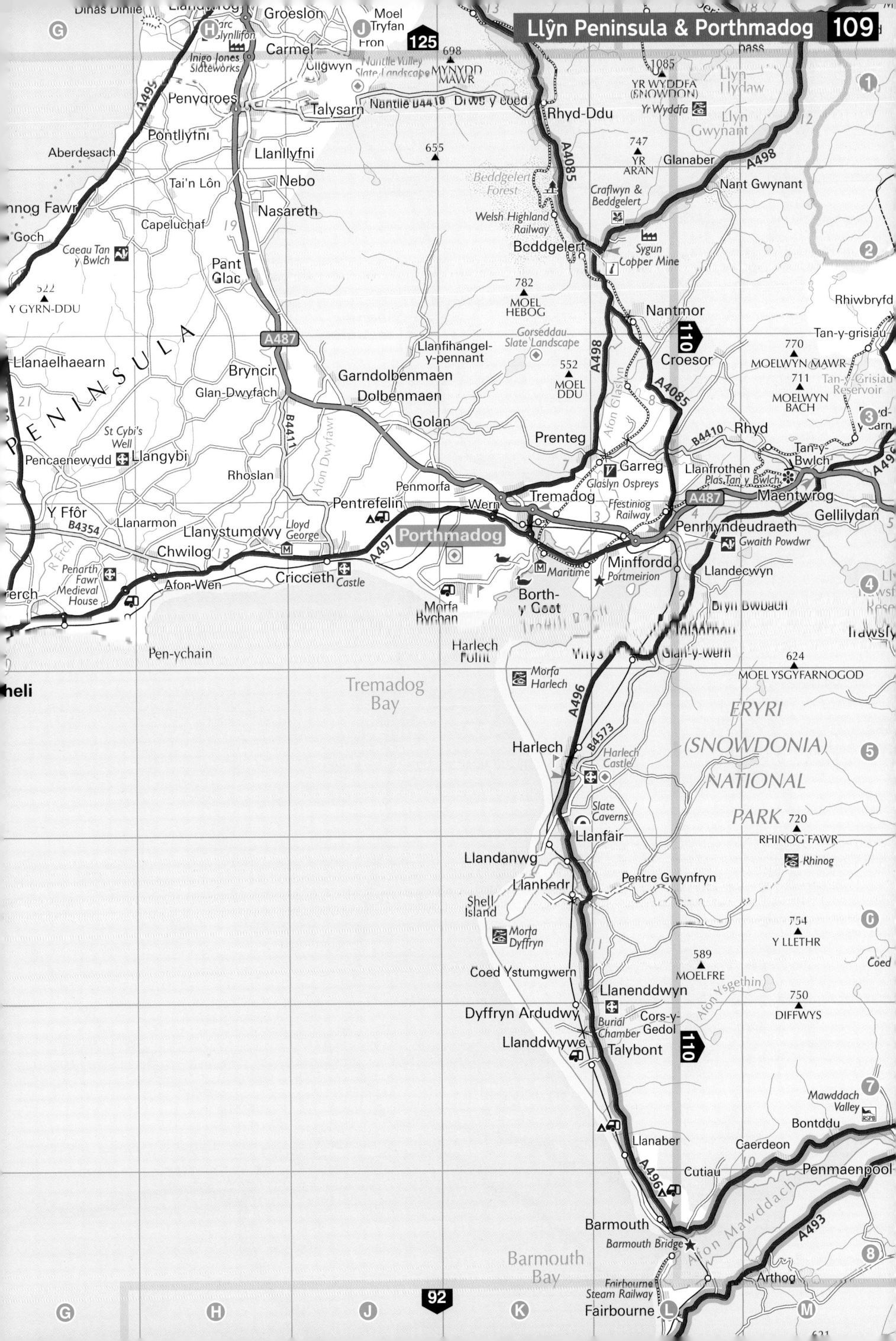

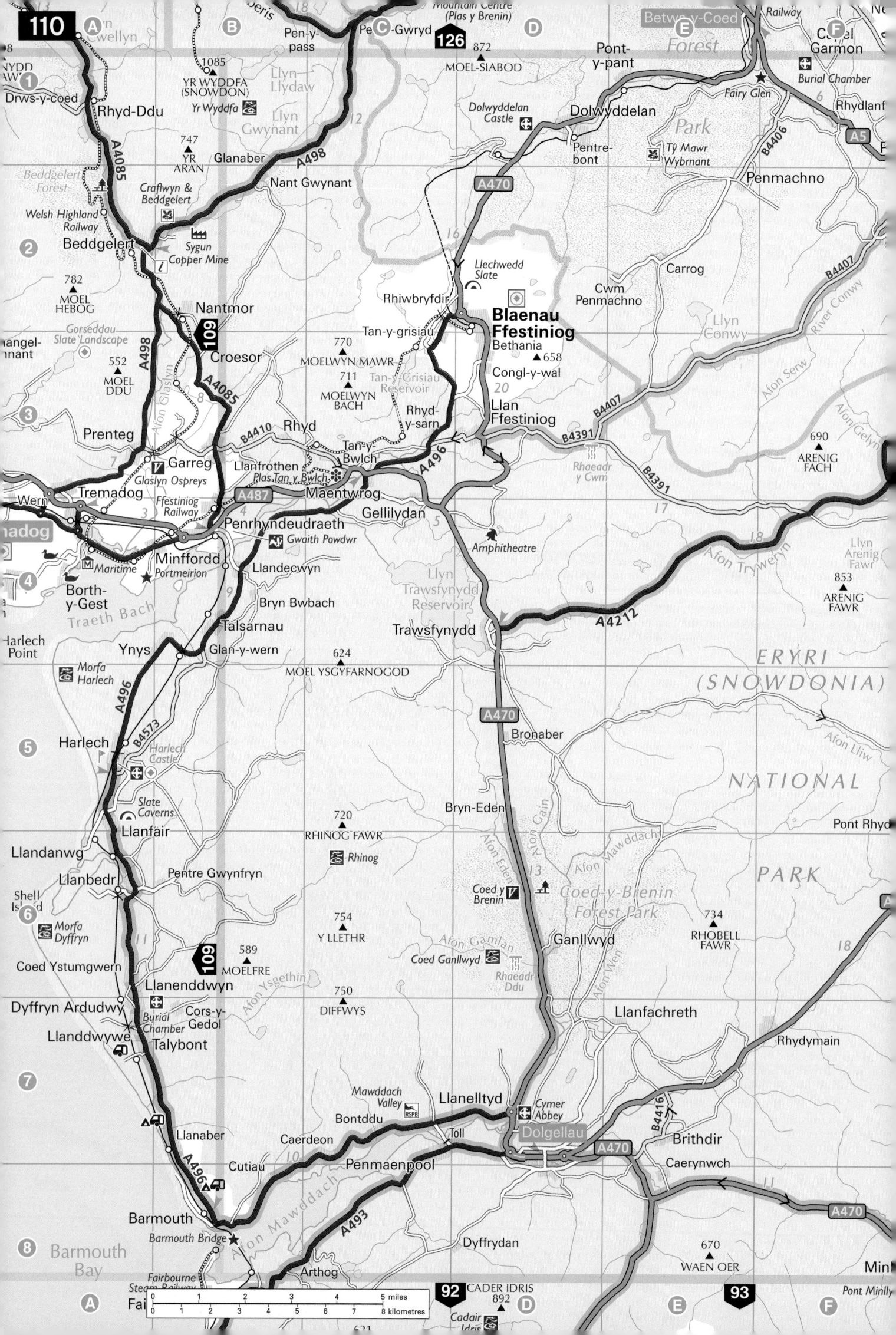

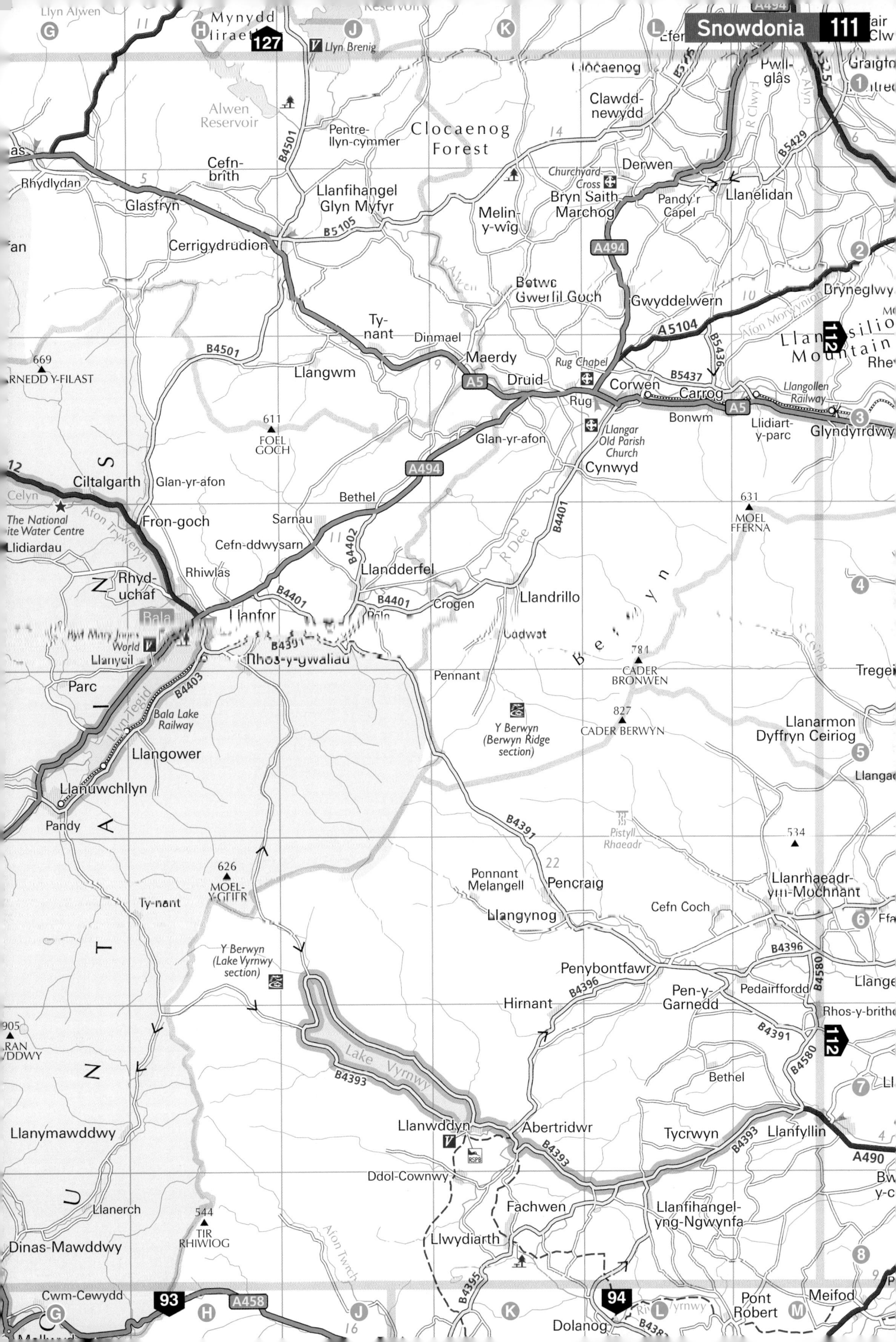

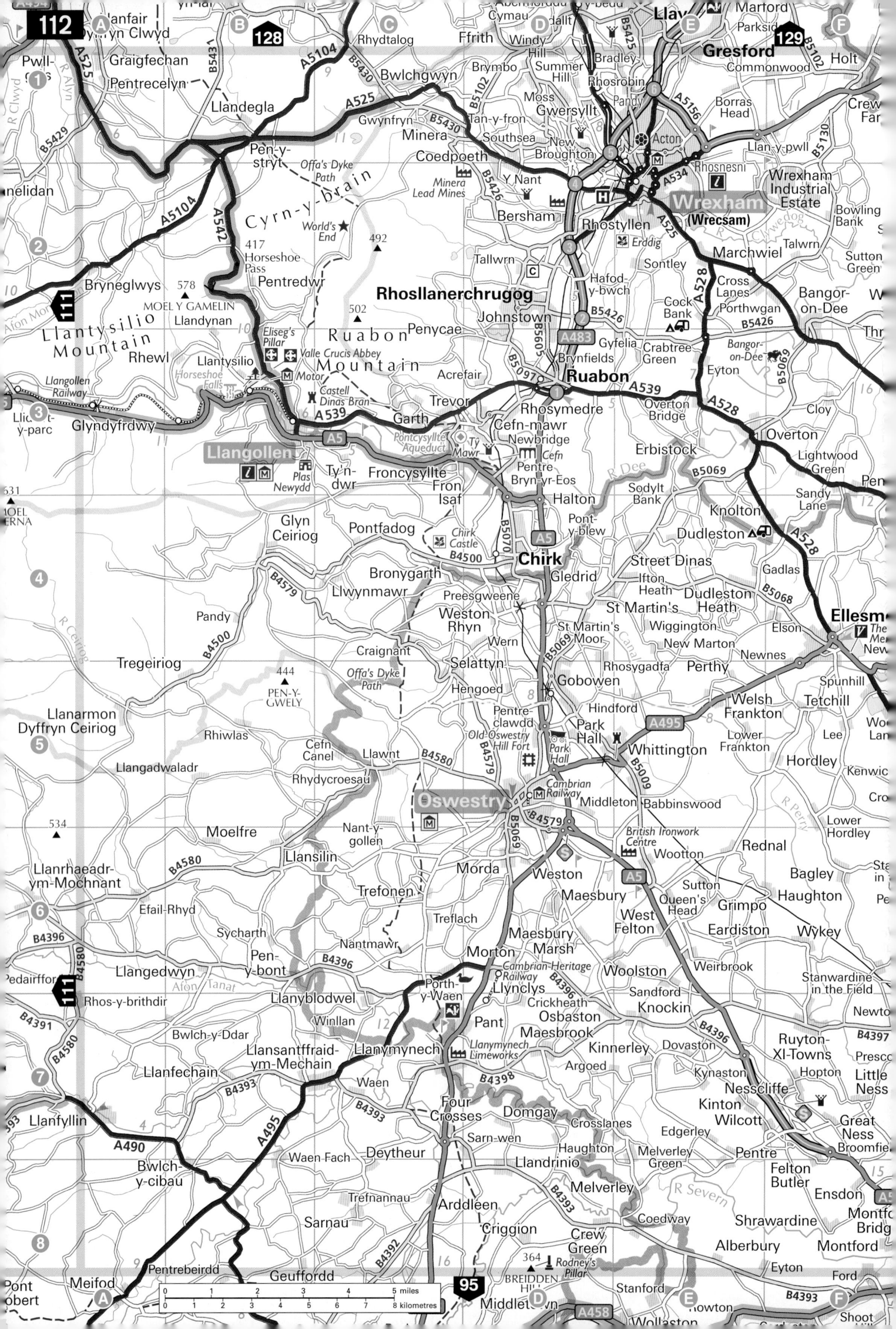

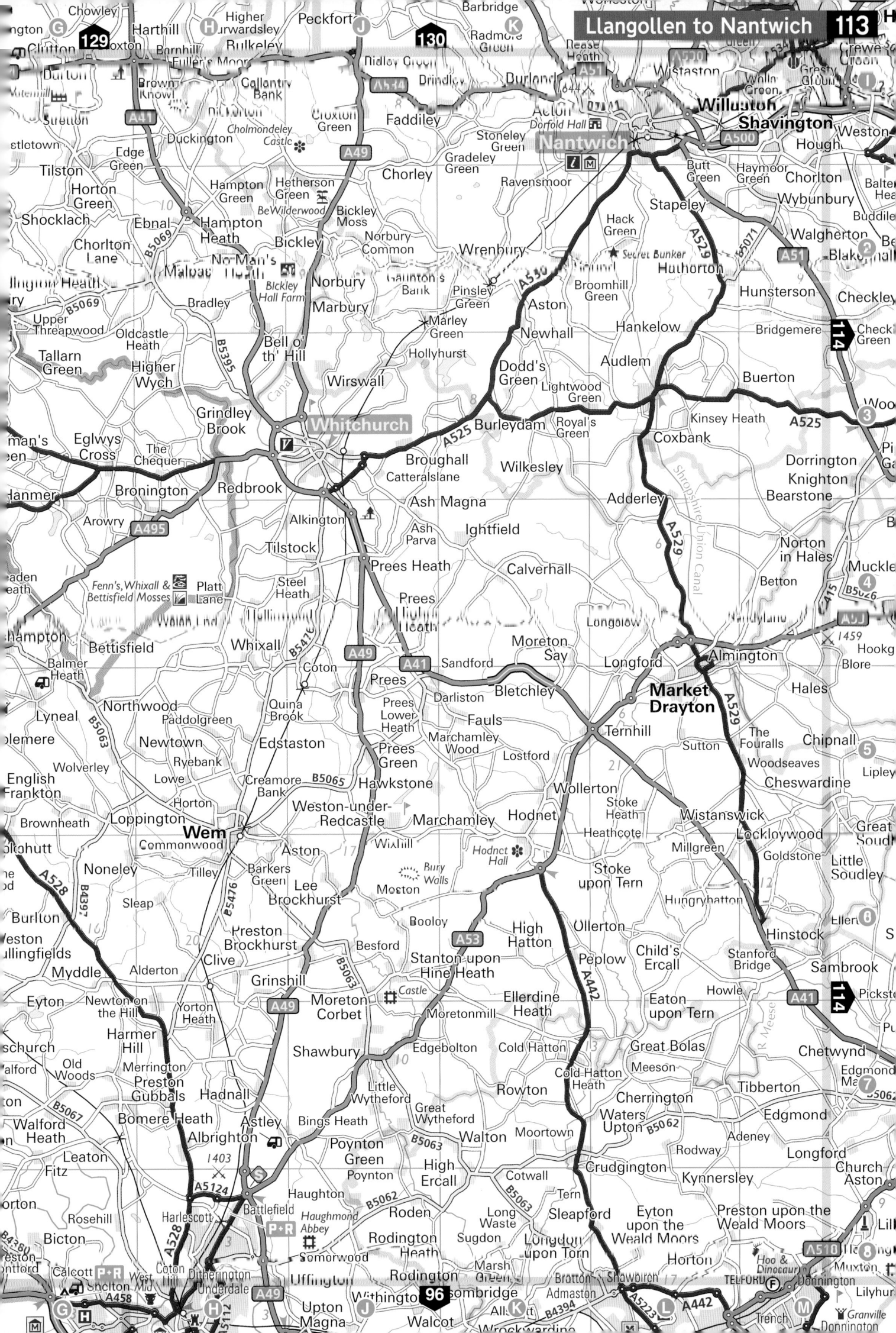

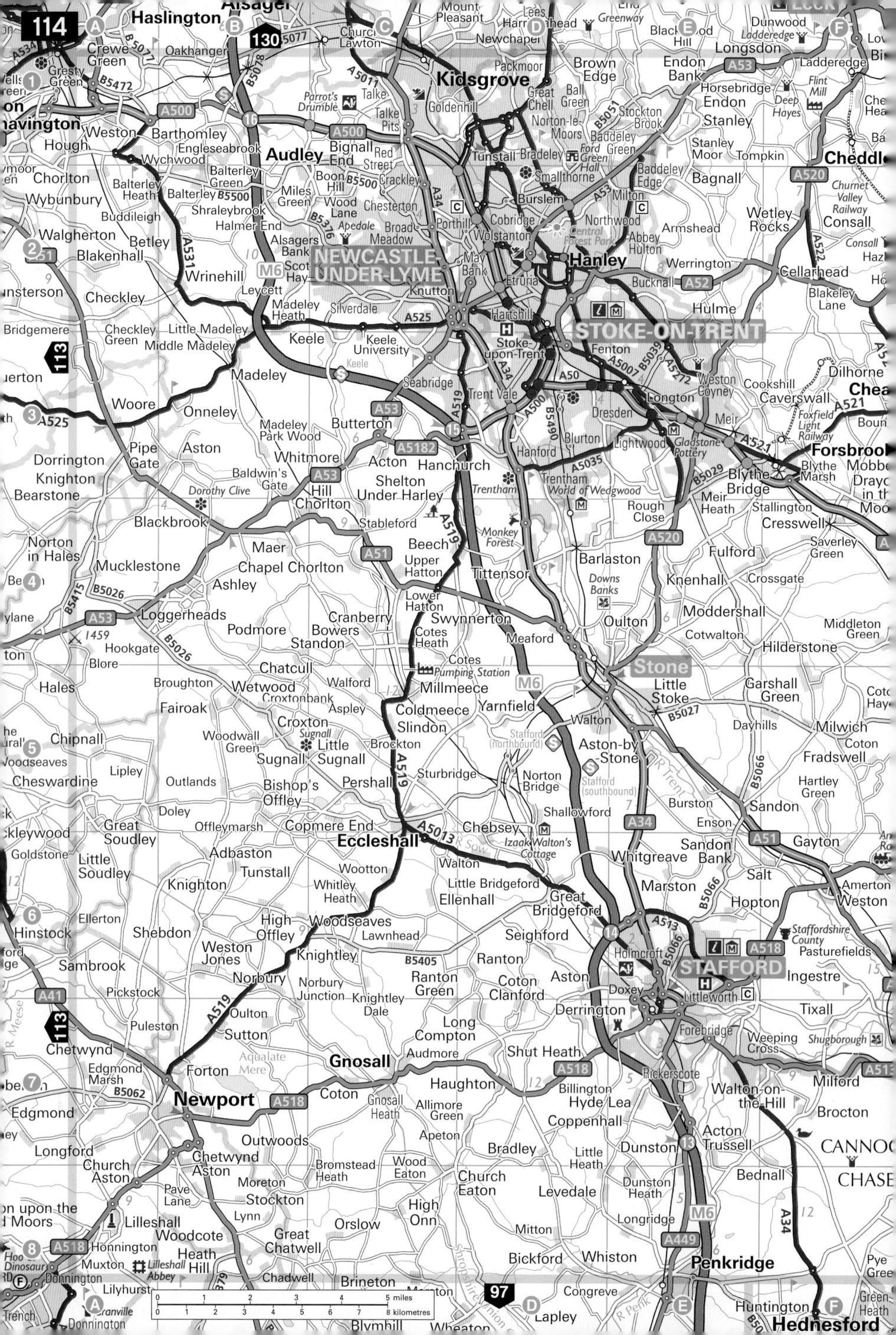

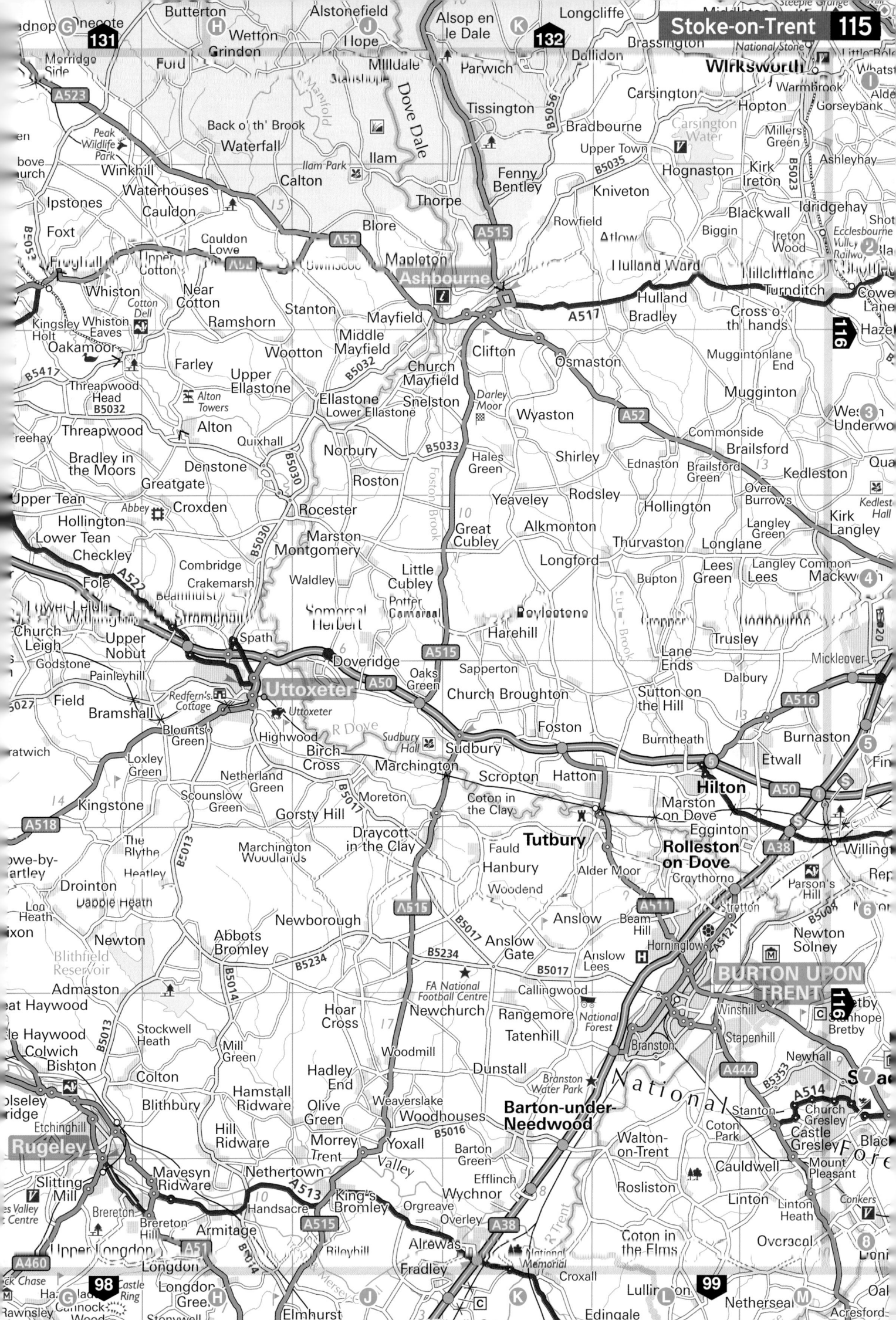

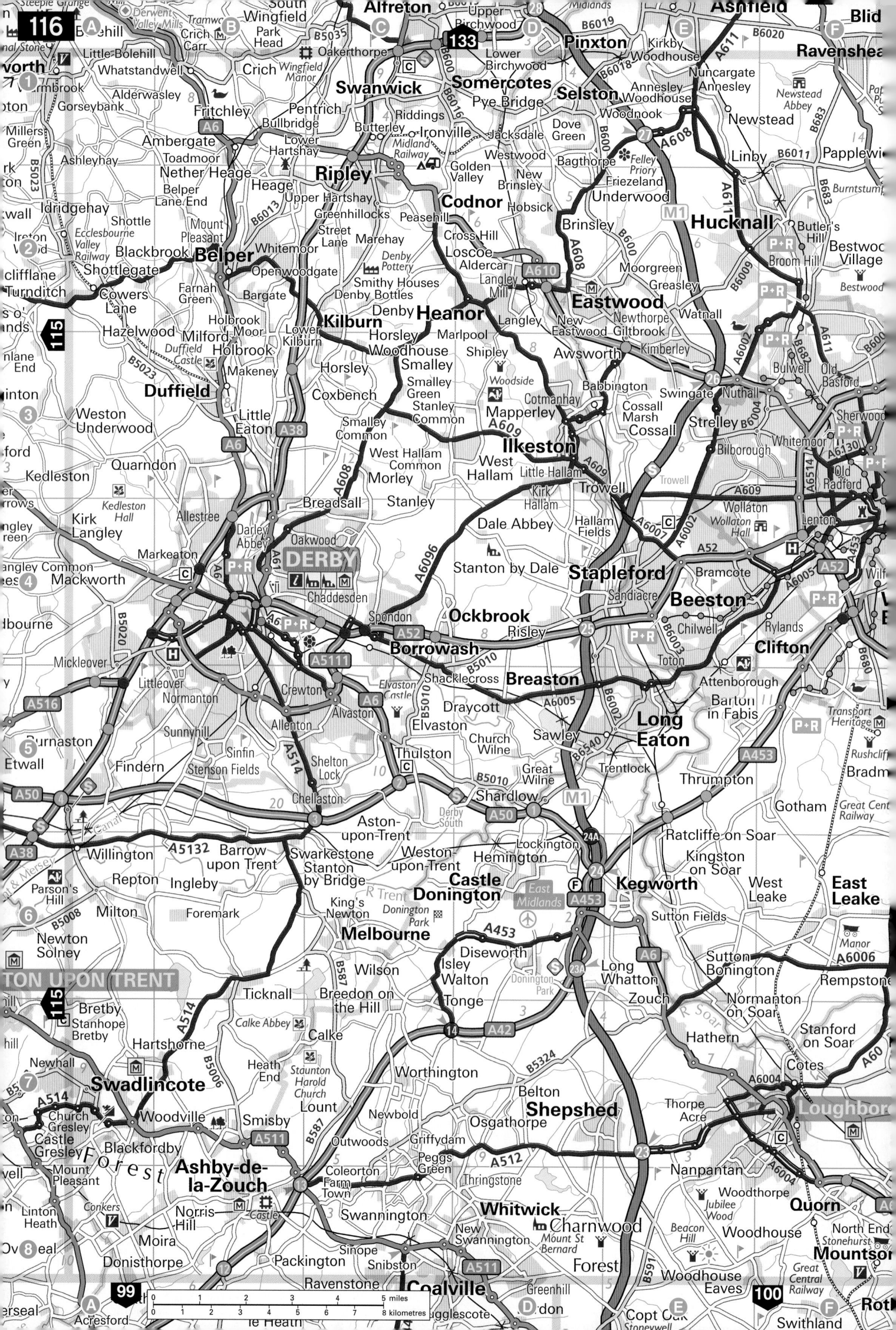

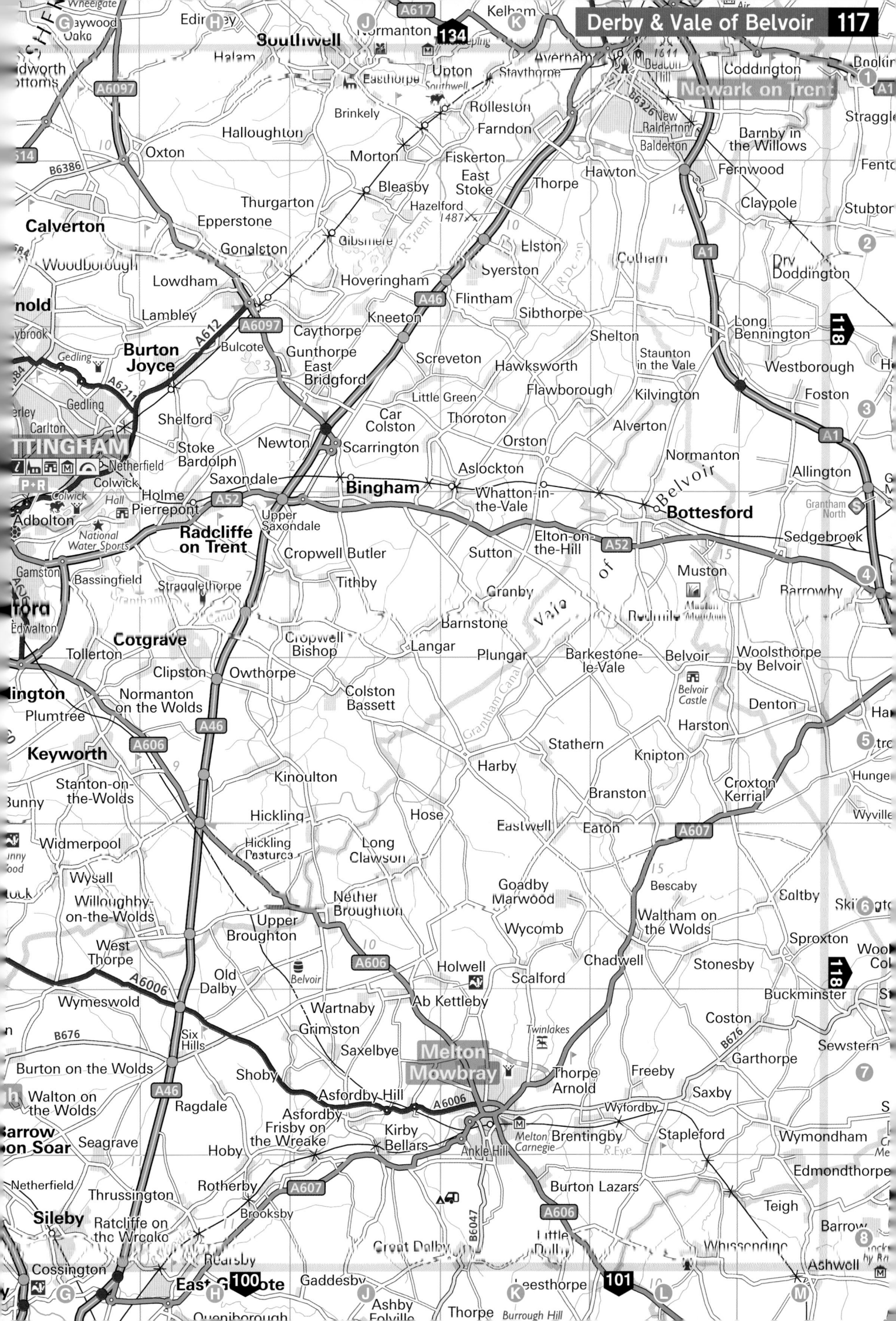

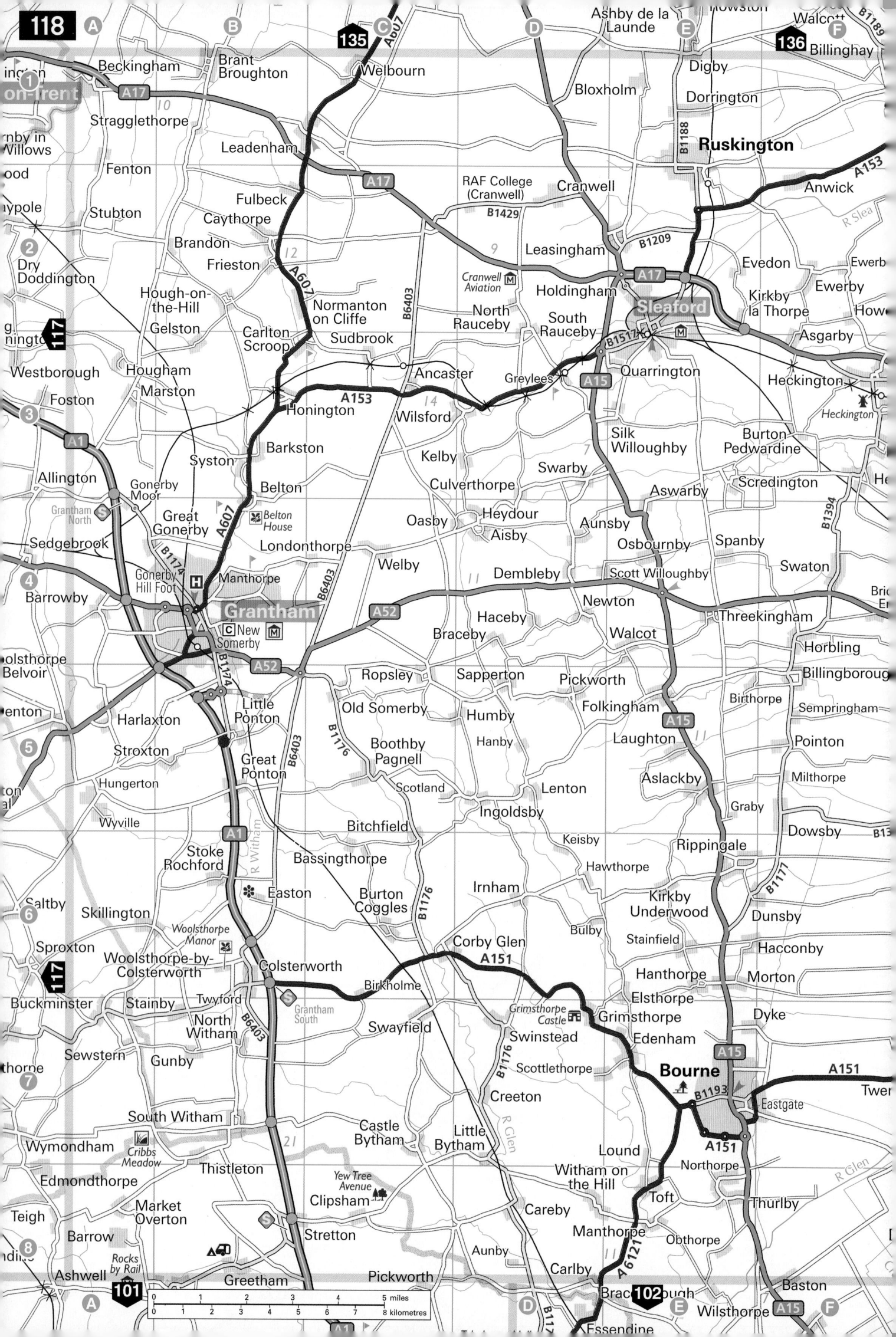

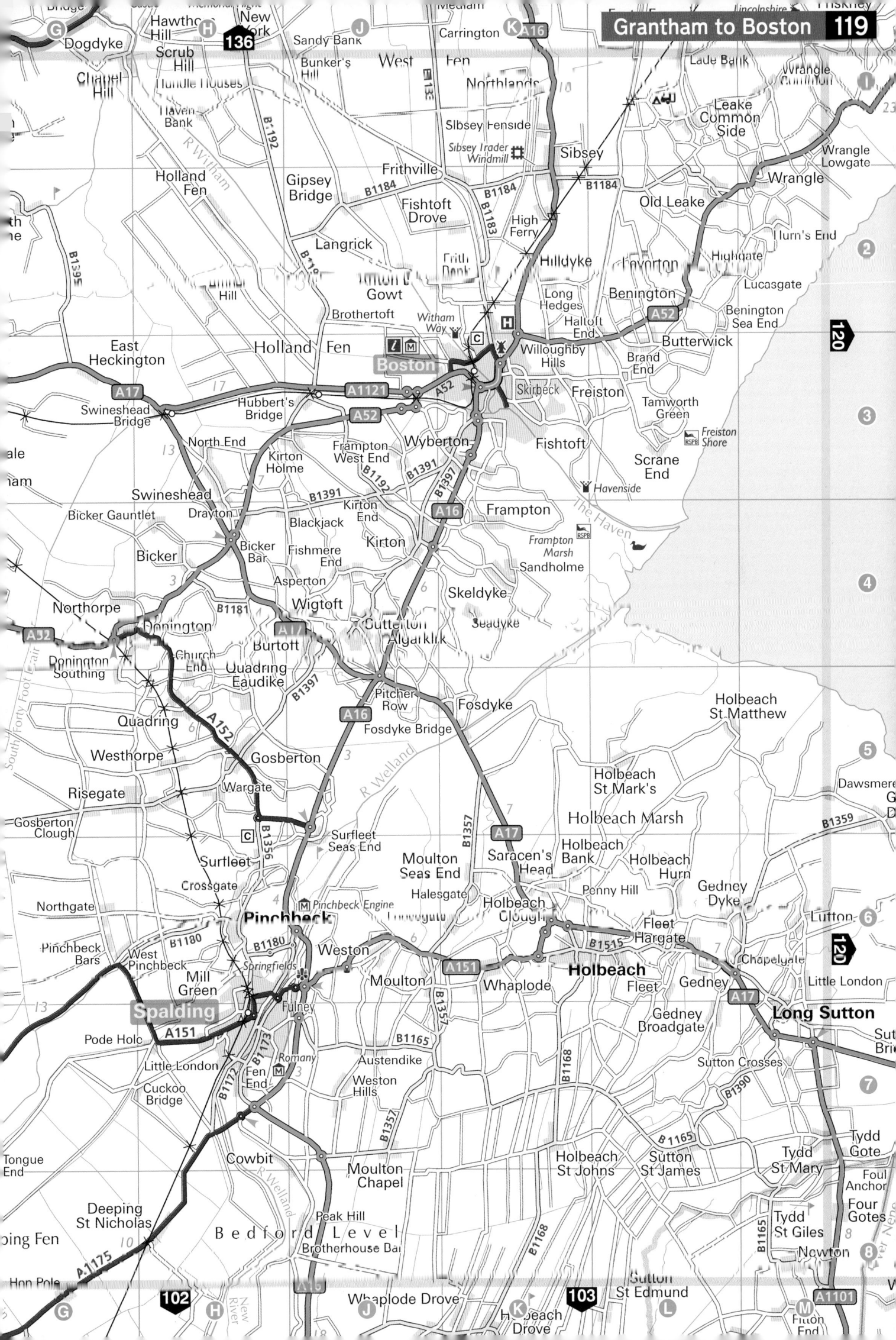

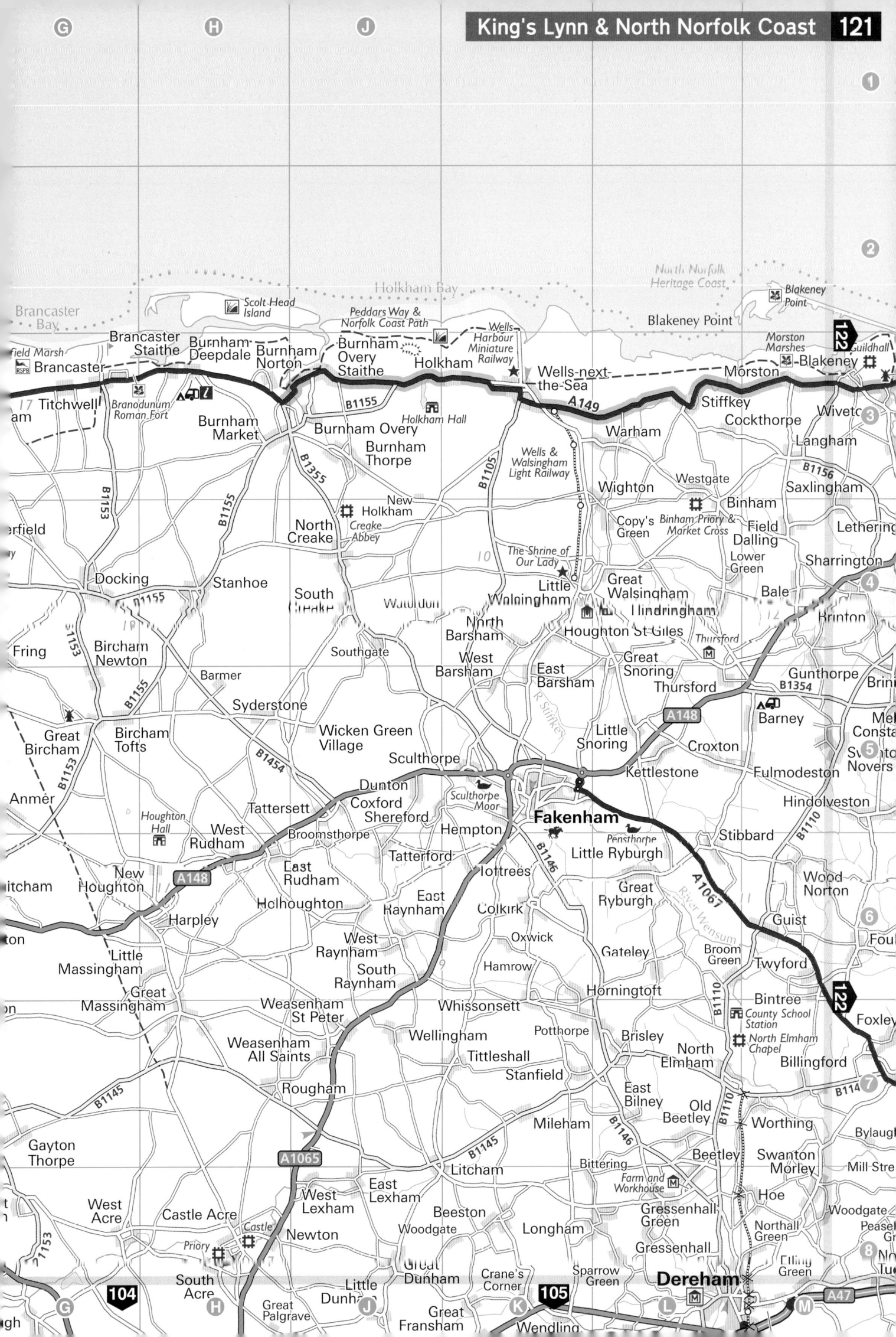

North Norfolk Heritage Coast

Holkham Bay

Brancaster Bay

Blakeney Point

field Marsh
RSPB

Brancaster

Brancaster Staithe

Burnham Deepdale

Burnham Norton

Scolt Head Island

Peddars Way & Norfolk Coast Path

Burnham Overy Staithe

Holkham

Wells Harbour Miniature Railway

Wells-next-the-Sea

A149

Morston

Morston Marshes

Blakeney Point

Blakeney

Guildhall

122

17 Titchwell

Branodunum Roman Fort

Burnham Market

Burnham Overy

Holkham Hall

B1155

Warham

Stiffkey

Cockthorpe

Wiveto

3

Burnham Thorpe

B1355

B1105

Wells & Walsingham Light Railway

Wighton

Westgate

Binham

Saxlingham

Langham

B1156

Lethering

erfield

B1153

B1355

New Holkham

Creake Abbey

North Creake

Copy's Green

Binham Priory & Market Cross

Field Dalling

Lower Green

Sharrington

Bale

4

ay

South Creake

Waterden

The Shrine of Our Lady

Little Walsingham

Great Walsingham

Hindringham

Thursford

Brinton

Fring

B1153

Docking

Stanhoe

B1155

18

Southgate

North Barsham

West Barsham

East Barsham

Houghton St Giles

Great Snoring

Thursford

12

Gunthorpe

Brin

5

Bircham Newton

Barmer

Syderstone

Snoring

A148

B1354

Barney

Me Consta

Sw to

Novers

Great Bircham

Bircham Tofts

Wicken Green Village

B1454

Sculthorpe

Little Snoring

Kettlestone

Croxton

Fulmodeston

Hindolveston

B1110

Anmer

B1153

Houghton Hall

Dunton Coxford Shereford

Sculthorpe Moor

Fakenham

Penthorpe

Stibbard

Wood Norton

Tattersett

Hempton

Little Ryburgh

A1067

River Wensum

Guist

6

itcham

New Houghton

A148

West Rudham

Broomsthorpe

Tatterford

Iottrees

B1146

Great Ryburgh

Broom Green

Twyford

Fou

Harpley

East Rudham

Holhoughton

East Raynham

Colkirk

Oxwick

Gateley

B1110

Bintree

122

Little Massingham

West Raynham

South Raynham

Hamrow

Great Ryburgh

County School Station

Foxley

Great Massingham

Weasenham St Peter

Whissonsett

Wellingham

Potthorpe

Horningtoft

Brisley

North Elmham

North Elmham Chapel

Billingford

Weasenham All Saints

Tittleshall

Stanfield

East Bilney

Old Beetley

B1110

B114

7

B1145

Rougham

Worthing

Bylaug

Gayton Thorpe

B1145

A1065

Litcham

West Lexham

East Lexham

Mileham

Beeston Woodgate

Longham

B1146

Bittering

Farm and Workhouse

Gressenhall Green

Gressenhall

Beetley

Swanton Morley

Hoe

Northall Green

Mill Stre

Woodgate

Pease Gr

West Acre

Castle Acre

Castle

Priory

Newton

Great Dunham

Crane's Corner

Sparrow Green

Dereham

Elling Green

No

Tu

8

gh

104

South Acre

Great Palgrave

Little Dunha

H

Great Fransham

J

105

Wendling

K

A47

L

M

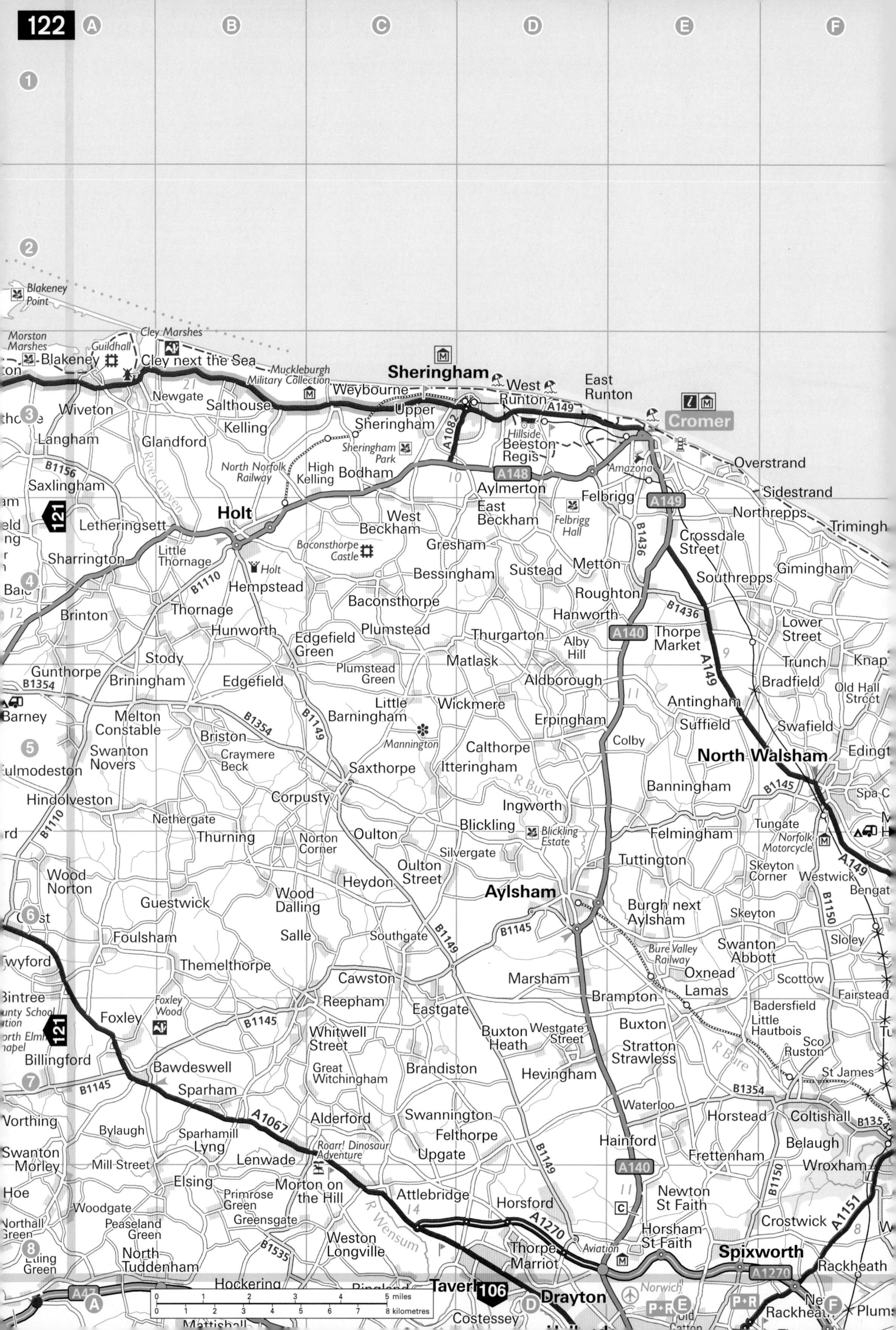

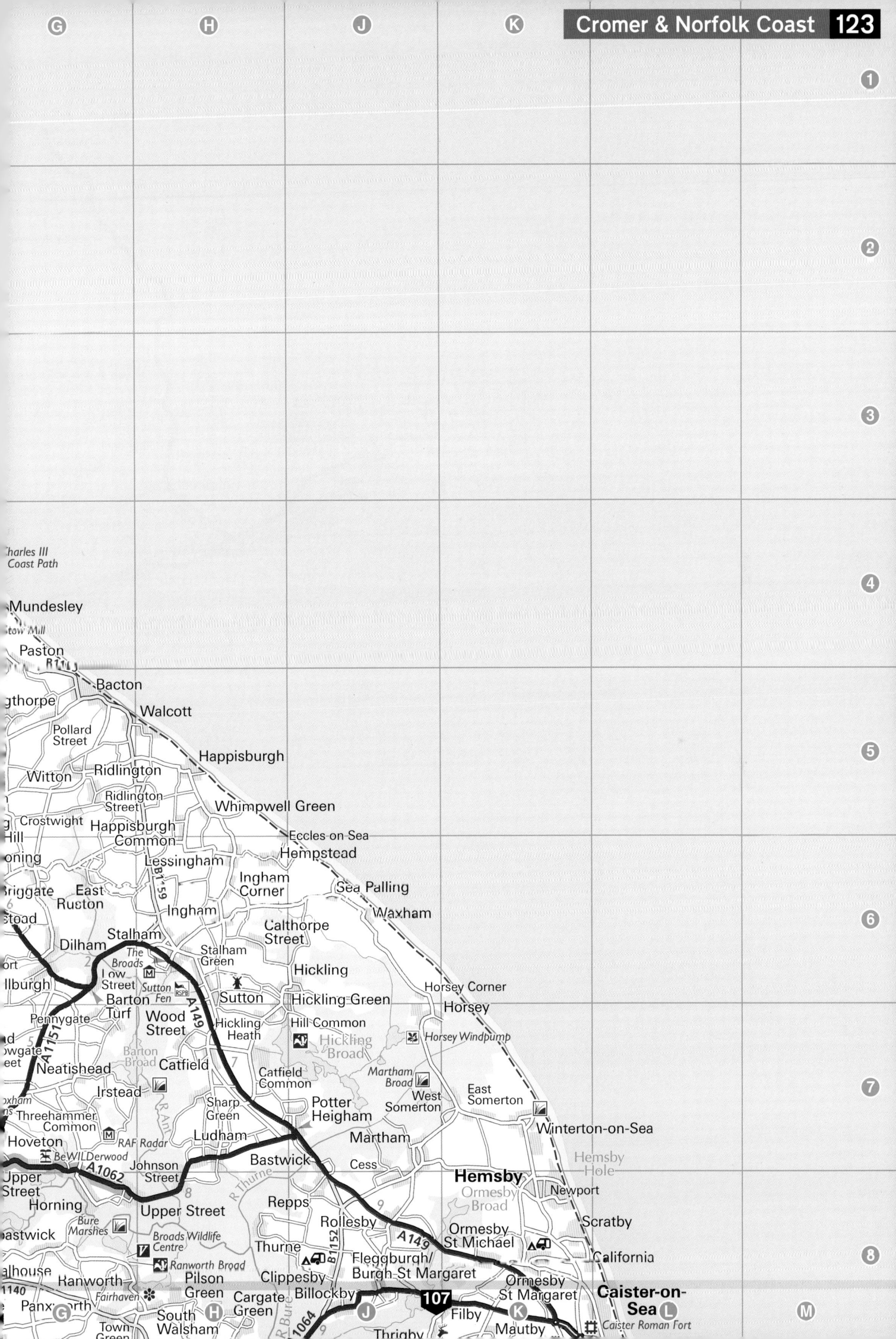

G   H   J   K

1
2
3
4
5
6
7
8

Charles III
Coast Path

Mundesley
tow Mill
Paston
Bacton
gthorpe
Walcott
Pollard
Street
Happisburgh
Witton
Ridlington
Ridlington
Street
Whimpwell Green
Crostwight
Hill
Happisburgh
Common
Eccles-on-Sea
oning
Lessingham
Hempstead
East
Ruston
Ingham
Corner
Sea Palling
Briggate
Ingham
Waxham
stoad
Stalham
Calthorpe
Street
Dilham
Stalham
Green
The Broads
Low
Street
Sutton
Fen
RSPB
Hickling
Horsey Corner
Ilburgh
Barton
Turf
Sutton
Hickling Green
Horsey
Pennygate
Wood
Street
Hickling
Heath
Hill Common
Hickling
Broad
Horsey Windpump
Barton
Broad
Catfield
Neatishead
Catfield
Common
Martham
Broad
East
Somerton
Irstead
Sharp
Green
Potter
Heigham
West
Somerton
oxham
Threehammer
Common
RAF Radar
Ludham
Winterton-on-Sea
Hoveton
BeWILDerwood
A1062
Johnson
Street
Bastwick
Cess
Hemsby
Hole
Upper
Street
Horning
Upper Street
Repps
Hemsby
Ormesby
Broad
Newport
astwick
Bure
Marshes
Rollesby
Scratby
Broads Wildlife
Centre
Thurne
Ormesby
St Michael
California
Ranworth Broad
Fleggburgh/
Burgh St Margaret
Clippesby
Ormesby
St Margaret
Caister-on-
Sea
Panx orth
Pilson
Green
Cargate
Green
Billockby
107
Filby
South
Walsham
Thrigby
Mautby
Caister Roman Fort

G   H   J   K   L   M

A B C D E F

1

The Skerries

North Anglesey
Heritage Coast

Wylfa
Head

Cem
Ba

Cemlyn
Bay

Hen
Borth

Cemaes

CARMEL HEAD

Tregele

Mynydd
Mechell

2

Dublin

Dublin
(Mar-Oct)

Holyhead
Bay

Church
Bay

Llanfairynghornwy

Swtan
Heritage

Llanrhyddlad

Porth
Tywynmawr

Llanfaethlu

Llanfflewyn

Llanba

Llanb

17

3

North Stack

Gogarth
Bay

Breakwater

South Stack

Holyhead Mountain
Heritage Coast

Ellins
Tower

Penrhyn Mawr

Holyhead
Maritime

Holyhead
(Caergybi)

Llaingoch

Holyhead Mountain
Hut Circles

Penrhos Feliw

Kingsland

Penrhos

Llanynghenedl

Llanfachraeth

Llanfwrog

Llanddeusant

Llynon
Mill

Elim

Stryd-y-
Facsen

Pen-llyn

Llanfigael

Llyn
Llywena

Presaddfed

B5109

4

HOLY ISLAND

Trearddur Bay

Trefignath

A5

A55

B4545

Four Mile
Bridge

Llanfair-yn-Neubwll

Valley

A5025

Caergeiliog

Llanfihangel
yn Nhowyn

RSPB
Valley

Llechylched

Capel Gwyn

Bodedern

Bryngwr

5

Rhoscolyn

Rhoscolyn
Head

Plas
Cymyran

Cymyran
Bay

Rhosneigr

A4080

Barclodiad
y Gawres

Porth Trecastell

Ty Newydd

Llanfaelog

Bryn Du

Ty
Croes

Pencarr

A4080

I·0·

6

Aberffraw

Anglesey
Circuit

Llang

Aberffraw
Bay

Aberffraw Bay
Heritage Coast

Malltraeth

7

C A E R N A R F O N

Llanddwyn Is

8

B A Y

0   1   2   3   4   5 miles
0 1 2 3 4 5 6 7 8 kilometres

A B C D E F

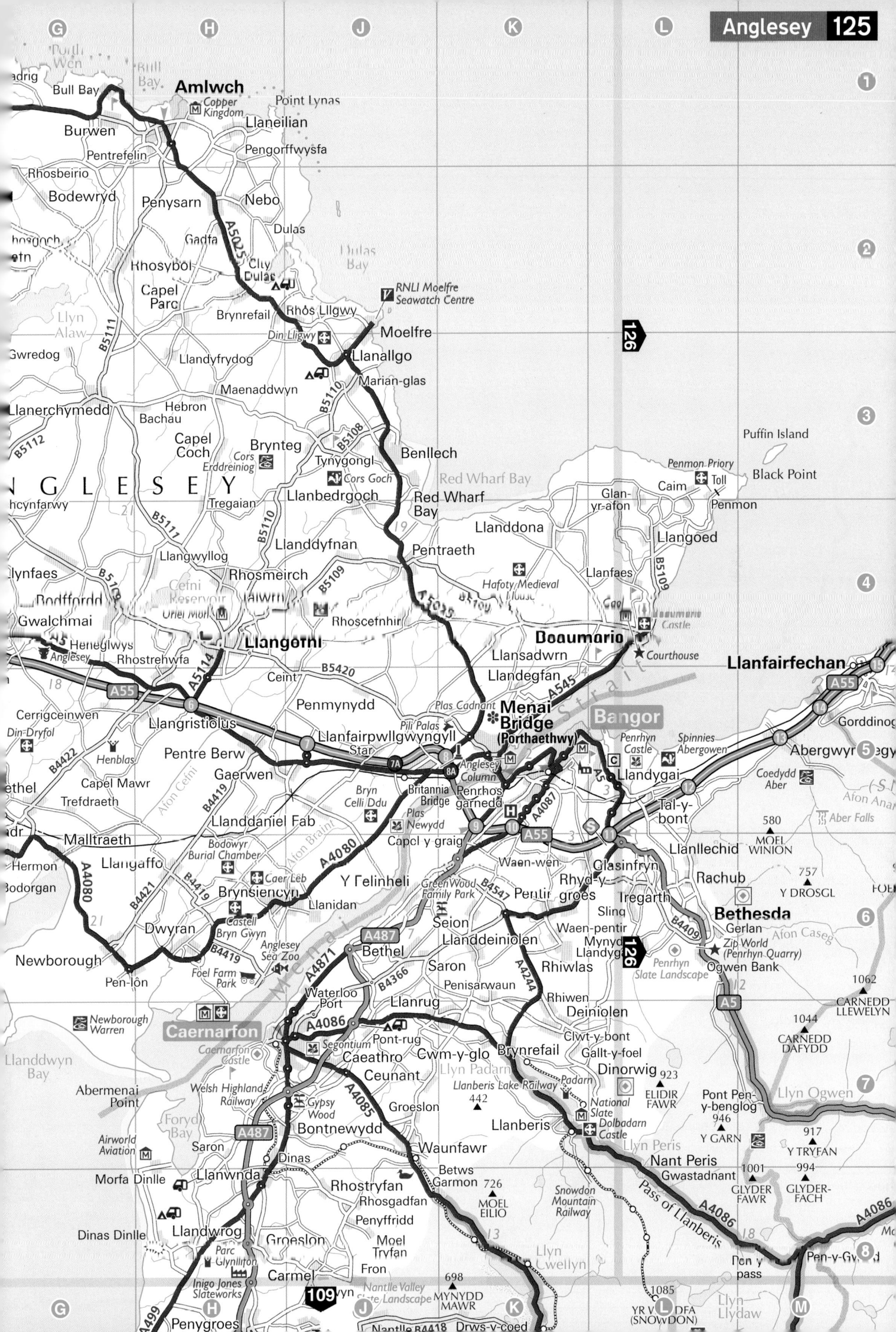

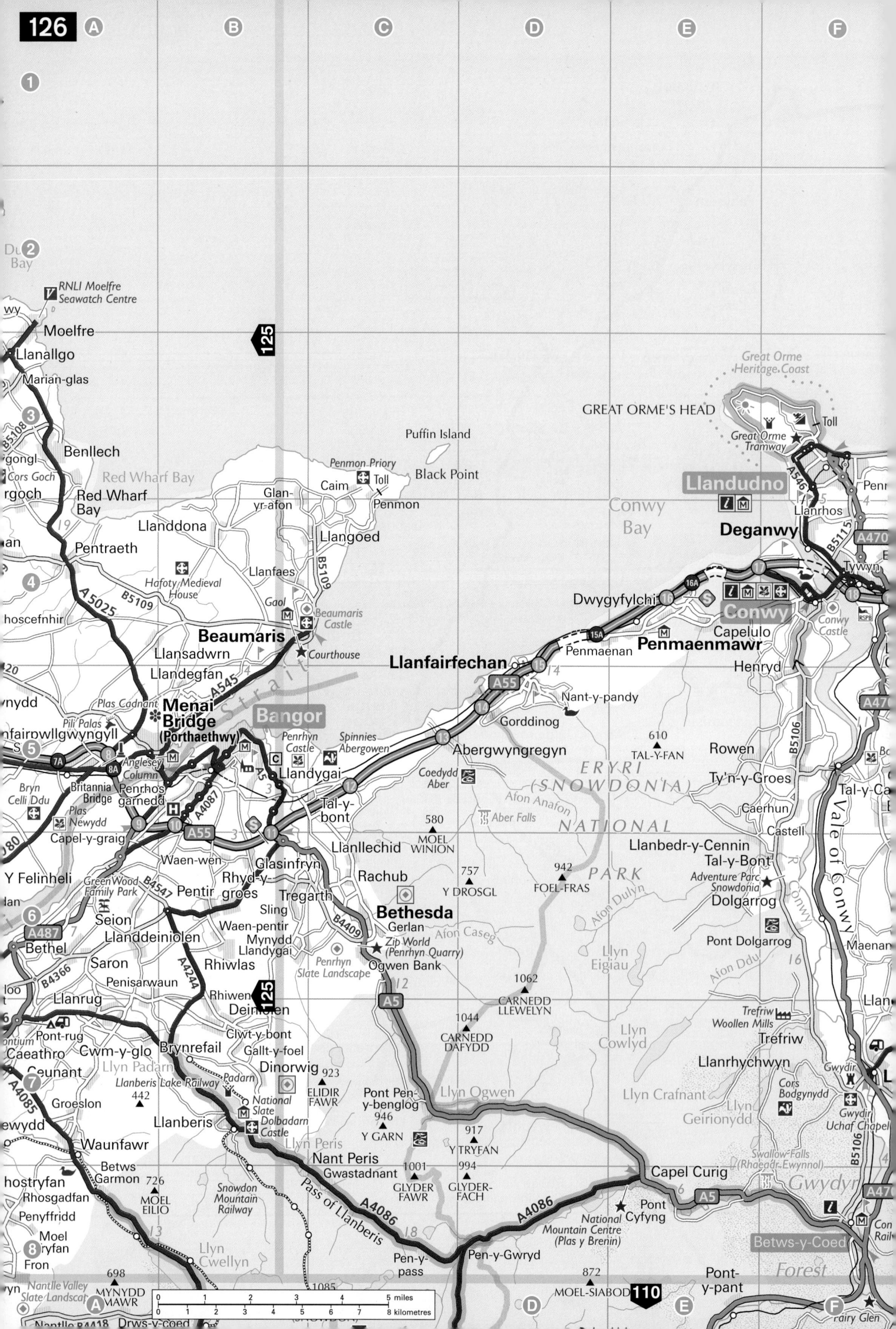

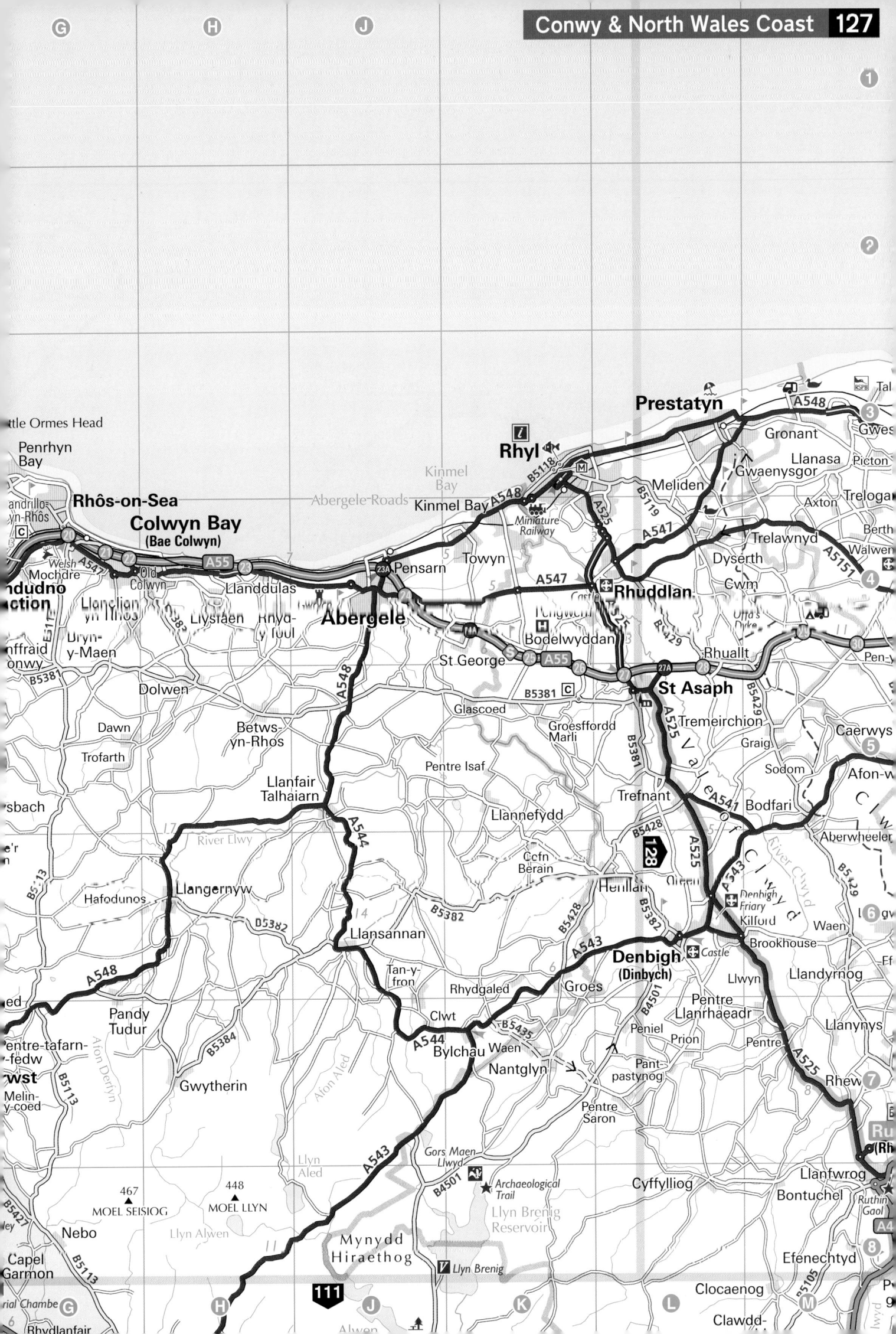

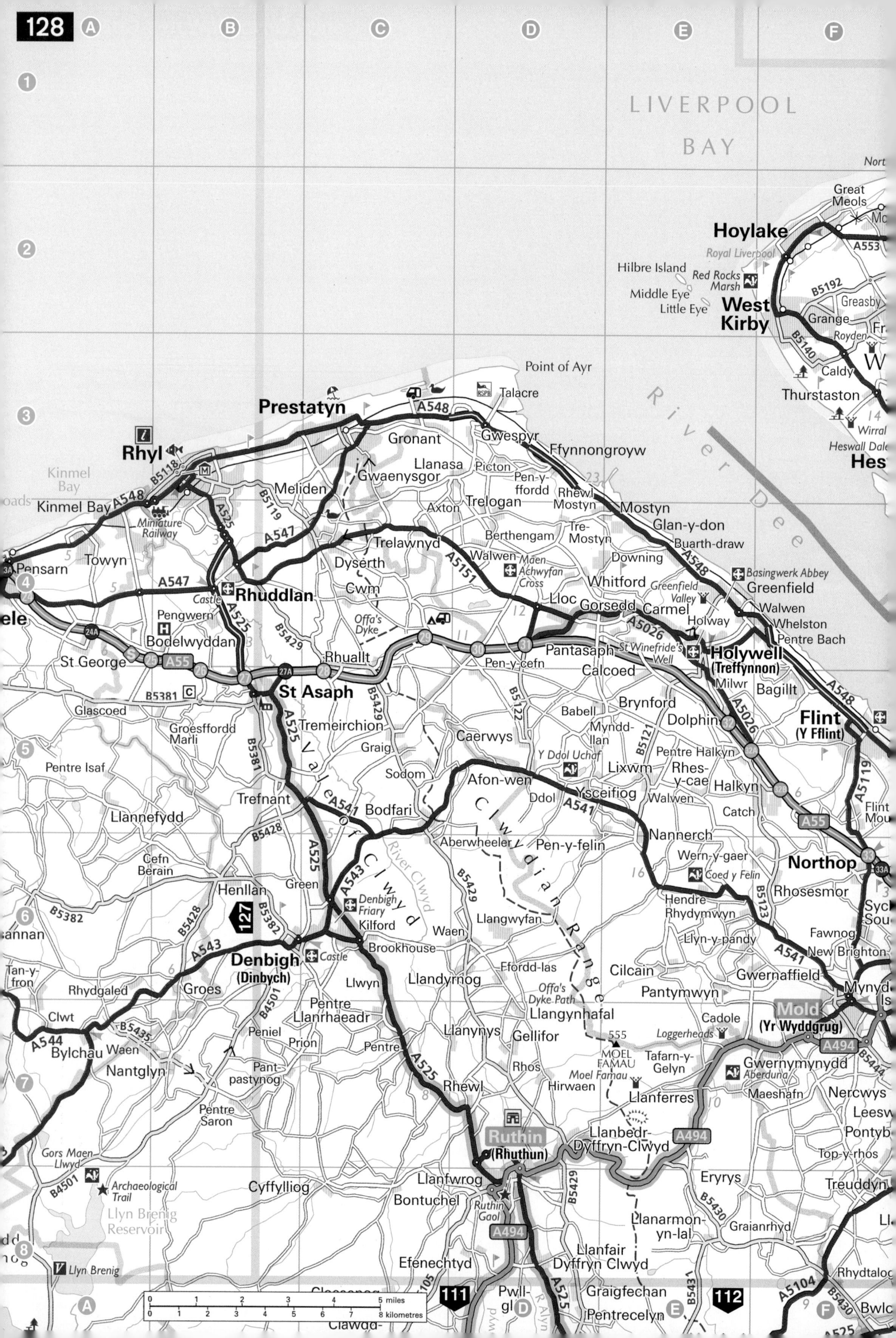

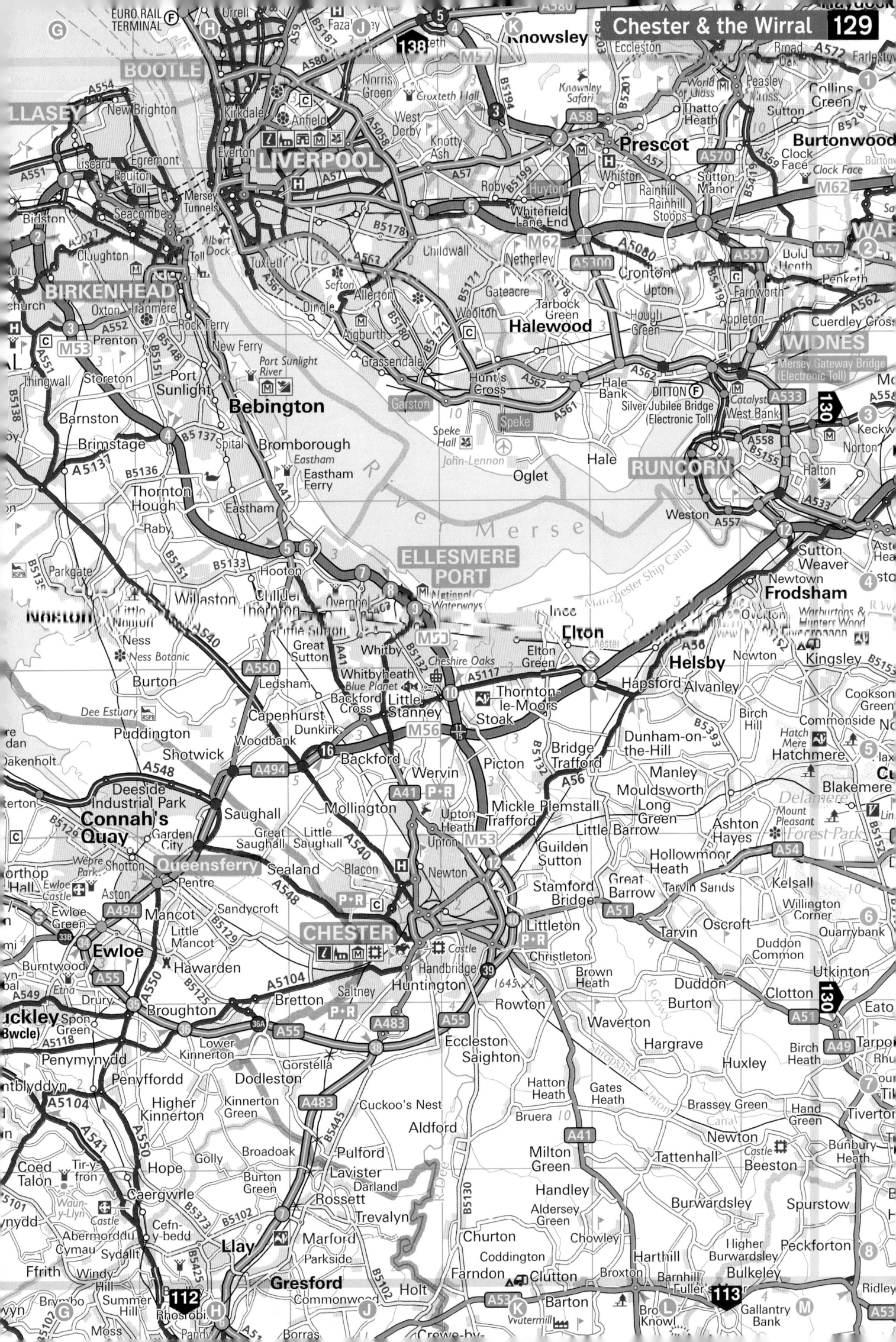

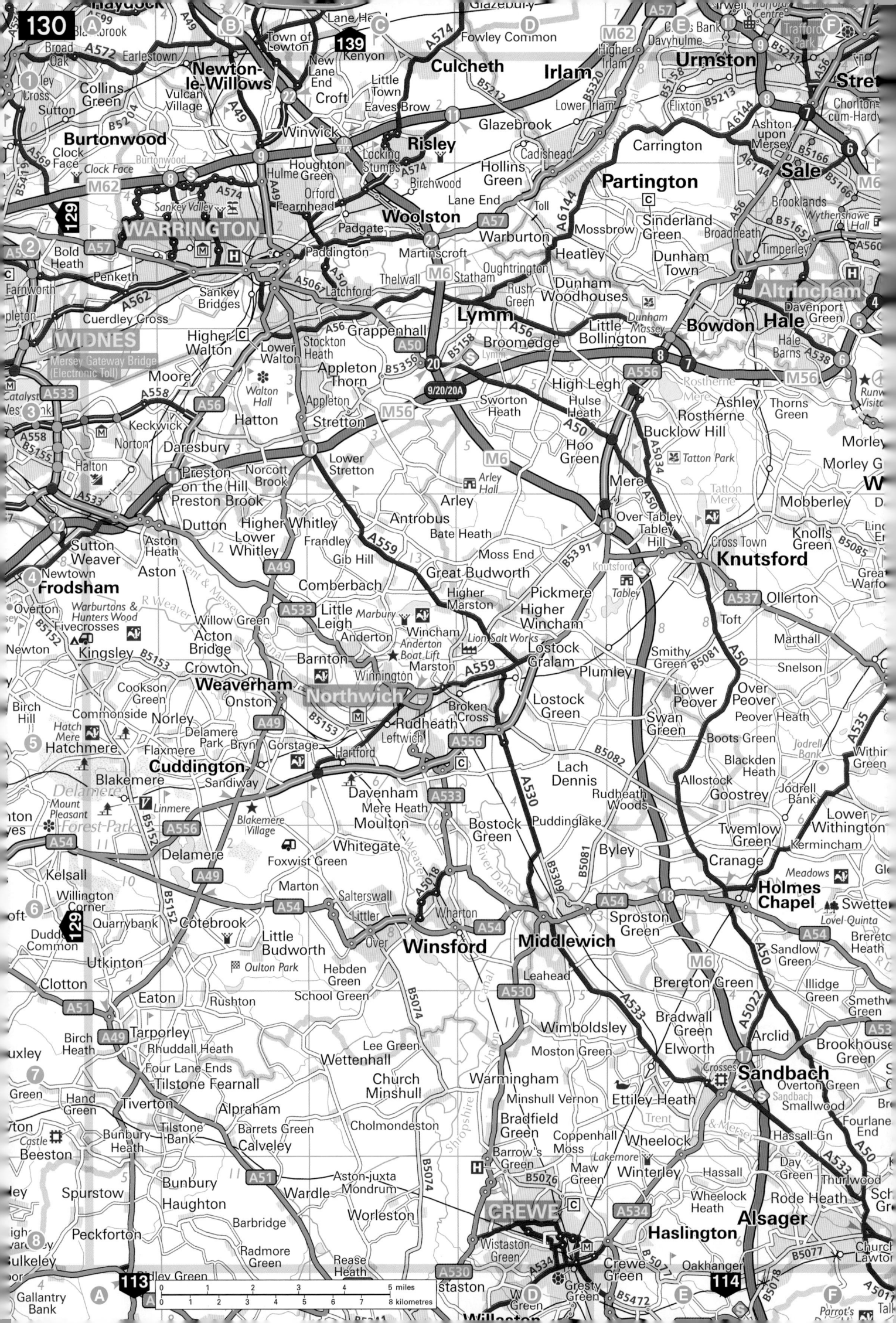

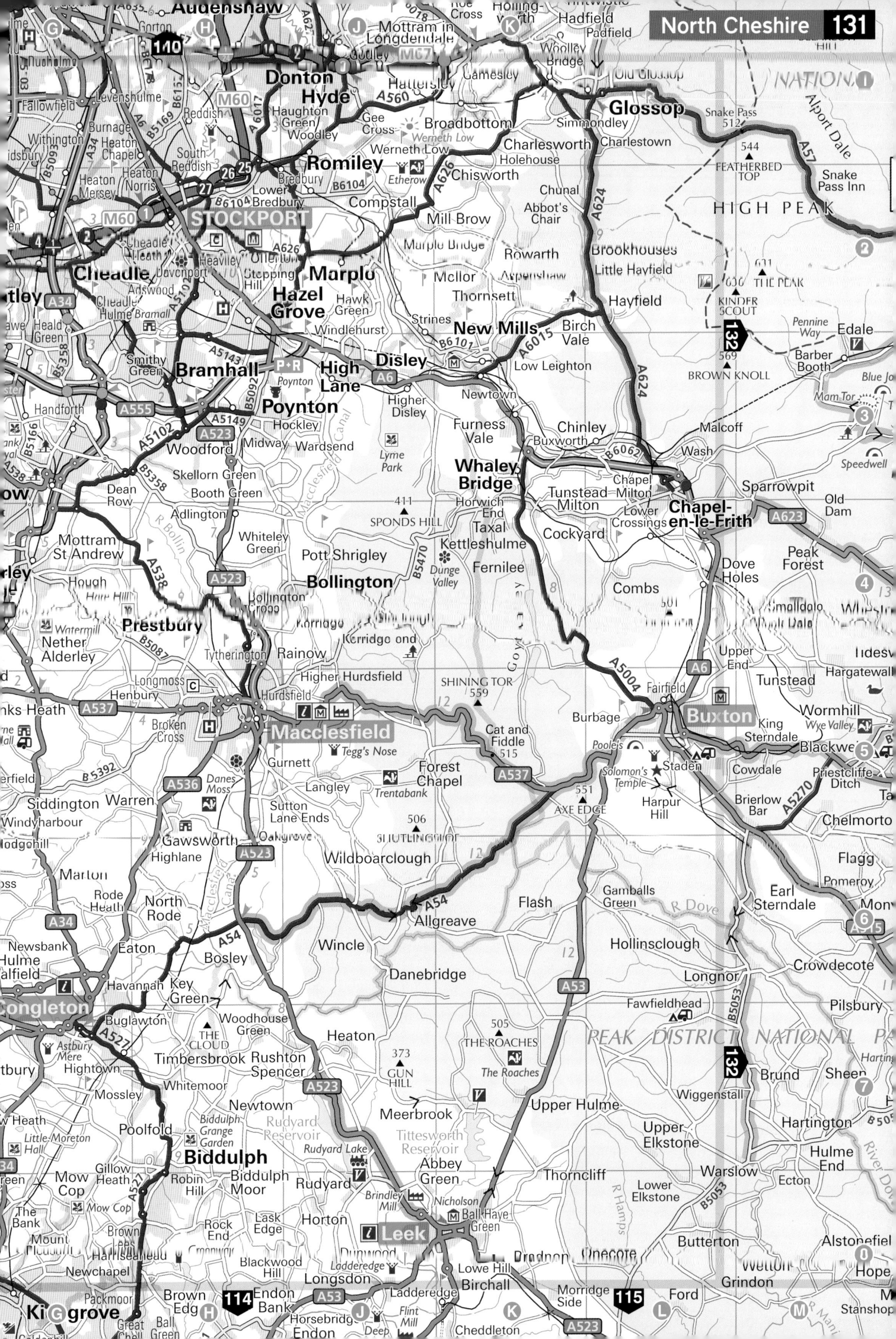

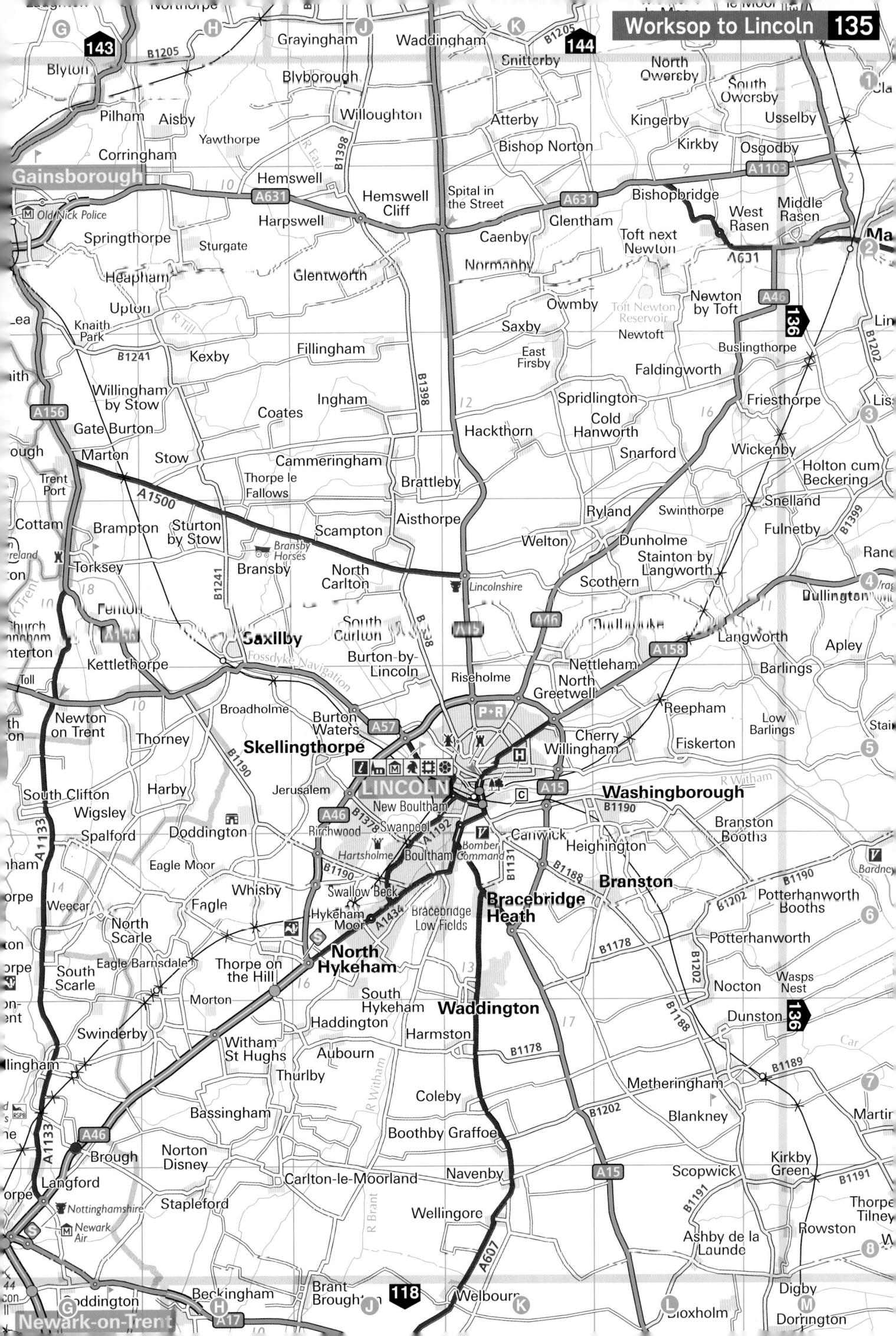

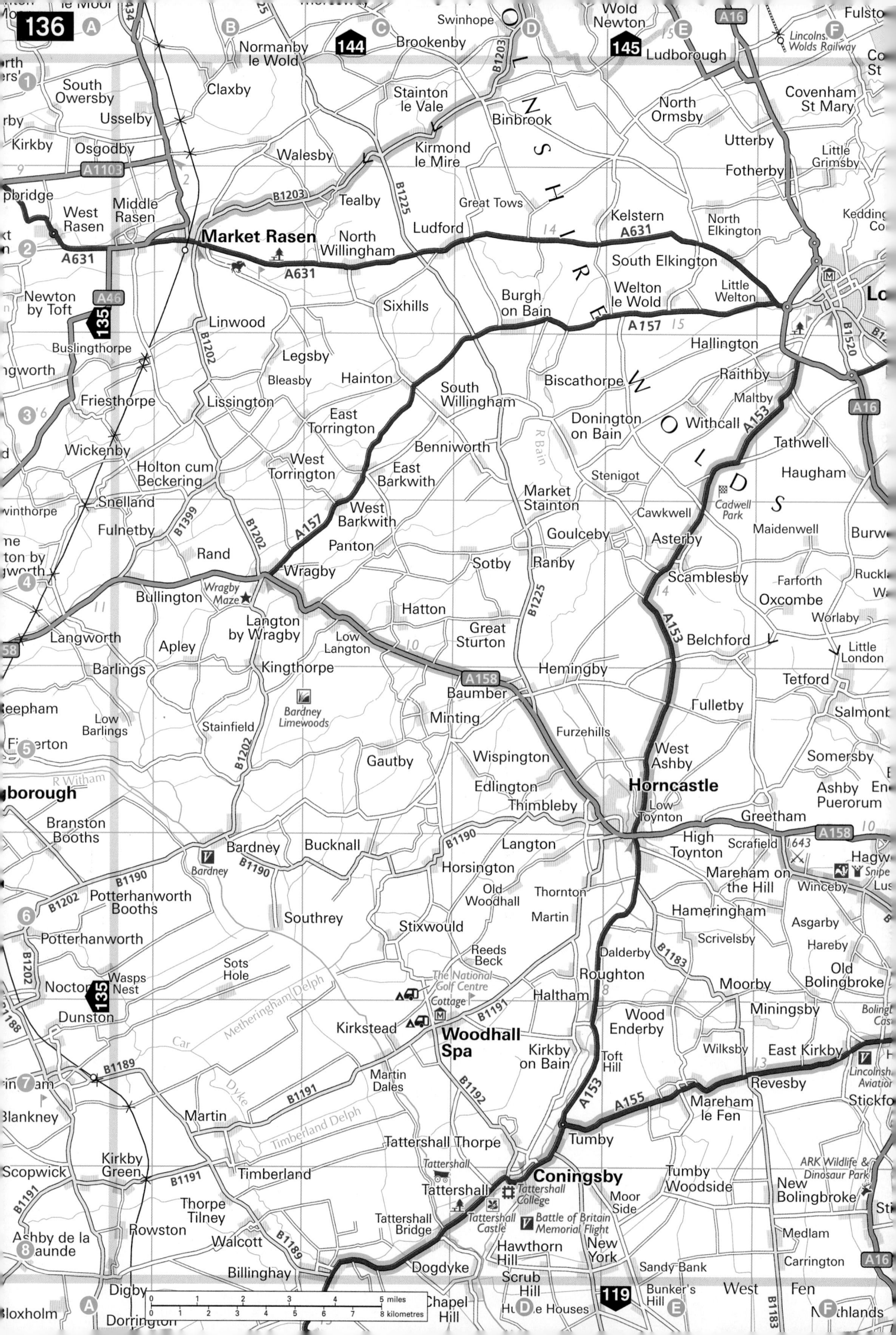

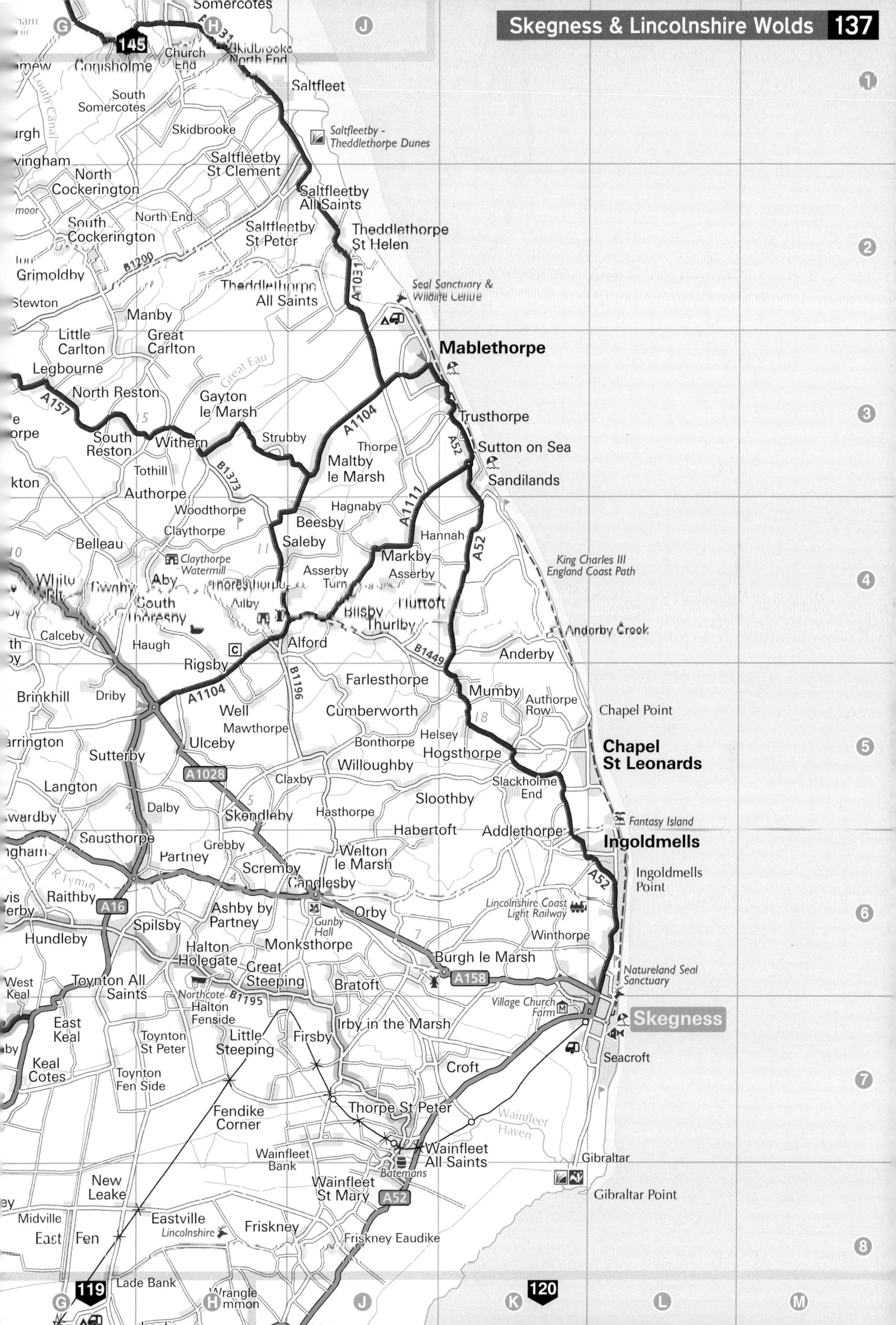

G · H 31 · J · 1 · 2 · 3 · 4 · 5 · 6 · 7 · 8

145

Somercotes

Conisholme

Church End

Skidbrooke North End

Saltfleet

Saltfleetby - Theddlethorpe Dunes

Saltfleetby St Clement

South Somercotes

Skidbrooke

burgh

vingham

North Cockerington

North End

Saltfleetby All Saints

Saltfleetby St Peter

Theddlethorpe St Helen

moor

South Cockerington

Theddlethorpe All Saints

Grimoldby

Stewton

Manby

B1200

Seal Sanctuary & Wildlife Centre

Mablethorpe

Little Carlton

Great Carlton

Legbourne

North Reston

A157

Gayton le Marsh

Great Eau

A1104

Trusthorpe

A52

Sutton on Sea

South Reston

Withern

Strubby

Thorpe

Maltby le Marsh

Sandilands

Tothill

B1373

A1111

Hagnaby

Authorpe

Woodthorpe

Beesby

Hannah

King Charles III England Coast Path

Belleau

Claythorpe

Claythorpe Watermill

Saleby

Markby

Aby

Thoresthorpe

Asserby Turn

Asserby

Huttoft

South Thoresby

Ailby

Bilsby

Thurlby

Andorby Crook

Calceby

Haugh

C

Alford

Anderby

Rigsby

Farlesthorpe

B1449

Anderby

Chapel Point

Brinkhill

Driby

A1104

Well

B1196

Mumby

Authorpe Row

Ulceby

Mawthorpe

Cumberworth

18

Chapel St Leonards

Sutterby

A1028

Bonthorpe

Helsey

Langton

Dalby

Claxby

Willoughby

Hogsthorpe

Skendleby

Hasthorpe

Sloothby

Slackholme End

Fantasy Island

Sausthorpe

Grebby

Habertoft

Addlethorpe

Ingoldmells

Partney

Welton le Marsh

Ingoldmells Point

Raithby

A16

Scremby

Lincolnshire Coast Light Railway

Spilsby

Ashby by Partney

Candlesby

Orby

Winthorpe

A52

Hundleby

Gunby Hall

Monksthorpe

Burgh le Marsh

A158

Natureland Seal Sanctuary

Halton Holegate

Great Steeping

Bratoft

Village Church Farm

M

Skegness

West Keal

Toynton All Saints

Northcote

Halton Fenside

B1195

Irby in the Marsh

East Keal

Toynton St Peter

Little Steeping

Firsby

Croft

Seacroft

Keal Cotes

Toynton Fen Side

Fendike Corner

Thorpe St Peter

Wainfleet Haven

by

New Leake

Wainfleet Bank

Wainfleet All Saints

Gibraltar

Batemans

Midville

Eastville

Wainfleet St Mary

A52

Gibraltar Point

East Fen

Lincolnshire

Friskney

Friskney Eaudike

Lade Bank

Wrangle mmon

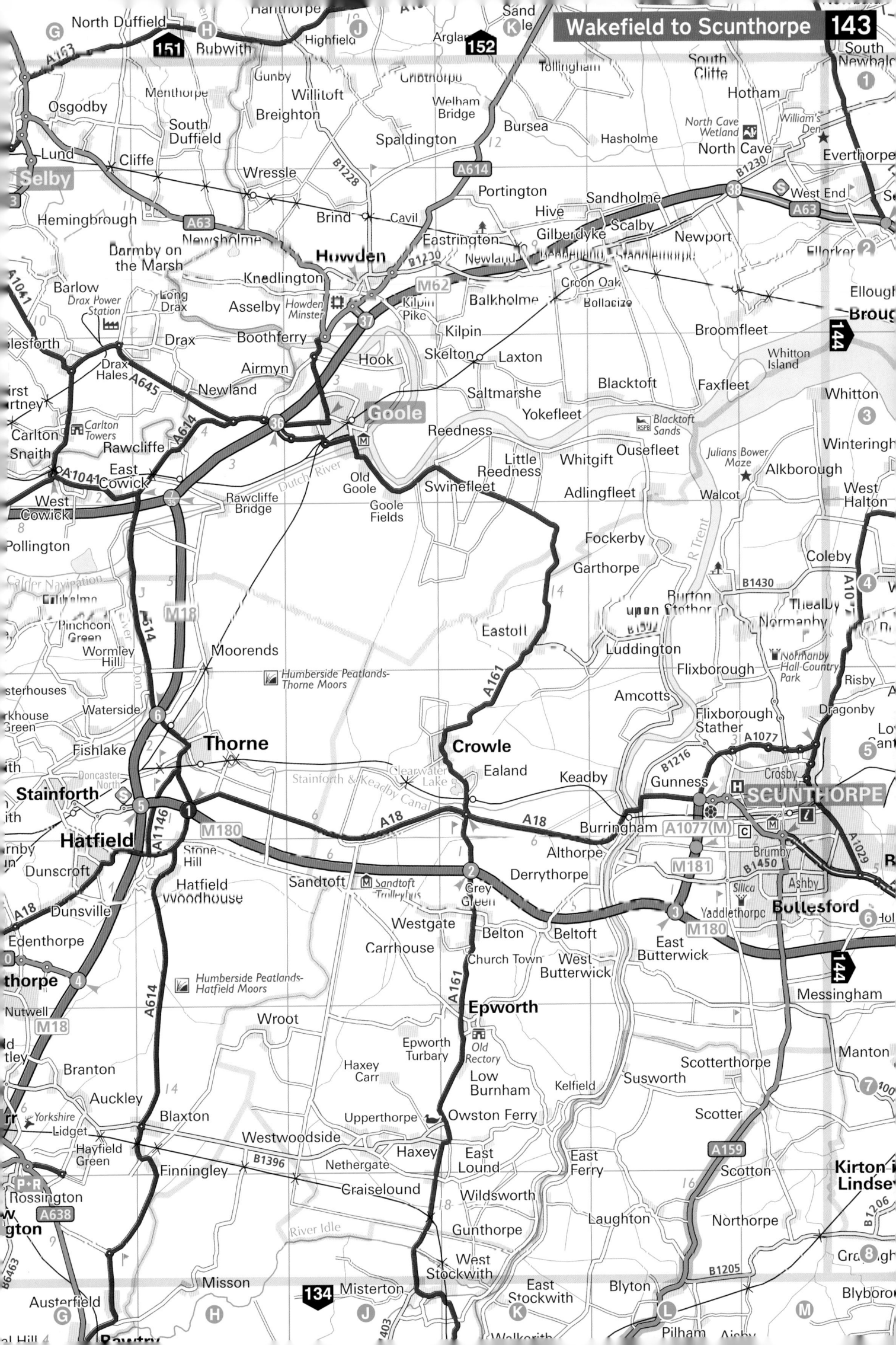

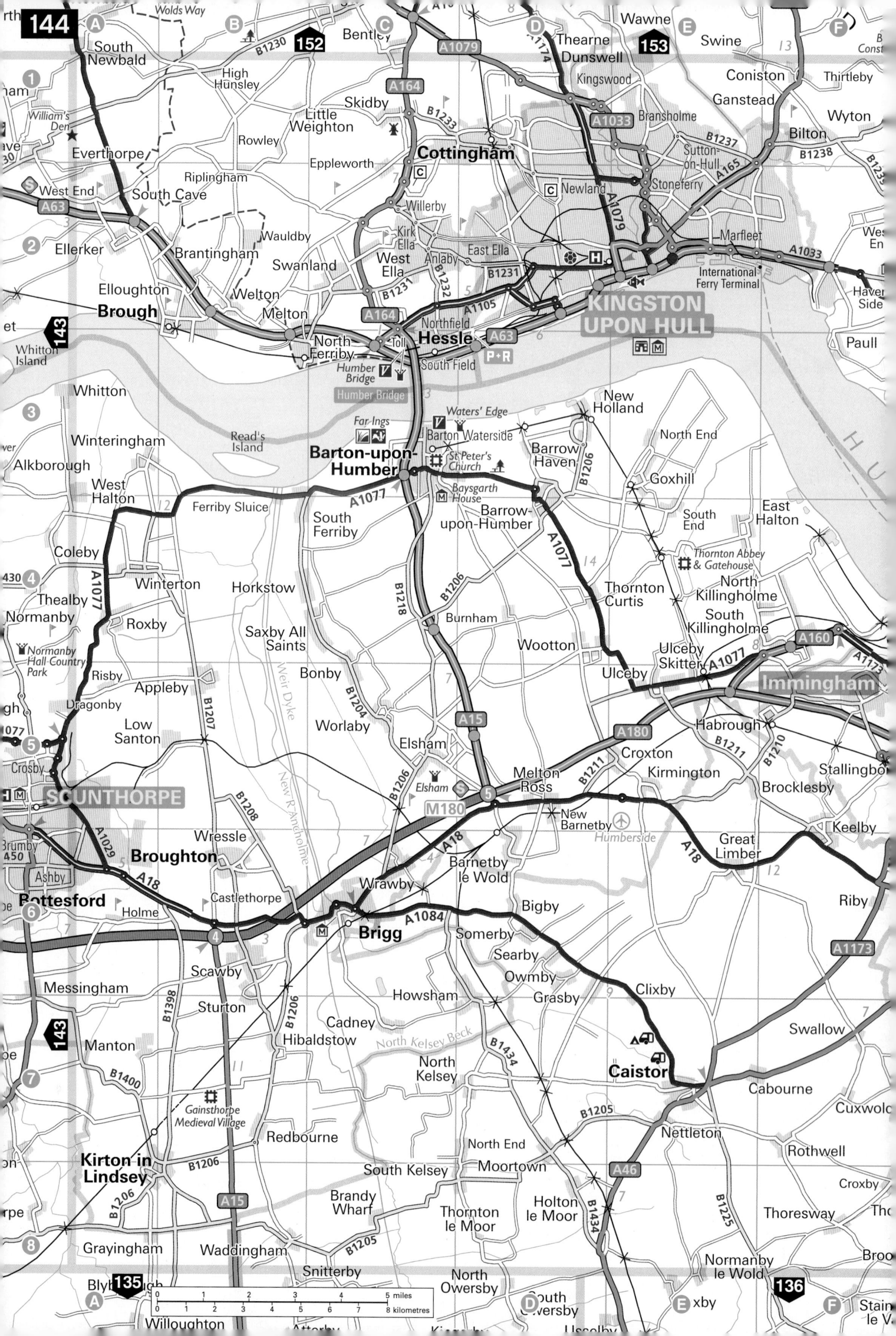

G H J

1

2

Withernsea

3

4

5

GRIMSBY

Cleethorpes

Humberston

6

New Waltham

Waltham

7

8

G H J K L M

SPURN HEAD

Rotterdam (Europoort)

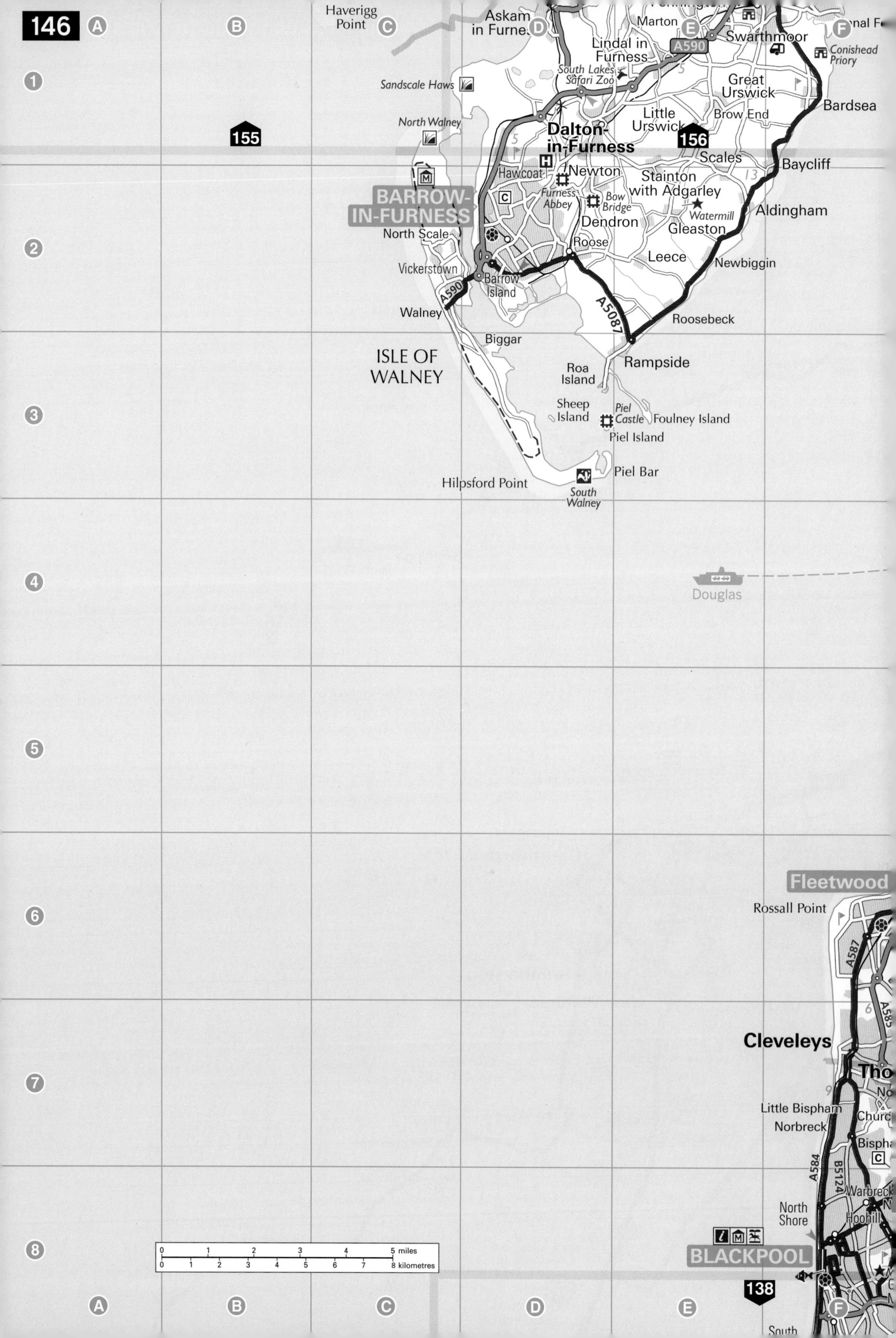

A B Haverigg Point C Askam in Furness D Pennington Marton E Swarthmoor F nal F

155 156

1
Lindal in Furness
South Lakes Safari Zoo
Sandscale Haws
North Walney
Great Urswick
Little Urswick
Brow End
Bardsea
Conishead Priory

2
BARROW-IN-FURNESS
Hawcoat Newton
North Scale
H M
C
Furness Abbey
Bow Bridge
Dendron
Stainton with Adgarley
Watermill
Gleaston
Scales
Baycliff
Aldingham
Leece
Newbiggin
Vickerstown
Barrow Island
Roose
A590
Walney
A5087

3
Biggar
ISLE OF WALNEY
Roosebeck
Rampside
Roa Island
Sheep Island
Piel Castle
Foulney Island
Piel Island
Hilpsford Point
Piel Bar
South Walney

4
Douglas

5

6
Fleetwood
Rossall Point
A587

7
Cleveleys
Tho
Little Bispham
Norbreck
Bispha
C
A584
B5124

8
North Shore
Warbreck
i M
BLACKPOOL
Hoohill

138

0 1 2 3 4 5 miles
0 1 2 3 4 5 6 7 8 kilometres

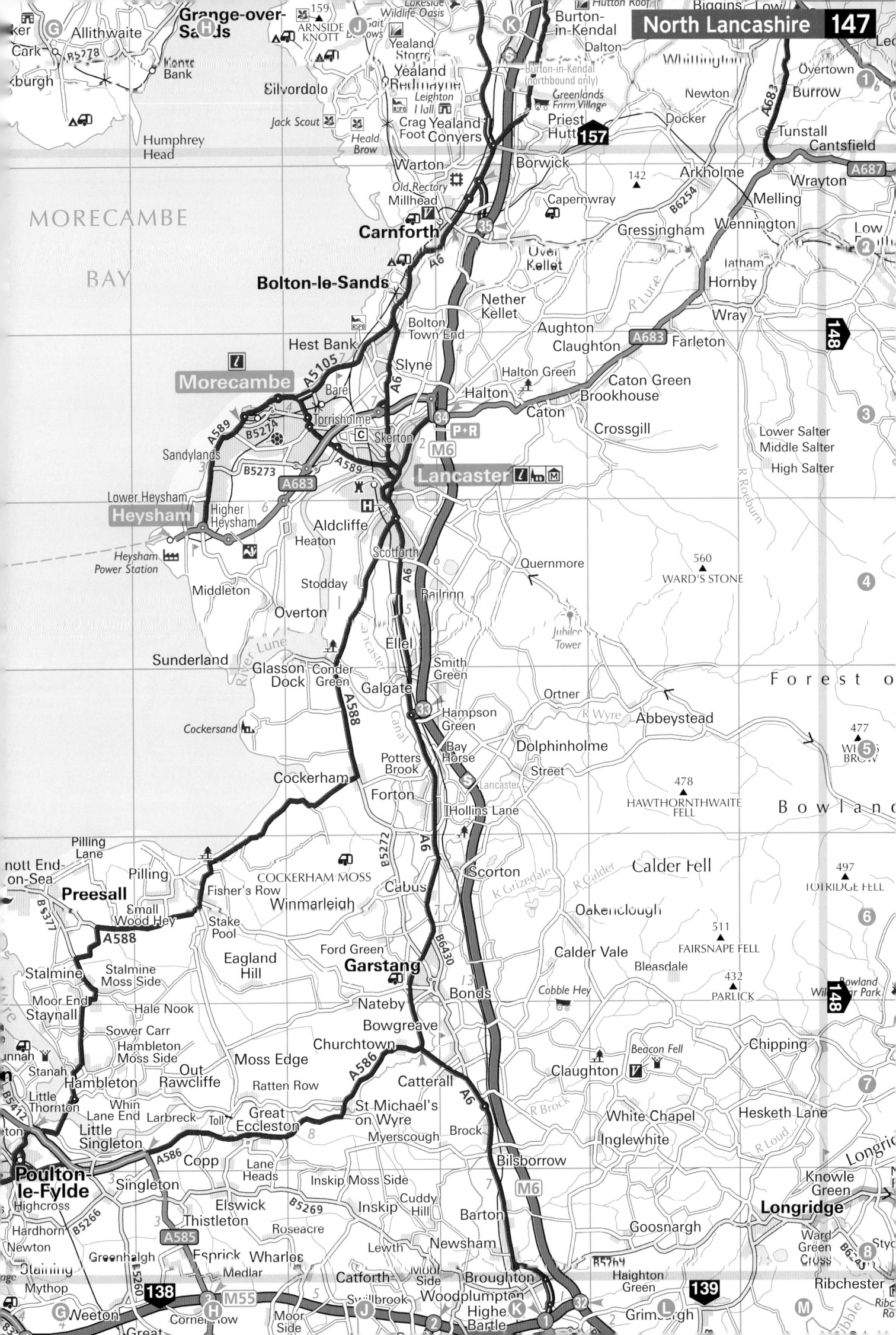

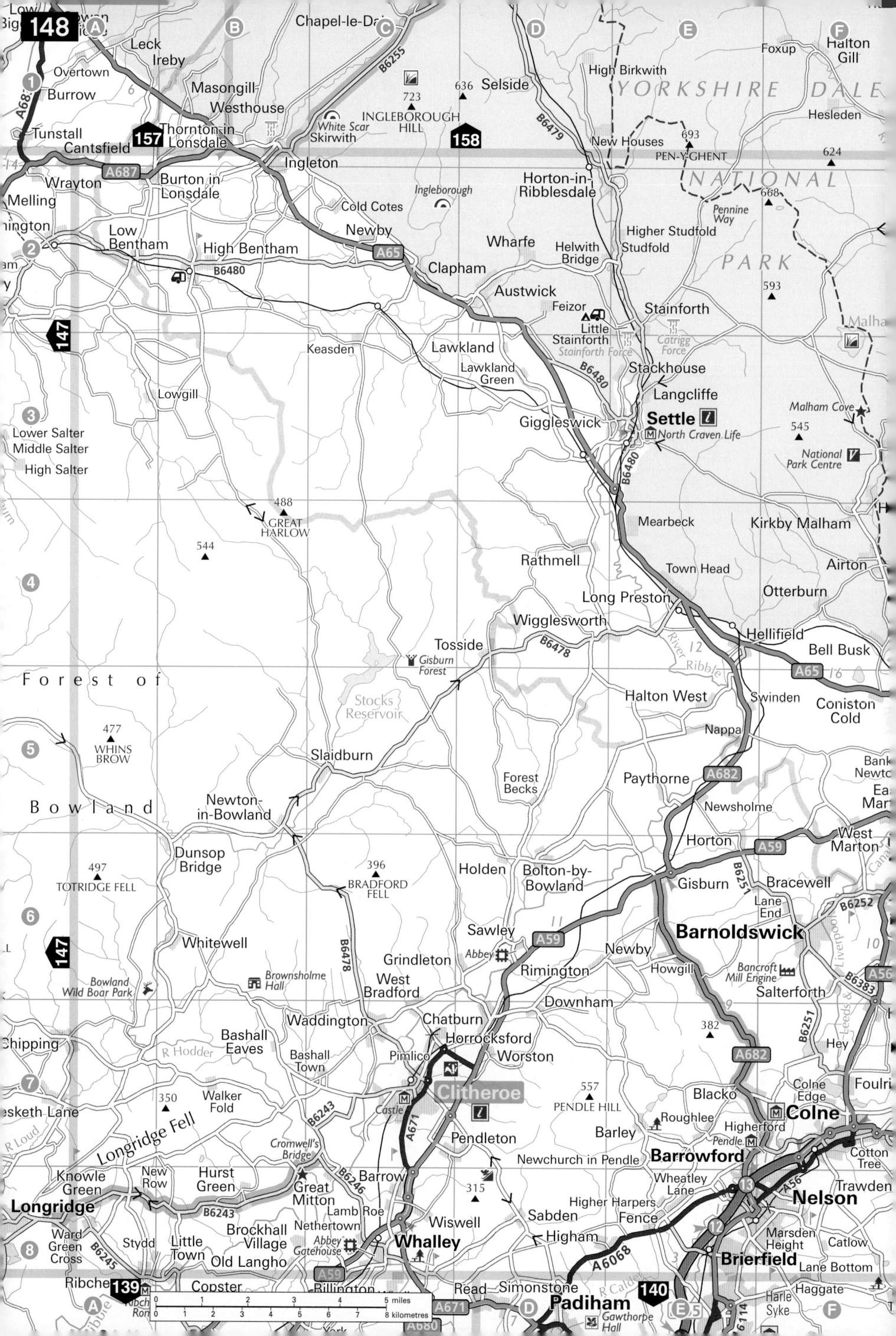

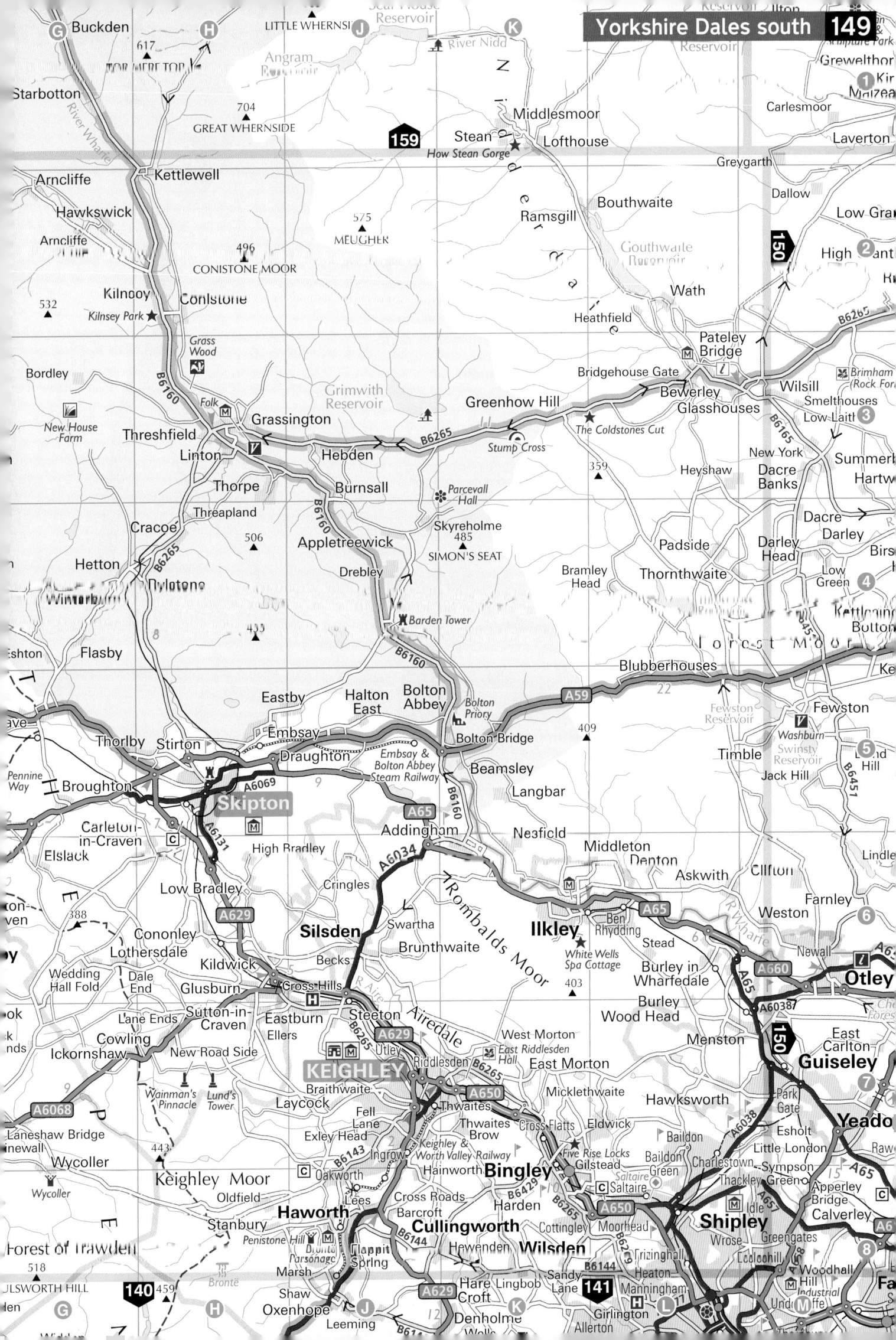

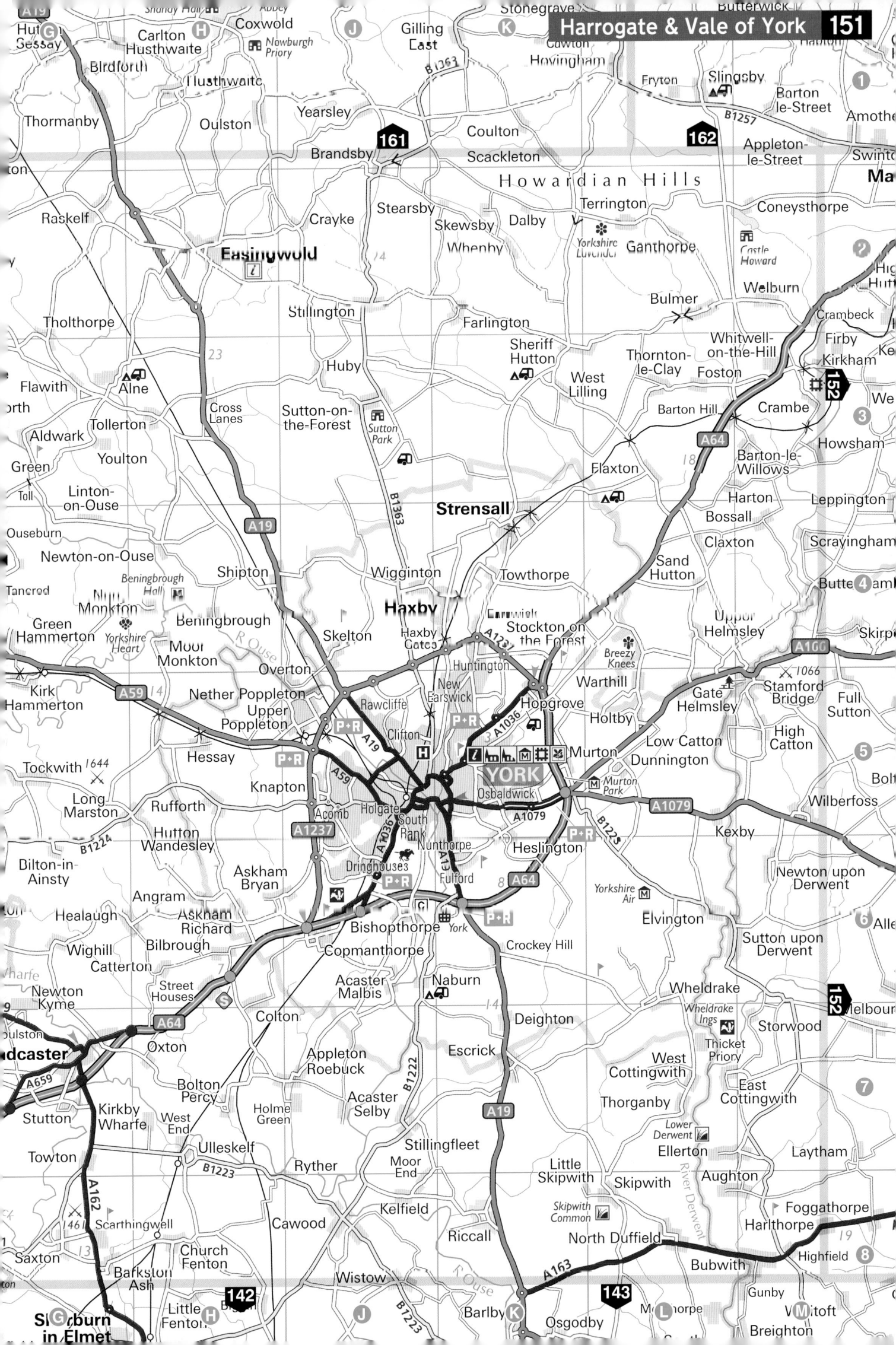

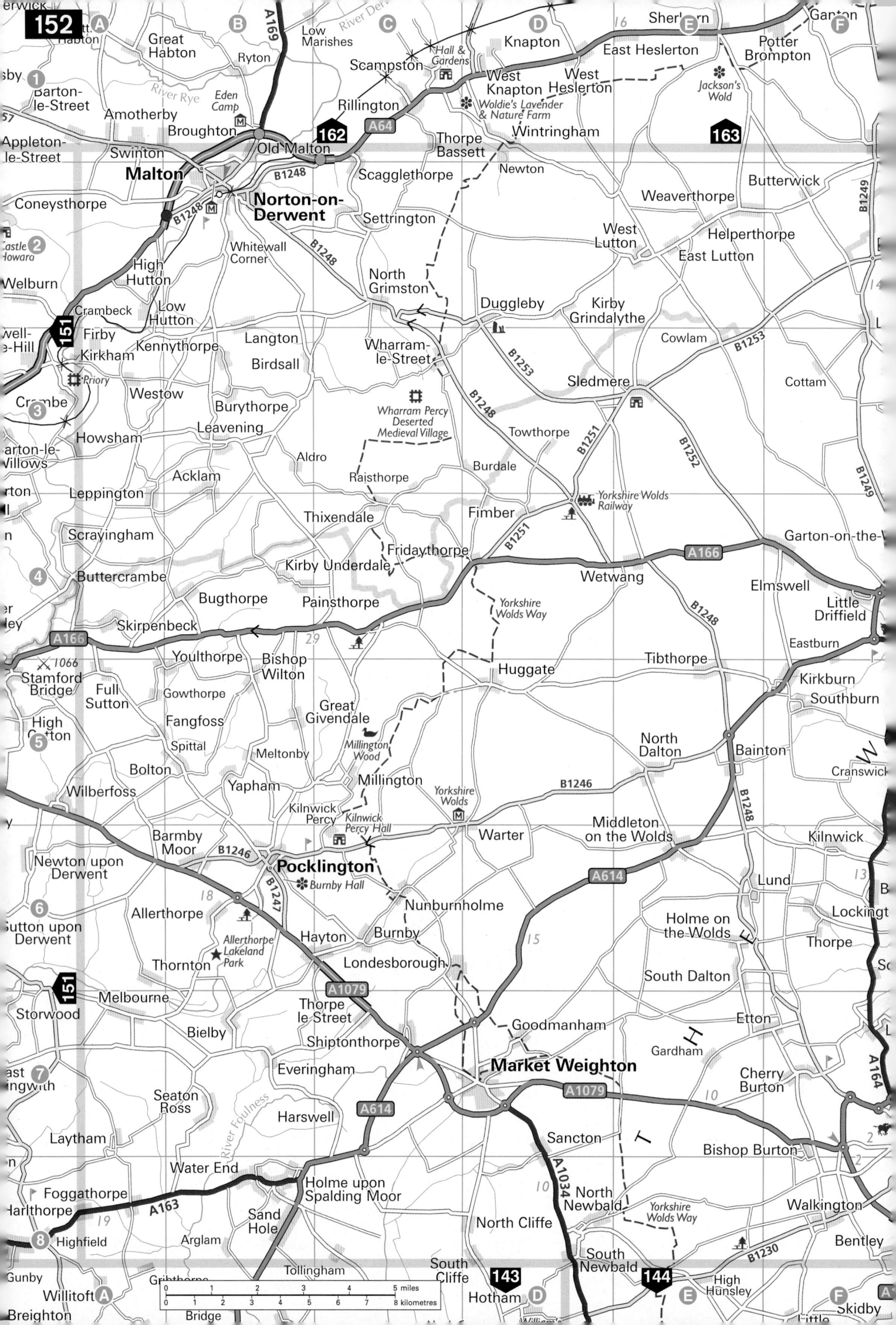

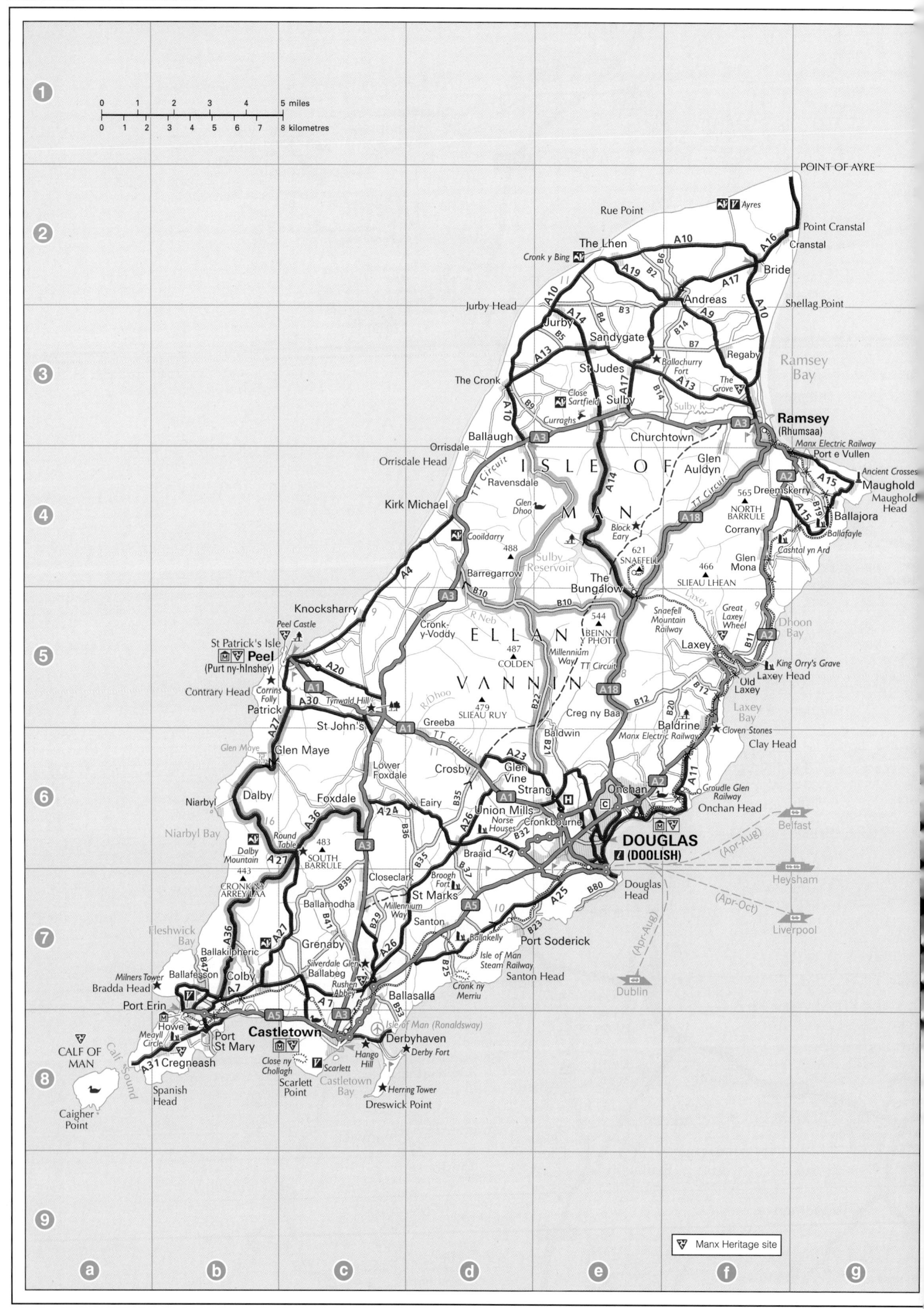

POINT OF AYRE

Rue Point

Ayres

The Lhen

Point Cranstal

Cranstal

A10

A16

A19

B6

B2

Cronk y Bing

Bride

A17

A2

Jurby Head

A10

Andreas

A9

Shellag Point

Jurby

A14

B4

B3

Sandygate

B14

A10

Ramsey Bay

A13

B5

St Judes

B7

Regaby

Ballachurry Fort

A17

The Grove

The Cronk

A10

B9

Close Sartfield

Sulby

B14

A13

Ramsey (Rhumsaa)

Currraghs

Sulby R.

A3

Manx Electric Railway

Ballaugh

Churchtown

A3

Port e Vullen

Orrisdale

A14

Glen Auldyn

A2

Ancient Crosses

Orrisdale Head

TT Circuit

Dreemskerry

A15

Maughold

ISLE OF

565

NORTH BARRULE

Maughold Head

Ravensdale

MAN

Ballajora

Kirk Michael

Glen Dhoo

Block Eary

A18

Corrany

A15

Ballafayle

Cooildarry

488

Sulby Reservoir

621 SNAEFELL

466

Glen Mona

Cashtal yn Ard

A4

Barregarrow

A3

B10

The Bungalow

SLIEAU LHEAN

B10

544

Snaefell Mountain Railway

Great Laxey Wheel

Dhoon Bay

Knocksharry

R. Neb

ELLAN

BEINN Y PHOTT

Laxey

A2

Peel Castle

Cronk-y-Voddy

487

Millennium Way

A18

B11

St Patrick's Isle

COLDEN

TT Circuit

B12

King Orry's Grave

Peel

A20

VANNIN

B22

Laxey Head

(Purt ny-hInshey)

A1

479 SLIEAU RUY

Old Laxey

Contrary Head

A30

R. Dhoo

B20

Laxey Bay

Corrins Folly

Tynwald Hill

Greeba

Creg ny Baa

B12

Clay Head

Patrick

St John's

Glen Vine

Baldwin

B21

Manx Electric Railway

Cloven Stones

Glen Maye

TT Circuit

Crosby

A23

Glen

Baldrine

Dalby

Lower Foxdale

Strang

A1

Onchan

A2

Groudle Glen Railway

Niarbyl

Glen Maye

A36

Foxdale

Eairy

A26

Union Mills

H

A11

Onchan Head

Niarbyl Bay

A24

Norse Houses

Cronkbourne

C

Dalby Mountain

Round Table

B35

B32

DOUGLAS (DOOLISH)

Belfast

483

B36

A3

Braaid

A24

(Apr-Aug)

SOUTH BARRULE

443

Closeclark

B35

Brough Fort

A25

Douglas Head

Heysham

CRONK NY ARREY LAA

A27

B39

B37

St Marks

A5

B80

(Apr-Oct)

Fleshwick Bay

A36

Ballamodha

Millennium Way

Santon

B23

Liverpool

Ballakilpheric

B41

Grenaby

A26

B25

Isle of Man Steam Railway

(Apr-Aug)

Silverdale Glen

Ballakelly

Port Soderick

Bradda Head

Ballafesson

Colby

Ballabeg

B25

Santon Head

Dublin

Milners Tower

A7

Rushen Abbey

Cronk ny Merriu

Ballasalla

B53

Port Erin

A5

A7

A3

Isle of Man (Ronaldsway)

Howe

Meayll Circle

Port St Mary

Castletown

Derbyhaven

CALF OF MAN

A31 Cregneash

Close ny Chollagh

Scarlett

Hango Hill

Derby Fort

Spanish Head

Scarlett Point

Castletown Bay

Herring Tower

Caigher Point

Dreswick Point

Manx Heritage site

Map labels

St Bees
Egremont
Lowes Court
Wilton
164
L A K E D
LANK K
L
HAYCOCK
PILLAR
KIRK FELL
GREAT GABLE
1

Thornhill
Carleton
Haile
Coulderton
Middletown
Nethertown
Beckermet
Blackbeck
692
SEATALLAN
Wasdale Head
Braystones
Ponsonby
Calder Bridge
River Bleng
978
SCAFELL PIKE
964
SCAFELL
R Eben
Calder
Cross
Wellington
Nether Wasdale
R Irt
Sollafield Station
B5344
Gosforth
Burnmoor Tarn
2

Santon
Santon Bridge
156
Hardknott Fort
Boot
Ha
River Mite
Seascale
Eskdale Green
Beckfoot
652
HARTER F
Hallsenna Moor
Drigg
Holmrook
Ravenglass & Eskdale Railway
Devoke Water
ESKDALE
3

Saltcoats
River Esk
L A K E   D I S T R I C T
Hall Dunnerdale
Ravenglass
Roman Bath House
Muncaster Castle, Hawk & Owl Centre
A595
N A T I O N A L
River
Newbiggin
Broad Oak
Waberthwaite
573
WHITFELL
Ulpha
4

Corney
Loganbeck
Broughton Mills
Hycemoor
Selker Bay
Beckfoot
Lower Hawthwaite
Swinside Stone Circle
Duddon Bridge
Bro
Hyton
Bootle
A595
5

Annaside
600
BLACK COMBE
Hallthwaites
Lady Hall
Foxfiel
Gutterby Spa
Whitbeck
The Green
Arnaby
Bridge End
King Charles III England Coast Path
Whicham
The Hill
Sand Side
156
Silecroft
Soutergate
6
A

Kirksanton
8
A5093
Millom
V
Steel Green
Borwick Rails
Hodbarrow
RSPB
Askam in Furness
Haverigg
Haverigg Point
Sandscale Haws
7

North Walney
Dalton-in-F
146
BARROW-IN-FURNESS
Hawcoat
Furness Abbey
C
M
Ne
North Scale
Vickerstown
row Island
A590
M
South Sa
8
G   H   J   K   L

Scale

0   1   2   3   4   5 miles
0   1   2   3   4   5   6   7   8 kilometres

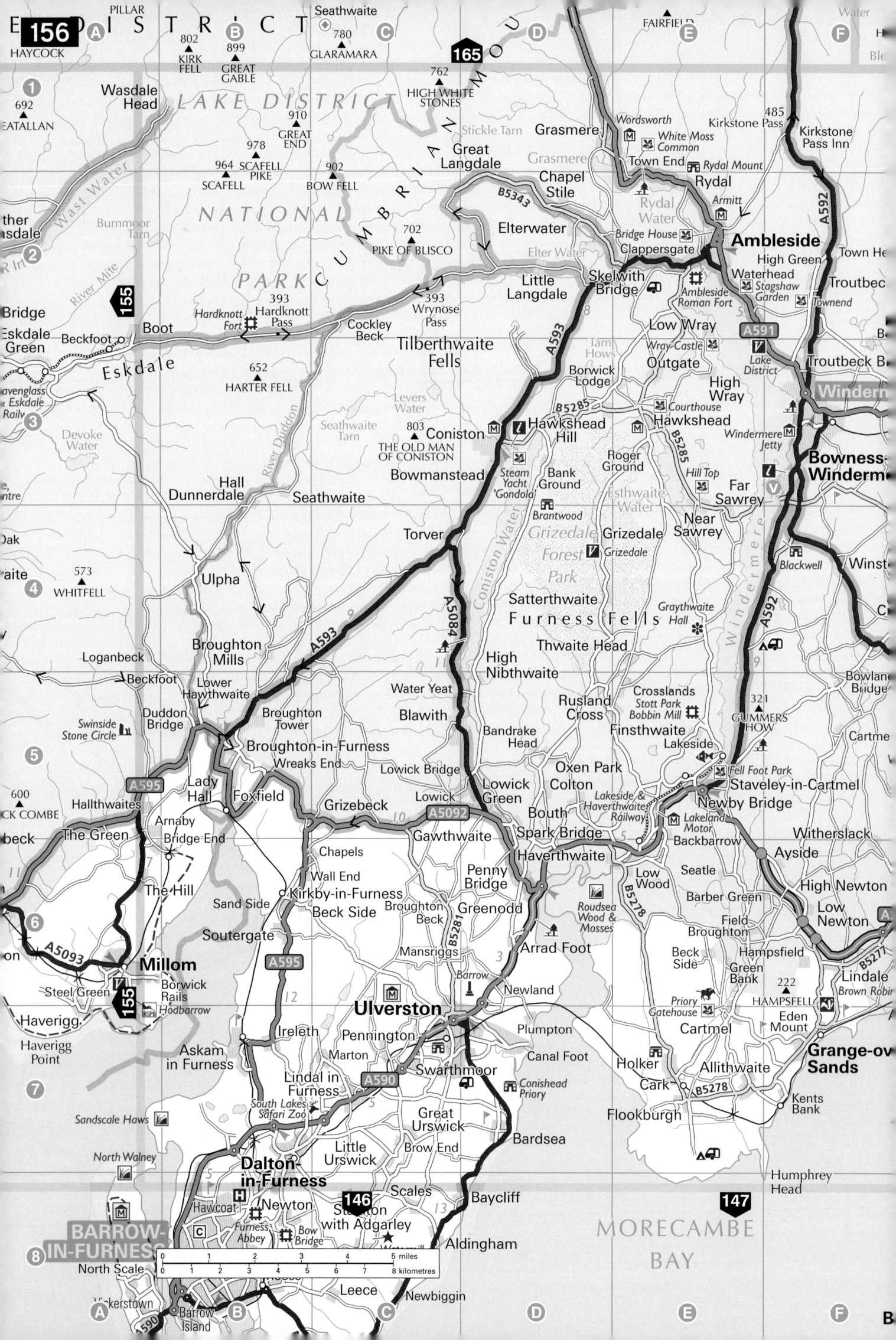

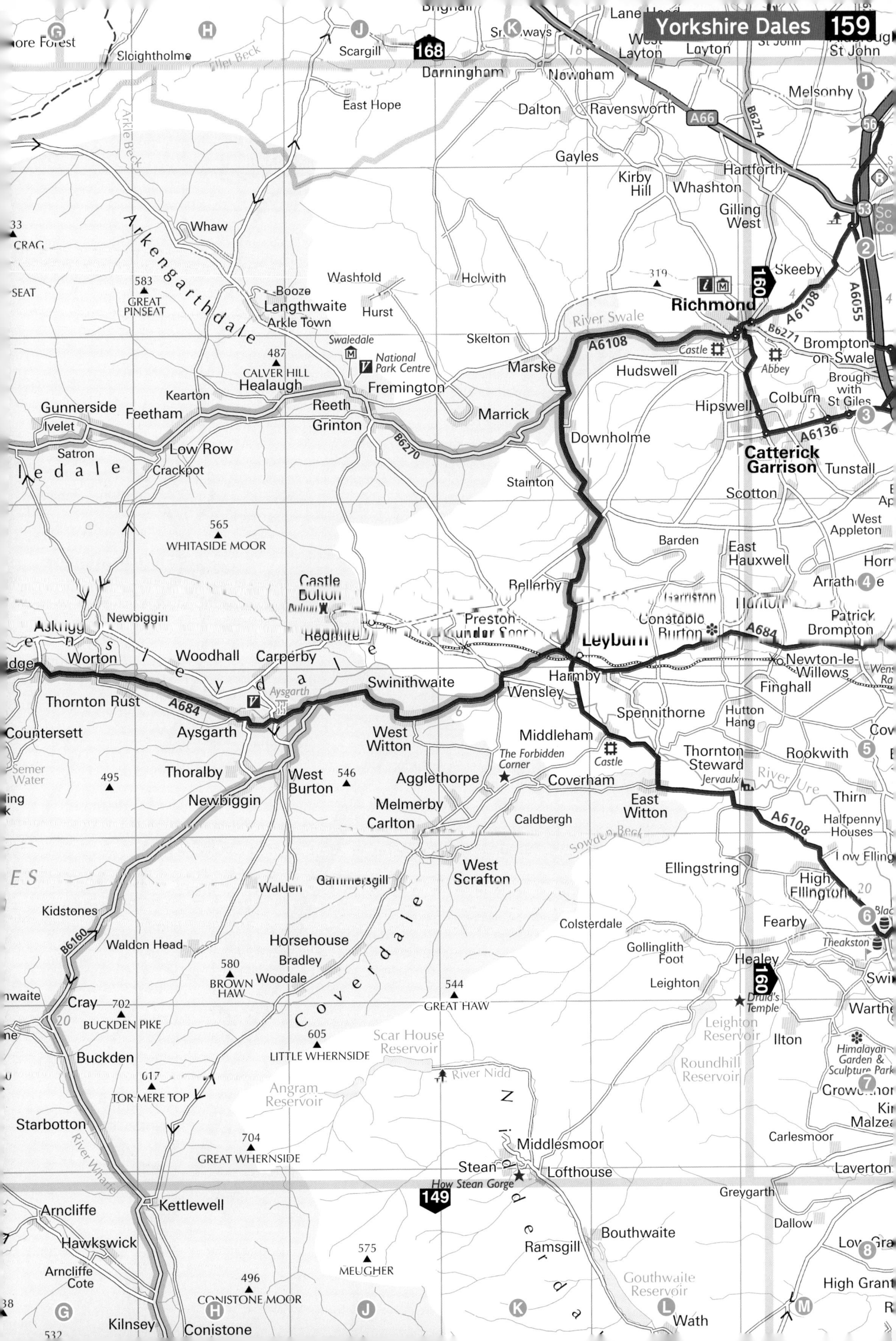

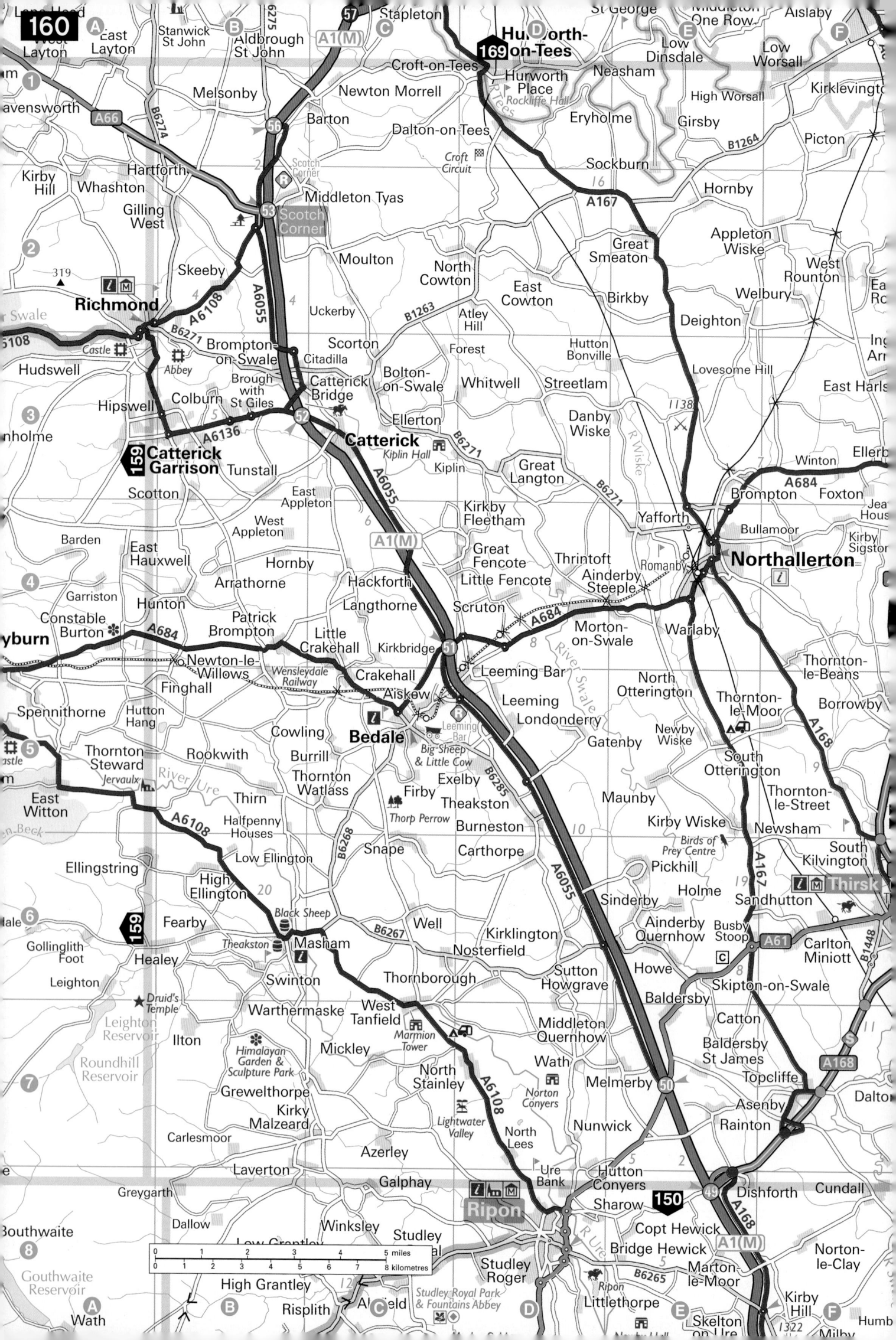

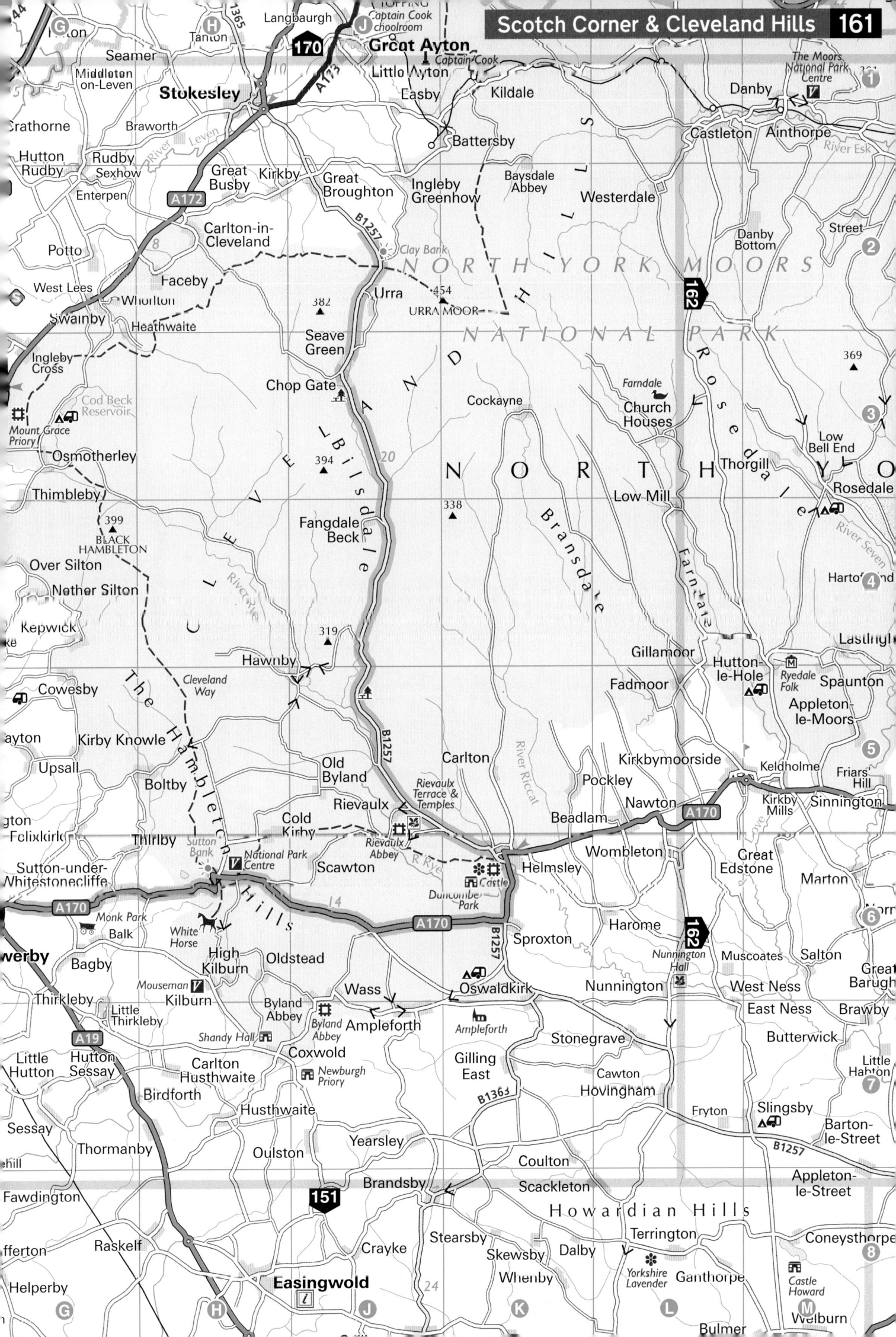

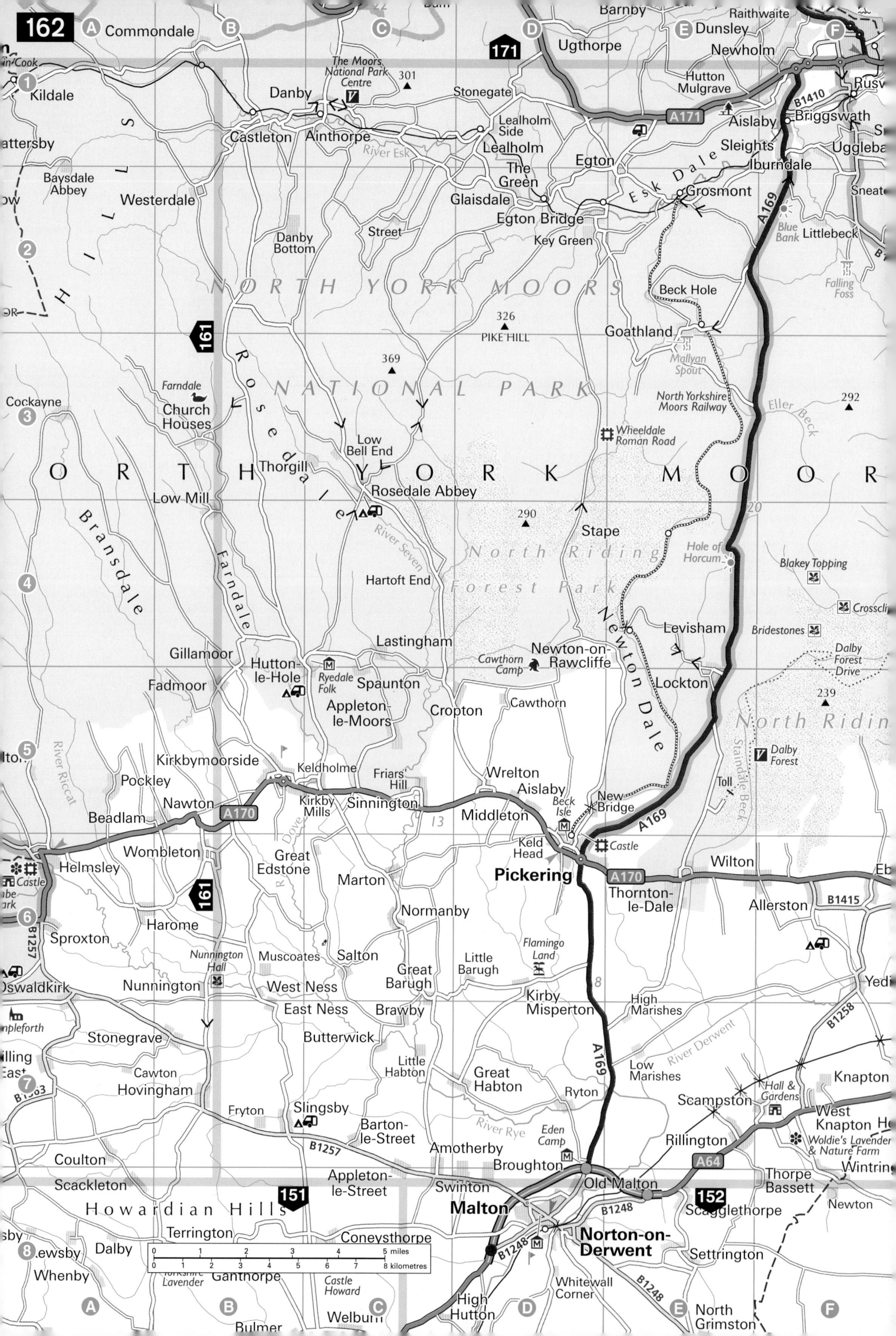

G H J

1

2

3

4

5

6

7

8

Scwick Bay

King Charles III
England Coast Path

ainsacre

High Hawsker

sker

B1447

Raw

Ness Point or
North Cheek

Robin Hood's Bay

Old Coastguard

Fylingthorpe

Robin
Hood's Bay

Old Peak or
South Cheek

Ravenscar

20

Staintondale

Hayburn
Wyke

Harwood
Dale

Cloughton
Newlands

Cloughton
Wyke

Cloughton

Burniston

Cromer Point

A165

Cleveland Way

ckley

Bluxa

Gilpho

Suffield

Scalby

Langdale
End

Hacknoss

Newby

North Bay Railway

Wrench
Green

Everley

A171

Castle

Forest Park

River Derwent

Sea Cut

Falsgrave

Scarborough

C

A170

Oliver's Mount

Bee Dale

Forge Valley
Wood

East
Ayton

H

Sawdon

West
Ayton

Betton

P+R

A165

P+R

Eastfield

Osgodby

Cayton
Bay

Ruston

Hutton
Buscel

Irton

Seamer

Crossgates

B1261

High
Killerby

Fair Collection

The
Wyke

Snainton

Wykeham

Cayton

Brompton-
by-Sawdon

B1261

Lebberston

Filey Brigg

A1039

Gristhorpe

Bird Garden
& Animal Park

Filey

A64

R Hertford

Muston

Folkton

A1039

Willerby

Flixton

West
Flotmanby

Filey Bay

Staxton

16

Sherburn

Ganton

Yorkshire
Wolds Way

Hunmanby

Flamborough Head
Heritage Coast

East Heslerton

Potter
Brompton

Fordon

Reighton

Jackson's
Wold

Speeton

B1229

Bempton
Cliffs

RSPB

Foxholes

Wold
Newton

153

Burton
Fleming

Buckton

Bempton

Butterwick

B1229

Weaverthorpe

B1249

Grindale

A165

Thwing

West
Lutton

Helperthorpe

Octon

C

Marton

B125

East Lutton

Sewerby

Hall &
Garden

Bondville

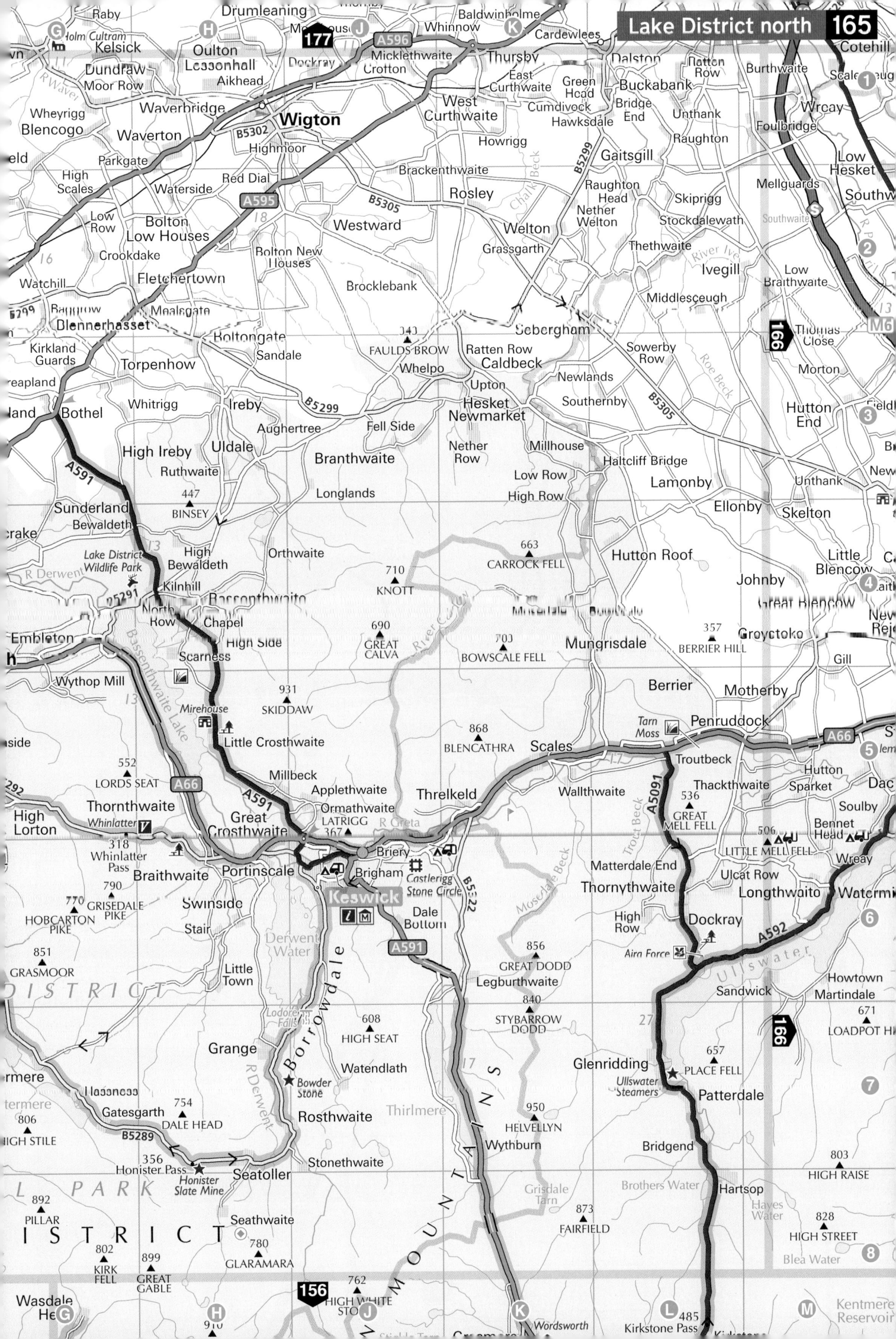

Raby
Drumleaning
Baldwinholme
G
Holm Cultram
H
Kelsick
Oulton
J
Whinnow
Cardewlees
K
Cotehill
Dundraw
Lessonhall
177
Dockray
Micklethwaite
A596
Thursby
Dalston
Hatton Row
Burthwaite
Scaleug
Moor Row
Aikhead
Crofton
East
Green
Buckabank
1
Waverbridge
Highmoor
Curthwaite
Head
Bridge
Unthank
Wreay
Wheyrigg
B5302
Wigton
West
Cumdivock
End
Raughton
Foulbridge
Blencogo
Waverton
Curthwaite
Hawksdale
Low
Parkgate
Howrigg
Hesket
High
Waterside
Red Dial
Brackenthwaite
B5299
Gaitsgill
Scales
A595
18
Rosley
Raughton
Skiprigg
Mellguards
Southw
Bolton
Westward
Head
Low Houses
B5305
Welton
Nether
Stockdalewath
Southwaite
S
2
Crookdake
Bolton New
Welton
Grassgarth
Thethwaite
River Ive
Fletchertown
Houses
Brocklebank
Ivegill
Low
M6
Blennerhasset
Sebergham
Sowerby
Braithwaite
166
Thomas
13
Kirkland
FAULDS BROW
Ratten Row
Row
Middlesceugh
Close
Guards
Sandale
Whelpo
Caldbeck
Newlands
Hutton
Morton
Torpenhow
Upton
Southernby
B5305
End
3
Bothel
Whitrigg
Ireby
B5299
Hesket
Field
Aughertree
Fell Side
Newmarket
Millhouse
New
High Ireby
Uldale
Nether
Haltcliff Bridge
Lamonby
Little
A591
Branthwaite
Row
Blencow
Ruthwaite
Longlands
Low Row
High Row
Ellonby
Skelton
Sunderland
447
663
Hutton Roof
Great Blencow
Bewaldeth
BINSEY
CARROCK FELL
Johnby
4
High
710
357
Groyctoko
Lake District
Bewaldeth
Orthwaite
KNOTT
BERRIER HILL
New
Wildlife Park
Kilnhill
690
703
Mungrisdale
Gill
R Derwent
B5291
Bassenthwaite
GREAT
Rej
North
CALVA
BOWSCALE FELL
Embleton
Row
Chapel
High Side
Berrier
Motherby
h
Scarness
931
868
Penruddock
Wythop Mill
SKIDDAW
BLENCATHRA
Tarn
A66
13
Moss
Mirehouse
Scales
Troutbeck
Hutton
5
side
Little Crosthwaite
Wallthwaite
Sparket
Dac
552
Thackthwaite
LORDS SEAT
Millbeck
A66
A5091
536
Soulby
High
Applethwaite
Threlkeld
GREAT
Bennet
Lorton
Thornthwaite
Ormathwaite
MELL FELL
506
Head
Whinlatter
V
Great
LATRIGG
R Greta
LITTLE MELL FELL
Wreay
318
Crosthwaite
367
Matterdale End
Longthwaite
Watermi
Whinlatter
Briery
Thornythwaite
Pass
Portinscale
Brigham
High
Dockray
6
Braithwaite
Castlerigg
Row
790
Keswick
Stone Circle
Aira Force
A592
Swinside
B5322
Ullswater
770
GRISEDALE
i
M
Dale
HOBCARTON
PIKE
Stair
856
Sandwick
Howtown
PIKE
Bottom
GREAT DODD
Martindale
851
Little
Legburthwaite
High
671
GRASMOOR
Derwent
Town
Row
LOADPOT H
DISTRICT
Water
840
STYBARROW
Glenridding
657
DODD
166
608
PLACE FELL
7
Grange
HIGH SEAT
Ullswater
Steamers
ermere
Borrowdale
Watendlath
17
Patterdale
R Derwent
950
Lodore
806
Falls
Bowder
HELVELLYN
Howtown
Stone
Thirlmere
Wythburn
Bridgend
termere
Gatesgarth
754
Rosthwaite
Brothers Water
803
806
DALE HEAD
Hartsop
HIGH RAISE
HIGH STILE
B5289
Stonethwaite
Grisdale
Hayes
356
Tarn
Water
828
Honister Pass
Seatoller
873
HIGH STREET
892
Honister
FAIRFIELD
Brothers Water
PILLAR
Slate Mine
Blea Water
8
PARK
Seathwaite
156
ISTRICT
780
802
899
GLARAMARA
762
485
KIRK
GREAT
HIGH WHITE
Kirkstone Pass
FELL
GABLE
STO
Wordsworth
L
M
Kentmere
Wasdale
G
910
H
J
K
Reservoir
He

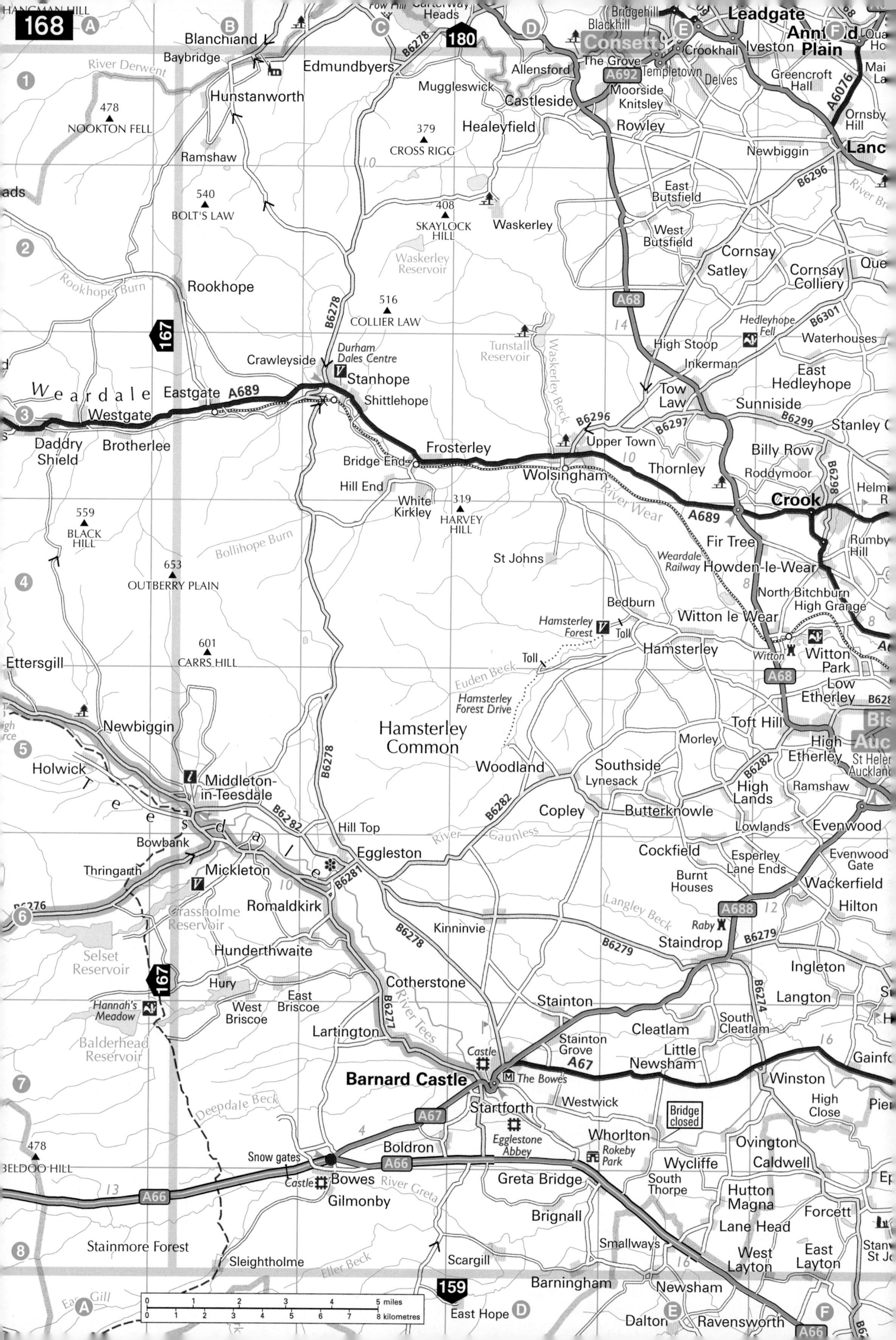

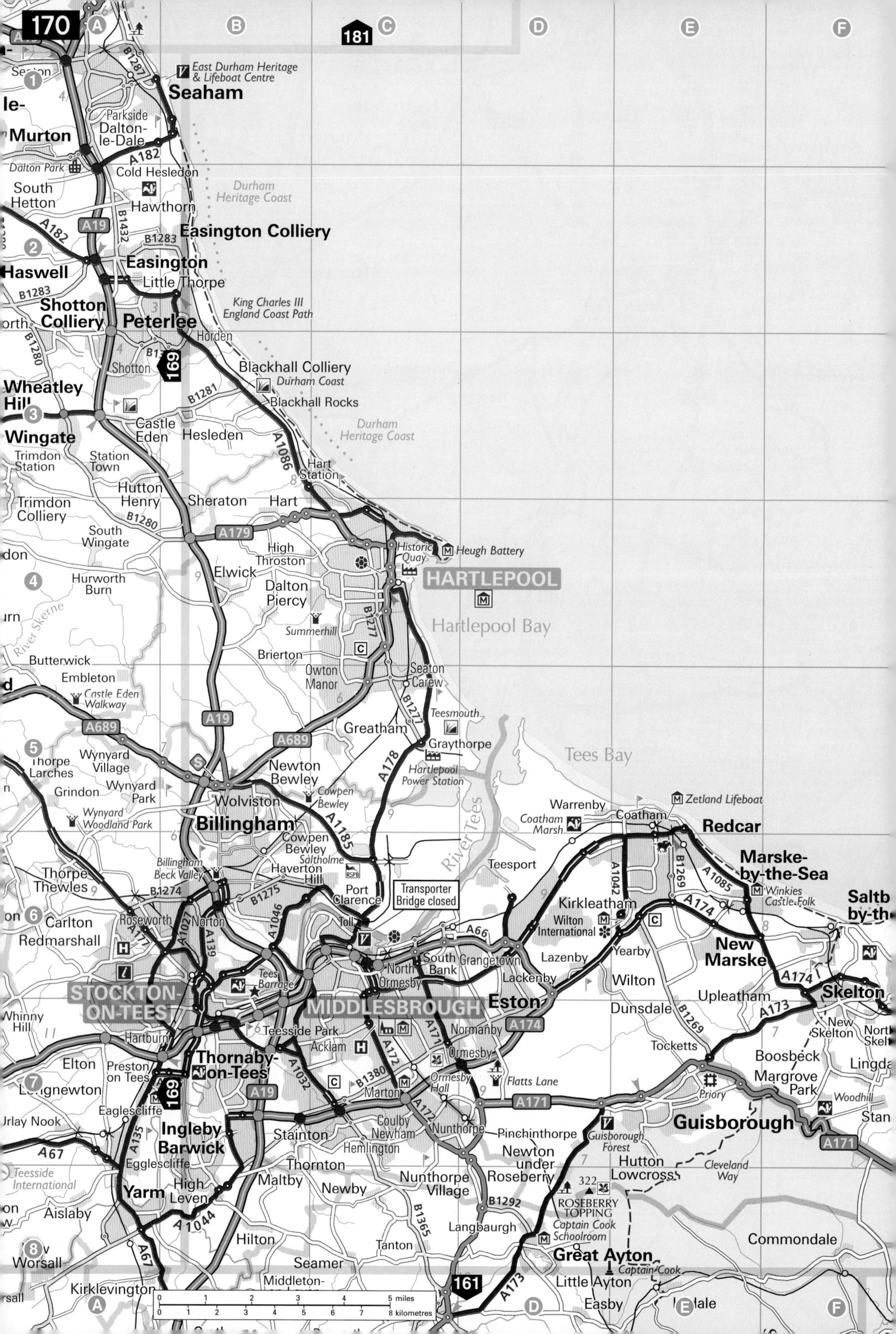

G   H   J

1
2
3
4
5
6
7
8

Hummersea Scar
Skinningrove
Ironstone Mining
Upton   Boulby
otton
Carlin How
Loftus   Staithes
Captain Cook & Staithes
Dalehouse
Easington   Port Mulgrave
ilton horpe   Liverton Mines   Hinderwell
iverton   Roxby   Newton Mulgrave   Runswick
Handale   Kettleness   Runswick Bay   North Yorkshire and Cleveland Heritage Coast
Borrowby   Goldsborough
oorsholm   Scaling   Ellerby   Overdale Wyke
B1366   B1266   A174   Lythe
Gerrick   Mickleby   Sandsend Wyke
Scaling Dam   West Barnby   East Barnby   Sandsend
Raithwaite   Whitby
Ugthorpe   Dunsley   Newholm   Abbey   Saltwick Bay
The Moors National Park Centre   162   Hutton Mulgrave   Ruswarp   King Charles III England Coast Path
anby   301   Stonegate   Aislaby   Briggswath   Sta acre
Lealholm   A171   G H J K 410 L M

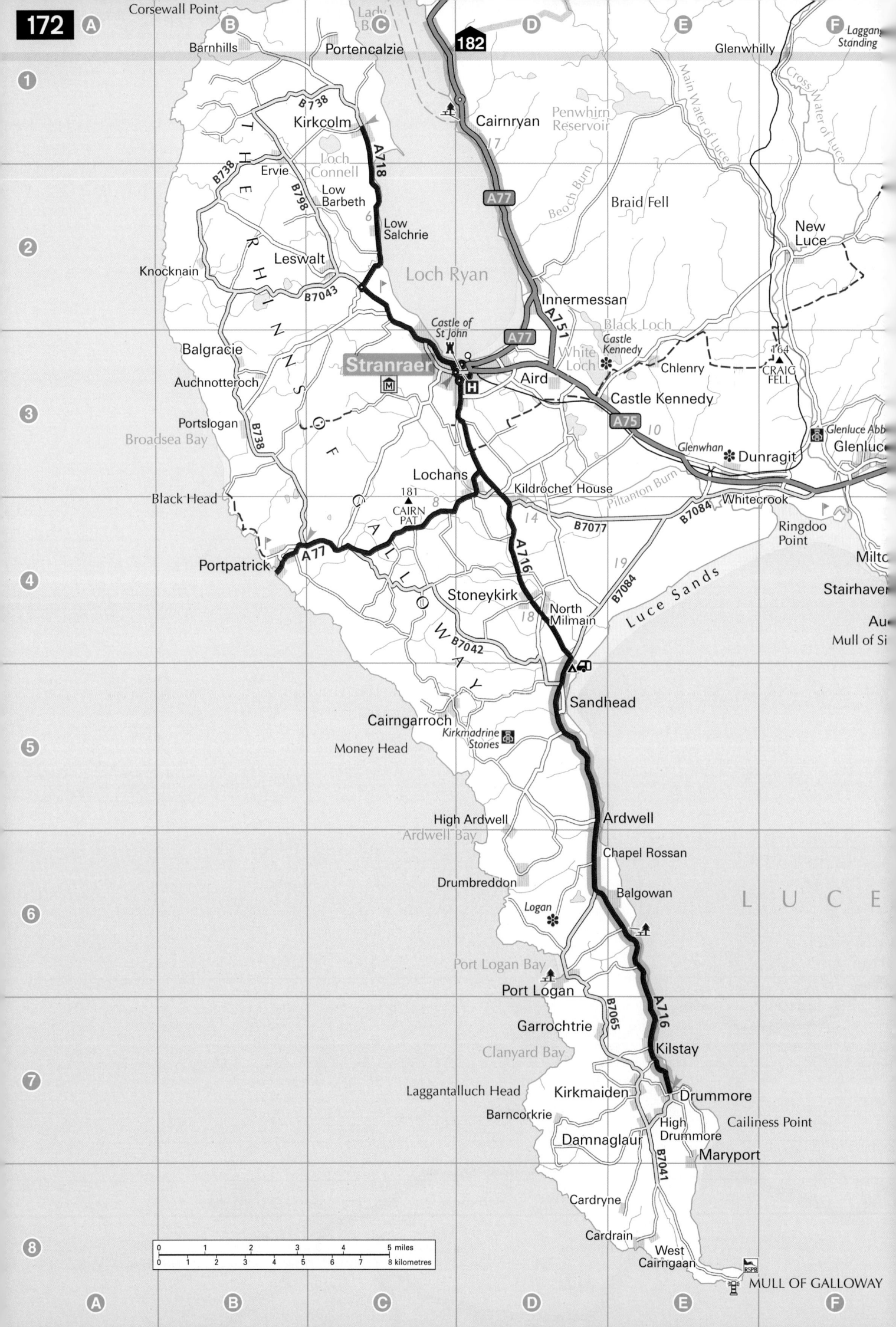

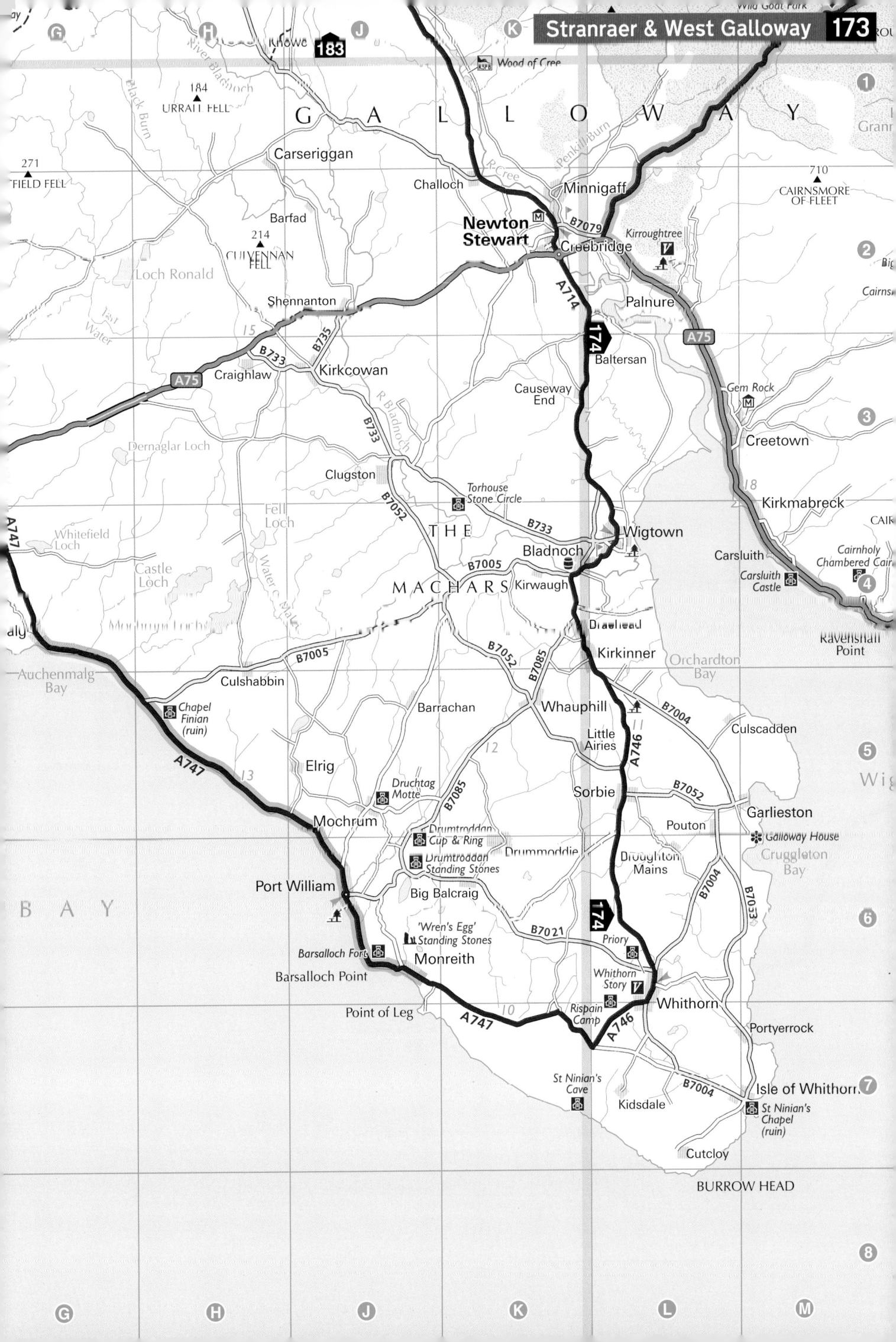

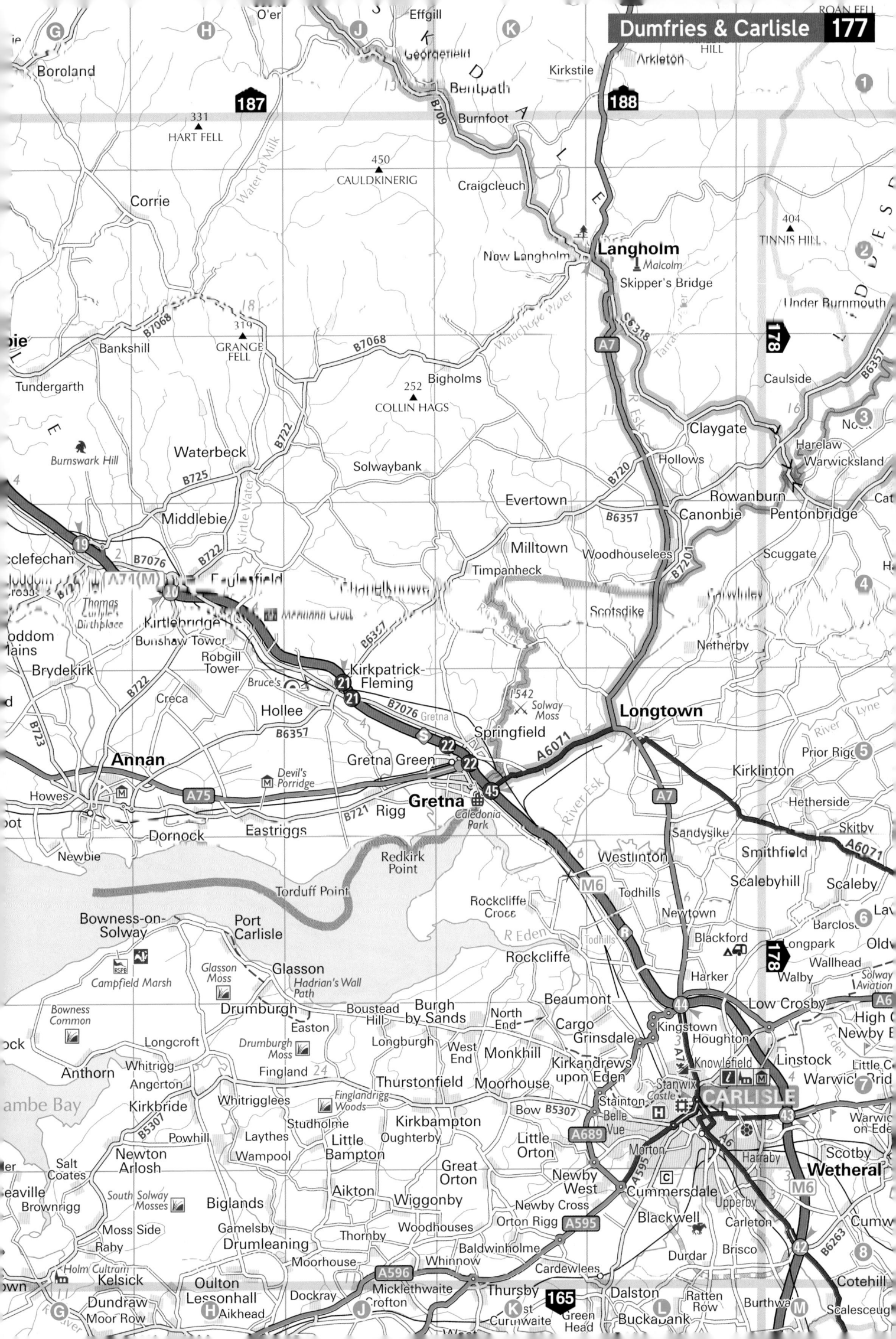

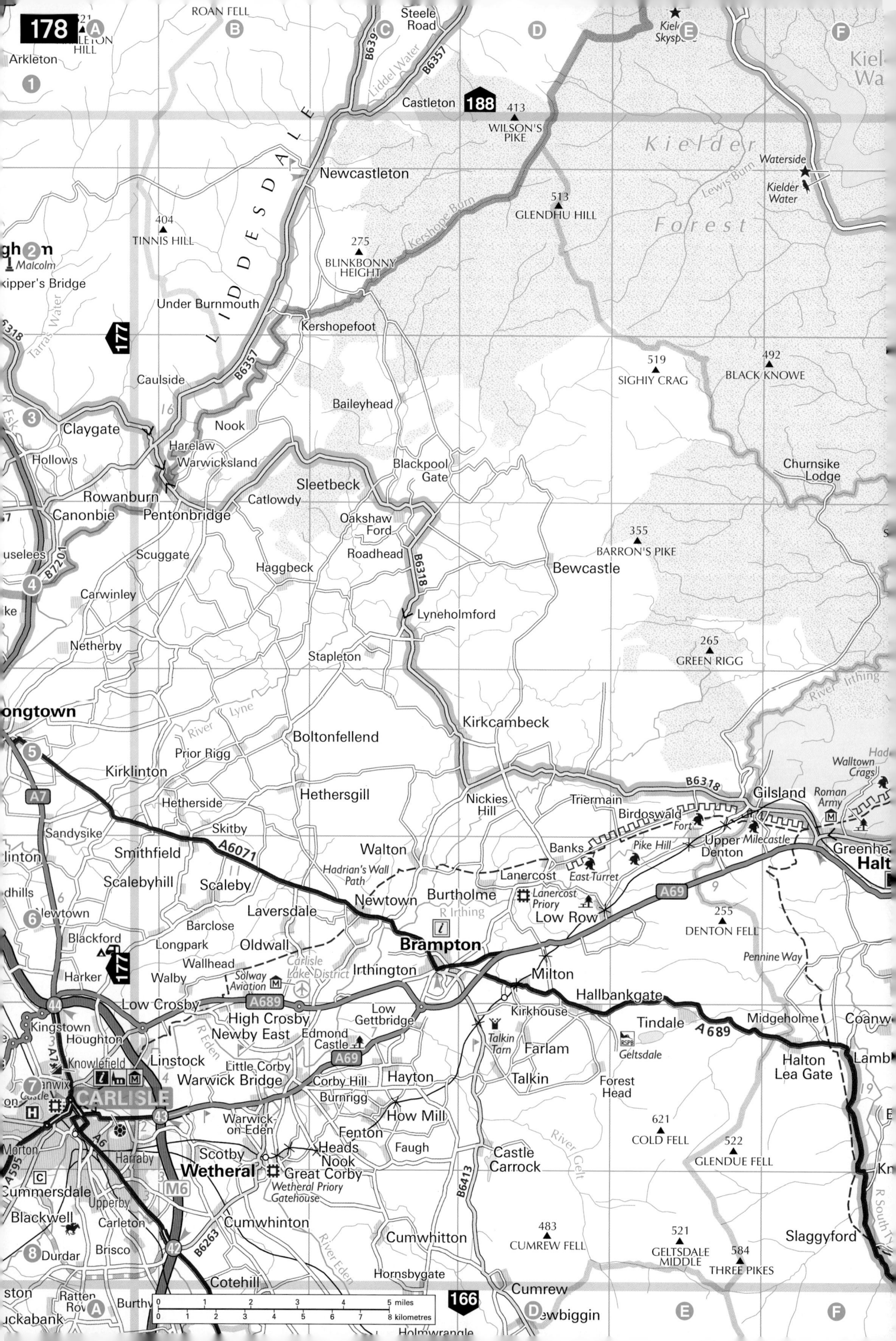

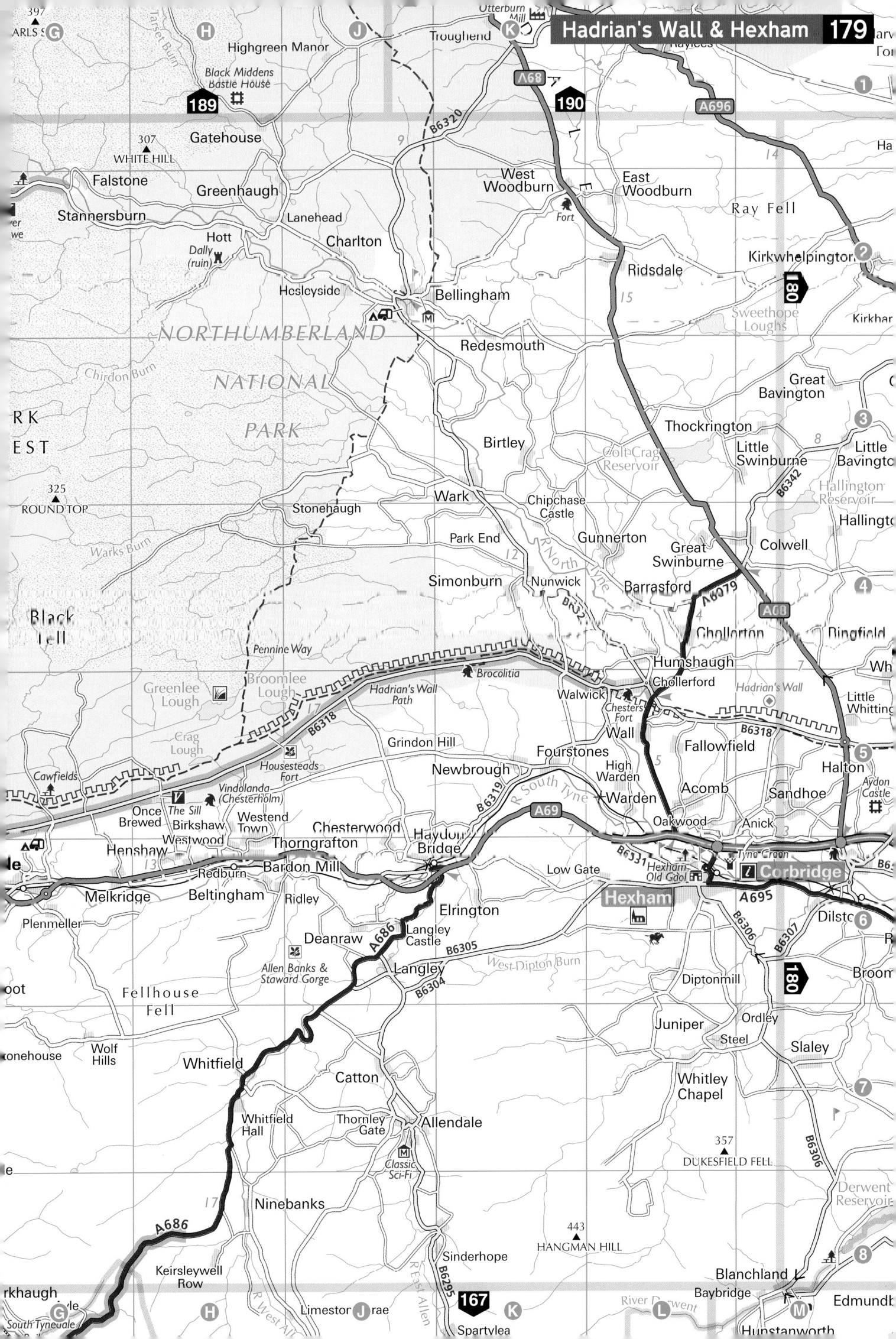

G H J K

397
ARLS S

Highgreen Manor

Troughend

Otterburn Mill

A68

190

A696

1

Black Middens
Bastle House

189

307 ▲
WHITE HILL

Gatehouse

B6320

9

West
Woodburn

East
Woodburn

Ray Fell

14

Falstone

Greenhaugh

Lanehead

Fort

Ridsdale

Kirkwhelpington

2

Stannersburn

Hott

Charlton

Bellingham

Redesmouth

ColtCrag
Reservoir

15

Sweethope
Loughs

Kirkhar

180

Dally
(ruin)

Heslcyside

M

NORTHUMBERLAND

Great
Bavington

Kirkwhelpington

3

Chirdon Burn

Birtley

Thockrington

Little
Swinburne

8

Little
Bavingto

Hallington
Reservoir

Hallingto

NATIONAL

Wark

Chipchase
Castle

Gunnerton

Great
Swinburne

Colwell

325 ▲
ROUND TOP

PARK

Stonehaugh

Park End

12

Simonburn

Nunwick

B632

Barrasford

A6079

A68

4

Black
Tell

Warks Burn

Pennine Way

Broomlee
Lough

Brocolitia

R North Tyne

Walwick

Chesters
Fort

Humshaugh

Chollerford

Hadrian's Wall

Chollerton

Ringfield

Wh

Greenlee
Lough

Hadrian's Wall
Path

17

B6318

Crag
Lough

Grindon Hill

Fourstones

Wall

B6318

Fallowfield

Little
Whitting

5

Cawfields

Housesteads
Fort

Newbrough

High
Warden

Acomb

Halton

Aydon
Castle

Vindolanda
(Chesterholm)

The Sill

V

Once
Brewed

Birkshaw

Westend
Town

Chesterwood

Warden

B6319

R South Tyne

Oakwood

Sandhoe

Anick

Henshaw

Westwood

Thorngrafton

Haydon
Bridge

A69

7

B6331

Hexham
Old Gaol

i Corbridge

A695

Melkridge

Redburn

13

Bardon Mill

Ridley

Beltingham

Elrington

Low Gate

Hexham

Tyne Croon

A695

Dilsto

Plenmeller

Deanraw

A686

Langley
Castle

B6305

West Dipton Burn

Diptonmill

B6306

B6307

180

6

Broon

Allen Banks &
Staward Gorge

Langley

B6304

Juniper

Ordley

Steel

Slaley

onehouse

Wolf
Hills

Fellhouse
Fell

Whitfield

Catton

Whitley
Chapel

7

oot

Whitfield
Hall

Thornley
Gate

Allendale

Classic
Sci-Fi

M

357 ▲
DUKESFIELD FELL

B6306

17

A686

Ninebanks

R East Allen

443 ▲
HANGMAN HILL

Blanchland

8

rkhaugh

South Tynedale

Keirsleywell
Row

G

Limestor J rae

H

B6295

167

K

Sinderhope

Spartvlea

River Derwent

L

Baybridge

Hunstanworth

M

Derwent
Reservoir

Edmundb

A1068 G
Linton • Ellington
Lynemouth

Woodhorn A189
Beacon Point
191
Woodhorn Demesne
ngton
QE2
A197 M
Hirst H
North
Seaton
Wansbeck
Riverside
epwash
Stakeford
West Sleekburn
North Seaton Colliery
Newbiggin-by-the-Sea

Guide
Post A147
Bomarsund
East
Sleekburn
Cambois
North Blyth

dlington
B1331
A193 C
Cowpen
Blyth
068
B1331
Bebside
Newsham

East
Hartford
A189
New
Delaval
South
Newsham
B1505
A192
Shankhouse
A1061
New
Hartley
Seaton
Sluice

lington
A192
East
Cramlington
A190
Seaton
Hartley
Seaton
Hall
ton
B1326
Seghill
A193
**Seaton
Delaval**
St Mary's
Holywell

Dudley
Annitsford
B132
A192
B1325
**Whitley
Bay**
eopel
Burradon
A1056
Backworth
Larsdon
A1142
Monkseaton
Cullercoats

Camperdown
B1317
Shiremoor
Murton
A193
South
Gosforth
Killingworth
A191
P+R
Forest-Hall
A191
New
York
C
H
Tynemouth

Jesmond
P+R
A19
Rising
Sun
A187
Tynemouth Priory
& Castle
- - - - - - - - - - - - - - - Amsterdam
(IJmuiden)

Longbenton
A1058
Willington
**North
Shields**
Int. Ferry
Terminal
**SOUTH
SHIELDS**

Heaton
Wallsend
M
Toll
Tyne Tunnel
(Electronic Toll)
i M
Westoe
Marsden
Bay
Walker
Jarrow
Jarrow
Hall
Harton
Souter Lighthouse
& The Leas
Byker
B1313
A185
Monkton
A19
C
Marsden
Whitburn Coastal Park
Souter Point
Hebburn
A1300
Cleadon
Park
Cleadon
A183
A184
Felling
Wardley
A194
Boldon
Colliery
West
Boldon
B1299
Whitburn
Shipley
M
GATESHEAD
3
A184
East
Boldon
A1018
A184
Whitburn
Bay
am
B1296
B1288
2
North-East
Land Sea
& Air
Hylton
Castle
Fulwell
Southwick
Seaburn
lley
A167
A194(M)
ow Wrekenton
Fell Bowes
Railway
H
Usworth
A195
A1290
A19
Wetland
Centre
Castletown
Roker
P+R
Monkwearmouth

Springwell
C
1
A1231
South
Hylton
C
H
SUNDERLAND
Birtley
66
65
WASHINGTON
Pennywell
A183
B1522
Hendon
Portobello
S
Washington
A195
Offerton
Penshaw
Monument
A183
High Newport
B1405
Grangetown
Urpeth
Ouston
64
Fatfield
Mount
Pleasant
A690
Herrington
New
Silksworth
B1286
Tunstall
Ryhope
Durham
Heritage Coast
Perkinsville
A167
63
A183
Penshaw
New Herrington
Philadelphia
Downat the Farm
693
R Wear
A182
Shiney Row
Newbottle
pelton
Houghton
Gate
Bournmoor
A1052
High
Dubmire
A19
A1018
East Durham Heritage
& Lifeboat Cent
B1287
**Chester-
le-Street**
B1284
Fence
Houses
**Houghton-
le-Spring**
Seaton
V
169
Chester
Colliery
Row
B1404
J
K
L
Seaham

1
2
3
4
5
6
7
8
G   H   J   K   M

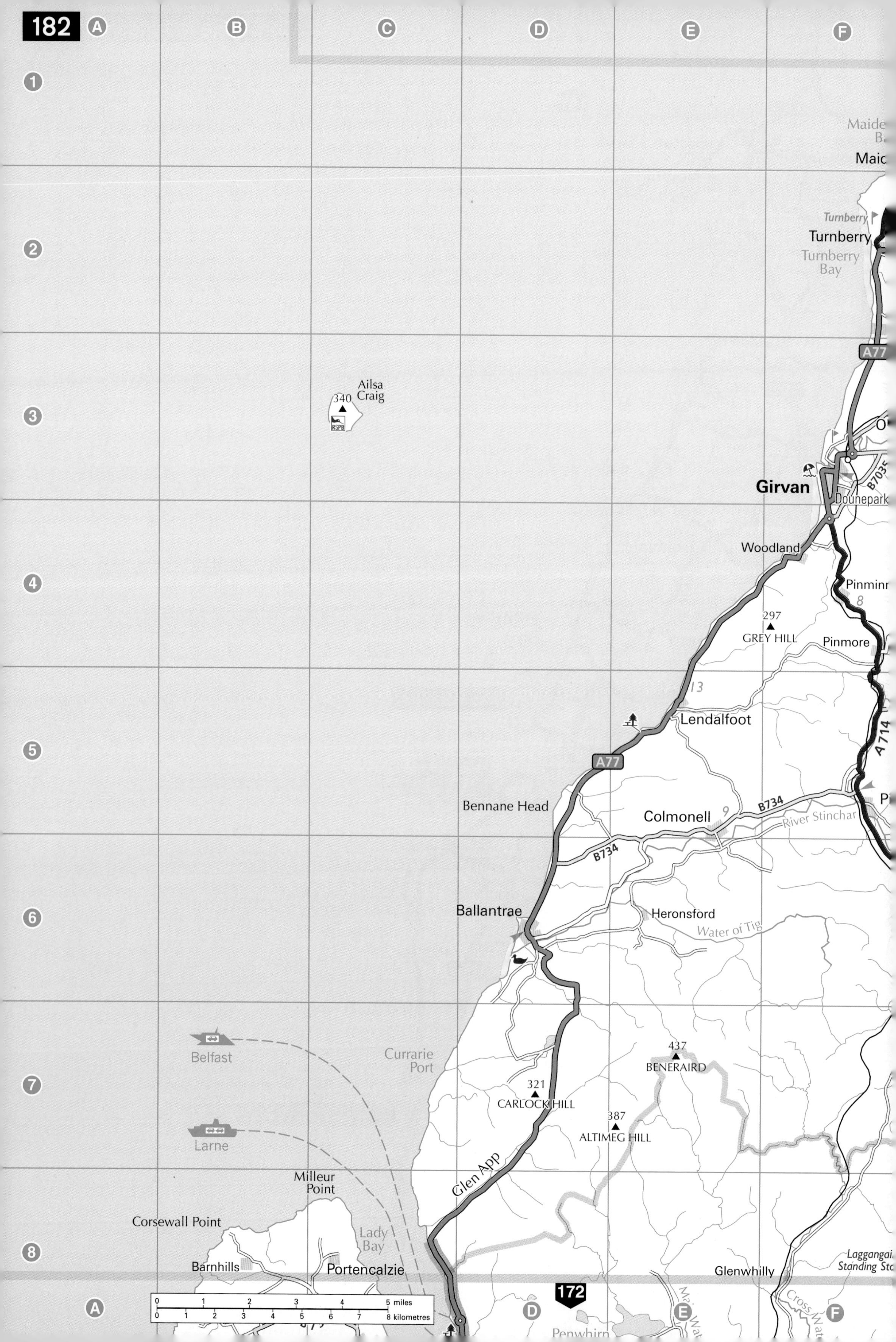

A B C D E F

1

2

Maide
B.

Maic

Turnberry

Turnberry

Turnberry
Bay

A77

3

Ailsa
Craig

340 ▲

RSPB

O

Girvan

Dounepark

B703

Woodland

4

Pinminn

8

297 ▲

GREY HILL

Pinmore

Pinmore

13

A714

5

Lendalfoot

A77

Bennane Head

Colmonell

9

B734

River Stinchar

P

B734

6

Ballantrae

Heronsford

Water of Tig

7

Belfast

Currarie
Port

437 ▲

BENERAIRD

321 ▲

CARLOCK HILL

Larne

387 ▲

ALTIMEG HILL

Milleur
Point

Glen App

Corsewall Point

Lady
Bay

Laggangai
Standing St

8

Barnhills

Portencalzie

Glenwhilly

A B C D E F

Penwhirn

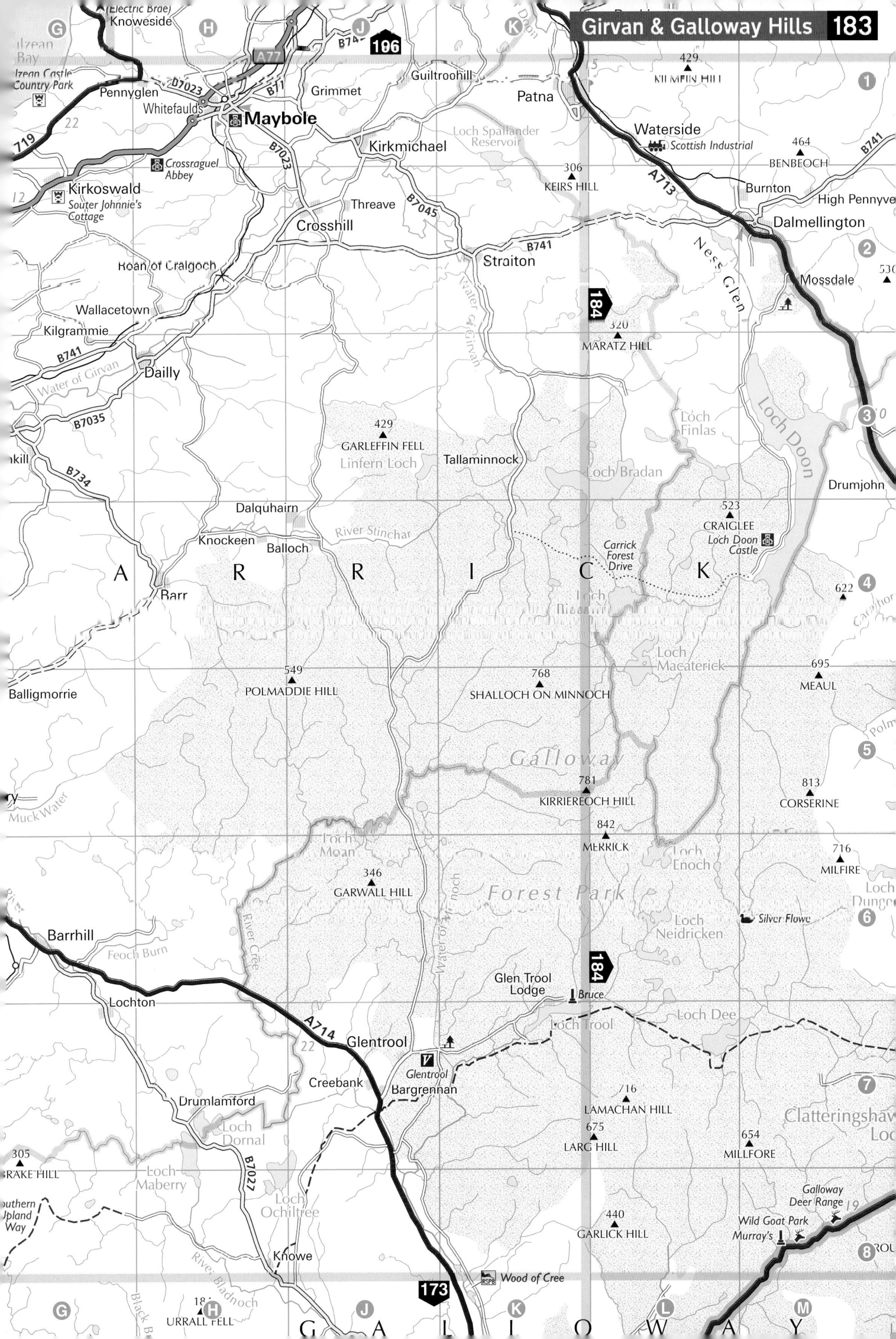

G   H   J   106   K   1

(Electric Brae)
Knoweside
Ailzean
Bay
Alzean Castle
Country Park
Pennyglen
A77
B71
B744
Guiltroohill
Patna
429
KILMEIN HILL
Whitefaulds
B7023
Grimmet
Waterside
Scottish Industrial
464
BENBEOCH
B741
Maybole
Crossraguel Abbey
Kirkmichael
306
KEIRS HILL
Burnton
High Pennyve
Kirkoswald
Souter Johnnie's Cottage
Threave
B7045
Crosshill
B7023
Straiton
B741
Dalmellington
Ness Glen
2
Roan of Craigoch
Wallacetown
184
320
MARATZ HILL
Mossdale
530
3
Kilgrammie
B741
Loch Finlas
Dailly
Water of Girvan
B7035
Loch Bradan
523
CRAIGLEE
Loch Doon Castle
Drumjohn
B734
429
GARLEFFIN FELL
Linfern Loch
Tallaminnock
Carrick Forest Drive
Dalquhairn
Knockeen
Balloch
River Stinchar
A   R   R   I   C   K
622
4
Barr
Loch Macaterick
549
POLMADDIE HILL
768
SHALLOCH ON MINNOCH
695
MEAUL
Balligmorrie
Galloway
5
Muck Water
781
KIRRIEREOCH HILL
813
CORSERINE
842
MERRICK
Loch Enoch
716
MILFIRE
Loch Moan
346
GARWALL HILL
Forest Park
Loch Neidricken
Silver Flowe
6
Barrhill
Feoch Burn
Water of Minnoch
River Cree
Loch Dee
Lochton
A714
22
Glen Trool Lodge
Bruce
184
Loch Trool
7
Glentrool
Creebank
Glentrool
Bargrennan
716
LAMACHAN HILL
Clatteringshaw
Loc
Drumlamford
675
LARG HILL
654
MILLFORE
305
BRAKE HILL
Loch Dornal
B7027
Galloway Deer Range
19
440
GARLICK HILL
Wild Goat Park
Murray's
Loch Maberry
Southern Upland Way
Loch Ochiltree
8
Knowe
173
Wood of Cree
RSPB
G   H   J   K   L   M
URRALL FELL
G   A   L   L   O   W   A   Y

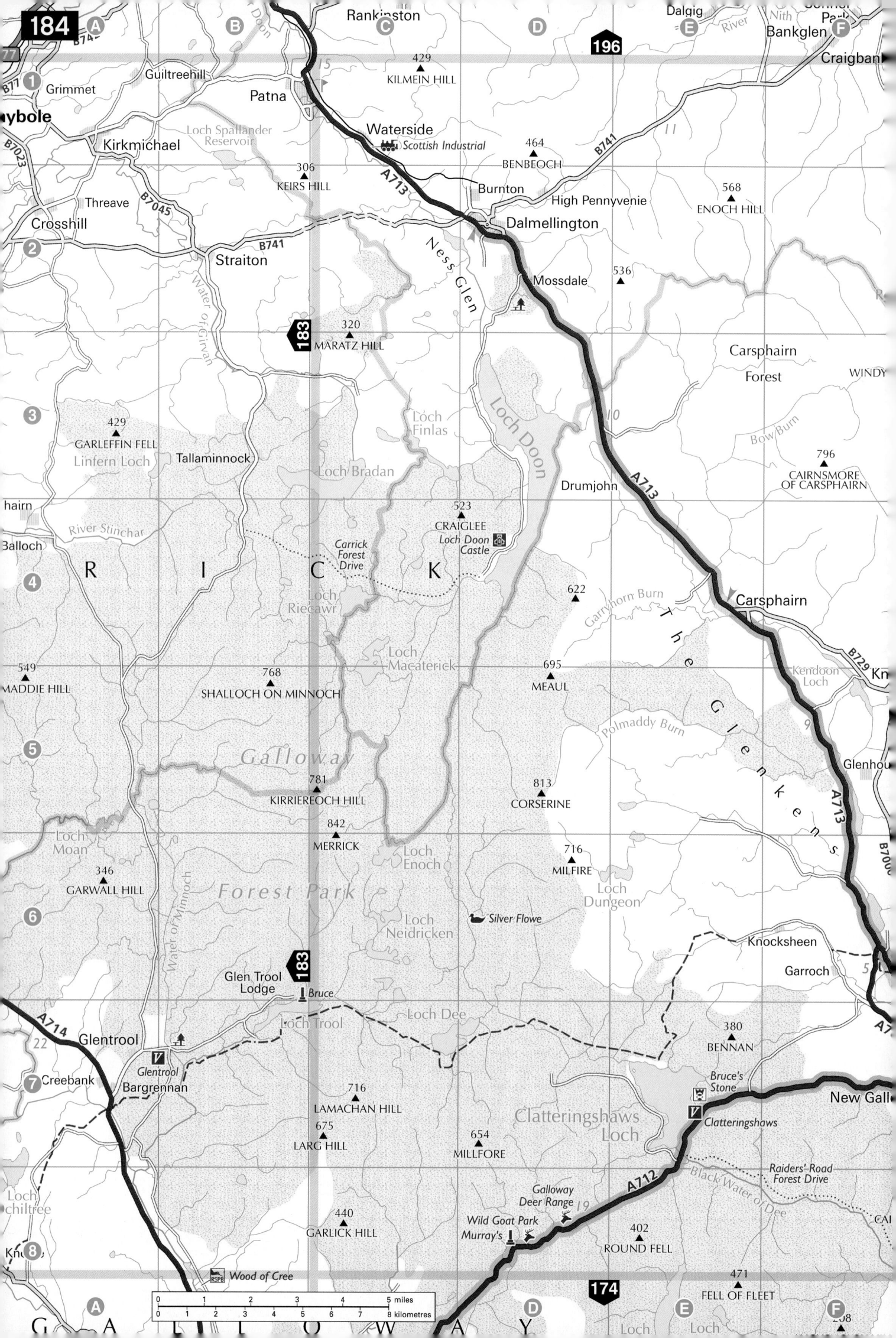

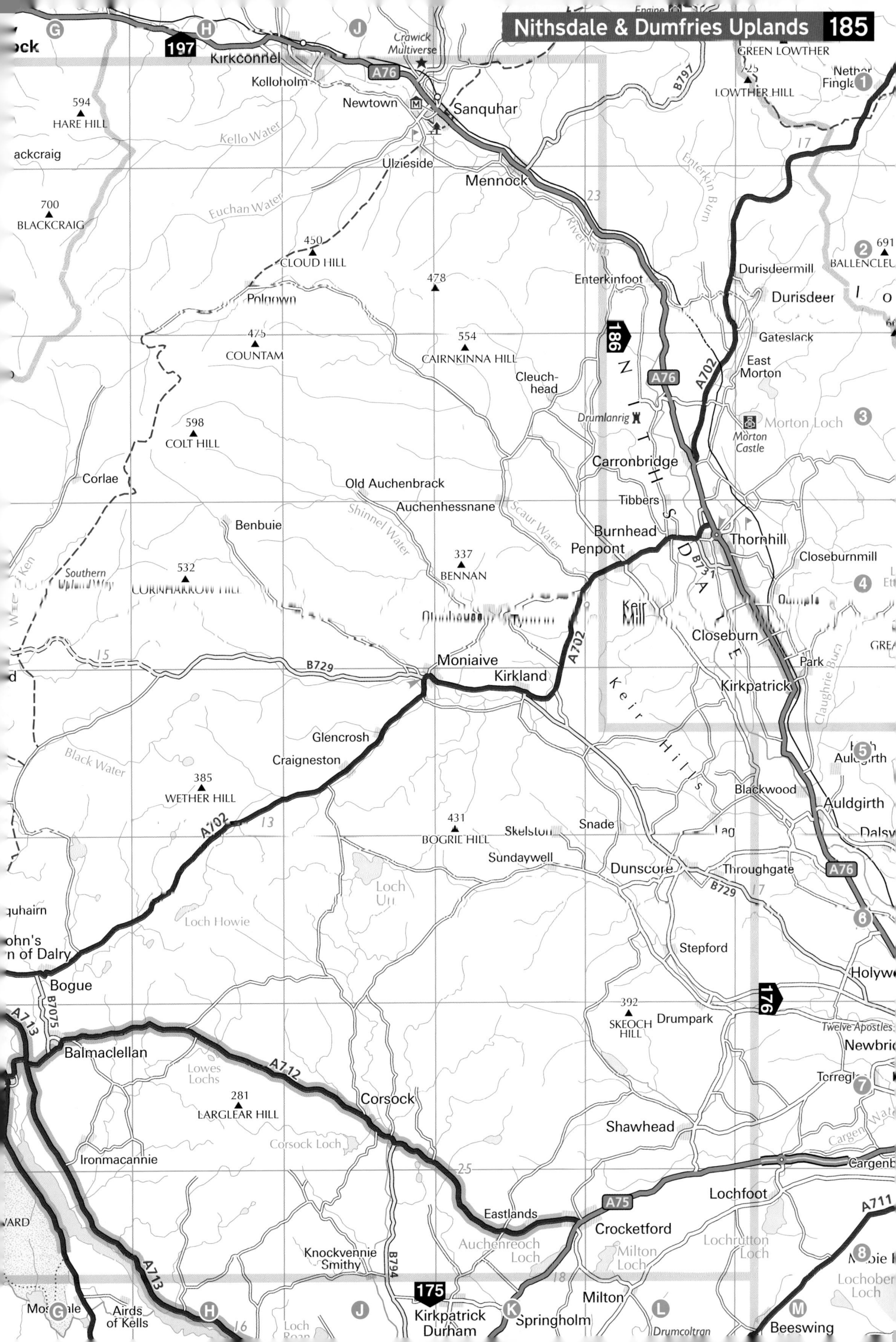

G H 197 J **Kirkconnel**

Crawick Multiverse

GREEN LOWTHER

Netho Fingla 1

Kolloholm

A76

Newtown

Sanquhar

B797

594 HARE HILL

LOWTHER HILL

ckcraig

Kello Water

Ulzieside

Mennock

River Nith

23

Durisdeermill

2 691 BALLENCLEU

Durisdeer

I o

700 BLACKCRAIG

Euchan Water

450 CLOUD HILL

Polgown

478

Enterkinfoot

Enterkin Burn

17

Gateslack

East Morton

475 COUNTAM

554 CAIRNKINNA HILL

Cleuch-head

186

Z

A76

A702

Drumlanrig

Durisdeer

3

Morton Loch

Morton Castle

598 COLT HILL

Old Auchenbrack

Carronbridge

Corlae

Auchenhessnane

Shinnel Water

Scaur Water

Tibbers

Benbuie

532 CORNHARROW HILL

337 BENNAN

Burnhead

Penpont

Thornhill

Closeburnmill

4

Southern Upland Way

Keir Mill

Closeburn

GREA

Wee Ken

Moniaive

Kirkland

A702

Park

15

B729

Glencrosh

Keir Hills

Kirkpatrick

5 Auldgirth

Black Water

Craigneston

385 WETHER HILL

431 BOGRIE HILL

Skelston

Snade

Blackwood

Auldgirth

Dalsv

A702

13

Sundaywell

Dunscore

Throughgate

A76

quhairn

Loch Urr

Loch Howie

Stepford

6

ohn's n of Dalry

Bogue

B7075

176

392 SKEOCH HILL

Drumpark

Holywo

A713

Balmaclellan

A712

Twelve Apostles

Newbri

Lowes Lochs

281 LARGLEAR HILL

Corsock

Shawhead

Terregl

7

Ironmacannie

Corsock Loch

25

Cargen Wate

Cargenb

Lochfoot

A711

WARD

A75

Crocketford

Lochrutton Loch

Eastlands

Auchenreoch Loch

Milton Loch

G Mo ale

Airds of Kells

H

16

Loch Roan

Knockvennie Smithy

B794

J

175

Kirkpatrick Durham

K Springholm

18

Milton

Drumcoltran

L

M Beeswing

8 ie L

Lochober Loch

A713

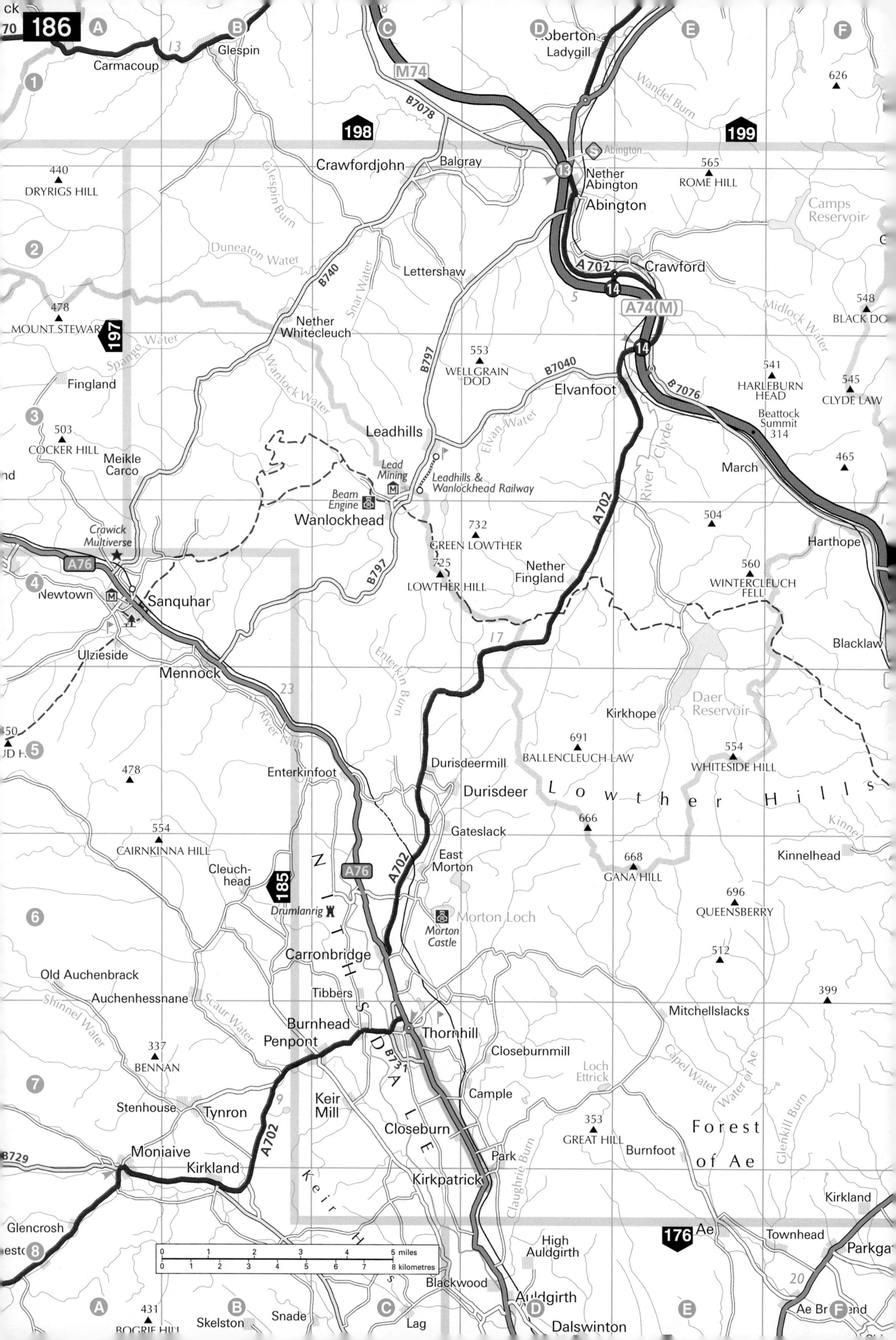

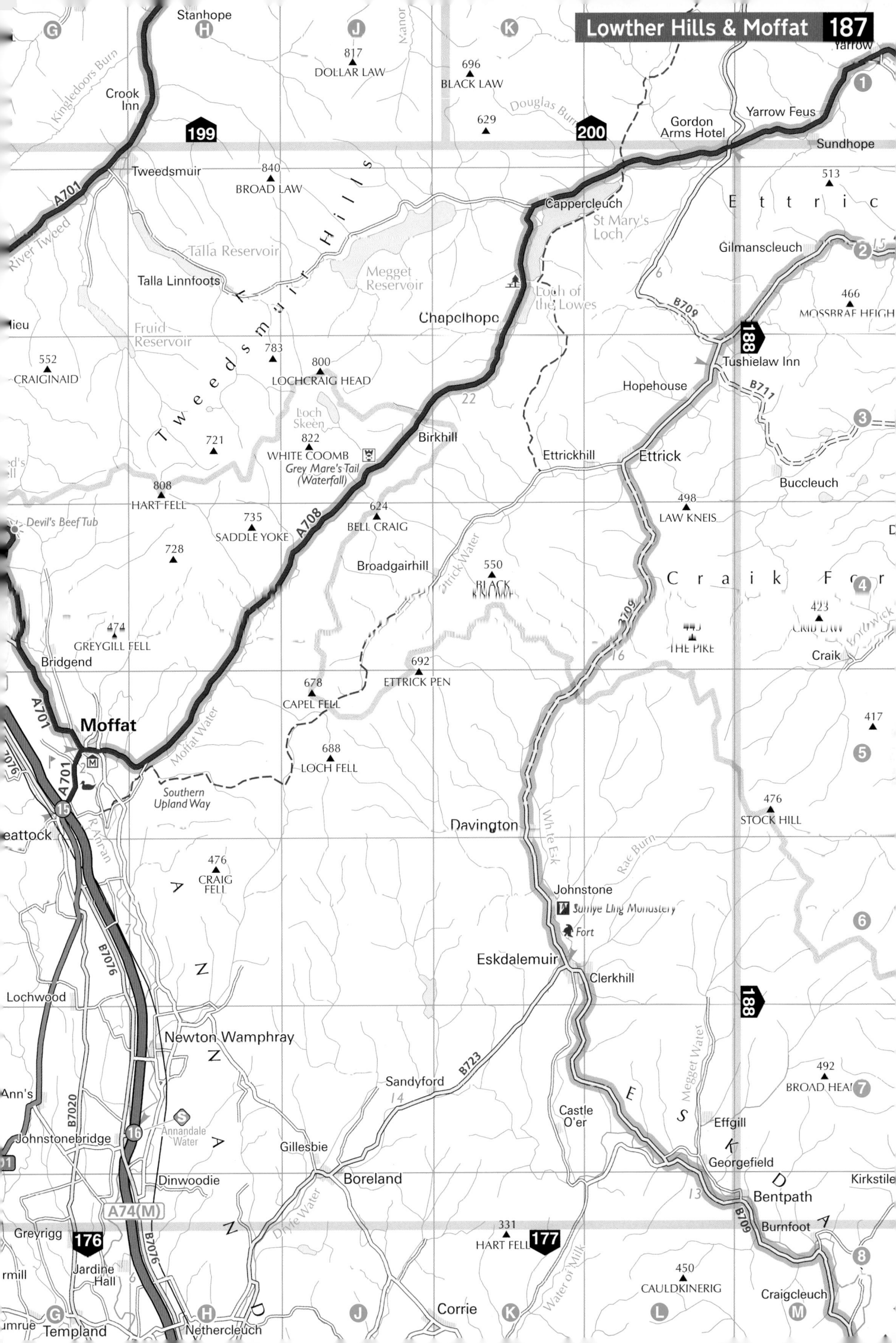

G
H Stanhope
J Manor
K
1 Yarrow

Crook Inn
Kingledoors Burn
817 DOLLAR LAW
696 BLACK LAW
Douglas Burn
Gordon Arms Hotel
Yarrow Feus
Sundhope

199
629
200

A701
Tweedsmuir
840 BROAD LAW
Cappercleuch
St Mary's Loch
Gilmanscleuch
513
E t t r i c

Talla Reservoir
Loch of the Lowes
B709
6
2

Talla Linnfoots
Megget Reservoir
466 MOSSBRAE HEIGH

River Tweed
Fruid Reservoir
Chapelhope
188
Tushielaw Inn

lieu
783
Hopehouse
B711

552 CRAIGINAID
800 LOCHCRAIG HEAD
Loch Skeen
3

721
822 WHITE COOMB
Birkhill
Ettrickhill
Ettrick
Buccleuch

Grey Mare's Tail (Waterfall)
498 LAW KNEIS

808 HART-FELL
735 SADDLE YOKE
624 BELL CRAIG
Ettrick Water
C r a i k F o r

Devil's Beef Tub
A708
Broadgairhill
550 BLACK KNOWE
423 CRIB LAW
4

728
692
THE PIKE
Craik

474 GREYGILL FELL
ETTRICK PEN
B709
16
417
5

Bridgend
678 CAPEL FELL

Moffat
688 LOCH FELL
476 STOCK HILL

A701
Southern Upland Way
Davington
White Esk
Rae Burn

15
Beattock
476 CRAIG FELL
Johnstone
Samye Ling Monastery
Fort
188

A74(M)
B7076
Z
Eskdalemuir
Clerkhill

Lochwood
Newton Wamphray
Z
B723
Megget Water
492 BROAD HEAD
7

Ann's
B7020
Sandyford
14
Castle O'er
E
Effgill
Georgefield

Johnstonebridge
16
Annandale Water
Gillesbie
S K
Bentpath
Kirkstile

Greyrigg
176
Dinwoodie
Boreland
Drive Water
13
B709
Burnfoot
8

Jardine Hall
B7076
331 HART FELL
177
Water of Milk
450 CAULDKINERIG
Craigcleuch

rmill
Templand
Nethercleuch
G
H
J
Corrie
K
L
M

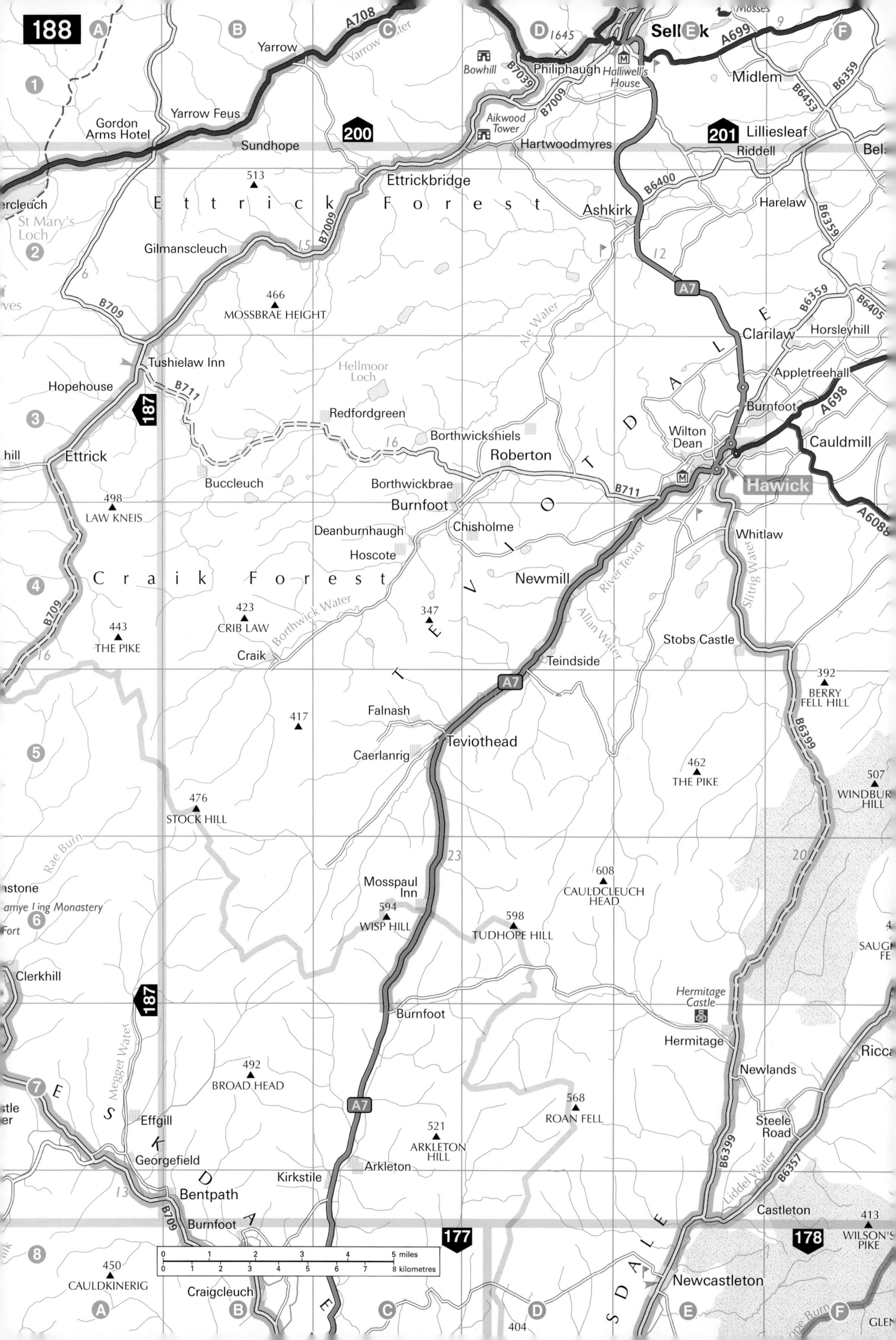

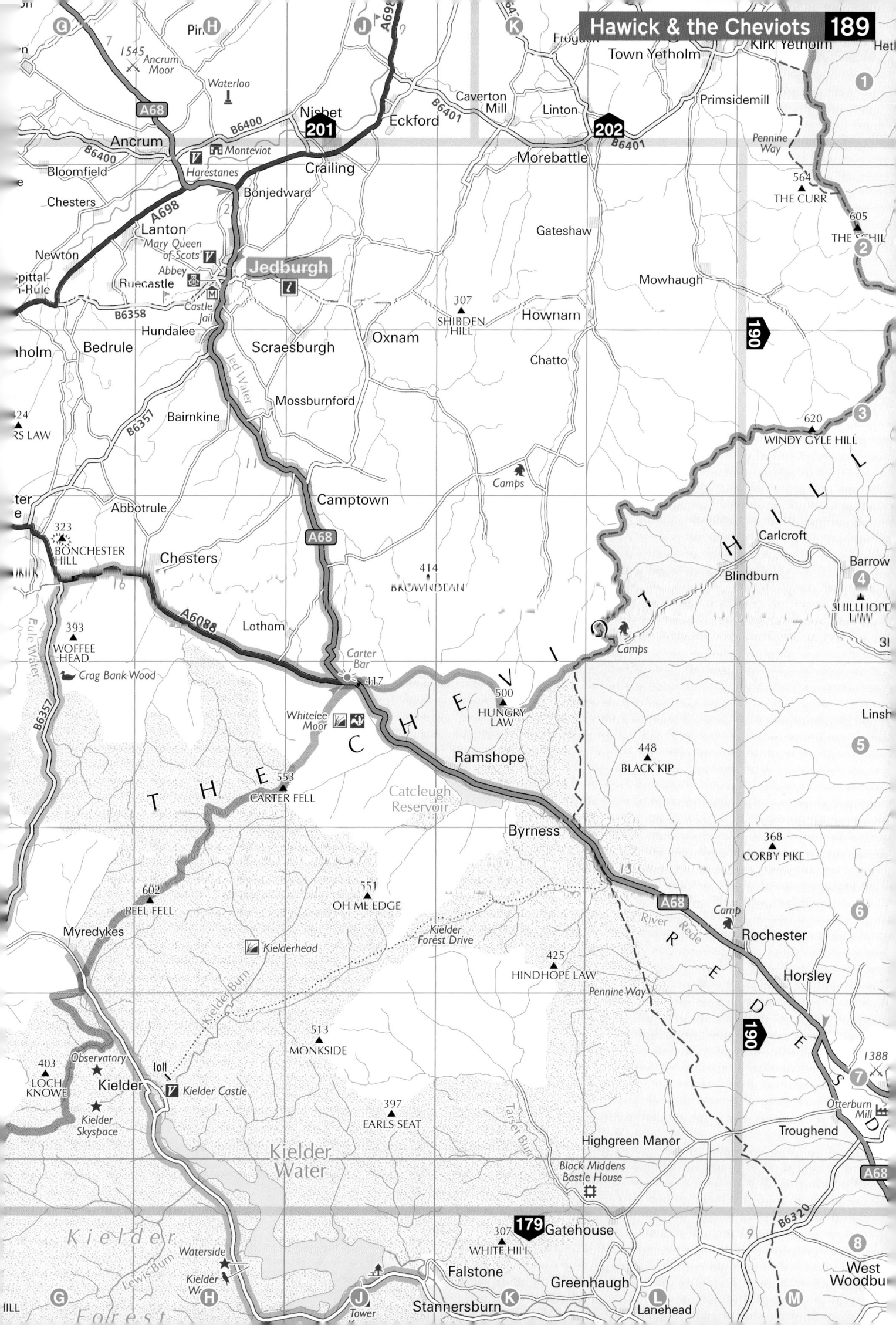

imacnar
Ballikline

J

792
BEINN NUIS

K

Glen Rosa

6
Merkland Point

G
Carradale
879
Port Righ

Waterfoot
Carradale
Point

Carradale
Bay

Glen Rosa

Brodick Castle, Garden
& Country Park

Brodick
Bay

1

A R R A N

Auchagallon
Stone Circle
Machrie

512
A'CHRUACH

M

Brodick

i

Strathwhillan

Corriegills

Machrie
Bay

Machrie Moor
Stone Circles

4

A841

H

Clauchlands
Point

2

Tormore

Moss Farm Road
Stone Circle

503
BEINN BHREAC

Lamlash

Margnaheglish

Balmichael

Lamlash
Bay

Holy Island

ddell
ay

Torbeg

B880

Shiskine

Gordon

K I L B R A N

Drumadoon
Point

Blackwaterfoot

Kilpatrick

Glen Scorrodale

Carn Ban

Auchencairn

Kingscross

Knockenkelly

Whiting

3

Kilpatrick Dun

Whiting Bay

Bay

194
Brown Head

Drumadoon
Bay

Glenashdale

(May-Sept,
Sat only)

V

Largymore

Corriecravie

Torr a' Chaisteal Fort

Sliddery

Kilmory Water

Largybeg

Dippin
Dippin Head

4

Kilmory

Bennan
Carn

Bennan

Khannan

195

Bennan Head

Hadda

Ballycastle
(Apr-Sept)

5

6

7

Ailsa
Craig

340

RSPB

8

G
H
J
K
L
M

A | B | C | D | E | F

206

Loch Ciàran
Loch Garasdale

Cock of Arran

1

Crossaig

Lochranza
Castle
247
CRUACH MHIC GOUGAIN
Catacol
Isle of Arran

264
CNOC AN T-SAMHLAIDH
Cour Bay
Glen Chalmadale
A841
8

Cour

Rhunahaorine
38

2

Grogport
Barmollack
Pirnmill
Penrioch
North Arran
834
CAISTEAL ABHAIL

205

Glen Catacol

Whitefarland
715
BEINN BHARRAIN
874
GOATFELL

354
CRUACH NAN GABHAR
Imachar
Glen Iorsa

3

dale

Water
39
B842
Carradale Water
Balliekine
792
BEINN NUIS
Glen Rosa

Carradale
Carradale Village
B879
Port Right
Iorsa Water

Bridgend
Dippen
Waterfoot
454
BEINN AN TUIRC
Torrisdale
Carradale Point
Carradale Bay

A R R A N

4

319

408
BÒRD MOR
Saddell Water
Auchagallon Stone Circle
Machrie
512
A'CHRUACH

Machrie Bay
Machrie Moor Stone Circles
B880

192

Saddell
Tormore
Moss Farm Road Stone Circle
503
BEINN BHREAC

Lussa Loch
396
SGREADAN HILL
Saddell Bay
Ugadale
Balmichael

5

Torbeg
Shiskine

N

Drumadoon Point
Blackwaterfoot
Glen Scorrodale

Glen Lussa
Kilpatrick
Carn Ban

6

Peninver
Ardnacross Bay
Drumadoon Bay
Kilpatrick Dun

Ki chael
B842
Brown Head
Corriecravie
Sliddery

193

Campbeltown
Campbeltown Loch
Island Davaar
Torr a' Chaisteal Fort
Kilmory
Lagg
Torrylin Cairn
Bennan

B842
V
Stewarton

Kilkerran
Kildalloig
Bennan Head

7

352
BEINN GHUILEAN
Achinhoan
Ballycastle (Apr-Sept)

8

Ru Stafnish

Glen Kerran

0 1 2 3 4 5 miles
0 1 2 3 4 5 6 7 8 kilometres

A | B | C | D | E | F

Polliwilline Bay

G H J 207 K

Gari H ty
Garroch Head
Little Cumbrae Island
Hunterston Power Station
12
Portencross
Farland Head
B7048
B7047
Seamill
A78
B781
Munnoch
B780
Drakemyre
Dalry
Hig
A737
1
C U N
B780
Dalgarven
7
Dalgarven Mill
2
B714
B778
Kilwinning
West **Kilbride**
Corrie
A78
A738
B78
Ardrossan
A78
Horse Isle
Stevenston
B780
Ardeer
Saltcoats 196
3
Irvine
Maritime
Merkland Point
Brodick Castle, Garden & Country Park
6
V
Fullar
Brodick Bay
Irvine Bay
Ga
i
F I R T H
Strathwhillan
O F
Corriegills
4
C L Y D L
4
Clauchlands Point
Margnaheglish
Lamlash Bay
V
Barn
Troon
Holy Island
Cordon
4
Royal
5
Lady Isle
Auchencairn
Kingscross
Knockenkelly
(May-Sept, Sat only)
(May-Sept)
Whiting Bay
hiting Bay
V
Pr
N
6
nashdale
Largymore
Largybeg
Dippin
Dippin Head
A
Kildonan
196
adda
Doonfoo
Heads of Ayr
Heads of Ayr
Burns Cott
Allo
Fisherton
A719
7
Dunure
Culroy
Drumshang
Croy Brae (Electric Brae)
Knoweside
Culzean Bay
8
Culzean Castle & Country Park
A77
Pennyglen
B70
M
Whitefaulds
May

G H 182 J K L

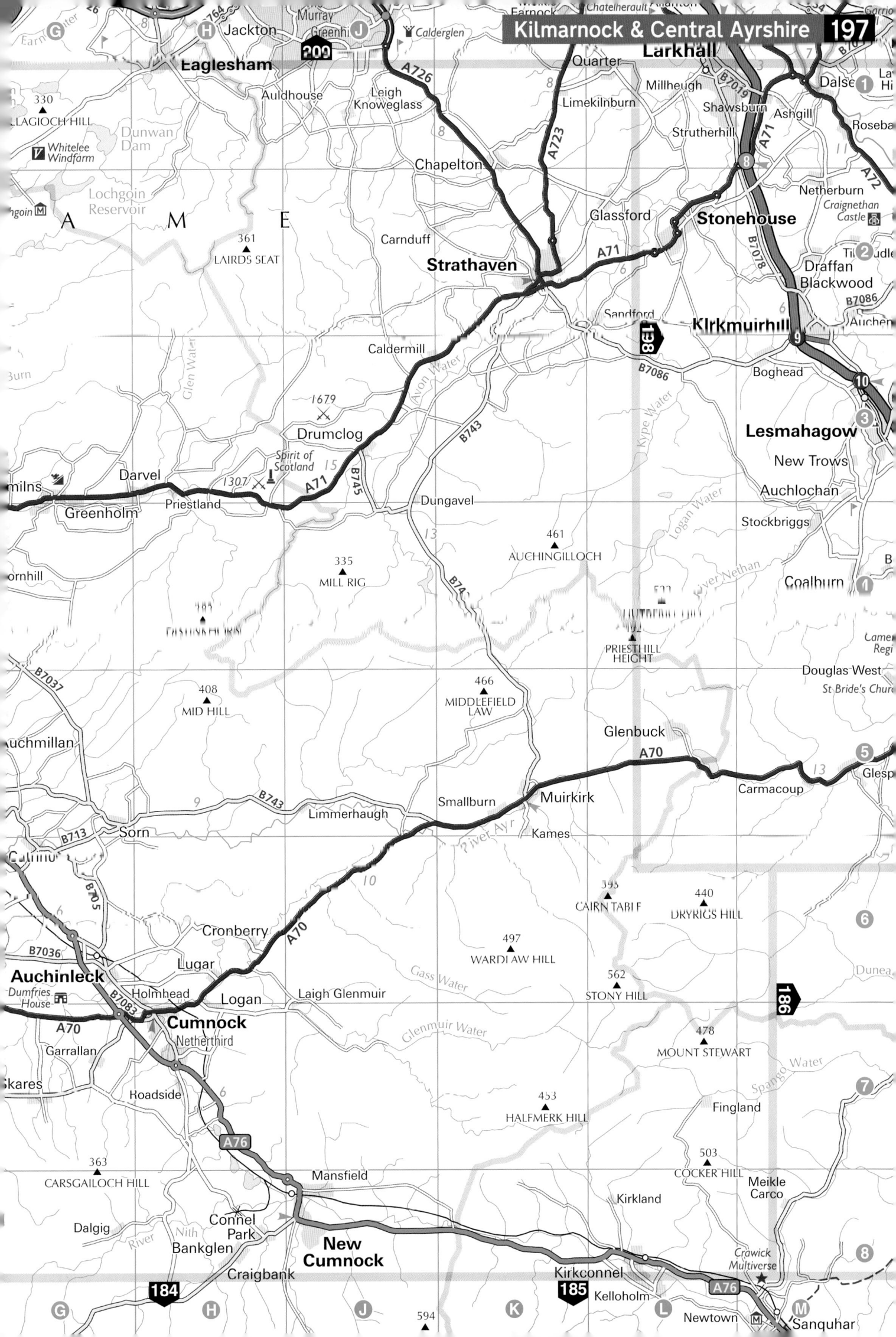

Murray
Greenhi
Jackton
Eaglesham
Auldhouse
Leigh
Knoweglass
Calderglen
A726
Quarter
Larkhall
Millheugh
Limekilnburn
Shawsburn
Ashgill
Roseba
Dalse
La
Hi
Strutherhill
Netherburn
Craignethan
Castle
A72

330
LAGIOCH HILL
Whitelee
Windfarm
A723
Chapelton
Glassford
A71
Stonehouse
Til udle
Draffan
Blackwood
Lochgoin
Reservoir
A M E
Dunwan
Dam
Carnduff
361
LAIRDS SEAT
Strathaven
Sandford
B7086
Auchen
Kirkmuirhill
9

Caldermill
Avon Water
B7086
Boghead
10
3

Burn
1679
Drumclog
B743
Kype Water
Lesmahagow
New Trows

milns
Darvel
1307
Spirit of
Scotland
A71
B745
Priestland
Greenholm
Dungavel
461
AUCHINGILLOCH
Logan Water
Auchlochan
Stockbriggs
Coalburn
ornhill
335
MILL RIG
13
B74
ASTONK HURN
522
RIVERHILL
PRIESTHILL
HEIGHT
River Nethan
Douglas West
St Bride's Churc
Camer
Regi

B7037
408
MID HILL
466
MIDDLEFIELD
LAW
Glenbuck
A70
5
Glesp

uchmillan
B743
9
Limmerhaugh
Smallburn
Muirkirk
Carmacoup
13
B713
Sorn
River Ayr
Kames
395
CAIRN TABLE
440
DRYRIGS HILL
6
alrmo
B705
10
Cronberry
A70
497
WARDLAW HILL
B7036
Lugar
562
STONY HILL
Dunea
Auchinleck
Holmhead
B7083
Logan
Laigh Glenmuir
Gass Water
Dumfries
House
A70
Cumnock
Netherthird
Glenmuir Water
478
MOUNT STEWART
186
Garrallan
Spango Water
Skares
Roadside
6
453
HALFMERK HILL
Fingland
7

363
CARSGAILOCH HILL
A76
Mansfield
Kirkland
503
COCKER HILL
Meikle
Carco
Dalgig
Connel
Park
Bankglen
Craigbank
**New
Cumnock**
Kirkconnel
185
Kelloholm
A76
Crawick
Multiverse
Newtown
Sanquhar
184
8

G H J K L M

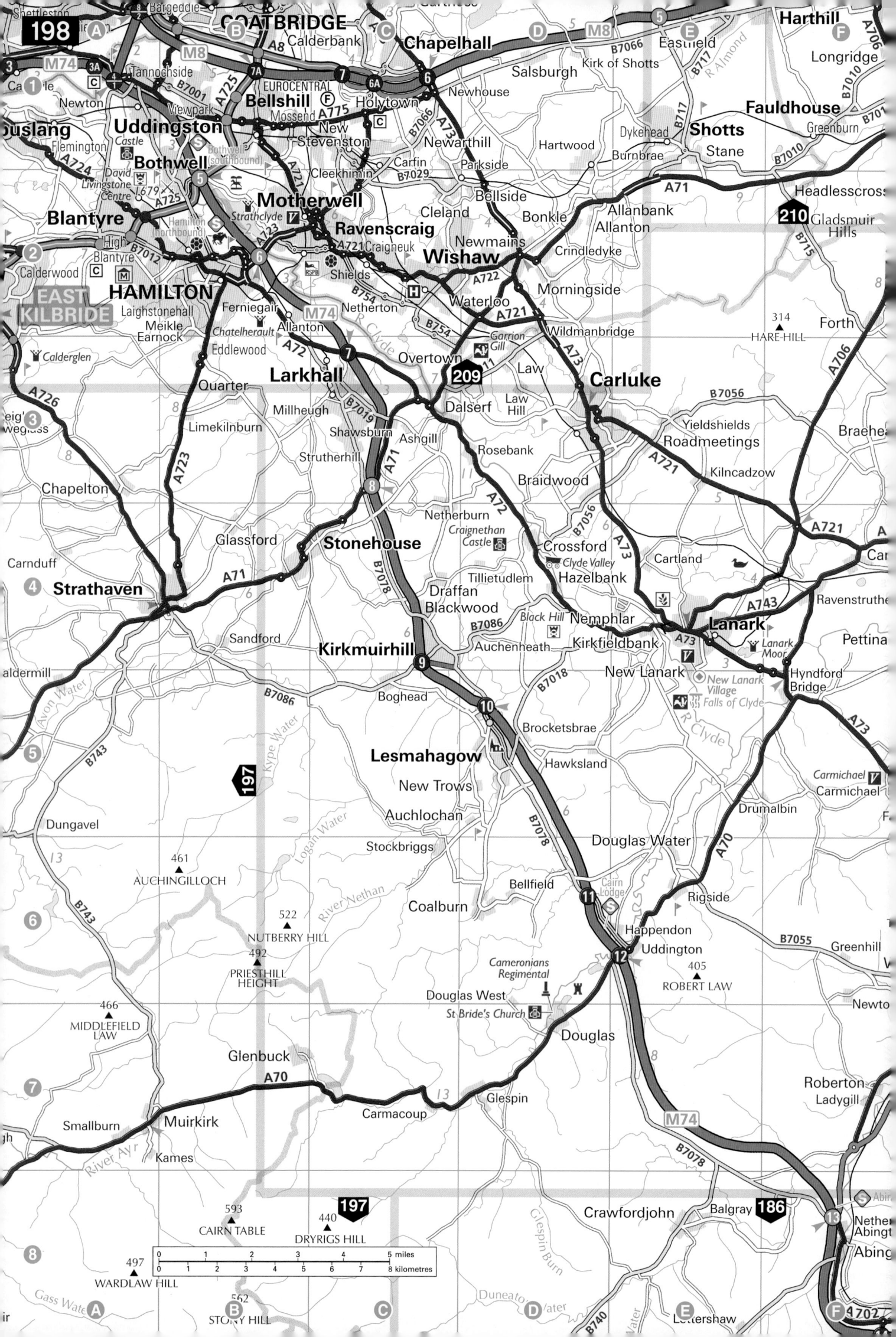

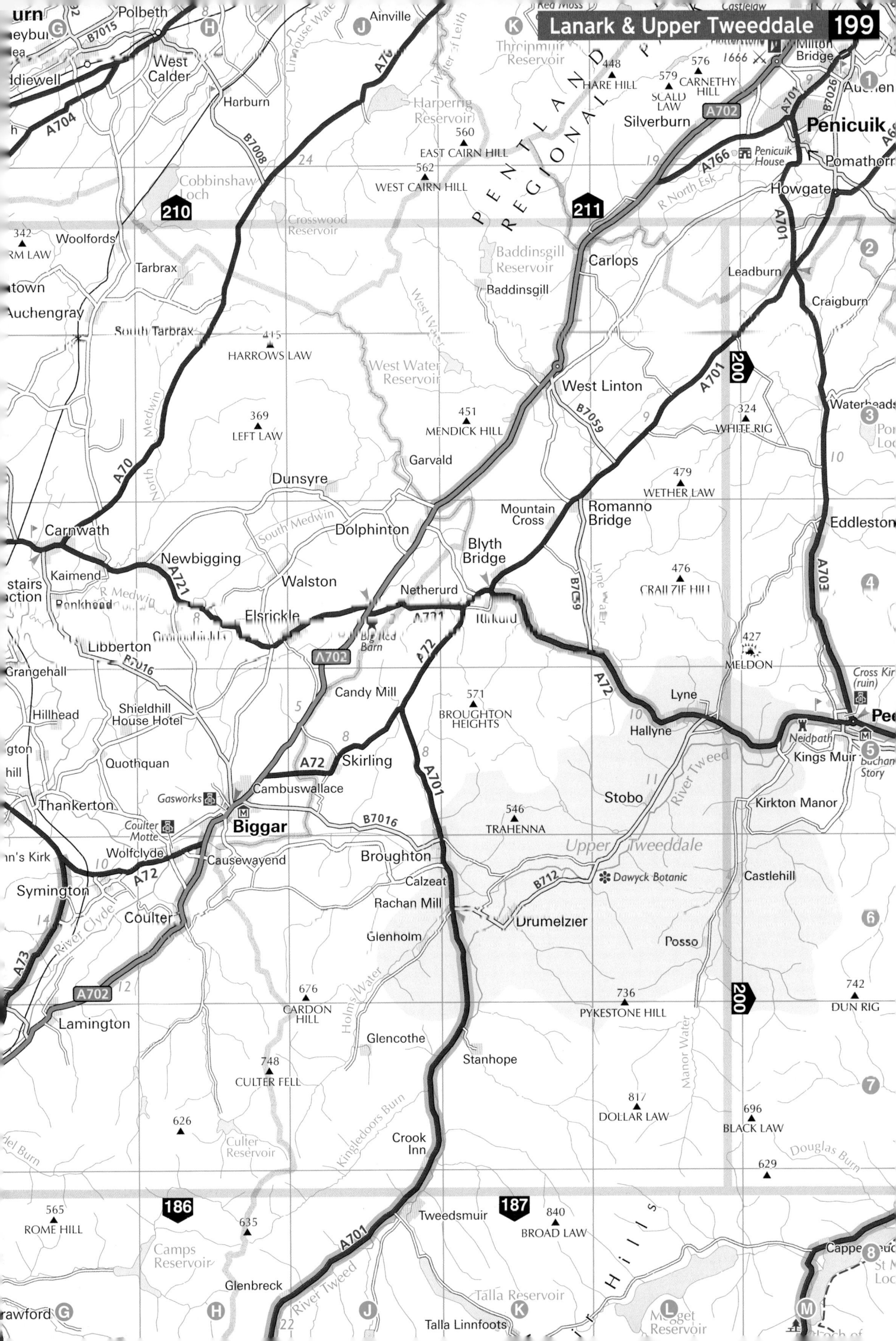

G   Polbeth   B7015   H   Ainville   J   Linhouse Water   Water of Leith   Red Moss   Castlelaw   K   Thriepmuir Reservoir   Flotterstone   Milton Bridge   1

eyburn   West Calder   Harburn   A70   Harperrig Reservoir   24   HARE HILL 448   SCALD LAW   579   CARNETHY HILL   576   1666   A702   Silverburn   A701   B7026   Auchen   Penicuik

diewell   A704   B7008   Cobbinshaw Loch   210   Crosswood Reservoir   EAST CAIRN HILL 560   WEST CAIRN HILL 562   211   A766   Penicuik House   Pomathorn   Howgate

342   Woolfords   RM LAW   Tarbrax   South Tarbrax   415   HARROWS LAW   West Water Reservoir   Baddingsill Reservoir   Baddinsgill   Carlops   R North Esk   A701   Leadburn   Craigburn   2

town   Auchengray   369   LEFT LAW   MENDICK HILL 451   Garvald   West Linton   B7059   9   A701   200   WHITE RIG 324   Waterheads   3   Pon Loc   10

Carnwath   A70   North Medwin   Dunsyre   Dolphinton   Mountain Cross   WETHER LAW 479   Romanno Bridge   CRAIL ZIE HILL 476   Eddleston   A703   4

Newbigging   A721   Walston   Netherurd   Blyth Bridge   B7059   Lyne Water   427   MELDON   Cross Kir (ruin)

Kaimend   Elsrickle   A701   Kirkurd   A72   10   Lyne   Pee

stairs ction   Parkhead   R Medwin   Libberton   B7016   Grangehall   Candy Mill   A702   B72   Big Red Barn   571   BROUGHTON HEIGHTS   10   Hallyne   River Tweed   Neidpath   5   Kings Muir   Story

Hillhead   Shieldhill House Hotel   Quothquan   A72   Skirling   A701   8   Stobo   Kirkton Manor   Upper Tweeddale   Castlehill

Thankerton   Gasworks   Cambuswallace   Biggar   B7016   546   TRAHENNA   Dawyck Botanic   6

n's Kirk   Coulter Motte   Wolfclyde   Causewayend   Broughton   B712   Drumelzier   Posso

Symington   A72   10   Coulter   Calzeat   Rachan Mill   Glenholm   742   DUN RIG

A73   River Clyde   A702   12   Lamington   676   CARDON HILL   Holms Water   Glencothe   Stanhope   736   PYKESTONE HILL   200   817   DOLLAR LAW   696   BLACK LAW   Douglas Burn   629   7

748   CULTER FELL   626   Culter Reservoir   Kingledoors Burn   Crook Inn   8

del Burn   565   ROME HILL   186   635   Camps Reservoir   A701   Tweedsmuir   187   840   BROAD LAW   M   Hills   Cappe   8

rawford   G   H   Glenbreck   River Tweed   22   J   Talla Linnfoots   Talla Reservoir   K   L   Reservoir   M

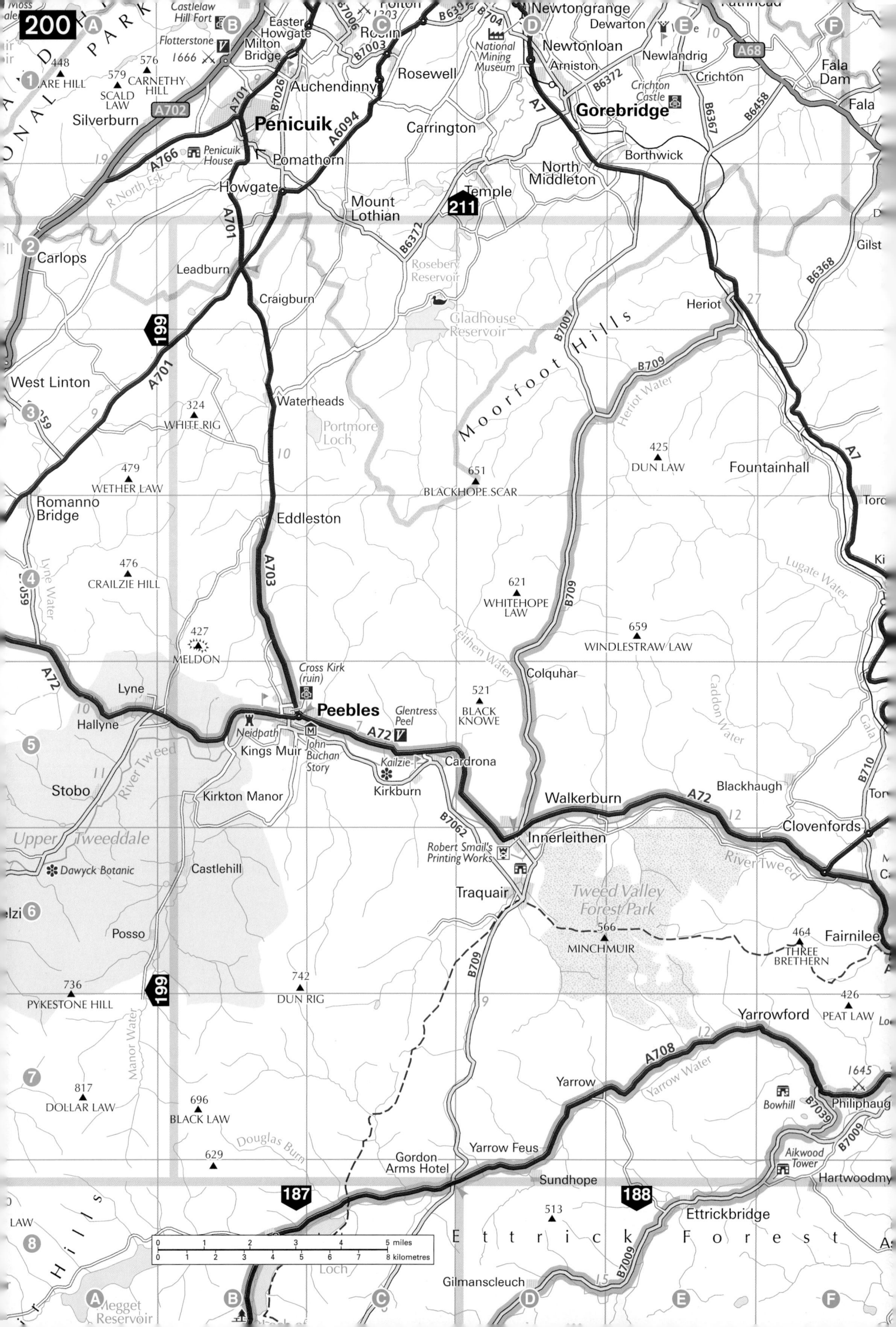

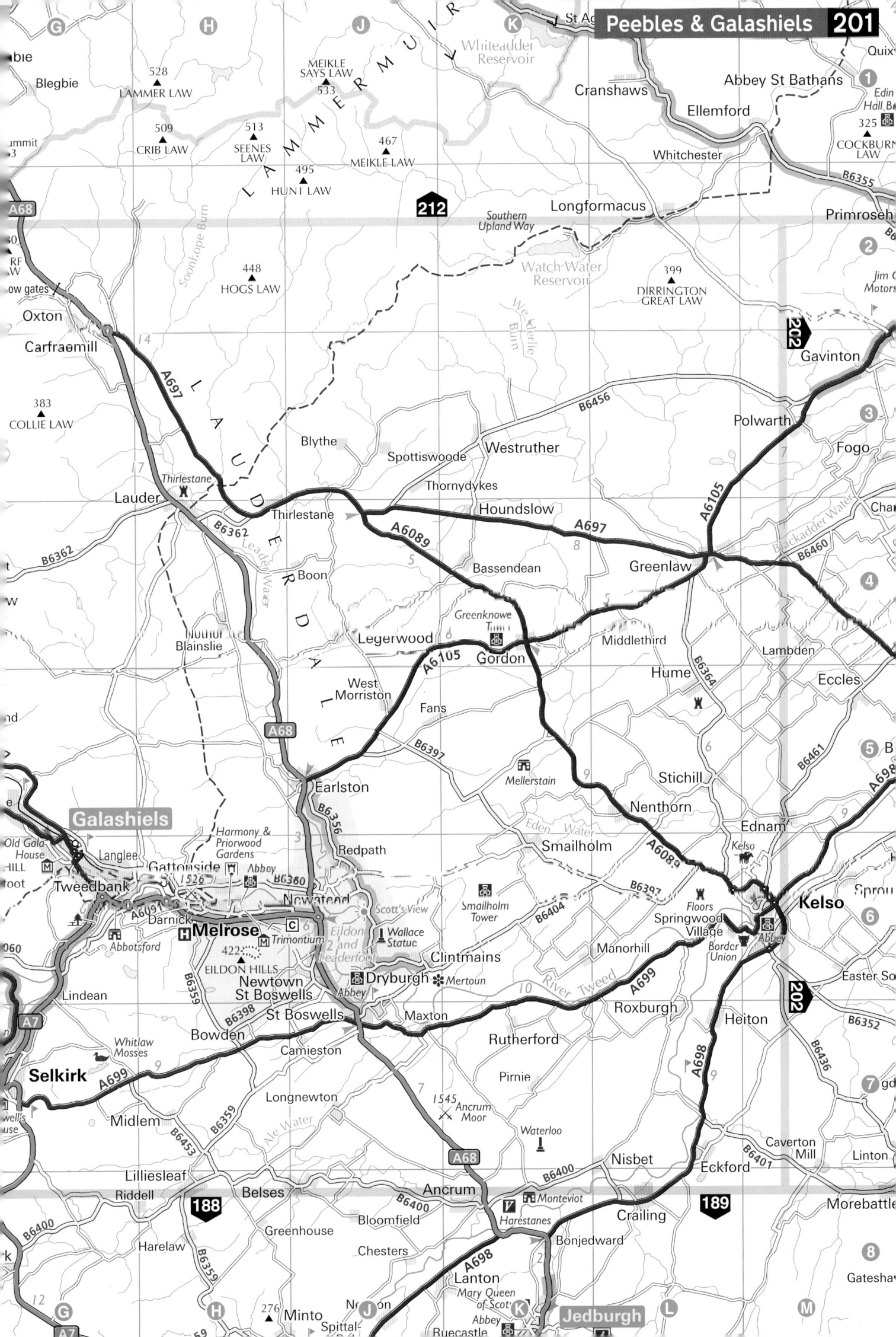

G   H   J   K   1

Blegbie

528 ▲
LAMMER LAW

MEIKLE
SAYS LAW
533 ▲

Cranshaws

Abbey St Bathans

Ellemford

Edin
Hall B

Whitchester

325 🏛
COCKBURN
LAW

B6355

Primroseh

509 ▲
CRIB LAW

513 ▲
SEENES
LAW

467 ▲
MEIKLE LAW

495 ▲
HUNT LAW

A68

LAMMERMUIR

212

Southern
Upland Way

Longformacus

2

448 ▲
HOGS LAW

Watch Water
Reservoir

399 ▲
DIRRINGTON
GREAT LAW

Jim C
Motor

RF
W
w gates

Oxton

Carfraemill

14

A697

Whiteadder
Reservoir

St Ag

Quix

B6456

202

Gavinton

383 ▲
COLLIE LAW

7

Thirlestane

Lauder

B6362

B6362

Blythe

Thirlestane

A6089

Boon

17

LEADERDALE

Leader Water

Spottiswoode

Thornydykes

Houndslow

Bassendean

5

Westruther

A697

8

Greenlaw

Polwarth

A6105

Fogo

3

Blackadder Water

B6460

Cha

4

Nether
Blainslie

Legerwood

A6105

Gordon

Greenknowe

Middlethird

Hume

B6364

Lambden

Eccles

A68

West
Morriston

Fans

B6397

Mellerstain

9

Stichill

Nenthorn

5

B6461

A698

B

Galashiels

Old Gala
House
HILL
oot

Langlee

M

Tweedbank

A6091

Darnick

Gattonside

1526

Harmony &
Priorwood
Gardens

Abbey
B6360

Earlston

B6356

Redpath

3

Newstead

Scott's View

Smailholm

Eden   Water

Smailholm
Tower

B6404

A6089

Kelso

Floors

Springwood
Village

Ednam

Border
Union

Abbey

Kelso

Sprou

6

H **Melrose**

C
Trimontium

6

422 ▲
EILDON HILLS

Abbotsford

B6359

Newtown
St Boswells

Dryburgh
Abbey

Eildon
2 and
Leaderfoot

Mertoun

Wallace
Statue

Clintmains

River Tweed

10

Manorhill

A699

Roxburgh

Heiton

202

Easter So

B6352

B6436

Lindean

A7

St Boswells

Bowden

Maxton

Rutherford

Whitlaw
Mosses

Camieston

Pirnie

A698

9

Caverton
Mill

Linton

Selkirk

A699

9

Midlem

B6453

Longnewton

7

1545 ×
Ancrum
Moor

Waterloo

Nisbet

Eckford

Crailing

Morebattle

well's
use

Lilliesleaf

Riddell

Belses

188

Greenhouse

Harelaw

B6359

Bloomfield

Chesters

B6400

Ancrum

B6400

V
Harestanes

A698

Montaviot

Bonjedward

189

8

Gateshay

B6400

12

G

A7

276 ▲

H   Minto

Spittal

J

Lanton

Mary Queen
of Scots
Abbey

Buccastle

Jedburgh

K

L

M

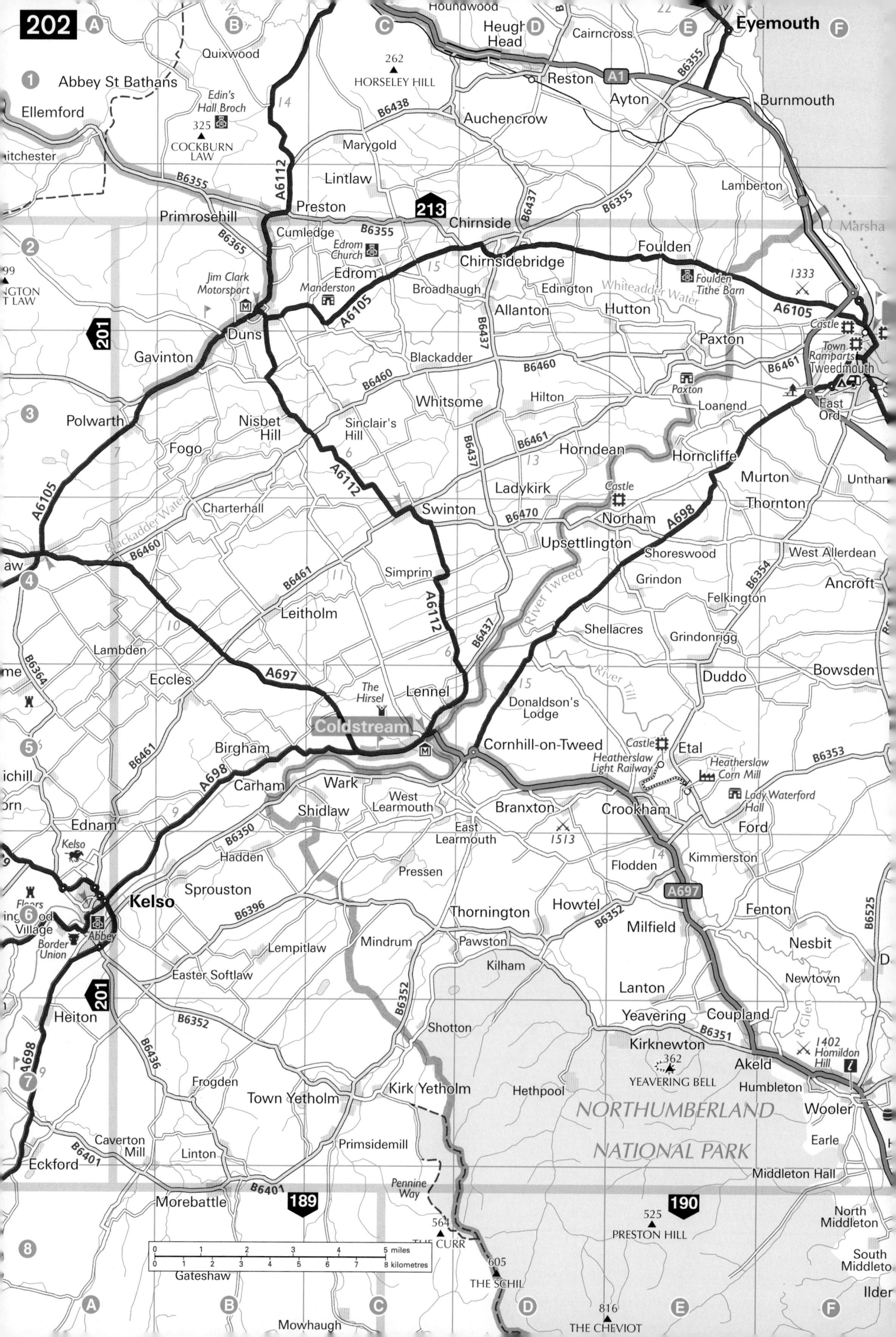

G   H   J

1
2
3
4
5
6
7
8

ws Bay

orthumberland
age Coast

ick-upon-Tweed

Huds
Head

merston

Cheswick

Goswick

Causeway flooded at high tide

HOLY ISLAND

Holy
Island

Lindisfarne
Castle

Lindisfarne
Priory

Castle Point

Fenham

Guile Point

B6353

West
Kyloe

Lowick

Fenwick

Buckton

Smeafield

Elwick

Ross

Detchant

Longstone

FARNE
ISLANDS

North Northumberland
Heritage Coast

Staple
Sound

Holburn

St Cuthbert's
Cave

Middleton

Low
Middleton

Easington

Budle
Bay

Bamburgh

B1342

Bamburgh

Inner
Sound

Hetton
Steads

Belford

Waren
Mill

Budle

Grace
Darling

New
Shoreston

North
Hazelrigg

Outchester

Spindlestone

Burton

Seahouses

ngton

South
Hazelrigg

B6349

Bradford

North Sunderland

West
orton

East
Horton

Bellshill

Warenton

Lucker

Elford

Beadnell

Chatton

B6348

Adderstone

Warenford

Newham

Newstead

Chathill

Swinhoe

Beadnell
Bay

348

efrin

h Head

Chillingham

Wild Cattle
Park

Ros Castle

Ellingham

Preston

Tughall

High Newton-by-the-Sea

Low Newton-by-the-Sea

River Till

Newtown

lburn
ower

190

Hepburn

267
▲
CATERAN HILL

Brownieside

Doxford

Preston
Tower

191

Brunton

Christon
Bank

Embleton &
Newton Links

Embleton

Old Bewick

B6346 Harehope

West
Ditchburn

South
Charlton

North
Charlton

Fallodon

B6347

B1339

Embleton
Bay

Dunstan
Steads

Dunstanburgh
Castle

Dunstan

G   H   J   K   L   M

A   B   C   D   E   F

214

Rubha
Bholsa

363
SGARB
BREA

Nave Island

Ardnave
Point

Gortantaoid
Point

Bunnahabhain

Tòn Mhòr

Kilnave

316
GUIR-
BHEINN

Sanaigmore

Loch Gruinart

Finlaggan

P
As

Eilean Mòr

Loch
Finlaggan

Keills

Rubha Lamanais

Loch
Gòrr

Lecht Gruinart

B8017

RSPB

Ballygrant

8

Lo
Bally

Saligo Bay

B8018

Gruinart

Gleann Mòr

A846

Loch
Los

Loch
Gorm

B8018

Coul Point

Sunderland

A847

Kilchoman

Machir
Bay

Loch
Indaal

Bridgend

Gartachossan

Bruichladdich

Kilchiaran Bay

Bowmore

Kilennan Burn

ISLAY

Islay Life

M

15

River Laggan

Port
Charlotte

231

BEINN TART A'MHILL

Laggan
Point

Duich R

B8016

A846

454

BEINN URARAIDH

Loch Ur

Lossit Bay

Nerabus

RHINNS OF ISLAY

A847

Rubha na
Faing

Glenegedale

A846

11

346

BEINN SHOLUM

Portnahaven

Port Wemyss

Laggan
Bay

Islay

Orsay

RHINNS
POINT

Rubha Mòr

Kintra

Port
Ellen

A846

Lagavuli

165

MAOL BUIDHE

Laphroaig

A

3

THE OA

Lower
Killeyan

Risabus

Texa

RSPB

Kilnaughton Bay

Kinnabus

American

Loch
Kinnabus

Ballycastle
(Apr-Sept)

MULL
OF OA

Rubha nan Leacan

0   1   2   3   4   5 miles
0   1   2   3   4   5   6   7   8 kilometres

A **B** **C** **D** **216** **E** **F**

1

Kilmahumaig
Bellanoch
B841
Dunadd Fort
Kilmichael Glassary
Bridgend
Loch
Asknish
B8000
Crinan Canal
Cairnbaan Rock Art
Argyll Beaver
Achnabreck Rock Art
Cairnbaan
Lochgair
Middle Kames

2
Carsaig Bay
Tayvallich
215
Knapdale
Knapdale
Achnamara
Kilmichael of Inverlussa
Taynish
Càm Loch
Lochgilphead
Kilmory Woodland Park
Carrick
CRUACH CHUILCEAC 435
Largiemore

Ardrishaig
Loch Gilp
Castleton
Otter Ferry
Kilmodan Sculptured Stones

3
Chapel
B8025
Loch Sween
466 CRUACH LUSACH
331 BEINN BHEAG
Brenfield
A83
Fearnoch

Kilbride Castle Sween
Inverneill

4
anna Island
Kilmory
Ellary
B8024
Erines
561 SLIABH GAOIL
Kilfinan Bay
Kilfinan
Drum
B8000
454 BEINN BHREAC

ory Bay
nap

5
Loch Caolisport
Druimdrishaig
Loch nan Torran
480 DUBH CHREAG
Glenralloch
Stonefield Castle Hotel
Glenan Bay
Auchenlochan
Tighna
Kames
Millhouse

Ormsary

6
Cretshengan
Coulaghailtro
Kilberry Sculptured Stones
Kilberry
Hea Point
213 CRUACH AIRDE
Tiretigan
Torinturk
Glenralloch
Tarbert
West Tarbert
A83
343 CRUACH AN T SORCHAIN
422 CNOC A' BHAILE-SHOIS
Kilbride Bay
Blair's Ferry
Portavadie
Ardlamont
207 CNOC NA CARRAIGE
Ardlamont Bay
Ardlamon Point
Kil

7
205
Ardpatrick
B8024
Kennacraig
Whitehouse
B8001
E
Castle
Skipness
Chapel
Skipness Point

Portachoillan
Clachan
Kilchamaig
B8001
Claonaig
B8001

8
Ronachan Point
Ronachan
Loch Ciàran
R
B842
Claonaig Bay
(Apr-Oct)
(Oct-Mar)
S o u n d

Loch Garasdale
Crossaig
194
Lochranza
Castle
Cock of Arran

Loch Stornoway

A **B** **C** **D** **E** **F**

| 0 | 1 | 2 | 3 | 4 | 5 miles |
| 0 | 1 | 2 | 3 | 4 | 5 | 6 | 7 | 8 kilometres |

CRUACH MHIC
264
Catacol

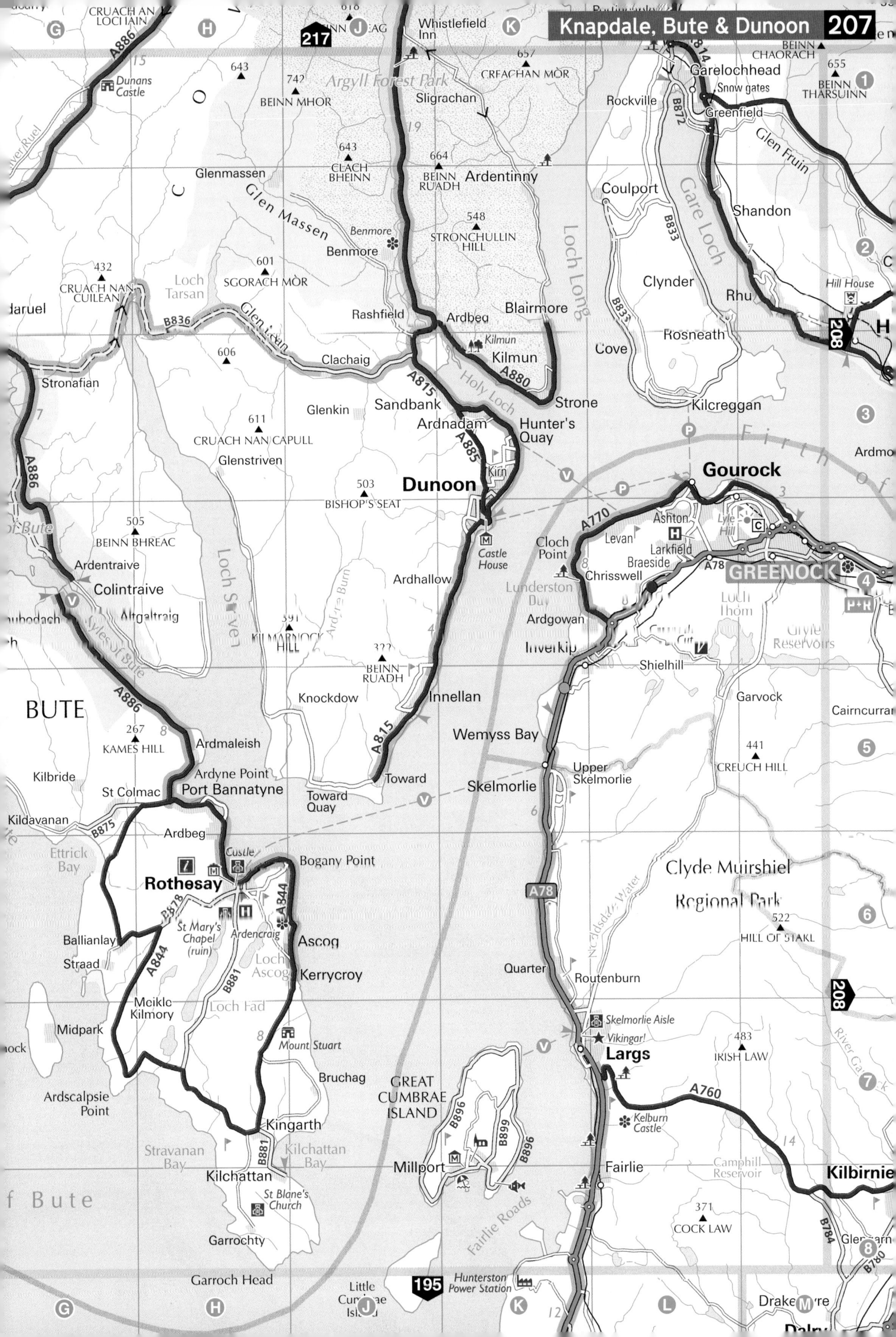

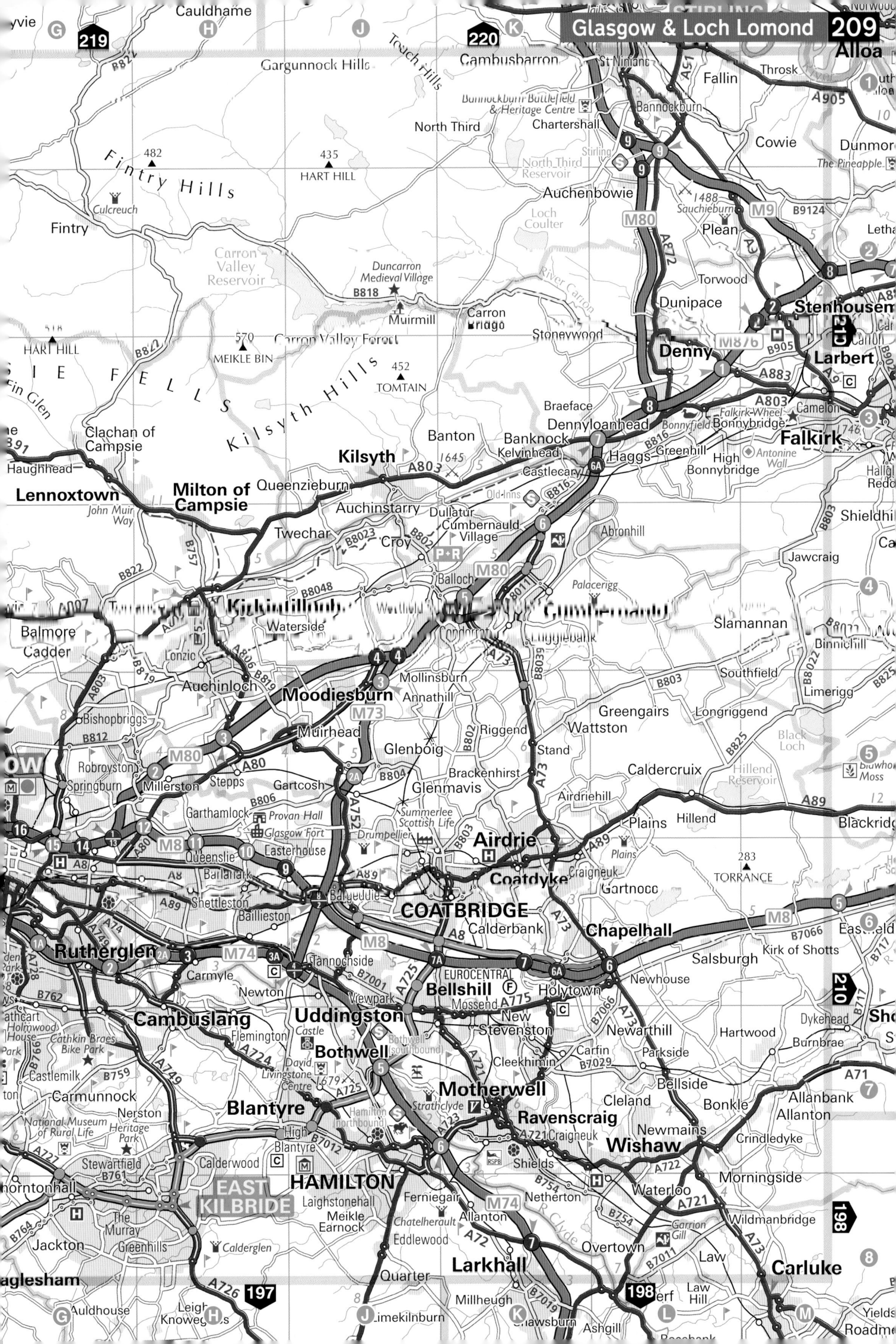

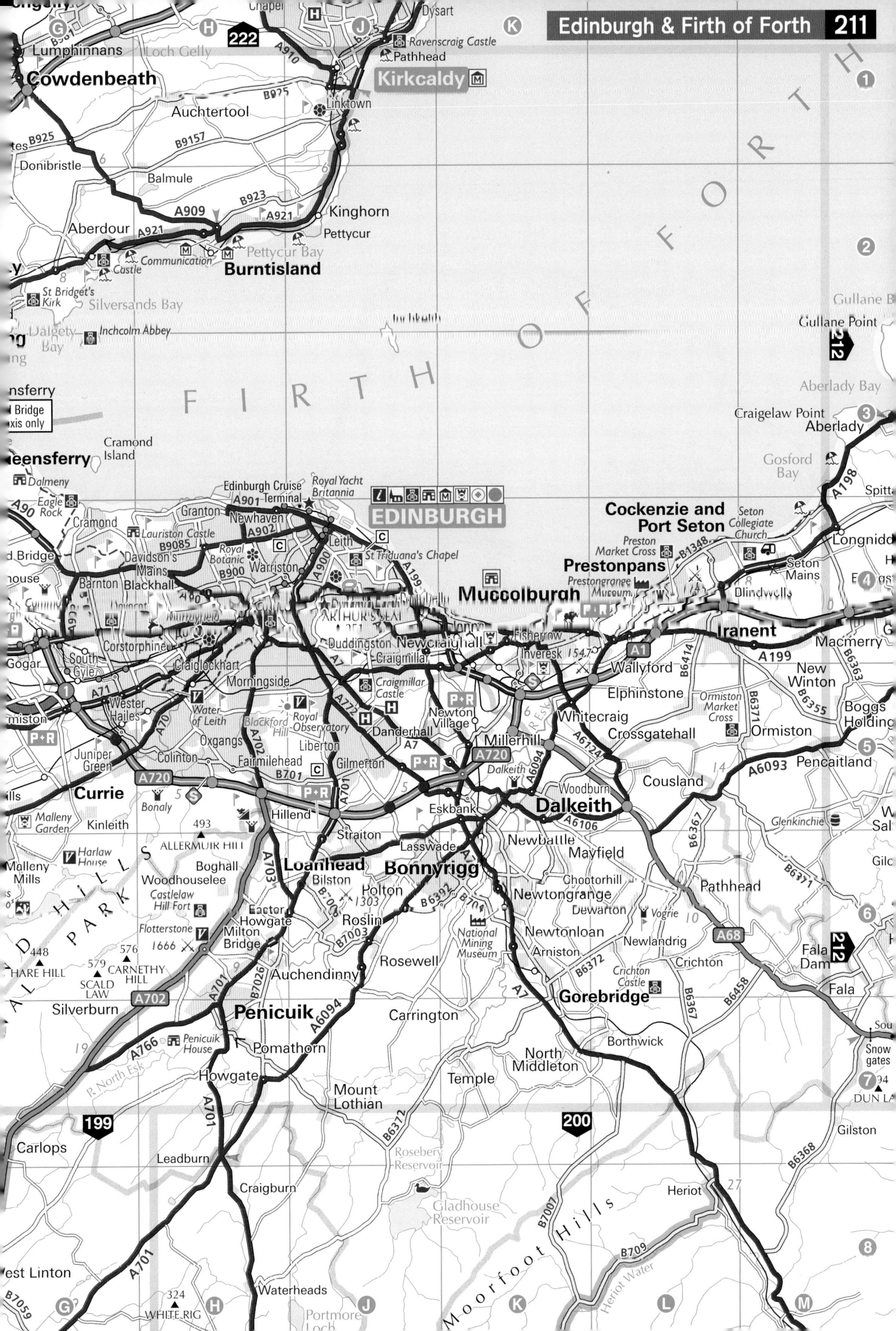

FIRTH OF FORTH

1

2

Gullane Point **212**

Aberlady Bay

Gosford Bay

Craigelaw Point
Aberlady 3

A198

Spitt

Cowdenbeath

Lumphinnans

G

B901

Loch Gelly

222

A910

H

J

5

Dysart

Ravenscraig Castle

Pathhead

K

Auchtertool

Kirkcaldy

Linktown

B925

B9157

Donibristle

B923

Balmule

A909

B921

A921

Kinghorn

Pettycur

Aberdour

A921

8

Castle

Communication

M

M

Pettycur Bay

Burntisland

St Bridget's Kirk

Silversands Bay

Dalgety Bay

Inchcolm Abbey

ng

nsferry

eensferry

Bridge
xis only

Cramond Island

Dalmeny

Eagle Rock

A90

d Bridge

house

Cramond

Davidson's Mains

Barnton

Blackhall

Lauriston Castle

B9085

Granton

A901

Newhaven

Edinburgh Cruise Terminal

Royal Yacht Britannia

A902

Leith

C

Royal Botanic

B900

Warriston

A900

St Triduana's Chapel

C

EDINBURGH

Cockenzie and Port Seton

Seton Collegiate Church

Preston Market Cross

B1348

Longnidd

Seton Mains

4

E as

Prestonpans

Prestongrange Museum

Dovecot

Corstorphine

South Gyle

Gogar

1

A71

A8

Murrayfield

ARTHUR'S SEAT

Dynamic Earth

Duddingston

Newcraighall

Craigmillar

Jeppo

Fisherrow

Inveresk 1547

Wallyford

Muccolburah

Iranent

A199

Macmerry

B6363

New Winton

B6355

Boggs Holding

A1

Elphinstone

B6414

Ormiston Market Cross

Whitecraig

Crossgatehall

Ormiston

5

B6371

Wester Hailes

A70

Water of Leith

Craiglockhart

Morningside

A772

Blackford Hill

Royal Observatory

H

V

Liberton

Danderhall

A7

Newton Village

P+R

Millerhill

A6094

A6124

Cousland

A6093

Pencaitland

miston

P+R

Juniper Green

Colinton

Oxgangs

A702

Fairmilehead

Gilmerton

B701

C

A701

A720

Dalkeith

A6094

Woodburn

Eskbank

Glenkinchie

W Sal

Dalkeith

A6106

Currie

Malleny Garden

Kinleith

493

Bonaly

S

Hillend

5

Newbattle

Mayfield

A720

Straiton

Lasswade

Ghootorhill

Pathhead

B6367

Malleny Mills

ls

V

Harlaw House

ALLERMUIR HILL

Boghall

Woodhouselee

Bilston

B700

Polton

1303

B6392

B701

Newtongrange

Dewarton

Vogrie

10

A68

s

Loanhead

Bonnyrigg

Newtonloan

Newlandrig

212

V

Castlelaw Hill Fort

Flotterstone

V

Milton Bridge

Roslin

B7003

Rosewell

National Mining Museum

Arniston

B6372

Crichton Castle

Crichton

Fala Dam

448

576

1666

Fala

HARE HILL

579

CARNETHY HILL

SCALD LAW

A702

Penicuik

Auchendinny

Rosebery Reservoir

North Middleton

B6372

Borthwick

B6458

B6367

Gorebridge

A68

Sou

Snow gates

Silverburn

A766

Penicuik House

A6094

Carrington

B7026

Pomathorn

Howgate

Mount Lothian

Temple

7

94

DUN LA

R North Esk

199

200

Gilston

Carlops

Leadburn

Craigburn

B7059

Gladhouse Reservoir

Heriot

27

est Linton

A701

B7007

B6368

Waterheads

324

Moorfoot Hills

B709

Heriot Water

8

G

H

WHITE RIG

J

Portmore

K

L

M

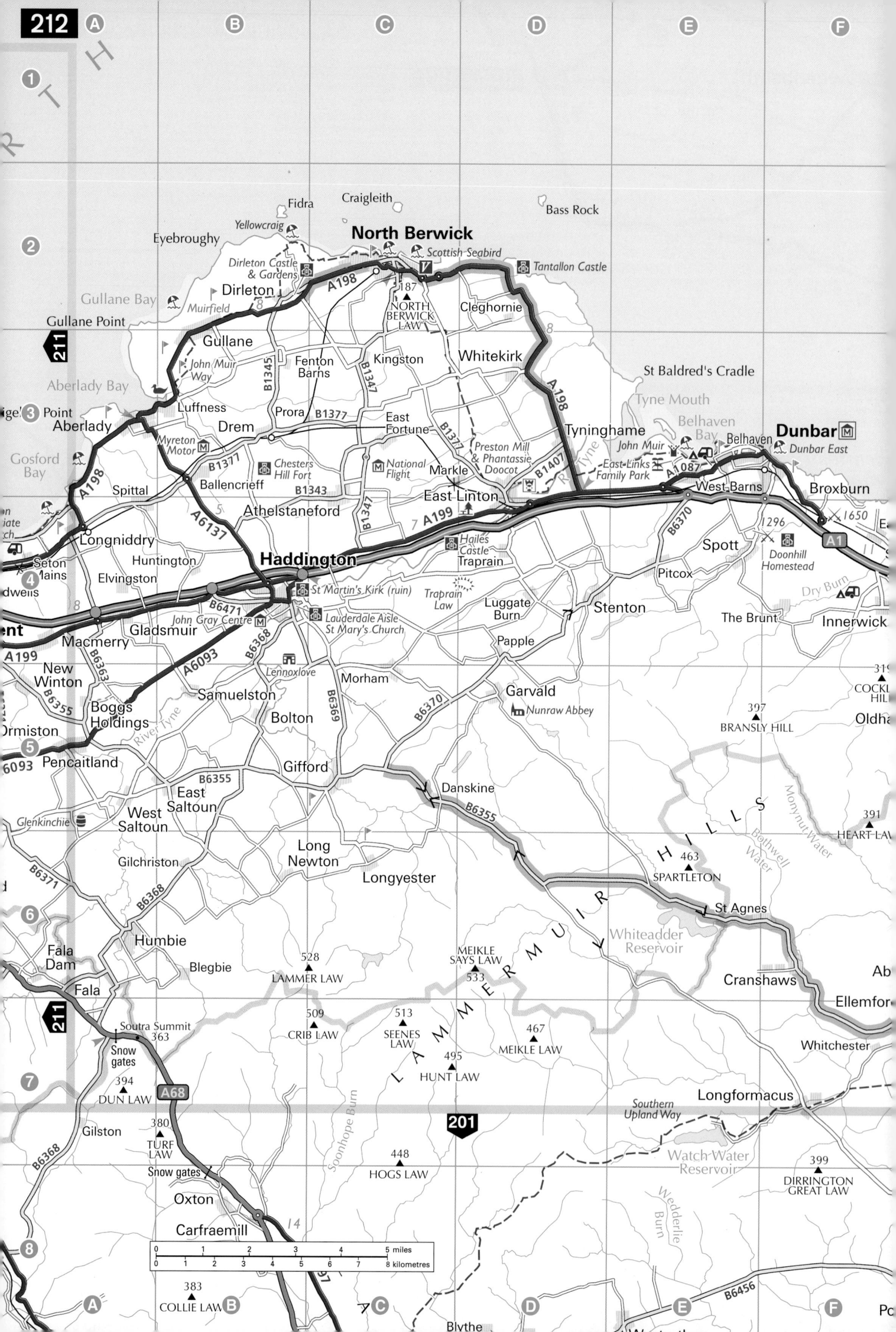

G H J

1

2

3

less

Chapel Point
Torness
Power Station
Thorntonloch

4

owhill

Dunglass
Collegiate
Church

ks

Point
Cove
Pease
Bay
Siccar
Point

Fast Castle Head

Cockburnspath
A1107
ST ABB'S HEAD

5

Pease Dean
196
BROWN RIG
Coldingham
Loch

Ecclaw

V
St Abbs

Southern
Upland Way
Grantshouse
Coldingham
Coldingham
Bay

Butterdean
B6438
A1107
22

Houndwood
Quixwood
Heugh
Head
Cairncross
Eyemouth

6

t Bathans
Edin's
Hall Broch
14
262
HORSELEY HILL
Reston
A1
B6355
Burnmouth

325
COCKBURN
LAW
B6438
Ayton

Marygold
Auchencrow

B6355
Lintlaw
A6112
B6437
Lamberton

7

B6355
Preston
Chirnside
Marshall Meadows Bay

Primrosehill
B6365
Cumledge
B6355
202
Foulden
North Northumberland
Heritage Coast

Edrom
Church
Chirnsidebridge
1333

Jim Clark
Motorsport
Edrom
15
Broadhaugh
Edington
Whiteadder Water
Foulden
Tithe Barn

Berwick-upo

Manderston
A6105
Hutton
A6105

Duns
Allanton
Paxton
Castle
Town
Ramparts
Barracks &
Main Guard

Gavinton
Blackadder
B6461
Tweedmouth

8

Nisbet
Hill
B6460
Hilton
Loanend
East
Ord
Spittal
Huds
Head

th
Sinclair's
Hill
Whitsome
Paxton
A1167
Scremerston

G H J K L M

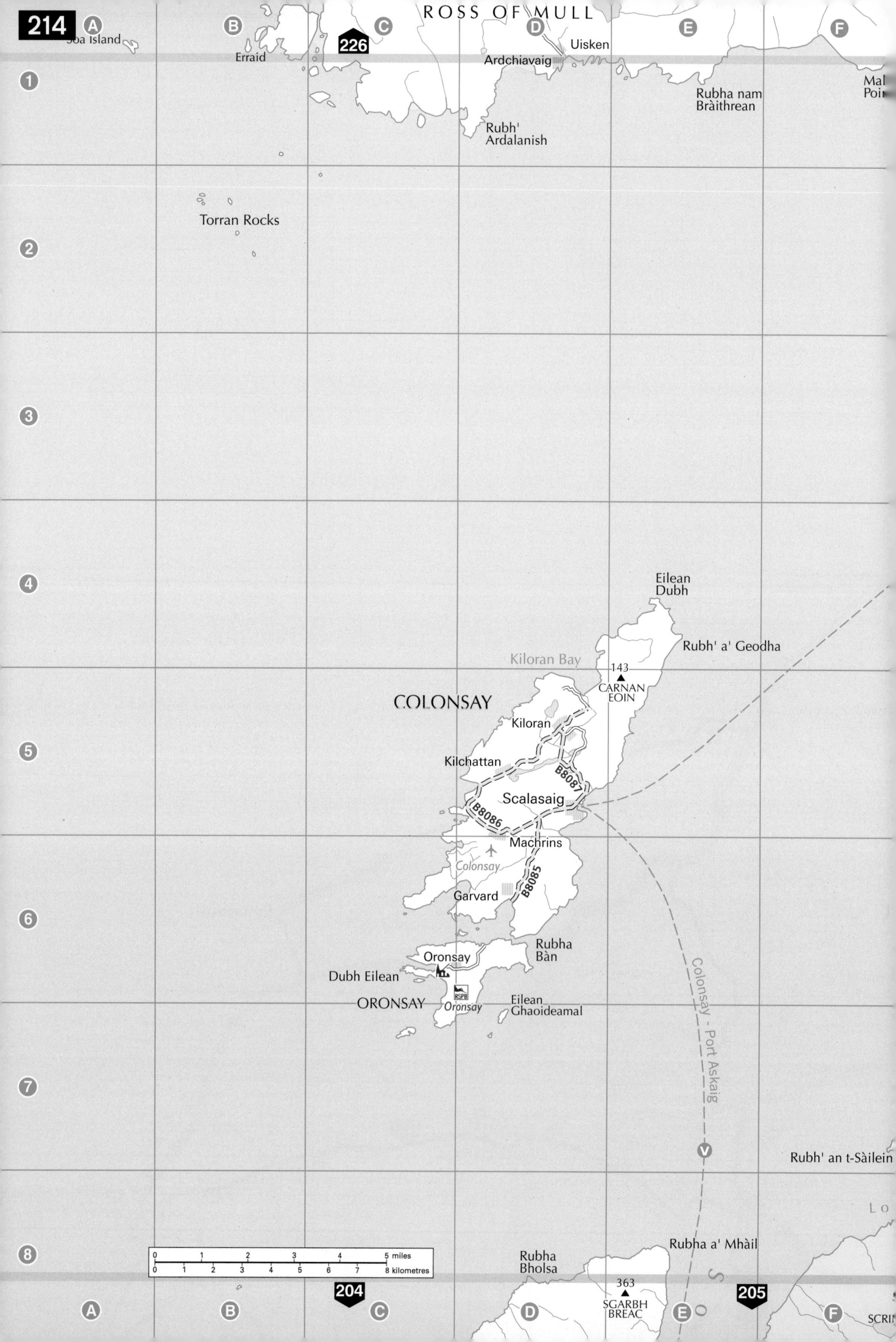

ROSS OF MULL

A B 226 C D E F

Soa Island

Erraid

Uisken

Ardchiavaig

Rubh'
Ardalanish

Rubha nam
Bràithrean

Mal
Poi

1

Torran Rocks

2

3

Eilean
Dubh

4

Kiloran Bay

Rubh' a' Geodha

143
CARNAN
EOIN

COLONSAY

Kiloran

Kilchattan

B8087

Scalasaig

B8086

Machrins

Colonsay

B8085

Garvard

5

Rubha
Bàn

Oronsay

Dubh Eilean

RSPB

ORONSAY

Oronsay

Eilean
Ghaoideamal

Colonsay - Port Askaig

6

Rubh' an t-Sàilein

7

V

Rubha a' Mhàil

0 1 2 3 4 5 miles
0 1 2 3 4 5 6 7 8 kilometres

204

Rubha
Bholsa

363
SGARBH
BREAC

205

SCRI

Lo

A B C D E F

8

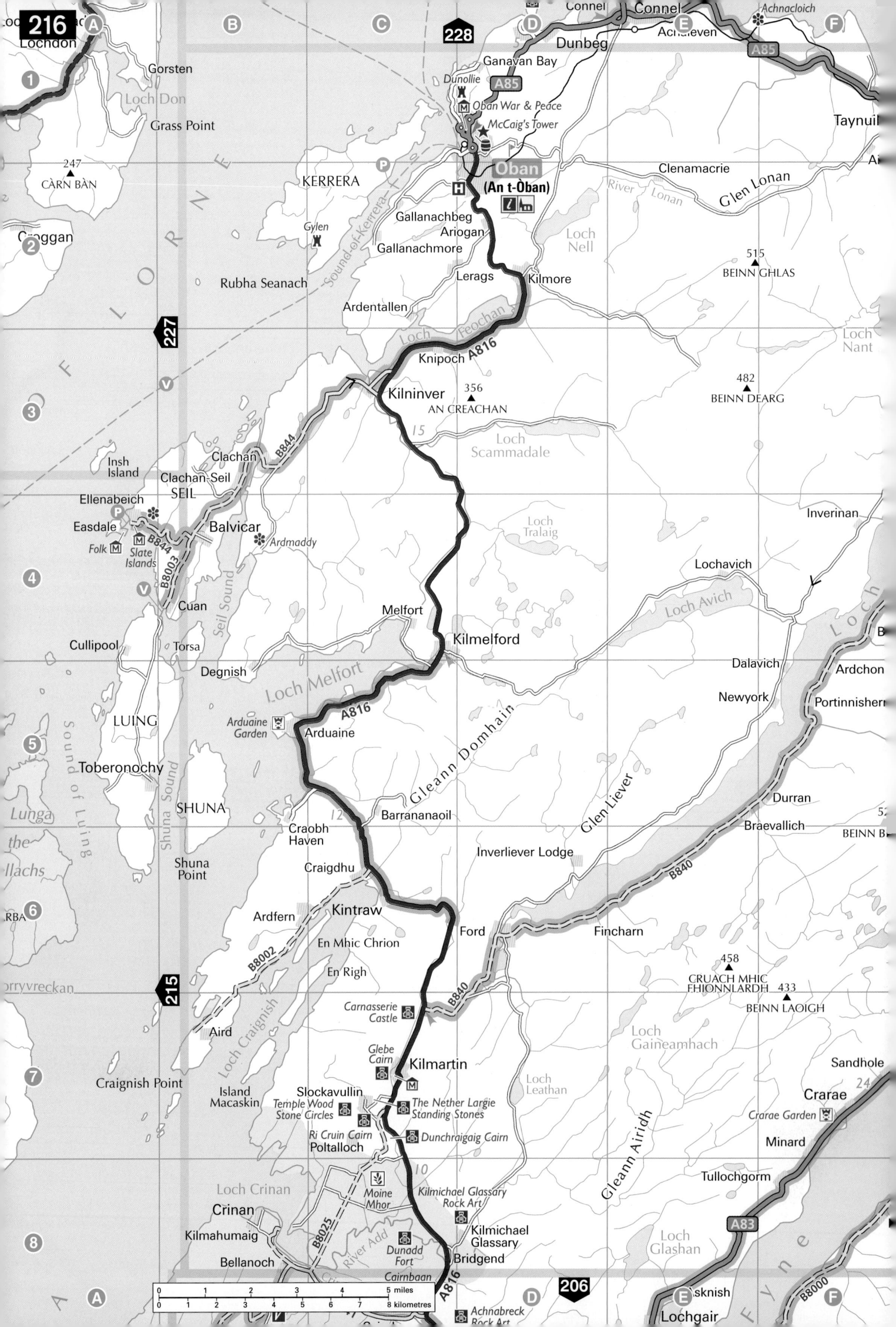

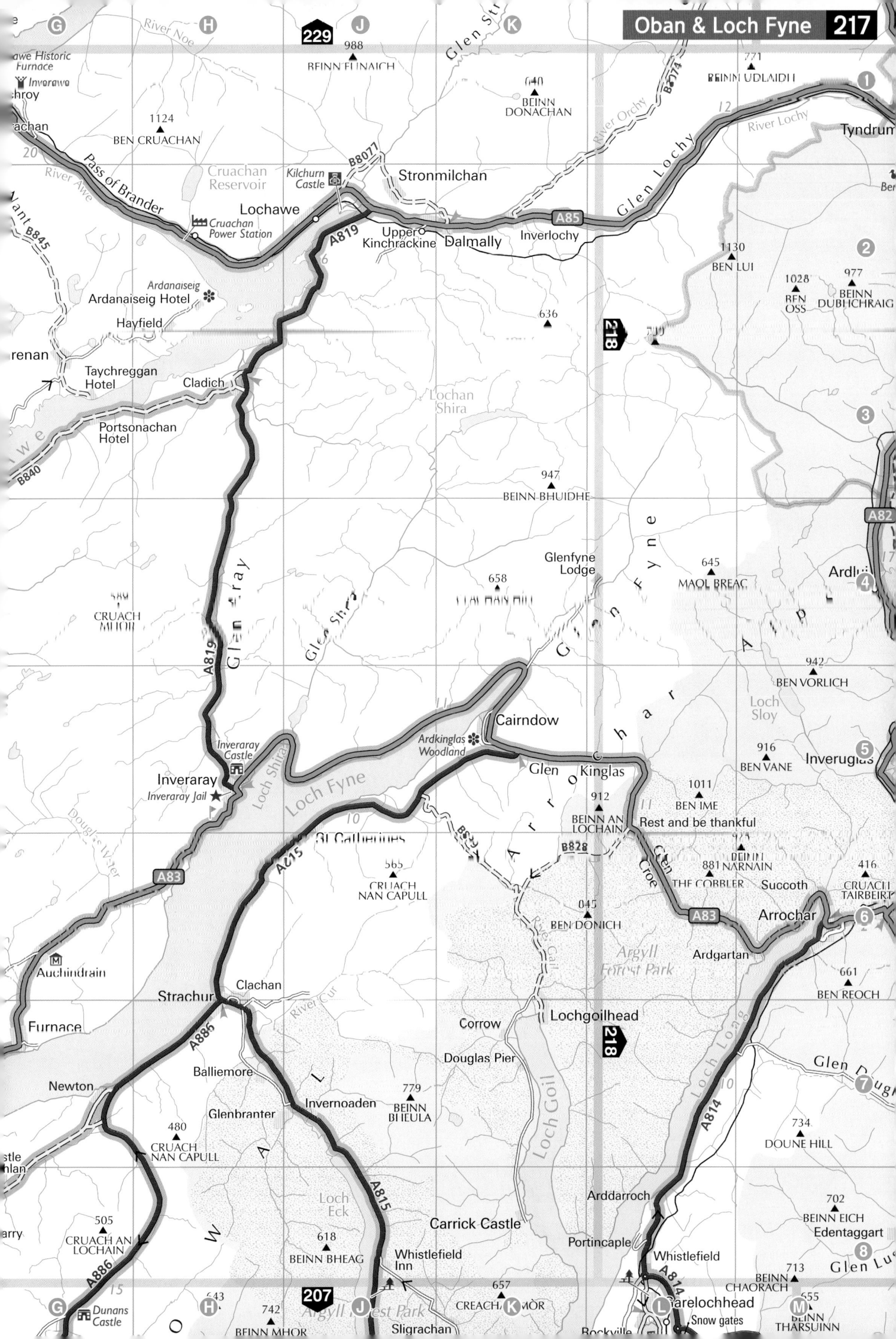

G
H
229
J
K

River Noe
988
BEINN FUNAICH
Glen Str
River Orchy
B8074
B EINN UDLAIDH
771
1

awe Historic
Furnace
Inverawe
chroy
640
BEINN DONACHAN
Tyndrum
River Lochy
12

1124
BEN CRUACHAN
River Orchy
20
Pass of Brander
Cruachan
Reservoir
B8077
Stronmilchan
A85
Glen Lochy
Inverlochy
BEN LUI
1130
2

Nant B845
River Awe
Kilchurn
Castle
Lochawe
Cruachan
Power Station
A819
Upper
Kinchrackine
Dalmally
1028
BEN OSS
BEINN DUBHCHRAIG
977

Ardanaiseig
Ardanaiseig Hotel
Hayfield
636
218
3

renan
Taychreggan
Hotel
Cladich
Lochan
Shira
A82

awe
B840
Portsonachan
Hotel
A819
Glen Aray
Glen Shira
BEINN BHUIDHE
947
Glen Fyne
4

Glenfyne
Lodge
MAOL BREAC
645
Ardlui

589
CRUACH
MHOR
658
CLAI NAN HILL
942
BEN VORLICH

Inveraray
Castle
Loch Shira
Cairndow
Ardkinglas
Woodland
Glen
Kinglas
Arrochar
Loch
Sloy
916
BEN VANE
Inveruglas
5

Inveraray
Inveraray Jail
Loch Fyne
912
BEINN AN
LOCHAIN
1011
BEN IME
Rest and be thankful
B828
Douglas Water
A83
A815
St Catherines
565
CRUACH
NAN CAPULL
B839
Glen Croe
881
NARNAIN
THE CORBLER
BEINN NARNAIN
Succoth
CRUACH
TAIRBEIRT
416
6

Auchindrain
045
BEN DONICH
River Gail
A83
Arrochar
Ardgartan
BEN REOCH
661

Furnace
Strachur
Clachan
River Cur
Argyll
Forest Park
Lochgoilhead
Corrow
218
Loch Goil
Loch Long
Glen Doug
7

Newton
A886
Balliemore
Glenbranter
Invernoaden
779
BEINN
BHEULA
Douglas Pier
A814
734
DOUNE HILL

480
CRUACH
NAN CAPULL
A
Loch
Eck
Arddarroch
702
BEINN EICH
Edentaggart
8

505
CRUACH AN
LOCHAIN
A886
arry
W
618
BEINN BHEAG
A815
Carrick Castle
Portincaple
Whistlefield
A814
BEINN
CHAORACH
713

stle
hlan
Dunans
Castle
742
BEINN MHOR
207
J
est Park
Sligrachan
657
CREACH MOR
K
arelochhead
Snow gates
M
655
BEINN
THARSUINN
L

G
H
J
K
L
M

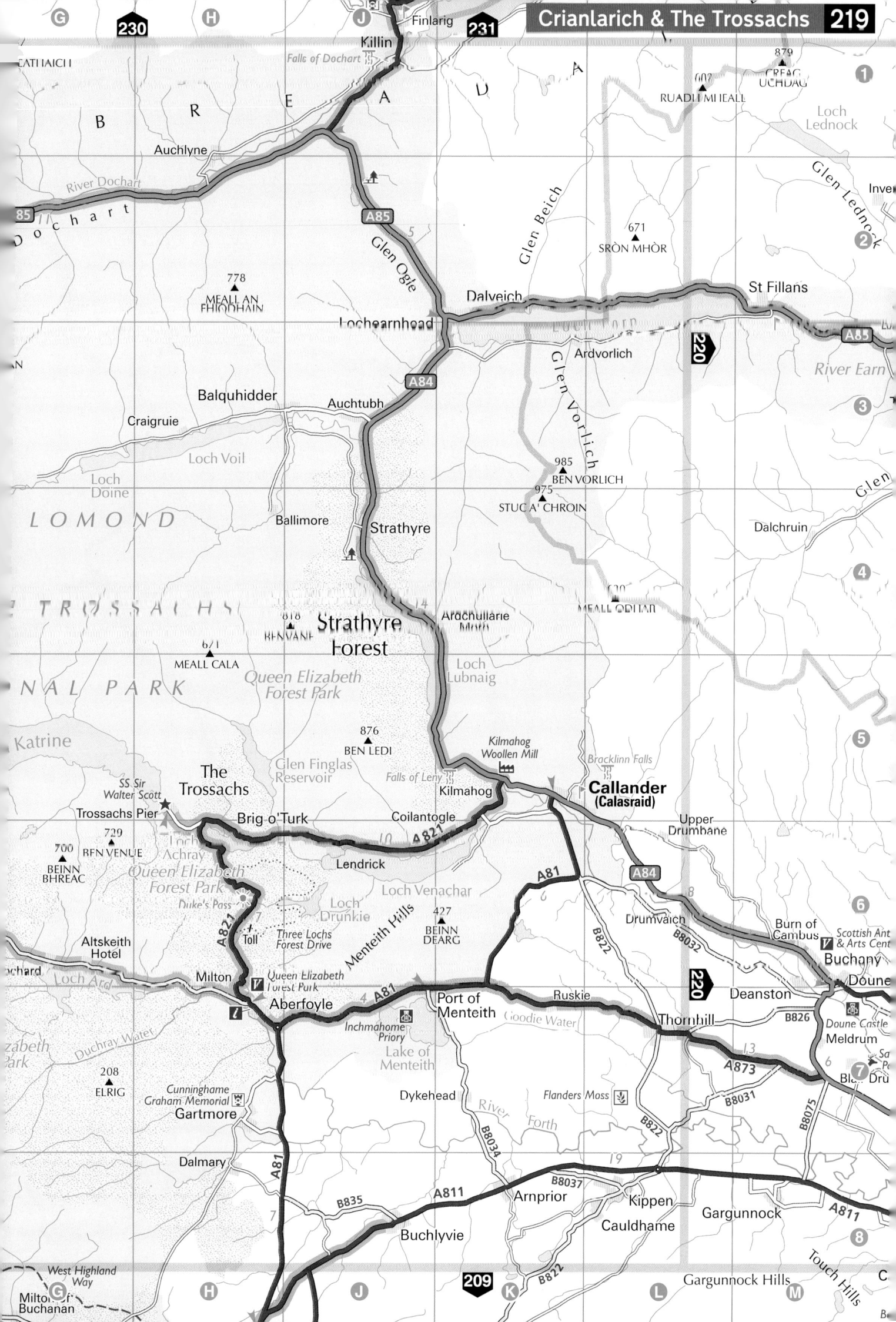

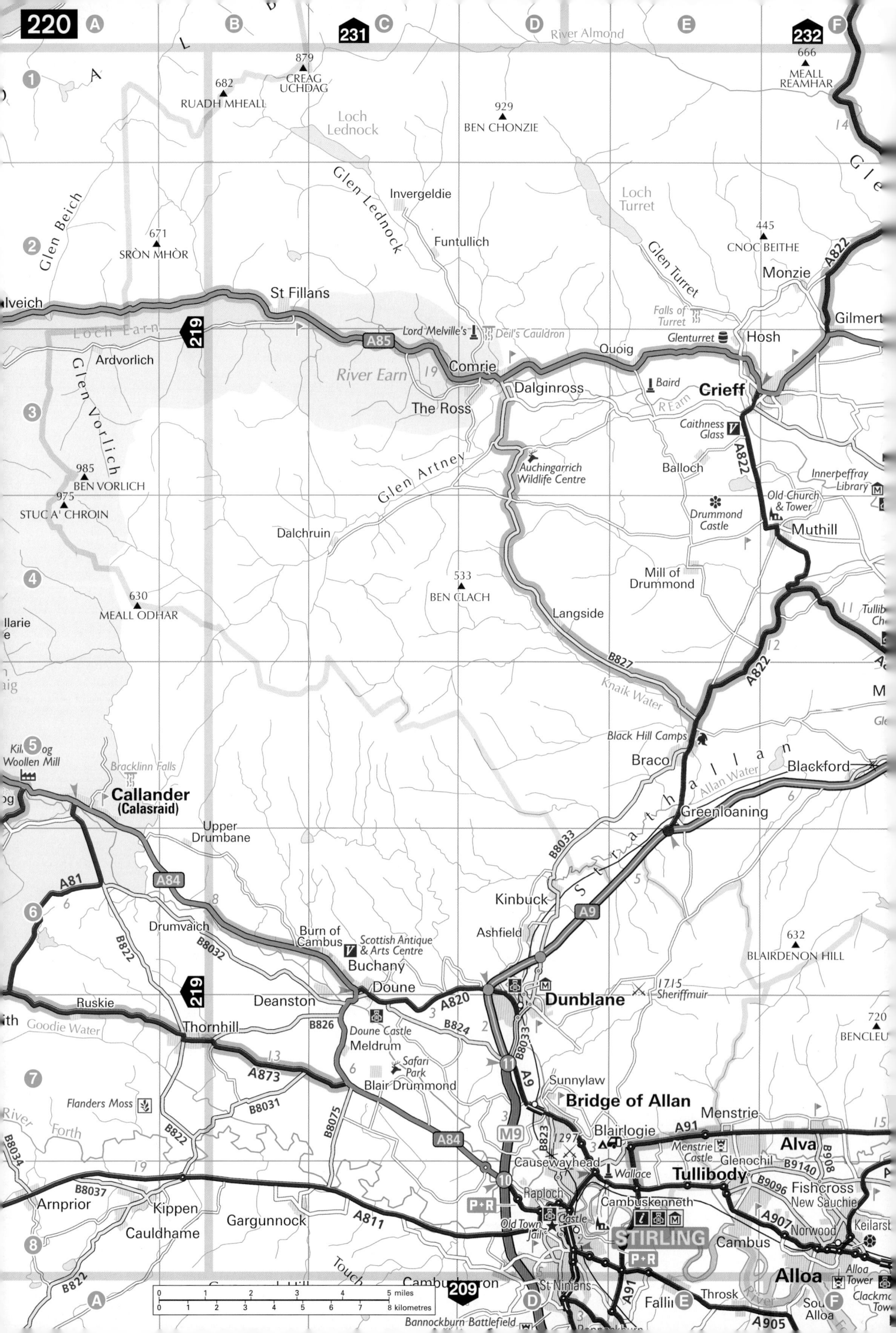

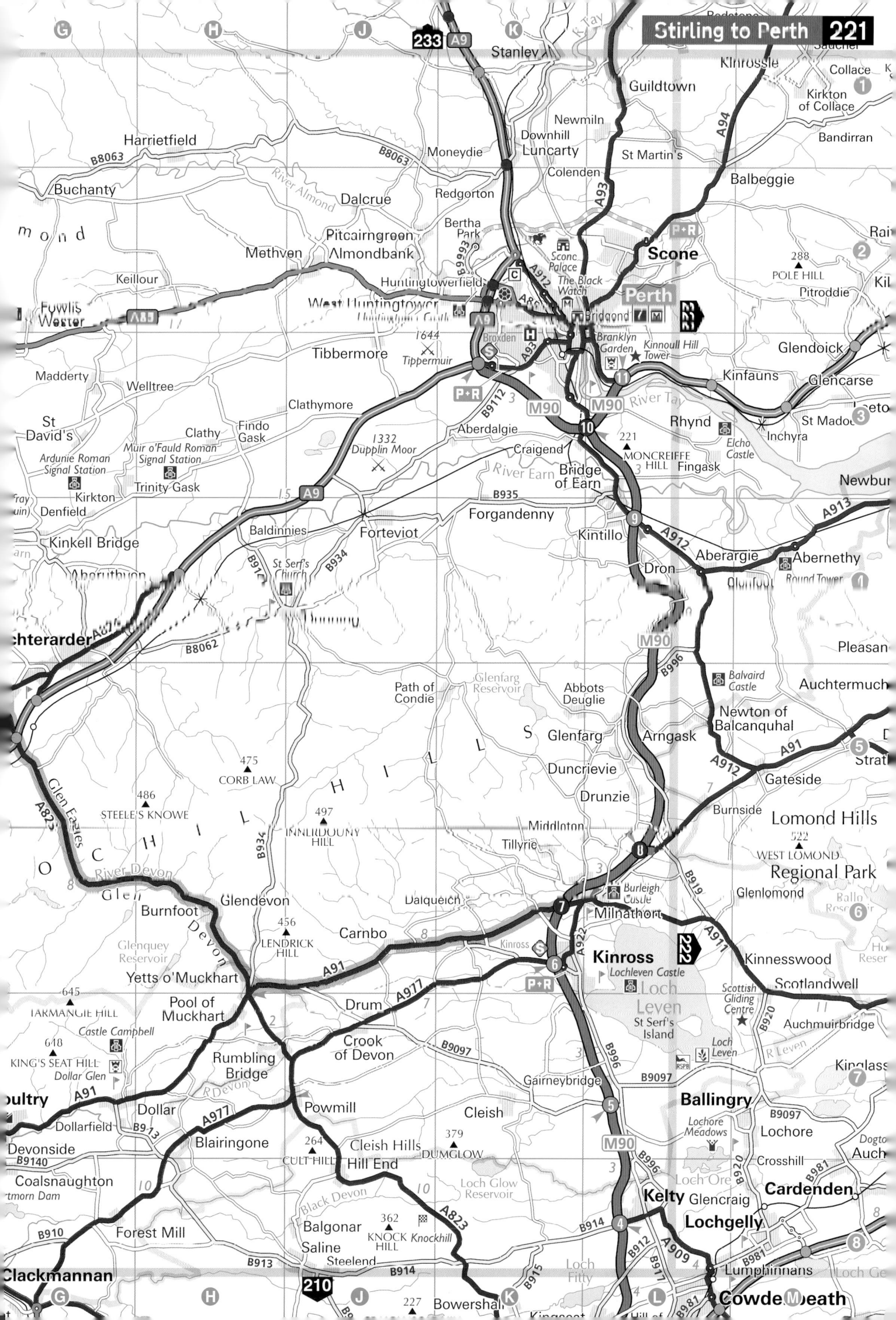

A B C D E F

1

2

3

Grishi
Clabhach

Hogh Bay   Ballyha

Totronalc

Bàgh a' Chaisteil
(Castlebay)   Coll   Acha

Feall   Arileod
Bay

Uig

RSPB

Calgary Point   Crossapol
                           Bay   Rubha
                                                   Fàsach

Gunna

Rubha Dubh

Caoles
                    B8069
                           Ruaig

Rubha Port   Clachan
Bhiosd   Mor Balephetrish
                           Bay
           Loch   B8068
Hough   Bhasapoll
Bay
      Ballevullin Cornoigmore   Kenovay   Gott
                                                        Bay
Kilkenneth   B8068   Tiree
                                                   Scarinish
      Moss   Heylipoll
Middleton   B8065
                   B8065   Crossapol   TIREE
Barrapoll
      Loch a'   Hynish Bay
      Phuill   B8067 Balemartine

                           Mannal

Rinn
Thorbhais   Balephuil   Hynish   Skerryvore
            Bay   Lighthouse

0   1   2   3   4   5 miles
0 1 2 3 4 5 6 7 8 kilometres

A B C D E F

G | H | J | K | L | 1

Sanna Point

Sanna
Sanna
Bay
Portuairk   Achnaha

Ardnamurchan   **Achosnich**
Point

B8007   2

BEINN NA SEILG

Ormsaigmore

236
Eilean Mòr

Bàgh a' Chaisteil
(Castlebay)
Loch Baghasdail
(Lochboisdale)
(Uct-Mal)

236

Ardmore   3
Point

Rubha
Mòr

Rubha
Sgor-innis

Bousd   Sorisdale

Cliad
Bay   Sorne
Point

Quinish Point   Glengorm Castle   Ru
nan

Tober or   4

Arinagour

COLL

Coll - Oban

'S AIRDE
BEINN

Eilean
Urnnay

Calnach Point

Dervaig
Achnadrish

Calgary
Art in
Nature   B8073

Calgary Bay   Old Byre   5   44

SPEINN

Treshnish Point   Ensay   342
CÀRN MÒR   Loch Frisa

Rubh' a' Chaoil   Burg   6

Fanmore   090
CNOC AN
DÀ CHINN

Fladda   Ballygown

226   Eas.Fors.

Lunga   Loch Tuath   BI
NAN

TRESHNISH   P
ISLES   Gometra   Oskamull   7

ULVA   Eorsa

Bac Mòr or Dutchman's Cap

Bac Beag   Loch

Little Colonsay   B8035 17

Inch Kenneth
Staffa   Inchkenneth Chapel
(ruin)

Loch na Keal   Balnahard   8
Fingal's   Isle of Mull

226

G | H | J | K | L | M

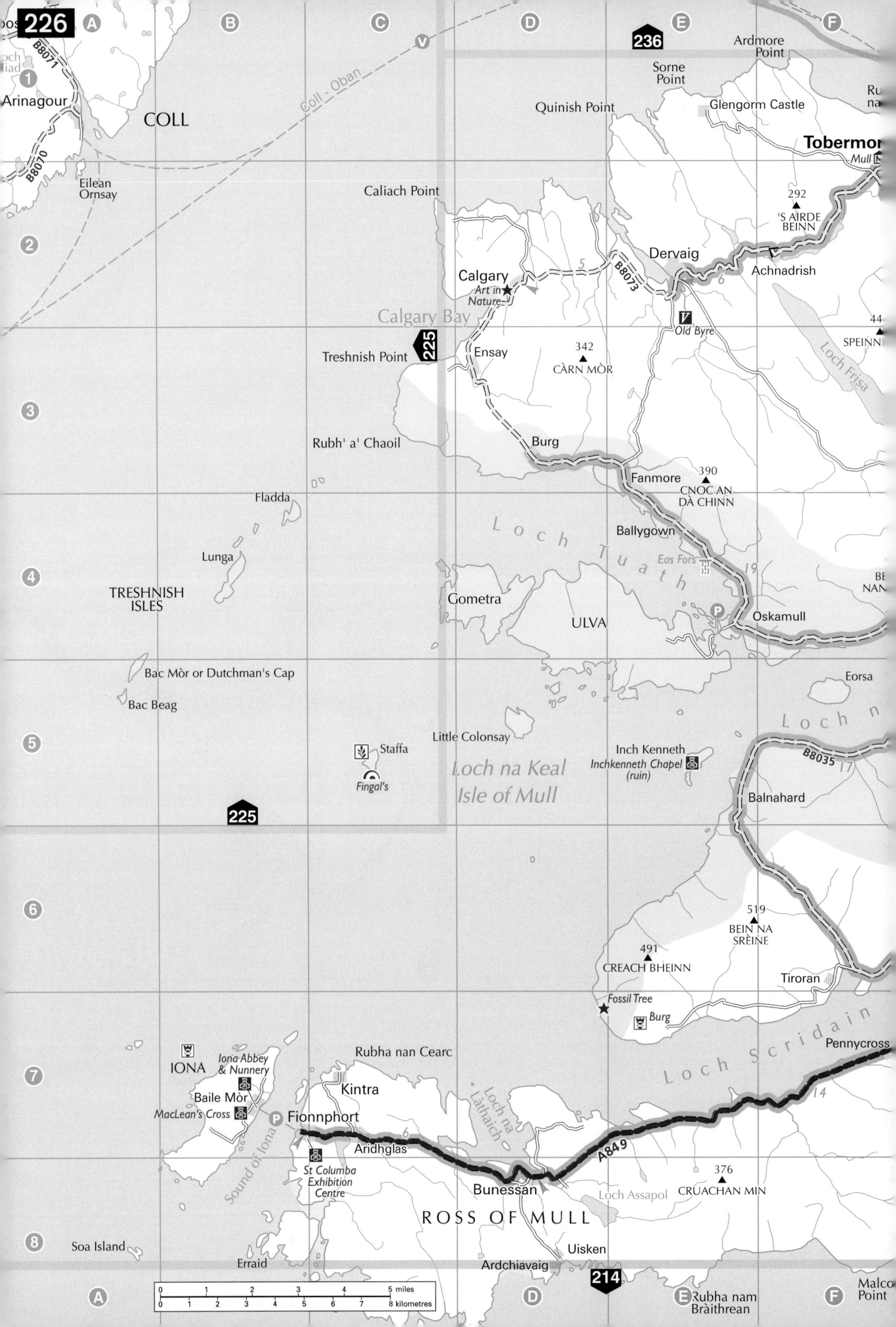

A B C D E F

1

Arinagour

COLL

Eilean
Ornsay

B8071

B8070

Coll - Oban

V

Quinish Point

Sorne
Point

Ardmore
Point

Glengorm Castle

Ru
na

Tobermor

Mull L

292 ▲

'S AIRDE
BEINN

2

Caliach Point

Calgary
Art in
Nature

Calgary Bay

★

5

B8073

Dervaig

Old Byre

V

Achnadrish

44

SPEINN

Loch Frisa

3

Treshnish Point

225

Ensay

342 ▲
CÀRN MÒR

Rubh' a' Chaoil

Burg

Fanmore

390 ▲
CNOC AN
DÀ CHINN

Ballygown

Loch Tuath

Eas Fors

19

4

Fladda

Lunga

TRESHNISH
ISLES

Gometra

ULVA

P

Oskamull

Eorsa

Loch n

5

Bac Mòr or Dutchman's Cap

Bac Beag

Staffa

Fingal's

Little Colonsay

Loch na Keal
Isle of Mull

Inch Kenneth
Inchkenneth Chapel
(ruin)

B8035 17

Balnahard

225

6

519 ▲
BEIN NA
SRÈINE

491 ▲
CREACH BHEINN

Tiroran

7

Iona Abbey
& Nunnery

IONA

Baile Mòr

MacLean's Cross

P

Fionnphort

St Columba
Exhibition
Centre

Rubha nan Cearc

Kintra

Aridhglas

Fossil Tree

★

Burg

Pennycross

Loch Scridain

Loch na Làthaich

6

A849

14

Bunessan

Loch Assapol

376 ▲
CRUACHAN MIN

ROSS OF MULL

8

Soa Island

Erraid

Uisken

Ardchiavaig

Rubha nam
Bràithrean

Malco
Point

A B C D E F

0   1   2   3   4   5 miles
0 1 2 3 4 5 6 7 8 kilometres

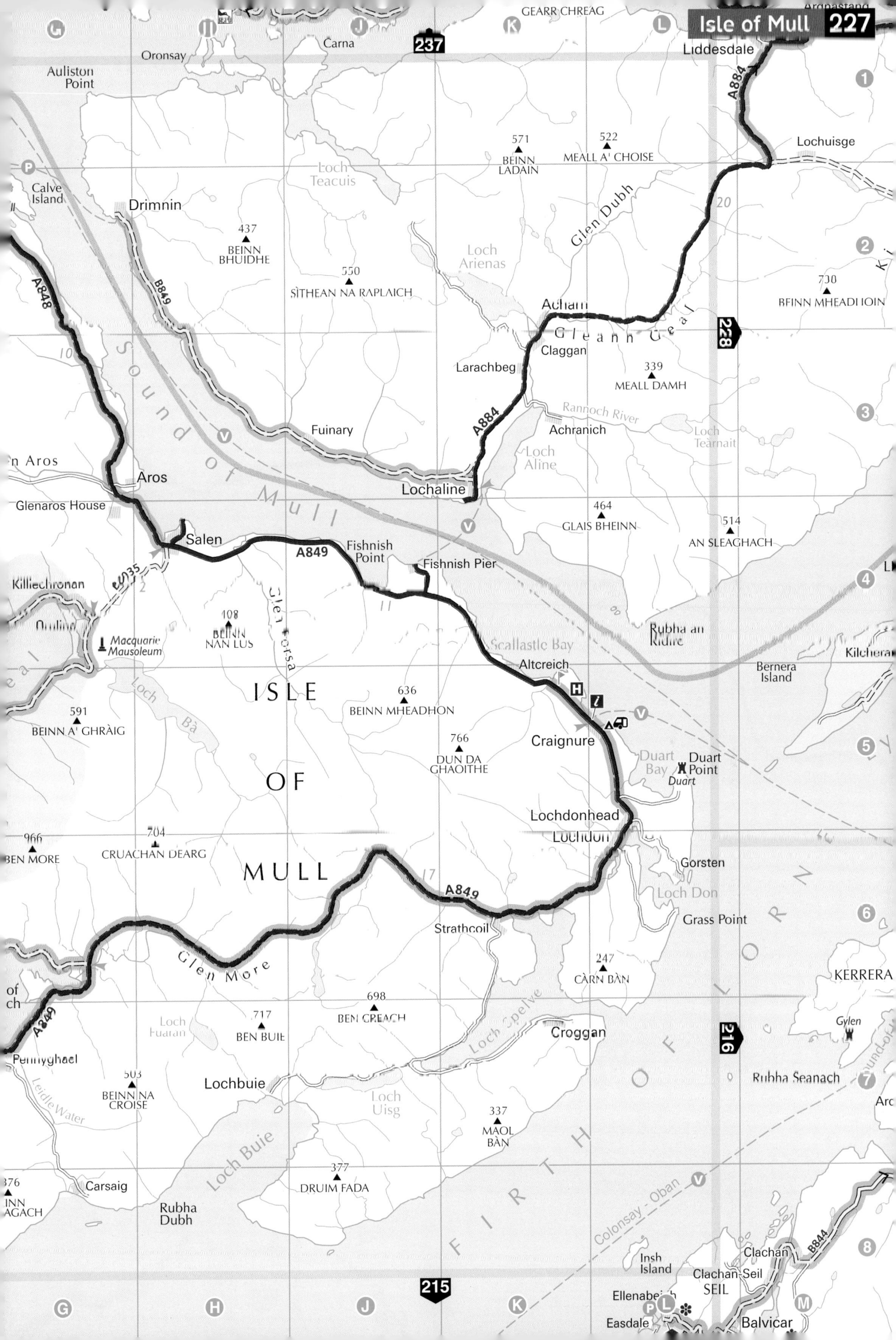

GEARR CHREAG

Argpastang

Liddesdale

Oronsay

Carna

237

K

L

1

Auliston
Point

571
BEINN
LADAIN

522
MEALL A' CHOISE

Lochuisge

20

A884

P

Loch
Teacuis

Calve
Island

Drimnin

437
BEINN
BHUIDHE

Loch
Arienas

Glen Dubh

2

730
BEINN MHEADHOIN

Ki

A848

B849

550
SÌTHEAN NA RAPLAICH

Acham

228

3

Gleann Geal

Claggan

339
MEALL DAMH

Fuinary

Larachbeg

A884

Loch
Achranich

Rannoch River

Loch
Teàrnait

n Aros

Aros

Loch
Aline

Lochaline

10

Sound

Glenaros House

464
GLAIS BHEINN

514
AN SLEAGHACH

Salen

A849

Fishnish
Point

Fishnish Pier

4

Killiechronan

B8035

2

of

Mull

V

Duline

108
BEINN
NAN LUS

Glen Forsa

Macquarie
Mausoleum

Scallastic Bay

Altcreich

Rubha an
Ridire

Bernera
Island

Kilchera

ISLE

636
BEINN MHEADHON

H

i

591
BEINN A' GHRÀIG

Loch Bà

OF

766
DUN DA
GHAOITHE

V

Craignure

5

Duart
Bay

Duart
Point

Duart

MULL

966
BEN MORE

704
CRUACHAN DEARG

Lochdonhead

Lochdon

Gorsten

Loch Don

Grass Point

17

A849

Strathcoil

247
CÀRN BÀN

6

Glen More

717
BEN BUIE

698
BEN CREACH

Loch Spelve

Croggan

216

KERRERA

of
ch

A849

Loch
Fuaran

Gylen

7

Pennyghael

503
BEINN NA
CROISE

Lochbuie

Loch
Uisg

Rubha Seanach

Ard

376
NN
AGACH

Carsaig

Rubha
Dubh

Loch Buie

377
DRUIM FADA

337
MAOL
BÀN

FIRTH OF LORN

Colonsay · Oban

V

B844

Clachan

8

Insh
Island

Clachan Seil
SEIL

Leidle Water

G

H

J

K

Ellenabeich

P L

Easdale

Balvicar

M

215

A · B · C · D · E · F

Kinlochmoidart

Brunery

Glen Forsian

Scamodale

664 ▲ BEN GAIRE

718 ▲ MEALL NAM DAMH

Glen G

Loch Shiel

Cona Glen

MOIDART

Langal

Dalelia

Glen Moidart

758 ▲ MEALL MÒR

Dalnabreck

Loch Shiel

754 ▲ SGOR AN TARMACHAIN

Polloch

Loch Doilet

Glen Hurich

Claish Moss

888 ▲ SGURR DHOMHNUILL

Glen Scaddle

237

SUNART

846 ▲ BEINN RESIPOL

Resipole Burn

12

Ariundle Oakwood

Glen Gour

Ard

Clovulin

Sunart

Anaheilt

884 ▲ GARBH BHEINN

A861

13

3

Glencripesdale

Woodend

Strontian

Achnalea

339 ▲ FÈARR CHREAG

Camasine

Ardnastang

A861

Glen Tarbert

Camasachoirce

Liddesdale

A884

Inversanda

Kentall

620 ▲ GLAS BHEINN

853 ▲ CREACH BHEINN

A82

4

522 ▲ MEALL A' CHOISE

Lochuisge

Cuil

Du

20

651 ▲ BEINN NA CILLE

Kingairloch

B8043

Salachan Gl

Glen Dubh

738 ▲ BEINN MHEADHOIN

Loch a' Choire

LOCH LINNHE

30

655 ▲ MEALL B

5

Gleann Geal

Claggan

568 ▲ SQURR A BHUIC

Shuna Island

339 ▲ MEALL DAMH

Portnacroish

Stalker

Fas

Inver L

Rannoch River

Achranich

Loch Tearnait

Appin

Glasdrum Wood

Port Ramsay

Inverfolla

Creagan Inn

6

464 ▲ GLAIS BHEINN

514 ▲ AN SLEAGHACH

Clachan

Port Appin

Eriska

North Shian

Loch Creran

Barcaldine

Tirefour (ruin)

Eilean Dubr

Lismore

LISMORE

South Shian

B8045

Barcaldine

A828

227

Rubha an Ridire

Bernera Island

Kilcheran

Achnacroish

Lynn of Lorne

Kiel Crofts

Benderloch

B845

7

creich

H

i

Benderloch

Ledaig

BENDERLOCH

V

Ardchattan Priory

Inver

Craignure

Duart Bay

Duart Point

Ardmucknish Bay

V

Dunstaffnage Castle & Chapel

Oban

Black Crofts

Achnacloich

8

Loc onhead

Duart

North Connel

Connel

Achaleven

A85

Lochdon

Dunbeg

216

Ganavan Bay

A85

Dunollie

Al

A · B · C · D · E · F

0   1   2   3   4   5 miles
0   1 2 3 4 5 6 7 8 kilometres

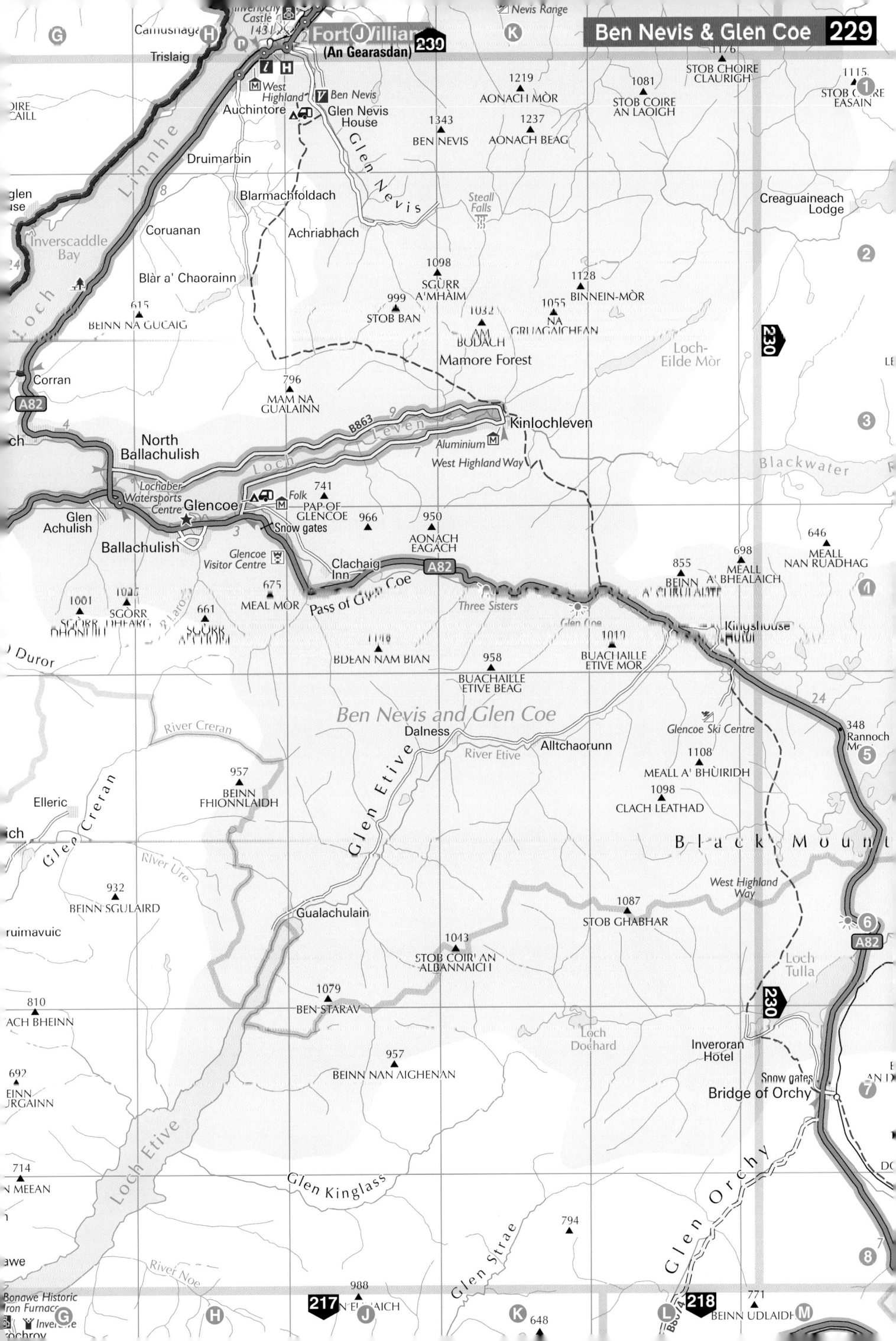

G H J K 1

Nevis Range

STOB CHOIRE
CLAURIGH 1176

1115 STOB COIRE
EASAIN

Camusnagaul
Trislaig

Inverlochy
Castle 143

Fort William
(An Gearasdan) 230

1219
AONACH MÒR

1081
STOB COIRE
AN LAOIGH

West Highland

Ben Nevis
Glen Nevis
House

1343
BEN NEVIS

1237
AONACH BEAG

Auchintore

Druimarbin

Creaguaineach
Lodge

2

Glen Nevis

Steall
Falls

Blarmachfoldach

Achriabhach

Inverscaddle
Bay

1098
SGÙRR
A'MHÀIM

1128
BINNEIN-MÒR

230

Blàr a' Chaorainn

999
STOB BAN

1032
AM
BODACH

1055
NA
GRUAGAICHEAN

Loch-
Eilde Mòr

615
BEINN NA GUCAIG

Coruanan

Corran

A82

4

796
MAM NA
GUALAINN

Mamore Forest

B863 9

Leven

Kinlochleven

3

North
Ballachulish

Loch

7

Aluminium

West Highland Way

Blackwater

Lochaber
Watersports
Centre

Glencoe

741

PAP OF
GLENCOE

966

950
AONACH
EAGACH

855
BEINN A' CHRULAISTE

698
MEALL
A' BHEALAICH

646
MEALL
NAN RUADHAG

4

Glen
Achulish

Ballachulish

Glencoe
Visitor Centre

Clachaig
Inn

Snow gates

Pass of Glen Coe

A82

Three Sisters

Glen Coe

Kingshouse
Hotel

1001

1025
SGÒRR
DHONUILL

661
SGÒRR
A' CHOIRE

675
MEAL MÒR

1110
BIDEAN NAM BIAN

958
BUACHAILLE
ETIVE BEAG

1019
BUACHAILLE
ETIVE MÒR

Glencoe Ski Centre

348
Rannoch
Moor 5

Duror

Ben Nevis and Glen Coe

Dalness

River Etive

Alltchaorunn

1108
MEALL A' BHÙIRIDH

1098
CLACH LEATHAD

River Creran

957
BEINN
FHIONNLAIDH

Glen Etive

Black Mount

Elleric

West Highland
Way

932
BEINN SGULAIRD

River Ure

Gualachulain

1087
STOB GHABHAR

6

A82

ruimavuic

1043
STOB COIR' AN
ALBANNAICH

Loch Tulla

810
ACH BHEINN

1079
BEN STARAV

230

Loch
Dochard

Inveroran
Hotel

692
EINN
URGAINN

957
BEINN NAN AIGHENAN

Glen Kinglass

Snow gates

7

Bridge of Orchy

714
MEEAN

Glen Creran

Glen Strae

794

Glen Orchy

Bonawe Historic
Iron Furnace

Inverawe
ochroy

988
N EUBHAICH

648

217 J K 771
BEINN UDLAIDH

218

L

M

8

Loch Etive

River Noe

Loch Linnhe

A · B · C · 240 · D · E · F

1176
STOB CHOIRE
CLAURIGH

TOB COIRE
AN LAOIGH

1115
STOB COIRE
EASAIN

1046 240
CHNO DEARG

Loch
Gulbin

1101
BEINN EIBHINN

1145
BEN ALDER

Creaguaineach
Lodge

Loch Treig

Glen Ossian

Loch Ossian

844
MEALL A'BHEALAICH

MÒR

229

Loch-
Eilde Mòr

Corrour
Station

952
SGÒR GAIBHRE

626
SRON A
CHLAONAIDH

906
LEUM UILLEIM

864
BEINN PHARIAGAIN

R Ericht

Blackwater   Reservoir

Rannoch
Station

Bridge
of Ericht

Dunan   Finnart
B846

646
MEALL
NAN RUADHAG

855
BEINN
A' CHRULAISTE

698
MEALL
A' BHEALAICH

738
A' CHRUACH

Loch
Laidon

Loch
Eigheach

Bridge
of Gaur

Kingshouse
Hotel

24

Glencoe Ski Centre

348
Rannoch
Moor

R a n n o c h   M o o r

AILLE
MOR

9

1108
MEALL A' BHÙIRIDH

Loch Bà

931
MEALL BUIDHE

1098
CLACH LEATHAD

B l a c k   M o u n t

Water of Tulla

Loch an
Daimh

West Highland
Way

087
HA R

A82

Loch Tulla

1079
BEINN A' CHREACHAIN

Pubil

229

996
BEINN
AN DÒTHAIDH

953
BEINN MHANACH

Loch
Lyon

1038
MEALL GHAORDIE

Inveroran
Hotel

Snow gates

Bridge of Orchy

1074
BEN
DORAIN

1076
BEINN HEASGARNICH

Glen Orchy

7

Glen Lochay

River Lochay

Falls of Lo

8

771
LINN UDL

818

218

937
BEINN CHEATHAIC

219

Glen Ossian

BEIN

CAN

0   1   2   3   4   5 miles
0 1 2 3 4 5 6 7 8 kilometres

A   B   C   D   E   F

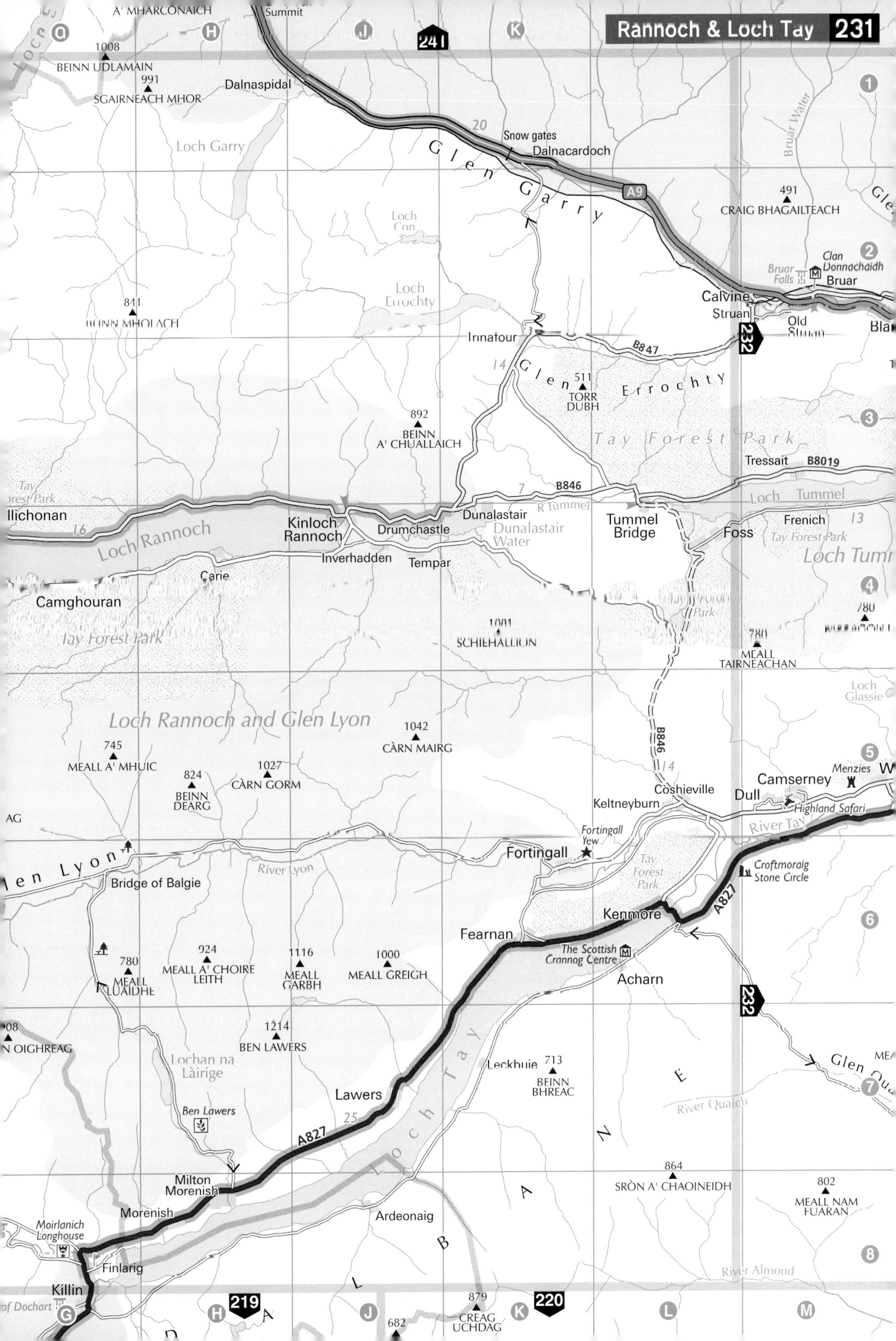

A' MHARCONAICH
Summit
H
J
241
K

1008
BEINN UDLAMAIN
Dalnaspidal

991
SGAIRNEACH MHOR

Loch Garry
20
Snow gates
Dalnacardoch

Glen Garry
A9

491
CRAIG BHAGAILTEACH

Loch Con

Loch Errochty

Clan
Donnachaidh
Bruar
Falls
Bruar

841
BEINN MHOLACH

Calvine
Struan
232
Old
Struan
Bla

Irinatour
B847
Glen Errochty

Tay Forest Park

511
TORR
DUBH

892
BEINN
A' CHUALLAICH

Tressait
B8019

Ilichonan
1.6
Loch Rannoch
Kinloch
Rannoch
Drumchastle
Dunalastair
7
B846
R Tummel
Tummel
Bridge
Foss
Loch Tummel
Frenich
Tay Forest Park
Loch Tumm

Inverhadden
Tempar

Carie

Camghouran
Tay Forest Park

1001
SCHIEHALLION

780
MEALL
TAIRNEACHAN

780

Loch
Glassie

Loch Rannoch and Glen Lyon

745
MEALL A' MHUIC

824
BEINN
DEARG

1027
CÀRN GORM

1042
CÀRN MAIRG

B846
14

Camserney
Dull
Menzies
W

Coshieville

Keltneyburn
Highland Safari

River Tay

AG

Glen Lyon
Bridge of Balgie
River Lyon

Fortingall
Yew
Fortingall
★

Tay
Forest
Park

Croftmoraig
Stone Circle

Kenmore
A827
232

780
MEALL
LUAIDHE

924
MEALL A' CHOIRE
LEITH

1116
MEALL
GARBH

1000
MEALL GREIGH

Fearnan

The Scottish
Crannog Centre

Acharn

Glen Qua

08
N OIGHREAG

1214
BEN LAWERS

Lochan na
Làirige

Leckbuie
713
BEINN
BHREAC

River Quaich

7

Ben Lawers

Lawers
A827
25

Loch Tay

864
SRÒN A' CHAOINEIDH

802
MEALL NAM
FUARAN

Milton
Morenish

Morenish

Ardeonaig

8

Moirlanich
Longhouse

Finlarig

River Almond

Killin
of Dochart
G
219
H
J
K
220
L
M

879
CREAG
UCHDAG

682

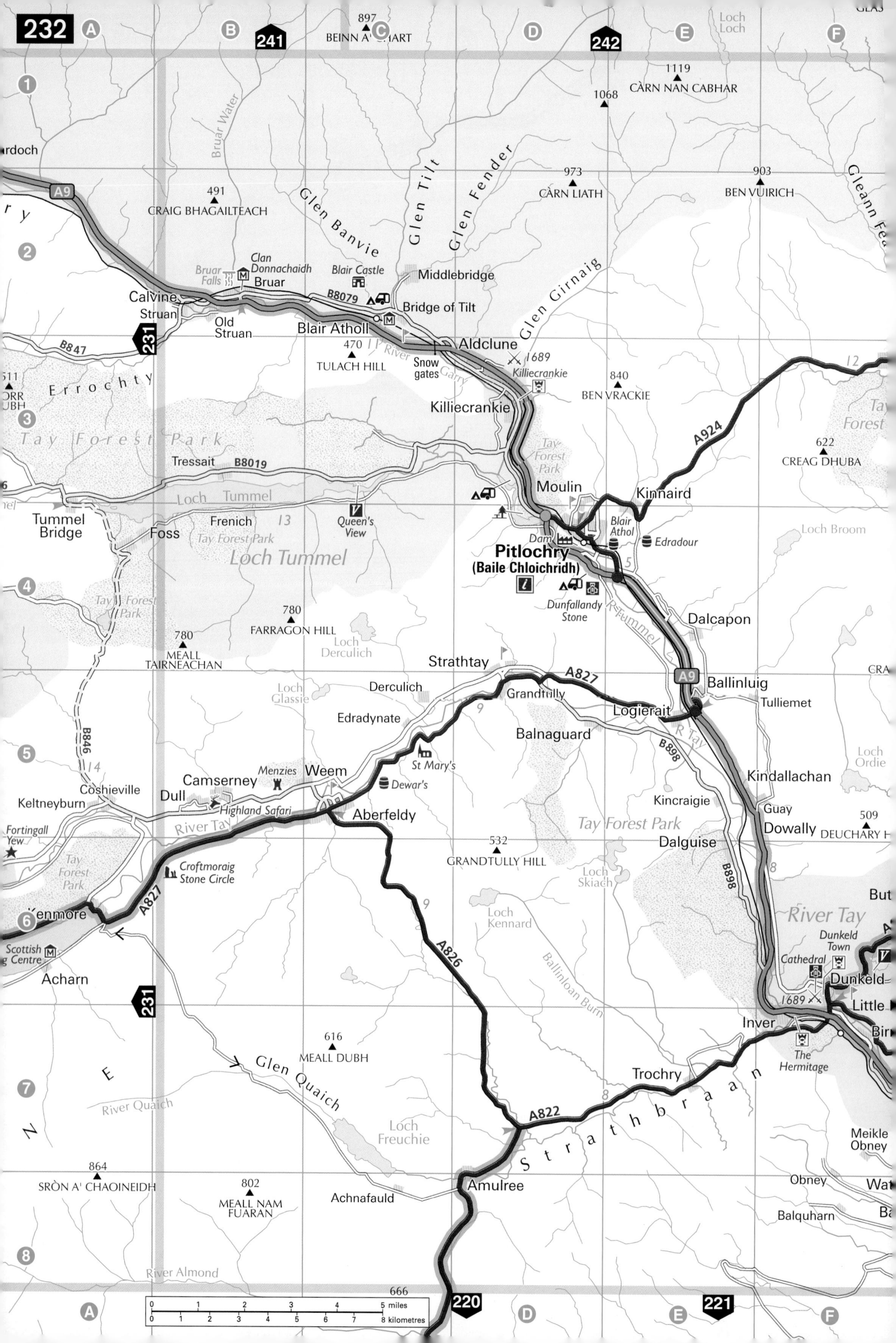

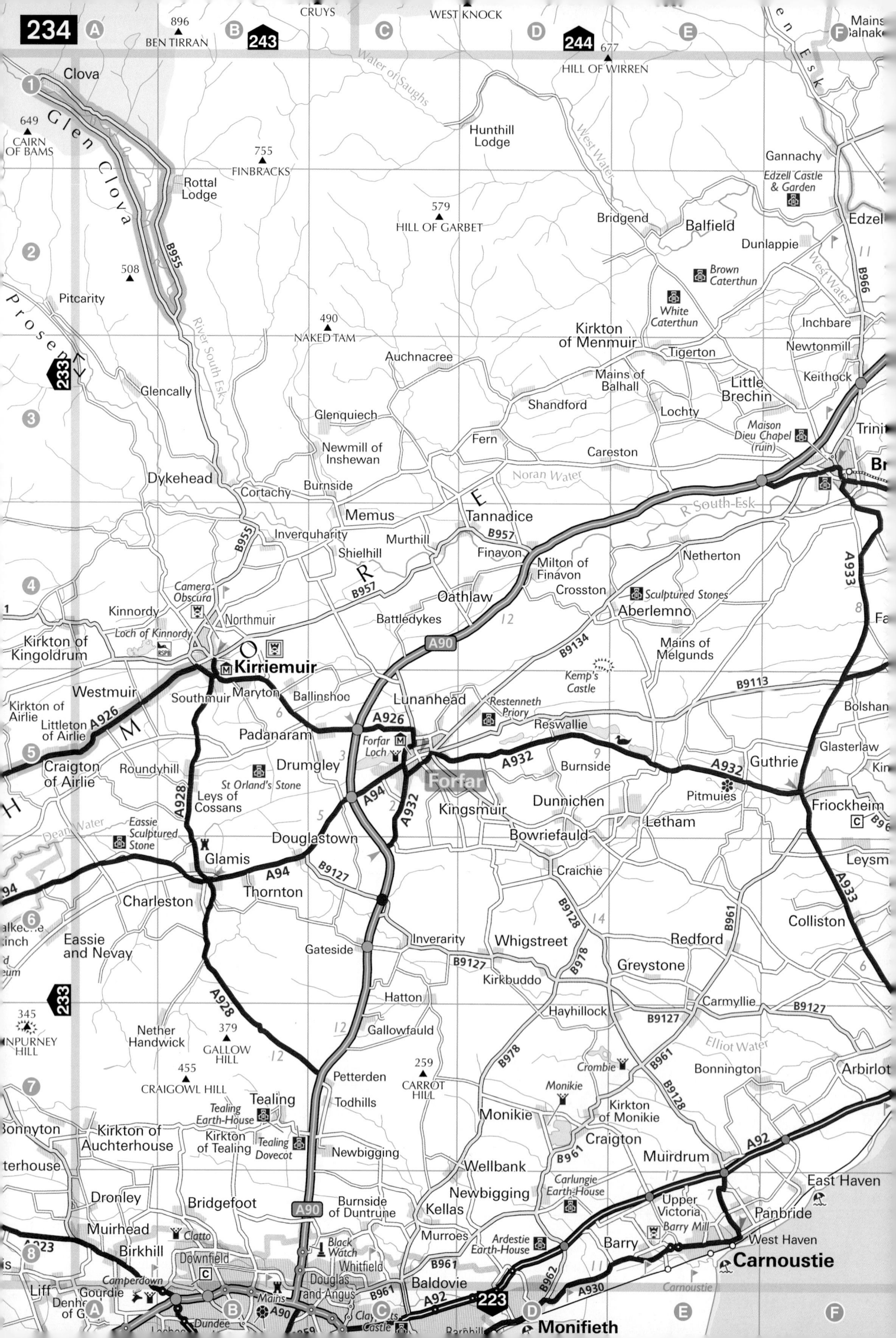

Pittarrow

Redmyre Arbuthnott Centre

244 **245**

Mains of
Haulkerton

Laurencekirk

Inverbervie

Bervie
Bay

Maritime

Gourdon

Sauchieburn

Redford

Benholm

Dykelands

Johnshaven

Logie
Pert

Milton Ness

Craigo Lochside Bush

Logie Morphie St Cyrus

Maryton

Hillside

A92

House of
Dun

Dun A935 Montrose Air Station

Bridge of Dun **Montrose**

Montrose
Basin

Barnhead

Maryton Scurdie Ness

A934 Forryden

Craig

Usan

Westerton
of Rossie

Braehead Boddin Point

Lunan

Lunan Bay

Inverkeilor

Chapelton

Cauldcots Red Head

Marywell

Auchmithie

Carlingheugh
Bay

Arbroath Abbey

The Deil's
Head

Arbroath

Signal Tower

| 0 | 1 | 2 | 3 | 4 | 5 miles |
| 0 | 1 | 2 | 3 | 4 | 5 | 6 | 7 | 8 kilometres |

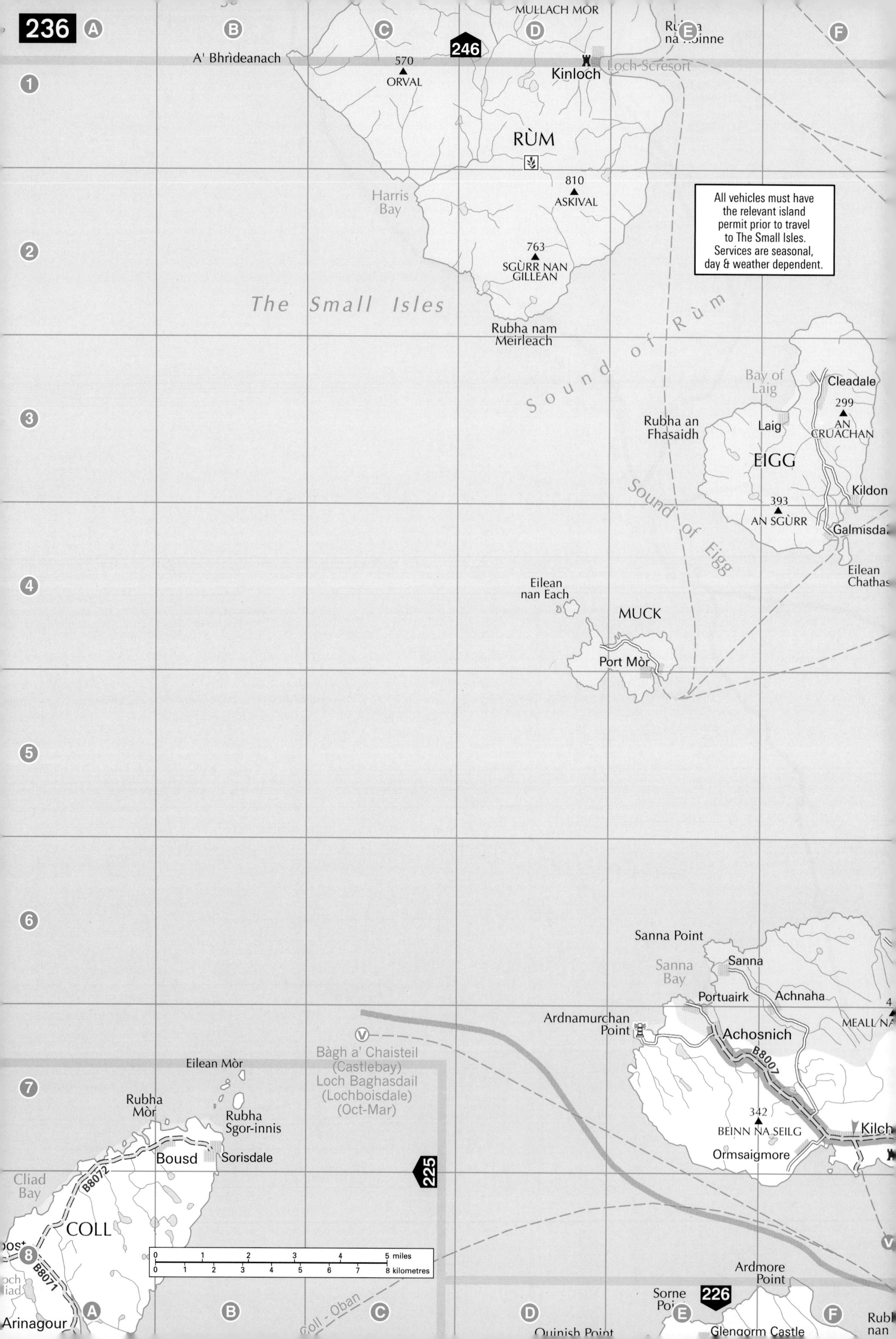

A B C **246** D E F

1

A' Bhrìdeanach
570
▲
ORVAL
Kinloch
Loch Scresort
Rubha
na Rinne
MULLACH MÒR

RÙM

Harris
Bay
810
▲
ASKIVAL

2

763
▲
SGÙRR NAN
GILLEAN

The Small Isles

Rubha nam
Meirleach

Sound of Rùm

Bay of
Laig
Cleadale
299
▲
AN
CRUACHAN

3

Rubha an
Fhasaidh
Laig

EIGG

Kildon
393
▲
AN SGÙRR
Galmisda
Sound of Eigg

Eilean
Chathas

4

Eilean
nan Each

MUCK

Port Mòr

5

6

Sanna Point
Sanna
Bay
Sanna
Portuairk
Achnaha
MEALL NA

7

Eilean Mòr
Rubha
Mòr
Rubha
Sgor-innis
Bàgh a' Chaisteil
(Castlebay)
Loch Baghasdail
(Lochboisdale)
(Oct-Mar)
Ardnamurchan
Point
Achosnich
B8007

Bousd
Sorisdale

V

225

342
▲
BEINN NA SEILG
Kilch
Ormsaigmore

Cliad
Bay
B8072

COLL

Ardmore
Point

B8071
ost
Ciad
Arinagour

0 1 2 3 4 5 miles
0 1 2 3 4 5 6 7 8 kilometres

Sorne
Poi
226
Rubh
nan

Coll - Oban
Quinish Point
Glengorm Castle

A B C D E F

8

G   H   J   V   K

KNOYD

Aird

Ard Thurinish

Point of Sleat

247

Sandai

Rubha Raonuill

Inverie Bay

1

Courteachan

Mallaigvaig

Mallaig (Malaig)

M

P

CÀRN A'GHOBHAIR   547

BEINN BH   85

Glasnacardoch Bay

Loch an Nostaire

437

SGÙRR BHUIDHE

Loch Nevis

P

Beoraidbeg

Morar

Bracorina

Tarbet

Ky   2   mo

Bracora

238   Swordland

Ky

Glenancross

A830

8

Loch   Morar

Bunacaimb

503   CÀRN A' MHÀDAIDH-RUAIDH

Meoble

3   71

Eilean Ighe

MEITH B

Loch nan Ceall

Back of Keppoch

600

River Meoble

Luinga Mhòr

Arisaig

SIDHEAN MÒR

9

Prince's Cairn

Rubh' Arisaig

Druimindarroch

Arisaig House

Kinlochnanuagh

Loch

103   CRUACH DOIRE

Loch nan Uamh

Polnish

Lochailort   4   Loch S

Sound of Arisaig

Rubha Choalais

Ardnish

Inverailort   Loch Eilt

877   ROIS-BHEINN

A861

712

5

Smirisary

Glenuig

664   BEINN GAIRE

21

Eilean Shona

Loch Moidart

Kinlochmoidart   Glen Forsian

Rubha Àird Druimnich

Tioram

Seven Men of Moidart

Brunery

6   Loch S

Morar, Moidart and Ardnamurchan

239   Ardmolich

BEINN BHREAC

Glen Moidart

MOIDART

Loch

Ockle Point

Ardtoe

Shielfoot

Langal

Dalelia

Kilmory   Ockle

BR044

Mingarrypark

Dalnabreck

Pollach

228

Loch Doile

356   BEINN BHREAC

Kentra

Blain

Branault

Arevegaig

Acharacle

Claish Moss

SUNART

ARDNAMURCHAN

437

846   BEINN RESIPOL

7

527   BEN HIANT

Natural History

Salen

Resipole Burn

Anaheilt

Glenbeg

512   BEN LAGA

A861

12

Ardslignish

Glenborrodale

Laga

B8007

Woodend

S

RSPB

Carna

339   GEÀRR CHREAG

Glencripesdale

Camasine

Ardnastang

Auliston Point

Oronsay

227

Camasachoirce

Liddesdale

A884

8

G   H   J   K   L   M

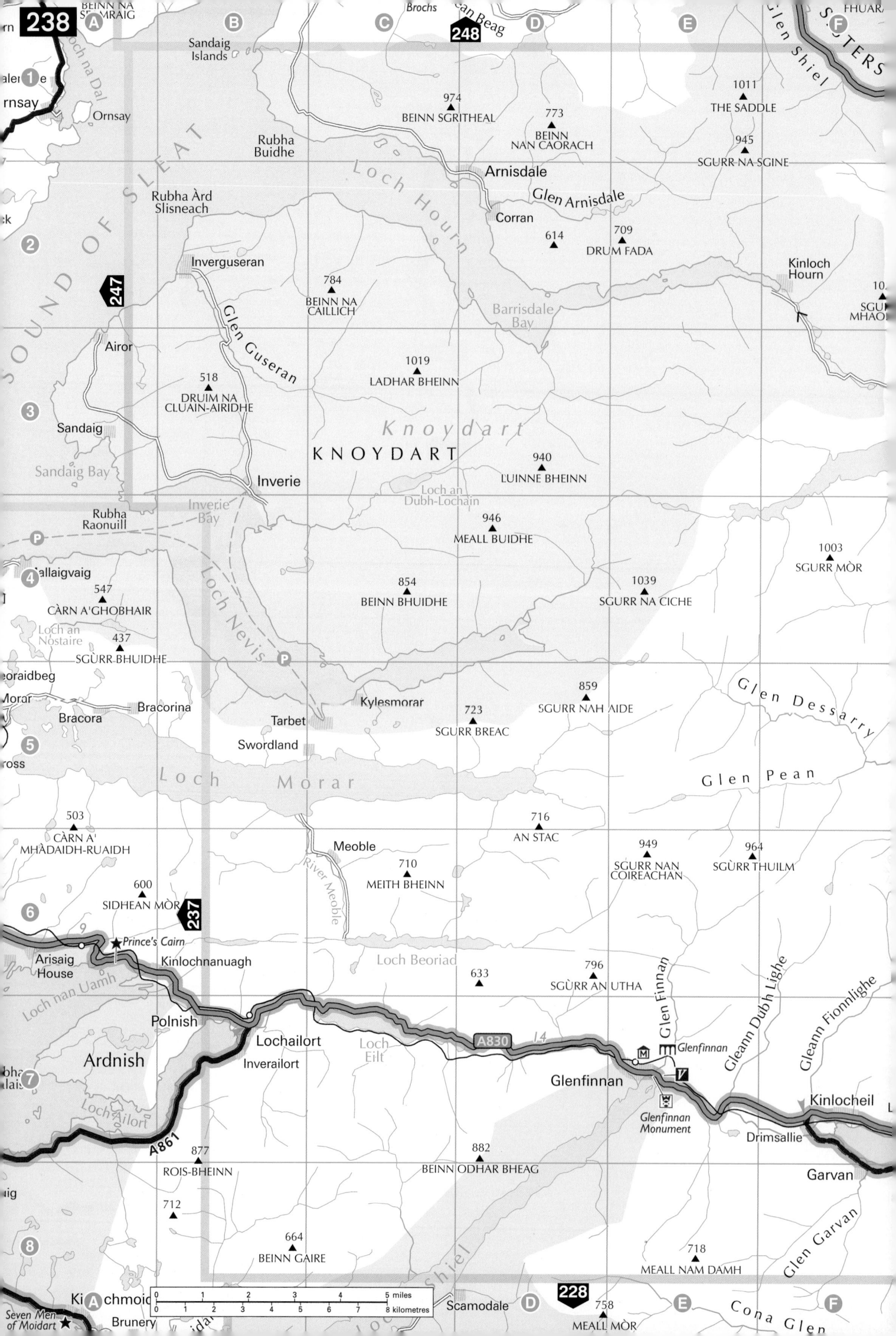

A B C D E F

1

BEINN NA
SEAMRAIG

Loch na Dal

Ornsay
Ornsay

Brochs

an Beag

FHUAR

Glen Shiel

S TERS

Sandaig
Islands

Rubha
Buidhe

Loch Hourn

▲ 974
BEINN SGRITHEAL

▲ 773
BEINN
NAN CAORACH

Arnisdale

Glen Arnisdale

▲ 1011
THE SADDLE

▲ 945
SGURR-NA-SGINE

2

SOUND OF SLEAT

Rubha Àrd
Slisneach

Inverguseran

Glen Guseran

247

Corran

▲ 614

▲ 709
DRUM FADA

Kinloch
Hourn

10.
▲ SGU
MHAO

3

Airor

Sandaig

Sandaig Bay

▲ 784
BEINN NA
CAILLICH

▲ 518
DRUIM NA
CLUAIN-AIRIDHE

Inverie

Knoydart

K N O Y D A R T

Barrisdale
Bay

▲ 1019
LADHAR BHEINN

▲ 940
LUINNE BHEINN

4

Rubha
Raonuill

Inverie
Bay

allaigvaig

▲ 547
CÀRN A'GHOBHAIR

Loch an Nòstaire

▲ 437
SGÙRR BHUIDHE

P

P

Loch Nevis

Loch an
Dubh-Lochain

▲ 946
MEALL BUIDHE

▲ 854
BEINN BHUIDHE

▲ 1039
SGURR NA CICHE

▲ 1003
SGURR MÒR

5

oraidbeg

Morar

Bracora

Bracorina

Tarbet

Swordland

Kylesmorar

Loch   Morar

▲ 723
SGURR BREAC

▲ 859
SGURR NAH AIDE

Glen Dessarry

Glen Pean

6

ross

▲ 503
CÀRN A'
MHÀDAIDH-RUAIDH

▲ 600
SIDHEAN MÒR

237

River Meoble

Meoble

▲ 710
MEITH BHEINN

Loch Beoriad

▲ 716
AN STAC

▲ 949
SGURR NAN
COIREACHAN

▲ 964
SGÙRR THUILM

7

Prince's Cairn

Arisaig
House

Loch nan Uamh

Kinlochnanuagh

Polnish

Ardnish

Lochailort

Inverailort

Loch
Eilt

▲ 633

A830

14

▲ 796
SGÙRR AN UTHA

Glen Finnan

M

Glenfinnan

Gleann Dubh Lighe

Gleann Fionnlighe

Glenfinnan

V

Glenfinnan
Monument

Drimsallie

Kinlocheil

bha
lais

Loch ilort

A861

▲ 877
ROIS-BHEINN

▲ 882
BEINN ODHAR BHEAG

Garvan

Glen Garvan

8

ig

▲ 712

▲ 664
BEINN GAIRE

Loch Shiel

228

▲ 718
MEALL NAM DAMH

Cona Glen

Ki achmoi

Brunery

Seven Men
of Moidart

A 0 1 2 3 4 5 miles
   0 1 2 3 4 5 6 7 8 kilometres

Scamodale

D

▲ 758
MEALL MÒR

E

F

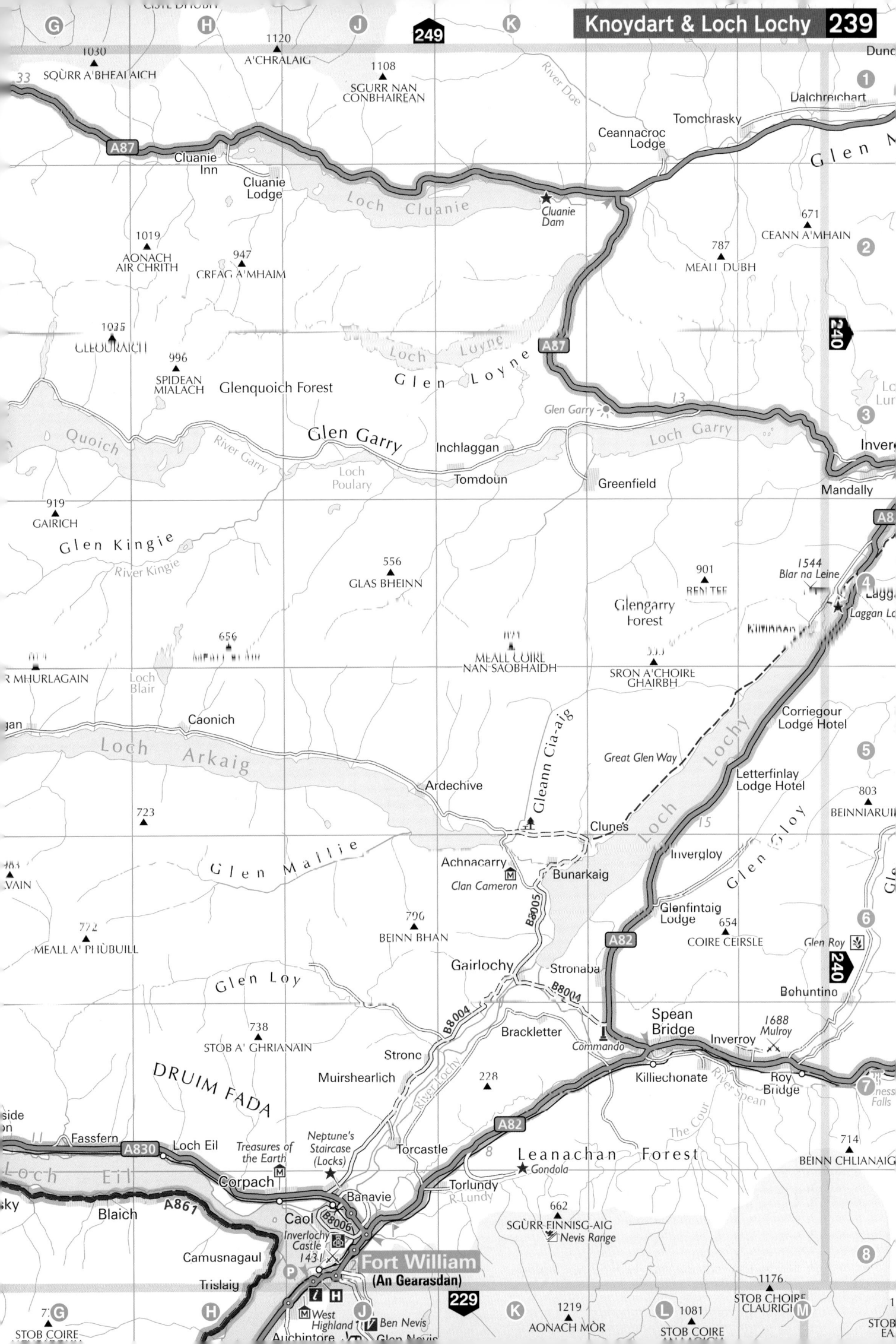

G · H · J · K

1030
SQÙRR A'BHEALAICH
33

1120
A'CHRALAIG

1108
SGURR NAN
CONBHAIREAN

River Doe

Dalchreichart
Dund

A87

Cluanie
Inn

Cluanie
Lodge

Loch Cluanie

Ceannacroc
Lodge

Tomchrasky

Glen M

Cluanie
Dam

671
CEANN A'MHAIN

1019
AONACH
AIR CHRITH

947
CREAG A'MHAIM

787
MEALL DUBH

1035
GLEOURAICH

996
SPIDEAN
MIALACH

Glenquoich Forest

Loch Loyne

Glen Loyne

A87

13

Glen Garry

Loch Garry

Quoich

Glen Garry

River Garry

Inchlaggan

Loch
Poulary

Tomdoun

Greenfield

Inver

Mandally

919
GAIRICH

Glen Kingie

River Kingie

556
GLAS BHEINN

901
BEN TEE

1544
Blar na Leine

A8

4
Lagg
Laggan Lo

Glengarry
Forest

656

MEALL BLAIR

R MHURLAGAIN

Loch
Blair

MEALL COIRE
NAN SAOBHAIDH

SRON A'CHOIRE
GHAIRBH

Kilfinnan

Corriegour
Lodge Hotel

Caonich

Loch Arkaig

Ardechive

Gleann Cia-aig

Great Glen Way

Clunes

Loch Lochy

15

Letterfinlay
Lodge Hotel

5

803
BEINNIARU

723

Glen Mallie

Achnacarry

Clan Cameron

B8005

Bunarkaig

Invergloy

Glen Gloy

Gle

654
COIRE CEIRSLE

Glen Roy

6

VAIN

722
MEALL A' PHUBUILL

796
BEINN BHAN

Gairlochy

A82

Stronaba

Glenfintaig
Lodge

240

Glen Loy

738
STOB A' GHRIANAIN

B8004

Brackletter

B8004

Commando

Spean
Bridge

Inverroy

1688
Mulroy

Bohuntino

Stronc

228

DRUIM FADA

Muirshearlich

River Lochy

Killiechonate

River Spean

Roy
Bridge

7
ness
Falls

side
on

Fassfern

A830

Loch Eil

Treasures
of the Earth

Neptune's
Staircase
(Locks)

Torcastle

8

Leanachan Forest

Gondola

714
BEINN CHLIANAIG

Loch Eil

Corpach

Torlundy

R. Lundy

The Cour

sky

Blaich

A861

Banavie

B8006

Caol

662
SGÙRR FINNISG-AIG

Nevis Range

1176
STOB CHOIRE
CLAURIGI

Camusnagaul

Inverlochy
Castle

1431

Fort William
(An Gearasdan)

Trislaig

229

7 G
STOB COIRE

H

West
Highland

J
Ben Nevis

Glen Nevis

K
1219
AONACH MÒR

L
1081
STOB COIRE

M
STOB
EA

Auchintore

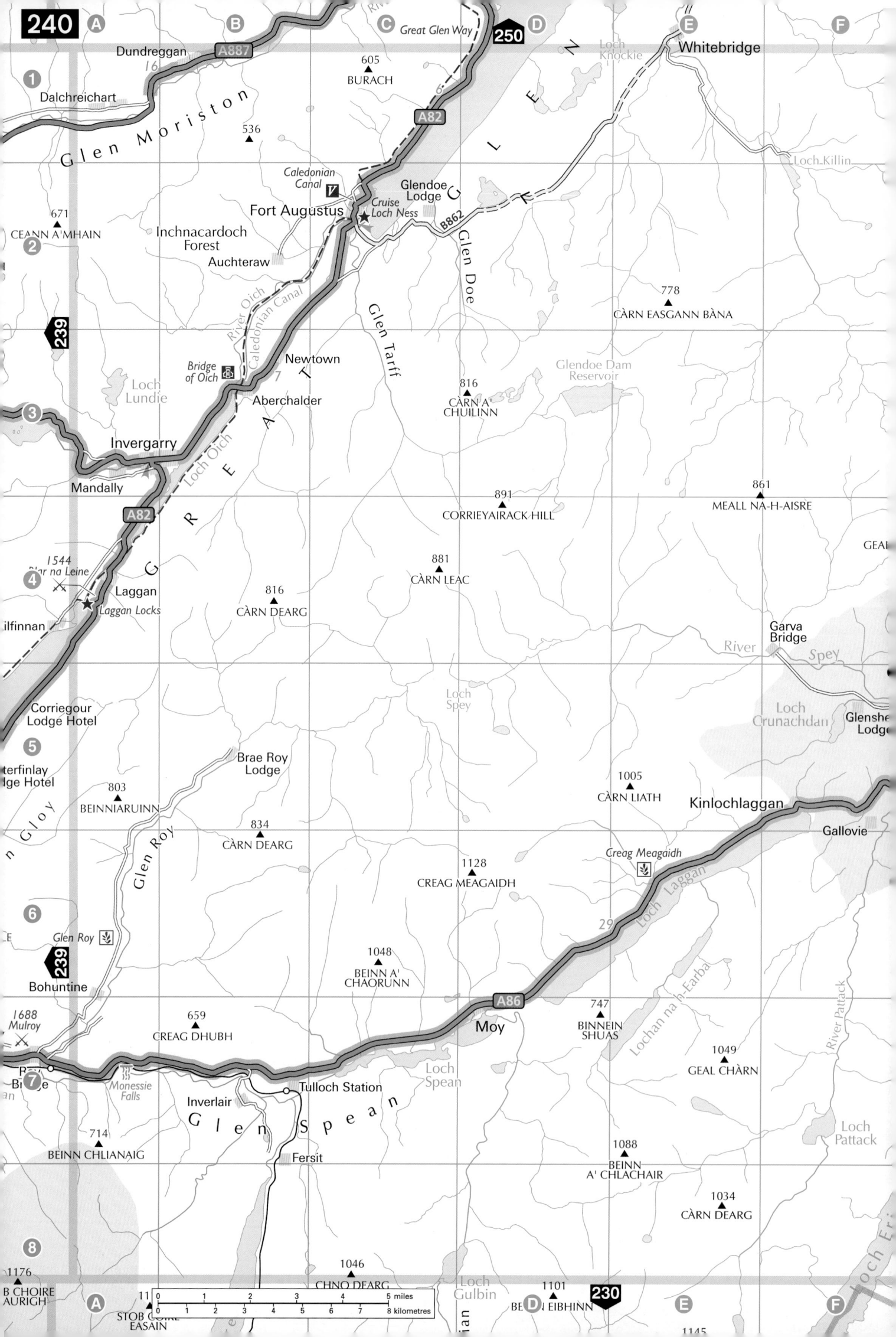

G | 251 | H | J | 252

810
ÀRN NA SAOBHAIDHE

790
CÀRN COIRE
NA H-EASGAINN

745
CNOC FRAING

712 **Avien**

810
ÀRN NA
HE MAOILE

824
GEAL-CHÀRN MÒR

Craigellachie

813
CALPA MÒR

729
CAIRN DULNAN

Loch Alvie

A9

B9152

River Eskin

M o n a d h l i a t h   M o u n t a i n s

878
CÀRN AN
FHREICEADAIN

Kingraig

Feshiebridge

855
SGARAMAN
NAM FIADH

928
A CHAILLEACH

Ralia Burn

Highland
Wildlife Park

*Loch
Insh*

Lagganlia

Farr

242

941
CÀRN BÀN

Lynchat

Insh

*Invereshie &
Inshriach*

Kingussie
Pitmain

Insh Marshes

Inveruglass

842
CÀRN AN
LETH-CHOIN

Newtonmore
(Baile Ur an t-Sleibh)

Ruthven

RSPB

Drumguish

Auchlean

Highland
Folk

*Ruthven
Barracks*

Ralia

A9

C A I R N G O R M S

River Tromie

Glen Feshie

River Feshie

Blargie   Laggan   Balgowan

Glentruim

MEALL BUIDHE

N A T I O N A L

MULLACH
A BH

A86

593
GARBH-
MHEALL MÒR

Catlodge   Snow gates

Etteridge

857
CÀRN DEARG MÒR

Glenfes

A86

768
MEALLACH MHÒR

Strathmashie
House

Crubenmore

P A R K

Loch
Caoidhair

A9

*Loch na
Cuaich*

A889

898
BAGHA-
CLOICHE

*Loch an
t-Seilich*

910
LEATHAD AN
TOABHAIN

Snow gates

Gaick Forest

242

R

Dalwhinnie

G

Glen Truim

Snow gates

941
CÀRN NA CAIM

Loch an Dùin

896
ALL
AIDH

769
CREAGAN
MÒR

1007
BEINN DEARG

975
A' MHARCONAICH

459
Drumochter
Summit

926
GLAS MHEALL MÒR

814
SRON A' CHLEIRICH

1008
JDLAMAIN

897
BEINN A' CHART

SGAIRNEACH MHOR

Dalnaspidal

H

J | 231 | K | L | 232 | M

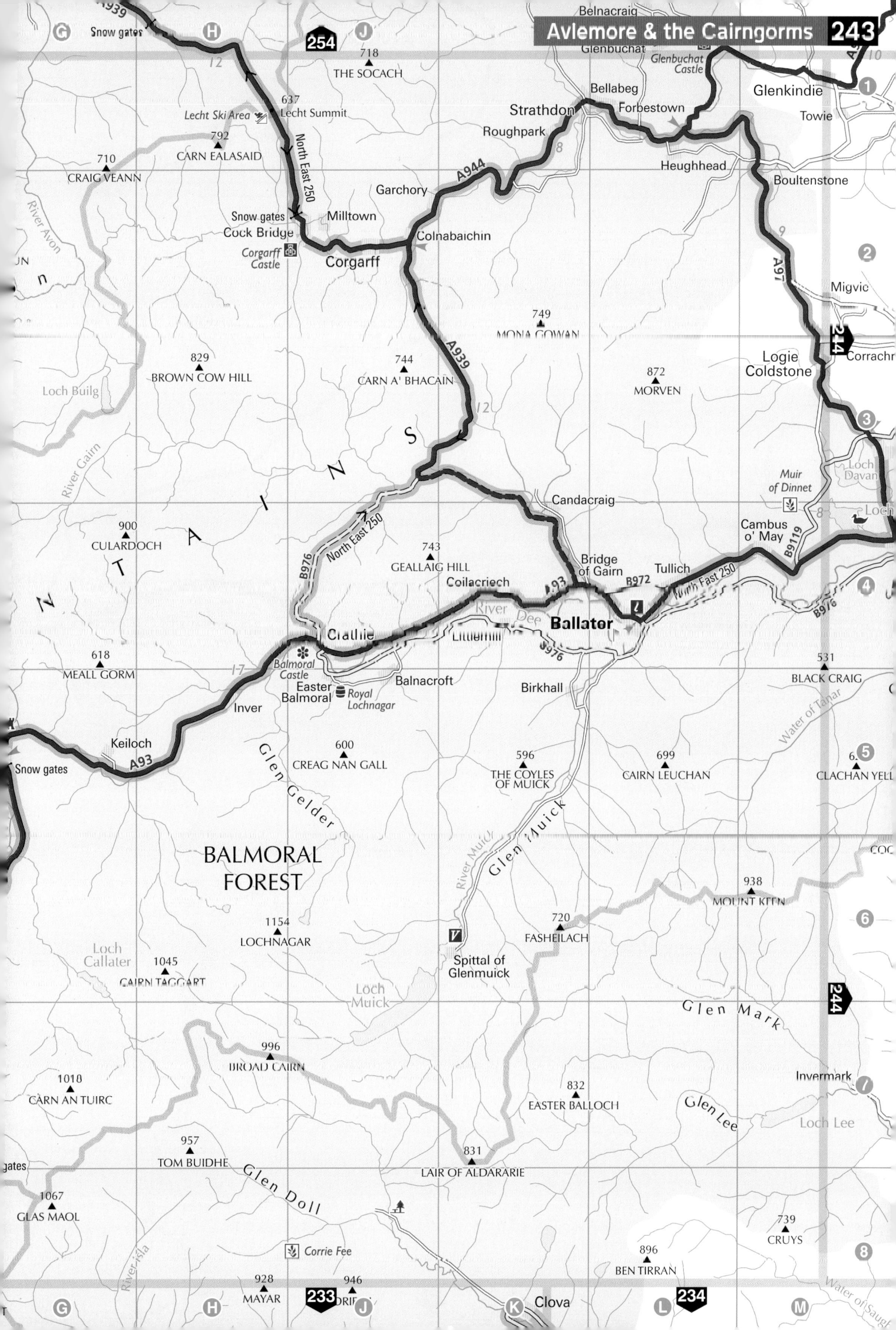

A939

G Snow gates

H 12

254 J

718 THE SOCACH

Belnacraig

Glenbuchat
Glenbuchat
Castle

Bellabeg
Forbestown

Strathdon

Roughpark

Garchory

637 Lecht Summit

Lecht Ski Area

North East 250

792 CARN EALASAID

710 CRAIG VEANN

River Avon

Snow gates

Cock Bridge

Corgarff Castle

Corgarff

Milltown

Colnabaichin

A944

8

Heughhead

Glenkindie

Towie

Boultenstone

A97

9

Migvic

Corrach

244

Logie Coldstone

Loch Davan

749 MONA GOWAN

Loch

Muir of Dinnet

8

N

T

A

I

N

S

A939

12

Loch Buig

Loch Builg

829 BROWN COW HILL

744 CARN A' BHACAIN

872 MORVEN

River Cairn

900 CULARDOCH

B976

North East 250

743 GEALLAIG HILL

Coilacriech

Candacraig

Bridge of Gairn

A93

B972

Tullich

North East 250

Cambus o' May

B9119

3

4

531 BLACK CRAIG

River Dee

Ballater

B976

618 MEALL GORM

1-7

Crathie

Littlemill

Balmoral Castle

Easter Balmoral

Royal Lochnagar

Balnacroft

Birkhall

596 THE COYLES OF MUICK

699 CAIRN LEUCHAN

6. 5 CLACHAN YELL

Inver

600 CREAG NAN GALL

Keiloch

A93

Snow gates

Glen Gelder

BALMORAL FOREST

Glen Muick

River Muick

938 MOUNT KEEN

6

Loch Callater

1154 LOCHNAGAR

1045 CAIRN TAGGART

Loch Muick

V

Spittal of Glenmuick

720 FASHEILACH

Glen Mark

244

Invermark

7

996 BROAD CAIRN

1010 CARN AN TUIRC

832 EASTER BALLOCH

Glen Lee

Loch Lee

1067 GLAS MAOL

957 TOM BUIDHE

Glen Doll

831 LAIR OF ALDARARIE

739 CRUYS

gates

River Isla

Corrie Fee

928 MAYAR

233

946 DRIFF

J

896 BEN TIRRAN

K Clova

234 L

M

Water of Saugh

8

G

H

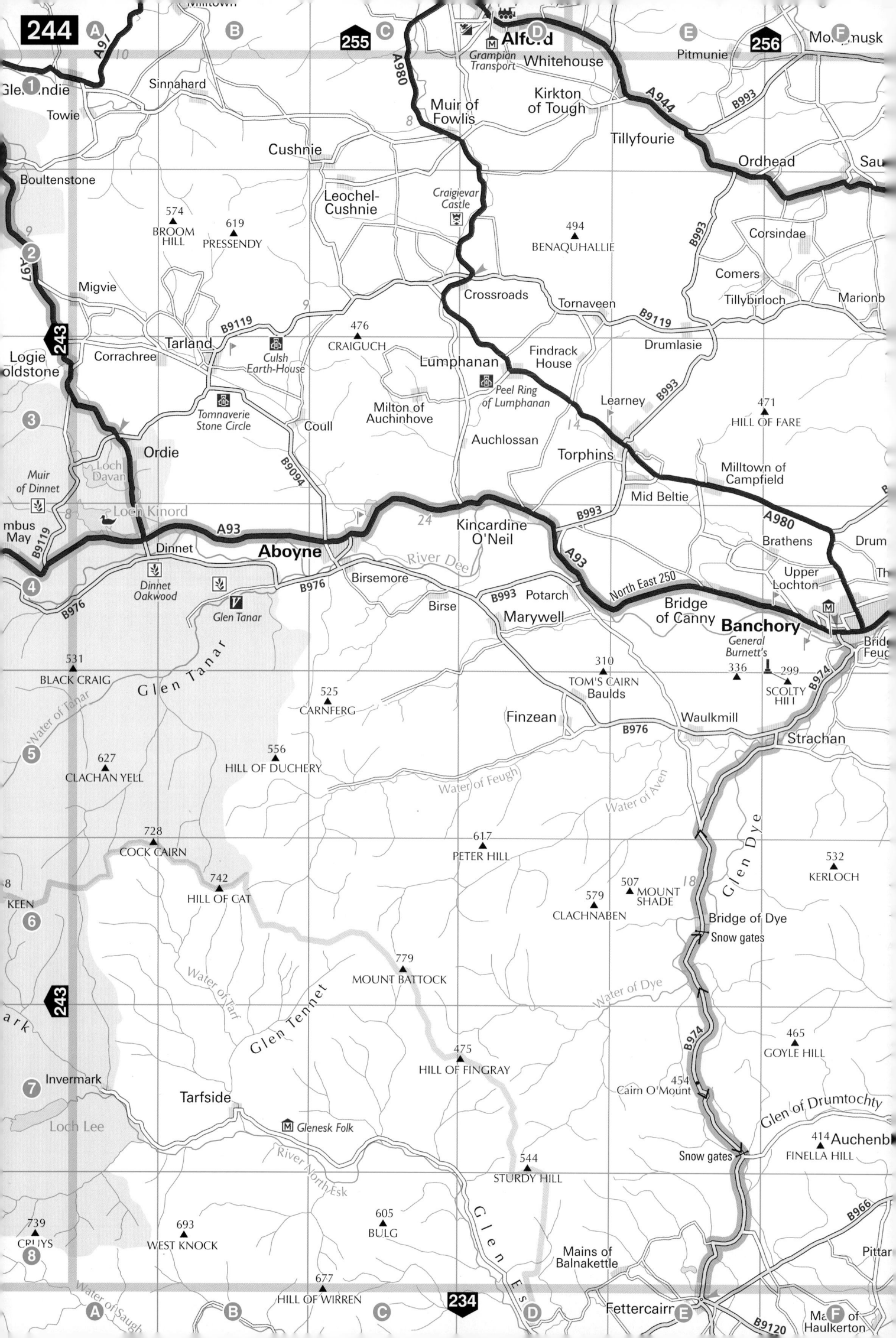

BHFAG

368
▲
BEINN NA
BOINEID

Harlosh Island
Colbost
Point
258
Tarner Island

Loch Bracadale

Wiay

Idrigill Point

Rubha nan Clach

Oronsay

Portnalong
Fiskavaig

Loch Harport
B8009

Fernilea

369
▲
ARNAVAL

Carbost

Talisker

Merkadale

Drynoch
A863
Glen Dryno

Talisker Bay

Talisker

Minginish

Glen Eynort

Dun Beag
Struan
Bracadale
Coillore

Oso
D

Loch Duagrich

439
▲
ROINEVAL

369
▲
BEINN BHR

Glen Brittle Forest

Fairy

447
▲
BEINN BHREAC

Grula

Loch Eynort

434
▲
AN CRUACHIN

Glenbrittle

Bualintur

Cu

97
SGU
A' GHEA

1

SC
ALA

Loch Brittle

225
▲
CEANN NA BEINNE

Rubha an Dùnain

Soay Sound

V
Loch Baghasdail
(Lochboisdale)

CUILLIN

Rub
Aongh

CANNA

210
▲
CÀRN A' GHAILL

Garrisdale Point

A'Chill

Canna Harbour

Sanday

Sound of Canna

Kilmory Bay

Rubha Shamhnan Insir

RÙM

302
▲
MULLACH MÒR

Rubha na Roinne

0   1   2   3   4   5 miles
0   1   2   3   4   5   6   7   8 kilometres

A Bhrideanach

236

570
▲
ORVAL

Kinloch

Loch Scresort

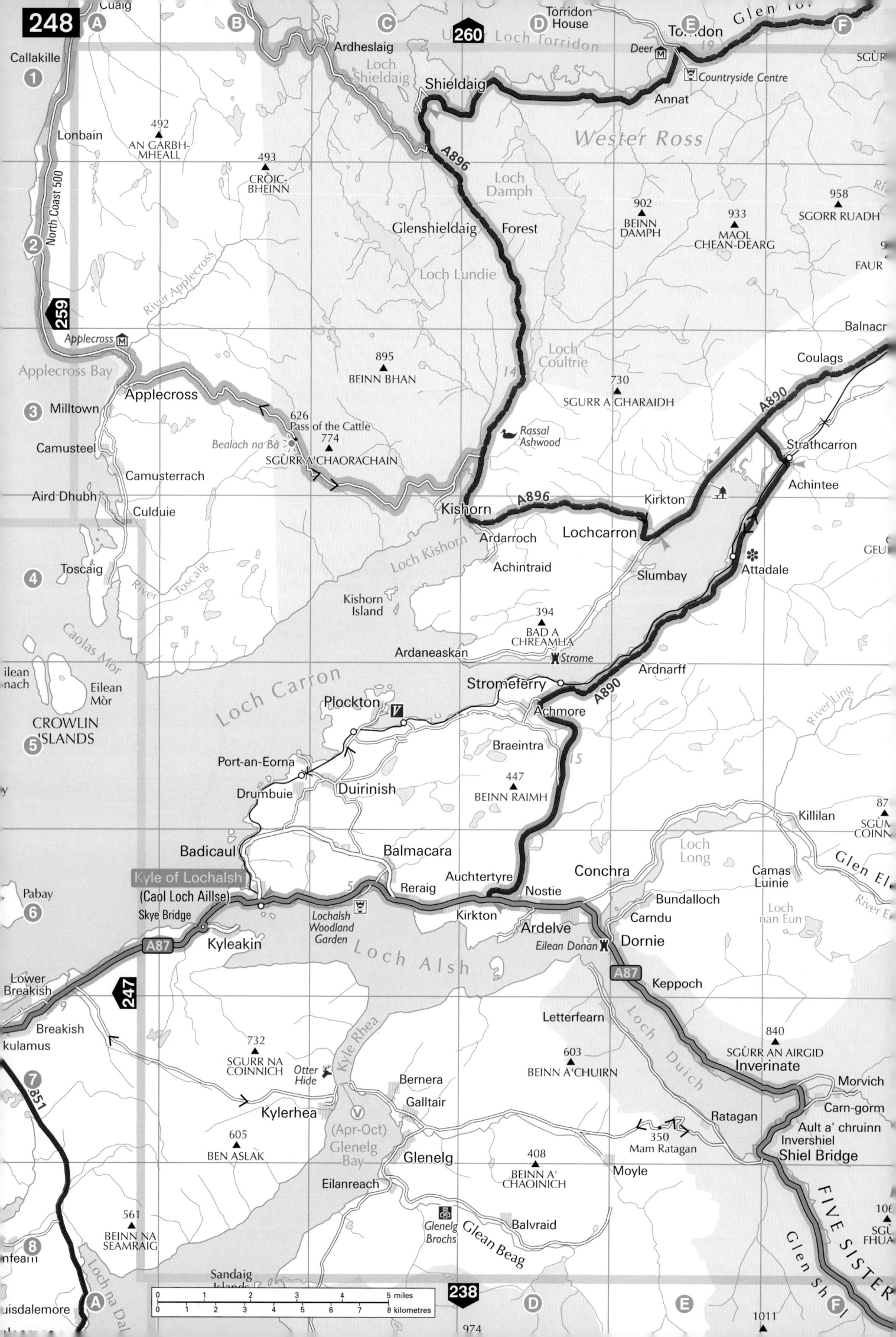

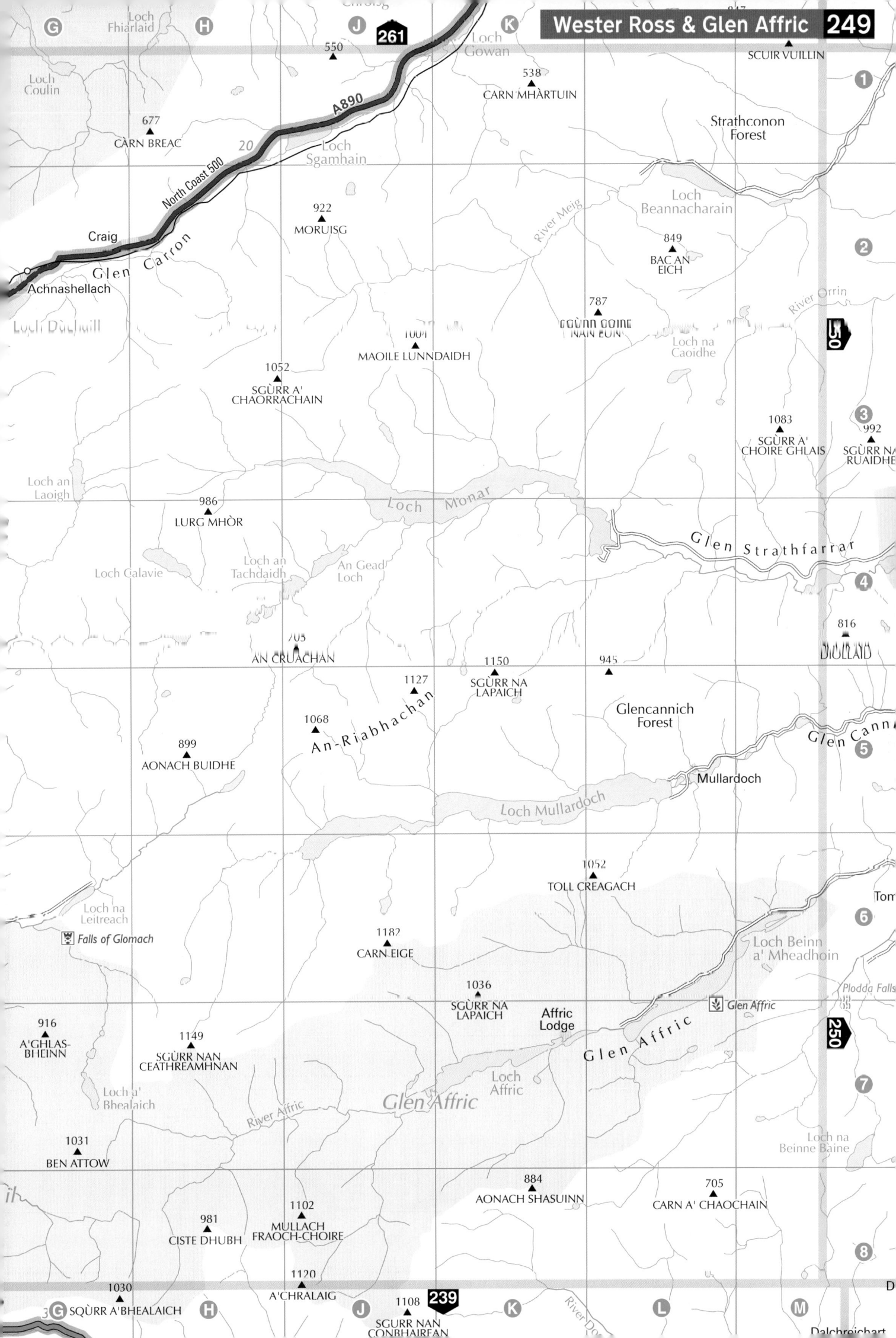

G H J **261** K

SCUIR VUILLIN

1

550▲

538▲
CARN MHÀRTUIN

Loch Gowan

Strathconon
Forest

A890

677▲
CÀRN BREAC

20

North Coast 500

Loch
Sgamhain

Loch
Beannacharain

849▲
BAC AN
EICH

2

Loch
Coulin

Loch
Fhiarlaid

Glen Carron

Craig

922▲
MORUISG

River Meig

River Orrin

Achnashellach

787▲
GOÙNN GOINE
NAN EÒN

Loch na
Caoidhe

50

1004▲
MAOILE LUNNDAIDH

1083▲
SGÙRR A'
CHOIRE GHLAIS

992▲
SGÙRR NA
RUAIDHE

3

Loch Ducliuill

1052▲
SGÙRR A'
CHAORRACHAIN

Loch an
Laoigh

986▲
LURG MHÒR

Loch Monar

Glen Strathfarrar

4

Loch Galavie

Loch an
Tachdaidh

An Gead
Loch

816▲
DIOLLAID

705▲
AN CRUACHAN

1127▲
An-Riabhachan

1150▲
SGÙRR NA
LAPAICH

945▲

Glencannich
Forest

Glen Cann

5

1068▲

899▲
AONACH BUIDHE

Mullardoch

Loch Mullardoch

1052▲
TOLL CREAGACH

6

Loch na
Leitreach

Falls of Glomach

1182▲
CARN EIGE

Loch Beinn
a' Mheadhoin

Plodda Falls

1036▲
SGÙRR NA
LAPAICH

Affric
Lodge

Glen Affric

Glen Affric

250

916▲
A'GHLAS-
BHEINN

1149▲
SGÙRR NAN
CEATHREAMHNAN

Loch a'
Bhealaich

Loch
Affric

Glen Affric

River Affric

Loch na
Beinne Baine

7

1031▲
BEN ATTOW

884▲
AONACH SHASUINN

705▲
CARN A' CHAOCHAIN

ih

1102▲
MULLACH
FRAOCH-CHOIRE

981▲
CISTE DHUBH

1120▲

8

1030▲
SQÙRR A'BHEALAICH

A'CHRALAIG

239

1108▲
SGURR NAN
CONBHAIREAN

River Do

Dalchreichart

G H J K L M D

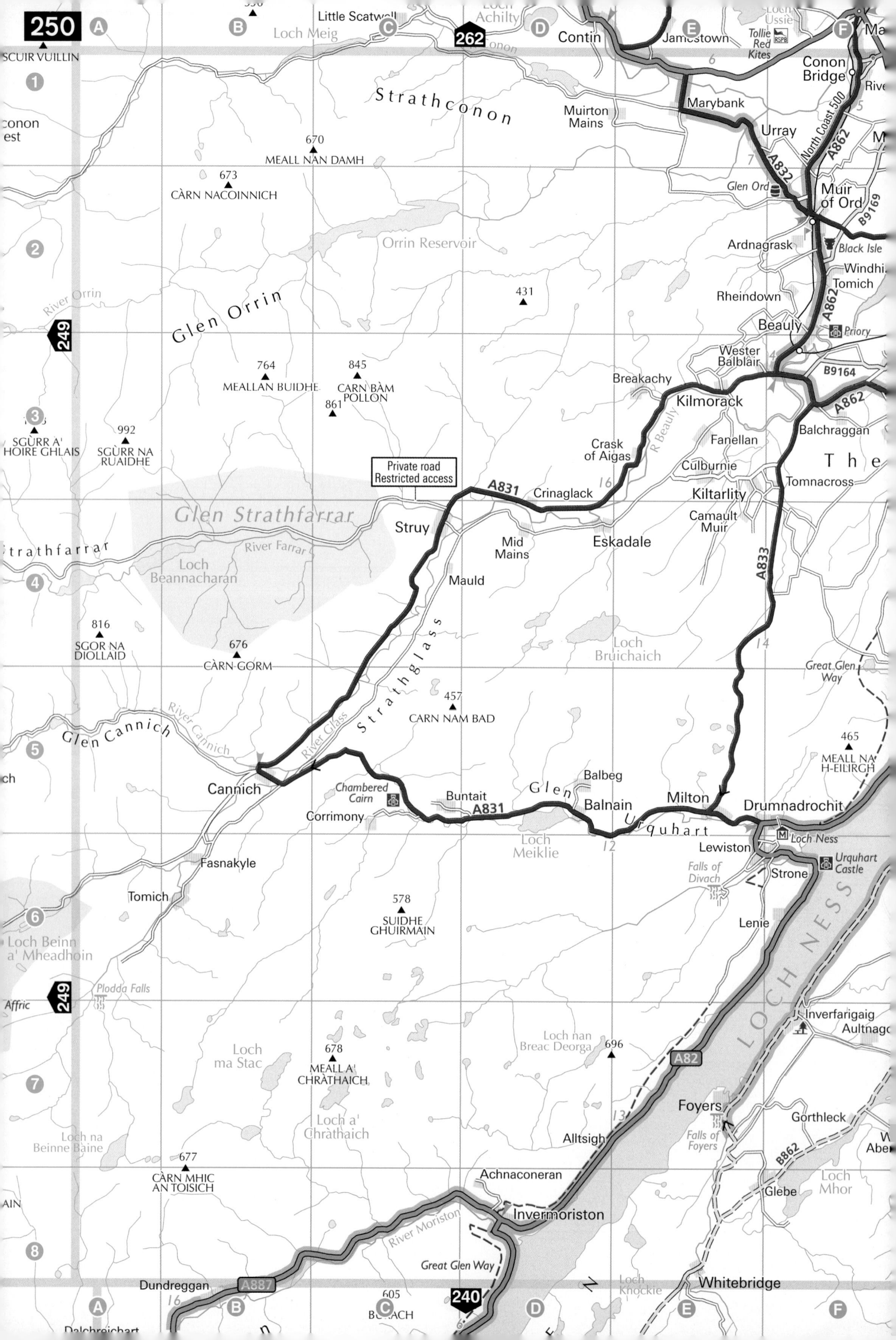

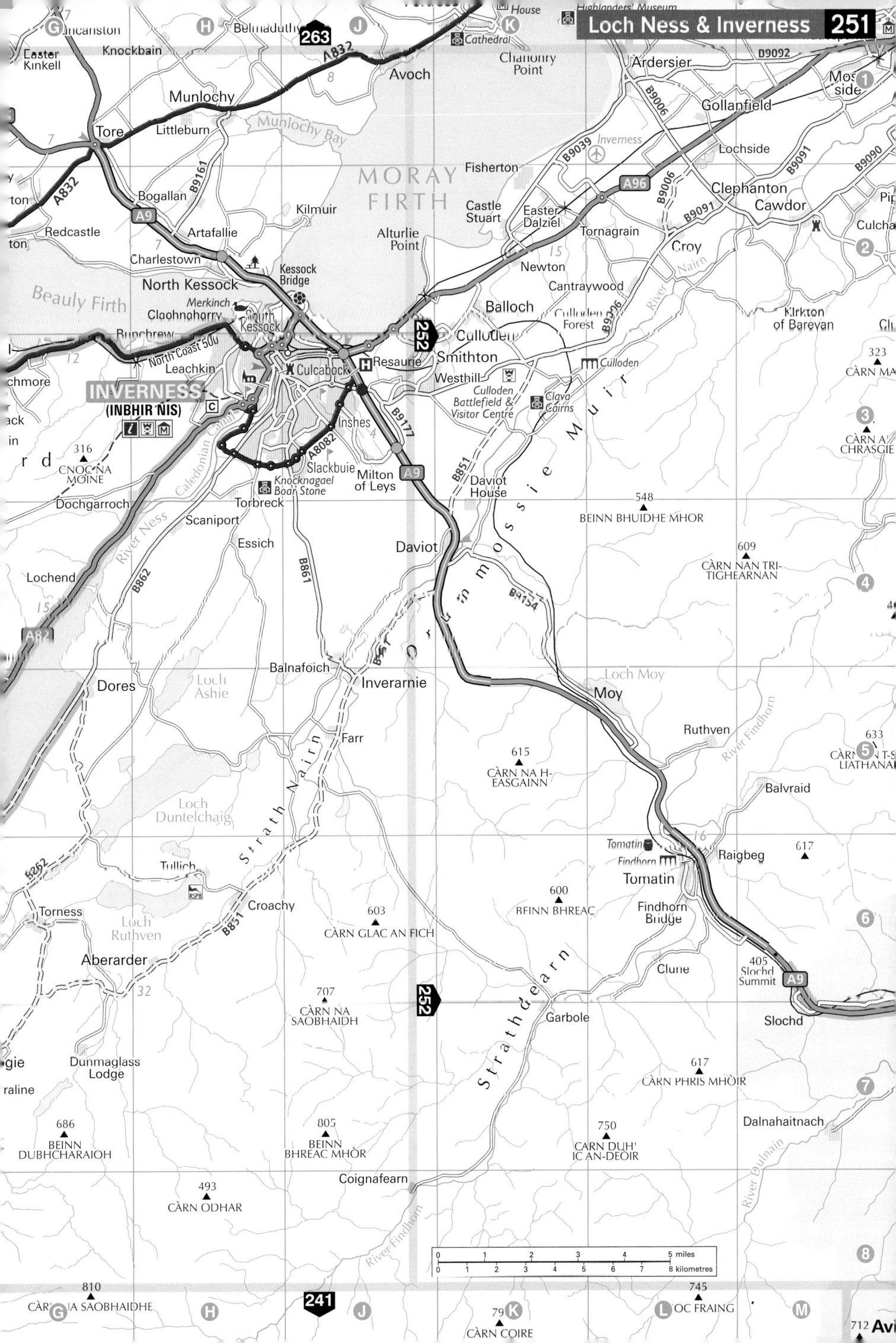

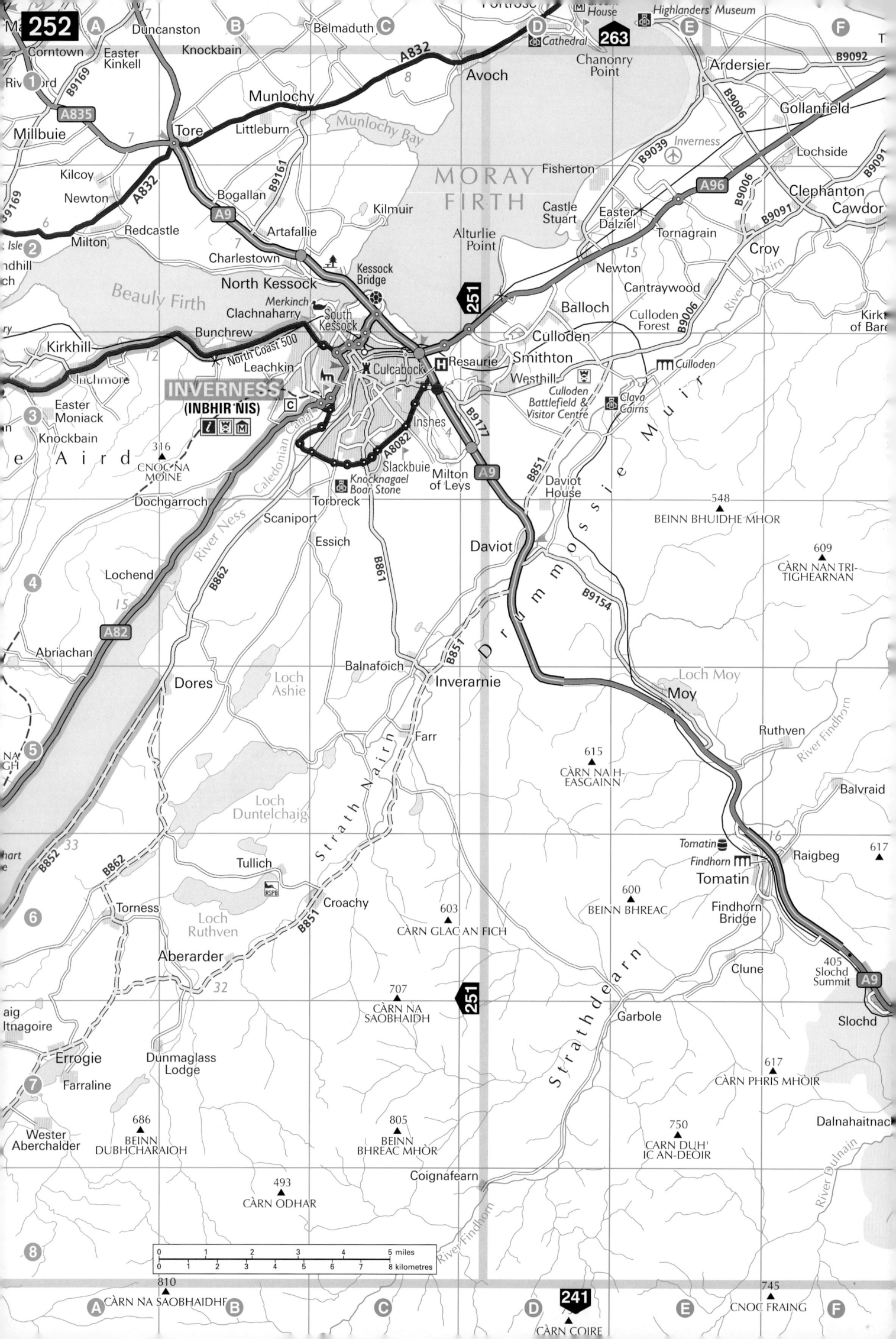

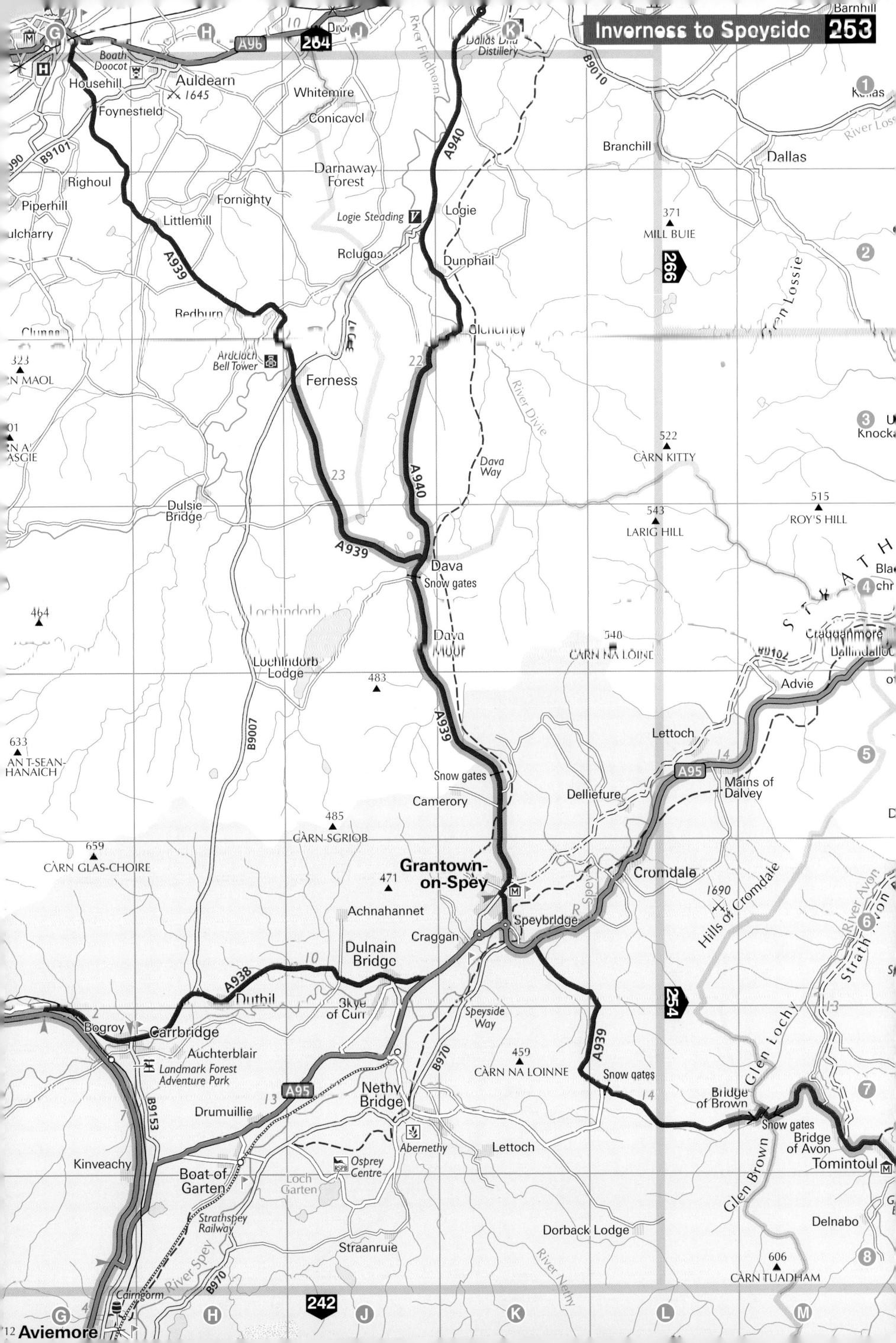

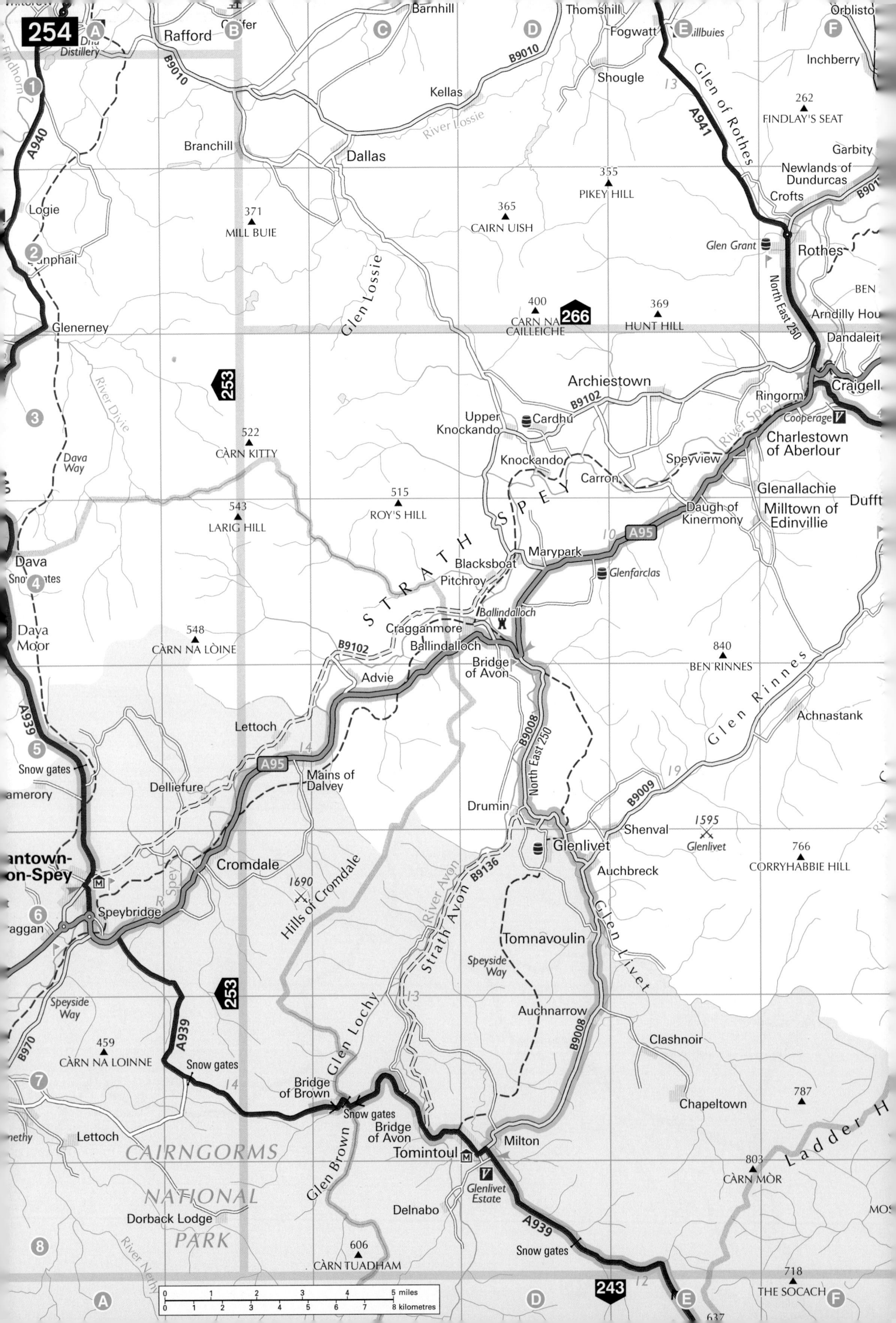

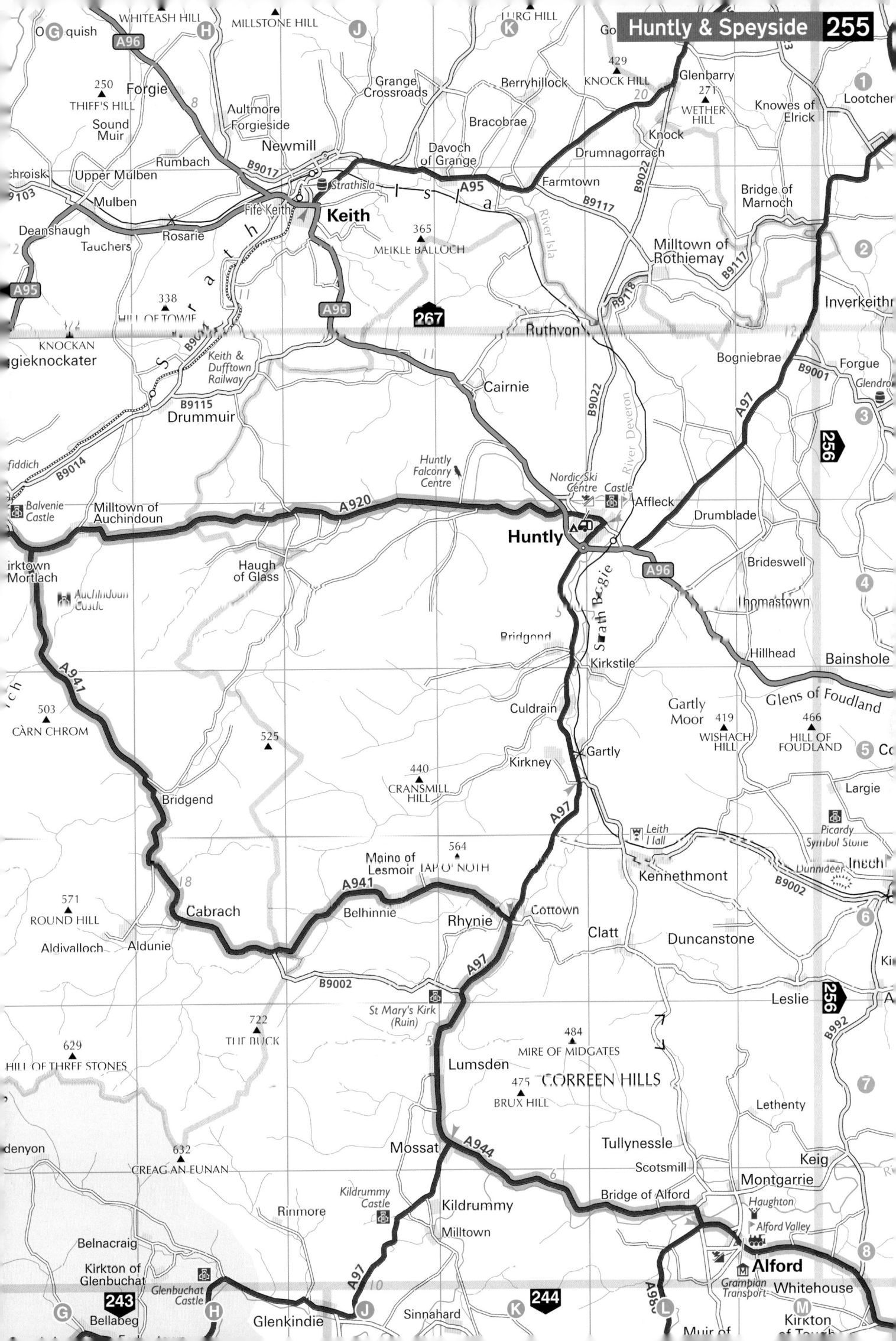

G quish
WHITEASH HILL
A96
H
MILLSTONE HILL
J
TURG HILL
K
Go
1
Lootcher

Forgie
250
THIFF'S HILL
Grange
Crossroads
Berryhillock
KNOCK HILL
20
429
Glenbarry
271
WETHER
HILL
Knowes of
Elrick

Sound
Muir
Aultmore
Forgieside
Bracobrae
Knock
Bridge of
Marnoch

chroisk
9103
Upper Mulben
Rumbach
Newmill
B9017
Davoch
of Grange
A95
Drumnagorrach
B9022
Milltown of
Rothiemay
2

Mulben
Strathisla
Isla
Farmtown
B9117

Deanshaugh
Tauchers
Rosarie
Fife Keith
Keith
River Isla
Inverkeithn

A95
gieknockater
KNOCKAN
338
HILL OF TOWIE
B9014
B904
Keith &
Dufftown
Railway
A96
267
365
MEIKLE BALLOCH
Ruthven
B9118
Bogniebrae
B9001
Forgue
Glendro
3
256

fiddich
B9115
Drummuir
Cairnie
B9022
River Deveron
A97

Balvenie
Castle
Milltown of
Auchindoun
A920
Huntly
Falconry
Centre
Nordic Ski
Centre
Castle
Affleck
Drumblade
4

irktown
Mortlach
14
Haugh
of Glass
Huntly
Strath Bogie
A96
Brideswell
Thomastown

Auchindoun
Castle
Bridgend
Kirkstile
Hillhead
Bainshole

A941
503
CÀRN CHROM
525
Culdrain
Gartly
Moor
419
WISHACH
HILL
466
HILL OF
FOUNDLAND
Glens of Foudland
5
Co

Bridgend
440
CRANSMILL
HILL
Kirkney
Gartly
A97
Largie

18
564
TAP O' NOTH
Leith
Hall
Picardy
Symbol Stone
Dunnideer
Insch

571
ROUND HILL
Cabrach
Maino of
Lesmoir
A941
Belhinnie
Rhynie
Cottown
Kennethmont
B9002
6

Aldivalloch
Aldunie
B9002
Clatt
Duncanstone
Leslie
256
A
B992

722
THE BUCK
St Mary's Kirk
(Ruin)
5
A97
484
MIRE OF MIDGATES

629
HILL OF THREE STONES
Lumsden
475
BRUX HILL
CORREEN HILLS
Lethenty
7

denyon
632
CREAG AN EUNAN
Mossat
A944
6
Tullynessle
Scotsmill
Keig
Montgarrie
Keig

Kildrummy
Castle
Kildrummy
Bridge of Alford
Haughton
Alford Valley

Belnacraig
Rinmore
Milltown
A97
Alford
Grampian
Transport
8

Kirkton of
Glenbuchat
G
243
Bellabeg
Glenbuchat
Castle
H
Glenkindie
J
Sinnahard
K
244
Muir
L
Kirkton
of Tough
M
Whitehouse
A980

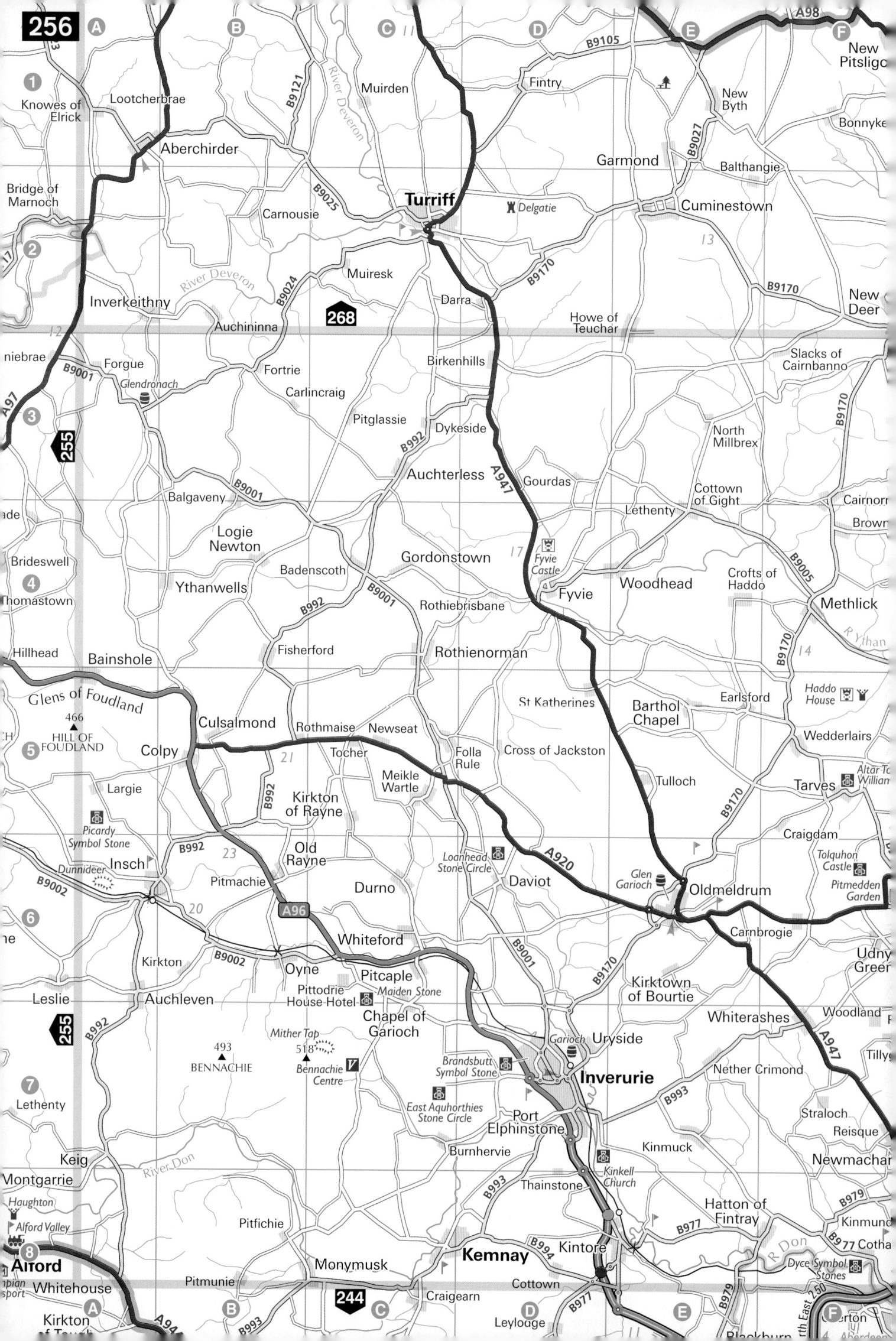

WAUGHTON HILL

Strichen

New Leeds

Crimond

Blackhill

North East 250

St Fergus

Scotstown Head

A90

Leys

Denhead

Backfolds

Kirktown

Fetterangus

Rora

Deer Abbey

Dunshillock

Aden

Mintlaw

Longside

Inverugie

Buchanhaven

Peterhead

Arbuthnot

Maud

Railway

B9029

Old Deer

Inverquhomery

A950

Peterhead Bay

Blackhill of Clackriach

Stuartfield

Hillhead of Cocklaw

Prison

Invernettie

Millbreck

Nether Kinmundy

Drymuir

Bulwark

Clola

Blackhill

Boddam

Nethermuir

Kinnadie

Stirling

Buchan Ness

Auchnagatt

Kinknockie

Lendrum Terrace

Inkhorn

Coldwells

Ardallie

Longhaven

A90

Arthrath

Mulltack

Bullers of Buchan

St Buchan

North Haven

Toll of Birness

Bogbrae

Slains

Cruden Bay

Birness

Chapel Hill

Bay of Cruden

Ythanbank

Artrochie

Whinnyfold

The Skares

Auchedly

Kinharrachie

Ellon

P+R

Ecclesmont

A920

B9005

Kirkton of Logie Buchan

Kirktown of Slains

Ilmedden

Logierieve

Collieston

Housieside

B9000

Forvie

Udny Station

B9000

Cultercullen

A90

Newburgh

Foveran

A975

North East 250

Delfrigs

B979

Causeyend

ngseat

Balmedie

Whitecairns

B999 B977

A90

Belhelvie

Balmedie

B977

Potterton

A90

245

B999

Black Dog

A92

| 0 | 1 | 2 | 3 | 4 | 5 miles |
| 0 | 1 2 3 4 | 5 6 | 7 | 8 kilometres |

A   B   C   D   E   F

Fladda-chùain

Rubha Hu

An Tairbeart
(Tarbert)

Lùb Score

Borneskitaig

Kilmuir

Kilva

Balgown

Loch nam Madadh
(Lochmaddy)

Lini

Totscore

Rubha Bhatairnis

Idrigill

Uig Bay

Ascrib
Islands

Loch Snizort

283
BEN
GEARY

Geary

Earlish

Trumpan

A87

Ardmore
Point

Gillen

Hallin

Waternish

DUNVEGAN
HEAD

Isay

Mingay

Stein

Lusta

Loch
Bay

214
BEN
DIUBAIG

Loch Greshornish

King

Claigan

Bay

Greshornish

22

Boreraig

Uig

327
BEINN BHREAC

B886

Flashader

Treaslane

A850

Loch
Pooltiel

Feriniquarrie

Glasphein

Upperglen

A850

Edinbane

Bernisdale

Oisgill
Bay

Glendale

Totaig

Milovaig

Lephin

B884

Colbost

Dunvegan

ISLE OF

Sk

Waterstein

Colbost Croft M

Dunvegan

A850

Skinidin

Giant Angus MacAskill

Kilmuir

271
CRUACHAN BEINN
A' CHEARCAILL

Neist
Point

Lonmore

Caroy River

265
BEN
AKETIL

SKYE

Moonen Bay

Roskhill

Duirnish

469
HEALAVAL
MORE

Roag

Orbost

Vatten

Ramasaig

Glen Ose

Hoe
Rape

Loch Caroy

A863

488
HEALAVAL
BHEAG

Harlosh

Ose

Hoe Point

368

Harlosh
Island

246

Colbost
Point

Dun
Beag

Bracadale

Tarner
Island

Coillore

The Little Minch

Loch Dunvegan

| 0 | 1 | 2 | 3 | 4 | 5 miles |
| 0 | 1 | 2 | 3 | 4 | 5 | 6 | 7 | 8 kilometres |

1

260

2

an Trodday

Kilmaluag

useum
nd Life

Flodigarry   Eilean Flodigarry

ta

542
MEAL NA
SUIREAMACH   Digg

Staffin
Bay   Staffin Island

3

Brogaig

464
BIODA
BUIDHE   Stenscholl   Staffin

Trotternish

Kilt Rock

Ellishader

Maligar

Marishader   Valtos

611
BEINN
EDRA   Garros   Rubha nam Brathairean

Culnaknock

4

Rubha
na Fearn

ry
an   Lealt

Ob
Chuaig

Iote

A855

Peinlich

608
CREAG A' LAIN

nisdal

5

C g

Callakille

451
BEINN A' SGÀ

RONA

Old Man
719 of Storr

Lonbain

mesnal   River Romesdal

THE
STORR

Eilean
Tigh

6

eyre

Kensaleyre

River Haultin

Loch
Cleathan

248

North Coast 500

16

Eilean
Fladday

Loch
Fada

B8036   Carbost   Borve

Manish
Point   Loch
Arnish   Torran

hader   Drumuie

A855   Arnish

7

Applecross

Glengrasco

312

Brochel

Applecross Bay

Ap

Torvaig

Portree

RAASAY

Milltown

Isle of Skye Candle

i

Camusteel

417
BEINN NA
GRÉINE   Penifiler   412
BEN
TIANAVAIG

Aird Dhubh

8

Ca

C

Glenmore

Glenvarragill

444

247   DÙN CAAN

Tianavaig
Bay

SOUND OF RAASAY

INNER SOUND

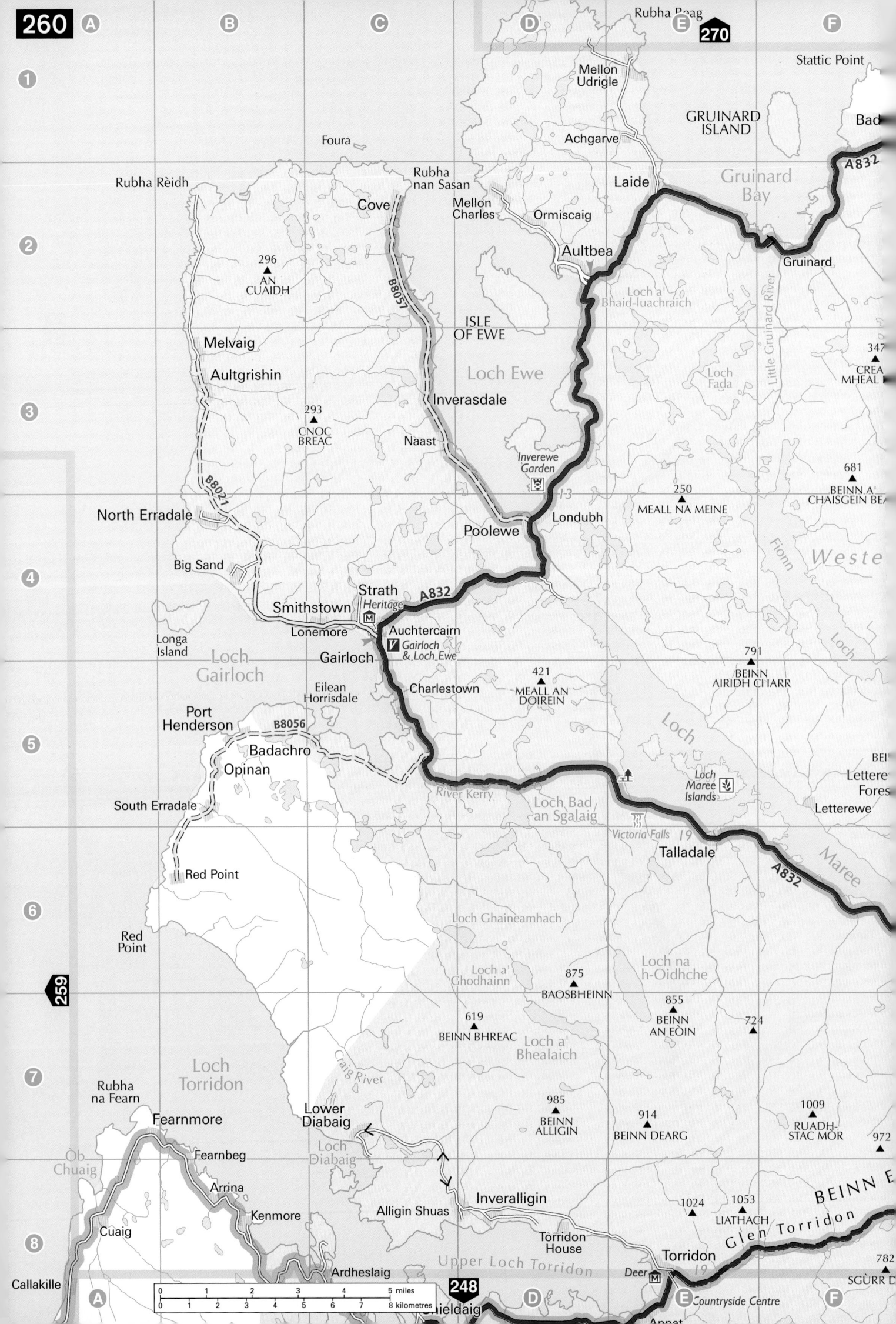

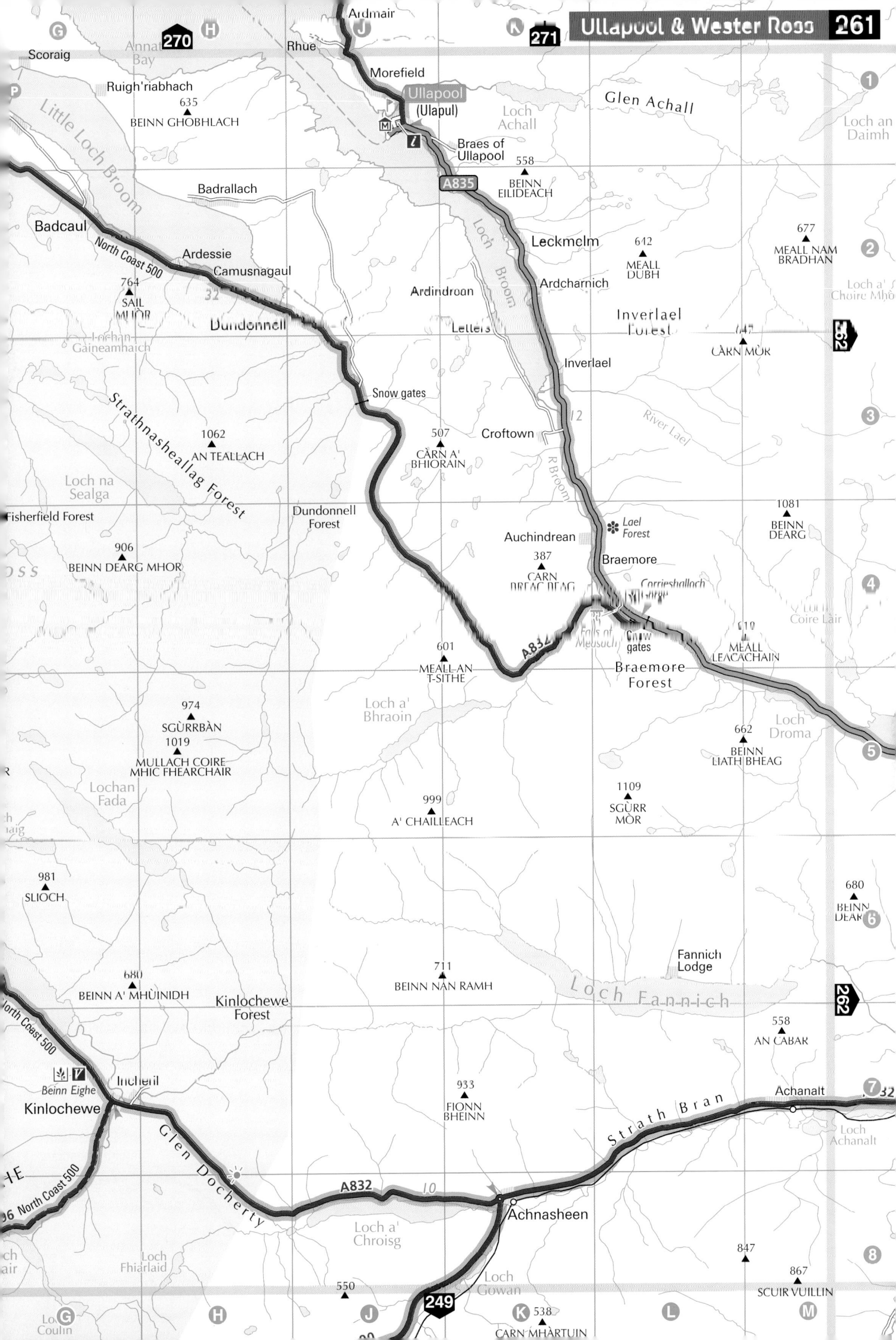

G H J K 271 1

270

Scoraig

Annat Bay

Rhue

Ardmair

Morefield

Ullapool
(Ulapul)

Braes of
Ullapool

A835

Glen Achall

Loch
Achall

Loch an
Daimh

Ruigh'riabhach

635

BEINN GHOBHLACH

Badrallach

558

BEINN
EILIDEACH

677

MEALL NAM
BRADHAN

2

Badcaul

North Coast 500

Ardessie

Camusnagaul

764

SAIL
MHÒR

Dundonnell

32

Lochan
Gaineamhaich

Leckmelm

Ardcharnich

642

MEALL
DUBH

Inverlael
Forest

647

CÀRN MÒR

262

Loch a'
Choire Mhò

Little Loch Broom

Ardindrean

Letters

Inverlael

Loch Broom

12

River Lael

3

Strathnasheallag Forest

Fisherfield Forest

1062

AN TEALLACH

Dundonnell
Forest

Snow gates

507

CÀRN A'
BHIORAIN

Croftown

R Broom

Lael
Forest

1081

BEINN
DEARG

ROSS

Loch na
Sealga

906

BEINN DEARG MHOR

Auchindrean

387

CARN
BREAC BEAG

Braemore

Corrieshalloch
Gorge

Falls of
Measach

Snow
gates

MEALL
LEACACHAIN

4

Loch
Coire Làir

601

MEALL AN
T-SITHE

A832

Braemore
Forest

619

974

SGÙRRBÀN

1019

MULLACH COIRE
MHIC FHEARCHAIR

Lochan
Fada

Loch a'
Bhraoin

662

BEINN
LIATH BHEAG

Loch
Droma

5

999

A' CHAILLEACH

1109

SGÙRR
MÒR

981

SLIOCH

680

BEINN
DEAR

6

h
Coulin

680

BEINN A' MHÙINIDH

Kinlochewe
Forest

711

BEINN NAN RAMH

Fannich
Lodge

Loch Fannich

262

North Coast 500

Beinn Eighe

V

Incheril

Kinlochewe

933

FIONN
BHEINN

558

AN CABAR

96 North Coast 500

Glen Docherty

A832

1.0

Strath Bran

Achanalt

32

7

Loch
Achanalt

E

847

Achnasheen

SE

Loch a'
Chroisg

Loch
Fhiarlaid

550

249

Loch
Gowan

538

CARN MHÀRTUIN

867

SCUIR VUILLIN

8

G H J K L M

Loch
Coulin

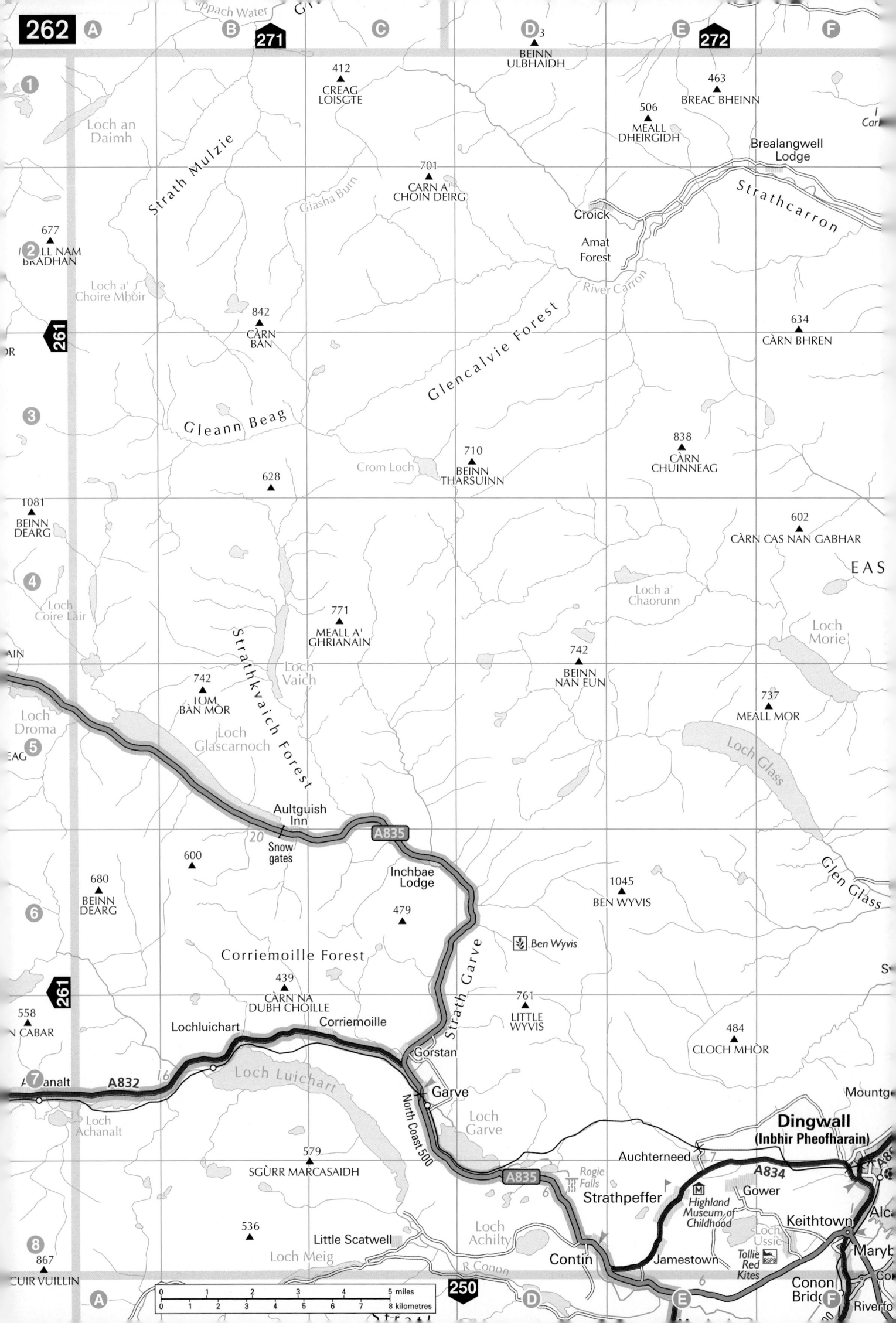

A B 271 C D 3 E 272 F

1

Loch an Daimh

Loch a' Choire Mhòir

Strath Mulzie

▲ 412
CREAG
LOISGTE

▲ BEINN
ULBHAIDH

▲ 463
BREAC BHEINN

▲ 506
MEALL
DHEIRGIDH

Brealangwell
Lodge

Strathcarron

2
▲ 677
LL NAM
BRADHAN

Giasha Burn

▲ 701
CARN A'
CHOIN DEIRG

Croick

Amat
Forest

River Carron

261

▲ 842
CÀRN
BÀN

Gleann Beag

Glencalvie Forest

▲ 634
CÀRN BHREN

3

▲ 1081
BEINN
DEARG

▲ 628

Crom Loch

▲ 710
BEINN
THARSUINN

▲ 838
CÀRN
CHUINNEAG

4

Loch
Coire Làir

▲ 771
MEALL A'
GHRIANAIN

Loch
Vaich

Loch a'
Chaorunn

▲ 602
CÀRN CAS NAN GABHAR

EAS

Loch
Morie

AIN

Strathkvaich Forest

▲ 742
BEINN
NAN EUN

5

Loch
Droma

▲ 742
TOM
BÀN MOR

Loch
Glascarnoch

▲ 737
MEALL MOR

Loch Glass

EAG

Aultguish
Inn

20

Snow
gates

A835

Inchbae
Lodge

Glen Glass

6

▲ 680
BEINN
DEARG

▲ 600

Corriemoille Forest

▲ 479

▲ 1045
BEN WYVIS

261

Ben Wyvis

▲ 439
CÀRN NA
DUBH CHOILLE

Strath Garve

7

▲ 558
N CABAR

analt

A832

16

Lochluichart

Corriemoille

Loch Luichart

Gorstan

▲ 761
LITTLE
WYVIS

▲ 484
CLOCH MHÒR

Loch
Achanalt

North Coast 500

Garve

Loch
Garve

Dingwall
(Inbhir Pheofharain)

Auchterneed

7

A834

8
▲ 867
CUIR VUILLIN

▲ 536

Little Scatwell

Loch Meig

▲ 579
SGÙRR MARCASAIDH

R Conon

Loch
Achilty

Rogie
Falls

Strathpeffer

6

Highland
Museum of
Childhood

Gower

Tollie
Red
Kites

Keithtown

Jamestown

Conon
Bridge

Maryb

Alc

Mountg

Riverfo

Con

0 1 2 3 4 5 miles
0 1 2 3 4 5 6 7 8 kilometres

A 250 D E F

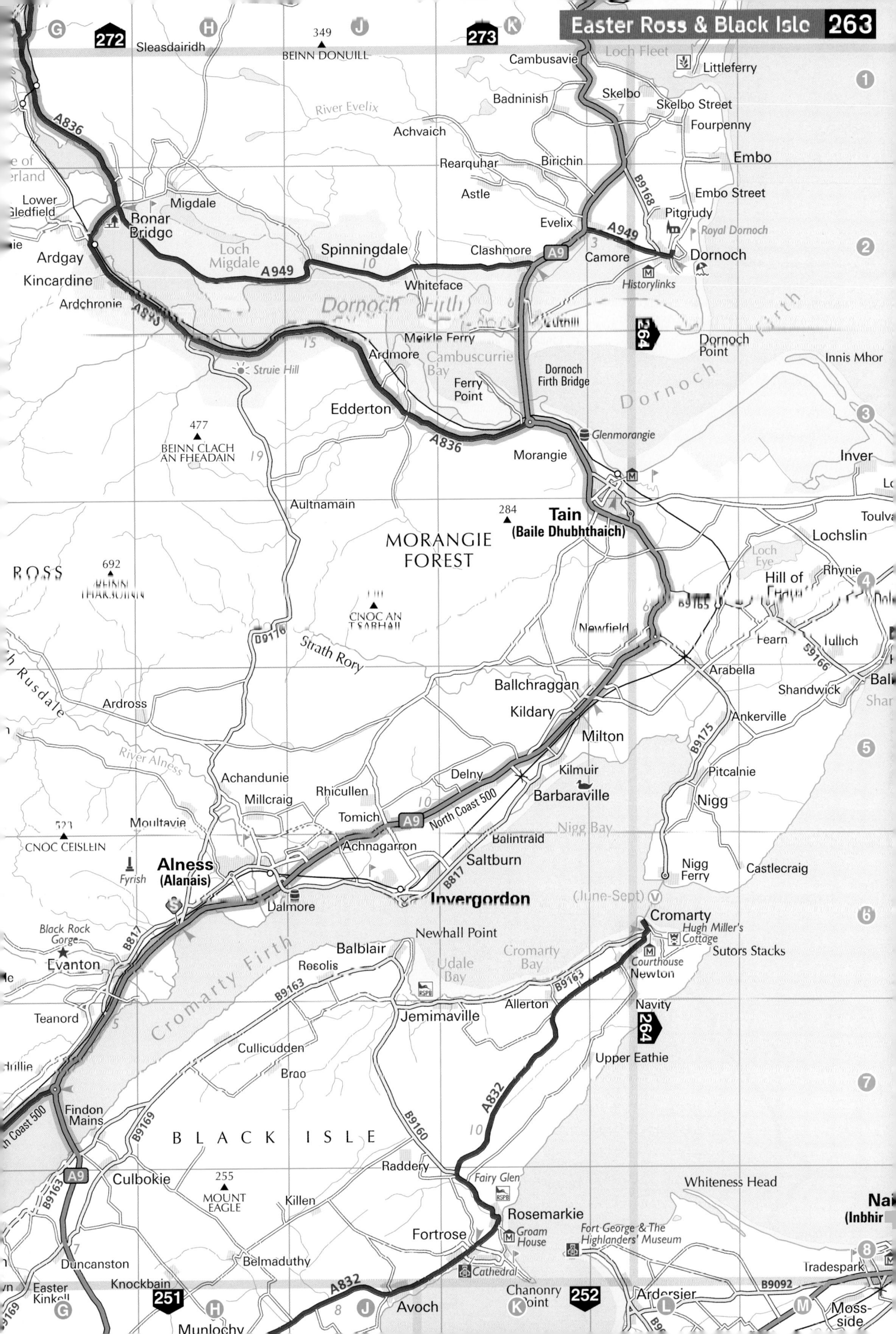

G **272** Sleasdairidh

349 ▲ J
BEINN DONUILL

273 K

Cambusavie

Loch Fleet

Littleferry

River Evelix

Badninish

Skelbo

Skelbo Street

Fourpenny

A836

Achvaich

Birichin

B9168

Embo

Rearquhar

Embo Street

Astle

Pitgrudy

Royal Dornoch

Lower Gledfield

Migdale

Evelix

A949

Camore

Dornoch

Bonar Bridge

Loch Migdale

A949

Spinningdale

10

Clashmore

A9

3

Historylinks

Ardgay

Whiteface

Kincardine

264

Dornoch Point

Innis Mhor

Ardchronie

A836

Dornoch Firth

Meikle Ferry

Cambuscurrie Bay

Dornoch Firth

Struie Hill

Ardmore

Ferry Point

Dornoch Firth Bridge

15

Edderton

A836

Glenmorangie

Inver

477 ▲
BEINN CLACH AN FHEADAIN

Morangie

19

Aultnamain

284 ▲

Tain
(Baile Dhubhthaich)

Loch Eye

Hill of Fearn

MORANGIE FOREST

Lochslin

B9116

Rhynie

R O S S

692 ▲
BEINN THARSUINN

4

CNOC AN T-SABHAIL

B9165

Fearn

Iullich

B9166

Strath Rory

Newfield

Arabella

Bal

Shandwick

Shar

Ardross

Ballchraggan

Ankerville

Rusdale

Kildary

B9175

Milton

River Alness

Achandunie

Delny

Kilmuir

Pitcalnie

521 ▲
CNOC CEISLEIN

Millcraig

Rhicullen

A9

Barbaraville

Nigg

Moultavie

Tomich

North Coast 500

10

Nigg Bay

Achnagarron

Balintraid

Nigg Ferry

Castlecraig

Alness
(Alanais)

Saltburn

B817

Fyrish

Dalmore

Invergordon

(June-Sept) V

Black Rock Gorge

Newhall Point

Cromarty

Hugh Miller's Cottage

Sutors Stacks

Evanton

B817

Balblair

Resolis

Cromarty Bay

Courthouse

Newton

Teanord

B9163

Udale Bay

RSPB

Allerton

B9163

Navity

Cullicudden

Cromarty Firth

Jemimaville

264

Brae

Upper Eathie

Coast 500

Findon Mains

B9169

B L A C K   I S L E

A832

A9

B9160

Raddery

10

B9163

Culbokie

255 ▲
MOUNT EAGLE

Killen

Fairy Glen

Whiteness Head

Duncanston

RSPB

Rosemarkie

Nai
(Inbhir

Easter Kinkell

Fortrose

Groam House

Fort George & The Highlanders' Museum

Tradespark

Knockbain

Belmaduthy

A832

Cathedral

Chanonry Point

252

Ardersier

B9092

Moss-side

251

G

H

Munlochy

8

J

Avoch

K

L

M

8

G   H   J   K   L

1

2

3

4

5

Fisheries &
Community

Branderburgh

Stotfield   **Lossiemouth**

Sealown

B9040

Burghead
Well   Hopeman   Burnside

Burghead   Cummingston   Duffus   St Peter's Kirk
& Parish Cross

B9012

B9013   Roseisle

B9012   Duffus
Castle

Loch
Spynie

6

6

A941

B9135

Spynie
Palace

B9102

Stonewells

Lochill

Kin
on

Burghead Bay   College of
Roseisle   Quarrywood   Viewfield

Findhorn   Hempriggs   Calcots

Innesmill

B9029   Bishopmill   Elgin

Urquhart

Findhorn
Bay   Kinloss   Newton   H   Lhanbryde

Coltfield   A96   Glen Moray   New Elgin

7

The
Lochs

9

Kincorth
House   Alves   Linkwood

Sueno's Stone   266   12   Mosstodloc

Grange Hall   Kilbuiack   A96   Croft
of Dippl

terow   **Forres**   Muir of
Miltonduff   Clackmarras

B9103

Longmorn

Pluscarden   Orbliston

8

Dallas Dhu
Distillery   Barnhill   Thomshill

Caliter   Fogwatt   Millbuies

Rafford   Inchberry

253   B9010   Kellas   Shougle   Glen

G   H   J   K   L   M   262

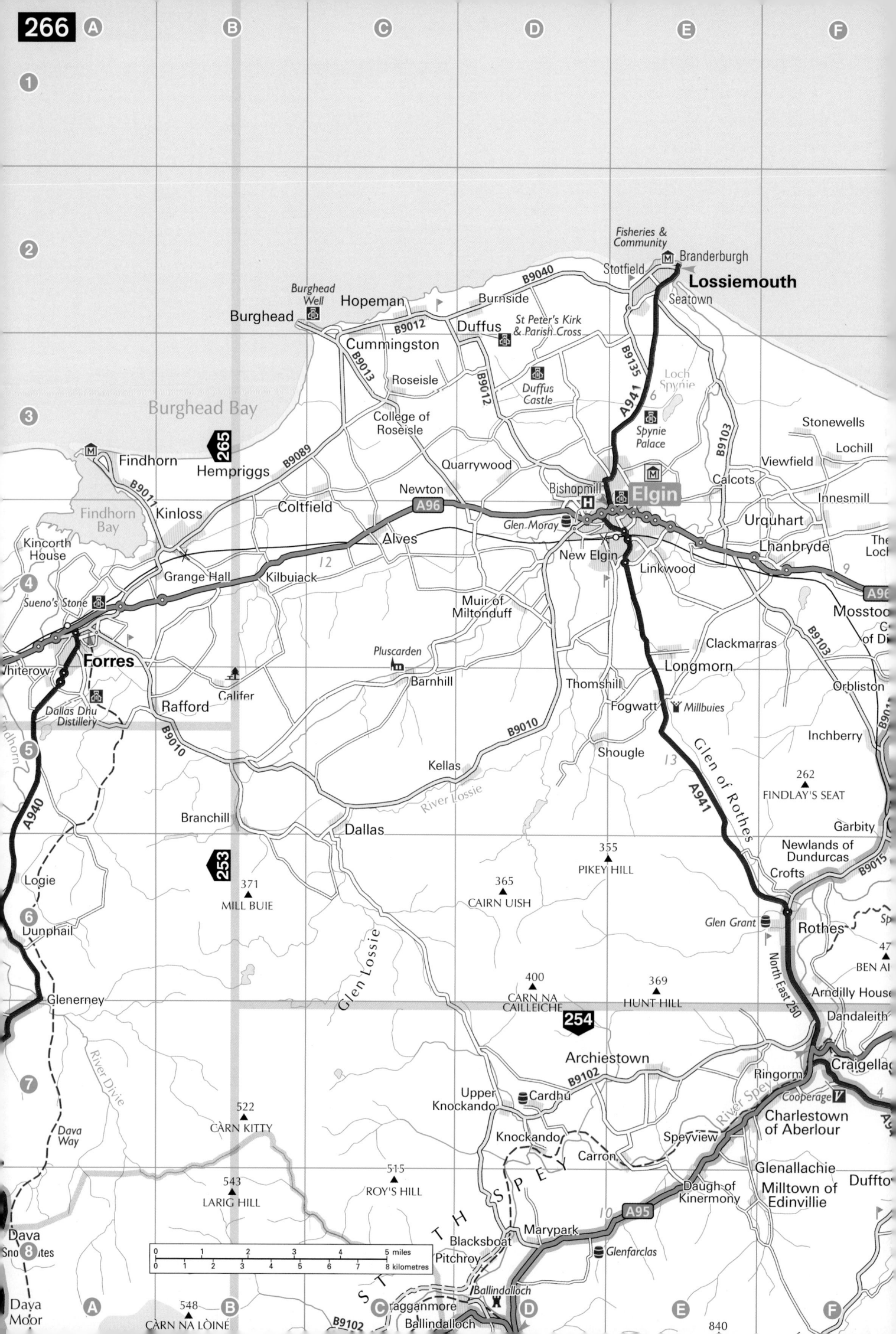

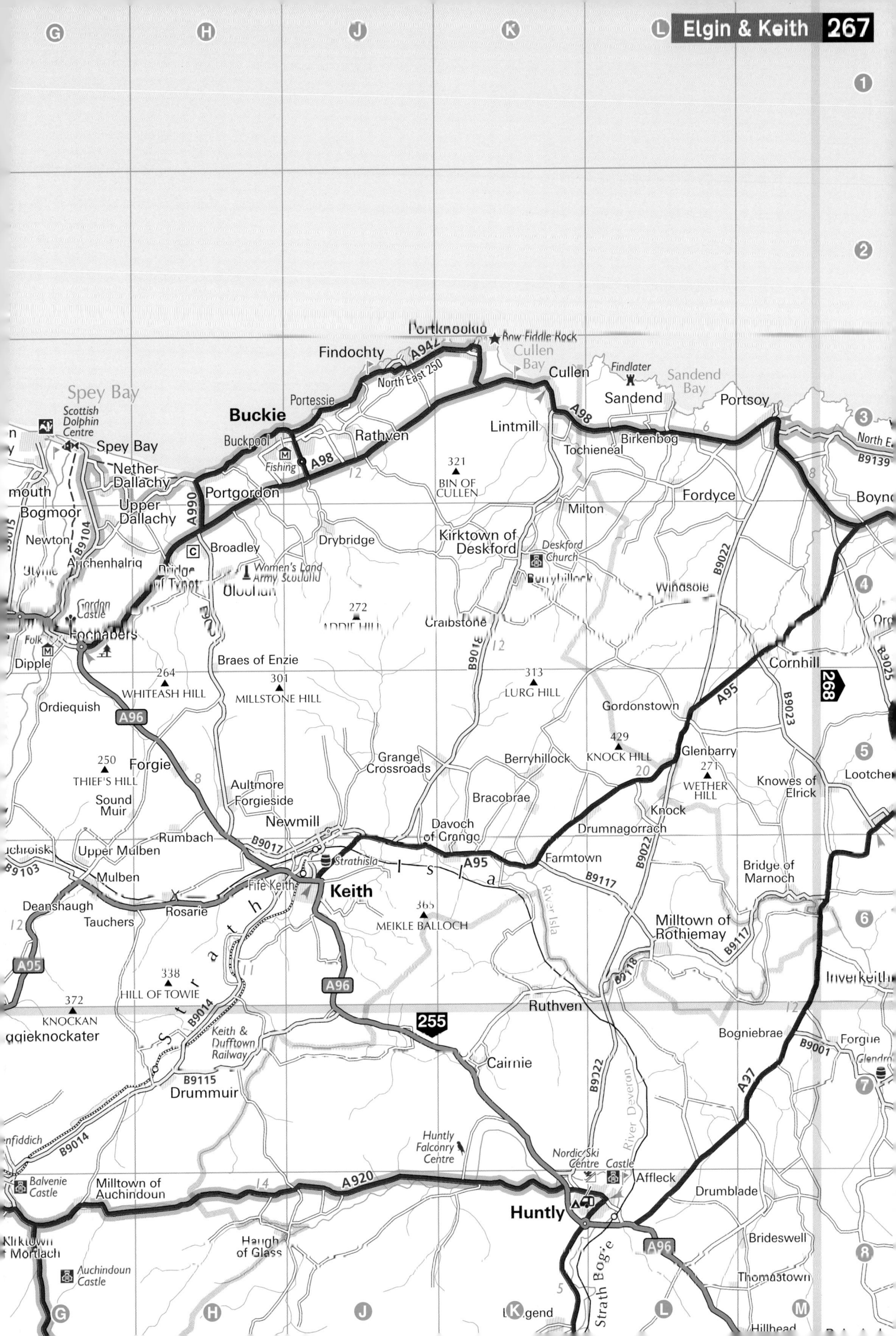

1

2

Portknockie
★ Bow Fiddle Rock
Findochty   A942   Cullen Bay
Spey Bay   North East 250   Cullen
Scottish Dolphin Centre   Portessie   Findlater   Sandend   Sandend Bay
Spey Bay   Buckie   Sandend   Portsoy   3
Nether Dallachy   Buckpool   Rathven   A98   Lintmill   6   North E
mouth   Fishing   A98   12   Tochieneal   Birkenbog   B9139
Bogmoor   Newton   A990   Portgordon   321 ▲ BIN OF CULLEN   Milton   Fordyce   Boynd
Glyne   Auchenhalrig   Broadley   Drybridge   Kirktown of Deskford   Deskford Church   4
C   Bridge of Tynet   Oldhall   Women's Land Army Scotland   Berryhillock   Winsole   B9022
Gordon Castle   272 ▲ ADDIE HILL   Craibstone   12   Cornhill   B9025
Folk   Fochabers   Braes of Enzie   B9018   313 ▲ LURG HILL   Gordonstown   A95   B9023   268
Dipple   264 ▲ WHITEASH HILL   301 ▲ MILLSTONE HILL   429 ▲ KNOCK HILL   Glenbarry   5
Ordiequish   A96   Grange Crossroads   Berryhillock   20   271 ▲ WETHER HILL   Knowes of Elrick   Lootche
250 ▲ Forgie   THIEF'S HILL   Aultmore Forgieside   Bracobrae   Knock   B9022   Bridge of Marnoch
Sound Muir   Newmill   Davoch of Grange   Drumnagorrach   6
chroisk   Upper Mulben   Rumbach   B9017   Strathisla   I s l a   A95   Farmtown   B9117   Milltown of Rothiemay
B9103   Mulben   Fife Keith   365 ▲ MEIKLE BALLOCH   River Isla   B9117   Inverkeith
Deanshaugh   Rosarie   Keith   B9118
12   A05   Tauchers   338 ▲ HILL OF TOWIE   Ruthven   12   Bogniebrae   B9001   Forgue   7
372 ▲ KNOCKAN   B9014   255   A37   Glendr
gieknockater   Keith & Dufftown Railway   Cairnie   B9922   River Deveron
B9115   Drummuir   Huntly Falconry Centre   Nordic Ski Centre   Castle   Affleck   Drumblade
nfiddich   B9014   Balvenie Castle   Milltown of Auchindoun   14   A920   Huntly   A96   Brideswell   8
Kirktown Mortlach   Auchindoun Castle   Haugh of Glass   Strath Bogie   5   A96   Thomastown
Hillhead

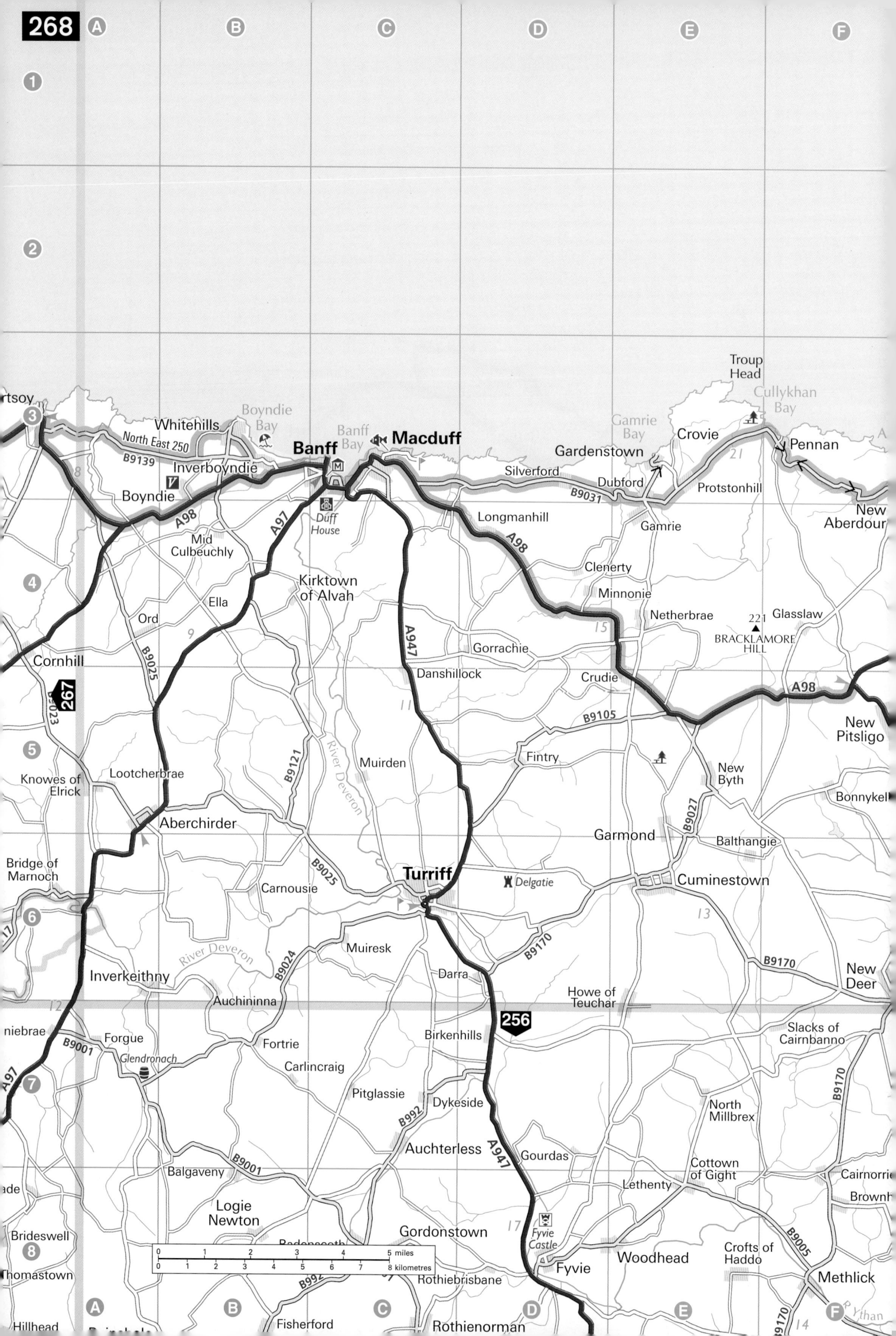

A   B   C   D   E   F

1

2

Troup
Head

3   tsoy   Whitehills   Boyndie   Banff   Macduff   Cullykhan
Bay
North East 250   Bay   Gardenstown   Crovie   Pennan
B9139   Inverboyndie   Silverford   21
Boyndie   Dubford   Protstonhill   New
Aberdour
A98   A97   Duff   Longmanhill   Gamrie
House   A98
Mid   Clenerty
Culbeuchly   Kirktown   Minnonie
of Alvah   221   Glasslaw
4   Ord   Ella   Netherbrae   BRACKLAMORE
HILL
Gorrachie   Crudie
Cornhill   Danshillock   15   New
267   A947   B9105   Pitsligo
5   Knowes of   Lootcherbrae   Muirden   Fintry   New
Elrick   Byth   Bonnykel
River Deveron   Garmond   B9027   Balthangie
Aberchirder   Cuminestown
Bridge of   Delgatie
Marnoch   Carnousie   Turriff   13
6   B9025   B9170
River Deveron   Muiresk   B9170   New
Inverkeithny   Darra   Deer
Auchininna   Howe of
12   Teuchar   Slacks of
niebrae   Forgue   Fortrie   Birkenhills   256   Cairnbanno
B9001   Carlincraig   North
7   Glendronach   Pitglassie   Dykeside   Millbrex
B992   Cottown
Balgaveny   B9001   Auchterless   A947   Gourdas   of Gight   Cairnorri
Lethenty   Brownh
Logie   B9005
Newton   17   Woodhead   Crofts of
8   Brideswell   Fyvie   Haddo
Castle   Methlick
homastown   B992   Fyvie
Fisherford   Rothiebrisbane   Rythan
Hillhead   Rothienorman   B9170   14

A   B   C   D   E   F

0   1   2   3   4   5 miles
0   1   2   3   4   5   6   7   8 kilometres

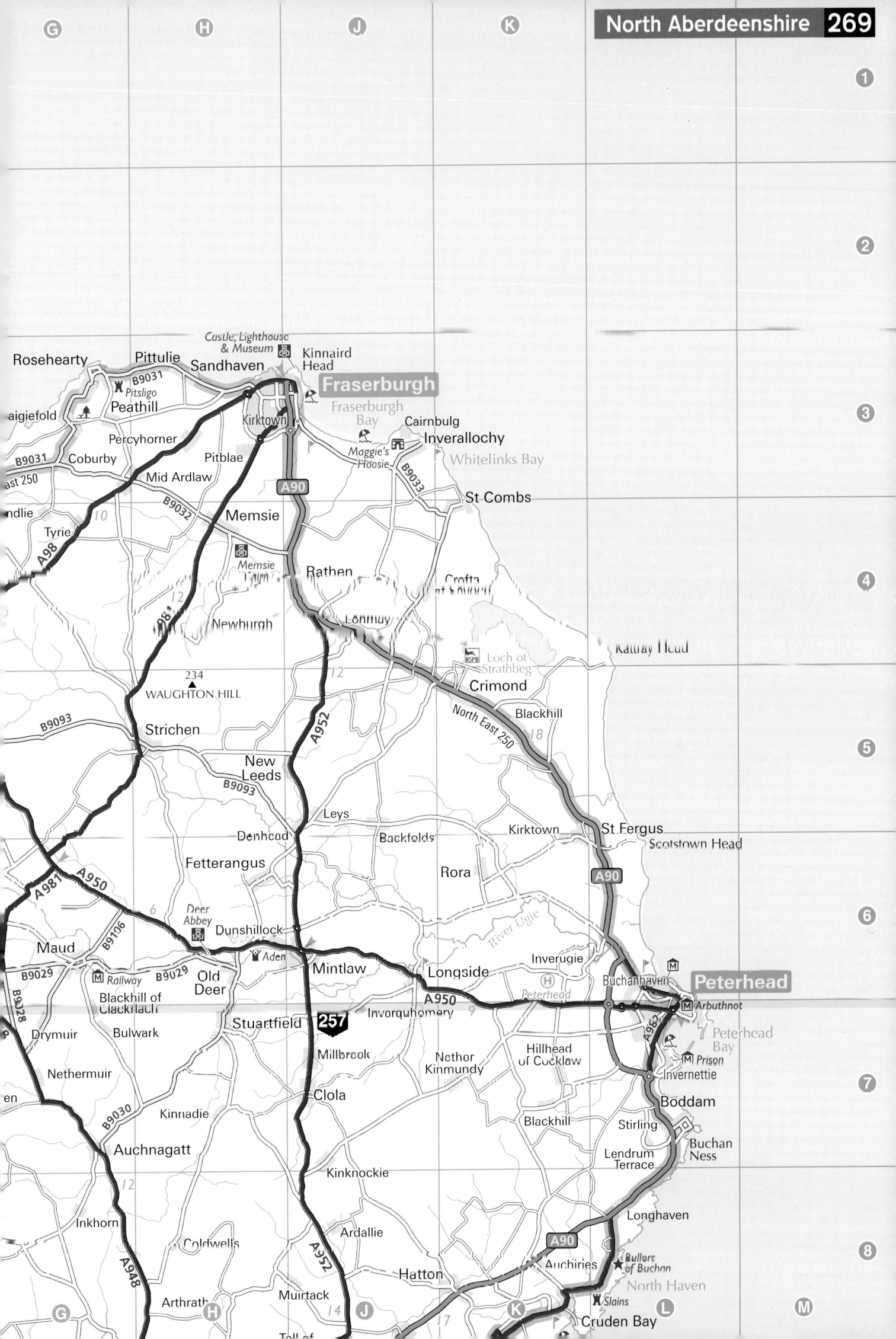

Roschearty
Pittulie
Sandhaven
Castle, Lighthouse & Museum
Kinnaird Head
Fraserburgh
Fraserburgh Bay
Cairnbulg
Inverallochy
Whitelinks Bay
B9031
Pitsligo
Peathill
aigiefold
Percyhorner
Kirktown
Maggie's Hoosie
B9033
St Combs
B9031
Coburby
Pitblae
Mid Ardlaw
B9032
Memsie
A90
East 250
ndlie
Tyrie
A98
Memsie Town
Rathen
Crofts
B9081
Newburgh
Lonmay
RSPB
Loch of Strathbeg
Rattray Head
234
WAUGHTON HILL
12
Crimond
Blackhill
B9093
Strichen
A952
North East 250
18
New Leeds
B9093
Leys
Kirktown
St Fergus
Scotstown Head
A90
Denhead
Backfolds
Fetterangus
Rora
A981
A950
River Ugie
Deer Abbey
Dunshillock
Inverugie
Buchanhaven
Peterhead
Maud
B9106
Aden
Mintlaw
Longside
Peterhead
Arbuthnot
B9029
Railway
B9029
Old Deer
A950
Peterhead Bay
Blackhill of Clackriach
Invorquhomery
Hillhead of Cocklaw
Prison
Invernettie
B9028
Stuartfield
257
Millbrook
Nether Kinmundy
Drymuir
Bulwark
Clola
Blackhill
Stirling
Boddam
Nethermuir
Kinnadie
Buchan Ness
B9030
Lendrum Terrace
Auchnagatt
12
Kinknockie
Longhaven
Inkhorn
Coldwells
Ardallie
A90
Bullers of Buchan
A948
Auchiries
North Haven
Arthrath
Muirtack
14
Hatton
Slains
Cruden Bay

G   H   J   K   L   M

1 2 3 4 5 6 7 8

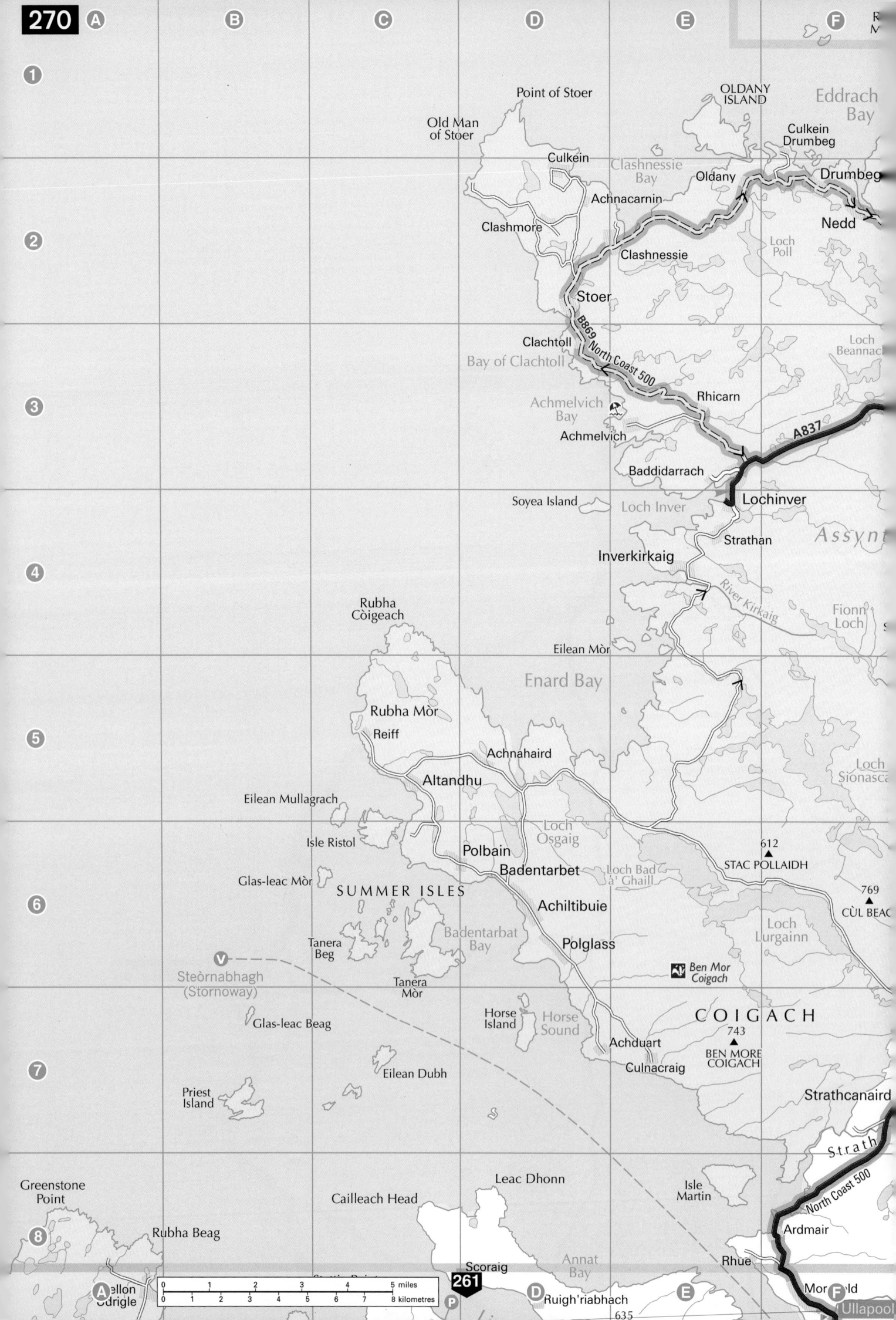

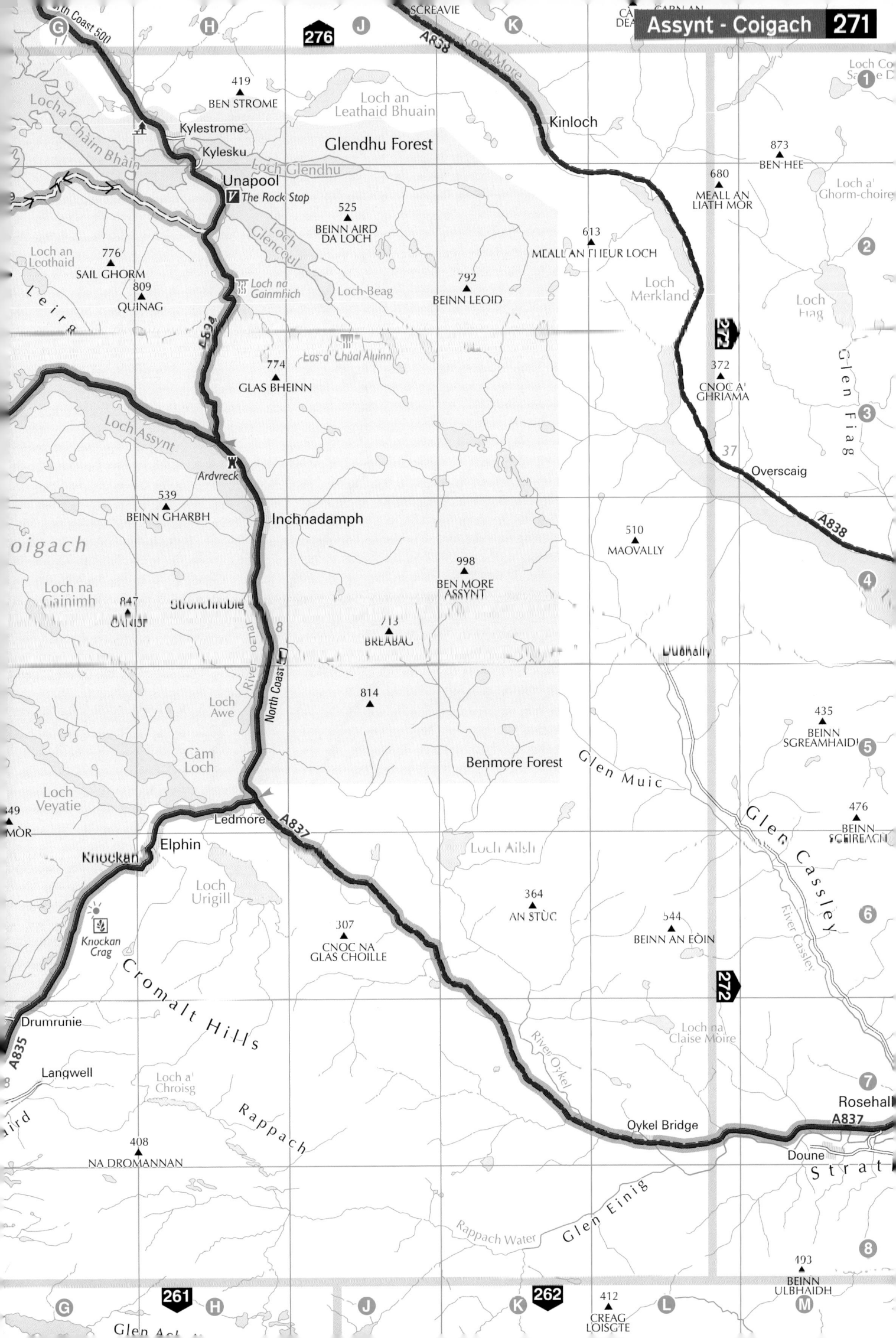

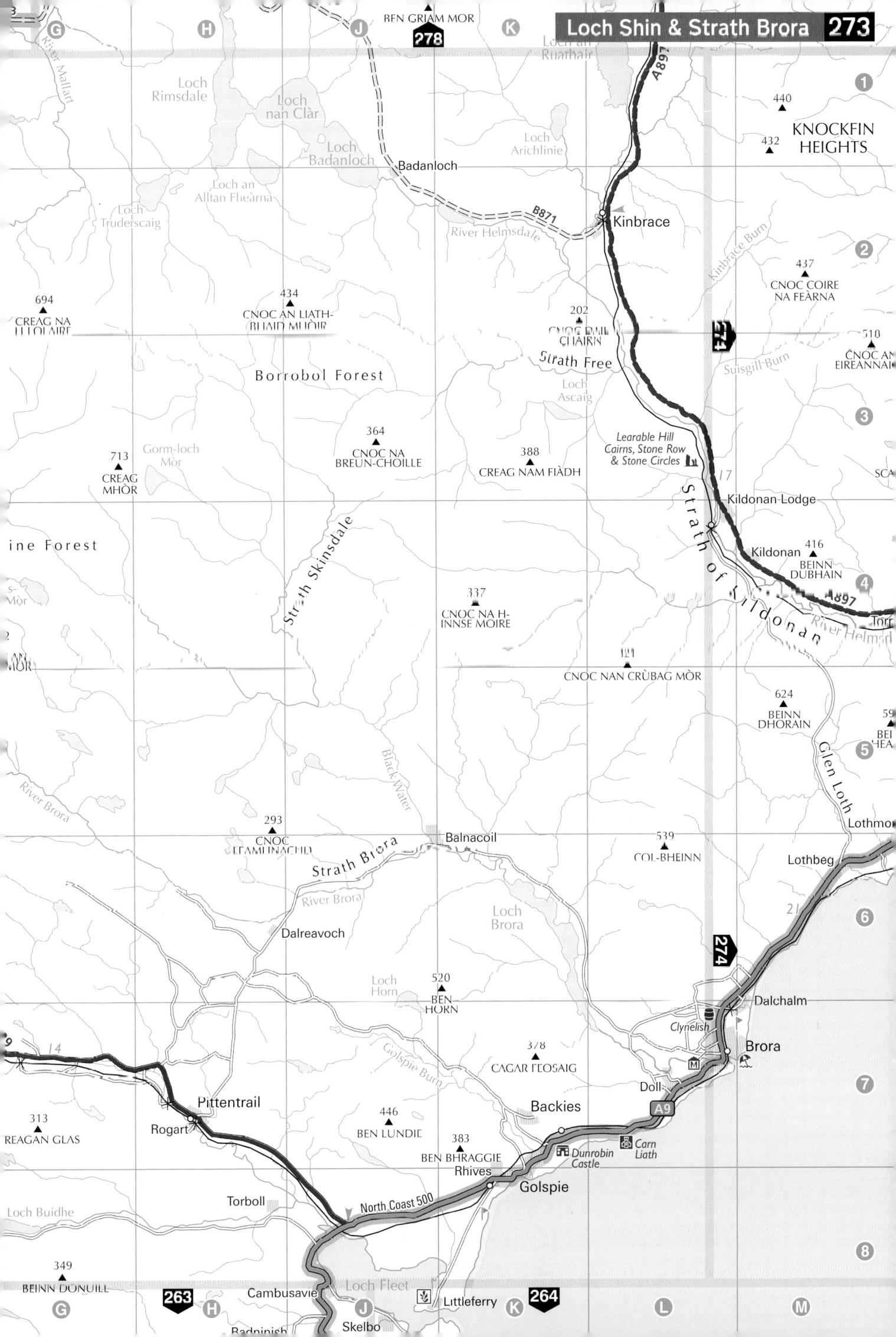

G   H   J   K

BEN GRIAM MOR

278

KNOCKFIN HEIGHTS

1

River Mallart

Loch Rimsdale

Loch nan Clàr

Loch Badanloch

Badanloch

Loch an Alltan Fheàrna

Loch Truderscaig

Loch Arichlinie

A897

440

432

Kinbrace Burn

2

B871

River Helmsdale

Kinbrace

437

CNOC COIRE NA FEÀRNA

694
CREAG NA
I I I OLAIRE

434
CNOC AN LIATH-
BHAID MHÒIR

Borrobol Forest

202
CNOC DAIL
CHAIRN

Strath Free

510
CNOC AN
EIREANNAI

713
CREAG
MHÒR

Gorm-loch
Mòr

364
CNOC NA
BREUN-CHOILLE

388
CREAG NAM FIÀDH

Loch
Ascaig

Suisgill Burn

SC

3

ine Forest

Strath Skinsdale

Learable Hill
Cairns, Stone Row
& Stone Circles

17

Strath of Kildonan

Kildonan-Lodge

Kildonan

416
BEINN
DUBHAIN

A897

4

s-
Mòr

337
CNOC NA H-
INNSE MOIRE

River Helm

Torr

2

624
BEINN
DHORAIN

59
BEI
HEA

CNOC NAN CRÙBAG MÒR

Glen Loth

5

River Brora

Black Water

Lothmo

293
CNOC
CEANN NACHD

539
COL-BHEINN

Lothbeg

Balnacoil

Strath Brora

River Brora

Loch
Brora

21

274

6

Dalreavoch

Loch
Horn

520
BEN
HORN

Dalchalm

Clynelish

Brora

9   14

Golspie Burn

3/8
CAGAR FEOSAIG

M

Doll

7

313
REAGAN GLAS

Pittentrail

Rogart

446
BEN LUNDIE

Backies

A9

383
BEN BHRAGGIE

Dunrobin
Castle

Carn
Liath

Torboll

Rhives

North Coast 500

Golspie

8

349
BEINN DONUILL

263

Loch Buidhe

Cambusavie

264

Loch Fleet

Littleferry

Skelbo

G   H   J   K   L   M

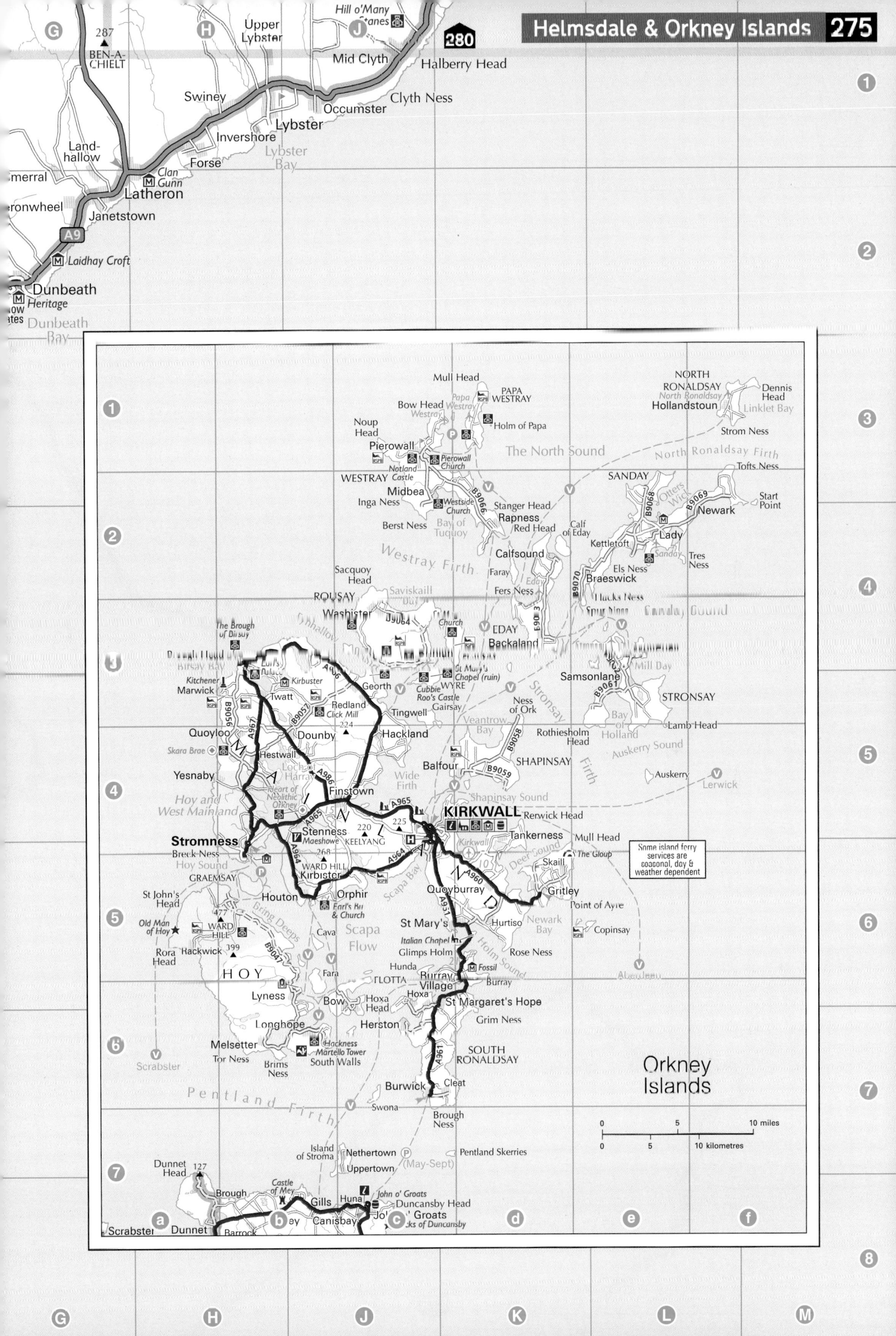

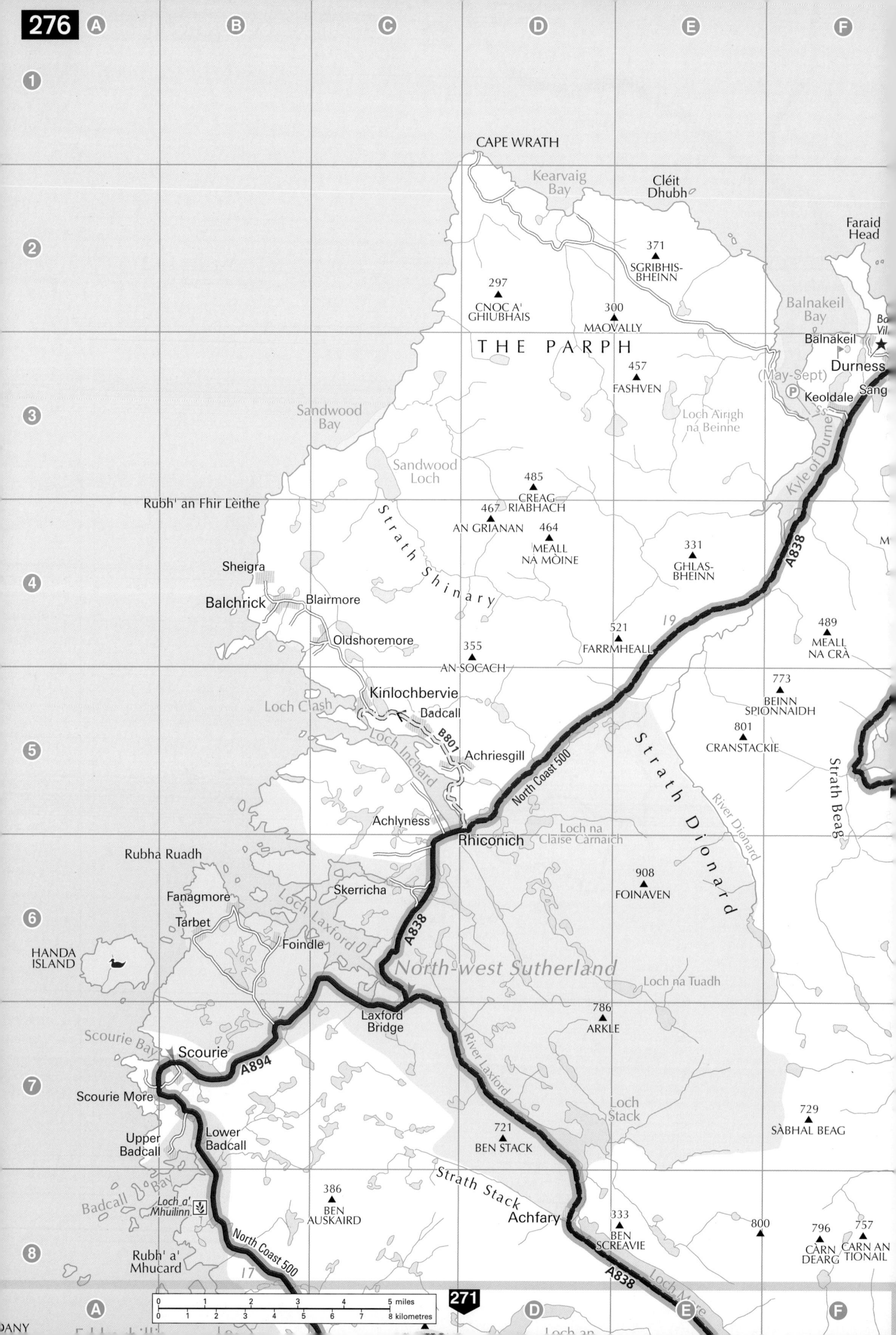

A B C D E F

1
2
3
4
5
6
7
8

CAPE WRATH

Kearvaig
Bay

Cléit
Dhubh ▲

Faraid
Head

371 ▲
SGRIBHIS-
BHEINN

Balnakeil
Bay

297 ▲
CNOC A'
GHIUBHAIS

300 ▲
MAOVALLY

T H E   P A R P H

Ba
Vil

Balnakeil
★

Durness

(May-Sept)

P Keoldale Sang

457 ▲
FASHVEN

Loch Àirigh
na Beinne

Sandwood
Bay

Sandwood
Loch

485 ▲
CREAG
RIABHACH

A838

331 ▲
GHLAS-
BHEINN

Rubh' an Fhir Lèithe

467 ▲
AN GRIANAN

464 ▲
MEALL
NA MÒINE

S t r a t h   S h i n a r y

19

489 ▲
MEALL
NA CRÀ

Sheigra

521 ▲
FARRMHEALL

773 ▲
BEINN
SPIONNAIDH

Balchrick

Blairmore

355 ▲
AN-SOCACH

801 ▲
CRANSTACKIE

Strath Beag

Oldshoremore

North Coast 500

S t r a t h   D i o n a r d

River Dionard

Kinlochbervie

Loch Clash

Badcall

B801

Achriesgill

Loch Inchard

Achlyness

Rhiconich

Loch na
Claise Càrnaich

908 ▲
FOINAVEN

Rubha Ruadh

Skerricha

A838

North-west Sutherland

Loch na Tuadh

Fanagmore

Tarbet

Foindle

Loch Laxford

HANDA
ISLAND

786 ▲
ARKLE

7

Laxford
Bridge

River Laxford

Scourie Bay

Scourie

A894

Loch
Stack

729 ▲
SÀBHAL BEAG

Scourie More

Upper
Badcall

Lower
Badcall

721 ▲
BEN STACK

Strath Stack

Achfary

333 ▲
BEN
SCREAVIE

800 ▲

796 ▲
CARN
DEARG

757 ▲
CARN AN
TIONAIL

386 ▲
BEN
AUSKAIRD

Badcall
Bay

Loch a'
Mhuilinn

North Coast 500

17

Rubh' a'
Mhucard

A838

Loch M

DANY

A B

D E F

0 1 2 3 4 5 miles
0 1 2 3 4 5 6 7 8 kilometres

Loch an

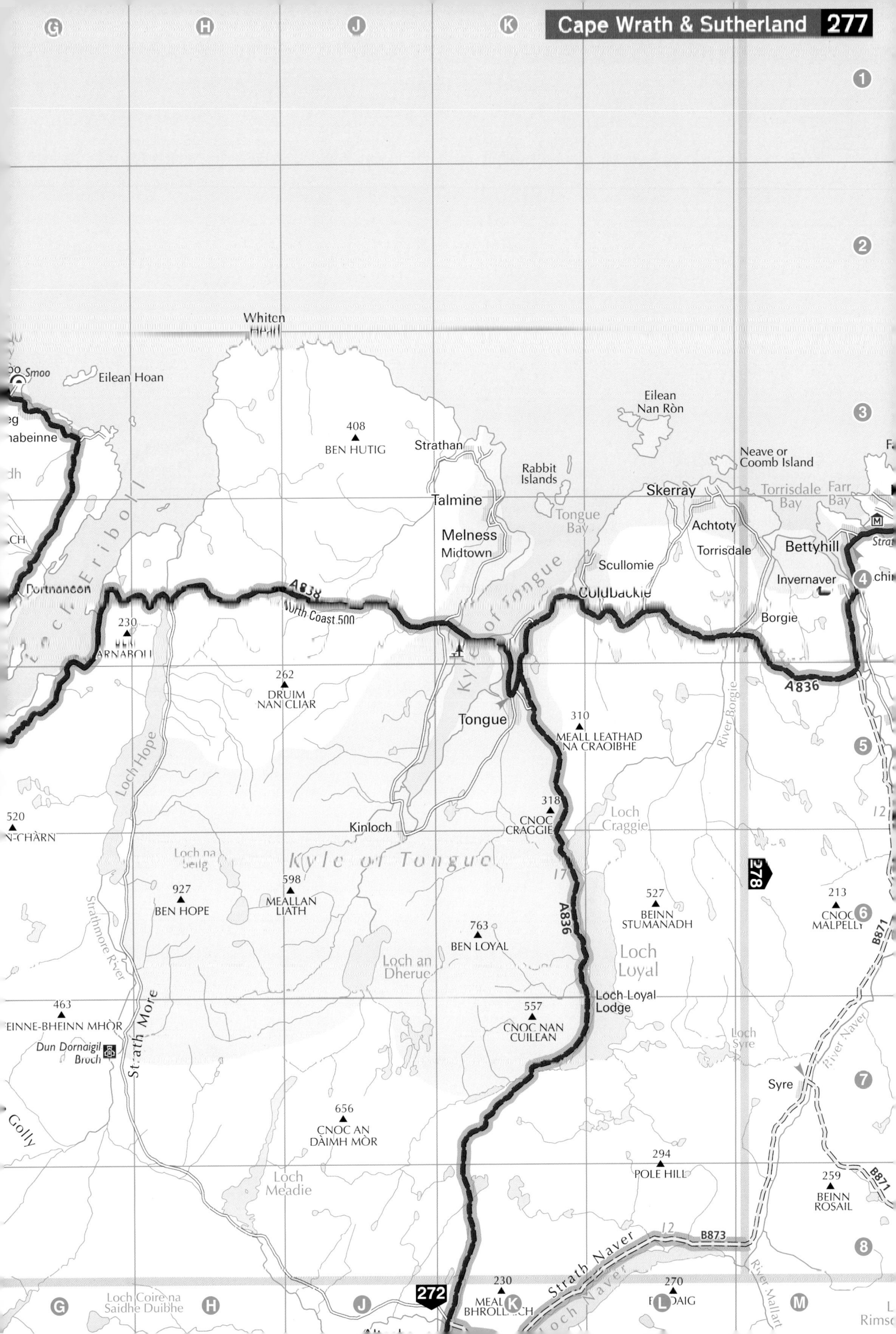

Whiten Hill

Smoo
Eilean Hoan

eg
habeinne

408
BEN HUTIG

Strathan

Rabbit
Islands

Eilean
Nan Ròn

Neave or
Coomb Island

Skerray

Achtoty

Torrisdale
Bay

Farr
Bay

M

Talmine

Melness
Midtown

Tongue
Bay

Scullomie

Torrisdale

Bettyhill

Invernaver

4

chi

ch

Portnancon

A838
North Coast 500

230
ARNABOU

Coldbackie

Borgie

A836

262
DRUIM
NAN CLIAR

Kyle of Tongue

Tongue

310
MEALL LEATHAD
NA CRAOIBHE

River Borgie

5

12

520
N-CHÀRN

Loch Hope

Loch na
Beilg

Kinloch

Kyle of Tongue

318
CNOC
CRAGGIE

Loch
Craggie

278

213
CNOC
MALPELLY

B871

6

927
BEN HOPE

598
MEALLAN
LIATH

17

527
BEINN
STUMANADH

Strathmore River

763
BEN LOYAL

Loch an
Dherue

A836

Loch
Loyal

463
EINNE-BHEINN MHÒR

Dun Dornaigil
Broch

Strath More

557
CNOC NAN
CUILEAN

Loch-Loyal
Lodge

Loch
Syre

River Naver

Syre

7

Golly

656
CNOC AN
DÀIMH MÒR

294
POLE HILL

259
BEINN
ROSAIL

B871

Loch
Meadie

272

230
MEAL
BHROLL CH

Strath Naver

12

B873

270
B DAIG

River Naver

River Mallart

Rimse

8

Loch Coire na
Saidhe Duibhe

Loch
Naver

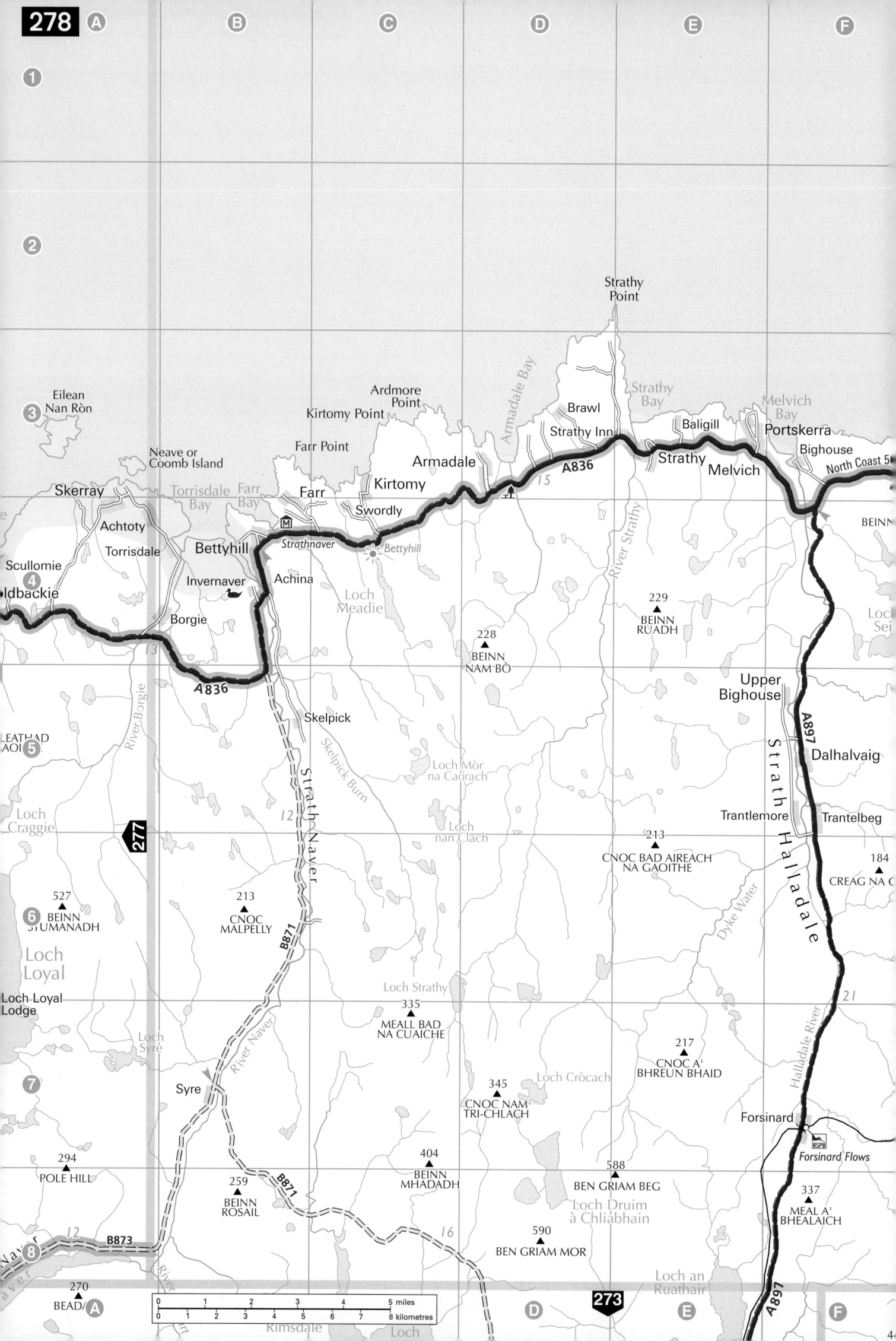

A B C D E F

1

2

Eilean
Nan Ròn
3

Neave or
Coomb Island

Skerray

Achtoty

Torrisdale

Scullomie

Idbackie
4

Borgie

A836

Torrisdale
Bay

Farr
Bay

Farr Point

Bettyhill

Strathnaver

Invernaver

Achina

Farr

Kirtomy Point

Swordly

Kirtomy

Ardmore
Point

Armadale

Bettyhill

Loch
Meadie

Armadale Bay

Strathy
Point

Brawl

Strathy Inn

A836

Strathy Bay

Baligill

Strathy
Melvich

Melvich
Bay

Portskerra

Bighouse

North Coast 5

BEINN

Loch
Sei

15

River Strathy

228
▲
BEINN
NAM BÒ

229
▲
BEINN
RUADH

Upper
Bighouse

A897

Dalhalvaig

Strath Halladale

Trantlemore

Trantelbeg

Skelpick

Strath Naver

Skelpick Burn

12

Loch Mòr
na Caorach

Loch
nan Clach

213
▲
CNOC BAD AIREACH
NA GAOITHE

184
▲
CREAG NA C

LEATHAD
AOI
5

Loch
Craggie

277

527
▲
BEINN
STUMANADH
6

Loch
Loyal

Loch Loyal
Lodge

Loch
Syre

Syre
7

River Naver

213
▲
CNOC
MALPELLY

B871

Loch Strathy

335
▲
MEALL BAD
NA CUAICHE

345
▲
CNOC NAM
TRI-CHLACH

Loch Cròcach

217
▲
CNOC A'
BHREUN BHAID

Dyke Water

21

Halladale River

Forsinard

RSPB

Forsinard Flows

337
▲
MEAL A'
BHEALAICH

294
▲
POLE HILL

259
▲
BEINN
ROSAIL

B871

16

404
▲
BEINN
MHADADH

590
▲
BEN GRIAM MOR

588
▲
BEN GRIAM BEG

Loch Druim
à Chliàbhain

Loch an
Ruathair

A897

Naver

12

B873

270
▲
BEAD
8

A

River

Rimsdale
Loch

0 1 2 3 4 5 miles
0 1 2 3 4 5 6 7 8 kilometres

273

D E F

4

G H J K

1

DUNNET HEAD
Briga Head
Dunnet
Head
121
DUNNET
HILL
Mary Ann's
Cottage
West Dunnet
Brough
St John's
Loch
B855
PENTL

2

Stromness
Holborn
Head
Clarden
Head
Dunnet
Bay
Dunnet

Brims Ness
St Mary's
Chapel (ruin)
Crosskirk
Scrabster
Thurso
Bay
Thurso
Muidh
Castlehill
Castletown

Forss
A836
A9
A836

Skiall
Lythmore
Sandside
Bay
Upper
Dounreay
Achreamie
Cnoc Freiceadain
Long Cairns
Glengolly
B874
Olrig
House
Tain

Isauld
A9
Weydale
280

Reay
Achvarasdal
Shebster
Westfield
Hilliclay
Bower
B876

3

Forss Water
Loch Calder
Sordale
Knockdee
Loch Scarmclate
Gillock
B874

242
BEINN
RATHA
Roadside
Glayock
A574

4

Brabster
Halkirk
Junction
Station
A882
B8

Shurrery
Scotscalder
Station
Harpsdale
176
SPITTAL
HILL
Loch Watten
B870
Watten

5

Shurrery
Lodge
Dorrery
Olgrinmore
Spittal
Mybster
Loch of
Toftingall
B8

290
BEIN NAM
BAD MHÒR
Loch
Scye
Westerdale
23

243
CNOC AN
HOARAIN BHÀIN
160
BRAIGH FÉITH HEMIGAL
132
DRUIM A'
CHRACAIRNIE
River Thurso
Strath Be

Loch
Shurrery
Loch Tuim
Ghlais
Loch
Caluim

6

203
CNOC PREAS
A'MHADAIDH
200
CNOC BEUL
NA FAIRE
106
BEINN CHÀITEAG
280

Altnabreac Station
A9

275
CNOC
N GALL
Loch
More
Loch
Ruard
Achavanich
Loch
Stemster

7

14
LLH
HII

Dalnawillan Lodge
Strathmore Water
Loch an
Thulachan
Loch
Sand
Loch
Rangag
226
COIRE
NA BEINNE
248
STEMSTER HILL

348
BEN ALISKY
287
BEN-A-
CHIELT

8

Glutt Water
Glutt Lodge
274
CNOCAN
K4
Swiney
U
Lyb

G H J L M

Rumsdale Water

PENTLAND FIRTH

ISLAND OF STROMA

Langaton Point
Nethertown
Mell Head
Uppertown

St Margaret's Hope

St John's Point
St John's Point

Inner Sound

Burwick (May-Sept)

DUNNET HEAD
Briga Head
Dunnet Head
127

Scarfskerry
Castle of Mey

Gills Bay
Gills

Kirkstyle
Huna
John o' Groats

DUNCANSBY HEAD

Muckle Stack

121
DUNNET HILL
Mary Ann's Cottage
Brough
Rattar
Mey
A836
Loch Mey
Gills

Canisbay
John o' Groats

Stacks of Duncansby

B855
West Dunnet
Dunnet
Barrock

A99

Clarden Head
Dunnet
Dunnet Bay
Castlehill
Inkstack
Brabstermire

Skirza
Skirza Head

279
Murkle
5
Castletown
Greenland
Loch Heilen
Gill Burn
Freswick
Freswick Bay

A836

Olrig House
Hilliclay
dale
Sordale
Tain
B876
Bowermadden
Slickly

Ness Head

side
Knockdee
Clayock
Gillock
Bower
Lyth
Sortat
Howe
Mireland

Auckengill
Nybster
Brough Head

Loch Scarmclate
Halcro
Kirk
16
North Coast 500
Keiss
A99

Georgemas Junction Station
A882
B874
B870
17

osdale
176
SPITTAL HILL
21
Loch Watten
Killimster
B876

Castle Sinclair Girnigoe
Noss Head
Sinclair's Bay

Spittal
B870
Watten
B874
Reiss
Winless

Mybster
Bilbster
A882
Wick River
Sibster
Ackergill

erdale
23
Haster
Milton
Wick
John o' Groats

Loch of Toftingall
Achairn Burn
Newton
A99
H
Wick Bay
Papigoe
Staxigoe

6
279
Badlipster
Loch Hempriggs
Old Wick
South Head
Whiterow
Castle of Old Wick

A9
Tannach
Thrumster

7
145
BALLHARN HILL
Grey Cairns of Camster
A99
Sarclet

Achavanich
Loch Stemster
212
HILL OF YARROWS
Loch of Yarrows

226
COIRE NA BEINNE
248
STEMSTER HILL
Cairn o'Get
Ulbster

8
287
BEN-A-CHIELT
Upper Lybster
275
Whaligoe
Whaligoe Steps
Bruan

Hill o'Many Stanes
Swiney
Mid Clyth
Halberry Head
Clyth Ness

0 1 2 3 4 5 miles
0 1 2 3 4 5 6 7 8 kilometres

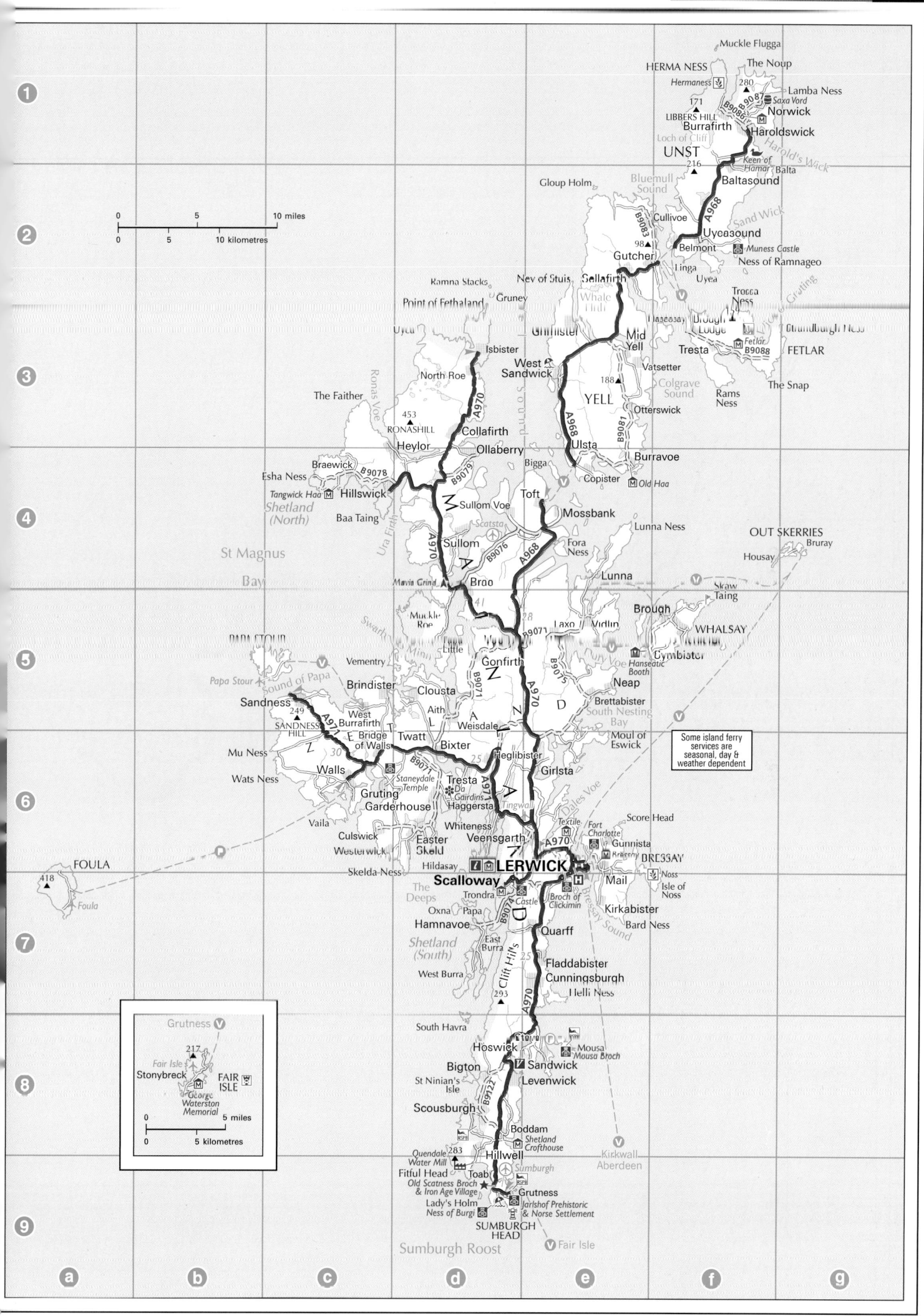

HERMA NESS
Muckle Flugga
The Noup
Hermaness
280
171
Lamba Ness
Saxa Vord
Norwick
LIBBERS HILL
Burrafirth
Haroldswick
Loch of Cliff
UNST
216
Keen of Hamar
Balta
Harold's Wick
Gloup Holm
Bluemull Sound
Baltasound
Sand Wick
Cullivoe
Uyeasound
B9083
Belmont
Muness Castle
Gutcher
Linga
Ness of Ramnageo
Ramna Stacks
Nev of Stuis
Sellafirth
Uyea
Trosca Ness
Gruney
Whale Firth
Dalsetter
Brough Lodge
Gaundburgh Ness
Point of Fethaland
Uyea
Gnifhister
Mid Yell
Tresta
FETLAR
Fetlar B9088
Isbister
West Sandwick
Vatsetter
North Roe
188
YELL
Colgrave Sound
The Snap
The Faither
Ronas Voe
453
RONASHILL
Collafirth
B9081
Otterswick
Rams Ness
A970
Ollaberry
Ulsta
Burravoe
Heylor
B9079
Bigga
Esha Ness
B9078
Copister
Old Haa
Braewick
Toft
Tangwick Haa
Hillswick
Sullom Voe
Mossbank
OUT SKERRIES
Shetland (North)
Baa Taing
Scatsta
Fora Ness
Lunna Ness
Bruray
Sullom
B9076
Housay
St Magnus Bay
Mavis Grind
Brae
A968
Lunna
41
Muckle Roe
Laxo
Vidlin
Brough
Skaw Taing
PAPA STOUR
Little Roe
B9071
Gonfirth
WHALSAY
Papa Stour
Vementry
A970
Symbister
Sound of Papa
Brindister
Hanseatic Booth
Sandness
West Burrafirth
Clousta
B9075
Neap
249
Aith
Brettabister
SANDNESS HILL
Twatt
Weisdale
South Nesting Bay
Mu Ness
A971
Bridge of Walls
Bixter
Moul of Eswick
Wats Ness
B9071
Heglibister
Girlsta
Some island ferry services are seasonal, day & weather dependent
Walls
30
Tresta
Staneydale Temple
Da Gairdins
Haggersta
Tingwall
Gruting
Garderhouse
Whiteness
Fort Charlotte
Score Head
Vaila
25
Veensgarth
A970
Gunnista
Culswick
Easter Skeld
Textile
Kraigeo
BRESSAY
Westerwick
Hildasay
LERWICK
Skelda Ness
Scalloway
Castle
Broch of Clickimin
Mail
The Deeps
Trondra
Isle of Noss
Noss
Oxna
Papa
Kirkabister
Bard Ness
Hamnavoe
B9074
Quarff
Shetland (South)
East Burra
Fladdabister
West Burra
Cunningburgh
Helli Ness
Clift Hills
293
A970
South Havra
Hoswick
Sandwick
Mousa
Bigton
Mousa Broch
St Ninian's Isle
Levenwick
Scousburgh
B9122
Boddam
Shetland Crofthouse
Kirkwall
Aberdeen
Quendale Water Mill
283
Hillwell
Sumburgh
Fitful Head
Toab
Old Scatness Broch & Iron Age Village
Grutness
Jarlshof Prehistoric & Norse Settlement
Lady's Holm
Ness of Burgi
SUMBURGH HEAD
Sumburgh Roost
Fair Isle

Grutness
217
Fair Isle
Stonybreck
FAIR ISLE
George Waterston Memorial
0   5 miles
0   5 kilometres

FOULA
418
Foula

0   5   10 miles
0   5   10 kilometres

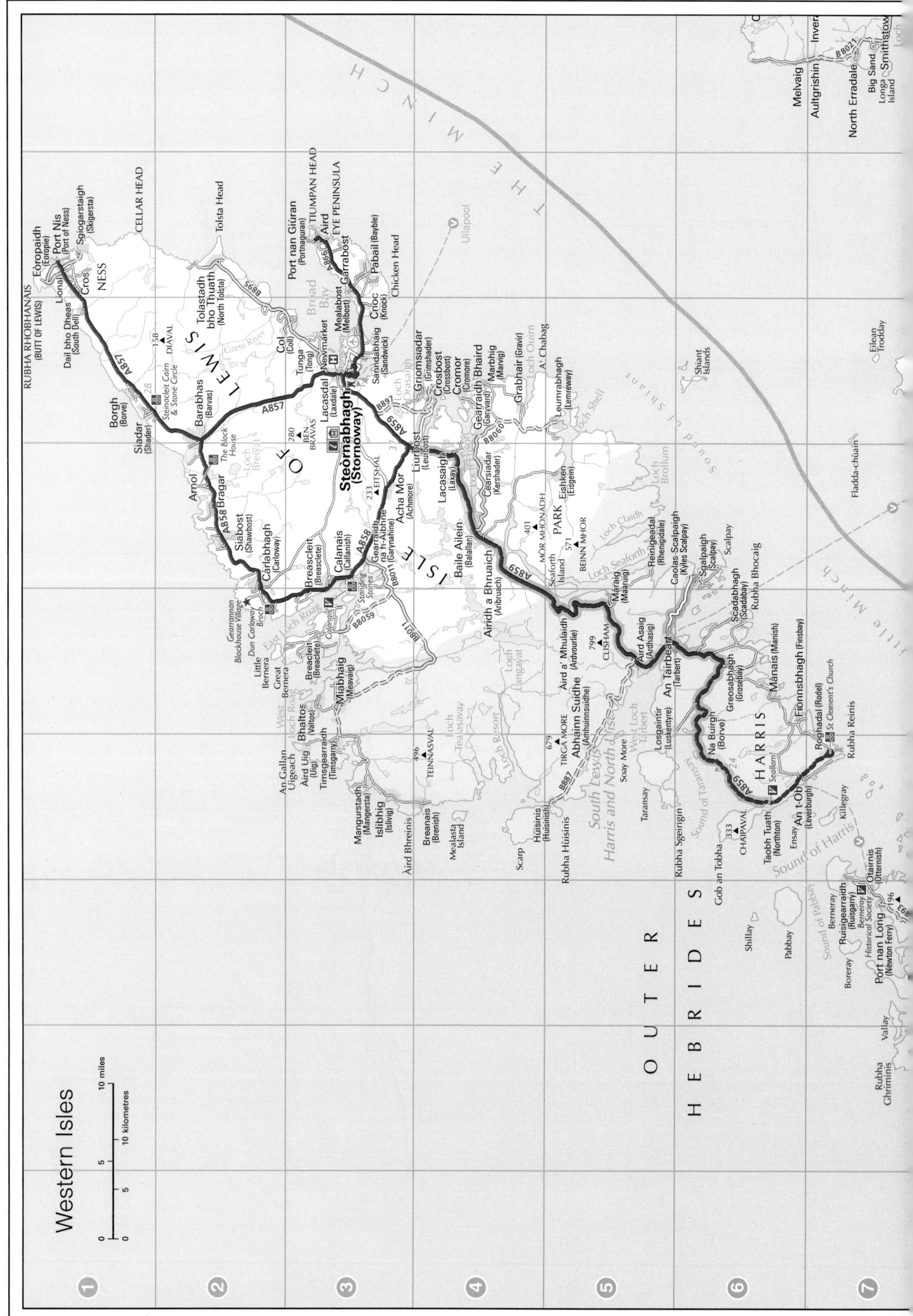

Western Isles

10 miles

10 kilometres

THE MINCH

Little Minch

THE MINCH

Sound of Shiant

Sound of Pabay

OUTER HEBRIDES

NESS

Rubha Rhobhanais
(BUTT OF LEWIS)

Eòropaidh
(Eoropie)

Port Nis
(Port of Ness)

Sgiogarstaigh
(Skigersta)

Lional

Dail bho Dheas
(South Dell)

Cros

Borgh
(Borve)

Siadar
(Shader)

Steinacleit Cairn
& Stone Circle

DIAVAL

CELLAR HEAD

Tolsta Head

Tolastadh
bho Thuath
(North Tolsta)

Barabhas
(Barvas)

A857

Arnol

The Black House

A858 Bragar

Gress River

Col
(Coll)

Tunga
(Tong)

Lacasdal
(Laxdale)

Newmarket

Steòrnabhagh
(Stornoway)

LEWIS

Loch Breugil

BEN BRAVAS

280

EITSHAL

233

A859

Siabost
(Shawbost)

Càrlabhagh
(Carloway)

Breasclett
(Breaclete)

Calanais
(Callanish)

Gearraidh
na h-Aibhne
(Garynahine)

Standing Stones

Gearrannan
Blackhouse Village

Dun Carloway
Broch

Little Bernera

Great Bernera

East Loch Roag

Colbost

B8059

B8011

B8011

Acha Mor
(Achmore)

A858

ISLE OF LEWIS

Liurbost
(Leurbost)

Lacasaigh
(Laxay)

Cearsiadar
(Kershader)

Baile Ailein
(Balallan)

Airidh a Bhruaich
(Aribruach)

Seaforth Island

401

MOR MHONADH

PARK

571

BEINN MHOR

Loch Seaforth

Màraig
(Maaruig)

Aird Asaig
(Ardhasig)

CLISHAM

799

An Tairbeart
(Tarbert)

Losgaintir
(Luskentyre)

West Loch Tarbert

Soay More

Taransay

TIRGA MORE

679

Abhainn Suidhe
(Amhuinnsuidhe)

Aird a' Mhulaidh
(Ardvourlie)

Na Buirgh
(Borve)

A859

Greosabhagh
(Grosebay)

24

Seallam!

An t-Ob
(Leverburgh)

Ensay

Killegray

Taobh Tuath
(Northton)

CHAIPAVAL

333

Gob an Tobha

Rubha Sgeirigin

Sound of Taransay

Sound of Harris

Rubha Ghriminis

Vallay

HARRIS

Mànais
(Manish)

Fionnsbhagh
(Finsbay)

Ròghadal
(Rodel)

St Clement's Church

Rubha Reinis

Scadabhagh
(Scadabay)

Rubha Bhocaig

Sgalpaigh
(Scalpay)

Reinigeadal
(Rhenigidale)

Caolas Scalpaigh
(Kyles Scalpay)

Scalpay

OUTER HEBRIDES

Pabbay

Shillay

Berneray

Rubha Ghriminis

Ruisigearraidh
(Ruisgarry)

Berneray

Historical Society

Port nan Long
(Newton Ferry)

Otairnis
(Otternish)

B893

196

Boreray

Sound of Pabbay

Harris and North Uist

South Uist

West Loch Tarbert

Loch Langavat

Loch Tealasavay

Loch Resort

Pairc Nis

EYE PENINSULA

Port nan Giùran
(Portnaguran)

TIUMPAN HEAD

Aird

A866

Garrabost

Pabail
(Bayble)

Cnòc
(Knock)

Chicken Head

Broad Bay

Mealabost
(Melbost)

Sanndabhaig
(Sandwick)

Griomsiadar
(Grimshader)

Crosbost
(Crossbost)

Cromor
(Cromore)

Gearraidh Bhaird
(Garyvard)

Marbhig
(Marvig)

Grabhair
(Gravir)

A' Chabag

Leumrabhagh
(Lemreway)

B8060

Eishken
(Eisgein)

Loch Shell

Loch Brollum

Loch Claidh

Loch Ourm

Ullapool

Eilean Troddav

Fladda-chuain

Shiant Islands

Melvaig

Aultgrishin

North Erradale

Big Sand

Longa Island

Smithstow

Inver

B8021

Ensay

A859

Loch Erisort

Loch Orasaigh

Loch Grimshader

158

28

37

496

TEINNASVAL

An Gallan
Uigeach

Aird Uig
(Uig)

Timsgearraidh
(Timsgarry)

Bhaltos
(Valtos)

Mangurstadh
(Mangersta)

Islibhig
(Islivig)

Breanais
(Brenish)

Mealasta
Island

Scarp

Aird Bhreinis

Hùisinis
(Huisinish)

Rubha Hùisinis

West Loch Roag

An Gallan

1
2
3
4
5
6
7

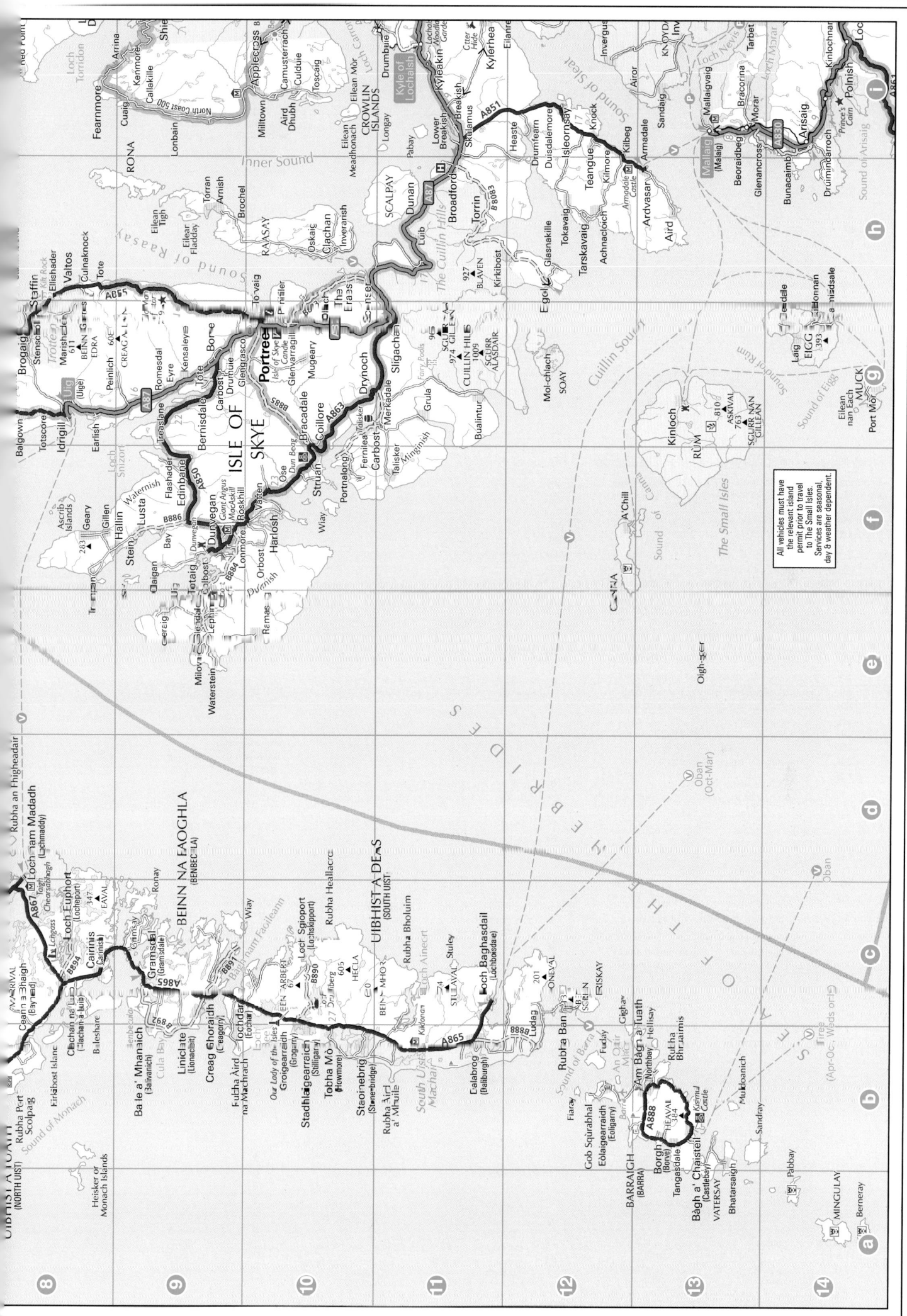

Motorway and primary route junctions which have access or exit restrictions are shown on the map pages thus:

M1 London - Leeds

Junction	Northbound	Southbound
2	Access only from A1 (northbound)	Exit only to A1 (southbound)
4	Access only from A41 (northbound)	Exit only to A41 (southbound)
6A	Access only from M25 (no link from A405)	Exit only to M25 (no link from A405)
7	Access only from A414	Exit only to A414
17	Exit only to M45	Access only from M45
19	Exit only to M6 (northbound)	Exit only to A14 (southbound)
21A	Exit only, no access	Access only, no exit
24A	Access only, no exit	Access only from A50 (eastbound)
35A	Exit only, no access	Access only, no exit
43	Exit only to M621	Access only from M621
48	Exit only to A1(M) (northbound)	Access only from A1(M) (southbound)

M2 Rochester - Faversham

Junction	Westbound	Eastbound
1	No exit to A2 (eastbound)	No access from A2 (westbound)

M3 Sunbury - Southampton

Junction	Northeastbound	Southwestbound
8	Access only from A303, no access	Exit only to A303, no access
10	Exit only, no access	Access only, no exit
14	Access from M27 only, no exit	No access to M27 (westbound)

M4 London - South Wales

Junction	Westbound	Eastbound
1	Access only from A4 (westbound)	Exit only to A4 (eastbound)
2	Access only from A4 (westbound)	Access only from A4 (eastbound)
21	Exit only to M48	Access only from M48
23	Access only from M48	Exit only to M48
25	Exit only, no access	Access only, no exit
25A	Exit only, no access	Access only, no exit
29	Exit only to A48(M)	Access only from A48(M)
38	Exit only, no access	No restriction
39	Access only, no exit	No access or exit
42	Exit only to A483	Access only from A483

M5 Birmingham - Exeter

Junction	Northeastbound	Southwestbound
10	Access only, no exit	Exit only, no access
11A	Access only from A417 (westbound)	Exit only to A417 (eastbound)
18A	Exit only to M49	Access only from M49
18	Exit only, no access	Access only, no exit

M6 Toll Motorway

Junction	Northwestbound	Southeastbound
T1	Access only, no exit	No access or exit
T2	No access or exit	Exit only, no access
T5	Access only, no exit	Exit only to A5148 (northbound), no access
T7	Exit only, no access	Access only, no exit
T8	Exit only, no access	Access only, no exit

M6 Rugby - Carlisle

Junction	Northbound	Southbound
3A	Exit only to M6 Toll	Access only from M6 Toll
4	Exit only to M42 (southbound) & A446	Exit only to A446
4A	Access only from M42 (southbound)	Exit only to M42
5	Exit only, no access	Access only, no exit
10A	Exit only to M54	Access only from M54
11A	Access only from M6 Toll	Exit only to M6 Toll
with M56 (jct 20A)	No restriction	Access only from M56 (eastbound)
20	Exit only to M56 (westbound)	Access only from M56 (eastbound)
24	Access only, no exit	Exit only, no access
25	Exit only, no access	Access only, no exit

30	Access only from M61	Exit only to M61
31A	Exit only, no access	Access only, no exit
45	Exit only, no access	Access only, no exit

M8 Edinburgh - Bishopton

Junction	Westbound	Eastbound
6	Exit only, no access	Access only, no exit
6A	Access only, no exit	Exit only, no access
7	Access only, no exit	Exit only, no access
7A	Exit only, no access	Access only from A725 (northbound), no exit
8	No access from M73 (southbound) or from A8 (eastbound) & A89	No exit to M73 (northbound) or to A8 (westbound) & A89
9	Access only, no exit	Exit only, no access
13	Access only from M80 (southbound)	Exit only to M80 (northbound)
14	Access only, no exit	Exit only, no access
16	Exit only to A804	Access only from A879
17	Exit only to A82	No restriction
18	Access only from A82 (eastbound)	Exit only to A814
19	No access from A814 (westbound)	Exit only to A814 (westbound)
20	Exit only, no access	Access only, no exit
21	Access only, no exit	Exit only to A8
22	Exit only to M77 (southbound)	Access only from M77 (northbound)
23	Exit only to B768	Access only from B768
25	No access or exit from or to A8	No access or exit from or to A8
25A	Exit only, no access	Access only, no exit
28	Exit only, no access	Access only, no exit
28A	Exit only to A737	Access only from A737
29A	Exit only to A8	Access only from A8

M9 Edinburgh - Dunblane

Junction	Northwestbound	Southeastbound
2	Access only, no exit	Exit only, no access
3	Exit only, no access	Access only, no exit
6	Access only, no exit	Exit only to A905
8	Exit only to M876 (southwestbound)	Access only from M876 (northeastbound)

M11 London - Cambridge

Junction	Northbound	Southbound
4	Access only from A406 (eastbound)	Exit only to A406
5	Exit only, no access	Access only, no exit
8A	Exit only, no access	No direct access, use jct 8
9	Exit only to A11	Access only from A11
13	Exit only, no access	Access only, no exit
14	Exit only, no access	Access only, no exit

M20 Swanley - Folkestone

Junction	Northwestbound	Southeastbound
2	Staggered junction; follow signs - access only	Staggered junction; follow signs - exit only
3	Exit only to M26 (westbound)	Access only from M26 (eastbound)
5	Access only from A20	For access follow signs - exit only to A20
6	No restriction	For exit follow signs
10	Access only, no exit	Exit only, no access
11A	Access only, no exit	Exit only, no access

M23 Hooley - Crawley

Junction	Northbound	Southbound
7	Exit only to A23 (northbound)	Access only from A23 (southbound)
10A	Access only, no exit	Exit only, no access

M25 London Orbital

Junction	Clockwise	Anticlockwise
1B	No direct access, use slip road to jct 2 Exit only	Access only, no exit
5	No exit to M26 (eastbound)	No access from M26
19	Exit only, no access	Access only, no exit
21	Access only from M1 (southbound) Exit only to M1 (northbound)	Access only from M1 (southbound) Exit only to M1 (northbound)
31	No exit (use slip road via jct 30), access only	No access (use slip road via jct 30), exit only

M26 Sevenoaks - Wrotham

Junction	Westbound	Eastbound
with M25 (jct 5)	Exit only to clockwise M25 (westbound)	Access only from anticlockwise M25 (eastbound)
with M20 (jct 3)	Access only from M20 (northwestbound)	Exit only to M20 (southeastbound)

M27 Cadnam - Portsmouth

Junction	Westbound	Eastbound
4	Staggered junction; follow signs - access only from M3 (southbound). Exit only to M3 (northbound)	Staggered junction; follow signs - access only from M3 (southbound). Exit only to M3 (northbound)
10	Exit only, no access	Access only, no exit
12	Staggered junction; follow signs - exit only to M275 (southbound)	Staggered junction; follow signs - access only from M275 (northbound)

M40 London - Birmingham

Junction	Northwestbound	Southeastbound
3	Exit only, no access	Access only, no exit
7	Exit only, no access	Access only, no exit
8	Exit only to M40/A40	Access only from M40/A40
13	Exit only, no access	Access only, no exit
14	Access only, no exit	Exit only, no access
16	Access only, no exit	Exit only, no access

M42 Bromsgrove - Measham

Junction	Northeastbound	Southwestbound
1	Access only, no exit	Exit only, no access
7	Exit only to M6 (northwestbound)	Access only from M6 (northwestbound)
7A	Exit only to M6 (southeastbound)	No access or exit
8	Access only from M6 (southeastbound)	Exit only to M6 (northwestbound)

M45 Coventry - M1

Junction	Westbound	Eastbound
Dunchurch (unnumbered)	Access only from A45	Exit only, no access
with M1 (jct 17)	Access only from M1 (northbound)	Exit only to M1 (southbound)

M48 Chepstow

Junction	Westbound	Eastbound
21	Access only from M4 (westbound)	Exit only to M4 (eastbound)
23	No exit to M4 (eastbound)	No access from M4 (westbound)

M53 Mersey Tunnel - Chester

Junction	Northbound	Southbound
11	Access only from M56 (westbound) Exit only to M56 (eastbound)	Access only from M56 (westbound) Exit only to M56 (eastbound)

M54 Telford - Birmingham

Junction	Westbound	Eastbound
with M6 (jct 10A)	Access only from M6 (northbound)	Exit only to M6 (southbound)

M56 Chester - Manchester

Junction	Westbound	Eastbound
1	Access only from M60 (westbound)	Exit only to M60 (eastbound) & A34 (northbound)
2	Exit only, no access	Access only, no exit
3	Access only, no exit	Exit only, no access
4	Exit only, no access	Access only, no exit
7	Exit only, no access	No restriction
8	Access only, no exit	No access or exit
9	No exit to M6 (southbound)	No access from M6 (northbound)
15	Exit only to M53	Access only from M53
16	No access or exit	No restriction

A57 Liverpool Outer Ring Road

Junction	Northwestbound	Southeastbound
3	Access only, no exit	Exit only, no access
5	Access only from A580 (westbound)	Exit only, no access

M60 Manchester Orbital

Junction	Clockwise	Anticlockwise
2	Access only, no exit	Exit only, no access
3	No access from M56	Access only from A34 (northbound)
4	Access only from A34 (northbound). Exit only to A34 (southbound)	Access only from M56 (eastbound). Exit only to A34 (southbound)
5	Access and exit only from and to A5103 (northbound)	Access and exit only from and to A5103 (southbound)
7	No direct access, use slip road to jct 8. Exit only to A56	Access only from A56. No exit, use jct 8
14	Access from A580 (eastbound)	Exit only to A580 (westbound)
16	Access only, no exit	Exit only, no access
20	Exit only, no access	Access only, no exit
22	No restriction	Exit only, no access
25	Exit only, no access	No restriction
26	No restriction	Exit only, no access
27	Access only, no exit	Exit only, no access

M61 Manchester - Preston

Junction	Northwestbound	Southeastbound
3	No access or exit	Exit only, no access
with M6 (jct 30)	Exit only to M6 (northbound)	Access only from M6 (southbound)

M62 Liverpool - Kingston upon Hull

Junction	Westbound	Eastbound
23	Access only, no exit	Exit only, no access
32A	No access to A1(M) (southbound)	No restriction

M65 Preston - Colne

Junction	Northeastbound	Southwestbound
9	Exit only, no access	Access only, no exit
11	Access only, no exit	Exit only, no access

M66 Bury

Junction	Northbound	Southbound
with A56	Exit only to A56 (northbound)	Access only from A56 (southbound)
1	Exit only, no access	Access only, no exit

M67 Hyde Bypass

Junction	Westbound	Eastbound
1A	Access only, no exit	Exit only, no access
2	Exit only, no access	Access only, no exit

M69 Coventry - Leicester

Junction	Northbound	Southbound
2	Access only, no exit	Exit only, no access

M73 East of Glasgow

Junction	Northbound	Southbound
1	No exit to A74 & A721	No exit to A74 & A721
2	No access from or exit to A89. No access from M8 (eastbound)	No access from or exit to A89. No exit to M8 (westbound)

M74 Glasgow - Abington

Junction	Northbound	Southbound
3	Exit only, no access	Access only, no exit
3A	Access only, no exit	Exit only, no access
4	No access from A74 & A721	Access only, no exit to A74 & A721
7	Access only, no exit	Exit only, no access
9	No access or exit	Exit only, no access
10	No restriction	Access only, no exit
11	Access only, no exit	Exit only, no access
12	Exit only, no access	Access only, no exit

M77 Glasgow - Kilmarnock

Junction	Northbound	Southbound
with M8 (jct 22)	No exit to M8 (westbound)	No access from M8 (eastbound)
4	Access only, no exit	Exit only, no access
6	Access only, no exit	Exit only, no access
7	Access only, no exit	No restriction
8	Exit only, no access	Exit only, no access

M80 Glasgow - Stirling

Junction	Northbound	Southbound
4A	Exit only, no access	Access only, no exit
6A	Access only, no exit	Exit only, no access
8	Exit only to M876 (northeastbound)	Access only from M876 (southwestbound)

M90 Edinburgh - Perth

Junction	Northbound	Southbound
1	No exit, access only	Exit only to A90 (eastbound)
2A	Exit only to A92 (eastbound)	Access only from A92 (westbound)
7	Access only, no exit	Exit only, no access
8	Exit only, no access	Access only, no exit
10	No access from A912. No exit to A912 (southbound)	No access from A912 (northbound) No exit to A912

M180 Doncaster - Grimsby

Junction	Westbound	Eastbound
1	Access only, no exit	Exit only, no access

M606 Bradford Spur

Junction	Northbound	Southbound
2	Exit only, no access	No restriction

M621 Leeds - M1

Junction	Clockwise	Anticlockwise
2A	Access only, no exit	Exit only, no access
4	No exit or access	No restriction
5	Access only, no exit	Exit only, no access
6	Exit only, no access	Access only, no exit
with M1 (jct 43)	Exit only to M1 (southbound)	Access only from M1 (northbound)

M876 Bonnybridge - Kincardine Bridge

Junction	Northeastbound	Southwestbound
with M80 (jct 5)	Access only from M80 (northeastbound)	Exit only to M80 (southwestbound)
with M9 (jct 8)	Exit only to M9 (eastbound)	Access only from M9 (westbound)

A1(M) South Mimms - Baldock

Junction	Northbound	Southbound
2	Exit only, no access	Access only, no exit
3	No restriction	Exit only, no access
5	Access only, no exit	No access or exit

A1(M) Pontefract - Bedale

Junction	Northbound	Southbound
40	Exit only to A162 (M62), no access	Access only, no exit
41	No access to M62 (eastbound)	No restriction
43	Access only from M1 (northbound)	Exit only to M1 (southbound)

A1(M) Scotch Corner - Newcastle upon Tyne

Junction	Northbound	Southbound
57	Exit only to A66(M) (eastbound)	Access only from A66(M) (westbound)
65	No access. Exit only to A194(M) & A1 (northbound)	No exit. Access only from A194(M) & A1 (southbound)

A3(M) Horndean - Havant

Junction	Northbound	Southbound
1	Access only from A3	Exit only to A3
4	Exit only, no access	Access only, no exit

A38(M) Birmingham, Victoria Road (Park Circus)

Junction	Northbound	Southbound
with B4132	No exit	No access

A48(M) Cardiff Spur

Junction	Westbound	Eastbound
29	Access only from M4 (westbound)	Exit only to M4 (eastbound)
29A	Exit only to A48 (westbound)	Access only from A48 (eastbound)

A57(M) Manchester, Brook Street (A34)

Junction	Westbound	Eastbound
with A34	No exit	No access

A58(M) Leeds, Park Lane and Westgate

Junction	Northbound	Southbound
with A58	No restriction	No access

A64(M) Leeds, Clay Pit Lane (A58)

Junction	Westbound	Eastbound
with A58	No exit (to Clay Pit Lane)	No access (from Clay Pit Lane)

A66(M) Darlington Spur

Junction	Westbound	Eastbound
with A1(M) (jct 57)	Exit only to A1(M) (southbound)	Access only from A1(M) (northbound)

A74(M) Gretna - Abington

Junction	Northbound	Southbound
18	Exit only, no access	Access only, no exit

A194(M) Gateshead

Junction	Northbound	Southbound
with A1(M) (jct 65)	Access only from A1(M) (northbound)	Exit only to A1(M) (southbound)

A12 M25 - Ipswich

Junction	Northeastbound	Southwestbound
13	Access only, no exit	No restriction
14	Exit only, no access	Access only, no exit
20A	Exit only, no access	Access only, no exit
20B	Access only, no exit	Exit only, no access
21	No restriction	Access only, no exit
23	Exit only, no access	Access only, no exit
24	Access only, no exit	Exit only, no access
27	Exit only, no access	Access only, no exit
Dedham & Stratford St Mary (unnumbered)	Exit only	Access only

A14 M1 - Felixstowe

Junction	Westbound	Eastbound
with M1/M6 (jct 19)	Exit only to M6 and M1 (northbound)	Access only from M6 and M1 (southbound)
4	Exit only, no access	Access only, no exit
21	Access only, no exit	Exit only, no access
22	Exit only, no access	Access only from A1 (southbound)
23	Access only, no exit	Exit only, no access
26	No restriction	Access only, no exit
34	Access only, no exit	Exit only, no access
36	Exit only to A11, access only from A1303	Access only from A11
38	Access only from A11	Exit only to A11
39	Exit only, no access	Access only, no exit
61	Access only, no exit	Exit only, no access

A55 Holyhead - Chester

Junction	Westbound	Eastbound
8A	Exit only, no access	Access only, no exit
23A	Access only, no exit	Exit only, no access
24A	Exit only, no access	No access or exit
27A	No restriction	No access or exit
33A	Exit only, no access	No access or exit
33B	Exit only, no access	Access only, no exit
36A	Exit only to A5104	Access only from A5104
39	Access only, no exit	Exit only, no access

Index to place names

This index lists places appearing in the main map section of the atlas in alphabetical order. The reference following each name gives the atlas page number and grid reference of the square in which the place appears. The map shows counties, unitary authorities and administrative areas, together with a list of the abbreviated name forms used in the index. In addition World Heritage sites are indexed in **green**, motorway services areas in **blue**, airports in blue *italic* and National Parks in green *italic.*

Scotland

Abers	Aberdeenshire
Ag & B	Argyll and Bute
Angus	Angus
Border	Scottish Borders
C Aber	City of Aberdeen
C Dund	City of Dundee
C Edin	City of Edinburgh
C Glas	City of Glasgow
Clacks	Clackmannanshire (1)
D & G	Dumfries & Galloway
E Ayrs	East Ayrshire
E Duns	East Dunbartonshire (2)
E Loth	East Lothian
E Rens	East Renfrewshire (3)
Falk	Falkirk
Fife	Fife
Highld	Highland
Inver	Inverclyde (4)
Mdloth	Midlothian (5)
Moray	Moray
N Ayrs	North Ayrshire
N Lans	North Lanarkshire (6)
Ork	Orkney Islands
P & K	Perth & Kinross
Rens	Renfrewshire (7)
S Ayrs	South Ayrshire
S Lans	South Lanarkshire
Shet	Shetland Islands
Stirlg	Stirling
W Duns	West Dunbartonshire (8)
W Isls	Western Isles (Na h-Eileanan an Iar)
W Loth	West Lothian

Wales

Blae G	Blaenau Gwent (9)
Brdgnd	Bridgend (10)
Caerph	Caerphilly (11)
Cardif	Cardiff
Carmth	Carmarthenshire
Cerdgn	Ceredigion
Conwy	Conwy
Denbgs	Denbighshire
Flints	Flintshire
Gwynd	Gwynedd
IoA	Isle of Anglesey
Mons	Monmouthshire
Myr Td	Merthyr Tydfil (12)
Neath	Neath Port Talbot (13)
Newpt	Newport (14)
Pembks	Pembrokeshire
Powys	Powys
Rhondd	Rhondda Cynon Taf (15)
Swans	Swansea
Torfn	Torfaen (16)
V Glam	Vale of Glamorgan (17)
Wrexhm	Wrexham

Channel Islands & Isle of Man

Guern	Guernsey
Jersey	Jersey
IoM	Isle of Man

England

BaNES	Bath & N E Somerset (18)
Barns	Barnsley (19)
BCP	Bournemouth, Christchurch and Poole (20)
Bed	Bedford
Birm	Birmingham
Bl w D	Blackburn with Darwen (21)
Bolton	Bolton (22)
Bpool	Blackpool
Br & H	Brighton & Hove (23)
Br For	Bracknell Forest (24)
Bristl	City of Bristol
Bucks	Buckinghamshire
Bury	Bury (25)
C Beds	Central Bedfordshire
C Brad	City of Bradford
C Derb	City of Derby
C KuH	City of Kingston upon Hull
C Leic	City of Leicester
C Nott	City of Nottingham
C Pete	City of Peterborough
C Plym	City of Plymouth
C Port	City of Portsmouth
C Sotn	City of Southampton
C Stke	City of Stoke-on-Trent
C York	City of York
Calder	Calderdale (26)
Cambs	Cambridgeshire
Ches E	Cheshire East
Ches W	Cheshire West and Chester
Cnwll	Cornwall
Covtry	Coventry
Cumb	Cumberland
Darltn	Darlington (27)
Derbys	Derbyshire
Devon	Devon
Donc	Doncaster (28)
Dorset	Dorset
Dudley	Dudley (29)
Dur	Durham
E R Yk	East Riding of Yorkshire
E Susx	East Sussex
Essex	Essex
Gatesd	Gateshead (30)
Gloucs	Gloucestershire
Gt Lon	Greater London
Halton	Halton (31)
Hants	Hampshire
Hartpl	Hartlepool (32)
Herefs	Herefordshire
Herts	Hertfordshire
IoS	Isles of Scilly
IoW	Isle of Wight
Kent	Kent
Kirk	Kirklees (33)
Knows	Knowsley (34)
Lancs	Lancashire
Leeds	Leeds
Leics	Leicestershire
Lincs	Lincolnshire
Lpool	Liverpool
Luton	Luton

M Keyn	Milton Keynes
Manch	Manchester
Medway	Medway
Middsb	Middlesbrough
N Linc	North Lincolnshire
N Nthn	North Northamptonshire
N Som	North Somerset
N Tyne	North Tyneside (35)
N u Ty	Newcastle upon Tyne
N York	North Yorkshire
NE Lin	North East Lincolnshire
Norfk	Norfolk
Notts	Nottinghamshire
Nthumb	Northumberland
Oldham	Oldham (36)
Oxon	Oxfordshire
R & Cl	Redcar & Cleveland
Readg	Reading
Rochdl	Rochdale (37)
Rothm	Rotherham (38)
Rutlnd	Rutland
S Glos	South Gloucestershire (39)
S on T	Stockton-on-Tees (40)
S Tyne	South Tyneside (41)
Salfd	Salford (42)
Sandw	Sandwell (43)
Sefton	Sefton (44)
Sheff	Sheffield
Shrops	Shropshire
Slough	Slough (45)
Solhll	Solihull (46)
Somset	Somerset
St Hel	St Helens (47)
Staffs	Staffordshire
Sthend	Southend-on-Sea
Stockp	Stockport (48)
Suffk	Suffolk
Sundld	Sunderland
Surrey	Surrey
Swindn	Swindon
Tamesd	Tameside (49)
Thurr	Thurrock (50)
Torbay	Torbay
Traffd	Trafford (51)
W & F	Westmorland & Furness
W & M	Windsor & Maidenhead (52)
W Berk	West Berkshire
W Nthn	West Northamptonshire
W Susx	West Sussex
Wakefd	Wakefield (53)
Warrtn	Warrington (54)
Warwks	Warwickshire
Wigan	Wigan (55)
Wilts	Wiltshire
Wirral	Wirral (56)
Wokham	Wokingham (57)
Wolves	Wolverhampton (58)
Worcs	Worcestershire
Wrekin	Telford & Wrekin (59)
Wsall	Walsall (60)

A

Abbas Combe Somset 32 B6
Abberley Worcs 81 H2
Abberley Common Worcs 81 G2
Abberton Essex 72 E3
Abberton Worcs 82 A4
Abberwick Nthumb 191 G3
Abbess Roding Essex 70 E5
Abbey Devon 14 D1
Abbeycwmhir Powys 78 E1
Abbeydale Sheff 132 F3
Abbey Dore Herefs 62 D1
Abbey Green Staffs 131 J8
Abbey Hill Somset 30 D7
Abbey Hulton C Stke. 114 E2
Abbey St Bathans Border 213 G6
Abbeystead Lancs 147 L5
Abbeytown Cumb 177 G8
Abbey Village Lancs 139 J3
Abbey Wood Gt Lon 52 A3
Abbotrule Border 189 G4
Abbots Bickington Devon 27 G8
Abbots Bromley Staffs 115 H6
Abbotsbury Dorset 16 A5
Abbot's Chair Derbys 131 K2
Abbots Deuglie P & K 221 K5
Abbotsham Devon 27 G5
Abbotskerswell Devon 8 C1
Abbots Langley Herts 68 E6
Abbotsleigh Devon 8 B5
Abbots Leigh N Som 45 G4
Abbotsley Cambs 86 E4
Abbots Morton Worcs 82 B4
Abbots Ripton Cambs 102 E7
Abbot's Salford Warwks 82 C5
Abbotstone Hants 35 H4
Abbotswood Hants 34 D6
Abbots Worthy Hants 35 G4
Abbotts Ann Hants 34 D2
Abbott Street Dorset 17 J3
Abcott Shrops 95 J7
Abdon Shrops 96 D6
Abenhall Gloucs 63 K4
Aberaeron Cerdgn 76 E3
Aberaman Rhondd 60 F7
Aberangell Gwynd 93 J2
Aber-arad Carmth 76 B7
Aberarder Highld 251 H6
Aberargie P & K 222 B4
Aberarth Cerdgn 76 E3
Aberavon Neath 57 K7
Aber-banc Cerdgn 76 C7
Aberbargoed Caerph 61 J7
Aberbeeg Blae G 61 K6
Abercanaid Myr Td 61 G6
Abercarn Caerph 43 K3
Abercastle Pembks 74 D5
Abercegir Powys 93 H3
Aberchalder Highld 240 B3
Aberchirder Abers 268 A5
Aber Clydach Powys 61 H3
Abercorn W Loth 210 E3
Abercraf Powys 59 M6
Abercregan Neath 42 C2
Abercwmboi Rhondd 60 F7
Abercych Pembks 75 M4
Abercynon Rhondd 43 G3
Aberdalgie P & K 221 K3
Aberdare Rhondd 60 F6
Aberdaron Gwynd 108 C6
Aberdeen C Aber 245 L2
Aberdeen Airport C Aber 245 J1
Aberdesach Gwynd 109 G1
Aberdour Fife 211 G2
Aberdulais Neath 57 L5
Aberdyfi Gwynd 92 D4
Aberedw Powys 78 F6
Abereiddy Pembks 74 C6
Abererch Gwynd 109 G4
Aberfan Myr Td 61 G7
Aberfeldy P & K 232 C5
Aberffraw IoA 124 F6
Aberffrwd Cerdgn 92 E7
Aberford Leeds 150 F8
Aberfoyle Stirlg 219 H7
Abergarw Brdgnd 42 D5
Abergarwed Neath 60 B6
Abergavenny Mons 62 C4
Abergele Conwy 127 J4
Aber-giar Carmth 76 F7
Abergorlech Carmth 59 G2
Abergwesyn Powys 78 A4
Abergwili Carmth 58 D5
Abergwydol Powys 93 G3
Abergwynfi Neath 42 D3
Abergwyngregyn Gwynd 126 C5
Abergynolwyn Gwynd 92 E2
Aberhafesp Powys 94 C5

Aberhosan Powys 93 H4
Aberkenfig Brdgnd 42 D5
Aberlady E Loth 212 A3
Aberlemno Angus 234 E4
Aberllefenni Gwynd 93 G2
Aberllynfi Powys 79 H7
Aberlour, Charlestown of
   Moray 254 E3
Abermagwr Cerdgn 92 E8
Aber-meurig Cerdgn 77 G4
Abermorddu Flints 129 G8
Abermule Powys 94 C4
Abernant Carmth 58 C4
Abernant Rhondd 60 F6
Abernethy P & K 222 C4
Abernyte P & K 222 D1
Aberporth Cerdgn 76 A5
Abersoch Gwynd 108 E6
Abersychan Torfn 62 B6
Aberthin V Glam 42 F6
Abertillery Blae G 61 K6
Abertridwr Caerph 43 H4
Abertridwr Powys 111 K7
Abertysswg Caerph 61 H6
Aberuthven P & K 221 H4
Aberwheeler Denbgs 128 C6
Aberyscir Powys 60 F1
Aberystwyth Cerdgn 92 C7
Abingdon-on-Thames Oxon 66 C7
Abinger Common Surrey 37 H2
Abinger Hammer Surrey 37 G2
Abington S Lans 186 D2
Abington W Nthn 84 F3
Abington Pigotts Cambs 86 F6
Abington Services S Lans 186 D1
Abingworth W Susx 21 J3
Ab Kettleby Leics 117 J7
Ab Lench Worcs 82 B5
Ablington Gloucs 65 G5
Ablington Wilts 33 K2
Abney Derbys 132 D4
Above Church Staffs 115 G2
Aboyne Abers 244 C4
Abhainn Suidhe W Isls 282 d5
Abram Wigan 139 J7
Abriachan Highld 250 F4
Abridge Essex 70 C7
Abronhill N Lans 209 L4
Abson S Glos 45 L4
Abthorpe W Nthn 84 C6
Aby Lincs 137 H4
Acaster Malbis C York 151 J6
Acaster Selby N York 151 J7
Accrington Lancs 139 M2
Acha Ag & B 224 F4
Achahoish Ag & B 206 B3
Achalader P & K 233 H6
Achaleven Ag & B 228 E8
Acha Mor W Isls 282 f3
Achanalt Highld 261 M7
Achandunie Highld 263 H5
Achany Highld 272 C2
Acharacle Highld 237 K7
Acharn Highld 227 K2
Acharn P & K 231 L6
Achavanich Highld 279 L7
Achduart Highld 270 D7
Achfary Highld 276 D8
Achgarve Highld 260 E1
A'Chill Highld 246 C7
Achiltibuie Highld 270 D6
Achina Highld 278 B4
Achinhoan Ag & B 192 F5
Achintee Highld 248 F3
Achintraid Highld 248 D5
Achlyness Highld 276 C5
Achmelvich Highld 270 E3
Achmore Highld 248 D5
Achmore W Isls 282 f3
Achnacarnin Highld 270 D2
Achnacarry Highld 239 K6
Achnacloich Highld 247 J2
Achnaconeran Highld 250 D8
Achnacroish Ag & B 228 C7
Achnadrish Ag & B 226 F2
Achnafauld P & K 232 C2
Achnagarron Highld 263 J6
Achnaha Highld 236 F6
Achnahaird Highld 270 D5
Achnahannet Highld 253 J6
Achnairn Highld 272 E5
Achnalea Highld 228 C3
Achnamara Ag & B 206 B2
Achnasheen Highld 261 K8
Achnashellach Highld 249 G2
Achnastank Moray 254 F5
Achosnich Highld 236 E7
Achranich Highld 227 L3
Achreamie Highld 279 H3
Achriabhach Highld 229 J2

Achriesgill Highld 276 D5
Achtoty Highld 277 M4
Achurch N Nthn 102 A6
Achvaich Highld 263 J1
Achvarasdal Highld 279 H3
Ackenthwaite W & F 157 H6
Ackergill Highld 280 E5
Acklam Middsb 170 C7
Acklam N York 152 B3
Ackleton Shrops 97 H4
Acklington Nthumb 191 J6
Ackton Wakefd 142 C3
Ackworth Moor Top Wakefd 142 C4
Acle Norfk 107 H1
Acock's Green Birm 98 E6
Acol Kent 41 J2
Acomb C York 151 J5
Acomb Nthumb 179 L5
Acombe Somset 30 B8
Aconbury Herefs 80 C8
Acre Lancs 140 B3
Acrefair Wrexhm 112 D3
Acresford Derbys 99 J1
Acton Ches E 113 K1
Acton Dorset 17 J7
Acton Gt Lon 51 G3
Acton Shrops 95 H6
Acton Staffs 114 C3
Acton Suffk 89 H6
Acton Worcs 81 J2
Acton Wrexhm 112 E1
Acton Beauchamp Herefs 80 F5
Acton Bridge Ches W 130 B4
Acton Burnell Shrops 96 C3
Acton Green Herefs 81 G5
Acton Pigott Shrops 96 C3
Acton Round Shrops 96 E4
Acton Scott Shrops 95 L5
Acton Trussell Staffs 114 E7
Acton Turville S Glos 46 A3
Adbaston Staffs 114 B6
Adber Dorset 31 K6
Adbolton Notts 117 G4
Adderbury Oxon 83 L8
Adderley Shrops 113 L3
Adderstone Nthumb 203 J7
Addiewell W Loth 210 C6
Addingham C Brad 149 K6
Addington Bucks 67 H2
Addington Gt Lon 51 K6
Addington Kent 52 E7
Addiscombe Gt Lon 51 J5
Addlestone Surrey 50 D6
Addlestonemoor Surrey 50 D6
Addlethorpe Lincs 137 K6
Adeney Wrekin 113 M7
Adeyfield Herts 68 D5
Adfa Powys 94 C3
Adforton Herefs 79 M1
Adisham Kent 41 H4
Adlestrop Gloucs 65 K2
Adlingfleet E R Yk 143 L3
Adlington Ches E 131 H4
Adlington Lancs 139 J5
Admaston Staffs 115 G7
Admaston Wrekin 96 E1
Admington Warwks 82 E6
Adpar Cerdgn 76 B7
Adsborough Somset 30 D5
Adscombe Somset 30 D5
Adstock Bucks 67 H1
Adstone W Nthn 84 B5
Adswood Stockp 131 H2
Adversane W Susx 37 G6
Advie Highld 254 C5
Adwalton Leeds 141 K2
Adwell Oxon 67 G7
Adwick le Street Donc 142 E6
Adwick upon Dearne Donc 142 D7
Ae D & G 176 C1
Ae Bridgend D & G 176 D2
Afan Forest Park Neath 42 C2
Affetside Bury 139 M5
Affleck Abers 255 L4
Affpuddle Dorset 16 F4
Affric Lodge Highld 249 K7
Afon-wen Flints 128 D5
Afon Wen Gwynd 109 H4
Afton Devon 8 C2
Afton IoW 18 E6
Agglethorpe N York 159 K5
Aigburth Lpool 129 J2
Aike E R Yk 153 G6
Aiketgate W & F 166 B1
Aikhead Cumb 165 H1
Aikton Cumb 177 J8
Ailby Lincs 137 H4
Ailey Herefs 79 L5
Ailsworth C Pete 102 C4
Ainderby Quernhow N York 160 E6

Ainderby Steeple N York 160 E4
Aingers Green Essex 73 G3
Ainsdale Sefton 138 C5
Ainsdale-on-Sea Sefton 138 C5
Ainstable W & F 166 C2
Ainsworth Bury 139 M5
Ainthorpe N York 162 C1
Aintree Sefton 138 D8
Ainville W Loth 210 F6
Aird Ag & B 216 B7
Aird D & G 172 D3
Aird Highld 247 J8
Aird W Isls 282 h3
Àird a' Mhulaidh W Isls 282 e5
Aird Asaig W Isls 282 e5
Aird Dhubh Highld 248 A4
Airdeny Ag & B 216 F1
Airdrie N Lans 209 K6
Airdriehill N Lans 209 K5
Airds of Kells D & G 175 G1
Àird Uig W Isls 282 d3
Airidh a bhruaich W Isls 282 f4
Airieland D & G 175 J3
Airlie Angus 233 M5
Airmyn E R Yk 143 J3
Airntully P & K 233 G8
Airor Highld 247 M7
Airth Falk 210 B2
Airton N York 148 F4
Aisby Lincs 118 D4
Aisby Lincs 135 H1
Aisgill W & F. 158 D3
Aish Devon 7 K3
Aish Devon 8 C3
Aisholt Somset 30 B4
Aiskew N York 160 C5
Aislaby N York 162 D5
Aislaby N York 162 F1
Aislaby S on T 169 L8
Aisthorpe Lincs 135 J4
Aith Shet 281 d5
Akeld Nthumb 202 E7
Akeley Bucks 84 D7
Akenham Suffk 90 D5
Albaston Cnwll 12 A8
Alberbury Shrops 112 E8
Albourne W Susx 22 C4
Albourne Green W Susx 22 C4
Albrighton Shrops 97 H3
Albrighton Shrops 113 H7
Alburgh Norfk 106 F6
Albury Herts 70 B2
Albury Oxon 67 G6
Albury Surrey 37 G2
Albury End Herts 70 B2
Albury Heath Surrey 37 G2
Alby Hill Norfk 122 D5
Alcaig Highld 263 G8
Alcaston Shrops 95 L6
Alcester Warwks 82 C4
Alciston E Susx 23 H6
Alcombe Somset 29 H2
Alcombe Wilts 46 A5
Alconbury Cambs 102 D8
Alconbury Weald Cambs 102 D8
Alconbury Weston Cambs 102 D7
Aldborough N York 150 F3
Aldborough Norfk 122 D5
Aldbourne Wilts 47 K4
Aldbrough E R Yk 153 L8
Aldbrough St John N York 169 G8
Aldbury Herts 68 B4
Aldcliffe Lancs 147 J4
Aldclune P & K 232 D3
Aldeburgh Suffk 91 K4
Aldeby Norfk 107 J5
Aldenham Herts 68 F7
Alderbury Wilts 33 L5
Aldercar Derbys 116 D2
Alderford Norfk 122 C7
Alderholt Dorset 33 K8
Alderley Gloucs 45 M1
Alderley Edge Ches E 131 G4
Aldermans Green Covtry 99 K6
Aldermaston W Berk 48 E6
Alderminster Warwks 82 F5
Alder Moor Staffs 115 L6
Aldersey Green Ches W 129 K8
Aldershot Hants 36 C1
Alderton Gloucs 82 B8
Alderton Shrops 113 H6
Alderton Suffk 91 H7
Alderton W Nthn 84 E6
Alderton Wilts 46 B2
Alderwasley Derbys 116 A1
Aldfield N York 150 C2
Aldford Ches W 129 K7
Aldgate Rutlnd 101 L3
Aldham Essex 72 C4
Aldham Suffk 90 B6

Aldingbourne W Susx 20 F5
Aldingham W & F 146 E2
Aldington Kent 40 E8
Aldington Worcs 82 C6
Aldington Corner Kent 40 E7
Aldivalloch Moray 255 G6
Aldochlay Ag & B 208 B1
Aldon Shrops 95 K7
Aldoth Cumb 164 F1
Aldreth Cambs 103 J8
Aldridge Wsall 98 D3
Aldringham Suffk 91 K3
Aldro N York 152 B3
Aldsworth Gloucs 65 H5
Aldsworth W Susx 20 C5
Aldunie Moray 255 G6
Aldwark Derbys 132 E8
Aldwark N York 151 H4
Aldwick W Susx 20 F7
Aldwincle N Nthn 101 M7
Aldworth W Berk 48 E3
Alexandria W Duns 208 C3
Aley Somset 30 B3
Alfardisworthy Devon 26 E8
Alfington Devon 14 D3
Alfold Surrey 36 F4
Alfold Bars W Susx 36 F4
Alfold Crossways Surrey 36 F4
Alford Abers 255 M8
Alford Lincs 137 H4
Alford Somset 31 K4
Alfreton Derbys 133 H8
Alfrick Worcs 81 H4
Alfrick Pound Worcs 81 G5
Alfriston E Susx 23 H6
Algarkirk Lincs 119 J4
Alhampton Somset 31 K4
Alkborough N Linc 143 M3
Alkerton Gloucs 63 M6
Alkerton Oxon 83 J6
Alkham Kent 41 H6
Alkington Shrops 113 H4
Alkmonton Derbys 115 K4
Allaleigh Devon 8 B4
Allanaquoich Abers 243 J5
Allanbank N Lans 209 M7
Allanton Border 202 D2
Allanton N Lans 209 M7
Allanton S Lans 209 K8
Allaston Gloucs 63 J6
Allbrook Hants 34 F6
All Cannings Wilts 46 F6
Allendale Nthumb 179 J7
Allen End Warwks 98 F4
Allenheads Nthumb 167 K2
Allensford Dur 168 D1
Allen's Green Herts 70 C4
Allensmore Herefs 80 B8
Allenton C Derb 116 B5
Aller Devon 28 D5
Aller Somset 30 F5
Allerby Cumb 164 E3
Allercombe Devon 14 B4
Aller Cross Devon 28 B5
Allerford Somset 28 F2
Allerston N York 162 F6
Allerthorpe E R Yk 152 B6
Allerton C Brad 141 H1
Allerton Highld 263 K6
Allerton Lpool 129 J2
Allerton Bywater Leeds 142 C2
Allerton Mauleverer N York 150 F4
Allesley Covtry 99 J7
Allestree C Derb 116 B4
Allet Cnwll 4 C5
Allexton Leics 101 H3
Allgreave Ches E 131 J6
Allhallows Medway 53 H3
Allhallows-on-Sea Medway 53 H3
Alligin Shuas Highld 260 D8
Allimore Green Staffs 114 D7
Allington Dorset 15 K4
Allington Kent 53 G7
Allington Lincs 117 M3
Allington Wilts 33 L3
Allington Wilts 46 C4
Allington Wilts 46 F6
Allithwaite W & F 156 E7
Alloa Clacks 220 F8
Allonby Cumb 164 E2
Allostock Ches W 130 E5
Alloway S Ayrs 196 C7
Allowenshay Somset 30 F8
All Saints South Elmham
  Suffk 107 G7
Allscott Shrops 97 G4
Allscott Wrekin 96 E1
All Stretton Shrops 95 L4
Alltami Flints 129 G6
Alltchaorunn Highld 229 K5

Alltmawr Powys 78 F6
Alltsigh Highld 250 D7
Alltwalis Carmth 58 E3
Alltwen Neath 57 K4
Alltyblaca Cerdgn 76 F6
Allwood Green Suffk 90 B1
Almeley Herefs 79 L5
Almeley Wooton Herefs 79 L5
Almer Dorset 17 H3
Almholme Donc 142 F6
Almington Staffs 113 M4
Almodington W Susx 20 D7
Almondbank P & K 221 J2
Almondbury Kirk 141 J5
Almondsbury S Glos 45 J2
Alne N York 151 G3
Alness Highld 263 H6
Alnham Nthumb 190 E4
Alnmouth Nthumb 191 J4
Alnwick Nthumb 191 H3
Alperton Gt Lon 50 F2
Alphamstone Essex 89 H8
Alpheton Suffk 89 H5
Alphington Devon 13 L4
Alpington Norfk 106 F3
Alport Derbys 132 D6
Alpraham Ches E 130 B7
Alresford Essex 72 F3
Alrewas Staffs 115 K8
Alsager Ches E 130 F8
Alsagers Bank Staffs 114 C2
Alsop en le Dale Derbys 132 C8
Alston Devon 15 G2
Alston W & F 167 G2
Alstone Gloucs 64 E1
Alstone Somset 30 D2
Alstonefield Staffs 132 C8
Alston Sutton Somset 44 E8
Alswear Devon 28 C6
Alt Oldham 140 E7
Altandhu Highld 270 C5
Altarnun Cnwll 11 J6
Altass Highld 272 D9
Altcreich Ag & B 227 K5
Altgaltraig Ag & B 207 G4
Althane Pembks 74 B4
Althorne Essex 72 F7
Althorpe N Linc 143 L6
Altnabreac Station Highld 279 H7
Altnaharra Highld 272 E1
Altofts Wakefd 142 B3
Alton Derbys 133 G6
Alton Hants 35 L3
Alton Staffs 115 H3
Alton Wilts 33 K2
Alton Barnes Wilts 47 G6
Alton Pancras Dorset 16 D2
Alton Priors Wilts 47 G6
Altrincham Traffd 130 E2
Altskeith Hotel Stirlg 219 G6
Alva Clacks 220 F7
Alvanley Ches W 129 L5
Alvaston C Derb 116 C5
Alvechurch Worcs 82 B1
Alvecote Warwks 99 H3
Alvediston Wilts 33 G4
Alveley Shrops 97 G6
Alverdiscott Devon 27 J6
Alverstoke Hants 19 K4
Alverstone IoW 19 K6
Alverthorpe Wakefd 141 M3
Alverton Notts 117 L3
Alves Moray 266 C4
Alvescot Oxon 65 K6
Alveston S Glos 45 J1
Alveston Warwks 82 F4
Alvingham Lincs 137 G2
Alvington Gloucs 63 J7
Alwalton C Pete 102 C4
Alweston Dorset 31 L8
Alwinton Nthumb 190 C5
Alwoodley Leeds 150 C7
Alwoodley Gates Leeds 150 D7
Alyth P & K 233 K5
Am Bàgh a Tuath W Isls 283 b13
Ambergate Derbys 116 B1
Amber Hill Lincs 119 H2
Amberley Gloucs 64 B6
Amberley W Susx 21 H4
Amber Row Derbys 133 G8
Amberstone E Susx 23 K5
Amble Nthumb 191 K5
Amblecote Dudley 97 K6
Ambler Thorn C Brad 141 H2
Ambleside W & F 156 E2
Ambleston Pembks 75 G7
Ambrosden Oxon 66 F3
Amcotts N Linc 143 L5
America Cambs 103 J7
Amersham Bucks 68 B7

Amersham Common Bucks 68 B7
Amersham Old Town Bucks 68 B7
Amersham on the Hill Bucks 68 B7
Amerton Staffs 114 F6
Amesbury Wilts 33 K3
Amhuinnsuidhe W Isls 282 d5
Amington Staffs 99 G3
Amisfield D & G 176 D2
Amlwch IoA 125 H1
Ammanford Carmth 59 H6
Amotherby N York 162 C7
Ampfield Hants 34 E6
Ampleforth N York 161 J7
Ampney Crucis Gloucs 64 F6
Ampney St Mary Gloucs 65 G6
Ampney St Peter Gloucs 65 G6
Amport Hants 34 C2
Ampthill C Beds 85 K7
Ampton Suffk 89 H1
Amroth Pembks 55 K5
Amulree P & K 232 D8
Amwell Herts 68 F4
Anaheilt Highld 228 C3
Ancaster Lincs 118 C3
Ancells Farm Hants 49 K7
Anchor Shrops 94 E6
Ancroft Nthumb 202 F4
Ancrum Border 189 H1
Ancton W Susx 21 G6
Anderby Lincs 137 K4
Anderby Creek Lincs 137 K4
Andersea Somset 30 E4
Andersfield Somset 30 C4
Anderson Dorset 17 G3
Anderton Ches W 130 C4
Anderton Cnwll 6 E4
Andover Hants 34 C2
Andover Down Hants 34 E2
Andoversford Gloucs 64 F3
Andreas IoM 154 f2
Anelog Gwynd 108 B6
Anerley Gt Lon 51 J5
Anfield Lpool 129 J1
Angarrack Cnwll 2 F3
Angarrick Cnwll 3 K4
Angelbank Shrops 96 B8
Angersleigh Somset 30 B7
Angerton Cumb 177 H7
Angle Pembks 54 D6
Anglesey IoA 125 G3
Angmering W Susx 21 H6
Angram N York 151 H6
Angram N York 158 F3
Angrouse Cnwll 3 H7
Anick Nthumb 179 L5
Ankerville Highld 264 C5
Ankle Hill Leics 117 K7
Anlaby E R Yk 144 C2
Anmer Norfk 121 G5
Anmore Hants 19 L1
Annan D & G 177 G5
Annandale Water Services
  D & G 187 H7
Annaside Cumb 155 K5
Annat Highld 248 E1
Annathill N Lans 209 J5
Anna Valley Hants 34 D2
Annbank S Ayrs 196 E6
Annesley Notts 116 E1
Annesley Woodhouse Notts 116 E1
Annfield Plain Dur 180 E8
Anniesland C Glas 208 F5
Annitsford N Tyne 181 G4
Annscroft Shrops 95 L2
Ansdell Lancs 138 D2
Ansford Somset 31 L4
Ansley Warwks 99 J5
Anslow Staffs 115 L6
Anslow Gate Staffs 115 K6
Anslow Lees Staffs 115 L6
Ansteadbrook Surrey 36 D4
Anstey Hants 35 L3
Anstey Herts 87 H8
Anstey Leics 100 C2
Anstruther Fife 223 K6
Ansty W Susx 37 L6
Ansty Warwks 99 L6
Ansty Wilts 33 G5
Ansty Cross Dorset 16 E2
An Tairbeart W Isls 282 e5
Anthill Common Hants 19 L1
Anthonys Surrey 50 C7
Anthorn Cumb 177 G7
Antingham Norfk 122 E5
An t-Ob W Isls 282 e6
Anton's Gowt Lincs 119 J2
Antony Cnwll 6 D4
Antrobus Ches W 130 C4
Anvil Corner Devon 11 M2

Anvil Green Kent 40 E5
Anwick Lincs 118 F2
Anwoth D & G 174 F4
Aperfield Gt Lon 51 L7
Apes Dale Worcs 82 A1
Apethorpe N Nthn 102 A4
Apeton Staffs 114 D7
Apley Lincs 136 B5
Apperknowle Derbys 133 H4
Apperley Gloucs 64 B2
Apperley Bridge C Brad 150 B8
Apperley Dene Nthumb 180 C7
Appersett N York 158 E4
Appin Ag & B 228 E6
Appleby N Linc 144 B5
Appleby-in-Westmorland
  W & F 166 F6
Appleby Magna Leics 99 J2
Appleby Parva Leics 99 J2
Appleby Street Herts 69 J6
Applecross Highld 248 G5
Appledore Devon 27 H5
Appledore Devon 29 K7
Appledore Kent 25 H2
Appledore Heath Kent 25 H1
Appleford Oxon 66 D8
Applegarth Town D & G 176 F2
Applehaigh Wakefd 142 A5
Applemore Hants 18 F2
Appleshaw Hants 34 C1
Applethwaite Cumb 165 J5
Appleton Halton 129 M2
Appleton Oxon 66 C6
Appleton Warrtn 130 B3
Appleton-le-Moors N York 162 C5
Appleton-le-Street N York 162 C7
Appleton Roebuck N York 151 J7
Appleton Thorn Warrtn 130 C3
Appleton Wiske N York 160 F2
Appletreehall Border 188 F3
Appletreewick N York 149 J4
Appley Somset 29 K6
Appley Bridge Lancs 139 G6
Apse Heath IoW 19 J7
Apsley End C Beds 86 C8
Apuldram W Susx 20 D6
Arabella Highld 264 C5
Arbirlot Angus 234 F7
Arborfield Wokham 49 H5
Arborfield Cross Wokham 49 J5
Arborfield Green Wokham 49 J6
Arbourthorne Sheff 133 G3
Arbroath Angus 235 G7
Arbuthnott Abers 245 H8
Arcadia Kent 39 L6
Archddu Carmth 56 E4
Archdeacon Newton Darltn 169 H7
Archencarroch W Duns 208 C3
Archiestown Moray 254 E3
Archirondel Jersey 9 f2
Arclid Ches E 130 F7
Ardallie Abers 257 J4
Ardanaiseig Hotel Ag & B 217 H2
Ardaneaskan Highld 248 D4
Ardarroch Highld 248 D4
Ardbeg Ag & B 204 F7
Ardbeg Ag & B 207 H5
Ardbeg Ag & B 207 K2
Ardcharnich Highld 261 K2
Ardchiavaig Ag & B 226 D8
Ardchonnell Ag & B 216 F5
Ardchronie Highld 263 G2
Ardchullarie More Stirlg 219 K4
Arddarroch Ag & B 218 C8
Arddleen Powys 112 C8
Ard Dorch Highld 247 J3
Ardechive Highld 239 J5
Ardeer N Ayrs 196 B3
Ardeley Herts 69 J2
Ardelve Highld 248 D6
Arden Ag & B 208 B2
Ardens Grafton Warwks 82 D4
Ardentallen Ag & B 216 C2
Ardentinny Ag & B 207 K2
Ardentraive Ag & B 207 G4
Ardeonaig Stirlg 231 J8
Ardersier Highld 252 E1
Ardessie Highld 261 H2
Ardfern Ag & B 216 C6
Ardfernal Ag & B 205 J2
Ardgartan Ag & B 218 D6
Ardgay Highld 263 G2
Ardgour Highld 229 G3
Ardgowan Inver 207 L4
Ardhallow Ag & B 207 K4
Ardhasig W Isls 282 e5
Ardheslaig Highld 260 C8
Ardindrean Highld 261 K2
Ardingly W Susx 38 A7
Ardington Oxon 48 B1

Ardington Wick Oxon....48 B1
Ardlamont Ag & B....206 F6
Ardleigh Essex....72 F1
Ardleigh Heath Essex....72 F1
Ardler P & K....233 L7
Ardley Oxon....66 D2
Ardley End Essex....70 D4
Ardlui Ag & B....218 D4
Ardlussa Ag & B....215 J6
Ardmair Highld....270 F8
Ardmaleish Ag & B....207 H5
Ardminish Ag & B....205 L6
Ardmolich Highld....237 K6
Ardmore Ag & B....208 A3
Ardmore Highld....263 J3
Ardnadam Ag & B....207 K3
Ardnagrask Highld....250 F2
Ardnamurchan Highld....237 H7
Ardnarff Highld....248 E4
Ardnastang Highld....228 B3
Ardpatrick Ag & B....206 B7
Ardrishaig Ag & B....206 D2
Ardross Highld....263 H5
Ardrossan N Ayrs....195 L3
Ardsley Barns....142 B6
Ardslignish Highld....237 H8
Ardtalla Ag & B....205 G5
Ardtoe Highld....237 J6
Arduaine Ag & B....216 B5
Ardullie Highld....263 G7
Ardvasar Highld....247 K7
Ardvorlich P & K....219 K3
Ardvourlie W Isls....282 e5
Ardwell D & G....172 D5
Ardwick Manch....140 C8
Areley Kings Worcs....81 H1
Arevegaig Highld....237 J7
Arford Hants....36 B3
Arglam E R Yk....152 B8
Argoed Caerph....61 J7
Argoed Shrops....112 E7
Argoed Mill Powys....78 D3
Argos Hill E Susx....23 J2
Argyll Forest Park Ag & B....218 C6
Aribruach W Isls....282 f4
Aridhglas Ag & B....226 C7
Arileod Ag & B....224 F4
Arinagour Ag & B....225 G4
Ariogan Ag & B....216 D2
Arisaig Highld....237 J3
Arisaig House Highld....237 K4
Arkendale N York....150 E4
Arkesden Essex....87 K8
Arkholme Lancs....147 L2
Arkleby Cumb....164 F3
Arkleton D & G....188 C7
Arkle Town N York....159 H2
Arkley Gt Lon....69 G7
Arksey Donc....142 F6
Arkwright Town Derbys....133 H5
Arle Gloucs....64 D2
Arlecdon Cumb....164 D7
Arlescote Warwks....83 J5
Arlesey C Beds....86 D7
Arleston Wrekin....96 F1
Arley Ches E....130 C3
Arlingham Gloucs....63 L5
Arlington Devon....27 L3
Arlington E Susx....23 J5
Arlington Gloucs....65 G5
Arlington Beccott Devon....27 L3
Armadale Highld....247 K7
Armadale Highld....278 D3
Armadale W Loth....210 B5
Armaside Cumb....164 F5
Armathwaite W & F....166 C2
Arminghall Norfk....106 E3
Armitage Staffs....115 H8
Armitage Bridge Kirk....141 H5
Armley Leeds....141 L1
Armscote Warwks....82 F6
Armshead Staffs....114 E2
Armston N Nthn....102 B6
Armthorpe Donc....143 G6
Arnabost Ag & B....225 G3
Arnaby Cumb....156 A5
Arncliffe N York....149 G2
Arncliffe Cote N York....149 G2
Arncroach Fife....223 J6
Arndilly House Moray....266 F6
Arne Dorset....17 J5
Arnesby Leics....100 D5
Arngask P & K....221 L5
Arnisdale Highld....238 D2
Arnish Highld....259 K7
Arniston Mdloth....211 K6
Arnol W Isls....282 f2
Arnold E R Yk....153 H7
Arnold Notts....117 G2
Arnprior Stirlg....219 K8

Arnside W & F....157 G7
Aros Ag & B....227 G3
Arowry Wrexhm....113 G4
Arrad Foot W & F....156 D6
Arram E R Yk....153 G7
Arran N Ayrs....194 E4
Arrathorne N York....160 B4
Arreton IoW....19 J6
Arrina Highld....260 B8
Arrington Cambs....87 H5
Arrochar Ag & B....218 D6
Arrow Warwks....82 C4
Arrowfield Top Worcs....98 C8
Arscott Shrops....95 K2
Artafallie Highld....251 H2
Arthington Leeds....150 C6
Arthingworth W Nthn....101 G7
Arthog Gwynd....110 C8
Arthrath Abers....257 H4
Arthursdale Leeds....150 E8
Arthrochie Abers....257 J5
Arundel W Susx....21 G5
Asby Cumb....164 E6
Ascog Ag & B....207 J6
Ascot W & M....50 A5
Ascott Warwks....83 H8
Ascott Earl Oxon....65 L3
Ascott-under-Wychwood Oxon....65 L3
Asenby N York....160 F7
Asfordby Leics....117 J7
Asfordby Hill Leics....117 J7
Asgarby Lincs....118 F3
Asgarby Lincs....136 F6
Ash Devon....8 C5
Ash Devon....12 C1
Ash Dorset....32 E8
Ash Kent....41 J4
Ash Kent....52 D6
Ash Somset....30 D6
Ash Somset....31 G6
Ash Surrey....36 D1
Ashampstead W Berk....48 E4
Ashampstead Green W Berk....48 E3
Ashbocking Suffk....90 E4
Ashbourne Derbys....115 K2
Ashbrittle Somset....29 J6
Ashburnham Place E Susx....24 C4
Ashburton Devon....13 H8
Ashbury Devon....12 C3
Ashbury Oxon....47 K2
Ashby N Linc....143 M6
Ashby by Partney Lincs....137 H6
Ashby cum Fenby NE Lin....145 H7
Ashby de la Launde Lincs....135 L8
Ashby-de-la-Zouch Leics....116 B8
Ashby Folville Leics....100 F1
Ashby Magna Leics....100 C5
Ashby Parva Leics....100 C5
Ashby Puerorum Lincs....136 F5
Ashby St Ledgers W Nthn....84 B2
Ashby St Mary Norfk....107 G3
Ashchurch Gloucs....81 L8
Ashcombe Devon....13 L6
Ashcombe N Som....44 C6
Ashcott Somset....31 G4
Ashdon Essex....88 B6
Ashdown Forest E Susx....38 C7
Ashe Hants....35 H1
Asheldham Essex....72 E6
Ashen Essex....88 E6
Ashendon Bucks....67 H4
Asheridge Bucks....68 B5
Ashfield Hants....34 E7
Ashfield Herefs....63 H2
Ashfield Stirlg....220 D6
Ashfield cum Thorpe Suffk....90 F3
Ashfield Green Suffk....88 F4
Ashfield Green Suffk....106 F8
Ashfold Crossways W Susx....37 K5
Ashford Devon....7 K5
Ashford Devon....27 J4
Ashford Kent....40 D6
Ashford Surrey....50 D4
Ashford Bowdler Shrops....80 C1
Ashford Carbonell Shrops....80 C1
Ashford Hill Hants....48 E6
Ashford in the Water Derbys....132 D5
Ashgill S Lans....198 C3
Ash Green Surrey....36 D1
Ash Green Warwks....99 J6
Ashill Devon....29 K8
Ashill Norfk....105 H3
Ashill Somset....30 D7
Ashingdon Essex....72 C8
Ashington BCP....17 K3
Ashington Nthumb....181 G1
Ashington Somset....31 J6
Ashington W Susx....21 K4
Ashkirk Border....188 E2
Ashlett Hants....19 G3

Ashleworth Gloucs....64 A2
Ashleworth Quay Gloucs....64 A2
Ashley Cambs....88 D3
Ashley Ches E....130 F3
Ashley Devon....28 B8
Ashley Dorset....18 A3
Ashley Gloucs....64 D8
Ashley Hants....18 C4
Ashley Hants....34 E4
Ashley Kent....41 J5
Ashley Nthn....101 H5
Ashley Staffs....114 B4
Ashley Wilts....46 B5
Ashley Worcs....81 B6
Ashley Green Bucks....68 B5
Ashleyhay Derbys....115 M1
Ashley Heath Dorset....17 M2
Ashley Moor Herefs....80 B2
Ash Magna Shrops....113 J4
Ashmansworth Hants....48 B7
Ashmansworthy Devon....26 F7
Ashmead Green Gloucs....63 M7
Ashmill Devon....11 M3
Ash Mill Devon....28 D6
Ashmore Dorset....32 F7
Ashmore Green W Berk....48 D5
Ashorne Warwks....83 G4
Ashover Derbys....133 G7
Ashover Hay Derbys....133 G7
Ash Parva Shrops....113 J4
Ashperton Herefs....80 E7
Ashprington Devon....8 B3
Ash Priors Somset....29 L5
Ashreigney Devon....27 L8
Ash Street Suffk....89 K6
Ashtead Surrey....50 F7
Ash Thomas Devon....29 H7
Ashton C Pete....102 B2
Ashton Cnwll....2 F5
Ashton Devon....13 K5
Ashton Hants....35 H7
Ashton Herefs....80 C2
Ashton Inver....207 L4
Ashton N Nthn....102 B5
Ashton Somset....30 C1
Ashton W Nthn....84 E5
Ashton Common Wilts....46 C7
Ashton Hayes Ches W....129 L6
Ashton Hill Wilts....46 C7
Ashton-in-Makerfield Wigan....139 H7
Ashton Keynes Wilts....64 F8
Ashton-on-Ribble Lancs....139 G2
Ashton under Hill Worcs....82 A7
Ashton-under-Lyne Tamesd....140 E7
Ashton upon Mersey Traffd....130 F1
Ashton Vale Bristl....45 H5
Ashurst Hants....18 E2
Ashurst Kent....38 D5
Ashurst Lancs....138 F6
Ashurst W Susx....21 L4
Ashurst Wood W Susx....38 B6
Ash Vale Surrey....49 L8
Ashwater Devon....11 M4
Ashwell Herts....86 F7
Ashwell Rutlnd....101 J1
Ashwell Somset....30 E7
Ashwell End Herts....86 E7
Ashwellthorpe Norfk....106 C4
Ashwick Somset....31 K1
Ashwicken Norfk....120 F7
Ashwood Staffs....97 K5
Askam in Furness W & F....156 B7
Askern Donc....142 F5
Askerswell Dorset....15 M4
Askett Bucks....67 K6
Askham Notts....134 E5
Askham W & F....166 C6
Askham Bryan C York....151 H6
Askham Richard C York....151 H6
Asknish Ag & B....206 E1
Askrigg N York....159 G4
Askwith N York....149 L6
Aslackby Lincs....118 E5
Aslacton Norfk....106 D5
Aslockton Notts....117 K3
Asney Somset....31 G3
Aspall Suffk....90 E2
Aspatria Cumb....164 F2
Aspenden Herts....69 K2
Aspenshaw Derbys....131 K2
Asperton Lincs....119 J4
Aspley Staffs....114 C5
Aspley Guise C Beds....85 J8
Aspley Heath C Beds....85 H8
Aspley Heath Warwks....82 C1
Aspull Wigan....139 J6
Aspull Common Wigan....139 J8
Asselby E R Yk....143 H2
Asserby Lincs....137 J4
Asserby Turn Lincs....137 J4

Assington Suffk....89 J7
Assington Green Suffk....88 F5
Astbury Ches E....131 G2
Astcote W Nthn....84 D4
Asterby Lincs....136 E4
Asterley Shrops....95 J2
Asterton Shrops....95 K5
Asthall Oxon....65 L5
Asthall Leigh Oxon....65 L4
Astle Highld....263 K2
Astley Shrops....113 H7
Astley Warwks....99 J5
Astley Wigan....139 L7
Astley Worcs....81 H2
Astley Abbots Shrops....96 F4
Astley Bridge Bolton....139 L5
Astley Cross Worcs....81 J1
Astley Green Wigan....139 L7
Aston Birm....98 D5
Aston Ches E....113 K2
Aston Ches W....130 A4
Aston Derbys....132 D3
Aston Flints....129 G6
Aston Herefs....80 B3
Aston Herts....69 H3
Aston Oxon....65 M6
Aston Rothm....133 J3
Aston Shrops....97 H5
Aston Shrops....113 H6
Aston Staffs....114 B3
Aston Staffs....114 D6
Aston Wokham....49 J2
Aston Wrekin....96 E2
Aston Abbotts Bucks....67 K3
Aston Botterell Shrops....96 E6
Aston-by-Stone Staffs....114 E5
Aston Cantlow Warwks....82 D3
Aston Clinton Bucks....67 L4
Aston Crews Herefs....63 K3
Aston Cross Gloucs....81 L8
Aston End Herts....69 H4
Aston-Eyre Shrops....96 E4
Aston Fields Worcs....81 M2
Aston Flamville Leics....100 A5
Aston Heath Ches W....130 A4
Aston Ingham Herefs....63 K3
Aston juxta Mondrum Ches E....130 C8
Aston le Walls W Nthn....83 L5
Aston Magna Gloucs....82 E8
Aston Munslow Shrops....96 C6
Aston-on-Carrant Gloucs....81 L8
Aston on Clun Shrops....95 J7
Aston Pigott Shrops....95 H2
Aston Rogers Shrops....95 H2
Aston Rowant Oxon....67 H7
Aston Sandford Bucks....67 J5
Aston Somerville Worcs....82 B7
Aston-sub-Edge Gloucs....82 D7
Aston Tirrold Oxon....48 E2
Aston-upon-Trent Derbys....116 C5
Aston Upthorpe Oxon....48 E2
Astrop W Nthn....83 L7
Astrope Herts....67 L4
Astwick C Beds....86 E7
Astwith Derbys....133 J6
Astwood M Keyn....85 J5
Astwood Worcs....81 L2
Astwood Bank Worcs....82 B3
Aswarby Lincs....118 E4
Aswardby Lincs....137 G5
Atcham Shrops....96 C2
Atch Lench Worcs....82 B5
Athelhampton Dorset....16 E4
Athelington Suffk....90 F1
Athelney Somset....30 E5
Athelstaneford E Loth....212 C4
Atherfield Green IoW....19 G7
Atherington Devon....27 L6
Atherington W Susx....21 G6
Atherstone Somset....30 F7
Atherstone Warwks....99 J4
Atherstone on Stour Warwks....82 F5
Atherton Wigan....139 K7
Atley Hill N York....160 D2
Atlow Derbys....115 L2
Attadale Highld....248 E4
Attenborough Notts....116 E5
Atterby Lincs....135 K1
Attercliffe Sheff....133 G2
Atterley Shrops....96 E4
Atterton Leics....99 K4
Attleborough Norfk....105 K5
Attleborough Warwks....99 K5
Attlebridge Norfk....122 C8
Attleton Green Suffk....88 E4
Atwick E R Yk....153 K5
Atworth Wilts....46 B6
Auberrow Herefs....80 C6
Aubourn Lincs....135 J7
Auchbreck Moray....254 D6

Auchedly Abers 257 G5
Auchenblae Abers 244 F7
Auchenbowie Stirlg 209 L2
Auchencairn D & G 175 K4
Auchencairn D & G 176 C2
Auchencairn N Ayrs 195 K5
Auchencrow Border 213 J7
Auchendinny Mdloth 211 H6
Auchengray S Lans 199 G2
Auchenhalrig Moray 267 H4
Auchenheath S Lans 198 D4
Auchenhessnane D & G 185 K4
Auchenlochan Ag & B 206 F4
Auchenmade N Ayrs 196 C2
Auchenmalg D & G 173 G4
Auchentiber N Ayrs 196 D2
Auchindrain Ag & B 217 G6
Auchindrean Highld 261 K4
Auchininna Abers 268 B6
Auchinleck E Ayrs 197 G6
Auchinloch N Lans 209 H6
Auchinstarry N Lans 209 J4
Auchintore Highld 229 H1
Auchiries Abers 257 K4
Auchlean Highld 241 M4
Auchlee Abers 245 K4
Auchleven Abers 256 A6
Auchlochan S Lans 198 D5
Auchlossan Abers 244 D3
Auchlyne Stirlg 219 H1
Auchmillan E Ayrs 197 G5
Auchmithie Angus 235 G6
Auchmuirbridge Fife 222 C7
Auchnacree Angus 234 C3
Auchnagatt Abers 257 G3
Auchnarrow Moray 254 D7
Auchnotteroch D & G 172 B3
Auchroisk Moray 267 G6
Auchterarder P & K 221 G4
Auchteraw Highld 240 B2
Auchterblair Highld 253 H7
Auchtercairn Highld 260 C4
Auchterderran Fife 222 C8
Auchterhouse Angus 233 M7
Auchterless Abers 256 C3
Auchtermuchty Fife 222 D7
Auchterneed Highld 262 F7
Auchtertool Fife 211 H1
Auchtertyre Highld 248 D6
Auchtubh Stirlg 219 J3
Auckengill Highld 280 E3
Auckley Donc 143 G7
Audenshaw Tamesd 140 D8
Audlem Ches E 113 L3
Audley Staffs 114 C2
Audley End Essex 87 L7
Audley End Essex 89 G7
Audley End Suffk 89 G4
Audmore Staffs 114 C7
Audnam Dudley 97 K6
Aughertree Cumb 165 H3
Aughton E R Yk 151 J8
Aughton Lancs 138 E6
Aughton Lancs 147 L2
Aughton Rothm 133 J2
Aughton Wilts 47 K7
Aughton Park Lancs 138 E6
Auldearn Highld 253 H1
Aulden Herefs 80 B4
Auldgirth D & G 176 B2
Auldhouse S Lans 197 J1
Ault a' chruinn Highld 248 F7
Aultbea Highld 260 D2
Aultgrishin Highld 260 B3
Aultguish Inn Highld 262 B6
Ault Hucknall Derbys 133 J6
Aultmore Moray 267 H5
Aultnagoire Highld 250 F7
Aultnamain Highld 263 J4
Aunby Lincs 118 D8
Aunk Devon 14 B3
Aunsby Lincs 118 D4
Aust S Glos 45 H1
Austendike Lincs 119 J7
Austerfield Donc 134 D1
Austerlands Oldham 140 E6
Austhorpe Leeds 142 B1
Austonley Kirk 141 H4
Austrey Warwks 99 J2
Austwick N York 148 D2
Authorpe Lincs 137 G3
Authorpe Row Lincs 137 K5
Avebury Wilts 47 G5
Avebury Wilts 47 G5
Avebury Trusloe Wilts 47 G5
Aveley Thurr 52 C3
Avening Gloucs 64 C7
Averham Notts 117 K1
Aveton Gifford Devon 7 K5
Aviemore Highld 242 B1

Avington W Berk 48 A5
Avoch Highld 251 J1
Avon Hants 18 A4
Avonbridge Falk 210 B4
Avon Dassett Warwks 83 K5
Avonmouth Bristl 45 G3
Avonwick Devon 7 K3
Awbridge Hants 34 D6
Awkley S Glos 45 H2
Awliscombe Devon 14 D2
Awre Gloucs 63 L5
Awsworth Notts 116 E3
Axborough Worcs 97 J7
Axbridge Somset 44 E8
Axford Hants 35 J2
Axford Wilts 47 K5
Axmansford Hants 48 F6
Axminster Devon 15 G3
Axmouth Devon 14 F4
Axton Flints 128 D4
Aycliffe Dur 169 H2
Aydon Nthumb 180 B5
Aylburton Gloucs 63 J6
Ayle Nthumb 167 G1
Aylesbeare Devon 14 B4
Aylesbury Bucks 67 K4
Aylesby NE Lin 145 G6
Aylesford Kent 52 F7
Aylesham Kent 41 H5
Aylestone C Leic 100 C3
Aylestone Park C Leic 100 D3
Aylmerton Norfk 122 D4
Aylsham Norfk 122 D6
Aylton Herefs 80 F7
Aylworth Gloucs 65 G3
Aymestrey Herefs 80 A2
Aynho W Nthn 83 L8
Ayot Green Herts 69 G4
Ayot St Lawrence Herts 69 G4
Ayot St Peter Herts 69 G4
Ayr S Ayrs 196 C6
Aysgarth N York 159 H5
Ayshford Devon 29 J7
Ayside W & F 156 F6
Ayston Rutlnd 101 J3
Aythorpe Roding Essex 70 F5
Ayton Border 213 K6
Azerley N York 160 C7

B

Babbacombe Torbay 8 D2
Babbington Notts 116 E3
Babbinswood Shrops 112 E5
Babbs Green Herts 69 K4
Babcary Somset 31 J5
Babel Carmth 59 M2
Babel Green Suffk 88 E5
Babell Flints 128 E5
Babeny Devon 12 F7
Bablock Hythe Oxon 66 B6
Babraham Cambs 87 K5
Babworth Notts 134 D3
Bachau IoA 125 H3
Bache Shrops 95 L7
Bacheldre Powys 94 F5
Bachelor's Bump E Susx 24 F5
Backaland Ork 275 d3
Backbarrow W & F 156 E5
Backe Carmth 58 A5
Backfolds Abers 269 J5
Backford Ches W 129 J5
Backford Cross Ches W 129 J5
Backies Highld 273 K7
Back of Keppoch Highld 237 J3
Back o' th' Brook Staffs 115 H1
Back Street Suffk 88 E3
Backwell N Som 44 F5
Backworth N Tyne 181 H4
Bacon's End Solhll 98 F6
Baconsthorpe Norfk 122 C4
Bacton Herefs 62 D1
Bacton Norfk 123 G5
Bacton Suffk 90 C2
Bacton Green Suffk 90 B2
Bacup Lancs 140 C3
Badachro Highld 260 C5
Badanloch Highld 273 J2
Badbury Swindn 47 J3
Badby W Nthn 84 A3
Badcall Highld 276 C5
Badcaul Highld 261 G2
Baddeley Edge C Stke 114 E1
Baddeley Green C Stke 114 E1
Baddesley Clinton Warwks 82 F1
Baddesley Ensor Warwks 99 H4
Baddidarrach Highld 270 E3
Baddinsgill Border 199 K2

Badenscoth Abers 256 C4
Badentarbet Highld 270 D6
Badenyon Abers 255 G7
Badersfield Norfk 122 E6
Badgall Cnwll 11 J5
Badgeney Cambs 103 J4
Badger Shrops 97 H3
Badger's Cross Cnwll 2 D4
Badgers Mount Kent 52 B6
Badgeworth Gloucs 64 C3
Badgworth Somset 44 E8
Badharlick Cnwll 11 J5
Badicaul Highld 248 B6
Badingham Suffk 91 G2
Badlesmere Kent 40 D4
Badlieu Border 187 G2
Badlipster Highld 280 B6
Badluarach Highld 261 G1
Badninish Highld 263 K1
Badrallach Highld 261 G1
Badroy Highld 283 f6
Badshot Lea Surrey 36 C1
Badsworth Wakefd 142 D5
Badwell Ash Suffk 89 K2
Badwell Green Suffk 89 K2
Bagber Dorset 32 C8
Bagby N York 161 G6
Bag Enderby Lincs 136 F5
Bagendon Gloucs 64 E5
Bagginswood Shrops 96 F7
Baggrow Cumb 165 G2
Bàgh a' Chaisteil W Isls 283 b13
Bagham Kent 40 E4
Bagillt Flints 128 F4
Baginton Warwks 99 K8
Baglan Neath 57 K6
Bagley Leeds 150 B8
Bagley Shrops 112 F6
Bagley Somset 31 G2
Bagmore Hants 35 K2
Bagnall Staffs 114 E1
Bagnor W Berk 48 C5
Bagshot Surrey 49 M6
Bagshot Wilts 47 L6
Bagstone S Glos 45 K2
Bagthorpe Notts 116 D1
Bagworth Leics 99 M2
Bagwyllydiart Herefs 62 F2
Baildon C Brad 149 L7
Baildon Green C Brad 149 L7
Baile Ailein W Isls 282 f4
Baile a' Mhanaich W Isls 283 c9
Baile Mòr Ag & B 226 B7
Bailey Green Hants 35 K5
Baileyhead Cumb 178 C3
Bailiff Bridge Calder 141 J3
Baillieston C Glas 209 H6
Bailrigg Lancs 147 J4
Bainbridge N York 159 G4
Bainshole Abers 256 A5
Bainton C Pete 102 B2
Bainton E R Yk 152 F5
Bainton Oxon 66 E2
Baintown Fife 222 F6
Bairnkine Border 189 H3
Baker's End Herts 69 L4
Baker Street Thurr 52 D3
Bakewell Derbys 132 D6
Bala Gwynd 111 H4
Balallan W Isls 282 f4
Balbeg Highld 250 D5
Balbeggie P & K 222 B1
Balblair Highld 263 J6
Balby Donc 142 E7
Balcary D & G 175 K5
Balchraggan Highld 250 F3
Balchrick Highld 276 B4
Balcombe W Susx 37 M5
Balcombe Lane W Susx 37 M4
Balcomie Links Fife 223 L5
Baldersby N York 160 E7
Baldersby St James N York 160 E7
Balderstone Lancs 139 J1
Balderstone Rochdl 140 D5
Balderton Notts 117 L1
Baldhu Cnwll 4 C6
Baldinnie Fife 223 G5
Baldinnies P & K 221 J4
Baldock Herts 86 E8
Baldock Services Herts 86 E7
Baldovie C Dund 234 C8
Baldrine IoM 154 f5
Baldslow E Susx 24 E4
Baldwin IoM 154 e6
Baldwinholme Cumb 177 K8
Baldwin's Gate Staffs 114 B3
Baldwin's Hill W Susx 38 B5
Bale Norfk 121 M4
Baledgarno P & K 222 D1
Balemartine Ag & B 224 C7

Balerno C Edin 211 G5
Balfarg Fife 222 D6
Balfield Angus 234 E5
Balfour Ork 275 d4
Balfron Stirlg 208 F1
Balgaveny Abers 256 C5
Balgonar Fife 221 J8
Balgowan D & G 172 E6
Balgowan Highld 241 H4
Balgown Highld 258 F3
Balgracie D & G 172 B3
Balgray S Lans 186 C2
Balham Gt Lon 51 H4
Balhary P & K 233 L6
Balholmie P & K 233 H8
Baligill Highld 278 E3
Balintore Angus 233 I4
Balintore Highld 264 D5
Balintraid Highld 263 K5
Balivanich W Isls 283 c9
Balk N York 161 G6
Balkeerie Angus 233 M6
Balkholme E R Yk 143 K2
Ballabeg IoM 154 c7
Ballachulish Highld 229 H4
Ballafesson IoM 154 b7
Ballajora IoM 154 g4
Ballakilpheric IoM 154 b7
Ballamodha IoM 154 c7
Ballantrae S Ayrs 182 D6
Ballards Gore Essex 72 C8
Ballards Green Warwks 99 H5
Ballasalla IoM 154 c7
Ballater Abers 243 L4
Ballaugh IoM 154 d3
Ballchraggan Highld 263 K5
Ballencrieff E Loth 212 B3
Ballevullin Ag & B 224 B6
Ball Green C Stke 114 D1
Ball Haye Green Staffs 131 K8
Ball Hill Hants 48 B6
Ballianlay Ag & B 207 G6
Ballidon Derbys 115 K1
Balliekine N Ayrs 194 D3
Balliemore Ag & B 217 H7
Ballimore Ag & B 192 9E
Ballimore Stirlg 219 H4
Ballindalloch Moray 254 D2
Ballindean P & K 222 D2
Ballingdon Suffk 89 H7
Ballinger Common Bucks 67 M6
Ballingham Herefs 63 H1
Ballingry Fife 222 B7
Ballinluig P & K 232 E5
Ballinshoe Angus 234 B5
Ballintuim P & K 233 L4
Balloch Highld 252 D2
Balloch N Lans 209 K4
Balloch P & K 220 E3
Balloch S Ayrs 183 J4
Balloch W Duns 208 C3
Balls Cross W Susx 36 E5
Balls Green E Susx 38 D6
Ball's Green Gloucs 64 B7
Ballygown Ag & B 226 E4
Ballygrant Ag & B 204 F3
Ballyhaugh Ag & B 224 C6
Balmacara Highld 248 C6
Balmaclellan D & G 185 G7
Balmae D & G 175 H6
Balmaha Stirlg 208 C1
Balmalcolm Fife 222 E5
Balmangan D & G 175 G5
Balmedie Abers 257 H8
Balmer Heath Shrops 113 G4
Balmerino Fife 222 F2
Balmerlawn Hants 18 D3
Balmichael N Ayrs 194 E5
Balmore E Duns 209 G4
Balmuchy Highld 264 D5
Balmule Fife 211 H2
Balmullo Fife 223 G3
Balnacoil Highld 273 K6
Balnacra Highld 248 E5
Balnacroft Abers 243 J5
Balnafoich Highld 251 J4
Balnaguard P & K 232 D5
Balnahard Ag & B 226 E5
Balnain Highld 250 D5
Balnakeil Highld 276 F3
Balne N York 142 F4
Balquharn P & K 232 F8
Balquhidder Stirlg 219 H3
Balsall Common Solhll 99 G8
Balsall Heath Birm 98 D6
Balsall Street Solhll 99 G8
Balscote Oxon 83 J6
Balsham Cambs 88 B5
Baltasound Shet 281 f1
Balterley Staffs 114 B2

Balterley Green Staffs 114 B2
Balterley Heath Staffs 114 B2
Baltersan D & G 174 C3
Balthangie Abers 268 E6
Baltonsborough Somset 31 J4
Balvicar Ag & B 216 J4
Balvraid Highld 248 D8
Balvraid Highld 252 F5
Balwest Cnwll 2 F5
Bamber Bridge Lancs 139 H3
Bamber's Green Essex 70 E3
Bamburgh Nthumb 203 K6
Bamford Derbys 132 D3
Bamford Rochdl 140 C5
Bampton Devon 29 G6
Bampton Oxon 65 L6
Bampton W & F 166 C7
Bampton Grange W & F 166 C7
Banavie Highld 239 J8
Banbury Oxon 83 K7
Bancffosfelen Carmth 58 E6
Banchory Abers 244 F4
Banchory-Devenick Abers 245 K3
Bancycapel Carmth 58 D6
Bancyfelin Carmth 58 B5
Banc-y-ffordd Carmth 76 D7
Bandirran P & K 222 C1
Bandrake Head W & F 156 D5
Banff Abers 268 C3
Bangor Gwynd 125 K5
Bangor-on-Dee Wrexhm 112 F2
Bangors Cnwll 11 H3
Bangor's Green Lancs 138 D6
Bangour Village W Loth 210 D5
Bangrove Suffk 89 J1
Banham Norfk 106 B6
Bank Hants 18 D2
Bankend D & G 176 D5
Bankfoot P & K 233 G8
Bankglen E Ayrs 197 H8
Bank Ground W & F 156 D3
Bankhead C Aber 245 K2
Bankhead S Lans 199 G4
Bank Newton N York 148 F5
Banknock Falk 209 K3
Banks Cumb 178 D6
Banks Lancs 138 E4
Banks Green Worcs 82 A2
Bankshill D & G 177 G3
Bank Street Worcs 80 E3
Bank Top Calder 141 H3
Bank Top Lancs 139 G6
Bannau Brycheiniog National
   Park 60 F2
Banningham Norfk 122 E5
Bannister Green Essex 71 G3
Bannockburn Stirlg 209 L1
Banstead Surrey 51 H7
Bantham Devon 7 K6
Banton N Lans 209 K3
Banwell N Som 44 E7
Bapchild Kent 40 B3
Bapton Wilts 33 G3
Barabhas W Isls 282 g2
Barassie S Ayrs 196 C4
Barbaraville Highld 263 K5
Barber Booth Derbys 132 B3
Barber Green W & F 156 F6
Barbieston S Ayrs 196 E7
Barbon W & F 157 K6
Barbridge Ches E 130 B8
Barbrook Devon 28 C2
Barby W Nthn 84 A1
Barcaldine Ag & B 228 F7
Barcheston Warwks 83 G7
Barclose Cumb 178 B6
Barcombe E Susx 22 F4
Barcombe Cross E Susx 23 G4
Barcroft C Brad 149 J8
Barden N York 159 L4
Barden Park Kent 38 F4
Bardfield End Green Essex 70 F1
Bardfield Saling Essex 71 G2
Bardney Lincs 136 B6
Bardon Leics 99 M1
Bardon Mill Nthumb 179 H6
Bardowie E Duns 209 G4
Bardown E Susx 39 G7
Bardrainney Inver 208 B4
Bardsea W & F 156 D7
Bardsey Leeds 150 E7
Bardsey Island Gwynd 108 A7
Bardsley Oldham 140 D7
Bardwell Suffk 105 J8
Bare Lancs 147 J3
Bareppa Cnwll 3 K5
Barfad D & G 173 J2
Barford Norfk 106 C2
Barford Warwks 83 G3
Barford St John Oxon 83 K8

Barford St Martin Wilts 33 J4
Barford St Michael Oxon 83 K8
Barfrestone Kent 41 H5
Bargate Derbys 116 B2
Bargeddie N Lans 209 J6
Bargoed Caerph 61 J7
Bargrennan D & G 183 J7
Barham Cambs 102 C8
Barham Kent 41 G5
Barham Suffk 90 D5
Bar Hill Cambs 87 H3
Barholm Lincs 102 B1
Barkby Leics 100 E2
Barkby Thorpe Leics 100 E2
Barkers Green Shrops 113 H6
Barkestone-le-Vale Leics 117 K4
Barkham Wokham 49 J5
Barking Gt Lon 51 L2
Barking Suffk 90 C4
Barking Riverside Gt Lon 52 A2
Barkingside Gt Lon 51 L1
Barking Tye Suffk 90 C4
Barkisland Calder 141 G4
Barkla Shop Cnwll 4 B5
Barkston Lincs 118 B3
Barkston Ash N York 151 G8
Barkway Herts 87 H8
Barlanark C Glas 209 H6
Barlaston Staffs 114 D4
Barlavington W Susx 21 G4
Barlborough Derbys 133 J4
Barlby N York 143 G1
Barlestone Leics 99 L2
Barley Herts 87 H7
Barley Lancs 148 E7
Barleycroft End Herts 70 B2
Barley Hole Rothm 142 B8
Barleythorpe Rutlnd 101 J2
Barling Essex 53 K1
Barlings Lincs 135 M5
Barlochan D & G 175 K3
Barlow Derbys 133 G5
Barlow Gatesd 180 E6
Barlow N York 143 G2
Barmby Moor E R Yk 152 B6
Barmby on the Marsh E R Yk 143 H2
Barmer Norfk 121 H5
Barming Heath Kent 39 J2
Barmollack Ag & B 194 C2
Barmouth Gwynd 109 L8
Barmpton Darltn 169 J7
Barmston E R Yk 153 J4
Barnaby Green Suffk 107 K7
Barnacarry Ag & B 216 F8
Barnack C Pete 102 B2
Barnacle Warwks 99 K6
Barnard Castle Dur 168 D7
Barnard Gate Oxon 66 B5
Barnardiston Suffk 88 E5
Barnbarroch D & G 175 L3
Barnburgh Donc 142 D7
Barnby Suffk 107 K5
Barnby Dun Donc 142 F6
Barnby in the Willows Notts 117 M1
Barnby Moor Notts 134 B3
Barncorkrie D & G 172 D7
Barnehurst Gt Lon 52 B4
Barnes Gt Lon 51 G4
Barnes Street Kent 39 G4
Barnet Gt Lon 69 H7
Barnetby le Wold N Linc 144 D6
Barnet Gate Gt Lon 69 G8
Barney Norfk 121 M5
Barnham Suffk 105 H7
Barnham W Susx 20 F6
Barnham Broom Norfk 106 B2
Barnhead Angus 235 G4
Barnhill C Dund 223 H1
Barnhill Ches W 113 H1
Barnhill Moray 266 C5
Barnhills D & G 182 B8
Barningham Dur 168 D8
Barningham Suffk 105 K8
Barnoldby le Beck NE Lin 145 G7
Barnoldswick Lancs 148 F6
Barnsdale Bar Donc 142 D5
Barns Green W Susx 37 H5
Barnsley Barns 142 A6
Barnsley Gloucs 65 G6
Barnsole Kent 41 J4
Barnstaple Devon 27 K4
Barnston Essex 70 F3
Barnston Wirral 129 G3
Barnstone Notts 117 J4
Barnt Green Worcs 98 C8
Barnton C Edin 211 G4
Barnton Ches W 130 C5
Barnwell All Saints N Nthn 102 A6
Barnwell St Andrew N Nthn 102 A6
Barnwood Gloucs 64 B3

Baron's Cross Herefs 80 B4
Baronwood W & F 166 C2
Barr S Ayrs 183 H4
Barra W Isls 283 b13
Barra Airport W Isls 283 b12
Barrachan D & G 173 J5
Barraigh W Isls 283 b13
Barrananaoil Ag & B 216 C5
Barrapoll Ag & B 224 B6
Barras W & F 167 J8
Barrasford Nthumb 179 L4
Barregarrow IoM 154 d4
Barrets Green Ches E 130 B7
Barrhead E Rens 208 E7
Barrhill S Ayrs 183 G6
Barrington Cambs 87 H5
Barrington Somset 30 F7
Barripper Cnwll 3 G3
Barmill N Ayrs 196 D1
Barrock Highld 280 C2
Barrow Gloucs 64 C2
Barrow Lancs 148 C8
Barrow Rutlnd 118 A8
Barrow Shrops 96 E3
Barrow Somset 32 B4
Barrow Suffk 88 F3
Barroway Drove Norfk 104 B3
Barrow Bridge Bolton 139 K5
Barrow Burn Nthumb 190 B4
Barrowby Lincs 118 A4
Barrow Common N Som 45 H5
Barrowden Rutlnd 101 L3
Barrowford Lancs 148 E7
Barrow Gurney N Som 45 G5
Barrow Haven N Linc 144 D3
Barrow Hill Derbys 133 H4
Barrow-in-Furness W & F 146 D2
Barrow Island W & F 146 D2
Barrow Nook Lancs 138 F7
Barrow's Green Ches E 130 D8
Barrows Green W & F 157 H5
Barrow Street Wilts 32 D5
Barrow-upon-Humber N Linc 144 D4
Barrow upon Soar Leics 116 F8
Barrow upon Trent Derbys 116 B6
Barrow Vale BaNES 45 J7
Barry Angus 234 E8
Barry V Glam 43 H7
Barry Island V Glam 43 H8
Barsby Leics 100 F1
Barsham Suffk 107 l15
Barston Solhll 99 G7
Bartestree Herefs 80 C7
Barthol Chapel Abers 256 E5
Bartholomew Green Essex 71 H3
Barthomley Ches E 114 B1
Bartley Hants 18 D1
Bartley Green Birm 98 C7
Bartlow Cambs 88 B6
Barton Cambs 87 H4
Barton Ches W 113 J1
Barton Gloucs 65 G2
Barton Herefs 79 K4
Barton Lancs 138 D6
Barton Lancs 147 K8
Barton N York 160 C1
Barton Oxon 66 E5
Barton Torbay 8 D2
Barton Warwks 82 D5
Barton Bendish Norfk 104 E2
Barton End Gloucs 64 B7
Barton Green Staffs 115 K7
Barton Hartshorn Bucks 66 F1
Barton Hill N York 151 L3
Barton in Fabis Notts 116 E5
Barton in the Beans Leics 99 L2
Barton-le-Clay C Beds 68 D1
Barton-le-Street N York 162 C7
Barton-le-Willows N York 151 M3
Barton Mills Suffk 104 E8
Barton-on-Sea Hants 18 C5
Barton-on-the-Heath Warwks 65 K1
Barton St David Somset 31 J4
Barton Seagrave N Nthn 101 J7
Barton Stacey Hants 34 F3
Barton Town Devon 28 B3
Barton Turf Norfk 123 G7
Barton-under-Needwood
   Staffs 115 K7
Barton-upon-Humber N Linc 144 C3
Barton upon Irwell Salfd 140 A8
Barton Waterside N Linc 144 C3
Barugh Barns 141 M6
Barugh Green Barns 141 M6
Barvas W Isls 282 g2
Barway Cambs 103 L8
Barwell Leics 99 L4
Barwick Devon 12 E1
Barwick Herts 69 K3
Barwick Somset 31 J8

Barwick in Elmet Leeds 150 F8
Baschurch Shrops 112 F7
Bascote Warwks 83 J3
Bascote Heath Warwks 83 J3
Base Green Suffk 89 L3
Basford Green Staffs 114 F1
Bashall Eaves Lancs 148 B7
Bashall Town Lancs 148 C7
Bashley Hants 18 C4
Basildon Essex 52 E1
Basingstoke Hants 48 F8
Baslow Derbys 132 E5
Bason Bridge Somset 30 D7
Bassaleg Newpt 44 B2
Bassendean Border 201 K4
Bassenthwaite Cumb 165 H4
Bassett C Sotn 34 F7
Bassingbourn-cum-
   Kneesworth Cambs 87 G6
Bassingfield Notts 117 G4
Bassingham Lincs 135 H7
Bassingthorpe Lincs 118 C6
Bassus Green Herts 69 J2
Basted Kent 38 F2
Baston Lincs 102 C1
Bastwick Norfk 123 J8
Batch Somset 44 C7
Batchworth Herts 68 D8
Batchworth Heath Herts 68 D8
Batcombe Dorset 16 B2
Batcombe Somset 31 M3
Bate Heath Ches E 130 D4
Batford Herts 68 F4
Bath BaNES 45 L6
Bath BaNES 45 L6
Bathampton BaNES 45 M5
Bathealton Somset 29 K6
Batheaston BaNES 45 M5
Bathford BaNES 46 A5
Bathgate W Loth 210 C5
Bathley Notts 134 F7
Bathpool Cnwll 11 K7
Bathpool Somset 30 C5
Bath Side Essex 73 K1
Bathville W Loth 210 B5
Bathway Somset 45 H8
Batley Kirk 141 K3
Batsford Gloucs 82 E8
Batson Devon 7 L7
Battersby N York 161 K1
Battersea Gt Lon 51 H4
Battisborough Cross Devon 7 H5
Battisford Suffk 90 C4
Battisford Tye Suffk 89 L4
Battle E Susx 24 D4
Battle Powys 60 F1
Battleborough Somset 30 E1
Battledown Gloucs 64 D3
Battledykes Angus 234 C4
Battlefield Shrops 113 H8
Battlesbridge Essex 71 J8
Battlesden C Beds 68 B2
Battleton Somset 29 G5
Battlies Green Suffk 89 H2
Battram Leics 99 L2
Battramsley Cross Hants 18 C4
Batt's Corner Hants 36 B3
Baughton Worcs 81 K6
Baughurst Hants 48 E6
Baulds Abers 244 D5
Baulking Oxon 47 L1
Baumber Lincs 136 D5
Baunton Gloucs 64 E6
Baveney Wood Shrops 96 F7
Baverstock Wilts 33 H4
Bawburgh Norfk 106 D2
Bawdeswell Norfk 122 A7
Bawdrip Somset 30 E3
Bawdsey Suffk 91 H7
Bawsey Norfk 120 E7
Bawtry Donc 134 C1
Baxenden Lancs 140 A2
Baxterley Warwks 99 H4
Baxter's Green Suffk 88 E4
Bay Highld 258 D6
Bayble W Isls 282 h3
Baybridge Hants 35 H6
Baybridge Nthumb 168 B1
Baycliff W & F 146 D7
Baydon Wilts 47 L3
Bayford Herts 69 J5
Bayford Somset 32 B5
Bayhead W Isls 283 b8
Bay Horse Lancs 147 K5
Bayley's Hill Kent 38 D3
Baylham Suffk 90 C5
Baynard's Green Oxon 66 E1
Baysdale Abbey N York 161 K1
Baysham Herefs 63 H2
Bayston Hill Shrops 96 B2

Baythorne End – Betws-yn-Rhos

293

Baythorne End Essex 88 E6
Bayton Worcs 96 F8
Bayton Common Worcs 81 G1
Bayworth Oxon 66 D6
Beach S Glos 45 L5
Beachampton Bucks 84 E7
Beachamwell Norfk 104 E2
Beachley Gloucs 45 H1
Beachy Head E Susx 23 K8
Beacon Devon 14 E2
Beacon End Essex 72 D2
Beacon Hill Kent 39 K6
Beacon Hill Notts 117 L1
Beacon Hill Surrey 36 C3
Beacon's Bottom Bucks 67 J8
Beaconsfield Bucks 50 B1
Beaconsfield Services Bucks 50 D1
Beadlam N York 161 L5
Beadlow C Beds 86 C7
Beadnell Nthumb 203 L7
Beaford Devon [illegible]
Beal N York 142 E3
Beal Nthumb 203 H4
Bealbury Cnwll 6 D2
Bealsmill Cnwll 11 L7
Beam Hill Staffs 115 L6
Beamhurst Staffs 115 H4
Beaminster Dorset 15 L2
Beamish Dur 180 F8
Beamsley N York 149 K5
Bean Kent 52 C4
Beanacre Wilts 46 C5
Beanley Nthumb 190 F3
Beardon Devon 12 C5
Beardwood Bl w D 139 K2
Beare Devon 14 A2
Beare Green Surrey 37 J2
Bearley Warwks 82 E3
Bearley Cross Warwks 82 E3
Bearpark Dur 169 G2
Bearsden E Duns 208 F4
Bearsted Kent 39 K2
Bearstone Shrops 114 A4
Bearwood BCP 17 L3
Bearwood Birm 98 C6
Bearwood Herefs 79 M4
Beattock D & G 187 G5
Beauchamp Roding Essex 70 E5
Beauchief Sheff 132 F3
Beaudesert Warwks 82 E2
Beaufort Blae G 61 J5
Beaulieu Essex 71 H5
Beaulieu Hants 18 F3
Beaulieu Road Station Hants 18 E2
Beauly Highld 250 F2
Beaumaris IoA 126 B4
Beaumaris Castle IoA 126 B4
Beaumont Cumb 177 K7
Beaumont Essex 73 H2
Beaumont Jersey 9 c3
Beaumont Hill Darltn 169 J7
Beaumont Leys C Leic 100 C2
Beausale Warwks 82 F1
Beauworth Hants 35 J5
Beaworthy Devon 12 B3
Beazley End Essex 71 H1
Bebington Wirral 129 H3
Bebside Nthumb 181 G3
Beccles Suffk 107 J5
Becconsall Lancs 138 F3
Beckbury Shrops 97 H3
Beckenham Gt Lon 51 K5
Beckermet Cumb 155 J1
Beckett End Norfk 104 F4
Beckfoot Cumb 155 L3
Beckfoot Cumb 156 B5
Beckfoot Cumb 164 E1
Beck Foot W & F 157 K3
Beckford Worcs 82 A8
Beckhampton Wilts 47 G5
Beck Hole N York 162 E2
Beckingham Lincs 118 A1
Beckingham Notts 134 F2
Beckington Somset 46 A8
Beckjay Shrops 95 J7
Beckley E Susx 24 F3
Beckley Hants 18 C4
Beckley Oxon 66 E5
Beck Row Suffk 104 D7
Becks C Brad 149 J6
Beck Side W & F 156 B6
Beck Side W & F 156 E6
Beckton Gt Lon 51 L3
Beckwithshaw N York 150 C5
Becontree Gt Lon 52 A2
Becquet Vincent Jersey 9 d2
Bedale N York 160 C5
Bedburn Dur 168 E4
Bedchester Dorset 32 E7
Beddau Rhondd 43 G4
Beddgelert Gwynd 109 L2
Beddingham E Susx 23 G5
Beddington Gt Lon 51 J6
Beddington Corner Gt Lon 51 H5
Bedfield Suffk 90 F2
Bedfield Little Green Suffk 90 F2
Bedford Bed 85 L5
Bedgebury Cross Kent 39 H6
Bedgrove Bucks 67 K4
Bedham W Susx 36 F6
Bedhampton Hants 20 A5
Bedingfield Suffk 90 E2
Bedingfield Green Suffk 90 E2
Bedlam N York 150 C3
Bedlington Nthumb 181 G3
Bedlinog Myr Td 61 H6
Bedminster Bristl 45 H5
Bedminster Down Bristl 45 H5
Bedmond Herts 68 E6
Bednall Staffs 114 E7
Bedrule Border 189 G3
Bedstone Shrops 95 J8
Bedwas Caerph 43 J4
Bedwellty Caerph 61 J7
Bedworth Warwks 99 K6
Bedworth Woodlands Warwks 99 K6
Beeby Leics 100 E2
Beech Hants 35 L3
Beech Staffs 114 D4
Beech Hill W Berk 49 G6
Beechingstoke Wilts 47 G7
Beedon W Berk 48 C3
Beedon Hill W Berk 48 C3
Beeford E R Yk 153 H5
Beeley Derbys 132 E6
Beelsby NE Lin 145 G7
Beenham W Berk 48 E5
Beenham's Heath W & M 49 K4
Beeny Cnwll 11 G4
Beer Devon 14 F5
Beer Somset 30 F4
Beercrocombe Somset 30 D6
Beer Hackett Dorset 31 K8
Beesands Devon 8 B6
Beesby Lincs 137 J4
Beeson Devon 8 B6
Beeston C Beds 86 D5
Beeston Ches W 129 M7
Beeston Leeds 141 L2
Beeston Norfk 121 K8
Beeston Notts 116 E4
Beeston Regis Norfk 122 D3
Beeswing D & G 176 A5
Beetham Somset 30 D8
Beetham W & F 157 H6
Beetley Norfk 121 L8
Began Cardif 43 K5
Begbroke Oxon 66 C4
Begdale Cambs 103 J2
Begelly Pembks 55 J5
Beggarington Hill Leeds 141 L3
Beggar's Bush Powys 79 J2
Beguildy Powys 94 F7
Beighton Norfk 107 H2
Beighton Sheff 133 J3
Beinn Na Faoghla W Isls 283 c9
Beith N Ayrs 208 B8
Bekesbourne Kent 41 G4
Bekesbourne Hill Kent 41 G4
Belaugh Norfk 122 F7
Belbroughton Worcs 97 L7
Belchalwell Dorset 16 F1
Belchalwell Street Dorset 16 F1
Belchamp Otten Essex 88 F6
Belchamp St Paul Essex 88 F6
Belchamp Walter Essex 89 G7
Belchford Lincs 136 E4
Belford Nthumb 203 H6
Belgrave C Leic 100 D2
Belhaven E Loth 212 E3
Belhelvie Abers 257 H8
Belhinnie Abers 255 J6
Bellabeg Abers 243 K1
Bellamore Herefs 79 M7
Bellanoch Ag & B 216 B8
Bellasize E R Yk 143 K2
Bellaty Angus 233 K3
Bell Bar Herts 69 H6
Bell Busk N York 148 F4
Belleau Lincs 137 G4
Bell End Worcs 97 L7
Bellerby N York 159 K4
Bellever Devon 12 F7
Belle Vue Cumb 177 L7
Belle Vue Wakefd 142 A4
Bellfield S Lans 198 D6
Bellfields Surrey 50 C8
Bell Heath Worcs 97 L7
Bell Hill Hants 35 M6
Bellingdon Bucks 68 B6
Bellingham Nthumb 179 J2
Belloch Ag & B 192 D1
Bellochantuy Ag & B 192 D2
Bell o' th' Hill Ches W 113 H2
Bellows Cross Dorset 33 J8
Bells Cross Suffk 90 D5
Bellshill N Lans 209 J7
Bellshill Nthumb 203 J7
Bellside N Lans 209 L7
Bellsquarry W Loth 210 E6
Bells Yew Green E Susx 38 F6
Belluton BaNES 45 J6
Belmaduthy Highld 263 H8
Belmesthorpe Rutlnd 102 A2
Belmont Bl w D 139 K4
Belmont Dur 169 J2
Belmont Gt Lon 51 H6
Belmont S Ayrs 196 C7
Belmont Shet 281 f2
Belnacraig Abers 255 H8
Belowda Cnwll 4 E3
Belper Derbys 116 B2
Belper Lane End Derbys 116 B2
Belph Derbys 133 L4
Belsay Nthumb 180 D3
Belses Border 201 J8
Belsford Devon 7 L3
Belsize Herts 68 D7
Belstead Suffk 90 D7
Belstone Devon 12 E4
Belthorn Bl w D 139 L3
Beltinge Kent 41 G2
Beltingham Nthumb 179 H6
Beltoft N Linc 143 K6
Belton Leics 116 D7
Belton Lincs 118 B3
Belton N Linc 143 K6
Belton Norfk 107 K3
Belton in Rutland Rutlnd 101 H3
Beltring Kent 39 H4
Belvedere Gt Lon 52 B3
Belvoir Leics 117 L5
Bembridge IoW 19 L6
Bemerton Wilts 33 K5
Bempton E R Yk 153 K2
Benacre Suffk 107 M6
Benbecula W Isls 283 c9
Benbecula Airport W Isls 283 c9
Benbuie D & G 185 H4
Benderloch Ag & B 228 D7
Benenden Kent 39 K6
Benfieldside Dur 180 D8
Benfleet Essex 53 G2
Bengate Norfk 122 F6
Bengeo Herts 69 J4
Bengeworth Worcs 82 B6
Benhall Green Suffk 91 J3
Benhall Street Suffk 91 H3
Benholm Abers 235 K2
Beningbrough N York 151 H4
Benington Herts 69 J2
Benington Lincs 119 L2
Benington Sea End Lincs 119 L2
Benllech IoA 125 J3
Benmore Ag & B 207 J2
Bennacott Cnwll 11 K4
Bennan N Ayrs 193 K4
Bennet Head W & F 166 B6
Bennetland E R Yk 143 L2
Bennett End Bucks 67 J7
Ben Nevis Highld 229 K1
Benniworth Lincs 136 D3
Benover Kent 39 H4
Ben Rhydding C Brad 149 L6
Benslie N Ayrs 196 C2
Benson Oxon 66 F8
Bentfield Green Essex 70 D2
Benthall Shrops 96 F3
Bentham Gloucs 64 C4
Benthoul C Aber 245 H3
Bentlawnt Shrops 95 H3
Bentley Donc 142 E6
Bentley E R Yk 152 F8
Bentley Hants 36 A2
Bentley Suffk 90 D7
Bentley Warwks 99 H4
Bentley Heath Herts 69 H7
Bentley Heath Solhll 98 F8
Benton Devon 28 B4
Bentpath D & G 188 B8
Bentwichen Devon 28 C4
Bentworth Hants 35 K3
Benvie Angus 222 E1
Benville Dorset 15 M2
Benwick Cambs 103 G5
Beoley Worcs 82 C1
Beoraidbeg Highld 237 K2
Bepton W Susx 20 D3
Berden Essex 70 C1
Berea Pembks 74 C6
Bere Alston Devon 6 E2
Bere Ferrers Devon 6 E2
Berepper Cnwll 3 G6
Bere Regis Dorset 17 G4
Bergh Apton Norfk 106 F3
Berhill Somset 31 G4
Berinsfield Oxon 66 E7
Berkeley Gloucs 63 K7
Berkeley Heath Gloucs 63 K7
Berkeley Road Gloucs 63 L7
Berkhamsted Herts 68 C5
Berkley Somset 32 D1
Berkswell Solhll 99 H7
Bermondsey Gt Lon 51 J3
Bermuda Warwks 99 K5
Bernera Highld 248 C7
Bernisdale Highld 258 F6
Berrick Prior Oxon 66 F8
Berrick Salome Oxon 66 F8
Berriedale Highld 274 F3
Berrier W & F 165 L5
Berriew Powys 94 E3
Berrington Nthumb 202 F4
Berrington Shrops 96 C2
Berrington Worcs 80 D2
Berrington Green Worcs 80 D2
Berrow Somset 44 C8
Berrow Worcs 81 H8
Berrow Green Worcs 81 H3
Berry Brow Kirk 141 H5
Berry Cross Devon 27 H7
Berry Down Cross Devon 27 K2
Berryfield Wilts 46 C6
Berryfields Bucks 67 J4
Berry Hill Gloucs 63 H4
Berry Hill Pembks 75 H4
Berryhillock Moray 267 K4
Berryhillock Moray 267 K5
Berrynarbor Devon 27 K2
Berry Pomeroy Devon 8 B3
Berry's Green Gt Lon 51 L7
Bersham Wrexhm 112 D2
Bersted W Susx 20 F6
Bertha Park P & K 221 K2
Berthengam Flints 128 D4
Berwick E Susx 23 H6
Berwick Bassett Wilts 47 G4
Berwick Hill Nthumb 180 E4
Berwick St James Wilts 33 J3
Berwick St John Wilts 32 F6
Berwick St Leonard Wilts 32 F4
Berwick Station E Susx 23 J6
Berwick-upon-Tweed Nthumb 202 F3
Bescaby Leics 117 L6
Bescar Lancs 138 E5
Besford Shrops 113 J6
Besford Worcs 81 L6
Bessacarr Donc 142 F7
Bessels Leigh Oxon 66 C6
Besses o' th' Barn Bury 140 B6
Bessingby E R Yk 153 J3
Bessingham Norfk 122 D4
Bestbeech Hill E Susx 38 F7
Besthorpe Norfk 106 B4
Besthorpe Notts 135 G6
Bestwood Village Notts 116 F2
Beswick E R Yk 152 F6
Betchcott Shrops 95 K4
Betchworth Surrey 37 K1
Bethania Cerdgn 77 G3
Bethania Gwynd 110 D3
Bethel Gwynd 111 J4
Bethel Gwynd 125 J6
Bethel IoA 125 G5
Bethel Powys 111 L7
Bethersden Kent 40 B7
Bethesda Gwynd 126 C6
Bethesda Gwynd 126 C6
Bethesda Pembks 55 J3
Bethlehem Carmth 59 J4
Bethnal Green Gt Lon 51 K2
Betley Staffs 114 B2
Betsham Kent 52 D4
Betteshanger Kent 41 J5
Bettiscombe Dorset 15 J3
Bettisfield Wrexhm 113 G4
Betton Shrops 113 M4
Betton Strange Shrops 96 C2
Bettws Brdgnd 42 D4
Bettws Newpt 44 C1
Bettws Cedewain Powys 94 D4
Bettws Ifan Cerdgn 76 B5
Bettws-Newydd Mons 62 D6
Bettyhill Highld 278 B4
Betws Carmth 59 H6
Betws Bledrws Cerdgn 77 H5
Betws Garmon Gwynd 125 K8
Betws Gwerfil Goch Denbgs 111 K2
Betws-y-Coed Conwy 126 F8
Betws-yn-Rhos Conwy 127 H5

Beulah Cerdgn 76 B6
Beulah Powys 78 C5
Bevendean Br & H 22 E6
Bevercotes Notts 134 D5
Beverley E R Yk 153 G7
Beverston Gloucs 64 B8
Bevington Gloucs 63 K7
Bewaldeth Cumb 165 H4
Bewcastle Cumb 178 D4
Bewdley Worcs 97 H8
Bewerley N York 149 L3
Bewholme E R Yk 153 J6
Bewlbridge Kent 39 H6
Bexhill-on-Sea E Susx 24 D5
Bexley Gt Lon 52 B4
Bexleyheath Gt Lon 52 A4
Bexleyhill W Susx 36 D6
Bexon Kent 53 J7
Bexwell Norfk 104 C3
Beyton Suffk 89 J3
Beyton Green Suffk 89 J3
Bhaltos W Isls 282 e3
Bhatarsaigh W Isls 283 b13
Bibstone S Glos 45 K1
Bibury Gloucs 65 G5
Bicester Oxon 66 E3
Bickenhill Solhll 99 G7
Bicker Lincs 119 H4
Bicker Bar Lincs 119 H4
Bicker Gauntlet Lincs 119 H4
Bickershaw Wigan 139 J7
Bickerstaffe Lancs 138 F7
Bickerton Ches E 113 H1
Bickerton Devon 8 B7
Bickerton N York 151 G5
Bickerton Nthumb 190 E6
Bickford Staffs 114 D8
Bickington Devon 13 J8
Bickington Devon 27 J4
Bickleigh Devon 7 G2
Bickleigh Devon 13 M1
Bickleton Devon 27 J5
Bickley Ches W 113 J2
Bickley Gt Lon 51 L5
Bickley N York 163 G4
Bickley Worcs 80 E1
Bickley Moss Ches W 113 J2
Bicknacre Essex 71 J2
Bicknoller Somset 29 K3
Bicknor Kent 53 J7
Bickton Hants 33 K8
Bicton Herefs 80 B2
Bicton Shrops 95 G6
Bicton Shrops 113 G8
Bidborough Kent 38 E5
Bidden Hants 35 L1
Biddenden Kent 39 L5
Biddenden Green Kent 39 M5
Biddenham Bed 85 K5
Biddestone Wilts 46 B4
Biddisham Somset 44 D8
Biddlesden Bucks 84 C7
Biddlestone Nthumb 190 D4
Biddulph Staffs 131 H7
Biddulph Moor Staffs 131 H8
Bideford Devon 27 H5
Bidford-on-Avon Warwks 82 D5
Bidston Wirral 129 G2
Bielby E R Yk 152 B7
Bieldside C Aber 245 K3
Bierley IoW 19 H8
Bierton Bucks 67 K4
Big Balcraig D & G 173 K6
Bigbury Devon 7 K5
Bigbury-on-Sea Devon 7 J6
Bigby Lincs 144 D6
Biggar S Lans 199 H5
Biggar W & F 146 D3
Biggin Derbys 115 L2
Biggin Derbys 132 C7
Biggin N York 142 E1
Biggin Hill Gt Lon 51 L7
Biggleswade C Beds 86 D6
Bigholms D & G 177 K3
Bighouse Highld 278 F3
Bighton Hants 35 J4
Biglands Cumb 177 H8
Bignall End Staffs 114 C1
Bignor W Susx 21 G4
Bigrigg Cumb 164 D8
Big Sand Highld 260 B4
Bigton Shet 281 d8
Bilborough C Nott 116 E3
Bilbrook Somset 29 J3
Bilbrook Staffs 97 K3
Bilbrough N York 151 H6
Bilbster Highld 280 C5
Bildershaw Dur 169 G6
Bildeston Suffk 89 K5
Billacott Cnwll 11 J4

Billericay Essex 71 G8
Billesdon Leics 100 F3
Billesley Warwks 82 D4
Billingborough Lincs 118 F5
Billinge St Hel 139 G7
Billingford Norfk 106 D7
Billingford Norfk 121 M7
Billingham S on T 170 B6
Billinghay Lincs 136 C6
Billingley Barns 142 C6
Billingshurst W Susx 37 G5
Billingsley Shrops 97 G6
Billington C Beds 68 B3
Billington Lancs 148 C8
Billington Staffs 114 D7
Billockby Norfk 107 J1
Billy Row Dur 168 F3
Bilsborrow Lancs 147 K7
Bilsby Lincs 137 J4
Bilsham W Susx 21 G6
Bilsington Kent 40 D8
Bilsthorpe Notts 134 C7
Bilsthorpe Moor Notts 134 C7
Bilston Mdloth 211 J6
Bilston Wolves 98 B4
Bilstone Leics 99 K2
Bilting Kent 40 D5
Bilton E R Yk 144 F1
Bilton N York 150 D4
Bilton Nthumb 191 J4
Bilton Warwks 100 B8
Bilton Banks Nthumb 191 J4
Bilton-in-Ainsty N York 151 G6
Binbrook Lincs 136 D1
Binchester Blocks Dur 169 G4
Bincombe Dorset 16 D5
Binegar Somset 31 K1
Bines Green W Susx 21 L3
Binfield Br For 49 K4
Binfield Heath Oxon 49 H3
Bingfield Nthumb 180 A4
Bingham Notts 117 J3
Bingham's Melcombe Dorset 16 E2
Bingley C Brad 149 K7
Bings Heath Shrops 113 J7
Binham Norfk 121 L4
Binley Covtry 99 K7
Binley Hants 48 B8
Binley Woods Warwks 99 L7
Binnegar Dorset 17 G5
Binniehill Falk 209 M4
Binscombe Surrey 36 E2
Binsey Oxon 66 C5
Binstead IoW 19 K5
Binsted Hants 36 A3
Binsted W Susx 21 G5
Binton Warwks 82 D4
Bintree Norfk 121 M7
Binweston Shrops 95 H3
Birch Essex 72 D3
Birch Rochdl 140 C6
Birchall Staffs 131 K8
Bircham Newton Norfk 121 G5
Bircham Tofts Norfk 121 G5
Birchanger Essex 70 D3
Birchanger Green Services
  Essex 70 D3
Birch Cross Staffs 115 J5
Birchencliffe Kirk 141 H4
Bircher Herefs 80 B2
Birchett's Green E Susx 39 G7
Birchfield Birm 98 D5
Birch Green Essex 72 D3
Birch Green Herts 69 J5
Birch Green Worcs 81 K6
Birchgrove Cardif 43 G5
Birchgrove Swans 57 K5
Birchgrove W Susx 38 B7
Birch Heath Ches W 130 A7
Birch Hill Ches W 129 M5
Birchington Kent 41 J2
Birchington-on-Sea Kent 41 J2
Birchley Heath Warwks 99 H4
Birchmoor Warwks 99 H3
Birchmoor Green C Beds 85 J8
Birchover Derbys 132 E7
Birch Services Rochdl 140 C6
Birch Vale Derbys 131 K2
Birchwood Lincs 135 J6
Birch Wood Somset 30 C8
Birchwood Warrtn 130 C2
Bircotes Notts 134 C2
Birdbrook Essex 88 E7
Birdforth N York 161 G7
Birdham W Susx 20 D6
Birdingbury Warwks 83 K2
Birdlip Gloucs 64 D4
Birdoswald Cumb 178 E5
Birdsall N York 152 B3
Birds Edge Kirk 141 K6

Birds Green Essex 70 E5
Birdsgreen Shrops 97 H6
Birdsmoorgate Dorset 15 J3
Bird Street Suffk 89 K5
Birdwell Barns 142 A7
Birdwood Gloucs 63 L3
Birgham Border 202 B5
Birichin Highld 263 K2
Birkacre Lancs 139 H5
Birkby N York 160 D2
Birkdale Sefton 138 C5
Birkenbog Abers 267 L3
Birkenhead Wirral 129 H2
Birkenhead (Queensway)
  Tunnel Lpool 129 H2
Birkenhills Abers 256 D3
Birkenshaw Kirk 141 K2
Birkhall Abers 243 K5
Birkhill Angus 234 A8
Birkhill D & G 187 J3
Birkholme Lincs 118 C6
Birkin N York 142 E2
Birks Leeds 141 L2
Birkshaw Nthumb 179 H5
Birley Herefs 80 B4
Birley Carr Sheff 133 G1
Birling Kent 52 E6
Birling Nthumb 191 K5
Birling Gap E Susx 23 J8
Birlingham Worcs 81 L6
Birmingham Birm 98 D6
Birmingham Airport Solhll 98 F6
Birnam P & K 232 F7
Birness Abers 257 H5
Birse Abers 244 C4
Birsemore Abers 244 C4
Birstall Kirk 141 K3
Birstall Leics 100 D2
Birstwith N York 150 B4
Birthorpe Lincs 118 E5
Birtley Gatesd 181 G2
Birtley Herefs 79 L2
Birtley Nthumb 179 K3
Birts Street Worcs 81 H7
Bisbrooke Rutlnd 101 J3
Biscathorpe Lincs 136 D3
Biscovey Cnwll 5 H4
Bisham W & M 49 K2
Bishampton Worcs 82 A5
Bish Mill Devon 28 C6
Bishop Auckland Dur 169 G5
Bishopbridge Lincs 135 L2
Bishopbriggs E Duns 209 G5
Bishop Burton E R Yk 152 F7
Bishop Middleham Dur 169 J4
Bishopmill Moray 266 E3
Bishop Monkton N York 150 D3
Bishop Norton Lincs 135 K1
Bishopsbourne Kent 41 G5
Bishops Cannings Wilts 46 F6
Bishop's Castle Shrops 95 H5
Bishop's Caundle Dorset 32 B8
Bishop's Cleeve Gloucs 64 D2
Bishop's Frome Herefs 80 F5
Bishops Gate Surrey 50 B5
Bishop's Green Essex 70 F3
Bishop's Green Hants 48 D6
Bishop's Hull Somset 30 B6
Bishop's Itchington Warwks 83 J4
Bishops Lydeard Somset 29 M5
Bishop's Norton Gloucs 64 B2
Bishop's Nympton Devon 28 D6
Bishop's Offley Staffs 114 B5
Bishop's Stortford Herts 70 C3
Bishop's Sutton Hants 35 J4
Bishop's Tachbrook Warwks 83 H3
Bishop's Tawton Devon 27 K5
Bishopsteignton Devon 13 L7
Bishopstoke Hants 34 F7
Bishopston Swans 57 G7
Bishopstone Bucks 67 J5
Bishopstone E Susx 23 G7
Bishopstone Herefs 80 A6
Bishopstone Kent 41 G2
Bishopstone Swindn 47 K2
Bishopstone Wilts 33 J5
Bishopstrow Wilts 32 E2
Bishop Sutton BaNES 45 H7
Bishop's Waltham Hants 35 H7
Bishopswood Somset 30 C8
Bishop's Wood Staffs 97 J2
Bishopsworth Bristl 45 H5
Bishop Thornton N York 150 C3
Bishopthorpe C York 151 J6
Bishopton Darltn 169 K6
Bishopton Rens 208 D5
Bishopton Warwks 82 E4
Bishop Wilton E R Yk 152 B5
Bishton Newpt 44 D2
Bishton Staffs 115 G7

Bisley Gloucs 64 C6
Bisley Surrey 50 B7
Bisley Camp Surrey 50 B7
Bispham Bpool 146 F7
Bispham Green Lancs 138 F5
Bissoe Cnwll 3 K3
Bisterne Hants 18 A3
Bitchet Green Kent 38 E3
Bitchfield Lincs 118 C6
Bittadon Devon 27 K3
Bittaford Devon 7 K3
Bittering Norfk 121 K8
Bitterley Shrops 96 D7
Bitterne C Sotn 34 F8
Bitteswell Leics 100 C6
Bitton S Glos 45 K5
Bix Oxon 49 H2
Bixter Shet 281 d6
Blaby Leics 100 C4
Blackadder Border 202 C3
Blackawton Devon 8 B5
Blackbeck Cumb 155 J1
Blackborough Devon 14 C1
Blackborough End Norfk 120 E8
Black Bourton Oxon 65 L6
Blackboys E Susx 23 J3
Blackbrook Derbys 116 B2
Blackbrook St Hel 139 G8
Blackbrook Staffs 114 B4
Blackbrook Surrey 37 J2
Blackburn Abers 245 J1
Blackburn Bl w D 139 K2
Blackburn Rothm 133 H1
Blackburn W Loth 210 C6
Blackburn with Darwen
  Services Bl w D 139 K3
Black Callerton N u Ty 180 E5
Black Carr Norfk 106 B4
Black Corner W Susx 37 L3
Blackcraig E Ayrs 185 G1
Black Crofts Ag & B 228 E3
Black Cross Cnwll 4 E3
Blackden Heath Ches E 130 F5
Blackdog Abers 245 L1
Black Dog Devon 13 J1
Blackdown Devon 12 C4
Blackdown Dorset 15 J2
Blackdyke Cumb 176 F8
Blacker Barns 142 A5
Blacker Hill Barns 142 B7
Blackfen Gt Lon 51 M4
Blackfield Hants 19 G3
Blackford Cumb 177 L6
Blackford P & K 220 F5
Blackford Somset 30 F2
Blackford Somset 31 L5
Blackfordby Leics 116 B7
Blackgang IoW 19 H8
Blackhall C Edin 211 H4
Blackhall Colliery Dur 170 B3
Blackhall Mill Gatesd 180 D7
Blackhall Rocks Dur 170 B3
Blackham E Susx 38 D5
Blackhaugh Border 200 F5
Blackheath Essex 72 E4
Blackheath Gt Lon 51 K4
Blackheath Sandw 98 B6
Blackheath Suffk 107 J8
Blackheath Surrey 36 F2
Black Heddon Nthumb 180 C4
Blackhill Abers 257 K3
Blackhill Abers 269 K5
Blackhill Dur 180 D8
Blackhill of Clackriach Abers 269 G7
Blackjack Lincs 119 H4
Blackland Wilts 46 E5
Black Lane Ends Lancs 149 G6
Blacklaw D & G 186 F4
Blackley Manch 140 C7
Blacklunans P & K 233 H3
Blackmarstone Herefs 80 C7
Blackmill Brdgnd 42 E4
Blackmoor Hants 36 A4
Black Moor Leeds 150 D7
Blackmoor N Som 44 E4
Blackmoorfoot Kirk 141 H5
Blackmoor Gate Devon 28 A2
Blackmore Essex 70 F6
Blackmore End Essex 71 H1
Blackmore End Herts 68 F4
Black Mountains 61 L2
Blackness Falk 210 E3
Blacknest Hants 36 B3
Blacknest W & M 50 B5
Black Notley Essex 71 J3
Blacko Lancs 148 E7
Black Pill Swans 57 H6
Blackpool Bpool 146 F8
Blackpool Devon 8 C5
Blackpool Devon 13 J7

Blackpool Gate Cumb 178 C3
Blackridge W Loth 210 A5
Blackrock Cnwll 3 G4
Blackrock Mons 61 K4
Blackrod Bolton 139 J5
Blacksboat Moray 254 D4
Blackshaw D & G 176 D5
Blackshaw Head Calder 140 E2
Blacksmith's Green Suffk 90 D2
Blacksnape Bl w D 139 L3
Blackstone W Susx 22 C4
Black Street Suffk 107 K6
Black Tar Pembks 55 G5
Blackthorn Oxon 66 F3
Blackthorpe Suffk 89 H3
Blacktoft E R Yk 143 L3
Blacktop C Aber 245 J3
Black Torrington Devon 12 B2
Blackwall Derbys 115 L2
Blackwall Tunnel Gt Lon 51 K3
Blackwater Cnwll 4 D5
Blackwater Hants 49 K7
Blackwater IoW 19 H6
Blackwater Somset 30 C7
Blackwaterfoot N Ayrs 194 D5
Blackwell Cumb 177 L8
Blackwell Darltn 169 H8
Blackwell Derbys 132 C5
Blackwell Derbys 133 J7
Blackwell Warwks 82 F6
Blackwell Worcs 82 A1
Blackwellsend Green Gloucs 63 M2
Blackwood Caerph 43 J2
Blackwood D & G 176 B2
Blackwood S Lans 198 C4
Blackwood Hill Staffs 131 H8
Blacon Ches W 129 J6
Bladbean Kent 41 G6
Bladnoch D & G 174 C4
Bladon Oxon 66 C4
Bladon Somset 30 F6
Blaenannerch Cerdgn 75 M2
Blaenau Ffestiniog Gwynd 110 D2
Blaenau Ffestiniog Gwynd 110 D2
Blaenavon Torfn 61 L5
Blaenavon Industrial Landscape Torfn 61 K5
Blaencwm Rhondd 60 D7
Blaen Dyryn Powys 78 C7
Blaenffos Pembks 75 L5
Blaengarw Brdgnd 42 D3
Blaengeuffordd Cerdgn 92 E7
Blaengwrach Neath 60 C6
Blaengwynfi Neath 42 D2
Blaenllechau Rhondd 42 F2
Blaenpennal Cerdgn 77 H2
Blaenplwyf Cerdgn 92 C8
Blaenporth Cerdgn 76 A5
Blaenrhondda Rhondd 60 D7
Blaenwaun Carmth 75 M6
Blaen-y-coed Carmth 58 C3
Blaen-y-cwm Blae G 61 H5
Blaenycwm Cerdgn 93 H8
Blagdon N Som 45 G7
Blagdon Somset 30 B7
Blagdon Torbay 8 C3
Blagdon Hill Somset 30 B7
Blagill W & F 167 G1
Blaguegate Lancs 138 F6
Blaich Highld 239 G8
Blain Highld 237 K6
Blaina Blae G 61 K5
Blair Atholl P & K 232 E3
Blair Drummond Stirlg 220 C7
Blairgowrie P & K 233 J6
Blairhall Fife 210 D1
Blairingone P & K 221 H7
Blairlogie Stirlg 220 E7
Blairmore Ag & B 207 K2
Blairmore Highld 276 B4
Blair's Ferry Ag & B 206 F5
Blaisdon Gloucs 63 K4
Blakebrook Worcs 97 J8
Blakedown Worcs 97 K7
Blake End Essex 71 H3
Blakeley Lane Staffs 114 F2
Blakemere Ches W 130 A5
Blakemere Herefs 79 L7
Blakemore Devon 7 M3
Blakenall Heath Wsall 98 C3
Blakeney Gloucs 63 K5
Blakeney Norfk 122 A3
Blakenhall Ches E 114 A2
Blakenhall Wolves 97 K4
Blakeshall Worcs 97 J7
Blakesley W Nthn 84 C5
Blanchland Nthumb 180 A8
Blandford Camp Dorset 17 H1
Blandford Forum Dorset 17 G1
Blandford St Mary Dorset 17 G2
Bland Hill N York 150 B5
Blanefield Stirlg 208 F3
Blankney Lincs 135 L7
Blantyre S Lans 209 J7
Blàr a' Chaorainn Highld 229 H2
Blarghour Ag & B 216 F4
Blargie Highld 241 G4
Blarmachfoldach Highld 229 H2
Blashford Hants 18 A2
Blaston Leics 101 H4
Blatherwycke N Nthn 101 L4
Blawith W & F 156 C5
Blawquhairn D & G 184 F6
Blaxhall Suffk 91 J4
Blaxton Donc 143 H7
Blaydon Gatesd 180 F6
Bleadney Somset 31 H2
Bleadon N Som 44 C7
Bleak Street Somset 32 C4
Blean Kent 40 F3
Bleasby Lincs 136 B3
Bleasby Notts 117 J2
Bleasdale Lancs 147 L6
Bleatarn W & F 167 G7
Bleathwood Herefs 80 D1
Blebocraigs Fife 223 G4
Bleddfa Powys 79 H2
Bledington Gloucs 65 K3
Bledlow Bucks 67 J6
Bledlow Ridge Bucks 67 J7
Bleet Wilts 46 C7
Blegbie E Loth 212 B6
Blencarn W & F 166 E4
Blencogo Cumb 165 G1
Blendworth Hants 35 L8
Blenheim Palace Oxon 66 B4
Blennerhasset Cumb 165 G2
Bletchingdon Oxon 66 D4
Bletchingley Surrey 38 A3
Bletchley M Keyn 85 G8
Bletchley Shrops 113 K5
Bletherston Pembks 55 H3
Bletsoe Bed 85 K4
Blewbury Oxon 48 D2
Blickling Norfk 122 D6
Blidworth Notts 134 D8
Blidworth Bottoms Notts 117 G1
Blindburn Nthumb 189 L4
Blindcrake Cumb 164 F4
Blindley Heath Surrey 38 A4
Blindwells E Loth 211 L4
Blisland Cnwll 10 F8
Blissford Hants 33 L8
Bliss Gate Worcs 81 G1
Blisworth W Nthn 84 D4
Blithbury Staffs 115 H7
Blitterlees Cumb 176 F8
Blockley Gloucs 82 E8
Blofield Norfk 107 G2
Blofield Heath Norfk 107 G1
Blo Norton Norfk 105 K7
Bloomfield Border 189 G2
Blore Staffs 114 A4
Blore Staffs 115 J2
Blounce Hants 35 L2
Blounts Green Staffs 115 H5
Blowick Sefton 138 D4
Bloxham Oxon 83 K8
Bloxholm Lincs 118 E1
Bloxwich Wsall 98 C3
Bloxworth Dorset 17 G4
Blubberhouses N York 149 L5
Blue Anchor Cnwll 4 E3
Blue Anchor Somset 29 J2
Blue Bell Hill Kent 52 F6
Blundellsands Sefton 138 C7
Blundeston Suffk 107 L4
Blunham C Beds 86 C5
Blunsdon St Andrew Swindn 47 H1
Bluntington Worcs 97 K8
Bluntisham Cambs 103 H8
Blunts Cnwll 6 C2
Blunts Green Warwks 82 D2
Blurton C Stke 114 D3
Blyborough Lincs 135 J1
Blyford Suffk 107 J8
Blymhill Staffs 97 H1
Blymhill Lawn Staffs 97 J1
Blyth Notts 134 C2
Blyth Nthumb 181 H3
Blyth Bridge Border 199 K4
Blythburgh Suffk 107 J8
Blythe Border 201 J3
Blythe Bridge Staffs 114 F3
Blythe End Warwks 99 G5
Blythe Marsh Staffs 114 F3
Blyth Services Notts 134 C2
Blyton Lincs 135 G1
Boarhills Fife 223 K4
Boarhunt Hants 19 K2
Boarley Kent 53 G7
Boarsgreave Lancs 140 C4
Boarshead E Susx 38 E6
Boar's Head Wigan 139 H6
Boars Hill Oxon 66 D6
Boarstall Bucks 66 F4
Boasley Cross Devon 12 C4
Boath Highld 263 G5
Boat of Garten Highld 253 H7
Bobbing Kent 53 J6
Bobbington Staffs 97 H5
Bobbingworth Essex 70 D6
Bocaddon Cnwll 5 L3
Bocking Essex 71 J2
Bocking Churchstreet Essex 71 J2
Bockleton Worcs 80 D3
Boconnoc Cnwll 5 K3
Boddam Abers 257 L3
Boddam Shet 281 d8
Boddington Gloucs 64 C2
Bodedern IoA 124 F4
Bodelwyddan Denbgs 127 K4
Bodenham Herefs 80 C5
Bodenham Wilts 33 L5
Bodenham Moor Herefs 80 D5
Bodewryd IoA 125 G2
Bodfari Denbgs 128 C5
Bodffordd IoA 125 G4
Bodham Norfk 122 C3
Bodiam E Susx 24 E2
Bodicote Oxon 83 K7
Bodieve Cnwll 10 D7
Bodinnick Cnwll 5 K4
Bodle Street Green E Susx 23 L4
Bodmin Cnwll 5 H2
Bodmin Moor Cnwll 11 H7
Bodney Norfk 105 G4
Bodorgan IoA 125 G6
Bodsham Kent 40 E6
Boduan Gwynd 108 E4
Bodwen Cnwll 5 H3
Bodymoor Heath Warwks 99 G4
Bogallan Highld 251 H2
Bogbrae Abers 257 J4
Bogend S Ayrs 196 D4
Boggs Holdings E Loth 212 A5
Boghall Mdloth 211 H6
Boghall W Loth 210 C5
Boghead S Lans 198 C5
Bogmoor Moray 267 G4
Bogmuir Abers 235 G1
Bogniebrae Abers 255 M3
Bognor Regis W Susx 20 F7
Bogroy Highld 253 G7
Bogue D & G 185 G6
Bohetherick Cnwll 6 E1
Bohortha Cnwll 3 L4
Bohuntine Highld 240 A6
Bojewyan Cnwll 2 B4
Bokiddick Cnwll 5 H2
Bolam Dur 169 G6
Bolam Nthumb 180 D2
Bolberry Devon 7 K7
Bold Heath St Hel 129 M2
Boldmere Birm 98 E4
Boldon Colliery S Tyne 181 J6
Boldre Hants 18 E4
Boldron Dur 168 C7
Bole Notts 134 F2
Bolehill Derbys 132 F8
Bole Hill Derbys 133 G5
Bolenowe Cnwll 3 H3
Bolham Devon 29 G7
Bolham Water Devon 29 L8
Bolingey Cnwll 4 C4
Bollington Ches E 131 J4
Bollington Cross Ches E 131 H4
Bollow Gloucs 63 L4
Bolney W Susx 37 L6
Bolnhurst Bed 86 B3
Bolnore W Susx 22 E3
Bolshan Angus 234 F5
Bolsover Derbys 133 J5
Bolster Moor Kirk 141 G5
Bolsterstone Sheff 141 L8
Boltby N York 161 H5
Bolter End Bucks 67 J8
Bolton Bolton 139 L6
Bolton E Loth 212 B5
Bolton E R Yk 152 B5
Bolton Nthumb 191 G3
Bolton W & F 166 E6
Bolton Abbey N York 149 K5
Bolton Bridge N York 149 K5
Bolton-by-Bowland Lancs 148 D6
Boltonfellend Cumb 178 B5
Boltongate Cumb 165 H3
Bolton-le-Sands Lancs 147 J2
Bolton Low Houses Cumb 165 H2
Bolton New Houses Cumb 165 H2
Bolton-on-Swale N York 160 C3
Bolton Percy N York 151 H7
Bolton Town End Lancs 147 J2
Bolton upon Dearne Barns 142 C7
Bolventor Cnwll 11 H7
Bomarsund Nthumb 181 G2
Bomere Heath Shrops 113 G7
Bonar Bridge Highld 263 G2
Bonawe Ag & B 228 F8
Bonby N Linc 144 C5
Boncath Pembks 75 L4
Bonchester Bridge Border 189 G4
Bonchurch IoW 19 K8
Bondleigh Devon 12 F2
Bonds Lancs 147 J6
Bonehill Devon 13 G7
Bonehill Staffs 99 G3
Bo'ness Falk 210 D3
Boney Hay Staffs 98 D2
Bonhill W Duns 208 C3
Boningale Shrops 97 J3
Bonjedward Border 189 H2
Bonkle N Lans 209 M7
Bonnington Angus 234 F7
Bonnington Kent 40 D8
Bonnybank Fife 222 F6
Bonnybridge Falk 209 L3
Bonnykelly Abers 268 F5
Bonnyrigg Mdloth 211 J6
Bonnyton Angus 233 M7
Bonsall Derbys 132 E8
Bonshaw Tower D & G 177 H4
Bont Mons 62 D3
Bontddu Gwynd 110 C7
Bont-Dolgadfan Powys 93 J3
Bont-goch Cerdgn 92 E6
Bonthorpe Lincs 137 J5
Bontnewydd Cerdgn 77 H2
Bontnewydd Gwynd 125 J7
Bontuchel Denbgs 128 C8
Bonvilston V Glam 43 G7
Bonwm Denbgs 111 L3
Bon-y-maen Swans [illegible]
Boode Devon 27 J3
Booker Bucks 49 K1
Booley Shrops 113 J6
Boon Border 201 J4
Boon Hill Staffs 114 C2
Boorley Green Hants 35 G8
Boosbeck R & Cl 170 F7
Boose's Green Essex 71 K1
Boot Cumb 155 M3
Booth Calder 141 G2
Boothby Graffoe Lincs 135 K7
Boothby Pagnell Lincs 118 C5
Boothferry E R Yk 143 J3
Booth Green Ches E 131 H3
Boothstown Salfd 139 L7
Boothtown Calder 141 G2
Boothville W Nthn 84 F2
Bootle Cumb 155 K5
Bootle Sefton 138 D8
Boots Green Ches W 130 E5
Boot Street Suffk 90 F5
Booze N York 159 H2
Boraston Shrops 80 E1
Bordeaux Guern 9 k2
Borden Kent 53 J6
Borden W Susx 36 B6
Border Cumb 177 G8
Bordesley Worcs 82 B1
Bordley N York 149 G3
Bordon Hants 36 B4
Boreham Essex 71 J5
Boreham Wilts 32 E2
Boreham Street E Susx 24 B5
Borehamwood Herts 69 G7
Boreland D & G 187 J8
Boreraig Highld 258 B6
Boreton Shrops 96 C2
Borgh W Isls 282 g1
Borgh W Isls 283 b13
Borgie Highld 278 B4
Borgue D & G 175 G5
Borgue Highld 274 F3
Borley Essex 89 G6
Borley Green Essex 89 G6
Borley Green Suffk 89 K3
Borneskitaig Highld 258 F2
Borness D & G 174 F5
Boroughbridge N York 150 E3
Borough Green Kent 38 F2
Borras Head Wrexhm 112 E1
Borrowash Derbys 116 C4
Borrowby N York 160 F5
Borrowby N York 171 H7
Borrowdale Cumb 165 J7
Borrowstoun Falk 210 D3
Borstal Medway 52 F5
Borth Cerdgn 92 D5

Borthwick Mdloth 211 L7
Borthwickbrae Border 188 C3
Borthwickshiels Border 188 D3
Borth-y-Gest Gwynd 109 K4
Borve Highld 259 G7
Borve W Isls 282 d6
Borve W Isls 282 g1
Borve W Isls 283 b13
Borwick Lancs 147 K1
Borwick Lodge W & F 156 E3
Borwick Rails Cumb 156 A6
Bosavern Cnwll 2 B5
Bosbury Herefs 80 F6
Boscarne Cnwll 5 H1
Boscastle Cnwll 10 F4
Boscombe BCP 17 M4
Boscombe Wilts 33 L3
Boscoppa Cnwll 5 H4
Bosham W Susx 20 C6
Bosham Hoe W Susx 20 D6
Bosherston Pembks 54 F7
Boskednan Cnwll 2 C4
Boskenna Cnwll 2 C6
Bosley Ches E 131 H6
Bosoughan Cnwll 4 E3
Bossall N York 151 M4
Bossiney Cnwll 10 F5
Bossingham Kent 40 F5
Bossington Somset 28 F1
Bostock Green Ches W 130 C6
Boston Lincs 119 K3
Boston Spa Leeds 150 F6
Boswarthan Cnwll 2 C4
Boswinger Cnwll 5 G6
Botallack Cnwll 2 B4
Botany Bay Gt Lon 69 J7
Botcheston Leics 100 B2
Botesdale Suffk 105 L8
Bothal Nthumb 180 F2
Bothampstead W Berk 48 D4
Bothamsall Notts 134 D5
Bothel Cumb 165 G3
Bothenhampton Dorset 15 L4
Bothwell S Lans 209 J7
Bothwell Services (southbound) S Lans 209 J7
Botley Bucks 68 B6
Botley Hants 35 G8
Botley Oxon 66 C6
Botolph Claydon Bucks 67 H2
Botolphs W Susx 21 L5
Botolph's Bridge Kent 40 F8
Bottesford Leics 117 L4
Bottesford N Linc 143 M6
Bottisham Cambs 87 L3
Bottomcraig Fife 222 F2
Bottom of Hutton Lancs 138 F2
Bottom o' th' Moor Bolton 139 K5
Bottoms Calder 140 D3
Bottoms Cnwll 2 B6
Botts Green Warwks 99 H5
Botusfleming Cnwll 6 E3
Botwnnog Gwynd 108 D5
Bough Beech Kent 38 D4
Boughrood Powys 79 G7
Boughspring Gloucs 63 H7
Boughton Norfk 104 D3
Boughton Notts 134 D6
Boughton W Nthn 84 E2
Boughton Aluph Kent 40 D6
Boughton End C Beds 85 J2
Boughton Green Kent 39 J3
Boughton Lees Kent 40 D6
Boughton Malherbe Kent 39 M3
Boughton Monchelsea Kent 39 J3
Boughton Street Kent 40 D3
Boulby R & Cl 171 H7
Boulder Clough Calder 140 F3
Bouldnor IoW 18 F5
Bouldon Shrops 96 H6
Boulmer Nthumb 191 K3
Boulston Pembks 55 G4
Boultenstone Abers 243 M2
Boultham Lincs 135 J6
Boundary Staffs 114 F3
Bourn Cambs 87 G4
Bournbrook Birm 98 D6
Bourne Lincs 118 E7
Bournebridge Essex 70 D8
Bourne End Bed 85 K3
Bourne End Bucks 49 L2
Bourne End C Beds 85 J6
Bourne End Herts 68 C6
Bournemouth BCP 17 L4
Bournemouth Airport BCP 17 M3
Bournes Green Gloucs 64 C6
Bournes Green Sthend 53 K2
Bournheath Worcs 98 B8
Bournmoor Dur 181 H8
Bournstream Gloucs 63 L8

Bournville Birm 98 D7
Bourton Dorset 32 C5
Bourton N Som 44 D6
Bourton Oxon 47 K2
Bourton Shrops 96 D4
Bourton Wilts 46 F6
Bourton on Dunsmore Warwks 83 K1
Bourton-on-the-Hill Gloucs 65 J1
Bourton-on-the-Water Gloucs 65 H3
Bousd Ag & B 225 H3
Boustead Hill Cumb 177 J7
Bouth W & F 156 D5
Bouthwaite N York 149 L2
Bouts Worcs 82 B3
Boveney Bucks 50 B3
Boveridge Dorset 33 J7
Bovey Tracey Devon 13 J7
Bovingdon Herts 68 C6
Bovingdon Green Bucks 49 K2
Bovinger Essex 70 D6
Bovington Dorset 16 E5
Bovington Camp Dorset 16 F5
Bow Cumb 177 K7
Bow Devon 8 B3
Bow Devon 13 G2
Bow Gt Lon 51 K2
Bow Ork 275 c6
Bowbank Dur 168 B6
Bow Brickhill M Keyn 85 H8
Bowbridge Gloucs 64 B6
Bowburn Dur 169 J3
Bowcombe IoW 19 H6
Bowd Devon 14 D4
Bowden Border 201 H7
Bowden Devon 8 C5
Bowden Hill Wilts 46 H5
Bowdon Traffd 130 E2
Bower Highld 280 B4
Bowerchalke Wilts 33 H6
Bowerhill Wilts 46 C6
Bower Hinton Somset 31 G7
Bower House Tye Suffk 89 K7
Bowermadden Highld 280 B3
Bowers Staffs 114 C4
Bowers Gifford Essex 53 G1
Bowershall Fife 210 E1
Bower's Row Leeds 142 B2
Bowes Dur 168 C7
Bowgreave Lancs 147 K7
Bowhouse D & G 176 D5
Bowithick Cnwll 11 H6
Bowker's Green Lancs 138 E6
Bowland Border 200 F5
Bowland Bridge W & F 156 F5
Bowley Herefs 80 C5
Bowley Town Herefs 80 C5
Bowlhead Green Surrey 36 D3
Bowling C Brad 141 J2
Bowling W Duns 208 D4
Bowling Bank Wrexhm 112 F2
Bowling Green Worcs 81 J5
Bowmanstead W & F 156 D3
Bowmore Ag & B 204 D4
Bowness-on-Solway Cumb 177 H6
Bowness-on-Windermere W & F 156 F3
Bow of Fife Fife 222 E4
Bowriefauld Angus 234 D6
Bowscale W & F 165 K4
Bowsden Nthumb 202 F5
Bowston W & F 157 H3
Bow Street Cerdgn 92 D6
Bow Street Norfk 105 K4
Bowthorpe Norfk 106 D2
Box Gloucs 64 B7
Box Wilts 46 B5
Boxbush Gloucs 63 K3
Boxbush Gloucs 63 L4
Box End Bed 85 K5
Boxford Suffk 89 K7
Boxford W Berk 48 B4
Boxgrove W Susx 20 E5
Box Hill Surrey 51 G8
Boxley Kent 53 G7
Boxmoor Herts 68 D6
Box's Shop Cnwll 11 H2
Boxted Essex 72 E1
Boxted Suffk 89 G5
Boxted Cross Essex 72 E1
Boxwell Gloucs 64 A8
Boxworth Cambs 87 G2
Boyden End Suffk 88 E4
Boyden Gate Kent 41 H2
Boylestone Derbys 115 K4
Boyndie Abers 268 B3
Boyndlie Abers 269 G4
Boynton E R Yk 153 J2
Boysack Angus 234 F5
Boys Hill Dorset 16 C1
Boythorpe Derbys 133 G5

Boyton Cnwll 11 L4
Boyton Suffk 91 J6
Boyton Wilts 32 F3
Boyton Cross Essex 70 F5
Boyton End Suffk 88 B7
Bozeat N Nthn 85 H3
Braaid IoM 154 d6
Brabling Green Suffk 91 G2
Brabourne Kent 40 E7
Brabourne Lees Kent 40 E7
Brabstermire Highld 280 D2
Bracadale Highld 246 E1
Braceborough Lincs 102 B1
Bracebridge Heath Lincs 135 K6
Bracebridge Low Fields Lincs 135 J6
Braceby Lincs 118 D4
Bracewell Lancs 148 F6
Brackenfield Derbys 133 G7
Brackenhirst N Lans 209 K5
Brackenthwaite Cumb 165 J1
Brackenthwaite N York 150 C5
Brackla Brdgnd 42 D5
Bracklesham W Susx 20 C7
Brackletter Highld 239 K7
Brackley W Nthn 84 B7
Brackley Hatch W Nthn 84 C7
Bracknell Br For 49 L5
Braco P & K 220 E5
Bracobrae Moray 267 K5
Bracon Ash Norfk 106 D3
Bracora Highld 237 L2
Bracorina Highld 237 L2
Bradaford Devon 11 M4
Bradbourne Derbys 115 K1
Bradbury Dur 169 J5
Bradden W Nthn 84 C5
Braddock Cnwll 5 K2
Bradeley C Stke 114 D1
Bradenham Bucks 67 K7
Bradenstoke Wilts 46 E3
Bradfield Devon 14 B1
Bradfield Essex 73 H1
Bradfield Norfk 122 F5
Bradfield Sheff 132 E1
Bradfield W Berk 48 F4
Bradfield Combust Suffk 89 H4
Bradfield Green Ches E 130 D7
Bradfield Heath Essex 73 H1
Bradfield St Clare Suffk 89 H4
Bradfield St George Suffk 89 H3
Bradfield Southend W Berk 48 E5
Bradford C Brad 141 J1
Bradford Cnwll 11 G7
Bradford Devon 12 A1
Bradford Nthumb 180 C3
Bradford Nthumb 203 H6
Bradford Abbas Dorset 31 K8
Bradford Leigh Wilts 46 B6
Bradford-on-Avon Wilts 46 B6
Bradford-on-Tone Somset 30 B6
Bradford Peverell Dorset 16 C4
Bradiford Devon 27 K4
Brading IoW 19 K6
Bradley Ches W 113 H2
Bradley Derbys 115 L2
Bradley Hants 35 K3
Bradley Kirk 141 J4
Bradley N York 159 J6
Bradley NE Lin 145 G6
Bradley Staffs 114 D7
Bradley Wolves 98 B4
Bradley Worcs 82 A3
Bradley Wrexhm 112 E1
Bradley Green Somset 30 C3
Bradley Green Warwks 99 H3
Bradley Green Worcs 82 A3
Bradley in the Moors Staffs 115 H3
Bradley Stoke S Glos 45 J3
Bradmore Notts 117 G5
Bradney Somset 30 E3
Bradninch Devon 14 A2
Bradninch Devon 27 L4
Bradnop Staffs 131 K8
Bradnor Green Herefs 79 K4
Bradpole Dorset 15 L4
Bradshaw Bolton 139 L5
Bradshaw Calder 141 G2
Bradshaw Kirk 141 G5
Bradstone Devon 11 M6
Bradwall Green Ches E 130 E7
Bradwell Derbys 132 C3
Bradwell Devon 27 J2
Bradwell Essex 71 K3
Bradwell M Keyn 85 G7
Bradwell Norfk 107 K3
Bradwell-on-Sea Essex 72 E5
Bradwell Waterside Essex 72 E5
Bradworthy Devon 26 E8
Brae Highld 263 H7
Brae Shet 281 d5

Braeface Falk 209 K3
Braehead Angus 235 H5
Braehead D & G 173 K4
Braehead S Lans 198 F3
Braeintra Highld 248 D5
Braemar Abers 243 G5
Braemore Highld 261 L4
Braemore Highld 274 E2
Brae Roy Lodge Highld 240 B5
Braeside Inver 207 L4
Braes of Coul Angus 233 L4
Braes of Enzie Moray 267 H4
Braes of Ullapool Highld 261 K1
Braeswick Ork 275 e2
Braevallich Ag & B 216 E5
Braewick Shet 281 c4
Brafferton Darltn 169 H6
Brafferton N York 150 F2
Brafield-on-the-Green W Nthn 84 F3
Bragar W Isls 282 f2
Bragbury End Herts 69 H3
Braidwood S Lans 198 D3
Brailsford Derbys 115 L3
Brailsford Green Derbys 115 L3
Brain's Green Gloucs 63 K5
Braintree Essex 71 J2
Braiseworth Suffk 90 D1
Braishfield Hants 34 E6
Braiswick Essex 72 E2
Braithwaite C Brad 149 J7
Braithwaite Cumb 165 H6
Braithwell Donc 133 K1
Braken Hill Wakefd 142 C4
Bramber W Susx 21 L5
Brambridge Hants 35 G6
Bramcote Notts 116 E4
Bramcote Warwks 99 L5
Bramdean Hants 35 J5
Bramerton Norfk 106 F2
Bramfield Herts 69 H4
Bramfield Suffk 107 H8
Bramford Suffk 90 D6
Bramhall Stockp 131 H3
Bramham Leeds 150 F7
Bramhope Leeds 150 C7
Bramley Hants 49 G8
Bramley Leeds 141 K1
Bramley Rothm 133 K1
Bramley Surrey 36 F2
Bramley Corner Hants 48 F7
Bramley Green Hants 49 G7
Bramley Head N York 149 L4
Bramling Kent 41 H4
Brampford Speke Devon 13 L3
Brampton Cambs 86 E1
Brampton Cumb 178 C6
Brampton Lincs 135 G4
Brampton Norfk 122 E6
Brampton Rothm 142 C7
Brampton Suffk 107 J7
Brampton W & F 166 F6
Brampton Abbotts Herefs 63 J2
Brampton Ash N Nthn 101 H6
Brampton Bryan Herefs 79 L1
Brampton-en-le-Morthen Rothm 133 J2
Bramshall Staffs 115 H5
Bramshaw Hants 34 C7
Bramshill Hants 49 H6
Bramshott Hants 36 C4
Bramwell Somset 31 G5
Branault Highld 237 G6
Brancaster Norfk 121 G3
Brancaster Staithe Norfk 121 H3
Brancepeth Dur 169 G3
Branchill Moray 266 B5
Brand End Lincs 119 L3
Branderburgh Moray 266 E2
Brandesburton E R Yk 153 H6
Brandeston Suffk 90 F3
Brand Green Gloucs 63 L2
Brandis Corner Devon 12 A2
Brandiston Norfk 122 C7
Brandon Dur 169 G3
Brandon Lincs 118 B2
Brandon Nthumb 190 F3
Brandon Suffk 104 F6
Brandon Warwks 99 L8
Brandon Bank Norfk 104 C5
Brandon Creek Norfk 104 C5
Brandon Parva Norfk 106 B2
Brandsby N York 151 J1
Brandy Wharf Lincs 144 C8
Brane Cnwll 2 B5
Bran End Essex 71 G2
Branksome BCP 17 L4
Branksome Park BCP 17 L4
Bransbury Hants 34 F2
Bransby Lincs 135 H4
Branscombe Devon 14 E5

Bransford Worcs 81 H5
Bransgore Hants 18 B4
Bransholme C KuH 144 E1
Bransley Shrops 96 E8
Branson's Cross Worcs 82 C1
Branston Leics 117 L6
Branston Lincs 135 L6
Branston Staffs 115 L6
Branston Booths Lincs 135 L6
Branstone IoW 19 J7
Brant Broughton Lincs 118 B1
Brantham Suffk 90 D8
Branthwaite Cumb 164 D6
Branthwaite Cumb 165 J3
Brantingham E R Yk 144 B2
Branton Donc 143 G7
Branton Nthumb 190 F3
Branton Green N York 150 F3
Branxton Nthumb 202 D5
Brassey Green Ches W 129 M1
Brassie Dur 169 H2
Brassington Derbys 115 L1
Brasted Kent 38 D2
Brasted Chart Kent 51 M8
Brathens Abers 244 F4
Bratoft Lincs 137 J6
Brattleby Lincs 135 J3
Bratton Somset 29 G2
Bratton Wilts 46 C8
Bratton Wrekin 96 E1
Bratton Clovelly Devon 12 B4
Bratton Fleming Devon 27 M3
Bratton Seymour Somset 31 L5
Braughing Herts 69 K2
Braughing Friars Herts 70 B2
Braunston Rutlnd 101 H2
Braunston W Nthn 84 A2
Braunstone Town Leics 100 C3
Braunton Devon 27 J4
Brawby N York 162 C7
Brawl Highld 278 D3
Braworth N York 161 H1
Bray W & M 49 L3
Braybrooke N Nthn 101 J4
Braydon Wilts 46 F1
Braydon Brook Wilts 64 E8
Braydon Side Wilts 46 E2
Brayford Devon 28 B4
Bray's Hill E Susx 24 B4
Bray Shop Cnwll 11 L7
Braystones Cumb 155 H2
Braythorn N York 150 C6
Brayton N York 142 F2
Braywick W & M 49 L3
Braywoodside W & M 49 L4
Brazacott Cnwll 11 K4
Breach Kent 41 G6
Breach Kent 53 H6
Breachwood Green Herts 68 F3
Breacleit W Isls 282 e3
Breaclete W Isle 282 e3
Breaden Heath Shrops 113 G4
Breadsall Derbys 116 B4
Breadstone Gloucs 63 L7
Breage Cnwll 3 G5
Breakachy Highld 250 E3
Breakish Highld 247 L4
Brealangwell Lodge Highld 262 F1
Bream Gloucs 63 J6
Breamore Hants 33 L7
Brean Somset 44 C7
Breanais W Isls 282 d4
Brearley Calder 140 F3
Brearton N York 150 D4
Breascleit W Isls 282 f3
Breasclete W Isls 282 f3
Breaston Derbys 116 D5
Brechfa Carmth 58 F3
Brechin Angus 234 F3
Breckles Norfk 105 J4
Brecon Powys 61 G2
Brecon Beacons National
Park 60 F2
Bredbury Stockp 131 H2
Brede E Susx 24 E4
Bredenbury Herefs 80 E4
Bredfield Suffk 91 G4
Bredgar Kent 53 J7
Bredhurst Kent 53 G6
Bredon Worcs 81 L7
Bredon's Hardwick Worcs 81 L7
Bredon's Norton Worcs 81 L7
Bredward Herefs 79 K4
Bredwardine Herefs 79 L6
Breedon on the Hill Leics 116 C7
Breich W Loth 210 C7
Breightmet Bolton 139 L6
Breighton E R Yk 143 H1
Breinton Herefs 80 B7
Breinton Herefs 80 B7
Bremhill Wilts 46 E4

Bremridge Devon 28 B5
Brenchley Kent 39 H5
Brendon Devon 11 L1
Brendon Devon 28 D1
Brendon Hill Somset 29 J4
Brenfield Ag & B 206 D3
Brenish W Isls 282 d4
Brenkley N u Ty 180 F4
Brent Cross Gt Lon 51 G2
Brent Eleigh Suffk 89 J5
Brentford Gt Lon 50 F3
Brentingby Leics 117 K7
Brent Knoll Somset 30 E1
Brent Mill Devon 7 K3
Brent Pelham Herts 70 B1
Brentwood Essex 70 E8
Brenzett Kent 25 J2
Brenzett Green Kent 25 J2
Brereton Staffs 115 G8
Brereton Green Ches E 130 F6
Brereton Heath Ches E 130 F6
Brereton Hill Staffs 115 G8
Bressay Shet 281 e6
Bressingham Norfk 106 B7
Bressingham Common Norfk 106 B7
Bretby Derbys 116 A7
Bretford Warwks 99 L7
Bretforton Worcs 82 C6
Bretherton Lancs 138 F4
Brettabister Shet 281 e5
Brettenham Norfk 105 J6
Brettenham Suffk 89 K4
Bretton C Pete 102 D3
Bretton Derbys 132 D4
Bretton Flints 129 H7
Brewers End Essex 70 E3
Brewer Street Surrey 51 J8
Brewood Staffs 97 K2
Briantspuddle Dorset 16 F4
Brick End Essex 70 E2
Brickendon Herts 69 J5
Bricket Wood Herts 68 E6
Brick Houses Sheff 132 F3
Brickkiln Green Essex 71 H1
Bricklehampton Worcs 82 A6
Bride IoM 154 f2
Bridekirk Cumb 164 F4
Bridell Pembks 75 L4
Bridestowe Devon 12 C5
Brideswell Abers 255 M4
Bridford Devon 13 J5
Bridge Kent 41 G4
Bridge End Cumb 156 A6
Bridge End Cumb 165 L1
Bridge End Devon 7 K5
Bridge End Dur 168 C3
Bridge End Essex 71 G1
Bridge End Lincs 118 F4
Bridgefoot Angus 234 B8
Bridgefoot Cumb 164 E5
Bridge Green Essex 87 K7
Bridgehampton Somset 31 J6
Bridge Hewick N York 150 D2
Bridgehill Dur 180 D8
Bridgehouse Gate N York 149 L3
Bridgemary Hants 19 K3
Bridgemere Ches E 113 M2
Bridgend Abers 255 K4
Bridgend Ag & B 194 B3
Bridgend Ag & B 204 E4
Bridgend Ag & B 216 C8
Bridgend Angus 234 E2
Bridgend Brdgnd 42 D5
Bridgend Cerdgn 75 L3
Bridgend D & G 187 G3
Bridgend Devon 7 G5
Bridgend Fife 223 G5
Bridgend Moray 255 H5
Bridgend P & K 221 L2
Bridgend W & F 165 L7
Bridgend W Loth 210 D4
Bridgend of Lintrathen Angus 233 L4
Bridge of Alford Abers 255 L8
Bridge of Allan Stirlg 220 D7
Bridge of Avon Moray 254 C7
Bridge of Avon Moray 254 D4
Bridge of Balgie P & K 231 G6
Bridge of Brewlands Angus 233 J3
Bridge of Brown Highld 254 C7
Bridge of Cally P & K 233 H5
Bridge of Canny Abers 244 E4
Bridge of Craigisla Angus 233 K4
Bridge of Dee D & G 175 J3
Bridge of Don C Aber 245 L2
Bridge of Dun Angus 235 G4
Bridge of Dye Abers 244 E6
Bridge of Earn P & K 221 L3
Bridge of Ericht P & K 230 F4
Bridge of Feugh Abers 244 F4
Bridge of Gairn Abers 243 K4

Bridge of Gaur P & K 230 F4
Bridge of Marnoch Abers 267 M6
Bridge of Muchalls Abers 245 K5
Bridge of Orchy Ag & B 230 B7
Bridge of Tilt P & K 232 C2
Bridge of Tynet Moray 267 H4
Bridge of Walls Shet 281 c6
Bridge of Weir Rens 208 C6
Bridge Reeve Devon 28 B8
Bridgerule Devon 11 K2
Bridges Shrops 95 J4
Bridge Sollers Herefs 80 A6
Bridge Street Suffk 89 H5
Bridgetown Cnwll 11 L5
Bridgetown Somset 29 G4
Bridge Trafford Ches W 129 K5
Bridge Yate S Glos 45 K4
Bridgham Norfk 105 J6
Bridgnorth Shrops 97 G5
Bridgwater Somset 30 D3
Bridgwater Services Somset 30 D4
Bridlington E R Yk 153 K3
Bridport Dorset 15 K4
Bridstow Herefs 63 H2
Brierfield Lancs 148 E8
Brierley Barns 142 B5
Brierley Gloucs 63 J4
Brierley Herefs 80 C4
Brierley Hill Dudley 97 L6
Brierlow Bar Derbys 132 B5
Brierton Hartpl 170 B5
Briery Cumb 165 J6
Brigg N Linc 144 C6
Briggate Norfk 123 G6
Briggswath N York 162 F1
Brigham Cumb 164 E4
Brigham Cumb 165 J6
Brigham E R Yk 153 H5
Brighouse Calder 141 J3
Brightgate Derbys 132 F7
Brighthampton Oxon 66 A6
Brightholmlee Sheff 132 F1
Brightley Devon 12 E3
Brightling E Susx 24 C3
Brightlingsea Essex 73 G4
Brighton Br & H 22 D6
Brighton Cnwll 4 E4
Brighton City Airport W Susx 22 B6
Brighton le Sands Sefton 138 C7
Brightons Falk 210 B3
Brightwalton W Berk 48 B3
Brightwalton Green W Berk 48 B3
Brightwalton Holt W Berk 48 B3
Brightwell Suffk 90 F6
Brightwell Baldwin Oxon 67 G8
Brightwell-cum-Sotwell Oxon 48 E1
Brightwell Upperton Oxon 67 G8
Brignall Dur 168 D8
Brig o'Turk Stirlg 219 J6
Brigsley NE Lin 145 H7
Brigsteer W & F 157 G5
Brigstock N Nthn 101 L6
Brill Bucks 67 G4
Brill Cnwll 3 J5
Brilley Herefs 79 J5
Brimfield Herefs 80 C2
Brimfield Cross Herefs 80 C2
Brimington Derbys 133 H5
Brimley Devon 13 J7
Brimpsfield Gloucs 64 D4
Brimpton W Berk 48 E6
Brimpton Common W Berk 48 E6
Brimscombe Gloucs 64 C6
Brimstage Wirral 129 G3
Brincliffe Sheff 132 F3
Brind E R Yk 143 J2
Brindham Somset 31 H3
Brindister Shet 281 c5
Brindle Lancs 139 J3
Brindley Ches E 113 K1
Brineton Staffs 97 H1
Bringhurst Leics 101 J5
Bringsty Common Herefs 81 G4
Brington Cambs 102 B8
Brinian Ork 275 c3
Briningham Norfk 122 A5
Brinkely Notts 117 J1
Brinkhill Lincs 137 G5
Brinkley Cambs 88 C4
Brinklow Warwks 99 L7
Brinkworth Wilts 46 E2
Brinscall Lancs 139 J4
Brinscombe Somset 44 E8
Brinsea N Som 44 F6
Brinsley Notts 116 D2
Brinsop Herefs 80 B6
Brinsworth Rothm 133 H2
Brinton Norfk 122 A4
Brisco Cumb 178 A8

Brisley Norfk 121 L7
Brislington Bristl 45 J5
Brissenden Green Kent 40 B7
Bristol Bristl 45 H4
Bristol Airport N Som 45 G6
Briston Norfk 122 B5
Brisworthy Devon 7 G2
Britannia Lancs 140 C3
Britford Wilts 33 L5
Brithdir Caerph 61 J6
Brithdir Gwynd 110 E7
British Legion Village Kent 52 F7
Briton Ferry Neath 57 K6
Britwell Salome Oxon 67 G8
Brixham Torbay 8 D4
Brixton Devon 7 G4
Brixton Gt Lon 51 J4
Brixton Deverill Wilts 32 E3
Brixworth W Nthn 84 E1
Brize Norton Oxon 65 L5
Brize Norton Airport Oxon 66 L5
Broad Alley Worcs 81 K2
Broad Blunsdon Swindn 47 H1
Broadbottom Tamesd 131 K1
Broadbridge W Susx 20 D6
Broadbridge Heath W Susx 37 H4
Broad Campden Gloucs 82 E7
Broad Carr Calder 141 H4
Broad Chalke Wilts 33 H5
Broad Clough Lancs 140 C3
Broadclyst Devon 14 A3
Broadfield Inver 208 B4
Broadfield Pembks 55 K6
Broadford Highld 247 K4
Broad Ford Kent 39 H5
Broadford Bridge W Susx 37 G6
Broadgairhill Border 187 K4
Broadgrass Green Suffk 89 K3
Broad Green Cambs 88 D3
Broad Green Essex 72 C2
Broad Green Worcs 81 H4
Broad Green Worcs 82 A1
Broadhaugh Border 202 D2
Broad Haven Pembks 54 D4
Broadheath Traffd 130 E2
Broadhembury Devon 14 C2
Broadhempston Devon 8 B2
Broad Hill Cambs 104 D8
Broad Hinton Wilts 47 G4
Broadholme Lincs 135 H5
Broadland Row E Susx 24 F3
Broadlay Carmth 56 C3
Broad Layings Hants 48 B6
Broadley Essex 70 B5
Broadley Lancs 140 C4
Broadley Moray 267 H4
Broadley Common Essex 70 B5
Broad Marston Worcs 82 D6
Broadmayne Dorset 16 D5
Broad Meadow Staffs 114 C2
Broadmere Hants 35 J2
Broadmoor Gloucs 63 J4
Broadmoor Pembks 55 J5
Broadnymett Devon 13 G2
Broad Oak Carmth 59 G4
Broad Oak Cumb 155 K4
Broadoak Dorset 15 K3
Broad Oak E Susx 23 K3
Broad Oak E Susx 24 F3
Broadoak Gloucs 63 K4
Broad Oak Hants 49 H8
Broad Oak Herefs 62 F3
Broad Oak Kent 41 G3
Broad Oak St Hel 139 G8
Broadoak Wrexhm 129 J7
Broad Road Suffk 106 F8
Broadsands Torbay 8 D3
Broad's Green Essex 71 G4
Broadstairs Kent 41 L2
Broadstone BCP 17 K3
Broadstone Mons 63 G6
Broadstone Shrops 96 C5
Broad Street E Susx 24 F4
Broad Street Essex 70 E4
Broad Street Kent 39 L2
Broad Street Kent 40 F7
Broad Street Medway 53 G4
Broad Street Wilts 47 G7
Broad Street Green Essex 71 L5
Broad Town Wilts 47 G3
Broadwas Worcs 81 H4
Broadwater Herts 69 H3
Broadwater W Susx 21 K6
Broadwaters Worcs 97 J7
Broadway Carmth 56 B3
Broadway Carmth 56 C3
Broadway Pembks 54 E4
Broadway Somset 30 D7
Broadway Suffk 107 H7
Broadway Worcs 82 C7

Broadwell Gloucs......63 H5
Broadwell Gloucs......65 J2
Broadwell Oxon......65 K6
Broadwell Warwks......83 K2
Broadwey Dorset......16 C2
Broadwindsor Dorset......15 K4
Broadwood Kelly Devon......12 E2
Broadwoodwidger Devon......12 A5
Brobury Herefs......79 L6
Brochel Highld......259 K7
Brochroy Ag & B......216 F1
Brock Lancs......147 K7
Brockamin Worcs......81 H4
Brockbridge Hants......35 J7
Brockdish Norfk......106 E7
Brockencote Worcs......97 K8
Brockenhurst Hants......18 D3
Brocketsbrae S Lans......198 D5
Brockford Green Suffk......90 D2
Brockford Street Suffk......90 D2
Brockhall W Nthn......84 C3
Brockhall Village Lancs......148 B8
Brockham Surrey......37 J1
Brockhampton Gloucs......64 D2
Brockhampton Gloucs......64 F3
Brockhampton Hants......20 B5
Brockhampton Herefs......63 H1
Brockhampton Green Dorset......16 D2
Brockholes Kirk......141 J5
Brockhurst Derbys......133 G6
Brockhurst Warwks......100 A6
Brocklebank Cumb......165 J2
Brocklesby Lincs......144 E5
Brockley N Som......44 F5
Brockley Suffk......89 G1
Brockley Green Suffk......88 E6
Brockley Green Suffk......89 G4
Brockleymoor W & F......166 C3
Brockmoor Dudley......97 K5
Brockscombe Devon......12 B4
Brock's Green Hants......48 D6
Brockton Shrops......95 H3
Brockton Shrops......95 H6
Brockton Shrops......96 D4
Brockton Shrops......97 G3
Brockton Staffs......114 C5
Brockweir Gloucs......63 G6
Brockwood Park Hants......35 K6
Brockworth Gloucs......64 C4
Brocton Cnwll......5 G1
Brocton Staffs......114 F7
Brodick N Ayrs......195 G4
Brodie Moray......264 F8
Brodsworth Donc......142 D6
Brogaig Highld......259 H3
Brogborough C Beds......85 J2
Brokenborough Wilts......46 D1
Broken Cross Ches E......131 H5
Broken Cross Ches W......130 D5
Brokerswood Wilts......46 B8
Bromborough Wirral......129 H3
Brome Suffk......106 C8
Brome Street Suffk......106 C8
Bromeswell Suffk......91 G5
Bromfield Cumb......165 G1
Bromfield Shrops......96 B8
Bromham Bed......85 K5
Bromham Wilts......46 D6
Bromley Barns......141 M7
Bromley Dudley......97 K5
Bromley Gt Lon......51 L5
Bromley Shrops......97 G4
Bromley Common Gt Lon......51 L5
Bromley Cross Bolton......139 L5
Bromley Cross Essex......72 F2
Bromley Green Kent......40 C8
Bromlow Shrops......95 H3
Brompton Medway......53 G5
Brompton N York......160 E3
Brompton-by-Sawdon N York......163 G6
Brompton-on-Swale N York......160 B3
Brompton Ralph Somset......29 K4
Brompton Regis Somset......29 G4
Bromsash Herefs......63 J2
Bromsberrow Gloucs......81 G8
Bromsberrow Heath Gloucs......81 G8
Bromsgrove Worcs......81 M1
Bromstead Heath Staffs......114 B8
Bromyard Herefs......80 F4
Bromyard Downs Herefs......80 F4
Bronaber Gwynd......110 D5
Bronant Cerdgn......77 H2
Broncroft Shrops......96 C6
Brongest Cerdgn......76 B6
Bronington Wrexhm......113 H3
Bronllys Powys......79 G8
Bronwydd Carmth......58 D4
Bronydd Powys......79 J6
Brongarth Shrops......112 C4
Brook Carmth......56 A3

Brook Hants......34 C8
Brook Hants......34 D5
Brook IoW......18 F6
Brook Kent......40 E6
Brook Surrey......36 D3
Brook Surrey......37 G2
Brooke Norfk......106 F3
Brooke Rutlnd......101 J2
Brookenby Lincs......145 G8
Brook End Bed......86 B3
Brook End C Beds......86 D5
Brook End Cambs......86 B1
Brook End M Keyn......85 H6
Brookfield Rens......208 C6
Brookhampton Oxon......66 F7
Brookhampton Somset......31 K5
Brook Hill Hants......34 C7
Brookhouse Denbgs......128 C6
Brookhouse Lancs......147 K3
Brookhouse Rothm......133 K2
Brookhouse Green Ches E......130 F7
Brookhouses Derbys......131 K2
Brookland Kent......25 J2
Brooklands Traffd......130 F2
Brookmans Park Herts......69 H6
Brooks Powys......94 E3
Brooks End Kent......41 J2
Brooks Green W Susx......37 H6
Brook Street Essex......70 E8
Brook Street Kent......40 B8
Brook Street Suffk......89 G5
Brook Street W Susx......22 D2
Brookthorpe Gloucs......64 B4
Brookville Norfk......104 E4
Brookwood Surrey......50 B7
Broom C Beds......86 D6
Broom Rothm......133 J1
Broom Warwks......82 C4
Broombank Worcs......80 F1
Broome Norfk......107 G5
Broome Shrops......95 K7
Broome Worcs......97 K7
Broomedge Warrtn......130 D3
Broome Park Nthumb......191 G4
Broomer's Corner W Susx......37 H6
Broomershill W Susx......21 H3
Broomfield Essex......71 H5
Broomfield Kent......39 L3
Broomfield Kent......41 G2
Broomfield Somset......30 B4
Broomfields Shrops......112 F1
Broomfleet E R Yk......143 M2
Broom Green Norfk......121 L6
Broomhall W & M......50 B5
Broomhaugh Nthumb......180 B6
Broom Hill Barns......142 C7
Broom Hill Dorset......17 K2
Broom Hill Notts......116 F2
Broomhill Nthumb......191 J6
Broom Hill Worcs......97 L8
Broomhill Green Ches E......113 K2
Broomley Nthumb......180 C6
Broompark Dur......169 H2
Broom's Green Gloucs......81 G8
Broomsthorpe Norfk......121 J6
Broom Street Kent......40 D3
Brora Highld......274 B7
Broseley Shrops......96 F3
Brotherhouse Bar Lincs......119 J8
Brotherlee Dur......167 L3
Brothertoft Lincs......119 J2
Brotherton N York......142 D3
Brotton R & Cl......170 F6
Broubster Highld......279 J4
Brough Derbys......132 D3
Brough E R Yk......144 B2
Brough Highld......280 B2
Brough Notts......135 G7
Brough Shet......281 f5
Brough W & F......167 J7
Broughall Shrops......113 J3
Brough Lodge Shet......281 f3
Brough Sowerby W & F......167 J8
Broughton Border......199 K6
Broughton Bucks......67 K4
Broughton Cambs......102 F7
Broughton Flints......129 H7
Broughton Hants......34 C4
Broughton Lancs......139 G1
Broughton M Keyn......85 H7
Broughton N Linc......144 B6
Broughton N Nthn......101 H8
Broughton N York......149 G5
Broughton N York......162 D8
Broughton Oxon......83 K7
Broughton Salfd......140 B7
Broughton Staffs......114 B5
Broughton V Glam......42 D7
Broughton Astley Leics......100 B5

Broughton Beck W & F......156 C6
Broughton Gifford Wilts......46 C6
Broughton Green Worcs......81 M3
Broughton Hackett Worcs......81 L4
Broughton-in-Furness W & F......156 B5
Broughton Mains D & G......174 C6
Broughton Mills W & F......156 B4
Broughton Moor Cumb......164 E4
Broughton Poggs Oxon......65 K6
Broughton Tower W & F......156 B5
Broughty Ferry C Dund......223 H1
Brough with St Giles N York......160 B3
Brow End W & F......156 C7
Brownber W & F......158 B2
Brown Candover Hants......35 J3
Brown Edge Lancs......138 D5
Brown Edge Staffs......114 E1
Brown Heath Ches W......129 K6
Brownheath Shrops......113 G5
Brownhill Abers......256 F4
Brownhills Fife......223 J4
Brownhills Wsall......98 D2
Brownieside Nthumb......191 H2
Browninghill Green Hants......48 E7
Brown Knowl Ches W......113 H1
Brown Lees Staffs......131 G8
Brownlow Heath Ches E......131 G7
Brownrigg Cumb......164 D6
Brownrigg Cumb......177 G8
Brownsea Island Dorset......17 K5
Brown's Green Birm......98 D5
Brownsham Devon......26 E5
Browns Hill Gloucs......64 C6
Brownsover Warwks......100 B7
Brownston Devon......7 K4
Brown Street Suffk......90 C3
Browston Green Norfk......107 K3
Broxa N York......163 G4
Broxbourne Herts......69 K5
Broxburn E Loth......212 F3
Broxburn W Loth......210 E4
Broxfield Nthumb......191 J3
Broxted Essex......70 E2
Broxton Ches W......113 H1
Broyle Side E Susx......23 G4
Bruan Highld......280 D8
Bruar P & K......232 B2
Bruchag Ag & B......207 J7
Bruera Ches W......129 K7
Bruern Abbey Oxon......65 K3
Bruichladdich Ag & B......204 C4
Bruisyard Suffk......91 H2
Bruisyard Street Suffk......91 H2
Brumby N Linc......143 M6
Brund Staffs......132 B7
Brundall Norfk......107 G2
Brundish Suffk......91 G1
Brundish Street Suffk......91 G1
Brunery Highld......237 L6
Brunnion Cnwll......2 D4
Brunslow Shrops......95 J6
Brunswick Village N u Ty......180 F4
Bruntcliffe Leeds......141 L2
Brunthwaite C Brad......149 J6
Bruntingthorpe Leics......100 D5
Brunton Fife......222 E3
Brunton Nthumb......191 J1
Brunton Wilts......47 K2
Brushford Devon......12 F1
Brushford Somset......29 G5
Bruton Somset......31 L4
Bryan's Green Worcs......81 K2
Bryanston Dorset......17 G1
Bryant's Bottom Bucks......67 L7
Brydekirk D & G......177 G5
Bryher IoS......10 b2
Brymbo Wrexhm......112 D1
Brympton Somset......31 H7
Bryn Carmth......57 G5
Bryn Ches W......130 B5
Bryn Neath......42 B3
Bryn Shrops......95 H6
Bryn Wigan......139 H7
Brynamman Carmth......59 K6
Brynberian Pembks......75 J5
Brynbryddan Neath......57 L6
Bryn Bwbach Gwynd......110 B4
Bryncae Rhondd......42 F5
Bryncethin Brdgnd......42 D5
Bryncir Gwynd......109 H3
Bryn-côch Neath......57 K5
Bryncroes Gwynd......108 C5
Bryncrug Gwynd......92 D3
Bryn Du IoA......124 F5
Bryn-Eden Gwynd......110 D5
Bryneglwys Denbgs......112 A2
Bryneglwys & Abergynolwyn
Slate Landscape Gwynd......92 E2
Brynfields Wrexhm......112 D3
Brynford Flints......128 E5

Bryn Gates Wigan......139 J7
Bryn Golau Rhondd......42 F4
Bryngwran IoA......124 F4
Bryngwyn Mons......62 D5
Bryngwyn Powys......79 H5
Bryn-Henllan Pembks......75 G4
Brynhoffnant Cerdgn......76 B5
Bryning Lancs......138 E2
Brynithel Blae G......61 K6
Brynmawr Blae G......61 J5
Bryn-mawr Gwynd......108 D5
Brynmenyn Brdgnd......42 D5
Brynmill Swans......57 H6
Brynna Rhondd......42 F5
Brynnau Gwynion Rhondd......42 E5
Bryn-penarth Powys......94 D3
Bryn Pydew Conwy......126 F4
Brynrefail Gwynd......125 K7
Brynrefail IoA......125 H2
Brynsadler Rhondd......42 F5
Bryn Saith Marchog Denbgs......111 L2
Brynsiencyn IoA......125 H6
Brynteg IoA......125 J3
Bryn-y-bal Flints......128 F6
Bryn-y-Maen Conwy......127 G4
Bryn-yr-Eos Wrexhm......112 D3
Bualintur Highld......246 F4
Buarth-draw Flints......128 E4
Bubbenhall Warwks......83 J1
Bubwith E R Yk......151 M8
Buccleuch Border......188 B3
Buchanan Smithy Stirlg......208 D1
Buchanhaven Abers......269 L6
Buchanty P & K......221 G2
Buchany Stirlg......220 C6
Buchlyvie Stirlg......219 J8
Buckabank Cumb......165 L1
Buckden Cambs......86 D2
Buckden N York......159 G7
Buckenham Norfk......107 G2
Buckerell Devon......14 D3
Buckfast Devon......7 L2
Buckfastleigh Devon......7 L2
Buckhaven Fife......222 F7
Buckholt Mons......63 G4
Buckhorn Devon......11 M3
Buckhorn Weston Dorset......32 C6
Buckhurst Hill Essex......69 L8
Buckie Moray......267 J3
Buckingham Bucks......84 D8
Buckland Bucks......67 L4
Buckland Devon......7 K6
Buckland Gloucs......82 C8
Buckland Hants......18 E4
Buckland Herts......87 G8
Buckland Kent......41 J6
Buckland Oxon......65 M7
Buckland Surrey......37 K1
Buckland Brewer Devon......27 G6
Buckland Common Bucks......68 A5
Buckland Dinham Somset......32 C1
Buckland Filleigh Devon......12 B1
Buckland in the Moor Devon......13 G7
Buckland Monachorum Devon......6 F1
Buckland Newton Dorset......16 D2
Buckland Ripers Dorset......16 C6
Buckland St Mary Somset......30 C7
Buckland-Tout-Saints Devon......7 L5
Bucklebury W Berk......48 E5
Bucklers Hard Hants......18 F4
Bucklesham Suffk......90 F6
Buckley Flints......129 G5
Buckley Green Warwks......82 E2
Bucklow Hill Ches E......130 E3
Buckminster Leics......118 A7
Bucknall C Stke......114 E2
Bucknall Lincs......136 C6
Bucknell Oxon......66 E2
Bucknell Shrops......95 J8
Buckpool Moray......267 H3
Bucksburn C Aber......245 K2
Buck's Cross Devon......26 F4
Bucks Green W Susx......37 G4
Buckshaw Village Lancs......139 H4
Bucks Hill Herts......68 D7
Bucks Horn Oak Hants......36 B3
Buck's Mills Devon......26 F6
Buckton E R Yk......153 K1
Buckton Herefs......95 J8
Buckton Nthumb......203 H5
Buckworth Cambs......102 C8
Budby Notts......134 C5
Buddileigh Staffs......114 B2
Bude Cnwll......11 H2
Budge's Shop Cnwll......6 C3
Budlake Devon......14 A3
Budle Nthumb......203 J6
Budleigh Salterton Devon......14 C6
Budlett's Common E Susx......23 H3
Budock Water Cnwll......3 K5

Buerton Ches E.............113 L3
Bugbrooke W Nthn.........84 D4
Bugford Devon.............8 B5
Buglawton Ches E.........131 G7
Bugle Cnwll...............5 G3
Bugley Dorset............32 C6
Bugthorpe E R Yk........152 B4
Buildwas Shrops..........96 E2
Builth Road Powys........78 E4
Builth Wells Powys.......78 E5
Bulbourne Herts..........68 B4
Bulbridge Wilts..........33 J5
Bulby Lincs.............118 D6
Bulcote Notts...........117 H3
Bulford Wilts............33 L2
Bulford Camp Wilts.......33 L2
Bulkeley Ches E.........113 J1
Bulkington Warwks........99 K6
Bulkington Wilts.........46 D2
Bulkworthy Devon.........27 K6
Bullamoor N York........160 F4
Bull Bay IoA............125 G1
Bullbridge Derbys.......116 B1
Bullbrook Br For.........49 L5
Bullen's Green Herts.....69 G6
Bulley Gloucs............63 M3
Bullgill Cumb...........164 E3
Bullingham Herefs........80 C7
Bullinghope Herefs.......80 C7
Bullington Hants.........34 F3
Bullington Lincs........136 A4
Bullockstone Kent........41 G2
Bull's Green Herts.......69 H4
Bull's Green Norfk......107 J4
Bulmer Essex............89 G7
Bulmer N York...........151 L2
Bulmer Tye Essex.........89 G7
Bulphan Thurr............52 D2
Bulstone Devon...........14 E4
Bulstrode Herts..........68 C6
Bulverhythe E Susx.......24 D5
Bulwark Abers...........257 G3
Bulwell C Nott..........116 F3
Bulwick N Nthn..........101 L4
Bumble's Green Essex.....69 L6
Bunacaimb Highld........237 J3
Bunarkaig Highld........239 K6
Bunbury Ches E..........130 A8
Bunbury Heath Ches E....130 A8
Bunchrew Highld.........251 H3
Buncton W Susx...........21 K4
Bundalloch Highld.......248 E6
Bunessan Ag & B.........226 D8
Bungay Suffk............107 G5
Bunker's Hill Lincs.....119 J1
Bunnahabhain Ag & B.....204 F2
Bunny Notts.............117 G5
Buntait Highld..........250 C5
Buntingford Herts........69 K1
Bunwell Norfk...........106 C4
Bunwell Hill Norfk......106 C5
Bupton Derbys...........115 J4
Burbage Derbys..........131 L5
Burbage Leics............99 L5
Burbage Wilts............47 K6
Burcher Herefs...........79 L3
Burchett's Green W & M...49 K3
Burcombe Wilts...........33 J5
Burcot Oxon..............66 E7
Burcot Worcs.............82 A1
Burcote Shrops...........97 G4
Burcott Bucks............67 K4
Burcott Bucks............67 L2
Burdale N York..........152 D3
Bures Essex.............89 H8
Burford Oxon.............65 K5
Burford Shrops...........80 D2
Burg Ag & B.............226 D3
Burgate Suffk...........106 R8
Burgates Hants...........36 A5
Burge End Herts..........68 F1
Burgess Hill W Susx......22 E3
Burgh Suffk..............90 F5
Burgh by Sands Cumb.....177 J6
Burgh Castle Norfk......107 K2
Burghclere Hants.........48 C6
Burghead Moray..........266 C2
Burghfield W Berk........49 G5
Burghfield Common W Berk.49 G5
Burgh Heath Surrey.......51 H7
Burgh Hill E Susx........24 C2
Burghill Herefs..........80 B6
Burgh Island Devon........7 J6
Burgh le Marsh Lincs....137 J6
Burgh next Aylsham Norfk.122 E6
Burgh on Bain Lincs.....136 D2
Burgh St Margaret Norfk.123 J8
Burgh St Peter Norfk....107 K5
Burghwallis Donc........142 E5
Burham Kent..............52 F6

Buriton Hants............20 B3
Burland Ches E..........113 K1
Burlawn Cnwll............10 D8
Burleigh Gloucs..........64 C6
Burlescombe Devon........29 K7
Burleston Dorset.........16 E4
Burlestone Devon..........8 B5
Burley Hants.............18 C3
Burley Rutlnd...........101 J1
Burley Shrops............96 B7
Burleydam Ches E........113 K3
Burley Gate Herefs.......80 E6
Burley in Wharfedale C Brad.149 L6
Burley Lawn Hants........18 C3
Burley Street Hants......18 B3
Burley Wood Head C Brad.149 L7
Burlingham Green Norfk..107 H1
Burlingjobb Powys........79 J4
Burlington Shrops........97 H1
Burlton Shrops..........113 G8
Burmarsh Kent............25 L1
Burmington Warwks........83 G7
Burn N York.............142 F2
Burnage Manch...........131 G1
Burnaston Derbys........115 M5
Burnbanks W & F.........166 C7
Burnbrae N Lans.........210 A7
Burn Bridge N York......150 D5
Burnby E R Yk...........152 C6
Burn Cross Sheff........142 A8
Burndell W Susx..........21 G6
Burnden Bolton..........139 L6
Burnedge Rochdl.........140 D5
Burneside W & F.........157 H3
Burneston N York........160 D5
Burnett BaNES............45 K6
Burnfoot Border.........188 C4
Burnfoot Border.........188 E3
Burnfoot D & G..........177 K1
Burnfoot D & G..........186 E7
Burnfoot D & G..........188 C6
Burnfoot P & K..........221 H6
Burnham Bucks............50 A3
Burnham N Linc..........144 D4
Burnham Deepdale Norfk..121 H3
Burnham Green Herts......69 H4
Burnham Market Norfk....121 H3
Burnham Norton Norfk....121 H3
Burnham-on-Crouch Essex..72 D7
Burnham-on-Sea Somset....30 D1
Burnham Overy Norfk.....121 J3
Burnham Overy Staithe Norfk.121 J3
Burnham Thorpe Norfk....121 J3
Burnhead D & G..........186 C7
Burnhervie Abers........256 C7
Burnhill Green Staffs....97 H3
Burnhope Dur............169 G1
Burnhouse N Ayrs........196 D1
Burniston N York........163 H4
Burnley Lancs...........140 C1
Burnmouth Border........213 L6
Burn Naze Lancs.........147 G7
Burn of Cambus Stirlg...220 C6
Burnopfield Dur.........180 E7
Burnrigg Cumb...........178 C7
Burnsall N York.........149 J3
Burnside Angus..........234 C3
Burnside Angus..........234 D5
Burnside Fife...........222 B5
Burnside Moray..........266 D2
Burnside of Duntrune Angus.234 C8
Burntcommon Surrey.......50 D8
Burntheath Derbys.......115 L5
Burnt Heath Essex........72 F2
Burnt Hill W Berk........48 E4
Burnthouse Cnwll..........3 K4
Burnt Houses Dur........168 L6
Burntisland Fife........211 H2
Burnt Oak E Susx.........23 H2
Burnton E Ayrs..........184 D2
Burntwood Flints........129 G6
Burntwood Staffs.........98 D2
Burntwood Green Staffs...98 D2
Burnt Yates N York......150 C4
Burnworthy Somset........30 B7
Burpham Surrey...........50 C8
Burpham W Susx...........21 H5
Burradon N Tyne.........181 G4
Burradon Nthumb.........190 D5
Burrafirth Shet.........281 f1
Burras Cnwll..............3 H4
Burraton Cnwll............6 E2
Burravoe Shet...........281 e4
Burray Village Ork......275 d6
Burrells W & F..........166 F7
Burrelton P & K.........233 J7
Burridge Devon...........15 H2
Burridge Devon...........27 K4
Burridge Hants...........19 J2
Burrill N York..........160 C5

Burringham N Linc.......143 L6
Burrington Devon.........27 L1
Burrington Herefs........80 B1
Burrington N Som.........44 F7
Burrough End Cambs.......88 C4
Burrough Green Cambs.....88 C4
Burrough on the Hill Leics.101 G1
Burrow Lancs............157 K7
Burrow Somset............29 G2
Burrow Bridge Somset.....30 C5
Burrowhill Surrey........50 B6
Burrows Cross Surrey.....37 G2
Burry Swans..............56 E6
Burry Green Swans........56 E6
Burry Port Carmth........56 E5
Burscough Lancs.........138 F5
Burscough Bridge Lancs..138 F5
Bursea E R Yk...........143 K1
Burshill E R Yk.........153 H6
Bursledon Hants..........19 H3
Burslem C Stke..........114 D2
Burstall Suffk...........90 C6
Burstock Dorset..........15 K2
Burston Norfk...........106 C6
Burston Staffs..........114 E5
Burstow Surrey...........37 M3
Burstwick E R Yk........145 G2
Burtersett N York.......158 F5
Burtholme Cumb..........178 D6
Burthorpe Green Suffk....88 F2
Burthwaite Cumb.........165 M1
Burthy Cnwll..............4 E4
Burtle Somset............30 F2
Burtle Hill Somset.......30 F2
Burtoft Lincs...........119 J4
Burton BCP...............18 B5
Burton Ches E...........129 H5
Burton Ches W...........129 L7
Burton Dorset............16 D4
Burton Nthumb...........203 K6
Burton Pembks............55 G5
Burton Somset............30 B2
Burton Somset............31 H8
Burton Wilts.............32 D4
Burton Wilts.............46 D3
Burton Agnes E R Yk.....153 H3
Burton Bradstock Dorset..15 L5
Burton-by-Lincoln Lincs.135 J5
Burton Coggles Lincs....118 C6
Burton Dassett Warwks....83 J5
Burton End Essex.........70 D2
Burton End Suffk.........88 D6
Burton Fleming E R Yk...153 H2
Burton Green Warwks......99 H8
Burton Green Wrexhm.....129 H7
Burton Hastings Warwks...99 L5
Burton Hill Wilts........46 D2
Burton-in-Kendal W & F..157 H7
Burton-in-Kendal Services
          W & F.........157 H7
Burton in Lonsdale N York.148 A2
Burton Joyce Notts......117 H3
Burton Latimer N Nthn...101 K8
Burton Lazars Leics.....117 K8
Burton Leonard N York...150 D3
Burton on the Wolds Leics.117 G7
Burton Overy Leics......100 E4
Burton Pedwardine Lincs.118 D3
Burton Pidsea E R Yk....145 H2
Burton Salmon N York....142 D2
Burton's Green Essex.....71 K2
Burton upon Stather N Linc.143 L4
Burton upon Trent Staffs.115 L6
Burton Waters Lincs.....135 J5
Burtonwood Warrtn.......130 A1
Burtonwood Services Warrtn.130 B2
Burwardsley Ches W......129 L8
Burwarton Shrops.........96 E6
Burwash E Susx...........24 B2
Burwash Common E Susx....23 L3
Burwash Weald E Susx.....23 L3
Burwell Cambs............88 B2
Burwell Lincs...........137 G4
Burwen IoA..............125 G1
Burwick Ork.............275 c6
Bury Bury...............140 B5
Bury Cambs..............102 F6
Bury Somset..............29 G5
Bury W Susx..............21 G4
Bury End C Beds..........86 C8
Bury Green Herts.........70 C3
Bury St Edmunds Suffk....89 G2
Burythorpe N York.......152 B3
Busby E Rens............208 F7
Busby Stoop N York......160 E6
Buscot Oxon..............65 J7
Bush Abers..............235 J2
Bush Cnwll..............11 J1
Bush Bank Herefs.........80 B5
Bushbury Wolves..........97 L3

Bushby Leics............100 E3
Bushey Herts.............68 E8
Bushey Heath Herts.......68 F8
Bush Green Norfk........106 E6
Bush Green Suffk.........89 H4
Bush Hill Park Gt Lon....69 J7
Bushley Worcs............81 K8
Bushley Green Worcs......81 K8
Bushmead Bed............86 C3
Bushmoor Shrops..........95 K6
Bushton Wilts............46 F3
Busk W & F..............166 E2
Buslingthorpe Lincs.....135 M3
Bussage Gloucs...........64 C6
Bussex Somset............30 E4
Butcher's Cross E Susx...23 J2
Butcombe N Som...........45 G6
Bute Ag & B.............207 G5
Butleigh Somset..........31 H4
Butleigh Wootton Somset..31 H4
Butlers Cross Bucks......67 K6
Butler's Cross Bucks.....67 K6
Butlers Marston Warwks...83 H5
Butley Suffk.............91 J5
Butley High Corner Suffk.91 J5
Buttercrambe N York.....152 A4
Butterdean Border.......213 H6
Butterknowle Dur........168 E5
Butterleigh Devon........14 A1
Butterley Derbys........116 C1
Buttermere Cumb.........165 G7
Buttermere Wilts.........47 M6
Buttershaw C Brad.......141 H2
Butterstone P & K.......233 G2
Butterton Staffs........114 C3
Butterton Staffs........131 L8
Butterwick Dur..........169 K3
Butterwick Lincs........119 L3
Butterwick N York.......152 F2
Butterwick N York.......162 C7
Butt Green Ches E.......113 L1
Buttington Powys.........95 G2
Buttonbridge Shrops......97 G7
Buttonoak Shrops.........97 G7
Buttsash Hants...........19 H2
Buttsbear Cross Cnwll....11 K2
Butt's Green Essex.......71 J6
Buxhall Suffk............89 K4
Buxhall Fen Street Suffk.89 K3
Buxted E Susx............23 H3
Buxton Derbys...........131 L5
Buxton Norfk............122 E7
Buxton Heath Norfk......122 D7
Buxworth Derbys.........131 K3
Bwlch Powys..............61 J3
Bwlchgwyn Wrexhm........112 C1
Bwlchllan Cerdgn.........77 G3
Bwlchnewydd Carmth.......58 C4
Bwlchtocyn Gwynd........108 E6
Bwlch-y-cibau Powys.....112 B8
Bwlch-y-Ddar Powys......112 B7
Bwlchyfadfa Cerdgn.......76 D5
Bwlch-y-llmdd Powys......94 C4
Bwlch-y-groes Pembks.....75 M5
Bwlchymyrdd Swans........57 G5
Bwlch-y-sarnau Powys.....94 B8
Byermoor Gatesd.........180 F7
Byers Green Dur.........169 G4
Byfield W Nthn...........83 M4
Byfleet Surrey...........50 D6
Byford Herefs............79 M6
Bygrave Herts............86 F7
Byker N u Ty............181 G6
Byland Abbey N York.....161 J6
Bylaugh Norfk...........122 A7
Bylchau Conwy...........127 K7
Byley Ches W............130 E6
Bynca Carmth.............57 G5
Byram N York............142 D3
Byrness Nthumb..........189 K6
Bystock Devon............14 B6
Bythorn Cambs...........102 B8
Byton Herefs.............79 L2
Bywell Nthumb...........180 C6
Byworth W Susx...........36 E6

C

Cabbacott Devon..........27 G6
Cabourne Lincs..........144 E7
Cabrach Ag & B..........205 H3
Cabrach Moray...........255 H6
Cabus Lancs.............147 J6
Cackle Street E Susx.....23 G2
Cackle Street E Susx.....24 C3
Cackle Street E Susx.....24 E3
Cadbury Devon............13 L2
Cadbury Barton Devon.....28 B7

Place	Page	Grid
Cadder E Duns	209	G4
Caddington C Beds	68	D3
Caddonfoot Border	200	F6
Cadeby Donc	142	E7
Cadeby Leics	99	L3
Cadeleigh Devon	13	L1
Cade Street E Susx	23	K3
Cadgwith Cnwll	3	J8
Cadham Fife	222	D6
Cadishead Salfd	130	D1
Cadle Swans	57	H5
Cadley Lancs	139	G2
Cadley Wilts	47	J5
Cadley Wilts	47	K8
Cadmore End Bucks	67	J8
Cadnam Hants	34	C8
Cadney N Linc	144	C7
Cadole Flints	128	E7
Cadoxton V Glam	43	H7
Cadoxton Juxta-Neath Neath	57	L5
Cadwst Denbgs	111	K4
Caeathro Gwynd	125	J7
Caehopkin Powys	59	M6
Caenby Lincs	135	K2
Caerau Brdgnd	42	C3
Caerau Cardif	43	H6
Cae'r-bont Powys	59	M6
Cae'r bryn Carmth	59	H6
Caerdeon Gwynd	110	C7
Caer Farchell Pembks	74	C6
Caergeiliog IoA	124	E4
Caergwrle Flints	129	G8
Caerhowel Powys	94	F4
Caerhun Conwy	126	F5
Caerlanrig Border	188	C5
Caerleon Newpt	44	D1
Caernarfon Gwynd	125	H7
Caernarfon Castle Gwynd	125	H7
Caerphilly Caerph	43	J4
Caersws Powys	94	B5
Caerwedros Cerdgn	76	C4
Caerwent Mons	44	F1
Caerwys Flints	128	D5
Caerynwch Gwynd	110	E8
Caggle Street Mons	62	D4
Caim IoA	126	C3
Caio Carmth	77	J7
Cairinis W Isls	283	c8
Cairnbaan Ag & B	206	C1
Cairnbulg Abers	269	J3
Cairncross Border	213	K6
Cairncurran Inver	208	A5
Cairndow Ag & B	217	K5
Cairneyhill Fife	210	D2
Cairngarroch D & G	172	C5
Cairngorms National Park	242	E3
Cairnie Abers	255	K3
Cairn Lodge Services S Lans	198	D6
Cairnorrie Abers	256	F3
Cairnryan D & G	172	D1
Cairnty Moray	267	G5
Caister-on-Sea Norfk	107	L1
Caistor Lincs	144	E7
Caistor St Edmund Norfk	106	E3
Cakebole Worcs	81	K1
Cake Street Norfk	106	B5
Calais Street Suffk	89	K7
Calanais W Isls	282	f3
Calbourne IoW	19	G6
Calceby Lincs	137	G4
Calcoed Flints	128	E5
Calcot Gloucs	65	G5
Calcot W Berk	49	G4
Calcot Row W Berk	49	G4
Calcots Moray	266	E3
Calcott Kent	41	G3
Calcott Shrops	113	G8
Calcutt N York	150	E4
Calcutt Wilts	65	G8
Caldbeck Cumb	165	K3
Caldbergh N York	159	K5
Caldecote Cambs	87	G4
Caldecote Cambs	102	C5
Caldecote Herts	86	E7
Caldecote W Nthn	84	D5
Caldecott N Nthn	85	K2
Caldecott Oxon	66	D7
Caldecott Rutlnd	101	J4
Caldecotte M Keyn	85	H8
Calder Cumb	155	J2
Calderbank N Lans	209	K6
Calder Bridge Cumb	155	J2
Calderbrook Rochdl	140	E4
Caldercruix N Lans	209	L5
Calder Grove Wakefd	141	M4
Caldermill S Lans	197	J3
Caldermore Rochdl	140	D4
Calder Vale Lancs	147	K6
Calderwood S Lans	209	H7
Caldey Island Pembks	55	K7
Caldicot Mons	44	F1
Caldmore Wsall	98	C4
Caldwell N York	168	F8
Caldy Wirral	128	F3
Calenick Cnwll	4	D6
Calford Green Suffk	88	D6
Calfsound Ork	275	d2
Calgary Ag & B	226	D2
Califer Moray	265	H8
California Falk	210	B4
California Norfk	123	K8
California Cross Devon	7	K4
Calke Derbys	116	B7
Callakille Highld	259	M5
Callander Stirlg	219	K5
Callanish W Isls	282	f3
Callaughton Shrops	96	E4
Callestick Cnwll	4	C5
Calligarry Highld	247	K7
Callington Cnwll	6	D1
Callingwood Staffs	115	K6
Callow Herefs	80	C8
Callow End Worcs	81	J5
Callow Hill Wilts	46	F2
Callow Hill Worcs	82	B2
Callow Hill Worcs	97	G8
Callows Grave Worcs	80	D2
Calmore Hants	34	D7
Calmsden Gloucs	64	F5
Calne Wilts	46	E5
Calow Derbys	133	H5
Calshot Hants	19	H3
Calstock Cnwll	6	E1
Calstone Wellington Wilts	46	F5
Calthorpe Norfk	122	D5
Calthorpe Street Norfk	123	H6
Calthwaite W & F	166	B3
Calton N York	148	F4
Calton Staffs	115	H2
Calveley Ches E	130	B7
Calver Derbys	132	E5
Calverhall Shrops	113	K4
Calver Hill Herefs	79	L5
Calverleigh Devon	29	G8
Calverley Leeds	150	B8
Calver Sough Derbys	132	E5
Calvert Bucks	67	G2
Calverton M Keyn	84	F7
Calverton Notts	117	G2
Calvine P & K	232	B2
Calvo Cumb	176	F8
Calzeat Border	199	K6
Cam Gloucs	63	M7
Camasachoirce Highld	228	B3
Camasine Highld	237	L8
Camas Luinie Highld	248	F6
Camastianavaig Highld	247	G1
Camault Muir Highld	250	E4
Camber E Susx	25	H3
Camberley Surrey	49	L6
Camberwell Gt Lon	51	J4
Camblesforth N York	143	G3
Cambo Nthumb	180	B2
Cambois Nthumb	181	H2
Camborne Cnwll	3	G3
Camborne & Redruth Mining District Cnwll	3	G3
Cambourne Cambs	87	G3
Cambridge Cambs	87	J3
Cambridge Gloucs	63	L6
Cambridge Airport Cambs	87	K4
Cambrose Cnwll	4	A5
Cambus Clacks	220	B8
Cambusavie Highld	263	L1
Cambusbarron Stirlg	209	K1
Cambuskenneth Stirlg	220	D8
Cambuslang S Lans	209	H7
Cambus o' May Abers	243	M4
Cambuswallace S Lans	199	H5
Camden Town Gt Lon	51	H2
Cameley BaNES	45	J7
Camelford Cnwll	10	F6
Camelon Falk	209	M3
Camerory Highld	253	K5
Camer's Green Worcs	81	H8
Camerton BaNES	45	K7
Camerton Cumb	164	D4
Camghouran P & K	231	G4
Camieston Border	201	J7
Cammachmore Abers	245	K4
Cammeringham Lincs	135	J3
Camore Highld	263	L2
Campbeltown Ag & B	192	E4
Campbeltown Airport Ag & B	192	D4
Camperdown N Tyne	181	G4
Cample D & G	186	D7
Campmuir P & K	233	K7
Camps W Loth	210	E5
Campsall Donc	142	E5
Campsea Ash Suffk	91	H4
Camps End Cambs	88	C6
Campton C Beds	86	C7
Camptown Border	189	J4
Camrose Pembks	54	F3
Camserney P & K	232	B5
Camusnagaul Highld	239	H8
Camusnagaul Highld	261	H2
Camusteel Highld	248	A3
Camusterrach Highld	248	A3
Canada Hants	34	C7
Canal Foot W & F	156	D7
Canaston Bridge Pembks	55	H4
Candacraig Abers	243	K4
Candlesby Lincs	137	H6
Candle Street Suffk	105	L8
Candover Green Shrops	96	C2
Candy Mill Border	199	J5
Cane End Oxon	49	G3
Canewdon Essex	72	C8
Canford Bottom Dorset	17	K3
Canford Cliffs BCP	17	L5
Canford Heath BCP	17	K4
Canford Magna BCP	17	K3
Canhams Green Suffk	90	C2
Canisbay Highld	280	D2
Canklow Rothm	133	H2
Canley Covtry	99	J7
Cann Dorset	32	E6
Canna Highld	246	B7
Cann Common Dorset	32	E6
Cannich Highld	250	B5
Cannington Somset	30	C3
Canning Town Gt Lon	51	L3
Cannock Staffs	98	B2
Cannock Chase Staffs	114	F7
Cannock Wood Staffs	98	D1
Cannon Bridge Herefs	80	A7
Canonbie D & G	177	L4
Canon Frome Herefs	80	F6
Canon Pyon Herefs	80	B5
Canons Ashby W Nthn	84	B5
Canonstown Cnwll	2	E4
Canterbury Kent	40	F4
Canterbury Cathedral Kent	40	F4
Cantley Norfk	107	H3
Cantlop Shrops	96	C2
Canton Cardif	43	J6
Cantraywood Highld	252	E2
Cantsfield Lancs	147	M1
Canvey Island Essex	53	G2
Canwick Lincs	135	K6
Canworthy Water Cnwll	11	J4
Caol Highld	239	J8
Caolas Scalpaigh W Isls	282	f6
Caoles Ag & B	224	D5
Caonich Highld	239	H5
Capel Kent	39	G4
Capel Surrey	37	J3
Capel Bangor Cerdgn	92	E7
Capel Betws Lleucu Cerdgn	77	H4
Capel Coch IoA	125	H3
Capel Curig Conwy	126	E8
Capel Cynon Cerdgn	76	C5
Capel Dewi Carmth	58	E5
Capel Dewi Cerdgn	76	C6
Capel-Dewi Cerdgn	92	D7
Capel Garmon Conwy	127	G8
Capel Green Suffk	91	J5
Capel Gwyn Carmth	58	E5
Capel Gwyn IoA	124	F4
Capel Gwynfe Carmth	59	K4
Capel Hendre Carmth	59	G6
Capel Isaac Carmth	59	G3
Capel Iwan Carmth	58	B2
Capel-le-Ferne Kent	41	H7
Capelles Guern	9	j2
Capel Llanilltern Cardif	43	H5
Capel Mawr IoA	125	G5
Capel Parc IoA	125	H2
Capel St Andrew Suffk	91	J5
Capel St Mary Suffk	90	C7
Capel Seion Cerdgn	92	D7
Capel Trisant Cerdgn	92	F8
Capeluchaf Gwynd	109	H2
Capelulo Conwy	126	E4
Capel-y-ffin Powys	61	L1
Capel-y-graig Gwynd	125	K6
Capenhurst Ches W	129	J5
Capernwray Lancs	147	K2
Cape Wrath Highld	276	D1
Capheaton Nthumb	180	C3
Caplaw E Rens	208	D7
Capon's Green Suffk	91	G2
Cappercleuch Border	187	K2
Capstone Medway	53	G6
Capton Devon	8	C4
Capton Somset	29	K3
Caputh P & K	233	G7
Caradon Mining District Cnwll	11	K7
Caradon Town Cnwll	11	K8
Carbeth Stirlg	208	E3
Carbis Cnwll	5	G3
Carbis Bay Cnwll	2	E3
Carbost Highld	246	E2
Carbost Highld	259	G7
Carbrook Sheff	133	G2
Carbrooke Norfk	105	J3
Carburton Notts	134	C5
Carclaze Cnwll	5	H4
Car Colston Notts	117	J3
Carcroft Donc	142	E6
Cardenden Fife	222	C8
Cardeston Shrops	95	J1
Cardewlees Cumb	177	K8
Cardhu Moray	254	D3
Cardiff Cardif	43	J6
Cardiff Airport V Glam	43	G8
Cardiff Gate Services Cardif	43	K5
Cardiff West Services Cardif	43	H5
Cardigan Cerdgn	75	L3
Cardinal's Green Cambs	88	C6
Cardington Bed	86	B5
Cardington Shrops	96	C4
Cardinham Cnwll	5	J1
Cardrain D & G	172	E8
Cardrona Border	200	C3
Cardross Ag & B	208	B3
Cardryne D & G	172	E8
Cardurnock Cumb	177	G7
Careby Lincs	118	D8
Careston Angus	234	E3
Carew Pembks	55	H6
Carew Cheriton Pembks	55	H6
Carew Newton Pembks	55	H6
Carey Herefs	63	H1
Carfin N Lans	209	K7
Carfraemill Border	201	G2
Cargate Green Norfk	107	H1
Cargenbridge D & G	176	C4
Cargill P & K	233	H8
Cargo Cumb	177	L7
Cargreen Cnwll	6	E2
Cargurrel Cnwll	3	M4
Carham Nthumb	202	B5
Carhampton Somset	29	H2
Carharrack Cnwll	4	B6
Carie P & K	231	H4
Carinish W Isls	283	c8
Carisbrooke IoW	19	H6
Cark W & F	156	D7
Carkeel Cnwll	6	E3
Càrlabhagh W Isls	282	e2
Carland Cross Cnwll	4	D4
Carlbury Darltn	169	G7
Carlby Lincs	102	A1
Carlcroft Nthumb	190	B4
Carlecotes Barns	141	J7
Carleen Cnwll	3	G5
Carlesmoor N York	160	B7
Carleton Cumb	155	J1
Carleton Cumb	178	A8
Carleton Lancs	147	G2
Carleton W & F	166	C5
Carleton Wakefd	142	D4
Carleton Forehoe Norfk	106	D2
Carleton-in-Craven N York	149	H6
Carleton Rode Norfk	106	C5
Carleton St Peter Norfk	107	G3
Carlidnack Cnwll	3	J6
Carlincraig Abers	256	B3
Carlingcott BaNES	45	K7
Carlin How R & Cl	171	G6
Carlisle Cumb	177	L7
Carlisle Lake District Airport Cumb	178	B6
Carloggas Cnwll	4	E2
Carlops Border	199	K2
Carloway W Isls	282	e2
Carlton Barns	142	B5
Carlton Bed	85	J4
Carlton Cambs	88	C4
Carlton Leeds	142	A2
Carlton Leics	99	L2
Carlton N York	143	G3
Carlton N York	159	J5
Carlton N York	161	K5
Carlton Notts	117	G3
Carlton S on T	169	K6
Carlton Suffk	91	J2
Carlton Colville Suffk	107	K5
Carlton Curlieu Leics	100	F4
Carlton Green Cambs	88	C5
Carlton Husthwaite N York	161	H7
Carlton-in-Cleveland N York	161	H2
Carlton in Lindrick Notts	134	B3
Carlton-le-Moorland Lincs	135	H8
Carlton Miniott N York	160	F6
Carlton-on-Trent Notts	134	D7

Carlton Scroop Lincs ... 118 B3
Carluke S Lans ... 198 D3
Carlyon Bay Cnwll ... 5 H4
Carmacoup S Lans ... 198 C7
Carmarthen Carmth ... 58 D5
Carmel Carmth ... 59 G5
Carmel Flints ... 128 E4
Carmel Gwynd ... 125 J8
Carmichael S Lans ... 198 F5
Carmunnock C Glas ... 209 G7
Carmyle C Glas ... 209 H6
Carmyllie Angus ... 234 E6
Carnaby E R Yk ... 153 J3
Carnbee Fife ... 223 J6
Carnbo P & K ... 221 J6
Carn Brea Cnwll ... 3 H3
Carnbrogie Abers ... 256 F6
Carndu Highld ... 248 E6
Carnduff S Lans ... 197 J2
Carne Cnwll ... 3 K8
Carne Cnwll ... 4 E7
Carne Cnwll ... 4 F3
Carnell E Ayrs ... 196 F4
Carnewas Cnwll ... 4 D1
Carnforth Lancs ... 147 K2
Carn-gorm Highld ... 248 F7
Carnhedryn Pembks ... 74 C6
Carnhell Green Cnwll ... 3 G4
Carnie Abers ... 245 H2
Carnkie Cnwll ... 3 H3
Carnkie Cnwll ... 3 H4
Carnkief Cnwll ... 4 C4
Carno Powys ... 93 L4
Carnock Fife ... 210 D1
Carnon Downs Cnwll ... 3 K3
Carnousie Abers ... 268 B6
Carnoustie Angus ... 234 E8
Carnsmerry Cnwll ... 5 G3
Carnwath S Lans ... 199 G4
Carnyorth Cnwll ... 2 B4
Carol Green Solhll ... 99 H7
Carpalla Cnwll ... 4 F4
Carperby N York ... 159 H5
Carr Rothm ... 133 K2
Carradale Ag & B ... 194 C3
Carradale Village Ag & B ... 194 B3
Carrbridge Highld ... 253 G7
Carrbrook Tamesd ... 140 E7
Carrefour Jersey ... 9 c2
Carreglefn IoA ... 125 G2
Carr Gate Wakefd ... 141 M3
Carrhouse N Linc ... 143 K6
Carrick Ag & B ... 206 E2
Carrick Castle Ag & B ... 217 K8
Carriden Falk ... 210 D3
Carrington Lincs ... 136 F8
Carrington Mdloth ... 211 K7
Carrington Traffd ... 130 E1
Carrog Conwy ... 110 E2
Carrog Denbgs ... 111 L3
Carron Falk ... 210 A3
Carron Moray ... 254 E3
Carronbridge D & G ... 186 C6
Carron Bridge Stirlg ... 209 K2
Carronshore Falk ... 210 A2
Carrow Hill Mons ... 44 E1
Carr Shield Nthumb ... 167 J1
Carrutherstown D & G ... 176 E4
Carruth House Inver ... 208 B6
Carr Vale Derbys ... 133 J5
Carrville Dur ... 169 J2
Carsaig Ag & B ... 227 G8
Carseriggan D & G ... 173 H1
Carsethorn D & G ... 176 C7
Carshalton Gt Lon ... 51 H6
Carsington Derbys ... 115 L1
Carskey Ag & B ... 192 D6
Carsluith D & G ... 174 D4
Carsphairn D & G ... 184 C4
Carstairs S Lans ... 198 F4
Carstairs Junction S Lans ... 198 F4
Carswell Marsh Oxon ... 65 L7
Carter's Clay Hants ... 34 C6
Carters Green Essex ... 70 D5
Carterton Oxon ... 65 L5
Carterway Heads Nthumb ... 180 C8
Carthew Cnwll ... 5 G4
Carthorpe N York ... 160 D6
Cartington Nthumb ... 190 E5
Cartland S Lans ... 198 E4
Cartledge Derbys ... 132 F4
Cartmel W & F ... 156 E7
Cartmel Fell W & F ... 156 F5
Carway Carmth ... 56 E3
Carwinley Cumb ... 177 L4
Cashe's Green Gloucs ... 64 B6
Cashmoor Dorset ... 33 G8
Cassington Oxon ... 66 C5
Cassop Dur ... 169 K3
Castallack Cnwll ... 2 C6

Castel Guern ... 9 j3
Castell Conwy ... 126 F6
Castell-y-bwch Torfn ... 62 B8
Casterton W & F ... 157 K6
Castle Cnwll ... 5 J3
Castle Acre Norfk ... 121 H8
Castle Ashby W Nthn ... 85 G3
Castlebay W Isls ... 283 b13
Castle Bolton N York ... 159 J4
Castle Bromwich Solhll ... 98 F5
Castle Bytham Lincs ... 118 C7
Castlebythe Pembks ... 75 H6
Castle Caereinion Powys ... 94 E2
Castle Camps Cambs ... 88 C6
Castle Carrock Cumb ... 178 D7
Castlecary N Lans ... 209 K3
Castle Cary Somset ... 31 L4
Castle Combe Wilts ... 46 B3
Castlecraig Highld ... 264 C6
Castle Donington Leics ... 116 H1
Castle Douglas D & G ... 175 J2
Castle Eaton Swindn ... 65 H7
Castle Eden Dur ... 169 L3
Castle End C Pete ... 102 C2
Castleford Wakefd ... 142 C3
Castle Frome Herefs ... 80 F6
Castle Gate Cnwll ... 2 D4
Castle Green Surrey ... 50 B6
Castle Green W & F ... 157 H4
Castle Gresley Derbys ... 115 M7
Castle Hedingham Essex ... 88 F8
Castlehill Border ... 200 B6
Castlehill Highld ... 280 B3
Castle Hill Kent ... 39 H5
Castle Hill Suffk ... 90 D6
Castlehill W Duns ... 208 C4
Castle Kennedy D & G ... 172 D3
Castle Lachlan Ag & B ... 217 G8
Castlemartin Pembks ... 54 E7
Castlemilk C Glas ... 209 G7
Castle Morris Pembks ... 74 L6
Castlemorton Worcs ... 81 H7
Castlemorton Common Worcs ... 81 H7
Castle Oer D & G ... 187 J6
Castle Rising Norfk ... 120 F6
Castleside Dur ... 168 D1
Castle Stuart Highld ... 252 D2
Castlethorpe M Keyn ... 84 F6
Castlethorpe N Linc ... 144 B6
Castleton Ag & B ... 206 D2
Castleton Border ... 188 E8
Castleton Derbys ... 132 C3
Castleton N York ... 162 B1
Castleton Newpt ... 43 L5
Castleton Rochdl ... 140 C5
Castletown Ches W ... 113 G1
Castletown Dorset ... 16 D7
Castletown Highld ... 280 A3
Castletown IoM ... 154 c8
Castletown Sundld ... 181 J7
Castley N York ... 150 C6
Caston Norfk ... 105 J4
Castor C Pete ... 102 C4
Caswell Bay Swans ... 57 G7
Catacol Ag & B ... 194 E1
Cat and Fiddle Derbys ... 131 K5
Catbrain S Glos ... 45 H3
Catbrook Mons ... 63 G6
Catch Flints ... 128 F5
Catchall Cnwll ... 2 C5
Catchem's Corner Solhll ... 99 H8
Catchgate Dur ... 180 E8
Catcliffe Rothm ... 133 H2
Catcomb Wilts ... 46 E4
Catcott Somset ... 30 F3
Caterham Surrey ... 51 J7
Catfield Norfk ... 123 H7
Catfield Common Norfk ... 123 H7
Catford Gt Lon ... 51 K4
Catforth Lancs ... 138 F1
Cathcart C Glas ... 209 G7
Cathedine Powys ... 61 J2
Cathcrine-de-Barnes Solhll ... 98 F7
Catherine Slack C Brad ... 141 G2
Catherington Hants ... 35 L8
Catherston Leweston Dorset ... 15 J4
Catherton Shrops ... 96 E7
Catisfield Hants ... 19 J2
Catley Herefs ... 80 F6
Catley Lane Head Rochdl ... 140 C4
Catlodge Highld ... 241 H5
Catlow Lancs ... 148 F8
Catlowdy Cumb ... 178 B3
Catmere End Essex ... 87 K7
Catmore W Berk ... 48 C3
Caton Devon ... 13 H8
Caton Lancs ... 147 K3
Caton Green Lancs ... 147 L3
Cator Court Devon ... 13 G7
Catrine E Ayrs ... 197 G6

Cat's Ash Newpt ... 44 D1
Catsfield E Susx ... 24 C4
Catsfield Stream E Susx ... 24 C4
Catsgore Somset ... 31 H5
Catsham Somset ... 31 J4
Catshill Worcs ... 98 B8
Catstree Shrops ... 97 G4
Cattadale Ag & B ... 192 D6
Cattal N York ... 150 F5
Cattawade Suffk ... 90 C8
Catterall Lancs ... 147 K7
Catterick N York ... 160 C3
Catterick Bridge N York ... 160 B3
Catterick Garrison N York ... 160 B3
Catterlen W & F ... 166 B4
Catterline Abers ... 245 J7
Catterton N York ... 151 H6
Catteshall Surrey ... 36 E2
Cattthorpe Leics ... 100 C7
Cattishall Suffk ... 89 H2
Cattistock Dorset ... 16 B3
Catton N York ... 160 E7
Catton Nthumb ... 179 J7
Catwick E R Yk ... 153 J6
Catworth Cambs ... 86 B1
Caudle Green Gloucs ... 64 D5
Caulcott C Beds ... 85 K6
Caulcott Oxon ... 66 D2
Cauldcots Angus ... 235 G6
Cauldhame Stirlg ... 219 L8
Cauldmill Border ... 188 F3
Cauldon Staffs ... 115 H2
Cauldon Lowe Staffs ... 115 H2
Cauldwell Derbys ... 115 L8
Caulkerbush D & G ... 176 B7
Caulside D & G ... 178 B3
Caundle Marsh Dorset ... 31 L8
Caunsall Worcs ... 97 J7
Caunton Notts ... 134 E7
Causeway Hants ... 35 M6
Causeway End D & G ... 173 K3
Causeway End Essex ... 71 G3
Causewayend S Lans ... 199 H6
Causeway End W & F ... 157 G5
Causewayhead Cumb ... 176 H8
Causewayhead Stirlg ... 220 D8
Causeyend Abers ... 257 H7
Causey Park Nthumb ... 191 H7
Causey Park Bridge Nthumb ... 191 H7
Cavendish Suffk ... 88 F6
Cavenham Suffk ... 88 F1
Caversfield Oxon ... 66 E2
Caversham Readg ... 49 H4
Caverswall Staffs ... 114 F3
Caverton Mill Border ... 202 A7
Cavil E R Yk ... 143 J2
Cawdor Highld ... 252 F2
Cawkwell Lincs ... 136 E4
Cawood N York ... 151 J8
Cawsand Cnwll ... 6 E5
Cawston Norfk ... 122 C6
Cawston Warwks ... 100 A8
Cawthorn N York ... 162 D5
Cawthorne Barns ... 141 L6
Cawton N York ... 161 K7
Caxton Cambs ... 86 F3
Caxton End Cambs ... 87 G4
Caxton Gibbet Cambs ... 86 F3
Caynham Shrops ... 80 D1
Caythorpe Lincs ... 118 B2
Caythorpe Notts ... 117 J2
Cayton N York ... 163 J6
Ceannabeinne Highld ... 277 G3
Ceann a Bhaigh W Isls ... 283 b8
Ceannacroc Lodge Highld ... 239 L2
Cearsiadar W Isls ... 282 f4
Ceciliford Mons ... 63 G6
Cefn Newpt ... 44 B1
Cefn Berain Conwy ... 127 K8
Cefn-brith Conwy ... 111 H2
Cefn-bryn-brain Carmth ... 59 K6
Cefn Byrle Powys ... 60 C5
Cefn Canel Powys ... 112 C5
Cefn Coch Powys ... 111 L6
Cefn-coed-y-cymmer Myr Td ... 60 F5
Cefn Cribwr Brdgnd ... 42 C5
Cefn Cross Brdgnd ... 42 C5
Cefn-ddwysarn Gwynd ... 111 J4
Cefn-Einion Shrops ... 95 G6
Cefneithin Carmth ... 59 G6
Cefngorwydd Powys ... 78 D4
Cefn-mawr Wrexhm ... 112 D3
Cefnpennar Rhondd ... 61 G7
Cefn-y-bedd Flints ... 129 H8
Cefn-y-pant Carmth ... 75 L7
Ceint IoA ... 125 J4
Cellan Cerdgn ... 77 H5
Cellardyke Fife ... 223 K6
Cellarhead Staffs ... 114 F2

Celleron W & F ... 166 C5
Celynen Caerph ... 43 K3
Cemaes IoA ... 124 F1
Cemmaes Powys ... 93 H2
Cemmaes Road Powys ... 93 H3
Cenarth Cerdgn ... 76 A7
Cerbyd Pembks ... 74 D6
Ceres Fife ... 223 G5
Cerne Abbas Dorset ... 16 C2
Cerney Wick Gloucs ... 65 J7
Cerrigceinwen IoA ... 125 G5
Cerrigydrudion Conwy ... 111 J2
Cess Norfk ... 123 J7
Ceunant Gwynd ... 125 J5
Chaceley Gloucs ... 64 B1
Chacewater Cnwll ... 4 B6
Chackmore Bucks ... 84 D8
Chacombe W Nthn ... 83 L6
Chadbury Worcs ... 82 B6
Chadderton Oldham ... 140 D6
Chadderton Fold Oldham ... 140 D6
Chaddesden C Derb ... 116 C4
Chaddesley Corbett Worcs ... 81 K1
Chaddlehanger Devon ... 12 B7
Chaddleworth W Berk ... 48 B3
Chadlington Oxon ... 65 M3
Chadshunt Warwks ... 83 H5
Chadwell Leics ... 117 K6
Chadwell Shrops ... 114 B3
Chadwell End Bed ... 86 B2
Chadwell Heath Gt Lon ... 52 A1
Chadwell St Mary Thurr ... 52 E3
Chadwick Worcs ... 81 J2
Chadwick End Solhll ... 99 G8
Chadwick Green St Hel ... 139 G7
Chaffcombe Somset ... 15 H1
Chafford Hundred Thurr ... 52 D3
Chagford Devon ... 13 G5
Chailey E Susx ... 22 F3
Chainbridge Cambs ... 103 J3
Chainhurst Kent ... 39 J4
Chalbury Dorset ... 17 K1
Chalbury Common Dorset ... 17 K1
Chaldon Surrey ... 51 J7
Chaldon Herring Dorset ... 16 F6
Chale IoW ... 19 H8
Chale Green IoW ... 19 H7
Chalfont Common Bucks ... 68 C8
Chalfont St Giles Bucks ... 68 C8
Chalfont St Peter Bucks ... 50 C1
Chalford Gloucs ... 64 C6
Chalford Oxon ... 67 H7
Chalford Wilts ... 32 E1
Chalgrave C Beds ... 68 C2
Chalgrove Oxon ... 66 F7
Chalk Kent ... 52 E4
Chalk End Essex ... 70 F5
Chalkhouse Green Oxon ... 49 H3
Chalkway Somset ... 15 J1
Chalkwell Kent ... 53 J6
Challaborough Devon ... 7 G7
Challacombe Devon ... 28 B3
Challoch D & G ... 173 K2
Challock Kent ... 40 C5
Chalmington Dorset ... 16 B2
Chalton C Beds ... 68 C2
Chalton C Beds ... 86 C5
Chalton Hants ... 20 B4
Chalvey Slough ... 50 B3
Chalvington E Susx ... 23 H5
Chambers Green Kent ... 40 B6
Chandler's Cross Herts ... 68 D7
Chandlers Cross Worcs ... 81 H7
Chandler's Ford Hants ... 34 F7
Channel's End Bed ... 86 C4
Channel Tunnel Terminal Kent ... 41 G7
Chantry Somset ... 32 B2
Chantry Suffk ... 90 D6
Chapel Cumb ... 165 H4
Chapel Fife ... 222 D8
Chapel Allerton Leeds ... 150 D8
Chapel Allerton Somset ... 30 F1
Chapel Amble Cnwll ... 10 D7
Chapel Brampton W Nthn ... 84 E2
Chapelbridge Cambs ... 102 F4
Chapel Chorlton Staffs ... 114 C4
Chapel Cross E Susx ... 23 K3
Chapel End Bed ... 86 B4
Chapel End C Beds ... 85 L6
Chapel End Cambs ... 102 C6
Chapel End Warwks ... 99 J5
Chapelend Way Essex ... 88 E7
Chapel-en-le-Frith Derbys ... 131 L3
Chapel Field Bury ... 140 B6
Chapelgate Lincs ... 119 L6
Chapel Green Warwks ... 83 L3
Chapel Green Warwks ... 99 H6
Chapel Haddlesey N York ... 142 F3
Chapelhall N Lans ... 209 K6
Chapel Hill Abers ... 257 K4

Chapel Hill Lincs......119 G1
Chapel Hill Mons......63 G7
Chapel Hill N York......150 D6
Chapelhope Border......187 K2
Chapelknowe D & G......177 K4
Chapel Lawn Shrops......95 H8
Chapel-le-Dale N York......158 C7
Chapel Leigh Somset......29 L5
Chapel Milton Derbys......131 L3
Chapel of Garioch Abers......256 C7
Chapel Rossan D & G......172 D6
Chapel Row E Susx......23 L5
Chapel Row Essex......71 J7
Chapel Row W Berk......48 E5
Chapels W & F......156 B6
Chapel St Leonards Lincs......137 K5
Chapel Stile W & F......156 D2
Chapelton Abers......245 K5
Chapelton Angus......234 F6
Chapelton Devon......27 K5
Chapelton S Lans......197 K1
Chapeltown Bl w D......139 L4
Chapel Town Cnwll......4 E4
Chapeltown Moray......254 E7
Chapeltown Sheff......142 A8
Chapmanslade Wilts......32 D1
Chapmans Well Devon......11 L4
Chapmore End Herts......69 J4
Chappel Essex......72 C2
Charaton Cnwll......6 B1
Chard Somset......15 H1
Chard Junction Somset......15 H2
Chardleigh Green Somset......30 D8
Chardstock Devon......15 G2
Charfield S Glos......63 L8
Chargrove Gloucs......64 D3
Charing Kent......40 B5
Charing Heath Kent......40 B5
Charing Hill Kent......40 B5
Charingworth Gloucs......82 E7
Charlbury Oxon......66 A3
Charlcombe BaNES......45 L5
Charlcutt Wilts......46 E4
Charlecote Warwks......83 G4
Charlemont Sandw......98 C4
Charles Devon......28 B4
Charleshill Surrey......36 D2
Charleston Angus......234 B6
Charlestown C Aber......245 L3
Charlestown C Brad......149 L8
Charlestown Calder......140 E2
Charlestown Cnwll......5 H4
Charlestown Cnwll......5 H4
Charlestown Derbys......131 L1
Charlestown Dorset......16 C6
Charlestown Fife......210 E2
Charlestown Highld......251 H2
Charlestown Highld......260 C5
Charlestown Salfd......140 B7
Charlestown of Aberlour
  Moray......254 E3
Charles Tye Suffk......89 L5
Charlesworth Derbys......131 K1
Charlinch Somset......30 C3
Charlottetown Fife......222 E5
Charlton Gt Lon......51 L3
Charlton Hants......34 D2
Charlton Herts......68 F2
Charlton Nthumb......179 J2
Charlton Somset......30 D5
Charlton Somset......31 K2
Charlton Somset......45 K8
Charlton Surrey......50 D5
Charlton W Nthn......83 M8
Charlton W Susx......20 E4
Charlton Wilts......32 F6
Charlton Wilts......46 D1
Charlton Worcs......81 J1
Charlton Worcs......82 B6
Charlton Wrekin......96 D1
Charlton Abbots Gloucs......64 F2
Charlton Adam Somset......31 J5
Charlton All Saints Wilts......33 L6
Charlton Down Dorset......16 C4
Charlton Hill Shrops......96 D2
Charlton Horethorne Somset......31 L6
Charlton Kings Gloucs......64 D3
Charlton Mackrell Somset......31 H5
Charlton Marshall Dorset......17 H2
Charlton Musgrove Somset......32 B5
Charlton-on-Otmoor Oxon......66 E4
Charlton on the Hill Dorset......17 H2
Charlton St Peter Wilts......47 G7
Charlwood Hants......35 K4
Charlwood Surrey......37 K3
Charminster Dorset......16 C4
Charmouth Dorset......15 H4
Charndon Bucks......67 G2
Charney Bassett Oxon......66 A8
Charnock Green Lancs......139 H4

Charnock Richard Lancs......139 H4
Charnock Richard Services
  Lancs......139 H5
Charsfield Suffk......90 F4
Chart Corner Kent......39 K3
Charter Alley Hants......48 E7
Charterhall Border......202 B4
Charterhouse Somset......45 G7
Chartershall Stirlg......209 L1
Charterville Allotments Oxon......65 L5
Chartham Kent......40 E4
Chartham Hatch Kent......40 E4
Chart Hill Kent......39 K3
Chartridge Bucks......68 B6
Chart Sutton Kent......39 K3
Chartway Street Kent......39 L3
Charvil Wokham......49 J4
Charwelton W Nthn......83 M4
Chase Cross Gt Lon......52 B1
Chase Terrace Staffs......98 D2
Chasetown Staffs......98 D2
Chastleton Oxon......65 K1
Chasty Devon......11 L2
Chatburn Lancs......148 D7
Chatcull Staffs......114 B4
Chatham Caerph......43 K4
Chatham Medway......53 G5
Chatham Green Essex......71 H4
Chathill Nthumb......203 K7
Chatley Worcs......81 J3
Chattenden Medway......53 G4
Chatter End Essex......70 C2
Chatteris Cambs......103 H6
Chatterton Lancs......140 B4
Chattisham Suffk......90 C6
Chatto Border......189 K3
Chatton Nthumb......203 G7
Chaul End C Beds......68 D3
Chawleigh Devon......28 C8
Chawley Oxon......66 C6
Chawston Bed......86 C4
Chawton Hants......35 L3
Chaxhill Gloucs......63 L4
Chazey Heath Oxon......49 G3
Cheadle Staffs......115 G3
Cheadle Stockp......131 G2
Cheadle Heath Stockp......131 H2
Cheadle Hulme Stockp......131 G2
Cheam Gt Lon......51 H6
Cheapside W & M......50 B5
Chearsley Bucks......67 H5
Chebsey Staffs......114 D6
Checkendon Oxon......49 G2
Checkley Ches E......114 A2
Checkley Herefs......80 E7
Checkley Staffs......115 G4
Checkley Green Ches E......114 A2
Chedburgh Suffk......88 F4
Cheddar Somset......44 F8
Cheddington Bucks......68 A4
Cheddleton Staffs......114 F1
Cheddleton Heath Staffs......114 F1
Cheddon Fitzpaine Somset......30 C5
Chedglow Wilts......64 D8
Chedgrave Norfk......107 H3
Chedington Dorset......15 L2
Chediston Suffk......107 G7
Chediston Green Suffk......107 G7
Chedworth Gloucs......64 F5
Chedzoy Somset......30 E3
Cheeseman's Green Kent......40 D7
Cheetham Hill Manch......140 C7
Cheldon Devon......28 C8
Chelford Ches E......130 F5
Chellaston C Derb......116 C5
Chellington Bed......85 J4
Chelmarsh Shrops......97 G5
Chelmer Village Essex......71 H5
Chelmick Shrops......95 L5
Chelmondiston Suffk......90 E7
Chelmorton Derbys......132 B5
Chelmsford Essex......71 H5
Chelmsley Wood Solhll......98 F6
Chelsea Gt Lon......51 H3
Chelsfield Gt Lon......52 A6
Chelsham Surrey......51 K7
Chelston Somset......29 L6
Chelsworth Suffk......89 K5
Cheltenham Gloucs......64 D3
Chelveston N Nthn......85 K1
Chelvey N Som......44 F5
Chelwood BaNES......45 J6
Chelwood Common E Susx......38 B7
Chelwood Gate E Susx......38 B7
Chelworth Wilts......64 C8
Chelworth Lower Green Wilts......65 G8
Chelworth Upper Green Wilts......65 G8
Cheney Longville Shrops......95 K6
Chenies Bucks......68 C7
Chepstow Mons......63 G8

Chequerbent Bolton......139 K6
Chequers Corner Norfk......103 K2
Cherhill Wilts......46 F5
Cherington Gloucs......64 C7
Cherington Warwks......83 G7
Cheriton Devon......28 C2
Cheriton Hants......35 J5
Cheriton Kent......41 G7
Cheriton Pembks......55 G7
Cheriton Swans......56 E6
Cheriton Bishop Devon......13 H4
Cheriton Fitzpaine Devon......13 K2
Cherrington Wrekin......113 L7
Cherry Burton E R Yk......152 F7
Cherry Hinton Cambs......87 K4
Cherry Orchard Worcs......81 K4
Cherry Willingham Lincs......135 L5
Chertsey Surrey......50 D5
Cherwell Valley Services Oxon......66 E2
Cheselbourne Dorset......16 E3
Chesham Bucks......68 B6
Chesham Bury......140 B5
Chesham Bois Bucks......68 B7
Cheshunt Herts......69 K6
Chesil Beach Dorset......16 B6
Chesley Kent......53 J6
Cheslyn Hay Staffs......98 B2
Chessetts Wood Warwks......99 G8
Chessington Gt Lon......50 F6
Chester Ches W......129 J6
Chesterblade Somset......31 L3
Chesterfield Derbys......133 G5
Chesterfield Staffs......98 E2
Chesterhill Mdloth......211 L6
Chester-le-Street Dur......181 G8
Chester Moor Dur......169 H7
Chesters Border......189 G2
Chesters Border......189 H4
Chester Services Ches W......129 K5
Chesterton Cambs......87 K3
Chesterton Cambs......102 C4
Chesterton Gloucs......64 E7
Chesterton Oxon......66 E3
Chesterton Shrops......97 H4
Chesterton Staffs......114 C2
Chesterton Green Warwks......83 H4
Chesterwood Nthumb......179 J6
Chestfield Kent......40 F2
Chestnut Street Kent......53 J6
Cheston Devon......7 K3
Cheswardine Shrops......114 A5
Cheswick Nthumb......203 G4
Cheswick Green Solhll......98 E8
Chetnole Dorset......16 B1
Chettiscombe Devon......29 H7
Chettisham Cambs......103 L6
Chettle Dorset......32 F8
Chetton Shrops......96 F5
Chetwode Bucks......66 F1
Chetwynd Wrekin......114 A7
Chetwynd Aston Wrekin......114 B8
Cheveley Cambs......88 D3
Chevening Kent......52 A7
Cheverton IoW......19 G6
Chevington Suffk......88 F3
Cheviot Hills......189 K5
Chevithorne Devon......29 H7
Chew Magna BaNES......45 H6
Chew Moor Bolton......139 K6
Chew Stoke BaNES......45 H6
Chewton Keynsham BaNES......45 K5
Chewton Mendip Somset......45 H8
Chichacott Devon......12 E3
Chicheley M Keyn......85 H6
Chichester W Susx......20 E6
Chickerell Dorset......16 C6
Chickering Suffk......106 E8
Chicklade Wilts......32 F4
Chicksands C Beds......86 C2
Chickward Herefs......79 K4
Chidden Hants......35 K7
Chiddingfold Surrey......36 E4
Chiddingly E Susx......23 L4
Chiddingstone Kent......38 D4
Chiddingstone Causeway Kent......38 E4
Chiddingstone Hoath Kent......38 D5
Chideock Dorset......15 K4
Chidham W Susx......20 C6
Chidswell Kirk......141 L3
Chieveley W Berk......48 C4
Chieveley Services W Berk......48 C4
Chignall St James Essex......71 G5
Chignall Smealy Essex......71 G5
Chigwell Essex......70 B8
Chigwell Row Essex......70 C8
Chilbolton Hants......34 E3
Chilcomb Hants......35 G5
Chilcombe Dorset......15 M4
Chilcompton Somset......45 J8
Chilcote Leics......99 H1

Childer Thornton Ches W......129 J4
Child Okeford Dorset......32 D8
Childrey Oxon......48 A2
Child's Ercall Shrops......113 L6
Childswickham Worcs......82 C7
Childwall Lpool......129 K2
Childwick Bury Herts......68 F5
Childwick Green Herts......68 F5
Chilfrome Dorset......16 B3
Chilgrove W Susx......20 D4
Chilham Kent......40 E4
Chilla Devon......12 B2
Chillaton Devon......12 B6
Chillenden Kent......41 J4
Chillerton IoW......19 H6
Chillesford Suffk......91 J5
Chillingham Nthumb......203 H3
Chillington Devon......8 B6
Chillington Somset......30 F8
Chilmark Wilts......33 G4
Chilmington Green Kent......40 C7
Chilson Oxon......65 L3
Chilsworthy Cnwll......12 A8
Chilsworthy Devon......11 L1
Chiltern Green C Beds......68 E3
Chiltern Hills......67 J7
Chilthorne Domer Somset......31 H7
Chilton Bucks......67 G5
Chilton Devon......13 K2
Chilton Dur......169 H5
Chilton Kent......41 J6
Chilton Oxon......48 C2
Chilton Suffk......89 H6
Chilton Candover Hants......35 J3
Chilton Cantelo Somset......31 J6
Chilton Foliat Wilts......47 L5
Chilton Polden Somset......30 E3
Chilton Street Suffk......88 E6
Chilton Trinity Somset......30 D3
Chilwell Notts......116 E4
Chilworth Hants......34 E7
Chilworth Surrey......36 F2
Chimney Oxon......65 M7
Chineham Hants......49 G7
Chingford Gt Lon......69 K8
Chinley Derbys......131 L3
Chinnor Oxon......67 J6
Chipchase Castle Nthumb......179 K6
Chipnall Shrops......114 A5
Chippenham Cambs......88 D1
Chippenham Wilts......46 D4
Chipperfield Herts......68 D6
Chipping Herts......69 K1
Chipping Lancs......147 M7
Chipping Campden Gloucs......82 E7
Chipping Hill Essex......71 K4
Chipping Norton Oxon......65 L2
Chipping Ongar Essex......70 E6
Chipping Sodbury S Glos......45 L3
Chipping Warden W Nthn......83 J5
Chipshop Devon......12 B7
Chipstable Somset......29 J5
Chipstead Kent......38 D2
Chipstead Surrey......51 H7
Chirbury Shrops......95 G4
Chirk Wrexhm......112 D4
Chirnside Border......202 D2
Chirnsidebridge Border......202 C2
Chirton Wilts......47 G7
Chisbury Wilts......47 K5
Chiselborough Somset......31 G7
Chiseldon Swindn......47 J3
Chiselhampton Oxon......66 E7
Chiserley Calder......140 F2
Chisholme Border......188 D4
Chislehurst Gt Lon......51 L5
Chislet Kent......41 H2
Chiswell Green Herts......68 E6
Chiswick Gt Lon......51 G3
Chiswick End Cambs......87 H6
Chisworth Derbys......131 K2
Chitcombe E Susx......24 E3
Chithurst W Susx......36 C6
Chittering Cambs......87 K1
Chitterne Wilts......33 G2
Chittlehamholt Devon......28 B6
Chittlehampton Devon......27 L5
Chittoe Wilts......46 D5
Chivelstone Devon......8 A7
Chivenor Devon......27 J4
Chiverton Cross Cnwll......4 B5
Chlenry D & G......172 E3
Chobham Surrey......50 B6
Cholderton Wilts......34 A2
Cholesbury Bucks......68 B5
Chollerford Nthumb......179 L5
Chollerton Nthumb......179 L4
Cholmondeston Ches E......130 C7
Cholsey Oxon......48 E2
Cholstrey Herefs......80 B3

Place	County	Page	Grid
Chop Gate	N York	161	J3
Choppington	Nthumb	181	G2
Chopwell	Gatesd	180	D7
Chorley	Ches E	113	J1
Chorley	Lancs	139	H4
Chorley	Shrops	96	F6
Chorley	Staffs	98	D1
Chorleywood	Herts	68	C7
Chorleywood West	Herts	68	C7
Chorlton	Ches E	114	A2
Chorlton-cum-Hardy	Manch	130	F1
Chorlton Lane	Ches W	113	G2
Choulton	Shrops	95	J5
Chowley	Ches W	129	L8
Chrishall	Essex	87	J7
Chrisswell	Inver	207	L4
Christchurch	BCP	18	B5
Christchurch	Cambs	103	K4
Christchurch	Gloucs	63	H4
Christchurch	Newpt	44	D1
Christian Malford	Wilts	46	D3
Christleton	Ches W	129	K6
Christmas Common	Oxon	67	H8
Christmas Pie	Surrey	36	D1
Christon	N Som	44	D7
Christon Bank	Nthumb	191	J2
Christow	Devon	13	J5
Christ's Hospital	W Susx	37	H5
Chuck Hatch	E Susx	38	D6
Chudleigh	Devon	13	K6
Chudleigh Knighton	Devon	13	K7
Chulmleigh	Devon	28	B8
Chunal	Derbys	131	L2
Church	Lancs	139	L2
Churcham	Gloucs	63	M3
Church Aston	Wrekin	114	A8
Church Brampton	W Nthn	84	D2
Church Brough	W & F	167	J7
Church Broughton	Derbys	115	K5
Church Cove	Cnwll	3	H8
Church Crookham	Hants	49	K8
Churchdown	Gloucs	64	C3
Church Eaton	Staffs	114	C0
Church End	Bed	85	L3
Church End	Bed	86	C3
Church End	Bed	87	H1
Church End	C Beds	68	C3
Church End	C Beds	68	C3
Church End	C Beds	85	J8
Church End	C Beds	85	K8
Church End	C Beds	86	D4
Church End	C Beds	86	D7
Church End	Cambs	102	B8
Church End	Cambs	102	E6
Church End	Cambs	103	G7
Church End	Essex	70	F3
Church End	Essex	71	H2
Church End	Essex	71	H4
Churchend	Essex	72	E8
Church End	Gloucs	81	K8
Church End	Gt Lon	51	H1
Church End	Herts	68	E8
Church End	Herts	69	H1
Church End	Herts	70	C3
Church End	Lincs	119	H5
Church End	Lincs	145	L8
Church End	Suffk	90	F8
Church End	Warwks	99	H5
Church End	Warwks	99	H5
Church Enstone	Oxon	66	A2
Church Fenton	N York	151	H8
Churchfield	Sandw	98	C5
Churchgate	Herts	69	K6
Churchgate Street	Essex	70	C5
Church Green	Devon	14	E3
Church Gresley	Derbys	115	M7
Church Hanborough	Oxon	66	B4
Church Hill	Staffs	98	C1
Church Houses	N York	161	J4
Churchill	Devon	15	G2
Churchill	Devon	27	L3
Churchill	N Som	44	E7
Churchill	Oxon	65	L2
Churchill	Worcs	81	L4
Churchill	Worcs	97	K7
Churchinford	Somset	30	B8
Church Knowle	Dorset	17	H6
Church Laneham	Notts	135	G4
Church Langton	Leics	100	F5
Church Lawford	Warwks	99	M8
Church Lawton	Ches E	130	F8
Church Leigh	Staffs	115	G4
Church Lench	Worcs	82	B5
Church Mayfield	Staffs	115	J3
Church Minshull	Ches E	130	C7
Church Norton	W Susx	20	E7
Churchover	Warwks	100	B7
Church Preen	Shrops	96	C4
Church Pulverbatch	Shrops	95	K3
Churchstanton	Somset	30	B7

Place	County	Page	Grid
Churchstoke	Powys	95	G4
Churchstow	Devon	7	K5
Church Stowe	W Nthn	84	C4
Church Street	Essex	88	F6
Church Street	Kent	52	F4
Church Street	Suffk	107	K6
Church Stretton	Shrops	95	L4
Churchthorpe	Lincs	145	J8
Churchtown	Bpool	146	F7
Churchtown	Cnwll	10	F7
Churchtown	Derbys	132	E7
Churchtown	Devon	28	B2
Churchtown	IoM	154	f3
Churchtown	Lancs	147	J7
Church Town	N Linc	143	K6
Churchtown	Sefton	138	D4
Church Village	Rhondd	43	H4
Church Warsop	Notts	133	L6
Church Wilne	Derbys	116	D5
Churnsike Lodge	Nthumb	178	F3
Churston Ferrers	Torbay	8	D1
Churt	Surrey	36	C3
Churton	Ches W	129	K8
Churwell	Leeds	141	L2
Chwilog	Gwynd	109	H4
Chyandour	Cnwll	2	D5
Chyanvounder	Cnwll	3	G6
Chyeowling	Cnwll	3	G6
Chyvarloe	Cnwll	3	G6
Cîl	Powys	94	E3
Cilcain	Flints	128	E6
Cilcennin	Cerdgn	76	F3
Cilcewydd	Powys	94	F3
Cilfrew	Neath	57	L5
Cilfynydd	Rhondd	43	H3
Cilgerran	Pembks	75	L4
Cilgwyn	Carmth	59	K3
Cilgwyn	Gwynd	109	J1
Ciliau-Aeron	Cerdgn	76	F4
Cilmaengwyn	Neath	57	K4
Cilmery	Powys	78	D5
Cilrhedyn	Pembks	58	A2
Cilsan	Carmth	59	H4
Ciltalgarth	Gwynd	111	G3
Cilycwm	Carmth	77	L7
Cimla	Neath	57	J7
Cinderford	Gloucs	63	K4
Cinder Hill	Wolves	97	L4
Cippenham	Slough	50	B3
Cirencester	Gloucs	64	F6
City	Gt Lon	51	J3
City	V Glam	42	F6
City Airport	Gt Lon	51	L3
City Dulas	IoA	125	H2
Clabhach	Ag & B	224	F3
Clachaig	Ag & B	207	J3
Clachaig Inn	Highld	229	J4
Clachan	Ag & B	206	B7
Clachan	Ag & B	216	B3
Clachan	Ag & B	217	H6
Clachan	Ag & B	228	D6
Clachan	Highld	247	H1
Clachan-a-Luib	W Isls	283	c8
Clachan Mor	Ag & B	224	C5
Clachan na Luib	W Isls	283	c8
Clachan of Campsie	E Duns	209	G3
Clachan-Seil	Ag & B	216	B3
Clachnaharry	Highld	251	H2
Clachtoll	Highld	270	D3
Clackmannan	Clacks	210	B1
Clackmannanshire Bridge Fife		210	B2
Clackmarras	Moray	266	E4
Clacton-on-Sea	Essex	73	J4
Cladich	Ag & B	217	H3
Cladswell	Worcs	82	C3
Claggan	Highld	227	K3
Claigan	Highld	258	C6
Clandown	BaNES	45	K7
Clanfield	Hants	35	L7
Clanfield	Oxon	65	L6
Clannaborough	Devon	13	H2
Clanville	Hants	34	D1
Clanville	Somset	31	K4
Claonaig	Ag & B	206	D7
Clapgate	Dorset	17	K2
Clapgate	Herts	70	C2
Clapham	Bed	85	K5
Clapham	Devon	13	L5
Clapham	Gt Lon	51	H4
Clapham	N York	148	C2
Clapham	W Susx	21	J5
Clapham Green	Bed	85	K4
Clap Hill	Kent	40	D7
Clappersgate	W & F	156	E2
Clapton	Somset	15	J1
Clapton	Somset	45	J8
Clapton-in-Gordano	N Som	44	F4

Place	County	Page	Grid
Clapton-on-the-Hill	Gloucs	65	H3
Clapworthy	Devon	28	B6
Clarach	Cerdgn	92	D6
Claravale	Gatesd	180	E6
Clarbeston	Pembks	55	H3
Clarbeston Road	Pembks	55	G3
Clarborough	Notts	134	E3
Clare	Suffk	88	F6
Clarebrand	D & G	175	J2
Clarencefield	D & G	176	E5
Clarewood	Nthumb	180	B5
Clarilaw	Border	188	F3
Clark's Green	Surrey	37	J3
Clarkston	E Rens	208	F7
Clashmore	Highld	263	K2
Clashmore	Highld	270	D2
Clashnessie	Highld	270	E2
Clashnoir	Moray	254	E7
Clathy	P & K	221	H3
Clathymore	P & K	221	H3
Clatt	Abers	255	L6
Clatter	Powys	94	B4
Clatterford End	Essex	70	F4
Clatworthy	Somset	29	J4
Claughton	Lancs	147	K7
Claughton	Lancs	147	L3
Claughton	Wirral	129	G2
Clavelshay	Somset	30	C4
Claverdon	Warwks	82	E2
Claverham	N Som	44	F5
Clavering	Essex	70	C1
Claverley	Shrops	97	H5
Claverton	BaNES	46	A6
Claverton Down	BaNES	45	M6
Clawdd-coch	V Glam	43	G6
Clawdd-newydd	Denbgs	111	L1
Clawthorpe	W & F	157	H7
Clawton	Devon	11	L3
Claxby	Lincs	136	B1
Claxby	Lincs	137	H5
Claxton	N York	151	L4
Claxton	Norfk	107	G3
Claybrooke Magna	Leics	100	D5
Clay Common	Suffk	107	K7
Clay Coton	W Nthn	100	D8
Clay Cross	Derbys	133	H7
Claydon	Oxon	83	K5
Claydon	Suffk	90	D5
Clay End	Herts	69	J2
Claygate	D & G	177	L3
Claygate	Kent	39	H4
Claygate	Surrey	50	F6
Claygate Cross	Kent	38	F2
Clayhall	Gt Lon	51	L1
Clayhanger	Devon	29	J6
Clayhanger	Wsall	98	D3
Clayhidon	Devon	29	L7
Clayhill	E Susx	24	F3
Clayhill	Hants	18	D2
Clayhithe	Cambs	87	K2
Clayock	Highld	279	L4
Claypit Hill	Cambs	87	G1
Claypits	Gloucs	63	M6
Claypole	Lincs	117	M2
Claythorpe	Lincs	137	H4
Clayton	C Brad	141	H2
Clayton	Donc	142	C6
Clayton	W Susx	22	D4
Clayton Green	Lancs	139	H3
Clayton-le-Moors	Lancs	139	M2
Clayton-le-Woods	Lancs	139	H3
Clayton West	Kirk	141	L5
Clayworth	Notts	134	E2
Cleadale	Highld	236	F3
Cleadon	S Tyne	181	J6
Cleadon Park	S Tyne	181	J6
Clearbrook	Devon	7	G2
Clearwell	Gloucs	63	H5
Cleasby	N York	169	H8
Cleat	Ork	275	c6
Cleatlam	Dur	168	E7
Cleator	Cumb	164	D7
Cleator Moor	Cumb	164	D7
Cleckheaton	Kirk	141	J3
Cleedownton	Shrops	96	D7
Cleehill	Shrops	96	D6
Cleekhimin	N Lans	209	K7
Clee St Margaret	Shrops	96	D6
Cleestanton	Shrops	96	D7
Cleethorpes	NE Lin	145	J6
Cleeton St Mary	Shrops	96	E7
Cleeve	N Som	44	F5
Cleeve	Oxon	48	F3
Cleeve Hill	Gloucs	64	E2
Cleeve Prior	Worcs	82	C5
Cleghornie	E Loth	212	D2
Clehonger	Herefs	80	B7
Cleish	P & K	221	K7
Cleland	N Lans	209	L7
Clement's End	C Beds	68	C4

Place	County	Page	Grid
Clement Street	Kent	52	B5
Clenamacrie	Ag & B	216	E2
Clench Common	Wilts	47	H6
Clenchwarton	Norfk	120	D7
Clenerty	Abers	268	D4
Clent	Worcs	97	L7
Cleobury Mortimer	Shrops	96	F8
Cleobury North	Shrops	96	E6
Cleongart	Ag & B	192	D2
Clephanton	Highld	252	F2
Clerkhill	D & G	187	L6
Cleuch-head	D & G	185	K3
Clevancy	Wilts	46	F4
Clevedon	N Som	44	E5
Cleveley	Oxon	66	B2
Cleveleys	Lancs	146	F7
Cleverton	Wilts	46	E2
Clewer	Somset	31	G1
Cley next the Sea	Norfk	122	A3
Cliburn	W & F	166	E5
Cliddesden	Hants	35	K1
Cliff	Warwks	99	G4
Cliffe	Lancs	139	L1
Cliffe	Medway	52	F4
Cliffe	N York	143	G2
Cliffe	N York	169	G7
Cliff End	E Susx	25	G4
Cliffe Woods	Medway	52	F4
Clifford	Herefs	79	J6
Clifford	Leeds	150	F7
Clifford Chambers	Warwks	82	E5
Clifford's Mesne	Gloucs	63	K2
Cliffsend	Kent	41	K2
Clifton	Bristl	45	H4
Clifton	C Beds	86	D7
Clifton	C Nott	116	F4
Clifton	C York	151	J5
Clifton	Calder	141	J3
Clifton	Derbys	115	K3
Clifton	Devon	27	L3
Clifton	Donc	142	E8
Clifton	Lancs	138	F2
Clifton	N York	150	B6
Clifton	Nthumb	180	F2
Clifton	Oxon	66	C1
Clifton	Wilts	180	B7
Clifton	W & F	166	C5
Clifton	Worcs	81	J6
Clifton Campville	Staffs	99	H1
Clifton Hampden	Oxon	66	D7
Clifton Reynes	M Keyn	85	H5
Clifton upon Dunsmore	Warwks	100	C8
Clifton upon Teme	Worcs	81	G3
Cliftonville	Kent	41	L1
Climping	W Susx	21	G6
Clink	Somset	32	C1
Clint	N York	150	C4
Clinterty	C Aber	245	J1
Clint Green	Norfk	105	L1
Clintmains	Border	201	J6
Clipiau	Gwynd	93	H1
Clippesby	Norfk	123	J8
Clipsham	Rutlnd	118	C8
Clipston	Notts	117	H5
Clipston	W Nthn	100	F7
Clipstone	C Beds	68	B2
Clipstone	Notts	134	B7
Clitheroe	Lancs	148	C7
Clive	Shrops	113	H6
Clixby	Lincs	144	F1
Cloatley	Wilts	46	E1
Clocaenog	Denbgs	111	L1
Clochan	Moray	267	H4
Clock Face	St Hel	129	M2
Cloddiau	Powys	94	F2
Clodock	Herefs	62	C2
Cloford	Somset	32	B2
Clola	Abers	257	J3
Clophill	C Beds	86	B7
Clopton	N Nthn	102	B7
Clopton	Suffk	90	F4
Clopton Corner	Suffk	90	F4
Clopton Green	Suffk	88	F4
Clopton Green	Suffk	89	K3
Clos du Valle	Guern	9	k1
Closeburn	D & G	186	D7
Closeburnmill	D & G	186	D7
Closeclark	IoM	154	c7
Closworth	Somset	16	A1
Clothall	Herts	69	H1
Clothall Common	Herts	86	E8
Clotton	Ches W	129	M6
Cloudesley Bush	Warwks	100	A6
Clouds	Herefs	80	D6
Clough	Oldham	140	E6
Clough Foot	Calder	140	D3
Clough Head	Calder	141	H4
Cloughton	N York	163	H4
Cloughton Newlands	N York	163	H3

Clousta Shet 281 d5
Clova Angus 233 M1
Clovelly Devon 26 E6
Clovenfords Border 200 F6
Clovulin Highld 228 F3
Clow Bridge Lancs 140 B2
Clowne Derbys 133 K4
Clows Top Worcs 81 G1
Cloy Wrexhm 112 F3
Cluanie Inn Highld 239 H1
Cluanie Lodge Highld.......239 H2
Clubworthy Cnwll 11 K4
Clugston D & G 173 J3
Clun Shrops 95 H7
Clunas Highld 253 G2
Clunbury Shrops 95 J7
Clunderwen Carmth 55 J3
Clune Highld 252 E6
Clunes Highld 239 K6
Clungunford Shrops 95 K7
Clunie P & K 233 H4
Clunton Shrops 95 H7
Cluny Fife 222 D8
Clutton BaNES 45 J7
Clutton Ches W 113 G1
Clutton Hill BaNES 45 J7
Clwt Conwy 127 J7
Clwt-y-bont Gwynd 125 K7
Clydach Mons 61 K4
Clydach Swans 57 J4
Clydach Vale Rhondd 42 E3
Clydebank W Duns 208 E5
Clydey Pembks 75 M5
Clyffe Pypard Wilts 47 G3
Clynder Ag & B 207 L2
Clyne Neath 60 B7
Clynnog Fawr Gwynd 109 G2
Clyro Powys 79 H6
Clyst Honiton Devon 14 A4
Clyst Hydon Devon 14 B2
Clyst St George Devon 14 A5
Clyst St Lawrence Devon 14 B3
Clyst St Mary Devon 14 A4
Cnoc W Isls 282 g3
Cnwch Coch Cerdgn 92 E8
Coad's Green Cnwll 11 K7
Coal Aston Derbys 133 G4
Coalbrookvale Blae G 61 K5
Coalburn S Lans 198 D6
Coalburns Gatesd 180 D6
Coalcy Gloucs 63 M6
Coalhill Essex 71 J7
Coalmoor Wrekin 96 F2
Coalpit Heath S Glos 45 K3
Coal Pool Wsall 98 C3
Coalport Wrekin 96 F3
Coalsnaughton Clacks 221 G8
Coal Street Suffk 90 F1
Coaltown of Balgonie Fife.....222 E7
Coaltown of Wemyss Fife ...222 E8
Coalville Leics 99 L1
Coanwood Nthumb 178 F7
Coat Somset 31 G6
Coatbridge N Lans 209 J6
Coatdyke N Lans 209 K6
Coate Swindn 47 J2
Coate Wilts 46 F6
Coates Cambs 102 F4
Coates Gloucs 64 E7
Coates Lincs 135 H3
Coates Notts 135 G3
Coates W Susx 21 G3
Coatham R & Cl 170 E5
Coatham Mundeville Darltn...169 H6
Cobbaton Devon 27 L5
Coberley Gloucs 64 D4
Cobhall Common Herefs 80 B8
Cobham Kent 52 E5
Cobham Surrey 50 E7
Cobham Services Surrey........50 E7
Coblers Green Essex 71 G3
Cobley Dorset 33 H6
Cobnash Herefs 80 B3
Cobo Guern 9 j2
Cobridge C Stke 114 D2
Coburby Abers 269 G3
Cock Alley Derbys 133 H5
Cockayne N York 161 K3
Cockayne Hatley C Beds......86 F5
Cock Bank Wrexhm 112 E2
Cock Bevington Warwks 82 C5
Cock Bridge Abers 243 J2
Cockburnspath Border 213 G5
Cock Clarks Essex 71 K6
Cock & End Suffk 88 E4
Cockenzie and Port Seton
     E Loth 211 L4
Cocker Bar Lancs 139 G3
Cocker Brook Lancs 139 L3
Cockerham Lancs 147 J5

Cockermouth Cumb 164 F4
Cockernhoe Herts 68 E2
Cockersdale Leeds 141 K2
Cockett Swans 57 H6
Cockfield Dur 168 D6
Cockfield Suffk 89 H4
Cockfosters Gt Lon 69 H7
Cock Green Essex 71 G3
Cocking W Susx 20 E3
Cocking Causeway W Susx ...20 E3
Cockington Torbay 8 D2
Cocklake Somset 31 G1
Cockley Beck W & F 156 C2
Cockley Cley Norfk 104 F3
Cock Marling E Susx 24 F3
Cockpole Green Wokham 49 J3
Cocks Cnwll 4 C4
Cockshutford Shrops 96 D6
Cockshutt Shrops 113 G5
Cock Street Kent 39 K3
Cockthorpe Norfk 121 L3
Cockwells Cnwll 2 E4
Cockwood Devon 13 M6
Cockwood Somset 30 B2
Cockyard Derbys 131 L4
Cockyard Herefs 80 A8
Coddenham Suffk 90 D4
Coddington Ches W 129 K6
Coddington Herefs 81 G6
Coddington Notts 117 L1
Codford St Mary Wilts 33 G3
Codford St Peter Wilts 33 G3
Codicote Herts 69 G3
Codmore Hill W Susx 21 H3
Codnor Derbys 116 C2
Codrington S Glos 45 L3
Codsall Staffs 97 K3
Codsall Wood Staffs 97 J2
Coed Darcy Neath 57 K5
Coedely Rhondd 42 F4
Coed Hirwaun Neath 42 B5
Coedkernew Newpt 44 B2
Coed Morgan Mons 62 D5
Coedpoeth Wrexhm 112 D1
Coed Talon Flints 129 G7
Coedway Powys 112 E8
Coed-y-Bryn Cerdgn 76 C6
Coed-y-caerau Newpt 44 D1
Coed-y-Cwm Rhondd 43 G3
Coed-y-paen Mons 62 C7
Coed-yr-ynys Powys 61 J3
Coed Ystumgwern Gwynd ...109 H6
Coelbren Powys 60 C5
Coffinswell Devon 8 D1
Coffle End Bed 85 K3
Cofton Devon 13 M6
Cofton Hackett Worcs 98 C8
Cogan V Glam 43 J7
Cogenhoe W Nthn 84 F3
Cogges Oxon 65 M5
Coggeshall Essex 71 K3
Coggin's Mill E Susx 23 K2
Coignafearn Highld 251 J8
Coilacriech Abers 243 K4
Coilantogle Stirlg 219 K5
Coillore Highld 246 E1
Coity Brdgnd 42 D5
Col W Isls 282 g3
Colaboll Highld 272 E6
Colan Cnwll 4 E3
Colaton Raleigh Devon 14 C5
Colbost Highld 258 C7
Colburn N York 160 B3
Colby IoM 154 b7
Colby Norfk 122 E5
Colby W & F 166 F6
Colchester Essex 72 E2
Cold Ash W Berk 48 D5
Cold Ashby W Nthn 100 E8
Cold Ashton S Glos 45 L4
Cold Aston Gloucs 65 H3
Coldbackie Highld 277 K4
Coldbeck W & F 158 C2
Cold Blow Pembks 55 J4
Cold Brayfield M Keyn 85 H5
Cold Cotes N York 148 C2
Coldean Br & H 22 E5
Coldeast Devon 13 J7
Colden Calder 140 E2
Colden Common Hants 35 G6
Coldfair Green Suffk 91 K3
Coldham Cambs 103 J3
Cold Hanworth Lincs 135 L3
Coldharbour Cnwll 4 B5
Coldharbour Devon 29 J4
Coldharbour Gloucs 63 H6
Cold Harbour Herts 68 F4
Cold Harbour Oxon 48 F3
Coldharbour Surrey 37 H2
Cold Hatton Wrekin 113 K7

Cold Hatton Heath Wrekin..........113 K7
Cold Hesledon Dur 169 L2
Cold Hiendley Wakefd 142 B5
Cold Higham W Nthn 84 C4
Coldingham Border 213 K6
Cold Kirby N York 161 H6
Coldmeece Staffs 114 D5
Cold Newton Leics 100 F2
Cold Northcott Cnwll 11 H5
Cold Norton Essex 71 K7
Cold Overton Leics 101 H2
Coldred Kent 41 J6
Coldridge Devon 13 G1
Coldstream Border 202 C5
Coldwaltham W Susx 21 H3
Coldwell Herefs 80 A8
Coldwells Abers 257 H4
Cold Weston Shrops 96 C6
Cole Somset 31 L4
Colebatch Shrops 95 H6
Colebrook C Plym 7 G3
Colebrook Devon 14 B2
Colebrooke Devon 13 H3
Coleby Lincs 135 K7
Coleby N Linc 143 M4
Cole End Warwks 99 G5
Coleford Devon 13 H2
Coleford Gloucs 63 H5
Coleford Somset 31 L1
Coleford Water Somset 29 L4
Colegate End Norfk 106 D6
Cole Green Herts 69 G5
Cole Green Herts 70 B1
Cole Henley Hants 34 F1
Colehill Dorset 17 K2
Coleman Green Herts 69 G4
Coleman's Hatch E Susx 38 C6
Colemere Shrops 113 G5
Colemore Hants 35 L5
Colemore Green Shrops 97 G4
Colenden P & K 221 K1
Coleorton Leics 116 C8
Colerne Wilts 46 B5
Colesbourne Gloucs 64 E4
Cole's Cross Devon 8 A5
Coles Cross Dorset 15 J2
Colesden Bed 86 C4
Coles Green Suffk 90 C7
Coleshill Bucks 68 B8
Coleshill Oxon 65 K8
Coleshill Warwks 99 G5
Colestocks Devon 14 C3
Coley BaNES 45 H7
Colgate W Susx 37 K4
Colinsburgh Fife 223 H6
Colinton C Edin 211 H5
Colintraive Ag & B 207 G4
Colkirk Norfk 121 K6
Coll Ag & B 225 G4
Coll W Isls 282 g3
Collace P & K 222 C1
Collafirth Shet 281 d3
Coll Airport Ag & B 224 F4
Collaton Devon 7 L7
Collaton St Mary Torbay 8 C3
College of Roseisle Moray ...266 C3
College Town Br For 49 K6
Collessie Fife 222 D4
Colleton Mills Devon 28 B7
Collett's Green Worcs 81 J5
Collier Row Gt Lon 52 B1
Collier's End Herts 69 K3
Collier's Green E Susx 24 E3
Colliers Green Kent 39 J5
Collier Street Kent 39 H4
Colliery Row Sundld 169 J1
Collieston Abers 257 J6
Collin D & G 176 D4
Collingbourne Ducis Wilts 47 K8
Collingbourne Kingston Wilts...47 K7
Collingham Leeds 150 E6
Collingham Notts 135 G7
Collington Herefs 80 F3
Collingtree W Nthn 84 E4
Collins Green Warrtn 130 A1
Collins Green Worcs 81 G4
Colliston Angus 234 F6
Colliton Devon 14 C2
Collyweston N Nthn 101 M3
Colmonell S Ayrs 182 E5
Colmworth Bed 86 C4
Colnabaichin Abers 243 J2
Colnbrook Slough 50 C3
Colne Cambs 103 H8
Colne Lancs 148 F7
Colne Bridge Kirk 141 J4
Colne Edge Lancs 148 F7
Colne Engaine Essex 71 K1
Colney Norfk 106 D2
Colney Heath Herts 69 G6

Colney Street Herts 68 F6
Coln Rogers Gloucs 65 G5
Coln St Aldwyns Gloucs 65 H6
Coln St Dennis Gloucs 65 G5
Colonsay Ag & B 214 D5
Colonsay Airport Ag & B 214 D6
Colpy Abers 256 B5
Colquhar Border 200 D5
Colquite Cnwll 10 E8
Colscott Devon 26 E7
Colsterdale N York 159 L6
Colsterworth Lincs 118 B6
Colston Bassett Notts 117 J5
Coltfield Moray 266 C3
Colt Hill Hants 49 H8
Coltishall Norfk 122 F7
Colton Leeds 142 B1
Colton N York 151 H6
Colton Norfk 106 C2
Colton Staffs 115 G7
Colton W & F 156 D5
Colt's Hill Kent 39 G4
Columbjohn Devon 13 M3
Colva Powys 79 H4
Colvend D & G 175 L4
Colwall Herefs 81 H6
Colwell Nthumb 179 M4
Colwich Staffs 115 G7
Colwick Notts 117 G3
Colwinston V Glam 42 E6
Colworth W Susx 20 F6
Colwyn Bay Conwy 127 G4
Colyford Devon 14 F4
Colyton Devon 14 F4
Combe Devon 7 L7
Combe Herefs 79 L3
Combe Oxon 66 B4
Combe W Berk 48 A6
Combe Almer Dorset 17 J3
Combe Common Surrey 36 E4
Combe Down BaNES 45 M6
Combe Fishacre Devon 8 C2
Combe Florey Somset 29 L4
Combe Hay BaNES 45 L7
Combeinteignhead Devon 13 L8
Combe Martin Devon 27 K2
Combe Raleigh Devon 14 E2
Comberbach Ches W 130 C4
Comberford Staffs 99 G2
Comberton Cambs 87 H4
Comberton Herefs 80 C2
Combe St Nicholas Somset ...30 D8
Combpyne Devon 15 G4
Combridge Staffs 115 H4
Combrook Warwks 83 H5
Combs Derbys 131 L4
Combs Suffk 90 B4
Combs Ford Suffk 90 B4
Combwich Somset 30 C2
Comers Abers 244 F2
Comeytrowe Somset 30 B6
Comhampton Worcs 81 J2
Commercial End Cambs 87 L3
Commins Coch Powys 93 J3
Commondale N York 170 F8
Common Edge Bpool 138 C1
Common End Cumb 164 D6
Common Moor Cnwll 6 A1
Common Platt Wilts 47 G2
Commonside Ches W 130 A5
Commonside Derbys 115 L3
Common Side Derbys 133 G4
Commonwood Shrops 113 H6
Commonwood Wrexhm 112 F1
Compass Somset 30 D4
Compstall Stockp 131 J2
Compstonend D & G 175 G4
Compton Devon 8 C2
Compton Hants 34 D5
Compton Hants 34 F1
Compton Staffs 97 J6
Compton Surrey 36 E2
Compton W Berk 48 D3
Compton W Susx 20 C4
Compton Wilts 47 H8
Compton Abbas Dorset 32 E7
Compton Abdale Gloucs 64 F4
Compton Bassett Wilts 46 F4
Compton Beauchamp Oxon ...47 K2
Compton Bishop Somset 44 E7
Compton Chamberlayne Wilts...33 H5
Compton Dando BaNES 45 J6
Compton Dundon Somset 31 H4
Compton Durville Somset 30 F7
Compton Greenfield S Glos ...45 H3
Compton Martin BaNES 45 H7
Compton Pauncefoot Somset...31 L5
Compton Valence Dorset 16 B4
Comrie Fife 210 D1
Comrie P & K 220 D3

Conaglen House Highld 229 G2
Conchra Highld 248 E6
Concraigie P & K 233 G6
Conder Green Lancs 147 J4
Conderton Worcs 81 M7
Condicote Gloucs 65 H2
Condorrat N Lans 209 K4
Condover Shrops 96 B2
Coney Hill Gloucs 64 B3
Coneyhurst W Susx 37 H6
Coneysthorpe N York 151 M2
Coneythorpe N York 150 E4
Coney Weston Suffk 105 J7
Conford Hants 36 B4
Congdon's Shop Cnwll 11 K7
Congerstone Leics 99 K2
Congham Norfk 120 F6
Congleton Ches E 131 G7
Congl-y-wal Gwynd 110 D3
Congresbury N Som 44 E6
Congreve Staffs 97 K1
Conheath D & G 176 C5
Conicavel Moray 253 J1
Coningsby Lincs 136 D8
Conington Cambs 87 G2
Conington Cambs 102 D6
Conisbrough Donc 142 D8
Conisholme Lincs 145 K8
Coniston E R Yk 144 F1
Coniston W & F 156 D3
Coniston Cold N York 148 F5
Conistone N York 149 H2
Connah's Quay Flints 129 G5
Connel Ag & B 228 E8
Connel Park E Ayrs 197 H8
Connor Downs Cnwll 2 F3
Conon Bridge Highld 250 F1
Cononley N York 149 H6
Consall Staffs 114 F2
Consett Dur 180 D8
Constable Burton N York 159 L4
Constable Lee Lancs 140 B3
Constantine Cnwll 3 J5
Constantine Bay Cnwll 10 D7
Contin Highld 260 D9
Conwy Conwy 126 F4
Conwy Castle Conwy 126 F4
Conyer Kent 40 C2
Conyer's Green Suffk 89 H2
Cooden E Susx 24 C6
Cookbury Devon 12 A2
Cookbury Wick Devon 11 M2
Cookham W & M 49 L2
Cookham Dean W & M 49 L2
Cookham Rise W & M 49 L2
Cookhill Worcs 82 C3
Cookley Suffk 107 G8
Cookley Worcs 97 J7
Cookley Green Oxon 49 G1
Cookney Abers 245 J5
Cooksbridge E Susx 22 F4
Cooksey Green Worcs 81 L1
Cook's Green Essex 73 J3
Cooks Green Suffk 89 K4
Cookshill Staffs 114 E3
Cooksland Cnwll 5 J1
Cooksmill Green Essex 70 F6
Cookson Green Ches W 130 B5
Coolham W Susx 37 H6
Cooling Medway 53 G4
Cooling Street Medway 52 F4
Coombe Cnwll 3 G3
Coombe Cnwll 3 L3
Coombe Cnwll 4 F4
Coombe Devon 13 J6
Coombe Devon 13 L7
Coombe Devon 14 C4
Coombe Gloucs 63 M8
Coombe Hants 35 K6
Coombe Wilts 33 K1
Coombe Bissett Wilts 33 K5
Coombe Cellars Devon 13 L8
Coombe Cross Hants 35 K6
Coombe Hill Gloucs 64 C2
Coombe Keynes Dorset 17 G6
Coombe Pafford Torbay 8 D2
Coombes W Susx 21 L5
Coombes-Moor Herefs 79 L3
Coombe Street Somset 32 C4
Coombeswood Dudley 98 B6
Coopersale Common Essex 70 C6
Coopersale Street Essex 70 C6
Cooper's Corner Kent 38 D3
Coopers Green E Susx 23 H3
Coopers Green Herts 69 G5
Cooper Street Kent 41 J3
Cooper Turning Bolton 139 J6
Cootham W Susx 21 J4
Copdock Suffk 90 D7
Copford Essex 72 D3

Copford Green Essex 72 D3
Copgrove N York 150 D3
Copister Shet 281 e4
Cople Bed 86 C5
Copley Calder 141 G3
Copley Dur 168 D5
Copley Tamesd 140 E8
Coplow Dale Derbys 132 C4
Copmanthorpe C York 151 J6
Copmere End Staffs 114 C5
Copp Lancs 147 H7
Coppathorne Cnwll 11 H3
Coppenhall Staffs 114 E7
Coppenhall Moss Ches E 130 D8
Copperhouse Cnwll 2 F3
Coppicegate Shrops 97 G7
Coppingford Cambs 102 D7
Coppins Corner Kent 40 B5
Copplestone Devon 13 H2
Coppull Lancs 139 H5
Coppull Moor Lancs 139 H5
Copsale W Susx 37 J6
Copster Green Lancs 139 K1
Copston Magna Warwks 99 M5
Cop Street Kent 41 J3
Copthall Green Essex 70 B7
Copt Heath Solhll 98 F7
Copt Hewick N York 150 D2
Copthorne Cnwll 11 K4
Copthorne W Susx 37 M3
Copt Oak Leics 100 B1
Copy's Green Norfk 121 L4
Copythorne Hants 34 C8
Coram Street Suffk 89 K6
Corbets Tey Gt Lon 52 C2
Corbière Jersey 9 a3
Corbridge Nthumb 180 B6
Corby N Nthn 101 K5
Corby Glen Lincs 118 C6
Corby Hill Cumb 178 B7
Cordon N Ayrs 195 G5
Cordwell Derbys 132 F4
Coreley Shrops 96 E8
Cores End Bucks 49 L2
Corfe Somset 30 C7
Corfe Castle Dorset 17 J6
Corfe Mullen Dorset 17 J3
Corfton Shrops 96 B6
Corgarff Abers 243 J2
Corhampton Hants 35 J6
Corks Pond Kent 39 G5
Corlae D & G 185 G3
Corley Warwks 99 J6
Corley Ash Warwks 99 J6
Corley Moor Warwks 99 H6
Corley Services Warwks 99 J6
Cormuir Angus 233 L2
Cornard Tye Suffk 89 H7
Corndon Devon 13 G5
Corner Row Lancs 138 E1
Corney Cumb 155 K4
Cornforth Dur 169 J4
Cornhill Abers 267 M4
Cornhill-on-Tweed Nthumb 202 D5
Cornholme Calder 140 D3
Cornish Hall End Essex 88 D7
Cornoigmore Ag & B 224 C6
Cornriggs Dur 167 K2
Cornsay Dur 168 F2
Cornsay Colliery Dur 168 F2
Corntown Highld 262 F8
Corntown V Glam 42 D6
Cornwall Airport Newquay Cnwll 4 E2
Cornwell Oxon 65 K2
Cornwood Devon 7 H3
Cornworthy Devon 8 B4
Corpach Highld 239 H8
Corpusty Norfk 122 C5
Corrachree Abers 244 B3
Corran Highld 229 G3
Corran Highld 238 D2
Corrany IoM 154 f4
Corrie D & G 177 G2
Corrie N Ayrs 195 G2
Corriecravie N Ayrs 193 J4
Corriegills N Ayrs 195 G4
Corriegour Lodge Hotel Highld 239 M5
Corriemoille Highld 262 C7
Corrimony Highld 250 C5
Corringham Lincs 135 H2
Corringham Thurr 52 F2
Corris Gwynd 93 G2
Corris Uchaf Gwynd 92 F2
Corrow Ag & B 217 K7
Corry Highld 247 K4
Corscombe Devon 12 E3
Corscombe Dorset 15 L2
Corse Gloucs 64 A2

Corse Lawn Gloucs 64 B1
Corsham Wilts 46 C5
Corsindae Abers 244 F2
Corsley Wilts 32 D2
Corsley Heath Wilts 32 D2
Corsock D & G 185 J7
Corston BaNES 45 K6
Corston Wilts 46 D2
Corstorphine C Edin 211 J4
Cors-y-Gedol Gwynd 109 L7
Cortachy Angus 234 B3
Corton Suffk 107 L4
Corton Wilts 32 F3
Corton Denham Somset 31 K6
Coruanan Highld 229 H2
Corwen Denbgs 111 L3
Coryates Dorset 16 B5
Coryton Devon 12 B6
Coryton Thurr 52 F2
Cosby Leics 100 C4
Coscote Dudley 97 J4
Cosford Shrops 97 H2
Cosgrove W Nthn 84 F6
Cosham C Port 19 L3
Cosheston Pembks 55 G6
Coshieville P & K 231 L5
Cossall Notts 116 E3
Cossall Marsh Notts 116 E3
Cossington Leics 100 D1
Cossington Somset 30 C3
Costessey Norfk 106 D1
Costock Notts 116 F6
Coston Leics 117 M7
Coston Norfk 106 B2
Cote Oxon 65 M6
Cote Somset 30 E2
Cotebrook Ches W 130 B6
Cotehill Cumb 166 B1
Cotes Leics 116 F7
Cotes Staffs 114 C4
Cotes W & F 157 G5
Cotesbach Leics 100 C7
Cotes Heath Staffs 114 C4
Cotford St Luke Somset 30 A5
Cotgrave Notts 117 H4
Cothal Abers 256 F8
Cotham Notts 117 L2
Cothelstone Somset 30 B4
Cotherstone Dur 168 C6
Cothill Oxon 66 C7
Cotleigh Devon 14 E2
Cotmanhay Derbys 116 D2
Coton Cambs 87 H3
Coton Shrops 113 J4
Coton Staffs 98 F2
Coton Staffs 114 C4
Coton Staffs 114 F5
Coton W Nthn 84 D1
Coton Clanford Staffs 114 D7
Coton Hayes Staffs 114 F5
Coton Hill Shrops 96 B1
Coton in the Clay Staffs 115 K5
Coton in the Elms Derbys 115 L8
Coton Park Derbys 115 M7
Cotswold Airport Wilts 64 D7
Cotswolds 64 E5
Cott Devon 8 B3
Cottam E R Yk 152 F3
Cottam Lancs 139 G1
Cottam Notts 135 G4
Cottenham Cambs 87 J2
Cotterdale N York 158 E4
Cottered Herts 69 J1
Cottcridge Birm 98 D7
Cotterstock N Nthn 102 A5
Cottesbrooke W Nthn 100 F8
Cottesmore Rutlnd 101 K1
Cottingham E R Yk 144 D1
Cottingham N Nthn 101 J3
Cottingley C Brad 149 K8
Cottisford Oxon 66 E1
Cotton Suffk 90 C2
Cotton End Bed 86 B6
Cotton Tree Lancs 148 F7
Cottown Abers 255 K6
Cottown Abers 256 D8
Cottown of Gight Abers 256 E6
Cotts Devon 6 E2
Cotwall Wrekin 113 K8
Cotwalton Staffs 114 E4
Couch's Mill Cnwll 5 K3
Coughton Herefs 63 H3
Coughton Warwks 82 C3
Coulaghailtro Ag & B 206 A6
Coulags Highld 248 E3
Coulby Newham Middsb 170 C7
Coulderton Cumb 155 H1
Coull Abers 244 B3
Coulport Ag & B 207 L2
Coulsdon Gt Lon 51 J7

Coulston Wilts 46 D8
Coulter S Lans 199 H6
Coultershaw Bridge W Susx 21 G3
Coultings Somset 30 C3
Coulton N York 161 K7
Coultra Fife 222 F3
Cound Shrops 96 D2
Coundlane Shrops 96 D2
Coundon Dur 169 G5
Coundon Grange Dur 169 G5
Countersett N York 159 G5
Countess Wilts 33 K2
Countess Cross Essex 72 C1
Countess Wear Devon 13 M5
Countesswells C Aber 245 J3
Countesthorpe Leics 100 D4
Countisbury Devon 28 C1
Coupar Angus P & K 233 K7
Coupe Green Lancs 139 H2
Coupland Nthumb 202 E7
Coupland W & F 167 J3
Cour Ag & B 194 C2
Court-at-Street Kent 40 E8
Courteachan Highld 237 K1
Courteenhall W Nthn 84 E4
Court Henry Carmth 59 G4
Courtsend Essex 72 F8
Courtway Somset 30 B4
Cousland Mdloth 211 L5
Cousley Wood E Susx 39 G6
Cove Ag & B 207 L3
Cove Border 213 G4
Cove Devon 29 G2
Cove Hants 49 L7
Cove Highld 260 C2
Cove Bay C Aber 245 L3
Cove Bottom Suffk 107 K7
Covehithe Suffk 107 L7
Coven Staffs 97 K2
Coveney Cambs 103 K7
Covenham St Bartholomew Lincs 136 F1
Covenham St Mary Lincs 136 F1
Coven Heath Staffs 97 K2
Coventry Covtry 99 J7
Coverack Cnwll 3 J0
Coverack Bridges Cnwll 3 H5
Coverham N York 159 K6
Covington Cambs 85 L1
Covington S Lans 199 G5
Cowan Bridge Lancs 157 K7
Cowbeech E Susx 23 K4
Cowbit Lincs 119 H7
Cowbridge V Glam 42 F6
Cowdale Derbys 132 B5
Cowden Kent 38 C5
Cowdenbeath Fife 211 G1
Cowden Pound Kent 38 C5
Cowden Station Kent 38 D5
Cowers Lane Derbys 116 A2
Cowes IoW 19 H4
Cowesby N York 161 G5
Cowesfield Green Wilts 34 B6
Cowfold W Susx 37 K6
Cowgill W & F 158 C5
Cow Green Suffk 90 C2
Cowhill S Glos 45 J1
Cowie Stirlg 209 M1
Cowlam E R Yk 152 E3
Cowley Devon 13 L3
Cowley Gloucs 64 D4
Cowley Gt Lon 50 D3
Cowley Oxon 66 D6
Cowling Lancs 139 J4
Cowling N York 149 H7
Cowling N York 160 C5
Cowlinge Suffk 88 E4
Cowmes Kirk 141 J4
Cowpe Lancs 140 C4
Cowpen Nthumb 181 H3
Cowpen Bewley S on T 170 B5
Cowplain Hants 19 M2
Cowshill Dur 167 K3
Cowslip Green N Som 44 F6
Cowthorpe N York 150 F5
Coxall Herefs 95 J8
Coxbank Ches E 113 L3
Coxbench Derbys 116 C3
Coxbridge Somset 31 J3
Cox Common Suffk 107 H7
Coxford Cnwll 11 H3
Coxford Norfk 121 J5
Coxgreen Staffs 97 H6
Cox Green Surrey 37 G4
Coxheath Kent 39 J3
Coxhoe Dur 169 J3
Coxley Somset 31 H2
Coxley Wakefd 141 L4
Coxley Wick Somset 31 H2
Coxpark Cnwll 12 A8

Coxtie Green Essex 70 E7
Coxwold N York 161 H7
Coychurch Brdgnd 42 E6
Coylton S Ayrs 196 E7
Coylumbridge Highld 242 B1
Coytrahen Brdgnd 42 D4
Crabbs Cross Worcs 82 B2
Crab Orchard Dorset 17 L1
Crabtree W Susx 37 K6
Crabtree Green Wrexhm 112 E3
Crackenthorpe W & F 166 F6
Crackington Haven Cnwll 11 G3
Crackley Staffs 114 C2
Crackley Warwks 99 J8
Crackleybank Shrops 97 G1
Crackpot N York 159 H3
Cracoe N York 149 H4
Craddock Devon 29 K8
Cradle End Herts 70 C3
Cradley Dudley 97 L6
Cradley Herefs 81 G6
Cradley Heath Sandw 97 L6
Cradoc Powys 60 F1
Crafthole Cnwll 6 D4
Crafton Bucks 67 L3
Crag Foot Lancs 157 G7
Craggan Highld 253 K6
Cragganmore Moray 254 D4
Cragg Hill Leeds 150 B8
Cragg Vale Calder 140 F3
Craghead Dur 180 F8
Crai Powys 60 D2
Craibstone Moray 267 K4
Craichie Angus 234 D6
Craig Angus 235 H4
Craig Highld 249 H2
Craigbank E Ayrs 197 H8
Craigburn Border 200 B2
Craig-cefn-parc Swans 57 J4
Craigcleuch D & G 177 K2
Craigdam Abers 256 F5
Craigdhu Ag & B 216 C6
Craigearn Abers 245 G1
Craigellachie Moray 254 F3
Craigend P & K 221 K3
Craigend Rens 208 D5
Craigendoran Ag & B 208 A3
Craigends Rens 208 C6
Craighlaw D & G 173 H3
Craighouse Ag & B 205 H3
Craigie P & K 233 H6
Craigie S Ayrs 196 E4
Craigiefold Abers 269 G3
Craigley D & G 175 J3
Craig Llangiwg Neath 57 K4
Craiglockhart C Edin 211 H5
Craigmillar C Edin 211 J4
Craignant Shrops 112 C4
Craigneston D & G 185 J5
Craigneuk N Lans 209 K6
Craigneuk N Lans 209 K7
Craignure Ag & B 227 L5
Craigo Angus 235 H3
Craig Penllyn V Glam 42 E6
Craigrothie Fife 222 F5
Craigruie Stirlg 219 H3
Craig's End Essex 88 E7
Craigton Angus 234 D7
Craigton C Aber 245 J3
Craigton E Rens 208 E8
Craigton of Airlie Angus 233 M5
Craig-y-Duke Neath 57 K4
Craig-y-nos Powys 60 C4
Craik Border 188 B4
Crail Fife 223 L5
Crailing Border 189 J1
Craiselound N Linc 143 J8
Crakehall N York 160 C5
Crakehill N York 160 F7
Crakemarsh Staffs 115 H4
Crambe N York 151 M3
Crambeck N York 151 M2
Cramlington Nthumb 181 G3
Cramond C Edin 211 G4
Cramond Bridge C Edin 211 G4
Crampmoor Hants 34 E6
Cranage Ches E 130 E6
Cranberry Staffs 114 C4
Cranborne Dorset 33 H8
Cranbourne Br For 50 A4
Cranbrook Devon 14 A4
Cranbrook Kent 39 J6
Cranbrook Common Kent 39 K5
Crane Moor Barns 141 M7
Crane's Corner Norfk 105 J1
Cranfield C Beds 85 J6
Cranford Devon 26 F6
Cranford Gt Lon 50 E4
Cranford St Andrew N Nthn 101 K7
Cranford St John N Nthn 101 K7

Cranham Gloucs 64 C4
Cranham Gt Lon 52 C2
Cranhill Warwks 82 D4
Crank St Hel 139 G7
Cranleigh Surrey 37 G3
Cranmer Green Suffk 89 L1
Cranmore IoW 18 F5
Cranmore Somset 31 L2
Cranoe Leics 101 K4
Cransford Suffk 91 H2
Cranshaws Border 212 F6
Cranstal IoM 154 f2
Cranswick E R Yk 152 F5
Crantock Cnwll 4 C3
Cranwell Lincs 118 D2
Cranwich Norfk 104 F4
Cranworth Norfk 105 K3
Craobh Haven Ag & B 216 B5
Crapstone Devon 6 F1
Crarae Ag & B 216 F7
Crask Inn Highld 272 D3
Crask of Aigas Highld 250 E3
Craster Nthumb 191 K2
Craswall Herefs 79 K8
Crateford Staffs 97 K2
Cratfield Suffk 107 G8
Crathes Abers 245 G4
Crathie Abers 243 J4
Crathie Highld 241 G5
Crathorne N York 161 G1
Craven Arms Shrops 95 K6
Crawcrook Gatesd 180 D6
Crawford Lancs 139 G2
Crawford S Lans 186 E2
Crawfordjohn S Lans 186 C2
Crawley Hants 34 F4
Crawley Oxon 65 M4
Crawley W Susx 37 L4
Crawley Down W Susx 38 A6
Crawleyside Dur 168 C3
Crawshawbooth Lancs 140 B3
Crawton Abers 245 J7
Craxe's Green Essex 72 D3
Cray N York 159 G6
Cray P & K 233 H3
Crayford Gt Lon 52 B4
Crayke N York 151 J2
Craymere Beck Norfk 122 B5
Crays Hill Essex 71 H8
Cray's Pond Oxon 48 F3
Craythorne Staffs 115 L6
Craze Lowman Devon 29 H8
Crazies Hill Wokham 49 J3
Creacombe Devon 28 E7
Creagan Inn Ag & B 228 F6
Creag Ghoraidh W Isls 283 c9
Creagorry W Isls 283 c9
Creaguaineach Lodge Highld 230 B2
Creamore Bank Shrops 113 H5
Creaton N Nthn 84 D1
Creca D & G 177 H5
Credenhill Herefs 80 B6
Crediton Devon 13 J3
Creebank D & G 183 J7
Creebridge D & G 173 K2
Creech Dorset 17 H6
Creech Heathfield Somset 30 D5
Creech St Michael Somset 30 C6
Creed Cnwll 4 F5
Creekmoor BCP 17 K4
Creekmouth Gt Lon 51 M3
Creeksea Essex 72 D7
Creeting St Mary Suffk 90 C4
Creeting St Peter Suffk 90 C3
Creeton Lincs 118 D7
Creetown D & G 174 D3
Cregneash IoM 154 b8
Creg ny Baa IoM 154 e5
Cregrina Powys 79 G5
Creich Fife 222 E3
Creigiau Cardif 43 G5
Cremyll Cnwll 6 E4
Cressage Shrops 96 D3
Cressbrook Derbys 132 C5
Cresselly Pembks 55 H5
Cressex Bucks 67 K8
Cressing Essex 71 J2
Cresswell Nthumb 191 K7
Cresswell Pembks 55 H5
Cresswell Staffs 114 F4
Creswell Derbys 133 K5
Creswell Green Staffs 98 D1
Cretingham Suffk 90 F3
Cretshengan Ag & B 206 A5
Crewe Ches E 130 D8
Crewe-by-Farndon Ches W 112 F1
Crewe Green Ches E 130 E8
Crew Green Powys 112 D8
Crewkerne Somset 15 K1
Crews Hill Gt Lon 69 J7

Crewton C Derb 116 C5
Crianlarich Stirlg 218 F2
Cribyn Cerdgn 76 F5
Criccieth Gwynd 109 J4
Crich Derbys 116 B1
Crich Carr Derbys 116 B1
Crichton Mdloth 211 L6
Crick Mons 44 F1
Crick Nhants 84 B1
Crickadarn Powys 78 F6
Cricket St Thomas Somset 15 J1
Crickheath Shrops 112 D7
Crickhowell Powys 61 K3
Cricklade Wilts 65 G8
Cricklewood Gt Lon 51 G2
Cridling Stubbs N York 142 E3
Crieff P & K 220 F1
Criggan Cnwll 5 G3
Criggion Powys 112 D8
Crigglestone Wakefd 141 M4
Crimble Rochdl 140 C5
Crimond Abers 269 K5
Crimplesham Norfk 104 C3
Crimscote Warwks 82 F5
Crinaglack Highld 250 D2
Crinan Ag & B 216 B8
Crindledyke N Lans 209 L7
Cringleford Norfk 106 D2
Cringles C Brad 149 J6
Crinow Pembks 55 K4
Cripplesease Cnwll 2 D4
Cripplestyle Dorset 33 J8
Cripp's Corner E Susx 24 D3
Croachy Highld 251 H6
Croanford Cnwll 10 E8
Crockenhill Kent 52 B5
Crocker End Oxon 49 J4
Crockerhill W Susx 20 F5
Crockernwell Devon 13 H4
Crocker's Ash Herefs 63 G4
Crockerton Wilts 32 E4
Crocketford D & G 185 K8
Crockey Hill C York 151 K6
Crockham Hill Kent 38 C3
Crockhurst Street Kent 39 G4
Crockleford Heath Essex 72 F2
Crock Street Somset 30 D8
Croeserw Neath 42 C3
Croes-goch Pembks 74 D6
Croes-lan Cerdgn 76 C6
Croesor Gwynd 110 B3
Croesyceiliog Carmth 58 D5
Croesyceiliog Torfn 62 C7
Croes-y-mwyalch Torfn 62 C8
Croes-y-pant Mons 62 C6
Croft Leics 100 B4
Croft Lincs 137 J7
Croft Warrtn 130 C1
Croftamie Stirlg 208 E2
Croft Mitchell Cnwll 3 H4
Crofton Cumb 165 J1
Crofton Wakefd 142 B4
Crofton Wilts 47 K6
Croft-on-Tees N York 160 D1
Croftown Highld 261 K3
Crofts Moray 266 F6
Crofts Bank Traffd 139 M8
Crofts of Dipple Moray 267 G4
Crofts of Haddo Abers 256 E4
Crofts of Savoch Abers 269 J4
Crofty Swans 56 F6
Crogen Gwynd 111 K4
Croggan Ag & B 227 K7
Croglin W & F 166 D1
Croick Highld 262 D2
Cromarty Highld 264 B6
Crombie Fife 210 E2
Cromdale Highld 253 L6
Cromer Herts 69 J2
Cromer Norfk 122 E3
Cromford Derbys 132 F8
Cromhall S Glos 45 K1
Cromhall Common S Glos 45 K1
Cromor W Isls 282 g4
Cromore W Isls 282 g4
Crompton Fold Oldham 140 E6
Cromwell Notts 134 F7
Cronberry E Ayrs 197 H6
Crondall Hants 36 B1
Cronkbourne IoM 154 e6
Cronk-y-Voddy IoM 154 d5
Cronton Knows 129 L2
Crook Dur 168 F4
Crook W & F 157 G4
Crookdake Cumb 165 G2
Crooke Wigan 139 H6
Crooked End Gloucs 63 J3
Crookedholm E Ayrs 196 E3
Crooked Soley Wilts 47 L4
Crookes Sheff 132 F2

Crookhall Dur 180 D8
Crookham Nthumb 202 E5
Crookham W Berk 48 D6
Crookham Village Hants 49 J8
Crook Inn Border 199 J7
Crooklands W & F 157 H6
Crook of Devon P & K 221 J7
Cropper Derbys 115 L4
Cropredy Oxon 83 L6
Cropston Leics 100 C1
Cropthorne Worcs 82 B6
Cropton N York 162 D5
Cropwell Bishop Notts 117 H4
Cropwell Butler Notts 117 J4
Cros W Isls 282 h1
Crosbost W Isls 282 g4
Crosby Cumb 164 E3
Crosby IoM 154 d6
Crosby N Linc 143 M5
Crosby Sefton 138 C8
Crosby Garret W & F 158 C1
Crosby Ravensworth W & F 166 E7
Crosby Villa Cumb 164 E3
Croscombe Somset 31 K2
Crosemere Shrops 113 G5
Crosland Edge Kirk 141 H5
Crosland Hill Kirk 141 H5
Cross Somset 44 E8
Crossaig Ag & B 194 C1
Crossapol Ag & B 224 C6
Cross Ash Mons 62 E3
Cross-at-Hand Kent 39 K4
Crossbost W Isls 282 g4
Crossbush W Susx 21 H5
Crosscanonby Cumb 164 E3
Cross Coombe Cnwll 4 B4
Crossdale Street Norfk 122 E4
Cross End Bed 85 L4
Cross End Essex 89 G8
Crossens Sefton 138 D4
Cross Flatts C Brad 149 K7
Crossford Fife 210 E2
Crossford S Lans 198 D4
Crossgate Cnwll 11 L5
Crossgate Lincs 119 H6
Crossgate Staffs 114 E4
Crossgatehall E Loth 211 L5
Crossgates E Ayrs 196 D2
Crossgates Fife 210 F1
Cross Gates Leeds 142 B1
Crossgates N York 163 J6
Crossgates Powys 78 F2
Crossgill Lancs 147 L3
Cross Green Devon 11 M5
Cross Green Leeds 141 M2
Cross Green Staffs 97 K4
Cross Green Suffk 89 G4
Cross Green Suffk 89 H4
Cross Green Suffk 89 K4
Crosshands Carmth 55 L2
Cross Hands Carmth 59 G6
Crosshands E Ayrs 196 F5
Cross Hands Pembks 55 H4
Cross Hill Derbys 116 C2
Crosshill Fife 222 B7
Crosshill S Ayrs 183 J2
Cross Hills N York 149 H6
Crosshouse E Ayrs 196 D3
Cross Houses Shrops 96 C2
Cross Houses Shrops 96 F5
Cross in Hand E Susx 23 J3
Cross Inn Cerdgn 76 G3
Cross Inn Cerdgn 77 G3
Cross Inn Pembks 55 G3
Cross Inn Rhondd 43 G3
Cross Keys Ag & B 208 B2
Crosskeys Caerph 43 K3
Cross Keys Wilts 46 C5
Crosskirk Highld 279 H2
Crosslands W & F 156 E5
Cross Lane IoW 19 H5
Cross Lane Head Shrops 97 G4
Cross Lanes Cnwll 3 H6
Cross Lanes Cnwll 4 C6
Cross Lanes N York 151 H3
Crosslanes Shrops 112 E7
Cross Lanes Wrexhm 112 E2
Crosslee Rens 208 C6
Crossley Kirk 141 K3
Crossmichael D & G 175 J2
Cross Oak Powys 61 G7
Cross of Jackston Abers 256 D5
Cross o' th' hands Derbys 115 M2
Crosspost W Susx 37 L6
Crossroads Abers 244 D2
Crossroads Abers 245 G5
Cross Roads C Brad 149 J8
Cross Street Suffk 106 D8
Crosston Angus 234 E4
Cross Town Ches E 130 E4

Crossway Mons ... 62 F3
Crossway Powys ... 78 E4
Crossway Green Mons ... 63 G8
Crossway Green Worcs ... 81 J2
Crossways Dorset ... 16 E5
Crosswell Pembks ... 75 J5
Crosthwaite W & F ... 156 F4
Croston Lancs ... 138 F4
Crostwick Norfk ... 122 H4
Crostwight Norfk ... 123 G5
Crouch Kent ... 38 F2
Crouch Kent ... 40 D4
Crouch End Gt Lon ... 51 J4
Croucheston Wilts ... 33 J6
Crouch Hill Dorset ... 32 B8
Crough House Green Kent ... 38 C4
Croughton W Nthn ... 84 A8
Crovie Abers ... 268 F3
Crow Hants ... 18 B3
Crowan Cnwll ... 3 G4
Crowborough E Susx ... 38 D7
Crowborough Warren E Susx ... 38 D7
Crowcombe Somset ... 29 L3
Crowdecote Derbys ... 132 B6
Crowden Derbys ... 141 G7
Crowden Devon ... 12 C3
Crowdhill Hants ... 35 G6
Crowdleham Kent ... 52 C7
Crow Edge Barns ... 141 J6
Crowell Oxon ... 67 H7
Crow End Cambs ... 87 G4
Crowfield Suffk ... 90 D4
Crowfield W Nthn ... 84 B7
Crowfield Green Suffk ... 90 D4
Crowgate Street Norfk ... 123 G7
Crow Green Essex ... 70 C4
Crowhill E Loth ... 213 G4
Crow Hill Herefs ... 63 J2
Crowhole Derbys ... 133 G4
Crowhurst E Susx ... 24 D5
Crowhurst Surrey ... 38 B4
Crowhurst Lane End Surrey ... 38 B4
Crowland Lincs ... 102 E2
Crowland Suffk ... 89 K1
Crowlas Cnwll ... 2 D5
Crowle N Linc ... 143 K5
Crowle Worcs ... 81 L4
Crowle Green Worcs ... 81 L4
Crowmarsh Gifford Oxon ... 48 F1
Crown Corner Suffk ... 90 F1
Crownhill C Plym ... 6 F3
Crownpits Surrey ... 36 E2
Crownthorpe Norfk ... 106 B3
Crowntown Cnwll ... 3 G5
Crows-an-Wra Cnwll ... 2 B5
Crow's Green Essex ... 71 G2
Crowshill Norfk ... 105 J2
Crow's Nest Cnwll ... 6 B1
Crowsnest Shrops ... 95 J3
Crowthorne Wokham ... 49 K6
Crowton Ches W ... 130 B5
Croxall Staffs ... 99 G1
Croxby Lincs ... 144 F8
Croxdale Dur ... 169 H3
Croxden Staffs ... 115 H4
Croxley Green Herts ... 68 D7
Croxteth Lpool ... 138 E8
Croxton Cambs ... 86 E3
Croxton N Linc ... 144 E5
Croxton Norfk ... 105 H6
Croxton Norfk ... 121 L5
Croxton Staffs ... 114 B5
Croxtonbank Staffs ... 114 B5
Croxton Green Ches E ... 113 J1
Croxton Kerrial Leics ... 117 L5
Croy Highld ... 252 E2
Croy N Lans ... 209 J4
Croyde Devon ... 27 H3
Croyde Bay Devon ... 27 G3
Croydon Cambs ... 87 G5
Croydon Gt Lon ... 51 J6
Crubenmore Highld ... 241 J5
Cruckmeole Shrops ... 95 K2
Cruckton Shrops ... 95 K1
Cruden Bay Abers ... 257 K4
Crudgington Wrekin ... 113 K7
Crudie Abers ... 268 E5
Crudwell Wilts ... 64 D8
Cruft Devon ... 12 C3
Crûg Powys ... 79 H1
Crugmeer Cnwll ... 10 C7
Crugybar Carmth ... 77 J7
Crug-y-byddar Powys ... 94 E7
Crumlin Caerph ... 43 K2
Crumplehorn Cnwll ... 5 L4
Crumpsall Manch ... 140 C7
Crundale Kent ... 40 E5
Crundale Pembks ... 54 F3
Crunwere Pembks ... 55 L5
Cruwys Morchard Devon ... 28 F8

Crux Easton Hants ... 48 B7
Cruxton Dorset ... 16 B3
Crwbin Carmth ... 58 E6
Cryers Hill Bucks ... 67 L7
Crymych Pembks ... 75 L5
Crynant Neath ... 60 B6
Crystal Palace Gt Lon ... 51 J5
Cuaig Highld ... 260 A8
Cuan Ag & B ... 215 L2
Cubbington Warwks ... 83 H2
Cubert Cnwll ... 4 C3
Cubley Barns ... 141 K7
Cublington Bucks ... 67 K3
Cublington Herefs ... 79 M7
Cuckfield W Susx ... 22 D2
Cucklington Somset ... 32 C5
Cuckney Notts ... 133 L5
Cuckoo Bridge Lincs ... 119 G7
Cuckoo's Corner Hants ... 35 M3
Cuckoo's Nest Ches W ... 129 J7
Cuddesdon Oxon ... 66 F6
Cuddington Bucks ... 67 H3
Cuddington Ches W ... 130 B5
Cuddington Heath Ches W ... 113 G2
Cuddy Hill Lancs ... 147 J8
Cudham Gt Lon ... 51 L7
Cudliptown Devon ... 12 C6
Cudnell BCP ... 17 L3
Cudworth Barns ... 142 B6
Cudworth Somset ... 30 F8
Cuerdley Cross Warrtn ... 130 A2
Cufaude Hants ... 49 G7
Cuffley Herts ... 69 J6
Cuil Highld ... 228 F4
Culbokie Highld ... 263 G7
Culbone Somset ... 28 E1
Culburnie Highld ... 250 E3
Culcabock Highld ... 251 J3
Culcharry Highld ... 253 G2
Culcheth Warrtn ... 130 C1
Culdrain Abers ... 255 L5
Culduie Highld ... 240 A1
Culford Suffk ... 89 G1
Culgaith W & F ... 166 E5
Culham Oxon ... 66 D6
Culkein Highld ... 270 D2
Culkein Drumbeg Highld ... 270 F1
Culkerton Gloucs ... 64 D7
Cullen Moray ... 267 K3
Cullercoats N Tyne ... 181 J4
Cullerlie Abers ... 245 G3
Cullicudden Highld ... 263 H7
Cullingworth C Brad ... 149 J8
Cuillin Hills Highld ... 247 G4
Cullipool Ag & B ... 215 L2
Cullivoe Shet ... 281 e2
Culloden Highld ... 252 D3
Cullompton Devon ... 14 B1
Cullompton Services Devon ... 14 B1
Culm Davy Devon ... 29 L7
Culmington Shrops ... 96 D7
Culmstock Devon ... 29 K8
Culnacraig Highld ... 270 E7
Culnaightrie D & G ... 175 J5
Culnaknock Highld ... 259 J4
Culpho Suffk ... 90 F5
Culrain Highld ... 263 G1
Culross Fife ... 210 C2
Culroy S Ayrs ... 196 C8
Culsalmond Abers ... 256 B5
Culscadden D & G ... 174 D5
Culshabbin D & G ... 173 H4
Culswick Shet ... 281 c6
Cultercullen Abers ... 257 G7
Cults C Aber ... 245 K3
Culverstone Green Kent ... 52 D6
Culverthorpe Lincs ... 118 D3
Culworth W Nthn ... 84 A6
Cumbernauld N Lans ... 209 K4
Cumbernauld Village N Lans ... 209 K4
Cumberworth Lincs ... 137 J5
Cumdivock Cumb ... 165 K1
Cuminestown Abers ... 268 E6
Cumledge Border ... 202 B2
Cummersdale Cumb ... 177 L8
Cummertrees D & G ... 176 F5
Cummingston Moray ... 266 C2
Cumnock E Ayrs ... 197 H7
Cumnor Oxon ... 66 C6
Cumrew Cumb ... 178 D8
Cumrue D & G ... 176 E2
Cumwhinton Cumb ... 178 B8
Cumwhitton Cumb ... 178 C8
Cundall N York ... 150 F1
Cunninghamhead N Ayrs ... 196 D3
Cunningsburgh Shet ... 281 e7
Cupar Fife ... 222 F4
Cupar Muir Fife ... 222 F4
Curbar Derbys ... 132 E5
Curbridge Hants ... 19 J1

Curbridge Oxon ... 65 M5
Curdridge Hants ... 35 H8
Curdworth Warwks ... 98 F5
Curland Somset ... 30 C7
Curridge W Berk ... 48 C4
Currie C Edin ... 211 G5
Curry Mallet Somset ... 30 E6
Curry Rivel Somset ... 30 F6
Curteis Corner Kent ... 39 L5
Curtisden Green Kent ... 39 J5
Curtisknowle Devon ... 7 L4
Cury Cnwll ... 3 H6
Cushnie Abers ... 244 C1
Cushuish Somset ... 30 B5
Cusop Herefs ... 79 J7
Cusworth Donc ... 142 L7
Cutcloy D & G ... 174 C7
Cutcombe Somset ... 29 G3
Cutgate Rochdl ... 140 C5
Cuthill Highld ... 263 K2
Cutiau Gwynd ... 110 B8
Cutler's Green Essex ... 70 F1
Cutmadoc Cnwll ... 5 J2
Cutmere Cnwll ... 6 C3
Cutnall Green Worcs ... 81 K2
Cutsdean Gloucs ... 65 G1
Cutthorpe Derbys ... 133 G5
Cuttivett Cnwll ... 6 D2
Cuxham Oxon ... 67 G8
Cuxton Medway ... 52 F5
Cuxwold Lincs ... 144 F7
Cwm Blae G ... 61 J6
Cwm Denbgs ... 128 C4
Cwmafan Neath ... 57 L6
Cwmaman Rhondd ... 60 F7
Cwmann Carmth ... 77 G6
Cwmavon Torfn ... 62 B6
Cwmbach Carmth ... 56 E4
Cwmbach Carmth ... 75 M7
Cwmbach Powys ... 79 G7
Cwmbach Rhondd ... 60 F6
Cwmbach Llechrhyd Powys ... 78 E4
Cwmbelan Powys ... 93 K7
Cwmbran Torfn ... 62 C8
Cwmbrwyno Cerdgn ... 92 F7
Cwm Capel Carmth ... 56 F4
Cwmcarn Caerph ... 43 K3
Cwmcarvan Mons ... 62 F5
Cwm-celyn Blae G ... 61 K5
Cwm-Cewydd Gwynd ... 93 J1
Cwm-cou Cerdgn ... 76 B6
Cwm Crawnon Powys ... 61 J3
Cwmdare Rhondd ... 60 F6
Cwmdu Carmth ... 59 H3
Cwmdu Powys ... 61 J2
Cwmdu Swans ... 57 H6
Cwmduad Carmth ... 58 C3
Cwm Dulais Swans ... 57 H4
Cwmdwr Carmth ... 59 K2
Cwmfelin Brdgnd ... 42 C4
Cwmfelin Myr Td ... 61 H6
Cwmfelin Boeth Carmth ... 55 L3
Cwmfelinfach Caerph ... 43 J3
Cwmfelin Mynach Carmth ... 75 L7
Cwmffrwd Carmth ... 58 D5
Cwmgiedd Powys ... 59 L6
Cwmgorse Carmth ... 57 K3
Cwm Gwaun Pembks ... 75 H5
Cwmgwili Carmth ... 57 G3
Cwmgwrach Neath ... 60 C6
Cwmhiraeth Carmth ... 76 C7
Cwmifor Carmth ... 59 J4
Cwm Irfon Powys ... 78 A5
Cwmisfael Carmth ... 58 F5
Cwm Llinau Powys ... 93 J2
Cwmllynfell Neath ... 59 K6
Cwmmawr Carmth ... 58 F6
Cwm Morgan Carmth ... 58 B2
Cwmorgan Rhondd ... 42 F3
Cwmpengraig Carmth ... 58 C2
Cwm Penmachno Conwy ... 110 E2
Cwmpennar Rhondd ... 61 G7
Cwmrhos Powys ... 61 J2
Cwmrhydyceirw Swans ... 57 J5
Cwmsychbant Cerdgn ... 76 E6
Cwmtillery Blae G ... 61 K6
Cwm-twrch Isaf Powys ... 57 L3
Cwm-twrch Uchaf Powys ... 59 L6
Cwm-y-glo Carmth ... 59 G6
Cwm-y-glo Gwynd ... 125 K7
Cwmyoy Mons ... 62 C3
Cwmystwyth Cerdgn ... 93 G8
Cwrt Gwynd ... 92 E3
Cwrtnewydd Cerdgn ... 76 E5
Cwrt-y-gollen Powys ... 61 K4
Cyffylliog Denbgs ... 128 C8
Cyfronydd Powys ... 94 E2
Cylibebyll Neath ... 57 K4
Cymau Flints ... 129 G8
Cymmer Neath ... 42 C3

Cymmer Rhondd ... 42 F3
Cyncoed Cardif ... 43 K5
Cynghordy Carmth ... 77 M7
Cynheidre Carmth ... 56 E3
Cynonville Neath ... 42 C3
Cynwyd Denbgs ... 111 K3
Cynwyl Elfed Carmth ... 58 C3

D

Daccombe Devon ... 8 D1
Dacre N York ... 150 B4
Dacre W & F ... 166 B5
Dacre Banks N York ... 150 B3
Daddry Shield Dur ... 167 K3
Dadford Bucks ... 84 C7
Dadlington Leics ... 99 L4
Dafen Carmth ... 56 F4
Daffy Green Norfk ... 105 J2
Dagenham Gt Lon ... 52 B2
Daglingworth Gloucs ... 64 E6
Dagnall Bucks ... 68 C4
Dagworth Suffk ... 89 L3
Dail bho Dheas W Isls ... 282 g1
Dailly S Ayrs ... 183 H3
Dainton Devon ... 8 C2
Dairsie Fife ... 223 G4
Daisy Hill Bolton ... 139 K6
Daisy Hill Leeds ... 141 L2
Dalabrog W Isls ... 283 b11
Dalavich Ag & B ... 216 F5
Dalbeattie D & G ... 175 L3
Dalbury Derbys ... 115 M5
Dalby IoM ... 154 b6
Dalby Lincs ... 137 H5
Dalby N York ... 151 K2
Dalcapon P & K ... 232 E4
Dalcham Highld ... 274 B6
Dalchreichart Highld ... 240 A1
Dalchruin P & K ... 220 C4
Dalcrue P & K ... 221 J2
Dalderby Lincs ... 136 E6
Dalditch Devon ... 14 B6
Dale Pembks ... 54 E5
Dale W & F ... 166 D2
Dale Abbey Derbys ... 116 D4
Dale Bottom Cumb ... 165 J6
Dale End Derbys ... 132 D7
Dale End N York ... 149 G6
Dale Hill E Susx ... 39 H7
Dalehouse N York ... 171 L6
Dalelia Highld ... 237 L6
Dalgarven N Ayrs ... 196 B2
Dalgety Bay Fife ... 211 G2
Dalgig E Ayrs ... 197 G8
Dalginross P & K ... 220 D3
Dalguise P & K ... 232 E6
Dalhalvaig Highld ... 278 F4
Dalham Suffk ... 88 E3
Daliburgh W Isls ... 283 b11
Dalkeith Mdloth ... 211 K5
Dallas Moray ... 266 C5
Dallinghoo Suffk ... 91 G4
Dallington E Susx ... 24 B3
Dallington W Nthn ... 84 E3
Dallow N York ... 150 B3
Dalmally Ag & B ... 217 K2
Dalmary Stirlg ... 219 H8
Dalmellington E Ayrs ... 184 D2
Dalmeny C Edin ... 210 F3
Dalmore Highld ... 263 H6
Dalmuir W Duns ... 208 E5
Dalnabreck Highld ... 237 K6
Dalnacardoch P & K ... 231 K1
Dalnahaitnach Highld ... 252 F7
Dalnaspidal P & K ... 231 J1
Dalnawillan Lodge Highld ... 279 H8
Dalness Highld ... 229 K3
Dalqueich P & K ... 221 K6
Dalquhairn S Ayrs ... 183 J4
Dalreavoch Highld ... 273 H6
Dalry N Ayrs ... 196 B1
Dalrymple E Ayrs ... 196 D8
Dalserf S Lans ... 198 C3
Dalsmeran Ag & B ... 192 D5
Dalston Cumb ... 165 L1
Dalston Gt Lon ... 51 J2
Dalswinton D & G ... 176 B2
Dalton D & G ... 176 D4
Dalton Lancs ... 139 G6
Dalton N York ... 159 K1
Dalton N York ... 160 F7
Dalton Nthumb ... 180 D4
Dalton Rothm ... 133 J1
Dalton W & F ... 157 H7
Dalton-in-Furness W & F ... 156 B7
Dalton-le-Dale Dur ... 169 L1
Dalton Magna Rothm ... 133 J1

Dalton-on-Tees N York	160	D1
Dalton Parva Rothm	133	J1
Dalton Piercy Hartpl	170	B4
Dalveich Stirlg	219	K2
Dalwhinnie Highld	241	H6
Dalwood Devon	14	F3
Damask Green Herts	69	H1
Damerham Hants	33	J7
Damgate Norfk	107	H2
Dam Green Norfk	105	L6
Damnaglaur D & G	172	E7
Danaway Kent	53	J6
Danbury Essex	71	J6
Danby N York	162	C1
Danby Bottom N York	162	B2
Danby Wiske N York	160	E3
Dandaleith Moray	254	F3
Danderhall Mdloth	211	J5
Danebridge Ches E	131	J6
Dane End Herts	69	J3
Danegate E Susx	38	E6
Danehill E Susx	22	F2
Dane Hills C Leic	100	C3
Danemoor Green Norfk	105	L2
Danesford Shrops	97	G5
Danesmoor Derbys	133	H7
Dane Street Kent	40	D5
Daniel's Water Kent	40	C7
Danshillock Abers	268	C5
Danskine E Loth	212	C5
Danthorpe E R Yk	145	H1
Danzey Green Warwks	82	D2
Dapple Heath Staffs	115	G6
Darby Green Hants	49	K7
Darcy Lever Bolton	139	L6
Dardy Powys	61	K3
Darenth Kent	52	C4
Daresbury Halton	130	B3
Darfield Barns	142	C6
Darfoulds Notts	133	L4
Dargate Kent	40	E3
Dargavel Rens	208	D5
Darite Cnwll	6	B1
Darland Medway	53	G6
Darland Wrexhm	129	J8
Darlaston Wsall	98	B4
Darlaston Green Wsall	98	B4
Darley N York	150	B4
Darley Abbey C Derb	116	B4
Darley Bridge Derbys	132	E7
Darley Dale Derbys	132	E7
Darley Green Solhll	98	F8
Darleyhall Herts	68	F3
Darley Head N York	150	B4
Darlingscott Warwks	82	F6
Darlington Darltn	169	H7
Darliston Shrops	113	J5
Darlton Notts	134	F5
Darnford Staffs	98	E2
Darnick Border	201	H6
Darowen Powys	93	H3
Darra Abers	268	D6
Darracott Devon	26	D7
Darracott Devon	27	H3
Darras Hall Nthumb	180	E5
Darrington Wakefd	142	D4
Darsham Suffk	91	K1
Darshill Somset	31	K2
Dartford Kent	52	B4
Dartford Crossing Kent	52	C4
Dartington Devon	8	B2
Dartmeet Devon	12	F7
Dartmoor National Park Devon	13	G6
Dartmouth Devon	8	C4
Darton Barns	141	M5
Darvel E Ayrs	197	H3
Darwell Hole E Susx	24	C3
Darwen Bl w D	139	K3
Datchet W & M	50	C3
Datchworth Herts	69	H3
Datchworth Green Herts	69	H3
Daubhill Bolton	139	L6
Daugh of Kinermony Moray	254	F6
Dauntsey Wilts	46	E3
Dava Highld	253	J4
Davenham Ches W	130	C5
Davenport Stockp	131	H2
Davenport Green Ches E	131	G4
Davenport Green Traffd	130	F2
Daventry W Nthn	84	B3
Davidson's Mains C Edin	211	H4
Davidstow Cnwll	11	G5
David Street Kent	52	E6
Davington D & G	187	K5
Davington Kent	40	D3
Daviot Abers	256	D6
Daviot Highld	252	D4
Daviot House Highld	252	D4
Davis's Town E Susx	23	J4
Davoch of Grange Moray	267	K6
Davyhulme Traffd	139	M8
Daw End Wsall	98	C3
Dawesgreen Surrey	37	K2
Dawley Wrekin	96	F2
Dawlish Devon	13	M7
Dawlish Warren Devon	13	M7
Dawn Conwy	127	G5
Daws Green Somset	30	B6
Daws Heath Essex	53	H1
Daw's House Cnwll	11	K6
Dawsmere Lincs	120	A5
Daybrook Notts	116	F3
Day Green Ches E	130	F8
Dayhills Staffs	114	F5
Dayhouse Bank Worcs	98	B7
Daylesford Gloucs	65	K2
Ddol Flints	128	D5
Ddol-Cownwy Powys	111	K8
Deal Kent	41	L5
Dean Cumb	164	E5
Dean Devon	7	L2
Dean Devon	27	L2
Dean Devon	28	C1
Dean Dorset	33	G7
Dean Hants	34	F4
Dean Hants	35	H7
Dean Lancs	140	C3
Dean Oxon	65	M3
Dean Somset	31	L2
Dean Bottom Kent	52	C5
Deanburnhaugh Border	188	C4
Deancombe Devon	7	L2
Dean Court Oxon	66	C6
Deane Bolton	139	K6
Deane Hants	35	H1
Dean End Dorset	33	G7
Dean Head Barns	141	L7
Deanhead Kirk	141	G4
Deanland Dorset	33	G7
Deanlane End W Susx	20	B4
Dean Prior Devon	7	L2
Deanraw Nthumb	179	J6
Dean Row Ches E	131	G3
Deans W Loth	210	D5
Deanscales Cumb	164	E5
Deanshanger W Nthn	84	E7
Deanshaugh Moray	267	G6
Deanston Stirlg	220	C6
Dean Street Kent	39	J3
Dearham Cumb	164	E3
Dearnley Rochdl	140	D4
Debach Suffk	90	F4
Debden Essex	70	C7
Debden Essex	87	L8
Debden Green Essex	70	E1
Debenham Suffk	90	E3
Deblin's Green Worcs	81	J5
Dechmont W Loth	210	D5
Deddington Oxon	66	C1
Dedham Essex	90	C8
Dedham Heath Essex	72	F1
Dedworth W & M	50	B4
Deene N Nthn	101	L5
Deenethorpe N Nthn	101	L5
Deepcar Sheff	141	L8
Deepcut Surrey	49	L7
Deepdale N York	158	F6
Deepdale W & F	158	C5
Deeping Gate C Pete	102	C2
Deeping St James Lincs	102	D2
Deeping St Nicholas Lincs	119	H8
Deerhurst Gloucs	64	C1
Deerhurst Walton Gloucs	64	C2
Deerton Street Kent	40	C3
Deeside Industrial Park Flints	129	G5
Defford Worcs	81	L6
Defynnog Powys	60	D2
Deganwy Conwy	126	F4
Degnish Ag & B	216	B5
Deighton C York	151	K7
Deighton N York	160	E2
Deiniolen Gwynd	125	K7
Delabole Cnwll	10	F6
Delamere Ches W	130	A6
Delamere Park Ches W	130	B5
Delfrigs Abers	257	H7
Delley Devon	27	K6
Delliefure Highld	253	L5
Dell Quay W Susx	20	D6
Delly End Oxon	65	M4
Delnabo Moray	254	C8
Delny Highld	263	K5
Delph Oldham	140	E6
Delves Dur	168	E1
Delvin End Essex	88	F8
Dembleby Lincs	118	D4
Demelza Cnwll	5	G2
Denaby Donc	142	D7
Denaby Main Donc	142	D7
Denbies Surrey	37	H1
Denbigh Denbgs	128	C6
Denbrae Fife	222	F3
Denbury Devon	8	B1
Denby Derbys	116	C2
Denby Bottles Derbys	116	C2
Denby Dale Kirk	141	K6
Denchworth Oxon	48	A1
Dendron W & F	146	D2
Denel End C Beds	85	K8
Denfield P & K	221	G4
Denford N Nthn	101	L8
Dengie Essex	72	E6
Denham Bucks	50	D2
Denham Suffk	88	E3
Denham Suffk	106	D8
Denham End Suffk	88	F3
Denham Green Bucks	50	D1
Denham Green Suffk	106	D8
Denhead Abers	269	J5
Denhead Fife	223	H4
Denhead of Gray C Dund	222	F1
Denholm Border	189	G3
Denholme C Brad	141	G1
Denholme Clough C Brad	141	G1
Denio Gwynd	108	F4
Denmead Hants	19	L1
Denmore C Aber	245	L1
Denne Park W Susx	37	J5
Dennington Suffk	91	G2
Denny Falk	209	L3
Dennyloanhead Falk	209	L3
Den of Lindores Fife	222	D4
Denshaw Oldham	140	E5
Denside of Durris Abers	245	H4
Densole Kent	41	G7
Denston Suffk	88	F5
Denstone Staffs	115	H3
Denstroude Kent	40	E3
Dent W & F	158	B5
Denton Cambs	102	C6
Denton Darltn	169	G7
Denton E Susx	23	G6
Denton Kent	41	G6
Denton Kent	52	E4
Denton Lincs	117	M5
Denton N York	149	L6
Denton Norfk	106	F5
Denton Oxon	66	C6
Denton Tamesd	131	H1
Denton W Nthn	85	G4
Denver Norfk	104	C3
Denwick Nthumb	191	J3
Deopham Norfk	105	L3
Deopham Green Norfk	105	L4
Depden Suffk	88	F4
Depden Green Suffk	88	F4
Deptford Gt Lon	51	K3
Deptford Wilts	33	H3
Derby C Derb	116	B4
Derby Devon	27	K4
Derbyhaven IoM	154	c8
Derculich P & K	232	C5
Dereham Norfk	105	K1
Deri Caerph	61	H6
Derril Devon	11	K2
Derringstone Kent	41	G5
Derrington Staffs	114	D7
Derriton Devon	11	L2
Derry Hill Wilts	46	D5
Derrythorpe N Linc	143	L6
Dersingham Norfk	120	F5
Dervaig Ag & B	226	E2
Derwen Denbgs	111	L2
Derwenlas Powys	92	F4
Derwent Valley Mills Derbys	132	F8
Derwent Water Cumb	165	J6
Derwydd Carmth	59	H5
Desborough N Nthn	101	H6
Desford Leics	100	B3
Detchant Nthumb	203	H6
Detling Kent	53	G7
Deuxhill Shrops	96	F6
Devauden Mons	62	F7
Devil's Bridge Cerdgn	92	F8
Devitts Green Warwks	99	H5
Devizes Wilts	46	E6
Devonport C Plym	6	E4
Devonside Clacks	221	G7
Devoran Cnwll	3	K3
Devoran & Perran Cnwll	3	K3
Dewarton Mdloth	211	L6
Dewlish Dorset	16	E3
Dewsbury Kirk	141	K3
Dewsbury Moor Kirk	141	K3
Deytheur Powys	112	C8
Dial N Som	45	G5
Dial Green W Susx	36	D5
Dial Post W Susx	21	K3
Dibberford Dorset	15	K2
Dibden Hants	18	F2
Dibden Purlieu Hants	18	F2
Dickens Heath Solhll	98	E8
Dickleburgh Norfk	106	D7
Didbrook Gloucs	64	F1
Didcot Oxon	48	D1
Diddington Cambs	86	D2
Diddlebury Shrops	96	C6
Didley Herefs	62	F1
Didling W Susx	20	D3
Didmarton Gloucs	46	B2
Didsbury Manch	131	G1
Didworthy Devon	7	K2
Digby Lincs	135	M8
Digg Highld	259	H3
Diggle Oldham	140	F6
Digmoor Lancs	139	G6
Digswell Herts	69	H4
Digswell Water Herts	69	H4
Dihewyd Cerdgn	76	E4
Dilham Norfk	123	G6
Dilhorne Staffs	114	F3
Dill Hall Lancs	139	M2
Dillington Cambs	86	C2
Dilston Nthumb	180	A6
Dilton Wilts	32	E1
Dilton Marsh Wilts	32	D1
Dilwyn Herefs	80	A4
Dimple Bolton	139	L4
Dimple Derbys	132	F7
Dinas Carmth	58	A3
Dinas Cnwll	10	C7
Dinas Gwynd	108	D4
Dinas Gwynd	125	H7
Dinas Rhondd	42	F3
Dinas Cross Pembks	75	G4
Dinas Dinlle Gwynd	125	H8
Dinas-Mawddwy Gwynd	111	G8
Dinas Powys V Glam	43	J7
Dinder Somset	31	J2
Dinedor Herefs	80	C7
Dingestow Mons	62	F5
Dingle Lpool	129	J2
Dingleden Kent	39	K7
Dingley N Nthn	101	G6
Dingwall Highld	262	F8
Dinmael Conwy	111	J3
Dinnet Abers	244	A4
Dinnington N u Ty	180	F4
Dinnington Rothm	133	K3
Dinnington Somset	30	F8
Dinorwig Gwynd	125	L7
Dinorwig Slate Landscape Gwynd	125	L7
Dinton Bucks	67	J5
Dinton Wilts	33	H4
Dinwoodie D & G	187	H8
Dinworthy Devon	26	E7
Dipford Somset	30	B6
Dipley Hants	49	H7
Dippen Ag & B	194	B3
Dippenhall Surrey	36	B2
Dippermill Devon	12	B1
Dippertown Devon	12	B5
Dippin N Ayrs	195	G6
Dipple Moray	267	G4
Dipple S Ayrs	182	F2
Diptford Devon	7	L3
Dipton Dur	180	E8
Diptonmill Nthumb	179	L6
Dirleton E Loth	212	B2
Dirt Pot Nthumb	167	K2
Discoed Powys	79	K2
Diseworth Leics	116	D6
Dishforth N York	160	E8
Disley Ches E	131	J3
Diss Norfk	106	C7
Disserth Powys	78	E4
Distington Cumb	164	D6
Ditchampton Wilts	33	J4
Ditcheat Somset	31	K4
Ditchingham Norfk	107	G5
Ditchling E Susx	22	E4
Ditherington Shrops	113	H8
Ditteridge Wilts	46	B5
Dittisham Devon	8	C4
Ditton Kent	52	F7
Ditton Green Cambs	88	C4
Ditton Priors Shrops	96	E5
Dixton Gloucs	64	E1
Dixton Mons	63	G4
Dizzard Cnwll	11	H3
Dobcross Oldham	140	F6
Dobwalls Cnwll	5	L2
Doccombe Devon	13	H6
Dochgarroch Highld	251	H3
Dockenfield Surrey	36	B3
Docker Lancs	157	J7
Docking Norfk	121	G4
Docklow Herefs	80	D4
Dockray Cumb	165	J1

Dockray W & F....165 L6
Dodbrooke Devon....7 L6
Doddinghurst Essex....70 E7
Doddington Cambs....103 H5
Doddington Kent....40 B4
Doddington Lincs....135 H5
Doddington Nthumb....202 F6
Doddington Shrops....96 E8
Doddiscombsleigh Devon....13 K5
Dodd's Green Ches E....113 K3
Doddshill Norfk....120 F5
Doddy Cross Cnwll....6 C2
Dodford W Nthn....84 B3
Dodford Worcs....97 L8
Dodington S Glos....45 L3
Dodington Somset....30 A3
Dodleston Ches W....129 J7
Dodscott Devon....27 K7
Dodside E Rens....200 C0
Dod's Leigh Staffs....115 G1
Dodworth Barns....141 M6
Dodworth Bottom Barns....141 M7
Dodworth Green Barns....141 M6
Doe Bank Birm....98 E4
Doe Lea Derbys....133 J6
Dogdyke Lincs....136 D8
Dogley Lane Kirk....141 J5
Dogmersfield Hants....49 J8
Dogridge Wilts....47 G2
Dogsthorpe C Pete....102 D3
Dog Village Devon....14 A3
Dolanog Powys....94 C1
Dolau Powys....79 G2
Dolaucothi Carmth....77 J7
Dolbenmaen Gwynd....109 J3
Doley Staffs....114 A5
Dolfach Powys....93 K3
Dol-fôr Powys....93 H2
Dolfor Powys....94 D6
Dolgarrog Conwy....126 E6
Dolgellau Gwynd....110 D7
Dolgoch Gwynd....92 E3
Dol-gran Carmth....58 D2
Doll Highld....273 L7
Dollar Clacks....221 G7
Dollarfield Clacks....221 G7
Dolley Green Powys....79 K2
Dollwen Cerdgn....92 E7
Dolphin Flints....128 E5
Dolphinholme Lancs....147 K5
Dolphinton S Lans....199 J4
Dolton Devon....27 K8
Dolwen Conwy....127 H5
Dolwyddelan Conwy....110 D1
Dolybont Cerdgn....92 D5
Dolyhir Powys....79 J4
Domgay Powys....112 D7
Donaldson's Lodge Nthumb....202 D5
Doncaster Donc....142 F7
Doncaster Docn Donc....142 F7
Doncaster North Services Donc....143 G5
Donhead St Andrew Wilts....32 F6
Donhead St Mary Wilts....32 F6
Donibristle Fife....211 J4
Doniford Somset....29 K2
Donington Lincs....119 H4
Donington on Bain Lincs....136 D3
Donington Park Services Leics....116 D6
Donington Southing Lincs....119 G5
Donisthorpe Leics....99 J1
Donkey Street Kent....25 L1
Donkey Town Surrey....50 B6
Donnington Gloucs....65 J2
Donnington Herefs....81 G8
Donnington Shrops....96 D2
Donnington W Berk....48 C5
Donnington W Susx....20 D6
Donnington Wrekin....113 M8
Donnington Wood Wrekin....97 G1
Donyatt Somset....30 E8
Doomsday Green W Susx....37 J5
Doonfoot S Ayrs....196 C7
Dora's Green Hants....36 B1
Dorback Lodge Highld....253 L8
Dorchester Dorset....16 D4
Dorchester-on-Thames Oxon....66 C7
Dordon Warwks....99 H3
Dore Sheff....132 F3
Dores Highld....251 G5
Dorking Surrey....37 J1
Dorking Tye Suffk....89 J7
Dormansland Surrey....38 B5
Dormans Park Surrey....38 B5
Dormington Herefs....80 D7
Dormston Worcs....82 A4
Dorn Gloucs....82 F8
Dorney Bucks....50 B3
Dorney Reach Bucks....50 A3

Dornie Highld....248 D6
Dornoch Highld....264 B2
Dornock D & G....177 H5
Dorrery Highld....279 J5
Dorridge Solhll....98 F8
Dorrington Lincs....118 E1
Dorrington Shrops....96 B3
Dorrington Shrops....114 A3
Dorsington Warwks....82 D5
Dorstone Herefs....79 K7
Dorton Bucks....67 G4
Dosthill Staffs....99 G3
Dothan IoA....124 F5
Dottery Dorset....15 K4
Doublebois Cnwll....5 L2
Doughton Gloucs....46 C1
Douglas IoM....154 e6
Douglas S Lans....198 D7
Douglas and Angus C Dund....234 C8
Douglas Pier Ag & B....217 K7
Douglastown Angus....234 B6
Douglas Water S Lans....198 E8
Douglas West S Lans....198 D7
Doulting Somset....31 L2
Dounby Ork....275 b4
Doune Highld....272 B7
Doune Stirlg....220 C6
Dounepark S Ayrs....182 F3
Dounie Highld....263 G2
Dousland Devon....7 G1
Dovaston Shrops....112 E7
Dove Dale Derbys....115 J1
Dove Green Notts....116 D1
Dove Holes Derbys....131 L4
Dovenby Cumb....164 E4
Dover Kent....41 K7
Dover Wigan....139 J7
Dovercourt Essex....73 K1
Doverdale Worcs....81 K2
Doveridge Derbys....115 J5
Doversgreen Surrey....37 L1
Dowally P & K....232 F5
Dowbridge Lancs....138 E2
Dowdeswell Gloucs....64 E3
Dowlais Myr Td....60 G4
Dowland Devon....12 D1
Dowlish Ford Somset....30 E8
Dowlish Wake Somset....30 E8
Down Ampney Gloucs....65 G7
Downderry Cnwll....6 C4
Downe Gt Lon....51 L6
Downend Gloucs....64 B7
Downend IoW....19 J6
Downend S Glos....45 K3
Downend W Berk....48 C4
Downfield C Dund....234 B8
Downgate Cnwll....11 K8
Downgate Cnwll....11 L8
Downham Essex....71 H7
Downham Gt Lon....51 K4
Downham Lancs....148 D7
Downham Market Norfk....104 C3
Down Hatherley Gloucs....64 C3
Downhead Somset....31 J6
Downhead Somset....32 A2
Downhill Cnwll....4 D1
Downhill P & K....221 K1
Downholland Cross Lancs....138 D6
Downholme N York....159 K3
Downicarey Devon....11 M4
Downies Abers....245 K4
Downing Flints....128 D4
Downley Bucks....67 K8
Down St Mary Devon....13 H2
Downside Somset....31 K2
Downside Somset....31 L1
Downside Surrey....50 E7
Down Thomas Devon....6 F5
Downton Hants....18 D5
Downton Wilts....33 L6
Dowsby Lincs....118 F5
Dowsdale Lincs....102 F2
Doxey Staffs....114 D6
Doxford Nthumb....191 H2
Doynton S Glos....45 L4
Draethen Caerph....43 K4
Draffan S Lans....198 C4
Dragonby N Linc....143 M5
Dragons Green W Susx....37 H6
Drakeholes Notts....134 D2
Drakelow Worcs....97 J7
Drakemyre N Ayrs....196 B1
Drakes Broughton Worcs....81 L5
Drakewalls Cnwll....12 B8
Draughton N York....149 J5
Draughton W Nthn....101 Q0
Drax N York....143 H3
Drax Hales N York....143 H3
Draycote Warwks....83 K1
Draycot Foliat Swindn....47 J3

Draycott Derbys....116 D5
Draycott Gloucs....82 E8
Draycott Shrops....97 H5
Draycott Somset....31 G1
Draycott Somset....31 J6
Draycott Worcs....81 K5
Draycott in the Clay Staffs....115 J6
Draycott in the Moors Staffs....114 F3
Drayford Devon....28 D8
Drayton C Port....19 L3
Drayton Leics....101 H5
Drayton Lincs....119 H4
Drayton Norfk....106 D1
Drayton Oxon....66 C8
Drayton Oxon....83 K7
Drayton Somset....30 F6
Drayton Somset....31 J7
Drayton Worcs....97 K0
Drayton Bassett Staffs....99 G3
Drayton Beauchamp Bucks....67 L5
Drayton Parslow Bucks....67 K0
Drayton St Leonard Oxon....66 F7
Drebley N York....149 J4
Dreemskerry IoM....154 g4
Dreen Hill Pembks....54 F4
Drefach Carmth....58 F6
Drefach Carmth....76 C7
Drefach Cerdgn....76 F6
Drefelin Carmth....76 C7
Dreghorn N Ayrs....196 C3
Drellingore Kent....41 H7
Drem E Loth....212 B3
Dresden C Stke....114 E3
Drewsteignton Devon....13 H4
Driby Lincs....137 G5
Driffield E R Yk....152 F4
Driffield Gloucs....65 G2
Driffield Cross Roads Gloucs....64 F7
Drift Cnwll....2 C5
Drigg Cumb....155 K3
Drighlington Leeds....141 K2
Drimnin Highld....227 G2
Drimpton Dorset....15 K2
Drimsallie Highld....238 F7
Drinkstone Suffk....89 J3
Drinkstone Green Suffk....89 J3
Drive End Dorset....16 B1
Driver's End Herts....69 G3
Drointon Staffs....115 G6
Droitwich Spa Worcs....81 K3
Dron P & K....221 L4
Dronfield Derbys....133 G4
Dronfield Woodhouse Derbys....133 G4
Drongan E Ayrs....196 E7
Dronley Angus....234 A8
Droop Dorset....16 E1
Dropping Well Rothm....133 H1
Droxford Hants....35 J7
Droylsden Tamesd....140 D8
Druid Derbys....111 K3
Druidston Pembks....54 C3
Druimarbin Highld....229 H1
Druimavuic Ag & B....229 G6
Druimdrishaig Ag & B....206 A5
Druimindarroch Highld....237 K4
Drum Ag & B....206 E4
Drum P & K....221 J7
Drumalbin S Lans....198 F5
Drumbeg Highld....270 F2
Drumblade Abers....255 M4
Drumbreddon D & G....172 D6
Drumbuie Highld....248 B5
Drumburgh Cumb....177 J7
Drumburn D & G....175 L4
Drumburn D & G....176 C6
Drumchapel C Glas....208 E5
Drumchastle P & K....231 J4
Drumclog S Lans....197 J3
Drumeldrie Fife....223 G6
Drumelzier Border....199 K6
Drumfearn Highld....247 L5
Drumfrennie Abers....244 F4
Drumgley Angus....234 C2
Drumguish Highld....241 L4
Drumin Moray....254 D5
Drumjohn D & G....184 E3
Drumlamford S Ayrs....183 H7
Drumlasie Abers....244 E2
Drumleaning Cumb....177 J8
Drumlemble Ag & B....192 D4
Drumlithie Abers....245 H7
Drummoddie D & G....173 K6
Drummore D & G....172 E7
Drummuir Moray....255 M4
Drumnadrochit Highld....250 E5
Drumnagorrach Moray....267 L5
Drumoak Abers....245 H4
Drumpark D & G....185 L7
Drumrunie Highld....271 G7

Drumshang S Ayrs....195 L8
Drumuie Highld....259 G7
Drumuillie Highld....253 H7
Drumvaich Stirlg....220 B6
Drunzie P & K....221 L5
Druridge Nthumb....191 K7
Drury Flints....129 G6
Drws-y-coed Gwynd....109 K1
Drybeck W & F....166 F7
Drybridge Moray....267 J4
Drybridge N Ayrs....196 D4
Drybrook Gloucs....63 J4
Dryburgh Border....201 J4
Dry Doddington Lincs....117 M2
Dry Drayton Cambs....87 H3
Dryhill Kent....38 D2
Drymen Stirlg....208 E1
Drymuir Abers....257 G3
Drynoch Highld....246 F2
Dry Sandford Oxon....66 C7
Dryslwyn Carmth....59 G5
Dry Street Essex....52 D0
Dryton Shrops....96 D2
Dubford Abers....268 E3
Dublin Suffk....90 E1
Duchally Highld....271 L4
Duck End Bed....85 L6
Duck End Cambs....86 E2
Duck End Essex....71 G2
Duck End Essex....88 D8
Duckend Green Essex....71 H3
Duckington Ches W....113 H1
Ducklington Oxon....65 M5
Duck's Cross Bed....86 C4
Duddenhoe End Essex....87 J7
Duddingston C Edin....211 J4
Duddington Nthumb....101 L3
Duddlestone Somset....30 C6
Duddleswell E Susx....38 C7
Duddlewick Shrops....96 F6
Duddo Nthumb....202 E4
Duddon Ches W....129 L6
Duddon Bridge Cumb....156 B5
Duddon Common Ches W....129 M6
Dudleston Shrops....112 E4
Dudleston Heath Shrops....112 F4
Dudley Dudley....97 L5
Dudley N Tyne....181 G4
Dudley Hill C Brad....141 J2
Dudley Port Sandw....98 B5
Dudnill Shrops....96 E8
Dudsbury Dorset....17 L3
Dudswell Herts....68 B5
Duffield Derbys....116 B3
Duffryn Neath....42 C3
Dufftown Moray....255 G5
Duffus Moray....266 D3
Dufton W & F....166 F5
Duggleby N York....152 D2
Duirinish Highld....248 C5
Duisdalemore Highld....247 L6
Duisky Highld....239 G8
Dukestown Blae G....61 J5
Duke Street Suffk....90 C6
Dukinfield Tamesd....140 H2
Dulas IoA....125 H2
Dulcote Somset....31 J2
Dulford Devon....14 C2
Dull P & K....232 B5
Dullatur N Lans....209 K4
Dullingham Cambs....88 C4
Dullingham Ley Cambs....88 C4
Dulnain Bridge Highld....253 J6
Duloe Bed....86 D3
Duloe Cnwll....5 M3
Dulsie Bridge Highld....253 H3
Dulverton Somset....29 G5
Dulwich Gt Lon....51 J4
Dumbarton W Duns....208 C4
Dumbleton Gloucs....82 B8
Dumfries D & G....176 C4
Dumgoyne Stirlg....208 E2
Dummer Hants....35 J2
Dumpton Kent....41 L2
Dun Angus....235 G3
Dunalastair P & K....231 K4
Dunan Highld....247 J3
Dunan P & K....230 E4
Dunaverty Ag & B....192 E6
Dunball Somset....30 D3
Dunbar E Loth....212 E3
Dunbeath Highld....275 G2
Dunbeg Ag & B....228 D8
Dunblane Stirlg....220 D7
Dunbog Fife....222 D4
Dunbridge Hants....34 D5
Duncanston Highld....263 G0
Duncanstone Abers....255 L6
Dunchideock Devon....13 K5
Dunchurch Warwks....83 L1

Duncote W Nthn....84 C5
Duncow D & G....176 C2
Duncrievie P & K....221 L5
Duncton W Susx....20 F3
Dundee C Dund....223 G1
Dundee Airport C Dund....222 F2
Dundon Somset....31 G4
Dundonald S Ayrs....196 D4
Dundonnell Highld....261 J2
Dundraw Cumb....165 H1
Dundreggan Highld....240 B1
Dundrennan D & G....175 J5
Dundry N Som....45 H5
Dunecht Abers....245 G2
Dunfermline Fife....210 E2
Dunfield Gloucs....65 H7
Dunford Bridge Barns....141 J4
Dungate Kent....40 B3
Dungavel S Lans....197 J3
Dunge Wilts....46 C8
Dungeness Kent....25 L4
Dungworth Sheff....132 E2
Dunham-on-the-Hill Ches W....129 L5
Dunham-on-Trent Notts....135 G5
Dunhampstead Worcs....81 L3
Dunhampton Worcs....81 J2
Dunham Town Traffd....130 E2
Dunham Woodhouses Traffd....130 E2
Dunholme Lincs....135 L4
Dunino Fife....223 J5
Dunipace Falk....209 L2
Dunkeld P & K....232 F6
Dunkerton BaNES....45 L7
Dunkeswell Devon....14 D1
Dunkeswick N York....150 D6
Dunkirk Ches W....129 J5
Dunkirk Kent....40 E3
Dunkirk S Glos....46 A2
Dunkirk Wilts....46 E6
Dunk's Green Kent....38 F3
Dunlappie Angus....234 F2
Dunley Hants....48 C8
Dunley Worcs....81 H2
Dunlop E Ayrs....196 E1
Dunmaglass Highld....251 G7
Dunmere Cnwll....5 H1
Dunmore Falk....210 A1
Dunnet Highld....280 B2
Dunnichen Angus....234 D5
Dunning P & K....221 J4
Dunnington C York....151 L5
Dunnington E R Yk....153 J5
Dunnington Warwks....82 C4
Dunnockshaw Lancs....140 B2
Dunn Street Kent....53 G6
Dunoon Ag & B....207 K4
Dunphail Moray....253 J2
Dunragit D & G....172 E3
Duns Border....202 B2
Dunsa Derbys....132 E5
Dunsby Lincs....118 E6
Dunscar Bolton....139 L5
Dunscore D & G....185 L6
Dunscroft Donc....143 G6
Dunsdale R & Cl....170 E6
Dunsden Green Oxon....49 H3
Dunsdon Devon....11 K1
Dunsfold Surrey....36 F4
Dunsford Devon....13 J5
Dunshalt Fife....222 D5
Dunshillock Abers....269 H6
Dunsill Notts....133 J7
Dunsley N York....171 K8
Dunsley Staffs....97 J6
Dunsmore Bucks....67 L6
Dunsop Bridge Lancs....148 B6
Dunstable C Beds....68 C3
Dunstall Staffs....115 K7
Dunstall Common Worcs....81 K6
Dunstall Green Suffk....88 E3
Dunstan Nthumb....191 K2
Dunstan Steads Nthumb....191 J2
Dunster Somset....29 H2
Duns Tew Oxon....66 C2
Dunston Gatesd....180 F6
Dunston Lincs....135 L7
Dunston Norfk....106 E3
Dunston Staffs....114 E8
Dunstone Devon....7 H4
Dunstone Devon....13 G7
Dunston Heath Staffs....114 E8
Dunsville Donc....143 G6
Dunswell E R Yk....144 D1
Dunsyre S Lans....199 J3
Dunterton Devon....11 M6
Dunthrop Oxon....65 M2
Duntisbourne Abbots Gloucs....64 E5
Duntisbourne Leer Gloucs....64 E5
Duntisbourne Rouse Gloucs....64 E6
Duntish Dorset....16 D2

Duntocher W Duns....208 E4
Dunton Bucks....67 K2
Dunton C Beds....86 E6
Dunton Norfk....121 J5
Dunton Bassett Leics....100 C5
Dunton Green Kent....38 D2
Dunton Wayletts Essex....52 E1
Duntulm Highld....259 G2
Dunure S Ayrs....195 L7
Dunvant Swans....57 G6
Dunvegan Highld....258 C7
Dunwich Suffk....91 L1
Dunwood Staffs....131 J8
Durdar Cumb....177 L8
Durgan Cnwll....3 K5
Durgates E Susx....39 G7
Durham Dur....169 H2
Durham Cathedral Dur....169 H2
Durham Services Dur....169 J3
Durisdeer D & G....186 C5
Durisdeermill D & G....186 C5
Durkar Wakefd....141 M4
Durleigh Somset....30 C4
Durley Hants....35 G7
Durley Wilts....47 K6
Durley Street Hants....35 H7
Durlock Kent....41 J2
Durlock Kent....41 J4
Durlow Common Herefs....80 E7
Durn Rochdl....140 E4
Durness Highld....276 F3
Durno Abers....256 C6
Duror Highld....228 F4
Durran Ag & B....216 F5
Durrington W Susx....21 J6
Durrington Wilts....33 K2
Dursley Gloucs....63 M7
Dursley Cross Gloucs....63 K3
Durston Somset....30 D5
Durweston Dorset....17 G1
Duston W Nthn....84 D3
Duthil Highld....253 H6
Dutlas Powys....94 F7
Duton Hill Essex....70 F2
Dutson Cnwll....11 L5
Dutton Ches W....130 B4
Duxford Cambs....87 K6
Duxford Oxon....66 A7
Dwygyfylchi Conwy....126 E4
Dwyran IoA....125 H6
Dyce C Aber....245 K1
Dyer's End Essex....88 E7
Dyfatty Carmth....56 E5
Dyffrydan Gwynd....110 D8
Dyffryn Brdgnd....42 C3
Dyffryn Myr Td....61 G6
Dyffryn V Glam....43 H7
Dyffryn Ardudwy Gwynd....109 K7
Dyffryn Castell Cerdgn....93 G7
Dyffryn Cellwen Neath....60 C5
Dyke Lincs....118 E7
Dyke Moray....264 F8
Dykehead Angus....233 K4
Dykehead Angus....234 B3
Dykehead N Lans....210 A7
Dykehead Stirlg....219 K7
Dykelands Abers....235 H2
Dykends Angus....233 K4
Dykeside Abers....256 C3
Dykes of Gray C Dund....222 F1
Dylife Powys....93 J4
Dymchurch Kent....25 L1
Dymock Gloucs....63 K1
Dyrham S Glos....45 L4
Dysart Fife....222 E8
Dyserth Denbgs....128 C4

E

Eachway Worcs....98 C8
Eachwick Nthumb....180 D4
Eagland Hill Lancs....147 H6
Eagle Lincs....135 H6
Eagle Barnsdale Lincs....135 H6
Eagle Moor Lincs....135 H6
Eaglescliffe S on T....169 L7
Eaglesfield Cumb....164 E5
Eaglesfield D & G....177 H4
Eaglesham E Rens....208 F8
Eagley Bolton....139 L5
Eairy IoM....154 d6
Eakring Notts....134 D7
Ealand N Linc....143 K5
Ealing Gt Lon....50 F3
Eals Nthumb....178 F7
Eamont Bridge W & F....166 C5
Earby Lancs....148 F6
Earcroft Bl w D....139 K3

Eardington Shrops....97 G5
Eardisland Herefs....80 A4
Eardisley Herefs....79 K5
Eardiston Shrops....112 E6
Eardiston Worcs....80 F2
Earith Cambs....103 H8
Earle Nthumb....202 F7
Earlestown St Hel....130 B1
Earley Wokham....49 H4
Earlham Norfk....106 D2
Earlish Highld....258 F4
Earls Barton N Nthn....85 G3
Earls Colne Essex....71 L1
Earls Common Worcs....81 M3
Earl's Croome Worcs....81 K6
Earlsditton Shrops....96 E8
Earlsdon Covtry....99 J7
Earl's Down E Susx....23 L3
Earlsferry Fife....223 H7
Earlsfield Gt Lon....51 H4
Earlsford Abers....256 E5
Earl's Green Suffk....90 B2
Earlsheaton Kirk....141 L3
Earl Shilton Leics....100 A4
Earl Soham Suffk....90 F3
Earl Sterndale Derbys....132 B6
Earlston Border....201 J5
Earlston E Ayrs....196 D4
Earl Stonham Suffk....90 D3
Earlswood Surrey....37 L1
Earlswood Warwks....98 E8
Earlswood Common Mons....62 F8
Earnley W Susx....20 D7
Earnshaw Bridge Lancs....139 G3
Earsdon N Tyne....181 H4
Earsdon Nthumb....191 J7
Earsham Norfk....107 G5
Earswick C York....151 K4
Eartham W Susx....20 F5
Earthcott S Glos....45 K2
Easby N York....161 J1
Easdale Ag & B....215 L1
Easebourne W Susx....36 D6
Easenhall Warwks....100 A7
Eashing Surrey....36 E2
Easington Bucks....67 G5
Easington Dur....169 L2
Easington E R Yk....145 K4
Easington Nthumb....203 J6
Easington Oxon....67 G7
Easington R & Cl....171 H7
Easington Colliery Dur....169 L2
Easington Lane Sundld....169 K2
Easingwold N York....151 H2
Easole Street Kent....41 H5
Eassie and Nevay Angus....233 M6
East Aberthaw V Glam....42 F8
East Allington Devon....7 M5
East Anstey Devon....28 F5
East Anton Hants....34 E1
East Appleton N York....160 C3
East Ardsley Leeds....141 M3
East Ashey IoW....19 K6
East Ashling W Susx....20 D5
East Aston Hants....34 F2
East Ayton N York....163 H5
East Balsdon Cnwll....11 K3
East Bank Blae G....61 K6
East Barkwith Lincs....136 C3
East Barming Kent....39 H3
East Barnby N York....171 J8
East Barnet Gt Lon....69 H8
East Barns E Loth....212 F4
East Barsham Norfk....121 K5
East Beckham Norfk....122 D4
East Bedfont Gt Lon....50 D4
East Bergholt Suffk....90 C8
East Bierley Kirk....141 J2
East Bilney Norfk....121 L7
East Blatchington E Susx....23 H7
East Bloxworth Dorset....17 H4
East Boldon S Tyne....181 J6
East Boldre Hants....18 F4
East Bolton Nthumb....191 G3
Eastbourne Darltn....169 J7
Eastbourne E Susx....23 K7
East Bower Somset....30 D3
East Bradenham Norfk....105 J2
East Brent Somset....44 D8
Eastbridge Suffk....91 K2
East Bridgford Notts....117 J3
East Briscoe Dur....168 B6
Eastbrook V Glam....43 J7
East Buckland Devon....28 B4
East Budleigh Devon....14 C5
Eastburn C Brad....149 J7
Eastburn E R Yk....152 F4
East Burnham Bucks....50 B2
East Burton Dorset....16 F5
Eastbury W Berk....47 M3

East Butsfield Dur....168 E2
East Butterwick N Linc....143 L6
Eastby N York....149 J5
East Calder W Loth....210 E5
East Carleton Norfk....106 D3
East Carlton Leeds....150 B7
East Carlton N Nthn....101 H5
East Chaldon Dorset....16 F6
East Challow Oxon....48 A1
East Charleton Devon....7 L5
East Chelborough Dorset....16 A2
East Chiltington E Susx....22 F4
East Chinnock Somset....31 H8
East Chisenbury Wilts....47 H8
East Cholderton Hants....34 C2
Eastchurch Kent....53 L5
East Clandon Surrey....50 D8
East Claydon Bucks....67 H2
East Clevedon N Som....44 E5
East Coker Somset....31 J8
Eastcombe Gloucs....64 C6
Eastcombe Somset....29 L4
East Compton Somset....31 K3
East Cornworthy Devon....8 C4
East Cote Cumb....176 F7
Eastcote Gt Lon....50 E1
Eastcote Solhll....99 G7
Eastcote W Nthn....84 D4
Eastcott Cnwll....26 D7
Eastcott Wilts....46 F7
East Cottingwith E R Yk....151 L7
Eastcourt Wilts....47 K6
Eastcourt Wilts....64 E8
East Cowes IoW....19 H4
East Cowick E R Yk....143 G3
East Cowton N York....160 D2
East Cramlington Nthumb....181 G4
East Cranmore Somset....31 L2
East Creech Dorset....17 H6
East Curthwaite Cumb....165 K1
East Dean E Susx....23 J7
East Dean Gloucs....63 K3
East Dean Hants....34 C5
East Dean W Susx....20 E4
Eastdown Devon....8 B5
East Down Devon....27 L3
East Drayton Notts....134 F4
East Dulwich Gt Lon....51 J4
East Dundry N Som....45 H5
East Ella C KuH....144 D2
East End Bed....86 C4
East End C Beds....85 J6
East End E R Yk....145 G2
East End E R Yk....145 H2
East End Essex....70 B5
Eastend Essex....72 D8
East End Hants....18 F4
East End Hants....48 B6
East End Herts....70 C2
East End Kent....39 L6
East End Kent....53 L4
East End M Keyn....85 J6
East End Oxon....66 B4
East End Somset....31 L2
East End Suffk....90 C8
Easter Balmoral Abers....243 J5
Easter Compton S Glos....45 H2
Easter Dalziel Highld....252 E2
Eastergate W Susx....20 F6
Easterhouse C Glas....209 J6
Easter Howgate Mdloth....211 H6
Easter Kinkell Highld....251 G1
Easter Moniack Highld....250 F3
Eastern Green Covtry....99 H7
Easter Ord Abers....245 J3
Easter Pitkierie Fife....223 K6
Easter Skeld Shet....281 d6
Easter Softlaw Border....202 B6
Easterton Wilts....46 F8
Eastertown Somset....44 D8
East Everleigh Wilts....47 J8
East Farleigh Kent....39 J3
East Farndon W Nthn....100 F6
East Ferry Lincs....143 K7
Eastfield N Lans....210 A6
Eastfield N York....163 J6
East Firsby Lincs....135 K3
East Fortune E Loth....212 D3
East Garforth Leeds....142 C1
East Garston W Berk....47 M4
Eastgate Dur....168 B3
Eastgate Lincs....118 F7
Eastgate Norfk....122 C7
East Ginge Oxon....48 C2
East Goscote Leics....100 E1
East Grafton Wilts....47 K6
East Green Suffk....91 K6
East Grimstead Wilts....34 B5
East Grinstead W Susx....38 B5
East Guldeford E Susx....25 H3

East Haddon W Nthn......84 C2
East Hagbourne Oxon......48 D1
East Halton N Linc......144 E4
East Ham Gt Lon......51 L2
Eastham Wirral......129 H4
Eastham Ferry Wirral......129 J3
Easthampton Herefs......80 A3
East Hanney Oxon......66 B8
East Hanningfield Essex......71 J6
East Hardwick Wakefd......142 D4
East Harling Norfk......105 K6
East Harlsey N York......160 F3
East Harnham Wilts......33 K5
East Harptree BaNES......45 H7
East Hartford Nthumb......181 G3
East Harting W Susx......20 C3
East Hatch Wilts......32 F5
East Hatley Cambs......86 F5
East Hauxwell N York......159 L1
East Haven Angus......234 F8
Eastheath Wokham......49 J3
East Heckington Lincs......119 G3
East Hedleyhope Dur......168 F3
East Helmsdale Highld......274 D5
East Hendred Oxon......48 C1
East Heslerton N York......163 G7
East Hewish N Som......44 E6
East Hoathly E Susx......23 H4
East Holme Dorset......17 H5
East Hope Dur......159 J1
Easthope Shrops......96 D4
Easthorpe Essex......72 C3
Easthorpe Notts......117 J1
East Horrington Somset......31 J2
East Horsley Surrey......50 E8
East Horton Nthumb......203 G7
East Howe BCP......17 L3
East Huntspill Somset......30 E2
East Hyde C Beds......68 E4
East Ilkerton Devon......28 C2
East Ilsley W Berk......34 A8
Eastington Devon......13 H1
Eastington Gloucs......63 M6
Eastington Gloucs......65 H4
East Keal Lincs......137 G7
East Kennett Wilts......47 G5
East Keswick Leeds......150 E7
East Kilbride S Lans......209 H8
East Kimber Devon......12 C3
East Kirkby Lincs......136 F7
East Knighton Dorset......16 F5
East Knowstone Devon......28 E6
East Knoyle Wilts......32 E5
East Lambrook Somset......31 G7
Eastlands D & G......185 K8
East Langdon Kent......41 K6
East Langton Leics......100 F5
East Lavant W Susx......20 D5
East Lavington W Susx......20 F4
East Layton N York......159 L1
Eastleach Martin Gloucs......65 J6
Eastleach Turville Gloucs......65 J6
East Leake Notts......116 F6
East Learmouth Nthumb......202 D5
East Leigh Devon......7 K4
East Leigh Devon......7 L3
East Leigh Devon......13 G2
Eastleigh Devon......27 J5
Eastleigh Hants......34 F4
East Lexham Norfk......121 J8
Eastling Kent......40 C4
East Linton E Loth......212 D3
East Liss Hants......36 A5
East Lockinge Oxon......48 B2
East Lound N Linc......143 K7
East Lulworth Dorset......17 G6
East Lutton N York......152 F2
East Lydeard Somset......30 B5
East Lydford Somset......31 J4
East Malling Kent......39 H2
East Malling Heath Kent......39 H2
East Marden W Susx......20 C4
East Markham Notts......134 E5
East Martin Hants......33 J7
East Marton N York......148 F5
East Meon Hants......35 L6
East Mere Devon......29 H7
East Mersea Essex......72 F4
East Midlands Airport Leics......116 D6
East Molesey Surrey......50 F5
Eastmoor Norfk......104 E3
East Morden Dorset......17 H4
East Morton C Brad......149 K7
East Morton D & G......186 C6
East Ness N York......162 B6
East Newton E R Yk......153 J4
Eastney C Port......19 L4
Eastnor Herefs......81 G7
East Norton Leics......101 G3
Eastoft N Linc......143 K4

East Ogwell Devon......13 J8
Easton Cambs......86 C1
Easton Cumb......177 J7
Easton Devon......13 G5
Easton Dorset......16 D8
Easton Hants......35 G4
Easton Lincs......118 B6
Easton Norfk......106 C1
Easton Somset......31 H2
Easton Suffk......91 G3
Easton W Berk......48 B4
Easton Wilts......46 C5
Easton Grey Wilts......46 C2
Easton-in-Gordano N Som......45 G4
Easton Maudit N Nthn......85 H3
Easton-on-the-Hill N Nthn......101 M3
Easton Royal Wilts......47 J7
East Orchard Dorset......32 D7
East Ord Nthumb......203 F5
East Panson Devon......11 L4
East Parley BCP......17 M3
East Peckham Kent......39 G4
East Pennard Somset......31 K3
East Portlemouth Devon......7 L7
East Prawle Devon......8 A7
East Preston W Susx......21 J6
East Pulham Dorset......16 D1
East Putford Devon......26 F7
East Quantoxhead Somset......29 L2
East Rainham Medway......53 H5
East Rainton Sundld......169 J1
East Ravendale NE Lin......145 G7
East Raynham Norfk......121 J6
Eastrea Cambs......102 F4
Eastriggs D & G......177 H5
East Rigton Leeds......150 E7
Eastrington E R Yk......143 K2
East Rolstone N Som......44 E6
East Rounton N York......160 F2
East Rudham Norfk......121 H6
East Runton Norfk......122 D3
East Ruston Norfk......123 G6
Eastry Kent......41 J4
East Saltoun E Loth......212 B5
Eastshaw W Susx......36 C6
East Sheen Gt Lon......51 G4
East Shefford W Berk......48 A4
East Sleekburn Nthumb......181 G2
East Somerton Norfk......123 K7
East Stockwith Lincs......134 F1
East Stoke Dorset......17 G5
East Stoke Notts......117 K2
East Stour Dorset......32 D6
East Stour Common Dorset......32 D6
East Stourmouth Kent......41 H3
East Stowford Devon......27 L5
East Stratton Hants......35 H3
East Studdal Kent......41 J5
East Sutton Kent......39 L3
East Taphouse Cnwll......5 L2
East-the-Water Devon......27 H5
East Thirston Nthumb......191 J6
East Tilbury Thurr......52 E3
East Tilbury Village Thurr......52 E3
East Tisted Hants......35 L4
East Torrington Lincs......136 B3
East Tuddenham Norfk......106 B1
East Tytherley Hants......34 C5
East Tytherton Wilts......46 D4
East Village Devon......13 K2
Eastville Brictl......45 J4
Eastville Lincs......137 H8
East Wall Shrops......96 C4
East Walton Norfk......121 G8
East Water Somset......31 J1
East Week Devon......12 F4
Eastwell Leics......117 K6
East Wellow Hants......34 C6
East Wemyss Fife......222 F7
East Whitburn W Loth......210 C6
Eastwick Herts......70 B5
East Wickham Gt Lon......51 M3
East Williamston Pembks......55 J6
East Winch Norfk......120 F8
East Winterslow Wilts......34 B4
East Wittering W Susx......20 C7
East Witton N York......159 L5
Eastwood Notts......116 D2
Eastwood Sthend......53 H1
East Woodburn Nthumb......179 L2
Eastwood End Cambs......103 J5
East Woodhay Hants......48 B6
East Woodlands Somset......32 C2
East Worldham Hants......35 M3
East Worlington Devon......27 K6
East Wretham Norfk......105 J5
East Youlstone Devon......26 D7
Eathorpe Warwks......83 J2
Eaton Ches E......131 G6

Eaton Ches W......130 B7
Eaton Leics......117 L5
Eaton Norfk......106 E2
Eaton Notts......134 E4
Eaton Oxon......66 C6
Eaton Shrops......95 J5
Eaton Shrops......96 B5
Eaton Bishop Herefs......80 B7
Eaton Bray C Beds......68 B3
Eaton Constantine Shrops......96 D2
Eaton Ford Cambs......86 D3
Eaton Green C Beds......68 B3
Eaton Hastings Oxon......65 K7
Eaton Mascott Shrops......96 C2
Eaton Socon Cambs......86 D3
Eaton upon Tern Shrops......113 L7
Eaves Brow Warrtn......130 C2
Eaves Green Solhll......99 H6
Ebberston N York......163 L8
Ebbesborne Wake Wilts......33 G6
Ebbsfleet Kent......52 D4
Ebbw Vale Blae G......61 J5
Ebchester Dur......180 D7
Ebdon N Som......44 D6
Ebernoe W Susx......36 E5
Ebford Devon......14 A5
Ebley Gloucs......64 B6
Ebnal Ches W......113 H2
Ebnall Herefs......80 B3
Ebrington Gloucs......82 E7
Ebsworthy Devon......12 C4
Ecchinswell Hants......48 D7
Ecclaw Border......213 G5
Ecclefechan D & G......177 G4
Eccles Border......202 B5
Eccles Kent......52 F6
Eccles Salfd......140 A8
Ecclesall Sheff......132 F3
Ecclesfield Sheff......133 G1
Eccles Green Herefs......79 L5
Eccleshall Staffs......114 C5
Eccleshill C Brad......149 MU
Ecclesmachan W Loth......210 E4
Eccles on Sea Norfk......123 K6
Eccles Road Norfk......105 L5
Eccleston Ches W......129 J7
Eccleston Lancs......139 G4
Eccleston St Hel......138 F8
Eccleston Green Lancs......139 G4
Echt Abers......245 G2
Eckford Border......201 L7
Eckington Derbys......133 H4
Eckington Worcs......81 L7
Ecton N Nthn......84 F3
Ecton Staffs......132 B8
Edale Derbys......132 B3
Eday Ork......275 d3
Eday Airport Ork......275 d2
Edburton W Susx......22 C5
Edderside Cumb......164 E2
Edderton Highld......263 J3
Eddington Cambs......87 J3
Eddington Kent......41 G2
Eddleston Border......200 B4
Eddlewood S Lans......209 J8
Edenbridge Kent......38 C4
Edenfield Lancs......140 B4
Edenhall W & F......166 D4
Edenham Lincs......118 E4
Eden Mount W & F......156 F7
Eden Park Gt Lon......51 K5
Edensor Derbys......132 C5
Edentaggart Ag & B......218 D8
Edenthorpe Donc......143 G6
Edern Gwynd......108 E4
Edgarley Somset......31 H3
Edgbaston Birm......98 D6
Edgcott Bucks......67 G3
Edgcott Somset......28 E3
Edgcumbe Cnwll......3 J4
Edge Gloucs......64 B6
Edge Shrops......95 K2
Edgebolton Shrops......113 J7
Edge End Gloucs......63 H4
Edgefield Norfk......122 B5
Edgefield Green Norfk......122 B4
Edgefold Bolton......139 L6
Edge Green Ches W......113 H1
Edgehill Warwks......83 J5
Edgerley Shrops......112 E7
Edgerton Kirk......141 H4
Edgeside Lancs......140 C3
Edgeworth Gloucs......64 D6
Edgeworthy Devon......28 E8
Edginswell Torbay......8 C2
Edgiock Worcs......82 B3
Edgmond Wrekin......114 A7
Edgmond Marsh Wrekin......114 A7
Edgton Shrops......95 J6
Edgware Gt Lon......51 G1

Edgworth Bl w D......139 L4
Edinbane Highld......258 E6
Edinburgh C Edin......211 J4
Edinburgh Airport C Edin......210 F4
Edinburgh Old & New Town C Edin......211 H4
Edingale Staffs......99 G1
Edingham D & G......175 L2
Edingley Notts......134 D8
Edingthorpe Norfk......123 G5
Edingthorpe Green Norfk......122 F5
Edington Border......202 D2
Edington Nthumb......180 E2
Edington Somset......30 F3
Edington Wilts......46 D8
Edingworth Somset......44 D8
Edithmead Somset......30 E1
Edith Weston Rutlnd......101 K3
Edlaston Derbys......90 D5
Edlesborough Bucks......68 B4
Edlingham Nthumb......191 G4
Edlington Lincs......136 D5
Edmond Castle Cumb......178 C7
Edmondsham Dorset......33 J8
Edmondsley Dur......169 G1
Edmondstown Rhondd......42 F4
Edmondthorpe Leics......117 M8
Edmonton Cnwll......10 D8
Edmonton Gt Lon......69 J8
Edmundbyers Dur......168 C1
Ednam Border......202 A5
Ednaston Derbys......115 L3
Edney Common Essex......71 G6
Edradynate P & K......232 C5
Edrom Border......202 C2
Edstaston Shrops......113 H5
Edstone Warwks......82 E3
Edvin Loach Herefs......80 F3
Edwalton Notts......117 G4
Edwardstone Suffk......89 J6
Edwardsville Myr Td......43 G2
Edwinsford Carmth......59 H8
Edwinstowe Notts......134 C6
Edworth C Beds......86 E7
Edwyn Ralph Herefs......80 F4
Edzell Angus......234 F3
Edzell Woods Abers......234 F2
Efail-fach Neath......57 L6
Efail Isaf Rhondd......43 H5
Efailnewydd Gwynd......108 F4
Efail-Rhyd Powys......112 A6
Efailwen Carmth......75 K7
Efenechtyd Denbgs......128 D8
Effgill D & G......187 L7
Effingham Surrey......50 E8
Effingham Junction Surrey......50 E8
Efflinch Staffs......115 K8
Efford Devon......13 K2
Egbury Hants......48 B8
Egdean W Susx......21 G3
Egerton Bolton......139 L5
Egerton Kent......40 B6
Egerton Forstal Kent......40 A6
Eggborough N York......142 E3
Eggbuckland C Plym......6 F3
Eggesford Devon......28 B8
Eggington C Beds......68 B2
Egginton Derbys......115 M6
Egglescliffe S on T......169 L7
Eggleston Dur......168 C6
Egham Surrey......50 C5
Egham Wick Surrey......50 B5
Egleton Rutlnd......101 J2
Eglingham Nthumb......191 G2
Egloshayle Cnwll......10 D8
Egloskerry Cnwll......11 K5
Eglwysbach Conwy......126 F5
Eglwys-Brewis V Glam......42 F7
Eglwys Cross Wrexhm......113 G3
Eglwys Fach Cerdgn......92 F4
Eglwyswrw Pembks......75 K4
Egmanton Notts......134 E6
Egremont Cumb......164 D8
Egremont Wirral......129 H1
Egton N York......162 E2
Egton Bridge N York......162 D2
Egypt Bucks......50 B2
Egypt Hants......34 F4
Eigg Highld......236 F3
Eight Ash Green Essex......72 D2
Eilanreach Highld......248 C8
Eisgein W Isls......282 f5
Eishken W Isls......282 f5
Eisteddfa Gurig Cerdgn......93 H6
Elan Valley Powys......78 B2
Elan Village Powys......78 C2
Elberton S Glos......45 J1
Elbridge W Susx......20 F6
Elburton C Plym......7 G4
Elcombe Swindn......47 H3

Elcot W Berk....................48 B5
Eldernell Cambs..............103 G4
Eldersfield Worcs..............64 A1
Elderslie Rens...................208 D6
Elder Street Essex............88 B8
Eldon Dur.........................169 G5
Eldwick C Brad...............149 L7
Elerch Cerdgn...................92 E6
Elfhill Abers....................245 H6
Elford Nthumb...............203 K7
Elford Staffs.....................98 F1
Elgin Moray....................266 E4
Elgol Highld....................247 H6
Elham Kent........................41 G6
Elie Fife..........................223 J7
Elilaw Nthumb...............190 D4
Elim IoA..........................124 F3
Eling Hants.......................18 F1
Elkesley Notts.................134 D4
Elkstone Gloucs................64 D4
Ella Abers.......................268 B4
Ellacombe Torbay..............8 D2
Elland Calder...................141 H4
Elland Lower Edge Calder ...141 H3
Ellary Ag & B..................206 A4
Ellastone Staffs..............115 J3
Ellel Lancs......................147 J4
Ellemford Border............212 F7
Ellenabeich Ag & B.........215 L1
Ellenborough Cumb........164 D3
Ellenbrook Salfd............139 L7
Ellenhall Staffs..............114 C6
Ellen's Green Surrey........37 G4
Ellerbeck N York............160 F3
Ellerby N York................171 J7
Ellerdine Heath Wrekin..113 K7
Ellerhayes Devon.............14 A2
Elleric Ag & B.................229 G5
Ellerker E R Yk...............144 A2
Ellers N York..................149 H7
Ellerton E R Yk...............151 L7
Ellerton N York...............160 C3
Ellerton Shrops..............114 A6
Ellesborough Bucks..........67 K6
Ellesmere Shrops............112 F4
Ellesmere Port Ches W....129 J4
Ellicombe Somset.............29 H2
Ellingham Hants...............18 A2
Ellingham Norfk..............107 H5
Ellingham Nthumb..........203 K8
Ellingstring N York.........159 M6
Ellington Cambs................86 D1
Ellington Nthumb...........191 K7
Ellington Thorpe Cambs....86 D1
Elliots Green Somset........32 D2
Ellisfield Hants.................35 K2
Ellishader Highld.............259 H3
Ellistown Leics.................99 L1
Ellon Abers....................257 H5
Ellonby W & F.................166 A4
Ellough Suffk..................107 J6
Elloughton E R Yk..........144 B2
Ellwood Gloucs.................63 H5
Elm Cambs.....................103 K2
Elmbridge Worcs..............81 K2
Elmdon Essex...................87 J7
Elmdon Solhll...................98 F6
Elmdon Heath Solhll........98 F7
Elmer W Susx....................21 G6
Elmers End Gt Lon...........51 K5
Elmer's Green Lancs........139 G6
Elmesthorpe Leics..........100 A4
Elm Green Essex...............71 J6
Elmhurst Staffs................98 E1
Elmington N Nthn...........102 B5
Elmley Castle Worcs.........82 A7
Elmley Lovett Worcs.........81 K1
Elmore Gloucs..................64 A4
Elmore Back Gloucs...........63 M4
Elm Park Gt Lon...............52 B2
Elmscott Devon................26 D6
Elmsett Suffk...................90 C6
Elms Green Worcs.............81 G2
Elmstead Heath Essex......72 F3
Elmstead Market Essex.....72 F2
Elmstead Row Essex.........72 F3
Elmsted Kent....................40 F6
Elmstone Kent.................41 H3
Elmstone Hardwicke
    Gloucs........................64 D2
Elmswell E R Yk..............152 H4
Elmswell Suffk..................89 K3
Elmton Derbys................133 K5
Elphin Highld.................271 H6
Elphinstone E Loth..........211 L5
Elrick Abers...................245 H2
Elrig D & G.....................173 J5
Elrington Nthumb............179 K6
Elsdon Nthumb...............190 C7
Elsecar Barns..................142 B7

Elsenham Essex................70 D2
Elsfield Oxon....................66 D5
Elsham N Linc................144 C5
Elsing Norfk...................122 B8
Elslack N York.................149 G6
Elson Hants.......................19 K3
Elson Shrops...................112 F4
Elsrickle S Lans...............199 J4
Elstead Surrey..................36 D2
Elsted W Susx....................20 D3
Elsted Marsh W Susx........20 D3
Elsthorpe Lincs...............118 E6
Elstob Dur......................169 J6
Elston Lancs....................139 J1
Elston Notts...................117 K2
Elston Wilts......................33 J2
Elstone Devon...................28 B7
Elstow Bed.......................85 L6
Elstree Herts....................68 F8
Elstronwick E R Yk..........145 G1
Elswick Lancs..................147 H8
Elswick N u Ty................180 F5
Elsworth Cambs................87 G3
Elterwater W & F............156 D2
Eltham Gt Lon..................51 L4
Eltisley Cambs..................86 F3
Elton Bury......................140 B5
Elton Cambs...................102 B4
Elton Ches W..................129 K4
Elton Derbys...................132 D7
Elton Gloucs.....................63 K4
Elton Herefs.....................80 B1
Elton S on T...................169 L7
Elton Green Ches W.........129 K5
Elton-on-the-Hill Notts...117 K4
Eltringham Nthumb........180 C6
Elvanfoot S Lans.............186 E3
Elvaston Derbys..............116 C5
Elveden Suffk.................105 G7
Elvetham Heath Hants......49 K7
Elvingston E Loth............212 A4
Elvington C York..............151 L6
Elvington Kent..................41 J5
Elwell Devon.....................28 B4
Elwick Hartpl..................170 B4
Elwick Nthumb...............203 J5
Elworth Ches E...............130 E7
Elworthy Somset...............29 K4
Ely Cambs......................103 L7
Ely Cardif.........................43 J6
Emberton M Keyn.............85 H5
Embleton Cumb..............165 G4
Embleton Dur.................169 L5
Embleton Nthumb..........191 J2
Embo Highld...................264 C1
Emborough Somset..........31 K1
Embo Street Highld.........264 C1
Embsay N York...............149 H5
Emery Down Hants...........18 D2
Emley Kirk.....................141 K5
Emley Moor Kirk.............141 K5
Emmbrook Wokham..........49 J5
Emmer Green Readg.........49 H4
Emmett Carr Derbys........133 J4
Emmington Oxon..............67 H6
Emneth Norfk.................103 K2
Emneth Hungate Norfk....103 K2
Empingham Rutlnd..........101 L2
Empshott Hants................35 M4
Empshott Green Hants......35 M5
Emsworth Hants...............20 B5
Enborne W Berk................48 B6
Enborne Row W Berk........48 C6
Enchmarsh Shrops............96 B4
Enderby Leics.................100 C3
Endmoor W & F...............157 H5
Endon Staffs...................114 E1
Endon Bank Staffs..........114 E1
Enfield Gt Lon..................69 K7
Enfield Lock Gt Lon..........69 K7
Enfield Wash Gt Lon.........69 K7
Enford Wilts......................47 H8
Engine Common S Glos......45 K2
England's Gate Herefs.......80 D5
Englefield W Berk..............48 F4
Englefield Green Surrey.....50 C4
Engleseabrook Ches E......114 B1
English Bicknor Gloucs......63 H4
Englishcombe BaNES........45 L6
English Frankton Shrops...113 G5
Engollan Cnwll..................10 B8
Enham Alamein Hants.......34 D1
Enmore Somset.................30 C4
Enmore Green Dorset........32 E6
Ennerdale Bridge
    Cumb........................164 E7
Enniscaven Cnwll................4 F3
Enochdhu P & K..............233 G3
Ensay Ag & B..................226 D3
Ensbury BCP....................17 L3

Ensdon Shrops................112 F8
Ensis Devon......................27 K5
Enson Staffs...................114 E6
Enstone Oxon....................66 A2
Enterkinfoot D & G.........186 C5
Enterpen N York..............161 G2
Enville Staffs.....................97 J6
Eochar W Isls...................283 b9
Eòlaigearraidh W Isls......283 b12
Eoligarry W Isls...............283 b12
Eòropaidh W Isls.............282 h1
Eoropie W Isls.................282 h1
Epney Gloucs....................63 M2
Epperstone Notts.............117 H2
Epping Essex.....................70 C6
Epping Green Essex...........70 B6
Epping Green Herts...........69 J5
Epping Upland Essex.........70 C6
Eppleby N York................168 F8
Eppleworth E R Yk..........144 C2
Epsom Surrey....................51 K6
Epwell Oxon......................83 H7
Epworth N Linc...............143 K7
Epworth Turbary N Linc...143 J7
Erbistock Wrexhm...........112 E3
Erdington Birm.................98 E5
Eridge Green E Susx..........38 E6
Eridge Station E Susx........38 E6
Erines Ag & B.................206 D4
Eriska Ag & B..................228 D6
Eriswell Suffk.................104 E7
Erith Gt Lon.....................52 B3
Erlestoke Wilts..................46 D8
Ermington Devon...............7 J4
Ernesettle C Plym...............6 E3
Erpingham Norfk.............122 D5
Erriottwood Kent...............40 D3
Errogie Highld.................250 F7
Errol P & K.....................222 D3
Erskine Rens...................208 D5
Erskine Bridge Rens.........208 D4
Ervie D & G....................172 B1
Erwarton Suffk..................90 F8
Erwood Powys...................78 F6
Eryholme N York.............160 D1
Eryri National Park..........110 F5
Eryrys Denbgs.................128 E8
Escalls Cnwll......................2 B5
Escomb Dur....................168 F4
Escott Somset...................29 K3
Escrick N York.................151 K7
Esgair Carmth...................58 C3
Esgair Cerdgn...................77 G2
Esgairgeiliog Powys..........93 G2
Esgerdawe Carmth............77 H7
Esgyryn Conwy...............126 F4
Esh Dur..........................169 G2
Esher Surrey.....................50 E6
Esholt C Brad..................150 A7
Eshott Nthumb...............191 J6
Eshton N York.................149 G5
Esh Winning Dur.............169 G2
Eskadale Highld..............250 D4
Eskbank Mdloth..............211 K5
Eskdale Green Cumb........155 L3
Eskdalemuir D & G.........187 K6
Eske E R Yk....................153 G7
Eskham Lincs..................145 K8
Eskholme Donc...............143 G4
Esperley Lane Ends
    Dur..........................168 E6
Esprick Lancs..................147 H8
Essendine Rutlnd.............102 A1
Essendon Herts.................69 H5
Essich Highld..................251 H4
Essington Staffs................98 B3
Esslemont Abers.............257 G6
Eston R & Cl...................170 D7
Etal Nthumb...................202 E5
Etchilhampton Wilts.........46 F7
Etchingham E Susx...........24 C2
Etchinghill Kent................41 G7
Etchinghill Staffs............115 G2
Etchingwood E Susx.........23 H3
Etling Green Norfk...........121 M8
Etloe Gloucs.....................63 K6
Eton W & M......................50 B3
Eton Wick W & M.............50 B3
Etruria C Stke.................114 D2
Etteridge Highld..............241 J5
Ettersgill Dur..................167 K5
Ettiley Heath
    Ches E.......................130 E7
Ettingshall Wolves............97 L4
Ettington Warwks.............83 G5
Etton C Pete...................102 A2
Etton E R Yk...................152 F7
Ettrick Border.................187 L3
Ettrickbridge
    Border.......................188 C1

Ettrickhill Border............187 L3
Etwall Derbys.................115 M5
Eudon George Shrops........96 F5
Euston Suffk...................105 H7
Euximoor Drove
    Cambs.......................103 K4
Euxton Lancs..................139 H4
Evancoyd Powys...............79 J3
Evanton Highld...............263 G6
Evedon Lincs...................118 E2
Evelith Shrops..................97 G2
Evelix Highld..................263 L2
Evenjobb Powys...............79 J3
Evenley W Nthn................84 B8
Evenlode Gloucs...............65 J1
Evenwood Dur................168 F5
Evenwood Gate Dur.........168 F6
Evercreech Somset............31 L3
Everingham E R Yk..........152 B7
Everleigh Wilts.................47 J8
Everley N York................163 H5
Eversholt C Beds..............85 K8
Evershot Dorset................16 A2
Eversley Hants..................49 J6
Eversley Cross Hants.........49 J6
Everthorpe E R Yk..........144 A2
Everton C Beds.................86 D5
Everton Hants...................18 D5
Everton Lpool.................129 H1
Everton Notts.................134 D2
Evertown D & G..............177 K4
Evesbatch Herefs..............80 C5
Evesham Worcs.................82 B6
Evington C Leic...............100 D3
Ewden Village Sheff.........141 L8
Ewell Surrey.....................51 K6
Ewell Minnis Kent............41 H6
Ewelme Oxon....................48 F1
Ewen Gloucs.....................64 E7
Ewenny V Glam................42 D6
Ewerby Lincs..................118 F2
Ewerby Thorpe Lincs.......118 F2
Ewhurst Surrey.................37 G3
Ewhurst Green E Susx......24 C2
Ewhurst Green Surrey.......37 G3
Ewloe Flints...................129 G6
Ewloe Green Flints..........129 G6
Ewood Bl w D.................139 K3
Ewood Bridge Lancs.........140 B4
Eworthy Devon.................12 B4
Ewshot Hants...................36 B1
Ewyas Harold Herefs.........62 D2
Exbourne Devon...............12 E2
Exbury Hants....................19 G4
Exceat E Susx...................23 H7
Exebridge Somset.............29 G6
Exelby N York.................160 D5
Exeter Devon...................13 L4
Exeter Airport Devon........14 A7
Exeter Services Devon.......13 M4
Exford Somset..................28 E3
Exfordsgreen Shrops.........95 L2
Exhall Warwks..................82 D4
Exhall Warwks..................99 K6
Exlade Street Oxon............49 G3
Exley Head C Brad...........149 J7
Exminster Devon...............13 M4
Exmoor National Park.......28 E3
Exmouth Devon................14 A6
Exning Suffk.....................88 C2
Exted Kent.......................41 G6
Exton Devon....................14 A5
Exton Hants.....................35 J6
Exton Rutlnd..................101 K1
Exton Somset...................29 G4
Exwick Devon..................13 L4
Eyam Derbys...................132 D4
Eydon W Nthn..................83 M5
Eye C Pete.....................102 E3
Eye Herefs.......................80 C2
Eye Suffk........................106 C8
Eye Green C Pete............102 E3
Eyemouth Border............213 L6
Eyeworth C Beds..............86 E6
Eyhorne Street Kent.........39 L2
Eyke Suffk........................91 H5
Eynesbury Cambs..............86 D3
Eynsford Kent...................52 C6
Eynsham Oxon..................66 B5
Eype Dorset......................15 K4
Eyre Highld....................259 G6
Eythorne Kent..................41 J5
Eyton Herefs....................80 B3
Eyton Shrops....................95 J6
Eyton Shrops..................112 F8
Eyton Shrops..................113 G7
Eyton Wrexhm................112 E3
Eyton on Severn Shrops....96 D2
Eyton upon the Weald Moors
    Wrekin......................113 L8

F

Faccombe Hants.....48 A7
Faceby N York.....161 H2
Fachwen Powys.....111 K8
Facit Lancs.....140 D4
Fackley Notts.....133 J7
Faddiley Ches E.....113 K1
Fadmoor N York.....161 L5
Faerdre Swans.....57 J4
Faifley W Duns.....208 E4
Failand N Som.....45 G4
Failford S Ayrs.....196 F5
Failsworth Oldham.....140 D7
Fairbourne Gwynd.....92 D1
Fairburn N York.....142 D2
Fair Field Derbys.....131 L5
Fairfield Kent.....25 H2
Fairfield Worcs.....97 L8
Fairfield Park Herts.....86 D8
Fairford Gloucs.....65 H6
Fairford Park Gloucs.....65 H6
Fairgirth D & G.....175 L3
Fair Green Norfk.....120 E8
Fairhaven Lancs.....138 C2
Fair Isle Shet.....281 b8
Fair Isle Airport Shet.....281 b8
Fairlands Surrey.....50 B8
Fairlie N Ayrs.....207 L8
Fairlight E Susx.....24 F5
Fairlight Cove E Susx.....24 F5
Fairmile Devon.....14 C3
Fairmile Surrey.....50 E6
Fairmilehead C Edin.....211 H5
Fairnilee Border.....200 F6
Fair Oak Hants.....35 G7
Fairoak Staffs.....114 B5
Fair Oak Green Hants.....49 G6
Fairseat Kent.....71 D6
Fairstead Essex.....71 J4
Fairstead Norfk.....120 E7
Fairstead Norfk.....122 F6
Fairwarp E Susx.....23 G2
Fairwater Cardif.....43 J6
Fairy Cross Devon.....27 G6
Fakenham Norfk.....121 K5
Fakenham Magna Suffk.....105 H8
Fala Mdloth.....211 M6
Fala Dam Mdloth.....211 M6
Falcut W Nthn.....84 B6
Faldingworth Lincs.....135 L3
Faldouët Jersey.....9 f2
Falfield S Glos.....63 K8
Falkenham Suffk.....91 G7
Falkirk Falk.....210 A3
Falkland Fife.....222 D5
Fallburn S Lans.....199 G5
Fallgate Derbys.....133 G7
Fallin Stirlg.....209 L1
Fallodon Nthumb.....191 H2
Fallowfield Manch.....131 G1
Fallowfield Nthumb.....179 L5
Falmer E Susx.....22 E5
Falmouth Cnwll.....3 K4
Falnash Border.....188 C5
Falsgrave N York.....163 J5
Falstone Nthumb.....179 G2
Fanagmore Highld.....276 B6
Fancott C Beds.....68 C2
Fanellan Highld.....250 E3
Fangdale Beck N York.....161 J4
Fangfoss E R Yk.....152 A3
Fanmore Ag & B.....226 E3
Fannich Lodge Highld.....261 L6
Fans Border.....201 J5
Far Bletchley M Keyn.....85 G8
Forest Combe.....102 D4
Far Cotton W Nthn.....84 E3
Farden Shrops.....96 D8
Fareham Hants.....19 K2
Farewell Staffs.....90 D1
Far Forest Worcs.....97 G8
Farforth Lincs.....136 F4
Far Green Gloucs.....63 M7
Faringdon Oxon.....65 L8
Farington Moss Lancs.....139 G3
Farlam Cumb.....178 D7
Farleigh N Som.....45 G5
Farleigh Surrey.....51 K7
Farleigh Hungerford Somset.....46 A7
Farleigh Wallop Hants.....35 J2
Farlesthorpe Lincs.....137 J5
Farleton Lancs.....147 L2
Farleton W & F.....157 H6
Farley Derbys.....132 F7
Farley Staffs.....115 H3
Farley Wilts.....34 B5
Farley Green Suffk.....88 E4
Farley Green Surrey.....37 G2

Farley Hill Wokham.....49 H6
Farleys End Gloucs.....63 M4
Farlington C Port.....19 M3
Farlington N York.....151 K2
Farlow Shrops.....96 E7
Farmborough BaNES.....45 K7
Farmbridge End Essex.....70 F5
Farmcote Gloucs.....64 F1
Farmcote Shrops.....97 H5
Farmington Gloucs.....65 H4
Farmoor Oxon.....66 C5
Far Moor Wigan.....139 G7
Farms Common Cnwll.....3 H4
Farm Town Leics.....116 C8
Farmtown Moray.....267 K6
Farnah Green Derbys.....116 D2
Farnborough Gt Lon.....51 L6
Farnborough Hants.....49 L8
Farnborough W Berk.....48 H7
Farnborough Warwks.....83 K5
Farnborough Park Hants.....49 L7
Farncombe Surrey.....36 F2
Farndish Bed.....85 H3
Farndon Ches W.....112 F1
Farndon Notts.....117 K1
Farne Islands Nthumb.....203 L5
Farnell Angus.....235 G4
Farnham Dorset.....33 G7
Farnham Essex.....70 C2
Farnham N York.....150 E4
Farnham Suffk.....91 H3
Farnham Surrey.....36 B2
Farnham Common Bucks.....50 B2
Farnham Green Essex.....70 C2
Farnham Royal Bucks.....50 B2
Farningham Kent.....52 C5
Farnley Leeds.....141 L1
Farnley N York.....150 B6
Farnley Tyas Kirk.....141 J5
Farnsfield Notts.....134 C8
Farnworth Bolton.....139 L7
Farnworth Halton.....129 L2
Far Oakridge Gloucs.....64 D6
Farr Highld.....241 L3
Farr Highld.....251 J5
Farr Highld.....278 B4
Farraline Highld.....251 G7
Farringdon Devon.....14 B4
Farrington Gurney BaNES.....45 J7
Far Sawrey W & F.....156 E4
Farsley Leeds.....141 K1
Farther Howegreen Essex.....71 K6
Farthing Green Kent.....39 K4
Farthinghoe W Nthn.....83 M7
Farthingloe Kent.....41 J7
Farthingstone W Nthn.....84 B4
Farthing Street Gt Lon.....51 L6
Fartown Kirk.....141 J4
Farway Devon.....14 E3
Fasnacloich Ag & B.....229 G6
Fasnakyle Highld.....250 B4
Fassfern Highld.....239 G7
Fatfield Sundld.....181 H7
Faugh Cumb.....178 C7
Fauld Staffs.....115 K6
Fauldhouse W Loth.....210 B6
Faulkbourne Essex.....71 J4
Faulkland Somset.....45 L8
Fauls Shrops.....113 K5
Faversham Kent.....40 D3
Fawdington N York.....150 F1
Fawdon N u Ty.....180 F5
Fawdon Nthumb.....190 F3
Fawfieldhead Staffs.....131 L7
Fawkham Green Kent.....52 C6
Fawler Oxon.....66 A4
Fawley Bucks.....49 J2
Fawley Hants.....19 G3
Fawley W Berk.....48 B3
Fawley Chapel Herefs.....63 H1
Fawnog Flints.....128 F6
Fawsley W Nthn.....84 A4
Faxfleet E R Yk.....143 L3
Faygate W Susx.....37 K4
Fazakerley Lpool.....138 D8
Fazeley Staffs.....99 G3
Fearby N York.....160 B6
Fearn Highld.....264 C4
Fearnan P & K.....231 K6
Fearnbeg Highld.....260 B7
Fearnhead Warrtn.....130 C2
Fearnmore Highld.....260 A7
Fearnoch Ag & B.....206 E3
Featherstone Staffs.....97 L2
Featherstone Wakefd.....142 C4
Feckenham Worcs.....82 B3
Feering Essex.....72 C3
Feetham N York.....159 H3
Feizor N York.....148 D2
Felbridge Surrey.....38 B5

Felbrigg Norfk.....122 E4
Felcourt Surrey.....38 B5
Felden Herts.....68 D6
Felindre Carmth.....59 G4
Felindre Carmth.....59 K5
Felindre Carmth.....76 C7
Felindre Cerdgn.....77 G4
Felindre Powys.....61 J2
Felindre Powys.....94 E7
Felindre Swans.....57 H4
Felindre Farchog Pembks.....75 J4
Felinfach Cerdgn.....76 F4
Felinfach Powys.....78 F8
Felinfoel Carmth.....56 F4
Felingwmisaf Carmth.....58 F4
Felingwmuchaf Carmth.....58 F4
Felixkirk N York.....161 G5
Felixstowe Suffk.....91 G8
Felixstowe Ferry Suffk.....91 H5
Felkington Nthumb.....202 F3
Felkirk Wakefd.....142 B5
Felling Gatesd.....181 G6
Fell Lane C Brad.....149 J7
Fell Side Cumb.....165 J3
Felmersham Bed.....85 K4
Felmingham Norfk.....122 E5
Felpham W Susx.....20 F7
Felsham Suffk.....89 J4
Felsted Essex.....71 G3
Feltham Gt Lon.....50 E4
Felthamhill Surrey.....50 E5
Felthorpe Norfk.....122 D4
Felton Herefs.....80 D5
Felton N Som.....45 G6
Felton Nthumb.....191 H6
Felton Butler Shrops.....112 F8
Feltwell Norfk.....104 E5
Fenay Bridge Kirk.....141 J4
Fence Lancs.....148 E8
Fence Rothm.....133 J2
Fence Houses Sundld.....169 J1
Fencott Oxon.....66 E4
Fendike Corner Lincs.....137 H7
Fen Ditton Cambs.....87 K3
Fen Drayton Cambs.....87 G2
Fen End Lincs.....119 H7
Fen End Solhll.....99 G8
Fenham Nthumb.....203 H5
Feniscliffe Bl w D.....139 K2
Feniscowles Bl w D.....139 K3
Feniton Devon.....14 D3
Feniton Court Devon.....14 D3
Fenn Green Shrops.....97 H6
Fenn Street Medway.....53 G4
Fenny Bentley Derbys.....115 K2
Fenny Bridges Devon.....14 D3
Fenny Compton Warwks.....83 K5
Fenny Drayton Leics.....99 K4
Fenny Stratford M Keyn.....85 G8
Fenrother Nthumb.....191 H7
Fenstanton Cambs.....87 G2
Fenstead End Suffk.....88 F5
Fen Street Norfk.....105 K4
Fen Street Suffk.....90 E3
Fenton C Stke.....114 D3
Fenton Cambs.....103 G7
Fenton Cumb.....178 C7
Fenton Lincs.....118 A1
Fenton Lincs.....135 G4
Fenton Notts.....134 F3
Fenton Nthumb.....202 F6
Fenton Barns E Loth.....212 B3
Fenwick Donc.....142 F4
Fenwick E Ayrs.....196 F2
Fenwick Nthumb.....180 C4
Fenwick Nthumb.....203 H5
Feock Cnwll.....3 L3
Feolin Ferry Ag & B.....205 G3
Fergushill N Ayrs.....196 C2
Feriniquarrie Highld.....258 B6
Fermain Bay Guern.....9 k3
Fern Angus.....234 D3
Ferndale Rhondd.....42 F2
Ferndown Dorset.....17 L3
Ferness Highld.....253 J3
Fernham Oxon.....65 L8
Fernhill Heath Worcs.....81 K3
Fernhurst W Susx.....36 D5
Fernie Fife.....222 E4
Ferniegair S Lans.....209 K8
Fernilea Highld.....246 E2
Fernilee Derbys.....131 K4
Fernwood Notts.....117 L2
Ferrensby N York.....150 E4
Ferriby Sluice N Linc.....144 B4
Ferrindonald Highld.....247 L7
Ferring W Susx.....21 J6
Ferrybridge Wakefd.....142 C4
Ferrybridge Services Wakefd.....142 D3

Ferryden Angus.....235 H4
Ferryhill Dur.....169 H4
Ferryhill Station Dur.....169 J4
Ferry Point Highld.....263 K3
Ferryside Carmth.....56 C3
Fersfield Norfk.....106 B6
Fersit Highld.....240 B7
Feshiebridge Highld.....241 M3
Fetcham Surrey.....50 F7
Fetlar Shet.....281 f3
Fetterangus Abers.....269 H6
Fettercairn Abers.....235 G1
Fewcott Oxon.....66 D2
Fewston N York.....150 B5
Ffairfach Carmth.....59 H4
Ffair Rhos Cerdgn.....77 K2
Ffald-y-Brenin Carmth.....77 H6
Ffarmers Carmth.....77 J6
Ffawyddog Powys.....61 K3
Fforest Carmth.....57 G4
Fforest Goch Neath.....57 K4
Ffostrasol Cerdgn.....76 C6
Ffrith Flints.....129 G8
Ffynnonddewi Cerdgn.....76 C4
Ffynnongroyw Flints.....128 D3
Ffynnon-oer Cerdgn.....76 F4
Fickleshole Surrey.....51 K6
Fiddington Gloucs.....64 D1
Fiddington Somset.....30 B3
Fiddleford Dorset.....32 D8
Fiddlers Green Cnwll.....4 D4
Fiddlers Hamlet Essex.....70 C6
Field Staffs.....115 G5
Field Broughton W & F.....156 E6
Field Dalling Norfk.....121 M4
Field Head Leics.....100 B2
Fieldhead W & F.....166 B3
Fifehead Magdalen Dorset.....32 C6
Fifehead Neville Dorset.....32 C8
Fifehead St Quintin Dorset.....16 E1
Fife Keith Moray.....267 J3
Fifield Oxon.....65 K3
Fifield W & M.....49 L4
Fifield Wilts.....33 K1
Figheldean Wilts.....33 K2
Filands Wilts.....46 D1
Filby Norfk.....107 K1
Filey N York.....163 L6
Filgrave M Keyn.....85 G5
Filkins Oxon.....65 K6
Filleigh Devon.....28 B5
Filleigh Devon.....28 C8
Fillingham Lincs.....135 J3
Fillongley Warwks.....99 H6
Filmore Hill Hants.....35 K5
Filton S Glos.....45 J3
Fimber E R Yk.....152 D4
Finavon Angus.....234 D4
Finberry Kent.....40 D7
Fincham Norfk.....104 D2
Finchampstead Wokham.....49 J4
Fincharn Ag & B.....216 D6
Finchdean Hants.....35 B4
Finchingfield Essex.....88 D8
Finchley Gt Lon.....51 H1
Findern Derbys.....116 A5
Findhorn Moray.....265 G7
Findhorn Bridge Highld.....252 E6
Findochty Moray.....267 J3
Findo Gask P & K.....221 H3
Findon Abers.....245 L4
Findon W Susx.....21 J5
Findon Mains Highld.....263 G7
Findon Valley W Susx.....21 K5
Findrack House Abers.....244 D3
Finedon N Nthn.....85 H1
Fingal Street Suffk.....90 F1
Fingask P & K.....222 E3
Fingest Bucks.....49 J1
Finghall N York.....160 D5
Fingland Cumb.....177 H7
Fingland D & G.....197 L2
Finglesham Kent.....41 K4
Fingringhoe Essex.....72 F3
Finkle Green Essex.....88 D7
Finkle Street Barns.....141 M7
Finlake Devon.....13 K6
Finlarig Stirlg.....231 G8
Finmere Oxon.....84 C8
Finnart P & K.....230 F4
Finningham Suffk.....90 C2
Finningley Donc.....143 H7
Finsbay W Isls.....282 e6
Finstall Worcs.....82 A1
Finsthwaite W & F.....156 E5
Finstock Oxon.....66 A4
Finstown Ork.....275 c4
Fintry Abers.....268 D5
Fintry Stirlg.....209 G2

Finzean Abers...244 D5
Fionnphort Ag & B...226 B7
Fionnsbhagh W Isls...282 e6
Firbank W & F...157 K4
Firbeck Rothm...133 L2
Firby N York...152 A3
Firby N York...160 C5
Firgrove Rochdl...140 D5
Firle E Susx...23 G6
Firsby Lincs...137 H7
Firsdown Wilts...34 B4
Fir Tree Dur...168 F4
Fishbourne IoW...19 J5
Fishbourne W Susx...20 D6
Fishburn Dur...169 K4
Fishcross Clacks...220 F8
Fisher W Susx...20 E6
Fisherford Abers...256 B4
Fisherrow E Loth...211 K4
Fisher's Pond Hants...35 G6
Fisher's Row Lancs...147 H6
Fisherstreet W Susx...36 E4
Fisherton Highld...252 D2
Fisherton S Ayrs...196 B7
Fisherton de la Mere Wilts...33 G3
Fisherwick Staffs...98 F2
Fishery W & M...49 L3
Fishguard Pembks...74 F5
Fishlake Donc...143 G5
Fishleigh Devon...12 D2
Fishmere End Lincs...119 J4
Fishnish Pier Ag & B...227 J4
Fishpond Bottom Dorset...15 J3
Fishponds Bristl...45 J4
Fishtoft Lincs...119 K3
Fishtoft Drove Lincs...119 K2
Fishwick Lancs...139 H2
Fiskavaig Highld...246 D2
Fiskerton Lincs...135 L5
Fiskerton Notts...117 K1
Fitling E R Yk...145 H1
Fittleton Wilts...33 K1
Fittleworth W Susx...21 G3
Fitton End Cambs...103 J1
Fitz Shrops...113 G7
Fitzhead Somset...29 L5
Fitzroy Somset...30 B5
Fitzwilliam Wakefd...142 C5
Five Ash Down E Susx...23 H3
Five Ashes E Susx...23 J2
Five Bells Somset...29 K2
Five Bridges Herefs...80 F6
Fivecrosses Ches W...129 M4
Fivehead Somset...30 E6
Fivelanes Cnwll...11 J6
Five Lanes Mons...44 F1
Five Oak Green Kent...39 G4
Five Oaks Jersey...9 e3
Five Oaks W Susx...37 G5
Five Roads Carmth...56 E4
Five Wents Kent...39 K3
Flack's Green Essex...71 J4
Flackwell Heath Bucks...49 L1
Fladbury Worcs...82 A6
Fladdabister Shet...281 e7
Flagg Derbys...132 C6
Flamborough E R Yk...153 K2
Flamborough Head E R Yk...153 L2
Flamstead Herts...68 D4
Flamstead End Herts...69 J6
Flansham W Susx...20 F6
Flanshaw Wakefd...141 M4
Flappit Spring C Brad...149 J8
Flasby N York...149 G4
Flash Staffs...131 K6
Flashader Highld...258 E6
Flaunden Herts...68 C7
Flawborough Notts...117 K3
Flawith N York...151 G3
Flax Bourton N Som...45 G5
Flaxby N York...150 E4
Flaxley Gloucs...63 K4
Flaxmere Ches W...130 A5
Flaxpool Somset...29 L4
Flaxton N York...151 L3
Fleckney Leics...100 E5
Flecknoe Warwks...83 M3
Fledborough Notts...134 F5
Fleet Dorset...16 C6
Fleet Hants...20 B6
Fleet Hants...49 K8
Fleet Lincs...119 L6
Fleet End Hants...19 H3
Fleet Hargate Lincs...119 L6
Fleet Services Hants...49 J7
Fleetwood Lancs...146 F6
Fleggburgh Norfk...123 J8
Flemingston V Glam...42 F7
Flemington S Lans...209 H7
Flempton Suffk...89 G1

Fletchersbridge Cnwll...5 J2
Fletcher's Green Kent...38 E3
Fletchertown Cumb...165 G2
Fletching E Susx...23 G3
Fleur-de-lis Caerph...43 J3
Flexbury Cnwll...11 J1
Flexford Surrey...36 D1
Flimby Cumb...164 D4
Flimwell E Susx...39 H7
Flint Flints...128 F5
Flint Cross Cambs...87 H6
Flintham Notts...117 K2
Flint Mountain Flints...128 F5
Flinton E R Yk...153 K8
Flint's Green Solhll...99 H7
Flishinghurst Kent...39 J6
Flitcham Norfk...120 F6
Flitch Green Essex...71 G3
Flitton C Beds...85 L8
Flitwick C Beds...85 K8
Flixborough N Linc...143 L5
Flixborough Stather N Linc...143 L5
Flixton N York...163 J6
Flixton Suffk...107 G6
Flixton Traffd...130 E1
Flockton Kirk...141 K5
Flockton Green Kirk...141 L5
Flodden Nthumb...202 E6
Flodigarry Highld...259 G2
Flookburgh W & F...156 E7
Flordon Norfk...106 D4
Flore Nthn...84 C3
Flotterton Nthumb...190 E5
Flowers Green E Susx...23 L5
Flowton Suffk...90 C6
Flushdyke Wakefd...141 L4
Flushing Cnwll...3 K4
Fluxton Devon...14 C4
Flyford Flavell Worcs...82 A4
Fobbing Thurr...52 F2
Fochabers Moray...267 G4
Fochriw Caerph...61 H6
Fockerby N Linc...143 L4
Foddington Somset...31 J5
Foel Powys...94 B1
Foelgastell Carmth...59 G6
Foel y Dyffryn Brdgnd...42 C3
Foggathorpe E R Yk...152 A8
Fogo Border...202 B3
Fogwatt Moray...266 E5
Foindle Highld...276 B6
Folda Angus...233 J3
Fole Staffs...115 G4
Foleshill Covtry...99 K7
Folke Dorset...31 L8
Folkestone Kent...41 H6
Folkestone Services Kent...40 F7
Folkingham Lincs...118 E5
Folkington E Susx...23 J6
Folksworth Cambs...102 C5
Folkton N York...163 J6
Folla Rule Abers...256 C5
Follifoot N York...150 D5
Folly Gate Devon...12 D3
Folly Hill Surrey...36 B1
Fonmon V Glam...43 G8
Fonthill Bishop Wilts...32 F4
Fonthill Gifford Wilts...32 F4
Fontmell Magna Dorset...32 E7
Fontmell Parva Dorset...32 D7
Fontwell W Susx...20 F5
Font-y-gary V Glam...43 G8
Foolow Derbys...132 D4
Foots Cray Gt Lon...52 A5
Forbestown Abers...243 L1
Forcett N York...168 F8
Ford Ag & B...216 D6
Ford Bucks...67 J5
Ford Derbys...133 H4
Ford Devon...7 J5
Ford Devon...8 B6
Ford Devon...27 G6
Ford Gloucs...65 G1
Ford Nthumb...202 E5
Ford Shrops...95 K1
Ford Somset...29 K5
Ford Somset...45 H8
Ford Staffs...115 H1
Ford W Susx...21 G6
Ford Wilts...33 L4
Ford Wilts...46 B4
Forda Devon...12 D4
Fordcombe Kent...38 E5
Fordell Fife...211 G1
Forden Powys...94 F3
Ford End Essex...71 G4
Forder Green Devon...8 B2
Ford Green Lancs...147 J6
Fordham Cambs...88 C1
Fordham Essex...72 D2

Fordham Norfk...104 C3
Fordham Heath Essex...72 D2
Ford Heath Shrops...95 K1
Fordingbridge Hants...33 K8
Fordon E R Yk...163 J7
Fordoun Abers...245 G8
Ford's Green Suffk...90 C2
Fordstreet Essex...72 D2
Ford Street Somset...29 L7
Fordton Devon...13 J3
Fordwells Oxon...65 L4
Fordwich Kent...41 G3
Fordyce Abers...267 L3
Forebridge Staffs...114 E7
Foremark Derbys...116 B6
Forest Guern...9 j4
Forest N York...160 C3
Forest Becks Lancs...148 D5
Forestburn Gate Nthumb...190 F7
Forest Chapel Ches E...131 J5
Forest Coal Pit Mons...62 B3
Forest Gate Gt Lon...51 L2
Forest Green Surrey...37 H3
Forest Hall N Tyne...181 G5
Forest Head Cumb...178 D7
Forest Hill Gt Lon...51 K4
Forest Hill Oxon...66 E5
Forest-in-Teesdale Dur...167 K4
Forest Lane Head N York...150 D4
Forest Mill Clacks...221 G8
Forest of Bowland Lancs...148 A5
Forest of Dean Gloucs...63 J5
Forest Row E Susx...38 C6
Forest Side IoW...19 H5
Forestside W Susx...20 C4
Forest Town Notts...133 L7
Forfar Angus...234 C5
Forgandenny P & K...221 K3
Forge Powys...93 G3
Forge Hammer Torfn...62 B7
Forge Side Torfn...61 L5
Forgie Moray...267 H5
Forgieside Moray...267 H5
Forgue Abers...256 A3
Forhill Worcs...98 D8
Formby Sefton...138 C6
Forncett End Norfk...106 C4
Forncett St Mary Norfk...106 D4
Forncett St Peter Norfk...106 D5
Fornham All Saints Suffk...89 G2
Fornham St Martin Suffk...89 G2
Fornham St Genevieve Suffk...89 G2
Fornighty Highld...253 H2
Forres Moray...265 G8
Forsbrook Staffs...114 F3
Forse Highld...275 H1
Forshaw Heath Warwks...98 E8
Forsinard Highld...278 F7
Forss Highld...279 J3
Forston Dorset...16 C3
Fort Augustus Highld...240 C2
Forteviot P & K...221 J4
Forth S Lans...198 F2
Forthampton Gloucs...64 B1
Fort Hommet Guern...9 i2
Forth Rail Bridge C Edin...210 F3
Forth Road Bridge Fife...210 F3
Fortingall P & K...231 K6
Forton Hants...34 F2
Forton Lancs...147 J5
Forton Shrops...113 G8
Forton Somset...15 H1
Forton Staffs...114 B7
Fort Richmond Guern...9 i2
Fortrie Abers...256 B3
Fortrose Highld...263 K8
Fortuneswell Dorset...16 D7
Fort William Highld...239 J8
Forty Green Bucks...68 B8
Forty Hill Gt Lon...69 J7
Forward Green Suffk...90 C3
Fosbury Wilts...47 L7
Foscot Oxon...65 K3
Foscote W Nthn...84 C6
Fosdyke Lincs...119 K5
Fosdyke Bridge Lincs...119 K5
Foss P & K...231 L4
Fossebridge Gloucs...65 G5
Foss-y-ffin Cerdgn...76 E3
Fosterhouses Donc...143 G5
Foster Street Essex...70 C5
Foston Derbys...115 K5
Foston Leics...100 D4
Foston Lincs...117 M3
Foston N York...151 L3
Foston on the Wolds E R Yk...153 H4
Fotherby Lincs...136 F2
Fothergill Cumb...164 D4
Fotheringhay N Nthn...102 B5
Foula Shet...281 a7

Foula Airport Shet...281 a7
Foul Anchor Cambs...120 A7
Foulbridge Cumb...165 M1
Foulby Wakefd...142 B4
Foulden Border...202 E2
Foulden Norfk...104 F4
Foul End Warwks...99 H4
Foul Mile E Susx...23 K4
Foulness Island Essex...53 L1
Foulridge Lancs...148 F7
Foulsham Norfk...122 A6
Fountainhall Border...200 F3
Four Ashes Solhll...98 F8
Four Ashes Staffs...97 H6
Four Ashes Staffs...97 L2
Four Ashes Suffk...89 K1
Four Cabots Guern...9 j3
Four Crosses Powys...112 C7
Four Crosses Staffs...98 B2
Four Elms Kent...38 C4
Four Foot Somset...31 J4
Four Forks Somset...30 C3
Four Gates Bolton...139 J6
Four Gotes Cambs...120 A8
Four Lane End Barns...141 L7
Four Lane Ends Ches W...130 A7
Four Lanes Cnwll...3 H3
Fourlanes End Ches E...130 F7
Four Marks Hants...35 K4
Four Mile Bridge IoA...124 E4
Four Oaks Birm...98 E4
Four Oaks E Susx...24 F7
Four Oaks Gloucs...63 K2
Four Oaks Solhll...99 H7
Fourpenny Highld...264 C1
Four Points W Berk...48 E3
Four Roads Carmth...56 E3
Four Shire Stone Warwks...65 K1
Fourstones Nthumb...179 K5
Four Throws Kent...39 J7
Four Wents Kent...38 E3
Fovant Wilts...33 H5
Foveran Abers...257 H7
Fowey Cnwll...5 K4
Fowley Common Warrtn...139 K8
Fowlhall Kent...39 H4
Fowlis Angus...233 M8
Fowlis Wester P & K...221 G2
Fowlmere Cambs...87 G3
Fownhope Herefs...80 D8
Foxbar Rens...208 D6
Foxcombe Devon...12 C5
Fox Corner Surrey...50 B7
Foxcote Gloucs...64 E3
Foxcote Somset...45 L7
Foxdale IoM...154 c6
Foxearth Essex...89 G6
Foxendown Kent...52 E5
Foxfield W & F...156 B5
Foxham Wilts...46 B3
Fox Hatch Essex...70 E7
Foxhills Hants...18 E1
Foxhole Cnwll...4 F4
Foxholes N York...163 H8
Foxhunt Green E Susx...23 J4
Foxley Norfk...122 A7
Foxley W Nthn...84 C5
Foxley Wilts...46 C2
Foxlydiate Worcs...82 B2
Fox Street Essex...72 F2
Foxt Staffs...115 G2
Foxton Cambs...87 H5
Foxton Dur...169 K5
Foxton Leics...100 F5
Foxton N York...160 F5
Foxup N York...158 F7
Foxwist Green Ches W...130 C6
Foxwood Shrops...96 E8
Foy Herefs...63 H2
Foyers Highld...250 F3
Foynesfield Highld...253 G1
Fraddam Cnwll...2 F4
Fraddon Cnwll...4 E3
Fradley Staffs...98 F1
Fradswell Staffs...114 F5
Fraisthorpe E R Yk...153 J3
Framfield E Susx...23 H3
Framingham Earl Norfk...106 F3
Framingham Pigot Norfk...106 F3
Framlingham Suffk...91 G3
Frampton Dorset...16 B4
Frampton Lincs...119 K4
Frampton Cotterell S Glos...45 K3
Frampton Mansell Gloucs...64 D6
Frampton-on-Severn Gloucs...63 L5
Frampton West End Lincs...119 J3
Framsden Suffk...90 E3
Framwellgate Moor Dur...169 H2
Franche Worcs...97 J7
Frandley Ches W...130 C4

Frankaborough Devon ...11 M4
Frankby Wirral ...128 F2
Frankfort Norfk ...122 F6
Franklands Gate Herefs ...80 C6
Frankley Worcs ...98 C7
Frankley Services Worcs ...98 C7
Franksbridge Powys ...78 F4
Frankton Warwks ...83 K1
Frant E Susx ...38 F6
Fraserburgh Abers ...269 J3
Frating Essex ...73 G3
Frating Green Essex ...73 G2
Fratton C Port ...19 L4
Freathy Cnwll ...6 D4
Freckenham Suffk ...88 D1
Freckleton Lancs ...138 E2
Freebirch Derbys ...132 F5
Freeby Leics ...117 L7
Freefolk Hants ...25 G1
Freehay Staffs ...115 G3
Freeland Oxon ...66 B4
Freethorpe Norfk ...107 H2
Freethorpe Common Norfk ...107 H2
Freiston Lincs ...119 L3
Fremington Devon ...27 J4
Fremington N York ...159 J3
Frenchay S Glos ...45 J3
Frenchbeer Devon ...12 F5
French Street Kent ...51 M8
Frenich P & K ...232 B4
Frensham Surrey ...36 C3
Freshfield Sefton ...138 C6
Freshford Wilts ...46 A7
Freshwater IoW ...18 E6
Freshwater Bay IoW ...18 E6
Freshwater East Pembks ...55 G7
Fressingfield Suffk ...106 F7
Freston Suffk ...90 E7
Freswick Highld ...280 E3
Fretherne Gloucs ...63 L5
Frettenham Norfk ...122 E8
Freuchie Fife ...222 D6
Freystrop Pembks ...54 F4
Friar Park Sandw ...98 C4
Friar's Gate E Susx ...38 D4
Friars' Hill N York ...162 C5
Friar Waddon Dorset ...16 C5
Friday Bridge Cambs ...103 K2
Friday Street Suffk ...90 F3
Friday Street Suffk ...91 H5
Friday Street Suffk ...91 J3
Friday Street Surrey ...37 H2
Fridaythorpe E R Yk ...152 D4
Friden Derbys ...132 C7
Friendly Calder ...141 G3
Friern Barnet Gt Lon ...69 H8
Friesthorpe Lincs ...135 M3
Frieston Lincs ...118 B2
Frieth Bucks ...49 J1
Friezeland Notts ...116 D2
Frilford Oxon ...66 C7
Frilsham W Berk ...48 E4
Frimley Surrey ...49 L7
Frimley Green Surrey ...49 L7
Frindsbury Medway ...52 F5
Fring Norfk ...121 G4
Fringford Oxon ...66 F1
Frinsted Kent ...40 A4
Frinton-on-Sea Essex ...73 K3
Friockheim Angus ...234 F5
Friog Gwynd ...92 D1
Frisby on the Wreake Leics ...117 J8
Friskney Lincs ...137 J8
Friskney Eaudike Lincs ...137 J8
Friston E Susx ...23 J7
Friston Suffk ...91 J3
Fritchley Derbys ...116 R1
Fritham Hants ...34 B8
Frith Bank Lincs ...119 K2
Frith Common Worcs ...80 F1
Frithelstock Devon ...27 H7
Frithelstock Stone Devon ...27 H7
Frithend Hants ...36 B3
Frithsden Herts ...68 C5
Frithville Lincs ...119 K2
Frittenden Kent ...39 K5
Frittiscombe Devon ...8 B6
Fritton Norfk ...106 C4
Fritton Norfk ...107 K3
Fritwell Oxon ...66 D1
Frizinghall C Brad ...149 L8
Frizington Cumb ...164 D7
Frocester Gloucs ...63 M6
Frodesley Shrops ...96 C3
Frodsham Ches W ...129 M4
Frogden Border ...202 B7
Frog End Cambs ...87 H6
Frog End Cambs ...87 L3
Froggatt Derbys ...132 E4
Froghall Staffs ...115 G2

Frogham Hants ...33 L8
Frogham Kent ...41 H5
Frogmore Devon ...7 M6
Frognall Lincs ...102 D2
Frogpool Cnwll ...3 J3
Frog Pool Worcs ...81 J2
Frogwell Cnwll ...6 C1
Frolesworth Leics ...100 B5
Frome Somset ...32 C1
Frome St Quintin Dorset ...16 B2
Fromes Hill Herefs ...80 F6
Fron Gwynd ...108 F4
Fron Gwynd ...109 J1
Fron Powys ...94 E4
Fron Powys ...94 F3
Froncysyllte Wrexhm ...112 C3
Fron-goch Gwynd ...111 H4
Fron Isaf Wrexhm ...112 C3
Frostenden Suffk ...107 K7
Frosterley Dur ...160 C7
Frostenhall Herefs ...85 J8
Froxfield Wilts ...47 L5
Froxfield Green Hants ...35 L5
Fryern Hill Hants ...34 F6
Fryerning Essex ...70 F7
Fryton N York ...162 B7
Fuinary Highld ...227 J3
Fulbeck Lincs ...118 B2
Fulbourn Cambs ...87 L4
Fulbrook Oxon ...65 K4
Fulflood Hants ...35 G5
Fulford C York ...151 K6
Fulford Somset ...30 B5
Fulford Staffs ...114 E4
Fulham Gt Lon ...51 H4
Fulking W Susx ...22 C5
Fullaford Devon ...28 B3
Fullarton N Ayrs ...196 C3
Fuller's End Essex ...70 D2
Fuller's Moor Ches W ...113 H1
Fuller Street Essex ...71 H4
Fuller Street Kent ...38 E2
Fullerton Hants ...34 E3
Fulletby Lincs ...136 E5
Fullready Warwks ...83 G6
Full Sutton E R Yk ...151 A3
Fullwood E Ayrs ...196 E1
Fulmer Bucks ...50 C2
Fulmodeston Norfk ...121 M5
Fulnetby Lincs ...136 B4
Fulney Lincs ...119 J6
Fulstone Kirk ...141 J6
Fulstow Lincs ...145 J8
Fulwell Oxon ...66 A3
Fulwell Sundld ...181 J7
Fulwood Lancs ...139 H2
Fulwood Notts ...133 J8
Fulwood Sheff ...132 F3
Fulwood Somset ...30 B6
Fundenhall Norfk ...106 C4
Funtington W Susx ...20 C5
Funtley Hants ...19 J2
Funtullich P & K ...220 C2
Furley Devon ...15 G2
Furnace Ag & B ...217 G7
Furnace Carmth ...56 E3
Furnace Cerdgn ...92 E4
Furnace End Warwks ...99 H5
Furner's Green E Susx ...22 F2
Furness Vale Derbys ...131 K3
Furneux Pelham Herts ...70 B2
Further Quarter Kent ...39 M5
Furtho W Nthn ...84 E6
Furzehill Devon ...29 G2
Furzehill Dorset ...17 K2
Furzehills Lincs ...136 E5
Furzeley Corner Hants ...19 L2
Furze Platt W & M ...49 L3
Furzley Hants ...34 C7
Fyfett Somset ...30 C7
Fyfield Essex ...70 E5
Fyfield Hants ...34 C2
Fyfield Oxon ...66 B7
Fyfield Wilts ...47 H5
Fyfield Wilts ...47 H6
Fyfield Bavant Wilts ...33 H6
Fylingthorpe N York ...163 G2
Fyning W Susx ...36 B6
Fyvie Abers ...256 D4

G

Gabroc Hill E Ayrs ...196 E1
Gaddesby Leics ...100 F1
Gaddesden Row Herts ...68 D4
Gadfa IoA ...125 H2
Gadgirth S Ayrs ...196 E6
Gadlas Shrops ...112 E4

Gaer Powys ...61 J3
Gaerllwyd Mons ...62 F7
Gaerwen IoA ...125 H5
Gagingwell Oxon ...66 B2
Gailes N Ayrs ...196 C4
Gailey Staffs ...97 K1
Gainford Dur ...168 F7
Gainsborough Lincs ...135 G2
Gainsborough Suffk ...90 E6
Gainsford End Essex ...88 E8
Gairloch Highld ...260 C4
Gairlochy Highld ...239 K6
Gairneybridge P & K ...221 J2
Gaisgill W & F ...157 K2
Gaitsgill Cumb ...165 L1
Galashiels Border ...201 G6
Galgate Lancs ...147 J6
Galhampton Somset ...31 K5
Gallanachbeg Ag & B ...216 C2
Gallanachmore Ag & B ...216 C2
Gallantry Bank Ches E ...113 H1
Gallatown Fife ...222 F8
Galley Common Warwks ...99 J5
Galleywood Essex ...71 H6
Gallovie Highld ...240 F5
Galloway Forest Park ...184 C6
Gallowfauld Angus ...234 C7
Gallowhill P & K ...233 J8
Gallows Green Essex ...72 C4
Gallows Green Worcs ...81 L3
Gallowstree Common Oxon ...49 G3
Galltair Highld ...248 C7
Gallt-y-foel Gwynd ...125 K7
Gallypot Street E Susx ...38 D6
Galmisdale Highld ...236 F4
Galmpton Devon ...7 K6
Galmpton Torbay ...8 D4
Galphay N York ...150 C1
Galston E Ayrs ...196 F4
Gamballs Green Staffs ...131 L6
Gamblesby W & F ...166 E3
Gambles Green Essex ...71 J4
Gamelsby Cumb ...177 H8
Gamesley Derbys ...131 K1
Gamlingay Cambs ...86 E5
Gamlingay Cinques Cambs ...86 F4
Gamlingay Great Heath Cambs ...86 E5
Gammersgill N York ...159 J6
Gamrie Abers ...268 E4
Gamston Notts ...117 G4
Gamston Notts ...134 E4
Ganarew Herefs ...63 G4
Ganavan Bay Ag & B ...216 D1
Gang Cnwll ...6 C1
Ganllwyd Gwynd ...110 D6
Gannachy Angus ...234 F1
Ganstead E R Yk ...144 F1
Ganthorpe N York ...151 L2
Ganton N York ...163 H7
Ganwick Corner Herts ...69 H7
Gappah Devon ...13 K7
Garabal Ag & B ...266 F5
Garboldisham Norfk ...105 K7
Garbole Highld ...252 D2
Garchory Abers ...243 J2
Garden City Flints ...129 H6
Gardeners Green Wokham ...49 K5
Gardenstown Abers ...268 E3
Garden Village Sheff ...141 L8
Garderhouse Shet ...281 d6
Gardham E R Yk ...152 E7
Gare Hill Somset ...32 C3
Garelochhead Ag & B ...207 L1
Garford Oxon ...66 B7
Garforth Leeds ...142 D1
Gargrave N York ...149 G5
Gargunnock Stirlg ...220 B8
Garlic Street Norfk ...106 E6
Garlieston D & G ...174 D5
Garlinge Kent ...41 K2
Garlinge Green Kent ...40 F5
Garlogie Abers ...245 H2
Garmond Abers ...268 E3
Garmouth Moray ...267 G3
Garmston Shrops ...96 E2
Garnant Carmth ...59 J6
Garndolbenmaen Gwynd ...109 J3
Garnett Bridge W & F ...157 H3
Garnfadryn Gwynd ...108 E5
Garnlydan Blae G ...61 J4
Garnswllt Swans ...57 H3
Garn-yr-erw Torfn ...61 K5
Garrabost W Isls ...282 h3
Garrallan E Ayrs ...197 G7
Garras Cnwll ...3 H6
Garreg Gwynd ...109 J3
Garrigill W & F ...167 H3
Garriston N York ...159 L4
Garroch D & G ...184 F6
Garrochtrie D & G ...172 D7

Garrochty Ag & B ...207 H8
Garros Highld ...259 H4
Garsdale W & F ...158 C5
Garsdale Head W & F ...158 D4
Garsdon Wilts ...46 D2
Garshall Green Staffs ...114 F5
Garsington Oxon ...66 E6
Garstang Lancs ...147 J6
Garston Herts ...68 E7
Garston Lpool ...129 J3
Garswood St Hel ...139 H7
Gartachossan Ag & B ...204 E4
Gartcosh N Lans ...209 J5
Garth Brdgnd ...42 C5
Garth Mons ...62 D8
Garth Powys ...78 C5
Garth Powys ...79 J1
Garth Wrexhm ...112 C3
Garthamlock C Glas ...209 H5
Garthbrengy Powys ...78 E8
Garthmyl Powys ...94 F3
Garthorpe Leics ...117 L7
Garthorpe N Linc ...143 L4
Garth Row W & F ...157 H3
Garths W & F ...157 H5
Gartly Abers ...255 K5
Gartmore Stirlg ...219 K7
Gartness N Lans ...209 K6
Gartness Stirlg ...208 E2
Gartocharn W Duns ...208 D2
Garton E R Yk ...145 H1
Garton-on-the-Wolds E R Yk ...152 F4
Gartymore Highld ...274 D5
Garva Bridge Highld ...240 F4
Garvald Border ...199 J3
Garvald E Loth ...212 D5
Garvan Highld ...238 F8
Garvard Ag & B ...214 D6
Garve Highld ...262 C7
Garvellachs Ag & B ...215 J2
Garvestone Norfk ...105 L2
Garvock Inver ...207 L5
Garway Herefs ...62 F3
Garway Common Herefs ...62 F3
Garway Hill Herefs ...62 F2
Garynahine W Isls ...282 f3
Garyvard W Isls ...282 g4
Gasper Wilts ...32 C4
Gastard Wilts ...46 C5
Gasthorpe Norfk ...105 K7
Gaston Green Essex ...70 D4
Gatcombe IoW ...19 H6
Gateacre Lpool ...129 K2
Gatebeck W & F ...157 J5
Gate Burton Lincs ...135 G3
Gateford Notts ...134 B3
Gateforth N York ...142 E2
Gatehead E Ayrs ...196 D4
Gate Helmsley N York ...151 L5
Gatehouse Nthumb ...179 H1
Gatehouse of Fleet D & G ...174 F4
Gateley Norfk ...121 L6
Gatenby N York ...160 D5
Gatesgarth Cumb ...165 G7
Gateshaw Border ...189 L2
Gateshead Gatesd ...181 G6
Gates Heath Ches W ...129 L7
Gateside Angus ...234 C6
Gateside E Rens ...208 E7
Gateside Fife ...222 B5
Gateside N Ayrs ...208 B8
Gateslack D & G ...186 C5
Gathurst Wigan ...139 G6
Gatley Stockp ...131 G2
Gatton Surrey ...51 H8
Gattonside Border ...201 H6
Gatwick Airport W Susx ...37 L3
Gaufron Powys ...78 D2
Gaulby Leics ...100 F3
Gauldry Fife ...222 F2
Gauldswell P & K ...233 K5
Gaulkthorn Lancs ...139 M3
Gaultree Norfk ...103 K2
Gaunt's Bank Ches E ...113 J2
Gaunt's Common Dorset ...17 K2
Gaunt's End Essex ...70 E2
Gautby Lincs ...136 C5
Gavinton Border ...202 B3
Gawber Barns ...141 M6
Gawcott Bucks ...67 G1
Gawsworth Ches E ...131 H5
Gawthorpe Wakefd ...141 L3
Gawthrop W & F ...158 B5
Gawthwaite W & F ...156 C1
Gay Bowers Essex ...71 J4
Gaydon Warwks ...83 J4
Gayhurst M Keyn ...85 G6
Gayle N York ...158 F5
Gayles N York ...159 L1

Gay Street W Susx 21 J3
Gayton Norfk 120 F7
Gayton Staffs 114 F6
Gayton W Nthn 84 D4
Gayton Wirral 129 G4
Gayton le Marsh Lincs 137 H3
Gayton Thorpe Norfk 121 G7
Gaywood Norfk 120 E7
Gazeley Suffk 88 E2
Gear Cnwll 3 J6
Gearraidh Bhaird W Isls 282 g4
Gearraidh na h-Aibhne W Isls... 282 f3
Geary Highld 258 D4
Gedding Suffk 89 J4
Geddington N Nthn 101 K6
Gedling Notts 117 G3
Gedney Lincs 119 L6
Gedney Broadgate Lincs 119 L7
Gedney Drove End Lincs 120 A5
Gedney Dyke Lincs 119 L6
Gedney Hill Lincs 103 G1
Gee Cross Tamesd 131 J1
Geeston Rutlnd 101 L3
Geirinis W Isls 283 c10
Geldeston Norfk 107 H5
Gelli Rhondd 42 E3
Gelli Torfn 62 B8
Gellideg Myr Td 60 F5
Gellifor Denbgs 128 D7
Gelligaer Caerph 43 H2
Gelligroes Caerph 43 J3
Gelligron Neath 57 K4
Gellilydan Gwynd 110 C4
Gellinudd Neath 57 K4
Gelly Pembks 55 J3
Gellyburn P & K 233 G7
Gellywen Carmth 58 A4
Gelston D & G 175 J3
Gelston Lincs 118 B3
Gembling E R Yk 153 H4
Gentleshaw Staffs 98 D1
Georgefield D & G 187 L7
George Green Bucks 50 C3
Georgeham Devon 27 H3
Georgemas Junction Station
   Highld 279 L4
George Nympton Devon 28 B6
Georgetown Blae G 61 J5
Georgia Cnwll 2 D4
Georth Ork 275 c3
Gerlan Gwynd 126 C6
Germansweek Devon 12 B4
Germoe Cnwll 2 F5
Gerrans Cnwll 3 M4
Gerrards Cross Bucks 50 C1
Gerrick R & Cl 171 G8
Gestingthorpe Essex 89 G7
Gethsemane Pembks 75 J4
Geuffordd Powys 112 B8
Gib Hill Ches W 130 C4
Gibraltar Lincs 137 K7
Gibsmere Notts 117 J2
Giddeahall Wilts 46 B4
Gidea Park Gt Lon 52 B1
Gidleigh Devon 12 F5
Giffnock E Rens 208 F7
Gifford E Loth 212 C5
Giffordtown Fife 222 E5
Giggleswick N York 148 D3
Gigha Ag & B 205 L6
Gilberdyke E R Yk 143 L2
Gilbert's End Worcs 81 J6
Gilbert Street Hants 35 K4
Gilchriston E Loth 212 B6
Gilcrux Cumb 164 F3
Gildersome Leeds 141 K2
Gildingwells Rothm 133 L3
Gilesgate Moor Dur 169 J2
Gileston V Glam 42 F8
Gilfach Caerph 43 J2
Gilfach Goch Brdgnd 42 E4
Gilfachrheda Cerdgn 76 D3
Gilgarran Cumb 164 D6
Gill W & F 166 B5
Gillamoor N York 162 B4
Gillan Cnwll 3 K6
Gillen Highld 258 D5
Gillesbie D & G 187 J7
Gilling East N York 161 K7
Gillingham Dorset 32 D5
Gillingham Medway 53 G5
Gillingham Norfk 107 H5
Gilling West N York 160 B2
Gillock Highld 280 B4
Gillow Heath Staffs 131 H7
Gills Highld 280 D2
Gill's Green Kent 39 J7
Gilmanscleuch Border 188 B2

Gilmerton C Edin 211 J5
Gilmerton P & K 220 F2
Gilmonby Dur 168 C8
Gilmorton Leics 100 C6
Gilsland Nthumb 178 E5
Gilson Warwks 99 G5
Gilstead C Brad 149 L7
Gilston Border 200 F2
Gilston Herts 70 C4
Gilston Park Herts 70 B4
Giltbrook Notts 116 E2
Gilwern Mons 61 L4
Gimingham Norfk 122 F4
Ginclough Ches E 131 J4
Gingers Green E Susx 23 K5
Gipping Suffk 90 C3
Gipsey Bridge Lincs 119 J2
Girdle Toll N Ayrs 196 C3
Girlington C Brad 141 H1
Girlsta Shet 281 e6
Girsby N York 160 E1
Girtford C Beds 86 D5
Girthon D & G 174 F4
Girton Cambs 87 J3
Girton Notts 135 G6
Girvan S Ayrs 182 F3
Gisburn Lancs 148 E6
Gisleham Suffk 107 K5
Gislingham Suffk 90 C1
Gissing Norfk 106 C6
Gittisham Devon 14 D3
Givons Grove Surrey 50 F7
Gladestry Powys 79 J4
Gladsmuir E Loth 212 A4
Glais Swans 57 K5
Glaisdale N York 162 D2
Glamis Angus 234 B6
Glanaber Gwynd 110 B1
Glanaman Carmth 59 J6
Glandford Norfk 122 A3
Glan-Duar Carmth 76 F6
Glandwr Pembks 75 L6
Glan-Dwyfach Gwynd 109 J3
Glandy Cross Carmth 75 K6
Glandyfi Cerdgn 92 F4
Glangrwyney Powys 61 K4
Glanllynfi Brdgnd 42 C3
Glanmule Powys 94 E5
Glanrhyd Pembks 75 K4
Glan-rhyd Powys 57 L3
Glanton Nthumb 190 F3
Glanton Pike Nthumb 190 F3
Glanvilles Wootton Dorset 16 C1
Glan-y-don Flints 128 E4
Glan-y-llyn Cardif 43 H5
Glan-y-nant Powys 93 K6
Glan-yr-afon Gwynd 111 H3
Glan-yr-afon Gwynd 111 K3
Glan-yr-afon IoA 126 B4
Glan-yr-afon Swans 57 H4
Glan-y-wern Gwynd 109 L4
Glapthorn N Nthn 101 M5
Glapwell Derbys 133 J6
Glasbury Powys 79 H7
Glascoed Denbgs 127 K5
Glascoed Mons 62 C6
Glascote Staffs 99 G3
Glascwm Powys 79 G5
Glasfryn Conwy 111 H2
Glasgow C Glas 209 G6
Glasgow Airport Rens 208 E5
Glasgow Prestwick Airport
   S Ayrs 196 D5
Glasinfryn Gwynd 125 K6
Glasnacardoch Bay Highld 237 K2
Glasnakille Highld 247 H6
Glasphein Highld 258 B6
Glaspwll Powys 92 F4
Glassenbury Kent 39 J6
Glassford S Lans 197 L2
Glasshoughton Wakefd 142 C3
Glasshouse Gloucs 63 L3
Glasshouse Hill Gloucs 63 L3
Glasshouses N York 149 L3
Glasslaw Abers 268 F4
Glasson Cumb 177 H6
Glassonby W & F 166 D3
Glasson Dock Lancs 147 J4
Glasterlaw Angus 234 F5
Glaston Rutlnd 101 K3
Glastonbury Somset 31 H3
Glatton Cambs 102 C6
Glazebrook Warrtn 130 D1
Glazebury Warrtn 139 K8
Glazeley Shrops 96 F5
Gleadless Sheff 133 G3
Gleadsmoss Ches E 130 F6
Gleaston W & F 146 E2
Glebe Highld 250 F8
Gledhow Leeds 150 D8

Gledpark D & G 175 G5
Gledrid Shrops 112 D4
Glemsford Suffk 89 G5
Glen Achulish Highld 229 G4
Glenallachie Moray 254 E3
Glenancross Highld 237 K2
Glenaros House Ag & B 227 G4
Glen Auldyn IoM 154 f4
Glenbarr Ag & B 192 D1
Glenbarry Abers 267 L5
Glenbeg Highld 237 H8
Glenbervie Abers 245 G7
Glenboig N Lans 209 J5
Glenborrodale Highld 237 H8
Glenbranter Ag & B 217 J7
Glenbreck Border 187 G2
Glenbrittle Highld 246 F4
Glenbuck E Ayrs 198 B7
Glencally Angus 234 A3
Glencaple D & G 176 C5
Glencarse P & K 222 C2
Glencoe Highld 229 H4
Glencothe Border 199 J7
Glencraig Fife 222 B8
Glencrosh D & G 185 J5
Glendale Highld 258 B6
Glendaruel Ag & B 206 F2
Glendevon P & K 221 H6
Glendoe Lodge Highld 240 C2
Glendoick P & K 222 C3
Glenduckie Fife 222 D3
Glenegedale Ag & B 204 E6
Glenelg Highld 248 C3
Glenerney Moray 253 K2
Glenfarg P & K 221 L5
Glenfield Leics 100 C2
Glenfinnan Highld 238 E7
Glenfintaig Lodge Highld 239 L6
Glenfoot P & K 222 B4
Glenfyne Lodge Ag & B 217 L4
Glengarnock N Ayrs 208 B8
Glengolly Highld 279 K3
Glengorm Castle Ag & B 226 E1
Glengrasco Highld 259 G7
Glenholm Border 199 J6
Glenhoul D & G 184 F5
Glenkin Ag & B 207 J3
Glenkindie Abers 243 M1
Glenlivet Moray 254 D6
Glenlochar D & G 175 J2
Glenlomond P & K 222 B6
Glenluce D & G 172 F3
Glenmassen Ag & B 207 H2
Glenmavis N Lans 209 K5
Glen Maye IoM 154 b6
Glen Mona IoM 154 f4
Glenmore Highld 259 G8
Glenmore Lodge Highld 242 C2
Glen Nevis House Highld 229 J1
Glenochil Clacks 220 F8
Glen Parva Leics 100 C4
Glenquiech Angus 234 C3
Glenralloch Ag & B 206 D5
Glenridding W & F 165 L7
Glenrothes Fife 222 D7
Glenshero Lodge Highld 240 F5
Glenstriven Ag & B 207 H3
Glentham Lincs 135 K2
Glentrool D & G 183 J7
Glen Trool Lodge D & G 183 K7
Glentrium Highld 241 J4
Glentworth Lincs 135 J2
Glenuig Highld 237 K5
Glenvarragill Highld 259 H8
Glen Vine IoM 154 d6
Glenwhilly D & G 182 F8
Glespin S Lans 198 D7
Glewstone Herefs 63 H3
Glinton C Pete 102 C2
Glooston Leics 101 G4
Glossop Derbys 131 L1
Gloster Hill Nthumb 191 K5
Gloucester Gloucs 64 B3
Gloucester Services Gloucs 64 B4
Gloucestershire Airport Gloucs 64 C3
Glusburn N York 149 H6
Glutt Lodge Highld 274 D1
Gluvian Cnwll 4 F2
Glympton Oxon 66 B3
Glynarthen Cerdgn 76 B5
Glyn Ceiriog Wrexhm 112 B4
Glyncoch Rhondd 43 G3
Glyncorrwg Neath 60 C7
Glynde E Susx 23 G5
Glyndebourne E Susx 23 G5
Glyndyfrdwy Denbgs 112 A3
Glynneath Neath 60 D5
Glynogwr Brdgnd 42 E4
Glyntaff Rhondd 43 H4
Glyntawe Powys 60 C4

Glynteg Carmth 76 C7
Gnosall Staffs 114 C7
Gnosall Heath Staffs 114 C7
Goadby Leics 101 G4
Goadby Marwood Leics 117 G6
Goatacre Wilts 46 F4
Goatham Green E Susx 24 E3
Goathill Dorset 31 L7
Goathland N York 162 E2
Goathurst Somset 30 C4
Goathurst Common Kent 38 D3
Goat Lees Kent 40 D6
Gobowen Shrops 112 D5
Godalming Surrey 36 E2
Goddard's Corner Suffk 91 G2
Goddard's Green Kent 39 K6
Goddards Green W Susx 22 D3
Godden Green Kent 38 E2
Godford Cross Devon 14 D2
Godington Oxon 66 F2
Godley Tamesd 140 E8
Godmanchester Cambs 86 E1
Godmanstone Dorset 16 C3
Godmersham Kent 40 D5
Godney Somset 31 H2
Godolphin Cross Cnwll 2 F5
Godre'r-graig Neath 57 L3
Godshill Hants 33 L7
Godshill IoW 19 J7
Godstone Staffs 115 G5
Godstone Surrey 51 K8
Godsworthy Devon 12 C7
Godwinscroft Hants 18 B4
Goetre Mons 62 C6
Goff's Oak Herts 69 J6
Gogar C Edin 211 G4
Goginan Cerdgn 92 E7
Golan Gwynd 109 J3
Golant Cnwll 5 K4
Golberdon Cnwll 11 L8
Golborne Wigan 139 J8
Golcar Kirk 141 H4
Goldcliff Newpt 44 D2
Golden Cross E Susx 23 J4
Golden Green Kent 39 G4
Golden Grove Carmth 59 G5
Goldenhill C Stke 114 D1
Golden Hill Pembks 55 G5
Golden Pot Hants 35 L2
Golden Valley Derbys 116 C1
Golders Green Gt Lon 51 H2
Goldfinch Bottom W Berk 48 D6
Goldhanger Essex 72 C5
Gold Hill Cambs 103 L5
Gold Hill Dorset 32 D6
Golding Shrops 96 C3
Goldington Bed 86 B5
Goldsborough N York 150 E4
Goldsborough N York 171 G3
Goldsithney Cnwll 2 E5
Goldstone Kent 41 J3
Goldstone Shrops 113 M6
Goldthorpe Barns 142 C7
Goldworthy Devon 27 G6
Golford Kent 39 K6
Golford Green Kent 39 K6
Gollanfield Highld 252 F1
Gollinglith Foot N York 159 L6
Golly Wrexhm 129 H7
Golsoncott Somset 29 J3
Golspie Highld 273 K8
Gomeldon Wilts 33 L4
Gomersal Kirk 141 K3
Gomshall Surrey 37 G1
Gonalston Notts 117 H2
Gonerby Hill Foot Lincs 118 B4
Gonerby Moor Lincs 118 A4
Gonfirth Shet 281 d5
Goodameavy Devon 7 G2
Good Easter Essex 70 F5
Gooderstone Norfk 104 F3
Goodleigh Devon 27 L4
Goodmanham E R Yk 152 D7
Goodmayes Gt Lon 51 M2
Goodnestone Kent 40 D3
Goodnestone Kent 41 H4
Goodrich Herefs 63 H3
Goodrington Torbay 8 D3
Goodshaw Lancs 140 B3
Goodshaw Fold Lancs 140 B3
Goodstone Devon 13 H8
Goodwick Pembks 74 F4
Goodwood W Susx 20 E5
Goodworth Clatford Hants 34 D2
Goodyers End Warwks 99 J6
Goole E R Yk 143 J3
Goole Fields E R Yk 143 J3
Goom's Hill Worcs 82 B4
Goonbell Cnwll 4 B5
Goonhavern Cnwll 4 C4

Goonvrea Cnwll........................4 B5
Goosecruives Abers.............245 G7
Gooseford Devon....................12 F4
Goose Green Essex................73 H2
Goose Green Kent..................39 G3
Goose Green Kent..................39 L6
Goose Green S Glos...............45 K4
Goose Green W Susx...............21 J3
Goose Green Wigan...............139 H7
Gooseham Cnwll.....................26 D7
Gooseham Mill Cnwll...............26 D7
Goosehill Green Worcs............81 L3
Goose Pool Herefs..................80 B7
Goosey Oxon..........................47 M1
Goosnargh Lancs..................147 L8
Goostrey Ches E..................130 F5
Gordano Services N Som..........45 G4
Gorddinog Conwy..................126 D5
Gordon Border......................201 K4
Gordon Arms Hotel Border.....200 C8
Gordonstown Abers...............256 C4
Gordonstown Abers...............267 L5
Gore Powys............................79 J3
Gorebridge Mdloth................211 K6
Gorefield Cambs....................103 J1
Gore Pit Essex.......................72 C3
Gores Wilts............................47 G7
Gore Street Kent....................41 J2
Gorey Jersey............................9 f3
Goring Oxon...........................48 F3
Goring-by-Sea W Susx.............21 J6
Goring Heath Oxon.................49 G3
Gorleston-on-Sea Norfk.........107 L3
Gorrachie Abers....................268 D4
Gorran Churchtown Cnwll.........5 G6
Gorran Haven Cnwll..................5 G6
Gorran High Lanes Cnwll..........5 G6
Gorrig Cerdgn.........................76 D6
Gors Cerdgn...........................92 D7
Gorsedd Flints.......................128 D4
Gorseddau Slate Landscape
  Gwynd.............................109 K3
Gorse Hill Swindn...................47 H2
Gorsgoch Cerdgn.....................57 G5
Gorseybank Derbys................115 M1
Gorsgoch Cerdgn.....................76 F5
Gorslas Carmth.......................59 G6
Gorsley Gloucs........................63 K2
Gorsley Common Herefs..........63 K2
Gorstage Ches W...................130 B5
Gorstan Highld......................262 C7
Gorstella Ches W...................129 H7
Gorsten Ag & B......................227 L6
Gorst Hill Worcs......................81 G1
Gorsty Hill Staffs..................115 H6
Gorthleck Highld...................250 F7
Gorton Manch.......................140 C8
Gosbeck Suffk.........................90 D4
Gosberton Lincs.....................119 H5
Gosberton Clough Lincs.........119 G5
Gosfield Essex.........................71 J1
Gosford Devon.........................14 C3
Gosford Oxon..........................66 D4
Gosforth Cumb......................155 J2
Gosforth N u Ty.....................180 F5
Gosling Street Somset.............31 J4
Gosmore Herts........................68 F2
Gospel End Staffs....................97 K4
Gospel Green W Susx...............36 D4
Gosport Hants.........................19 K4
Gossard's Green C Beds............85 J6
Gossington Gloucs...................63 L6
Goswick Nthumb...................203 G4
Gotham Notts........................116 F5
Gotherington Gloucs...............64 D1
Gotton Somset........................30 C5
Goudhurst Kent.......................39 H6
Goulceby Lincs......................136 E4
Gourdas Abers......................256 D3
Gourdie C Dund....................222 F1
Gourdon Abers......................235 K1
Gourock Inver.......................207 L3
Govan C Glas.........................208 F6
Goveton Devon.........................7 L5
Govilon Mons..........................61 L4
Gowdall E R Yk......................143 G3
Gower Highld........................262 E8
Gower Swans..........................56 F6
Gowerton Swans......................57 G5
Gowkhall Fife.......................210 E1
Gowthorpe E R Yk..................152 A5
Goxhill E R Yk.......................153 K6
Goxhill N Linc.......................144 E3
Goytre Neath..........................57 L7
Grabhair W Isls.....................282 g4
Graby Lincs...........................118 E5
Grade Cnwll..............................3 H8
Gradeley Green Ches E...........113 K1
Graffham W Susx.....................20 F3
Grafham Cambs.......................86 D2

Grafham Surrey.......................36 F3
Grafton Herefs........................80 C7
Grafton Oxon..........................65 K7
Grafton Shrops......................113 G7
Grafton Worcs.........................80 D3
Grafton Worcs.........................82 A7
Grafton Flyford Worcs.............81 M4
Grafton Regis W Nthn..............84 E6
Grafton Underwood N Nthn....101 K7
Grafty Green Kent...................39 L4
Graianrhyd Denbgs...............128 F8
Graig Conwy..........................126 F5
Graig Denbgs.........................128 C5
Graigfechan Denbgs...............112 A1
Grain Medway..........................53 J4
Grains Bar Oldham................140 E6
Grainsby Lincs.......................145 H1
Grainthorpe Lincs.................145 K8
Grampound Cnwll......................4 F3
Grampound Road Cnwll............4 E5
Gramsdal W Isls.....................283 c9
Gramsdale W Isls...................283 c9
Granborough Bucks.................67 J2
Granby Notts.........................117 K4
Grandborough Warwks.............83 L2
Grand Chemins Jersey...............9 e3
Grandes Rocques Guern.............9 j2
Grandtully P & K...................232 D5
Grange Cumb.........................165 H1
Grange Medway........................53 G5
Grange P & K.........................222 D2
Grange Wirral........................128 F2
Grange Crossroads Moray......267 K5
Grange Hall Moray.................265 H7
Grangehall S Lans..................199 G4
Grange Hill Essex....................70 C8
Grangemill Derbys.................132 E8
Grange Moor Kirk..................141 K4
Grangemouth Falk.................210 B3
Grange of Lindores Fife..........222 D4
Grange-over-Sands W & F.......156 F7
Grangepans Falk....................210 D3
Grange Park W Nthn.................84 E4
Grangetown R & Cl................170 D6
Grangetown Sundld................181 K8
Grange Villa Dur....................180 F8
Gransmoor E R Yk..................153 H4
Gransmore Green Essex...........71 G3
Granston Pembks.....................74 E5
Grantchester Cambs.................87 J4
Grantham Lincs.....................118 B4
Granton C Edin......................211 H4
Grantown-on-Spey Highld.....253 K6
Grantsfield Herefs...................80 C3
Grantshouse Border...............213 H6
Grappenhall Warrtn...............130 C2
Grasby Lincs.........................144 D6
Grasmere W & F.....................156 D1
Grasscroft Oldham.................140 E6
Grassendale Lpool.................129 J3
Grassgarth Cumb...................165 K2
Grass Green Essex...................88 F7
Grassington N York................149 H3
Grassmoor Derbys.................133 H6
Grassthorpe Notts.................134 F6
Grateley Hants........................34 C3
Gratwich Staffs.....................115 G5
Graveley Cambs.......................86 E3
Graveley Herts........................69 G2
Gravelly Hill Birm...................98 E5
Gravelsbank Shrops................95 H3
Graveney Kent........................40 D3
Gravesend Kent.......................52 C4
Gravir W Isls.........................282 g4
Grayingham Lincs..................144 A8
Grayrigg W & F......................157 J3
Grays Thurr............................52 D3
Grayshott Hants......................36 C4
Grayson Green Cumb.............164 C5
Grayswood Surrey...................36 D4
Graythorpe Hartpl.................170 C5
Grazeley Wokham....................49 G5
Greasbrough Rothm...............142 C8
Greasby Wirral......................128 F2
Greasley Notts......................116 E2
Great Abington Cambs.............87 L5
Great Addington N Nthn........101 L8
Great Alne Warwks..................82 D3
Great Altcar Lancs.................138 C6
Great Amwell Herts..................69 K4
Great Asby W & F...................166 F8
Great Ashfield Suffk................89 K2
Great Ayton N York................170 D8
Great Baddow Essex.................71 H6
Great Badminton S Glos...........46 A2
Great Bardfield Essex...............71 G1
Great Barford Bed....................86 C5
Great Barr Sandw....................98 D4
Great Barrington Gloucs...........65 J4
Great Barrow Ches W.............129 L6

Great Barton Suffk..................89 H2
Great Barugh N York..............162 C6
Great Bavington Nthumb.......180 B3
Great Bealings Suffk.................90 F5
Great Bedwyn Wilts.................47 K6
Great Bentley Essex.................73 J4
Great Billing W Nthn................84 F3
Great Bircham Norfk..............121 G5
Great Blakenham Suffk............90 D5
Great Blencow W & F.............166 B4
Great Bolas Wrekin................113 L7
Great Bookham Surrey.............50 E8
Great Bosullow Cnwll................2 C4
Great Bourton Oxon.................83 K6
Great Bowden Leics................101 G5
Great Bradley Suffk..................88 D4
Great Braxted Essex.................72 B4
Great Bricett Suffk...................90 B5
Great Brickhill Bucks................67 L1
Great Bridge Sandw..................98 C5
Great Bridgeford Staffs..........114 D6
Great Brington W Nthn............84 C2
Great Bromley Essex.................73 G2
Great Broughton Cumb..........164 E4
Great Broughton N York.........161 J2
Great Budworth Ches W.........130 C4
Great Burdon Darltn..............169 J7
Great Burstead Essex...............71 G8
Great Busby N York................161 J1
Great Canfield Essex................70 E3
Great Carlton Lincs................137 H3
Great Casterton Rutlnd..........101 M2
Great Chalfield Wilts................46 B6
Great Chart Kent.....................40 C7
Great Chatwell Staffs.............114 B8
Great Chell C Stke..................114 D1
Great Chesterford Essex...........87 K6
Great Cheverell Wilts...............46 E8
Great Chishill Cambs................87 J7
Great Clacton Essex.................73 J4
Great Cliff Wakefd..................141 M4
Great Clifton Cumb................164 D5
Great Coates NE Lin...............145 G6
Great Comberton Worcs...........81 L6
Great Comp Kent......................39 G2
Great Corby Cumb..................178 B7
Great Cornard Suffk.................89 H7
Great Cowden E R Yk.............153 L7
Great Coxwell Oxon.................65 K8
Great Cransley N Nthn...........101 H8
Great Cressingham Norfk.......105 G3
Great Crosthwaite Cumb........165 H4
Great Cubley Derbys...............115 K4
Great Cumbrae Island N Ayrs..207 K7
Great Dalby Leics...................117 K8
Great Denham Bed...................85 K5
Great Doddington N Nthn........85 H2
Great Doward Herefs................63 G4
Great Dunham Norfk..............121 J8
Great Dunmow Essex...............70 F3
Great Durnford Wilts...............33 K3
Great Easton Essex...................70 F2
Great Easton Leics..................101 J5
Great Eccleston Lancs............147 H1
Great Edstone N York.............162 C6
Great Ellingham Norfk...........105 L4
Great Elm Somset....................32 C1
Great Everdon W Nthn............84 B4
Great Eversden Cambs.............87 H4
Great Fencote N York.............160 D4
Greatfield Wilts........................47 G2
Great Finborough Suffk............89 K4
Greatford Lincs.....................102 B1
Great Fransham Norfk............105 H1
Great Gaddesden Herts............68 C5
Greatgate Staffs....................115 G3
Great Gidding Cambs.............102 C6
Great Givendale E R Yk..........152 B5
Great Glemham Suffk...............91 H3
Great Glen Leics....................100 E4
Great Gonerby Lincs...............118 B4
Great Gransden Cambs............86 F4
Great Green Cambs...................86 F5
Great Green Norfk..................106 F5
Great Green Suffk....................89 J2
Great Green Suffk....................89 J4
Great Habton N York..............162 D7
Great Hale Lincs....................118 F3
Great Hallingbury Essex...........70 D3
Greatham Hants.......................36 A5
Greatham Hartpl....................170 C5
Greatham W Susx....................21 H4
Great Hampden Bucks..............67 K6
Great Harrowden N Nthn.........85 G1
Great Harwood Lancs.............139 L1
Great Haseley Oxon..................66 F6
Great Hatfield E R Yk.............153 K7
Great Haywood Staffs............114 F7
Great Heck N York.................142 F3
Great Henny Essex....................89 H7

Great Hinton Wilts...................46 C7
Great Hockham Norfk.............105 J5
Great Holland Essex.................73 J3
Great Hollands Br For.............49 L5
Great Horkesley Essex.............72 E1
Great Hormead Herts...............69 L1
Great Horton C Brad..............141 J2
Great Horwood Bucks..............67 J1
Great Houghton Barns...........142 C6
Great Houghton W Nthn..........84 F3
Great Hucklow Derbys...........132 D4
Great Kelk E R Yk..................153 H4
Great Kimble Bucks.................67 K6
Great Kingshill Bucks..............67 L7
Great Langdale W & F.............156 D2
Great Langton N York.............160 D3
Great Leighs Essex...................71 H4
Great Limber Lincs................144 E6
Great Linford M Keyn...............85 G6
Great Livermere Suffk.............89 H1
Great Longstone Derbys.........132 D5
Great Lumley Dur...................169 J1
Great Lyth Shrops....................95 L2
Great Malvern Worcs................81 H6
Great Maplestead Essex...........89 G8
Great Marton Bpool................138 C1
Great Massingham Norfk........121 H7
Great Melton Norfk................106 C2
Great Meols Wirral.................128 F2
Great Milton Oxon...................66 F6
Great Missenden Bucks............67 L6
Great Mitton Lancs................148 C8
Great Mongeham Kent.............41 K5
Great Moulton Norfk.............106 D5
Great Munden Herts.................69 K2
Great Musgrave W & F...........167 H7
Great Ness Shrops..................112 F7
Great Notley Essex...................71 H3
Great Oak Mons......................62 D5
Great Oakley Essex...................73 J2
Great Oakley N Nthn..............101 J6
Great Offley Herts....................68 F2
Great Ormside W & F.............167 H7
Great Orton Cumb.................177 K7
Great Ouseburn N York..........150 F3
Great Oxendon W Nthn..........100 F6
Great Oxney Green Essex.........71 G6
Great Palgrave Norfk.............105 G1
Great Pardon Essex...................70 B5
Great Paxton Cambs.................86 E3
Great Plumpton Lancs............138 D1
Great Plumstead Norfk..........106 F2
Great Ponton Lincs................118 B5
Great Potheridge Devon..........27 J7
Great Preston Leeds...............142 B2
Great Purston W Nthn.............83 M7
Great Raveley Cambs..............102 E7
Great Rissington Gloucs...........65 J4
Great Rollright Oxon...............65 L1
Great Ryburgh Norfk..............121 L6
Great Ryle Nthumb................190 E4
Great Ryton Shrops.................96 B3
Great Saling Essex....................71 G2
Great Salkeld W & F...............166 D3
Great Sampford Essex..............88 C8
Great Saredon Staffs................98 B2
Great Saughall Ches W...........129 H5
Great Saxham Suffk..................88 F3
Great Shefford W Berk.............48 A4
Great Shelford Cambs...............87 J5
Great Smeaton N York............160 E2
Great Snoring Norfk...............121 L4
Great Somerford Wilts.............46 D2
Great Soudley Shrops.............114 A5
Great Stainton Darltn............169 J6
Great Stambridge Essex............53 J1
Great Staughton Cambs...........86 C2
Great Steeping Lincs...............137 H6
Great Stonar Kent....................41 K3
Greatstone-on-Sea Kent...........25 K3
Great Strickland W & F...........166 D6
Great Stukeley Cambs.............102 E8
Great Sturton Lincs................136 D4
Great Sutton Ches W..............129 J4
Great Sutton Shrops.................96 C6
Great Swinburne Nthumb.......179 L4
Great Tew Oxon........................66 B1
Great Tey Essex........................72 C2
Great Thurlow Suffk.................88 D5
Great Torrington Devon...........27 J7
Great Tosson Nthumb.............190 E6
Great Totham Essex..................72 B5
Great Totham Essex..................72 C4
Great Tows Lincs....................136 D2
Great Urswick W & F..............156 C7
Great Wakering Essex...............53 K2
Great Waldingfield Suffk..........89 H6
Great Walsingham Norfk........121 L4
Great Waltham Essex...............71 G4

Great Warford Ches E.........130 F4
Great Warley Essex..........52 C1
Great Washbourne Gloucs........82 A8
Great Weeke Devon.........13 G5
Great Welnetham Suffk.........89 H3
Great Wenham Suffk..........90 C7
Great Whittington Nthumb....180 B5
Great Wigborough Essex........72 D4
Great Wilbraham Cambs......87 L4
Great Wilne Derbys.........116 D5
Great Wishford Wilts..........33 J4
Great Witchingham Norfk....122 C7
Great Witcombe Gloucs.......64 D4
Great Witley Worcs.........81 H2
Great Wolford Warwks........82 F8
Greatworth W Nthn.........84 A6
Great Wratting Suffk.........88 D5
Great Wymondley Herts.......69 G2
Great Wyrley Staffs.........98 C2
Great Wytheford Shrops....113 J7
Great Yarmouth Norfk......107 L2
Great Yeldham Essex........88 F7
Grebby Lincs.........137 H6
Greeba IoM.........154 d6
Green Denbgs.........128 C6
Green Bank W & F.........156 E6
Greenbottom Cnwll.........4 C6
Greenburn W Loth.........210 B7
Greencroft Hall Dur.........168 F1
Green Cross Surrey.........36 C3
Green Down Somset.........45 H8
Green End Bed.........85 K5
Green End Bed.........86 B2
Green End Bed.........86 B3
Green End Bed.........86 C5
Green End Cambs.........87 H4
Green End Cambs.........87 K2
Green End Cambs.........87 K3
Green End Cambs.........102 D6
Green End Cambs.........102 E8
Green End Herts.........69 H1
Green End Herts.........69 J3
Green End Herts.........87 G8
Greenend Oxon.........65 L3
Green End Warwks.........99 H6
Greenfield Ag & B.........207 L1
Greenfield C Beds.........85 L8
Greenfield Flints.........128 E4
Greenfield Highld.........239 L3
Greenfield Oldham.........140 F7
Greenfield Oxon.........49 H1
Greenford Gt Lon.........50 F3
Greengairs N Lans.........209 L5
Greengates C Brad.........150 B8
Greengill Cumb.........164 F3
Greenhalgh Lancs.........147 H8
Greenham Somset.........29 K6
Greenham W Berk.........48 C6
Green Hammerton N York.........151 G4
Greenhaugh Nthumb.........179 J2
Green Head Cumb.........165 L1
Greenhead Nthumb.........178 F6
Green Heath Staffs.........98 C1
Greenheys Salfd.........139 L7
Greenhill D & G.........176 F3
Greenhill Falk.........209 L3
Greenhill Herefs.........81 G5
Greenhill Kent.........40 F2
Greenhill Leics.........99 M1
Greenhill S Lans.........198 F6
Green Hill Wilts.........46 F2
Greenhillocks Derbys.........116 C2
Greenhills S Lans.........209 G8
Greenhithe Kent.........52 C4
Greenholm E Ayrs.........197 G3
Greenholme W & F.........157 J2
Greenhouse Border.........188 F2
Greenhow Hill N York.........149 K3
Greenland Highld.........280 B3
Greenland Sheff.........133 H2
Greenlands Bucks.........49 J2
Green Lane Devon.........13 H7
Green Lane Worcs.........82 C2
Greenlaw Border.........201 L4
Greenlea D & G.........176 D4
Greenloaning P & K.........220 E5
Green Moor Barns.........141 L7
Greenmount Bury.........140 A5
Green Oak E R Yk.........143 K2
Greenock Inver.........207 M4
Greenodd W & F.........156 D6
Green Ore Somset.........31 J1
Green Park Readg.........49 H5
Green Quarter W & F.........157 G2
Greensgate Norfk.........122 B8
Greenshields S Lans.........199 H4
Greenside Gatesd.........180 E6
Greenside Kirk.........141 H6
Greens Norton W Nthn.........84 C5
Greenstead Green Essex.........71 K2

Greensted Essex.........70 D6
Green Street E Susx.........24 D5
Green Street Gloucs.........64 C4
Green Street Herts.........69 G7
Green Street Herts.........70 C3
Green Street Worcs.........81 K5
Green Street Green Gt Lon.........51 M6
Green Street Green Kent.........52 C5
Greenstreet Green Suffk.........90 B5
Green Tye Herts.........70 C3
Greenway Gloucs.........81 G8
Greenway Somset.........30 D6
Greenway V Glam.........43 G7
Greenway Worcs.........81 G1
Greenwich Gt Lon.........51 K3
Greenwich Maritime Gt Lon.........51 K3
Greet Gloucs.........64 F1
Greete Shrops.........80 D1
Greetham Lincs.........136 F5
Greetham Rutlnd.........118 B8
Greetland Calder.........141 G3
Gregson Lane Lancs.........139 J2
Greinton Somset.........30 F4
Grenaby IoM.........154 c7
Grendon N Nthn.........85 G3
Grendon Warwks.........99 H3
Grendon Green Herefs.........80 E4
Grendon Underwood Bucks.........67 G3
Grenofen Devon.........12 C8
Grenoside Sheff.........133 G1
Greosabhagh W Isls.........282 e6
Gresford Wrexhm.........112 E1
Gresham Norfk.........122 D4
Greshornish Highld.........258 E6
Gressenhall Norfk.........121 L8
Gressenhall Green Norfk.........121 L8
Gressingham Lancs.........147 L2
Gresty Green Ches E.........113 M1
Greta Bridge Dur.........168 D8
Gretna D & G.........177 K5
Gretna Green D & G.........177 K5
Gretna Services D & G.........177 J5
Gretton Gloucs.........64 E1
Gretton N Nthn.........101 K4
Gretton Shrops.........96 C4
Grewelthorpe N York.........160 C7
Grey Friars Suffk.........91 L1
Greygarth N York.........150 A1
Grey Green N Linc.........143 K6
Greylake Somset.........30 F4
Greylees Lincs.........118 D3
Greyrigg D & G.........176 E1
Greys Green Oxon.........49 H2
Greysouthen Cumb.........164 E5
Greystoke W & F.........166 B4
Greystone Angus.........234 E6
Greywell Hants.........35 L1
Gribb Dorset.........15 J2
Gribthorpe E R Yk.........143 J1
Griff Warwks.........99 K5
Griffithstown Torfn.........62 C7
Griffydam Leics.........116 C7
Griggs Green Hants.........36 B4
Grimeford Village Lancs.........139 J5
Grimesthorpe Sheff.........133 G2
Grimethorpe Barns.........142 C6
Grimister Shet.........281 e3
Grimley Worcs.........81 J3
Grimmet S Ayrs.........183 J1
Grimoldby Lincs.........137 G2
Grimpo Shrops.........112 E6
Grimsargh Lancs.........139 H1
Grimsby NE Lin.........145 H5
Grimscote W Nthn.........84 C4
Grimscott Cnwll.........11 J1
Grimshader W Isls.........282 g4
Grimshaw Bl w D.........139 L3
Grimshaw Green Lancs.........139 G5
Grimsthorpe Lincs.........118 D7
Grimston E R Yk.........145 H1
Grimston Leics.........117 J7
Grimston Norfk.........120 F7
Grimstone Dorset.........16 C4
Grimstone End Suffk.........89 J2
Grinacombe Moor Devon.........12 A4
Grindale E R Yk.........153 J2
Grindle Shrops.........97 G3
Grindleford Derbys.........132 E4
Grindleton Lancs.........148 D6
Grindley Brook Shrops.........113 H3
Grindlow Derbys.........132 D4
Grindon Nthumb.........202 L4
Grindon S on T.........169 K5
Grindon Staffs.........115 H1
Grindon Hill Nthumb.........179 J5
Grindonrigg Nthumb.........202 L4
Gringley on the Hill Notts.........134 E2
Grinsdale Cumb.........177 L7
Grinshill Shrops.........113 H6
Grinton N York.........159 J3

Griomsiadar W Isls.........282 g4
Grishipoll Ag & B.........224 F3
Grisling Common E Susx.........23 G3
Gristhorpe N York.........163 K6
Griston Norfk.........105 J4
Gritley Ork.........275 d5
Grittenham Wilts.........46 F2
Grittleton Wilts.........46 B3
Grizebeck W & F.........156 C5
Grizedale W & F.........156 D4
Groby Leics.........100 B2
Groes Conwy.........127 K6
Groes-faen Rhondd.........43 G5
Groesffordd Gwynd.........108 D4
Groesffordd Powys.........61 G2
Groesffordd Marli Denbgs.........127 K5
Groeslon Gwynd.........125 H8
Groeslon Gwynd.........125 J7
Groes-lwyd Powys.........94 F1
Groes-Wen Caerph.........43 H4
Grogarry W Isls.........283 c10
Grogport Ag & B.........194 C2
Groigearraidh W Isls.........283 c10
Gromford Suffk.........91 J3
Gronant Flints.........128 C3
Groombridge E Susx.........38 C6
Grosebay W Isls.........282 e6
Grosmont Mons.........62 E2
Grosmont N York.........162 E2
Groton Suffk.........89 J7
Grotton Oldham.........140 F6
Grouville Jersey.........9 e3
Grove Bucks.........67 M3
Grove Dorset.........16 D8
Grove Kent.........41 H3
Grove Notts.........134 E4
Grove Oxon.........48 B1
Grove Pembks.........55 G6
Grove Green Kent.........39 K2
Grovenhurst Kent.........39 H5
Grove Park Gt Lon.........51 L4
Grovesend S Glos.........45 K1
Grovesend Swans.........57 G6
Grubb Street Kent.........52 C5
Gruinard Highld.........260 F2
Gruinart Ag & B.........204 D3
Grula Highld.........246 E3
Gruline Ag & B.........227 G4
Grumbla Cnwll.........2 C5
Grundisburgh Suffk.........90 F5
Gruting Shet.........281 c6
Grutness Shet.........281 d9
Gualachulain Highld.........229 J6
Guanockgate Lincs.........103 H2
Guardbridge Fife.........223 H3
Guarlford Worcs.........81 J6
Guay P & K.........232 F5
Guernsey Guern.........9 j3
Guernsey Airport Guern.........9 i3
Guestling Green E Susx.........24 F4
Guestling Thorn E Susx.........24 F4
Guestwick Norfk.........122 B6
Guide Bridge Tamesd.........140 D8
Guide Post Nthumb.........181 G2
Guilden Morden Cambs.........86 F6
Guilden Sutton Ches W.........129 K6
Guildford Surrey.........36 F1
Guildstead Kent.........53 H6
Guildtown P & K.........221 L1
Guilsborough W Nthn.........84 D1
Guilsfield Powys.........94 F1
Guilton Kent.........41 J4
Guiltreehill S Ayrs.........183 J1
Guineaford Devon.........27 K3
Guisborough R & Cl.........170 E7
Guiseley Leeds.........150 B7
Guist Norfk.........121 M6
Guiting Power Gloucs.........65 G2
Gullane E Loth.........212 B2
Gulling Green Suffk.........89 G4
Gulval Cnwll.........2 D5
Gulworthy Devon.........12 B8
Gumfreston Pembks.........55 J6
Gumley Leics.........100 F5
Gummow's Shop Cnwll.........4 C5
Gunby E R Yk.........143 H1
Gunby Lincs.........118 B7
Gundleton Hants.........35 J4
Gun Green Kent.........39 J7
Gun Hill E Susx.........23 J4
Gun Hill Warwks.........99 H5
Gunn Devon.........27 L4
Gunnerside N York.........159 G3
Gunnerton Nthumb.........179 L4
Gunness N Linc.........143 L5
Gunnislake Cnwll.........12 B8
Gunnista Shet.........281 e6
Gunthorpe C Pete.........102 D3
Gunthorpe N Linc.........143 K8
Gunthorpe Norfk.........121 M4

Gunthorpe Notts.........117 H
Gunton Suffk.........107 L
Gunwalloe Cnwll.........3 G
Gupworthy Somset.........29 H
Gurnard IoW.........19 H
Gurnett Ches E.........131 H
Gurney Slade Somset.........31 K
Gurnos Powys.........57 L
Gushmere Kent.........40 D
Gussage All Saints Dorset.........33 G
Gussage St Andrew Dorset.........33 G
Gussage St Michael Dorset.........33 G
Guston Kent.........41 K
Gutcher Shet.........281 e
Guthrie Angus.........234 E
Guyhirn Cambs.........103 H
Guyhirn Gull Cambs.........103 H
Guy's Marsh Dorset.........32 D
Guyzance Nthumb.........191 J
Gwaenysgor Flints.........128 C
Gwalchmai IoA.........125 G4
Gwastadnant Gwynd.........126 C
Gwaun-Cae-Gurwen Carmth.........59 J6
Gwbert on Sea Cerdgn.........75 K2
Gwealavellan Cnwll.........2 F3
Gweek Cnwll.........3 H
Gwehelog Mons.........62 D6
Gwenddwr Powys.........78 E6
Gwennap Cnwll.........3 J3
Gwennap Mining District Cnwll.........4 B6
Gwenter Cnwll.........3 J7
Gwernaffield Flints.........128 F6
Gwernesney Mons.........62 E6
Gwernogle Carmth.........58 F2
Gwernymynydd Flints.........128 F7
Gwersyllt Wrexhm.........112 D1
Gwespyr Flints.........128 D3
Gwindra Cnwll.........4 F4
Gwinear Cnwll.........2 F4
Gwithian Cnwll.........2 F3
Gwredog IoA.........125 G3
Gwrhay Caerph.........61 J7
Gwyddelwern Denbgs.........111 L2
Gwyddgrug Carmth.........58 E2
Gwynfryn Wrexhm.........112 C1
Gwystre Powys.........78 E2
Gwytherin Conwy.........127 H7
Gyfelia Wrexhm.........112 E3
Gyrn Goch Gwynd.........109 G2

H

Habberley Shrops.........95 K3
Habberley Worcs.........97 H7
Habergham Lancs.........140 B1
Habertoft Lincs.........137 J6
Habin W Susx.........36 B6
Habrough NE Lin.........144 F5
Hacconby Lincs.........118 E6
Haceby Lincs.........118 D4
Hacheston Suffk.........91 G3
Hackbridge Gt Lon.........51 H5
Hackenthorpe Sheff.........133 H3
Hackford Norfk.........106 B3
Hackforth N York.........160 C4
Hack Green Ches E.........113 L2
Hackland Ork.........275 c4
Hackleton W Nthn.........84 F4
Hacklinge Kent.........41 K4
Hackman's Gate Worcs.........97 K7
Hackness N York.........163 H4
Hackness Somset.........30 E2
Hackney Gt Lon.........51 K2
Hackthorn Lincs.........135 K3
Hackthorpe W & F.........166 C4
Hacton Gt Lon.........52 C2
Hadden Border.........202 B6
Haddenham Bucks.........67 H5
Haddenham Cambs.........103 J8
Haddington E Loth.........212 B4
Haddington Lincs.........135 H7
Haddiscoe Norfk.........107 J4
Haddon Cambs.........102 C5
Hade Edge Kirk.........141 J6
Hadfield Derbys.........140 F8
Hadham Cross Herts.........70 B3
Hadham Ford Herts.........70 B3
Hadleigh Essex.........53 H2
Hadleigh Suffk.........89 L6
Hadleigh Heath Suffk.........89 K7
Hadley Worcs.........81 K2
Hadley Wrekin.........96 F1
Hadley End Staffs.........115 J7
Hadley Wood Gt Lon.........69 H7
Hadlow Kent.........39 G3
Hadlow Down E Susx.........23 J2
Hadnall Shrops.........113 H7
Hadrian's Wall.........179 M5

Hadstock Essex...........88 B6
Hadston Nthumb.........191 K6
Hadzor Worcs............81 L3
Haffenden Quarter Kent....39 M5
Hafodunos Conwy........127 H6
Hafod-y-bwch Wrexhm.....112 D2
Hafod-y-coed Blae G.......61 K7
Hafodyrynys Caerph........61 K7
Haggate Lancs..........140 C1
Haggbeck Cumb.........178 B4
Haggersta Shet.........281 d6
Haggerston Nthumb......203 G4
Haggington Hill Devon.....27 K2
Haggs Falk............209 L3
Hagley Herefs...........80 D7
Hagley Worcs...........97 K7
Hagmore Green Suffk......89 J7
Hagnaby Lincs.........136 F7
Hagnaby Lincs.........137 J4
Hagworthingham Lincs....136 F6
Haigh Wigan...........139 J6
Haighton Green Lancs.....139 H1
Haile Cumb............155 J1
Hailes Gloucs...........64 F1
Hailey Herts...........69 K5
Hailey Oxon............48 F2
Hailey Oxon............65 M4
Hailsham E Susx........23 K5
Hail Weston Cambs........86 D3
Hainault Gt Lon.........70 C8
Haine Kent............41 K2
Hainford Norfk.........122 E7
Hainton Lincs.........136 C3
Hainworth C Brad.......149 J8
Haisthorpe E R Yk......153 H3
Hakin Pembks...........54 E5
Halam Notts...........117 H1
Halbeath Fife.........210 F1
Halberton Devon........29 H8
Halcro Highld.........280 B4
Hale Halton..........129 L3
Hale Hants............33 L7
Hale Somset...........32 C5
Hale Surrey...........36 C1
Hale Traffd..........130 F2
Hale W & F...........157 H7
Hale Bank Halton.......129 L3
Hale Barns Traffd......130 F3
Hale Green E Susx.......23 J4
Hale Nook Lancs.......147 G7
Hales Norfk...........107 H4
Hales Staffs.........113 M5
Halesgate Lincs.......119 K6
Hales Green Derbys.....115 K3
Halesowen Dudley.......98 B6
Hales Place Kent........40 F3
Hale Street Kent........39 G3
Halesville Essex.......72 C8
Halesworth Suffk.......107 H7
Halewood Knows.......129 K3
Halford Devon..........13 J7
Halford Shrops.........95 K6
Halford Warwks.........83 G6
Halfpenny W & F.......157 H5
Halfpenny Green Staffs....97 J5
Halfpenny Houses N York...160 B5
Halfway Carmth.........59 J3
Halfway Carmth.........59 M2
Halfway Sheff.........133 J3
Halfway W Berk.........48 B5
Halfway Bridge W Susx....36 D6
Halfway House Shrops.....95 H1
Halfway Houses Kent.....53 K4
Halifax Calder........141 H3
Halket E Ayrs.........208 D8
Halkirk Highld.........279 K4
Halkyn Flints.........128 F5
Hall E Rens..........208 C8
Hallam Fields Derbys....116 D4
Halland E Susx.........23 H4
Hallaton Leics........101 H4
Hallatrow BaNES........45 J7
Hallbankgate Cumb......178 D7
Hallbeck W & F.......157 H7
Hall Cliffe Wakefd.....141 L4
Hall Cross Lancs......138 E2
Hall Dunnerdale W & F....156 B3
Hallen S Glos..........45 H3
Hall End Bed...........85 K6
Hall End C Beds........86 B7
Hallfield Gate Derbys....133 H8
Hallgarth Dur.........169 J2
Hallglen Falk.........210 A3
Hall Green Birm........98 E7
Hallin Highld.........258 C5
Halling Medway.........52 F6
Hallington Lincs......136 F3
Hallington Nthumb......180 B4
Halliwell Bolton......139 L5
Halloughton Notts......117 J1

Hallow Worcs...........81 J3
Hallow Heath Worcs......81 J3
Hallsands Devon.........8 B7
Hall's Green Essex......69 L5
Hall's Green Herts......69 H2
Hallthwaites Cumb......156 A5
Hallworthy Cnwll.......11 H5
Hallyne Border........199 L5
Halmer End Staffs......114 B2
Halmond's Frome Herefs...80 F5
Halmore Gloucs.........63 K6
Halnaker W Susx........20 E5
Halsall Lancs.........138 D5
Halse Somset...........29 L5
Halse W Nthn...........84 A7
Halsetown Cnwll.........2 D3
Halsham E R Yk.......145 H2
Halsinger Devon........27 J3
Halstead Essex.........71 K1
Halstead Kent.........52 A6
Halstead Leics.......101 G2
Halstock Dorset........15 M1
Halsway Somset.........29 L3
Haltcliff Bridge W & F...165 L3
Haltham Lincs.........136 D7
Haltoft End Lincs......119 L3
Halton Bucks...........67 L5
Halton Halton.........129 M3
Halton Lancs.........147 K3
Halton Leeds.........142 A1
Halton Nthumb........180 B5
Halton Wrexhm........112 D3
Halton East N York....149 J5
Halton Fenside Lincs....137 H7
Halton Gill N York....158 F7
Halton Green Lancs.....147 K3
Halton Holegate Lincs...137 H6
Halton Lea Gate Nthumb..178 F7
Halton Quay Cnwll.......6 E2
Halton Shields Nthumb...180 B5
Halton West N York....148 E5
Haltwhistle Nthumb.....179 G6
Halvana Cnwll.........11 J6
Halvergate Norfk......107 J2
Halwell Devon..........8 A4
Halwill Devon.........12 B3
Halwill Junction Devon...12 B3
Ham Devon............14 F2
Ham Gloucs............63 K7
Ham Gloucs............64 E3
Ham Gt Lon............50 F4
Ham Kent.............41 K4
Ham Somset............30 D6
Ham Somset............31 L1
Ham Wilts............47 L6
Hambleden Bucks........49 J2
Hambledon Hants........35 K7
Hambledon Surrey.......36 E3
Hamble-le-Rice Hants....19 H2
Hambleton Lancs.......147 G7
Hambleton N York......142 E2
Hambleton Moss Side Lancs..147 G7
Hambridge Somset.......30 F6
Hambrook S Glos........45 J3
Hambrook W Susx........20 C5
Ham Common Dorset......32 D5
Hameringham Lincs.....136 F6
Hamerton Cambs.......102 C7
Ham Green Herefs.......81 H6
Ham Green Kent.........25 G2
Ham Green Kent.........53 H5
Ham Green N Som........45 G4
Ham Green Worcs........82 B3
Ham Hill Kent.........52 F6
Hamilton S Lans......209 J7
Hamilton Services
  (northbound) S Lans....209 J7
Hamlet Dorset.........16 B1
Hammer W Susx.........36 C4
Hammerpot W Susx.......21 H5
Hammersmith Gt Lon.....51 G3
Hammer Vale Hants......36 C4
Hammerwich Staffs......98 D2
Hammerwood E Susx......38 C5
Hammond Street Herts....69 J6
Hammoon Dorset........32 D7
Hamnavoe Shet........281 d7
Hampden Park E Susx....23 K6
Hamperden End Essex....70 E1
Hampnett Gloucs........65 G4
Hampole Donc.........142 D5
Hampreston Dorset......17 L3
Hampsfield W & F......156 F6
Hampson Green Lancs....147 J5
Hampstead Gt Lon.......51 H2
Hampstead Norreys W Berk..48 D4
Hampsthwaite N York....150 C4
Hampton Devon.........15 G3
Hampton Gt Lon.........50 F5
Hampton Kent..........40 F2

Hampton Shrops.........97 G6
Hampton Swindn.........65 J8
Hampton Worcs.........82 B6
Hampton Bishop Herefs...80 D7
Hampton Fields Gloucs....64 C7
Hampton Green Ches W...113 H2
Hampton Hargate C Pete..102 D4
Hampton Heath Ches W...113 H2
Hampton-in-Arden Solhll...99 G7
Hampton Loade Shrops....97 G6
Hampton Lovett Worcs....81 K2
Hampton Lucy Warwks....83 G4
Hampton Magna Warwks....83 G2
Hampton on the Hill Warwks..82 F2
Hampton Park Wilts......33 K4
Hampton Poyle Oxon.....66 D4
Hampton Vale C Pete....102 D4
Hampton Wick Gt Lon....50 F5
Hamptworth Wilts.......34 B7
Hamrow Norfk.........121 K6
Hamsey E Susx.........22 F5
Hamsey Green Surrey....51 K7
Hamstall Ridware Staffs..115 H7
Hamstead Birm.........98 D5
Hamstead IoW..........18 F5
Hamstead Marshall W Berk..48 B6
Hamsterley Dur........168 E4
Hamsterley Dur........180 D7
Hamsterley Mill Dur....180 E7
Hamstreet Kent.........40 C8
Ham Street Somset......31 J4
Hamwood N Som.........44 D7
Hamworthy BCP.........17 K4
Hanbury Staffs.......115 K6
Hanbury Worcs.........81 M2
Hanby Lincs.........118 D5
Hanchet End Suffk......88 C6
Hanchurch Staffs......114 C3
Handa Island Highld....276 A6
Handale R & Cl.......171 G7
Hand and Pen Devon.....14 B3
Handbridge Ches W......112 A8
Handcross W Susx.......37 L5
Handforth Ches E......131 G3
Hand Green Ches W......130 A7
Handley Ches W.......129 L8
Handley Derbys.......133 G7
Handley Green Essex.....71 G6
Handsacre Staffs......115 H8
Handsworth Birm........98 D5
Handsworth Sheff......133 H2
Handy Cross Bucks......49 K1
Hanford C Stke.......114 D3
Hanford Dorset........32 D8
Hanging Heaton Kirk....141 L3
Hanging Houghton W Nthn..84 E1
Hanging Langford Wilts...33 H3
Hangleton Br & H.......22 D6
Hangleton W Susx.......21 J6
Hanham S Glos.........45 J4
Hankelow Ches E.......113 L2
Hankerton Wilts........46 E1
Hankham E Susx.........23 K6
Hanley C Stke.......114 D2
Hanley Broadheath Worcs..80 F2
Hanley Castle Worcs.....81 J6
Hanley Child Worcs......80 F2
Hanley Swan Worcs......81 J6
Hanley William Worcs....80 F2
Hanlith N York.......148 F3
Hanmer Wrexhm........113 G4
Hannaford Devon........27 L5
Hannah Lincs.........137 J4
Hannington Hants.......48 D7
Hannington Swindn......65 H8
Hannington W Nthn......84 F1
Hannington Wick Swindn..65 H8
Hanscombe End C Beds....86 C8
Hanslope M Keyn........84 H6
Hanthorpe Lincs......118 E6
Hanwell Gt Lon........50 F3
Hanwell Oxon..........83 K6
Hanwood Shrops........95 K2
Hanworth Gt Lon........50 E5
Hanworth Norfk.......122 D4
Happendon S Lans......198 E6
Happisburgh Norfk.....123 H5
Happisburgh Common Norfk..123 H5
Hapsford Ches W.......129 L5
Hapton Lancs.........140 B2
Hapton Norfk.........106 D4
Harberton Devon.........8 A3
Harbertonford Devon......8 A4
Harbledown Kent........40 F4
Harborne Birm.........98 C6
Harborough Magna Warwks..100 A8
Harbottle Nthumb......190 C5
Harbourneford Devon.....7 K2
Harbours Hill Worcs.....81 M2
Harbridge Hants........18 A2

Harbridge Green Hants....33 K8
Harburn W Loth........210 D6
Harbury Warwks.........83 J3
Harby Leics.........117 K5
Harby Notts.........135 H5
Harcombe Devon........13 K6
Harcombe Devon........14 D4
Harcombe Bottom Devon...15 H3
Harden C Brad.........149 K8
Harden Wsall..........98 C3
Hardendale W & F......166 D7
Hardenhuish Wilts......46 C4
Hardgate Abers.......245 H3
Hardgate D & G.......175 K2
Hardgate N York......150 C3
Hardgate W Duns......208 E4
Hardham W Susx.........21 H3
Hardhorn Lancs.......147 G8
Hardingham Norfk......105 L3
Hardingstone W Nthn....84 E4
Hardington Somset......45 L8
Hardington Mandeville Somset..31 H0
Hardington Marsh Somset..31 H7
Hardington Moor Somset...31 H8
Hardisworthy Devon.....26 D6
Hardley Hants.........19 G3
Hardley Street Norfk...107 H3
Hardmead M Keyn........85 H5
Hardraw N York.......158 F4
Hardsough Lancs.......140 B4
Hardstoft Derbys......133 J7
Hardway Hants.........19 K3
Hardway Somset........32 B4
Hardwick Bucks........67 K3
Hardwick Cambs........87 H3
Hardwick N Nthn........85 G1
Hardwick Norfk.......106 E5
Hardwick Oxon.........66 A6
Hardwick Oxon.........66 E1
Hardwick Rothm.......133 K2
Hardwick Wsall........98 D4
Hardwicke Gloucs.......64 A4
Hardwicke Gloucs.......64 D2
Hardwick Village Notts..134 C4
Hardy's Green Essex....72 D3
Harebeating E Susx.....23 K5
Hareby Lincs.........136 F6
Hare Croft C Brad.....149 K8
Harefield Gt Lon.......50 D1
Hare Green Essex.......73 G2
Hare Hatch Wokham......49 J3
Harehill Derbys......115 K4
Harehills Leeds......141 M1
Harehope Nthumb......191 G2
Harelaw Border.......188 F2
Harelaw D & G.......178 B3
Harelaw Dur..........180 E8
Hareplain Kent........39 L5
Haresceugh W & F......166 E2
Harescombe Gloucs......64 B5
Haresfield Gloucs......64 A5
Harestock Hants........34 F4
Hare Street Essex......70 D5
Hare Street Essex......70 D7
Hare Street Herts......69 K1
Harewood Leeds.......150 D6
Harewood End Herefs....63 G2
Harford Devon..........7 J3
Hargate Norfk.......106 C5
Hargatewall Derbys....132 B4
Hargrave Ches W.......129 L7
Hargrave N Nthn........85 K1
Hargrave Suffk.........88 F3
Harker Cumb.........177 L6
Harkstead Suffk........90 E8
Harlaston Staffs.......99 G1
Harlaxton Lincs......118 A5
Harlech Gwynd.......109 K5
Harlech Castle Gwynd...109 K5
Harlescott Shrops.....113 H8
Harlesden Gt Lon.......51 G2
Harlesthorpe Derbys....133 K4
Harleston Devon.........8 B6
Harleston Norfk.......106 E6
Harleston Suffk........89 L3
Harlestone W Nthn......84 D2
Harle Syke Lancs......140 C1
Harley Rothm.........142 B8
Harley Shrops.........96 D3
Harling Road Norfk....105 K6
Harlington C Beds......68 D1
Harlington Donc......142 D7
Harlington Gt Lon......50 E3
Harlosh Highld.......258 D8
Harlow Essex..........70 C5
Harlow Hill Nthumb....180 C5
Harlthorpe E R Yk.....151 M8
Harlton Cambs.........87 H5
Harlyn Cnwll..........10 B7
Harman's Cross Dorset...17 J6

Place	Area	Page	Grid
Harmby	N York	159	L5
Harmer Green	Herts	69	H4
Harmer Hill	Shrops	113	H7
Harmondsworth	Gt Lon	50	D3
Harmston	Lincs	135	K7
Harnage	Shrops	96	D3
Harnham	Nthumb	180	C3
Harnhill	Gloucs	64	F7
Harold Hill	Gt Lon	70	D8
Haroldston West	Pembks	54	D4
Haroldswick	Shet	281	f1
Harold Wood	Gt Lon	52	C1
Harome	N York	161	L6
Harpenden	Herts	68	E4
Harpford	Devon	14	C4
Harpham	E R Yk	153	H3
Harpley	Norfk	121	H6
Harpley	Worcs	80	F3
Harpole	W Nthn	84	D3
Harpsdale	Highld	279	K5
Harpsden	Oxon	49	J3
Harpswell	Lincs	135	J2
Harpurhey	Manch	140	C7
Harpur Hill	Derbys	131	L5
Harraby	Cumb	177	M7
Harracott	Devon	27	K5
Harrapool	Highld	247	K4
Harras	Cumb	164	C7
Harrietfield	P & K	221	H1
Harrietsham	Kent	39	L3
Harringay	Gt Lon	51	J1
Harrington	Cumb	164	C5
Harrington	Lincs	137	G5
Harrington	N Nthn	101	G7
Harringworth	N Nthn	101	K4
Harris	W Isls	282	e6
Harriseahead	Staffs	131	G6
Harriston	Cumb	165	G2
Harrogate	N York	150	D5
Harrold	Bed	85	J4
Harrop Dale	Oldham	140	F6
Harrow	Gt Lon	50	F1
Harrowbarrow	Cnwll	11	M8
Harrowden	Bed	86	B5
Harrowgate Village	Darltn	169	H7
Harrow Green	Suffk	89	H4
Harrow Hill	Gloucs	63	K4
Harrow on the Hill	Gt Lon	50	F2
Harrow Weald	Gt Lon	50	F1
Harston	Cambs	87	J5
Harston	Leics	117	L5
Harswell	E R Yk	152	C7
Hart	Hartpl	170	B4
Hartburn	Nthumb	180	D2
Hartburn	S on T	169	L7
Hartest	Suffk	89	G5
Hartfield	E Susx	38	D6
Hartford	Cambs	86	E1
Hartford	Ches W	130	C5
Hartford	Somset	29	G5
Hartfordbridge	Hants	49	J7
Hartford End	Essex	71	G3
Harthill	N York	159	L2
Hartgrove	Dorset	32	D7
Harthill	Ches W	129	L8
Harthill	N Lans	210	B6
Harthill	Rothm	133	K3
Harthope	D & G	186	F4
Hartington	Derbys	132	C7
Hartington	Nthumb	180	B1
Hartland	Devon	26	D6
Hartland Quay	Devon	26	C6
Hartlebury	Worcs	81	J1
Hartlepool	Hartpl	170	C4
Hartley	Kent	39	J6
Hartley	Kent	52	D5
Hartley	Nthumb	181	H4
Hartley	W & F	158	D1
Hartley Green	Kent	52	D5
Hartley Green	Staffs	114	F5
Hartley Wespall	Hants	49	G7
Hartley Wintney	Hants	49	J7
Hartlip	Kent	53	H6
Hartoft End	N York	162	C4
Harton	N York	151	L3
Harton	S Tyne	181	J6
Harton	Shrops	96	B5
Hartpury	Gloucs	64	A2
Hartshead	Kirk	141	J3

Hartshead Moor Services

Place	Area	Page	Grid
Calder		141	J3
Hartshead Moor Top	Kirk	141	J3
Hartshill	C Stke	114	D2
Hartshill	Warwks	99	J4
Hartshorne	Derbys	116	B7
Hartside	Nthumb	190	D3
Hartsop	W & F	165	L8
Hart Station	Hartpl	170	B3
Hartswell	Somset	29	K5
Hartwell	W Nthn	84	F5

Place	Area	Page	Grid
Hartwith	N York	150	B3
Hartwood	N Lans	209	M7
Hartwoodmyres	Border	188	D1
Harvel	Kent	52	E6
Harvington	Worcs	82	C5
Harvington	Worcs	97	K8
Harwell	Notts	134	D2
Harwell	Oxon	48	C1
Harwich	Essex	73	K1
Harwood	Bolton	139	L5
Harwood	Dur	167	J4
Harwood	Nthumb	190	E8
Harwood Dale	N York	163	H3
Harwood Lee	Bolton	139	L5
Harworth	Notts	134	C2
Hasbury	Dudley	98	B6
Hascombe	Surrey	36	F3
Haselbech	W Nthn	100	F7
Haselbury Plucknett	Somset	31	G8
Haseley	Warwks	82	F2
Haseley Green	Warwks	82	F1
Haseley Knob	Warwks	82	F1
Haselor	Warwks	82	D4
Hasfield	Gloucs	64	B2
Hasguard	Pembks	54	D5
Hasholme	E R Yk	143	L1
Haskayne	Lancs	138	D6
Hasketon	Suffk	90	F5
Hasland	Derbys	133	H5
Haslemere	Surrey	36	D4
Haslingden	Lancs	140	B3
Haslingfield	Cambs	87	H5
Haslington	Ches E	130	E8
Hassall	Ches E	130	E8
Hassall Green	Ches E	130	F7
Hassell Street	Kent	40	E6
Hassingham	Norfk	107	H2
Hassness	Cumb	165	G7
Hassocks	W Susx	22	D4
Hassop	Derbys	132	D5
Haste Hill	Surrey	36	D4
Hasthorpe	Lincs	137	J5
Hastingleigh	Kent	40	E6
Hastings	E Susx	24	E5
Hastings	Somset	30	D7
Hastingwood	Essex	70	C5
Hastoe	Herts	68	A5
Haswell	Dur	169	K2
Haswell Plough	Dur	169	K2
Hatch	C Beds	86	D5
Hatch Beauchamp	Somset	30	D6
Hatch End	Bed	86	B3
Hatch End	Gt Lon	50	E1
Hatchet Gate	Hants	18	F3
Hatching Green	Herts	68	E4
Hatchmere	Ches W	130	A5
Hatch Warren	Hants	35	J1
Hatcliffe	NE Lin	145	G7
Hatfield	Donc	143	G6
Hatfield	Herefs	80	E3
Hatfield	Herts	69	G5
Hatfield	Worcs	81	K5
Hatfield Broad Oak	Essex	70	E4
Hatfield Heath	Essex	70	D4
Hatfield Peverel	Essex	71	J5
Hatfield Woodhouse	Donc	143	H6
Hatford	Oxon	65	M8
Hatherden	Hants	34	D1
Hatherleigh	Devon	12	D2
Hathern	Leics	116	E7
Hatherop	Gloucs	65	H6
Hathersage	Derbys	132	E3
Hathersage Booths	Derbys	132	E3
Hatherton	Ches E	113	L2
Hatherton	Staffs	98	B1
Hatley St George	Cambs	86	F5
Hatt	Cnwll	6	D2
Hattersley	Tamesd	131	K1
Hattingley	Hants	35	K3
Hatton	Abers	257	K4
Hatton	Angus	234	C6
Hatton	Derbys	115	L5
Hatton	Gt Lon	50	E4
Hatton	Lincs	136	C4
Hatton	Shrops	95	L5
Hatton	Warrtn	130	B3
Hatton	Warwks	82	F2
Hatton Heath	Ches W	129	K7
Hatton of Fintray	Abers	256	F8
Hatton Park	Warwks	82	F2
Haugh	E Ayrs	196	F6
Haugh	Lincs	137	H4
Haugh	Rochdl	140	E5
Haugham	Lincs	136	F3
Haughhead	E Duns	209	G3
Haugh Head	Nthumb	202	F7
Haughley	Suffk	89	L3
Haughley Green	Suffk	89	L2
Haugh of Glass	Moray	255	H4

Place	Area	Page	Grid
Haugh of Urr	D & G	175	K2
Haughs of Kinnaird	Angus	235	G4
Haughton	Ches E	130	B8
Haughton	Notts	134	D5
Haughton	Powys	112	D7
Haughton	Shrops	96	F4
Haughton	Shrops	97	G2
Haughton	Shrops	112	F6
Haughton	Shrops	113	J8
Haughton	Staffs	114	D7
Haughton Green	Tamesd	131	J1
Haughton le Skerne	Darltn	169	J7
Haultwick	Herts	69	J3
Haunton	Staffs	99	L1
Hautes Croix	Jersey	9	d1
Hauxton	Cambs	87	J5
Havannah	Ches E	131	G6
Havant	Hants	20	B5
Haven	Herefs	79	M4
Haven Bank	Lincs	119	H1
Haven Side	E R Yk	144	F2
Havenstreet	IoW	19	J5
Havercroft	Wakefd	142	B5
Haverfordwest	Pembks	54	F4
Haverhill	Suffk	88	D6
Haverigg	Cumb	155	L7
Havering-atte-Bower	Gt Lon	70	D8
Havering's Grove	Essex	71	G8
Haversham	M Keyn	84	F6
Haverthwaite	W & F	156	E6
Haverton Hill	S on T	170	C6
Havyatt	N Som	44	F6
Havyatt	Somset	31	H3
Hawarden	Flints	129	H6
Hawbridge	Worcs	81	L5
Hawbush Green	Essex	71	J3
Hawcoat	W & F	146	E2
Hawen	Cerdgn	76	C6
Hawes	N York	158	F5
Hawe's Green	Norfk	106	E4
Hawford	Worcs	81	J3
Hawick	Border	188	E3
Hawkchurch	Devon	15	H3
Hawkedon	Suffk	88	F4
Hawkenbury	Kent	39	K4
Hawkeridge	Wilts	46	B8
Hawkerland	Devon	14	C5
Hawker's Cove	Cnwll	10	C7
Hawkesbury	S Glos	45	M2
Hawkesbury	Warwks	99	K6
Hawkesbury Upton	S Glos	45	M2
Hawkes End	Covtry	99	J6
Hawk Green	Stockp	131	J2
Hawkhead	Rens	208	E6
Hawkhill	Nthumb	191	J4
Hawkhurst	Kent	39	J7
Hawkhurst Common	E Susx	23	J4
Hawkinge	Kent	41	H7
Hawkley	Hants	35	M5
Hawkley	Wigan	139	H7
Hawkridge	Somset	28	F5
Hawksdale	Cumb	165	L1
Hawkshaw	Bury	139	M5
Hawkshead	W & F	156	E3
Hawkshead Hill	W & F	156	D3
Hawksland	S Lans	198	D5
Hawkspur Green	Essex	71	G1
Hawkstone	Shrops	113	J5
Hawkswick	N York	149	G2
Hawksworth	Leeds	149	L7
Hawksworth	Notts	117	K3
Hawkwell	Essex	53	J1
Hawkwell	Nthumb	180	C4
Hawley	Hants	49	K7
Hawley	Kent	52	C4
Hawling	Gloucs	64	F3
Hawnby	N York	161	J5
Haworth	C Brad	149	J8
Hawridge	Bucks	68	B6
Hawstead	Suffk	89	G3
Hawstead Green	Suffk	89	H3
Hawthorn	Dur	169	L2
Hawthorn	Hants	35	K4
Hawthorn	Rhondd	43	H4
Hawthorn Hill	Br For	49	L4
Hawthorn Hill	Lincs	136	D8
Hawthorpe	Lincs	118	D6
Hawton	Notts	117	L1
Haxby	C York	151	K4
Haxby Gates	C York	151	K4
Haxey	N Linc	143	J7
Haxey Carr	N Linc	143	J7
Haxted	Surrey	38	C4
Haxton	Wilts	33	K1
Hay	Cnwll	4	F4
Hay	Cnwll	10	D8
Haydock	St Hel	139	H8
Haydon	BaNES	45	K8
Haydon	Dorset	31	L7
Haydon	Somset	30	C6

Place	Area	Page	Grid
Haydon Bridge	Nthumb	179	J6
Haydon Wick	Swindn	47	H2
Haye	Cnwll	11	L8
Hayes	Gt Lon	50	E3
Hayes	Gt Lon	51	L5
Hayes End	Gt Lon	50	D3
Hayfield	Ag & B	217	H2
Hayfield	Derbys	131	L2
Hayfield Green	Donc	143	G7
Haygate	Wrekin	96	E1
Hay Green	Norfk	120	C7
Hayhillock	Angus	234	E7
Hayle	Cnwll	2	E4
Hayle Port	Cnwll	2	F4
Hayley Green	Dudley	98	B6
Hayling Island	Hants	20	B6
Haymoor Green	Ches E	113	L2
Hayne	Devon	13	H5
Hayne	Devon	29	G7
Haynes	C Beds	86	B6
Haynes Church End	C Beds	86	B7
Haynes West End	C Beds	85	L7
Hay-on-Wye	Powys	79	J6
Hayscastle	Pembks	74	E7
Hayscastle Cross	Pembks	74	E7
Hay Street	Herts	69	K2
Hayton	Cumb	164	F2
Hayton	Cumb	178	C7
Hayton	E R Yk	152	C6
Hayton	Notts	134	E3
Hayton's Bent	Shrops	96	C7
Haytor Vale	Devon	13	H7
Haytown	Devon	26	F7
Haywards Heath	W Susx	22	E2
Haywood	Donc	142	F5
Haywood	Herefs	80	B8
Haywood Oaks	Notts	134	C8
Hazards Green	E Susx	24	C5
Hazelbank	S Lans	198	D4
Hazelbury Bryan	Dorset	16	E1
Hazeleigh	Essex	71	K6
Hazeley	Hants	49	H7
Hazelford	Notts	117	J2
Hazel Grove	Stockp	131	H2
Hazelhurst	Tamesd	140	E7
Hazelslade	Staffs	98	C1
Hazel Street	Kent	39	H5
Hazel Stub	Suffk	88	D6
Hazelton Walls	Fife	222	E3
Hazelwood	Derbys	116	B2
Hazlemere	Bucks	67	L8
Hazlerigg	N u Ty	180	F4
Hazles	Staffs	114	F2
Hazleton	Gloucs	65	G3
Heacham	Norfk	120	E4
Headbourne Worthy	Hants	35	G4
Headbrook	Herefs	79	K4
Headcorn	Kent	39	L4
Headingley	Leeds	150	C8
Headington	Oxon	66	D5
Headlam	Dur	168	F7
Headlesscross	N Lans	210	B7
Headless Cross	Worcs	82	B2
Headley	Hants	36	B4
Headley	Hants	48	D6
Headley	Surrey	51	G8
Headley Down	Hants	36	B4
Headley Heath	Worcs	98	D8
Headon	Devon	11	M2
Headon	Notts	134	E4
Heads Nook	Cumb	178	C7
Heage	Derbys	116	B2
Healaugh	N York	151	G6
Healaugh	N York	159	H3
Heald Green	Stockp	131	G3
Heale	Devon	28	A2
Heale	Somset	30	C6
Heale	Somset	30	F5
Healey	N York	160	B6
Healey	Nthumb	180	B7
Healey	Rochdl	140	D4
Healey	Wakefd	141	L4
Healeyfield	Dur	168	D1
Healing	NE Lin	145	G5
Heamoor	Cnwll	2	D5
Heanor	Derbys	116	D2
Heanton Punchardon	Devon	27	J4
Heapham	Lincs	135	H2
Hearn	Hants	36	B3

Heart of Scotland Services

Place	Area	Page	Grid
N Lans		210	B6
Hearts Delight	Kent	53	J6
Heasley Mill	Devon	28	C4
Heaste	Highld	247	K5
Heath	Derbys	133	J6
Heath	Wakefd	142	A4
Heath and Reach	C Beds	68	B2
Heath Common	W Susx	21	J4
Heathcote	Derbys	132	C7
Heathcote	Shrops	113	L6

Heath End Bucks 67 L7
Heath End Hants 48 B6
Heath End Leics 116 B7
Heath End Warwks 82 F3
Heather Leics 99 K1
Heathfield Cambs 87 J6
Heathfield Devon 13 J7
Heathfield E Susx 23 K3
Heathfield N York 149 L2
Heathfield Somset 29 L5
Heathfield Village Oxon 66 D4
Heath Green Worcs 82 C1
Heath Hall D & G 176 C3
Heath Hayes & Wimblebury
Staffs 98 C2
Heath Hill Shrops 97 H1
Heath House Somset 30 F2
Heathrow Airport Gt Lon 50 D4
Heathstock Devon 14 F2
Heathton Shrops 97 H5
Heath Town Wolves 97 L3
Heathwaite N York 161 G2
Heatley Staffs 115 H6
Heatley Warrtn 130 D2
Heaton Bolton 139 L6
Heaton C Brad 149 L8
Heaton Lancs 147 J4
Heaton N u Ty 181 G5
Heaton Staffs 131 J7
Heaton Chapel Stockp 131 H1
Heaton Mersey Stockp 131 G2
Heaton Norris Stockp 131 H1
Heaton's Bridge Lancs 138 E5
Heaverham Kent 52 C7
Heaviley Stockp 131 H2
Heavitree Devon 13 L4
Hebburn S Tyne 181 H6
Hebden N York 149 J3
Hebden Bridge Calder 140 F2
Hebden Green Ches W 130 C6
Hebing End Herts 69 J4
Hebron Carmth 75 L6
Hebron IoA 125 H3
Hebron Nthumb 191 J8
Heckfield Hants 49 H0
Heckfield Green Suffk 106 D8
Heckfordbridge Essex 72 D3
Heckington Lincs 118 F3
Heckmondwike Kirk 141 K3
Heddington Wilts 46 E5
Heddon-on-the-Wall Nthumb 180 D5
Hedenham Norfk 107 G5
Hedge End Hants 19 H1
Hedgerley Bucks 50 B2
Hedgerley Green Bucks 50 B2
Hedging Somset 30 D5
Hedley on the Hill Nthumb 180 C7
Hednesford Staffs 98 C1
Hedon E R Yk 145 F2
Hedsor Bucks 49 L2
Heeley Sheff 133 G2
Hegdon Hill Herefs 80 D4
Heglibister Shet 281 d6
Heighington Darltn 169 H6
Heighington Lincs 135 L6
Heightington Worcs 81 H1
Heiton Border 201 L7
Hele Devon 13 H8
Hele Devon 14 A2
Hele Devon 27 J2
Hele Somset 30 B6
Helebridge Cnwll 11 J2
Hele Lane Devon 28 D8
Helensburgh Ag & B 208 A3
Helenton S Ayrs 196 G5
Helford Cnwll 3 J6
Helford Passage Cnwll 3 J5
Helhoughton Norfk 121 J6
Helions Bumpstead Essex 88 C7
Hellaby Rothm 133 K1
Helland Cnwll 10 F8
Hellandbridge Cnwll 10 F8
Hell Corner W Berk 48 A4
Hellescott Cnwll 11 K5
Hellesdon Norfk 106 E1
Hellesveor Cnwll 2 D3
Hellidon W Nthn 83 H4
Hellifield N York 148 E4
Hellingly E Susx 23 K5
Hellington Norfk 107 G3
Helm Nthumb 191 H7
Helmdon W Nthn 84 B6
Helme Kirk 141 H5
Helmingham Suffk 90 E4
Helmington Row Dur 168 E2
Helmsdale Highld 274 D5
Helmshore Lancs 140 B3
Helmsley N York 161 K6
Helperby N York 150 F2
Helperthorpe N York 152 E2

Helpringham Lincs 118 F3
Helpston C Pete 102 C2
Helsby Ches W 129 L4
Helsey Lincs 137 K5
Helston Cnwll 3 H5
Helstone Cnwll 10 F6
Helton W & F 166 C6
Helwith N York 159 K2
Helwith Bridge N York 148 D2
Hemblington Norfk 107 G1
Hembridge Somset 31 K3
Hemel Hempstead Herts 68 D5
Hemerdon Devon 7 H3
Hemingbrough N York 143 H2
Hemingby Lincs 136 D5
Hemingfield Barns 142 B7
Hemingford Abbots Cambs 86 F1
Hemingford Grey Cambs 86 F1
Hemingstone Suffk 90 D4
Hemington Leics 116 D5
Hemington N Nthn 102 D6
Hemington Somset 45 L8
Hemley Suffk 91 G6
Hemlington Middsb 170 D6
Hempholme E R Yk 153 H5
Hempnall Norfk 106 E4
Hempnall Green Norfk 106 E5
Hempriggs Moray 266 C3
Hempstead Essex 88 C7
Hempstead Medway 53 G6
Hempstead Norfk 122 C4
Hempstead Norfk 123 H6
Hempsted Gloucs 64 B4
Hempton Norfk 121 K5
Hempton Oxon 66 C1
Hemsby Norfk 123 K8
Hemswell Lincs 135 J2
Hemswell Cliff Lincs 135 J2
Hemsworth Wakefd 142 C5
Hemyock Devon 29 L8
Henbury Bristl 38 H2
Henbury Ches E 131 H6
Hendham Devon 7 L5
Hendomen Powys 94 F4
Hendon Gt Lon 51 G1
Hendon Sundld 181 K7
Hendra Cnwll 3 J4
Hendra Cnwll 10 E7
Hendre Brdgnd 42 E5
Hendre Flints 128 E6
Hendredenny Caerph 43 H4
Hendy Carmth 57 G4
Heneglwys IoA 125 G4
Henfield W Susx 22 C4
Henford Devon 11 M4
Henfynyw Cerdgn 76 E3
Henghurst Kent 40 B8
Hengoed Caerph 43 J3
Hengoed Powys 79 J4
Hengoed Shrops 112 D5
Hengrave Suffk 89 G2
Henham Essex 70 F2
Heniarth Powys 94 D2
Henlade Somset 30 C6
Henley Dorset 16 D2
Henley Gloucs 64 C4
Henley Shrops 95 L5
Henley Shrops 96 C8
Henley Somset 30 F4
Henley Suffk 90 E5
Henley W Susx 36 D5
Henley Green Covtry 99 K7
Henley-in-Arden Warwks 82 E2
Henley-on-Thames Oxon 49 J2
Henley Park Surrey 50 B8
Henley's Down E Susx 24 D5
Henley Street Kent 52 E5
Henllan Cerdgn 76 C7
Henllan Denbgs 127 L6
Henllan Amgoed Carmth 55 L3
Henllys Torfn 44 B1
Henlow C Beds 86 D7
Henlow Camp C Beds 86 D7
Hennock Devon 13 J6
Henny Street Essex 89 H7
Henryd Conwy 126 F5
Henry's Moat (Castell
Hendre) Pembks 75 H6
Hensall N York 142 F3
Henshaw Nthumb 179 H6
Hensingham Cumb 164 C7
Henstead Suffk 107 K6
Hensting Hants 35 G6
Henstridge Somset 32 B7
Henstridge Ash Somset 32 B6
Henstridge Marsh Somset 32 B6
Henton Oxon 67 J6
Henton Somset 31 H2
Henwick Worcs 81 J4
Henwood Cnwll 11 K7

Henwood Oxon 66 C6
Heolgerrig Myr Td 60 F6
Heol-las Swans 57 J5
Heol Senni Powys 60 D2
Heol-y-Cyw Brdgnd 42 E5
Hepburn Nthumb 190 F1
Hepple Nthumb 190 E6
Hepscott Nthumb 180 F2
Heptonstall Calder 140 E2
Hepworth Kirk 141 J6
Hepworth Suffk 105 K8
Herbrandston Pembks 54 E5
Hereford Herefs 80 C7
Hereson Kent 41 L2
Heribusta Highld 258 F3
Heriot Border 200 E2
Hermiston C Edin 211 G5
Hermitage Border 188 E7
Hermitage Dorset 16 C1
Hermitage W Berk 48 D4
Hermon Carmth 58 C3
Hermon IoA 125 G6
Hermon Pembks 75 L6
Herne Kent 41 G2
Herne Bay Kent 41 G2
Herne Common Kent 41 G2
Herne Hill Gt Lon 51 J4
Herne Pound Kent 39 G3
Herner Devon 27 K5
Hernhill Kent 40 E3
Herodsfoot Cnwll 5 L3
Heronden Kent 41 J4
Herongate Essex 52 D1
Heronsford S Ayrs 182 E6
Heronsgate Herts 68 C8
Herriard Hants 35 K2
Herringfleet Suffk 107 K4
Herring's Green Bed 86 B6
Herringswell Suffk 88 E1
Herringthorpe Rothm 133 J1
Herrington Sundld 181 J0
Hersden Kent 41 G3
Hersham Cnwll 11 J1
Hersham Surrey 50 E6
Herstmonceux E Susx 23 L5
Herston Dorset 17 K6
Herston Ork 275 c6
Hertford Herts 69 J4
Hertford Heath Herts 69 K5
Hertingfordbury Herts 69 J5
Hesketh Bank Lancs 138 F3
Hesketh Lane Lancs 147 M7
Hesket Newmarket Cumb 165 K3
Heskin Green Lancs 139 G4
Hesleden Dur 170 B3
Hesleden N York 158 F7
Hesley Donc 134 C1
Hesleyside Nthumb 179 J2
Heslington C York 151 K5
Hessay C York 151 H5
Hessenford Cnwll 6 C3
Hessett Suffk 89 J3
Hessle E R Yk 144 C3
Hessle Wakefd 142 C4
Hest Bank Lancs 147 J3
Hestley Green Suffk 90 D2
Heston Gt Lon 50 E3
Heston Services Gt Lon 50 E3
Hestwall Ork 275 b4
Heswall Wirral 129 G3
Hethe Oxon 66 E1
Hethersett Norfk 106 C2
Hethersgill Cumb 178 B5
Hetherside Cumb 178 B5
Hetherson Green Ches W 113 H2
Hethpool Nthumb 202 D7
Hett Dur 169 H3
Hetton N York 149 G4
Hetton-le-Hole Sundld 169 K1
Hetton Steads Nthumb 203 G6
Heugh Nthumb 180 D4
Heughhead Abers 243 L1
Heugh Head Border 213 J6
Heveningham Suffk 91 H1
Hever Kent 38 D4
Heversham W & F 157 H6
Hevingham Norfk 122 D7
Hewas Water Cnwll 4 F5
Hewelsfield Gloucs 63 H6
Hewenden C Brad 149 K8
Hewish N Som 44 E6
Hewish Somset 15 K1
Hewood Dorset 15 H2
Hexham Nthumb 179 L6
Hextable Kent 52 B5
Hexthorpe Donc 142 F7
Hexton Herts 68 E1
Hexworthy Cnwll 11 L6

Hexworthy Devon 12 F8
Hey Lancs 148 F7
Heybridge Essex 70 F7
Heybridge Essex 71 L5
Heybridge Basin Essex 72 C5
Heybrook Bay Devon 6 F5
Heydon Cambs 87 J7
Heydon Norfk 122 C6
Heydour Lincs 118 D4
Hey Houses Lancs 138 D2
Heyliphol Ag & B 224 B6
Heylor Shet 281 d4
Heyrod Tamesd 140 E7
Heysham Lancs 147 H4
Heyshaw N York 149 L3
Heyshott W Susx 20 E3
Heyside Oldham 140 D6
Heytesbury Wilts 32 F2
Heythrop Oxon 65 M2
Heywood Rochdl 140 C5
Heywood Wilts 46 C8
Hibaldstow N Linc 144 B7
Hickleton Donc 142 D6
Hickling Norfk 123 J6
Hickling Notts 117 J6
Hickling Green Norfk 123 H6
Hickling Heath Norfk 123 H7
Hickling Pastures Notts 117 H6
Hickmans Green Kent 40 E4
Hicks Forstal Kent 41 G3
Hickstead W Susx 22 D3
Hidcote Bartrim Gloucs 82 E6
Hidcote Boyce Gloucs 82 E6
High Ackworth Wakefd 142 C4
Higham Barns 141 M6
Higham Derbys 133 H7
Higham Kent 38 F4
Higham Kent 52 F5
Higham Lancs 148 E8
Higham Suffk 88 E2
Higham Suffk 89 L8
Higham Dykes Nthumb 180 D4
Higham Ferrers N Nthn 85 J3
Higham Gobion C Beds 86 C8
Higham Hill Gt Lon 51 K1
Higham on the Hill Leics 99 K4
Highampton Devon 12 C2
Highams Park Gt Lon 69 K8
High Angerton Nthumb 180 D2
High Ardwell D & G 172 D5
High Auldgirth D & G 176 B1
High Bankhill W & F 166 D2
High Barnet Gt Lon 69 H7
High Beach Essex 69 L7
High Bentham N York 148 B2
High Bewaldeth Cumb 165 H4
High Bickington Devon 27 L6
High Biggins W & F 157 K7
High Birkwith N York 158 D7
High Blantyre S Lans 209 H7
High Bonnybridge Falk 209 L3
High Borrans W & F 156 F3
High Bradley N York 149 H6
High Bray Devon 28 B4
Highbridge Hants 34 F6
Highbridge Somset 30 D2
Highbrook W Susx 38 A7
High Brooms Kent 38 F5
High Bullen Devon 27 J6
Highburton Kirk 141 J5
Highbury Gt Lon 51 J2
Highbury Somset 31 M1
High Buston Nthumb 191 J4
High Callerton Nthumb 180 F5
High Casterton W & F 157 K7
High Catton E R Yk 151 M5
Highclere Hants 48 B7
Highcliffe BCP 18 C5
High Close Dur 168 F7
High Cogges Oxon 66 A5
High Common Norfk 105 K2
High Coniscliffe Darltn 169 G7
High Crosby Cumb 178 B6
High Cross Cnwll 3 J5
High Cross E Ayrs 196 D2
High Cross Hants 35 L5
High Cross Herts 69 K3
Highcross Lancs 147 G8
High Cross W Susx 22 C4
High Cross Warwks 82 E2
High Drummore D & G 172 E7
High Dubmire Sundld 169 J1
High Easter Essex 70 F4
High Eggborough N York 142 F3
High Ellington N York 160 B6
Higher Alham Somset 31 L3
Higher Ansty Dorset 16 E2
Higher Ballam Lancs 138 D2
Higher Bartle Lancs 139 G1
Higher Berry End C Beds 85 J8

Place	County	Page	Grid
Higher Bockhampton	Dorset	16	D4
Higher Brixham	Torbay	8	D4
Higher Burrowton	Devon	14	B3
Higher Burwardsley	Ches W	129	M8
High Ercall	Wrekin	113	K8
Higher Chillington	Somset	15	J1
Higher Clovelly	Devon	26	E6
Highercombe	Somset	28	F5
Higher Coombe	Dorset	15	M4
Higher Disley	Ches E	131	J3
Higher Folds	Wigan	139	K7
Higherford	Lancs	148	F7
Higher Gabwell	Devon	8	D1
Higher Halstock Leigh	Dorset	15	L1
Higher Harpers	Lancs	148	E8
Higher Heysham	Lancs	147	H4
Higher Hurdsfield	Ches E	131	J5
Higher Irlam	Salfd	130	E1
Higher Kingcombe	Dorset	15	M3
Higher Kinnerton	Flints	129	H7
Higher Marston	Ches W	130	C4
Higher Muddiford	Devon	27	K3
Higher Nyland	Dorset	32	B6
Higher Ogden	Rochdl	140	E5
Higher Pentire	Cnwll	3	G6
Higher Penwortham	Lancs	139	G2
Higher Prestacott	Devon	11	M3
Higher Studfold	N York	148	E2
Higher Town	Cnwll	4	C6
Higher Town	Cnwll	5	G3
Higher Town	IoS	10	c2
Higher Tregantle	Cnwll	6	D4
Higher Walton	Lancs	139	H2
Higher Walton	Warrtn	130	B3
Higher Wambrook	Somset	15	G1
Higher Waterston	Dorset	16	D3
Higher Whatcombe	Dorset	17	G2
Higher Wheelton	Lancs	139	J3
Higher Whitley	Ches W	130	B4
Higher Wincham	Ches W	130	D4
Higher Wraxhall	Dorset	16	A2
Higher Wych	Ches W	113	H3
High Etherley	Dur	168	F5
High Ferry	Lincs	119	K2
Highfield	E R Yk	151	M8
Highfield	Gatesd	180	E7
Highfield	N Ayrs	196	C1
Highfields	Donc	142	E6
Highfields Caldecote	Cambs	87	G3
High Flats	Kirk	141	K6
High Garrett	Essex	71	J2
Highgate	E Susx	38	C5
Highgate	Gt Lon	51	H2
Highgate	Kent	39	J7
Highgate	Lincs	119	L2
High Grange	Dur	168	F4
High Grantley	N York	150	B2
High Green	Kirk	141	K5
High Green	Norfk	106	C2
High Green	Norfk	106	D5
High Green	Sheff	142	A8
High Green	Shrops	96	F6
High Green	Suffk	89	G3
High Green	W & F	156	F2
High Green	Worcs	81	K6
Highgreen Manor	Nthumb	189	L7
High Halden	Kent	40	A7
High Halstow	Medway	53	G4
High Ham	Somset	30	H4
High Harrington	Cumb	164	D5
High Harrogate	N York	150	D5
High Haswell	Dur	169	K2
High Hatton	Shrops	113	K6
High Hauxley	Nthumb	191	K5
High Hawsker	N York	163	G1
High Hesket	W & F	166	B2
High Hoyland	Barns	141	L5
High Hunsley	E R Yk	144	B1
High Hurstwood	E Susx	23	H1
High Hutton	N York	152	A2
High Ireby	Cumb	165	H3
High Kelling	Norfk	122	C3
High Kilburn	N York	161	H6
High Killerby	N York	163	J6
High Knipe	W & F	166	C6
High Lands	Dur	168	E5
Highlane	Ches E	131	H6
Highlane	Derbys	133	H3
High Lane	Stockp	131	J3
High Lanes	Cnwll	2	F4
High Laver	Essex	70	D5
Highlaws	Cumb	164	F1
Highleadon	Gloucs	63	M2
High Legh	Ches E	130	D3
Highleigh	W Susx	20	D7
High Leven	S on T	170	B8
Highley	Shrops	97	G6
High Littleton	BaNES	45	J7
High Lorton	Cumb	165	G5
High Marishes	N York	162	E7

Place	County	Page	Grid
High Marnham	Notts	134	F5
High Melton	Donc	142	D7
High Mickley	Nthumb	180	C6
Highmoor	Cumb	165	J1
Highmoor	Oxon	49	H2
Highmoor Cross	Oxon	49	H2
Highmoor Hill	Mons	44	F1
High Moorsley	Sundld	169	J2
High Newport	Sundld	181	J8
High Newton	W & F	156	F6
High Newton-by-the-Sea	Nthumb	203	L8
High Nibthwaite	W & F	156	D5
High Offley	Staffs	114	B6
High Ongar	Essex	70	E6
High Onn	Staffs	114	C8
High Park Corner	Essex	72	F3
High Pennyvenie	E Ayrs	184	D2
High Pittington	Dur	169	J2
Highridge	N Som	45	H5
High Post	Wilts	33	K4
High Roding	Essex	70	F4
High Row	Cumb	165	K3
High Row	W & F	165	K6
High Salter	Lancs	147	M3
High Salvington	W Susx	21	K5
High Scales	Cumb	165	G2
High Seaton	Cumb	164	D4
High Shaw	N York	158	F4
High Side	Cumb	165	H4
High Spen	Gatesd	180	E7
Highstead	Kent	41	G2
Highsted	Kent	40	B3
High Stoop	Dur	168	E3
High Street	Cnwll	5	G4
High Street	Kent	39	J7
Highstreet	Kent	40	E3
High Street	Suffk	91	J1
High Street	Suffk	91	K4
Highstreet Green	Essex	88	F8
Highstreet Green	Surrey	36	E4
Hightae	D & G	176	E3
Highter's Heath	Birm	98	E7
High Throston	Hartpl	170	C4
Hightown	Ches E	131	G7
Hightown	Hants	18	B3
Hightown	Sefton	138	C7
High Town	Staffs	98	C1
Hightown Green	Suffk	89	K4
High Toynton	Lincs	136	E5
High Trewhitt	Nthumb	190	E5
High Urpeth	Dur	181	G8
High Valleyfield	Fife	210	D2
High Warden	Nthumb	179	L5
Highway	Herefs	80	D7
Highway	Wilts	46	F4
Highweek	Devon	13	K8
High Westwood	Dur	180	D7
Highwood	Essex	70	F6
Highwood	Staffs	115	H5
Highwood	W Susx	37	J5
Highwood Hill	Gt Lon	69	G8
Highwoods	Essex	72	E2
High Woolaston	Gloucs	63	H7
High Worsall	N York	160	F1
Highworth	Swindn	65	J8
High Wray	W & F	156	E3
High Wych	Herts	70	C4
High Wycombe	Bucks	67	L8
Hilborough	Norfk	105	G3
Hilcote	Derbys	133	J8
Hilcott	Wilts	47	G7
Hildenborough	Kent	38	E4
Hilden Park	Kent	38	F4
Hildersham	Cambs	87	L5
Hilderstone	Staffs	114	E4
Hilderthorpe	E R Yk	153	J3
Hilfield	Dorset	16	C2
Hilgay	Norfk	104	C4
Hill	S Glos	63	J8
Hill	Warwks	83	K2
Hillam	N York	142	D2
Hillbeck	W & F	167	H7
Hillborough	Kent	41	G2
Hill Brow	Hants	36	B5
Hillbutts	Dorset	17	K2
Hill Chorlton	Staffs	114	B4
Hillclifflane	Derbys	115	M2
Hill Common	Norfk	123	H7
Hill Common	Somset	29	L5
Hill Deverill	Wilts	32	E3
Hilldyke	Lincs	119	K2
Hill End	Dur	168	C3
Hillend	Fife	210	F2
Hill End	Fife	221	J8
Hill End	Gloucs	81	K7
Hillend	Mdloth	211	H5
Hillend	N Lans	209	L5
Hillend	Swans	56	D6

Place	County	Page	Grid
Hillersland	Gloucs	63	H4
Hillerton	Devon	13	G3
Hillesden	Bucks	67	G1
Hillesley	Gloucs	45	M1
Hillfarrance	Somset	29	L6
Hill Green	Kent	53	H6
Hillgrove	W Susx	36	D5
Hillhampton	Herefs	80	D6
Hillhead	Abers	255	M4
Hillhead	Devon	8	D4
Hill Head	Hants	19	J3
Hillhead	S Lans	199	G5
Hillhead of Cocklaw	Abers	257	K3
Hilliard's Cross	Staffs	98	F1
Hilliclay	Highld	279	L3
Hillingdon	Gt Lon	50	D2
Hillington	C Glas	208	E6
Hillington	Norfk	120	F6
Hillis Corner	IoW	19	H5
Hillmorton	Warwks	100	C8
Hillock Vale	Lancs	140	A2
Hill of Beath	Fife	210	F1
Hill of Fearn	Highld	264	C4
Hillowton	D & G	175	J2
Hillpool	Worcs	97	K8
Hillpound	Hants	35	J7
Hill Ridware	Staffs	115	H8
Hillside	Abers	245	K4
Hillside	Angus	235	H3
Hillside	Devon	7	K3
Hill Side	Kirk	141	J4
Hill Side	Worcs	81	H3
Hills Town	Derbys	133	J5
Hillstreet	Hants	34	D7
Hillswick	Shet	281	c4
Hill Top	Dur	168	C6
Hill Top	Hants	18	F3
Hill Top	Kirk	141	G5
Hill Top	Rothm	133	H1
Hill Top	Sandw	98	C5
Hill Top	Wakefd	142	A4
Hillwell	Shet	281	d8
Hilmarton	Wilts	46	E4
Hilperton	Wilts	46	C7
Hilperton Marsh	Wilts	46	C7
Hilsea	C Port	19	L3
Hilston	E R Yk	145	H1
Hiltingbury	Hants	34	F6
Hilton	Border	202	D3
Hilton	Cambs	86	F2
Hilton	Derbys	115	L5
Hilton	Dorset	16	E2
Hilton	Dur	168	F6
Hilton	S on T	170	B8
Hilton	Shrops	97	H4
Hilton	W & F	167	G6
Hilton of Cadboll	Highld	264	D4
Hilton Park Services	Staffs	98	B2
Himbleton	Worcs	81	L3
Himley	Staffs	97	K5
Hincaster	W & F	157	H5
Hinchley Wood	Surrey	50	F6
Hinckley	Leics	99	L4
Hinderclay	Suffk	105	L8
Hinderwell	N York	171	J7
Hindford	Shrops	112	E5
Hindhead	Surrey	36	C4
Hindhead Tunnel	Surrey	36	C4
Hindle Fold	Lancs	139	L1
Hindley	Nthumb	180	C7
Hindley	Wigan	139	J6
Hindley Green	Wigan	139	J7
Hindlip	Worcs	81	K3
Hindolveston	Norfk	122	A5
Hindon	Wilts	32	F4
Hindringham	Norfk	121	L4
Hingham	Norfk	105	L3
Hinksford	Staffs	97	K5
Hinstock	Shrops	113	M6
Hintlesham	Suffk	90	C6
Hinton	Gloucs	63	K6
Hinton	Hants	18	C4
Hinton	Herefs	79	L7
Hinton	S Glos	45	L4
Hinton	Shrops	95	K2
Hinton	Shrops	96	E7
Hinton	W Nthn	83	M5
Hinton Admiral	Hants	18	C4
Hinton Ampner	Hants	35	J5
Hinton Blewett	BaNES	45	H7
Hinton Charterhouse	BaNES	45	M7
Hinton Cross	Worcs	82	B7
Hinton-in-the-Hedges	W Nthn	84	A7
Hinton Marsh	Hants	35	J5
Hinton Martell	Dorset	17	K2
Hinton on the Green	Worcs	82	B7
Hinton Parva	Swindn	47	K2
Hinton St George	Somset	30	F8
Hinton St Mary	Dorset	32	C7
Hinton Waldrist	Oxon	66	A7

Place	County	Page	Grid
Hints	Shrops	96	E8
Hints	Staffs	98	F3
Hinwick	Bed	85	J3
Hinxhill	Kent	40	D6
Hinxton	Cambs	87	K6
Hinxworth	Herts	86	E7
Hipperholme	Calder	141	H3
Hipsburn	Nthumb	191	J4
Hipswell	N York	160	B3
Hirn	Abers	245	G3
Hirnant	Powys	111	K7
Hirst	Nthumb	181	G2
Hirst Courtney	N York	142	F3
Hirwaen	Denbgs	128	D7
Hirwaun	Rhondd	60	C6
Hiscott	Devon	27	K5
Histon	Cambs	87	J3
Hitcham	Suffk	89	K5
Hitcham Causeway	Suffk	89	K5
Hitcham Street	Suffk	89	K5
Hitchin	Herts	68	F1
Hither Green	Gt Lon	51	K4
Hittisleigh	Devon	13	G3
Hive	E R Yk	143	K2
Hixon	Staffs	114	F6
Hoaden	Kent	41	J3
Hoar Cross	Staffs	115	J7
Hoarwithy	Herefs	63	G1
Hoath	Kent	41	G2
Hoathly	Kent	39	G6
Hobarris	Shrops	95	H7
Hobbles Green	Suffk	88	D4
Hobbs Cross	Essex	70	C7
Hobbs Cross	Essex	70	D5
Hobkirk	Border	189	G4
Hobland Hall	Norfk	107	K3
Hobsick	Notts	116	D2
Hobson	Dur	180	E7
Hoby	Leics	117	H8
Hoccombe	Somset	29	K5
Hockering	Norfk	106	B1
Hockerton	Notts	134	E8
Hockley	Ches E	131	J3
Hockley	Covtry	99	H7
Hockley	Essex	71	K8
Hockley	Staffs	99	G3
Hockley Heath	Solhll	82	E1
Hockliffe	C Beds	68	B2
Hockwold cum Wilton	Norfk	104	E6
Hockworthy	Devon	29	J7
Hoddesdon	Herts	69	K5
Hoddlesden	Bl w D	139	L3
Hoddom Cross	D & G	177	G4
Hoddom Mains	D & G	177	G4
Hodgehill	Ches E	131	G5
Hodgeston	Pembks	55	H7
Hodnet	Shrops	113	K6
Hodsock	Notts	134	C3
Hodsoll Street	Kent	52	D6
Hodson	Swindn	47	H3
Hodthorpe	Derbys	133	L4
Hoe	Hants	35	H7
Hoe	Norfk	121	M8
Hoe Benham	W Berk	48	B5
Hoe Gate	Hants	35	K8
Hoff	W & F	166	F2
Hogben's Hill	Kent	40	D4
Hoggards Green	Suffk	89	H4
Hoggeston	Bucks	67	K2
Hoggrill's End	Warwks	99	G5
Hog Hill	E Susx	25	G4
Hoghton	Lancs	139	J2
Hoghton Bottoms	Lancs	139	J2
Hognaston	Derbys	115	L2
Hogsthorpe	Lincs	137	K5
Holbeach	Lincs	119	K6
Holbeach Bank	Lincs	119	K6
Holbeach Clough	Lincs	119	K6
Holbeach Drove	Lincs	103	G1
Holbeach Hurn	Lincs	119	L6
Holbeach St Johns	Lincs	119	K7
Holbeach St Mark's	Lincs	119	L5
Holbeach St Matthew	Lincs	119	L5
Holbeck	Notts	133	L5
Holbeck Woodhouse	Notts	133	L5
Holberrow Green	Worcs	82	B3
Holbeton	Devon	7	J5
Holborn	Gt Lon	51	J3
Holborough	Kent	52	F6
Holbrook	Derbys	116	B3
Holbrook	Sheff	133	J3
Holbrook	Suffk	90	E7
Holbrook Moor	Derbys	116	B3
Holbrooks	Covtry	99	J6
Holburn	Nthumb	203	G6
Holbury	Hants	19	G3
Holcombe	Devon	13	M7
Holcombe	Somset	31	L1
Holcombe Rogus	Devon	29	J7
Holcot	W Nthn	84	F1

Place	County	Page	Grid
Holden	Lancs	148	D6
Holdenby	W Nthn	84	D2
Holden Gate	Calder	140	D3
Holder's Green	Essex	70	F1
Holdgate	Shrops	96	D5
Holdingham	Lincs	118	E2
Holditch	Dorset	15	H2
Holdsworth	Calder	141	G2
Holehouse	Derbys	131	K1
Hole-in-the-Wall	Herefs	63	J2
Holemoor	Devon	12	A2
Hole Street	W Susx	21	K4
Holford	Somset	29	L3
Holgate	C York	151	K5
Holker	W & F	156	E7
Holkham	Norfk	121	K3
Hollacombe	Devon	11	M2
Holland Fen	Lincs	119	H2
Holland Lees	Lancs	139	G6
Holland-on-Sea	Essex	73	J4
Hollandstoun	Ork	275	f1
Hollee	D & G	177	J5
Hollesley	Suffk	91	H6
Hollicombe	Torbay	8	D2
Hollingbourne	Kent	39	L2
Hollingbury	Br & H	22	D5
Hollingdon	Bucks	67	L2
Hollingrove	E Susx	24	C3
Hollingthorpe	Leeds	142	B2
Hollington	Derbys	115	L4
Hollington	Staffs	115	G4
Hollingworth	Tamesd	140	F8
Hollins	Bury	140	B6
Hollins	Derbys	132	F5
Hollins	Staffs	114	F2
Hollinsclough	Staffs	131	L6
Hollins End	Sheff	133	H3
Hollins Green	Warrtn	130	D2
Hollins Lane	Lancs	147	K5
Hollinswood	Wrekin	96	F2
Hollinwood	Shrops	113	H4
Hollocombe	Devon	27	L8
Holloway	Derbys	132	F8
Holloway	Gt Lon	51	J2
Holloway	Wilts	32	E5
Hollowell	W Nthn	84	D1
Hollowmoor Heath	Ches W	129	L6
Hollows	D & G	177	L3
Hollybush	Caerph	61	J6
Hollybush	E Ayrs	196	D7
Hollybush	Herefs	81	H7
Holly End	Norfk	103	K2
Holly Green	Worcs	81	K7
Hollyhurst	Ches E	113	J3
Hollym	E R Yk	145	J3
Hollywater	Hants	36	B4
Hollywood	Worcs	98	D7
Holmbridge	Kirk	141	H6
Holmbury St Mary	Surrey	37	H2
Holmbush	Cnwll	5	H4
Holmcroft	Staffs	114	E6
Holme	Cambs	102	D6
Holme	Kirk	141	H6
Holme	N Linc	144	A6
Holme	N York	160	E6
Holme	Notts	134	F7
Holme	W & F	157	H7
Holme Chapel	Lancs	140	C2
Holme Green	N York	151	J7
Holme Hale	Norfk	105	H2
Holme Lacy	Herefs	80	D8
Holme Marsh	Herefs	79	L4
Holme next the Sea	Norfk	120	F3
Holme on the Wolds	E R Yk	152	E6
Holme Pierrepont	Notts	117	G4
Holmer	Herefs	80	C6
Holmer Green	Bucks	67	L7
Holme St Cuthbert	Cumb	164	F1
Holmes Chapel	Ches E	130	E6
Holmesfield	Derbys	132	F4
Holmes Hill	E Susx	23	J4
Holmeswood	Lancs	138	F4
Holmethorpe	Surrey	51	H8
Holme upon Spalding Moor	E R Yk	152	B8
Holmewood	Derbys	133	H6
Holmfield	Calder	141	G2
Holmfirth	Kirk	141	H6
Holmgate	Derbys	133	G6
Holmhead	E Ayrs	197	H7
Holmpton	E R Yk	145	K3
Holmrook	Cumb	155	K3
Holmshurst	E Susx	23	L2
Holmside	Dur	169	G1
Holmwrangle	Cumb	166	C1
Holne	Devon	7	K1
Holnest	Dorset	16	C1
Holnicote	Somset	29	G2
Holsworthy	Devon	11	L2
Holsworthy Beacon	Devon	11	L1
Holt	Dorset	17	K2
Holt	Norfk	122	B4
Holt	Wilts	46	B6
Holt	Worcs	81	J3
Holt	Wrexhm	112	F1
Holtby	C York	151	L5
Holt End	Worcs	82	C1
Holt Fleet	Worcs	81	J3
Holt Green	Lancs	138	E6
Holt Heath	Dorset	17	L2
Holt Heath	Worcs	81	J3
Holton	Oxon	66	F5
Holton	Somset	31	L5
Holton	Suffk	107	H7
Holton cum Beckering	Lincs	136	B3
Holton Heath	Dorset	17	J4
Holton Hill	E Susx	24	B2
Holton le Clay	Lincs	145	H7
Holton le Moor	Lincs	144	D8
Holton St Mary	Suffk	90	C7
Holt Street	Kent	41	H5
Holtye	E Susx	38	C9
Holway	Flints	128	E4
Holwell	Dorset	32	B8
Holwell	Herts	86	D8
Holwell	Leics	117	J6
Holwell	Oxon	65	K5
Holwick	Dur	167	L5
Holworth	Dorset	16	E6
Holybourne	Hants	35	M3
Holy Cross	Worcs	97	L7
Holyfield	Essex	69	K6
Holyhead	IoA	124	D3
Holy Island	IoA	124	D3
Holy Island	Nthumb	203	J4
Holy Island	Nthumb	203	J5
Holymoorside	Derbys	133	G6
Holyport	W & M	49	L3
Holystone	Nthumb	190	D5
Holytown	N Lans	209	K6
Holywell	C Beds	60	G1
Holywell	Cambs	87	G1
Holywell	Cnwll	4	C3
Holywell	Dorset	16	B2
Holywell	Flints	128	F4
Holywell	Nthumb	181	H4
Holywell	Warwks	82	F2
Holywell Green	Calder	141	G4
Holywell Lake	Somset	29	K6
Holywell Row	Suffk	104	E7
Holywood	D & G	176	B3
Holywood Village	D & G	176	C3
Homer	Shrops	96	E3
Homer Green	Sefton	138	D7
Homersfield	Suffk	106	F6
Homescales	W & F	157	J5
Hom Green	Herefs	63	H3
Homington	Wilts	33	K5
Honeyborough	Pembks	54	F5
Honeybourne	Worcs	82	D6
Honeychurch	Devon	12	E2
Honey Hill	Kent	40	F3
Honeystreet	Wilts	47	G6
Honey Tye	Suffk	89	J8
Honiley	Warwks	82	F1
Honing	Norfk	123	G6
Honingham	Norfk	106	C1
Honington	Lincs	118	B3
Honington	Suffk	105	H8
Honington	Warwks	83	G6
Honiton	Devon	14	E3
Honley	Kirk	141	H5
Honnington	Wrekin	114	A8
Hoo	Kent	41	J2
Hoobrook	Worcs	97	J8
Hood Green	Barns	141	M7
Hood Hill	Rothm	142	B8
Hooe	C Plym	6	F4
Hooe	E Susx	24	C5
Hoo End	Herts	68	F3
Hoo Green	Ches E	130	D3
Hoohill	Bpool	146	F8
Hook	Cambs	103	J6
Hook	Devon	15	G2
Hook	E R Yk	143	J3
Hook	Gt Lon	50	F6
Hook	Hants	19	H3
Hook	Hants	49	H8
Hook	Pembks	55	G4
Hook	Wilts	47	G2
Hook-a-Gate	Shrops	95	L2
Hook Bank	Worcs	81	J7
Hooke	Dorset	15	M3
Hook End	Essex	70	E7
Hookgate	Staffs	114	A4
Hook Green	Kent	39	G6
Hook Green	Kent	52	D5
Hook Norton	Oxon	83	H8
Hook Street	Gloucs	63	K7
Hook Street	Wilts	47	G2
Hookway	Devon	13	K3
Hookwood	Surrey	37	L2
Hooley	Surrey	51	H7
Hooley Bridge	Rochdl	140	C5
Hoo Meavy	Devon	7	G2
Hoo St Werburgh	Medway	53	G4
Hooton	Ches W	129	J4
Hooton Levitt	Rothm	133	K2
Hooton Pagnell	Donc	142	D6
Hooton Roberts	Rothm	142	D8
Hopcrofts Holt	Oxon	66	C2
Hope	Derbys	132	C3
Hope	Devon	7	K6
Hope	Flints	129	G7
Hope	Powys	95	G2
Hope	Shrops	95	H3
Hope	Staffs	132	B8
Hope Bagot	Shrops	96	D8
Hope Bowdler	Shrops	95	L5
Hope End Green	Essex	70	F?
Hopehouse	Border	187	L3
Hopeman	Moray	266	C2
Hope Mansell	Herefs	63	J3
Hopesay	Shrops	95	J6
Hopetown	Wakefd	142	B3
Hope under Dinmore	Herefs	80	C5
Hopgrove	C York	151	K5
Hopperton	N York	150	F4
Hop Pole	Lincs	102	D1
Hopsford	Warwks	99	L6
Hopstone	Shrops	97	H4
Hopton	Derbys	115	L1
Hopton	Shrops	112	F7
Hopton	Staffs	114	E6
Hopton	Suffk	105	K7
Hopton Cangeford	Shrops	96	C3
Hopton Castle	Shrops	95	J7
Hoptonheath	Shrops	95	J7
Hopton on Sea	Norfk	107	L3
Hopton Wafers	Shrops	96	C8
Hopwas	Staffs	98	F2
Hopwood	Rochdl	140	C6
Hopwood	Worcs	98	C8
Hopwood Park Services	Worcs	98	D8
Horam	E Susx	23	K4
Horbling	Lincs	118	F4
Horbury	Wakefd	141	L4
Horcott	Gloucs	65	H7
Horden	Dur	170	B3
Horderley	Shrops	95	K6
Hordle	Hants	18	D4
Hordley	Shrops	112	F5
Horeb	Carmth	56	F4
Horeb	Cerdgn	76	D6
Horfield	Bristl	45	H4
Horham	Suffk	90	F1
Horkesley Heath	Essex	72	E1
Horkstow	N Linc	144	B4
Horley	Oxon	83	K6
Horley	Surrey	37	L2
Hornblotton Green	Somset	31	K4
Hornby	Lancs	147	L2
Hornby	N York	160	B3
Hornby	N York	160	E2
Horncastle	Lincs	136	E6
Hornchurch	Gt Lon	52	B2
Horncliffe	Nthumb	202	E5
Horndean	Border	202	D3
Horndean	Hants	35	L8
Horndon	Devon	12	C6
Horndon on the Hill	Thurr	52	E2
Horne	Surrey	38	A4
Horner	Somset	28	F2
Horne Row	Essex	71	J6
Horners Green	Suffk	89	K7
Horney Common	E Susx	23	G2
Horn Hill	Bucks	68	C8
Horning	Norfk	123	G8
Horninghold	Leics	101	H4
Horninglow	Staffs	115	L6
Horningsea	Cambs	87	K3
Horningsham	Wilts	32	D3
Horningtoft	Norfk	121	K6
Horningtops	Cnwll	6	D3
Hornsbury	Somset	30	E8
Hornsby	Cumb	166	C1
Hornsbygate	Cumb	166	C1
Horns Cross	Devon	27	G6
Horns Cross	E Susx	24	E3
Hornsea	E R Yk	153	K6
Hornsey	Gt Lon	51	L2
Horn's Green	Gt Lon	51	M7
Horn Street	Kent	41	G8
Hornton	Oxon	83	J6
Horpit	Swindn	47	J2
Horrabridge	Devon	7	G1
Horringer	Suffk	89	G3
Horringford	IoW	19	J6
Horrocks Fold	Bolton	139	L5
Horrocksford	Lancs	148	C7
Horsacott	Devon	27	J4
Horsebridge	Devon	12	A7
Horsebridge	E Susx	23	K5
Horsebridge	Hants	34	D5
Horsebridge	Shrops	95	J2
Horsebridge	Staffs	114	F1
Horsebrook	Staffs	97	K1
Horsecastle	N Som	44	E5
Horsedown	Cnwll	3	G4
Horsehay	Wrekin	96	F2
Horseheath	Cambs	88	C5
Horsehouse	N York	159	J6
Horsell	Surrey	50	C7
Horseman's Green	Wrexhm	113	G3
Horsenden	Bucks	67	J6
Horsey	Norfk	123	J7
Horsey	Somset	30	D3
Horsey Corner	Norfk	123	J6
Horsford	Norfk	122	D8
Horsforth	Leeds	150	B8
Horsham	W Susx	37	J4
Horsham	Worcs	81	G4
Horsham St Faith	Norfk	122	E8
Horsington	Lincs	136	C6
Horsington	Somset	32	B6
Horsley	Derbys	116	C3
Horsley	Gloucs	64	B7
Horsley	Nthumb	180	D5
Horsley	Nthumb	190	B6
Horsley Cross	Essex	73	H2
Horsleycross Street	Essex	73	G1
Horsley-Gate	Derbys	132	F4
Horsleyhill	Border	188	F2
Horsley's Green	Bucks	67	J8
Horsley Woodhouse	Derbys	116	C3
Horsmonden	Kent	39	H5
Horspath	Oxon	66	E6
Horstead	Norfk	122	E7
Horsted Keynes	W Susx	22	F2
Horton	Bucks	68	A3
Horton	Dorset	17	K1
Horton	Lancs	148	E6
Horton	S Glos	45	MJ
Horton	Shrops	113	H5
Horton	Somset	30	D7
Horton	Staffs	131	J8
Horton	Surrey	71	H6
Horton	Swans	56	F7
Horton	W & M	50	C4
Horton	W Nthn	84	F4
Horton	Wilts	46	F6
Horton	Wrekin	113	L4
Horton Cross	Somset	30	E7
Horton-cum-Studley	Oxon	66	F4
Horton Green	Ches W	113	G2
Horton Heath	Hants	35	G7
Horton-in-Ribblesdale	N York	148	D2
Horton Kirby	Kent	52	C5
Horwich	Bolton	139	J5
Horwich End	Derbys	131	K3
Horwood	Devon	27	J5
Hoscar	Lancs	138	F5
Hoscote	Border	188	C4
Hose	Leics	117	J5
Hosey Hill	Kent	51	M8
Hosh	P & K	220	E3
Hoswick	Shet	281	e8
Hotham	E R Yk	143	M1
Hothfield	Kent	40	C6
Hoton	Leics	116	F7
Hott	Nthumb	179	H2
Hough	Ches E	113	M1
Hough	Ches E	131	G4
Hougham	Lincs	118	A3
Hough End	Leeds	141	L1
Hough Green	Halton	129	L2
Hough-on-the-Hill	Lincs	118	B2
Houghton	Cambs	86	F1
Houghton	Cumb	177	L2
Houghton	Hants	34	D4
Houghton	Nthumb	180	D5
Houghton	Pembks	55	G5
Houghton	W Susx	21	H4
Houghton Conquest	C Beds	85	L7
Houghton Gate	Dur	181	H8
Houghton Green	E Susx	25	G3
Houghton Green	Warrtn	130	C1
Houghton le Side	Darltn	169	G6
Houghton-le-Spring	Sundld	169	J1
Houghton on the Hill	Leics	100	E3
Houghton Regis	C Beds	68	C2
Houghton St Giles	Norfk	121	K4
Houlton	Warwks	100	C8
Hound Green	Hants	49	H7
Houndslow	Border	201	K4
Houndsmoor	Somset	29	L5
Houndwood	Border	213	J6
Hounslow	Gt Lon	50	F4
Househill	Highld	253	G1
Houses Hill	Kirk	141	K4

Housieside Abers 257 G6
Houston Rens 208 C5
Houstry Highld 275 G1
Houton Ork 275 b5
Hove Br & H 22 D6
Hove Edge Calder 141 H3
Hoveringham Notts 117 J2
Hoveton Norfk 122 F7
Hovingham N York 161 L7
Howbrook Barns 141 M8
How Caple Herefs 63 J1
Howden E R Yk 143 J2
Howden-le-Wear Dur 168 F4
Howe Highld 280 D4
Howe IoM 154 b8
Howe N York 160 E6
Howe Norfk 106 F3
Howe Bridge Wigan 139 K7
Howe Green Essex 71 H6
Howegreen Essex 71 K6
Howell Lincs 118 F2
How End C Beds 85 K7
Howe of Teuchar Abers 268 E6
Howes D & G 177 G5
Howe Street Essex 71 G4
Howe Street Essex 88 D8
Howey Powys 78 E3
Howgate Cumb 164 C6
Howgate Mdloth 211 H7
Howgill Lancs 148 E6
Howick Nthumb 191 K3
Howle Wrekin 113 M6
Howle Hill Herefs 63 J3
Howlett End Essex 88 B8
Howley Somset 15 G1
How Mill Cumb 178 C7
Howmore W Isls 283 b10
Hownam Border 189 L2
Howrigg Cumb 165 K1
Howsham N Linc 144 D6
Howsham N York 151 M3
Howtel Nthumb 202 D6
Howt Green Kent 53 J6
Howton Herefs 62 E1
Howtown W & F 166 B6
How Wood Herts 68 F6
Howwood Rens 208 C7
Hoxa Ork 275 c6
Hoxne Suffk 106 D7
Hoy Ork 275 b5
Hoylake Wirral 128 F2
Hoyland Barns 142 B7
Hoyland Common Barns ... 142 B7
Hoylandswaine Barns 141 L6
Hoyle W Susx 20 E3
Hoyle Mill Barns 142 B6
Hubberholme N York 159 G7
Hubberston Pembks 54 E5
Hubbert's Bridge Lincs ... 119 J3
Huby N York 150 C6
Huby N York 151 J3
Huccaby Devon 12 F8
Hucclecote Gloucs 64 C4
Hucking Kent 53 H7
Hucknall Notts 116 F2
Huddersfield Kirk 141 H4
Huddington Worcs 81 L4
Hudnall Herts 68 C4
Hudswell N York 159 L3
Huggate E R Yk 152 D5
Hugglescote Leics 99 L1
Hughenden Valley Bucks 67 L7
Hughley Shrops 96 D4
Hugh Town IoS 10 c3
Huish Devon 27 J8
Huish Wilts 47 H6
Huish Champflower Somset . 29 J5
Huish Episcopi Somset 31 G5
Hùisinis W Isls 282 d5
Huisinish W Isls 282 d5
Hulcote C Beds 85 J7
Hulcote W Nthn 84 D5
Hulcott Bucks 67 K4
Hulham Devon 14 B6
Hulland Derbys 115 L2
Hulland Ward Derbys 115 L2
Hullavington Wilts 46 C3
Hull Bridge E R Yk 153 G7
Hullbridge Essex 71 K8
Hull, Kingston upon C KuH . 144 D2
Hulme Manch 140 C4
Hulme Staffs 114 E2
Hulme Warrtn 130 B2
Hulme End Staffs 132 B7
Hulme Walfield Ches E 131 G6
Hulse Heath Ches E 130 E3
Hulton Lane Ends Bolton .. 139 K6
Hulverstone IoW 18 F6
Hulver Street Norfk 105 J1
Hulver Street Suffk 107 K6

Humber Devon 13 L7
Humber Herefs 80 C4
Humber Bridge N Linc 144 C3
Humberside Airport N Linc . 144 E5
Humberston NE Lin 145 J6
Humberstone C Leic 100 E2
Humberton N York 150 F2
Humbie E R Yk 145 G1
Humbie E Loth 212 A6
Humbleton E R Yk 145 G1
Humbleton Nthumb 202 F7
Humby Lincs 118 D5
Hume Border 201 L5
Humshaugh Nthumb 179 L4
Huna Highld 280 E2
Huncoat Lancs 140 A2
Huncote Leics 100 B4
Hundalee Border 189 H3
Hundall Derbys 133 H4
Hundleby Lincs 137 G6
Hundle Houses Lincs 119 H1
Hundleton Pembks 54 F6
Hundon Suffk 88 E5
Hundred End Lancs 138 E3
Hundred House Powys 78 F4
Hungarton Leics 100 F2
Hungerford Hants 33 L8
Hungerford Somset 29 J3
Hungerford W Berk 47 M5
Hungerford Newtown W Berk 47 M4
Hunger Hill Bolton 139 K6
Hunger Hill Lancs 139 G5
Hungerstone Herefs 80 B8
Hungerton Lincs 118 A5
Hungryhatton Shrops 113 L6
Hunmanby N York 163 K7
Hunningham Warwks 83 J2
Hunnington Worcs 98 B7
Hunsbury Hill W Nthn 84 E4
Hunsdon Herts 69 L4
Hunsdonbury Herts 69 L4
Hunsingore N York 150 F5
Hunslet Leeds 141 M2
Hunsonby W & F 166 D4
Hunstanton Norfk 120 E3
Hunstanworth Dur 168 B1
Hunsterson Ches E 113 M2
Hunston Suffk 89 K2
Hunston W Susx 20 D6
Hunston Green Suffk 89 K2
Hunstrete BaNES 45 J6
Hunsworth Kirk 141 J2
Hunt End Worcs 82 B2
Hunter's Inn Devon 28 B1
Hunter's Quay Ag & B 207 K3
Huntham Somset 30 E5
Hunthill Lodge Angus 234 D1
Huntingdon Cambs 86 E1
Huntingfield Suffk 107 G8
Huntingford Dorset 32 D5
Huntington C York 151 K4
Huntington Ches W 129 K6
Huntington E Loth 212 B4
Huntington Herefs 79 J4
Huntington Herefs 80 B6
Huntington Staffs 98 B1
Huntingtowerfield P & K .. 221 K2
Huntley Gloucs 63 L3
Huntly Abers 255 L4
Hunton Hants 35 G3
Hunton Kent 39 H3
Hunton N York 160 B4
Hunton Bridge Herts 68 D7
Hunt's Corner Norfk 105 L5
Huntscott Somset 29 G2
Hunt's Cross Lpool 129 K3
Hunts Green Bucks 67 L6
Hunts Green Warwks 98 F4
Huntsham Devon 29 H6
Huntshaw Devon 27 J6
Huntshaw Cross Devon 27 J6
Huntspill Somset 30 D2
Huntstile Somset 30 C4
Huntworth Somset 30 D4
Hunwick Dur 168 F4
Hunworth Norfk 122 B4
Hurcott Somset 30 F7
Hurdcott Wilts 33 L4
Hurdsfield Ches E 131 H5
Hurley W & M 49 K2
Hurley Warwks 99 H4
Hurley Bottom W & M 49 K2
Hurley Common Warwks 99 H4
Hurlford E Ayrs 196 E4
Hurlston Green Lancs 138 E5
Hurn BCP 18 A4
Hurn's End Lincs 119 M2
Hursley Hants 34 F6
Hurst Dorset 16 F4
Hurst N York 159 J2

Hurst Somset 31 G7
Hurst Wokham 49 J4
Hurstbourne Priors Hants ... 34 F2
Hurstbourne Tarrant Hants .. 48 A8
Hurst Green E Susx 24 D2
Hurst Green Essex 73 G4
Hurst Green Lancs 148 B8
Hurst Green Surrey 38 B3
Hurst Hill Dudley 97 L4
Hurstley Herefs 79 L5
Hurstpierpoint W Susx 22 D4
Hurst Wickham W Susx 22 D4
Hurstwood Lancs 140 C2
Hurtiso Ork 275 d5
Hurtmore Surrey 36 E2
Hurworth Burn Dur 169 L4
Hurworth-on-Tees Darltn .. 169 J8
Hurworth Place Darltn 160 D1
Hury Dur 168 B6
Husbands Bosworth Leics .. 100 E6
Husborne Crawley C Beds ... 85 J8
Husthwaite N York 161 H7
Hutcherleigh Devon 8 A5
Hut Green N York 142 F3
Huthwaite Notts 133 J7
Huttoft Lincs 137 K4
Hutton Border 202 E2
Hutton E R Yk 152 F5
Hutton Essex 70 F8
Hutton Lancs 139 G2
Hutton N Som 44 D7
Hutton W & F 166 B5
Hutton Bonville N York 160 E3
Hutton Buscel N York 163 H6
Hutton Conyers N York 160 D7
Hutton Cranswick E R Yk .. 153 G5
Hutton End W & F 166 B3
Hutton Hang N York 159 L5
Hutton Henry Dur 169 L3
Hutton-le-Hole N York 162 B4
Hutton Lowcross R & Cl ... 170 E7
Hutton Magna Dur 168 E8
Hutton Mulgrave N York ... 162 E1
Hutton Roof W & F 157 J7
Hutton Roof W & F 165 L4
Hutton Rudby N York 161 G2
Hutton Sessay N York 161 G7
Hutton Wandesley N York .. 151 H5
Huxham Devon 13 M3
Huxham Green Somset 31 K4
Huxley Ches W 129 L7
Huyton Knows 129 K2
Hycemoor Cumb 155 K5
Hyde Gloucs 64 C6
Hyde Hants 33 L8
Hyde Tamesd 131 J1
Hyde Heath Bucks 68 B7
Hyde Lea Staffs 114 E7
Hydestile Surrey 36 E3
Hykeham Moor Lincs 135 J6
Hyndford Bridge S Lans 198 F5
Hynish Ag & B 224 C7
Hyssington Powys 95 H4
Hystfield Gloucs 63 K7
Hythe Essex 72 E2
Hythe Hants 19 G2
Hythe Kent 41 G8
Hythe Somset 44 F8
Hythe End W & M 50 C4
Hyton Cumb 155 K5

I

Ibberton Dorset 16 F1
Ible Derbys 132 E8
Ibsley Hants 18 A2
Ibstock Leics 99 L2
Ibstone Bucks 67 J8
Ibthorpe Hants 48 A8
Iburndale N York 162 F1
Ibworth Hants 48 F7
Icelton N Som 44 D6
Ichrachan Ag & B 217 G1
Ickburgh Norfk 105 G4
Ickenham Gt Lon 50 D2
Ickford Bucks 66 F5
Ickham Kent 41 H4
Ickleford Herts 68 F1
Icklesham E Susx 24 F4
Ickleton Cambs 87 K6
Icklingham Suffk 88 F1
Ickornshaw N York 149 G7
Ickwell Green C Beds 86 C6
Icomb Gloucs 65 J3
Idbury Oxon 65 K3
Iddesleigh Devon 12 D1
Ide Devon 13 L4
Ideford Devon 13 K7

Ide Hill Kent 38 D1
Iden E Susx 25 G3
Iden Green Kent 39 J6
Iden Green Kent 39 K7
Idle C Brad 149 M8
Idless Cnwll 4 D5
Idlicote Warwks 83 G6
Idmiston Wilts 33 L3
Idole Carmth 58 D5
Idridgehay Derbys 115 M2
Idrigill Highld 258 F4
Idstone Oxon 47 K2
Iffley Oxon 66 D6
Ifield W Susx 37 K3
Ifold W Susx 36 F4
Iford BCP 18 A5
Iford E Susx 22 F5
Ifton Mons 44 F1
Ifton Heath Shrops 112 E4
Ightfield Shrops 113 K4
Ightham Kent 38 F2
Iken Suffk 91 J4
Ilam Staffs 115 J2
Ilchester Somset 31 H6
Ilderton Nthumb 190 E2
Ilford Gt Lon 51 L2
Ilford Somset 30 E7
Ilfracombe Devon 27 J2
Ilkeston Derbys 116 D3
Ilketshall St Andrew Suffk . 107 H6
Ilketshall St John Suffk ... 107 H6
Ilketshall St Lawrence Suffk 107 H6
Ilketshall St Margaret Suffk 107 G6
Ilkley C Brad 149 K6
Illand Cnwll 11 K7
Illey Dudley 98 B7
Illidge Green Ches E 130 F7
Illingworth Calder 141 G2
Illogan Cnwll 3 H2
Illston on the Hill Leics ... 100 F3
Ilmer Bucks 67 J4
Ilmington Warwks 82 F6
Ilminster Somset 30 E7
Ilsington Devon 13 H7
Ilsington Dorset 16 E4
Ilston Swans 57 G6
Ilton N York 160 B7
Ilton Somset 30 E7
Imachar N Ayrs 194 D3
Immingham NE Lin 144 F5
Immingham Dock NE Lin ... 145 G4
Impington Cambs 87 J3
Ince Ches W 129 K4
Ince Blundell Sefton 138 C7
Ince-in-Makerfield Wigan .. 139 J6
Inchbae Lodge Highld 262 C6
Inchbare Angus 234 F2
Inchberry Moray 266 F5
Incheril Highld 261 G7
Inchinnan Rens 208 E6
Inchlaggan Highld 239 K3
Inchmichael P & K 222 D2
Inchmore Highld 251 G3
Inchnadamph Highld 271 J4
Inchture P & K 222 D2
Inchyra P & K 222 C3
Indian Queens Cnwll 4 E3
Ingatestone Essex 70 F7
Ingbirchworth Barns 141 K6
Ingerthorpe N York 150 C3
Ingestre Staffs 114 F6
Ingham Lincs 135 J3
Ingham Norfk 123 H6
Ingham Suffk 89 G1
Ingham Corner Norfk 123 H6
Ingleborough Norfk 120 B8
Ingleby Derbys 116 B6
Ingleby Arncliffe N York .. 161 G3
Ingleby Barwick S on T 170 B7
Ingleby Cross N York 161 G3
Ingleby Greenhow N York .. 161 J2
Ingleigh Green Devon 12 E1
Inglesbatch BaNES 45 L6
Inglesham Swindn 65 J7
Ingleston D & G 176 C6
Ingleton Dur 168 F6
Ingleton N York 158 B8
Inglewhite Lancs 147 L7
Ingmanthorpe N York 150 F5
Ingoe Nthumb 180 C4
Ingol Lancs 139 G1
Ingoldisthorpe Norfk 120 F5
Ingoldmells Lincs 137 K6
Ingoldsby Lincs 118 D5
Ingram Nthumb 190 E3
Ingrave Essex 52 D1
Ingrow C Brad 149 J7
Ings W & F 157 G3
Ingst S Glos 45 H2
Ingthorpe Rutlnd 101 M2

Ingworth Norfk.................122 D5
Inkberrow Worcs.................82 B4
Inkerman Dur.................168 E3
Inkersall Green Derbys.................133 H5
Inkhorn Abers.................257 G4
Inkpen W Berk.................48 A4
Inkstack Highld.................280 C2
Inmarsh Wilts.................46 D6
Innellan Ag & B.................207 J5
Innerleithen Border.................200 D6
Innerleven Fife.................222 F7
Innermessan D & G.................172 D2
Innerwick E Loth.................212 F4
Innesmill Moray.................266 F2
Innsworth Gloucs.................64 B3
Insch Abers.................256 A6
Insh Highld.................241 L3
Inshes Highld.................251 J3
Inskip Lancs.................147 J4
Inskip Moss Side Lancs.................147 J4
Inslow Devon.................27 H5
Insworke Cnwll.................6 E4
Intake Sheff.................133 H3
Inver Abers.................243 H5
Inver Highld.................264 D3
Inver P & K.................232 F7
Inverailort Highld.................238 B7
Inveralligin Highld.................260 D8
Inverallochy Abers.................269 K4
Inveran Highld.................272 E8
Inveraray Ag & B.................217 H5
Inverarish Highld.................247 H2
Inverarity Angus.................234 C8
Inverarnan Stirlg.................218 D3
Inverarnie Highld.................251 J5
Inverasdale Highld.................260 C3
Inverbeg Ag & B.................218 E2
Inverbervie Abers.................235 K1
Inverboyndie Abers.................268 B3
Invercreran Lodge Ag & B.................229 G6
Inverdruie Highld.................242 D1
Inveresk E Loth.................211 K5
Inveresragan Ag & B.................228 F8
Inverey Abers.................242 E5
Inverfarigaig Highld.................250 F7
Inverfolla Ag & D.................228 F6
Invergarry Highld.................240 A3
Invergeldie P & K.................220 C2
Invergloy Highld.................239 L6
Invergordon Highld.................263 J6
Invergowrie P & K.................222 F1
Inverguseran Highld.................238 B2
Inverhadden P & K.................231 J4
Inverie Highld.................238 B3
Inverinan Ag & B.................216 F4
Inverinate Highld.................248 E7
Inverkeilor Angus.................235 K4
Inverkeithing Fife.................210 F2
Inverkeithny Abers.................268 A6
Inverkip Inver.................207 K4
Inverkirkaig Highld.................270 E4
Inverlael Highld.................261 K3
Inverlair Highld.................240 B7
Inverliever Lodge Ag & B.................216 E4
Inverlochy Ag & B.................217 K2
Invermark Angus.................244 A7
Invermoriston Highld.................250 D8
Invernaver Highld.................278 B4
Inverneill Ag & B.................206 D3
Inverness Highld.................251 H3
Inverness Airport Highld.................252 E1
Invernettie Abers.................257 L3
Invernoaden Ag & B.................217 J7
Inveroran Hotel Ag & B.................229 M7
Inverquharity Angus.................234 B4
Inverquhomery Abers.................257 J2
Inverroy Highld.................239 M7
Inversanda Highld.................228 E3
Invershiel Highld.................248 F7
Invershin Highld.................272 E8
Invershore Highld.................275 H1
Inversnaid Hotel Stirlg.................218 E5
Inverugie Abers.................269 L6
Inveruglas Ag & B.................218 D3
Inveruglass Highld.................241 L3
Inverurie Abers.................256 D7
Inwardleigh Devon.................12 D3
Inworth Essex.................72 C3
Iochdar W Isls.................283 b9
Iona Ag & B.................226 B7
Iping W Susx.................36 C6
iPort Logistics Park Donc.................142 F8
Ipplepen Devon.................8 B2
Ipsden Oxon.................48 F2
Ipstones Staffs.................115 G2
Ipswich Suffk.................90 E6
Irby Wirral.................128 F3
Irby in the Marsh Lincs.................137 J7
Irby upon Humber NE Lin.................145 G6
Irchester N Nthn.................85 H2

Ireby Cumb.................165 H3
Ireby Lancs.................157 L7
Ireland C Beds.................86 C7
Ireleth W & F.................156 B7
Ireshopeburn Dur.................167 K3
Ireton Wood Derbys.................115 M2
Irlam Salfd.................130 E1
Irnham Lincs.................118 D6
Iron Acton S Glos.................45 K2
Iron Bridge Cambs.................103 K4
Ironbridge Wrekin.................96 F3
Ironbridge Gorge Wrekin.................96 F3
Iron Cross Warwks.................82 C5
Ironmacannie D & G.................185 G7
Irons Bottom Surrey.................37 K2
Ironville Derbys.................116 D1
Irstead Norfk.................123 H7
Irthington Cumb.................178 C6
Irthlingborough N Nthn.................85 J1
Irton N York.................163 L6
Irvine N Ayrs.................196 D3
Isauld Highld.................279 G3
Isbister Shet.................281 d3
Isbister Shet.................281 f5
Isfield E Susx.................23 G4
Isham N Nthn.................101 J8
Isington Hants.................36 A2
Islandpool Worcs.................97 K7
Islay Ag & B.................204 F5
Islay Airport Ag & B.................204 E6
Isle Abbotts Somset.................30 E6
Isle Brewers Somset.................30 E6
Isleham Cambs.................104 C8
Isle of Dogs Gt Lon.................51 K3
Isle of Grain Medway.................53 J4
Isle of Lewis W Isls.................282 f3
Isle of Man IoM.................154 e5
Isle of Man Ronaldsway
    Airport IoM.................154 c8
Isle of Mull Ag & B.................227 H5
Isle of Portland Dorset.................17 L7
Isle of Sheppey Kent.................40 C2
Isle of Skye Highld.................246 F1
Isle of Thanet Kent.................41 K2
Isle of Walney W & F.................146 D3
Isle of Whithorn D & G.................174 D7
Isle of Wight IoW.................19 J6
Isleornsay Highld.................247 L6
Isles of Scilly IoS.................10 c2
Isles of Scilly St Mary's
    Airport IoS.................10 c3
Islesteps D & G.................176 C4
Islet Village Guern.................9 k2
Isleworth Gt Lon.................50 F4
Isley Walton Leics.................116 C6
Islibhig W Isls.................282 d3
Islington Gt Lon.................51 J2
Islip N Nthn.................101 L7
Islip Oxon.................66 D4
Islivig W Isls.................282 d3
Isombridge Wrekin.................96 E1
Istead Rise Kent.................52 D5
Itchen Abbas Hants.................35 H4
Itchen Stoke Hants.................35 H4
Itchingfield W Susx.................37 H5
Itchington S Glos.................45 K2
Itteringham Norfk.................122 C5
Itton Devon.................12 F3
Itton Mons.................62 F8
Itton Common Mons.................62 F7
Ivegill W & F.................165 M2
Ivelet N York.................159 G3
Iver Bucks.................50 D3
Iver Heath Bucks.................50 C2
Iveston Dur.................168 E1
Ivinghoe Bucks.................68 B4
Ivinghoe Aston Bucks.................68 B3
Ivington Herefs.................80 B4
Ivington Green Herefs.................80 B4
Ivybridge Devon.................7 J4
Ivychurch Kent.................25 J2
Ivy Cross Dorset.................32 E6
Ivy Hatch Kent.................38 F3
Ivy Todd Norfk.................105 H2
Iwade Kent.................40 A2
Iwerne Courtney Dorset.................32 E8
Iwerne Minster Dorset.................32 E8
Ixworth Suffk.................89 J1
Ixworth Thorpe Suffk.................89 J1

J

Jack Green Lancs.................139 J3
Jack Hill N York.................150 B5
Jack-in-the-Green Devon.................14 B3
Jack's Bush Hants.................34 C3
Jacksdale Notts.................116 D1
Jackson Bridge Kirk.................141 J6

Jackton S Lans.................209 G8
Jacobstow Cnwll.................11 H3
Jacobstowe Devon.................12 E2
Jacobs Well Surrey.................50 C8
Jameston Pembks.................55 H7
Jamestown Highld.................262 E8
Jamestown W Duns.................208 C3
Janetstown Highld.................275 G2
Jardine Hall D & G.................176 E1
Jarrow S Tyne.................181 H6
Jarvis Brook E Susx.................38 E7
Jasper's Green Essex.................71 H2
Jawcraig Falk.................209 M4
Jaywick Essex.................73 H4
Jealott's Hill Br For.................49 L4
Jeater Houses N York.................160 F4
Jedburgh Border.................189 H2
Jeffreyston Pembks.................55 J5
Jemimaville Highld.................263 K7
Jerbourg Guern.................9 k4
Jersey Jersey.................9 b2
Jersey Airport Jersey.................9 b2
Jersey Marine Neath.................57 K6
Jerusalem Lincs.................135 J5
Jesmond N u Ty.................181 G5
Jevington E Susx.................23 J7
Jingle Street Mons.................62 F5
Jockey End Herts.................68 D4
Jodrell Bank Ches E.................130 F5
Jodrell Bank Ches E.................130 F5
Johnby W & F.................166 B4
John Lennon Airport Lpool.................129 K3
John o' Groats Highld.................280 E2
Johns Cross E Susx.................24 D3
Johnshaven Abers.................235 K2
Johnson Street Norfk.................123 H8
Johnston Pembks.................54 F5
Johnstone D & G.................187 K6
Johnstone Rens.................208 D6
Johnstonebridge D & G.................187 G2
Johnstown Carmth.................58 D5
Johnstown Wrexhm.................112 H3
Joppa C Edin.................211 K4
Joppa Cerdgn.................77 G2
Joppa S Ayrs.................196 E7
Jordans Bucks.................50 B1
Jordanston Pembks.................74 F5
Jordanthorpe Sheff.................133 G3
Joyden's Wood Kent.................52 B4
Jubilee Corner Kent.................39 L4
Jump Barns.................142 B7
Jumper's Town E Susx.................38 C6
Juniper Nthumb.................179 L7
Juniper Green C Edin.................211 G5
Jura Ag & B.................215 G7
Jurassic Coast Devon.................15 H5
Jurby IoM.................154 e3
Jurston Devon.................13 G5

K

Kaber W & F.................167 J8
Kaimend S Lans.................199 G4
Kames Ag & B.................206 F5
Kames E Ayrs.................197 K5
Kea Cnwll.................4 C6
Keadby N Linc.................143 L5
Keal Cotes Lincs.................137 G7
Kearby Town End N York.................150 E6
Kearsley Bolton.................139 M6
Kearsley Nthumb.................180 B4
Kearsney Kent.................41 J6
Kearstwick W & F.................157 K6
Kearton N York.................159 H3
Keasden N York.................148 C3
Keaton Devon.................7 J4
Keckwick Halton.................130 B3
Keddington Lincs.................136 F2
Keddington Corner Lincs.................137 G2
Kedington Suffk.................88 E6
Kedleston Derbys.................116 A3
Keelby Lincs.................144 F5
Keele Staffs.................114 C3
Keele Services Staffs.................114 C3
Keele University Staffs.................114 C3
Keeley Green Bed.................85 K6
Keelham C Brad.................141 G1
Keeres Green Essex.................70 F4
Keeston Pembks.................54 E3
Keevil Wilts.................46 D7
Kegworth Leics.................116 E6
Kehelland Cnwll.................3 G3
Keig Abers.................256 A7
Keighley C Brad.................149 J7
Keilarsbrae Clacks.................220 F8
Keillour P & K.................221 H2
Keiloch Abers.................243 G5
Keils Ag & B.................205 H2

Keinton Mandeville Somset.................31 J5
Keir Mill D & G.................186 C7
Keirsleywell Row Nthumb.................179 H8
Keisby Lincs.................118 D6
Keisley W & F.................167 G6
Keiss Highld.................280 D4
Keith Moray.................267 J6
Keithick P & K.................233 J7
Keithock Angus.................234 F3
Keithtown Highld.................262 F8
Kelbrook Lancs.................148 F5
Kelby Lincs.................118 D3
Keld N York.................158 F3
Keld W & F.................166 D7
Keld Head N York.................162 D5
Keldholme N York.................162 C5
Kelfield N Linc.................143 L7
Kelfield N York.................151 J8
Kelham Notts.................134 F8
Kelhead D & G.................176 F5
Kellacott Devon.................12 A3
Kellamergh Lancs.................147 H5
Kellas Angus.................234 C8
Kellas Moray.................266 D5
Kellaton Devon.................8 B7
Kelleth W & F.................157 L2
Kelling Norfk.................122 B3
Kellingley N York.................142 E3
Kellington N York.................142 E3
Kelloe Dur.................169 K3
Kelloholm D & G.................185 J1
Kells Cumb.................164 C7
Kelly Devon.................11 M6
Kelly Bray Cnwll.................11 L8
Kelmarsh W Nthn.................101 G7
Kelmscott Oxon.................65 K7
Kelsale Suffk.................91 J2
Kelsall Ches W.................129 M6
Kelshall Herts.................87 G7
Kelsick Cumb.................165 G1
Kelso Border.................201 M6
Kelstedge Derbys.................133 G7
Kelstern Lincs.................136 F1
Kelsterton Flints.................129 G5
Kelston BaNES.................45 K5
Keltneyburn P & K.................231 L5
Kelton D & G.................176 C3
Kelty Fife.................221 L8
Kelvedon Essex.................72 C3
Kelvedon Hatch Essex.................70 E7
Kelvinhead N Lans.................209 K3
Kelynack Cnwll.................2 B5
Kemacott Devon.................28 B2
Kemback Fife.................223 G4
Kemberton Shrops.................97 G3
Kemble Gloucs.................64 E7
Kemble Wick Gloucs.................64 E7
Kemerton Worcs.................81 L7
Kemeys Commander Mons.................62 D6
Kemnay Abers.................256 D8
Kempe's Corner Kent.................40 D6
Kempley Gloucs.................63 K1
Kempley Green Gloucs.................63 K1
Kempsey Worcs.................81 J5
Kempsford Gloucs.................65 H7
Kemps Green Warwks.................82 D1
Kempshott Hants.................35 J1
Kempston Bed.................85 K5
Kempston Hardwick Bed.................85 K6
Kempton Shrops.................95 J6
Kemp Town Br & H.................22 E6
Kemsing Kent.................52 C7
Kemsley Kent.................40 B2
Kemsley Street Kent.................53 H6
Kenardington Kent.................25 H1
Kenchester Herefs.................80 B6
Kencot Oxon.................65 K6
Kendal W & F.................157 H4
Kenderchurch Herefs.................62 F2
Kendleshire S Glos.................45 K3
Kenfig Brdgnd.................42 B5
Kenfig Hill Brdgnd.................42 C5
Kenilworth Warwks.................83 G1
Kenley Gt Lon.................51 J7
Kenley Shrops.................96 D3
Kenmore Highld.................260 B8
Kenmore P & K.................231 L6
Kenn Devon.................13 L5
Kenn N Som.................44 E5
Kennacraig Ag & B.................206 C6
Kennall Vale Cnwll.................3 J3
Kennards House Cnwll.................11 K6
Kenneggy Cnwll.................2 F5
Kennerleigh Devon.................13 J1
Kennet Clacks.................210 B1
Kennethmont Abers.................255 L6
Kennett Cambs.................88 D2
Kennford Devon.................13 L5
Kenninghall Norfk.................105 L6
Kennington Kent.................40 D6

Kennington Oxon......66 D6
Kennington Lees Kent......40 D6
Kennoway Fife......222 F6
Kenny Somset......30 D7
Kenny Hill Suffk......104 D7
Kennythorpe N York......152 B3
Kenovay Ag & B......224 C6
Kensaleyre Highld......259 G6
Kensington Gt Lon......51 H3
Kensworth Common C Beds......68 C3
Kentallen Highld......228 F4
Kentchurch Herefs......62 E2
Kentford Suffk......88 E2
Kent Green Ches E......131 G8
Kentisbeare Devon......14 C1
Kentisbury Devon......27 L2
Kentisbury Ford Devon......27 L2
Kentish Town Gt Lon......51 H2
Kentmere W & F......157 G2
Kenton Devon......13 M6
Kenton Gt Lon......50 F1
Kenton N u Ty......180 F5
Kenton Suffk......90 E2
Kenton Bankfoot N u Ty......180 F5
Kentra Highld......237 J6
Kents Bank W & F......156 F7
Kentsboro Hants......34 C3
Kent's Green Gloucs......63 L2
Kent's Oak Hants......34 D6
Kent Street E Susx......24 E4
Kent Street Kent......39 G2
Kenwick Shrops......112 F5
Kenwyn Cnwll......4 D5
Kenyon Warrtn......139 J8
Keoldale Highld......276 F3
Keppoch Highld......248 E6
Kepwick N York......161 G4
Keresley Covtry......99 J6
Kermincham Ches E......130 F6
Kernborough Devon......8 B6
Kerne Bridge Herefs......63 H3
Kerrera Ag & B......216 C2
Kerridge Ches E......131 J4
Kerridge-end Ches E......131 J4
Kerris Cnwll......2 C5
Kerry Powys......94 E5
Kerrycroy Ag & B......207 J6
Kersall Notts......134 E7
Kersbrook Devon......14 C6
Kerscott Devon......27 L5
Kersey Suffk......89 K6
Kersey Tye Suffk......89 K6
Kersey Upland Suffk......89 K6
Kershader W Isls......282 f4
Kershopefoot Cumb......178 B2
Kersoe Worcs......82 A7
Kerswell Devon......14 C2
Kerswell Green Worcs......81 K6
Kerthen Wood Cnwll......2 F4
Kesgrave Suffk......90 F6
Kessingland Suffk......107 L6
Kessingland Beach Suffk......107 L6
Kestle Cnwll......5 G5
Kestle Mill Cnwll......4 D3
Keston Gt Lon......51 L6
Keswick Cumb......165 J6
Keswick Norfk......106 E2
Ketsby Lincs......137 G4
Kettering N Nthn......101 J7
Ketteringham Norfk......106 D3
Kettins P & K......233 K7
Kettlebaston Suffk......89 K6
Kettlebridge Fife......222 E5
Kettlebrook Staffs......99 G3
Kettleburgh Suffk......91 G3
Kettle Green Herts......69 L3
Kettleholm D & G......176 F3
Kettleness N York......171 J7
Kettleshulme Ches E......131 K4
Kettlesing N York......150 B4
Kettlesing Bottom N York......150 B4
Kettlestone Norfk......121 L5
Kettlethorpe Lincs......135 G4
Kettletoft Ork......275 e2
Kettlewell N York......149 H2
Ketton Rutlnd......101 L3
Kew Gt Lon......50 F4
Kew Royal Botanic Gardens
  Gt Lon......50 F4
Kewstoke N Som......44 C6
Kexbrough Barns......141 M6
Kexby C York......151 L5
Kexby Lincs......135 H3
Key Green Ches E......131 H7
Key Green N York......162 D2
Keyham Leics......100 E2
Keyhaven Hants......18 D5
Keyingham E R Yk......145 H3
Keymer W Susx......22 D4
Keynsham BaNES......45 K5

Keysoe Bed......86 B3
Keysoe Row Bed......86 B3
Keyston Cambs......102 A8
Keyworth Notts......117 G5
Kibbear Somset......30 B6
Kibblesworth Gatesd......181 G7
Kibworth Beauchamp Leics......100 F4
Kibworth Harcourt Leics......100 F4
Kidbrooke Gt Lon......51 L4
Kidburngill Cumb......164 E6
Kiddemore Green Staffs......97 J2
Kidderminster Worcs......97 H8
Kiddington Oxon......66 B3
Kidd's Moor Norfk......106 C3
Kidlington Oxon......66 D4
Kidmore End Oxon......49 G3
Kidsdale D & G......174 C7
Kidsgrove Staffs......131 G8
Kidstones N York......159 G6
Kidwelly Carmth......56 D3
Kiel Crofts Ag & B......228 D7
Kielder Nthumb......189 H7
Kielder Forest......178 E2
Kiells Ag & B......204 F3
Kilbarchan Rens......208 C6
Kilbeg Highld......247 K7
Kilberry Ag & B......206 A6
Kilbirnie N Ayrs......208 A8
Kilbride Ag & B......207 G5
Kilbride Ag & B......215 L8
Kilbuiack Moray......266 B4
Kilburn Derbys......116 C2
Kilburn Gt Lon......51 H2
Kilburn N York......161 H6
Kilby Leics......100 D4
Kilchamaig Ag & B......206 C6
Kilchattan Ag & B......207 H8
Kilchattan Ag & B......214 D5
Kilcheran Ag & B......228 C7
Kilchoan Highld......236 F7
Kilchoman Ag & B......204 B4
Kilchrenan Ag & B......217 G3
Kilconquhar Fife......223 H6
Kilcot Gloucs......63 K2
Kilcoy Highld......251 G2
Kilcreggan Ag & B......207 L3
Kildale N York......161 K1
Kildalloig Ag & B......192 F4
Kildary Highld......263 K5
Kildavaig Ag & B......206 F6
Kildavanan Ag & B......207 G5
Kildonan Highld......274 B4
Kildonan N Ayrs......195 G6
Kildonan Lodge Highld......274 B4
Kildonnan Highld......236 F3
Kildrochet House D & G......172 D4
Kildrummy Abers......255 J8
Kildwick N York......149 H6
Kilfinan Ag & B......206 E3
Kilfinnan Highld......239 M4
Kilford Denbgs......128 C6
Kilgetty Pembks......55 K5
Kilgrammie S Ayrs......183 G3
Kilgwrrwg Common Mons......62 F7
Kilham E R Yk......153 G3
Kilham Nthumb......202 D6
Kilkenneth Ag & B......224 B6
Kilkenzie Ag & B......192 D3
Kilkerran Ag & B......192 E4
Kilkhampton Cnwll......26 D8
Killamarsh Derbys......133 J4
Killay Swans......57 H6
Killearn Stirlg......208 E2
Killen Highld......263 J8
Killerby Darltn......169 G6
Killerton Devon......14 A3
Killichonan P & K......231 G4
Killiechonate Highld......239 L7
Killiechronan Ag & B......227 G4
Killiecrankie P & K......232 D3
Killilan Highld......248 F5
Killimster Highld......280 D5
Killin Stirlg......231 G8
Killinghall N York......150 C4
Killington Devon......28 B2
Killington W & F......157 K5
Killington Lake Services W & F......157 J4
Killingworth N Tyne......181 G5
Killiow Cnwll......4 C6
Killochyett Border......200 F4
Kilmacolm Inver......208 B5
Kilmahog Stirlg......219 K5
Kilmahumaig Ag & B......216 B8
Kilmaluag Highld......259 G2
Kilmany Fife......222 F3
Kilmarnock E Ayrs......196 E3
Kilmartin Ag & B......216 C7
Kilmaurs E Ayrs......196 E3
Kilmelford Ag & B......216 C4

Kilmersdon Somset......45 K8
Kilmeston Hants......35 J5
Kilmichael Ag & B......192 E4
Kilmichael Glassary Ag & B......216 D8
Kilmichael of Inverlussa
  Ag & B......206 B2
Kilmington Devon......15 G3
Kilmington Wilts......32 C4
Kilmington Common Wilts......32 C4
Kilmington Street Wilts......32 C4
Kilmorack Highld......250 E3
Kilmore Ag & B......216 D2
Kilmore Highld......247 K7
Kilmory Ag & B......205 M2
Kilmory Highld......237 G6
Kilmory N Ayrs......193 K4
Kilmuir Highld......251 J2
Kilmuir Highld......258 D7
Kilmuir Highld......258 F3
Kilmuir Highld......263 K5
Kilmun Ag & B......207 K3
Kilnave Ag & B......204 D2
Kilncadzow S Lans......198 E3
Kilndown Kent......39 H6
Kiln Green Wokham......49 K3
Kilnhill Cumb......165 H4
Kilnhurst Rothm......142 C8
Kilninver Ag & B......216 C3
Kiln Pit Hill Nthumb......180 C7
Kilnsea E R Yk......145 L4
Kilnsey N York......149 H2
Kilnwick E R Yk......152 F6
Kilnwick Percy E R Yk......152 C6
Kilnwood Vale W Susx......37 K4
Kiloran Ag & B......214 D5
Kilpatrick N Ayrs......194 D5
Kilpeck Herefs......62 F1
Kilpin E R Yk......143 K2
Kilpin Pike E R Yk......143 J2
Kilrenny Fife......223 K6
Kilsby W Nthn......84 A1
Kilspindie P & K......222 C2
Kilstay D & G......172 E7
Kilsyth N Lans......209 J3
Kiltarlity Highld......250 E3
Kilton R & Cl......171 G7
Kilton Somset......29 L2
Kilton Thorpe R & Cl......171 G7
Kilvaxter Highld......258 F3
Kilve Somset......29 L2
Kilvington Notts......117 L3
Kilwinning N Ayrs......196 B2
Kimberley Norfk......106 B3
Kimberley Notts......116 E3
Kimberworth Rothm......133 H1
Kimblesworth Dur......169 H1
Kimble Wick Bucks......67 J5
Kimbolton Cambs......86 B2
Kimbolton Herefs......80 C3
Kimcote Leics......100 D6
Kimmeridge Dorset......17 H6
Kimmerston Nthumb......202 E6
Kimpton Hants......34 C2
Kimpton Herts......68 F3
Kimworthy Devon......26 E8
Kinbrace Highld......273 L2
Kinbuck Stirlg......220 D6
Kincaple Fife......223 H3
Kincardine Fife......210 B2
Kincardine Highld......263 G2
Kincardine Bridge Fife......210 B2
Kincardine O'Neil Abers......244 D4
Kinclaven P & K......233 H7
Kincorth C Aber......245 L3
Kincorth House Moray......265 G7
Kincraig Highld......241 M2
Kincraigie P & K......232 E5
Kindallachan P & K......232 E5
Kinerarach Ag & B......205 L5
Kineton Gloucs......65 G2
Kineton Warwks......83 H5
Kinfauns P & K......222 B3
Kingarth Ag & B......207 H7
Kingcausie Abers......245 J3
Kingcoed Mons......62 E6
Kingerby Lincs......135 L1
Kingford Devon......11 K2
Kingham Oxon......65 K2
Kingholm Quay D & G......176 C4
Kinghorn Fife......211 J2
Kinglassie Fife......222 C7
Kingoodie P & K......222 F1
King's Acre Herefs......80 B7
Kingsand Cnwll......6 E5
Kingsash Bucks......67 L6
Kingsbarns Fife......223 K5
Kingsborough Kent......53 L4
Kingsbridge Devon......7 L6
Kingsbridge Somset......29 H3
Kingsbridge Swans......57 G5

King's Bromley Staffs......115 J8
Kingsbrook Bucks......67 K4
Kingsburgh Highld......258 F5
Kingsbury Gt Lon......51 G1
Kingsbury Warwks......99 G4
Kingsbury Episcopi Somset......31 G6
King's Caple Herefs......63 H2
Kingsclere Hants......48 D7
King's Cliffe N Nthn......101 M4
Kings Clipstone Notts......134 C6
Kingscote Gloucs......64 B7
Kingscott Devon......27 K7
King's Coughton Warwks......82 C3
Kingscross N Ayrs......195 G5
Kingsdon Somset......31 H5
Kingsdown Kent......41 L5
Kingsdown Swindn......47 H1
Kingsdown Wilts......46 A5
Kingseat Abers......257 G7
Kingseat Fife......210 F1
Kingsey Bucks......67 H6
Kingsfold W Susx......37 J4
Kingsford C Aber......245 J2
Kingsford E Ayrs......196 E2
Kingsford Worcs......97 J7
Kingsgate Kent......41 L1
Kings Green Gloucs......81 H8
Kingshall Street Suffk......89 J3
Kingsheanton Devon......27 K3
King's Heath Birm......98 D7
Kings Hill Kent......39 H2
King's Hill Wsall......98 C4
Kingshouse Hotel Highld......229 L4
Kingshurst Solhll......98 F5
Kingside Hill Cumb......177 G8
Kingskerswell Devon......8 C1
Kingskettle Fife......222 E5
Kingsland Dorset......15 K3
Kingsland Herefs......80 B3
Kingsland IoA......124 D3
Kings Langley Herts......68 D6
Kingsley Ches W......130 A5
Kingsley Hants......36 B3
Kingsley Staffs......115 G2
Kingsley Green W Susx......36 D5
Kingsley Holt Staffs......115 G2
Kingsley Park W Nthn......84 E3
Kingslow Shrops......97 H4
King's Lynn Norfk......120 D7
Kings Meaburn W & F......166 C4
Kingsmead Hants......35 J8
King's Mills Guern......9 i3
King's Moss St Hel......139 G7
Kingsmuir Angus......234 E3
Kings Muir Border......200 B5
Kingsmuir Fife......223 J5
Kings Newnham Warwks......99 M7
King's Newton Derbys......116 C6
Kingsnorth Kent......40 C7
King's Norton Birm......98 D7
King's Norton Leics......100 F3
Kings Nympton Devon......28 B5
King's Pyon Herefs......80 B5
Kings Ripton Cambs......102 F8
King's Somborne Hants......34 D4
King's Stag Dorset......32 B8
King's Stanley Gloucs......64 A6
King's Sutton W Nthn......83 L8
Kingstanding Birm......98 D6
Kingsteignton Devon......13 K8
Kingsteps Highld......264 E8
King Sterndale Derbys......132 B5
Kingsthorne Herefs......63 G1
Kingsthorpe W Nthn......84 E3
Kingston Cambs......87 G4
Kingston Cnwll......11 L7
Kingston Devon......7 J5
Kingston Devon......14 C5
Kingston Dorset......16 E1
Kingston Dorset......17 J6
Kingston E Loth......212 C3
Kingston Hants......18 A3
Kingston IoW......19 H7
Kingston Kent......41 G6
Kingston W Susx......21 J6
Kingston Bagpuize Oxon......66 B7
Kingston Blount Oxon......67 H7
Kingston by Sea W Susx......22 C6
Kingston Deverill Wilts......32 C3
Kingstone Herefs......80 A8
Kingstone Somset......30 E8
Kingstone Staffs......115 H5
Kingston Winslow Oxon......47 K2
Kingston Lisle Oxon......47 L2
Kingston near Lewes E Susx......22 F5
Kingston on Soar Notts......116 D6
Kingston on Spey Moray......267 G3
Kingston Russell Dorset......16 A4
Kingston St Mary Somset......30 B5
Kingston Seymour N Som......44 E5

Kingston Stert Oxon 67 H7
Kingston upon Hull C KuH ...144 D2
Kingston upon Thames Gt Lon ...50 F5
Kingstown Cumb 177 L7
King's Walden Herts ...68 F2
Kingswear Devon 8 C4
Kingswells C Aber ...245 J2
Kings Weston Bristl ...45 G3
Kingswinford Dudley ...97 K5
Kingswood Bucks ...67 G3
Kingswood C KuH ...144 D1
Kingswood Gloucs ...63 L8
Kingswood Kent ...39 L3
Kingswood Powys ...94 F3
Kingswood S Glos ...45 J4
Kingswood Somset ...29 K3
Kingswood Surrey ...51 L8
Kingswood Warrtn ...82 E1
Kingswood Brook Warwks ...82 E1
Kingswood Common Herefd ...79 H4
Kingswood Common Staffs ...97 J3
Kings Worthy Hants ...35 G4
Kingthorpe Lincs ...136 B4
Kington Herefs ...79 K4
Kington S Glos ...45 J1
Kington Worcs ...82 A4
Kington Langley Wilts ...46 D3
Kington Magna Dorset ...32 C6
Kington St Michael Wilts ...46 C3
Kingussie Highld ...241 K3
Kingweston Somset ...31 H5
Kinharrachie Abers ...257 J3
Kinharvie D & G ...176 B5
Kinkell Bridge P & K ...221 G4
Kinknockie Abers ...257 J3
Kinleith C Edin ...211 K5
Kinlet Shrops ...97 G7
Kinloch Highld ...246 E8
Kinloch Highld ...271 K1
Kinloch Highld ...277 J5
Kinloch P & K ...233 H6
Kinlochard Stirlg ...219 G6
Kinlochbervie Highld ...276 C5
Kinlocheil Highld ...238 F7
Kinlochewe Highld ...261 G7
Kinloch Hourn Highld ...238 F2
Kinlochlaggan Highld ...240 F5
Kinlochleven Highld ...229 K3
Kinlochmoidart Highld ...237 K6
Kinlochnanuagh Highld ...237 L4
Kinloch Rannoch P & K ...231 J4
Kinloss Moray ...265 H3
Kinmel Bay Conwy ...127 K4
Kinmuck Abers ...256 E7
Kinmundy Abers ...256 F8
Kinnabus Ag & B ...204 D7
Kinnadie Abers ...257 H3
Kinnaird P & K ...232 E4
Kinneff Abers ...245 J8
Kinnelhead D & G ...186 F6
Kinnell Angus ...234 F5
Kinnerley Shrops ...112 E7
Kinnersley Herefs ...79 L5
Kinnersley Worcs ...81 K6
Kinnerton Powys ...79 J3
Kinnerton Shrops ...95 J4
Kinnerton Green Flints ...129 H7
Kinnesswood P & K ...222 B6
Kinninvie Dur ...168 D6
Kinnordy Angus ...234 B4
Kinoulton Notts ...117 H5
Kinross P & K ...221 K8
Kinrossie P & K ...222 C1
Kinross Services P & K ...221 K6
Kinsbourne Green Herts ...68 E4
Kinsey Heath Ches E ...113 L3
Kinsham Herefs ...79 L2
Kinsham Worcs ...81 L8
Kinsley Wakefd ...142 H2
Kinson BCP ...17 L3
Kintail Highld ...249 G8
Kintbury W Berk ...48 A5
Kintessack Moray ...264 F7
Kintillo P & K ...221 L4
Kinton Herefs ...95 K8
Kinton Shrops ...112 E7
Kintore Abers ...256 E8
Kintour Ag & B ...205 G6
Kintra Ag & B ...204 D6
Kintra Ag & B ...226 C7
Kintraw Ag & B ...216 C6
Kintyre Ag & B ...194 A3
Kinveachy Highld ...253 G7
Kinver Staffs ...97 J6
Kiplin N York ...160 C3
Kippax Leeds ...142 C2
Kippen Stirlg ...219 L8
Kippford D & G ...175 L4
Kipping's Cross Kent ...39 G5
Kirbister Ork ...275 c5

Kirby Bedon Norfk ...106 F2
Kirby Bellars Leics ...117 J7
Kirby Cane Norfk ...107 H5
Kirby Corner Covtry ...99 J8
Kirby Cross Essex ...73 J3
Kirby Fields Leics ...100 B3
Kirby Green Norfk ...107 H4
Kirby Grindalythe N York ...152 D2
Kirby Hill N York ...150 E2
Kirby Hill N York ...159 L2
Kirby Knowle N York ...161 G5
Kirby-le-Soken Essex ...73 J3
Kirby Misperton N York ...162 D6
Kirby Muxloe Leics ...100 B3
Kirby Sigston N York ...160 F4
Kirby Underdale E R Yk ...152 B4
Kirby Wiske N York ...160 E5
Kirdford W Susx ...36 F5
Kirk Highld ...280 C4
Kirkabister Shet ...281 e7
Kirkandrews D & G ...174 F5
Kirkandrews upon Eden Cumb ...177 K7
Kirkbampton Cumb ...177 J7
Kirkbean D & G ...176 C7
Kirk Bramwith Donc ...143 G5
Kirkbride Cumb ...177 H7
Kirkbridge N York ...160 C4
Kirkbuddo Angus ...234 D6
Kirkburn Border ...200 C5
Kirkburn E R Yk ...152 F5
Kirkburton Kirk ...141 K5
Kirkby Knows ...138 E7
Kirkby Lincs ...135 L1
Kirkby N York ...161 H2
Kirkby Fleetham N York ...160 D4
Kirkby Green Lincs ...136 A8
Kirkby-in-Ashfield Notts ...133 K8
Kirkby-in-Furness W & F ...156 B6
Kirkby la Thorpe Lincs ...118 E2
Kirkby Lonsdale W & F ...157 K7
Kirkby Malham N York ...148 F4
Kirkby Mallory Leics ...99 M3
Kirkby Malzeard N York ...160 C7
Kirkby Mills N York ...162 C6
Kirkbymoorside N York ...162 B5
Kirkby on Bain Lincs ...136 D7
Kirkby Overblow N York ...150 D6
Kirkby Stephen W & F ...158 D1
Kirkby Thore W & F ...166 E5
Kirkby Underwood Lincs ...118 E6
Kirkby Wharf N York ...151 H7
Kirkby Woodhouse Notts ...116 E1
Kirkcaldy Fife ...211 J1
Kirkcambeck Cumb ...178 C5
Kirkchrist D & G ...175 G4
Kirkcolm D & G ...172 C1
Kirkconnel D & G ...197 L8
Kirkconnell D & G ...176 C5
Kirkcowan D & G ...173 J3
Kirkcudbright D & G ...175 H5
Kirkdale Lpool ...129 H1
Kirk Deighton N York ...150 F5
Kirk Ella E R Yk ...144 C2
Kirkfieldbank S Lans ...198 E4
Kirkgunzeon D & G ...175 L2
Kirk Hallam Derbys ...116 D3
Kirkham Lancs ...138 E1
Kirkham N York ...151 M3
Kirkhamgate Wakefd ...141 L3
Kirk Hammerton N York ...151 G5
Kirkharle Nthumb ...180 B2
Kirkhaugh Nthumb ...167 G1
Kirkheaton Kirk ...141 J4
Kirkheaton Nthumb ...180 B3
Kirkhill Highld ...250 F3
Kirkhope S Lans ...186 E5
Kirkhouse Cumb ...178 D7
Kirkhouse Green Donc ...143 G5
Kirkibost Highld ...247 H5
Kirkinch P & K ...233 L6
Kirkinner D & G ...174 C4
Kirkintilloch E Duns ...209 H4
Kirk Ireton Derbys ...115 M2
Kirkland Cumb ...164 E7
Kirkland D & G ...185 K5
Kirkland D & G ...186 F8
Kirkland D & G ...197 L8
Kirkland W & F ...166 F4
Kirkland Guards Cumb ...165 G3
Kirk Langley Derbys ...115 M4
Kirkleatham R & Cl ...170 E6
Kirklevington S on T ...160 F1
Kirkley Suffk ...107 L5
Kirklington N York ...160 D6
Kirklington Notts ...134 D8
Kirklinton Cumb ...178 B5
Kirkliston C Edin ...210 F4
Kirkmabreck D & G ...174 D4
Kirkmaiden D & G ...172 E7
Kirk Merrington Dur ...169 H4

Kirk Michael IoM ...154 d4
Kirkmichael P & K ...233 G3
Kirkmichael S Ayrs ...183 J1
Kirkmuirhill S Lans ...198 C4
Kirknewton Nthumb ...202 E7
Kirknewton W Loth ...210 F5
Kirkney Abers ...255 K5
Kirk of Shotts N Lans ...209 M6
Kirkoswald S Ayrs ...183 G2
Kirkoswald W & F ...166 D3
Kirkpatrick D & G ...186 D8
Kirkpatrick Durham D & G ...175 K1
Kirkpatrick-Fleming D & G ...177 J5
Kirk Sandall Donc ...142 F6
Kirksanton Cumb ...155 L6
Kirk Smeaton N York ...142 E4
Kirkstall Leeds ...150 C8
Kirkstead Lincs ...136 C7
Kirkstile Abers ...255 L5
Kirkstile D & G ...186 D5
Kirkstyle Highld ...280 D2
Kirkthorpe Wakefd ...142 D3
Kirkton Abers ...256 B6
Kirkton D & G ...176 C3
Kirkton Fife ...222 F2
Kirkton Highld ...248 C6
Kirkton Highld ...248 E3
Kirkton P & K ...221 G3
Kirkton Manor Border ...200 B5
Kirkton of Airlie Angus ...233 M5
Kirkton of Auchterhouse
  Angus ...234 A7
Kirkton of Barevan Highld ...252 F2
Kirkton of Collace P & K ...222 C1
Kirkton of Durris Abers ...245 G4
Kirkton of Glenbuchat Abers ...255 H8
Kirkton of Glenisla Angus ...233 K3
Kirkton of Kingoldrum Angus ...233 M4
Kirkton of Lethendy P & K ...233 H7
Kirkton of Logie Buchan
  Abers ...257 H8
Kirkton of Maryculter Abers ...245 J4
Kirkton of Menmuir Angus ...234 E3
Kirkton of Monikie Angus ...234 D7
Kirkton of Rayne Abers ...256 C5
Kirkton of Skene Abers ...245 H2
Kirkton of Tealing Angus ...234 B7
Kirkton of Tough Abers ...244 D1
Kirktown Abers ...269 J3
Kirktown Abers ...269 K6
Kirktown of Alvah Abers ...268 B4
Kirktown of Bourtie Abers ...256 E6
Kirktown of Deskford Moray ...267 K4
Kirktown of Fetteresso Abers ...245 J6
Kirktown of Mortlach Moray ...255 G4
Kirktown of Slains Abers ...257 J6
Kirkurd Border ...199 K4
Kirkwall Ork ...275 c4
Kirkwall Airport Ork ...275 d5
Kirkwhelpington Nthumb ...180 B2
Kirk Yetholm Border ...202 C7
Kirmington N Linc ...144 E5
Kirmond le Mire Lincs ...136 C1
Kirn Ag & B ...207 K3
Kirriemuir Angus ...234 B4
Kirstead Green Norfk ...106 F4
Kirtlebridge D & G ...177 H4
Kirtling Cambs ...88 D4
Kirtling Green Cambs ...88 D4
Kirtlington Oxon ...66 D3
Kirtomy Highld ...278 C3
Kirton Lincs ...119 J4
Kirton Notts ...134 D6
Kirton Suffk ...91 G7
Kirton End Lincs ...119 J3
Kirtonhill W Duns ...208 C4
Kirton Holme Lincs ...119 J3
Kirton in Lindsey N Linc ...144 A8
Kirwaugh D & G ...173 K4
Kishorn Highld ...248 D4
Kislingbury W Nthn ...84 D3
Kitebrook Warwks ...65 K1
Kite Green Warwks ...82 E2
Kites Hardwick Warwks ...83 L2
Kitleigh Cnwll ...11 J3
Kitt Green Wigan ...139 H6
Kittisford Somset ...29 K6
Kittle Swans ...57 G7
Kitt's Green Birm ...98 F6
Kittybrewster C Aber ...245 K2
Kitwood Hants ...35 K4
Kivernoll Herefs ...62 F1
Kiveton Park Rothm ...133 K3
Knaith Lincs ...135 G3
Knaith Park Lincs ...135 G3
Knap Corner Dorset ...32 D6
Knaphill Surrey ...50 B7
Knapp Somset ...30 D5
Knapp Hill Hants ...34 E6

Knapthorpe Notts ...134 E7
Knapton C York ...151 J5
Knapton N York ...162 F7
Knapton Norfk ...122 F5
Knapton Green Herefs ...80 B5
Knapwell Cambs ...87 G3
Knaresborough N York ...150 E4
Knarsdale Nthumb ...178 F8
Knaven Abers ...257 G3
Knayton N York ...160 F5
Knebworth Herts ...69 H3
Knedlington E R Yk ...143 J2
Kneesall Notts ...134 D6
Kneeton Notts ...117 J2
Knelston Swans ...56 E7
Knenhall Staffs ...114 E4
Knettishall Suffk ...105 K7
Knightacott Devon ...28 B3
Knightcote Warwks ...83 J4
Knightley Staffs ...114 C6
Knightley Dale Staffs ...114 C6
Knighton BCP ...17 L8
Knighton C Leic ...100 D3
Knighton Devon ...7 G5
Knighton Dorset ...31 K8
Knighton Powys ...79 K1
Knighton Somset ...30 B2
Knighton Staffs ...114 A3
Knighton Staffs ...114 B6
Knighton Wilts ...47 L4
Knighton on Teme Worcs ...80 E1
Knightsbridge Gloucs ...64 C2
Knightsmill Cnwll ...10 F6
Knightwick Worcs ...81 G4
Knill Herefs ...79 K3
Knipoch Ag & B ...216 C3
Knipton Leics ...117 L5
Knitsley Dur ...168 E1
Kniveton Derbys ...115 K2
Knock Highld ...247 L6
Knock Moray ...267 L5
Knock W & F ...166 F5
Knock W Isls ...282 g3
Knockally Highld ...274 F2
Knockan Highld ...271 H6
Knockando Moray ...254 D3
Knockbain Highld ...250 F3
Knockbain Highld ...263 H0
Knockdee Highld ...279 L4
Knockdow Ag & B ...207 J5
Knockdown Wilts ...46 B1
Knockeen S Ayrs ...183 H4
Knockenkelly N Ayrs ...195 G5
Knockentiber E Ayrs ...196 D3
Knockhall Kent ...52 C4
Knockholt Kent ...51 M7
Knockholt Pound Kent ...52 A7
Knockin Shrops ...112 E7
Knockinlaw E Ayrs ...196 E3
Knockmill Kent ...52 C6
Knocknain D & G ...172 A2
Knockrome Ag & B ...205 J2
Knocksharry IoM ...154 c5
Knocksheen D & G ...184 F6
Knockvennie Smithy D & G ...185 J8
Knodishall Suffk ...91 K3
Knodishall Common Suffk ...91 K3
Knole Somset ...31 G6
Knole Park S Glos ...45 J4
Knolls Green Ches E ...130 F4
Knolton Wrexhm ...112 F4
Knook Wilts ...32 F3
Knossington Leics ...101 H2
Knott End-on-Sea Lancs ...147 G6
Knotting Bed ...85 K3
Knotting Green Bed ...85 K3
Knottingley Wakefd ...142 D3
Knotty Ash Lpool ...129 J1
Knotty Green Bucks ...68 B8
Knowbury Shrops ...96 D8
Knowe D & G ...183 H8
Knowehead D & G ...184 F5
Knoweside S Ayrs ...195 L8
Knowes of Elrick Abers ...268 A5
Knowle Bristl ...45 J5
Knowle Devon ...13 H2
Knowle Devon ...14 B1
Knowle Devon ...14 B6
Knowle Devon ...27 J3
Knowle Shrops ...96 D8
Knowle Solhll ...98 F8
Knowle Somset ...29 H2
Knowle Cross Devon ...14 B3
Knowlefield Cumb ...177 L7
Knowle Green Lancs ...148 A8
Knowle Hill Surrey ...50 C5
Knowle St Giles Somset ...30 E8
Knowle Village Hants ...19 J2
Knowle Wood Calder ...140 D3
Knowl Green Essex ...88 F7

Place	County	Page	Grid
Knowl Hill	W & M	49	K3
Knowlton	Dorset	17	K1
Knowlton	Kent	41	J4
Knowsley	Knows	138	E8
Knowstone	Devon	28	E6
Knox	N York	150	C4
Knox Bridge	Kent	39	K5
Knoydart	Highld	238	C3
Knucklas	Powys	95	G8
Knuston	N Nthn	85	H2
Knutsford	Ches E	130	E4
Knutsford Services	*Ches E*	*130*	*E4*
Knutton	Staffs	114	C2
Krumlin	Calder	141	G4
Kuggar	Cnwll	3	J7
Kyleakin	Highld	248	B6
Kyle of Lochalsh	Highld	248	B6
Kylerhea	Highld	248	C7
Kylesku	Highld	271	H1
Kylesmorar	Highld	238	C5
Kyles Scalpay	W Isls	282	f6
Kylestrome	Highld	271	H1
Kynaston	Herefs	80	E8
Kynaston	Shrops	112	E7
Kynnersley	Wrekin	113	L8
Kyre Green	Worcs	80	E3
Kyre Park	Worcs	80	E3
Kyrewood	Worcs	80	E2
Kyrle	Somset	29	J6

L

Place	County	Page	Grid
La Bellieuse	Guern	9	j3
Lacasaigh	W Isls	282	f4
Lacasdal	W Isls	282	g3
Laceby	NE Lin	145	G6
Lacey Green	Bucks	67	K7
Lach Dennis	Ches W	130	D5
Lackenby	R & Cl	170	D6
Lackford	Suffk	88	F1
Lackford Green	Suffk	88	F1
Lacock	Wilts	46	C5
Ladbroke	Warwks	83	K3
Ladderedge	Staffs	114	F1
Laddingford	Kent	39	H4
Lade Bank	Lincs	119	L1
Ladock	Cnwll	4	E5
Lady	Ork	275	e2
Ladybank	Fife	222	E5
Ladycross	Cnwll	11	L5
Ladygill	S Lans	198	F7
Lady Hall	Cumb	156	B5
Ladykirk	Border	202	D3
Ladyridge	Herefs	63	H1
Lady's Green	Suffk	88	E3
Ladywood	Birm	98	D6
Ladywood	Worcs	81	K3
La Fontenelle	Guern	9	k1
La Fosse	Guern	9	j4
Lag	D & G	185	L5
Laga	Highld	237	J8
Lagavulin	Ag & B	204	F7
Lagg	N Ayrs	193	K4
Laggan	Highld	240	A4
Laggan	Highld	241	G5
Lagganlia	Highld	241	M3
La Greve	Guern	9	k2
La Grève de Lecq	Jersey	9	b1
La Hougue Bie	Jersey	9	e3
La Houguette	Guern	9	h3
Laid	Highld	277	G4
Laide	Highld	260	E2
Laig	Highld	236	F3
Laigh Clunch	E Ayrs	196	F2
Laigh Fenwick	E Ayrs	196	F3
Laigh Glenmuir	E Ayrs	197	J7
Laighstonehall	S Lans	209	J8
Laindon	Essex	52	E1
Lairg	Highld	272	E6
Laisterdyke	C Brad	141	J1
Laithes	W & F	166	B4
Lake	Devon	12	C5
Lake	Devon	27	K4
Lake	IoW	19	K7
Lake	Wilts	33	K4
Lake District	*Cumb*	*165*	*H8*
Lake District National Park *Cumb*		*165*	*H8*
Lakenham	Norfk	106	E2
Lakenheath	Suffk	104	E6
Laker's Green	Surrey	36	F4
Lakes End	Norfk	103	L4
Lakeside	W & F	156	E5
Laleham	Surrey	50	D5
Laleston	Brdgnd	42	C5
Lamanva	Cnwll	3	J5
Lamarsh	Essex	89	H8
Lamas	Norfk	122	E7
Lambden	Border	202	A4
Lamberhurst	Kent	39	H6
Lamberhurst Down	Kent	39	G6
Lamberton	Border	213	L7
Lambeth	Gt Lon	51	J3
Lambfair Green	Suffk	88	E4
Lambley	Notts	117	H2
Lambley	Nthumb	178	F7
Lambourn	W Berk	47	L3
Lambourne End	Essex	70	C8
Lambourn Woodlands	W Berk	47	L4
Lamb Roe	Lancs	148	C8
Lambs Green	W Susx	37	K3
Lambston	Pembks	54	E3
Lamellion	Cnwll	6	A2
Lamerton	Devon	12	B7
Lamesley	Gatesd	181	G7
Lamington	S Lans	199	G7
Lamlash	N Ayrs	195	G5
Lamonby	W & F	165	L3
Lamorick	Cnwll	5	H1
Lamorna	Cnwll	2	C6
Lamorran	Cnwll	4	E6
Lampen	Cnwll	5	L2
Lampeter	Cerdgn	77	G5
Lampeter Velfrey	Pembks	55	K4
Lamphey	Pembks	55	G6
Lamplugh	Cumb	164	E6
Lamport	W Nthn	101	G8
Lamyatt	Somset	31	L4
Lana	Devon	11	K1
Lana	Devon	11	L3
Lanark	S Lans	198	E4
Lancaster	Lancs	147	J3
Lancaster Services	*Lancs*	*147*	*K5*
Lancaut	Gloucs	63	G7
Lanchester	Dur	168	F1
Lancing	W Susx	21	L6
L'Ancresse	Guern	9	k1
Landbeach	Cambs	87	K2
Landcross	Devon	27	H6
Landerberry	Abers	245	G3
Landford	Wilts	34	B7
Land-hallow	Highld	275	G2
Landimore	Swans	56	E6
Landkey	Devon	27	L4
Landore	Swans	57	J5
Landrake	Cnwll	6	D3
Landscove	Devon	7	M2
Land's End	Cnwll	2	A6
Land's End Airport	*Cnwll*	*2*	*B5*
Landshipping	Pembks	55	G4
Landue	Cnwll	11	L6
Landulph	Cnwll	6	E3
Landwade	Suffk	88	C2
Lane	Cnwll	4	D3
Lane Bottom	Lancs	140	C1
Lane End	Bucks	49	K1
Lane End	Cnwll	5	H1
Lane End	Hants	35	H5
Lane End	Kent	52	C4
Lane End	Lancs	148	F6
Lane End	Warrtn	130	D2
Lane End	Wilts	32	D2
Lane Ends	Derbys	115	L4
Lane Ends	Lancs	140	B2
Lane Ends	N York	149	H7
Lane Green	Staffs	97	K3
Laneham	Notts	134	F4
Lanehead	Dur	167	J2
Lane Head	Dur	168	E8
Lanehead	Nthumb	179	H2
Lane Head	Wigan	139	J8
Lane Head	Wsall	98	B3
Lane Heads	Lancs	147	H1
Lanercost	Cumb	178	D6
Laneshaw Bridge	Lancs	149	G7
Lane Side	Lancs	140	B3
Langaford	Devon	12	A3
Langal	Highld	237	K6
Langaller	Somset	30	C5
Langar	Notts	117	J4
Langbank	Rens	208	C4
Langbar	N York	149	K5
Langbaurgh	N York	170	D8
Langcliffe	N York	148	E3
Langdale End	N York	163	G4
Langdon	Cnwll	11	K5
Langdon Beck	Dur	167	K4
Langdon Hills	Essex	52	E2
Langdown	Hants	19	G2
Langdyke	Fife	222	E6
Langenhoe	Essex	72	E3
Langford	C Beds	86	D7
Langford	Devon	14	D3
Langford	Essex	71	K5
Langford	N Som	44	F6
Langford	Notts	135	G7
Langford	Oxon	65	K6
Langford	Somset	30	B5
Langford Budville	Somset	29	K6
Langham	Dorset	32	C5
Langham	Essex	72	F1
Langham	Norfk	121	M3
Langham	Rutlnd	101	J1
Langham	Suffk	89	K1
Langho	Lancs	139	L1
Langholm	D & G	177	L2
Langland	Swans	57	H7
Langlee	Border	201	G6
Langley	Ches E	131	J5
Langley	Derbys	116	D2
Langley	Gloucs	64	E2
Langley	Hants	19	G3
Langley	Herts	69	G3
Langley	Kent	39	K3
Langley	Nthumb	179	J6
Langley	Oxon	65	L4
Langley	Rochdl	140	C6
Langley	Slough	50	C3
Langley	Somset	29	K5
Langley	W Susx	36	B5
Langley	Warwks	82	E3
Langley Burrell	Wilts	46	D4
Langley Castle	Nthumb	179	J6
Langley Common	Derbys	115	M4
Langley Green	Derbys	115	M4
Langley Green	Essex	72	C3
Langley Green	Warwks	82	E3
Langley Heath	Kent	39	K3
Langley Lower Green	Essex	87	J8
Langley Marsh	Somset	29	K5
Langley Mill	Derbys	116	D2
Langley Moor	Dur	169	H3
Langley Park	Dur	169	G2
Langley Street	Norfk	107	H3
Langley Upper Green	Essex	87	J8
Langney	E Susx	23	L6
Langold	Notts	134	B2
Langore	Cnwll	11	K5
Langport	Somset	30	F5
Langrick	Lincs	119	J2
Langridge	BaNES	45	L5
Langridgeford	Devon	27	K6
Langrigg	Cumb	165	G2
Langrish	Hants	35	L6
Langsett	Barns	141	K7
Langside	P & K	220	D4
Langstone	Hants	20	B6
Langstone	Newpt	44	D1
Langthorne	N York	160	C4
Langthorpe	N York	150	E2
Langthwaite	N York	159	H2
Langtoft	E R Yk	152	F3
Langtoft	Lincs	102	C1
Langton	Dur	168	F6
Langton	Lincs	136	D6
Langton	Lincs	137	G5
Langton	N York	152	B2
Langton by Wragby	Lincs	136	C4
Langton Green	Kent	38	E5
Langton Green	Suffk	106	C8
Langton Herring	Dorset	16	B6
Langton Long Blandford Dorset		17	H2
Langton Matravers	Dorset	17	K6
Langtree	Devon	27	H7
Langtree Week	Devon	27	H7
Langwathby	W & F	166	D4
Langwell	Highld	271	K6
Langwell House	Highld	274	F3
Langwith	Derbys	133	K5
Langwith Junction	Derbys	133	K6
Langworth	Lincs	135	L4
Lanivet	Cnwll	5	H2
Lanjeth	Cnwll	5	G4
Lank	Cnwll	10	F7
Lanlivery	Cnwll	5	J3
Lanner	Cnwll	3	J3
Lanoy	Cnwll	11	K7
Lanreath	Cnwll	5	L3
Lansallos	Cnwll	5	K4
Lanteglos	Cnwll	10	F6
Lanteglos Highway	Cnwll	5	K4
Lanton	Border	189	G2
Lanton	Nthumb	202	F6
La Passee	Guern	9	j2
Lapford	Devon	13	G1
Laphroaig	Ag & B	204	F7
Lapley	Staffs	97	K1
La Pulente	Jersey	9	a3
Lapworth	Warwks	82	E1
Larachbeg	Highld	227	K3
Larbert	Falk	209	M3
Larbreck	Lancs	147	H7
Largie	Abers	256	A5
Largiemore	Ag & B	206	E2
Largoward	Fife	223	H5
Largs	N Ayrs	207	K7
Largybeg	N Ayrs	195	G6
Largymore	N Ayrs	195	G6
Larkbeare	Devon	14	C3
Larkfield	Inver	207	L4
Larkfield	Kent	52	F7
Larkhall	S Lans	198	C3
Larkhill	Wilts	33	K2
Larling	Norfk	105	K5
La Rocque	Jersey	9	f4
La Rousaillerie	Guern	9	j2
Lartington	Dur	168	C7
Lasborough	Gloucs	64	B8
Lasham	Hants	35	K2
Lashbrook	Devon	12	A1
Lashbrook	Devon	12	B2
Lashenden	Kent	39	L5
Lask Edge	Staffs	131	H8
Lasswade	Mdloth	211	J6
Lastingham	N York	162	C4
Latcham	Somset	31	G2
Latchford	Herts	69	K3
Latchford	Oxon	67	G6
Latchingdon	Essex	72	C7
Latchley	Cnwll	12	A7
Lately Common	Warrtn	139	K8
Lathbury	M Keyn	85	G6
Latheron	Highld	275	G2
Latheronwheel	Highld	275	G2
Lathom	Lancs	138	F5
Lathones	Fife	223	H5
Latimer	Bucks	68	C7
Latteridge	S Glos	45	K2
Lattiford	Somset	32	B5
Latton	Wilts	65	G7
Lauder	Border	201	H4
Laugharne	Carmth	56	B3
Laughterton	Lincs	135	G4
Laughton	E Susx	23	H4
Laughton	Leics	100	E5
Laughton	Lincs	118	E5
Laughton	Lincs	143	L8
Laughton Common	Rothm	133	K2
Laughton-en-le-Morthen Rothm		133	K2
Launcells	Cnwll	11	K2
Launcells Cross	Cnwll	11	K2
Launceston	Cnwll	11	L5
Launton	Oxon	66	F3
Laurencekirk	Abers	235	H1
Laurieston	D & G	175	H2
Laurieston	Falk	210	B3
Lavendon	M Keyn	85	H4
Lavenham	Suffk	89	J5
Lavernock	V Glam	43	J8
Laversdale	Cumb	178	B6
Laverstock	Wilts	33	L5
Laverstoke	Hants	35	G1
Laverton	Gloucs	82	C8
Laverton	N York	160	B7
Laverton	Somset	45	M8
La Villette	Guern	9	j3
Lavister	Wrexhm	129	J8
Law	S Lans	209	L8
Lawers	P & K	231	J7
Lawford	Essex	73	G1
Lawford	Somset	29	L4
Law Hill	S Lans	209	L8
Lawhitton	Cnwll	11	L6
Lawkland	N York	148	D3
Lawkland Green	N York	148	D3
Lawley	Wrekin	96	F2
Lawnhead	Staffs	114	C6
Lawrence Weston	Bristl	45	H3
Lawrenny	Pembks	55	G5
Lawrenny Quay	Pembks	55	G5
Lawshall	Suffk	89	H4
Lawshall Green	Suffk	89	H4
Lawton	Herefs	80	B3
Laxay	W Isls	282	f4
Laxdale	W Isls	282	g3
Laxey	IoM	154	f5
Laxfield	Suffk	91	G1
Laxford Bridge	Highld	276	C7
Laxo	Shet	281	e5
Laxton	E R Yk	143	K3
Laxton	N Nthn	101	L4
Laxton	Notts	134	E6
Laycock	C Brad	149	J7
Layer Breton	Essex	72	D3
Layer-de-la-Haye	Essex	72	D3
Layer Marney	Essex	72	D4
Layham	Suffk	89	L7
Laymore	Dorset	15	J2
Layter's Green	Bucks	50	C1
Laytham	E R Yk	152	K4
Laythes	Cumb	177	H7
Lazenby	R & Cl	170	D6
Lazonby	W & F	166	D3

Lea Derbys 132 F8
Lea Herefs 63 K3
Lea Lincs 135 G2
Lea Shrops 95 J5
Lea Shrops 95 K2
Lea Wilts 46 D2
Leachkin Highld 251 H3
Leadburn Border 200 B2
Leadenham Lincs 118 B1
Leaden Roding Essex 70 E4
Leadgate Dur 180 D8
Leadgate Nthumb 180 D7
Leadgate W & F 167 G2
Leadhills S Lans 186 C3
Leadingcross Green Kent 39 M3
Leadmill Derbys 132 E4
Leafield Oxon 65 L4
Leagrave Luton 68 D2
Lea Green Ches W 130 D6
Leahead Ches W 130
Lea Heath Staffs 114 C6
Leake N York 160 F4
Leake Common Side Lincs 119 L1
Lealholm N York 162 D1
Lealholm Side N York 162 D1
Lealt Highld 259 H4
Leam Derbys 132 E4
Lea Marston Warwks 99 G5
Leamington Hastings Warwks 83 K2
Leamington Spa Warwks 83 H2
Leamside Dur 169 J1
Leap Cross E Susx 23 K5
Learney Abers 244 E3
Leasgill W & F 157 H6
Leasingham Lincs 118 E2
Leasingthorne Dur 169 H4
Leatherhead Surrey 50 F7
Leathley N York 150 B6
Leaton Shrops 113 G7
Leaton Wrekin 96 E1
Lea Town Lancs 130 F2
Leaveland Kent 40 C4
Leavenheath Suffk 89 J7
Leavening N York 152 B3
Leaves Green Gt Lon 51 L6
Lea Yeat W & F 158 D5
Lebberston N York 163 K6
Le Bigard Guern 9 i4
Le Bourg Guern 9 j4
Le Bourg Jersey 9 f4
Lechlade on Thames Gloucs 65 J7
Lecht Gruinart Ag & B 204 D3
Leck Lancs 157 K7
Leckbuie P & K 231 K7
Leckford Hants 34 E3
Leckhampstead Bucks 84 D7
Leckhampstead W Berk 48 B4
Leckhampstead Thicket W Berk 48 B4
Leckhampton Gloucs 64 D3
Leckmelm Highld 261 K2
Leckwith V Glam 43 J6
Leconfield E R Yk 152 F7
Ledaig Ag & B 228 E7
Ledburn Bucks 67 L3
Ledbury Herefs 81 G7
Leddington Gloucs 80 F8
Ledgemoor Herefs 79 M5
Ledicot Herefs 80 A3
Ledmore Highld 271 H5
Ledsham Ches W 129 H5
Ledsham Leeds 142 C2
Ledston Leeds 142 C2
Ledstone Devon 7 L5
Ledston Luck Leeds 142 C2
Ledwell Oxon 66 B2
Lee Devon 27 H2
Lee Gt Lon 51 K4
Lee Hants 34 D7
Lee Shrops 112 F5
Leebotwood Shrops 96 B4
Lee Brockhurst Shrops 113 J6
Leece W & F 146 E2
Lee Chapel Essex 52 C2
Lee Clump Bucks 67 M6
Lee Common Bucks 67 M6
Leeds Kent 39 K3
Leeds Leeds 141 L1
Leeds Bradford Airport Leeds 150 B7
Leeds Skelton Lake Services
  Leeds 142 A2
Leedstown Cnwll 2 F4
Lee Green Ches E 130 C7
Leek Staffs 131 K8
Leek Wootton Warwks 83 G2
Lee Mill Devon 7 H4
Leeming C Brad 141 G1
Leeming N York 160 D5
Leeming Bar N York 160 D4
Leeming Bar Rest Area N York 160 D5
Lee Moor Devon 7 H3
Lee-on-the-Solent Hants 19 J3

Lees C Brad 149 J8
Lees Derbys 115 L4
Lees Oldham 140 E6
Lees Green Derbys 115 L4
Leesthorpe Leics 101 H1
Leeswood Flints 129 G7
Leetown P & K 222 C3
Leftwich Ches W 130 C5
Legar Powys 61 K4
Legbourne Lincs 137 G3
Legburthwaite Cumb 165 K6
Legerwood Border 201 J4
Le Gron Guern 9 i3
Legsby Lincs 136 B3
Le Haguais Jersey 9 e4
Le Hocq Jersey 9 e4
Leicester C Leic 100 D3
Leicester Forest East Leics 100 B3
Leicester Forest East
  services 100 C3
Leigh Devon 28 C8
Leigh Dorset 16 B1
Leigh Gloucs 64 C2
Leigh Kent 38 E4
Leigh Shrops 95 H3
Leigh Surrey 37 K2
Leigh Wigan 139 K7
Leigh Wilts 64 F8
Leigh Worcs 81 H4
Leigh Beck Essex 53 H2
Leigh Delamere Wilts 46 C3
Leigh Delamere Services Wilts 46 C3
Leigh Green Kent 40 A8
Leigh Knoweglass S Lans 197 J1
Leighland Chapel Somset 29 J4
Leigh-on-Sea Sthend 53 H2
Leigh Park Dorset 17 K3
Leigh Park Hants 20 B5
Leigh Sinton Worcs 81 H5
Leighswood Wsall 98 D3
Leighterton Gloucs 46 B1
Leighton N York 159 L6
Leighton Powys 94 F2
Leighton Shrops 96 E2
Leighton Somset 32 B2
Leighton Bromswold Cambs 102 C8
Leighton Buzzard C Beds 68 A2
Leigh upon Mendip Somset 31 M2
Leigh Woods N Som 45 H4
Leinthall Earls Herefs 80 B2
Leinthall Starkes Herefs 80 A1
Leintwardine Herefs 95 K8
Leire Leics 100 B5
Leiston Suffk 91 K3
Leith C Edin 211 J4
Leitholm Border 202 B4
Lelant Cnwll 2 E4
Lelley E R Yk 145 G1
Lem Hill Worcs 97 G8
Lempitlaw Border 202 B6
Lemreway W Isls 282 g5
Lemsford Herts 69 G4
Lenchwick Worcs 82 B6
Lendalfoot S Ayrs 182 E5
Lendrick Stirlg 219 J6
Lendrum Terrace Abers 257 L3
Lenham Kent 40 A5
Lenham Heath Kent 40 B5
Lenie Highld 250 F6
Lennel Border 202 C5
Lennox Plunton D & G 174 F4
Lennoxtown E Duns 209 G3
Lent Bucks 50 A3
Lenton C Nott 116 F4
Lenton Lincs 118 D5
Lenwade Norfk 122 B7
Lenzie E Duns 209 H4
Leochel-Cushnie Abers 244 C2
Leomansley Staffs 98 E2
Leominster Herefs 80 C3
Leonard Stanley Gloucs 64 A6
Leoville Jersey 9 b1
Lepe Hants 19 G4
Lephin Highld 258 B6
Leppington N York 152 A4
Lepton Kirk 141 K5
Lerags Ag & B 216 C2
L'Erée Guern 9 h3
Lerryn Cnwll 5 K3
Lerwick Shet 281 e6
Les Arquêts Guern 9 h3
Lesbury Nthumb 191 J4
Les Hubits Guern 9 k3
Leslie Abers 255 M6
Leslie Fife 222 D6
Les Lohiers Guern 9 i3
Lesmahagow S Lans 198 D5
Les Murchez Guern 9 i4
Lesnewth Cnwll 11 G4
Les Nicolles Guern 9 j4

Les Quartiers Guern 9 j2
Les Quennevais Jersey 9 b3
Les Sages Guern 9 i3
Lessingham Norfk 123 H6
Lessonhall Cumb 165 H1
Lestowder Cnwll 3 K6
Les Villets Guern 9 i4
Leswalt D & G 172 C2
L'Etacq Jersey 9 a2
Letchmore Heath Herts 68 F7
Letchworth Garden City Herts 86 E8
Letcombe Bassett Oxon 48 A2
Letcombe Regis Oxon 48 A2
Letham Angus 234 E5
Letham Border 189 J4
Letham Falk 210 B2
Letham Fife 222 E4
Letham Grange Angus 235 G6
Lethenty Abers 255 M7
Lethenty Abers 256 E4
Letheringham Suffk 91 G4
Letheringsett Norfk 122 B4
Lettaford Devon 13 G6
Letterewe Highld 260 F5
Letterfearn Highld 248 D7
Letterfinlay Lodge Hotel Highld 239 L5
Letters Highld 261 K2
Lettershaw S Lans 186 D2
Letterston Pembks 74 F2
Lettoch Highld 253 K7
Lettoch Highld 254 B5
Letton Herefs 79 L1
Letton Herefs 79 L6
Lett's Green Kent 51 M7
Letty Green Herts 69 H5
Letwell Rothm 133 L2
Leuchars Fife 223 H1
Leumrabhagh W Isls 282 g5
Leurbost W Isls 282 g4
Levalsa Meor Cnwll 5 G5
Levan Inver 207 L4
Levedale Staffs 114 D8
Level's Green Essex 70 C2
Leven E R Yk 153 H6
Leven Fife 222 F7
Levens W & F 157 G5
Levens Green Herts 69 K3
Levenshulme Manch 131 G1
Levenwick Shet 281 d8
Leverburgh W Isls 282 d6
Leverington Cambs 103 J1
Leverstock Green Herts 68 D5
Leverton Lincs 119 L2
Le Villocq Guern 9 j2
Levington Suffk 90 F7
Levisham N York 162 E4
Lew Oxon 65 L6
Lewannick Cnwll 11 K6
Lewdown Devon 12 B5
Lewes E Susx 22 F5
Leweston Pembks 54 F2
Lewisham Gt Lon 51 K4
Lewiston Highld 250 F6
Lewistown Brdgnd 42 E4
Lewis Wych Herefs 79 L4
Lewknor Oxon 67 H7
Leworthy Devon 11 L2
Leworthy Devon 28 B3
Lewson Street Kent 40 C3
Lewth Lancs 147 J8
Lewtrenchard Devon 12 B5
Lexden Essex 72 D2
Lexworthy Somset 30 C4
Ley Cnwll 5 K2
Leybourne Kent 52 E7
Leyburn N York 159 K4
Leycett Staffs 114 B2
Leygreen Herts 68 F2
Ley Hill Bucks 68 C6
Leyland Lancs 139 H3
Leyland Green St Hel 139 H7
Leylodge Abers 245 G1
Leys Abers 269 J5
Leys P & K 233 K7
Leysdown-on-Sea Kent 53 M5
Leysmill Angus 234 F6
Leys of Cossans Angus 234 B5
Leysters Herefs 80 D2
Leyton Gt Lon 51 K2
Leytonstone Gt Lon 51 K2
Lezant Cnwll 11 L6
Lezerea Cnwll 3 H4
Leziate Norfk 120 E7
Lhanbryde Moray 266 F4
Libanus Powys 60 F2
Libberton S Lans 199 G4
Libbery Worcs 81 L4
Liberton C Edin 211 J5
Lichfield Staffs 98 E2
Lickey Worcs 98 C8

Lickey End Worcs 81 M1
Lickey Rock Worcs 98 B8
Lickfold W Susx 36 D5
Liddaton Green Devon 12 B6
Liddesdale Highld 228 B3
Liddington Swindn 47 J3
Lidgate Derbys 132 F4
Lidgate Suffk 88 E4
Lidget Donc 143 G7
Lidgett Notts 134 C6
Lidham Hill E Susx 24 F4
Lidlington C Beds 85 K7
Lidsey W Susx 20 F6
Lidsing Kent 53 G6
Liff Angus 222 E1
Lifford Birm 98 D7
Lifton Devon 11 M5
Liftondown Devon 11 M5
Lighthorne Warwks 83 H4
Lighthorne Heath Warwks 83 H4
Lightwater Surrey 50 B6
Lightwood C Stke 114 F2
Lightwood Green Ches E 113 L3
Lightwood Green Wrexhm 112 F3
Lilbourne W Nthn 100 C8
Lilburn Tower Nthumb 190 E1
Lilford N Nthn 102 A6
Lilleshall Wrekin 114 A8
Lilley Herts 68 E2
Lilley W Berk 48 C3
Lilliesleaf Border 201 H8
Lillingstone Dayrell Bucks 84 D7
Lillingstone Lovell Bucks 84 D7
Lillington Dorset 31 K8
Lilliput BCP 17 K5
Lilstock Somset 29 L2
Lilyhurst Shrops 97 G1
Limbrick Lancs 139 J4
Limbury Luton 68 D2
Limebrook Herefs 79 L2
Limefield Bury 140 B5
Limekilnburn S Lans 197 K1
Limekilns Fife 210 E1
Limerigg Falk 209 M5
Limerstone IoW 19 G7
Limestone Brae Nthumb 167 J1
Lime Street Worcs 81 A1
Limington Somset 31 J6
Limmerhaugh E Ayrs 197 J5
Limpenhoe Norfk 107 H3
Limpley Stoke Wilts 45 M6
Limpsfield Surrey 51 L8
Limpsfield Chart Surrey 51 L8
Linby Notts 116 F1
Linchmere W Susx 36 C5
Lincluden D & G 176 C3
Lincoln Lincs 135 K5
Lincomb Worcs 81 J2
Lincombe Devon 7 L6
Lincombe Devon 27 J2
Lindale W & F 156 F6
Lindal in Furness W & F 156 C7
Lindean Border 201 G6
Lindfield W Susx 22 E2
Lindford Hants 36 B4
Lindley Kirk 141 H4
Lindley N York 150 B6
Lindores Fife 222 D4
Lindow End Ches E 130 E4
Lindridge Worcs 80 F2
Lindsell Essex 70 F2
Lindsey Suffk 89 K6
Lindsey Tye Suffk 89 K6
Liney Somset 30 C4
Linford Hants 18 B2
Linford Thurr 52 E3
Lingbob C Brad 149 K8
Lingdale R & Cl 170 F7
Lingen Herefs 79 L2
Lingfield Surrey 38 B4
Lingfield Common Surrey 38 B4
Lingwood Norfk 107 G2
Liniclate W Isls 283 c9
Linicro Highld 258 E3
Linkend Worcs 64 B1
Linkenholt Hants 48 A7
Linkhill Kent 24 E2
Linkinhorne Cnwll 11 L7
Linktown Fife 211 J1
Linkwood Moray 266 E4
Linley Shrops 95 J5
Linley Green Herefs 80 F4
Linleygreen Shrops 96 F4
Linlithgow W Loth 210 C4
Linshiels Nthumb 190 C5
Linsidemore Highld 272 C3
Linslade C Beds 67 M2
Linstead Parva Suffk 107 G7
Linstock Cumb 178 A7
Linthurst Worcs 82 B1

Linthwaite Kirk 141 H5
Lintlaw Border 213 H7
Lintmill Moray 267 K3
Linton Border 202 B7
Linton Cambs 88 B6
Linton Derbys 115 M8
Linton Herefs 63 K2
Linton Kent 39 J3
Linton Leeds 150 E6
Linton N York 149 H3
Linton Nthumb 191 K7
Linton Heath Derbys 115 M8
Linton Hill Herefs 63 K2
Linton-on-Ouse N York 151 G4
Linwood Hants 18 G2
Linwood Lincs 136 B2
Linwood Rens 208 D6
Lionacleit W Isls 283 c9
Lional W Isls 282 h1
Lions Green E Susx 23 J4
Liphook Hants 36 C4
Lipley Shrops 114 A5
Liscard Wirral 129 G1
Liscombe Somset 28 F4
Liskeard Cnwll 6 B2
Lismore Ag & B 228 C7
Liss Hants 36 A5
Lissett E R Yk 153 J4
Liss Forest Hants 36 A5
Lissington Lincs 136 B3
Liston Essex 89 G6
Lisvane Cardif 43 J5
Liswerry Newpt 44 D2
Litcham Norfk 121 J8
Litchborough W Nthn 84 C4
Litchfield Hants 48 C8
Litherland Sefton 138 D8
Litlington Cambs 87 G6
Litlington E Susx 23 J7
Little Abington Cambs 87 L5
Little Addington N Nthn 101 L8
Little Airies D & G 173 K5
Little Almshoe Herts 69 G2
Little Alne Warwks 82 D3
Little Altcar Sefton 138 C6
Little Amwell Herts 69 K5
Little Asby W & F 158 B1
Little Aston Staffs 98 E3
Little Atherfield IoW 19 G7
Little Ayton N York 170 D8
Little Baddow Essex 71 J5
Little Badminton S Glos 46 A2
Little Bampton Cumb 177 J7
Little Bardfield Essex 71 G1
Little Barford Bed 86 D4
Little Barningham Norfk 122 C5
Little Barrington Gloucs 65 J4
Little Barrow Ches W 129 L5
Little Barugh N York 162 D6
Little Bavington Nthumb 180 B3
Little Bealings Suffk 90 F5
Littlebeck N York 162 F2
Little Bedwyn Wilts 47 L5
Little Bentley Essex 73 G2
Little Berkhamsted Herts 69 H5
Little Billing W Nthn 84 F3
Little Billington C Beds 68 B3
Little Birch Herefs 63 G1
Little Bispham Bpool 146 F7
Little Blakenham Suffk 90 C5
Little Blencow W & F 166 B4
Little Bloxwich Wsall 98 C3
Little Bognor W Susx 21 G3
Little Bolehill Derbys 116 A1
Little Bollington Ches E 130 E2
Little Bookham Surrey 50 E8
Littleborough Devon 28 E8
Littleborough Notts 135 G3
Littleborough Rochdl 140 E4
Littlebourne Kent 41 G6
Little Bourton Oxon 83 K6
Little Bowden Leics 101 G6
Little Bradley Suffk 88 D5
Little Brampton Herefs 79 K3
Little Brampton Shrops 95 J7
Little Braxted Essex 71 K4
Little Brechin Angus 234 F3
Littlebredy Dorset 16 B5
Little Brickhill M Keyn 67 L1
Little Bridgeford Staffs 114 D6
Little Brington W Nthn 84 C3
Little Bromley Essex 73 G2
Little Broughton Cumb 164 E4
Little Budworth Ches W 130 B6
Littleburn Highld 251 H1
Little Burstead Essex 71 G8
Littlebury Essex 87 L7
Littlebury Green Essex 87 K7
Little Bytham Lincs 118 D7
Little Canfield Essex 70 E3

Little Carlton Lincs 137 G3
Little Carlton Notts 134 F8
Little Casterton Rutlnd 101 M2
Little Catwick E R Yk 153 H6
Little Catworth Cambs 86 B1
Little Cawthorpe Lincs 137 G3
Little Chalfont Bucks 68 C7
Little Chart Kent 40 B6
Little Chesterford Essex 87 L7
Little Cheveney Kent 39 H4
Little Cheverell Wilts 46 E8
Little Chishill Cambs 87 J7
Little Clacton Essex 73 H3
Little Clanfield Oxon 65 K6
Little Clifton Cumb 164 E5
Little Coates NE Lin 145 H6
Little Comberton Worcs 81 M6
Little Common E Susx 24 C5
Little Comp Kent 39 G2
Little Compton Warwks 65 K1
Little Corby Cumb 178 B7
Little Cornard Suffk 89 H7
Littlecott Wilts 47 H8
Little Cowarne Herefs 80 E5
Little Coxwell Oxon 65 L8
Little Crakehall N York 160 C4
Little Cransley N Nthn 101 H8
Little Cressingham Norfk 105 H3
Little Crosby Sefton 138 C7
Little Crosthwaite Cumb 165 H5
Little Cubley Derbys 115 J4
Little Dalby Leics 117 K8
Littledean Gloucs 63 K4
Little Dewchurch Herefs 63 G1
Little Ditton Cambs 88 D3
Little Doward Herefs 63 G4
Littledown Hants 47 M7
Little Downham Cambs 103 L6
Little Driffield E R Yk 152 F4
Little Dunham Norfk 105 H1
Little Dunkeld P & K 232 F7
Little Dunmow Essex 71 G3
Little Durnford Wilts 33 K4
Little Easton Essex 70 F2
Little Eaton Derbys 116 B3
Little Ellingham Norfk 105 K3
Little Elm Somset 32 B2
Little Everdon W Nthn 84 B4
Little Eversden Cambs 87 H4
Little Faringdon Oxon 65 J6
Little Fencote N York 160 D4
Little Fenton N York 142 E1
Littleferry Highld 264 C1
Little Fransham Norfk 105 H1
Little Gaddesden Herts 68 C4
Little Garway Herefs 62 F2
Little Gidding Cambs 102 C7
Little Glemham Suffk 91 H4
Little Gorsley Herefs 63 K2
Little Gransden Cambs 86 F4
Little Green Notts 117 J3
Little Green Somset 32 B1
Little Grimsby Lincs 136 F2
Little Gringley Notts 134 E3
Little Habton N York 162 C7
Little Hadham Herts 70 B3
Little Hale Lincs 118 F3
Little Hallam Derbys 116 D3
Little Hallingbury Essex 70 D4
Littleham Devon 14 B6
Littleham Devon 27 H6
Little Hampden Bucks 67 L6
Littlehampton W Susx 21 H6
Little Hanford Dorset 32 D8
Little Harrowden N Nthn 85 G1
Little Haseley Oxon 66 F7
Little Hatfield E R Yk 153 J7
Little Hautbois Norfk 122 E7
Little Haven Pembks 54 D4
Littlehaven W Susx 37 J4
Little Hay Staffs 98 E3
Little Hayfield Derbys 131 K2
Little Haywood Staffs 115 G7
Little Heath Staffs 114 D6
Little Heath W Berk 49 G4
Littlehempston Devon 8 B2
Little Hereford Herefs 80 D2
Little Horkesley Essex 72 D1
Little Hormead Herts 69 L2
Little Horsted E Susx 23 G4
Little Horton C Brad 141 J2
Little Horton Wilts 46 F6
Little Horwood Bucks 67 J1
Little Houghton Barns 142 C6
Littlehoughton Nthumb 191 J3
Little Houghton N Nthn 84 F3
Little Hucklow Derbys 132 C4
Little Hulton Salfd 139 L7
Little Hungerford W Berk 48 D4
Little Hutton N York 161 G7

Little Irchester N Nthn 85 H2
Little Kelk E R Yk 153 H4
Little Keyford Somset 32 C2
Little Kimble Bucks 67 K5
Little Kineton Warwks 83 H5
Little Kingshill Bucks 67 L7
Little Knox D & G 175 K3
Little Langdale W & F 156 D2
Little Langford Wilts 33 H4
Little Laver Essex 70 E5
Little Leigh Ches W 130 B4
Little Leighs Essex 71 H4
Little Lever Bolton 139 M6
Little Linford M Keyn 85 G3
Little Load Somset 31 G6
Little London Bucks 66 F4
Little London Cambs 103 J4
Little London E Susx 23 J3
Little London Essex 70 C1
Little London Essex 88 D8
Little London Gloucs 63 L3
Little London Hants 34 E1
Little London Hants 48 F7
Little London Leeds 150 B7
Little London Lincs 119 H7
Little London Lincs 119 M6
Little London Lincs 136 F5
Little London Norfk 120 C7
Little London Powys 94 C5
Little Longstone Derbys 132 D5
Little Madeley Staffs 114 B3
Little Malvern Worcs 81 H7
Little Mancot Flints 129 H6
Little Maplestead Essex 89 G8
Little Marcle Herefs 80 F7
Little Marland Devon 27 J8
Little Marlow Bucks 49 L2
Little Massingham Norfk 121 H6
Little Melton Norfk 106 D2
Littlemill Abers 243 K4
Littlemill Highld 253 H2
Little Mill Mons 62 C6
Little Milton Oxon 66 F7
Little Missenden Bucks 68 A7
Little Mongeham Kent 41 K5
Littlemoor Derbys 133 G7
Little Moor Somset 30 D4
Littlemore Oxon 66 D6
Little Musgrave W & F 167 H8
Little Ness Shrops 112 F7
Little Neston Ches W 129 G4
Little Newcastle Pembks 75 G6
Little Newsham Dur 168 F7
Little Norton Somset 31 G7
Little Oakley Essex 73 J1
Little Oakley N Nthn 101 K6
Little Odell Bed 85 J4
Little Offley Herts 68 E2
Little Ormside W & F 167 G7
Little Orton Cumb 177 K7
Little Ouse Cambs 104 C5
Little Ouseburn N York 150 F4
Littleover C Derb 116 B5
Little Oxendon W Nthn 100 F6
Little Packington Warwks 99 G6
Little Pattenden Kent 39 J4
Little Paxton Cambs 86 D3
Little Petherick Cnwll 10 C8
Little Plumpton Lancs 138 D1
Little Plumstead Norfk 107 G1
Little Ponton Lincs 118 B5
Littleport Cambs 104 B6
Littleport Bridge Cambs 104 B6
Little Posbrook Hants 19 J3
Little Potheridge Devon 27 J8
Little Preston Leeds 142 B2
Little Preston W Nthn 84 B4
Littler Ches W 130 C6
Little Raveley Cambs 102 E7
Little Reedness E R Yk 143 K3
Little Ribston N York 150 E5
Little Rissington Gloucs 65 J3
Little Rollright Oxon 65 L1
Little Rowsley Derbys 132 E6
Little Ryburgh Norfk 121 L6
Little Ryle Nthumb 190 E4
Little Ryton Shrops 96 B3
Little Salkeld W & F 166 C3
Little Sampford Essex 88 C8
Little Sandhurst Br For 49 K6
Little Saredon Staffs 97 L2
Little Saughall Ches W 129 J4
Little Saxham Suffk 88 F3
Little Scatwell Highld 262 C8
Little Shelford Cambs 87 J5
Little Shrewley Warwks 82 F3
Little Silver Devon 13 L1
Little Singleton Lancs 147 G7
Little Skipwith N York 151 K8
Little Smeaton N York 142 E4

Little Snoring Norfk 121 L5
Little Sodbury S Glos 45 M2
Little Sodbury End S Glos 45 L2
Little Somborne Hants 34 E4
Little Somerford Wilts 46 D2
Little Soudley Shrops 114 A6
Little Stainforth N York 148 E2
Little Stainton Darltn 169 K6
Little Stanion N Nthn 101 K6
Little Stanney Ches W 129 J5
Little Staughton Bed 86 B3
Little Steeping Lincs 137 H7
Little Stoke Staffs 114 E5
Littlestone-on-Sea Kent 25 K2
Little Stonham Suffk 90 D3
Little Stretton Leics 100 E3
Little Stretton Shrops 95 K5
Little Strickland W & F 166 D6
Little Stukeley Cambs 102 E8
Little Sugnall Staffs 114 C5
Little Sutton Ches W 129 J4
Little Sutton Ches W 96 C6
Little Swinburne Nthumb 179 M3
Little Sypland D & G 175 H4
Little Tew Oxon 66 A2
Little Tey Essex 72 C2
Little Thetford Cambs 103 L8
Little Thirkleby N York 161 G7
Little Thornage Norfk 122 B4
Little Thornton Lancs 147 G7
Little Thorpe Dur 169 L2
Littlethorpe Leics 100 C4
Littlethorpe N York 150 D2
Little Thurlow Suffk 88 D5
Little Thurlow Green Suffk 88 D5
Little Thurrock Thurr 52 D3
Littleton BaNES 45 H6
Littleton Ches W 129 K6
Littleton D & G 175 G4
Littleton Dorset 17 H2
Littleton Hants 34 F4
Littleton Somset 31 H5
Littleton Surrey 36 E2
Littleton Surrey 50 D5
Littleton Drew Wilts 46 B3
Littleton of Airlie Angus 234 A5
Littleton-on-Severn S Glos 45 H1
Littleton Panell Wilts 46 E8
Little Torrington Devon 27 J7
Little Totham Essex 72 C5
Little Town Cumb 165 H6
Littletown Dur 169 J2
Little Town Lancs 148 B8
Little Town Warrtn 130 C1
Little Twycross Leics 99 J2
Little Urswick W & F 156 C7
Little Wakering Essex 53 K1
Little Walden Essex 87 L7
Little Waldingfield Suffk 89 J6
Little Walsingham Norfk 121 K4
Little Waltham Essex 71 H4
Little Warley Essex 52 D1
Little Washbourne Gloucs 82 A8
Little Weighton E R Yk 144 B1
Little Welnetham Suffk 89 H3
Little Welton Lincs 136 F2
Little Wenham Suffk 90 C7
Little Wenlock Wrekin 96 E2
Little Weston Somset 31 K5
Little Whitefield IoW 19 K5
Little Whittingham Green
  Suffk 106 F8
Little Whittington Nthumb 180 B5
Littlewick Green W & M 49 K3
Little Wilbraham Cambs 87 L3
Littlewindsor Dorset 15 K2
Little Witcombe Gloucs 64 C4
Little Witley Worcs 81 H3
Little Wittenham Oxon 66 E8
Little Wolford Warwks 83 G8
Littlewood Staffs 98 C2
Little Woodcote Gt Lon 51 H6
Littleworth Bucks 67 L3
Littleworth Oxon 65 L7
Littleworth Staffs 98 C1
Littleworth Staffs 114 E7
Littleworth W Susx 21 L3
Littleworth Worcs 81 K5
Littleworth Worcs 82 B3
Littleworth Common Bucks 50 B2
Little Wratting Suffk 88 D5
Little Wymington Bed 85 J2
Little Wymondley Herts 69 G2
Little Wyrley Staffs 98 C2
Little Wytheford Shrops 113 J7
Little Yeldham Essex 88 F7
Littley Green Essex 71 G4
Litton Derbys 132 C4
Litton N York 158 F7
Litton Somset 45 H8

Litton Cheney Dorset ...15 M4
Liurbost W Isls ...282 g4
Liverpool Lpool ...129 H2
Liversedge Kirk ...141 J3
Liverton Devon ...13 J7
Liverton R & Cl ...171 G7
Liverton Mines R & Cl ...171 G7
Liverton Street Kent ...39 L3
Livingston W Loth ...210 E5
Livingston Village W Loth ...210 D5
Lixwm Flints ...128 E5
Lizard Cnwll ...3 H8
Llaingoch IoA ...124 D3
Llaithddu Powys ...94 C7
Llan Powys ...93 J3
Llanaber Gwynd ...109 L7
Llanaelhaearn Gwynd ...109 G3
Llanafan Cerdgn ...77 J1
Llanafan-Fawr Powys ...78 D4
Llanallgo IoA ...124 H1
Llanarmon Gwynd ...107 G1
Llanarmon Dyffryn Ceiriog
  Wrexhm ...112 A5
Llanarmon-yn-Ial Denbgs ...128 E8
Llanarth Cerdgn ...76 D4
Llanarth Mons ...62 D5
Llanarthne Carmth ...58 F5
Llanasa Flints ...128 D3
Llanbabo IoA ...124 F2
Llanbadarn Fawr Cerdgn ...92 D7
Llanbadarn Fynydd Powys ...94 D7
Llanbadarn-y-garreg Powys ...78 F5
Llanbadoc Mons ...62 D7
Llanbadrig IoA ...124 F1
Llanbeder Newpt ...44 D1
Llanbedr Gwynd ...109 K6
Llanbedr Powys ...61 K3
Llanbedr Powys ...79 G6
Llanbedr-Dyffryn-Clwyd
  Denbgs ...128 D7
Llanbedrgoch IoA ...125 G4
Llanbedrog Gwynd ...108 E5
Llanbedr-y-Cennin Conwy ...126 F6
Llanberis Gwynd ...125 J7
Llanbethêry V Glam ...43 G7
Llanbister Powys ...94 D8
Llanblethian V Glam ...42 F7
Llanboidy Carmth ...55 L2
Llanbradach Caerph ...43 J4
Llanbrynmair Powys ...93 K3
Llancadle V Glam ...42 F8
Llancarfan V Glam ...43 G7
Llancayo Mons ...62 D6
Llancloudy Herefs ...63 G3
Llancynfelyn Cerdgn ...92 E5
Llandaff Cardif ...43 J6
Llandanwg Gwynd ...109 K6
Llandarcy Neath ...57 K6
Llandawke Carmth ...58 A6
Llanddaniel Fab IoA ...125 J5
Llanddarog Carmth ...58 F5
Llanddeiniol Cerdgn ...77 G1
Llanddeiniolen Gwynd ...125 K6
Llandderfel Gwynd ...111 J4
Llanddeusant Carmth ...59 L4
Llanddeusant IoA ...124 F3
Llanddew Powys ...61 J1
Llanddewi Swans ...56 E7
Llanddewi Brefi Cerdgn ...77 J4
Llanddewi'r Cwm Powys ...78 E5
Llanddewi Rhydderch Mons ...62 D4
Llanddewi Velfrey Pembks ...55 K3
Llanddewi Ystradenni Powys ...78 F2
Llanddoged Conwy ...126 F7
Llanddona IoA ...125 K4
Llanddowror Carmth ...58 A6
Llanddulas Conwy ...127 H4
Llanddwywe Gwynd ...109 K7
Llanddyfnan IoA ...125 J4
Llandecwyn Gwynd ...110 B4
Llandefaelog Powys ...60 F1
Llandefaelog-Tre'r-Graig
  Powys ...61 H1
Llandefalle Powys ...78 F8
Llandegfan IoA ...125 K5
Llandegla Denbgs ...112 B1
Llandegley Powys ...79 G2
Llandegveth Mons ...62 C8
Llandegwning Gwynd ...108 D5
Llandeilo Carmth ...59 H4
Llandeilo Graban Powys ...78 F6
Llandeilo'r Fan Powys ...78 B8
Llandeloy Pembks ...74 D6
Llandenny Mons ...62 E6
Llandevaud Newpt ...44 F1
Llandevenny Mons ...44 E2
Llandinabo Herefs ...63 G2
Llandinam Powys ...94 B5
Llandissilio Pembks ...55 J3
Llandogo Mons ...63 G6

Llandough V Glam ...42 F7
Llandough V Glam ...43 J7
Llandovery Carmth ...59 L2
Llandow V Glam ...42 E7
Llandre Carmth ...77 J6
Llandre Cerdgn ...92 D6
Llandre Isaf Pembks ...75 K6
Llandrillo Denbgs ...111 K4
Llandrillo-yn-Rhôs Conwy ...127 G4
Llandrindod Wells Powys ...78 E3
Llandrinio Powys ...112 D8
Llandudno Conwy ...126 F3
Llandudno Junction Conwy ...126 F4
Llandulas Powys ...78 B7
Llandwrog Gwynd ...125 H8
Llandybie Carmth ...59 H6
Llandyfaelog Carmth ...58 D6
Llandyfan Carmth ...59 H5
Llandyfriog Cerdgn ...76 B7
Llandyfrydog IoA ...125 H2
Llandygai Conwy ...126 D5
Llandygwydd Cerdgn ...75 M3
Llandynan Denbgs ...112 B3
Llandyrnog Denbgs ...128 D6
Llandyssil Powys ...94 F4
Llandysul Cerdgn ...76 D7
Llanedeyrn Cardif ...43 K5
Llanedi Carmth ...57 G3
Llaneglwys Powys ...78 E7
Llanegryn Gwynd ...92 D2
Llanegwad Carmth ...58 F4
Llaneilian IoA ...125 H1
Llanelian-yn-Rhôs Conwy ...127 G4
Llanelidan Denbgs ...111 L2
Llanelieu Powys ...79 H8
Llanellen Mons ...62 C5
Llanelli Carmth ...56 F5
Llanelltyd Gwynd ...110 D7
Llanelly Mons ...61 K4
Llanelly Hill Mons ...61 K4
Llanelwedd Powys ...78 E3
Llanenddwyn Gwynd ...109 L6
Llanengan Gwynd ...108 F6
Llanerch Powys ...111 G8
Llanerch Conwy ...95 H4
Llanerchymedd IoA ...125 G3
Llanerfyl Powys ...94 B2
Llanfabon Caerph ...43 H3
Llanfachraeth IoA ...124 E3
Llanfachreth Gwynd ...110 E7
Llanfaelog IoA ...124 F5
Llanfaelrhys Gwynd ...108 C6
Llanfaenor Mons ...62 E4
Llanfaes IoA ...126 B4
Llanfaes Powys ...61 G2
Llanfaethlu IoA ...124 E2
Llanfair Gwynd ...109 K5
Llanfair Caereinion Powys ...94 D2
Llanfair Clydogau Cerdgn ...77 H5
Llanfair Dyffryn Clwyd Denbgs ...128 D8
Llanfair-fechan Conwy ...126 D5
Llanfair Kilgeddin Mons ...62 D5
Llanfair-Nant-Gwyn Pembks ...75 K5
Llanfairpwllgwyngyll IoA ...125 J5
Llanfair Talhaiarn Conwy ...127 J5
Llanfair Waterdine Shrops ...94 F8
Llanfairynghornwy IoA ...124 E2
Llanfair-yn-Neubwll IoA ...124 E4
Llanfallteg Carmth ...55 K3
Llanfallteg West Carmth ...55 K3
Llanfarian Cerdgn ...92 D7
Llanfechain Powys ...112 B7
Llanfechan Powys ...78 D5
Llanfechell IoA ...124 F2
Llanferres Denbgs ...128 C6
Llan Ffestiniog Gwynd ...110 D3
Llanfflewyn IoA ...124 F2
Llanfigael IoA ...124 F3
Llanfihangel-ar-arth Carmth ...76 E7
Llanfihangel Glyn Myfyr
  Conwy ...111 J2
Llanfihangel Nant Bran Powys ...78 C8
Llanfihangel-nant-Melan
  Powys ...79 H4
Llanfihangel Rhydithon Powys ...79 G2
Llanfihangel Rogiet Mons ...44 F2
Llanfihangel Tal-y-llyn Powys ...61 H2
Llanfihangel-uwch-Gwili
  Carmth ...58 E4
Llanfihangel-y-Creuddyn
  Cerdgn ...92 E8
Llanfihangel-yng-Ngwynfa
  Powys ...111 L8
Llanfihangel yn Nhowyn IoA ...124 E4
Llanfihangel-y-pennant Gwynd ...92 E2
Llanfihangel-y-pennant
  Gwynd ...109 J3
Llanfilo Powys ...78 F8
Llanfoist Mons ...62 B4
Llanfor Gwynd ...111 H4

Llanfrechfa Torfn ...62 C8
Llanfrothen Gwynd ...110 B3
Llanfrynach Powys ...61 G2
Llanfwrog Denbgs ...128 D8
Llanfwrog IoA ...124 E3
Llanfyllin Powys ...112 A7
Llanfynydd Carmth ...59 G3
Llanfynydd Flints ...129 G8
Llanfyrnach Pembks ...75 L4
Llangadfan Powys ...94 B1
Llangadog Carmth ...56 D3
Llangadog Carmth ...59 K3
Llangadwaladr IoA ...125 G6
Llangadwaladr Powys ...112 B5
Llangaffo IoA ...125 H6
Llangain Carmth ...58 C5
Llangammarch Wells Powys ...78 C6
Llangan V Glam ...42 E6
Llangarron Herefs ...63 G3
Llangasty-Talyllyn Powys ...61 H2
Llangathen Carmth ...59 G4
Llangattock Powys ...61 K3
Llangattock Lingoed Mons ...62 D3
Llangattock-Vibon-Avel Mons ...62 F4
Llangedwyn Powys ...112 B6
Llangefni IoA ...125 H4
Llangeinor Brdgnd ...42 D4
Llangeitho Cerdgn ...77 H3
Llangeler Carmth ...76 C7
Llangelynin Gwynd ...92 C2
Llangennech Carmth ...57 G4
Llangennith Swans ...56 D6
Llangenny Powys ...61 K3
Llangernyw Conwy ...127 H6
Llangian Gwynd ...108 E5
Llangiwg Neath ...57 K4
Llangloffan Pembks ...74 E5
Llanglydwen Carmth ...75 L6
Llangoed IoA ...126 C4
Llangoedmor Cerdgn ...75 L3
Llangollen Denbgs ...112 B3
Llangolman Pembks ...75 H4
Llangors Powys ...61 H2
Llangorwen Cerdgn ...92 D6
Llangovan Mons ...62 F6
Llangower Gwynd ...111 G5
Llangranog Cerdgn ...76 B4
Llangristiolus IoA ...125 H5
Llangrove Herefs ...63 G3
Llangua Mons ...62 E2
Llangunllo Powys ...79 H1
Llangunnor Carmth ...58 D5
Llangurig Powys ...93 K7
Llangwm Conwy ...111 J3
Llangwm Mons ...62 E7
Llangwm Pembks ...55 G5
Llangwnnadl Gwynd ...108 C5
Llangwyfan Denbgs ...128 D6
Llangwyllog IoA ...125 H4
Llangwyryfon Cerdgn ...77 H1
Llangybi Cerdgn ...77 H4
Llangybi Gwynd ...109 G3
Llangybi Mons ...62 D7
Llangyfelach Swans ...57 H5
Llangyndeyrn Carmth ...58 E6
Llangynhafal Denbgs ...128 D7
Llangynidr Powys ...61 J3
Llangynin Carmth ...55 M3
Llangynllo Cerdgn ...76 C6
Llangynog Carmth ...58 C6
Llangynog Powys ...111 L6
Llangynwyd Brdgnd ...42 C4
Llanhamlach Powys ...61 H2
Llanharan Rhondd ...42 F5
Llanharry Rhondd ...42 F5
Llanhennock Mons ...62 D8
Llanhilleth Blae G ...61 K7
Llanidan IoA ...125 J6
Llanidloes Powys ...93 L6
Llaniestyn Gwynd ...108 D5
Llanigon Powys ...79 H7
Llanilar Cerdgn ...92 D8
Llanilid Rhondd ...42 E5
Llanina Cerdgn ...76 D3
Llanio Cerdgn ...77 H4
Llanishen Cardif ...43 J5
Llanishen Mons ...62 F6
Llanllechid Gwynd ...126 C6
Llanlleonfel Powys ...78 C5
Llanllowell Mons ...62 D7
Llanllugan Powys ...94 C3
Llanllwch Carmth ...58 C5
Llanllwchaiarn Powys ...94 D5
Llanllwni Carmth ...76 F7
Llanllyfni Gwynd ...109 H1
Llanmadoc Swans ...56 D6
Llanmaes V Glam ...42 E7
Llanmartin Newpt ...44 E1
Llanmerewig Powys ...94 E5
Llanmihangel V Glam ...42 E7

Llanmiloe Carmth ...55 M5
Llanmorlais Swans ...56 F6
Llannefydd Conwy ...127 K5
Llannon Carmth ...56 F3
Llannor Gwynd ...108 F4
Llanon Cerdgn ...76 F2
Llanover Mons ...62 C5
Llanpumsaint Carmth ...58 D3
Llanrhaeadr-ym-Mochnant
  Powys ...111 M6
Llanrhian Pembks ...74 D6
Llanrhidian Swans ...56 F6
Llanrhos Conwy ...126 F4
Llanrhychwyn Conwy ...126 F7
Llanrhyddlad IoA ...124 F2
Llanrhystud Cerdgn ...76 F1
Llanrothal Herefs ...62 F3
Llanrug Gwynd ...125 J7
Llanrumney Cardif ...43 K5
Llanrwst Conwy ...126 F7
Llansadurnen Carmth ...56 A3
Llansadwrn Carmth ...59 J5
Llansadwrn IoA ...125 K4
Llansaint Carmth ...56 C3
Llansamlet Swans ...57 J5
Llansanffraid Glan Conwy
  Conwy ...126 F4
Llansannan Conwy ...127 J6
Llansannor V Glam ...42 F6
Llansantffraed Powys ...61 H2
Llansantffraed-Cwmdeuddwr
  Powys ...78 D2
Llansantffraed-in-Elvel Powys ...78 F4
Llansantffraid Cerdgn ...76 F2
Llansantffraid-ym-Mechain
  Powys ...112 C7
Llansawel Carmth ...59 H2
Llansilin Powys ...112 B6
Llansoy Mons ...62 E6
Llanspyddid Powys ...60 F2
Llanstadwell Pembks ...54 F6
Llansteffan Carmth ...56 C3
Llanstephan Powys ...78 F7
Llantarnam Torfn ...62 C8
Llanteg Pembks ...55 L5
Llanthewy Skirrid Mons ...62 D4
Llanthony Mons ...62 B2
Llantilio-Crossenny Mons ...62 E4
Llantilio Pertholey Mons ...62 C4
Llantood Pembks ...75 K4
Llantrisant IoA ...124 F3
Llantrisant Mons ...62 D7
Llantrisant Rhondd ...43 G5
Llantrithyd V Glam ...43 G7
Llantwit Fardre Rhondd ...43 G4
Llantwit Major V Glam ...42 E7
Llantysilio Denbgs ...112 B3
Llanuwchllyn Gwynd ...111 G5
Llanvaches Newpt ...44 E1
Llanvair Discoed Mons ...62 F8
Llanvapley Mons ...62 D4
Llanvetherine Mons ...62 D4
Llanveynoe Herefs ...62 C1
Llanvihangel Crucorney Mons ...62 C3
Llanvihangel Gobion Mons ...62 D5
Llanvihangel-Ystern-Llewern
  Mons ...62 E4
Llanwarne Herefs ...63 G2
Llanwddyn Powys ...111 K7
Llanwenarth Mons ...62 B4
Llanwenog Cerdgn ...76 F6
Llanwern Newpt ...44 D2
Llanwinio Carmth ...58 A4
Llanwnda Gwynd ...125 H8
Llanwnda Pembks ...74 F4
Llanwnnen Cerdgn ...76 F6
Llanwnog Powys ...94 B4
Llanwonno Rhondd ...42 F3
Llanwrda Carmth ...59 K3
Llanwrin Powys ...93 G3
Llanwrthwl Powys ...78 D3
Llanwrtyd Powys ...78 B5
Llanwrtyd Wells Powys ...78 B6
Llanwyddelan Powys ...94 C3
Llanyblodwel Shrops ...112 C7
Llanybri Carmth ...58 B6
Llanybydder Carmth ...76 F6
Llanycefn Pembks ...55 J2
Llanychaer Pembks ...75 G5
Llanycil Gwynd ...111 H4
Llanycrwys Carmth ...77 H6
Llanymawddwy Gwynd ...111 G7
Llanymynech Powys ...112 C7
Llanynghenedl IoA ...124 E3
Llanynys Denbgs ...128 C7
Llan-y-pwll Wrexhm ...112 F1
Llanyre Powys ...78 F3
Llanystumdwy Gwynd ...109 H4
Llanywern Powys ...61 H2
Llawhaden Pembks ...55 H3

Llawnt Shrops....................112 C5
Llawryglyn Powys..................93 K5
Llay Wrexhm......................129 H8
Llechcynfarwy IoA................125 G3
Llechfaen Powys...................61 G2
Llechrhyd Caerph..................61 H5
Llechryd Cerdgn...................75 L3
Llechylched IoA..................124 F4
Lledrod Cerdgn....................77 H1
Llidiardau Gwynd.................111 G4
Llidiartnenog Carmth..............77 G7
Llidiart-y-parc Denbgs...........111 M3
Llithfaen Gwynd..................108 F3
Lloc Flints......................128 D4
Llowes Powys......................79 H7
Llwydcoed Rhondd..................60 F6
Llwydiarth Powys.................111 K8
Llwyn Denbgs.....................128 C6
Llwyncelyn Cerdgn.................76 E3
Llwyndafydd Cerdgn................76 C4
Llwynderw Powys...................94 F3
Llwyn-drain Pembks................58 A2
Llwyn-du Mons.....................62 C4
Llwyndyrys Gwynd.................108 F3
Llwyngwril Gwynd..................92 D2
Llwynhendy Carmth.................56 F5
Llwynmawr Wrexhm.................112 C4
Llwyn-on Myr Td...................60 F5
Llwyn-y-brain Carmth..............55 L4
Llwyn-y-groes Cerdgn..............77 G4
Llwynypia Rhondd..................42 F3
Llynclys Shrops..................112 D6
Llynfaes IoA.....................125 G4
Llŷn Peninsula Gwynd.............108 E4
Llyn-y-pandy Flints..............128 E6
Llysfaen Conwy...................127 H4
Llyswen Cerdgn....................76 E3
Llyswen Powys.....................79 G7
Llysworney V Glam.................42 E6
Llys-y-frân Pembks................55 H2
Llywel Powys......................60 C1
Load Brook Sheff.................132 E2
Loan Falk........................210 C4
Loanend Nthumb...................202 E3
Loanhead Mdloth..................211 J6
Loaningfoot D & G................176 C7
Loans S Ayrs.....................196 C4
Lobb Devon........................27 H3
Lobhillcross Devon................12 B5
Lochailort Highld................238 B7
Lochaline Highld.................227 K3
Lochans D & G....................172 D3
Locharbriggs D & G...............176 C3
Lochavich Ag & B.................216 E4
Lochawe Ag & B...................217 J2
Loch Baghasdail W Isls...........283 c11
Lochboisdale W Isls..............283 c11
Lochbuie Ag & B..................227 H7
Lochcarron Highld................248 E4
Lochdon Ag & B...................227 L6
Lochdonhead Ag & B...............227 L5
Lochead Ag & B...................206 B3
Lochearnhead Stirlg..............219 K2
Lochee C Dund....................222 F1
Loch Eil Highld..................239 H7
Locheilside Station Highld.......239 G7
Lochend Highld...................251 G4
Lochead W Isls...................283 c8
Loch Euphort W Isls..............283 c8
Lochfoot D & G...................176 B4
Lochgair Ag & B..................206 E1
Lochgelly Fife...................222 C8
Lochgilphead Ag & B..............206 D2
Lochgoilhead Ag & B..............217 K7
Lochieheads Fife.................222 D4
Lochill Moray....................266 F3
Lochindorb Lodge Highld..........253 J4
Lochinver Highld.................270 E4
Loch Lomond and The
  Trossachs National Park........219 G4
Loch Loyal Lodge Highld..........277 L7
Lochluichart Highld..............262 B7
Lochmaben D & G..................176 E2
Lochmaddy W Isls.................283 d8
Loch nam Madadh W Isls...........283 d8
Loch Ness Highld.................250 F6
Lochore Fife.....................222 B7
Loch Portain W Isls..............283 d8
Lochportain W Isls...............283 d8
Lochranza N Ayrs.................194 E1
Loch Sgioport W Isls.............283 c10
Lochside Abers...................235 J3
Lochside D & G...................176 C3
Lochside Highld..................252 F1
Lochskipport W Isls..............283 c10
Lochslin Highld..................264 C4
Lochton S Ayrs...................183 G7
Lochty Angus.....................234 E3
Lochty Fife......................223 J5
Lochuisge Highld.................228 B4

Lochwinnoch Rens.................208 B7
Lochwood D & G...................187 G6
Lockengate Cnwll...................5 H3
Lockerbie D & G..................176 F3
Lockeridge Wilts..................47 H5
Lockerley Hants...................34 C5
Locking N Som.....................44 D7
Locking Stumps Warrtn............130 C1
Lockington E R Yk................152 F6
Lockington Leics.................116 D6
Lockleywood Shrops...............113 M6
Locksbottom Gt Lon................51 L6
Locksgreen IoW....................19 G5
Locks Heath Hants.................19 H2
Lockton N York...................162 E5
Loddington Leics.................101 H3
Loddington N Nthn................101 H7
Loddiswell Devon...................7 L5
Loddon Norfk.....................107 H4
Lode Cambs........................87 L3
Lode Heath Solhll.................98 F7
Loders Dorset.....................15 L4
Lodsworth W Susx..................36 D6
Lofthouse Leeds..................142 A3
Lofthouse N York.................159 K8
Lofthouse Gate Wakefd............142 A3
Loftus R & Cl....................171 G7
Logan E Ayrs.....................197 H6
Loganbeck Cumb...................156 A4
Loganlea W Loth..................210 C6
Loggerheads Staffs...............114 A4
Logie Angus......................235 M3
Logie Fife.......................223 G3
Logie Moray......................253 K2
Logie Coldstone Abers............243 M3
Logie Newton Abers...............256 D3
Logie Pert Angus.................235 G3
Logierait P & K..................232 E5
Logierieve Abers.................257 G6
Login Carmth......................55 K2
Lolworth Cambs....................87 H2
Lonbain Highld...................259 M6
Londesborough E R Yk.............152 C6
London Gt Lon.....................51 J3
London Apprentice Cnwll............5 G5
London Ashford Airport Kent.......25 K3
London Beach Kent.................39 M6
London City Airport Gt Lon........51 J3
London Colney Herts...............68 F6
Londonderry N York...............160 D5
London Gateway Services
  Gt Lon...........................69 G8
London Gatwick Airport W Susx.....37 L3
London Heathrow Airport
  Gt Lon...........................50 D4
London Luton Airport Luton........68 E3
London Oxford Airport Oxon........66 C4
London Southend Airport
  Essex............................53 J1
London Stansted Airport Essex.....70 E2
Londonthorpe Lincs...............118 C4
Londubh Highld...................260 D4
Lonemore Highld..................260 C4
Long Ashton N Som.................45 H5
Long Bank Worcs...................97 H8
Long Bennington Lincs............117 L3
Longbenton N Tyne................181 G6
Longborough Gloucs................65 J1
Long Bredy Dorset.................16 A4
Longbridge Birm...................98 C7
Longbridge Warwks.................83 G3
Longbridge Deverill Wilts.........32 E3
Long Buckby W Nthn................84 C2
Longburgh Cumb...................177 J7
Longburton Dorset.................31 L8
Long Cause Devon...................8 B3
Long Clawson Leics...............117 J6
Longcliffe Derbys................132 D8
Longcombe Devon....................8 C3
Long Common Hants.................35 G7
Long Compton Staffs..............114 D7
Long Compton Warwks...............83 G8
Longcot Oxon......................47 K1
Long Crendon Bucks................67 G5
Long Crichel Dorset...............17 J1
Longcroft Cumb...................177 H7
Longcross Surrey..................50 C6
Longden Shrops....................95 K2
Longden Common Shrops.............95 K2
Long Ditton Surrey................50 F5
Longdon Staffs...................115 H8
Longdon Worcs.....................81 J7
Longdon Green Staffs..............98 D1
Longdon Heath Worcs...............81 J7
Longdon upon Tern Wrekin.........113 K8
Longdown Devon....................13 K4
Longdowns Cnwll....................3 J4
Long Drax N York.................143 H2
Long Duckmanton Derbys...........133 J5
Long Eaton Derbys................116 E5

Longfield Kent....................52 D5
Longford Covtry...................99 K6
Longford Derbys..................115 L4
Longford Gloucs...................64 B3
Longford Gt Lon...................50 D4
Longford Kent.....................38 D2
Longford Shrops..................113 L5
Longford Wrekin..................114 A7
Longforgan P & K.................222 E1
Longformacus Border..............212 F7
Longframlington Nthumb...........191 G6
Long Green Ches W................129 L5
Long Green Worcs..................81 J8
Longham Dorset....................17 L3
Longham Norfk....................121 L8
Long Hanborough Oxon..............66 C4
Longhaven Abers..................257 L4
Long Hedges Lincs................119 K2
Longhirst Nthumb.................191 J8
Longhope Gloucs...................63 K3
Longhope Ork.....................275 b6
Longhorsley Nthumb...............191 H7
Longhoughton Nthumb..............191 J3
Long Itchington Warwks............83 K2
Longlands Cumb...................165 J3
Longlane Derbys..................115 L4
Long Lawford Warwks..............100 A8
Longlevens Gloucs.................64 B3
Longley Calder..................141 G3
Longley Kirk.....................141 J6
Longley Green Worcs...............81 G5
Longleys P & K...................233 J6
Long Load Somset..................31 G6
Longmanhill Abers................268 D4
Long Marston Herts................67 L4
Long Marston N York..............151 H5
Long Marston Warwks...............82 E5
Long Marton W & F................166 F5
Long Meadowend Shrops.............95 K7
Long Melford Suffk................89 H6
Longmoor Camp Hants...............36 B4
Longmorn Moray...................266 E4
Longmoss Ches E..................131 H5
Long Newnton Gloucs...............64 C8
Long Newton Border...............201 J7
Long Newton E Loth...............212 B6
Longnewton S on T................169 K7
Longney Gloucs....................63 M4
Longniddry E Loth................212 A4
Longnor Shrops....................96 B3
Longnor Staffs...................132 B6
Longparish Hants..................34 F2
Longpark Cumb....................178 A6
Long Preston N York..............148 E4
Longridge Lancs..................147 M8
Longridge Staffs.................114 E8
Longridge W Loth.................210 C6
Longriggend N Lans...............209 L5
Long Riston E R Yk...............153 H7
Longrock Cnwll.....................2 D5
Longsdon Staffs..................114 F1
Longshaw Wigan...................139 G7
Longside Abers...................269 J6
Long Sight Oldham................140 D6
Longslow Shrops..................113 L4
Longstanton Cambs.................87 H2
Longstock Hants...................34 D3
Longstone Pembks..................55 K5
Longstowe Cambs...................86 F4
Long Stratton Norfk..............106 D5
Long Street M Keyn................84 F5
Longstreet Wilts..................47 H8
Long Sutton Hants.................35 M2
Long Sutton Lincs................119 M7
Long Sutton Somset................31 G6
Longthorpe C Pete................102 D4
Long Thurlow Suffk................89 K2
Longthwaite W & F................166 B6
Longton C Stke...................114 E3
Longton Lancs....................138 F3
Longtown Cumb....................177 L5
Longtown Herefs...................62 C1
Longueville Jersey.................9 e3
Longville in the Dale Shrops......96 C4
Long Waste Wrekin................113 K8
Long Whatton Leics...............116 D6
Longwick Bucks....................67 J4
Long Wittenham Oxon...............66 E8
Longwitton Nthumb................180 C1
Longwood D & G...................175 H3
Longwood Shrops...................96 D2
Longworth Oxon....................66 A7
Longyester E Loth................212 C6
Lôn-las Swans.....................57 K5
Lonmay Abers.....................269 J4
Lonmore Highld...................258 D7
Looe Cnwll.........................6 B4
Loose Kent........................39 J3
Loosebeare Devon..................13 G2
Loosegate Lincs..................119 K6

Loosley Row Bucks.................67 K7
Lootcherbrae Abers...............268 A5
Lopcombe Corner Wilts.............34 B4
Lopen Somset......................30 F8
Loppington Shrops................113 G5
Lorbottle Nthumb.................190 E5
Lordington W Susx.................20 C5
Lordsbridge Norfk................104 B1
Lordshill C Sotn..................34 E7
Lords Wood Medway.................53 G6
Lornty P & K.....................233 J6
Loscoe Derbys....................116 C2
Loscombe Dorset...................15 L3
Losgaintir W Isls................282 e6
Lossiemouth Moray................266 E2
Lostford Shrops..................113 K5
Lostock Gralam Ches W............130 D5
Lostock Green Ches W.............130 D5
Lostock Hall Lancs...............139 H3
Lostock Hall Fold Bolton.........139 K6
Lostock Junction Bolton..........139 K6
Lostwithiel Cnwll..................5 J3
Lothbeg Highld...................274 C6
Lothersdale N York...............149 G6
Lothmore Highld..................274 C6
Loudwater Bucks...................49 L1
Loudwater Herts...................68 D7
Loughborough Leics...............116 C7
Loughor Swans.....................57 G5
Loughton Essex....................70 B7
Loughton M Keyn...................85 G7
Loughton Shrops...................96 E6
Lound Lincs......................118 E7
Lound Notts......................134 D2
Lound Suffk......................107 K4
Lounston Devon....................13 J7
Lount Leics......................116 C7
Louth Lincs......................136 F2
Loveclough Lancs.................140 B2
Lovedean Hants....................19 M1
Lover Wilts.......................34 B6
Loversall Donc...................142 F8
Loves Green Essex.................70 F6
Lovesome Hill N York.............160 E3
Loveston Pembks...................55 J5
Lovington Somset..................31 K5
Low Ackworth Wakefd..............142 C4
Low Angerton Nthumb..............180 D2
Lowbands Gloucs...................63 M1
Low Barbeth D & G................172 C2
Low Barlings Lincs...............136 A5
Low Bell End N York..............162 C3
Low Bentham N York...............148 A2
Low Biggins W & F................157 K7
Low Borrowbridge W & F...........157 K2
Low Bradfield Sheff..............132 E2
Low Bradley N York...............149 H6
Low Braithwaite W & F............166 A2
Low Burnham N Linc...............143 K7
Low Buston Nthumb................191 J5
Lowca Cumb.......................164 C6
Low Catton E R Yk................151 L5
Low Coniscliffe Darltn...........169 H7
Low Crosby Cumb..................178 B7
Lowdham Notts....................117 H2
Low Dinsdale Darltn..............169 K8
Lowe Shrops......................113 H5
Lowe Hill Staffs.................131 K8
Low Ellington N York.............160 B6
Lower Aisholt Somset..............30 B4
Lower Ansty Dorset................16 E2
Lower Apperley Gloucs.............64 B2
Lower Arboll Highld..............264 D3
Lower Arncott Oxon................66 F3
Lower Ashton Devon................13 K4
Lower Assendon Oxon...............49 H2
Lower Badcall Highld.............276 B7
Lower Ballam Lancs...............138 D2
Lower Bartle Lancs...............139 G1
Lower Basildon W Berk.............48 F3
Lower Bearwood Herefs.............79 M4
Lower Beeding W Susx..............37 K5
Lower Benefield N Nthn...........101 L4
Lower Bentley Worcs...............82 A2
Lower Beobridge Shrops............97 H5
Lower Birchwood Derbys...........116 D1
Lower Boddington N Nthn...........83 L5
Lower Boscaswell Cnwll.............2 B4
Lower Bourne Surrey...............36 C2
Lower Brailes Warwks..............83 H7
Lower Breakish Highld............247 L4
Lower Bredbury Stockp............131 H2
Lower Broadheath Worcs............81 J4
Lower Broxwood Herefs............79 L4
Lower Buckenhill Herefs...........80 E8
Lower Bullingham Herefs..........80 C7
Lower Burgate Hants...............33 K7
Lower Burrowton Devon............14 B3
Lower Burton Herefs...............80 A4
Lower Caldecote C Beds............86 D6

Lower Cam Gloucs 63 L7
Lower Canada N Som 44 D7
Lower Catesby W Nthn 83 M3
Lower Chapel Powys 78 E8
Lower Chicksgrove Wilts 33 G5
Lower Chute Wilts 47 L8
Lower Clapton Gt Lon 51 K2
Lower Clent Worcs 97 L7
Lower Common Hants 49 J6
Lower Compton Wilts 46 E5
Lower Creedy Devon 13 K2
Lower Crossings Derbys 131 L4
Lower Cumberworth Kirk 141 K6
Lower Darwen Bl w D 139 K3
Lower Dean Bed 85 L2
Lower Denby Kirk 141 K6
Lower Diabaig Highld 260 C7
Lower Dicker E Susx 23 J5
Lower Dinchope Shrops 95 L6
Lower Down Shrops 95 H5
Lower Dunsforth N York 150 F3
Lower Egleton Herefs 80 E6
Lower Elkstone Staffs 131 L8
Lower Ellastone Staffs 115 J3
Lower End Bucks 67 G5
Lower End M Keyn 85 H7
Lower End N Nthn 85 H3
Lower End W Nthn 84 F3
Lower Everleigh Wilts 47 J8
Lower Exbury Hants 19 G4
Lower Eythorne Kent 41 J5
Lower Failand N Som 45 G4
Lower Farringdon Hants 35 L4
Lower Feltham Gt Lon 50 E4
Lower Fittleworth W Susx 21 G3
Lower Foxdale IoM 154 c6
Lower Frankton Shrops 112 E5
Lower Freystrop Pembks 54 F4
Lower Froyle Hants 35 M2
Lower Gabwell Devon 8 D1
Lower Gledfield Highld 263 G2
Lower Godney Somset 31 G2
Lower Gornal Dudley 97 L5
Lower Gravenhurst C Beds 86 C8
Lower Green Herts 86 D8
Lower Green Herts 87 J8
Lower Green Kent 38 E5
Lower Green Kent 39 G5
Lower Green Norfk 121 L4
Lower Green Staffs 97 K2
Lower Green Suffk 88 E2
Lower Hacheston Suffk 91 H4
Lower Halstock Leigh Dorset 15 M1
Lower Halstow Kent 53 J5
Lower Hamworthy BCP 17 K4
Lower Hardres Kent 40 F5
Lower Harpton Herefs 79 K3
Lower Hartlip Kent 53 H6
Lower Hartshay Derbys 116 C1
Lower Hartwell Bucks 67 J4
Lower Hatton Staffs 114 C4
Lower Hawthwaite W & F 156 B5
Lower Haysden Kent 38 F4
Lower Hergest Herefs 79 K4
Lower Heyford Oxon 66 C2
Lower Heysham Lancs 147 H4
Lower Higham Kent 52 F4
Lower Holbrook Suffk 90 E8
Lower Hordley Shrops 112 F5
Lower Horncroft W Susx 21 G3
Lowerhouse Lancs 140 B1
Lower Houses Kirk 141 J5
Lower Howsell Worcs 81 H5
Lower Irlam Salfd 130 D1
Lower Kilburn Derbys 116 C3
Lower Kilcott Gloucs 46 A1
Lower Killeyan Ag & B 204 D7
Lower Kingcombe Dorset 16 A3
Lower Kingswood Surrey 51 H8
Lower Kinnerton Ches W 129 H7
Lower Langford N Som 44 F6
Lower Largo Fife 223 G6
Lower Leigh Staffs 115 G4
Lower Lemington Gloucs 82 F8
Lower Llanfadog Powys 78 C2
Lower Lovacott Devon 27 J5
Lower Loxhore Devon 27 L3
Lower Lydbrook Gloucs 63 H6
Lower Lye Herefs 79 M2
Lower Machen Newpt 43 K4
Lower Maes-coed Herefs 62 D1
Lower Mannington Dorset 17 L2
Lower Marston Somset 32 C2
Lower Meend Gloucs 63 H6
Lower Merridge Somset 30 B4
Lower Middleton Cheney W Nthn 83 L7
Lower Milton Somset 31 J2
Lower Moor Worcs 82 A6
Lower Morton S Glos 63 J8

Lower Nazeing Essex 69 K6
Lower Norton Warwks 82 F3
Lower Nyland Dorset 32 C6
Lower Oddington Gloucs 65 K2
Lower Penarth V Glam 43 J7
Lower Penn Staffs 97 K4
Lower Pennington Hants 18 E5
Lower Penwortham Lancs 139 G2
Lower Peover Ches E 130 E5
Lower Place Rochdl 140 D5
Lower Pollicott Bucks 67 H4
Lower Quinton Warwks 82 E6
Lower Rainham Medway 53 H5
Lower Raydon Suffk 90 B7
Lower Roadwater Somset 29 J3
Lower Salter Lancs 147 M3
Lower Seagry Wilts 46 D3
Lower Shelton C Beds 85 K6
Lower Shiplake Oxon 49 J3
Lower Shuckburgh Warwks 83 L5
Lower Slaughter Gloucs 65 H3
Lower Soothill Kirk 141 L3
Lower Soudley Gloucs 63 K5
Lower Standen Kent 41 H7
Lower Stanton St Quintin Wilts 46 D3
Lower Stoke Medway 53 H4
Lower Stondon C Beds 86 C8
Lower Stone Gloucs 63 K8
Lower Stonnall Staffs 98 D3
Lower Stow Bedon Norfk 105 K4
Lower Street Dorset 17 G3
Lower Street E Susx 24 C5
Lower Street Norfk 122 F4
Lower Street Suffk 88 F5
Lower Street Suffk 90 D5
Lower Stretton Warrtn 130 C3
Lower Stroud Dorset 15 K3
Lower Sundon C Beds 68 D2
Lower Swanwick Hants 19 H2
Lower Swell Gloucs 65 H2
Lower Tadmarton Oxon 83 J7
Lower Tale Devon 14 C2
Lower Tasburgh Norfk 106 D4
Lower Town Cnwll 115 G4
Lower Thurlton Norfk 107 J3
Lower Town Cnwll 3 G5
Lower Town Devon 13 G8
Lower Town Herefs 80 E6
Lower Town IoS 10 c1
Lower Town Pembks 74 F5
Lower Trebullett Cnwll 11 L7
Lower Treluswell Cnwll 3 K4
Lower Tysoe Warwks 83 H6
Lower Ufford Suffk 91 G5
Lower Upcott Devon 13 K6
Lower Upham Hants 35 H7
Lower Upnor Medway 53 G5
Lower Vexford Somset 29 L4
Lower Walton Warrtn 130 B3
Lower Waterston Dorset 16 E4
Lower Weare Somset 44 E8
Lower Weedon W Nthn 84 C3
Lower Welson Herefs 79 K5
Lower Westmancote Worcs 81 L7
Lower Whatcombe Dorset 17 G2
Lower Whatley Somset 32 B2
Lower Whitley Ches W 130 B4
Lower Wick Gloucs 63 L7
Lower Wick Worcs 81 J5
Lower Wield Hants 35 K3
Lower Willingdon E Susx 23 K6
Lower Withington Ches E 130 F5
Lower Woodend Bucks 49 K2
Lower Woodford Wilts 33 K4
Lower Wraxhall Dorset 16 A2
Lower Wyche Worcs 81 H6
Lower Wyke C Brad 141 J3
Lowesby Leics 100 F2
Lowestoft Suffk 107 L5
Loweswater Cumb 164 F6
Low Etherley Dur 168 F5
Low Fell Gatesd 181 G7
Lowfield Heath W Susx 37 L3
Low Gartachorrans Stirlg 208 D2
Low Gate Nthumb 179 L6
Low Gettbridge Cumb 178 C7
Lowgill Lancs 148 A3
Lowgill W & F 157 K3
Low Grantley N York 150 B2
Low Green N York 150 B4
Low Habberley Worcs 97 H7
Low Ham Somset 30 F5
Low Harrogate N York 150 C5
Low Hawsker N York 163 G1
Low Hesket W & F 166 B2
Low Hutton N York 152 A2
Lowick N Nthn 101 L7
Lowick Nthumb 203 G5
Lowick W & F 156 D5

Lowick Bridge W & F 156 D5
Lowick Green W & F 156 D5
Low Knipe W & F 166 C6
Low Laithe N York 150 B3
Lowlands Dur 168 C5
Lowlands Torfn 62 C7
Low Langton Lincs 136 C4
Low Leighton Derbys 131 K3
Low Lorton Cumb 164 F5
Low Marishes N York 162 E7
Low Marnham Notts 134 F6
Low Middleton Nthumb 203 H6
Low Mill N York 161 L4
Low Moor C Brad 141 J2
Low Moorsley Sundld 169 J2
Low Moresby Cumb 164 C6
Low Newton W & F 156 F6
Low Newton-by-the-Sea Nthumb 191 J1
Low Pittington Dur 169 J2
Low Row Cumb 165 G2
Low Row Cumb 170 D6
Low Row N York 159 H3
Low Salchrie D & G 172 C2
Low Santon N Linc 144 B5
Lowsonford Warwks 82 E2
Low Street Norfk 123 G6
Low Street Thurr 52 E3
Low Tharston Norfk 106 D4
Lowther W & F 166 D6
Lowthorpe E R Yk 153 H4
Lowton Devon 12 F2
Lowton Somset 30 B7
Lowton Wigan 139 J8
Lowton Common Wigan 139 J8
Lowton St Mary's Wigan 139 J8
Low Torry Fife 210 D2
Low Toynton Lincs 136 E5
Low Valley Barns 142 B7
Low Wood W & F 156 E6
Low Worsall N York 160 F1
Low Wray W & F 156 E2
Loxbeare Devon 29 G7
Loxhill Surrey 36 F3
Loxhore Devon 27 L3
Loxhore Cott Devon 27 L3
Loxley Warwks 83 G4
Loxley Green Staffs 115 H5
Loxter Herefs 81 G7
Loxton N Som 44 D7
Loxwood W Susx 36 F4
Lubenham Leics 100 F6
Lucasgate Lincs 119 M2
Lucas Green Surrey 50 B7
Luccombe Somset 29 G2
Luccombe Village IoW 19 K7
Lucker Nthumb 203 J7
Luckett Cnwll 11 M7
Lucking Street Essex 89 G3
Luckington Wilts 46 B2
Lucklawhill Fife 223 G3
Lucknam Wilts 46 D4
Luckwell Bridge Somset 28 F3
Lucton Herefs 80 B2
Lucy Cross N York 169 G8
Ludag W Isls 283 c12
Ludborough Lincs 145 H8
Ludbrook Devon 7 J4
Ludchurch Pembks 55 K4
Luddenden Calder 141 G3
Luddenden Foot Calder 141 G3
Luddenham Court Kent 40 C3
Luddesdown Kent 52 E5
Luddington N Linc 143 L4
Luddington Warwks 82 E5
Luddington in the Brook N Nthn 102 C6
Ludford Lincs 136 D2
Ludford Shrops 96 C8
Ludgershall Bucks 67 G4
Ludgershall Wilts 34 B1
Ludgvan Cnwll 2 D4
Ludham Norfk 123 H7
Ludlow Shrops 96 C8
Ludney Somset 30 F8
Ludwell Wilts 32 F6
Ludworth Dur 169 K2
Luffenhall Herts 69 J1
Luffincott Devon 11 L4
Luffness E Loth 212 B3
Lugar E Ayrs 197 H6
Luggate Burn E Loth 212 D4
Lugg Green Herefs 80 B3
Luggiebank N Lans 209 K4
Lugton E Ayrs 208 C8
Lugwardine Herefs 80 D7
Luib Highld 247 J3
Luing Ag & B 215 L2
Lulham Herefs 80 A7

Lullington Derbys 99 H1
Lullington E Susx 23 J6
Lullington Somset 45 M8
Lulsgate Bottom N Som 45 G6
Lulsley Worcs 81 G4
Lulworth Camp Dorset 16 E6
Lumb Calder 140 F3
Lumb Lancs 140 C3
Lumbutts Calder 140 E3
Lumby N York 142 D2
Lumphanan Abers 244 D3
Lumphinnans Fife 222 B8
Lumsden Abers 255 K7
Lunan Angus 235 H5
Lunanhead Angus 234 D5
Luncarty P & K 221 K1
Lund E R Yk 152 E6
Lund N York 143 G1
Lundie Angus 233 L8
Lundin Links Fife 223 G6
Lundin Mill Fife 223 G6
Lundy Devon 26 B9
Lunga Ag & B 215 K3
Lunna Shet 281 e4
Lunsford Kent 52 F7
Lunsford's Cross E Susx 24 C5
Lunt Sefton 138 D6
Luntley Herefs 79 M4
Luppitt Devon 14 E1
Lupridge Devon 7 L4
Lupset Wakefd 141 M4
Lupton W & F 157 J6
Lurgashall W Susx 36 D5
Lurley Devon 29 G7
Lusby Lincs 136 F6
Luscombe Devon 8 B3
Luskentyre W Isls 282 e6
Luson Devon 7 H5
Luss Ag & B 218 E8
Lussagiven Ag & B 215 J7
Lusta Highld 258 D5
Lustleigh Devon 13 H6
Luston Herefs 80 B3
Luthermuir Abers 235 G2
Luthrie Fife 222 E3
Lutley Dudley 97 L6
Luton Devon 13 L8
Luton Devon 14 C2
Luton Luton 68 E3
Luton Medway 53 G5
Luton Airport Luton 68 E3
Lutterworth Leics 100 C6
Lutton Devon 7 H3
Lutton Devon 7 K3
Lutton Lincs 119 M6
Lutton N Nthn 102 C6
Luxborough Somset 29 H3
Luxulyan Cnwll 5 H3
Luxulyan Valley Cnwll 5 H3
Luzley Tamesd 140 E7
Lybster Highld 275 H1
Lydbury North Shrops 95 J6
Lydcott Devon 28 B4
Lydd Kent 25 K3
Lydd Airport Kent 25 K3
Lydden Kent 41 H6
Lydden Kent 41 K2
Lyddington Rutlnd 101 J4
Lydd-on-Sea Kent 25 K3
Lydeard St Lawrence Somset 29 L4
Lyde Green Hants 49 H7
Lyde Green S Glos 45 K3
Lydford Devon 12 C5
Lydford on Fosse Somset 31 J5
Lydgate Calder 140 D3
Lydgate Rochdl 140 E4
Lydham Shrops 95 H5
Lydiard Green Wilts 47 G2
Lydiard Millicent Wilts 47 G2
Lydiard Tregoze Swindn 47 G2
Lydiate Sefton 138 D7
Lydiate Ash Worcs 98 B8
Lydlinch Dorset 32 B8
Lydney Gloucs 63 J6
Lydstep Pembks 55 J7
Lye Dudley 97 L6
Lye Cross N Som 44 F6
Lye Green Bucks 68 B6
Lye Green E Susx 38 D6
Lye Green Warwks 82 G2
Lye Head Worcs 97 G8
Lye's Green Wilts 32 D2
Lyford Oxon 66 B8
Lymbridge Green Kent 40 F6
Lyme Regis Dorset 15 H4
Lyminge Kent 40 F7
Lymington Hants 18 E4
Lyminster W Susx 21 H6
Lymm Warrtn 130 D2

Lymm Services Warrtn ... 130 C3
Lympne Kent ... 40 F8
Lympsham Somset ... 44 C8
Lympstone Devon ... 14 A6
Lynbridge Devon ... 28 C1
Lynchat Highld ... 241 L3
Lynch Green Norfk ... 106 C2
Lyndhurst Hants ... 18 D2
Lyndon Rutlnd ... 101 K3
Lyndon Green Birm ... 98 F6
Lyne Border ... 199 L5
Lyne Surrey ... 50 C5
Lyneal Shrops ... 113 G5
Lyne Down Herefs ... 63 J1
Lyneham Oxon ... 65 K3
Lyneham Wilts ... 46 F3
Lyneholmford Cumb ... 178 C4
Lynemouth Nthumb ... 191 K7
Lyne of Skene Abers ... 245 G2
Lynesack Dur ... 168 E5
Lyness Ork ... 275 b6
Lyng Norfk ... 122 B7
Lyng Somset ... 30 E5
Lynmouth Devon ... 28 C1
Lynn Staffs ... 98 D3
Lynn Wrekin ... 114 B8
Lynsted Kent ... 40 B3
Lynstone Cnwll ... 11 H2
Lynton Devon ... 28 C1
Lynton Cross Devon ... 27 K2
Lyon's Gate Dorset ... 16 C2
Lyonshall Herefs ... 79 L4
Lytchett Matravers Dorset ... 17 J3
Lytchett Minster Dorset ... 17 J4
Lyth Highld ... 280 C4
Lytham Lancs ... 138 D2
Lytham St Annes Lancs ... 138 D2
Lythbank Shrops ... 95 L2
Lythe N York ... 171 K8
Lythmore Highld ... 279 J3

M

Maaruig W Isls ... 282 e5
Mabe Burnthouse Cnwll ... 3 J4
Mablethorpe Lincs ... 137 J3
Macclesfield Ches E ... 131 H5
Macduff Abers ... 268 C3
Macharioch Ag & B ... 192 E6
Machen Caerph ... 43 K4
Machrie N Ayrs ... 194 D4
Machrihanish Ag & B ... 192 D4
Machrins Ag & B ... 214 D5
Machroes Gwynd ... 108 E6
Machynlleth Powys ... 93 G3
Machynys Carmth ... 56 F5
Mackworth Derbys ... 116 A4
Macmerry E Loth ... 211 M4
Maddaford Devon ... 12 D4
Madderty P & K ... 221 G3
Maddington Wilts ... 33 J2
Maddiston Falk ... 210 B4
Madehurst W Susx ... 21 G5
Madeley Staffs ... 114 B3
Madeley Wrekin ... 96 F3
Madeley Heath Staffs ... 114 B2
Madeley Park Wood Staffs ... 114 B3
Madford Devon ... 29 L8
Madingley Cambs ... 87 H3
Madley Herefs ... 80 A7
Madresfield Worcs ... 81 J5
Madron Cnwll ... 2 C5
Maenaddwyn IoA ... 125 H3
Maenan Conwy ... 126 F6
Maenclochog Pembks ... 75 J6
Maendy V Glam ... 42 F6
Maenporth Cnwll ... 3 K5
Maentwrog Gwynd ... 110 C3
Maen-y-groes Cerdgn ... 76 C3
Maer Cnwll ... 11 H1
Maer Staffs ... 114 B4
Maerdy Carmth ... 59 J3
Maerdy Conwy ... 111 K3
Maerdy Rhondd ... 42 E2
Maesbrook Shrops ... 112 D7
Maesbury Shrops ... 112 D6
Maesbury Marsh Shrops ... 112 D6
Maes-glas Newpt ... 44 C2
Maesgwynne Carmth ... 55 L2
Maeshafn Denbgs ... 128 E7
Maesllyn Cerdgn ... 76 C6
Maesmynis Powys ... 78 D6
Maesmynis Powys ... 78 E5
Maesteg Brdgnd ... 42 C3
Maesybont Carmth ... 59 G5
Maesycwmmer Caerph ... 43 J3
Magdalen Laver Essex ... 70 D5
Maggieknockater Moray ... 254 F3

Maggots End Essex ... 70 C2
Magham Down E Susx ... 23 K5
Maghull Sefton ... 138 D7
Magna Park Leics ... 100 B6
Magor Mons ... 44 E2
Magor Services Mons ... 44 E1
Maidenbower W Susx ... 37 L4
Maiden Bradley Wilts ... 32 D3
Maidencombe Torbay ... 8 D1
Maidenhayne Devon ... 15 G3
Maiden Head N Som ... 45 H5
Maidenhead W & M ... 49 L3
Maiden Law Dur ... 168 F1
Maiden Newton Dorset ... 16 B3
Maidens S Ayrs ... 182 F1
Maiden's Green Br For ... 49 L4
Maidenwell Lincs ... 136 F4
Maiden Wells Pembks ... 55 G7
Maidford W Nthn ... 84 B5
Maids Moreton Bucks ... 84 D8
Maidstone Kent ... 39 J2
Maidstone Services Kent ... 39 K2
Maidwell W Nthn ... 101 G8
Mail Shet ... 281 e6
Maindee Newpt ... 44 C1
Mainland Ork ... 275 c4
Mainland Shet ... 281 d6
Mainsforth Dur ... 169 J4
Mains of Balhall Angus ... 234 D3
Mains of Balnakettle Abers ... 244 E8
Mains of Dalvey Highld ... 254 B5
Mains of Haulkerton Abers ... 235 H1
Mains of Lesmoir Abers ... 255 J6
Mains of Melgunds Angus ... 234 E4
Mainsriddle D & G ... 176 B7
Mainstone Shrops ... 95 G6
Maisemore Gloucs ... 64 A3
Major's Green Worcs ... 98 E7
Makeney Derbys ... 116 B3
Malborough Devon ... 7 K7
Malcoff Derbys ... 131 L3
Malden Rushett Gt Lon ... 50 F6
Maldon Essex ... 71 K5
Malham N York ... 148 F3
Maligar Highld ... 259 H4
Mallaig Highld ... 237 K1
Mallaigvaig Highld ... 237 K1
Malleny Mills C Edin ... 211 G6
Mallows Green Essex ... 70 C2
Malltraeth IoA ... 125 G6
Mallwyd Gwynd ... 93 J1
Malmesbury Wilts ... 46 D2
Malmsmead Devon ... 28 D1
Malpas Ches W ... 113 H2
Malpas Cnwll ... 4 D6
Malpas Newpt ... 44 C1
Malshanger Hants ... 48 E8
Malswick Gloucs ... 63 L2
Maltby Lincs ... 136 F3
Maltby Rothm ... 133 K1
Maltby S on T ... 170 B7
Maltby le Marsh Lincs ... 137 J3
Malting Green Essex ... 72 E3
Maltman's Hill Kent ... 40 A6
Malton N York ... 152 B2
Malvern Worcs ... 81 H6
Malvern Hills ... 81 H6
Malvern Link Worcs ... 81 H5
Malvern Wells Worcs ... 81 H6
Mamble Worcs ... 80 F1
Mamhilad Mons ... 62 C6
Manaccan Cnwll ... 3 J6
Manafon Powys ... 94 D3
Mànais W Isls ... 282 e6
Manaton Devon ... 13 H6
Manby Lincs ... 137 G2
Mancetter Warwks ... 99 J4
Manchester Manch ... 140 C8
Manchester Airport Manch ... 130 F3
Mancot Flints ... 129 H6
Mandally Highld ... 240 A3
Manea Cambs ... 103 K5
Maney Birm ... 98 E4
Manfield N York ... 169 G8
Mangersta W Isls ... 282 d3
Mangerton Dorset ... 15 L3
Mangotsfield S Glos ... 45 K4
Mangrove Green Herts ... 68 C2
Mangurstadh W Isls ... 282 d3
Manhay Cnwll ... 3 H5
Manish W Isls ... 282 e6
Mankinholes Calder ... 140 E4
Manley Ches W ... 129 L5
Manmoel Caerph ... 61 J6
Mannal Ag & B ... 224 C7
Manningford Bohune Wilts ... 47 H7
Manningford Bruce Wilts ... 47 H7
Manningham C Brad ... 141 J1
Mannings Heath W Susx ... 37 K5
Mannington Dorset ... 17 L2

Manningtree Essex ... 73 G1
Mannofield C Aber ... 245 K3
Manorbier Pembks ... 55 H7
Manorbier Newton Pembks ... 55 H6
Manordeilo Carmth ... 59 J4
Manorhill Border ... 201 K6
Manorowen Pembks ... 74 F5
Manor Park Gt Lon ... 51 L2
Mansell Gamage Herefs ... 79 M6
Mansell Lacy Herefs ... 80 A6
Mansergh W & F ... 157 K6
Mansfield E Ayrs ... 197 J8
Mansfield Notts ... 133 K7
Mansfield Woodhouse Notts ... 133 K7
Mansriggs W & F ... 156 D6
Manston Dorset ... 32 D7
Manston Kent ... 41 K2
Manston Leeds ... 142 B1
Manswood Dorset ... 17 J1
Manthorpe Lincs ... 118 B4
Manthorpe Lincs ... 118 E8
Manton N Linc ... 144 A7
Manton Notts ... 134 C4
Manton Rutlnd ... 101 J3
Manton Wilts ... 47 H5
Manuden Essex ... 70 C2
Manwood Green Essex ... 70 E4
Maperton Somset ... 31 L5
Maplebeck Notts ... 134 E7
Maple Cross Herts ... 68 C8
Mapledurham Oxon ... 49 G4
Mapledurwell Hants ... 49 G8
Maplehurst W Susx ... 37 J6
Maplescombe Kent ... 52 C6
Mapleton Derbys ... 115 K2
Mapleton Kent ... 38 C3
Mapperley Derbys ... 116 D3
Mapperley Park C Nott ... 117 G3
Mapperton Dorset ... 15 L3
Mappleborough Green Warwks ... 82 C2
Mappleton E R Yk ... 153 K7
Mapplewell Barns ... 141 M5
Mappowder Dorset ... 16 E2
Màraig W Isls ... 282 e5
Marazanvose Cnwll ... 4 C5
Marazion Cnwll ... 2 E5
Marbhig W Isls ... 282 g4
Marbury Ches E ... 113 J2
March Cambs ... 103 J4
March S Lans ... 186 E3
Marcham Oxon ... 66 C7
Marchamley Shrops ... 113 K5
Marchamley Wood Shrops ... 113 K5
Marchington Staffs ... 115 J5
Marchington Woodlands Staffs ... 115 J6
Marchwiel Wrexhm ... 112 E2
Marchwood Hants ... 18 F2
Marcross V Glam ... 42 D7
Marden Herefs ... 80 C6
Marden Kent ... 39 J4
Marden Wilts ... 47 G7
Marden Ash Essex ... 70 E6
Marden Beech Kent ... 39 J4
Marden's Hill E Susx ... 38 D7
Marden Thorn Kent ... 39 J5
Mardlebury Herts ... 69 H3
Mardy Mons ... 62 D5
Marefield Leics ... 101 G2
Mareham le Fen Lincs ... 136 E7
Mareham on the Hill Lincs ... 136 E6
Marehay Derbys ... 116 C2
Marehill W Susx ... 21 H3
Maresfield E Susx ... 23 G2
Marfleet C KuH ... 144 E2
Marford Wrexhm ... 129 H8
Margam Neath ... 57 L7
Margaret Marsh Dorset ... 32 D7
Margaret Roding Essex ... 70 F5
Margaretting Essex ... 71 G6
Margaretting Tye Essex ... 71 G7
Margate Kent ... 41 K1
Margnaheglish N Ayrs ... 195 G4
Margrie D & G ... 174 F5
Margrove Park R & Cl ... 170 F7
Marham Norfk ... 104 E2
Marhamchurch Cnwll ... 11 J2
Marham Park Suffk ... 89 G2
Marholm C Pete ... 102 C3
Marian-glas IoA ... 125 J3
Mariansleigh Devon ... 28 C6
Marine Town Kent ... 53 K4
Marishader Highld ... 259 H4
Maristow Devon ... 6 F2
Marjoriebanks D & G ... 176 E2
Mark Somset ... 30 F1
Markbeech Kent ... 38 D5
Markby Lincs ... 137 J4
Mark Causeway Somset ... 30 E2

Mark Cross E Susx ... 38 F7
Markeaton C Derb ... 116 B4
Market Bosworth Leics ... 99 L3
Market Deeping Lincs ... 102 C2
Market Drayton Shrops ... 113 L5
Market Harborough Leics ... 100 F6
Market Lavington Wilts ... 46 E8
Market Overton Rutlnd ... 118 A8
Market Rasen Lincs ... 136 B2
Market Stainton Lincs ... 136 D4
Market Warsop Notts ... 133 L6
Market Weighton E R Yk ... 152 D7
Market Weston Suffk ... 105 K7
Markfield Leics ... 100 B2
Markham Caerph ... 61 J6
Markham Moor Notts ... 134 E5
Markinch Fife ... 222 E6
Markington N York ... 150 C3
Markle E Loth ... 212 C3
Marksbury BaNES ... 45 K6
Mark's Corner IoW ... 19 H5
Marks Tey Essex ... 72 C2
Markwell Cnwll ... 6 D3
Markyate Herts ... 68 D4
Marlborough Wilts ... 47 J5
Marlbrook Herefs ... 80 C4
Marlbrook Worcs ... 98 B8
Marlcliff Warwks ... 82 C5
Marldon Devon ... 8 C2
Marle Green E Susx ... 23 K4
Marlesford Suffk ... 91 H3
Marley Kent ... 41 G5
Marley Kent ... 41 K4
Marley Green Ches E ... 113 J2
Marley Hill Gatesd ... 180 F7
Marlingford Norfk ... 106 C2
Marloes Pembks ... 54 C5
Marlow Bucks ... 49 K2
Marlow Herefs ... 95 K8
Marlow Bottom Bucks ... 49 K1
Marlpit Hill Kent ... 38 C4
Marlpits E Susx ... 24 C4
Marlpits E Susx ... 38 C7
Marlpool Derbys ... 116 D3
Marnhull Dorset ... 32 C7
Marple Stockp ... 131 J2
Marple Bridge Stockp ... 131 J2
Marr Donc ... 142 E6
Marrick N York ... 159 K3
Marros Carmth ... 55 L5
Marsden Kirk ... 141 G5
Marsden S Tyne ... 181 K6
Marsden Height Lancs ... 148 F8
Marsett N York ... 158 F5
Marsh Bucks ... 67 K5
Marsh C Brad ... 149 J8
Marsh Devon ... 30 C8
Marshall's Heath Herts ... 68 F4
Marshalswick Herts ... 68 F5
Marsham Norfk ... 122 D6
Marsh Baldon Oxon ... 66 E7
Marsh Benham W Berk ... 48 B5
Marshborough Kent ... 41 J4
Marshbrook Shrops ... 95 K5
Marshchapel Lincs ... 145 K7
Marsh Farm Luton ... 68 D2
Marshfield Newpt ... 43 L5
Marshfield S Glos ... 45 M4
Marshgate Cnwll ... 11 G4
Marsh Gibbon Bucks ... 66 F3
Marsh Green Devon ... 14 B4
Marsh Green Kent ... 38 C4
Marsh Green Wrekin ... 113 K8
Marshland St James Norfk ... 103 L2
Marsh Lane Derbys ... 133 H4
Marsh Lane Gloucs ... 63 H5
Marshside Sefton ... 138 D4
Marsh Street Somset ... 29 H2
Marshwood Dorset ... 15 J3
Marske N York ... 159 K3
Marske-by-the-Sea R & Cl ... 170 E6
Marsland Green Wigan ... 139 K7
Marston Ches W ... 130 D5
Marston Herefs ... 79 L4
Marston Lincs ... 118 A3
Marston Oxon ... 66 D5
Marston Staffs ... 97 J1
Marston Staffs ... 114 E6
Marston Warwks ... 99 G4
Marston Wilts ... 46 D7
Marston Green Solhll ... 98 F6
Marston Jabbet Warwks ... 99 K5
Marston Magna Somset ... 31 K6
Marston Meysey Wilts ... 65 H7
Marston Montgomery Derbys ... 115 J4
Marston Moretaine C Beds ... 85 K7
Marston on Dove Derbys ... 115 L5
Marston St Lawrence W Nthn ... 84 A7
Marston Stannett Herefs ... 80 D4
Marston Trussell W Nthn ... 100 F6

Marstow Herefs 63 H3
Marsworth Bucks 68 A4
Marten Wilts 47 L7
Marthall Ches E 130 F4
Martham Norfk 123 J7
Martin Hants 33 J7
Martin Kent 41 K6
Martin Lincs 136 B7
Martin Lincs 136 D6
Martindale W & F 166 B6
Martin Dales Lincs 136 C7
Martin Drove End Hants 33 H6
Martinhoe Devon 28 B1
Martin Hussingtree Worcs 81 K3
Martinscroft Warrtn 130 C2
Martinstown Dorset 16 C5
Martlesham Suffk 90 F6
Martlesham Heath Suffk 90 F6
Martletwy Pembks 55 I15
Martley Worcs 81 H1
Martock Somset 31 G7
Marton Ches E 131 G6
Marton Ches W 130 C6
Marton E R Yk 153 J7
Marton E R Yk 153 K2
Marton Lincs 135 G3
Marton Middsb 170 C7
Marton N York 162 C6
Marton Shrops 95 G3
Marton W & F 156 C7
Marton Warwks 83 J2
Marton-cum-Grafton N York 150 F3
Marton-le-Moor N York 150 E2
Martyr's Green Surrey 50 E7
Martyr Worthy Hants 35 G4
Marvig W Isls 282 g4
Marwick Ork 275 b3
Marwood Devon 27 K3
Marybank Highld 250 E1
Maryburgh Highld 263 F9
Marygold Border 213 H7
Maryhill C Glas 208 F5
Marykirk Abers 235 H2
Maryland Mons 63 G6
Marylebone Gt Lon 51 H3
Marylebone Wigan 139 H6
Marypark Moray 254 D4
Maryport Cumb 164 D3
Maryport D & G 172 E7
Marystow Devon 12 B6
Mary Tavy Devon 12 C6
Maryton Angus 234 B5
Maryton Angus 235 H4
Marywell Abers 244 D4
Marywell Abers 245 L4
Marywell Angus 235 G6
Masham N York 160 B6
Mashbury Essex 71 G5
Masongill N York 157 L7
Mastin Moor Derbys 133 J4
Matching Essex 70 D5
Matching Green Essex 70 D5
Matching Tye Essex 70 D5
Matfen Nthumb 180 C4
Matfield Kent 39 G5
Mathern Mons 45 G1
Mathon Herefs 81 G6
Mathry Pembks 74 E6
Matlask Norfk 122 C4
Matlock Derbys 132 F7
Matlock Bank Derbys 132 F7
Matlock Bath Derbys 132 F8
Matlock Dale Derbys 132 F7
Matson Gloucs 64 B4
Matterdale End W & F 165 L6
Mattersey Notts 134 D2
Mattersey Thorpe Notts 134 D2
Mattingley Hants 49 H7
Mattishall Norfk 105 L1
Mattishall Burgh Norfk 105 L1
Mauchline E Ayrs 196 F5
Maud Abers 269 C6
Maufant Jersey 9 e2
Maugersbury Gloucs 65 J2
Maughold IoM 154 g4
Mauld Highld 250 C4
Maulden C Beds 85 L7
Maulds Meaburn W & F 166 E7
Maunby N York 160 E5
Maund Bryan Herefs 80 D5
Maundown Somset 29 J5
Mautby Norfk 107 K1
Mavesyn Ridware Staffs 115 H8
Mavis Enderby Lincs 137 G6
Mawbray Cumb 164 E1
Mawdesley Lancs 139 G5
Mawdlam Brdgnd 42 B5
Mawgan Cnwll 3 H6
Mawgan Porth Cnwll 4 D2
Maw Green Ches E 130 D8

Mawla Cnwll 4 A5
Mawnan Cnwll 3 K5
Mawnan Smith Cnwll 3 K5
Mawsley W Nthn 101 H8
Mawthorpe Lincs 137 J5
Maxey C Pete 102 C2
Maxstoke Warwks 99 G6
Maxted Street Kent 40 F6
Maxton Border 201 J7
Maxton Kent 41 J7
Maxwelltown D & G 176 C4
Maxworthy Cnwll 11 J4
Mayals Swans 57 H6
May Bank Staffs 114 D2
Maybole S Ayrs 183 H1
Maybury Surrey 50 C7
Mayes Green Surrey 37 H3
Mayfield E Susx 23 K2
Mayfield Mdloth 211 K6
Mayfield Staffs 115 J2
Mayford Surrey 50 C7
May Hill Gloucs 63 L1
Mayland Essex 72 D6
Maylandsea Essex 72 C6
Maynard's Green E Susx 23 K3
Maypole Birm 98 D7
Maypole Kent 41 G2
Maypole Mons 62 F4
Maypole Green Norfk 107 J4
Maypole Green Suffk 89 J3
Maypole Green Suffk 91 G2
May's Green Oxon 49 H3
May's Green Surrey 50 E7
Mead Devon 26 C7
Meadgate BaNES 45 K7
Meadle Bucks 67 K6
Meadowfield Dur 169 H3
Meadowtown Shrops 95 H3
Meadwell Devon 12 A6
Meaford Staffs 114 D4
Mealabost W Isls 282 g3
Meal Bank W & F 157 H4
Mealrigg Cumb 164 F2
Mealsgate Cumb 165 H2
Meanwood Leeds 150 C8
Mearbeck N York 148 E4
Meare Somset 31 G2
Meare Green Somset 30 D6
Meare Green Somset 30 E5
Mearns E Rens 208 F7
Mears Ashby N Nthn 85 G2
Measham Leics 99 J1
Meath Green Surrey 37 L2
Meathop W & F 156 F6
Meaux E R Yk 153 H7
Meavaig W Isls 282 e3
Meavy Devon 7 G2
Medbourne Leics 101 H5
Medburn Nthumb 180 D5
Meddon Devon 26 D7
Meden Vale Notts 134 B5
Medlam Lincs 136 F8
Medlar Lancs 147 H8
Medmenham Bucks 49 K2
Medomsley Dur 180 D7
Medstead Hants 35 K3
Medway Services Medway 53 H6
Meerbrook Staffs 131 K7
Meer Common Herefs 79 L5
Meesden Herts 70 B1
Meeson Wrekin 113 L7
Meeth Devon 12 D1
Meeting Green Suffk 88 C4
Meeting House Hill Norfk 122 F6
Meidrim Carmth 58 B5
Meifod Powys 94 E1
Meigle P & K 233 L6
Meikle Carco D & G 186 A3
Meikle Earnock S Lans 209 J8
Meikle Ferry Highld 263 K2
Meikle Kilmory Ag & B 207 G6
Meikle Obney P & K 232 F7
Meikleour P & K 233 J7
Meikle Wartle Abers 256 C5
Meinciau Carmth 56 E3
Meir C Stke 114 E3
Meir Heath Staffs 114 E3
Melbost W Isls 282 g3
Melbourn Cambs 87 H6
Melbourne Derbys 116 C6
Melbourne E R Yk 152 A7
Melbourne Essex 71 G5
Melbur Cnwll 4 F4
Melbury Devon 26 F7
Melbury Abbas Dorset 32 E6
Melbury Bubb Dorset 16 B2
Melbury Osmond Dorset 16 A1
Melbury Sampford Dorset 16 A2
Melchbourne Bed 85 K2
Melcombe Bingham Dorset 16 E2

Meldon Devon 12 D4
Meldon Nthumb 180 D2
Meldon Park Nthumb 180 D2
Meldreth Cambs 87 H6
Meldrum Stirlg 220 C7
Melfort Ag & B 216 C4
Meliden Denbgs 128 C3
Melinau Pembks 55 K4
Melin-byrhedyn Powys 93 H4
Melincourt Neath 60 B6
Melin-y-coed Conwy 127 G7
Melin-y-ddol Powys 94 D2
Melin-y-wig Denbgs 111 K2
Melkinthorpe W & F 166 D5
Melkridge Nthumb 179 G6
Melksham Wilts 46 C6
Mellangoose Cnwll 3 H5
Mell Green W Berk 48 C3
Mellguards W & F 166 B2
Melling Lancs 147 M2
Melling Sefton 138 F7
Melling Mount Sefton 138 E7
Mellis Suffk 106 B8
Mellon Charles Highld 260 D2
Mellon Udrigle Highld 260 E1
Mellor Lancs 139 K2
Mellor Stockp 131 K2
Mellor Brook Lancs 139 J2
Mells Somset 32 B1
Mells Suffk 107 H8
Melmerby N York 159 K5
Melmerby N York 160 E7
Melmerby W & F 166 E3
Melness Highld 277 K4
Melon Green Suffk 89 G4
Melplash Dorset 15 L3
Melrose Border 201 H6
Melsetter Ork 275 b6
Melsonby N York 160 B1
Meltham Kirk 141 H5
Meltham Mills Kirk 141 H5
Melton E R Yk 152 H7
Melton Suffk 91 G5
Meltonby E R Yk 152 B5
Melton Constable Norfk 122 A5
Melton Mowbray Leics 117 K7
Melton Ross N Linc 144 D5
Melvaig Highld 260 B4
Melverley Shrops 112 E8
Melverley Green Shrops 112 E7
Melvich Highld 278 E3
Membury Devon 15 G2
Memsie Abers 269 H4
Memus Angus 234 C4
Menabilly Cnwll 5 J4
Menagissey Cnwll 4 B5
Menai Bridge IoA 125 K5
Mendham Suffk 106 F6
Mendip Hills 45 G8
Mendlesham Suffk 90 D2
Mendlesham Green Suffk 90 C3
Menheniot Cnwll 6 B2
Menithwood Worcs 81 G2
Menna Cnwll 4 E4
Mennock D & G 185 K2
Menston C Brad 149 L7
Menstrie Clacks 220 E7
Menthorpe N York 143 H1
Mentmore Bucks 67 M3
Meoble Highld 238 C6
Meole Brace Shrops 96 R1
Meonstoke Hants 35 J7
Meon Vale Warwks 82 E6
Meopham Kent 52 D5
Meopham Green Kent 52 D5
Meopham Station Kent 52 D5
Mepal Cambs 103 J7
Meppershall C Beds 86 C2
Merbach Herefs 79 K6
Mere Ches E 130 E3
Mere Wilts 32 D4
Mere Brow Lancs 138 E4
Mereclough Lancs 140 C2
Mere Green Birm 98 E4
Mere Green Worcs 81 L3
Mere Heath Ches W 130 C5
Meresborough Medway 53 H6
Mereworth Kent 39 G3
Meriden Solhll 99 G7
Merkadale Highld 246 E2
Merley BCP 17 K3
Merlin's Bridge Pembks 54 F4
Merrington Shrops 113 G7
Merrion Pembks 54 F7
Merriott Somset 31 G8
Merrivale Devon 12 D7
Merrow Surrey 36 F1
Merry Field Hill Dorset 17 K2
Merry Hill Herts 68 E8

Merryhill Wolves 97 K4
Merry Lees Leics 100 A2
Merrymeet Cnwll 6 B2
Mersea Island Essex 72 F4
Mersey Gateway Bridge
Halton 129 M3
Mersham Kent 40 D7
Merstham Surrey 51 H8
Merston W Susx 20 E6
Merstone IoW 19 J6
Merther Cnwll 4 D6
Merthyr Carmth 58 C5
Merthyr Cynog Powys 78 D7
Merthyr Dyfan V Glam 43 H7
Merthyr Mawr Brdgnd 42 D6
Merthyr Tydfil Myr Td 61 G6
Merthyr Vale Myr Td 61 G7
Merton Devon 27 J8
Merton Gt Lon 51 H5
Merton Norfk 105 H4
Merton Oxon 66 E3
Meshaw Devon 28 D7
Messing Essex 72 C3
Messingham N Linc 143 M6
Metal Bridge Dur 169 J4
Metfield Suffk 106 F7
Metherell Cnwll 6 E1
Metheringham Lincs 135 L7
Methil Fife 222 F7
Methilhill Fife 222 F7
Methley Leeds 142 B2
Methley Junction Leeds 142 B3
Methlick Abers 256 F4
Methven P & K 221 J2
Methwold Norfk 104 E4
Methwold Hythe Norfk 104 E4
Mettingham Suffk 107 H5
Metton Norfk 122 D4
Mevagissey Cnwll 5 G6
Mexborough Donc 142 D7
Mey Highld 280 C2
Meysey Hampton Gloucs 65 G7
Miabhaig W Isls 282 e3
Michaelchurch Herefs 63 G3
Michaelchurch Escley Herefs 79 K8
Michaelchurch-on-Arrow
Powys 79 J5
Michaelstone-y-Fedw Newpt 43 K5
Michaelston-le-Pit V Glam 43 J7
Michaelstow Cnwll 10 F6
Michaelwood Services Gloucs 63 L8
Michelcombe Devon 7 K1
Micheldever Hants 35 G3
Micheldever Station Hants 35 G2
Michelmersh Hants 34 D5
Mickfield Suffk 90 D3
Micklebring Donc 133 K1
Mickleby N York 171 J8
Micklefield Leeds 142 C1
Micklefield Green Herts 68 D5
Mickleham Surrey 50 F8
Mickleover C Derb 116 A5
Micklethwaite C Brad 149 K7
Micklethwaite Cumb 165 J1
Mickleton Dur 168 B6
Mickleton Gloucs 82 E6
Mickletown Leeds 142 B2
Mickle Trafford Ches W 129 K5
Mickley Derbys 132 F4
Mickley N York 160 C7
Mickley Green Suffk 89 G4
Mickley Square Nthumb 180 C6
Mid Ardlaw Abers 269 H3
Midbea Ork 275 e2
Mid Beltie Abers 244 E3
Mid Bockhampton BCP 18 B4
Mid Calder W Loth 210 E5
Mid Clyth Highld 280 C8
Mid Culbeuchly Abers 268 B4
Middle Assendon Oxon 49 H2
Middle Aston Oxon 66 C2
Middle Barton Oxon 66 B2
Middlebie D & G 177 H4
Middlebridge P & K 232 C2
Middle Chinnock Somset 31 G8
Middle Claydon Bucks 67 H2
Middlecliffe Barns 142 C6
Middlecott Devon 13 G5
Middlecroft Derbys 133 H5
Middle Duntisbourne Gloucs 64 E6
Middleham N York 159 L5
Middle Handley Derbys 133 H4
Middle Harling Norfk 105 K6
Middlehill Cnwll 6 B1
Middlehill Wilts 46 B5
Middlehope Shrops 96 B5
Middle Kames Ag & B 206 E1
Middle Littleton Worcs 82 C6
Middle Madeley Staffs 114 B3
Middle Maes-coed Herefs 79 L8

Middlemarsh Dorset......16 C1
Middle Mayfield Staffs......115 J3
Middle Mill Pembks......74 C7
Middlemoor Devon......12 C8
Middle Quarter Kent......40 A7
Middle Rasen Lincs......136 A2
Middle Rocombe Devon......8 D1
Middle Salter Lancs......147 M3
Middlesbrough Middsb......170 C6
Middlesceugh W & F......165 L2
Middleshaw W & F......157 J5
Middlesmoor N York......159 K7
Middle Stoford Somset......30 B6
Middle Stoke Medway......53 H4
Middlestone Dur......169 H4
Middlestone Moor Dur......169 H4
Middle Stoughton Somset......30 F1
Middlestown Wakefd......141 L4
Middle Street Gloucs......63 M6
Middle Taphouse Cnwll......5 K2
Middlethird Border......201 L4
Middleton Ag & B......224 B6
Middleton Derbys......132 D7
Middleton Derbys......132 E8
Middleton Essex......89 H7
Middleton Hants......34 F2
Middleton Herefs......80 D1
Middleton Lancs......147 H4
Middleton Leeds......141 M2
Middleton N Nthn......101 J5
Middleton N York......149 L6
Middleton N York......162 D5
Middleton Norfk......120 E8
Middleton Nthumb......180 C2
Middleton Nthumb......203 H6
Middleton P & K......221 L6
Middleton Rochdl......140 C6
Middleton Shrops......96 C7
Middleton Shrops......112 D5
Middleton Suffk......91 K2
Middleton Swans......56 D7
Middleton W & F......157 K5
Middleton Warwks......98 F4
Middleton Cheney W Nthn......83 L7
Middleton Green Staffs......114 F4
Middleton Hall Nthumb......202 F8
Middleton-in-Teesdale Dur......168 B5
Middleton Moor Suffk......91 J2
Middleton One Row Darltn......169 K8
Middleton-on-Leven N York......161 G1
Middleton-on-Sea W Susx......20 F6
Middleton on the Hill Herefs......80 C2
Middleton on the Wolds
    E R Yk......152 E6
Middleton Park C Aber......245 K1
Middleton Priors Shrops......96 E5
Middleton Quernhow N York......160 E7
Middleton St George Darltn......169 K8
Middleton Scriven Shrops......96 F6
Middleton Stoney Oxon......66 D2
Middleton Tyas N York......160 B2
Middletown Cumb......155 H1
Middle Town IoS......10 b3
Middletown N Som......44 F4
Middletown Powys......95 H1
Middle Tysoe Warwks......83 H6
Middle Wallop Hants......34 C3
Middlewich Ches E......130 D6
Middle Winterslow Wilts......34 B4
Middlewood Cnwll......11 K7
Middlewood Herefs......79 K6
Middle Woodford Wilts......33 K4
Middlewood Green Suffk......90 C3
Middle Yard Gloucs......64 B6
Middlezoy Somset......30 E4
Middridge Dur......169 H5
Midford BaNES......45 M6
Midge Hall Lancs......139 G3
Midgeholme Cumb......178 E7
Midgham W Berk......48 E5
Midgley Calder......140 F3
Midgley Wakefd......141 L5
Mid Holmwood Surrey......37 J2
Midhopestones Sheff......141 K7
Midhurst W Susx......36 C6
Mid Lavant W Susx......20 D5
Midlem Border......201 H7
Mid Mains Highld......250 D4
Midney Somset......31 H5
Midpark Ag & B......207 G7
Midsomer Norton BaNES......45 K8
Midtown Highld......277 K4
Midville Lincs......137 G8
Midway Ches E......131 H3
Mid Yell Shet......281 e3
Migdale Highld......263 H2
Migvie Abers......244 A2
Milborne Port Somset......31 L7
Milborne St Andrew Dorset......16 F3
Milborne Wick Somset......31 L6

Milbourne Nthumb......180 D4
Milbourne Wilts......46 D2
Milburn W & F......166 F5
Milbury Heath S Glos......45 K1
Milby N York......150 F2
Milcombe Oxon......83 K8
Milden Suffk......89 J6
Mildenhall Suffk......104 E8
Mildenhall Wilts......47 J5
Milebrook Powys......79 K1
Milebush Kent......39 J4
Mile Elm Wilts......46 E5
Mile End Gloucs......63 H5
Mile End Suffk......107 G5
Mileham Norfk......121 K7
Mile Oak Br & H......22 C5
Mile Oak Kent......39 H4
Mile Oak Staffs......98 F3
Miles Green Staffs......114 C2
Miles Hope Herefs......80 D2
Milesmark Fife......210 E1
Miles Platting Manch......140 C7
Mile Town Kent......53 K4
Milfield Nthumb......202 E6
Milford Derbys......116 B3
Milford Devon......26 D6
Milford Powys......94 D5
Milford Staffs......114 F7
Milford Surrey......36 E2
Milford Haven Pembks......54 E5
Milford on Sea Hants......18 D5
Milkwall Gloucs......63 H5
Millais Jersey......9 a1
Milland W Susx......36 B5
Milland Marsh W Susx......36 C5
Mill Bank Calder......140 F3
Millbeck Cumb......165 H5
Millbreck Abers......257 J3
Millbridge Surrey......36 C2
Millbrook C Beds......85 K7
Millbrook C Sotn......34 E8
Millbrook Cnwll......6 E4
Millbrook Jersey......9 c3
Millbrook Tamesd......140 E7
Mill Brow Stockp......131 J2
Millbuie Abers......245 H2
Millbuie Highld......250 F1
Millcombe Devon......8 B5
Mill Common Norfk......107 G3
Mill Common Suffk......107 H7
Millcorner E Susx......24 E3
Millcraig Highld......263 H5
Mill Cross Devon......7 L3
Milldale Staffs......115 J1
Mill End Bucks......49 J2
Millend Gloucs......63 L7
Mill End Herts......87 G8
Millerhill Mdloth......211 K5
Miller's Dale Derbys......132 C5
Millers Green Derbys......115 M1
Miller's Green Essex......70 E5
Millerston C Glas......209 H5
Millgate Lancs......140 D4
Mill Green Cambs......88 C6
Mill Green Essex......70 F6
Mill Green Herts......69 G5
Mill Green Lincs......119 H6
Mill Green Norfk......106 C6
Millgreen Shrops......113 L6
Mill Green Staffs......98 D3
Mill Green Staffs......115 H7
Mill Green Suffk......89 J6
Mill Green Suffk......89 K4
Mill Green Suffk......90 D3
Mill Green Suffk......91 H3
Millhalf Herefs......79 K6
Millhayes Devon......14 F2
Millhead Lancs......147 K2
Millheugh S Lans......198 B3
Mill Hill E Susx......23 L6
Mill Hill Gt Lon......69 G8
Millhouse Ag & B......206 F5
Millhouse W & F......165 K3
Millhousebridge D & G......176 F2
Millhouse Green Barns......141 K7
Millhouses Barns......142 C6
Millhouses Sheff......133 G3
Milliken Park Rens......208 C6
Millin Cross Pembks......55 G4
Millington E R Yk......152 C5
Mill Lane Hants......36 A1
Millmeece Staffs......114 C6
Millness W & F......157 H6
Mill of Drummond P & K......220 E4
Mill of Haldane W Duns......208 C3
Millom Cumb......155 M6
Millook Cnwll......11 H3
Millpool Cnwll......2 F5
Millpool Cnwll......11 G8
Millport N Ayrs......207 K8

Mill Side W & F......157 G6
Mill Street Kent......39 H2
Mill Street Norfk......122 B7
Mill Street Suffk......90 C1
Millthorpe Derbys......132 F4
Millthrop W & F......157 L4
Milltimber C Aber......245 J3
Milltown Abers......243 J2
Milltown Abers......255 J8
Milltown Cnwll......5 J3
Milltown D & G......177 K4
Milltown Derbys......133 G7
Milltown Devon......27 K3
Milltown Highld......248 A3
Milltown of Auchindoun
    Moray......255 G4
Milltown of Campfield Abers......244 E3
Milltown of Edinvillie Moray......254 F4
Milltown of Rothiemay Moray......267 L6
Milnathort P & K......221 K6
Milngavie E Duns......208 F4
Milnrow Rochdl......140 D5
Milnthorpe W & F......157 H6
Milnthorpe Wakefd......142 A4
Milovaig Highld......258 B6
Milson Shrops......80 E1
Milstead Kent......40 A3
Milston Wilts......33 L2
Milthorpe Lincs......118 F5
Milthorpe W Nthn......84 B6
Milton C Stke......114 E2
Milton Cambs......87 K3
Milton Cumb......178 D6
Milton D & G......172 F4
Milton D & G......175 L1
Milton Derbys......116 A6
Milton Highld......250 E5
Milton Highld......251 G2
Milton Highld......263 K5
Milton Highld......280 D6
Milton Inver......208 B5
Milton Kent......52 E4
Milton Moray......254 D7
Milton Moray......267 K4
Milton N Som......44 D6
Milton Newpt......44 D1
Milton Notts......134 E5
Milton Oxon......66 C8
Milton Oxon......83 K8
Milton P & K......233 G3
Milton Pembks......55 H6
Milton Somset......31 G6
Milton Stirlg......219 H7
Milton W Duns......208 D4
Milton Abbas Dorset......16 F2
Milton Abbot Devon......12 A6
Milton Bridge Mdloth......211 H6
Milton Bryan C Beds......68 B1
Milton Clevedon Somset......31 L3
Milton Combe Devon......6 F2
Milton Common Oxon......67 G6
Milton Damerel Devon......27 G8
Milton End Gloucs......63 L5
Milton End Gloucs......65 H7
Milton Ernest Bed......85 K4
Milton Green Ches W......129 K7
Milton Heights Oxon......48 C1
Milton Hill Oxon......48 C1
Milton Keynes M Keyn......85 G7
Milton Lilbourne Wilts......47 J7
Milton Malsor W Nthn......84 E4
Milton Morenish P & K......231 H8
Milton of Auchinhove Abers......244 C3
Milton of Balgonie Fife......222 E7
Milton of Buchanan Stirlg......208 D1
Milton of Campsie E Duns......209 H4
Milton of Finavon Angus......234 D4
Milton of Leys Highld......251 J3
Milton of Murtle C Aber......245 J3
Milton on Stour Dorset......32 D5
Milton Regis Kent......40 A2
Milton Street E Susx......23 J6
Milton-under-Wychwood
    Oxon......65 K3
Milverton Somset......29 L5
Milverton Warwks......83 H2
Milwich Staffs......114 F5
Milwr Flints......128 E5
Minard Ag & B......216 F7
Minchington Dorset......33 G7
Minchinhampton Gloucs......64 C7
Mindenhurst Surrey......49 M7
Mindrum Nthumb......202 C6
Minehead Somset......29 H2
Minera Wrexhm......112 C1
Minety Wilts......46 F1
Minffordd Gwynd......109 L4
Mingarrypark Highld......237 K6
Miningsby Lincs......136 F6
Minions Cnwll......11 J8

Minishant S Ayrs......196 C8
Minllyn Gwynd......111 G8
Minnigaff D & G......173 K2
Minnonie Abers......268 D4
Minshull Vernon Ches E......130 D7
Minskip N York......150 E3
Minstead Hants......18 D2
Minsted W Susx......20 D3
Minster Kent......41 J2
Minsterley Shrops......95 J2
Minster Lovell Oxon......65 L5
Minster-on-Sea Kent......53 L4
Minsterworth Gloucs......64 A4
Minterne Magna Dorset......16 C2
Minterne Parva Dorset......16 C2
Minting Lincs......136 C5
Mintlaw Abers......269 J6
Minto Border......188 F2
Minton Shrops......95 K5
Minwear Pembks......55 H4
Minworth Birm......98 F5
Mirehouse Cumb......164 C7
Mireland Highld......280 D4
Mirfield Kirk......141 K4
Miserden Gloucs......64 D5
Miskin Rhondd......43 G3
Miskin Rhondd......43 G5
Misson Notts......134 D1
Misterton Leics......100 C6
Misterton Notts......134 F1
Misterton Somset......15 K1
Mistley Essex......73 G1
Mistley Heath Essex......73 H1
Mitcham Gt Lon......51 H5
Mitcheldean Gloucs......63 K3
Mitchell Cnwll......4 D4
Mitchellslacks D & G......186 E7
Mitchel Troy Mons......62 F5
Mitford Nthumb......180 E2
Mithian Cnwll......4 B5
Mitton Staffs......114 D8
Mixbury Oxon......84 B8
Mixenden Calder......141 G2
Moats Tye Suffk......90 B4
Mobberley Ches E......130 F4
Mobberley Staffs......115 G3
Moccas Herefs......79 L6
Mochdre Conwy......127 G4
Mochdre Powys......94 C5
Mochrum D & G......173 J5
Mockbeggar Hants......18 B2
Mockbeggar Kent......39 H4
Mockerkin Cumb......164 E5
Modbury Devon......7 J4
Moddershall Staffs......114 E4
Moelfre IoA......125 J2
Moelfre Powys......112 B6
Moel Tryfan Gwynd......125 J8
Moffat D & G......187 G5
Mogador Surrey......51 H8
Moggerhanger C Beds......86 C5
Moira Leics......116 A8
Molash Kent......40 D5
Mol-chlach Highld......246 F6
Mold Flints......128 F7
Moldgreen Kirk......141 J4
Molehill Green Essex......70 E2
Molehill Green Essex......71 H3
Molescroft E R Yk......152 F7
Molesden Nthumb......180 E2
Molesworth Cambs......102 B8
Moll Highld......247 J3
Molland Devon......28 E5
Mollington Ches W......129 J5
Mollington Oxon......83 K5
Mollinsburn N Lans......209 J5
Monachty Cerdgn......76 F3
Mondynes Abers......245 H7
Monewden Suffk......90 F3
Moneydie P & K......221 L3
Moneyrow Green W & M......49 L3
Moniaive D & G......185 J5
Monifieth Angus......223 J1
Monikie Angus......234 D7
Monimail Fife......222 E4
Monington Pembks......75 K3
Monk Bretton Barns......142 B6
Monken Hadley Gt Lon......69 H7
Monk Fryston N York......142 D2
Monkhide Herefs......80 E6
Monkhill Cumb......177 K7
Monkhopton Shrops......96 E5
Monkland Herefs......80 B4
Monkleigh Devon......27 H6
Monknash V Glam......42 D7
Monkokehampton Devon......12 E2
Monkseaton N Tyne......181 J4
Monks Eleigh Suffk......89 K5
Monk's Gate W Susx......37 K5
Monks Heath Ches E......131 G5

Monk Sherborne – Mylor Bridge 337

Monk Sherborne Hants 48 F7
Monks Horton Kent 40 E7
Monksilver Somset 29 K3
Monks Kirby Warwks 100 A6
Monk Soham Suffk 90 F2
Monkspath Solhll 98 E8
Monks Risborough Bucks 67 K6
Monksthorpe Lincs 137 H6
Monk Street Essex 70 F2
Monkswood Mons 62 D6
Monkton Devon 14 E2
Monkton Kent 41 J2
Monkton S Ayrs 196 D5
Monkton S Tyne 181 H6
Monkton V Glam 42 D7
Monkton Combe BaNES 45 M6
Monkton Deverill Wilts 32 E3
Monkton Farleigh Wilts 46 A6
Monkton Heathfield Somset 30 C5
Monkton Up Wimborne Dorset 33 H8
Monkton Wyld Dorset 13 H3
Monkwearmouth Sundld 181 K7
Monkwood Hants 35 K5
Monmore Green Wolves 97 L4
Monmouth Mons 63 G4
Monnington on Wye Herefs 79 L6
Monreith D & G 173 J6
Montacute Somset 31 H7
Montcliffe Bolton 139 K5
Montford Shrops 112 F8
Montford Bridge Shrops 113 G8
Montgarrie Abers 255 L8
Montgomery Powys 94 F4
Monton Salfd 140 A7
Montrose Angus 235 H4
Mont Saint Guern 9 i3
Monxton Hants 34 C2
Monyash Derbys 132 C6
Monymusk Abers 256 C8
Monzie P & K 220 F2
Moodiesburn N Lans 209 J5
Moonzie Fife 222 F4
Moor Allerton Leeds 150 D8
Moorbath Dorset 15 K4
Moorby Lincs 136 F6
Moorcot Herefs 79 L4
Moor Crichel Dorset 17 K1
Moordown BCP 17 L4
Moore Halton 130 B3
Moor End C Beds 68 B3
Moor End Calder 141 G2
Moor End Devon 12 F1
Moorend Gloucs 63 L6
Moor End Lancs 147 G6
Moor End N York 151 J8
Moorends Donc 143 H4
Moorgreen Hants 35 G7
Moor Green Herts 69 J2
Moorgreen Notts 116 E2
Moorhall Derbys 132 F5
Moorhampton Herefs 79 M6
Moorhead C Brad 149 L8
Moor Head Leeds 141 K2
Moorhouse Cumb 177 H8
Moorhouse Cumb 177 K7
Moorhouse Donc 142 D5
Moorhouse Notts 134 E6
Moorhouse Bank Surrey 51 L8
Moorland Somset 30 E4
Moorlinch Somset 30 F3
Moor Monkton N York 151 H4
Moor Row Cumb 164 D7
Moor Row Cumb 165 H1
Moorsholm R & Cl 170 F7
Moorside Dorset 32 D7
Moorside Dur 168 D1
Moor Side Lancs 138 E1
Moor Side Lancs 147 K8
Moorside Leeds 150 C8
Moor Side Lincs 136 E8
Moorside Oldham 140 F6
Moorstock Kent 40 E7
Moor Street Medway 53 H6
Moorswater Cnwll 5 M2
Moorthorpe Wakefd 142 C5
Moortown Devon 12 C7
Moortown Hants 18 A3
Moortown IoW 19 G7
Moortown Leeds 150 D7
Moortown Lincs 144 D7
Moortown Wrekin 113 K7
Morangie Highld 263 K3
Morar Highld 237 K2
Morborne Cambs 102 C5
Morchard Bishop Devon 13 H1
Morchard Road Devon 13 H2
Morcombelake Dorset 15 J4
Morcott Rutlnd 101 K3
Morda Shrops 112 D6
Morden Dorset 17 H3
Morden Gt Lon 51 H5
Mordiford Herefs 80 D7
Mordon Dur 169 J5
More Shrops 95 H5
Morebath Devon 29 G6
Morebattle Border 189 K1
Morecambe Lancs 147 H3
Moredon Swindn 47 H2
Morefield Highld 261 J1
Morehall Kent 41 G7
Moreleigh Devon 7 L4
Morenish P & K 231 H8
Moresby Parks Cumb 164 C6
Morestead Hants 35 G6
Moreton Dorset 16 F5
Moreton Essex 70 D5
Moreton Herefs 80 C2
Moreton Oxon 67 G6
Moreton Staffs 114 D8
Moreton Staffs 115 J5
Moreton Wirral 129 [illegible]
Moreton Corbet Shrops 113 J8
Moreton Hall Suffk 89 H2
Moretonhampstead Devon 13 H5
Moreton-in-Marsh Gloucs 65 J1
Moreton Jeffries Herefs 80 E5
Moretonmill Shrops 113 J7
Moreton Morrell Warwks 83 H4
Moreton on Lugg Herefs 80 C6
Moreton Paddox Warwks 83 H4
Moreton Pinkney W Nthn 84 B5
Moreton Say Shrops 113 L4
Moreton Valence Gloucs 63 M5
Morfa Cerdgn 76 B4
Morfa Bychan Gwynd 109 K4
Morfa Dinlle Gwynd 125 H8
Morfa Glas Neath 60 C6
Morfa Nefyn Gwynd 108 E3
Morganstown Cardif 43 H5
Morgan's Vale Wilts 33 L6
Morham E Loth 212 C5
[illegible]
Morland W & F 166 E6
Morley Ches E 130 F3
Morley Derbys 116 C3
Morley Dur [illegible]
Morley Leeds 141 L2
Morley Green Ches E 130 F3
Morley St Botolph Norfk 106 B3
Mornick Cnwll 11 L8
Morningside C Edin 211 H5
Morningside N Lans 209 L7
Morningthorpe Norfk 106 E5
Morpeth Nthumb 180 F2
Morphie Abers 235 H3
Morrey Staffs 115 J7
Morridge Side Staffs 115 G1
Morriston Swans 57 J5
Morston Norfk 121 M3
Mortehoe Devon 27 H2
Morthen Rothm 133 J2
Mortimer W Berk 49 G6
Mortimer Common W Berk 49 G6
Mortimer's Cross Herefs 80 A3
Mortimer West End Hants 48 F6
Mortlake Gt Lon 51 G4
Morton Cumb 177 L7
Morton Derbys 133 H7
Morton IoW 19 K6
Morton Lincs 118 E6
Morton Lincs 134 F1
Morton Lincs 135 H7
Morton Notts 117 J1
Morton Shrops 112 D6
Morton W & F 166 B3
Morton-on-Swale N York 160 D4
Morton on the Hill Norfk 122 C8
Morton Tinmouth Dur 168 F6
Morvah Cnwll 2 B4
Morval Cnwll 6 D3
Morvich Highld 248 F7
Morville Shrops 96 F4
Morville Heath Shrops 96 F4
Morwenstow Cnwll 26 C7
Mosborough Sheff 133 H3
Moscow E Ayrs 196 F3
Mose Shrops 97 G5
Mosedale W & F 165 K4
Moseley Birm 98 D6
Moseley Wolves 97 L4
Moseley Worcs 81 J3
Moses Gate Bolton 139 L6
Moss Ag & B 224 B6
Moss Donc 142 F5
Moss Wrexhm 112 D1
Mossat Abers 255 K7
Mossbank Shet 281 e4
Moss Bank St Hel 139 G8
Mossbay Cumb 164 C5
Mossblown S Ayrs 196 D6
Mossbrow Traffd 130 D2
Mossburnford Border 189 H3
Mossdale D & G 175 G1
Mossdale E Ayrs 184 D2
Moss Edge Lancs 147 H7
Moss End Ches E 130 D4
Mossend N Lans 209 K7
Mosser Mains Cumb 164 F5
Mossley Ches E 131 H7
Mossley Tamesd 140 E7
Mosspaul Inn Border 188 C6
Moss Side Cumb 177 G8
Moss-side Highld 253 G1
Moss Side Lancs 138 D2
Moss Side Sefton 138 D7
Mosstodloch Moray 267 G4
Mossyard D & G 174 E4
Mossy Lea Lancs 139 G5
Mosterton Dorset 15 K2
Moston Manch 140 C7
Moston Shrops 113 J6
Moston Green Ches E 130 F7
Mostyn Flints 128 F4
Motcombe Dorset 32 E6
Mothecombe Devon 7 H5
Motherby W & F 166 A5
Motherwell N Lans 209 K7
Motspur Park Gt Lon 51 G5
Mottingham Gt Lon 51 L4
Mottisfont Hants 34 D5
Mottistone IoW 18 F7
Mottram in Longdendale Tamesd 140 F8
Mottram St Andrew Ches E 131 G4
Mouilpied Guern 9 j3
Mouldsworth Ches W 129 L5
Moulin P & K 232 D3
Moulsecoomb Br & H 22 E6
Moulsford Oxon 48 E2
Moulsoe M Keyn 85 H7
Moultavie Highld 263 H5
Moulton Ches W 130 C5
Moulton Lincs 119 J6
Moulton N York 160 C2
Moulton Suffk 88 D2
Moulton V Glam 43 G7
Moulton W Nthn 84 F2
Moulton Chapel Lincs 119 J7
Moulton St Mary Norfk 107 H2
Moulton Seas End Lincs 119 K6
Mount Cnwll 4 C4
Mount Cnwll 5 K1
Mount Kirk 141 H4
Mountain C Brad 141 G2
Mountain Ash Rhondd 61 G7
Mountain Cross Border 199 K4
Mountain Street Kent 40 E5
Mount Ambrose Cnwll 4 B6
Mount Bures Essex 89 H8
Mountfield E Susx 24 D3
Mountgerald Highld 263 G7
Mount Hawke Cnwll 4 B5
Mount Hermon Cnwll 3 H7
Mountjoy Cnwll 4 E3
Mount Lothian Mdloth 200 C2
Mountnessing Essex 70 F7
Mounton Mons 63 G8
Mount Pleasant Ches E 131 G8
Mount Pleasant Derbys 115 M8
Mount Pleasant Derbys 116 B2
Mount Pleasant Dur 169 H4
Mount Pleasant E R Yk 153 L7
Mount Pleasant E Susx 23 G4
Mount Pleasant Norfk 105 K4
Mount Pleasant Suffk 88 E5
Mount Pleasant Sundld 181 H8
Mount Pleasant Worcs 82 B2
Mountsorrel Leics 116 F8
Mount Sorrel Wilts 33 H6
Mount Tabor Calder 141 G2
Mousehole Cnwll 2 D5
Mouswald D & G 176 E4
Mowbray W Susx 37 J4
Mow Cop Ches E 131 G8
Mowhaugh Border 189 L2
Mowmacre Hill C Leic 100 D2
Mowsley Leics 100 E5
Moy Highld 240 D7
Moy Highld 252 E5
Moyle Highld 248 D7
Moylegrove Pembks 75 J3
Muasdale Ag & B 205 L8
Muchalls Abers 245 K5
Much Birch Herefs 63 G1
Much Cowarne Herefs 80 E6
Much Dewchurch Herefs 62 F1
Muchelney Somset 30 F6
Muchelney Ham Somset 31 G6
Much Hadham Herts 70 B3
Much Hoole Lancs 138 F3
Much Hoole Town Lancs 138 F3
Muchlarnick Cnwll 5 L3
Much Marcle Herefs 63 K1
Much Wenlock Shrops 96 E3
Muck Highld 236 E4
Mucking Thurr 52 E3
Muckleford Dorset 16 C4
Mucklestone Staffs 114 A4
Muckley Shrops 96 E4
Muckton Lincs 137 G3
Muddiford Devon 27 K3
Muddles Green E Susx 23 J4
Mudeford BCP 18 B5
Mudford Somset 31 J7
Mudford Sock Somset 31 J7
Mudgley Somset 31 G2
Mud Row Kent 53 M4
Mugdock Stirlg 208 F4
Mugeary Highld 246 F1
Mugginton Derbys 115 M3
Muggintonlane End Derbys 115 M3
Muggleswick Dur 168 D1
Muirden Abers 268 C5
Muirdrum Angus 234 E7
Muiresk Abers 268 C6
Muirhead Angus 233 M8
Muirhead Fife 222 D6
Muirhead N Lans 209 J5
Muirhouses Falk 210 D3
Muirkirk E Ayrs 197 K5
Muirmill Stirlg 209 J2
Muir of Fowlis Abers 244 C1
Muir of Miltonduff Moray 266 D4
Muir of Ord Highld 250 F2
Muirshearlich Highld 239 J7
Muirtack Abers 257 J4
Muirton P & K 221 G5
Muirton Mains Highld 250 E1
Muirton of Ardblair P & K 233 J6
Muker N York 158 F3
Mulbarton Norfk 106 D3
Mulben Moray 267 G6
Mulfra Cnwll 2 [illegible]
Mull Ag & B 227 H5
Mullacott Cross Devon 27 J2
Mullardoch Highld 242 L5
Mullion Cnwll 3 H7
Mullion Cove Cnwll 3 H7
Mumby Lincs 137 K5
Munderfield Row Herefs 80 F5
Munderfield Stocks Herefs 80 F5
Mundesley Norfk 123 G4
Mundford Norfk 104 F4
Mundham Norfk 107 G4
Mundon Essex 72 C6
Mundy Bois Kent 40 B6
Mungrisdale W & F 165 L4
Munlochy Highld 251 H1
Munnoch N Ayrs 195 L1
Munsley Herefs 80 F7
Munslow Shrops 96 C6
Murchington Devon 13 G5
Murcot Worcs 82 C7
Murcott Oxon 66 F4
Murcott Wilts 46 D1
Murkle Highld 279 L3
Murlaggan Highld 239 G5
Murrell Green Hants 49 H7
Murroes Angus 234 C8
Murrow Cambs 103 H2
Mursley Bucks 67 K2
Murston Kent 40 B3
Murthill Angus 234 C4
Murthly P & K 233 G7
Murton C York 151 K5
Murton Dur 169 K1
Murton N Tyne 181 H5
Murton Nthumb 202 F3
Murton Swans 57 G7
Murton W & F 167 G6
Musbury Devon 15 G4
Muscoates N York 162 B6
Musselburgh E Loth 211 K4
Muston Leics 117 L4
Muston N York 163 K6
Mustow Green Worcs 97 K8
Muswell Hill Gt Lon 51 H1
Mutehill D & G 175 H5
Mutford Suffk 107 K5
Muthill P & K 220 F4
Mutterton Devon 14 B2
Muxton Wrekin 114 A8
Mybster Highld 279 L5
Myddfai Carmth 59 L3
Myddle Shrops 113 G6
Mydroilyn Cerdgn 76 E4
Myerscough Lancs 147 K7
Myland Essex 72 E2
Mylor Cnwll 3 L4
Mylor Bridge Cnwll 3 K4

Mynachlog ddu Pembks 75 K6
Myndd-llan Flints 128 D5
Myndtown Shrops 95 J5
Mynydd Bach Cerdgn 92 F8
Mynydd-bach Mons 62 F8
Mynydd-Bach Swans 57 J5
Mynyddgarreg Carmth 56 D3
Mynydd Isa Flints 128 F7
Mynydd Llandygai Gwynd 126 B6
Mynydd Mechell IoA 124 F2
Mynytho Gwynd 108 E5
Myrebird Abers 245 G4
Myredykes Border 189 G6
Mytchett Surrey 49 L7
Mytholm Calder 140 E2
Mytholmroyd Calder 140 F3
Mythop Lancs 138 D1
Myton-on-Swale N York 150 F3

N

Naast Highld 260 C3
Nab's Head Lancs 139 J2
Na Buirgh W Isls 282 d6
Naburn C York 151 J6
Naccolt Kent 40 D6
Nackington Kent 40 F4
Nacton Suffk 90 F7
Nafferton E R Yk 153 G4
Nag's Head Gloucs 64 C7
Nailbridge Gloucs 63 J4
Nailsbourne Somset 30 B5
Nailsea N Som 44 F5
Nailstone Leics 99 L2
Nailsworth Gloucs 64 B7
Nairn Highld 264 D8
Nalderswood Surrey 37 K2
Nancegollan Cnwll 3 D4
Nancledra Cnwll 2 D4
Nanhoron Gwynd 108 E5
Nannerch Flints 128 E5
Nanpantan Leics 116 E8
Nanpean Cnwll 4 F4
Nanquidno Cnwll 2 B5
Nanstallon Cnwll 5 H2
Nant-ddu Powys 60 F4
Nanternis Cerdgn 76 C4
Nantgaredig Carmth 58 F4
Nantgarw Rhondd 43 H4
Nant-glas Powys 78 D2
Nantglyn Denbgs 127 K7
Nantgwyn Powys 93 L8
Nant Gwynant Gwynd 110 B2
Nantlle Gwynd 109 J1
Nantlle Valley Slate
 Landscape Gwynd 109 J1
Nantmawr Shrops 112 C6
Nantmel Powys 78 E2
Nantmor Gwynd 109 L2
Nant Peris Gwynd 126 B7
Nantwich Ches E 113 L1
Nant-y-Bwch Blae G 61 H5
Nantycaws Carmth 58 E5
Nant-y-derry Mons 62 C6
Nant-y-ffin Carmth 59 G3
Nantyffyllon Brdgnd 42 C3
Nantyglo Blae G 61 K5
Nant-y-gollen Shrops 112 C5
Nant-y-moel Brdgnd 42 D3
Nant-y-pandy Conwy 126 D5
Naphill Bucks 67 K7
Napleton Worcs 81 K5
Nappa N York 148 E5
Napsbury Park Herts 68 F6
Napton on the Hill Warwks 83 L3
Narberth Pembks 55 J4
Narborough Leics 100 C4
Narborough Norfk 104 E1
Narkurs Cnwll 6 C4
Nasareth Gwynd 109 H2
Naseby W Nthn 100 F7
Nash Bucks 84 F8
Nash Gt Lon 51 L6
Nash Herefs 79 K3
Nash Newpt 44 D2
Nash Shrops 80 E1
Nash End Worcs 97 H7
Nashes Green Hants 35 K2
Nash Lee Bucks 67 K5
Nash Street Kent 52 D5
Nassington N Nthn 102 B4
Nastend Gloucs 64 A6
Nasty Herts 69 K2
Nateby Lancs 147 J7
Nateby W & F 158 D1
Natland W & F 157 H5
Naughton Suffk 89 L5
Naunton Gloucs 65 G2

Naunton Worcs 81 K7
Naunton Beauchamp Worcs 81 M5
Navenby Lincs 135 K8
Navestock Essex 70 D7
Navestock Side Essex 70 E7
Navidale Highld 274 D5
Navity Highld 264 B7
Nawton N York 161 L5
Nayland Suffk 89 K8
Nazeing Essex 69 L6
Nazeing Gate Essex 69 L6
Neacroft Hants 18 B4
Neal's Green Warwks 99 J6
Neap Shet 281 e5
Near Cotton Staffs 115 H2
Near Sawrey W & F 156 E3
Neasden Gt Lon 51 L2
Neasham Darltn 169 J8
Neat Enstone Oxon 66 A2
Neath Neath 57 L5
Neatham Hants 35 M3
Neatishead Norfk 123 G7
Nebo Cerdgn 77 G2
Nebo Conwy 127 G8
Nebo Gwynd 109 H2
Nebo IoA 125 H2
Necton Norfk 105 H2
Nedd Highld 270 F2
Nedderton Nthumb 180 F2
Nedging Suffk 89 K5
Nedging Tye Suffk 89 L5
Needham Norfk 106 E7
Needham Market Suffk 90 C4
Needham Street Suffk 88 C2
Needingworth Cambs 87 G1
Neen Savage Shrops 96 F7
Neen Sollars Shrops 80 F1
Neenton Shrops 96 E6
Nefyn Gwynd 108 E3
Neilston E Rens 208 E7
Nelson Caerph 43 H3
Nelson Lancs 148 F8
Nemphlar S Lans 198 E4
Nempnett Thrubwell BaNES 45 G7
Nenthall W & F 167 H2
Nenthead W & F 167 H2
Nenthorn Border 201 L5
Neopardy Devon 13 J3
Nep Town W Susx 22 B4
Nerabus Ag & B 204 C5
Nercwys Flints 128 F7
Nerston S Lans 209 H7
Nesbit Nthumb 202 F6
Nesfield N York 149 K6
Ness Ches W 129 G4
Nesscliffe Shrops 112 F7
Neston Ches W 129 G4
Neston Wilts 46 B5
Netchwood Shrops 96 E5
Nether Abington S Lans 186 D2
Nether Alderley Ches E 131 G4
Netheravon Wilts 33 K1
Nether Blainslie Border 201 H4
Netherbrae Abers 268 E4
Nether Broughton Leics 117 J6
Netherburn S Lans 198 C4
Netherbury Dorset 15 L3
Netherby Cumb 177 L4
Netherby N York 150 D6
Nether Cerne Dorset 16 C3
Nethercleuch D & G 176 F2
Nether Compton Dorset 31 K7
Nethercote Warwks 83 M2
Nethercott Devon 11 L3
Nethercott Devon 27 H3
Nether Crimond Abers 256 F7
Nether Dallachy Moray 267 G3
Netherend Gloucs 63 H7
Nether Exe Devon 13 L3
Netherfield E Susx 24 C3
Netherfield Leics 117 G8
Netherfield Notts 117 G3
Nether Fingland S Lans 186 D4
Nethergate N Linc 143 J7
Nethergate Norfk 122 B5
Netherhampton Wilts 33 K5
Nether Handley Derbys 133 H4
Nether Handwick Angus 234 B7
Nether Haugh Rothm 142 C8
Netherhay Dorset 15 J2
Nether Headon Notts 134 E4
Nether Heage Derbys 116 B2
Nether Heyford W Nthn 84 C3
Nether Kellet Lancs 147 K2
Nether Kinmundy Abers 257 K3
Netherland Green Staffs 115 H5
Nether Langwith Notts 133 K5
Netherley Abers 245 J5
Netherley Lpool 129 K2
Nethermill D & G 176 D1

Nethermuir Abers 257 G3
Netherne-on-the-Hill Surrey 51 K6
Netheroyd Hill Kirk 141 H4
Nether Padley Derbys 132 E4
Nether Poppleton C York 151 J5
Nether Row Cumb 165 K3
Netherseal Derbys 99 H1
Nether Silton N York 161 G4
Nether Skyborry Shrops 95 G8
Nether Stowey Somset 30 B3
Nether Street Essex 70 E5
Netherstreet Wilts 46 E6
Netherthird E Ayrs 197 H7
Netherthong Kirk 141 H6
Netherthorpe Derbys 133 J5
Netherton Angus 234 E4
Netherton Devon 13 L8
Netherton Dudley 97 L5
Netherton Hants 48 A7
Netherton Herefs 63 G2
Netherton Kirk 141 H5
Netherton N Lans 209 K8
Netherton Nthumb 190 E4
Netherton Oxon 66 B7
Netherton P & K 233 H5
Netherton Sefton 138 D7
Netherton Shrops 97 G6
Netherton Stirlg 208 F3
Netherton Wakefd 141 L4
Netherton Worcs 82 A7
Nethertown Cumb 155 H1
Nethertown Highld 280 E1
Nethertown Lancs 148 C8
Nethertown Staffs 115 J8
Netherurd Border 199 J4
Nether Wallop Hants 34 C4
Nether Wasdale Cumb 155 L2
Nether Welton Cumb 165 K2
Nether Westcote Gloucs 65 J3
Nether Whitacre Warwks 99 G5
Nether Whitecleuch S Lans 186 B2
Nether Winchendon Bucks 67 H4
Netherwitton Nthumb 191 G8
Nethy Bridge Highld 253 J7
Netley Hants 19 G2
Netley Marsh Hants 34 D8
Nettlebed Oxon 49 G2
Nettlebridge Somset 31 L1
Nettlecombe Dorset 15 L3
Nettlecombe IoW 19 J8
Nettleden Herts 68 C5
Nettleham Lincs 135 K4
Nettlestead Kent 39 H3
Nettlestead Green Kent 39 H3
Nettlestone IoW 19 L5
Nettlesworth Dur 169 H1
Nettleton Lincs 144 E7
Nettleton Wilts 46 B3
Nettleton Shrub Wilts 46 B3
Netton Devon 7 G5
Netton Wilts 33 K3
Neuadd Carmth 59 K4
Neuadd-ddu Powys 93 K8
Nevendon Essex 53 G1
Nevern Pembks 75 J4
Nevill Holt Leics 101 H4
New Abbey D & G 176 C5
New Aberdour Abers 268 F3
New Addington Gt Lon 51 K6
Newall Leeds 150 B6
New Alresford Hants 35 J4
New Alyth P & K 233 K7
Newark C Pete 102 E3
Newark Ork 275 f2
Newark-on-Trent Notts 117 L1
New Arley Warwks 99 J5
New Arram E R Yk 153 G7
Newarthill N Lans 209 L7
New Ash Green Kent 52 D6
New Balderton Notts 117 L1
Newbarn Kent 40 F7
New Barn Kent 52 D5
New Barnet Gt Lon 69 H7
New Barnetby N Linc 144 D5
New Barton N Nthn 85 G2
Newbattle Mdloth 211 K6
New Bewick Nthumb 190 F2
Newbie D & G 177 G2
Newbiggin Cumb 155 K4
Newbiggin Dur 167 L5
Newbiggin Dur 168 F1
Newbiggin N York 159 G4
Newbiggin N York 159 H5
Newbiggin W & F 146 E2
Newbiggin W & F 166 B5
Newbiggin W & F 166 D1
Newbiggin W & F 166 E5
Newbiggin-by-the-Sea
 Nthumb 181 H1
Newbigging Angus 233 L7

Newbigging Angus 234 C7
Newbigging Angus 234 D5
Newbigging S Lans 199 H4
Newbiggin-on-Lune W & F 158 C2
New Bilton Warwks 100 B8
Newbold Derbys 133 G5
Newbold Leics 116 C7
Newbold on Avon Warwks 100 B7
Newbold on Stour Warwks 82 F6
Newbold Pacey Warwks 83 G4
Newbold Revel Warwks 99 M7
Newbold Verdon Leics 99 L3
New Bolingbroke Lincs 136 F8
Newborough C Pete 102 D2
Newborough IoA 125 G6
Newborough Staffs 115 J6
Newbottle Sundld 181 H8
Newbottle W Nthn 83 M7
New Boultham Lincs 135 K5
Newbourne Suffk 91 G6
New Bradwell M Keyn 84 F7
New Brampton Derbys 133 G5
New Brancepeth Dur 169 G2
Newbridge C Edin 210 F4
Newbridge Caerph 43 G7
Newbridge Cerdgn 76 F3
Newbridge Cnwll 2 C5
Newbridge Cnwll 4 C6
Newbridge D & G 176 C3
Newbridge Hants 34 C7
Newbridge IoW 18 F6
New Bridge N York 162 D5
Newbridge Oxon 66 B6
Newbridge Wrexhm 112 D3
Newbridge Green Worcs 81 J7
Newbridge-on-Usk Mons 62 D8
Newbridge-on-Wye Powys 78 E4
New Brighton Flints 128 F6
New Brighton Wirral 129 G1
New Brinsley Notts 116 D2
Newbrough Nthumb 179 K5
New Broughton Wrexhm 112 D1
New Buckenham Norfk 106 B5
Newbuildings Devon 13 J2
Newburgh Abers 257 J6
Newburgh Abers 269 H4
Newburgh Fife 222 C3
Newburgh Lancs 138 F4
Newburn N u Ty 180 E6
New Bury Bolton 139 L6
Newbury Somset 32 B1
Newbury W Berk 48 C5
Newbury Wilts 32 D3
Newbury Park Gt Lon 51 L1
Newby Lancs 148 E6
Newby N York 148 C2
Newby N York 163 J5
Newby N York 170 C8
Newby W & F 166 E6
Newby Bridge W & F 156 E5
Newby Cross Cumb 177 L8
Newby East Cumb 178 B7
Newby Head W & F 166 E6
New Byth Abers 268 E5
Newby West Cumb 177 L8
Newby Wiske N York 160 E5
Newcastle Mons 62 F4
Newcastle Shrops 95 G6
Newcastle Airport Nthumb 180 E4
Newcastle Emlyn Carmth 76 B7
Newcastle Great Park N u Ty 180 F5
Newcastleton Border 178 C2
Newcastle-under-Lyme Staffs 114 C2
Newcastle upon Tyne N u Ty 181 G6
Newchapel Pembks 75 L4
Newchapel Staffs 131 G6
Newchapel Surrey 38 A5
Newchurch Blae G 61 J5
Newchurch Herefs 79 L5
Newchurch IoW 19 J6
Newchurch Kent 25 K1
Newchurch Mons 62 F7
Newchurch Powys 79 H5
Newchurch Staffs 115 J7
Newchurch in Pendle Lancs 148 E7
New Costessey Norfk 106 D2
New Cowper Cumb 164 F2
Newcraighall C Edin 211 K4
New Crofton Wakefd 142 B4
New Cross Cerdgn 92 D8
New Cross Gt Lon 51 K4
New Cross Somset 30 F7
New Cumnock E Ayrs 197 J8
New Cut E Susx 24 E4
New Deer Abers 268 F6
New Delaval Nthumb 181 H3
New Delph Oldham 140 F6
New Denham Bucks 50 D2
Newdigate Surrey 37 J3
New Duston W Nthn 84 D3

New Earswick C York 151 K5
New Eastwood Notts 116 D2
New Edlington Donc 142 E7
New Elgin Moray 266 E4
New Ellerby E R Yk 153 J7
Newell Green Br For 49 L5
New Eltham Gt Lon 51 L4
New End Worcs 82 C3
Newenden Kent 24 F2
New England C Pete 102 D3
New England Essex 88 E6
Newent Gloucs 63 L2
New Farnley Leeds 141 L2
New Ferry Wirral 129 H3
Newfield Dur 169 G4
Newfield Dur 181 G8
Newfield Highld 264 B4
New Fletton C Pete 102 D4
New Forest National Park 18 D2
Newfound Hants 48 F8
New Fryston Wakefd 142 C2
Newgale Pembks 54 D2
New Galloway D & G 185 G7
Newgate Norfk 122 A3
Newgate Street Herts 69 J6
New Gilston Fife 223 G5
New Grimsby IoS 10 b2
Newhall Ches E 113 K2
Newhall Derbys 115 M7
Newham Nthumb 203 K7
New Hartley Nthumb 181 H3
Newhaven C Edin 211 H4
Newhaven Derbys 132 C7
Newhaven E Susx 23 G7
New Haw Surrey 50 D6
New Hedges Pembks 55 K6
New Herrington Sundld 181 H8
Newhey Rochdl 140 D5
New Holkham Norfk 121 J4
New Holland N Linc 144 D3
Newholm N York 171 K8
New Houghton Derbys 133 K6
New Houghton Norfk 121 H6
Newhouse N Lans 209 L6
New Houses N York 158 D7
New Hutton W & F 157 J1
New Hythe Kent 52 F7
Newick E Susx 22 F3
Newingreen Kent 40 H8
Newington Kent 41 G7
Newington Kent 53 J6
Newington Oxon 66 F7
Newington Shrops 95 K6
Newington Bagpath Gloucs 64 B8
New Inn Carmth 58 E2
New Inn Pembks 75 H6
New Inn Torfn 62 C7
New Invention Shrops 95 H8
New Lanark S Lans 198 E4
New Lanark Village S Lans 198 E5
Newland C KuH 144 D2
Newland E R Yk 143 K2
Newland Gloucs 63 H5
Newland N York 143 H3
Newland Oxon 66 A5
Newland Somset 28 E3
Newland W & F 156 D6
Newland Worcs 81 H5
Newlandrig Mdloth 211 L6
Newlands Border 188 E7
Newlands Nthumb 180 D7
Newlands W & F 165 K3
Newlands of Dundurcas Moray 266 F6
New Lane Lancs 138 E5
New Lane End Warrtn 130 C1
New Langholm D & G 177 K2
New Leake Lincs 137 G8
New Leeds Abers 269 H5
New Lodge Barns 142 A6
New Longton Lancs 139 G3
New Luce D & G 172 F2
Newlyn Cnwll 2 D5
Newmachar Abers 256 F7
Newmains N Lans 209 L7
New Malden Gt Lon 51 G5
Newman's End Essex 70 D4
Newman's Green Suffk 89 H6
Newmarket Suffk 88 C3
Newmarket W Isls 282 g3
New Marske R & Cl 170 E6
New Marston Oxon 66 D5
New Marton Shrops 112 E4
New Mill Abers 245 H7
Newmill Border 188 D4
New Mill Cnwll 2 D4
New Mill Herts 68 A4
New Mill Kirk 141 J6
Newmill Moray 267 J5
Newmillerdam Wakefd 142 A4

Newmill of Inshewan Angus 234 C3
Newmills C Edin 211 G5
New Mills Cnwll 4 E4
New Mills Derbys 131 K3
Newmills Fife 210 D2
Newmills Mons 63 G5
New Mills Powys 94 D3
Newmiln P & K 221 L1
Newmilns E Ayrs 197 G3
New Milton Hants 18 C4
New Mistley Essex 73 H1
New Moat Pembks 75 H7
Newnes Shrops 112 F5
Newney Green Essex 71 G5
Newnham Hants 49 H8
Newnham Herts 86 E7
Newnham Kent 40 B4
Newnham W Nthn 84 B3
Newnham Bridge Worcs 80 E2
Newnham on Severn Gloucs 63 K5
New Ollerton Notts 134 D6
New Oscott Birm 98 E4
New Passage S Glos 45 G2
New Pitsligo Abers 268 F5
New Polzeath Cnwll 10 C6
Newport Cnwll 11 L5
Newport Dorset 17 G4
Newport E R Yk 143 L2
Newport Essex 87 L8
Newport Gloucs 63 K7
Newport Highld 274 F3
Newport IoW 19 H6
Newport Newpt 44 C1
Newport Norfk 123 K8
Newport Pembks 75 H4
Newport Wrekin 114 A7
Newport-on-Tay Fife 223 G2
Newport Pagnell M Keyn 85 G6
Newport Pagnell Services M Keyn 85 G6
Newpound Common W Susx 37 G5
New Prestwick S Ayrs 196 C6
New Quay Cerdgn 76 D3
Newquay Cnwll 4 D3
New Quay Essex 72 F2
New Rackheath Norfk 106 F1
New Radnor Powys 79 H3
New Rent W & F 166 B3
New Ridley Nthumb 180 C7
New Road Side N York 149 H7
New Romney Kent 25 K2
New Rossington Donc 143 G8
New Row Cerdgn 92 F8
New Row Lancs 148 A8
New Sauchie Clacks 220 F8
Newsbank Ches E 131 G6
Newseat Abers 256 C5
Newsham Lancs 147 K8
Newsham N York 160 E5
Newsham N York 168 E8
Newsham Nthumb 181 H3
New Sharlston Wakefd 142 B4
Newsholme E R Yk 143 H2
Newsholme Lancs 148 E5
New Shoreston Nthumb 203 K6
New Silksworth Sundld 181 J8
New Skelton R & Cl 170 F7
Newsome Kirk 141 J5
New Somerby Lincs 118 B4
New Springs Wigan 139 J6
Newstead Border 201 H6
Newstead Notts 116 E1
Newstead Nthumb 203 J7
New Stevenston N Lans 209 K7
New Street Herefs 79 L4
New Swanage Dorset 17 K6
New Swannington Leics 116 D8
Newthorpe N York 142 D1
Newthorpe Notts 116 E2
New Thundersley Essex 53 G1
Newtimber W Susx 22 D4
Newtoft Lincs 135 L2
Newton Ag & B 217 G7
Newton Border 189 G2
Newton Brdgnd 42 C6
Newton C Beds 86 E6
Newton Cambs 87 J5
Newton Cambs 119 M8
Newton Cardif 43 K6
Newton Ches W 129 J6
Newton Ches W 129 L7
Newton Ches W 129 M4
Newton Derbys 133 J7
Newton Herefs 79 L1
Newton Herefs 79 L8
Newton Herefs 80 C4
Newton Highld 251 G2
Newton Highld 252 D2
Newton Highld 263 L6
Newton Highld 280 D6

Newton Lancs 147 G8
Newton Lancs 157 J7
Newton Lincs 118 D4
Newton Moray 266 C3
Newton Moray 267 K3
Newton N Nthn 101 J6
Newton N York 152 D1
Newton Norfk 121 H8
Newton Notts 117 J3
Newton Nthumb 180 C6
Newton Nthumb 190 D5
Newton S Lans 198 F6
Newton S Lans 209 H6
Newton Sandw 98 C4
Newton Shrops 112 F4
Newton Somset 29 K3
Newton Somset 115 G6
Newton Suffk 89 J7
Newton W & F 146 D2
Newton W Loth 210 E3
Newton Warwks 100 C7
Newton Wilts 34 B6
Newton Abbot Devon 13 K8
Newton Arlosh Cumb 177 G7
Newton Aycliffe Dur 169 H5
Newton Bewley Hartpl 170 B5
Newton Blossomville M Keyn 85 H5
Newton Bromswold N Nthn 85 K2
Newton Burgoland Leics 99 K2
Newton by Toft Lincs 135 L2
Newton Ferrers Devon 7 G5
Newton Ferry W Isls 282 c7
Newton Flotman Norfk 106 E4
Newtongrange Mdloth 211 K6
Newton Green Mons 45 G1
Newton Harcourt Leics 100 E4
Newton Heath Manch 140 C7
Newtonhill Abers 245 K5
Newton Hill Wakefd 141 M3
Newton-in-Bowland Lancs 148 B5
Newton Kyme N York 151 G7
Newton-le-Willows N York 160 B5
Newton-le-Willows St Hel 139 H8
Newtonloan Mdloth 211 K6
Newton Longville Bucks 67 K1
Newton Mearns E Rens 208 F7
Newtonmill Angus 234 F3
Newtonmore Highld 241 J4
Newton Morrell N York 160 C1
Newton Mountain Pembks 55 G5
Newton Mulgrave N York 171 H7
Newton of Balcanquhal P & K 222 B5
Newton of Balcormo Fife 223 J6
Newton of Belltrees Rens 208 C7
Newton-on-Ayr S Ayrs 196 C6
Newton-on-Ouse N York 151 H4
Newton-on-Rawcliffe N York 162 E4
Newton on the Hill Shrops 113 H7
Newton-on-the-Moor Nthumb 191 H5
Newton on Trent Lincs 135 G5
Newton Poppleford Devon 14 C5
Newton Purcell Oxon 66 F1
Newton Regis Warwks 99 H2
Newton Reigny W & F 166 B3
Newton St Cyres Devon 13 K3
Newton St Faith Norfk 122 E8
Newton St Loe BaNES 45 L6
Newton St Petrock Devon 27 G8
Newton Solney Derbys 115 M6
Newton Stacey Hants 34 E3
Newton Stewart D & G 173 K2
Newton Tony Wilts 34 B7
Newton Tracey Devon 27 J5
Newton under Roseberry R & Cl 170 D8
Newton Underwood Nthumb 180 E2
Newton upon Derwent E R Yk 151 M6
Newton Valence Hants 35 L4
Newton Village Mdloth 211 K5
Newton Wamphray D & G 187 H7
Newton with Scales Lancs 138 F2
Newtown BCP 17 K4
Newtown Blae G 61 J5
Newtown Ches W 129 M4
Newtown Cnwll 2 F5
Newtown Cnwll 11 K7
Newtown Cumb 164 L1
Newtown Cumb 177 L6
Newtown Cumb 178 C6
Newtown D & G 185 J1
Newtown Derbys 131 K3
Newtown Devon 14 C3
Newtown Devon 28 D6
Newtown Dorset 15 L2
New Town Dorset 17 K1
New Town Dorset 32 F7
New Town Dorset 33 G7
New Town E Susx 23 H3
Newtown Gloucs 63 K6
Newtown Hants 18 D2

Newtown Hants 35 J8
Newtown Hants 48 C6
Newtown Herefs 80 B4
Newtown Herefs 80 C8
Newtown Herefs 80 C8
Newtown Highld 240 B3
Newtown IoW 19 G5
Newtown Nthumb 190 E6
Newtown Nthumb 202 F6
Newtown Nthumb 203 G8
Newtown Powys 94 D5
Newtown Rhondd 61 G7
Newtown Shrops 112 F5
Newtown Shrops 113 H5
Newtown Somset 30 C8
Newtown Staffs 98 C3
Newtown Staffs 131 H5
Newtown W & F 166 C6
Newtown Wigan 139 H6
Newtown Wilts 32 F5
Newtown Wilts 47 J6
Newtown Worcs 81 K4
Newtown Worcs 98 D7
Newtown in St Martin Cnwll 3 J6
Newtown Linford Leics 100 B2
Newtown St Boswells Border 201 J6
Newtown Unthank Leics 100 B3
New Tredegar Caerph 61 J6
New Trows S Lans 198 D5
New Tupton Derbys 133 H6
Newtyle Angus 233 L7
New Walsoken Cambs 103 K2
New Waltham NE Lin 145 H6
New Whittington Derbys 133 H4
New Winton E Loth 211 M5
New Yatt Oxon 66 A4
Newyears Green Gt Lon 50 D1
Newyork Ag & B 216 F5
New York Lincs 136 D8
New York N Tyne 181 H5
New York N York 150 B3
New Zealand Wilts 46 F3
Nextend Herefs 79 L4
Neyland Pembks 54 F6
Niarbyl IoM 154 b6
Nibley Gloucs 45 K3
Nibley S Glos 45 K3
Nibley Green Gloucs 63 L7
Nicholashayne Devon 29 K7
Nicholaston Swans 56 F7
Nickies Hill Cumb 178 D5
Nidd N York 150 D4
Nigg C Aber 245 L3
Nigg Highld 264 C5
Nigg Ferry Highld 264 B6
Nimlet BaNES 45 L5
Ninebanks Nthumb 179 H8
Nine Elms Swindn 47 G2
Nine Wells Pembks 74 C7
Ninfield E Susx 24 C5
Ningwood IoW 18 F6
Nisbet Border 201 L8
Nisbet Hill Border 202 B3
Niton IoW 19 H8
Nitshill C Glas 208 E7
Noah's Ark Kent 52 C7
Noak Bridge Essex 52 E1
Noak Hill Gt Lon 70 D8
Noblethorpe Barns 141 L6
Nobold Shrops 95 L2
Nobottle W Nthn 84 D3
Nocton Lincs 135 L6
Nogdam End Norfk 107 H3
Noke Oxon 66 E1
Nolton Pembks 54 E3
Nolton Haven Pembks 54 D3
No Man's Heath Ches W 113 H2
No Man's Heath Warwks 99 H2
No Man's Land Cnwll 6 B3
Nomansland Devon 28 E8
Nomansland Wilts 34 B7
Noneley Shrops 113 H6
Nonington Kent 41 H5
Nook Cumb 178 B3
Nook W & F 157 H6
Norbiton Gt Lon 51 G5
Norbreck Bpool 146 F7
Norbridge Herefs 81 G6
Norbury Ches E 113 J2
Norbury Derbys 115 J3
Norbury Gt Lon 51 J5
Norbury Shrops 95 J5
Norbury Staffs 114 B6
Norbury Common Ches E 113 J2
Norbury Junction Staffs 114 D7
Norchard Worcs 81 J2
Norcott Brook Ches W 130 B4
Norcross Lancs 146 F7
Nordelph Norfk 103 L3
Norden Rochdl 140 C5

Nordley Shrops......96 F4
Norfolk Broads Norfk......107 J2
Norham Nthumb......202 D4
Norland Calder......141 G3
Norley Ches W......130 B5
Norleywood Hants......18 E4
Norlington E Susx......23 G4
Normanby Lincs......135 K2
Normanby N Linc......143 M4
Normanby N York......162 C6
Normanby R & Cl......170 D7
Normanby le Wold Lincs......136 B1
Norman Cross Cambs......102 D5
Normandy Surrey......50 B8
Normans Bay E Susx......24 C6
Norman's Green Devon......14 C2
Normanton C Derb......116 B5
Normanton Leics......117 L3
Normanton Notts......134 E8
Normanton Rutlnd......101 K2
Normanton Wakefd......142 B3
Normanton Wilts......33 K3
Normanton le Heath Leics......99 K1
Normanton on Cliffe Lincs......118 B2
Normanton on Soar Notts......116 E7
Normanton on the Wolds
    Notts......117 G5
Normanton on Trent Notts......134 F6
Normoss Lancs......147 G8
Norney Surrey......36 D2
Norrington Common Wilts......46 C6
Norris Green Cnwll......6 E1
Norris Green Lpool......129 J1
Norris Hill Leics......116 B8
Norristhorpe Kirk......141 K3
Northacre Norfk......105 J4
Northall Bucks......68 B3
Northallerton N York......160 E4
Northall Green Norfk......121 M8
Northam C Sotn......19 G1
Northam Devon......27 H5
Northampton W Nthn......84 E3
Northampton Worcs......81 J2
Northampton Services W Nthn......84 D4
North Anston Rothm......133 K3
North Ascot Br For......49 M5
North Aston Oxon......66 C1
Northaw Herts......69 H6
Northay Somset......30 D8
North Baddesley Hants......34 E6
North Ballachulish Highld......229 G3
North Barrow Somset......31 K5
North Barsham Norfk......121 K4
Northbay W Isls......283 b13
North Benfleet Essex......53 G1
North Berwick E Loth......212 C2
North Bitchburn Dur......168 F4
North Blyth Nthumb......181 H2
North Boarhunt Hants......19 K2
North Bockhampton BCP......18 B4
Northborough C Pete......102 C2
Northbourne Kent......41 K5
North Bovey Devon......13 H6
North Bradley Wilts......46 B7
North Brentor Devon......12 C6
North Brewham Somset......32 B3
North Bridge Surrey......36 E3
Northbridge Street E Susx......24 D2
Northbrook Hants......35 G3
Northbrook Oxon......66 D3
North Brook End Cambs......86 F6
North Buckland Devon......27 H3
North Burlingham Norfk......107 H2
North Cadbury Somset......31 K5
North Carlton Lincs......135 J4
North Carlton Notts......134 B3
North Cave E R Yk......143 M1
North Cerney Gloucs......64 E5
North Chailey E Susx......22 F3
Northchapel W Susx......36 E5
North Charford Hants......33 L7
North Charlton Nthumb......191 H2
North Cheam Gt Lon......51 G6
North Cheriton Somset......31 M5
North Chideock Dorset......15 K4
Northchurch Herts......68 B5
North Cliffe E R Yk......152 D8
North Clifton Notts......135 G5
North Close Dur......169 H4
North Cockerington Lincs......137 G2
North Connel Ag & B......228 E8
North Cornelly Brdgnd......42 B5
North Corner Cnwll......3 K7
North Cotes Lincs......145 J7
Northcott Devon......11 L4
Northcott Devon......14 D1
Northcott Devon......29 K8
North Country Cnwll......4 A6
Northcourt Oxon......66 D7
North Cove Suffk......107 K5

North Cowton N York......160 D2
North Crawley M Keyn......85 H6
North Cray Gt Lon......52 A4
North Creake Norfk......121 J4
North Curry Somset......30 D6
North Dalton E R Yk......152 E5
North Deighton N York......150 E5
Northdown Kent......41 L1
North Downs......40 B4
North Duffield N York......151 L8
Northedge Derbys......133 G6
North Elham Kent......41 G6
North Elkington Lincs......136 L3
North Elmham Norfk......121 L7
North Elmsall Wakefd......142 D5
Northend Bucks......67 H8
North End C Port......19 L3
North End Cumb......177 K7
North End Dorset......32 D5
North End E R Yk......145 H2
North End E R Yk......153 K7
North End Essex......71 G3
North End Hants......33 J7
North End Hants......35 J5
North End Leics......116 F8
North End Lincs......119 H3
North End Lincs......137 H2
North End Lincs......144 D7
North End Lincs......145 J7
North End N Linc......144 E3
North End N Nthn......85 J2
North End N Som......44 B5
North End Norfk......105 K5
North End Nthumb......191 G6
North End Sefton......138 C6
North End W Susx......21 G6
North End W Susx......21 J5
Northend Warwks......83 J5
Northenden Manch......131 G2
Northend Woods Bucks......49 L1
North Erradale Highld......260 B4
North Evington C Leic......100 D3
North Fambridge Essex......71 K7
North Featherstone Wakefd......142 C3
North Ferriby E R Yk......144 B3
Northfield Birm......98 C7
Northfield C Aber......245 K2
Northfield E R Yk......144 C2
Northfields Lincs......102 A2
Northfleet Kent......52 D4
North Frodingham E R Yk......153 H5
Northgate Lincs......119 G6
North Gorley Hants......33 L8
North Green Norfk......106 E5
North Green Suffk......91 G3
North Green Suffk......91 J2
North Greetwell Lincs......135 K5
North Grimston N York......152 C2
North Halling Medway......52 F6
North Hayling Hants......20 B6
North Hazelrigg Nthumb......203 G6
North Heasley Devon......28 C4
North Heath W Susx......37 G6
North Hele Devon......29 J6
North Hill Cnwll......11 K7
North Hillingdon Gt Lon......50 D2
North Hinksey Village Oxon......66 D6
North Holmwood Surrey......37 J2
North Huish Devon......7 K3
North Hykeham Lincs......135 J6
Northiam E Susx......24 E2
Northill C Beds......86 C6
Northington Gloucs......63 L5
Northington Hants......35 H3
North Kelsey Lincs......144 D7
North Kessock Highld......251 H2
North Killingholme N Linc......144 F4
North Kilvington N York......160 F5
North Kilworth Leics......100 D6
North Kingston Hants......18 B3
North Kyme Lincs......118 F1
North Lancing W Susx......21 L5
North Landing E R Yk......153 L2
Northlands Lincs......119 K1
Northleach Gloucs......65 G4
North Lee Bucks......67 K5
North Lees N York......160 D7
Northleigh Devon......14 E3
Northleigh Devon......27 L4
North Leigh Kent......40 F6
North Leigh Oxon......66 A4
North Leverton with
    Habblesthorpe Notts......134 F3
Northlew Devon......12 C3
North Littleton Worcs......82 C5
Northload Bridge Somset......31 H3
North Lopham Norfk......105 L6
North Luffenham Rutlnd......101 K3
North Marden W Susx......20 C4
North Marston Bucks......67 J3

North Middleton Mdloth......211 K7
North Middleton Nthumb......190 E1
North Millbrex Abers......256 E3
North Milmain D & G......172 D4
North Molton Devon......28 C5
Northmoor Oxon......66 B6
North Moreton Oxon......48 E1
Northmuir Angus......234 B4
North Mundham W Susx......20 E6
North Muskham Notts......134 F7
North Newbald E R Yk......152 D8
North Newington Oxon......83 K7
North Newnton Wilts......47 H7
North Newton Somset......30 D4
Northney Hants......20 B6
North Nibley Gloucs......63 L7
North Oakley Hants......48 D8
North Ockendon Gt Lon......52 C2
Northolt Gt Lon......50 E2
Northolt Airport Gt Lon......50 E2
Northop Flints......128 F6
Northop Hall Flints......129 G6
North Ormesby Middsb......170 C6
North Ormsby Lincs......136 E1
Northorpe Kirk......141 K3
Northorpe Lincs......118 E8
Northorpe Lincs......119 G4
Northorpe Lincs......143 M8
North Otterington N York......160 E5
Northover Somset......31 H3
Northover Somset......31 H6
North Owersby Lincs......135 L1
Northowram Calder......141 H2
North Perrott Somset......15 L1
North Petherton Somset......30 D4
North Petherwin Cnwll......11 K5
North Pickenham Norfk......105 H1
North Piddle Worcs......81 M4
North Poorton Dorset......15 M3
Northport Dorset......17 H5
North Poulner Hants......18 B2
North Queensferry Fife......210 F3
North Radworthy Devon......28 C4
North Rauceby Lincs......118 D2
Northrepps Norfk......122 E4
North Reston Lincs......137 G3
North Rigton N York......150 C6
North Ripley Hants......18 B4
North Rode Ches E......131 H6
North Roe Shet......281 d3
North Ronaldsay Ork......275 f1
North Ronaldsay Airport Ork......275 f1
North Row Cumb......165 H4
North Runcton Norfk......120 E8
North Scale W & F......146 C2
North Scarle Lincs......135 G6
North Seaton Nthumb......181 H2
North Seaton Colliery Nthumb......181 H2
North Shian Ag & B......228 E6
North Shields N Tyne......181 J5
North Shoebury Sthend......53 K2
North Shore Bpool......146 F8
North Side C Pete......102 F3
North Side Cumb......164 C5
North Skelton R & Cl......170 F7
North Somercotes Lincs......145 L8
North Stainley N York......160 D7
North Stainmore W & F......167 J2
North Stifford Thurr......52 D3
North Stoke BaNES......45 L5
North Stoke Oxon......48 F2
North Stoke W Susx......21 H5
Northstowe Cambs......87 H2
North Street Cambs......88 B2
North Street Hants......33 K7
North Street Hants......35 K4
North Street Kent......40 D4
North Street Medway......53 H4
North Street W Berk......48 F4
North Sunderland Nthumb......203 K6
North Tamerton Cnwll......11 K3
North Tawton Devon......12 F2
North Third Stirlg......209 K1
North Thoresby Lincs......145 H8
North Togston Nthumb......191 K5
North Tolsta W Isls......282 h2
Northton W Isls......282 d6
North Town Devon......12 C1
North Town Somset......31 J2
North Town W & M......49 L3
North Tuddenham Norfk......122 A8
North Uist W Isls......283 b8
*Northumberland National
    Park* Nthumb......179 J3
North Walbottle N u Ty......180 E5
North Walsham Norfk......122 F5
North Waltham Hants......35 H2
North Warnborough Hants......35 M1
Northway Somset......29 L5
North Weald Bassett Essex......70 D6

North Wheatley Notts......134 F3
North Whilborough Devon......8 C2
Northwich Ches W......130 C5
North Wick BaNES......45 H6
Northwick S Glos......45 H4
Northwick Somset......30 E1
Northwick Worcs......81 J4
North Widcombe BaNES......45 H7
North Willingham Lincs......136 C2
North Wingfield Derbys......133 H6
North Witham Lincs......118 B7
Northwold Norfk......104 E4
Northwood C Stke......114 D2
Northwood Derbys......132 E6
Northwood Gt Lon......50 E1
Northwood IoW......19 H5
Northwood Shrops......113 H5
Northwood Worcs......97 H7
Northwood Green Gloucs......63 L4
North Wootton Dorset......31 L7
North Wootton Norfk......120 E6
North Wootton Somset......31 J3
North Wraxall Wilts......46 B4
North Wroughton Swindn......47 H3
*North York Moors National
    Park*......162 C3
Norton Donc......142 E5
Norton E Susx......23 G7
Norton Gloucs......64 B2
Norton Halton......130 A3
Norton Hants......34 F3
Norton Herts......86 E8
Norton IoW......18 E6
Norton Mons......62 F3
Norton N Som......44 D6
Norton Notts......133 L5
Norton Powys......79 K2
Norton S on T......170 B6
Norton Sheff......133 G3
Norton Shrops......95 G2
Norton Shrops......96 D2
Norton Shrops......96 E6
Norton Shrops......97 G3
Norton Suffk......89 J2
Norton Swans......57 H7
Norton W Nthn......84 B3
Norton W Susx......20 F5
Norton Wilts......46 C2
Norton Worcs......81 K5
Norton Worcs......82 B5
Norton Bavant Wilts......32 F2
Norton Bridge Staffs......114 C7
Norton Canes Staffs......98 C2
Norton Canes Services Staffs......98 C2
Norton Canon Herefs......79 M6
Norton Corner Norfk......122 B6
Norton Disney Lincs......135 H7
Norton Ferris Wilts......32 C4
Norton Fitzwarren Somset......30 B5
Norton Green IoW......18 E6
Norton Hawkfield BaNES......45 H6
Norton Heath Essex......70 F6
Norton in Hales Shrops......113 M4
Norton-Juxta-Twycross Leics......99 J2
Norton-le-Clay N York......150 F2
Norton-le-Moors C Stke......114 D1
Norton Lindsey Warwks......82 F3
Norton Little Green Suffk......89 K2
Norton Malreward BaNES......45 J6
Norton Mandeville Essex......70 E6
Norton-on-Derwent N York......152 B2
Norton St Philip Somset......45 M7
Norton Subcourse Norfk......107 H4
Norton sub Hamdon Somset......31 G7
Norton Wood Herefs......79 L5
Norwell Notts......134 F7
Norwell Woodhouse Notts......134 E7
Norwich Norfk......106 E2
Norwich Airport Norfk......106 E1
Norwick Shet......281 f1
Norwood Clacks......220 F8
Norwood Derbys......133 J3
Norwood Kent......25 K1
Norwood End Essex......70 E5
Norwood Green Calder......141 H2
Norwood Green Gt Lon......50 E3
Norwood Hill Surrey......37 K2
Norwoodside Cambs......103 H4
Noseley Leics......101 G4
Noss Mayo Devon......7 G5
Nosterfield N York......160 C6
Nosterfield End Cambs......88 C6
Nostie Highld......248 D6
Notgrove Gloucs......65 G3
Nottage Brdgnd......42 B6
Notter Cnwll......6 D3
Nottingham C Nott......116 F4
Nottington Dorset......16 C6
Notton Wakefd......142 A5
Notton Wilts......46 C5

Nounsley Essex....71 J5
Noutard's Green Worcs....81 J2
Nowton Suffk....89 H3
Nox Shrops....95 K1
Nuffield Oxon....49 G2
Nunburnholme E R Yk....152 C6
Nuncargate Notts....116 E1
Nunclose W & F....166 C2
Nuneaton Warwks....99 K5
Nuneham Courtenay Oxon....66 E7
Nunhead Gt Lon....51 K4
Nunkeeling E R Yk....153 J6
Nun Monkton N York....151 H4
Nunney Somset....32 B2
Nunney Catch Somset....32 B2
Nunnington Herefs....80 D6
Nunnington N York....161 L6
Nunsthorpe NE Lin....145 H6
Nunthorpe C York....151 J6
Nunthorpe Middsb....170 C7
Nunthorpe Village Middsb....170 D8
Nunton Wilts....33 K5
Nunwick N York....160 D3
Nunwick Nthumb....179 K1
Nupdown S Glos....63 J7
Nup End Bucks....67 L3
Nupend Gloucs....64 A5
Nuptown Br For....49 L4
Nursling Hants....34 E7
Nursted Hants....36 A6
Nursteed Wilts....46 F6
Nurton Staffs....97 J3
Nutbourne W Susx....20 C6
Nutbourne W Susx....21 J3
Nutfield Surrey....37 M1
Nuthall Notts....116 E3
Nuthampstead Herts....87 H8
Nuthurst W Susx....37 J5
Nutley E Susx....23 G2
Nutley Hants....35 J2
Nuttall Bury....140 B6
Nutwell Donc....143 G7
Nybster Highld....280 E3
Nyetimber W Susx....20 F7
Nyewood W Susx....36 B6
Nymet Rowland Devon....13 G1
Nymet Tracey Devon....13 G3
Nympsfield Gloucs....64 A7
Nynehead Somset....29 L6
Nythe Somset....30 F4
Nyton W Susx....20 F5

O

Oadby Leics....100 D3
Oad Street Kent....53 J6
Oakall Green Worcs....81 J3
Oakamoor Staffs....115 G3
Oakbank W Loth....210 E5
Oak Cross Devon....12 D3
Oakdale Caerph....43 J2
Oake Somset....29 L6
Oaken Staffs....97 J3
Oakenclough Lancs....147 K6
Oakengates Wrekin....96 F1
Oakenholt Flints....129 G5
Oakenshaw Dur....169 G3
Oakenshaw Kirk....141 J2
Oakerthorpe Derbys....133 H8
Oakford Cerdgn....76 E4
Oakford Devon....29 G6
Oakfordbridge Devon....29 G6
Oakgrove Ches E....131 H6
Oakham Rutlnd....101 J2
Oakhanger Ches E....114 B1
Oakhanger Hants....36 A4
Oakhill Somset....31 K2
Oakhurst Kent....38 E3
Oakington Cambs....87 H2
Oaklands Herts....69 H3
Oaklands Powys....78 E5
Oakle Street Gloucs....63 M4
Oakley BCP....17 K3
Oakley Bed....85 K4
Oakley Bucks....66 F4
Oakley Fife....210 D1
Oakley Hants....35 H1
Oakley Oxon....67 H7
Oakley Suffk....106 D7
Oakley Green W & M....50 A4
Oakley Park Powys....93 L6
Oakridge Lynch Gloucs....64 C6
Oaks Lancs....139 K1
Oaks Green Derbys....115 J5
Oaksey Wilts....64 E8
Oakshaw Ford Cumb....178 C4
Oakshott Hants....35 M5

Oakthorpe Leics....99 J1
Oak Tree Darltn....169 K8
Oakwood C Derb....116 C4
Oakwood Nthumb....179 L5
Oakworth C Brad....149 J8
Oare Kent....40 C3
Oare Somset....28 D2
Oare Wilts....47 H6
Oasby Lincs....118 D4
Oath Somset....30 F5
Oathlaw Angus....234 D4
Oatlands Park Surrey....50 E6
Oban Ag & B....216 D1
Oban Airport Ag & B....228 E8
Obley Shrops....95 H7
Obney P & K....232 F8
Oborne Dorset....31 L7
Obthorpe Lincs....118 E8
Occold Suffk....90 D1
Occumster Highld....275 J1
Ochiltree E Ayrs....196 F6
Ockbrook Derbys....116 C4
Ocker Hill Sandw....98 B4
Ockeridge Worcs....81 H3
Ockham Surrey....50 D7
Ockle Highld....237 G6
Ockley Surrey....37 H3
Ocle Pychard Herefs....80 E6
Octon E R Yk....153 G2
Odcombe Somset....31 H7
Odd Down BaNES....45 L6
Oddendale W & F....166 E8
Oddingley Worcs....81 L3
Oddington Oxon....66 E4
Odell Bed....85 J4
Odham Devon....12 C2
Odiham Hants....35 M1
Odsal C Brad....141 J2
Odsey Cambs....86 F7
Odstock Wilts....33 K5
Odstone Leics....99 K2
Offchurch Warwks....83 J2
Offenham Worcs....82 C6
Offerton Stockp....131 H2
Offerton Sundld....181 J7
Offham E Susx....22 F5
Offham Kent....39 G2
Offham W Susx....21 H5
Offleymarsh Staffs....114 B5
Offord Cluny Cambs....86 E2
Offord D'Arcy Cambs....86 E2
Offton Suffk....90 C5
Offwell Devon....14 E3
Ogbourne Maizey Wilts....47 J4
Ogbourne St Andrew Wilts....47 J4
Ogbourne St George Wilts....47 J4
Ogden Calder....141 G2
Ogle Nthumb....180 E3
Oglet Lpool....129 K3
Ogmore V Glam....42 D6
Ogmore-by-Sea V Glam....42 C6
Ogmore Vale Brdgnd....42 E4
Ogwen Bank Gwynd....126 C6
Okeford Fitzpaine Dorset....32 D8
Okehampton Devon....12 E4
Oker Side Derbys....132 E7
Okewood Hill Surrey....37 H3
Olchard Devon....13 K7
Old W Nthn....84 F1
Old Aberdeen C Aber....245 L2
Old Alresford Hants....35 J4
Oldany Highld....270 E2
Old Arley Warwks....99 H5
Old Auchenbrack D & G....185 J3
Old Basford C Nott....116 F3
Old Basing Hants....49 G8
Old Beetley Norfk....121 L7
Oldberrow Warwks....82 D2
Old Bewick Nthumb....190 F2
Old Bolingbroke Lincs....136 F6
Old Boxted Essex....89 K8
Old Bramhope Leeds....150 B7
Old Brampton Derbys....133 G5
Old Bridge of Urr D & G....175 J1
Old Buckenham Norfk....106 B5
Old Burghclere Hants....48 C7
Oldbury Kent....38 F2
Oldbury Sandw....98 C5
Oldbury Shrops....97 G5
Oldbury Warwks....99 J4
Oldbury Naite S Glos....63 J8
Oldbury-on-Severn S Glos....63 J8
Oldbury on the Hill Gloucs....46 B1
Old Byland N York....161 J5
Old Cantley Donc....143 G7
Old Cassop Dur....169 J3
Oldcastle Mons....62 C2
Oldcastle Heath Ches W....113 G2
Old Catton Norfk....106 E1
Old Churchstoke Powys....95 G4

Old Clee NE Lin....145 H6
Old Cleeve Somset....29 J3
Old Colwyn Conwy....127 H4
Oldcotes Notts....134 B2
Old Coulsdon Gt Lon....51 J7
Old Dailly S Ayrs....183 G3
Old Dalby Leics....117 H6
Old Dam Derbys....132 B4
Old Deer Abers....269 H6
Old Ditch Somset....31 H1
Old Edlington Donc....142 E8
Old Eldon Dur....169 H5
Old Ellerby E R Yk....153 J8
Old Felixstowe Suffk....91 H8
Oldfield C Brad....149 H8
Oldfield Worcs....81 J2
Old Fletton C Pete....102 D4
Oldford Somset....32 C1
Old Forge Herefs....63 H3
Old Furnace Herefs....62 F2
Old Glossop Derbys....131 L1
Old Goole E R Yk....143 J1
Old Grimsby IoS....10 b2
Old Hall Green Herts....69 K3
Oldhall Green Suffk....89 H4
Old Hall Street Norfk....122 F5
Oldham Oldham....140 D6
Oldhamstocks E Loth....213 G5
Old Harlow Essex....70 C5
Old Heath Essex....72 E3
Old Hunstanton Norfk....120 F3
Old Hurst Cambs....102 F7
Old Hutton W & F....157 J5
Old Inns Services N Lans....209 K4
Old Kea Cnwll....4 D6
Old Kilpatrick W Duns....208 D4
Old Knebworth Herts....69 G3
Old Lakenham Norfk....106 E2
Oldland S Glos....45 K4
Old Langho Lancs....148 B8
Old Laxey IoM....154 f5
Old Leake Lincs....119 L3
Old Malton N York....152 B1
Oldmeldrum Abers....256 E6
Oldmill Cnwll....11 M7
Old Milverton Warwks....83 G2
Oldmixon N Som....44 C7
Old Newton Suffk....90 B3
Old Oxted Surrey....51 K8
Old Philpstoun W Loth....210 E4
Old Portlethen Abers....245 L4
Old Quarrington Dur....169 J3
Old Radford C Nott....116 F3
Old Radnor Powys....79 J3
Old Rayne Abers....256 B6
Old Romney Kent....25 J2
Old Shoreham W Susx....22 B6
Oldshoremore Highld....276 C4
Old Soar Kent....38 F3
Old Sodbury S Glos....45 L3
Old Somerby Lincs....118 C5
Oldstead N York....161 H6
Old Stratford W Nthn....84 E7
Old Struan P & K....232 B2
Old Swarland Nthumb....191 H6
Old Swinford Dudley....97 K6
Old Tebay W & F....157 K2
Old Thirsk N York....160 F6
Old Town Calder....140 F2
Old Town E Susx....23 K7
Old Town IoS....10 c3
Old Town W & F....157 K1
Old Town W & F....166 B2
Old Trafford Traffd....140 B8
Old Tupton Derbys....133 H6
Oldwall Cumb....178 B6
Oldwalls Swans....56 E6
Old Warden C Beds....86 C6
Oldways End Somset....28 H6
Old Weston Cambs....102 B7
Old Wick Highld....280 E6
Old Windsor W & M....50 C4
Old Wives Lees Kent....40 E4
Old Woking Surrey....50 C4
Old Wolverton M Keyn....84 F7
Old Woodhall Lincs....136 D6
Old Woods Shrops....113 G6
Olgrinmore Highld....279 K5
Olive Green Staffs....115 J7
Oliver's Battery Hants....34 F5
Ollaberry Shet....281 d4
Ollach Highld....247 H1
Ollerton Ches E....130 F4
Ollerton Notts....134 D6
Ollerton Shrops....113 L6
Olmarch Cerdgn....77 H4
Olmstead Green Cambs....88 C7
Olney M Keyn....85 H5
Olrig House Highld....279 L3
Olton Solhll....98 E7

Olveston S Glos....45 J2
Ombersley Worcs....81 J2
Ompton Notts....134 D6
Once Brewed Nthumb....179 H5
Onchan IoM....154 e6
Onecote Staffs....131 L8
Onehouse Suffk....89 K3
Onen Mons....62 E4
Ongar Street Herefs....79 M2
Onibury Shrops....95 L7
Onich Highld....229 G3
Onllwyn Neath....60 C5
Onneley Staffs....114 B3
Onslow Green Essex....71 G3
Onslow Village Surrey....36 E1
Onston Ches W....130 B5
Openwoodgate Derbys....116 B2
Opinan Highld....260 B5
Orbliston Moray....266 F5
Orbost Highld....258 D7
Orby Lincs....137 J6
Orchard Portman Somset....30 B7
Orcheston Wilts....33 J2
Orcop Herefs....62 F2
Orcop Hill Herefs....62 F2
Ord Abers....268 A4
Ordhead Abers....244 E2
Ordie Abers....244 A3
Ordiequish Moray....267 G5
Ordley Nthumb....179 L7
Ordsall Notts....134 D4
Ore E Susx....24 F5
Oreleton Common Herefs....80 B2
Oreton Shrops....96 E7
Orford Suffk....91 K5
Orford Warrtn....130 B2
Organford Dorset....17 H4
Orgreave Staffs....115 J8
Orkney Islands Ork....275 c4
Orkney Neolithic Ork....275 b4
Orlestone Kent....40 C8
Orleton Herefs....80 A1
Orleton Worcs....81 G2
Orlingbury N Nthn....85 G1
Ormathwaite Cumb....165 J5
Ormesby R & Cl....170 C7
Ormesby St Margaret Norfk....123 K8
Ormesby St Michael Norfk....123 K8
Ormiscaig Highld....260 D2
Ormiston E Loth....211 M5
Ormsaigmore Highld....236 F7
Ormsary Ag & B....206 A4
Ormskirk Lancs....138 E6
Ornsby Hill Dur....168 F1
Oronsay Ag & B....214 C6
Orphir Ork....275 b5
Orpington Gt Lon....51 M5
Orrell Sefton....138 D8
Orrell Wigan....139 G7
Orrell Post Wigan....139 G6
Orrisdale IoM....154 d4
Orroland D & G....175 J5
Orsett Thurr....52 D3
Orsett Heath Thurr....52 D3
Orslow Staffs....114 C8
Orston Notts....117 K3
Orthwaite Cumb....165 H2
Ortner Lancs....147 K5
Orton N Nthn....101 H7
Orton Staffs....97 K4
Orton W & F....157 K1
Orton Longueville C Pete....102 D4
Orton-on-the-Hill Leics....99 J3
Orton Rigg Cumb....177 K8
Orton Waterville C Pete....102 C4
Orwell Cambs....87 H5
Osbaldeston Lancs....139 K2
Osbaldeston Green Lancs....139 K1
Osbaldwick C York....151 K5
Osbaston Leics....99 L3
Osbaston Mons....63 G4
Osbaston Shrops....112 D7
Osborne IoW....19 H5
Osbournby Lincs....118 C4
Oscroft Ches W....129 L6
Ose Highld....258 E8
Osgathorpe Leics....116 D7
Osgodby Lincs....135 M1
Osgodby N York....143 G1
Osgodby N York....163 J5
Oskaig Highld....247 H1
Oskamull Ag & B....226 E4
Osmaston Derbys....115 K3
Osmington Dorset....16 D6
Osmington Mills Dorset....16 D6
Osmondthorpe Leeds....142 A1
Osmotherley N York....161 G3
Osney Oxon....66 D6
Ospringe Kent....40 C3
Ossett Wakefd....141 L4

Ossington Notts............134 E6
Ostend Essex............72 D7
Osterley Gt Lon............50 F3
Oswaldkirk N York............161 K6
Oswaldtwistle Lancs............139 L2
Oswestry Shrops............112 D5
Otairnis W Isls............282 c7
Otford Kent............52 B7
Otham Kent............39 K3
Otham Hole Kent............39 K3
Othery Somset............30 F4
Otley Leeds............150 B6
Otley Suffk............90 E4
Otley Green Suffk............90 E4
Otterbourne Hants............34 F6
Otterburn N York............148 F4
Otterburn Nthumb............190 C7
Otter Ferry Ag & B............206 E2
Otterham Cnwll............11 H4
Otterhampton Somset............30 C2
Otterham Quay Kent............53 H5
Otterham Station Cnwll............11 G5
Otternish W Isls............282 c7
Ottershaw Surrey............50 C6
Otterswick Shet............281 e3
Otterton Devon............14 C5
Otterwood Hants............18 F3
Ottery St Mary Devon............14 C3
Ottinge Kent............41 G6
Ottringham E R Yk............145 H3
Oughterby Cumb............177 J7
Oughtershaw N York............158 F6
Oughterside Cumb............164 F3
Oughtibridge Sheff............132 F1
Oughtrington Warrtn............130 D2
Oulston N York............161 J7
Oulton Cumb............177 H8
Oulton Leeds............142 B2
Oulton Norfk............122 C6
Oulton Staffs............114 B7
Oulton Staffs............114 E4
Oulton Suffk............107 L4
Oulton Broad Suffk............107 L5
Oulton Street Norfk............122 C6
Oundle N Nthn............102 A5
Ounsdale Staffs............97 K5
Ousby W & F............166 E4
Ousden Suffk............88 E3
Ousefleet E R Yk............143 L3
Ouston Dur............181 G8
Outchester Nthumb............203 J6
Out Elmstead Kent............41 G5
Outgate W & F............156 E3
Outhgill W & F............158 D2
Outhill Warwks............82 D2
Outlands Staffs............114 B5
Outlane Kirk............141 G4
Out Newton E R Yk............145 K3
Out Rawcliffe Lancs............147 H7
Out Skerries Shet............281 g4
Outwell Norfk............103 K3
Outwick Hants............33 K7
Outwood Surrey............37 M2
Outwood Wakefd............142 A3
Outwood Gate Bury............140 B6
Outwoods Leics............116 C7
Outwoods Staffs............114 B7
Ouzlewell Green Leeds............142 A3
Ovenden Calder............141 G2
Over Cambs............87 H1
Over Ches W............130 C6
Over Gloucs............64 A3
Over S Glos............45 H2
Over Burrows Derbys............115 L4
Overbury Worcs............81 M7
Overcombe Dorset............16 D6
Over Compton Dorset............31 K7
Over End Cambs............102 B5
Overgreen Derbys............132 F5
Over Green Warwks............98 F4
Over Haddon Derbys............132 D6
Over Hulton Bolton............139 K6
Over Kellet Lancs............147 K2
Over Kiddington Oxon............66 B3
Overleigh Somset............31 G4
Overley Staffs............115 J8
Over Monnow Mons............63 G4
Over Norton Oxon............65 L2
Over Peover Ches E............130 F5
Overpool Ches W............129 J4
Overscaig Highld............272 B3
Overseal Derbys............115 M8
Over Silton N York............161 G4
Oversland Kent............40 D4
Oversley Green Warwks............82 C4
Overstone W Nthn............84 F2
Overstrand Norfk............122 E3
Over Stratton Somset............31 G7
Overstreet Wilts............33 J3
Over Tabley Ches E............130 E4
Overthorpe W Nthn............83 L7
Overton C Aber............245 J1
Overton Ches W............129 M4
Overton Hants............35 G1
Overton Lancs............147 H4
Overton N York............151 J5
Overton Shrops............80 C1
Overton Swans............56 E7
Overton Wakefd............141 L4
Overton Wrexhm............112 E3
Overton Bridge Wrexhm............112 E3
Overton Green Ches E............130 F7
Overtown Lancs............140 C2
Overtown Lancs............157 K7
Overtown N Lans............209 L8
Overtown Swindn............47 H3
Overtown Wakefd............142 A4
Over Wallop Hants............34 C3
Over Whitacre Warwks............99 H5
Over Woodhouse Derbys............133 J5
Over Worton Oxon............66 B1
Overy Oxon............66 E8
Oving Bucks............67 J3
Oving W Susx............20 E6
Ovingdean Br & H............22 E6
Ovingham Nthumb............180 D6
Ovington Dur............168 E7
Ovington Essex............88 F6
Ovington Hants............35 H4
Ovington Norfk............105 J3
Ovington Nthumb............180 C6
Ower Hants............19 H3
Ower Hants............34 D7
Owermoigne Dorset............16 E5
Owlbury Shrops............95 H5
Owlerton Sheff............133 G2
Owlpen Gloucs............64 A7
Owl's Green Suffk............91 G1
Owlsmoor Br For............49 K6
Owlswick Bucks............67 J2
Owmby Lincs............135 K2
Owmby Lincs............144 D6
Owslebury Hants............35 G6
Owston Donc............142 E5
Owston Leics............101 G2
Owston Ferry N Linc............143 K7
Owstwick E R Yk............145 H1
Owthorne E R Yk............145 J2
Owthorpe Notts............117 H5
Owton Manor Hartpl............170 C5
Oxborough Norfk............104 E3
Oxbridge Dorset............15 L3
Oxcombe Lincs............136 F4
Oxcroft Derbys............133 J5
Oxen End Essex............71 G1
Oxenholme W & F............157 H5
Oxenhope C Brad............140 F1
Oxen Park W & F............156 D5
Oxenpill Somset............31 G3
Oxenton Gloucs............64 D1
Oxenwood Wilts............47 L7
Oxford Oxon............66 D6
Oxford Airport Oxon............66 C4
Oxford Services Oxon............66 F6
Oxgangs C Edin............211 H5
Oxhey Herts............68 E8
Oxhill Dur............180 F8
Oxhill Warwks............83 H6
Oxley Wolves............97 K3
Oxley Green Essex............72 C4
Oxley's Green E Susx............24 C3
Oxlode Cambs............103 K6
Oxnam Border............189 J3
Oxnead Norfk............122 E6
Oxshott Surrey............50 F6
Oxshott Heath Surrey............50 E6
Oxspring Barns............141 L7
Oxted Surrey............51 K8
Oxton Border............201 G2
Oxton N York............151 H7
Oxton Notts............117 G1
Oxton Wirral............129 G2
Oxwich Swans............56 F7
Oxwich Green Swans............56 F7
Oxwick Norfk............121 K6
Oykel Bridge Highld............271 L7
Oyne Abers............256 B6
Oystermouth Swans............57 H7
Ozleworth Gloucs............64 A8

P

Pabail W Isls............282 h3
Packers Hill Dorset............16 D1
Packington Leics............116 B8
Packmoor C Stke............114 D1
Packmores Warwks............83 G2

Padanaram Angus............234 C5
Padbury Bucks............67 H1
Paddington Gt Lon............51 H3
Paddington Warrtn............130 C2
Paddlesworth Kent............41 G7
Paddlesworth Kent............52 E6
Paddock Wood Kent............39 G4
Paddolgreen Shrops............113 H5
Padfield Derbys............140 F8
Padgate Warrtn............130 C2
Padhams Green Essex............70 F7
Padiham Lancs............140 B1
Padside N York............149 L6
Padstow Cnwll............10 C7
Padworth W Berk............48 F5
Page Bank Dur............169 G4
Pagham W Susx............20 E7
Paglesham Essex............72 D8
Paignton Torbay............8 C3
Pailton Warwks............100 A7
Paine's Cross E Susx............23 K3
Painleyhill Staffs............115 G5
Painscastle Powys............79 G6
Painshawfield Nthumb............180 C6
Painsthorpe E R Yk............152 B4
Painswick Gloucs............64 C5
Painter's Forstal Kent............40 C3
Paisley Rens............208 E6
Pakefield Suffk............107 L5
Pakenham Suffk............89 J2
Pale Gwynd............111 J4
Pale Green Essex............88 D6
Palestine Hants............34 B3
Paley Street W & M............49 L4
Palfrey Wsall............98 C4
Palgrave Suffk............106 C7
Pallington Dorset............16 F4
Palmarsh Kent............40 F8
Palmers Green Gt Lon............69 J8
Palmerston E Ayrs............196 F7
Palmerstown V Glam............43 H7
Palnackie D & G............175 K3
Palnure D & G............174 C2
Palterton Derbys............133 J6
Pamber End Hants............48 F7
Pamber Green Hants............48 F7
Pamber Heath Hants............48 F6
Pamington Gloucs............81 L8
Pamphill Dorset............17 K3
Pampisford Cambs............87 K5
Panborough Somset............31 G2
Panbride Angus............234 E8
Pancrasweek Devon............11 K2
Pancross V Glam............43 G7
Pandy Gwynd............92 D3
Pandy Gwynd............111 G5
Pandy Mons............62 D3
Pandy Powys............93 K3
Pandy Wrexhm............112 B4
Pandy Wrexhm............112 E1
Pandy'r Capel Denbgs............111 L2
Pandy Tudur Conwy............127 G6
Panfield Essex............71 H2
Pangbourne W Berk............48 F4
Pangdean W Susx............22 D5
Panks Bridge Herefs............80 E5
Pannal N York............150 D5
Pannal Ash N York............150 C5
Pant Shrops............112 D7
Pantasaph Flints............128 E4
Panteg Pembks............74 F5
Pantersbridge Cnwll............5 K1
Pant-ffrwyth Brdgnd............42 E5
Pant Glas Gwynd............109 H2
Pantglas Powys............93 G4
Pant-Gwyn Carmth............59 G4
Pant-lasau Swans............57 J5
Pant Mawr Powys............93 J7
Panton Lincs............136 C4
Pant-pastynog Denbgs............128 B7
Pantperthog Gwynd............93 G3
Pantside Caerph............43 K2
Pant-y-caws Carmth............75 K7
Pant-y-dwr Powys............93 L8
Pant-y-ffridd Powys............94 B3
Pantyffynnon Carmth............57 H3
Pantygaseg Torfn............61 L7
Pantygelli Mons............62 C3
Pant-y-gog Brdgnd............42 D3
Pantymwyn Flints............128 E6
Panxworth Norfk............107 J3
Papa Stour Shet............281 c5
Papa Stour Airport Shet............281 c5
Papa Westray Ork............275 d1
Papa Westray Airport Ork............275 d1
Papcastle Cumb............164 F4
Papigoe Highld............280 E6
Papple E Loth............212 D4
Papplewick Notts............116 F1
Papworth Everard Cambs............86 F3

Papworth St Agnes Cambs............86 F2
Par Cnwll............5 H4
Paramour Street Kent............41 J3
Parbold Lancs............139 G5
Parbrook Somset............31 J4
Parbrook W Susx............37 G6
Parc Gwynd............111 G5
Parcllyn Cerdgn............75 M2
Parc Seymour Newpt............44 E1
Pardown Hants............35 J1
Pardshaw Cumb............164 E5
Parham Suffk............91 G3
Park D & G............186 D7
Park Nthumb............178 F6
Park Bottom Cnwll............3 H3
Park Bridge Tamesd............140 E7
Park Corner E Susx............38 E6
Park Corner Oxon............49 G1
Park Corner W & M............49 K2
Park End Bed............85 K4
Parkend Gloucs............63 J5
Park End Nthumb............179 K4
Parker's Green Kent............38 F4
Parkeston Essex............73 K1
Parkeston Quay Essex............90 F8
Park Farm Kent............40 D7
Parkgate Ches W............129 G4
Parkgate Cumb............165 H1
Parkgate D & G............176 D1
Parkgate E Susx............24 C4
Parkgate Essex............71 G1
Park Gate Hants............19 J2
Parkgate Kent............39 L6
Parkgate Kent............52 B6
Park Gate Leeds............150 A7
Parkgate Surrey............37 K2
Park Gate Worcs............81 L1
Park Green Essex............70 C2
Park Green Suffk............90 D2
Park Hall Shrops............112 D5
Parkhall W Duns............208 E4
Parkham Devon............27 G6
Parkham Ash Devon............26 F6
Park Head Derbys............116 B1
Parkhill Dur............169 J3
Park Hill Gloucs............63 H7
Parkhouse Mons............63 G6
Parkmill Swans............57 G2
Park Royal Gt Lon............51 G3
Parkside Dur............169 L1
Parkside N Lans............209 L7
Parkside Wrexhm............129 J8
Parkstone BCP............17 K4
Park Street Herts............68 F6
Park Street W Susx............37 H4
Parkway Herefs............81 G8
Parley Green BCP............17 M3
Parmoor Bucks............49 J1
Parracombe Devon............28 B2
Parrog Pembks............75 H4
Parsonby Cumb............164 F3
Parson Cross Sheff............133 G1
Parson Drove Cambs............103 H2
Parson's Heath Essex............72 F2
Parson's Hill Derbys............116 A6
Partick C Glas............208 F5
Partington Traffd............130 D2
Partney Lincs............137 H6
Parton Cumb............164 C6
Partridge Green W Susx............22 B3
Partrishow Powys............62 B3
Parwich Derbys............115 K7
Paslow Wood Common Essex............70 E6
Passenham W Nthn............84 F7
Passfield Hants............36 B4
Passingford Bridge Essex............70 D7
Paston C Pete............102 D3
Paston Norfk............123 G4
Pasturefields Staffs............114 F6
Patchacott Devon............12 B3
Patcham Br & H............22 D5
Patchetts Green Herts............68 F7
Patching W Susx............21 J5
Patchole Devon............27 L2
Patchway S Glos............45 J3
Pateley Bridge N York............149 L3
Paternoster Heath Essex............72 F4
Pathe Somset............30 F4
Pathhead Fife............222 E8
Pathhead Mdloth............211 L6
Pathlow Warwks............82 K3
Path of Condie P & K............221 K5
Patmore Heath Herts............70 B2
Patna E Ayrs............183 K1
Patney Wilts............47 G7
Patrick IoM............154 c5
Patrick Brompton N York............160 B4
Patricroft Salfd............139 M8
Patrington E R Yk............145 J3
Patrington Haven E R Yk............145 J3

Patrixbourne Kent 41 G4
Patterdale W & F 165 L7
Pattingham Staffs 97 J4
Pattishall W Nthn 84 C4
Pattiswick Green Essex 71 K4
Patton Shrops 96 D4
Patton Bridge W & F 157 J3
Paul Cnwll 2 D5
Paulerspury W Nthn 84 D6
Paull E R Yk 144 F3
Paulton BaNES 45 K7
Paunton Herefs 80 F5
Pauperhaugh Nthumb 191 G6
Pave Lane Wrekin 114 B8
Pavenham Bed 85 K4
Pawlett Somset 30 D2
Pawston Nthumb 202 C6
Paxford Gloucs 82 E7
Paxton Border 202 E3
Payden Street Kent 40 B4
Paynembury Devon 14 C2
Poynter's Lane End Cnwll 3 H2
Paythorne Lancs 148 L5
Payton Herefs 80 A1
Peacehaven E Susx 22 F7
Peak Dale Derbys 132 B4
Peak District National Park 132 D2
Peak Forest Derbys 132 B4
Peak Hill Lincs 119 J8
Peakirk C Pete 102 D2
Pearson's Green Kent 39 H4
Peartree Green Herefs 80 E5
Peasedown St John BaNES 45 K7
Peasehill Derbys 116 C2
Peaseland Green Norfk 122 B8
Peasemore W Berk 48 C3
Peasenhall Suffk 91 H2
Pease Pottage W Susx 37 L4
Pease Pottage Services W Susx 37 L4
Peaslake Surrey 37 G2
Peasley Cross St Hel 129 M1
Peasmarsh E Susx 25 G3
Peasmarsh Somset 30 L0
Peasmarsh Surrey 36 E2
Peathill Abers 269 G3
Peat Inn Fife 223 H5
Peatling Magna Leics 100 D5
Peatling Parva Leics 100 D5
Peaton Shrops 96 C6
Pebmarsh Essex 89 G8
Pebsham E Susx 24 D5
Pebworth Worcs 82 D6
Pecket Well Calder 140 F2
Peckforton Ches E 129 M8
Peckham Gt Lon 51 J4
Peckleton Leics 100 A3
Pedairffordd Powys 111 M6
Pedlinge Kent 40 F8
Pedmore Dudley 97 K7
Pedwell Somset 30 F4
Peebles Border 200 B5
Peel IoM 154 c5
Peel Lancs 138 D2
Peel Common Hants 19 K3
Peene Kent 41 G7
Peening Quarter Kent 39 M7
Peggs Green Leics 116 C7
Pegsdon C Beds 68 E1
Pegswood Nthumb 180 F2
Pegwell Kent 41 K3
Peinchorran Highld 247 H2
Peinlich Highld 259 G5
Pelcomb Pembks 54 F3
Pelcomb Bridge Pembks 54 F3
Pelcomb Cross Pembks 54 F3
Peldon Essex 72 E4
Pell Green E Susx 39 G6
Pelsall Wsall 98 C3
Pelsall Wood Wsall 98 C3
Pelton Dur 181 G8
Pelton Fell Dur 181 G8
Pelutho Cumb 164 F1
Pelynt Cnwll 5 L4
Pemberton Carmth 56 F5
Pemberton Wigan 139 H7
Pembles Cross Kent 39 M4
Pembrey Carmth 56 D4
Pembridge Herefs 79 M4
Pembroke Pembks 55 G6
Pembroke Dock Pembks 54 F6
Pembrokeshire Coast National Park Pembks 54 D3
Pembury Kent 39 G5
Pen-allt Herefs 63 H1
Penallt Mons 63 G5
Penally Pembks 55 J7
Penare Cnwll 5 G6
Penarth V Glam 43 J7
Penblewin Pembks 55 J4
Pen-bont Rhydybeddau Cerdgn 92 E6

Penbryn Cerdgn 76 B5
Pencader Carmth 58 E2
Pencaenewydd Gwynd 109 G3
Pencaitland E Loth 212 A5
Pencarnisiog IoA 124 F5
Pencarreg Carmth 76 F6
Pencarrow Cnwll 10 F6
Pencelli Powys 61 H2
Penclawdd Swans 57 G5
Pencoed Brdgnd 42 E5
Pencombe Herefs 80 E5
Pencoyd Herefs 63 G2
Pencraig Herefs 63 H3
Pencraig Powys 111 K6
Pendeen Cnwll 2 B4
Penderyn Rhondd 60 E5
Pendine Carmth 55 L5
Pendlebury Salfd 140 B7
Pendleton Lancs 148 D7
Pendock Worcs 81 H0
Pendoggett Cnwll 10 E6
Pendomer Somset 31 H8
Pendoylan V Glam 43 G6
Penegoes Powys 93 G3
Penelewey Cnwll 3 K3
Pen-ffordd Pembks 55 J2
Pengam Caerph 43 J2
Pengam Cardif 43 K6
Penge Gt Lon 51 K5
Pengelly Cnwll 10 F6
Pengenffordd Powys 61 J1
Pengorffwysfa IoA 125 H1
Pengover Green Cnwll 6 B2
Pen-groes-oped Mons 62 C5
Pengwern Denbgs 127 K4
Penhale Cnwll 3 H7
Penhale Cnwll 4 E3
Penhale Cnwll 5 J3
Penhale Cnwll 6 E4
Penhallow Cnwll 4 C4
Penhalurick Cnwll 3 H3
Penhalvean Cnwll 3 H3
Penhill Swindn 47 H1
Penhow Newpt 44 E1
Penhurst E Susx 24 C4
Peniarth Gwynd 92 D2
Penicuik Mdloth 211 H7
Peniel Carmth 58 D4
Peniel Denbgs 127 L7
Penifiler Highld 259 H8
Peninver Ag & B 192 F3
Penisarwaun Gwynd 125 K7
Penistone Barns 141 K7
Penjerrick Cnwll 3 K5
Penketh Warrtn 130 A2
Penkill S Ayrs 183 G3
Penkridge Staffs 97 L1
Penlean Cnwll 11 H3
Penleigh Wilts 32 E1
Penley Wrexhm 112 F3
Penllergaer Swans 57 H5
Pen-llyn IoA 124 F3
Penllyn V Glam 42 E6
Pen-lôn IoA 125 G6
Penmachno Conwy 110 E2
Penmaen Caerph 43 J2
Penmaen Swans 56 F7
Penmaenan Conwy 126 E4
Penmaenmawr Conwy 126 E4
Penmaenpool Gwynd 110 C7
Penmark V Glam 43 G7
Penmon IoA 126 C3
Penmorfa Gwynd 109 K3
Penmynydd IoA 125 J5
Penn Bucks 67 M8
Penn Wolves 97 K4
Pennal Gwynd 92 F3
Pennan Abers 268 F3
Pennant Cerdgn 76 F3
Pennant Denbgs 111 K5
Pennant Powys 93 J4
Pennant-Melangell Powys 111 K6
Pennar Pembks 54 F6
Pennard Swans 57 G7
Pennerley Shrops 95 J3
Pennicott Devon 13 K2
Pennines 140 E1
Pennington Hants 18 D4
Pennington W & F 156 C7
Pennington Green Wigan 139 J6
Pennorth Powys 61 H2
Penn Street Bucks 68 A7
Pennsylvania S Glos 45 L4
Penny Bridge W & F 156 D6
Pennycross Ag & B 226 F7
Pennygate Norfk 123 G7
Pennyghael Ag & B 227 G7
Pennyglen S Ayrs 183 H1
Penny Green Derbys 133 L4
Penny Hill Lincs 119 K6

Pennymoor Devon 28 F8
Pennywell Sundld 181 J7
Penparc Cerdgn 75 L3
Penparcau Cerdgn 92 D7
Penpedairheol Caerph 43 J2
Penpedairheol Mons 62 C6
Penpergwm Mons 62 C5
Penperlleni Mons 62 C6
Penpethy Cnwll 10 F5
Penpillick Cnwll 5 J4
Penpol Cnwll 3 K3
Penpoll Cnwll 5 K4
Penponds Cnwll 3 G3
Penpont D & G 186 C7
Penpont Powys 60 E2
Penquit Devon 7 J4
Penrest Cnwll 11 L7
Penrherber Carmth 76 B7
Pen-rhiw Pembks 75 M4
Penrhiwceiber Rhondd 43 G2
Pen Rhiwfawr Neath 57 K3
Penrhiwgoch Carmth 59 G5
Penrhiwllan Cerdgn 76 C6
Penrhiwpal Cerdgn 76 C6
Penrhos Gwynd 108 F5
Penrhos IoA 124 D3
Penrhos Mons 62 E5
Penrhos Powys 59 L6
Penrhos garnedd Gwynd 125 K5
Penrhyn Bay Conwy 127 G3
Penrhyn-coch Cerdgn 92 E6
Penrhyndeudraeth Gwynd 109 L4
Penrhyn-side Conwy 126 F3
Penrhyn Slate Landscape Gwynd 126 C6
Penrhys Rhondd 42 F3
Penrice Swans 56 F7
Penrioch N Ayrs 194 D2
Penrith W & F 166 C4
Penrose Cnwll 10 B8
Penruddock W & F 166 A5
Penryn Cnwll 3 K4
Pensarn Conwy 127 J4
Pensax Worcs 81 G2
Pensby Wirral 129 G3
Penselwood Somset 32 C4
Pensford BaNES 45 J6
Pensham Worcs 81 L6
Penshaw Sundld 181 H8
Penshurst Kent 38 E4
Penshurst Station Kent 38 E4
Pensilva Cnwll 11 K8
Pensnett Dudley 97 K5
Penstone Devon 13 H3
Penstrowed Powys 94 C5
Pentewan Cnwll 5 G5
Pentir Gwynd 125 K6
Pentire Cnwll 4 C3
Pentlepoir Pembks 55 J5
Pentlow Essex 89 G6
Pentlow Street Essex 89 G6
Pentney Norfk 120 F8
Penton Grafton Hants 34 D2
Penton Mewsey Hants 34 D2
Pentraeth IoA 125 J4
Pentre Denbgs 128 C6
Pentre Flints 129 H6
Pentre Mons 62 C6
Pentre Mons 62 E7
Pentre Powys 94 C6
Pentre Powys 94 E5
Pentre Powys 95 G5
Pentre Rhondd 42 E2
Pentre Shrops 112 E7
Pentre Wrexhm 112 D3
Pentre-bâch Cerdgn 77 G6
Pentre Bach Flints 128 F4
Pentrebach Myr Td 61 G6
Pentre-bach Powys 78 B8
Pentrebeirdd Powys 94 E1
Pentre Berw IoA 125 H5
Pentre-bont Conwy 110 D1
Pentre-cagel Carmth 76 C7
Pentrecelyn Denbgs 112 A1
Pentre-celyn Powys 93 J2
Pentre-chwyth Swans 57 J6
Pentre-clawdd Shrops 112 D5
Pentre-cwrt Carmth 76 D7
Pentredwr Denbgs 112 B2
Pentrefelin Gwynd 109 J4
Pentrefelin IoA 125 H1
Pentre Ffwrndan Flints 128 F5
Pentrefoelas Conwy 111 G4
Pentregalar Pembks 75 L6
Pentregat Cerdgn 76 C5
Pentre-Gwenlais Carmth 59 H5
Pentre Gwynfryn Gwynd 109 L6
Pentre Halkyn Flints 128 E5

Pentre Hodrey Shrops 95 H7
Pentre Isaf Conwy 127 K5
Pentre Llanrhaeadr Denbgs 128 C7
Pentre Llifior Powys 94 E4
Pentrellwyn Denbgs 76 D6
Pentre-llwyn-llwyd Powys 78 C4
Pentre-llyn Cerdgn 92 D8
Pentre-llyn-cymmer Conwy 111 J1
Pentre-Maw Powys 93 J3
Pentre Meyrick V Glam 42 E6
Pentre-piod Torfn 62 B6
Pentre-poeth Newpt 44 B2
Pentre'rbryn Cerdgn 76 D2
Pentre'r-felin Cerdgn 77 H5
Pentre'r Felin Conwy 126 F6
Pentre'r-felin Powys 60 D1
Pentre Saron Denbgs 127 L7
Pentre-tafarn-y-fedw Conwy 126 F7
Pentre ty gwyn Carmth 59 M2
Pentrich Derbys 116 C1
Pentridge Dorset 33 H7
Pen-twyn Caerph 61 K7
Pentwyn Cardif 43 K5
Pen-twyn Mons 63 G5
Pen-twyn Torfn 61 L6
Pentwynmaur Caerph 43 K2
Pentyrch Cardif 43 H5
Penwithick Cnwll 5 H4
Penwood Hants 48 C6
Penwyllt Powys 60 C4
Penybanc Carmth 59 H4
Penybont Powys 78 F2
Pen-y-bont Powys 112 B6
Penybontfawr Powys 111 L6
Pen-y-bryn Pembks 75 L4
Pen-y-cae Powys 60 C4
Penycae Wrexhm 112 D3
Pen-y-cae-mawr Mons 62 E8
Penycaerau Gwynd 108 C6
Pen-y-cefn Flints 128 D4
Pen-y-clawdd Mons 62 F5
Pen-y-coedcae Rhondd 43 G4
Penycwn Pembks 54 D2
Pen-y-fai Brdgnd 42 D5
Pen-y-felin Flints 128 D5
Pen-y-ffordd Flints 100 D0
Penyffordd Flints 129 G7
Penyffridd Gwynd 125 J8
Pen-y-garn Cerdgn 92 D6
Pen-y-Garnedd Powys 111 L6
Pen-y-graig Gwynd 108 C5
Penygraig Rhondd 42 F3
Penygroes Carmth 59 G6
Penygroes Gwynd 109 H1
Penygroeslon Gwynd 108 C5
Pen-y-Gwryd Gwynd 126 D8
Pen-y-lan V Glam 42 F6
Pen-y-Mynydd Carmth 56 E4
Penymynydd Flints 129 G7
Pen-y-pass Gwynd 126 C8
Pen-yr-Heol Mons 62 E5
Penysarn IoA 125 H2
Pen-y-stryt Denbgs 112 B1
Penywaun Rhondd 60 E6
Penzance Cnwll 2 D5
Peopleton Worcs 81 L5
Peover Heath Ches E 130 F5
Peper Harow Surrey 36 D2
Peplow Shrops 113 K6
Pepper's Green Essex 70 F5
Pepperstock C Beds 68 D3
Perceton N Ayrs 196 C3
Percyhorner Abers 269 H3
Perelle Guern 9 i3
Perham Down Wilts 34 B1
Periton Somset 29 G2
Perivale Gt Lon 50 F2
Perkins Village Devon 14 B4
Perkinsville Dur 181 G8
Perlethorpe Notts 134 C5
Perranarworthal Cnwll 3 K4
Perranporth Cnwll 4 B4
Perranuthnoe Cnwll 2 D5
Perranwell Cnwll 3 K3
Perranwell Cnwll 4 C4
Perran Wharf Cnwll 3 K3
Perranzabuloe Cnwll 4 C4
Perrott's Brook Gloucs 64 E6
Perry Birm 98 D5
Perry Cambs 86 C2
Perry Barr Birm 98 D5
Perry Green Essex 71 K3
Perry Green Herts 70 B4
Perry Green Wilts 46 E1
Perrystone Hill Herefs 63 H1
Perry Street Somset 15 H2
Pershall Staffs 114 C5
Pershore Worcs 81 L6
Pertenhall Bed 86 B2
Perth P & K 221 K3

Perthy Shrops	112	E5	
Perton Herefs	80	E7	
Perton Staffs	97	J3	
Pertwood Wilts	32	E4	
Peterborough C Pete	102	D4	
Peterborough Services Cambs	102	C5	
Peterchurch Herefs	79	L7	
Peterculter C Aber	245	J3	
Peterhead Abers	257	L2	
Peterlee Dur	169	L2	
Petersfield Hants	35	M6	
Peter's Green Herts	68	F3	
Petersham Gt Lon	50	F4	
Peters Marland Devon	27	H8	
Peterstone Wentlooge Newpt	43	L5	
Peterston-super-Ely V Glam	43	G6	
Peterstow Herefs	63	H2	
Peters Village Kent	52	F6	
Peter Tavy Devon	12	C7	
Petham Kent	40	F5	
Petherwin Gate Cnwll	11	K5	
Petrockstow Devon	12	C1	
Petsoe End M Keyn	85	H5	
Pet Street Kent	40	E6	
Pett E Susx	24	F4	
Pettaugh Suffk	90	E3	
Pett Bottom Kent	40	F5	
Petterden Angus	234	C7	
Pettinain S Lans	198	F4	
Pettistree Suffk	91	G4	
Petton Devon	29	H6	
Petton Shrops	113	G6	
Petts Wood Gt Lon	51	M5	
Pettycur Fife	211	J2	
Petty France S Glos	46	A2	
Pettymuk Abers	257	G7	
Petworth W Susx	36	E6	
Pevensey E Susx	23	L6	
Pevensey Bay E Susx	24	B6	
Pewsey Wilts	47	H7	
Pewsham Wilts	46	D4	
Pheasant's Hill Bucks	49	J2	
Phepson Worcs	81	L3	
Philadelphia Sundld	181	H8	
Philham Devon	26	D6	
Philiphaugh Border	200	F7	
Phillack Cnwll	2	F3	
Philleigh Cnwll	3	L3	
Philpot End Essex	70	F3	
Philpstoun W Loth	210	D4	
Phocle Green Herefs	63	J2	
Phoenix Green Hants	49	J7	
Pibsbury Somset	31	G5	
Pica Cumb	164	D6	
Piccadilly Warwks	99	G4	
Piccotts End Herts	68	D5	
Pickburn Donc	142	E6	
Pickering N York	162	D6	
Picket Piece Hants	34	E2	
Picket Post Hants	18	B2	
Picket Twenty Hants	34	E2	
Pickford Covtry	99	H7	
Pickford Green Covtry	99	H7	
Pickhill N York	160	E6	
Picklescott Shrops	95	K3	
Pickmere Ches E	130	D4	
Pickney Somset	30	B5	
Pickstock Wrekin	114	A6	
Pickup Bank Bl w D	139	L3	
Pickwell Devon	27	H3	
Pickwell Leics	101	G1	
Pickwick Wilts	46	B5	
Pickworth Lincs	118	D5	
Pickworth Rutlnd	101	L1	
Picton Ches W	129	K5	
Picton Flints	128	D3	
Picton N York	160	F1	
Piddinghoe E Susx	23	G6	
Piddington Bucks	67	K8	
Piddington Oxon	66	F4	
Piddington W Nthn	84	F4	
Piddlehinton Dorset	16	D3	
Piddletrenthide Dorset	16	D3	
Pidley Cambs	103	G7	
Piercebridge Darltn	169	G7	
Pierowall Ork	275	c1	
Piff's Elm Gloucs	64	C2	
Pigdon Nthumb	180	E1	
Pigeon Green Warwks	82	F3	
Pig Oak Dorset	17	K2	
Pig Street Herefs	79	L5	
Pikehall Derbys	132	D7	
Pilford Dorset	17	K2	
Pilgrims Hatch Essex	70	E7	
Pilham Lincs	135	H1	
Pill N Som	45	G4	
Pillaton Cnwll	6	D2	
Pillatonmill Cnwll	6	D2	
Pillerton Hersey Warwks	83	G5	
Pillerton Priors Warwks	83	G5	
Pilleth Powys	79	J2	
Pilley Barns	142	A7	
Pilley Hants	18	E4	
Pilley Bailey Hants	18	E4	
Pillgwenlly Newpt	44	C2	
Pillhead Devon	27	H5	
Pilling Lancs	147	H6	
Pilling Lane Lancs	147	G6	
Pilning S Glos	45	H2	
Pilot Inn Kent	25	K4	
Pilsbury Derbys	132	B7	
Pilsdon Dorset	15	J3	
Pilsgate C Pete	102	B2	
Pilsley Derbys	132	E5	
Pilsley Derbys	133	H7	
Pilson Green Norfk	107	H1	
Piltdown E Susx	23	G3	
Pilton Devon	27	K4	
Pilton N Nthn	101	M6	
Pilton Rutlnd	101	K3	
Pilton Somset	31	K4	
Pilton Green Swans	56	E7	
Pimbo Lancs	139	G7	
Pimlico Herts	68	E6	
Pimlico Lancs	148	C1	
Pimlico W Nthn	84	B7	
Pimperne Dorset	17	H1	
Pinchbeck Lincs	119	H6	
Pinchbeck Bars Lincs	119	G6	
Pincheon Green Donc	143	G4	
Pinchinthorpe R & Cl	170	D7	
Pincock Lancs	139	H4	
Pinfold Lancs	138	E5	
Pinford End Suffk	89	L3	
Pinged Carmth	56	D4	
Pingewood W Berk	49	G5	
Pin Green Herts	69	H2	
Pinhoe Devon	13	M4	
Pinkett's Booth Covtry	99	H7	
Pinkney Wilts	46	B2	
Pinkneys Green W & M	49	L3	
Pinley Covtry	99	K7	
Pinley Green Warwks	82	F2	
Pin Mill Suffk	90	E7	
Pinminnoch S Ayrs	182	F4	
Pinmore S Ayrs	182	F4	
Pinn Devon	14	C5	
Pinner Gt Lon	50	E1	
Pinner Green Gt Lon	50	E1	
Pinsley Green Ches E	113	K2	
Pinvin Worcs	81	M5	
Pinwherry S Ayrs	182	F5	
Pinxton Derbys	133	J8	
Pipe and Lyde Herefs	80	C6	
Pipe Aston Herefs	80	B1	
Pipe Gate Shrops	114	A3	
Pipehill Staffs	98	E2	
Piperdam Angus	233	L8	
Piperhill Highld	253	G2	
Pipers Pool Cnwll	11	J6	
Pipewell N Nthn	101	J6	
Pippacott Devon	27	J3	
Pippin Street Lancs	139	H3	
Pipton Powys	79	G7	
Pirbright Surrey	50	B7	
Pirbright Camp Surrey	50	B7	
Pirnie Border	201	K7	
Pirnmill N Ayrs	194	D2	
Pirton Herts	68	F1	
Pirton Worcs	81	K5	
Pisgah Cerdgn	92	E7	
Pishill Oxon	49	H1	
Pistyll Gwynd	108	E3	
Pitblae Abers	269	H3	
Pitcairngreen P & K	221	J2	
Pitcalnie Highld	264	C5	
Pitcaple Abers	256	C6	
Pitcarity Angus	233	M2	
Pitchcombe Gloucs	64	B5	
Pitchcott Bucks	67	J3	
Pitcher Row Lincs	119	J5	
Pitchford Shrops	96	C3	
Pitch Green Bucks	67	J6	
Pitch Place Surrey	36	C3	
Pitch Place Surrey	50	B8	
Pitchroy Moray	254	D4	
Pitcombe Somset	31	L4	
Pitcot V Glam	42	D6	
Pitcox E Loth	212	E4	
Pitfichie Abers	256	B8	
Pitglassie Abers	256	C3	
Pitgrudy Highld	264	B2	
Pitlessie Fife	222	E5	
Pitlochry P & K	232	D4	
Pitmachie Abers	256	B6	
Pitmain Highld	241	K3	
Pitmedden Abers	256	F6	
Pitminster Somset	30	B7	
Pitmuies Angus	234	E5	
Pitmunie Abers	256	B8	
Pitney Somset	31	G5	
Pitroddie P & K	222	D2	
Pitscottie Fife	223	G4	
Pitsea Essex	52	F1	
Pitses Oldham	140	E7	
Pitsford W Nthn	84	E2	
Pitstone Bucks	68	B4	
Pitt Devon	29	J7	
Pitt Hants	34	F5	
Pittarrow Abers	245	G8	
Pitt Court Gloucs	63	L7	
Pittentrail Highld	273	H7	
Pittenweem Fife	223	K6	
Pitteuchar Fife	222	D7	
Pittodrie House Hotel Abers	256	C6	
Pitton Wilts	34	B4	
Pitt's Wood Kent	38	F3	
Pittulie Abers	269	H3	
Pityme Cnwll	10	C7	
Pity Me Dur	169	H2	
Pivington Kent	40	B6	
Pixey Green Suffk	106	E8	
Pixham Surrey	37	J1	
Plains N Lans	209	L5	
Plain Street Cnwll	10	D6	
Plaish Shrops	96	C4	
Plaistow Gt Lon	51	L2	
Plaistow W Susx	36	F5	
Plaitford Hants	34	C7	
Plank Lane Wigan	139	J7	
Plas Cymyran IoA	124	E4	
Plastow Green Hants	48	D6	
Platt Bridge Wigan	139	J7	
Platt Lane Shrops	113	H4	
Platts Heath Kent	39	L3	
Plawsworth Dur	169	H1	
Plaxtol Kent	38	F3	
Playden E Susx	25	G3	
Playford Suffk	90	F5	
Play Hatch Oxon	49	H4	
Playing Place Cnwll	4	C2	
Playley Green Gloucs	63	M1	
Plealey Shrops	95	K2	
Plean Stirlg	209	M2	
Pleasance Fife	222	C4	
Pleasington Bl w D	139	J2	
Pleasley Derbys	133	K6	
Pleasleyhill Notts	133	K6	
Pleck Dorset	32	B8	
Pledgdon Green Essex	70	E2	
Pledwick Wakefd	142	A4	
Pleinheaume Guern	9	j2	
Plemont Jersey	9	a1	
Plemstall Ches W	129	K5	
Plenmeller Nthumb	179	G6	
Plesheyy Essex	71	G4	
Plockton Highld	248	C5	
Plowden Shrops	95	J6	
Plox Green Shrops	95	J3	
Pluckley Kent	40	B6	
Pluckley Station Kent	40	B6	
Pluckley Thorne Kent	40	B6	
Plucks Gutter Kent	41	J3	
Plumbland Cumb	164	F3	
Plumgarths W & F	157	G4	
Plumley Ches E	130	E5	
Plump Hill Gloucs	63	K4	
Plumpton E Susx	22	E4	
Plumpton W & F	156	D7	
Plumpton W & F	166	C3	
Plumpton W Nthn	84	B5	
Plumpton End W Nthn	84	D6	
Plumpton Green E Susx	22	E4	
Plumpton Head W & F	166	C4	
Plumstead Gt Lon	51	L3	
Plumstead Norfk	122	C4	
Plumstead Green Norfk	122	C4	
Plumtree Notts	117	G5	
Plumtree Green Kent	39	K4	
Plungar Leics	117	K5	
Plurenden Kent	40	B7	
Plush Dorset	16	D2	
Plusha Cnwll	11	J6	
Plushabridge Cnwll	11	K5	
Plwmp Cerdgn	76	C5	
Plymouth C Plym	6	F4	
Plympton C Plym	7	G4	
Plymstock C Plym	7	G4	
Plymtree Devon	14	B2	
Pockley N York	161	K5	
Pocklington E R Yk	152	B6	
Pode Hole Lincs	119	H7	
Podimore Somset	31	J6	
Podington Bed	85	J3	
Podmore Staffs	114	B4	
Point Clear Essex	73	G4	
Pointon Lincs	118	F5	
Pokesdown BCP	18	A5	
Polbain Highld	270	C6	
Polbathic Cnwll	6	C3	
Polbeth W Loth	210	D6	
Polbrock Cnwll	5	G1	
Poldark Mine Cnwll	3	H5	
Polebrook N Nthn	102	B6	
Pole Elm Worcs	81	J5	
Polegate E Susx	23	K6	
Pole Moor Kirk	141	G4	
Polesworth Warwks	99	H3	
Polgigga Cnwll	2	B6	
Polglass Highld	270	G8	
Polgooth Cnwll	5	G5	
Polgown D & G	185	H2	
Poling W Susx	21	H6	
Poling Corner W Susx	21	H6	
Polkerris Cnwll	5	J4	
Pollard Street Norfk	123	G5	
Pollington E R Yk	142	F4	
Polloch Highld	228	B2	
Pollok C Glas	208	F6	
Pollokshaws C Glas	208	F6	
Pollokshields C Glas	208	F6	
Polmassick Cnwll	5	G5	
Polmear Cnwll	5	J4	
Polmont Falk	210	B3	
Polnish Highld	237	L4	
Polperro Cnwll	5	L4	
Polruan Cnwll	5	K5	
Polsham Somset	31	H2	
Polstead Suffk	89	K7	
Polstead Heath Suffk	89	K7	
Poltalloch Ag & B	216	C7	
Poltescoe Cnwll	3	J7	
Poltimore Devon	13	M3	
Polton Mdloth	211	J6	
Polwarth Border	202	A3	
Polyphant Cnwll	11	J6	
Polzeath Cnwll	10	C5	
Pomathorn Mdloth	211	H7	
Pomeroy Derbys	132	B6	
Ponde Powys	78	F7	
Pondersbridge Cambs	102	F5	
Ponders End Gt Lon	69	K7	
Ponsanooth Cnwll	3	J3	
Ponsonby Cumb	155	J2	
Ponsongath Cnwll	3	J7	
Ponsworthy Devon	13	G7	
Pont Abraham Services Carmth	57	G3	
Pontac Jersey	9	e4	
Pontamman Carmth	59	H6	
Pontantwn Carmth	58	E6	
Pontardawe Neath	57	K4	
Pontarddulais Swans	57	G4	
Pont-ar-gothi Carmth	58	F4	
Pont-ar-Hydfer Powys	60	C2	
Pont-ar-llechau Carmth	59	K4	
Pontarsais Carmth	58	E3	
Pontblyddyn Flints	129	G2	
Pont Cyfyng Conwy	126	E8	
Pontcysyllte Aqueduct Wrexhm	112	C3	
Pont Dolgarrog Conwy	126	F6	
Pontdolgoch Powys	94	B5	
Pont-Ebbw Newpt	44	C2	
Pontefract Wakefd	142	C3	
Ponteland Nthumb	180	E4	
Ponterwyd Cerdgn	93	G7	
Pontesbury Shrops	95	K2	
Pontesbury Hill Shrops	95	K2	
Pontesford Shrops	95	K2	
Pontfadog Wrexhm	112	C4	
Pontfaen Pembks	75	G5	
Pont-faen Powys	78	C6	
Pontgarreg Cerdgn	76	B4	
Pontgarreg Pembks	75	K4	
Pont Henri Carmth	56	E3	
Ponthir Torfn	62	C2	
Ponthirwaun Cerdgn	76	A6	
Pontllanfraith Caerph	43	J3	
Pontlliw Swans	57	H5	
Pontllyfni Gwynd	109	H1	
Pontlottyn Caerph	61	H6	
Pont Morlais Carmth	56	F3	
Pontnêddféchan Neath	60	D5	
Pontnewydd Torfn	62	B7	
Pontnewynydd Torfn	62	B6	
Pont Pen-y-benglog Gwynd	126	C7	
Pontrhydfendigaid Cerdgn	77	K2	
Pont Rhyd-sarn Gwynd	111	G6	
Pont Rhyd-y-cyff Brdgnd	42	C4	
Pontrhydyfen Neath	42	B3	
Pont-rhyd-y-groes Cerdgn	77	K1	
Pontrhydyrun Torfn	62	C7	
Pontrilas Herefs	62	E2	
Pont Robert Powys	94	D1	
Pont-rug Gwynd	125	J7	
Ponts Green E Susx	24	B4	
Pontshill Herefs	63	J3	
Pontsian Cerdgn	76	D6	
Pontsticill Myr Td	61	G5	
Pont Walby Neath	60	D6	

Place	County	Page	Grid
Pontwelly	Carmth	76	D7
Pontyates	Carmth	56	E3
Pontyberem	Carmth	58	F6
Pont-y-blew	Wrexhm	112	D4
Pontybodkin	Flints	129	G7
Pontyclun	Rhondd	42	F5
Pontycymer	Brdgnd	42	D3
Pontyglasier	Pembks	75	K5
Pontygwaith	Rhondd	42	F3
Pontygynon	Pembks	75	K5
Pontymister	Caerph	43	K4
Pont-y-pant	Conwy	110	E1
Pontypool	Torfn	62	B7
Pontypridd	Rhondd	43	G4
Pont-yr-hafod	Pembks	74	E7
Pont-yr-Rhyl	Brdgnd	42	D4
Pontywaun	Caerph	43	K3
Pool	Cnwll	3	H3
Poole	BCP	17	K4
Poole Keynes	Gloucs	64	E8
Poolewe	Highld	260	D6
Pooley Bridge	W & F	166	B6
Pooley Street	Norfk	105	L7
Poolfold	Staffs	131	H7
Pool Head	Herefs	80	D5
Poolhill	Gloucs	63	L1
Pool in Wharfedale	Leeds	150	C6
Pool of Muckhart	Clacks	221	H7
Pool Quay	Powys	95	G1
Pool Street	Essex	88	F7
Pootings	Kent	38	C3
Popes Hill	Gloucs	63	K4
Popham	Hants	35	H2
Poplar	Gt Lon	51	K3
Poplar Street	Suffk	91	K2
Porchfield	IoW	19	G5
Poringland	Norfk	106	F3
Porkellis	Cnwll	3	H4
Porlock	Somset	28	F2
Porlock Weir	Somset	28	F1
Portachoillan	Ag & B	206	B7
Port-an-Eorna	Highld	248	B5
Port Appin	Ag & B	229	H6
Port Askaig	Ag & B	205	C3
Portavadie	Ag & B	206	E5
Port Bannatyne	Ag & B	207	H5
Portbury	N Som	44	G4
Port Carlisle	Cumb	177	H6
Port Charlotte	Ag & B	204	C4
Portchester	Hants	19	K3
Port Clarence	S on T	170	C6
Port Driseach	Ag & B	206	F4
Port Ellen	Ag & B	204	E7
Port Elphinstone	Abers	256	D7
Portencalzie	D & G	182	C8
Portencross	N Ayrs	195	K1
Port Erin	IoM	154	b8
Portesham	Dorset	16	B5
Portessie	Moray	267	J3
Port e Vullen	IoM	154	g4
Port Eynon	Swans	56	E7
Portfield Gate	Pembks	54	F4
Portgate	Devon	12	A5
Port Gaverne	Cnwll	10	D6
Port Glasgow	Inver	208	B4
Portgordon	Moray	267	H3
Portgower	Highld	274	D5
Porth	Cnwll	4	D2
Porth	Rhondd	42	F3
Porthallow	Cnwll	3	K6
Porthallow	Cnwll	5	L4
Porthcawl	Brdgnd	42	B6
Porthcothan	Cnwll	10	B8
Porthcurno	Cnwll	2	B6
Porthdinllaen	Gwynd	108	D3
Port Henderson	Highld	260	B5
Porthgain	Pembks	74	D5
Porthgwarra	Cnwll	2	B6
Porthill	Staffs	114	D2
Porthkea	Cnwll	4	D6
Porthkerry	V Glam	43	G8
Porthleven	Cnwll	3	G6
Porthmadog	Gwynd	109	K4
Porthmadog	Gwynd	109	K4
Porthmeor	Cnwll	2	C4
Porth Navas	Cnwll	3	J5
Portholland	Cnwll	4	F6
Porthoustock	Cnwll	5	K6
Porthpean	Cnwll	5	H5
Porthtowan	Cnwll	4	A5
Porthwgan	Wrexhm	112	F2
Porthyrhyd	Carmth	58	F5
Porth-y-Waen	Shrops	112	C6
Portincaple	Ag & B	218	C8
Portinfer	Jersey	9	a1
Portington	E R Yk	143	K2
Portinnisherrich	Ag & B	216	F5
Portinscale	Cumb	165	H6
Port Isaac	Cnwll	10	D6
Portishead	N Som	44	F4
Portknockie	Moray	267	K3
Portland	Dorset	16	D8
Portlethen	Abers	245	K4
Portling	D & G	175	L4
Portloe	Cnwll	4	F7
Port Logan	D & G	172	D6
Portlooe	Cnwll	6	A4
Portmahomack	Highld	264	E3
Port Mary	D & G	175	J5
Portmellon	Cnwll	5	G6
Port Mòr	Highld	236	E4
Portmore	Hants	18	E4
Port Mulgrave	N York	171	J7
Portnacroish	Ag & B	228	E6
Portnaguran	W Isls	282	h3
Portnahaven	Ag & B	204	B6
Portnalong	Highld	246	D2
Portnancon	Highld	277	G4
Port nan Giùran	W Isls	282	h3
Port nan Long	W Isls	282	c7
Port Nis	W Isls	282	h1
Portobello	C Edin	211	J4
Portobello	Gatesd	181	G7
Portobello	Wolves	90	D4
Port of Menteith	Stirlg	219	J7
Port of Ness	W Isls	282	h1
Porton	Wilts	33	L4
Portontown	Devon	12	A7
Portpatrick	D & G	172	B4
Port Quin	Cnwll	10	D6
Port Ramsay	Ag & B	228	D6
Portreath	Cnwll	3	G2
Portreath Harbour	Cnwll	3	G2
Portree	Highld	259	H7
Port Righ	Ag & B	194	C3
Port St Mary	IoM	154	b8
Portscatho	Cnwll	3	M4
Portsea	C Port	19	L4
Portskerra	Highld	278	E3
Portskewett	Mons	45	G1
Portslade	Br & H	22	C6
Portslade-by-Sea	Br & H	22	C6
Portsmouth	C Port	19	L4
Portsmouth	Calder	140	D3
Portsmouth Arms	Devon	27	L7
Port Soderick	IoM	154	d7
Port Solent	C Port	19	L3
Portsonachan Hotel	Ag & B	217	G3
Portsoy	Abers	267	M3
Port Sunlight	Wirral	129	H3
Portswood	C Sotn	34	F8
Port Talbot	Neath	57	L7
Port Tennant	Swans	57	J6
Portuairk	Highld	236	E7
Portway	Herefs	80	B6
Portway	Herefs	80	C8
Portway	Sandw	98	B6
Portway	Worcs	82	C1
Port Wemyss	Ag & B	204	B6
Port William	D & G	173	J6
Portwrinkle	Cnwll	6	D4
Portyerrock	D & G	174	D7
Posbury	Devon	13	J3
Posenhall	Shrops	96	E3
Poslingford	Suffk	88	F5
Posso	Border	199	L6
Postbridge	Devon	12	F6
Postcombe	Oxon	67	H7
Post Green	Dorset	17	J4
Postling	Kent	40	F7
Postwick	Norfk	106	F2
Potarch	Abers	244	D4
Potsgrove	C Beds	68	B1
Pullen End	Herts	68	C5
Potten Street	Kent	41	H2
Potter Brompton	N York	163	H7
Pottergate Street	Norfk	106	D5
Potterhanworth	Lincs	135	L6
Potterhanworth Booths	Lincs	135	M6
Potter Heigham	Norfk	123	J7
Potterne	Wilts	46	E7
Potterne Wick	Wilts	46	E7
Potter Row	Bucks	67	L6
Potters Bar	Herts	69	H6
Potters Brook	Lancs	147	J5
Potters Corner	Kent	40	C6
Potter's Cross	Staffs	97	J6
Potters Crouch	Herts	68	E6
Potter's Forstal	Kent	39	M4
Potters Green	Covtry	99	K7
Potter's Green	E Susx	23	H3
Potter's Green	Herts	69	K3
Pottersheath	Herts	69	G3
Potters Marston	Leics	100	B4
Potter Somersal	Derbys	115	J4
Potterspury	W Nthn	84	E6
Potter Street	Essex	70	C5
Potterton	Abers	257	G8
Potterton	Leeds	150	F8
Potthorpe	Norfk	121	L7
Pottle Street	Wilts	32	D3
Potto	N York	161	G2
Potton	C Beds	86	E5
Pott Row	Norfk	120	F7
Pott's Green	Essex	72	C3
Pott Shrigley	Ches E	131	J4
Poughill	Cnwll	11	J1
Poughill	Devon	13	K1
Poulner	Hants	18	B2
Poulshot	Wilts	46	E7
Poulton	Gloucs	65	G7
Poulton	Wirral	129	G2
Poulton-le-Fylde	Lancs	147	G6
Poulton Priory	Gloucs	65	G7
Pound Bank	Worcs	97	G8
Poundbury	Dorset	16	C4
Poundffald	Swans	57	G6
Poundgate	E Susx	38	D7
Pound Green	E Susx	23	H3
Pound Green	Suffk	88	E4
Pound Green	Worcs	97	G7
Pound Hill	W Susx	37	L3
Poundon	Bucks	66	F2
Poundsbridge	Kent	38	B4
Poundsgate	Devon	13	G8
Poundstock	Cnwll	11	H3
Pound Street	Hants	48	C6
Pounsley	E Susx	23	J3
Pouton	D & G	174	C5
Pouy Street	Suffk	91	H1
Povey Cross	Surrey	37	L3
Powburn	Nthumb	190	F3
Powderham	Devon	13	M5
Powerstock	Dorset	15	L3
Powfoot	D & G	176	F5
Pow Green	Herefs	81	G6
Powhill	Cumb	177	H7
Powick	Worcs	81	J5
Powmill	P & K	221	J7
Poxwell	Dorset	16	E6
Poyle	Slough	50	G4
Poynings	W Susx	22	E5
Poyntington	Dorset	31	L6
Poynton	Ches E	131	H3
Poynton	Wrekin	113	J8
Poynton Green	Wrekin	113	J7
Poyston Cross	Pembks	55	G3
Poystreet Green	Suffk	89	K4
Praa Sands	Cnwll	2	F5
Pratt's Bottom	Gt Lon	52	A6
Praze-an-Beeble	Cnwll	2	F5
Predannack Wollas	Cnwll	3	H7
Prees	Shrops	113	J5
Preesall	Lancs	147	G6
Prees Green	Shrops	113	J5
Preesgweene	Shrops	112	D4
Prees Heath	Shrops	113	J4
Prees Higher Heath	Shrops	113	J4
Prees Lower Heath	Shrops	113	J5
Prendwick	Nthumb	190	E4
Pren-gwyn	Cerdgn	76	D6
Prenteg	Gwynd	109	K3
Prenton	Wirral	129	G2
Prescot	Knows	129	L1
Prescott	Devon	29	K8
Prescott	Shrops	96	F7
Prescott	Shrops	112	F7
Presnerb	Angus	233	J2
Pressen	Nthumb	202	C6
Prestatyn	Denbgs	128	C3
Prestbury	Ches E	131	H4
Prestbury	Gloucs	64	E2
Presteigne	Powys	79	K2
Prestleigh	Somset	31	K3
Prestolee	Bolton	139	M6
Preston	Border	213	H7
Preston	Br & H	22	D6
Preston	Devon	13	K7
Preston	Dorset	16	D6
Preston	E R Yk	144	F2
Preston	Gloucs	64	F7
Preston	Herts	68	F2
Preston	Kent	40	D3
Preston	Kent	41	H3
Preston	Lancs	139	G4
Preston	Nthumb	203	K8
Preston	Rutlnd	101	J3
Preston	Shrops	96	C1
Preston	Somset	29	K4
Preston	Torbay	8	D3
Preston	Wilts	46	F3
Preston	Wilts	47	K4
Preston Bagot	Warwks	82	F2
Preston Bissett	Bucks	67	G1
Preston Bowyer	Somset	29	L5
Preston Brockhurst	Shrops	113	J6
Preston Brook	Halton	130	B4
Preston Candover	Hants	35	J3
Preston Capes	W Nthn	84	B4
Preston Crowmarsh	Oxon	48	F1
Preston Deanery	W Nthn	84	F4
Preston Green	Warwks	82	E2
Preston Gubbals	Shrops	113	H7
Preston Montford	Shrops	113	G8
Preston on Stour	Warwks	82	F4
Preston on Tees	S on T	169	L7
Preston on the Hill	Halton	130	B3
Preston on Wye	Herefs	79	M7
Prestonpans	E Loth	211	L4
Preston Patrick	W & F	157	H6
Preston Plucknett	Somset	31	H7
Preston St Mary	Suffk	89	J5
Preston Street	Kent	41	J5
Preston-under-Scar	N York	159	K4
Preston upon the Weald Moors	Wrekin	113	L8
Preston Wynne	Herefs	80	D6
Prestwich	Bury	140	B6
Prestwick	Nthumb	180	E4
Prestwick	S Ayrs	196	D6
Prestwick Airport	S Ayrs	196	D6
Prestwood	Bucks	67	L7
Prestwood	Staffs	97	K6
Price Town	Brdgnd	42	E3
Prickwillow	Cambs	104	B7
Priddy	Somset	31	H1
Priestacott	Devon	12	B1
Priestcliffe	Derbys	132	C5
Priestcliffe Ditch	Derbys	132	C5
Priest Hutton	Lancs	157	H7
Priestland	E Ayrs	197	H3
Priestley Green	Calder	141	H3
Priest Weston	Shrops	95	H4
Priestwood Green	Kent	52	E6
Primethorpe	Leics	100	B3
Primrose Green	Norfk	122	B8
Primrosehill	Border	213	H7
Primrose Hill	Cambs	103	H5
Primrose Hill	Derbys	133	J8
Primrose Hill	Dudley	97	L6
Primrose Hill	Lancs	138	E6
Primrosehill	Border	202	C3
Prince of Wales Bridge	Mons	45	G2
Princes Gate	Pembks	55	K4
Princes Risborough	Bucks	67	K6
Princethorpe	Warwks	83	J1
Princetown	Devon	12	E7
Prinsted	W Susx	20	C5
Prion	Denbgs	128	C7
Prior Rigg	Cumb	178	B5
Priors Halton	Shrops	96	B8
Priors Hardwick	Warwks	83	L4
Priorslee	Wrekin	97	G1
Priors Marston	Warwks	83	L4
Priors Norton	Gloucs	64	C2
Priors Park	Gloucs	64	C1
Priory Wood	Herefs	79	J6
Prisk	V Glam	42	F6
Priston	BaNES	45	K7
Pristow Green	Norfk	106	C5
Prittlewell	Sthend	53	J2
Privett	Hants	35	L5
Prixford	Devon	27	K3
Probus	Cnwll	4	E5
Prora	E Loth	212	B3
Prospect	Cumb	164	F5
Prospidnick	Cnwll	3	G5
Protstonhill	Abers	268	E3
Prudhoe	Nthumb	180	D6
Prussia Cove	Cnwll	2	F5
Pubil	P & K	230	E7
Publow	BaNES	45	J6
Puckeridge	Herts	69	K2
Puckington	Somset	30	E7
Pucklechurch	S Glos	45	K4
Puckrup	Gloucs	81	K7
Puddinglake	Ches W	130	E5
Puddington	Ches W	129	H5
Puddington	Devon	28	E8
Puddledock	Norfk	105	L5
Puddletown	Dorset	16	E4
Pudleston	Herefs	80	D3
Pudsey	Leeds	141	K1
Pulborough	W Susx	21	H3
Puleston	Wrekin	114	A7
Pulford	Ches W	129	J7
Pulham	Dorset	16	D1
Pulham Market	Norfk	106	D6
Pulham St Mary	Norfk	106	E6
Pullens Green	S Glos	63	J8
Pulloxhill	C Beds	85	L8
Pumpherston	W Loth	210	E5
Pumsaint	Carmth	77	J7
Puncheston	Pembks	75	J5
Puncknowle	Dorset	15	M5
Punnett's Town	E Susx	23	K3
Purbrook	Hants	19	M2
Purfleet-on-Thames	Thurr	52	C3

Puriton Somset........................30 D3
Purleigh Essex........................71 K6
Purley Gt Lon........................51 J6
Purley on Thames W Berk......49 G4
Purlogue Shrops......................95 G7
Purlpit Wilts........................46 C5
Purls Bridge Cambs................103 K6
Purse Caundle Dorset..............32 B7
Purshull Green Worcs..............81 K1
Purslow Shrops........................95 J7
Purston Jaglin Wakefd........142 C4
Purtington Somset..................15 J1
Purton Gloucs........................63 K6
Purton Gloucs........................63 K6
Purton Wilts........................47 G2
Purton Stoke Wilts................47 G1
Pury End W Nthn......................84 D6
Pusey Oxon........................65 M7
Putley Herefs........................80 E7
Putley Green Herefs..............80 F7
Putloe Gloucs........................64 A5
Putney Gt Lon........................51 G4
Putsborough Devon................27 H3
Puttenham Herts......................67 L4
Puttenham Surrey....................36 D2
Puttock End Essex..................89 G7
Putton Dorset........................16 C6
Putts Corner Devon................14 D3
Puxley W Nthn........................84 E6
Puxton N Som........................44 E6
Pwll Carmth........................56 E4
Pwllcrochan Pembks................54 F6
Pwll-du Mons........................61 L5
Pwll-glâs Denbgs..................111 M1
Pwllgloyw Powys......................78 E8
Pwllheli Gwynd......................108 F4
Pwllmeyric Mons......................63 G8
Pwll-trap Carmth....................58 A5
Pwll-y-glaw Neath..................42 B3
Pye Bridge Derbys................116 D1
Pyecombe W Susx......................22 D4
Pye Corner Newpt....................44 D2
Pye Green Staffs..................114 F8
Pyle Brdgnd........................42 B5
Pyleigh Somset........................29 L5
Pylle Somset........................31 K3
Pymoor Cambs........................103 K6
Pymore Dorset........................15 L4
Pyrford Surrey........................50 D7
Pyrton Oxon........................67 G7
Pytchley N Nthn......................101 J8
Pyworthy Devon........................11 K2

Q

Quabbs Shrops........................94 F7
Quadring Lincs......................119 H5
Quadring Eaudike Lincs......119 H5
Quainton Bucks........................67 H3
Quaker's Yard Myr Td..............43 H3
Quaking Houses Dur..............180 F8
Quantock Hills Somset..........30 A3
Quarff Shet........................281 e7
Quarley Hants........................34 C2
Quarndon Derbys....................116 B3
Quarr Hill IoW........................19 K5
Quarrier's Village Inver......208 B5
Quarrington Lincs................118 E3
Quarrington Hill Dur............169 J3
Quarrybank Ches W................130 A6
Quarry Bank Dudley................97 L6
Quarrywood Moray................266 D3
Quarter N Ayrs......................207 K6
Quarter S Lans......................197 L1
Quatford Shrops......................97 G5
Quatt Shrops........................97 G5
Quebec Dur........................168 J2
Quedgeley Gloucs....................64 A4
Queen Adelaide Cambs..........104 B7
Queenborough Kent..................53 K4
Queen Camel Somset................31 K6
Queen Charlton BaNES............45 J5
Queen Dart Devon....................28 E7
Queen Elizabeth Forest Park
  Stirlg........................219 H6
Queen Elizabeth II Bridge
  Thurr........................52 C4
Queenhill Worcs......................81 K7
Queen Oak Dorset....................32 C4
Queen's Bower IoW..................19 J6
Queensbury C Brad................141 H2
Queensferry Flints................129 H6
Queensferry Crossing Fife......210 F3
Queen's Head Shrops..............112 E6
Queen's Hills Norfk..............106 D1
Queenslie C Glas..................209 H6
Queen's Park Bed....................85 L5
Queen's Park Essex..................71 G7

Queen's Park W Nthn..............84 E3
Queen Street Kent..................39 H4
Queen Street Wilts................46 F2
Queenzieburn N Lans............209 J3
Quendon Essex........................70 D1
Queniborough Leics..............100 E1
Quenington Gloucs..................65 H6
Quernmore Lancs..................147 K4
Queslett Birm........................98 D4
Quethiock Cnwll........................6 C2
Quick's Green W Berk..............48 E4
Quidenham Norfk....................105 L6
Quidhampton Hants..................35 G1
Quidhampton Wilts..................33 K5
Quina Brook Shrops..............113 H5
Quinbury End W Nthn..............84 B5
Quinton Dudley........................98 C6
Quinton W Nthn......................84 E4
Quinton Green W Nthn............84 F4
Quintrell Downs Cnwll..............4 D3
Quixhall Staffs......................115 H3
Quixwood Border....................213 H6
Quoditch Devon........................12 A3
Quoig P & K........................220 E3
Quorn Leics........................116 F8
Quothquan S Lans..................199 G5
Quoyburray Ork......................275 d5
Quoyloo Ork........................275 b4

R

Raasay Highld........................259 K8
Rabbit's Cross Kent................39 K4
Rableyheath Herts..................69 G3
Raby Cumb........................177 D6
Raby Wirral........................129 H4
Rachan Mill Border................199 K6
Rachub Gwynd......................126 C6
Rackenford Devon..................28 E7
Rackham W Susx......................21 H4
Rackheath Norfk....................106 F1
Racks D & G........................176 D4
Rackwick Ork........................275 a5
Radbourne Derbys................115 M4
Radcliffe Bury......................140 B6
Radcliffe Nthumb................191 K5
Radcliffe on Trent Notts......117 H4
Radclive Bucks........................84 D8
Radcot Oxon........................65 L7
Raddery Highld......................263 J7
Raddington Somset..................29 J5
Radernie Fife......................223 H5
Radford Covtry........................99 J7
Radford Semele Warwks..........83 H2
Radlet Somset........................30 B3
Radlett Herts........................68 F7
Radley Devon........................28 C6
Radley Oxon........................66 D7
Radley W Berk........................48 A5
Radley Green Essex................70 F6
Radmore Green Ches E..........130 B8
Radnage Bucks........................67 J7
Radstock BaNES......................45 K8
Radstone W Nthn......................84 B7
Radway Warwks........................83 J3
Radwell Bed........................85 K4
Radwell Herts........................86 E8
Radwinter Essex......................88 C7
Radwinter End Essex..............88 C7
Radyr Cardif........................43 H5
RAF College (Cranwell) Lincs......118 D2
Rafford Moray......................265 H8
Ragdale Leics......................117 H7
Ragdon Shrops........................95 L5
Raginnis Cnwll........................2 D6
Raglan Mons........................62 E5
Ragnall Notts......................134 F2
Raigbeg Highld......................252 F6
Rainbow Hill Worcs................81 K4
Rainford St Hel....................138 F7
Rainford Junction St Hel......138 F7
Rainham Gt Lon......................52 B3
Rainham Medway......................53 H6
Rainhill St Hel......................129 L2
Rainhill Stoops St Hel..........129 L2
Rainow Ches E......................131 J4
Rainsough Bury......................140 B7
Rainton N York......................160 E7
Rainworth Notts....................134 B8
Raisbeck W & F......................157 K1
Raise W & F........................167 G2
Raisthorpe N York................152 C3
Rait P & K........................222 C2
Raithby Lincs......................136 F3
Raithby Lincs......................137 G6
Raithwaite N York................171 K8
Rake Hants........................36 B5
Rakewood Rochdl....................140 E5

Ralia Highld........................241 J4
Ram Carmth........................77 G6
Ramasaig Highld....................258 B7
Rame Cnwll..........................3 J4
Rame Cnwll..........................6 E5
Ram Hill S Glos......................45 K3
Ram Lane Kent........................40 C6
Rampisham Dorset....................16 A2
Rampside W & F......................146 E3
Rampton Cambs........................87 J2
Rampton Notts......................134 F4
Ramsbottom Bury..................140 B4
Ramsbury Wilts........................47 L5
Ramscraigs Highld................274 F3
Ramsdean Hants......................35 L6
Ramsdell Hants........................48 E7
Ramsden Oxon........................65 M4
Ramsden Worcs........................81 L6
Ramsden Bellhouse Essex......71 H8
Ramsden Heath Essex..............71 H7
Ramsey Cambs......................102 F6
Ramsey Essex........................73 J1
Ramsey IoM........................154 f3
Ramsey Forty Foot Cambs......102 F6
Ramsey Heights Cambs..........102 E6
Ramsey Island Pembks............74 A7
Ramsey Mereside Cambs..........102 F5
Ramsey St Mary's Cambs......102 E6
Ramsgate Kent........................41 L2
Ramsgill N York....................149 K2
Ramshaw Dur........................168 B1
Ramshaw Dur........................168 F5
Ramsholt Suffk........................91 H7
Ramshope Nthumb................189 K5
Ramshorn Staffs....................115 H3
Ramsley Devon........................12 F4
Ramsnest Common Surrey......36 E4
Ranby Lincs........................136 D4
Ranby Notts........................134 C3
Rand Lincs........................136 B4
Randwick Gloucs......................64 B5
Ranfurly Rens......................208 C6
Rangemore Staffs..................115 K7
Rangeworthy S Glos................45 K2
Rankinston E Ayrs................196 E8
Ranksborough Rutlnd..............101 H1
Rank's Green Essex................71 H3
Rannoch Station P & K..........230 D7
Ranscombe Somset..................29 G2
Ranskill Notts......................134 C2
Ranton Staffs......................114 D6
Ranton Green Staffs..............114 D7
Ranworth Norfk....................123 G8
Raploch Stirlg......................220 D8
Rapness Ork........................275 d2
Rapps Somset........................30 E7
Rascarrel D & G....................175 K5
Rashfield Ag & B..................207 J2
Rashwood Worcs......................81 L2
Raskelf N York......................151 G2
Rassau Blae G........................61 J5
Rastrick Calder....................141 H3
Ratagan Highld......................248 E7
Ratby Leics........................100 B2
Ratcliffe Culey Leics..............99 J3
Ratcliffe on Soar Notts......116 E6
Ratcliffe on the Wreake Leics......117 G8
Rathen Abers......................269 J4
Rathillet Fife......................222 F3
Rathmell N York....................148 D4
Ratho C Edin........................210 F5
Ratho Station C Edin............210 F4
Rathven Moray......................267 J3
Ratlake Hants........................34 E6
Ratley Warwks........................83 J5
Ratling Kent........................41 H4
Ratlinghope Shrops................95 K4
Rattar Highld......................280 C2
Ratten Row Cumb....................165 K3
Ratten Row Cumb....................165 L1
Ratten Row Lancs..................147 H7
Rattery Devon........................7 L3
Rattlesden Suffk......................89 K3
Ratton Village E Susx............23 K7
Rattray P & K........................233 J6
Raughton Cumb......................165 L1
Raughton Head Cumb..............165 L2
Raunds N Nthn......................85 K1
Ravenfield Rothm..................133 J1
Ravenglass Cumb..................155 K3
Ravenhills Green Worcs..........81 G4
Raveningham Norfk................107 H4
Ravenscar N York..................163 H2
Ravenscraig N Lans..............209 K7
Ravensdale IoM......................154 e4
Ravensden Bed........................86 B4
Ravenseat N York..................158 E2
Ravenshead Notts..................133 L8
Ravensmoor Ches E................113 K2
Ravensthorpe Kirk................141 C1

Ravensthorpe W Nthn..............84 C1
Ravenstone Leics....................99 L1
Ravenstone M Keyn..................85 G5
Ravenstonedale W & F..........158 C2
Ravenstruther S Lans............198 F4
Ravensworth N York..............159 L1
Raw N York........................163 G2
Rawcliffe C York..................151 J5
Rawcliffe E R Yk..................143 H3
Rawcliffe Bridge E R Yk......143 H3
Rawdon Leeds......................150 B7
Rawling Street Kent................40 B3
Rawmarsh Rothm....................142 C4
Rawnsley Staffs......................98 C1
Rawreth Essex........................71 J8
Rawridge Devon........................14 E2
Rawtenstall Lancs................140 B3
Raydon Suffk........................90 B7
Raylees Nthumb....................190 C7
Rayleigh Essex........................53 H1
Raymond's Hill Devon............15 H3
Rayne Essex........................71 H3
Raynes Park Gt Lon................51 G5
Reach Cambs........................88 B2
Read Lancs........................140 A3
Reading Readg........................49 H4
Reading Services W Berk......49 G5
Reading Street Kent................25 G1
Reading Street Kent................41 L2
Reagill W & F......................166 E7
Rearquhar Highld..................263 K1
Rearsby Leics......................117 H8
Rease Heath Ches E................113 L1
Reawla Cnwll..........................2 F4
Reay Highld........................279 G3
Reculver Kent........................41 H2
Red Ball Devon........................29 K7
Redberth Pembks......................55 J6
Redbourn Herts........................68 E4
Redbourne N Linc..................144 B4
Redbrook Gloucs......................63 G5
Redbrook Wrexhm..................113 H3
Redbrook Street Kent..............40 B8
Redburn Highld......................253 H2
Redburn Nthumb....................179 H6
Redcar R & Cl......................170 E6
Redcastle D & G....................175 K2
Redcastle Highld..................251 G2
Red Dial Cumb......................165 H2
Redding Falk........................210 B3
Reddingmuirhead Falk............210 B3
Reddish Stockp......................131 H1
Redditch Worcs........................82 B2
Rede Suffk........................88 F4
Redenhall Norfk....................106 F6
Redenham Hants......................34 C1
Redesmouth Nthumb..............179 K3
Redford Abers......................235 J2
Redford Angus......................234 E6
Redford W Susx......................36 C5
Redfordgreen Border..............188 C3
Redgate Rhondd......................42 F4
Redgorton P & K....................221 K2
Redgrave Suffk......................105 L7
Redhill Abers......................245 H3
Red Hill BCP........................17 L3
Redhill Herts........................86 F8
Redhill N Som........................45 G6
Redhill Surrey........................37 L1
Red Hill Warwks......................82 D4
Redisham Suffk......................107 H6
Redland Bristl........................45 H4
Redland Ork........................275 c3
Redlingfield Suffk..................90 E1
Redlingfield Green Suffk......90 E1
Red Lodge Suffk......................88 D1
Red Lumb Rochdl..................140 C4
Redlynch Somset......................32 B4
Redlynch Wilts........................33 L6
Redmain Cumb......................164 F4
Redmarley Worcs......................81 H2
Redmarley D'Abitot Gloucs......63 L1
Redmarshall S on T................169 K6
Redmile Leics......................117 L4
Redmire N York......................159 J4
Redmyre Abers......................245 G8
Rednal Birm........................98 C8
Rednal Shrops......................112 C6
Redpath Border......................201 J6
Red Point Highld..................260 B6
Red Post Cnwll........................11 K2
Red Rice Hants........................34 D2
Red Rock Wigan....................139 H6
Red Roses Carmth....................55 L4
Red Row Nthumb....................191 K6
Redruth Cnwll..........................4 C4
Redstocks Wilts......................46 D6
Redstone P & K......................233 J8
Redstone Cross Pembks............55 J4
Red Street Staffs..................114 C1

Redvales Bury 140 B6
Red Wharf Bay IoA 125 J3
Redwick Newpt 44 E2
Redwick S Glos 45 H2
Redworth Darltn 169 G6
Reed Herts 87 H8
Reedham Norfk 107 J3
Reedness E R Yk 143 K3
Reeds Beck Lincs 136 D6
Reeds Holme Lancs 140 B3
Reepham Lincs 135 L5
Reepham Norfk 122 B7
Reeth N York 159 J3
Reeves Green Solhll 99 H7
Regaby IoM 154 f3
Regil N Som 45 G6
Reiff Highld 270 C5
Reigate Surrey 37 L1
Reighton N York 163 L7
Reinigeadal W Isls 282 f5
Reisque Abers 256 F7
Reiss Highld 280 D5
Relerran Cnwll 4 C4
Releath Cnwll 3 G4
Relubbus Cnwll 2 F4
Relugas Moray 253 J2
Remenham Wokham 49 J2
Remenham Hill Wokham 49 J2
Rempstone Notts 116 F6
Rendcomb Gloucs 64 E5
Rendham Suffk 91 H2
Rendlesham Suffk 91 H4
Renfrew Rens 208 E5
Renhold Bed 86 B5
Renishaw Derbys 133 J4
Rennington Nthumb 191 J3
Renton W Duns 208 C3
Renwick W & F 166 E2
Repps Norfk 123 J8
Repton Derbys 116 A6
Reraig Highld 248 C6
Resaurie Highld 251 J3
Rescassa Cnwll .... 3 AA
Rescorla Cnwll 5 G5
Resipole Burn Highld 237 L7
Reskadinnick Cnwll 3 G3
Resolis Highld 263 J6
Resolven Neath 60 C6
Rest and be thankful Ag & B 218 C5
Reston Border 213 J6
Restronguet Cnwll 3 K4
Reswallie Angus 234 D5
Reterth Cnwll 4 F2
Retford Notts 134 D3
Retire Cnwll 5 G2
Rettendon Common Essex 71 J7
Rettendon Village Essex 71 J7
Retyn Cnwll 4 E3
Revesby Lincs 136 E7
Rew Devon 7 K7
Rew Devon 13 H8
Rewe Devon 13 M3
Rew Street IoW 19 H5
Rexon Devon 12 A5
Reydon Suffk 107 K7
Reymerston Norfk 105 L2
Reynalton Pembks 55 J5
Reynoldston Swans 56 E6
Rezare Cnwll 11 L7
Rhadyr Mons 62 D6
Rhandirmwyn Carmth 77 L6
Rhayader Powys 78 D2
Rheindown Highld 250 F2
Rhenigidale W Isls 282 f5
Rhes-y-cae Flints 128 E5
Rhewl Denbgs 112 B3
Rhewl Denbgs 128 D7
Rhewl Mostyn Flints 128 D4
Rhicarn Highld 270 E3
Rhiconich Highld 276 D5
Rhicullen Highld 263 J5
Rhigos Rhondd 60 D6
Rhives Highld 273 K7
Rhiwbina Cardif 43 J5
Rhiwbrytdir Gwynd 110 D2
Rhiwderyn Newpt 43 L4
Rhiwen Gwynd 125 K7
Rhiwinder Rhondd 42 F4
Rhiwlas Gwynd 111 H4
Rhiwlas Gwynd 125 K6
Rhiwlas Powys 112 B5
Rhiwsaeson Rhondd 43 G5
Rhode Somset 30 C4
Rhoden Green Kent 39 H4
Rhodesia Notts 133 L4
Rhodes Minnis Kent 40 F6
Rhodiad-y-brenin Pembks 74 C6
Rhonehouse D & G 175 J3
Rhoose V Glam 43 G8
Rhos Carmth 58 C2

Rhos Denbgs 128 D7
Rhos Neath 57 K4
Rhosaman Carmth 59 K6
Rhosbeirio IoA 125 G2
Rhoscefnhir IoA 125 J4
Rhoscolyn IoA 124 D4
Rhoscrowther Pembks 54 E6
Rhosesmor Flints 128 F6
Rhos-fawr Gwynd 109 G4
Rhosgadfan Gwynd 125 J8
Rhosgoch IoA 125 G2
Rhosgoch Powys 79 H5
Rhos Haminiog Cerdgn 76 F2
Rhoshill Pembks 75 L4
Rhoshirwaun Gwynd 108 C5
Rhoslan Gwynd 109 H3
Rhoslefain Gwynd 92 C2
Rhosllanerchrugog Wrexhm 112 D2
Rhôs Lligwy IoA 125 J2
Rhosmaen Carmth 59 H4
Rhosmeirch IoA 125 H4
Rhosneigr IoA 124 F3
Rhosnesni Wrexhm 112 L2
Rhôs-on-Sea Conwy 127 G1
Rhosrobin Wrexhm 112 E1
Rhossili Swans 56 D7
Rhostrehwfa IoA 125 H5
Rhostryfan Gwynd 125 J8
Rhostyllen Wrexhm 112 D2
Rhosybol IoA 125 G2
Rhos-y-brithdir Powys 111 M7
Rhosygadfa Shrops 112 D4
Rhos-y-garth Cerdgn 77 H1
Rhos-y-gwaliau Gwynd 111 H4
Rhos-y-llan Gwynd 108 D4
Rhosymedre Wrexhm 112 D3
Rhos-y-meirch Powys 79 K1
Rhu Ag & B 207 M2
Rhuallt Denbgs 128 C5
Rhubodach Ag & B 207 G4
Rhuddall Heath Ches W 130 A7
Rhuddlan Cerdgn 76 F6
Rhuddlan Denbgs 127 L4
Rhue Highld 270 E8
Rhulen Powys 79 G5
Rhunahaorine Ag & B 205 M6
Rhyd Gwynd 110 B3
Rhydargaeau Carmth 58 D4
Rhydcymerau Carmth 77 G7
Rhydd Worcs 81 J6
Rhyd-Ddu Gwynd 109 K1
Rhydding Neath 57 K5
Rhydgaled Conwy 127 K6
Rhydlanfair Conwy 110 F1
Rhydlewis Cerdgn 76 C3
Rhydlios Gwynd 108 C5
Rhydlydan Conwy 111 G2
Rhydowen Cerdgn 76 E6
Rhydroser Cerdgn 77 G2
Rhydspence Herefs 79 J5
Rhydtalog Flints 128 F8
Rhyd-uchaf Gwynd 111 G4
Rhyd-y-clafdy Gwynd 108 E4
Rhydycroesau Shrops 112 C5
Rhydyfelin Cerdgn 92 D7
Rhydyfelin Rhondd 43 H4
Rhyd-y-foel Conwy 127 H4
Rhydyfro Neath 57 K4
Rhyd-y-groes Gwynd 125 K6
Rhydymain Gwynd 110 F7
Rhyd-y-meirch Mons 62 C5
Rhydymwyn Flints 128 E6
Rhyd-y-pennau Cerdgn 92 D6
Rhyd-yr-onnen Gwynd 92 D3
Rhyd-y-sarn Gwynd 110 C3
Rhyl Denbgs 127 K3
Rhymney Caerph 61 H5
Rhynd P & K 222 B3
Rhynie Abers 255 K6
Rhynie Highld 264 C4
Ribbesford Worcs 97 H8
Ribbleton Lancs 139 H2
Ribby Lancs 138 E2
Ribchester Lancs 139 K1
Riber Derbys 132 F7
Riby Lincs 144 F6
Riccall N York 151 K8
Riccarton Border 188 F7
Riccarton E Ayrs 196 E4
Richards Castle Herefs 80 C1
Richings Park Bucks 50 D3
Richmond Gt Lon 50 F4
Richmond N York 159 M2
Richmond Sheff 133 H3
Richmond Park Kent 41 J6
Rich's Holford Somset 29 L4
Rickerscote Staffs 114 E7
Rickford N Som 44 F7
Rickham Devon 7 L7
Rickinghall Suffk 105 L8

Rickling Essex 70 D1
Rickling Green Essex 70 D1
Rickmansworth Herts 68 D8
Riddell Border 188 E1
Riddings Derbys 116 C1
Riddlecombe Devon 27 L8
Riddlesden C Brad 149 K7
Ridge BaNES 45 H7
Ridge Dorset 17 H5
Ridge Herts 69 G7
Ridge Wilts 33 G2
Ridgebourne Powys 78 E3
Ridge Green Surrey 37 L1
Ridge Lane Warwks 99 J4
Ridge Row Kent 41 G6
Ridgeway Derbys 133 H3
Ridgeway Worcs 82 B3
Ridgeway Cross Herefs 81 G5
Ridgewell Essex 88 E7
Ridgewood E Susx 23 H3
Ridgmont C Beds 85 J8
Riding Mill Nthumb 180 D6
Ridley Kent 52 D6
Ridley Nthumb 179 H6
Ridley Green Ches E 113 J1
Ridlington Norfk 123 G5
Ridlington Rutlnd 101 J3
Ridlington Street Norfk 123 G5
Ridsdale Nthumb 179 L2
Rievaulx N York 161 J5
Rigg D & G 177 J5
Riggend N Lans 209 K5
Righoul Highld 253 G2
Rigmadon Park W & F 157 K5
Rigsby Lincs 137 H4
Rigside S Lans 198 E6
Riley Green Lancs 139 J3
Rileyhill Staffs 115 J8
Rilla Mill Cnwll 11 K7
Rillaton Cnwll 11 K7
Rillington N York 162 E7
Rimington Lancs 148 D6
Rimpton Somset 31 K6
Rimswell E R Yk 145 J2
Rinaston Pembks 75 G7
Rindleford Shrops 97 G4
Ringford D & G 175 H3
Ringinglow Sheff 132 F3
Ringland Norfk 106 C1
Ringles Cross E Susx 23 H3
Ringlestone Kent 39 L2
Ringley Bolton 139 M6
Ringmer E Susx 23 G5
Ringmore Devon 7 J5
Ringmore Devon 13 L8
Ringorm Moray 254 E3
Ring's End Cambs 103 H3
Ringsfield Suffk 107 H5
Ringsfield Corner Suffk 107 H6
Ringshall Herts 68 C4
Ringshall Suffk 90 B4
Ringshall Stocks Suffk 90 D5
Ringstead N Nthn 101 L8
Ringstead Norfk 120 F3
Ringwood Hants 18 A3
Ringwould Kent 41 K5
Rinmore Abers 255 H8
Rinsey Cnwll 2 F5
Rinsey Croft Cnwll 2 F5
Ripe E Susx 23 H5
Ripley Derbys 116 C2
Ripley Hants 18 B4
Ripley N York 150 C4
Ripley Surrey 50 D7
Riplingham E R Yk 144 B2
Riplington Hants 35 K6
Ripon N York 150 D2
Rippingale Lincs 118 E6
Ripple Kent 41 K5
Ripple Worcs 81 K7
Ripponden Calder 140 F4
Risabus Ag & B 204 D7
Risbury Herefs 80 D4
Risby N Linc 144 A5
Risby Suffk 88 F2
Risca Caerph 43 K3
Rise E R Yk 153 J7
Riseden E Susx 38 F7
Riseden Kent 39 H6
Risegate Lincs 119 H5
Riseholme Lincs 135 K5
Risehow Cumb 164 D4
Riseley Bed 85 L3
Riseley Wokham 49 H6
Rishangles Suffk 90 E2
Rishton Lancs 139 L2
Rishworth Calder 140 F4
Rising Bridge Lancs 140 A3
Risley Derbys 116 D4
Risley Warrtn 130 C1

Risplith N York 150 B2
Rivar Wilts 47 L6
Rivenhall End Essex 71 K4
River Kent 41 J6
River W Susx 36 D6
River Bank Cambs 87 L2
Riverford Highld 250 F1
Riverhead Kent 38 D2
Rivers Corner Dorset 32 C8
Rivington Lancs 139 J5
Rivington Services Lancs 139 J5
Roachill Devon 28 E6
Roade N Nthn 84 E5
Road Green Norfk 106 F3
Roadhead Cumb 178 C4
Roadmeetings S Lans 198 E3
Roadside E Ayrs 197 H7
Roadside Highld 279 L4
Roadwater Somset 29 J3
Roag Highld 258 D7
Roa Island W & F 146 D3
Roan of Craigoch S Ayrs 183 H3
Roast Green Essex 87 J8
Roath Cardif 43 K6
Roberton Border 188 D3
Roberton S Lans 198 F7
Robertsbridge E Susx 24 D3
Robertstown Kirk 141 J3
Robeston Wathen Pembks 55 J4
Robgill Tower D & G 177 H4
Robin Hill Staffs 131 H8
Robin Hood Lancs 139 G5
Robin Hood Leeds 141 M2
Robinhood End Essex 88 E7
Robin Hood's Bay N York 163 G2
Roborough Devon 6 F2
Roborough Devon 27 K7
Robroyston C Glas 209 H5
Roby Knows 129 K2
Roby Mill Lancs 139 G6
Rocester Staffs 115 J4
Roch Pembks 54 E3
Rochdale Rochdl 140 D5
Roche Cnwll 5 G3
Rochester Medway 52 F5
Rochester Nthumb 180 M2
Rochford Essex 53 J1
Rochford Worcs 80 E2
Roch Gate Pembks 54 E3
Rock Cnwll 10 C7
Rock Neath 57 L6
Rock Nthumb 191 J4
Rock W Susx 21 K4
Rock Worcs 81 G1
Rockbeare Devon 14 B4
Rockbourne Hants 33 K7
Rockcliffe Cumb 177 K6
Rockcliffe D & G 175 L4
Rockcliffe Cross Cumb 177 K6
Rock End Staffs 131 H8
Rockend Torbay 8 D2
Rock Ferry Wirral 129 H2
Rockfield Highld 264 E3
Rockfield Mons 62 F4
Rockford Devon 28 D1
Rockford Hants 18 B2
Rockgreen Shrops 96 C8
Rockhampton S Glos 63 K8
Rockhead Cnwll 10 F5
Rockhill Shrops 95 G7
Rock Hill Worcs 81 L1
Rockingham N Nthn 101 J5
Rockland All Saints Norfk 105 K4
Rockland St Mary Norfk 107 G3
Rockland St Peter Norfk 105 K4
Rockley Notts 134 C5
Rockley Wilts 47 H4
Rockliffe Lancs 140 C3
Rockville Ag & B 207 L1
Rockwell End Bucks 49 J8
Rockwell Green Somset 29 L6
Rodborough Gloucs 64 B6
Rodbourne Swindn 47 H2
Rodbourne Wilts 46 D2
Rodd Herefs 79 K3
Roddam Nthumb 190 E2
Rodden Dorset 16 B5
Roddymoor Dur 168 F3
Rode Somset 46 A8
Rode Heath Ches E 130 F8
Rode Heath Ches E 131 G6
Rodel W Isls 282 d7
Roden Wrekin 113 J8
Rodhuish Somset 29 J3
Rodington Wrekin 113 K8
Rodington Heath Wrekin 113 K8
Rodley Gloucs 63 L5
Rodley Leeds 150 B8
Rodmarton Gloucs 64 D7
Rodmell E Susx 22 F6

Rodmersham Kent....40 B3
Rodmersham Green Kent....40 B3
Rodney Stoke Somset....31 H1
Rodsley Derbys....115 K3
Rodway Somset....30 C3
Rodway Wrekin....113 L7
Roecliffe N York....150 E3
Roe Cross Tamesd....140 E8
Roe Green Herts....69 G5
Roe Green Herts....87 G8
Roe Green Salfd....139 L7
Roehampton Gt Lon....51 G4
Roffey W Susx....37 J4
Rogart Highld....273 H7
Rogate W Susx....36 B6
Roger Ground W & F....156 E3
Rogerstone Newpt....44 B2
Roghadal W Isls....282 d7
Rogiet Mons....44 F2
Roke Oxon....66 F8
Roker Sundld....181 K7
Rollesby Norfk....123 J8
Rolleston Leics....100 F3
Rolleston Notts....117 K1
Rolleston Wilts....33 J2
Rolleston on Dove Staffs....115 L6
Rolston E R Yk....153 K6
Rolstone N Som....44 D6
Rolvenden Kent....39 L7
Rolvenden Layne Kent....39 L7
Romaldkirk Dur....168 C6
Romanby N York....160 E4
Romanno Bridge Border....199 K3
Romansleigh Devon....28 C6
Romden Castle Kent....40 A7
Romesdal Highld....258 F6
Romford Dorset....17 L1
Romford Gt Lon....52 B1
Romiley Stockp....131 J2
Romney Street Kent....52 C6
Romsey Cambs....87 K4
Romsey Hants....34 D6
Romsley Shrops....97 H6
Romsley Worcs....98 B7
Rona Highld....259 L5
Ronachan Ag & B....206 B8
Rood Ashton Wilts....46 C7
Rookhope Dur....167 L2
Rookley IoW....19 H6
Rookley Green IoW....19 H7
Rooks Bridge Somset....44 D8
Rooks Nest Somset....29 K4
Rookwith N York....160 B5
Roos E R Yk....145 H2
Roose W & F....146 D2
Roosebeck W & F....146 E2
Roothams Green Bed....86 B4
Ropley Hants....35 K4
Ropley Dean Hants....35 K4
Ropley Soke Hants....35 K4
Ropsley Lincs....118 C5
Rora Abers....269 K6
Rorrington Shrops....95 H3
Rosarie Moray....267 H6
Rose Cnwll....4 C4
Roseacre Lancs....147 H8
Rose Ash Devon....28 D6
Rosebank S Lans....198 D3
Rosebush Pembks....75 J6
Rosecare Cnwll....11 H3
Rosecliston Cnwll....4 D3
Rosedale Abbey N York....162 C3
Rose Green Essex....72 C2
Rose Green Suffk....89 J7
Rose Green Suffk....89 K6
Rose Green W Susx....20 E7
Rosehall Highld....272 C7
Rosehearty Abers....269 G3
Rose Hill E Susx....23 G4
Rose Hill Lancs....140 B2
Rosehill Shrops....113 G8
Roseisle Moray....266 C3
Roselands E Susx....23 K7
Rosemarket Pembks....54 F5
Rosemarkie Highld....263 K8
Rosemary Lane Devon....29 L7
Rosemount P & K....233 J6
Rosenannon Cnwll....4 F2
Rosenithon Cnwll....3 K6
Roser's Cross E Susx....23 J3
Rosevean Cnwll....5 H3
Rosevine Cnwll....3 M4
Rosewarne Cnwll....2 F4
Rosewell Mdloth....211 J6
Roseworth S on T....169 L6
Roseworthy Cnwll....3 G3
Rosgill W & F....166 D7
Roskestal Cnwll....2 B6
Roskhill Highld....258 D7
Roskorwell Cnwll....3 K6

Rosley Cumb....165 K2
Roslin Mdloth....211 J6
Rosliston Derbys....115 L8
Rosneath Ag & B....207 L2
Ross D & G....175 G6
Ross Nthumb....203 J5
Rossett Wrexhm....129 J8
Rossett Green N York....150 D5
Rossington Donc....143 G8
Ross-on-Wye Herefs....63 J2
Roster Highld....280 C8
Rostherne Ches E....130 E3
Rosthwaite Cumb....165 H7
Roston Derbys....115 J3
Rosudgeon Cnwll....2 E5
Rosyth Fife....210 F2
Rothbury Nthumb....190 F6
Rotherby Leics....117 H8
Rotherfield E Susx....38 E7
Rotherfield Greys Oxon....49 H3
Rotherfield Peppard Oxon....49 H3
Rotherham Rothm....133 H1
Rothersthorpe W Nthn....84 D4
Rotherwick Hants....49 H7
Rothes Moray....266 F6
Rothesay Ag & B....207 H6
Rothiebrisbane Abers....256 D4
Rothiemurchus Lodge Highld....242 C2
Rothienorman Abers....256 C4
Rothley Leics....100 D1
Rothley Nthumb....180 C1
Rothmaise Abers....256 B5
Rothwell Leeds....142 A2
Rothwell Lincs....144 F7
Rothwell N Nthn....101 H7
Rotsea E R Yk....153 G5
Rottal Lodge Angus....234 B2
Rottingdean Br & H....22 F6
Rottington Cumb....164 C8
Roucan D & G....176 D3
Roud IoW....19 H7
Rougham Norfk....121 H7
Rougham Suffk....89 H3
Rough Close Staffs....114 E4
Rough Common Kent....40 F3
Roughlee Lancs....148 E7
Roughpark Abers....243 K1
Roughton Lincs....136 D6
Roughton Norfk....122 E4
Roughton Shrops....97 G4
Roughway Kent....38 F3
Roundbush Essex....72 B6
Round Bush Herts....68 F7
Roundbush Green Essex....70 E6
Round Green Luton....68 E3
Roundham Somset....15 K1
Roundhay Leeds....150 D8
Rounds Green Sandw....98 C5
Round Street Kent....52 E5
Roundstreet Common W Susx....37 G5
Roundswell Devon....27 K4
Roundway Wilts....46 E6
Roundyhill Angus....234 B5
Rousay Ork....275 c3
Rousdon Devon....15 G4
Rousham Oxon....66 C2
Rous Lench Worcs....82 B4
Routenburn N Ayrs....207 K6
Routh E R Yk....153 H7
Rout's Green Bucks....67 J7
Row Cnwll....10 F7
Row W & F....157 G5
Row W & F....166 E4
Rowanburn D & G....177 L3
Rowardennan Stirlg....218 E7
Rowarth Derbys....131 K2
Row Ash Hants....35 H8
Rowberrow Somset....44 F7
Rowborough IoW....19 G6
Rowde Wilts....46 E6
Rowden Devon....12 F3
Rowen Conwy....126 E5
Rowfield Derbys....115 K2
Rowfoot Nthumb....178 F6
Rowford Somset....30 C5
Row Green Essex....71 H2
Rowhedge Essex....72 F3
Rowhook W Susx....37 H4
Rowington Warwks....82 F2
Rowland Derbys....132 D5
Rowland's Castle Hants....20 B5
Rowlands Gill Gatesd....180 E7
Rowledge Surrey....36 B2
Rowley Dur....168 E1
Rowley E R Yk....144 B1
Rowley Shrops....95 H2
Rowley Hill Kirk....141 J5
Rowley Regis Sandw....98 B6

Rowlstone Herefs....62 D2
Rowly Surrey....37 G3
Rowner Hants....19 K3
Rowney Green Worcs....82 B1
Rownhams Hants....34 E7
Rownhams Services Hants....34 E7
Rowrah Cumb....164 E7
Rowsham Bucks....67 K3
Rowsley Derbys....132 E6
Rowstock Oxon....48 C1
Rowston Lincs....136 A8
Rowthorne Derbys....133 J6
Rowton Ches W....129 K6
Rowton Shrops....95 J1
Rowton Shrops....95 K7
Rowton Wrekin....113 K7
Row Town Surrey....50 D6
Roxburgh Border....201 L7
Roxby N Linc....144 A4
Roxby N York....171 H7
Roxton Bed....86 C4
Roxwell Essex....70 F5
Royal Leamington Spa Warwks....83 H2
Royal Oak Darltn....169 G3
Royal Oak Lancs....138 E7
Royal's Green Ches E....113 K3
Royal Sutton Coldfield Birm....98 E4
Royal Tunbridge Wells Kent....38 F5
Royal Wootton Bassett Wilts....46 F3
Roy Bridge Highld....239 M7
Roydhouse Kirk....141 K5
Roydon Essex....69 L5
Roydon Norfk....106 C7
Roydon Norfk....120 F7
Roydon Hamlet Essex....69 L5
Royston Barns....142 B5
Royston Herts....87 G7
Royton Oldham....140 D6
Rozel Jersey....9 e2
Ruabon Wrexhm....112 D3
Ruaig Ag & B....224 D6
Ruan High Lanes Cnwll....4 E6
Ruan Lanihorne Cnwll....4 E6
Ruan Major Cnwll....3 H7
Ruan Minor Cnwll....3 J8
Ruardean Gloucs....63 J3
Ruardean Hill Gloucs....63 J4
Ruardean Woodside Gloucs....63 J4
Rubery Birm....98 C7
Rubha Ban W Isls....283 c12
Ruckcroft W & F....166 C2
Ruckhall Herefs....80 B7
Ruckinge Kent....40 D8
Ruckland Lincs....136 F4
Ruckley Shrops....96 C3
Rudbaxton Pembks....54 F3
Rudby N York....161 G1
Rudchester Nthumb....180 D5
Ruddington Notts....116 F5
Ruddle Gloucs....63 K5
Ruddlemoor Cnwll....5 G4
Rudford Gloucs....63 M3
Rudge Somset....46 B8
Rudgeway S Glos....45 J2
Rudgwick W Susx....37 G4
Rudhall Herefs....63 J2
Rudheath Ches W....130 D5
Rudheath Woods Ches E....130 E5
Rudley Green Essex....71 K6
Rudloe Wilts....46 B5
Rudry Caerph....43 K4
Rudston E R Yk....153 H2
Rudyard Staffs....131 J8
Ruecastle Border....189 G2
Rufford Lancs....138 F4
Rufforth C York....151 H5
Rug Denbgs....111 K3
Rugby Warwks....100 B8
Rugby Services Warwks....100 B7
Rugeley Staffs....115 G7
Ruigh'riabhach Highld....261 G1
Ruisgarry W Isls....282 d7
Ruishton Somset....30 C6
Ruisigearraidh W Isls....282 d7
Ruislip Gt Lon....50 E2
Rùm Highld....236 D1
Rumbach Moray....267 H5
Rumbling Bridge P & K....221 J7
Rumburgh Suffk....107 G7
Rumby Hill Dur....168 F4
Rumford Cnwll....10 B8
Rumford Falk....210 B4
Rumney Cardif....43 K6
Rumwell Somset....30 B6
Runcorn Halton....129 L3
Runcton W Susx....20 E6
Runcton Holme Norfk....104 C2

Runfold Surrey....36 C2
Runhall Norfk....105 L2
Runham Norfk....107 J1
Runham Norfk....107 L2
Runnington Somset....29 L6
Runsell Green Essex....71 J6
Runshaw Moor Lancs....139 G4
Runswick N York....171 J7
Runtaleave Angus....233 L2
Runwell Essex....71 J8
Ruscombe Wokham....49 J4
Rushall Herefs....80 E8
Rushall Norfk....106 D6
Rushall Wilts....47 H7
Rushall Wsall....98 C3
Rushbrooke Suffk....89 H3
Rushbury Shrops....96 C5
Rushden Herts....69 J1
Rushden N Nthn....85 J2
Rushenden Kent....53 K5
Rusher's Cross E Susx....38 F7
Rushford Devon....12 B7
Rushford Norfk....105 J7
Rush Green Essex....73 H4
Rush Green Gt Lon....52 B2
Rush Green Herts....69 G2
Rush Green Warrtn....130 D2
Rushlake Green E Susx....23 L3
Rushmere Suffk....107 K6
Rushmere St Andrew Suffk....90 E6
Rushmoor Surrey....36 C3
Rushock Herefs....79 K3
Rushock Worcs....81 K1
Rusholme Manch....131 G1
Rushton Ches W....130 B7
Rushton N Nthn....101 J6
Rushton Shrops....96 D2
Rushton Spencer Staffs....131 J7
Rushwick Worcs....81 J4
Rushyford Dur....169 H5
Ruskie Stirlg....219 K7
Ruskington Lincs....118 E1
Rusland Cross W & F....156 E5
Rusper W Susx....37 K3
Ruspidge Gloucs....63 K5
Russell Green Essex....71 J4
Russell's Water Oxon....49 H1
Russel's Green Suffk....90 F1
Russ Hill Surrey....37 K3
Rusthall Kent....38 E5
Rustington W Susx....21 H6
Ruston N York....163 G6
Ruston Parva E R Yk....153 G3
Ruswarp N York....162 F1
Ruthall Shrops....96 D5
Rutherford Border....201 K7
Rutherglen S Lans....209 G6
Ruthernbridge Cnwll....5 G2
Ruthin Denbgs....128 D8
Ruthrieston C Aber....245 K3
Ruthven Abers....267 K6
Ruthven Angus....233 L5
Ruthven Highld....241 K4
Ruthven Highld....252 F5
Ruthvoes Cnwll....4 F3
Ruthwaite Cumb....165 L3
Ruthwell D & G....176 E5
Ruxley Gt Lon....52 A5
Ruxton Green Herefs....63 G3
Ruyton-XI-Towns Shrops....112 F7
Ryal Nthumb....180 B4
Ryall Dorset....15 J4
Ryall Worcs....81 K7
Ryarsh Kent....52 E7
Rycote Oxon....67 G6
Rydal W & F....156 E2
Ryde IoW....19 H5
Rye E Susx....25 G3
Ryebank Shrops....113 H5
Ryeford Herefs....63 J3
Rye Foreign E Susx....25 G3
Rye Harbour E Susx....25 H3
Ryehill E R Yk....145 G3
Ryeish Green Wokham....49 H5
Rye Street Worcs....81 H8
Ryhall Rutlnd....102 A1
Ryhill Wakefd....142 B5
Ryhope Sundld....181 K8
Rylah Derbys....133 J6
Ryland Lincs....135 K4
Rylands Notts....116 F4
Rylstone N York....149 H4
Ryme Intrinseca Dorset....31 J8
Ryther N York....151 J7
Ryton Gatesd....180 E6
Ryton N York....162 D7
Ryton Shrops....97 G3
Ryton Warwks....99 L6
Ryton-on-Dunsmore Warwks....99 K8
Ryton Woodside Gatesd....180 E6

S

Sabden Lancs 148 D8
Sabine's Green Essex 70 E7
Sacombe Herts 69 J3
Sacombe Green Herts 69 J3
Sacriston Dur 169 G1
Sadberge Darltn 169 J7
Saddell Ag & B 194 B4
Saddington Leics 100 E5
Saddlebow Norfk 120 D8
Saddlescombe W Susx 22 C5
Sadgill W & F 157 G2
Saffron Walden Essex 87 L7
Sageston Pembks 55 H6
Saham Hills Norfk 105 H3
Saham Toney Norfk 105 H3
Saighton Ches W 129 K7
St Abbs Border 213 K5
St Agnes Border 212 H6
St Agnes Cnwll 4 D3
St Agnes IoS 10 b3
St Agnes Mining District Cnwll ...4 D6
St Albans Herts 68 F5
St Allen Cnwll 4 D5
St Andrew Guern 9 j3
St Andrews Fife 223 J4
St Andrews Major V Glam 43 H7
St Andrews Well Dorset 15 L4
St Anne's Lancs 138 C2
St Ann's D & G 187 G7
St Ann's Chapel Cnwll 12 A8
St Ann's Chapel Devon 7 J5
St Anthony-in-Meneage Cnwll ...3 K6
St Anthony's Hill E Susx 23 L7
St Arvans Mons 63 G7
St Asaph Denbgs 128 B5
St Athan V Glam 42 F8
St Aubin Jersey 9 c3
St Austell Cnwll 5 G4
St Bees Cumb 164 C8
St Blazey Cnwll 5 H4
St Blazey Gate Cnwll 5 H4
St Boswells Border 201 J7
St Brelade Jersey 9 b3
St Brelade's Bay Jersey 9 b3
St Breock Cnwll 10 D8
St Breward Cnwll 10 F7
St Briavels Gloucs 63 H6
St Brides Pembks 54 C5
St Brides Major V Glam 42 F6
St Brides Netherwent Mons ..44 E1
St Brides-super-Ely V Glam ..43 H6
St Brides Wentlooge Newpt ..44 C3
St Budeaux C Plym 6 D5
Saintbury Gloucs 82 D7
St Buryan Cnwll 2 C6
St Catherine BaNES 45 M5
St Catherines Ag & B 217 J5
St Chloe Gloucs 64 B6
St Clears Carmth 58 A5
St Cleer Cnwll 6 A1
St Clement Cnwll 4 D6
St Clement Jersey 9 e4
St Clether Cnwll 11 H5
St Colmac Ag & B 207 G5
St Columb Major Cnwll 4 D2
St Columb Minor Cnwll 4 D2
St Columb Road Cnwll 4 E3
St Combs Abers 269 K4
St Cross South Elmham Suffk ..106 F6
St Cyrus Abers 235 J2
St David's P & K 221 G3
St Davids Pembks 74 B7
St Day Cnwll 4 B6
St Decumans Somset 29 K2
St Dennis Cnwll 4 F3
St Devereux Herefs 62 E1
St Dogmaels Pembks 75 K3
St Dogwells Pembks 75 G6
St Dominick Cnwll 6 D1
St Donats V Glam 42 E8
St Edith's Marsh Wilts 46 H4
St Endellion Cnwll 10 D6
St Enoder Cnwll 4 E3
St Erme Cnwll 4 D5
St Erney Cnwll 6 D3
St Erth Cnwll 2 E4
St Erth Praze Cnwll 2 F4
St Ervan Cnwll 10 B8
St Eval Cnwll 4 D1
St Ewe Cnwll 5 G5
St Fagans Cardif 43 H6
St Fergus Abers 269 K6
St Fillans P & K 220 B2
St Florence Pembks 55 J6
St Gennys Cnwll 11 G3
St George Conwy 127 K4
St Georges N Som 44 D6

St George's V Glam 43 H6
St George's Hill Surrey 50 D6
St Germans Cnwll 6 D3
St Giles in the Wood Devon ...27 J7
St Giles-on-the-Heath Devon ..11 L4
St Gluvia's Cnwll 3 K4
St Harmon Powys 78 D1
St Helen Auckland Dur 168 F5
St Helens Cumb 164 D8
St Helen's E Susx 24 E5
St Helens IoW 19 L6
St Helens St Hel 139 G8
St Helier Gt Lon 51 H5
St Helier Jersey 9 d3
St Hilary Cnwll 2 E5
St Hilary V Glam 42 F7
Saint Hill Devon 14 C1
Saint Hill W Susx 38 B6
St Illtyd Blae G 61 K6
St Ippolyts Herts 69 G2
St Ishmael's Pembks 54 C5
St Issey Cnwll 10 A8
St Ive Cnwll 6 C2
St Ive Cross Cnwll 6 C2
St Ives Cambs 87 G1
St Ives Cnwll 2 E3
St Ives Dorset 17 M2
St James Norfk 122 F7
St James's End W Nthn 84 E3
St James South Elmham Suffk ..107 G7
St Jidgey Cnwll 4 F1
St John Cnwll 6 E4
St John Jersey 9 c1
St Johns Dur 168 D4
St John's E Susx 38 D7
St John's IoM 154 c5
St John's Kent 38 E2
St Johns Surrey 50 C7
St Johns Worcs 81 J4
St John's Chapel Devon 27 J4
St John's Chapel Dur 167 K3
St John's Fen End Norfk 120 L1
St John's Highway Norfk 120 C8
St John's Kirk S Lans 199 G6
St John's Town of Dalry D & G ..184 F6
St John's Wood Gt Lon 51 H2
St Judes IoM 154 e3
St Just Cnwll 2 B5
St Just-in-Roseland Cnwll 3 L4
St Just Mining District Cnwll ..2 B4
St Katherines Abers 256 D5
St Keverne Cnwll 3 K6
St Kew Cnwll 10 E7
St Kew Highway Cnwll 10 E7
St Keyne Cnwll 6 A3
St Lawrence Cnwll 5 H7
St Lawrence Essex 72 D6
St Lawrence IoW 19 J8
St Lawrence Jersey 9 c2
St Lawrence Kent 41 K2
St Lawrence Bay Essex 72 D6
St Leonards Bucks 67 M5
St Leonards Dorset 17 M2
St Leonards E Susx 24 E5
St Leonard's Street Kent 39 H2
St Levan Cnwll 2 B6
St Luke's Park Essex 71 J7
St Lythans V Glam 43 H7
St Mabyn Cnwll 10 E7
St Madoes P & K 222 C3
St Margarets Herefs 79 L8
St Margarets Herts 69 K5
St Margaret's at Cliffe Kent ..41 K6
St Margaret's Hope Ork 275 c6
St Margaret South Elmham Suffk ..107 G6
St Marks IoM 154 d7
St Martin Cnwll 3 J6
St Martin Cnwll 6 B4
St Martin Guern 9 J3
St Martin Jersey 9 e2
St Martin's IoS 10 c1
St Martin's P & K 221 L1
St Martin's Shrops 112 D4
St Martin's Moor Shrops 112 D4
St Mary Jersey 9 c2
St Mary Bourne Hants 34 F1
St Marychurch Torbay 8 D2
St Mary Church V Glam 42 F7
St Mary Cray Gt Lon 52 A5
St Mary Hill V Glam 42 F6
St Mary in the Marsh Kent ...25 K2
St Mary's IoS 10 c3
St Mary's Ork 275 d5
St Mary's Bay Kent 25 K2
St Mary's Hoo Medway 53 H4
St Mary's Platt Kent 39 G2
St Maughans Mons 62 F4
St Maughans Green Mons 62 F4
St Mawes Cnwll 3 L4

St Mawgan Cnwll 4 E2
St Mellion Cnwll 6 D2
St Mellons Cardif 43 K5
St Merryn Cnwll 10 B7
St Mewan Cnwll 5 G4
St Michael Caerhays Cnwll 4 F6
St Michael Church Somset 30 D5
St Michael Penkevil Cnwll 4 D6
St Michaels Kent 39 M6
St Michaels Worcs 80 D2
St Michael's on Wyre Lancs ...147 J7
St Michael South Elmham
  Suffk 107 G6
St Minver Cnwll 10 D7
St Monans Fife 223 J6
St Neot Cnwll 5 L1
St Neots Cambs 86 D3
St Newlyn East Cnwll 4 D3
St Nicholas Pembks 74 E5
St Nicholas V Glam 43 H6
St Nicholas at Wade Kent 41 J2
St Ninians Stirlg 209 L1
St Olaves Norfk 107 J4
St Osyth Essex 73 H4
St Ouen Jersey 9 b2
St Owen's Cross Herefs 63 G2
St Paul's Cray Gt Lon 52 A5
St Paul's Walden Herts 69 G3
St Peter Jersey 9 b2
St Peter Port Guern 9 k3
St Peter's Guern 9 i3
St Peter's Kent 41 L2
St Peter's Hill Cambs 86 E1
St Petrox Pembks 55 G7
St Pinnock Cnwll 5 L2
St Quivox S Ayrs 196 D6
St Ruan Cnwll 3 J8
St Sampson Guern 9 k2
St Saviour Guern 9 i3
St Saviour Jersey 9 d3
St Stephen Cnwll 4 F4
St Stephens Cnwll 6 D1
St Stephens Cnwll 11 L5
St Teath Cnwll 10 F6
St Thomas Devon 13 L4
St Margaret's Bay Kent 41 K6
St Tudy Cnwll 10 F7
St Twynnells Pembks 54 F7
St Veep Cnwll 5 K4
St Vigeans Angus 235 G6
St Wenn Cnwll 5 G2
St Weonards Herefs 63 G2
St Winnow Cnwll 5 J3
St y-Nyll V Glam 43 H6
Salcombe Devon 7 L7
Salcombe Regis Devon 14 D5
Salcott-cum-Virley Essex 72 D4
Sale Trafld 130 F2
Saleby Lincs 137 J5
Sale Green Worcs 81 L4
Salehurst E Susx 24 D2
Salem Carmth 59 H1
Salem Cerdgn 92 E6
Salen Ag & B 227 H4
Salen Highld 237 K7
Salesbury Lancs 139 K1
Salford C Beds 85 H7
Salford Oxon 65 L2
Salford Salfd 140 B8
Salford Priors Warwks 82 C5
Salfords Surrey 37 L2
Salhouse Norfk 123 G8
Saline Fife 221 J8
Salisbury Wilts 33 K5
Salisbury Plain Wilts 33 J2
Salkeld Dykes W & F 166 D3
Sallachy Highld 272 D6
Salle Norfk 122 C6
Salmonby Lincs 136 F5
Salperton Gloucs 65 G3
Salph End Bed 86 B5
Salsburgh N Lans 209 L6
Salt Staffs 114 F6
Salta Cumb 164 E2
Saltaire C Brad 149 L8
Saltaire C Brad 149 L8
Saltash Cnwll 6 D3
Saltburn Highld 263 K6
Saltburn-by-the-Sea R & Cl ..170 F6
Saltby Leics 117 M6
Salt Coates Cumb 177 G8
Saltcoats Cumb 155 K3
Saltcoats N Ayrs 195 L3
Saltcotes Lancs 138 D2
Saltdean Br & H 22 F6
Salterbeck Cumb 164 C5
Salterforth Lancs 148 F6
Salterswall Ches W 130 C6
Salterton Wilts 33 K4
Saltfleet Lincs 137 H1

Saltfleetby All Saints Lincs ..137 H2
Saltfleetby St Clement Lincs ..137 J1
Saltfleetby St Peter Lincs ..137 H2
Saltford BaNES 45 K5
Salthouse Norfk 122 B3
Saltley Birm 98 E5
Saltmarsh Newpt 44 D2
Saltmarshe E R Yk 143 K3
Saltney Flints 129 J6
Salton N York 162 C6
Saltrens Devon 27 H6
Saltwick Nthumb 180 E3
Saltwood Kent 40 F8
Salvington W Susx 21 K6
Salwarpe Worcs 81 K3
Salway Ash Dorset 15 K3
Sambourne Warwks 82 C3
Sambrook Wrekin 113 M6
Samlesbury Lancs 139 H2
Samlesbury Bottoms Lancs ..139 J2
Sampford Arundel Somset 29 K7
Sampford Brett Somset 29 K3
Sampford Courtenay Devon ...13 H1
Sampford Moor Somset 29 K7
Sampford Peverell Devon 29 J8
Sampford Spiney Devon 12 D8
Samsonlane Ork 275 e3
Samson's Corner Essex 73 G3
Samuelston E Loth 212 B5
Sanaigmore Ag & B 204 C2
Sancreed Cnwll 2 C5
Sancton E R Yk 152 D7
Sand Somset 31 G2
Sandaig Highld 247 M8
Sandale Cumb 165 H3
Sandal Magna Wakefd 142 A4
Sanday Ork 275 e2
Sanday Airport Ork 275 e2
Sandbach Ches E 130 E7
Sandbach Services Ches E ..130 F7
Sandbank Ag & B 207 K3
Sandbanks BCP 17 K5
Sandend Abers 267 L3
Sanderstead Gt Lon 51 J6
Sandford Devon 13 J2
Sandford Dorset 17 H5
Sandford Hants 18 B3
Sandford IoW 19 J7
Sandford N Som 44 E7
Sandford S Lans 197 L2
Sandford Shrops 112 E6
Sandford Shrops 113 J5
Sandford W & F 167 G7
Sandford-on-Thames Oxon ...66 D6
Sandford Orcas Dorset 31 K6
Sandford St Martin Oxon 66 B2
Sandgate Kent 41 G8
Sandhaven Abers 269 H3
Sandhead D & G 172 D5
Sandhill Rothm 142 C8
Sandhills Dorset 16 B3
Sandhills Dorset 31 L8
Sand Hills Leeds 150 E7
Sandhills Oxon 66 E5
Sandhills Surrey 36 D3
Sandhoe Nthumb 180 A5
Sandhole Ag & B 216 F7
Sand Hole E R Yk 152 B8
Sandholme E R Yk 143 L2
Sandholme Lincs 119 K4
Sandhurst Br For 49 K6
Sandhurst Gloucs 64 B2
Sandhurst Kent 39 K7
Sandhurst Cross Kent 24 E2
Sand Hutton N York 151 L4
Sandhutton N York 160 E6
Sandiacre Derbys 116 F4
Sandilands Lincs 137 K3
Sandiway Ches W 130 B5
Sandleheath Hants 33 K7
Sandleigh Oxon 66 C5
Sandley Dorset 32 C6
Sandling Kent 53 G7
Sandlow Green Ches E 130 F6
Sandness Shet 281 c5
Sandon Essex 71 H6
Sandon Herts 87 G8
Sandon Staffs 114 E5
Sandon Bank Staffs 114 E6
Sandown IoW 19 K6
Sandplace Cnwll 6 A3
Sandridge Herts 68 F5
Sandridge Wilts 46 D6
Sandringham Norfk 120 F5
Sands Bucks 67 K8
Sandsend N York 171 K8
Sand Side W & F 156 B6
Sandside W & F 157 G6
Sandtoft N Linc 143 J6
Sandway Kent 39 M3

Sandwich Kent......41 K4
Sandwich Bay Kent......41 K4
Sandwick Shet......281 e8
Sandwick W & F......166 A6
Sandwick W Isls......282 g3
Sandwith Cumb......164 C7
Sandwith Newtown Cumb......164 C7
Sandy C Beds......86 D5
Sandy Bank Lincs......136 E4
Sandycroft Flints......129 H6
Sandy Cross E Susx......23 K3
Sandy Cross Herefs......80 F4
Sandyford D & G......187 J2
Sandygate Devon......13 K7
Sandygate IoM......154 e3
Sandy Haven Pembks......54 D5
Sandyhills D & G......175 M4
Sandylands Lancs......147 H3
Sandy Lane C Brad......149 K8
Sandylane Staffs......113 M4
Sandylane Swans......57 G2
Sandy Lane Wilts......46 D5
Sandy Lane Wrexhm......112 F3
Sandy Park Devon......13 G5
Sandysike Cumb......177 L5
Sandyway Herefs......63 D7
Sangobeg Highld......277 G3
Sangomore Highld......276 F3
Sankey Bridges Warrtn......130 B2
Sankyn's Green Worcs......81 H2
Sanna Highld......236 E6
Sanndabhaig W Isls......282 g3
Sannox N Ayrs......195 G2
Sanquhar D & G......185 K1
Santon Cumb......155 K2
Santon IoM......154 d7
Santon Bridge Cumb......155 K2
Santon Downham Suffk......105 G6
Sapcote Leics......100 B5
Sapey Common Herefs......81 G2
Sapiston Suffk......105 J8
Sapley Cambs......102 E8
Sapperton Derbys......115 K4
Sapperton Gloucs......64 D6
Sapperton Lincs......118 D5
Saracen's Head Lincs......119 K6
Sarclet Highld......280 D7
Sarisbury Hants......19 H2
Sarn Brdgnd......42 D5
Sarn Powys......94 F5
Sarnau Carmth......58 B5
Sarnau Cerdgn......76 B5
Sarnau Gwynd......111 J4
Sarnau Powys......78 E8
Sarnau Powys......112 C8
Sarn Bach Gwynd......108 E6
Sarnesfield Herefs......79 L5
Sarn Mellteyrn Gwynd......108 D5
Sarn Park Services Brdgnd......42 D5
Sarn-wen Powys......112 D7
Saron Carmth......59 H6
Saron Carmth......76 C7
Saron Gwynd......125 H7
Saron Gwynd......125 J6
Sarratt Herts......68 D7
Sarre Kent......41 H2
Sarsden Oxon......65 L3
Sarson Hants......34 C2
Satley Dur......168 E2
Satmar Kent......41 H7
Satron N York......159 G3
Satterleigh Devon......28 B6
Satterthwaite W & F......156 D4
Satwell Oxon......49 H2
Sauchen Abers......244 F1
Saucher P & K......233 J8
Sauchieburn Abers......235 G2
Saughall Ches W......129 H5
Saul Gloucs......63 L5
Saundby Notts......134 F2
Saundersfoot Pembks......55 K6
Saunderton Bucks......67 J6
Saunderton Station Bucks......67 K7
Saunton Devon......27 H3
Sausthorpe Lincs......137 G6
Saverley Green Staffs......114 F4
Savile Town Kirk......141 K4
Sawbridge Warwks......83 L2
Sawbridgeworth Herts......70 C4
Sawdon N York......163 G5
Sawley Derbys......116 D5
Sawley Lancs......148 D6
Sawley N York......150 C2
Sawston Cambs......87 K5
Sawtry Cambs......102 D6
Saxby Leics......117 L7
Saxby Lincs......135 K3
Saxby All Saints N Linc......144 C4
Saxelbye Leics......117 J7
Saxham Street Suffk......90 C3

Saxilby Lincs......135 H4
Saxlingham Norfk......122 A4
Saxlingham Green Norfk......106 E4
Saxlingham Nethergate Norfk......106 E4
Saxlingham Thorpe Norfk......106 E4
Saxmundham Suffk......91 J3
Saxondale Notts......117 H3
Saxon Street Cambs......88 D3
Saxtead Suffk......91 G2
Saxtead Green Suffk......90 F2
Saxtead Little Green Suffk......90 F2
Saxthorpe Norfk......122 C5
Saxton N York......151 G8
Sayers Common W Susx......22 D4
Scackleton N York......161 L8
Scadabay W Isls......282 e6
Scadabhagh W Isls......282 e6
Scafell Pike Cumb......156 B1
Scaftworth Notts......134 D2
Scagglethorpe N York......152 C1
Scalasaig Ag & B......214 D5
Scalby E R Yk......143 L2
Scalby N York......163 H4
Scald End Bed......85 L4
Scaldwell N Nthn......84 E1
Scaleby Cumb......178 B6
Scalebyhill Cumb......178 B6
Scale Houses W & F......166 E2
Scales W & F......146 E2
Scales W & F......165 K5
Scalesceugh Cumb......166 B1
Scalford Leics......117 K6
Scaling N York......171 H7
Scaling Dam R & Cl......171 H8
Scalloway Shet......281 d7
Scalpay Highld......247 J2
Scalpay W Isls......282 f6
Scamblesby Lincs......136 E4
Scammonden Kirk......141 G4
Scamodale Highld......228 C1
Scampston N York......162 F7
Scampton Lincs......135 J4
Scaniport Highld......251 H4
Scapegoat Hill Kirk......141 G4
Scarba Ag & B......215 K3
Scarborough N York......163 J5
Scarcewater Cnwll......4 F4
Scarcliffe Derbys......133 K6
Scarcroft Leeds......150 E7
Scarfskerry Highld......280 C2
Scargill Dur......168 D8
Scarinish Ag & B......224 D6
Scarisbrick Lancs......138 D5
Scarness Cumb......165 H4
Scarning Norfk......105 J1
Scarrington Notts......117 J3
Scarth Hill Lancs......138 E6
Scarthingwell N York......151 G8
Scartho NE Lin......145 H6
Scatsta Airport Shet......281 d4
Scaur D & G......175 L4
Scawby N Linc......144 B6
Scawsby Donc......142 E6
Scawthorpe Donc......142 E6
Scawton N York......161 J6
Scayne's Hill W Susx......22 F3
Scethrog Powys......61 H2
Scholar Green Ches E......131 G8
Scholes Kirk......141 J3
Scholes Kirk......141 J6
Scholes Leeds......150 E8
Scholes Rothm......142 B8
Scholes Wigan......139 J6
School Aycliffe Dur......169 H6
School Green C Brad......141 H1
School Green Ches W......130 C6
Schoolgreen Wokham......49 H5
School House Dorset......15 J2
Scissett Kirk......141 K5
Scleddau Pembks......74 F5
Scofton Notts......134 C4
Scole Norfk......106 C7
Scone P & K......221 L2
Sconser Highld......247 H2
Scoonie Fife......222 F6
Scopwick Lincs......135 M8
Scoraig Highld......261 G1
Scorborough E R Yk......152 F6
Scorrier Cnwll......4 B6
Scorriton Devon......7 K1
Scorton Lancs......147 K6
Scorton N York......160 C3
Sco Ruston Norfk......122 F7
Scotby Cumb......178 B7
Scotch Corner N York......160 B2
Scotch Corner Rest Area N York......160 B2
Scotforth Lancs......147 J4
Scot Hay Staffs......114 B2
Scothern Lincs......135 L4

Scotland Lincs......118 C5
Scotland Gate Nthumb......181 G2
Scotlandwell P & K......222 C7
Scot Lane End Bolton......139 J6
Scotscalder Station Highld......279 K5
Scotsdike Cumb......177 L4
Scot's Gap Nthumb......180 C2
Scotsmill Abers......255 L7
Scotstoun C Glas......208 F5
Scotswood N u Ty......180 F6
Scotter Lincs......143 M7
Scotterthorpe Lincs......143 L7
Scottlethorpe Lincs......118 D7
Scotton Lincs......143 M7
Scotton N York......150 D4
Scotton N York......160 B3
Scottow Norfk......122 F6
Scott Willoughby Lincs......118 D4
Scoulton Norfk......105 K3
Scounslow Green Staffs......115 H5
Scourie Highld......276 B7
Scourie More Highld......276 A7
Scousburgh Shet......281 d8
Scouthead Oldham......140 E6
Scrabster Highld......279 K2
Scraesburgh Border......189 J3
Scrafield Lincs......136 F6
Scrainwood Nthumb......190 D4
Scrane End Lincs......119 L3
Scraptoft Leics......100 E2
Scratby Norfk......123 K8
Scrayingham N York......152 A4
Scrays E Susx......24 D3
Scredington Lincs......118 E3
Scremby Lincs......137 H6
Scremerston Nthumb......202 F3
Screveton Notts......117 J3
Scrivelsby Lincs......136 E6
Scriven N York......150 E4
Scrooby Notts......134 C2
Scropton Derbys......115 K5
Scrub Hill Lincs......136 D8
Scruton N York......160 D4
Scuggate Cumb......178 B4
Scullomie Highld......277 L4
Sculthorpe Norfk......121 K5
Scunthorpe N Linc......143 M5
Scurlage Swans......56 E7
Sea Somset......30 E8
Seaborough Dorset......15 K2
Seabridge Staffs......114 C3
Seabrook Kent......41 G8
Seaburn Sundld......181 K6
Seacombe Wirral......129 H2
Seacroft Leeds......150 E8
Seacroft Lincs......137 L7
Seadyke Lincs......119 K4
Seafield W Loth......210 D6
Seaford E Susx......23 H7
Seaforth Sefton......138 C8
Seagrave Leics......117 G8
Seagry Heath Wilts......46 D3
Seaham Dur......169 L1
Seahouses Nthumb......203 L6
Seal Kent......38 E2
Sealand Flints......129 H6
Seale Surrey......36 D1
Seamer N York......163 J6
Seamer N York......170 C8
Seamill N Ayrs......195 K2
Sea Palling Norfk......123 J6
Searby Lincs......144 D6
Seasalter Kent......40 E2
Seascale Cumb......155 J2
Seathwaite Cumb......165 H8
Seathwaite W & F......156 B3
Seatle W & F......156 E6
Seatoller Cumb......165 H7
Seaton Cnwll......6 C4
Seaton Cumb......164 D4
Seaton Devon......14 F4
Seaton Dur......169 L1
Seaton E R Yk......153 J6
Seaton Kent......41 H3
Seaton Nthumb......181 H3
Seaton Rutlnd......101 K4
Seaton Burn N Tyne......181 G4
Seaton Carew Hartpl......170 C5
Seaton Delaval Nthumb......181 H4
Seaton Ross E R Yk......152 B7
Seaton Sluice Nthumb......181 H3
Seatown Dorset......15 K4
Seatown Moray......266 E2
Seave Green N York......161 J3
Seaview IoW......19 L5
Seaville Cumb......177 G8
Seavington St Mary Somset......30 F7
Seavington St Michael Somset......30 F7
Sebastopol Torfn......62 C7
Seborgham Cumb......165 K2

Seckington Warwks......99 H2
Second Severn Crossing Mons......45 G2
Sedbergh W & F......157 L4
Sedbury Gloucs......63 H8
Sedbusk N York......158 F4
Sedgeberrow Worcs......82 B7
Sedgebrook Lincs......117 M4
Sedge Fen Suffk......104 D6
Sedgefield Dur......169 K5
Sedgeford Norfk......120 F4
Sedgehill Wilts......32 E5
Sedgemoor Services Somset......44 D8
Sedgley Dudley......97 L4
Sedgley Park Bury......140 B7
Sedgwick W & F......157 H5
Sedlescombe E Susx......24 E4
Sedrup Bucks......67 J5
Seed Kent......40 B4
Seend Wilts......46 D6
Seend Cleeve Wilts......46 D6
Seer Green Bucks......68 B8
Seething Norfk......107 G4
Sefton Sefton......138 D7
Seghill Nthumb......181 G4
Seighford Staffs......114 D6
Seion Gwynd......125 K6
Seisdon Staffs......97 J4
Selattyn Shrops......112 C5
Selborne Hants......35 M4
Selby N York......142 F1
Selham W Susx......20 F3
Selhurst Gt Lon......51 J5
Selkirk Border......201 G7
Sellack Herefs......63 H2
Sellafield Station Cumb......155 J2
Sellafirth Shet......281 e2
Sellan Cnwll......2 C5
Sellick's Green Somset......30 B7
Sellindge Kent......40 E7
Selling Kent......40 D4
Sells Green Wilts......46 D6
Selly Oak Birm......98 D7
Selmeston E Susx......23 H6
Selsdon Gt Lon......51 K6
Selsey W Susx......20 D8
Selsfield Common W Susx......38 A6
Selside N York......158 D7
Selside W & F......157 H3
Selsley Gloucs......64 B6
Selsted Kent......41 H6
Selston Notts......116 D1
Selworthy Somset......29 G2
Semer Suffk......89 K6
Semington Wilts......46 C6
Semley Wilts......32 E5
Sempringham Lincs......118 F5
Send Surrey......50 C7
Send Marsh Surrey......50 D7
Senghenydd Caerph......43 H3
Sennen Cnwll......2 B6
Sennen Cove Cnwll......2 B6
Sennybridge Powys......60 D2
Serlby Notts......134 C2
Sessay N York......161 G7
Setchey Norfk......104 C1
Setley Hants......18 D3
Seton Mains E Loth......211 M4
Settle N York......148 E3
Settrington N York......152 C2
Seven Ash Somset......29 L4
Sevenhampton Gloucs......64 F3
Sevenhampton Swindn......47 J2
Seven Kings Gt Lon......51 M2
Sevenoaks Kent......38 E2
Sevenoaks Weald Kent......38 E3
Seven Sisters Neath......60 B5
Seven Springs Gloucs......64 C4
Seven Star Green Essex......72 D2
Severn Beach S Glos......45 G2
Severn Bridge S Glos......45 H1
Severn Stoke Worcs......81 K6
Severn View Services S Glos......45 H1
Sevick End Bed......86 B4
Sevington Kent......40 D7
Sewards End Essex......88 B3
Sewardstonebury Essex......69 K7
Sewell C Beds......68 C3
Sewerby E R Yk......153 K2
Seworgan Cnwll......3 H5
Sewstern Leics......118 A7
Sexhow N York......161 G2
Sgalpaigh W Isls......282 f6
Sgiogarstaigh W Isls......282 h1
Shabbington Bucks......67 G5
Shackerley Shrops......97 J2
Shackerstone Leics......99 K2
Shacklecross Derbys......116 C5
Shackleford Surrey......36 D2
Shade Calder......140 D3
Shader W Isls......282 g1

Shadforth Dur 169 J3
Shadingfield Suffk 107 J6
Shadoxhurst Kent 40 C7
Shadwell Leeds 150 D7
Shadwell Norfk 105 J6
Shaftenhoe End Herts 87 H7
Shaftesbury Dorset 32 E6
Shaftholme Donc 142 F6
Shafton Barns 142 B5
Shafton Two Gates Barns 142 B5
Shakerley Wigan 139 K7
Shalbourne Wilts 47 L6
Shalcombe IoW 18 F6
Shalden Hants 35 L3
Shalden Green Hants 35 L2
Shaldon Devon 13 L8
Shalfleet IoW 18 F6
Shalford Essex 71 H1
Shalford Surrey 36 F2
Shalford Green Essex 71 H2
Shallowford Staffs 114 D5
Shalmsford Street Kent 40 F4
Shalstone Bucks 84 C7
Shamley Green Surrey 36 F2
Shandford Angus 234 D3
Shandon Ag & B 207 L2
Shandwick Highld 264 D5
Shangton Leics 100 F4
Shankhouse Nthumb 181 G3
Shanklin IoW 19 K7
Shantron Ag & B 208 B2
Shap W & F 166 D7
Shapinsay Ork 275 d4
Shapwick Dorset 17 H2
Shapwick Somset 30 F3
Shard End Birm 98 F6
Shardlow Derbys 116 D5
Shareshill Staffs 97 L2
Sharlston Wakefd 142 B4
Sharlston Common Wakefd 142 B4
Sharmans Cross Solhll 98 E7
Sharnal Street Medway 52 C4
Sharnbrook Bed 85 K3
Sharneyford Lancs 140 C3
Sharnford Leics 100 B5
Sharnhill Green Dorset 16 D2
Sharoe Green Lancs 139 G1
Sharow N York 150 D2
Sharpenhoe C Beds 68 D1
Sharperton Nthumb 190 D5
Sharp Green Norfk 123 H7
Sharpness Gloucs 63 K6
Sharpthorne W Susx 38 B6
Sharptor Cnwll 11 J8
Sharpway Gate Worcs 81 L2
Sharrington Norfk 122 A4
Shatterford Worcs 97 H7
Shatterling Kent 41 J4
Shatton Derbys 132 D3
Shaugh Prior Devon 7 G2
Shave Cross Dorset 15 J3
Shavington Ches E 113 M1
Shaw C Brad 140 F1
Shaw Oldham 140 D8
Shaw Swindn 47 G2
Shaw W Berk 48 C5
Shaw Wilts 46 G5
Shawbirch Wrekin 113 L8
Shawbost W Isls 282 f2
Shawbury Shrops 113 J7
Shawclough Rochdl 140 F6
Shaw Common Gloucs 63 K2
Shawdon Hill Nthumb 190 F3
Shawell Leics 100 C7
Shawford Hants 34 F6
Shawforth Lancs 140 D4
Shaw Green Herts 69 J1
Shaw Green Lancs 139 G4
Shaw Green N York 150 C7
Shawhead D & G 185 L7
Shaw Mills N York 150 C3
Shawsburn S Lans 198 C3
Shear Cross Wilts 32 E3
Shearington D & G 176 D5
Shearsby Leics 100 D5
Shearston Somset 30 D5
Shebbear Devon 12 B5
Shebdon Staffs 114 B6
Shebster Highld 279 H3
Shedfield Hants 35 H8
Sheen Staffs 132 B7
Sheepbridge Derbys 133 G5
Sheep Hill Dur 180 E7
Sheepridge Kirk 141 J4
Sheepscar Leeds 141 M1
Sheepscombe Gloucs 64 C5
Sheepstor Devon 7 G1
Sheepwash Devon 12 C2
Sheepwash Nthumb 181 G5
Sheepway N Som 45 G4

Sheepy Magna Leics 99 J3
Sheepy Parva Leics 99 J3
Sheering Essex 70 D4
Sheerness Kent 53 K4
Sheerwater Surrey 50 C6
Sheet Hants 36 A6
Sheffield Cnwll 2 D5
Sheffield Sheff 133 G2
Sheffield Bottom W Berk 49 G5
Sheffield Green E Susx 22 F2
Shefford C Beds 86 C7
Shefford Woodlands W Berk 48 A4
Sheigra Highld 276 B3
Sheinton Shrops 96 E3
Shelderton Shrops 95 K7
Sheldon Birm 98 F6
Sheldon Derbys 132 C6
Sheldon Devon 14 D1
Sheldwich Kent 40 D4
Sheldwich Lees Kent 40 D4
Shelf Calder 141 H2
Shelfanger Norfk 106 D6
Shelfield Warwks 82 D3
Shelfield Wsall 98 C3
Shelfield Green Warwks 82 D3
Shelford Notts 117 H3
Shelford Warwks 99 L5
Shellacres Nthumb 202 H4
Shelley Essex 70 E6
Shelley Kirk 141 K5
Shelley Suffk 89 L7
Shelley Far Bank Kirk 141 K5
Shellingford Oxon 65 L8
Shellow Bowells Essex 70 F5
Shelsley Beauchamp Worcs 81 G3
Shelsley Walsh Worcs 81 G3
Shelton Bed 85 K2
Shelton Norfk 106 E5
Shelton Notts 117 K3
Shelton Shrops 95 L1
Shelton Green Norfk 106 E5
Shelton Lock C Derb 116 D5
Shelton Under Harley Staffs 114 C4
Shelve Shrops 95 H4
Shelwick Herefs 80 C6
Shenfield Essex 70 F8
Shenington Oxon 83 J6
Shenley Herts 68 F7
Shenley Brook End M Keyn 85 G8
Shenleybury Herts 68 F6
Shenley Church End M Keyn 85 G7
Shenmore Herefs 79 M7
Shennanton D & G 173 J2
Shenstone Staffs 98 E3
Shenstone Worcs 97 J8
Shenstone Woodend Staffs 98 E3
Shenton Leics 99 K3
Shenval Moray 254 E6
Shepeau Stow Lincs 102 F1
Shephall Herts 69 H2
Shepherd's Bush Gt Lon 51 G3
Shepherd's Green Oxon 49 H2
Shepherds Patch Gloucs 63 L6
Shepherdswell Kent 41 H5
Shepley Kirk 141 J6
Shepperdine S Glos 63 J8
Shepperton Surrey 50 D5
Shepperton Green Surrey 50 D5
Shepreth Cambs 87 H5
Shepshed Leics 116 E7
Shepton Beauchamp Somset 30 F7
Shepton Mallet Somset 31 K2
Shepton Montague Somset 31 L4
Shepway Kent 39 J3
Sheraton Dur 170 B4
Sherborne Dorset 31 L7
Sherborne Gloucs 65 H4
Sherborne Somset 45 H7
Sherborne St John Hants 49 H4
Sherbourne Warwks 83 G3
Sherburn Dur 169 J2
Sherburn N York 163 G7
Sherburn Hill Dur 169 J2
Sherburn in Elmet N York 142 D1
Shere Surrey 37 G1
Shereford Norfk 121 K5
Sherfield English Hants 34 C6
Sherfield on Loddon Hants 49 G7
Sherfin Lancs 140 B3
Sherford Devon 7 G4
Sherford Devon 8 A7
Sherford Dorset 17 H4
Sheriffhales Shrops 97 G1
Sheriff Hutton N York 151 K3
Sheringham Norfk 122 D3
Sherington M Keyn 85 H6
Shermanbury W Susx 22 B3
Shernborne Norfk 120 F5
Sherrington Wilts 33 G3
Sherston Wilts 46 B2

Sherwood C Nott 116 F3
Sherwood Forest Notts 134 C7
Shetland Islands Shet 281 d6
Shettleston C Glas 209 H6
Shevington Wigan 139 H6
Shevington Moor Wigan 139 H5
Shevington Vale Wigan 139 G6
Sheviock Cnwll 6 D4
Shibden Head C Brad 141 H2
Shide IoW 19 H6
Shidlaw Nthumb 202 C5
Shiel Bridge Highld 248 F7
Shieldaig Highld 248 C1
Shieldhill D & G 176 D2
Shieldhill Falk 210 B4
Shieldhill House Hotel S Lans 199 G5
Shields N Lans 209 K7
Shielfoot Highld 237 J6
Shielhill Angus 234 C4
Shielhill Inver 207 L4
Shifford Oxon 66 A6
Shifnal Shrops 97 G2
Shilbottle Nthumb 191 J4
Shildon Dur 169 G5
Shillford E Rens 208 D7
Shillingford Devon 29 H6
Shillingford Oxon 66 E8
Shillingford Abbot Devon 13 L5
Shillingford St George Devon 13 L5
Shillingstone Dorset 32 D8
Shillington C Beds 86 C8
Shillmoor Nthumb 190 B4
Shilton Oxon 65 K5
Shilton Warwks 99 L6
Shimpling Norfk 106 D6
Shimpling Suffk 89 H5
Shimpling Street Suffk 89 H4
Shincliffe Dur 169 H3
Shiney Row Sundld 181 H8
Shinfield Wokham 49 H5
Shingay Cambs 86 F6
Shingle Street Suffk 91 H6
Shinnersbridge Devon 8 B2
Shinness Highld 272 D5
Shipbourne Kent 38 F3
Shipdham Norfk 105 J2
Shipham Somset 44 E7
Shiphay Torbay 8 D2
Shiplake Oxon 49 J3
Shiplake Row Oxon 49 H3
Shiplate N Som 44 D7
Shipley C Brad 149 L8
Shipley Derbys 116 D3
Shipley Shrops 97 H4
Shipley W Susx 37 H6
Shipley Bridge Surrey 37 M3
Shipley Hatch Kent 40 C7
Shipmeadow Suffk 107 H5
Shippea Hill Station Cambs 104 C6
Shippon Oxon 66 C7
Shipston-on-Stour Warwks 83 G7
Shipton Bucks 67 J2
Shipton Gloucs 64 F3
Shipton N York 151 H4
Shipton Shrops 96 D5
Shipton Bellinger Hants 34 B2
Shipton Gorge Dorset 15 L4
Shipton Green W Susx 20 C7
Shipton Moyne Gloucs 46 C1
Shipton-on-Cherwell Oxon 66 C4
Shiptonthorpe E R Yk 152 C7
Shipton-under-Wychwood
  Oxon 65 L3
Shirburn Oxon 67 G7
Shirdley Hill Lancs 138 D5
Shire W & F 166 E4
Shirebrook Derbys 133 K6
Shiregreen Sheff 133 G1
Shirehampton Bristl 45 G4
Shiremoor N Tyne 181 H4
Shirenewton Mons 62 F8
Shire Oak Wsall 98 D3
Shireoaks Notts 133 L3
Shirkoak Kent 40 B8
Shirland Derbys 133 H8
Shirlett Shrops 96 E4
Shirley C Sotn 34 E8
Shirley Derbys 115 L3
Shirley Gt Lon 51 K6
Shirley Solhll 98 E7
Shirl Heath Herefs 80 A3
Shirrell Heath Hants 35 H8
Shirwell Devon 27 L3
Shiskine N Ayrs 194 E5
Shittlehope Dur 168 C3
Shobdon Herefs 79 M3
Shobley Hants 18 B2
Shobrooke Devon 13 K2
Shoby Leics 117 H7
Shocklach Ches W 113 G2

Shocklach Green Ches W 113 G2
Shoeburyness Sthend 53 K2
Sholden Kent 41 K5
Sholing C Sotn 19 G2
Shoot Hill Shrops 95 K1
Shop Cnwll 10 B7
Shop Cnwll 26 D7
Shopwyke W Susx 20 E6
Shore Rochdl 140 D4
Shoreditch Gt Lon 51 J2
Shoreditch Somset 30 C6
Shoreham Kent 52 B6
Shoreham-by-Sea W Susx 22 C6
Shoreswood Nthumb 202 E4
Shorley Hants 35 J5
Shorncote Gloucs 64 F7
Shorne Kent 52 E5
Shortacross Cnwll 6 B3
Shortbridge E Susx 23 G3
Shortfield Common Surrey 36 C2
Shortgate E Susx 23 H4
Short Heath Birm 98 L5
Shortheath Hants 36 A4
Short Heath Wsall 98 B3
Shortlanesend Cnwll 4 C5
Shortlees E Ayrs 196 E4
Shortstown Bed 86 B6
Shorwell IoW 19 G7
Shoscombe BaNES 45 L7
Shotesham Norfk 106 E4
Shotgate Essex 71 J8
Shotley Suffk 90 F8
Shotley Bridge Dur 180 D8
Shotleyfield Nthumb 180 C8
Shotley Gate Suffk 90 F8
Shottenden Kent 40 D4
Shottermill Surrey 36 C4
Shottery Warwks 82 E4
Shotteswell Warwks 83 K6
Shottisham Suffk 91 H6
Shottle Derbys 116 A2
Shottlegate Derbys 116 A2
Shotton Dur 169 K5
Shotton Dur 169 L3
Shotton Flints 129 H6
Shotton Nthumb 180 F3
Shotton Nthumb 202 C7
Shotton Colliery Dur 169 K3
Shotts N Lans 210 A7
Shotwick Ches W 129 H5
Shougle Moray 266 D5
Shouldham Norfk 104 D2
Shouldham Thorpe Norfk 104 D2
Shoulton Worcs 81 J3
Shover's Green E Susx 39 G7
Shraleybrook Staffs 114 B2
Shrawardine Shrops 112 F8
Shrawley Worcs 81 J2
Shreding Green Bucks 50 C3
Shrewley Warwks 82 F2
Shrewsbury Shrops 96 B1
Shrewton Wilts 33 J2
Shripney W Susx 20 F6
Shrivenham Oxon 47 K1
Shropham Norfk 105 K5
Shroton Dorset 32 E8
Shrub End Essex 72 E2
Shucknall Herefs 80 D6
Shudy Camps Cambs 88 C6
Shuna Ag & B 216 B5
Shurdington Gloucs 64 D3
Shurlock Row W & M 49 K4
Shurnock Worcs 82 B3
Shurrery Highld 279 J4
Shurrery Lodge Highld 279 J5
Shurton Somset 30 B2
Shustoke Warwks 99 G5
Shute Devon 13 L3
Shute Devon 14 F3
Shuthonger Gloucs 81 K8
Shutlanger W Nthn 84 L5
Shutterton Devon 13 M6
Shutt Green Staffs 97 K2
Shuttington Warwks 99 H2
Shuttlewood Derbys 133 K6
Shuttleworth Bury 140 B4
Siabost W Isls 282 f2
Siadar W Isls 282 g1
Sibbertoft W Nthn 100 E6
Sibdon Carwood Shrops 95 K6
Sibford Ferris Oxon 83 H7
Sibford Gower Oxon 83 H7
Sible Hedingham Essex 88 C8
Sibley's Green Essex 70 F2
Siblyback Cnwll 11 J8
Sibsey Lincs 119 G3
Sibsey Fenside Lincs 119 K1
Sibson Cambs 102 B4

Sibson Leics	99	K3	
Sibster Highld	280	D5	
Sibthorpe Notts	117	K2	
Sibthorpe Notts	134	E5	
Sibton Suffk	91	J2	
Sicklesmere Suffk	89	H3	
Sicklinghall N York	150	E6	
Sidbrook Somset	30	C5	
Sidbury Devon	14	D4	
Sidbury Shrops	96	F6	
Sid Cop Barns	142	B6	
Sidcot N Som	44	E7	
Sidcup Gt Lon	51	M4	
Siddick Cumb	164	D4	
Siddington Ches E	131	G5	
Siddington Gloucs	64	F7	
Sidemoor Worcs	81	L1	
Sidestrand Norfk	122	F3	
Sidford Devon	14	D4	
Sidlesham W Susx	20	D7	
Sidlesham Common W Susx	20	D6	
Sidley E Susx	24	D5	
Sidmouth Devon	14	D5	
Siefton Shrops	96	B6	
Sigford Devon	13	H7	
Sigglesthorne E R Yk	153	J6	
Sigingstone V Glam	42	E7	
Signet Oxon	65	K5	
Silchester Hants	48	H6	
Sileby Leics	117	G8	
Silecroft Cumb	155	L6	
Silfield Norfk	106	C3	
Silian Cerdgn	77	G5	
Silkstead Hants	34	F6	
Silkstone Barns	141	L6	
Silkstone Common Barns	141	L6	
Silk Willoughby Lincs	118	E3	
Silloth Cumb	176	F8	
Silpho N York	163	H4	
Silsden C Brad	149	J6	
Silsoe C Beds	86	B8	
Silton Dorset	32	C5	
Silverburn Mdloth	211	G7	
Silverdale Lancs	157	G7	
Silverdale Staffs	114	C2	
Silver End Essex	71	K3	
Silverford Abers	268	D3	
Silvergate Norfk	122	D6	
Silver Jubilee Bridge Halton	129	L3	
Silverlace Green Suffk	91	H3	
Silverley's Green Suffk	106	F8	
Silverstone W Nthn	84	C6	
Silver Street Kent	53	J7	
Silver Street Somset	31	J4	
Silverton Devon	13	M2	
Silverwell Cnwll	4	B5	
Silvington Shrops	96	E7	
Simister Bury	140	C6	
Simmondley Derbys	131	K1	
Simonburn Nthumb	179	K4	
Simonsbath Somset	28	D3	
Simonsburrow Devon	29	L7	
Simonstone Lancs	140	A1	
Simonstone N York	158	F4	
Simprim Border	202	C4	
Simpson M Keyn	85	H8	
Simpson Cross Pembks	54	E3	
Sinclair's Hill Border	202	C3	
Sinclairston E Ayrs	196	F7	
Sinderby N York	160	E6	
Sinderhope Nthumb	179	K8	
Sinderland Green Traffd	130	E2	
Sindlesham Wokham	49	J5	
Sinfin C Derb	116	B5	
Singleborough Bucks	67	J1	
Single Street Gt Lon	51	L7	
Singleton Kent	40	C7	
Singleton Lancs	147	G8	
Singleton W Susx	20	E4	
Singlewell Kent	52	F6	
Sinkhurst Green Kent	39	K5	
Sinnahard Abers	244	B1	
Sinnington N York	162	C5	
Sinope Leics	116	C8	
Sinton Worcs	81	J3	
Sinton Worcs	81	J3	
Sinton Green Worcs	81	J3	
Sipson Gt Lon	50	D3	
Sirhowy Blae G	61	J5	
Sissinghurst Kent	39	K6	
Siston S Glos	45	K4	
Sitcott Devon	11	L4	
Sithney Cnwll	3	G5	
Sithney Common Cnwll	3	G5	
Sithney Green Cnwll	3	G5	
Sittingbourne Kent	40	B3	
Six Ashes Shrops	97	H5	
Six Bells Blae G	61	K6	
Six Hills Leics	117	H7	
Sixhills Lincs	136	C2	
Six Mile Bottom Cambs	88	B4	
Sixmile Cottages Kent	40	F6	
Sixpenny Handley Dorset	33	G7	
Six Rues Jersey	9	c2	
Sizewell Suffk	91	L3	
Skaill Ork	275	d5	
Skara Brae Ork	275	b4	
Skares E Ayrs	197	G7	
Skateraw Abers	245	K5	
Skateraw E Loth	213	G4	
Skeabost Highld	259	G7	
Skeeby N York	160	B2	
Skeffington Leics	101	G3	
Skeffling E R Yk	145	K4	
Skegby Notts	133	K7	
Skegby Notts	134	F5	
Skegness Lincs	137	L7	
Skelbo Highld	264	B1	
Skelbo Street Highld	264	B1	
Skelbrooke Donc	142	D5	
Skeldyke Lincs	119	K4	
Skellingthorpe Lincs	135	J5	
Skellorn Green Ches E	131	H3	
Skellow Donc	142	E5	
Skelmanthorpe Kirk	141	K5	
Skelmersdale Lancs	138	F6	
Skelmorlie N Ayrs	207	K5	
Skelpick Highld	278	B5	
Skelston D & G	185	K6	
Skelton C York	151	J4	
Skelton E R Yk	143	J3	
Skelton N York	159	K3	
Skelton R & Cl	170	F7	
Skelton W & F	166	B4	
Skelton on Ure N York	150	E2	
Skelwith Bridge W & F.	156	E2	
Skendleby Lincs	137	H5	
Skene House Abers	245	G2	
Skenfrith Mons	62	F3	
Skerne E R Yk	153	G5	
Skerray Highld	277	L4	
Skerricha Highld	276	C6	
Skerton Lancs	147	J3	
Sketchley Leics	99	L5	
Sketty Swans	57	H6	
Skewen Neath	57	K5	
Skewsby N York	151	K2	
Skeyton Norfk	122	E6	
Skeyton Corner Norfk	122	E6	
Skiall Highld	279	H3	
Skidbrooke Lincs	137	H1	
Skidbrooke North End Lincs	137	H1	
Skidby E R Yk	144	C1	
Skigersta W Isls	282	h1	
Skilgate Somset	29	H5	
Skillington Lincs	118	A6	
Skinburness Cumb	176	F7	
Skinflats Falk	210	B2	
Skinidin Highld	258	C7	
Skinners Green W Berk	48	C6	
Skinningrove R & Cl	171	G6	
Skipness Ag & B	206	E7	
Skipper's Bridge D & G.	177	L2	
Skiprigg Cumb	165	L2	
Skipsea E R Yk	153	J5	
Skipsea Brough E R Yk	153	J5	
Skipton N York	149	H5	
Skipton-on-Swale N York	160	E6	
Skipwith N York	151	L8	
Skirbeck Lincs	119	K3	
Skirlaugh E R Yk	153	J7	
Skirling Border	199	J3	
Skirmett Bucks	49	J1	
Skirpenbeck E R Yk	152	A4	
Skirwith N York	158	C7	
Skirwith W & F	166	E4	
Skirza Highld	280	E3	
Skitby Cumb	178	B5	
Skittle Green Bucks	67	J6	
Skokholm Island Pembks	54	B6	
Skomer Island Pembks	54	B5	
Skulamus Highld	247	L4	
Skyborry Green Shrops	95	G8	
Skye Green Essex	72	C3	
Skye of Curr Highld	253	J6	
Skyreholme N York	149	J4	
Slack Calder	140	E2	
Slackbuie Highld	251	J3	
Slackcote Oldham	140	E6	
Slack Head W & F.	157	G6	
Slackholme End Lincs	137	K5	
Slacks of Cairnbanno Abers	256	F3	
Slad Gloucs	64	C5	
Slade Devon	14	D1	
Slade Devon	27	J2	
Slade Devon	28	E5	
Slade End Oxon	48	E1	
Slade Green Gt Lon	52	B4	
Slade Heath Staffs	97	L2	
Slade Hooton Rothm	133	K2	
Sladesbridge Cnwll	10	E8	
Slades Green Worcs	81	J8	
Slaggyford Nthumb	178	F8	
Slaidburn Lancs	148	C5	
Slaithwaite Kirk	141	G5	
Slaley Derbys	132	E8	
Slaley Nthumb	180	A7	
Slamannan Falk	209	M4	
Slapton Bucks	68	B3	
Slapton Devon	8	B6	
Slapton W Nthn	84	C6	
Slattocks Rochdl	140	D6	
Slaugham W Susx	37	L5	
Slaughterford Wilts	46	B4	
Slawston Leics	101	G4	
Sleaford Hants	36	B3	
Sleaford Lincs	118	E2	
Sleagill W & F	166	E6	
Sleap Shrops	113	H6	
Sleapford Wrekin	113	L8	
Sleapshyde Herts	69	G3	
Sleasdairidh Highld	272	F8	
Slebech Pembks	55	H4	
Sledge Green Worcs	81	J8	
Sledmere E R Yk	152	E3	
Sleetbeck Cumb	178	C3	
Sleight Dorset	17	J3	
Sleightholme Dur	168	B8	
Sleights N York	162	F1	
Slepe Dorset	17	H4	
Slickly Highld	280	C3	
Sliddery N Ayrs	193	J4	
Sligachan Highld	247	G3	
Sligrachan Ag & B	207	K1	
Slimbridge Gloucs	63	L6	
Slindon Staffs	114	C5	
Slindon W Susx	20	L5	
Slinfold W Susx	37	H4	
Sling Gloucs	63	H5	
Sling Gwynd	126	B6	
Slingsby N York	162	B7	
Slip End C Beds	68	D3	
Slip End Herts	86	F7	
Slipton N Nthn	101	L7	
Slitting Mill Staffs	115	G8	
Slochd Highld	252	F7	
Slockavullin Ag & B	216	C7	
Sloley Norfk	122	F6	
Sloncombe Devon	13	H5	
Sloothby Lincs	137	J5	
Slough Slough	50	C3	
Slough Green Somset	30	C7	
Slough Green W Susx	37	L5	
Slumbay Highld	248	E4	
Slyfield Surrey	50	C8	
Slyne Lancs	147	J3	
Smailholm Border	201	K6	
Smallbridge Rochdl	140	D5	
Smallbrook Devon	13	K3	
Smallbrook Gloucs	63	H7	
Smallburgh Norfk	123	G6	
Smallburn E Ayrs	197	K5	
Smalldale Derbys	132	B4	
Smalldale Derbys	132	C3	
Small Dole W Susx	22	C5	
Smalley Derbys	116	C3	
Smalley Common Derbys	116	C3	
Smalley Green Derbys	116	C3	
Smallfield Surrey	37	M2	
Smallford Herts	69	G5	
Small Heath Birm	98	E6	
Small Hythe Kent	25	G1	
Smallridge Devon	15	G2	
Smallthorne C Stke	114	D2	
Smallways N York	168	E8	
Smallwood Ches E	130	F7	
Small Wood Hey Lancs	147	H6	
Smallworth Norfk	105	K7	
Smannell Hants	34	E1	
Smardale W & F	158	C1	
Smarden Kent	39	L5	
Smarden Bell Kent	39	L5	
Smart's Hill Kent	38	E5	
Smeafield Nthumb	203	H5	
Smeatharpe Devon	14	E1	
Smeeth Kent	40	E7	
Smeeton Westerby Leics	100	E5	
Smelthouses N York	150	B3	
Smerral Highld	275	G2	
Smestow Staffs	97	J5	
Smethwick Sandw	98	C6	
Smethwick Green Ches E	130	F7	
Smirisary Highld	237	J5	
Smisby Derbys	116	B7	
Smith End Green Worcs	81	H5	
Smith Green Lancs	147	J5	
Smithies Barns	142	A6	
Smithincott Devon	29	J8	
Smith's End Herts	87	H7	
Smith's Green Essex	70	E3	
Smith's Green Essex	88	D7	
Smithstown Highld	260	C4	
Smithton Highld	252	D3	
Smithy Bridge Rochdl	140	D5	
Smithy Green Ches E	130	E5	
Smithy Green Stockp	131	G3	
Smithy Houses Derbys	116	C2	
Smockington Leics	99	M5	
Smoo Highld	277	G3	
Smythe's Green Essex	72	D3	
Snade D & G	185	L3	
Snailbeach Shrops	95	J3	
Snailwell Cambs	88	C2	
Snainton N York	163	G6	
Snaith E R Yk	143	G3	
Snake Pass Inn Derbys	132	B2	
Snape N York	160	C6	
Snape Suffk	91	J3	
Snape Green Lancs	138	D5	
Snape Street Suffk	91	J4	
Snaresbrook Gt Lon	51	L1	
Snarestone Leics	99	K2	
Snarford Lincs	135	L3	
Snargate Kent	25	J2	
Snave Kent	25	J1	
Sneachill Worcs	81	L4	
Snead Powys	95	H5	
Sneath Common Norfk	106	D5	
Sneaton N York	162	F1	
Sneatonthorpe N York	162	F2	
Snelland Lincs	135	M4	
Snelson Ches E	130	F5	
Snelston Derbys	115	J3	
Snetterton Norfk	105	K5	
Snettisham Norfk	120	F4	
Snibston Leics	116	C8	
Snig's End Gloucs	64	A1	
Snitter Nthumb	190	E5	
Snitterby Lincs	135	K1	
Snitterfield Warwks	82	F3	
Snitterton Derbys	132	E7	
Snitton Shrops	96	D8	
Snoadhill Kent	40	B6	
Snodhill Herefs	79	K7	
Snodland Kent	52	F6	
Snoll Hatch Kent	39	G4	
Snowden Hill Barns	141	L7	
Snowdon Gwynd	109	L1	
Snowdon Kent	41	H5	
Snowdonia National Park	110	F5	
Snow End Herts	69	L1	
Snowshill Gloucs	82	C8	
Snow Street Norfk	106	C3	
Soake Hants	19	L2	
Soar Cardif	43	H5	
Soar Devon	7	K7	
Soar Powys	60	E1	
Soay Highld	246	F6	
Soberton Hants	35	J7	
Soberton Heath Hants	35	J8	
Sockbridge W & F	166	C5	
Sockburn Darltn	160	E1	
Sodom Denbgs	128	C5	
Sodylt Bank Shrops	112	G3	
Soham Cambs	104	B8	
Soham Cotes Cambs	104	B8	
Solas W Isls	282	c7	
Solbury Pembks	54	E4	
Soldon Devon	26	E8	
Soldon Cross Devon	26	E8	
Soldridge Hants	35	K4	
Sole Street Kent	40	E5	
Sole Street Kent	52	E5	
Solihull Solhll	98	F7	
Sollas W Isls	282	c7	
Sollers Dilwyn Herefs	80	A4	
Sollers Hope Herefs	80	E8	
Sollom Lancs	138	F4	
Solva Pembks	74	C7	
Solwaybank D & G	177	J3	
Somerby Leics	101	G1	
Somerby Lincs	144	D6	
Somercotes Derbys	116	C1	
Somerford BCP	18	B5	
Somerford Keynes Gloucs	64	E8	
Somerley W Susx	20	D7	
Somerleyton Suffk	107	K4	
Somersal Herbert Derbys	115	J5	
Somersby Lincs	136	F5	
Somersham Cambs	103	G7	
Somersham Suffk	90	C5	
Somerton Oxon	66	C2	
Somerton Somset	31	H5	
Somerton Suffk	89	G4	
Somerwood Shrops	113	J8	
Sompting W Susx	21	K6	
Sompting Abbotts W Susx	21	K5	
Sonning Wokham	49	J4	
Sonning Common Oxon	49	H3	

Sonning Eye Oxon......49 H4
Sontley Wrexhm......112 E2
Sopley Hants......18 B4
Sopwell Herts......68 F6
Sopworth Wilts......46 B2
Sorbie D & G......174 C5
Sordale Highld......279 L4
Sorisdale Ag & B......225 H3
Sorn E Ayrs......197 G5
Sornhill E Ayrs......197 G5
Sortat Highld......280 C4
Sotby Lincs......136 D4
Sots Hole Lincs......136 B6
Sotterley Suffk......107 J6
Soughton Flints......128 F6
Soulbury Bucks......67 L2
Soulby W & F......166 B5
Soulby W & F......167 H8
Souldern Oxon......66 D1
Souldrop Bed......85 J3
Sound Ches E......113 K2
Sound Muir Moray......267 G5
Soundwell S Glos......45 J4
Sourton Devon......12 D4
Soutergate W & F......156 B6
South Acre Norfk......121 H8
South Alkham Kent......41 H7
Southall Gt Lon......50 E3
South Allington Devon......8 B7
South Alloa Falk......210 A1
Southam Gloucs......64 E2
Southam Warwks......83 K3
South Ambersham W Susx......20 F3
Southampton C Sotn......19 G1
Southampton Airport Hants......34 F7
South Anston Rothm......133 K3
South Ascot W & M......50 A5
South Ashford Kent......40 C7
South Baddesley Hants......18 E4
South Bank C York......151 J5
South Bank R & Cl......170 C6
South Barrow Somset......31 K5
South Beddington Gt Lon......51 H6
South Beer Cnwll......11 K4
South Benfleet Essex......53 G2
South Bersted W Susx......18 B6
Southborough Gt Lon......51 L5
Southborough Kent......38 F7
Southbourne BCP......18 A5
Southbourne W Susx......20 C5
South Bowood Dorset......15 K3
South Bramwith Donc......143 G6
South Brent Devon......7 K3
South Brewham Somset......32 B4
South Broomhill Nthumb......191 K6
Southburgh Norfk......105 K2
South Burlingham Norfk......107 H2
Southburn E R Yk......152 F5
South Cadbury Somset......31 K5
South Carlton Lincs......135 J4
South Carlton Notts......134 B3
South Cave E R Yk......144 A2
South Cerney Gloucs......64 F7
South Chailey E Susx......22 F4
South Chard Somset......15 H2
South Charlton Nthumb......191 H2
South Cheriton Somset......32 B6
South Church Dur......169 H4
Southchurch Sthend......53 J2
South Cleatlam Dur......168 E7
South Cliffe E R Yk......152 D8
South Clifton Notts......135 G5
South Cockerington Lincs......137 G2
South Cornelly Brdgnd......42 B5
Southcott Cnwll......11 H3
Southcott Devon......12 D4
Southcott Devon......13 H6
Southcott Devon......27 H7
Southcott Wilts......47 H7
Southcourt Bucks......67 K5
South Cove Suffk......107 K7
South Creake Norfk......121 J4
South Crosland Kirk......141 H5
South Croxton Leics......100 F2
South Dalton E R Yk......152 E6
South Darenth Kent......52 C5
South Dell W Isls......282 g1
South Downs National Park......22 E5
South Duffield N York......143 H1
South Earlswood Surrey......37 L1
Southease E Susx......23 G6
South Elkington Lincs......136 E2
South Elmsall Wakefd......142 D5
Southend Ag & B......192 E6
South End E R Yk......145 K4
South End Hants......33 J7
South End Herefs......81 G6
South End N Linc......144 E4
South End Norfk......105 K5
Southend Wilts......47 J4

Southend Airport Essex......53 J1
Southend-on-Sea Sthend......53 J2
Southernby W & F......165 L3
Southernden Kent......39 L4
Southerndown V Glam......42 D7
Southerness D & G......176 C7
South Erradale Highld......260 B5
Southerton Devon......14 C4
Southery Norfk......104 C4
South Fambridge Essex......72 B8
South Fawley W Berk......48 A3
South Ferriby N Linc......144 B4
South Field E R Yk......144 C3
Southfield Falk......209 M4
Southfleet Kent......52 D5
Southford IoW......19 J7
Southgate Gt Lon......69 J8
Southgate Norfk......120 E5
Southgate Norfk......121 J4
Southgate Norfk......122 C6
Southgate Swans......57 G7
South Godstone Surrey......38 A1
South Gorley Hants......18 B2
South Gosforth N u Ty......181 G5
South Green Essex......71 G8
South Green Essex......72 F3
South Green Kent......53 J7
South Green Norfk......105 L1
South Green Suffk......106 D8
South Gyle C Edin......211 G4
South Hanningfield Essex......71 H7
South Harting W Susx......20 C3
South Hayling Hants......20 B6
South Hazelrigg Nthumb......203 G6
South Heath Bucks......67 M6
South Heighton E Susx......23 G6
South Hetton Dur......169 K2
South Hiendley Wakefd......142 B5
South Hill Cnwll......11 L8
South Hill Somset......31 G5
South Hinksey Oxon......66 D6
South Hole Devon......26 C6
South Holmwood Surrey......37 J2
South Hornchurch Gt Lon......52 B2
South Horrington Somset......31 J2
South Huish Devon......7 K6
South Hykeham Lincs......135 J6
South Hylton Sundld......181 J7
Southill C Beds......86 C6
Southington Hants......35 G1
South Kelsey Lincs......144 D8
South Kessock Highld......251 H2
South Killingholme N Linc......144 F4
South Kilvington N York......160 F6
South Kilworth Leics......100 D7
South Kirkby Wakefd......142 C5
South Knighton Devon......13 J8
South Kyme Lincs......119 G2
Southleigh Devon......14 E4
South Leigh Oxon......66 B5
South Leverton Notts......134 F3
South Littleton Worcs......82 C6
South Lopham Norfk......105 L7
South Luffenham Rutlnd......101 K3
South Lynn Norfk......120 D7
South Malling E Susx......23 G5
South Marston Swindn......47 J2
South Merstham Surrey......51 H8
South Middleton Nthumb......190 E2
South Milford N York......142 D2
South Milton Devon......7 K6
South Mimms Herts......69 G6
South Mimms Services Herts......69 G7
Southminster Essex......72 D7
South Molton Devon......28 C5
South Moor Dur......180 F8
Southmoor Oxon......66 B7
South Moreton Oxon......48 E1
Southmuir Angus......234 B5
South Mundham W Susx......20 F6
South Muskham Notts......134 F8
South Newbald E R Yk......152 D8
South Newington Oxon......83 J8
South Newsham Nthumb......181 H3
South Newton Wilts......33 J4
South Nitshill C Glas......208 E7
South Normanton Derbys......133 J8
South Norwood Gt Lon......51 J5
South Nutfield Surrey......37 M1
South Ockendon Thurr......52 D2
Southoe Cambs......86 D2
Southolt Suffk......90 E2
South Ormsby Lincs......137 G4
Southorpe C Pete......102 B3
South Ossett Wakefd......141 L4
South Otterington N York......160 E5
Southover Dorset......16 B4
Southover E Susx......24 B2
South Owersby Lincs......135 L1
Southowram Calder......141 H3

South Park Surrey......37 K1
South Perrott Dorset......15 L1
South Petherton Somset......31 G7
South Petherwin Cnwll......11 K6
South Pickenham Norfk......105 K3
South Pill Cnwll......6 E3
South Pool Devon......7 M6
South Poorton Dorset......15 M3
Southport Sefton......138 D4
South Queensferry C Edin......210 F3
South Radworthy Devon......28 C4
South Rauceby Lincs......118 D2
South Raynham Norfk......121 J6
South Reddish Stockp......131 H1
Southrepps Norfk......122 E4
South Reston Lincs......137 G3
Southrey Lincs......136 B6
South Ronaldsay Ork......275 c6
Southrop Gloucs......65 J6
Southrope Hants......35 K2
South Runcton Norfk......104 C2
South Scarle Notts......135 G6
Southsea C Port......19 L4
Southsea Wrexhm......112 D1
South Shian Ag & B......228 E7
South Shields S Tyne......181 J5
South Shore Bpool......138 C1
Southside Dur......168 E5
South Somercotes Lincs......137 H1
South Stainley N York......150 D3
South Stifford Thurr......52 D3
South Stoke BaNES......45 L4
South Stoke Oxon......48 F2
South Stoke W Susx......21 H5
South Stour Kent......40 D7
South Street Kent......40 D4
South Street Kent......40 F2
South Street Kent......52 D6
South Tarbrax S Lans......199 H3
South Tawton Devon......12 F4
South Tehidy Cnwll......3 G3
South Thoresby Lincs......137 G4
South Thorpe Dur......168 E7
South Town Hants......35 K4
Southtown Norfk......107 L2
Southwaite Cumb......165 J2
South Uist W Isls......283 c10
Southwaite W & F......166 B2
Southwaite Services W & F......166 B2
South Walsham Norfk......107 H1
Southwark Gt Lon......51 J3
South Warnborough Hants......35 L2
Southwater W Susx......37 J5
Southwater Street W Susx......37 J5
Southway C Plym......6 F3
Southway Somset......31 H2
South Weald Essex......70 E8
Southwell Dorset......16 D8
Southwell Notts......117 J1
South Weston Oxon......67 H7
South Wheatley Cnwll......11 J4
South Wheatley Notts......134 F3
Southwick Hants......19 L2
Southwick N Nthn......101 M5
Southwick Somset......30 E2
Southwick Sundld......181 J7
Southwick W Susx......22 C5
Southwick Wilts......46 B7
South Widcombe BaNES......45 H7
South Wigston Leics......100 D4
South Willingham Lincs......136 C3
South Wingate Dur......169 L4
South Wingfield Derbys......133 G8
South Witham Lincs......118 B7
Southwold Suffk......107 K8
South Wonston Hants......34 F4
Southwood Norfk......107 H2
Southwood Somset......31 J4
South Woodham Ferrers Essex......71 K7
South Wootton Norfk......120 F7
South Wraxall Wilts......46 B6
South Zeal Devon......12 F4
Sovereign Harbour E Susx......23 L6
Sowerby Calder......141 G3
Sowerby N York......160 F6
Sowerby Bridge Calder......141 G3
Sowerby Row W & F......165 L3
Sower Carr Lancs......147 G2
Sowerhill Somset......28 F6
Sowhill Torfn......62 B7
Sowley Green Suffk......88 D5
Sowood Calder......141 G4
Sowton Devon......6 F2
Sowton Devon......14 A4
Soyland Town Calder......140 F4
Spa Common Norfk......122 F5
Spain's End Essex......88 D7
Spalding Lincs......119 H7
Spaldington E R Yk......143 J1
Spaldwick Cambs......86 C1

Spalford Notts......135 G6
Spanby Lincs......118 E4
Spanish Green Hants......49 G7
Sparham Norfk......122 B7
Sparhamill Norfk......122 B7
Spark Bridge W & F......156 D5
Sparket W & F......166 B5
Sparkford Somset......31 K5
Sparkhill Birm......98 E6
Sparkwell Devon......7 H3
Sparrow Green Norfk......121 L8
Sparrowpit Derbys......132 B3
Sparrows Green E Susx......39 G6
Sparsholt Hants......34 F4
Sparsholt Oxon......47 M2
Spartylea Nthumb......167 K1
Spath Staffs......115 H4
Spaunton N York......162 C5
Spaxton Somset......30 C3
Spean Bridge Highld......239 L7
Spear Hill W Susx......21 K3
Speddoch D & G......177 J6
Speen Bucks......67 K7
Speen W Berk......48 C5
Speeton N York......163 L7
Speke Lpool......129 K3
Speldhurst Kent......38 E5
Spellbrook Herts......70 C4
Spelmonden Kent......39 H6
Spelsbury Oxon......65 M3
Spen Kirk......141 K3
Spencers Wood Wokham......49 H5
Spen Green Ches E......130 F7
Spennithorne N York......159 L5
Spennymoor Dur......169 H4
Spernall Warwks......82 C3
Spetchley Worcs......81 K4
Spetisbury Dorset......17 H2
Spexhall Suffk......107 H7
Spey Bay Moray......267 G3
Speybridge Highld......253 K6
Speyview Moray......254 E3
Spilsby Lincs......137 G6
Spindlestone Nthumb......203 J6
Spinkhill Derbys......133 J4
Spinningdale Highld......263 J7
Spion Kop Notts......133 L6
Spirthill Wilts......46 E4
Spital Wirral......129 H3
Spital Hill Donc......134 C1
Spital in the Street Lincs......135 K2
Spithurst E Susx......23 G4
Spittal E Loth......212 A4
Spittal E R Yk......152 B5
Spittal Highld......279 L5
Spittal Nthumb......202 F3
Spittal Pembks......55 G2
Spittalfield P & K......233 H7
Spittal of Glenmuick Abers......243 K6
Spittal of Glenshee P & K......233 H2
Spittal-on-Rule Border......189 G2
Spixworth Norfk......122 E8
Splatt Cnwll......10 C7
Splatt Cnwll......11 J5
Splatt Devon......12 E2
Splayne's Green E Susx......23 G2
Splott Cardif......43 K6
Spofforth N York......150 E5
Spondon C Derb......116 C4
Spon Green Flints......129 G7
Spooner Row Norfk......106 B4
Sporle Norfk......105 G1
Spott E Loth......212 E4
Spottiswoode Border......201 J3
Spratton W Nthn......84 D1
Spreakley Surrey......36 B3
Spreyton Devon......13 G3
Spriddlestone Devon......7 G4
Spridlington Lincs......135 K3
Springburn C Glas......209 G5
Springfield D & G......177 K5
Springfield Essex......71 H5
Springfield Fife......222 F5
Springhill Staffs......98 B3
Springhill Staffs......98 D2
Springholm D & G......175 K1
Springside N Ayrs......196 D3
Springthorpe Lincs......135 H2
Spring Vale Barns......141 L7
Springwell Sundld......181 G7
Springwood Village Border......201 L6
Sproatley E R Yk......145 F1
Sproston Green Ches W......130 E6
Sprotbrough Donc......142 E7
Sproughton Suffk......90 D6
Sprouston Border......202 B6
Sprowston Norfk......106 E1
Sproxton Leics......117 M6
Sproxton N York......161 K6
Spunhill Shrops......112 F5

Spurstow Ches E 130 A8
Spyway Dorset 15 M4
Square and Compass Pembks 74 D6
Stableford Shrops 97 G4
Stableford Staffs 114 C4
Stacey Bank Sheff 132 F2
Stackhouse N York 148 E3
Stackpole Pembks 55 G7
Stackpole Elidor Pembks 55 G7
Stacksford Norfk 105 L5
Stacksteads Lancs 140 C3
Staddiscombe C Plym 7 G4
Staddlethorpe E R Yk 143 L2
Staden Derbys 131 L5
Stadhampton Oxon 66 F7
Stadhlaigearraidh W Isls 283 b10
Staffield W & F 166 D2
Staffin Highld 259 H3
Stafford Staffs 114 E7
Stafford Services (northbound) Staffs 114 D5
Stafford Services (southbound) Staffs 114 D5
Stagsden Bed 85 J5
Stainborough Barns 141 M7
Stainburn Cumb 164 D5
Stainburn N York 150 C6
Stainby Lincs 118 B7
Staincross Barns 141 M5
Staindrop Dur 168 E6
Staines-upon-Thames Surrey 50 D5
Stainfield Lincs 118 B4
Stainfield Lincs 136 B5
Stainforth Donc 143 G5
Stainforth N York 148 E2
Staining Lancs 147 G8
Stainland Calder 141 G4
Stainsacre N York 163 G1
Stainsby Derbys 133 J6
Stainton Cumb 177 L7
Stainton Donc 133 L1
Stainton Dur 168 D7
Stainton Middsb 170 B7
Stainton N York 159 K3
Stainton W & F 157 H5
Stainton W & F 166 C5
Stainton by Langworth Lincs 135 L4
Staintondale N York 163 H3
Stainton Grove Dur 168 D7
Stainton le Vale Lincs 136 C1
Stainton with Adgarley W & F 146 E1
Stair Cumb 165 H6
Stair E Ayrs 196 E6
Stairfoot Barns 142 B6
Stairhaven D & G 172 F4
Staithes N York 171 H7
Stakeford Nthumb 181 G2
Stake Pool Lancs 147 H6
Stakes Hants 19 M2
Stalbridge Dorset 32 B7
Stalbridge Weston Dorset 32 B7
Stalham Norfk 123 H6
Stalham Green Norfk 123 H6
Stalisfield Green Kent 40 B5
Stalland Common Norfk 105 L4
Stallen Dorset 31 K7
Stallingborough NE Lin 145 G5
Stalling Busk N York 159 G5
Stallington Staffs 114 E4
Stalmine Lancs 147 G6
Stalmine Moss Side Lancs 147 G6
Stalybridge Tamesd 140 E8
Stambourne Essex 88 E7
Stambourne Green Essex 88 D7
Stamford Lincs 102 A2
Stamford Nthumb 191 J2
Stamford Bridge Ches W 129 L6
Stamford Bridge E R Yk 151 M5
Stamfordham Nthumb 180 C4
Stamford Hill Gt Lon 51 J2
Stanah Lancs 147 G7
Stanborough Herts 69 G5
Stanbridge C Beds 68 B2
Stanbridge Dorset 17 K2
Stanbury C Brad 149 H8
Stand Bury 140 B6
Stand N Lans 209 K5
Standburn Falk 210 B4
Standeford Staffs 97 K2
Standen Kent 39 L5
Standen Street Kent 39 K7
Standerwick Somset 32 D1
Standford Hants 36 B4
Standingstone Cumb 164 D4
Standish Gloucs 64 A5
Standish Wigan 139 H5
Standish Lower Ground Wigan 139 H6
Standlake Oxon 66 B6
Standon Hants 34 F5
Standon Herts 69 K3

Standon Staffs 114 C4
Standon Green End Herts 69 K3
Standwell Green Suffk 90 D1
Stane N Lans 210 A7
Stanfield Norfk 121 K7
Stanford C Beds 86 D7
Stanford Kent 40 F7
Stanford Shrops 95 H1
Stanford Bishop Herefs 80 F5
Stanford Bridge Worcs 81 G2
Stanford Bridge Wrekin 113 M6
Stanford Dingley W Berk 48 E4
Stanford in the Vale Oxon 65 M8
Stanford le Hope Thurr 52 E3
Stanford on Avon W Nthn 100 D7
Stanford on Soar Notts 116 F7
Stanford on Teme Worcs 81 G2
Stanford Rivers Essex 70 D7
Stanfree Derbys 133 J5
Stanghow R & Cl 170 F7
Stanground C Pete 102 D4
Stanhill Lancs 139 L2
Stanhoe Norfk 121 H4
Stanhope Border 199 K7
Stanhope Dur 168 C3
Stanhope Kent 40 C7
Stanhope Bretby Derbys 116 A7
Stanion N Nthn 101 K6
Stanklin Worcs 97 J8
Stanley Derbys 116 C3
Stanley Dur 180 F8
Stanley Notts 133 J7
Stanley P & K 221 K1
Stanley Shrops 97 G6
Stanley Staffs 114 E1
Stanley Wakefd 142 A3
Stanley Common Derbys 116 C3
Stanley Crook Dur 168 F3
Stanley Ferry Wakefd 142 A3
Stanley Gate Lancs 138 F6
Stanley Moor Staffs 114 E1
Stanley Pontlarge Gloucs 64 E1
Stanmer Br & H 22 E5
Stanmore Gt Lon 68 F8
Stanmore Hants 34 F5
Stanmore W Berk 48 C3
Stannersburn Nthumb 179 G2
Stanningfield Suffk 89 H4
Stanningley Leeds 141 K1
Stannington Nthumb 180 F3
Stannington Sheff 132 F2
Stannington Station Nthumb 180 F3
Stansbatch Herefs 79 L3
Stansfield Suffk 88 F5
Stanshope Staffs 115 J1
Stanstead Suffk 89 G5
Stanstead Abbotts Herts 69 K5
Stansted Kent 52 D6
Stansted Airport Essex 70 E2
Stansted Mountfitchet Essex 70 D2
Stanton Derbys 115 M7
Stanton Gloucs 82 C8
Stanton Mons 62 C3
Stanton Nthumb 191 G8
Stanton Staffs 115 J2
Stanton Suffk 105 K8
Stanton by Bridge Derbys 116 B6
Stanton by Dale Derbys 116 D4
Stanton Cross N Nthn 85 H2
Stanton Drew BaNES 45 H6
Stanton Fitzwarren Swindn 47 J1
Stanton Harcourt Oxon 66 B6
Stanton Hill Notts 133 J7
Stanton in Peak Derbys 132 E6
Stanton Lacy Shrops 96 F7
Stanton Lees Derbys 132 E7
Stanton Long Shrops 96 D5
Stanton-on-the-Wolds Notts 117 G5
Stanton Prior BaNES 45 K6
Stanton St Bernard Wilts 47 G6
Stanton St John Oxon 66 E5
Stanton St Quintin Wilts 46 C3
Stanton Street Suffk 89 J2
Stanton under Bardon Leics 100 A1
Stanton upon Hine Heath Shrops 113 J6
Stanton Wick BaNES 45 J6
Stantway Gloucs 63 L4
Stanwardine in the Field Shrops 112 F6
Stanwardine in the Wood Shrops 113 G6
Stanway Essex 72 D2
Stanway Gloucs 64 F1
Stanway Green Essex 72 D2
Stanway Green Suffk 90 F1
Stanwell Surrey 50 D4
Stanwell Moor Surrey 50 D4
Stanwick N Nthn 85 J1
Stanwick St John N York 168 F8

Stanwix Cumb 177 L7
Staoinebrig W Isls 283 b10
Stape N York 162 D4
Stapehill Dorset 17 L3
Stapeley Ches E 113 L2
Stapenhill Staffs 115 L7
Staple Kent 41 J4
Staple Cross Devon 29 J6
Staplecross E Susx 24 E3
Staplefield W Susx 37 L5
Staple Fitzpaine Somset 30 C7
Stapleford Cambs 87 K5
Stapleford Herts 69 J4
Stapleford Leics 117 L7
Stapleford Lincs 135 H8
Stapleford Notts 116 E4
Stapleford Wilts 33 J3
Stapleford Abbotts Essex 70 D8
Stapleford Tawney Essex 70 D7
Staplegrove Somset 30 B5
Staplehay Somset 30 B6
Staple Hill Worcs 98 B8
Staplehurst Kent 39 K5
Staplers IoW 19 K7
Staplestreet Kent 40 D3
Stapleton Cumb 178 C4
Stapleton Herefs 79 L2
Stapleton Leics 99 L4
Stapleton N York 169 H8
Stapleton Shrops 95 L3
Stapleton Somset 31 G6
Staploe Bed 86 C3
Staplow Herefs 80 F7
Star Fife 222 E6
Star IoA 125 J3
Star Pembks 75 M5
Star Somset 44 E7
Starbeck N York 150 D4
Starbotton N York 159 G6
Starcross Devon 13 M6
Stareton Warwks 83 H1
Starkholmes Derbys 132 F7
Starlings Green Essex 70 C1
Starr's Green E Susx 24 D4
Starston Norfk 106 E6
Start Devon 8 B6
Startforth Dur 168 D7
Startley Wilts 46 D3
Statenborough Kent 41 J4
Statham Warrtn 130 D2
Stathe Somset 30 E5
Stathern Leics 117 K5
Station Town Dur 169 L3
Staughton Green Cambs 86 C2
Staughton Highway Cambs 86 C2
Staunton Gloucs 63 H4
Staunton Gloucs 64 A1
Staunton in the Vale Notts 117 L3
Staunton on Arrow Herefs 79 L3
Staunton on Wye Herefs 79 L6
Staveley Derbys 133 H5
Staveley N York 150 E3
Staveley W & F 157 G3
Staveley-in-Cartmel W & F 156 E5
Staverton Devon 8 B2
Staverton Gloucs 64 C2
Staverton W Nthn 83 M3
Staverton Wilts 46 B6
Staverton Bridge Gloucs 64 C3
Stawell Somset 30 E3
Stawley Somset 29 J6
Staxigoe Highld 280 E5
Staxton N York 163 J6
Staylittle Cerdgn 92 E5
Staylittle Powys 93 J5
Staynall Lancs 147 G7
Staythorpe Notts 117 K1
Stead C Brad 149 L6
Stean N York 159 K8
Stearsby N York 151 K2
Steart Somset 30 C2
Stebbing Essex 71 G2
Stebbing Green Essex 71 G2
Stechford Birm 98 E6
Stede Quarter Kent 39 L5
Stedham W Susx 36 C6
Steel Nthumb 179 L7
Steel Cross E Susx 38 E7
Steelend Fife 210 D1
Steele Road Border 188 F7
Steel Green Cumb 155 L6
Steel Heath Shrops 113 J4
Steen's Bridge Herefs 80 C4
Steep Hants 35 M6
Steephill IoW 19 J8
Steep Lane Calder 140 F3
Steeple Dorset 17 H6
Steeple Essex 72 D6
Steeple Ashton Wilts 46 C7

Steeple Aston Oxon 66 C2
Steeple Barton Oxon 66 C2
Steeple Bumpstead Essex 88 D7
Steeple Claydon Bucks 67 H2
Steeple Gidding Cambs 102 C2
Steeple Langford Wilts 33 H3
Steeple Morden Cambs 86 F6
Steep Marsh Hants 35 M5
Steeton C Brad 149 J7
Stein Highld 258 D5
Stella Gatesd 180 E6
Stelling Minnis Kent 40 F6
Stembridge Somset 30 F6
Stenalees Cnwll 5 G3
Stenhouse D & G 185 K4
Stenhousemuir Falk 210 A2
Stenigot Lincs 136 D3
Stenness Ork 275 b4
Stenscholl Highld 259 H3
Stenson Fields Derbys 116 B5
Stenton E Loth 212 D4
Steòrnabhagh W Isls 282 g3
Stepaside Pembks 55 K5
Stepford D & G 185 L6
Stepney Gt Lon 51 K3
Stepping Hill Stockp 131 H2
Steppingley C Beds 85 K8
Stepps N Lans 209 H5
Sternfield Suffk 91 J3
Stert Wilts 46 F7
Stetchworth Cambs 88 C3
Stevenage Herts 69 J2
Steven's Crouch E Susx 24 C4
Stevenston N Ayrs 196 B3
Steventon Hants 35 H1
Steventon Oxon 66 C6
Steventon End Essex 88 B6
Stevington Bed 85 K4
Stewartby Bed 85 K6
Stewartfield S Lans 209 G7
Stewarton Ag & B 192 E4
Stewarton E Ayrs 196 E2
Stewkley Bucks 67 K2
Stewley Somset 30 D7
Stewton Lincs 137 G2
Steyne Cross IoW 19 L6
Steyning W Susx 21 L4
Steynton Pembks 54 E5
Stibb Cnwll 26 C8
Stibbard Norfk 121 L6
Stibb Cross Devon 27 G7
Stibb Green Wilts 47 J6
Stibbington Cambs 102 B4
Stichill Border 201 L5
Sticker Cnwll 5 G5
Stickford Lincs 136 F7
Sticklepath Devon 12 F4
Sticklepath Somset 29 J4
Stickling Green Essex 87 K8
Stickney Lincs 136 F8
Stiffkey Norfk 121 L3
Stifford Clays Thurr 52 D3
Stifford's Bridge Herefs 81 G3
Stiff Street Kent 53 J6
Stile Bridge Kent 39 J4
Stileway Somset 31 G3
Stilligarry W Isls 283 b10
Stillingfleet N York 151 J7
Stillington N York 151 J2
Stillington S on T 169 K6
Stilton Cambs 102 D5
Stinchcombe Gloucs 63 L7
Stinsford Dorset 16 D4
Stiperstones Shrops 95 J3
Stirchley Birm 98 D7
Stirchley Wrekin 96 F2
Stirling Abers 257 L3
Stirling Stirlg 220 D8
Stirling Services Stirlg 209 L1
Stirtloe Cambs 86 D2
Stirton N York 149 H5
Stisted Essex 71 J2
Stitchcombe Wilts 47 K5
Stithians Cnwll 3 J4
Stivichall Covtry 99 J8
Stixwould Lincs 136 C6
St Michaels Fife 223 H3
Stoak Ches W 129 K5
Stobo Border 199 L5
Stoborough Dorset 17 H5
Stoborough Green Dorset 17 H5
Stobs Castle Border 188 E4
Stobswood Nthumb 191 J7
Stock Essex 71 G7
Stock N Som 44 F6
Stockbridge Hants 34 D4
Stockbridge W Susx 20 D6
Stockbriggs S Lans 198 C6
Stockbury Kent 53 H6
Stockcross W Berk 48 B5

Stockdalewath Cumb 165 L2
Stocker's Head Kent 40 C5
Stockerston Leics 101 H4
Stock Green Worcs 82 A3
Stocking Herefs 63 J1
Stockingford Warwks 99 J5
Stocking Pelham Herts 70 C1
Stockland Devon 14 F2
Stockland Bristol Somset 30 C2
Stockland Green Kent 38 E5
Stockleigh English Devon 13 K2
Stockleigh Pomeroy Devon 13 K2
Stockley Wilts 46 E5
Stockley Hill Herefs 79 L7
Stocklinch Somset 30 F7
Stockmoor Herefs 79 M4
Stockport Stockp 131 H2
Stocksbridge Sheff 141 L8
Stocksfield Nthumb 180 C6
Stocksmoor Kirk 141 J5
Stockton Herefs 80 C3
Stockton Norfk 107 H1
Stockton Shrops 95 G3
Stockton Shrops 97 G3
Stockton Warwks 83 K3
Stockton Wilts 33 G3
Stockton Wrekin 114 B8
Stockton Brook Staffs 114 E1
Stockton Heath Warrtn 130 B3
Stockton-on-Tees S on T 170 B6
Stockton on Teme Worcs 81 G2
Stockton on the Forest C York ...151 L4
Stockwell Gloucs 64 D4
Stockwell End Wolves 97 K3
Stockwell Heath Staffs 115 G7
Stockwood Bristl 45 J5
Stockwood Dorset 16 B1
Stock Wood Worcs 82 B3
Stodday Lancs 147 J4
Stodmarsh Kent 41 H3
Stody Norfk 122 B4
Stoer Highld 270 D2
Stoford Somset 31 J8
Stoford Wilts 33 J4
Stogumber Somset 29 K3
Stogursey Somset 30 K7
Stoke Covtry 99 K7
Stoke Devon 26 D6
Stoke Hants 20 B6
Stoke Hants 48 B8
Stoke Medway 53 H4
Stoke Abbott Dorset 15 K3
Stoke Albany N Nthn 101 H5
Stoke Ash Suffk 90 D1
Stoke Bardolph Notts 117 H3
Stoke Bliss Worcs 80 E7
Stoke Bruerne W Nthn 84 E5
Stoke-by-Clare Suffk 88 E6
Stoke-by-Nayland Suffk 89 K7
Stoke Canon Devon 13 L3
Stoke Charity Hants 35 G3
Stoke Climsland Cnwll 11 L7
Stoke Cross Herefs 80 E5
Stoke D'Abernon Surrey 50 E7
Stoke Doyle N Nthn 102 M6
Stoke Dry Rutlnd 101 J4
Stoke Edith Herefs 80 E7
Stoke End Warwks 98 F4
Stoke Farthing Wilts 33 H5
Stoke Ferry Norfk 104 D3
Stoke Fleming Devon 8 C5
Stokeford Dorset 17 G5
Stoke Gabriel Devon 8 C3
Stoke Gifford S Glos 45 J3
Stoke Golding Leics 99 L4
Stoke Goldington M Keyn 85 G5
Stoke Green Bucks 50 B3
Stokeham Notts 134 F4
Stoke Hammond Bucks 67 L1
Stoke Heath Shrops 113 L5
Stoke Heath Worcs 81 L2
Stoke Holy Cross Norfk 106 E3
Stokeinteignhead Devon 13 L4
Stoke Lacy Herefs 80 E5
Stoke Lyne Oxon 66 E2
Stoke Mandeville Bucks 67 K5
Stokenchurch Bucks 67 J7
Stoke Newington Gt Lon 51 J2
Stokenham Devon 8 B6
Stoke-on-Trent C Stke 114 D2
Stoke Orchard Gloucs 64 D2
Stoke Poges Bucks 50 B2
Stoke Pound Worcs 81 M2
Stoke Prior Herefs 80 C4
Stoke Prior Worcs 81 L2
Stoke Rivers Devon 27 L4
Stoke Rochford Lincs 118 B6
Stoke Row Oxon 49 G2
Stoke St Gregory Somset 30 E5
Stoke St Mary Somset 30 C6

Stoke St Michael Somset 31 L2
Stoke St Milborough Shrops 96 D7
Stokesay Shrops 95 K7
Stokesby Norfk 107 J1
Stokesley N York 161 H1
Stoke sub Hamdon Somset 31 G7
Stoke Talmage Oxon 67 G7
Stoke Trister Somset 32 B5
Stoke upon Tern Shrops 113 L6
Stoke-upon-Trent C Stke 114 D3
Stoke Wake Dorset 16 E1
Stoke Wharf Worcs 81 L2
Stolford Somset 30 C2
Stondon Massey Essex 70 E7
Stone Bucks 67 J4
Stone Gloucs 63 K8
Stone Kent 52 C4
Stone Rothm 133 L2
Stone Somset 31 J4
Stone Staffs 114 E5
Stone Worcs 97 J8
Stonea Cambs 103 J5
Stone Allerton Somset 30 F1
Ston Easton Somset 45 J8
Stonebridge N Som 44 D7
Stonebridge Norfk 105 J5
Stonebridge Warwks 99 G6
Stone Bridge Corner C Pete 102 F3
Stonebroom Derbys 133 H7
Stone Chair Calder 141 H2
Stone Cross E Susx 23 K6
Stone Cross E Susx 38 D7
Stone Cross E Susx 39 G7
Stone Cross Kent 38 E5
Stone Cross Kent 40 D7
Stone Cross Kent 41 K4
Stonecross Green Suffk 89 G4
Stonecrouch Kent 39 H6
Stone-edge-Batch N Som 44 F4
Stoneferry C KuH 125 K4
Stonefield Castle Hotel Ag & B ...206 D5
Stonegate E Susx 39 G7
Stonegate N York 162 D1
Stonegrave N York 161 L2
Stonehall Worcs 81 K5
Stonehaugh Nthumb 179 J8
Stonehaven Abers 245 J6
Stonehenge Wilts 33 K2
Stone Hill Donc 143 H6
Stonehouse C Plym 6 F4
Stonehouse Gloucs 64 A6
Stonehouse Nthumb 179 G7
Stonehouse S Lans 198 C4
Stone House W & F 158 D5
Stone in Oxney Kent 25 H2
Stoneleigh Warwks 83 H1
Stoneley Green Ches E 113 K1
Stonely Cambs 86 C2
Stoner Hill Hants 35 M5
Stonesby Leics 117 L6
Stonesfield Oxon 66 B4
Stones Green Essex 73 H2
Stone Street Kent 38 F2
Stone Street Suffk 89 K6
Stone Street Suffk 89 K7
Stone Street Suffk 107 H7
Stonestreet Green Kent 40 E7
Stonethwaite Cumb 165 J7
Stonewells Moray 266 F3
Stonewood Kent 52 D4
Stoneybridge W Isls 283 b10
Stoneybridge Worcs 97 L8
Stoneyburn W Loth 210 C6
Stoney Cross Hants 18 D1
Stoneygate C Leic 100 D3
Stoneyhills Essex 72 D7
Stoneykirk D & G 172 D1
Stoney Middleton Derbys 132 E4
Stoney Stanton Leics 100 B4
Stoney Stoke Somset 32 D4
Stoney Stratton Somset 31 L3
Stoney Stretton Shrops 95 J2
Stoneywood C Aber 245 K1
Stoneywood Falk 209 L2
Stonham Aspal Suffk 90 D3
Stonnall Staffs 98 D3
Stonor Oxon 49 H1
Stonton Wyville Leics 101 G4
Stonybreck Shet 281 b8
Stony Cross Herefs 80 D2
Stony Cross Herefs 81 G5
Stonyford Hants 34 D7
Stony Houghton Derbys 133 K6
Stony Stratford M Keyn 84 F7
Stonywell Staffs 98 D1
Stoodleigh Devon 28 B4
Stoodleigh Devon 29 G7
Stopham W Susx 21 H3
Stopsley Luton 68 E2
Stoptide Cnwll 10 C4

Storeton Wirral 129 G3
Storeyard Green Herefs 81 G6
Storey Arms Powys 60 E3
Stornoway W Isls 282 g3
Stornoway Airport W Isls 282 g3
Storridge Herefs 81 H5
Storrington W Susx 21 J4
Storth W & F 157 G6
Storwood E R Yk 151 M7
Stotfield Moray 266 E2
Stotfold C Beds 86 E7
Stottesdon Shrops 96 F6
Stoughton Leics 100 E3
Stoughton Surrey 50 C8
Stoughton W Susx 20 C4
Stoulton Worcs 81 L5
Stourbridge Dudley 97 K6
Stourpaine Dorset 17 G1
Stourport-on-Severn Worcs 81 J1
Stour Provost Dorset 32 C6
Stour Row Dorset 32 D6
Stourton Leeds 141 M2
Stourton Staffs 97 K6
Stourton Warwks 83 G7
Stourton Wilts 32 C4
Stourton Caundle Dorset 32 B7
Stout Somset 31 G4
Stove Shet 281 e8
Stoven Suffk 107 J7
Stow Border 200 F4
Stow Lincs 135 H3
Stow Bardolph Norfk 104 C2
Stow Bedon Norfk 105 J4
Stowbridge Norfk 104 B2
Stow-cum-Quy Cambs 87 L3
Stowe Gloucs 63 H5
Stowe Shrops 95 H8
Stowe-by-Chartley Staffs 114 F6
Stowehill W Nthn 84 C3
Stowell Somset 31 L6
Stowey BaNES 45 H7
Stowford Devon 12 B3
Stowford Devon 12 B5
Stowford Devon 14 D5
Stowford Devon 28 B3
Stowlangtoft Suffk 89 J2
Stow Longa Cambs 86 C1
Stow Maries Essex 71 K7
Stowmarket Suffk 90 B3
Stow-on-the-Wold Gloucs 65 J2
Stowting Kent 40 F7
Stowting Common Kent 40 F6
Stowupland Suffk 90 C3
Straad Ag & B 207 G6
Straanruie Highld 253 J8
Strachan Abers 244 F5
Strachur Ag & B 217 H7
Stradbroke Suffk 106 E8
Stradbrook Wilts 46 D8
Stradishall Suffk 88 E5
Stradsett Norfk 104 D2
Stragglethorpe Lincs 118 D1
Stragglethorpe Notts 117 H4
Straight Soley Wilts 47 L4
Straiton Mdloth 211 J5
Straiton S Ayrs 183 K2
Straloch Abers 256 F7
Straloch P & K 232 F3
Stramshall Staffs 115 H4
Strang IoM 154 e6
Strangeways Salfd 140 B7
Strangford Herefs 63 H2
Stranraer D & G 172 C3
Strata Florida Cerdgn 77 K2
Stratfield Mortimer W Berk 49 G6
Stratfield Saye Hants 49 G6
Stratfield Turgis Hants 49 G7
Stratford C Beds 86 D5
Stratford Gt Lon 51 K2
Stratford St Andrew Suffk 91 H3
Stratford St Mary Suffk 90 B8
Stratford sub Castle Wilts 33 K4
Stratford Tony Wilts 33 J5
Stratford-upon-Avon Warwks 82 H4
Strath Highld 260 C4
Strathan Highld 270 E4
Strathan Highld 277 K3
Strathaven S Lans 197 K2
Strathblane Stirlg 208 F3
Strathcanaird Highld 270 F7
Strathcarron Highld 248 E3
Strathcoil Ag & B 227 K6
Strathdon Abers 243 K1
Strathkinness Fife 223 H4
Strathloanhead W Loth 210 M4
Strathmashie House Highld 241 G5
Strathmiglo Fife 222 C5
Strathpeffer Highld 262 E8
Strathtay P & K 232 D4
Strathwhillan N Ayrs 195 G4

Strathy Highld 278 E3
Strathy Inn Highld 278 E3
Strathyre Stirlg 219 J4
Stratton Cnwll 11 J1
Stratton Dorset 16 C4
Stratton Gloucs 64 E6
Stratton Audley Oxon 66 F2
Stratton-on-the-Fosse Somset ...31 L1
Stratton St Margaret Swindn 47 H2
Stratton St Michael Norfk 106 D4
Stratton Strawless Norfk 122 E7
Stream Somset 29 K3
Streat E Susx 22 E4
Streatham Gt Lon 51 J4
Streatley C Beds 68 D2
Streatley W Berk 48 E3
Street Devon 14 E5
Street Lancs 147 K5
Street N York 162 C2
Street Somset 31 H3
Street Ashton Warwks 99 M7
Street Dinas Shrops 112 L7
Street End E Susx 23 K3
Street End Kent 40 F4
Street End W Susx 20 D7
Street Gate Gatesd 180 F7
Streethay Staffs 98 F1
Street Houses N York 151 H6
Streetlam N York 160 D3
Street Lane Derbys 116 C2
Streetly Wsall 98 D4
Streetly End Cambs 88 C5
Street on the Fosse Somset 31 K3
Strefford Shrops 95 K6
Strelitz P & K 233 J8
Strelley Notts 116 E3
Strensall C York 151 K4
Strensham Worcs 81 L7
Strensham Services
  (northbound) Worcs 81 K7
Strensham Services
  (southbound) Worcs 81 L7
Stretcholt Somset 30 D2
Strete Devon 8 C4
Stretford Herefs 80 B4
Stretford Herefs 80 F4
Stretford Traffd 130 F1
Stretchall Essex 87 K7
Stretham Cambs 103 K8
Strettington W Susx 20 E5
Stretton Ches W 113 G1
Stretton Derbys 133 H7
Stretton Rutlnd 118 B8
Stretton Staffs 97 K1
Stretton Staffs 115 L6
Stretton Warrtn 130 C3
Stretton en le Field Leics 99 J1
Stretton Grandison Herefs 80 E6
Stretton-on-Dunsmore
  Warwks 83 J1
Stretton on Fosse Warwks 82 F7
Stretton Sugwas Herefs 80 B6
Stretton under Fosse Warwks 99 M7
Stretton Westwood Shrops 96 D4
Strichen Abers 269 H5
Strines Stockp 131 J2
Stringston Somset 30 B2
Strixton N Nthn 85 H3
Stroat Gloucs 63 H7
Strollamus Highld 247 J3
Stroma Highld 280 E1
Stromeferry Highld 248 D5
Stromness Ork 275 b4
Stronaba Highld 239 L6
Stronachlachar Stirlg 218 F5
Stronafian Ag & B 207 G3
Stronchrubie Highld 271 H4
Strone Ag & B 207 K3
Strone Highld 239 J7
Strone Highld 250 F6
Stronmilchan Ag & B 217 J2
Stronsay Ork 275 e3
Stronsay Airport Ork 275 e3
Strontian Highld 228 C3
Strood Kent 39 L7
Strood Medway 52 F5
Strood Green Surrey 37 J1
Strood Green W Susx 36 F6
Stroud Gloucs 64 B6
Stroud Hants 35 L6
Stroude Surrey 50 C5
Stroud Green Essex 53 J1
Stroud Green Gloucs 64 A5
Stroxton Lincs 118 B5
Struan Highld 246 D1
Struan P & K 232 B2
Strubby Lincs 137 H3
Strumpshaw Norfk 107 G2
Strutherhill S Lans 198 C3
Struthers Fife 222 F5

Place	Region	Page	Grid
Struy	Highld	250	C4
Stryd-y-Facsen	IoA	124	F3
Stuartfield	Abers	257	H3
Stubbers Green	Wsall	98	D3
Stubbington	Hants	19	J3
Stubbins	Lancs	140	B4
Stubbs Cross	Kent	40	C7
Stubbs Green	Norfk	106	E4
Stubhampton	Dorset	32	F8
Stubley	Derbys	133	G4
Stubshaw Cross	Wigan	139	H7
Stubton	Lincs	118	A2
Stuckton	Hants	33	L8
Studfold	N York	148	E2
Stud Green	W & M	49	L3
Studham	C Beds	68	C4
Studholme	Cumb	177	H7
Studland	Dorset	17	K6
Studlands Park	Suffk	88	C2
Studley	Warwks	82	C2
Studley	Wilts	46	D4
Studley Common	Warwks	82	C2
Studley Roger	N York	150	C2
Studley Royal	N York	150	C2
Studley Royal Park & Fountains Abbey	N York	150	C2
Stuntney	Cambs	103	L7
Stunts Green	E Susx	23	K4
Sturbridge	Staffs	114	C5
Sturgate	Lincs	135	H2
Sturmer	Essex	88	D6
Sturminster Common	Dorset	32	C8
Sturminster Marshall	Dorset	17	J3
Sturminster Newton	Dorset	32	C8
Sturry	Kent	41	G3
Sturton	N Linc	144	B7
Sturton by Stow	Lincs	135	H4
Sturton le Steeple	Notts	134	F3
Stuston	Suffk	106	C7
Stutton	N York	151	G7
Stutton	Suffk	90	D8
Styal	Ches E	131	G3
Stydd	Lancs	148	A8
Stynie	Moray	267	G4
Styrrup	Notts	134	C2
Succoth	Ag & B	218	D6
Suckley	Worcs	81	G5
Suckley Green	Worcs	81	G4
Sudborough	N Nthn	101	L7
Sudbourne	Suffk	91	J4
Sudbrook	Lincs	118	C3
Sudbrook	Mons	45	G2
Sudbrooke	Lincs	135	L4
Sudbury	Derbys	115	K5
Sudbury	Gt Lon	50	F2
Sudbury	Suffk	89	H7
Sudden	Rochdl	140	C5
Sudgrove	Gloucs	64	D5
Suffield	N York	163	H4
Suffield	Norfk	122	E5
Sugdon	Wrekin	113	K8
Sugnall	Staffs	114	B5
Sugwas Pool	Herefs	80	B6
Suisnish	Highld	247	J5
Sulby	IoM	154	e3
Sulgrave	W Nthn	84	A6
Sulham	W Berk	48	F4
Sulhamstead	W Berk	48	F5
Sulhamstead Abbots	W Berk	48	F5
Sulhamstead Bannister	W Berk	48	F5
Sullington	W Susx	21	J4
Sullom	Shet	281	d4
Sullom Voe	Shet	281	d4
Sully	V Glam	43	J8
Sumburgh Airport	Shet	281	d9
Summerbridge	N York	150	B3
Summercourt	Cnwll	4	E4
Summerfield	Norfk	121	G4
Summerfield	Worcs	97	J8
Summer Heath	Bucks	49	H1
Summerhill	Pembks	55	K5
Summerhill	Staffs	98	D2
Summer Hill	Wrexhm	112	D1
Summerhouse	Darltn	169	G6
Summerlands	W & F	157	H5
Summerley	Derbys	133	G4
Summersdale	W Susx	20	D5
Summerseat	Bury	140	B5
Summertown	Oxon	66	D5
Summit	Oldham	140	D6
Summit	Rochdl	140	E4
Sunbiggin	W & F	157	L1
Sunbury-on-Thames	Surrey	50	E5
Sundaywell	D & G	185	K6
Sunderland	Ag & B	204	C3
Sunderland	Cumb	165	G4
Sunderland	Lancs	147	H4
Sunderland	SundId	181	K7
Sunderland Bridge	Dur	169	H3
Sundhope	Border	200	D8
Sundon Park	Luton	68	D2
Sundridge	Kent	38	D2
Sunk Island	E R Yk	145	H4
Sunningdale	W & M	50	B5
Sunninghill	W & M	50	B5
Sunningwell	Oxon	66	D7
Sunniside	Dur	168	F3
Sunniside	Gatesd	180	F7
Sunny Brow	Dur	169	G4
Sunnyhill	C Derb	116	B5
Sunnyhurst	Bl w D	139	K3
Sunnylaw	Stirlg	220	D7
Sunnymead	Oxon	66	D5
Sunton	Wilts	47	K8
Surbiton	Gt Lon	50	F5
Surfleet	Lincs	119	H6
Surfleet Seas End	Lincs	119	J6
Surlingham	Norfk	107	G2
Surrex	Essex	72	C3
Sustead	Norfk	122	D4
Susworth	Lincs	143	L7
Sutcombe	Devon	26	F8
Sutcombemill	Devon	26	F8
Suton	Norfk	106	B4
Sutterby	Lincs	137	G5
Sutterton	Lincs	119	J4
Sutton	C Beds	86	E5
Sutton	C Pete	102	B4
Sutton	Cambs	103	J7
Sutton	Devon	7	K6
Sutton	Devon	13	G2
Sutton	Donc	142	E6
Sutton	E Susx	23	H7
Sutton	Gt Lon	51	H6
Sutton	Kent	41	K5
Sutton	N York	142	D3
Sutton	Norfk	123	H6
Sutton	Notts	117	K4
Sutton	Oxon	66	B6
Sutton	Pembks	54	E4
Sutton	Shrops	96	C1
Sutton	Shrops	97	G6
Sutton	Shrops	112	E6
Sutton	Shrops	113	L5
Sutton	St Hel	129	M1
Sutton	Staffs	114	B7
Sutton	Suffk	91	G6
Sutton	W Susx	21	G4
Sutton Abinger	Surrey	37	H2
Sutton-at-Hone	Kent	52	C5
Sutton Bassett	N Nthn	101	G5
Sutton Benger	Wilts	46	D3
Sutton Bingham	Somset	31	J8
Sutton Bonington	Notts	116	E6
Sutton Bridge	Lincs	120	B7
Sutton Cheney	Leics	99	L3
Sutton Coldfield	Birm	98	E4
Sutton Courtenay	Oxon	66	D8
Sutton Crosses	Lincs	119	M7
Sutton cum Lound	Notts	134	D3
Sutton Fields	Notts	116	E6
Sutton Green	Surrey	50	C8
Sutton Green	Wrexhm	112	D2
Sutton Heath	Suffk	91	H5
Sutton Howgrave	N York	160	D6
Sutton-in-Ashfield	Notts	133	K7
Sutton-in-Craven	N York	149	H7
Sutton in the Elms	Leics	100	B4
Sutton Lane Ends	Ches E	131	H5
Sutton Maddock	Shrops	97	G3
Sutton Mallet	Somset	30	C4
Sutton Mandeville	Wilts	33	G5
Sutton Manor	St Hel	129	L2
Sutton Marsh	Herefs	80	D6
Sutton Montis	Somset	31	K6
Sutton-on-Hull	C KuH	144	E1
Sutton on Sea	Lincs	137	K3
Sutton-on-the-Forest	N York	151	J3
Sutton on the Hill	Derbys	115	L5
Sutton on Trent	Notts	134	F6
Sutton Poyntz	Dorset	16	D6
Sutton St Edmund	Lincs	103	H1
Sutton St James	Lincs	119	L7
Sutton St Nicholas	Herefs	80	C6
Sutton Scotney	Hants	34	F3
Sutton Street	Kent	39	K2
Sutton-under-Whitestonecliffe	N York	161	G6
Sutton upon Derwent	E R Yk	151	L6
Sutton Valence	Kent	39	K3
Sutton Veny	Wilts	32	F3
Sutton Waldron	Dorset	32	E7
Sutton Weaver	Ches W	130	A4
Sutton Wick	BaNES	45	H7
Sutton Wick	Oxon	66	C8
Swaby	Lincs	137	G4
Swadlincote	Derbys	116	A7
Swaffham	Norfk	105	G2
Swaffham Bulbeck	Cambs	87	L3
Swaffham Prior	Cambs	88	B2
Swafield	Norfk	122	F5
Swainby	N York	161	G2
Swainshill	Herefs	80	B7
Swainsthorpe	Norfk	106	E3
Swainswick	BaNES	45	M5
Swalcliffe	Oxon	83	J7
Swalecliffe	Kent	40	F2
Swallow	Lincs	144	F7
Swallow Beck	Lincs	135	J6
Swallowcliffe	Wilts	33	G5
Swallowfield	Wokham	49	H6
Swallownest	Rothm	133	J3
Swallows Cross	Essex	70	F7
Swampton	Hants	34	E1
Swanage	Dorset	17	K6
Swanbourne	Bucks	67	K2
Swanbridge	V Glam	43	J8
Swancote	Shrops	97	G4
Swan Green	Ches W	130	E5
Swanland	E R Yk	144	F2
Swanley	Kent	52	B5
Swanley Village	Kent	52	B5
Swanmore	Hants	35	J7
Swannington	Leics	116	C2
Swannington	Norfk	122	C7
Swanpool	Lincs	135	J6
Swanscombe	Kent	52	D4
Swansea	Swans	57	J6
Swansea Airport	*Swans*	*57*	*G6*
Swansea West Services	*Swans*	*57*	*H5*
Swan Street	Essex	72	C2
Swanton Abbot	Norfk	122	F6
Swanton Morley	Norfk	121	M8
Swanton Novers	Norfk	121	M5
Swanton Street	Kent	53	J7
Swan Valley	W Nthn	84	D4
Swan Village	Sandw	98	C5
Swanwick	Derbys	116	C1
Swanwick	Hants	19	H2
Swarby	Lincs	118	D3
Swardeston	Norfk	106	D3
Swarkestone	Derbys	116	B6
Swarland	Nthumb	191	H5
Swarraton	Hants	35	H3
Swartha	C Brad	149	J6
Swarthmoor	W & F	156	C7
Swaton	Lincs	118	F4
Swavesey	Cambs	87	G2
Sway	Hants	18	D4
Swayfield	Lincs	118	C7
Swaythling	C Sotn	34	F7
Sweet Green	Worcs	80	F3
Sweetham	Devon	13	K3
Sweethaws	E Susx	38	D7
Sweetlands Corner	Kent	39	K4
Sweets	Cnwll	11	G3
Sweetshouse	Cnwll	5	J3
Swefling	Suffk	91	H3
Swepstone	Leics	99	K1
Swerford	Oxon	66	A1
Swettenham	Ches E	130	F6
Swffryd	Blae G	61	K7
Swift's Green	Kent	39	L4
Swilland	Suffk	90	E4
Swillbrook	Lancs	138	F1
Swillington	Leeds	142	B2
Swimbridge	Devon	27	L5
Swimbridge Newland	Devon	27	L5
Swinbrook	Oxon	65	L4
Swincliffe	Kirk	141	K2
Swincliffe	N York	150	C5
Swincombe	Devon	28	B3
Swindale	W & F	166	C8
Swinden	N York	148	F5
Swinderby	Lincs	135	H7
Swindon	Gloucs	64	D2
Swindon	Nthumb	190	D6
Swindon	Staffs	97	J5
Swindon	Swindn	47	H2
Swine	E R Yk	153	J8
Swinefleet	E R Yk	143	J3
Swineford	S Glos	45	K5
Swineshead	Bed	85	L2
Swineshead	Lincs	119	H3
Swineshead Bridge	Lincs	119	H3
Swiney	Highld	275	H1
Swinford	Leics	100	C7
Swinford	Oxon	66	C5
Swingate	Notts	116	E3
Swingfield Minnis	Kent	41	H6
Swingfield Street	Kent	41	H6
Swingleton Green	Suffk	89	K6
Swinhoe	Nthumb	203	K7
Swinhope	Lincs	145	G2
Swinithwaite	N York	159	J5
Swinmore Common	Herefs	80	F7
Swinscoe	Staffs	115	J2
Swinside	Cumb	165	H6
Swinstead	Lincs	118	D7
Swinthorpe	Lincs	135	L4
Swinton	Border	202	C4
Swinton	N York	160	B6
Swinton	N York	162	D8
Swinton	Rothm	142	C7
Swinton	Salfd	140	A7
Swiss Valley	Carmth	56	F4
Swithland	Leics	100	C1
Swordale	Highld	263	G6
Swordland	Highld	238	B5
Swordly	Highld	278	C4
Sworton Heath	Ches E	130	D3
Swydffynnon	Cerdgn	77	J2
Swyncombe	Oxon	49	G1
Swynnerton	Staffs	114	D4
Swyre	Dorset	15	M5
Sycharth	Powys	112	B6
Sychdyn	Flints	128	F6
Sychnant	Powys	93	L7
Sychtyn	Powys	94	B7
Sydallt	Wrexhm	129	H8
Syde	Gloucs	64	D5
Sydenham	Gt Lon	51	K4
Sydenham	Oxon	67	H6
Sydenham Damerel	Devon	12	A7
Sydenhurst	Surrey	36	E4
Syderstone	Norfk	121	H5
Sydling St Nicholas	Dorset	16	C3
Sydmonton	Hants	48	C7
Sydnal Lane	Shrops	97	H2
Syerston	Notts	117	K2
Syke	Rochdl	140	C4
Sykehouse	Donc	143	G4
Syleham	Suffk	106	E7
Sylen	Carmth	56	F3
Symbister	Shet	281	e5
Symington	S Ayrs	196	D5
Symington	S Lans	199	G6
Symondsbury	Dorset	15	K4
Symonds Yat (East)	Herefs	63	H4
Symonds Yat (West)	Herefs	63	H4
Sympson Green	C Brad	150	A8
Synderford	Dorset	15	J2
Synod Inn	Cerdgn	76	D2
Syre	Highld	278	B7
Syreford	Gloucs	64	F3
Syresham	W Nthn	84	C7
Syston	Leics	100	D1
Syston	Lincs	118	B3
Sytchampton	Worcs	81	J2
Sywell	N Nthn	84	F2

T

Place	Region	Page	Grid
Tabley Hill	Ches E	130	E4
Tackley	Oxon	66	C3
Tacolneston	Norfk	106	C4
Tadcaster	N York	151	G7
Taddington	Derbys	132	C5
Taddington	Gloucs	65	G1
Taddiport	Devon	27	H7
Tadley	Hants	48	F6
Tadlow	Cambs	86	F5
Tadmarton	Oxon	83	J7
Tadpole	Swindn	47	G1
Tadwick	BaNES	45	L5
Tadworth	Surrey	51	G7
Tafarnaubach	Blae G	61	H5
Tafarn-y-bwlch	Pembks	75	J3
Tafarn-y-Gelyn	Denbgs	128	E7
Taff's Well	Cardif	43	H5
Tafolwern	Powys	93	J3
Taibach	Neath	57	L7
Tain	Highld	263	L3
Tain	Highld	280	B3
Tai'n Lôn	Gwynd	109	H2
Tai'r Bull	Powys	60	F2
Tairgwaith	Neath	59	K6
Takeley	Essex	70	E3
Takeley Street	Essex	70	E3
Talachddu	Powys	78	F8
Talacre	Flints	128	D3
Talaton	Devon	14	C3
Talbenny	Pembks	54	D4
Talbot Green	Rhondd	43	G5
Talbot Village	BCP	17	L4
Taleford	Devon	14	C3
Talerddig	Powys	93	K3
Talgarreg	Cerdgn	76	D3
Talgarth	Powys	79	G8
Talisker	Highld	246	D3
Talke	Staffs	114	C1
Talke Pits	Staffs	114	C1
Talkin	Cumb	178	D7
Talladale	Highld	260	E6
Talla Linnfoots	Border	187	H2
Tallaminnock	S Ayrs	183	K3
Tallarn Green	Wrexhm	113	G3

Tallentire Cumb 164 F4
Talley Carmth 59 H2
Tallington Lincs 102 B2
Tallwrn Wrexhm 112 D2
Talmine Highld 277 K4
Talog Carmth 58 B4
Talsarn Cerdgn 77 G4
Talsarnau Gwynd 109 L4
Talskiddy Cnwll 4 E2
Talwrn IoA 125 J4
Talwrn Wrexhm 112 F2
Tal-y-bont Cerdgn 92 E5
Tal-y-Bont Conwy 126 F6
Talybont Gwynd 109 L7
Tal-y-bont Gwynd 126 C5
Talybont-on-Usk Powys 61 H3
Tal-y-Cafn Conwy 126 F5
Tal-y-coed Mons 62 E4
Tal-y-garn Rhondd 42 F5
Tal-y-llyn Gwynd 92 F2
Talysarn Gwynd 109 J1
Tal-y-Waun Torfn 61 L6
Talywern Powys 93 H3
Tamar Valley Mining District
Devon 6 E2
Tamer Lane End Wigan 139 J7
Tamerton Foliot C Plym 6 F3
Tamworth Staffs 99 G3
Tamworth Green Lincs 119 L3
Tamworth Services Warwks 99 H3
Tancred N York 151 G4
Tancredston Pembks 74 E7
Tandridge Surrey 38 B3
Tanfield Dur 180 F7
Tanfield Lea Dur 180 F8
Tangasdale W Isls 283 b13
Tangiers Pembks 54 F3
Tangley Hants 47 L8
Tangmere W Susx 20 E5
Tan Hill N York 158 F1
Tankerness Ork 275 d4
Tankersley Barns 140 A7
Tankerton Kent 40 F2
Tannach Highld 280 D6
Tannachie Abers 245 H6
Tannadice Angus 234 D4
Tanner's Green Worcs 98 D8
Tannington Suffk 90 F2
Tannochside N Lans 209 J6
Tansley Derbys 132 F7
Tansor N Nthn 102 B5
Tantobie Dur 180 E7
Tanton N York 170 C8
Tanwood Worcs 97 K8
Tanworth in Arden Warwks 82 D1
Tan-y-Bwlch Gwynd 110 C3
Tan-y-fron Conwy 127 J6
Tan-y-fron Wrexhm 112 D1
Tan-y-grisiau Gwynd 110 C3
Tan-y-groes Cerdgn 76 B5
Taobh Tuath W Isls 282 d6
Taplow Bucks 49 M3
Tarbert Ag & B 205 L6
Tarbert Ag & B 206 D5
Tarbert W Isls 282 e5
Tarbet Ag & B 218 D6
Tarbet Highld 238 C5
Tarbet Highld 276 B6
Tarbock Green Knows 129 K2
Tarbolton S Ayrs 196 E5
Tarbrax S Lans 199 H2
Tardebigge Worcs 82 B2
Tarfside Angus 244 B7
Tarland Abers 244 B3
Tarleton Lancs 138 F4
Tarlscough Lancs 138 E5
Tarlton Gloucs 64 D7
Tarnock Somset 44 D8
Tarns Cumb 164 F1
Tarnside W & F 156 F4
Tarporley Ches W 130 A7
Tarr Somset 28 F4
Tarrant Crawford Dorset 17 H2
Tarrant Gunville Dorset 32 F8
Tarrant Hinton Dorset 32 F8
Tarrant Keyneston Dorset 17 H2
Tarrant Launceston Dorset 17 J1
Tarrant Monkton Dorset 17 J1
Tarrant Rawston Dorset 17 H1
Tarrant Rushton Dorset 17 H2
Tarring Neville E Susx 23 G6
Tarrington Herefs 80 E7
Tarskavaig Highld 247 J6
Tarves Abers 256 F5
Tarvin Ches W 129 L6
Tarvin Sands Ches W 129 L6
Tasburgh Norfk 106 E4
Tasley Shrops 96 F4
Taston Oxon 65 M3
Tatenhill Staffs 115 K7

Tathall End M Keyn 84 F6
Tatham Lancs 147 M2
Tathwell Lincs 136 F3
Tatsfield Surrey 51 L7
Tattenhall Ches W 129 L7
Tatterford Norfk 121 J6
Tattersett Norfk 121 J5
Tattershall Lincs 136 D8
Tattershall Bridge Lincs 136 C8
Tattershall Thorpe Lincs 136 D7
Tattingstone Suffk 90 D7
Tattingstone White Horse
Suffk 90 D7
Tatworth Somset 15 H2
Tauchers Moray 267 H6
Taunton Somset 30 C6
Taunton Deane Services
Somset 30 B6
Taverham Norfk 106 D1
Taverners Green Essex 70 E3
Tavernspite Pembks 55 L4
Tavistock Devon 12 C7
Tavistock Devon 12 C7
Taw Green Devon 12 F3
Tawstock Devon 27 K5
Taxal Derbys 131 K4
Tay Bridge C Dund 223 G1
Taychreggan Hotel Ag & B 217 G3
Tay Forest Park P & K 231 L3
Tayinloan Ag & B 205 M7
Taynton Gloucs 63 L3
Taynton Oxon 65 K4
Taynuilt Ag & B 216 F1
Tayport Fife 223 H2
Tayvallich Ag & B 215 L7
Tealby Lincs 136 C2
Tealing Angus 234 B7
Team Valley Gatesd 181 G7
Teangue Highld 247 K6
Teanord Highld 263 G7
Tebay W & F 157 K2
Tebay Services W & F 157 K1
Tebworth C Beds 68 C2
Tedburn St Mary Devon 13 J4
Teddington Gloucs 81 M8
Teddington Gt Lon 50 I6
Tedstone Delamere Herefs 80 F3
Tedstone Wafer Herefs 80 F3
Teesport R & Cl 170 D6
Teesside International Airport
S on T 169 K8
Teesside Park S on T 170 B7
Teeton W Nthn 84 D1
Teffont Evias Wilts 33 G4
Teffont Magna Wilts 33 G4
Tegryn Pembks 75 L5
Teigh Rutlnd 117 M8
Teigncombe Devon 12 F5
Teigngrace Devon 13 K7
Teignmouth Devon 13 L8
Teindside Border 188 D4
Telford Wrekin 96 F2
Telford Services Shrops 97 G2
Telham E Susx 24 D4
Tellisford Somset 46 A7
Telscombe E Susx 22 F6
Telscombe Cliffs E Susx 22 F7
Tempar P & K 231 J4
Templand D & G 176 E2
Temple Cnwll 11 G7
Temple Mdloth 211 K7
Temple Balsall Solhll 99 G8
Temple Bar Cerdgn 76 F4
Temple Cloud BaNES 45 J7
Templecombe Somset 32 B6
Temple End Suffk 88 D5
Temple Ewell Kent 41 J6
Temple Grafton Warwks 82 D4
Temple Guiting Gloucs 65 G2
Temple Herdewyke Warwks 83 J5
Temple Hirst N York 142 F3
Temple Normanton Derbys 133 H6
Temple of Fiddes Abers 245 H7
Temple Sowerby W & F 166 E5
Templeton Devon 28 F8
Templeton Pembks 55 J4
Templetown Dur 168 E1
Tempsford C Beds 86 D4
Tenbury Wells Worcs 80 E2
Tenby Pembks 55 K6
Tendring Essex 73 H2
Tendring Green Essex 73 H2
Tendring Heath Essex 73 H2
Ten Mile Bank Norfk 104 B4
Tenpenny Heath Essex 73 G3
Tenterden Kent 39 M6
Terling Essex 71 J4
Tern Wrekin 113 K8
Ternhill Shrops 113 L5
Terregles D & G 176 B3

Terrington N York 151 L2
Terrington St Clement Norfk 120 C7
Terrington St John Norfk 104 A1
Terry's Green Warwks 98 E8
Teston Kent 39 H3
Testwood Hants 34 D7
Tetbury Gloucs 64 C8
Tetbury Upton Gloucs 64 C8
Tetchill Shrops 112 F5
Tetcott Devon 11 L3
Tetford Lincs 136 F5
Tetney Lincs 145 J7
Tetney Lock Lincs 145 J7
Tetsworth Oxon 67 G6
Tettenhall Wolves 97 K3
Tettenhall Wood Wolves 97 K3
Teversal Notts 133 J2
Teversham Cambs 87 K3
Teviothead Border 188 C5
Tewin Herts 69 H4
Tewin Wood Herts 69 H4
Tewkesbury Gloucs 81 K6
Teynham Kent 40 B3
Thackley C Brad 149 M8
Thackthwaite Cumb 164 F6
Thackthwaite W & F 166 A5
Thainstone Abers 256 D8
Thakeham W Susx 21 J3
Thame Oxon 67 H6
Thames Ditton Surrey 50 F5
Thamesmead Gt Lon 52 A3
Thamesport Medway 53 J4
Thanington Kent 40 F4
Thankerton S Lans 199 G5
Tharston Norfk 106 D4
Thatcham W Berk 48 D5
Thatto Heath St Hel 129 L1
Thaxted Essex 70 F1
Theakston N York 160 D5
Thealby N Linc 143 M4
Theale Somset 31 G2
Theale W Berk 48 F4
Thearne E R Yk 153 G8
The Bank Ches E 131 G8
The Beeches Gloucs 64 F8
The Blythe Staffs 115 G6
The Bog Shrops 95 J4
The Bourne Worcs 82 A4
The Braes Highld 247 H2
The Bratch Staffs 97 K4
The Bridge Kent 52 C4
The Broad Herefs 80 C3
The Broads 107 K2
The Brunt E Loth 212 F4
The Bryn Mons 62 C5
The Bungalow IoM 154 e5
The Burf Worcs 81 J2
The Camp Gloucs 64 C5
The Chequer Wrexhm 113 H3
The City Bed 86 C3
The City Bucks 67 J7
The Common Oxon 65 L2
The Common Wilts 34 B4
The Common Wilts 46 F2
The Corner Kent 39 H5
The Cronk IoM 154 d3
Theddingworth Leics 100 E6
Theddlethorpe All Saints
Lincs 137 J2
Theddlethorpe St Helen Lincs 137 J2
The Den N Ayrs 196 C1
The Forge Herefs 79 L3
The Forstal Kent 40 D7
The Fouralls Shrops 113 L5
The Green Cumb 156 A5
The Green Essex 71 J3
The Green N York 162 D2
The Green Wilts 32 E4
The Grove Dur 168 E1
The Grove Worcs 81 K7
The Haven W Susx 37 G5
The Haw Gloucs 64 B2
The Hendre Mons 62 F4
The Hill Cumb 156 A6
The Holt Wokham 49 K3
The Hundred Herefs 80 C2
Thelbridge Cross Devon 28 D8
The Leacon Kent 40 C8
The Lee Bucks 67 L6
The Lhen IoM 154 e2
Thelnetham Suffk 105 L7
The Lochs Moray 266 F4
Thelveton Norfk 106 D7
Thelwall Warrtn 130 C2
The Marsh Powys 95 H4
Themelthorpe Norfk 122 B6
The Middles Dur 180 F8
The Moor Kent 39 J7
The Mumbles Swans 57 H7

The Murray S Lans 209 H8
The Mythe Gloucs 81 K8
The Narth Mons 63 G6
The Neuk Abers 245 G4
Thenford W Nthn 83 M7
Theobald's Green Wilts 46 F5
The Quarry Gloucs 63 L7
The Quarter Kent 39 M4
The Reddings Gloucs 64 C3
Therfield Herts 87 G7
The Rhôs Powys 61 J1
The Ross P & K 220 D3
The Sands Surrey 36 C2
The Shoe Wilts 46 A4
The Smithies Shrops 96 F4
The Spring Warwks 83 G1
The Square Torfn 62 B7
The Stair Kent 38 F4
The Stocks Kent 25 G2
The Straits Hants 36 A3
The Strand Wilts 46 D7
Thetford Norfk 105 H6
Thetford Forest Park 104 F5
Thethwaite Cumb 165 L2
The Towans Cnwll 2 F5
The Town IoS 10 b2
The Vauld Herefs 80 C5
The Wyke Shrops 97 G2
Theydon Bois Essex 70 C7
Theydon Mount Essex 70 C7
Thicket Priory N York 151 L7
Thickwood Wilts 46 B4
Thimbleby Lincs 136 D5
Thimbleby N York 161 G6
Thingwall Wirral 129 G3
Thirkleby N York 161 G6
Thirlby N York 161 G6
Thirlestane Border 201 H4
Thirn N York 160 B5
Thirsk N York 160 F6
Thirtleby E R Yk 144 F1
Thistleton Lancs 147 H1
Thistleton Rutlnd 118 B7
Thistley Green Suffk 104 D8
Thixendale N York 152 C4
Thockrington Nthumb 179 M1
Tholomas Drove Cambs 103 H2
Tholthorpe N York 151 G2
Thomas Chapel Pembks 55 J5
Thomas Close W & F 166 B3
Thomastown Abers 255 L4
Thompson Norfk 105 J4
Thomshill Moray 266 D5
Thong Kent 52 E5
Thongsbridge Kirk 141 J6
Thoralby N York 159 H6
Thoresby Notts 134 C5
Thoresthorpe Lincs 137 J4
Thoresway Lincs 144 F8
Thorganby Lincs 145 G8
Thorganby N York 151 L7
Thorgill N York 162 C3
Thorington Suffk 107 J8
Thorington Street Suffk 89 K8
Thorlby N York 149 H5
Thorley Herts 70 C3
Thorley IoW 18 F6
Thorley Houses Herts 70 C3
Thorley Street IoW 18 F6
Thormanby N York 161 H7
Thornaby-on-Tees S on T 170 B7
Thornage Norfk 122 B4
Thornborough Bucks 84 E8
Thornborough N York 160 D6
Thornbury C Brad 141 J1
Thornbury Devon 12 A1
Thornbury Herefs 80 E3
Thornbury S Glos 45 J1
Thornby Cumb 177 J8
Thornby W Nthn 100 D8
Thorncliff Staffs 131 K7
Thorncombe Dorset 15 J2
Thorncombe Street Surrey 36 F2
Thorncott Green C Beds 86 C5
Thorncross IoW 19 G7
Thorndon Suffk 90 D1
Thorndon Cross Devon 12 D4
Thorne Donc 143 H5
Thorne Coffin Somset 31 H7
Thornecroft Devon 7 M2
Thornehillhead Devon 27 G7
Thorner Leeds 150 E7
Thornes Staffs 98 D3
Thornes Wakefd 141 M4
Thorne St Margaret Somset 29 K6
Thorney Bucks 50 D3
Thorney C Pete 102 F3
Thorney Notts 135 G5
Thorney Somset 30 F6
Thorney Hill Hants 18 B4

Thorney Island W Susx 20 C6
Thorney Toll Cambs 103 G3
Thornfalcon Somset 30 D6
Thornford Dorset 31 K8
Thorngrafton Nthumb 179 H6
Thorngrove Somset 30 E4
Thorngumbald E R Yk 145 G3
Thornham Norfk 121 G3
Thornham Magna Suffk 90 C1
Thornham Parva Suffk 90 D1
Thornhaugh C Pete 102 B3
Thornhill C Sotn 19 G1
Thornhill Caerph 43 J5
Thornhill Cumb 155 H1
Thornhill D & G 186 C7
Thornhill Derbys 132 D3
Thornhill Kirk 141 L4
Thornhill Stirlg 219 L7
Thornhill Lees Kirk 141 K4
Thornhills Calder 141 J3
Thornholme E R Yk 153 H3
Thornicombe Dorset 17 G2
Thornington Nthumb 202 D6
Thornley Dur 168 E3
Thornley Dur 169 K3
Thornley Gate Nthumb 179 J7
Thornliebank E Rens 208 F7
Thorns Suffk 88 E4
Thornsett Derbys 131 K2
Thorns Green Ches E 130 F3
Thornthwaite Cumb 165 H5
Thornthwaite N York 149 L4
Thornton Angus 234 B6
Thornton Bucks 84 E8
Thornton C Brad 141 H1
Thornton E R Yk 152 A6
Thornton Fife 222 E7
Thornton Lancs 146 F7
Thornton Leics 100 A2
Thornton Lincs 136 D6
Thornton Middsb 170 B7
Thornton Nthumb 202 E4
Thornton Pembks 54 E5
Thornton Sefton 138 D7
Thornton Curtis N Linc 144 D4
Thorntonhall S Lans 209 G7
Thornton Heath Gt Lon 51 J5
Thornton Hough Wirral 129 G3
Thornton-in-Craven N York 148 F6
Thornton in Lonsdale N York 158 B8
Thornton-le-Beans N York 160 F4
Thornton-le-Clay N York 151 L3
Thornton-le-Dale N York 162 E6
Thornton le Moor Lincs 144 D8
Thornton-le-Moor N York 160 F5
Thornton-le-Moors Ches W 129 K5
Thornton-le-Street N York 160 F5
Thorntonloch E Loth 213 G4
Thornton Rust N York 159 G5
Thornton Steward N York 160 A5
Thornton Watlass N York 160 C5
Thornwood Common Essex 70 C6
Thornydykes Border 201 J3
Thornythwaite W & F 165 L6
Thoroton Notts 117 K3
Thorp Arch Leeds 150 F6
Thorpe Derbys 115 J2
Thorpe E R Yk 152 F6
Thorpe Lincs 137 J3
Thorpe N York 149 H3
Thorpe Norfk 107 J4
Thorpe Notts 117 K2
Thorpe Surrey 50 C5
Thorpe Abbotts Norfk 106 D7
Thorpe Acre Leics 116 E7
Thorpe Arnold Leics 117 K7
Thorpe Audlin Wakefd 142 D4
Thorpe Bassett N York 162 F8
Thorpe Bay Sthend 53 K2
Thorpe by Water Rutlnd 101 K4
Thorpe Common Rothm 133 G1
Thorpe Constantine Staffs 99 H2
Thorpe End Norfk 106 F1
Thorpe Green Essex 73 H3
Thorpe Green Lancs 139 H3
Thorpe Green Suffk 89 J4
Thorpe Hesley Rothm 142 B8
Thorpe in Balne Donc 142 F5
Thorpe Langton Leics 101 G5
Thorpe Larches Dur 169 K5
Thorpe Lea Surrey 50 C5
Thorpe le Fallows Lincs 135 H4
Thorpe-le-Soken Essex 73 J3
Thorpe le Street E R Yk 152 C7
Thorpe Malsor N Nthn 101 H7
Thorpe Mandeville W Nthn 83 M6
Thorpe Market Norfk 122 E4
Thorpe Marriot Norfk 122 D8
Thorpe Morieux Suffk 89 J4
Thorpeness Suffk 91 L3

Thorpe on the Hill Leeds 141 M2
Thorpe on the Hill Lincs 135 H6
Thorpe St Andrew Norfk 106 F2
Thorpe St Peter Lincs 137 J7
Thorpe Salvin Rothm 133 K3
Thorpe Satchville Leics 100 F1
Thorpe Thewles S on T 169 L6
Thorpe Tilney Lincs 136 B8
Thorpe Underwood N Nthn 101 H7
Thorpe Underwood N York 151 G4
Thorpe Waterville N Nthn 102 A7
Thorpe Willoughby N York 142 F2
Thorpland Norfk 104 C2
Thorrington Essex 73 G3
Thorverton Devon 13 L2
Thrales End C Beds 68 E4
Thrandeston Suffk 106 C8
Thrapston N Nthn 101 M7
Threapland Cumb 165 G3
Threapland N York 149 H4
Threapwood Ches W 113 G3
Threapwood Staffs 115 G3
Threapwood Head Staffs 115 G3
Threave S Ayrs 183 J2
Three Ashes Herefs 63 G3
Three Bridges W Susx 37 L3
Three Burrows Cnwll 4 B5
Three Chimneys Kent 39 K5
Three Cocks Powys 79 G7
Three Crosses Swans 57 G6
Three Cups Corner E Susx 23 L3
Three Gates Worcs 80 F3
Threehammer Common Norfk 123 G7
Three Hammers Cnwll 11 J5
Three Holes Norfk 103 K3
Threekingham Lincs 118 E4
Three Leg Cross E Susx 39 H7
Three Legged Cross Dorset 17 L2
Three Mile Cross Wokham 49 H5
Threemilestone Cnwll 4 C6
Threemiletown W Loth 210 E4
Three Oaks E Susx 24 F4
Threlkeld W & F 165 K5
Threshers Bush Essex 70 D5
Threshfield N York 149 H3
Thrigby Norfk 107 J1
Thringarth Dur 167 L6
Thringstone Leics 116 D8
Thrintoft N York 160 D4
Thriplow Cambs 87 J6
Throapham Rothm 133 K2
Throckenhalt Lincs 103 G2
Throcking Herts 69 J1
Throckley N u Ty 180 E5
Throckmorton Worcs 82 A5
Throop BCP 17 M3
Throop Dorset 16 F4
Throphill Nthumb 180 D2
Thropton Nthumb 190 E5
Throsk Stirlg 209 M1
Througham Gloucs 64 D5
Throughgate D & G 185 L6
Throwleigh Devon 12 F4
Throwley Kent 40 C4
Throwley Forstal Kent 40 C4
Thrumpton Notts 116 E5
Thrumpton Notts 134 D4
Thrumster Highld 280 D7
Thrunscoe NE Lin 145 J6
Thrunton Nthumb 190 F4
Thrup Oxon 65 L7
Thrupp Gloucs 64 B6
Thrupp Oxon 66 C4
Thrushelton Devon 12 B5
Thrussington Leics 117 H8
Thruxton Hants 34 C2
Thruxton Herefs 80 B8
Thrybergh Rothm 142 D8
Thulston Derbys 116 C5
Thundersley Essex 53 G1
Thurcaston Leics 100 C1
Thurcroft Rothm 133 K2
Thurdon Cnwll 26 D8
Thurgarton Norfk 122 D4
Thurgarton Notts 117 J2
Thurgoland Barns 141 L7
Thurlaston Leics 100 B4
Thurlaston Warwks 83 L1
Thurlbear Somset 30 C6
Thurlby Lincs 118 E8
Thurlby Lincs 135 H7
Thurlby Lincs 137 J4
Thurleigh Bed 85 L3
Thurlestone Devon 7 K6
Thurloxton Somset 30 C5
Thurlstone Barns 141 K7
Thurlton Norfk 107 J4
Thurlwood Ches E 130 F8
Thurmaston Leics 100 D2
Thurnby Leics 100 E3

Thurne Norfk 123 H8
Thurnham Kent 53 H7
Thurning N Nthn 102 B6
Thurning Norfk 122 B5
Thurnscoe Barns 142 C6
Thurrock Services Thurr 52 C3
Thursby Cumb 165 K1
Thursden Lancs 140 D1
Thursford Norfk 121 L5
Thursley Surrey 36 D3
Thurso Highld 279 K3
Thurstaston Wirral 128 F3
Thurston Suffk 89 J2
Thurston Clough Oldham 140 E6
Thurstonfield Cumb 177 K7
Thurstonland Kirk 141 J5
Thurston Planche Suffk 89 J2
Thurton Norfk 107 G3
Thurvaston Derbys 115 L4
Thuxton Norfk 105 L2
Thwaite N York 158 F3
Thwaite Suffk 90 D2
Thwaite Head W & F 156 E4
Thwaites C Brad 149 K7
Thwaite St Mary Norfk 107 G4
Thwaites Brow C Brad 149 K7
Thwing E R Yk 153 G2
Tibbermore P & K 221 J3
Tibbers D & G 186 C6
Tibberton Gloucs 63 M3
Tibberton Worcs 81 L4
Tibberton Wrekin 113 L7
Tibenham Norfk 106 C5
Tibshelf Derbys 133 J7
Tibshelf Services Derbys 133 J7
Tibthorpe E R Yk 152 E5
Ticehurst E Susx 39 H7
Tichborne Hants 35 H5
Tickencote Rutlnd 101 L2
Tickenham N Som 44 F4
Tickford End M Keyn 85 H6
Tickhill Donc 134 B1
Ticklerton Shrops 96 B5
Ticknall Derbys 116 B6
Tickton E R Yk 153 H3
Tidbury Green Solhll 98 E8
Tidcombe Wilts 47 L7
Tiddington Oxon 67 G6
Tiddington Warwks 82 F4
Tiddleywink Wilts 46 C4
Tidebrook E Susx 38 F7
Tideford Cnwll 6 C3
Tideford Cross Cnwll 6 C3
Tidenham Gloucs 63 H7
Tideswell Derbys 132 C4
Tidmarsh W Berk 48 F4
Tidmington Warwks 83 G7
Tidpit Hants 33 J7
Tidworth Wilts 34 B1
Tiers Cross Pembks 54 E5
Tiffield W Nthn 84 D5
Tigerton Angus 234 E3
Tigh a' Ghearraidh W Isls 283 b8
Tigharry W Isls 283 b8
Tighnabruaich Ag & B 206 F4
Tigley Devon 7 L3
Tilbrook Cambs 86 B2
Tilbury Thurr 52 D4
Tibury Dock Thurr 52 D4
Tilbury Green Essex 88 E7
Tilbury Juxta Clare Essex 88 F7
Tile Cross Birm 98 F4
Tile Hill Covtry 99 H7
Tilehouse Green Solhll 98 F8
Tilehurst Readg 49 G4
Tilford Surrey 36 C2
Tilgate W Susx 37 L4
Tilgate Forest Row W Susx 37 L4
Tilham Street Somset 31 J4
Tillers Green Gloucs 80 E7
Tilley Shrops 113 H6
Tillicoultry Clacks 221 G7
Tillietudlem S Lans 198 D4
Tillingham Essex 72 E6
Tillington Herefs 80 B6
Tillington W Susx 36 E6
Tillington Common Herefs 80 B6
Tillybirloch Abers 244 F2
Tillyfourie Abers 244 E1
Tillygreig Abers 256 F7
Tillyrie P & K 221 K6

Tilsworth C Beds 68 B2
Tilton on the Hill Leics 101 G2
Tiltups End Gloucs 64 B7
Tilty Essex 70 E2
Timberland Lincs 136 B7
Timbersbrook Ches E 131 H7
Timberscombe Somset 29 G2
Timble N York 149 M5
Timewell Devon 29 H5
Timpanheck D & G 177 K4
Timperley Traffd 130 F2
Timsbury BaNES 45 K7
Timsbury Hants 34 C6
Timsgarry W Isls 282 d3
Timsgearraidh W Isls 282 d3
Timworth Suffk 89 H2
Timworth Green Suffk 89 H2
Tincleton Dorset 16 E4
Tindale Cumb 178 E7
Tingewick Bucks 84 C8
Tingley Leeds 141 L5
Tingrith C Beds 68 C1
Tingwall Airport Shet 281 e6
Tingwell Ork 275 c3
Tinhay Devon 12 A5
Tinker's Hill Hants 34 E2
Tinkersley Derbys 132 E6
Tinsley Sheff 133 H2
Tinsley Green W Susx 37 L3
Tintagel Cnwll 10 F5
Tintern Mons 63 G7
Tintinhull Somset 31 H7
Tintwistle Derbys 140 F8
Tinwald D & G 176 D3
Tinwell Rutlnd 101 M2
Tippacott Devon 28 D2
Tipp's End Norfk 103 K4
Tiptoe Hants 18 C4
Tipton Sandw 98 B5
Tipton Green Sandw 98 B5
Tipton St John Devon 14 C4
Tiptree Essex 72 C4
Tiptree Heath Essex 72 C4
Tirabad Powys 78 B2
Tircoed Swans 57 H5
Tiree Ag & B 224 C6
Tiree Airport Ag & B 224 C6
Tiretigan Ag & B 206 A6
Tirley Gloucs 64 B2
Tiroran Ag & B 226 F6
Tirphil Caerph 61 H6
Tirril W & F 166 C5
Tir-y-fron Flints 129 G7
Tisbury Wilts 32 F5
Tisman's Common W Susx 37 G4
Tissington Derbys 115 K1
Titchberry Devon 26 D5
Titchfield Hants 19 J3
Titchfield Common Hants 19 J2
Titchmarsh N Nthn 102 A7
Titchwell Norfk 121 G3
Tithby Notts 117 J4
Tithebarn Devon 14 A4
Titley Herefs 79 L3
Titmore Green Herts 69 G2
Titsey Surrey 51 L7
Titson Cnwll 11 J2
Tittensor Staffs 114 D6
Tittleshall Norfk 121 K7
Titton Worcs 81 J1
Tiverton Ches W 130 A7
Tiverton Devon 29 G8
Tivetshall St Margaret Norfk 106 D6
Tivetshall St Mary Norfk 106 D6
Tivington Somset 29 G2
Tivy Dale Barns 141 L6
Tixall Staffs 114 F7
Tixover Rutlnd 101 L3
Toab Shet 281 d9
Toadhole Derbys 133 H8
Toadmoor Derbys 116 B1
Tobermory Ag & B 226 F1
Toberonochy Ag & B 215 L3
Tobha Mòr W Isls 283 b10
Tocher Abers 256 C5
Tochieneal Moray 267 K3
Tockenham Wilts 46 F3
Tockenham Wick Wilts 46 F3
Tocketts R & Cl 170 E7
Tockholes Bl w D 139 K3
Tockington S Glos 45 J2
Tockwith N York 151 G5
Todber Dorset 32 D7
Todburn Nthumb 191 G7
Toddington C Beds 68 C2
Toddington Gloucs 64 F1
Toddington Services C Beds 68 C1
Todds Green Herts 69 G2
Todenham Gloucs 82 F8
Todhills Angus 234 C7

Todhills Cumb......177 L6
Todhills Dur......169 G4
Todhills Rest Area Cumb......177 L6
Todmorden Calder......140 E3
Todwick Rothm......133 K3
Toft Cambs......87 G4
Toft Ches E......130 E4
Toft Lincs......118 E8
Toft Shet......281 e4
Toft Warwks......83 L1
Toft Hill Dur......168 F5
Toft Hill Lincs......136 D7
Toft Monks Norfk......107 J4
Toft next Newton Lincs......135 L2
Toftrees Norfk......121 K6
Toftwood Norfk......105 K1
Togston Nthumb......191 K6
Tokavaig Highld......247 J6
Tokers Green Oxon......49 H3
Tolastadh bho Thuath W Isls......282 h2
Toldish Cnwll......4 F3
Tolland Somset......29 K4
Tollard Farnham Dorset......32 F7
Tollard Royal Wilts......32 F7
Toll Bar Donc......142 E6
Tollbar End Covtry......99 K8
Toller Fratrum Dorset......16 B3
Toller Porcorum Dorset......16 A3
Tollerton N York......151 H4
Tollerton Notts......117 G4
Toller Whelme Dorset......15 L2
Tollesbury Essex......72 D5
Tolleshunt D'Arcy Essex......72 D5
Tolleshunt Knights Essex......72 D4
Tolleshunt Major Essex......72 C5
Tollingham E R Yk......152 C8
Toll of Birness Abers......257 J5
Tolpuddle Dorset......16 F4
Tolworth Gt Lon......51 G5
Tomatin Highld......252 E6
Tomchrasky Highld......239 M1
Tomdoun Highld......239 K2
Tomich Highld......250 B6
Tomich Highld......250 F2
Tomich Highld......263 J5
Tomich Highld......272 E7
Tomintoul Moray......254 D7
Tomlow Warwks......83 K3
Tomnacross Highld......250 F3
Tomnavoulin Moray......254 D6
Tompkin Staffs......114 E1
Ton Mons......62 C6
Ton Mons......62 D7
Tonbridge Kent......38 F4
Tondu Brdgnd......42 D5
Tonedale Somset......29 L6
Tonfanau Gwynd......92 C3
Tong C Brad......141 K2
Tong Kent......40 C4
Tong Shrops......97 H2
Tong W Isls......282 q3
Tonge Leics......116 C7
Tong Green Kent......40 C4
Tongham Surrey......36 C1
Tongland D & G......175 H4
Tong Norton Shrops......97 H2
Tongue Highld......277 K5
Tongue End Lincs......119 J2
Tongwynlais Cardif......43 H5
Tonmawr Neath......42 B2
Tonna Neath......57 L5
Ton-teg Rhondd......43 H4
Tonwell Herts......69 J4
Tonypandy Rhondd......42 F3
Tonyrefail Rhondd......42 F4
Toot Baldon Oxon......66 F7
Toot Hill Essex......70 D6
Toothill Hants......34 E7
Toothill Swindn......47 G2
Tooting Gt Lon......51 H5
Tooting Bec Gt Lon......51 H4
Topcliffe N York......160 F7
Topcroft Norfk......106 F5
Topcroft Street Norfk......106 F5
Top End Bed......85 L3
Topham Donc......143 G4
Top of Hebers Rochdl......140 C6
Toppesfield Essex......88 E7
Toprow Norfk......106 D4
Topsham Devon......13 M5
Top-y-rhos Flints......128 F7
Torbeg N Ayrs......194 D5
Torboll Highld......273 H8
Torbreck Highld......251 H3
Torbryan Devon......8 B2
Torcastle Highld......239 J7
Torcross Devon......8 B6
Tore Highld......251 G1
Torfrey Cnwll......5 J4
Torinturk Ag & B......206 C6

Torksey Lincs......135 G4
Torlundy Highld......239 K8
Tormarton S Glos......45 M3
Tormore N Ayrs......194 D4
Tornagrain Highld......252 E2
Tornaveen Abers......244 D2
Torness Highld......251 G6
Toronto Dur......169 G4
Torpenhow Cumb......165 G3
Torphichen W Loth......210 C4
Torphins Abers......244 E3
Torpoint Cnwll......6 E4
Torquay Torbay......8 D2
Torquhan Border......200 F3
Torr Devon......7 H4
Torran Highld......259 K6
Torrance E Duns......209 G4
Torranyard N Ayrs......196 D2
Torre Somset......29 J3
Torridon Highld......260 E8
Torridon House Highld......260 D8
Torrin Highld......247 J4
Torrisdale Ag & B......191 K1
Torrisdale Highld......278 B4
Torrish Highld......274 C4
Torrisholme Lancs......147 J3
Torrobull Highld......272 E7
Torry C Aber......245 L3
Torryburn Fife......210 D2
Torteval Guern......9 h4
Torthorwald D & G......176 D3
Tortington W Susx......21 G6
Torton Worcs......81 J1
Tortworth S Glos......63 L8
Torvaig Highld......259 H7
Torver W & F......156 C4
Torwood Falk......209 M2
Torwoodlee Border......201 G5
Torworth Notts......134 D4
Tosberry Devon......26 D6
Toscaig Highld......247 L1
Toseland Cambs......86 LJ
Tosside Lancs......148 D4
Tostock Suffk......89 J3
Totaig Highld......258 B6
Tote Highld......259 G6
Tote Highld......259 J4
Tote Hill W Susx......36 C6
Totford Hants......35 H3
Tothill Lincs......137 H3
Totland IoW......18 E6
Totley Sheff......132 F4
Totley Brook Sheff......132 F4
Totnes Devon......8 B3
Toton Notts......116 E4
Totronald Ag & B......224 F4
Totscore Highld......258 F3
Tottenham Gt Lon......51 J1
Tottenhill Norfk......104 C1
Totteridge Gt Lon......69 H8
Totternhoe C Beds......68 C3
Tottington Bury......140 A6
Tottleworth Lancs......139 L2
Totton Hants......34 D8
Touchen End W & M......49 L4
Toulston N York......151 G7
Toulton Somset......30 B4
Toulvaddie Highld......264 D4
Tovil Kent......39 J3
Towan Cnwll......5 G5
Towan Cnwll......10 B7
Toward Ag & B......207 J5
Toward Quay Ag & B......207 J5
Towcester W Nthn......84 D5
Towednack Cnwll......2 D3
Tower of London Gt Lon......51 J3
Towersey Oxon......67 H6
Towie Abers......244 A1
Tow Law Dur......168 E3
Town End Cambs......103 J4
Town End W & F......156 E1
Town End W & F......156 F6
Town End W & F......166 F5
Townend W Duns......208 C4
Towngate Lincs......102 C1
Towngate W & F......166 C1
Town Green Lancs......138 E6
Town Green Norfk......107 G1
Townhead Barns......141 J7
Townhead Cumb......164 E3
Townhead D & G......176 D1
Town Head N York......148 E4
Town Head W & F......156 F2
Townhead W & F......166 E4
Townhead of Greenlaw D & G......175 J2
Townhill Fife......210 F1
Town Kelloe Dur......169 K3
Townlake Devon......12 A7
Town Lane Wigan......139 K7
Town Littleworth E Susx......22 F4

Town of Lowton Wigan......139 J8
Town Row E Susx......38 E7
Towns End Hants......48 E7
Townsend Somset......30 E7
Townshend Cnwll......2 F4
Town Street Suffk......104 F6
Townwell S Glos......45 K1
Town Yetholm Border......202 C7
Towthorpe C York......151 K4
Towthorpe E R Yk......152 D3
Towton N York......151 G7
Towyn Conwy......127 K4
Toxteth Lpool......129 H2
Toynton All Saints Lincs......137 G7
Toynton Fen Side Lincs......137 G7
Toynton St Peter Lincs......137 G7
Toy's Hill Kent......38 D3
Trabboch E Ayrs......196 E6
Trabbochburn E Ayrs......196 F6
Traboe Cnwll......3 J6
Tracebridge Somset......29 H8
Tradespark Highld......264 C8
Trafford Park Traffd......140 B8
Trallong Powys......60 E1
Tranent E Loth......211 L4
Tranmere Wirral......129 H2
Trantelbeg Highld......278 F6
Trantlemore Highld......278 F5
Tranwell Nthumb......180 F2
Trap Carmth......59 J5
Traprain E Loth......212 D4
Trap's Green Warwks......82 D1
Trapshill W Berk......48 A6
Traquair Border......200 D6
Trash Green W Berk......49 G5
Trawden Lancs......148 F8
Trawscoed Cerdgn......77 J1
Trawsfynydd Gwynd......110 D4
Trealaw Rhondd......42 F3
Treales Lancs......138 F1
Trearddur Bay IoA......124 D4
Treator Cnwll......10 C7
Tre Aubrey V Glam......43 G7
Trebanog Rhondd......42 F4
Trebanos Neath......57 K4
Trebartha Cnwll......11 K7
Trebarwith Cnwll......10 E5
Trebeath Cnwll......11 J5
Trebetherick Cnwll......10 C7
Treborough Somset......29 H4
Trebudannon Cnwll......4 E3
Trebullett Cnwll......11 L7
Treburgett Cnwll......10 E6
Treburley Cnwll......11 L7
Treburrick Cnwll......10 B8
Trebyan Cnwll......5 J2
Trecastle Powys......60 C1
Trecogo Cnwll......11 K6
Trecott Devon......12 F3
Trecwn Pembks......74 F5
Trecynon Rhondd......60 F6
Tredaule Cnwll......11 J6
Tredavoe Cnwll......2 C5
Tredegar Blae G......61 J5
Tredethy Cnwll......10 F8
Tredington Gloucs......64 C1
Tredington Warwks......83 G6
Tredinnick Cnwll......5 H3
Tredinnick Cnwll......5 K2
Tredinnick Cnwll......5 M3
Tredinnick Cnwll......6 B3
Tredinnick Cnwll......10 C8
Tredomen Powys......61 H1
Tredrizzick Cnwll......10 D7
Tredunnock Mons......62 D8
Tredustan Powys......61 H1
Treen Cnwll......2 B6
Treen Cnwll......2 C3
Treesmill Cnwll......5 J4
Treeton Rothm......133 J2
Trefasser Pembks......74 E4
Trefdraeth IoA......125 G5
Trefecca Powys......61 J1
Trefechan Myr Td......61 G5
Trefeglwys Powys......93 L5
Trefenter Cerdgn......77 H2
Treffgarne Pembks......54 F2
Treffgarne Owen Pembks......74 E7
Treffynnon Pembks......74 D6
Trefil Blae G......61 H4
Trefilan Cerdgn......77 G4
Trefin Pembks......74 D5
Treflach Shrops......112 C6
Trefnannau Powys......112 C8
Trefnant Denbgs......128 C5
Trefonen Shrops......112 C6
Trefor Gwynd......108 F2
Trefor IoA......124 F4
Treforest Rhondd......43 G4
Trefrew Cnwll......10 F5

Trefriw Conwy......126 F7
Tregadillett Cnwll......11 K6
Tre-gagle Mons......63 G5
Tregaian IoA......125 H4
Tregare Mons......62 E5
Tregarne Cnwll......3 K6
Tregaron Cerdgn......77 J3
Tregarth Gwynd......126 B6
Tregaswith Cnwll......4 E5
Tregatta Cnwll......10 F5
Tregawne Cnwll......5 G2
Tregeare Cnwll......11 J5
Tregeiriog Wrexhm......112 B5
Tregele IoA......124 E1
Tregellist Cnwll......10 E7
Tregenna Cnwll......4 E6
Tregeseal Cnwll......2 B5
Tregew Cnwll......3 K4
Tre-Gibbon Rhondd......60 F6
Tregidden Cnwll......3 K6
Tregiskey Cnwll......5 G5
Treglemais Pembks......74 D6
Tregole Cnwll......11 H3
Tregolls Cnwll......3 J4
Tregonce Cnwll......10 C7
Tregonetha Cnwll......4 F2
Tregonning & Gwinear
   Mining District Cnwll......2 F5
Tregony Cnwll......4 F6
Tregoodwell Cnwll......11 G6
Tregorrick Cnwll......5 G4
Tregoss Cnwll......4 F3
Tregoyd Powys......79 H7
Tregrehan Mills Cnwll......5 H4
Tre-groes Cerdgn......76 D6
Tregullon Cnwll......5 H2
Tregunna Cnwll......10 D7
Tregunnon Cnwll......11 J6
Tregurrian Cnwll......4 D2
Tregynon Powys......94 D4
Tre-gynwr Carmth......58 D5
Trehafod Rhondd......43 G3
Trehan Cnwll......6 D3
Treharris Myr Td......43 H2
Treharrock Cnwll......10 E6
Trehemborne Cnwll......10 B7
Treherbert Carmth......77 G6
Treherbert Rhondd......42 C2
Trehunist Cnwll......6 C2
Trekenner Cnwll......11 L7
Treknow Cnwll......10 E5
Trelan Cnwll......3 J7
Trelash Cnwll......11 H4
Trelassick Cnwll......4 E4
Trelawne Cnwll......5 L4
Trelawnyd Flints......128 C4
Treleague Cnwll......3 K6
Treleaver Cnwll......3 K7
Trelech Carmth......58 A3
Trelech a'r Betws Carmth......58 B3
Treleddyd-fawr Pembks......74 B6
Trelew Cnwll......3 K4
Trelewis Myr Td......43 H2
Treligga Cnwll......10 E6
Trelights Cnwll......10 D6
Trelill Cnwll......10 E7
Trelinnoe Cnwll......11 K6
Trelion Cnwll......4 F4
Trelissick Cnwll......3 L3
Trellech Mons......63 G6
Trelleck Grange Mons......62 F6
Trelogan Flints......128 D4
Trelow Cnwll......4 F1
Trelowarren Cnwll......3 J6
Trelowia Cnwll......6 B3
Treluggan Cnwll......3 M3
Trelystan Powys......95 G3
Tremadog Gwynd......109 K3
Tremail Cnwll......11 H5
Tremain Cerdgn......75 M3
Tremaine Cnwll......11 J5
Tremar Cnwll......6 B1
Trematon Cnwll......6 D3
Trembraze Cnwll......6 B2
Tremeirchion Denbgs......128 C5
Tremethick Cross Cnwll......2 C5
Tremore Cnwll......5 G2
Tre-Mostyn Flints......128 D4
Trenance Cnwll......3 K6
Trenance Cnwll......4 D1
Trenance Cnwll......10 C6
Trenarren Cnwll......5 H5
Trench Wrekin......96 F1
Trench Green Oxon......49 G3
Trendeal Cnwll......4 E4
Trendrine Cnwll......2 D3
Treneague Cnwll......10 D8
Trenear Cnwll......3 H5
Treneglos Cnwll......11 H5
Trenerth Cnwll......2 F4

Trenewan Cnwll 5 K4
Trenewth Cnwll 10 F7
Trengune Cnwll 11 H4
Treninnick Cnwll 4 D3
Trenowah Cnwll 4 C3
Trenoweth Cnwll 3 J4
Trent Dorset 31 K7
Trentham C Stke 114 D3
Trentishoe Devon 28 A1
Trentlock Derbys 116 E5
Trent Port Lincs 135 G3
Trent Vale C Stke 114 D3
Trenwheal Cnwll 3 G4
Treoes V Glam 42 E6
Treorchy Rhondd 42 E2
Trequite Cnwll 10 E7
Tre'r-ddol Cerdgn 92 E5
Trerhyngyll V Glam 42 F6
Trerulefoot Cnwll 6 C3
Tresaith Cerdgn 76 A5
Tresawle Cnwll 4 E5
Tresco IoS 10 b2
Trescott Staffs 97 J4
Trescowe Cnwll 2 F5
Tresean Cnwll 4 C3
Tresham Gloucs 46 A1
Treshnish Isles Ag & B 225 H7
Tresillian Cnwll 4 E5
Tresinney Cnwll 10 F6
Treskinnick Cross Cnwll 11 H3
Tresmeer Cnwll 11 J5
Tresparrett Cnwll 11 G4
Tressait P & K 232 B3
Tresta Shet 281 d6
Tresta Shet 281 f3
Treswell Notts 134 F4
Treswithian Cnwll 3 G3
Tre Taliesin Cerdgn 92 E5
Trethevey Cnwll 10 F5
Trethewey Cnwll 2 B6
Trethomas Caerph 43 J4
Trethosa Cnwll 4 F4
Trethurgy Cnwll 5 H4
Tretio Pembks 74 C6
Tretire Herefs 63 G2
Tretower Powys 61 J3
Treuddyn Flints 128 F8
Trevadlock Cnwll 11 K6
Trevalga Cnwll 10 F4
Trevalyn Wrexhm 129 J8
Trevanger Cnwll 10 D7
Trevanson Cnwll 10 D8
Trevarrack Cnwll 2 D5
Trevarren Cnwll 4 E3
Trevarrian Cnwll 4 D2
Trevarrick Cnwll 5 G6
Trevarth Cnwll 3 J3
Trevaughan Carmth 55 L4
Tre-vaughan Carmth 58 D4
Treveal Cnwll 2 C3
Treveal Cnwll 4 C3
Treveighan Cnwll 10 F6
Trevellas Downs Cnwll 4 B4
Trevelmond Cnwll 5 L2
Trevemper Cnwll 4 D3
Treveor Cnwll 5 G6
Treverbyn Cnwll 4 E5
Treverbyn Cnwll 5 G3
Treverva Cnwll 3 J5
Trevescan Cnwll 2 B6
Trevethin Torfn 62 B6
Trevia Cnwll 10 F6
Trevigro Cnwll 6 C1
Trevilla Cnwll 3 L3
Trevilson Cnwll 4 D4
Treviscoe Cnwll 4 F4
Treviskey Cnwll 4 F6
Trevithick Cnwll 4 E2
Trevithick Cnwll 4 F4
Trevoll Cnwll 4 D3
Trevone Cnwll 10 B7
Trevor Wrexhm 112 C3
Trevorgans Cnwll 2 B6
Trevorrick Cnwll 10 C7
Trevose Cnwll 10 B7
Trew Cnwll 3 G5
Trewalder Cnwll 10 F6
Trewalkin Powys 61 J1
Trewarmett Cnwll 10 F5
Trewassa Cnwll 11 G5
Trewavas Cnwll 2 F5
Trewavas Mining District Cnwll 2 F5
Treween Cnwll 11 J6
Trewellard Cnwll 2 B4
Trewen Cnwll 11 J6
Trewennack Cnwll 3 H5
Trewent Pembks 55 G7
Trewern Powys 95 G1
Trewetha Cnwll 10 E6
Trewethern Cnwll 10 E7

Trewidland Cnwll 6 B3
Trewillis Cnwll 3 K7
Trewint Cnwll 6 B2
Trewint Cnwll 11 J6
Trewithian Cnwll 3 M4
Trewoodloe Cnwll 11 L8
Trewoon Cnwll 3 H7
Trewoon Cnwll 5 G4
Treworga Cnwll 4 E6
Treworgan Cnwll 4 D5
Treworlas Cnwll 4 E7
Treworld Cnwll 11 G4
Treworthal Cnwll 3 M3
Tre-wyn Mons 62 C3
Treyarnon Cnwll 10 B7
Treyford W Susx 20 D3
Trickett's Cross Dorset 17 L2
Triermain Cumb 178 E5
Triffleton Pembks 75 G7
Trillacott Cnwll 11 K4
Trimdon Dur 169 K4
Trimdon Colliery Dur 169 K3
Trimdon Grange Dur 169 K3
Trimdon Station Dur 169 K3
Trimingham Norfk 122 F4
Trimley Lower Street Suffk 91 G7
Trimley St Martin Suffk 91 G7
Trimley St Mary Suffk 91 G7
Trimpley Worcs 97 H7
Trimsaran Carmth 56 E4
Trims Green Herts 70 C4
Trimstone Devon 27 J2
Trinafour P & K 231 K3
Trinant Caerph 61 K7
Tring Herts 68 A5
Tringford Herts 67 M4
Tring Wharf Herts 68 A4
Trinity Angus 234 F3
Trinity Jersey 9 d2
Trinity Gask P & K 221 G3
Triscombe Somset 29 L4
Trislaig Highld 239 H8
Trispen Cnwll 4 D5
Tritlington Nthumb 191 J7
Troan Cnwll 4 E5
Trochry P & K 232 E7
Troedrhiwfuwch Caerph 61 H6
Troedyraur Cerdgn 76 B6
Troedyrhiw Myr Td 61 G6
Trofarth Conwy 127 G5
Trois Bois Jersey 9 c2
Troon Cnwll 3 G3
Troon S Ayrs 196 C5
Trossachs Stirlg 219 H5
Trossachs Pier Stirlg 219 H5
Troston Suffk 89 H1
Troswell Cnwll 11 J4
Trotshill Worcs 81 K4
Trottiscliffe Kent 52 D7
Trotton W Susx 36 B6
Troughend Nthumb 190 B7
Trough Gate Lancs 140 D3
Troutbeck W & F 156 F2
Troutbeck W & F 165 L5
Troutbeck Bridge W & F 156 F3
Troway Derbys 133 H4
Trowbridge Wilts 46 B7
Trowell Notts 116 E3
Trowell Services Notts 116 E3
Trowle Common Wilts 46 B7
Trowley Bottom Herts 68 D4
Trowse Newton Norfk 106 E2
Troy Leeds 150 C8
Trudoxhill Somset 32 C2
Trull Somset 30 B6
Trumfleet Donc 142 F5
Trumpan Highld 258 C4
Trumpet Herefs 80 F7
Trumpington Cambs 87 J4
Trumpsgreen Surrey 50 C5
Trunch Norfk 122 F4
Trunnah Lancs 147 G7
Truro Cnwll 4 B6
Truscott Cnwll 11 K5
Trusham Devon 13 K6
Trusley Derbys 115 L4
Trusthorpe Lincs 137 K3
Trysull Staffs 97 J4
Tubney Oxon 66 B7
Tuckenhay Devon 8 B4
Tuckhill Shrops 97 H5
Tuckingmill Cnwll 3 G3
Tuckingmill Wilts 32 F5
Tuckton BCP 18 A5
Tucoyse Cnwll 4 F5
Tuddenham Suffk 88 E1
Tuddenham St Martin Suffk 90 E5
Tudeley Kent 38 F4
Tudhoe Dur 169 H3
Tudorville Herefs 63 H3

Tudweiliog Gwynd 108 D4
Tuesley Surrey 36 E3
Tuffley Gloucs 64 B4
Tufton Hants 34 F2
Tufton Pembks 75 H6
Tugby Leics 101 G3
Tugford Shrops 96 D6
Tughall Nthumb 203 K7
Tullibody Clacks 220 E8
Tullich Abers 243 L4
Tullich Highld 251 H6
Tullich Highld 264 D4
Tulliemet P & K 232 F5
Tulloch Abers 256 E5
Tullochgorm Ag & B 216 F8
Tulloch Station Highld 240 B7
Tullymurdoch P & K 233 J5
Tullynessle Abers 255 L7
Tulse Hill Gt Lon 51 J4
Tumble Carmth 58 F6
Tumbler's Green Essex 71 K2
Tumby Lincs 136 D7
Tumby Woodside Lincs 136 E8
Tummel Bridge P & K 231 L4
Tunbridge Wells Kent 38 F5
Tundergarth D & G 177 G3
Tunga W Isls 282 g3
Tungate Norfk 122 F5
Tunley BaNES 45 K7
Tunstall C Stke 114 D1
Tunstall E R Yk 145 J2
Tunstall Kent 40 A3
Tunstall Lancs 157 K8
Tunstall N York 160 B3
Tunstall Norfk 107 J2
Tunstall Staffs 114 B6
Tunstall Suffk 91 H4
Tunstall Sundld 181 J8
Tunstead Derbys 132 B5
Tunstead Norfk 122 F7
Tunstead Milton Derbys 131 K4
Tunworth Hants 35 K1
Tupsley Herefs 80 C7
Turgis Green Hants 49 G7
Turkdean Gloucs 65 G4
Tur Langton Leics 100 F4
Turleigh Wilts 46 A6
Turleygreen Shrops 97 H6
Turn Lancs 140 B4
Turnastone Herefs 79 L7
Turnberry S Ayrs 182 F2
Turnchapel C Plym 6 F4
Turnditch Derbys 116 A2
Turner Green Lancs 139 J2
Turner's Green E Susx 23 L3
Turner's Green Warwks 82 E2
Turners Hill W Susx 38 A6
Turners Puddle Dorset 16 F4
Turnford Herts 69 K6
Turnhouse C Edin 211 G4
Turnworth Dorset 16 F1
Turriff Abers 268 C6
Turton Bottoms Bl w D 139 L4
Turves Cambs 103 G4
Turvey Bed 85 J5
Turville Bucks 49 J1
Turville Heath Bucks 49 H1
Turweston Bucks 84 B7
Tushielaw Inn Border 187 L3
Tutbury Staffs 115 L6
Tutnall Worcs 82 A1
Tutshill Gloucs 63 G8
Tuttington Norfk 122 E6
Tutts Clump W Berk 48 E5
Tutwell Cnwll 11 M7
Tuxford Notts 134 E5
Twatt Ork 275 b3
Twatt Shet 281 d6
Twechar E Duns 209 J4
Tweedbank Border 201 H6
Tweedmouth Nthumb 202 F3
Tweedsmuir Border 187 G1
Twelveheads Cnwll 4 B6
Twelve Oaks E Susx 24 C3
Twemlow Green Ches E 130 F6
Twenty Lincs 118 F7
Twerton BaNES 45 L6
Twickenham Gt Lon 50 F4
Twigworth Gloucs 64 B3
Twineham W Susx 22 C3
Twineham Green W Susx 22 C3
Twinhoe BaNES 45 L7
Twinstead Essex 89 H7
Twitchen Devon 28 D5
Twitchen Shrops 95 J2
Twitham Kent 41 H4
Two Bridges Devon 12 E7
Two Dales Derbys 132 E7
Two Gates Staffs 99 G3
Two Mile Ash W Susx 37 H5

Two Mile Oak Cross Devon 8 C1
Two Pots Devon 27 J2
Two Waters Herts 68 D6
Twycross Leics 99 J2
Twyford Bucks 67 G2
Twyford Hants 35 G6
Twyford Leics 100 F2
Twyford Lincs 118 B6
Twyford Norfk 121 M6
Twyford Wokham 49 J4
Twyford Common Herefs 80 C8
Twyn-carno Caerph 61 H5
Twynholm D & G 175 G4
Twyning Gloucs 81 K7
Twynllanan Carmth 59 L4
Twyn-yr-Odyn V Glam 43 H7
Twyn-y-Sheriff Mons 62 E6
Twywell N Nthn 101 L7
Tyberton Herefs 79 M7
Tyburn Birm 98 E5
Tycroes Carmth 57 H3
Ty Croes IoA 124 F5
Tycrwyn Powys 111 L7
Tydd Gote Lincs 120 A7
Tydd St Giles Cambs 119 M8
Tydd St Mary Lincs 119 M7
Tye Hants 20 B6
Tye Green Essex 70 D2
Tye Green Essex 71 J4
Tye Green Essex 88 B8
Tyersal C Brad 141 J1
Tyldesley Wigan 139 K7
Tyler Hill Kent 40 F3
Tylers Green Bucks 67 L8
Tyler's Green Essex 70 D6
Tylers Green Surrey 51 K8
Tylorstown Rhondd 42 F3
Tylwch Powys 93 L7
Ty-nant Conwy 111 J3
Ty-nant Gwynd 111 H6
Tyncelyn Cerdgn 77 H3
Tyndrum Stirlg 218 E1
Ty'n-dwr Denbgs 112 C3
Tyneham Dorset 17 G6
Tynemouth N Tyne 181 J5
Tyne Tunnel S Tyne 181 H5
Tynewydd Rhondd 60 E7
Tyninghame E Loth 212 D3
Tynron D & G 185 K4
Ty'n-y-bryn Rhondd 42 F4
Ty'n-y-coedcae Caerph 43 K4
Tynygongl IoA 125 J3
Tynygraig Cerdgn 77 J1
Ty'n-y-Groes Conwy 126 F5
Tyn-y-nant Rhondd 43 G4
Tyrie Abers 269 G4
Tyringham M Keyn 85 G6
Tyseley Birm 98 E6
Tythegston Brdgnd 42 C6
Tytherington Ches E 131 H4
Tytherington S Glos 45 K1
Tytherington Somset 32 C2
Tytherington Wilts 32 F3
Tytherleigh Devon 15 H2
Tytherton Lucas Wilts 46 D4
Tyttenhanger Herts 68 F6
Tywardreath Cnwll 5 J4
Tywardreath Highway Cnwll 5 J4
Tywyn Conwy 126 F4
Tywyn Gwynd 92 C3

U

Ubbeston Green Suffk 91 H1
Ubley BaNES 45 G7
Uckerby N York 160 C2
Uckfield E Susx 23 H3
Uckinghall Worcs 81 K7
Uckington Gloucs 64 C2
Uckington Shrops 96 D2
Uddingston S Lans 209 J6
Uddington S Lans 198 E2
Udimore E Susx 24 F3
Udny Green Abers 256 F6
Udny Station Abers 257 G6
Uffcott Wilts 47 H3
Uffculme Devon 29 K8
Uffington Lincs 102 B2
Uffington Oxon 47 L1
Uffington Shrops 96 C1
Ufford C Pete 102 B3
Ufford Suffk 91 G5
Ufton Warwks 83 J3
Ufton Nervet W Berk 48 F5
Ugadale Ag & B 194 B5
Ugborough Devon 7 K4
Uggeshall Suffk 107 J7
Ugglebarnby N York 162 F1

Ughill Sheff 132 E2
Ugley Essex 70 D2
Ugley Green Essex 70 D2
Ugthorpe N York 171 J8
Uibhist A Deas W Isls 283 c10
Uibhist A Tuath W Isls 283 b8
Uig Ag & B 224 F4
Uig Highld 258 B6
Uig Highld 258 F4
Uig W Isls 282 d3
Uigshader Highld 259 G7
Uisken Ag & B 226 D8
Ulbster Highld 280 D7
Ulcat Row W & F 165 L6
Ulceby Lincs 137 H5
Ulceby N Linc 144 E5
Ulceby Skitter N Linc 144 E5
Ulcombe Kent 39 L4
Uldale Cumb 165 H3
Uley Gloucs 62 M7
Ulgham Nthumb 191 J7
Ullapool Highld 271 H2
Ullenhall Warwks 82 D2
Ullenwood Gloucs 64 D4
Ulleskelf N York 151 H7
Ullesthorpe Leics 100 B6
Ulley Rothm 133 J2
Ullingswick Herefs 80 E5
Ullock Cumb 164 E6
Ullswater W & F 166 A6
Ulnes Walton Lancs 139 G4
Ulpha Cumb 156 B4
Ulpha W & F 157 G6
Ulrome E R Yk 153 J4
Ulsta Shet 281 e4
Ulting Wick Essex 71 K5
Ulva Ag & B 226 D4
Ulverley Green Solhll 98 E7
Ulverston W & F 156 C7
Ulwell Dorset 17 K6
Ulzieside D & G 185 J1
Umberleigh Devon 27 L0
Unapool Highld 271 H2
Underbarrow W & F 157 G4
Under Burnmouth Border 179 M0
Undercliffe C Brad 141 J1
Underdale Shrops 96 B1
Underling Green Kent 39 J4
Underriver Kent 38 E3
Underwood Newpt 44 D1
Underwood Notts 116 D2
Undley Suffk 104 D7
Undy Mons 44 E2
Union Mills IoM 154 e6
Union Street E Susx 39 H7
Unst Shet 281 f2
Unstone Derbys 133 G4
Unstone Green Derbys 133 G4
Unthank Cumb 165 L1
Unthank Derbys 132 F4
Unthank Nthumb 202 F3
Unthank W & F 166 B3
Unthank W & F 166 E3
Upavon Wilts 47 H7
Up Cerne Dorset 16 C2
Upchurch Kent 53 H5
Upcott Devon 28 D5
Upcott Herefs 79 K5
Upend Cambs 88 D3
Up Exe Devon 13 L2
Upgate Norfk 122 C7
Upgate Street Norfk 106 C7
Upgate Street Norfk 106 F5
Uphall Dorset 16 A2
Uphall W Loth 210 E5
Upham Devon 13 K1
Upham Hants 35 H6
Uphampton Herefs 79 M3
Uphampton Worcs 81 J2
Uphill N Som 44 C7
Up Holland Lancs 139 G6
Uplawmoor E Rens 208 D8
Upleadon Gloucs 63 L2
Upleatham R & Cl 170 E6
Uplees Kent 40 C2
Uploders Dorset 15 L4
Uplowman Devon 29 J7
Uplyme Devon 15 H4
Up Marden W Susx 20 C4
Upminster Gt Lon 52 C2
Up Mudford Somset 31 J7
Up Nately Hants 49 G6
Upottery Devon 14 E1
Upper Affcot Shrops 95 K6
Upper Arley Worcs 97 H7
Upper Arncott Oxon 66 F4
Upper Astrop W Nthn 83 L7
Upper Badcall Highld 276 B7
Upper Basildon W Berk 48 F4
Upper Batley Kirk 141 K3

Upper Beeding W Susx 22 B5
Upper Benefield N Nthn 101 L5
Upper Bentley Worcs 82 B2
Upper Bighouse Highld 278 F5
Upper Birchwood Derbys 133 J8
Upper Boat Rhondd 43 H4
Upper Boddington W Nthn 83 L5
Upper Borth Cerdgn 92 D5
Upper Brailes Warwks 83 G7
Upper Breinton Herefs 80 B7
Upper Broadheath Worcs 81 J4
Upper Broughton Notts 117 J6
Upper Bucklebury W Berk 48 D5
Upper Burgate Hants 33 K7
Upper Bush Medway 52 E5
Upperby Cumb 177 L8
Upper Caldecote C Beds 86 D6
Upper Canada N Som 44 D7
Upper Canterton Hants 18 D1
Upper Catesby W Nthn 83 M3
Upper Catshill Worcs 98 B8
Upper Chapel Powys 79 D7
Upper Cheddon Somset 30 C5
Upper Chicksgrove Wilts 33 G5
Upper Chute Wilts 47 L8
Upper Clapton Gt Lon 51 K2
Upper Clatford Hants 34 D2
Upper Coberley Gloucs 64 E4
Upper Cotton Staffs 115 G6
Upper Cound Shrops 96 C2
Upper Cudworth Barns 142 B6
Upper Cumberworth Kirk 141 K6
Upper Dallachy Moray 267 G6
Upper Deal Kent 41 K5
Upper Dean Bed 85 L2
Upper Denby Kirk 141 K6
Upper Denton Cumb 178 C6
Upper Dicker E Susx 23 J5
Upper Dinchope Shrops 95 L6
Upper Dounreay Highld 279 H3
Upper Dovercourt Essex 73 K6
Upper Brailes/Drumbane Stirlg .218 I6
Upper Dunsforth N York 150 F3
Upper Eashing Surrey 36 E2
Upper Egleton Herefs 80 E6
Upper Elkstone Staffs 131 I7
Upper Ellastone Staffs 115 J3
Upper End Derbys 132 B4
Upper Enham Hants 34 E1
Upper Farmcote Shrops 97 H5
Upper Farringdon Hants 35 L4
Upper Framilode Gloucs 63 L5
Upper Froyle Hants 35 M2
Upperglen Highld 258 E6
Upper Godney Somset 31 J4
Upper Gravenhurst C Beds 86 C8
Upper Green Mons 62 D3
Upper Green Suffk 88 E2
Upper Green W Berk 48 A6
Upper Grove Common Herefs 63 H2
Upper Hackney Derbys 132 F7
Upper Hale Surrey 36 B1
Upper Halliford Surrey 50 E5
Upper Halling Medway 52 E6
Upper Hambleton Rutlnd 101 K2
Upper Harbledown Kent 40 F4
Upper Hardres Court Kent 40 F5
Upper Hardwick Herefs 79 M4
Upper Hartfield E Susx 38 C6
Upper Hartshay Derbys 116 C2
Upper Hatherley Gloucs 64 D3
Upper Hatton Staffs 114 C4
Upper Haugh Rothm 142 C8
Upper Hayton Shrops 96 C7
Upper Heaton Kirk 141 J4
Upper Helmsley N York 151 L4
Upper Hergest Herefs 79 J4
Upper Heyford Oxon 66 D2
Upper Heyford W Nthn 84 C2
Upper Hill Herefs 80 B4
Upper Hockenden Kent 52 B5
Upper Hopton Kirk 141 K4
Upper Howsell Worcs 81 H5
Upper Hulme Staffs 131 K7
Upper Ifold Surrey 36 F4
Upper Inglesham Swindn 65 J7
Upper Kilcott Gloucs 46 A1
Upper Killay Swans 57 G6
Upper Kinchrackine Ag & B 217 J2
Upper Knockando Moray 254 D3
Upper Lambourn W Berk 47 L3
Upper Landywood Staffs 98 C2
Upper Langford N Som 44 F7
Upper Langwith Derbys 133 K5
Upper Largo Fife 223 G6
Upper Layham Suffk 90 B7
Upper Leigh Staffs 115 G4
Upper Littleton N Som 45 H6
Upper Lochton Abers 244 F4

Upper Longdon Staffs 115 H8
Upper Ludstone Shrops 97 H4
Upper Lybster Highld 275 H1
Upper Lydbrook Gloucs 63 J4
Upper Lyde Herefs 80 C6
Upper Lye Herefs 79 M2
Upper Maes-coed Herefs 79 L8
Upper Marham Norfk 104 E2
Upper Midhope Sheff 141 K7
Uppermill Oldham 140 F6
Upper Milton Worcs 81 J1
Upper Minety Wilts 46 E1
Upper Moor Worcs 81 M5
Upper Moor Side Leeds 141 K2
Upper Mulben Moray 267 G6
Upper Netchwood Shrops 96 E5
Upper Nobut Staffs 115 G4
Upper Norwood W Susx 20 F3
Upper Oddington Gloucs 65 J2
Upper Padley Derbys 132 E4
Upper Pennington Hants 19 K4
Upper Poppleton C York 151 J5
Upper Quinton Warwks 82 E6
Upper Ratley Hants 34 D6
Upper Rissington Gloucs 65 J3
Upper Rochford Worcs 80 E2
Upper Ruscoe D & G 174 E3
Upper Sapey Herefs 80 F3
Upper Saxondale Notts 117 H4
Upper Seagry Wilts 46 D3
Upper Shelton C Beds 85 K6
Upper Sheringham Norfk 122 C3
Upper Skelmorlie N Ayrs 207 K5
Upper Slaughter Gloucs 65 H3
Upper Soudley Gloucs 63 K5
Upper Spond Herefs 79 K4
Upper Standen Kent 41 H7
Upper Staploe Bed 86 C3
Upper Stoke Norfk 106 E3
Upper Stondon C Beds 86 C8
Upper Stowe W Nthn 84 C4
Upper Street Hants 33 K7
Upper Street Norfk 106 D7
Upper Street Norfk 123 G7
Upper Street Norfk 123 G8
Upper Street Suffk 88 F5
Upper Street Suffk 90 C5
Upper Street Suffk 90 D8
Upper Strensham Worcs 81 K7
Upper Sundon C Beds 68 D2
Upper Swell Gloucs 65 H2
Upper Tankersley Barns 142 A7
Upper Tean Staffs 115 G4
Upperthong Kirk 141 H6
Upperthorpe Derbys 133 J4
Upperthorpe N Linc 143 J7
Upper Threapwood Ches W 113 G2
Upperton W Susx 36 E6
Upper Town Derbys 115 L1
Uppertown Derbys 132 F6
Upper Town Dur 168 D3
Upper Town Herefs 80 D5
Uppertown Highld 280 D1
Upper Town N Som 45 G6
Upper Town Suffk 89 J2
Upper Tumble Carmth 59 G6
Upper Tysoe Warwks 83 H6
Upper Ufford Suffk 91 G4
Upperup Gloucs 64 F7
Upper Upham Wilts 47 J3
Upper Upnor Medway 53 G5
Upper Victoria Angus 234 E8
Upper Vobster Somset 32 B1
Upper Wardington Oxon 83 L6
Upper Weald M Keyn 84 F7
Upper Weedon W Nthn 84 B3
Upper Welland Worcs 81 H7
Upper Wellingham E Susx 23 G7
Upper Weston BaNES 45 L5
Upper Weybread Suffk 106 F7
Upper Wick Worcs 81 J5
Upper Wield Hants 35 K3
Upper Winchendon Bucks 67 H4
Upperwood Derbys 132 F8
Upper Woodford Wilts 33 K3
Upper Woolhampton W Berk 48 E5
Upper Wootton Hants 48 E7
Upper Wraxall Wilts 46 A4
Upper Wyche Worcs 81 H6
Uppincott Devon 13 L2
Uppingham Rutlnd 101 J3
Uppington Dorset 17 K2
Uppington Shrops 96 D2
Upsall N York 161 G5
Upsettlington Border 202 D4
Upshire Essex 69 L7
Up Somborne Hants 34 E4
Upstreet Kent 41 H3
Up Sydling Dorset 16 B2

Upthorpe Suffk 89 K1
Upton Bucks 67 J5
Upton C Pete 102 C3
Upton Cambs 102 D7
Upton Ches W 129 J6
Upton Cnwll 11 J6
Upton Cnwll 11 K8
Upton Cumb 165 K3
Upton Devon 7 K6
Upton Devon 14 C2
Upton Dorset 16 E6
Upton Dorset 17 J4
Upton E R Yk 153 J5
Upton Halton 129 L2
Upton Hants 34 E7
Upton Hants 47 M7
Upton Leics 99 K3
Upton Lincs 135 H2
Upton Norfk 107 H1
Upton Notts 117 J1
Upton Notts 134 F4
Upton Oxon 48 D3
Upton Pembks 55 G6
Upton R & Cl 171 G6
Upton Slough 50 B3
Upton Somset 29 H5
Upton Somset 31 G5
Upton W Nthn 84 D3
Upton Wakefd 142 D5
Upton Warwks 82 D4
Upton Wilts 32 E4
Upton Wirral 129 G2
Upton Bishop Herefs 63 K2
Upton Cheyney S Glos 45 K5
Upton Cressett Shrops 96 E5
Upton Crews Herefs 63 J2
Upton Cross Cnwll 11 K8
Upton End C Beds 86 C8
Upton Grey Hants 35 L1
Upton Heath Ches W 129 J5
Upton Hellions Devon 13 K2
Upton Lovell Wilts 33 G3
Upton Magna Shrops 96 C1
Upton Noble Somset 32 B3
Upton Pyne Devon 13 L3
Upton St Leonards Gloucs 64 B4
Upton Scudamore Wilts 32 E1
Upton Snodsbury Worcs 81 L4
Upton Towans Cnwll 2 F3
Upton-upon-Severn Worcs 81 K7
Upton Warren Worcs 81 L2
Upwaltham W Susx 20 F4
Upware Cambs 87 L1
Upwell Norfk 103 K3
Upwey Dorset 16 C5
Upwick Green Herts 70 C5
Upwood Cambs 102 E6
Urchfont Wilts 46 F7
Urdimarsh Herefs 80 C5
Ure Bank N York 150 D1
Urlay Nook S on T 169 L7
Urmston Traffd 130 E1
Urpeth Dur 181 G7
Urquhart Moray 266 F4
Urra N York 161 J2
Urray Highld 250 E1
Ury Abers 245 J6
Uryside Abers 256 D7
Usan Angus 235 H4
Ushaw Moor Dur 169 G2
Usk Mons 62 D7
Usselby Lincs 136 A1
Usworth Sundld 181 H7
Utkinton Ches W 130 A6
Utley C Brad 149 J2
Uton Devon 13 J3
Utterby Lincs 136 F1
Uttoxeter Staffs 115 H6
Uwchmynydd Gwynd 108 B6
Uxbridge Gt Lon 50 D2
Uyeasound Shet 281 I2
Uzmaston Pembks 54 F4

V

Vale Guern 9 k2
Valley IoA 124 E4
Valley End Surrey 50 B6
Valley Truckle Cnwll 10 F6
Valtos Highld 259 J4
Valtos W Isls 282 e3
Vange Essex 52 F2
Varteg Torfn 61 L6
Vatsetter Shet 281 e3
Vatten Highld 258 D7
Vaynor Myr Td 61 G5
Vazon Bay Guern 9 i2

Veensgarth Shet....281 e6
Velindre Powys....79 H7
Yellow Somset....29 K3
Velly Devon....26 E6
Venngreen Devon....26 F8
Vennington Shrops....95 H2
Venn Ottery Devon....14 C4
Venny Tedburn Devon....13 J3
Venterdon Cnwll....11 L7
Ventnor IoW....19 J8
Venton Devon....7 H3
Vernham Dean Hants....47 M7
Vernham Street Hants....47 M7
Vernolds Common Shrops....95 L7
Verwood Dorset....17 L1
Veryan Cnwll....4 E7
Veryan Green Cnwll....4 F6
Vicarage Devon....14 E5
Vickerstown W & F....146 C2
Victoria Barns....141 J6
Victoria Blae G....61 J5
Victoria Cnwll....5 G3
Vidlin Shet....281 e5
Viewfield Moray....266 F3
Viewpark N Lans....209 J6
Vigo Kent....52 D6
Village de Putron Guern....9 k3
Ville la Bas Jersey....9 a1
Villiaze Guern....9 i3
Vinehall Street E Susx....24 D3
Vines Cross E Susx....23 K4
Virginia Water Surrey....50 C5
Virginstow Devon....11 M4
Vobster Somset....32 B1
Voe Shet....281 d5
Vowchurch Herefs....79 L7
Vulcan Village St Hel....130 B1

W

Waberthwaite Cumb....155 K4
Wackerfield Dur....168 F6
Wacton Norfk....106 D5
Wadborough Worcs....81 K5
Waddesdon Bucks....67 H4
Waddeton Devon....8 C3
Waddicar Sefton....138 E7
Waddingham Lincs....144 B8
Waddington Lancs....148 C7
Waddington Lincs....135 K6
Waddon Devon....13 K6
Waddon Dorset....16 B5
Waddon Gt Lon....51 J6
Wadebridge Cnwll....10 D8
Wadeford Somset....30 D8
Wadenhoe N Nthn....101 M6
Wadesmill Herts....69 K4
Wadhurst E Susx....39 G7
Wadshelf Derbys....132 F5
Wadswick Wilts....46 B5
Wadworth Donc....142 F8
Waen Denbgs....127 K7
Waen Denbgs....128 D6
Waen Powys....112 C7
Waen Fach Powys....112 B8
Waen-pentir Gwynd....125 K6
Waen-wen Gwynd....125 K6
Wagbeach Shrops....95 J3
Wainfelin Torfn....62 B6
Wainfleet All Saints Lincs....137 J7
Wainfleet Bank Lincs....137 J7
Wainfleet St Mary Lincs....137 J8
Wainford Norfk....107 G5
Wainhouse Corner Cnwll....11 H3
Wainscott Medway....52 F5
Wain's Hill N Som....44 E5
Wainstalls Calder....141 G2
Waitby W & F....158 C1
Waithe Lincs....145 H7
Wakefield Wakefd....142 A4
Wake Green Birm....98 E6
Wakerley N Nthn....101 L3
Wakes Colne Essex....72 C2
Walberswick Suffk....107 K8
Walberton W Susx....21 G5
Walbottle N u Ty....180 E5
Walbutt D & G....175 J1
Walby Cumb....178 B6
Walcombe Somset....31 J2
Walcot Lincs....118 E4
Walcot N Linc....143 M3
Walcot Shrops....95 J6
Walcot Shrops....96 D1
Walcot Swindn....47 H2
Walcote Leics....100 C6
Walcote Warwks....82 D4
Walcot Green Norfk....106 C7
Walcott Lincs....136 B8

Walcott Norfk....123 G5
Walden N York....159 H6
Walden Head N York....159 H6
Walden Stubbs N York....142 E4
Walderslade Medway....53 G6
Walderton W Susx....20 C5
Walditch Dorset....15 L4
Waldley Derbys....115 J4
Waldridge Dur....169 H1
Waldringfield Suffk....91 G6
Waldron E Susx....23 J3
Wales Rothm....133 J3
Wales Somset....31 K6
Walesby Lincs....136 B1
Walesby Notts....134 D5
Walford Herefs....63 H3
Walford Herefs....79 M1
Walford Shrops....113 G7
Walford Staffs....114 C5
Walford Heath Shrops....113 G7
Walgherton Ches E....113 M2
Walgrave W Nthn....84 F1
Walhampton Hants....18 E4
Walkden Salfd....139 L7
Walker N u Ty....181 H6
Walkerburn Border....200 D5
Walker Fold Lancs....148 B7
Walkeringham Notts....134 F1
Walkerith Lincs....134 F1
Walkern Herts....69 H2
Walker's Green Herefs....80 C5
Walker's Heath Birm....98 D7
Walkerton Fife....222 C7
Walkford BCP....18 C5
Walkhampton Devon....7 G1
Walkington E R Yk....152 F8
Walkley Sheff....133 G2
Walk Mill Lancs....140 C2
Walkwood Worcs....82 B2
Wall Nthumb....179 L5
Wall Staffs....98 E2
Wallacetown S Ayrs....183 H2
Wallacetown S Ayrs....196 C6
Wallands Park E Susx....22 F5
Wallasey Wirral....129 G1
Wallasey (Kingsway) Tunnel
  Wirral....129 H2
Wall End Herefs....80 B4
Wallend Medway....53 J4
Wall End W & F....156 B6
Waller's Green Herefs....80 F7
Wallhead Cumb....178 B6
Wall Heath Dudley....97 K5
Wall Houses Nthumb....180 C5
Wallingford Oxon....48 F1
Wallington Gt Lon....51 H6
Wallington Hants....19 K2
Wallington Herts....86 F8
Wallington Heath Wsall....98 C3
Wallis Pembks....75 G7
Wallisdown BCP....17 L4
Walliswood Surrey....37 H3
Walls Shet....281 c6
Wallsend N Tyne....181 H5
Wallthwaite W & F....165 K5
Wall under Haywood Shrops....96 C5
Wallyford E Loth....211 L4
Walmer Kent....41 L5
Walmer Bridge Lancs....138 F3
Walmersley Bury....140 B5
Walmestone Kent....41 H3
Walmley Birm....98 F5
Walmley Ash Birm....98 F5
Walmsgate Lincs....137 G4
Walney W & F....146 C2
Walpole Somset....30 D3
Walpole Suffk....107 H8
Walpole Cross Keys Norfk....120 B7
Walpole Highway Norfk....120 B8
Walpole St Andrew Norfk....120 B8
Walpole St Peter Norfk....120 B8
Walrow Somset....30 E2
Walsall Wsall....98 C4
Walsall Wood Wsall....98 D3
Walsden Calder....140 D3
Walsgrave on Sowe Covtry....99 K7
Walsham le Willows Suffk....89 K1
Walshaw Bury....140 A5
Walshford N York....150 F5
Walsoken Norfk....103 K1
Walston S Lans....199 H4
Walsworth Herts....69 G1
Walter's Ash Bucks....67 K7
Walters Green Kent....38 D5
Walterston V Glam....43 G7
Walterstone Herefs....62 D2
Waltham Kent....40 E5
Waltham NE Lin....145 H7
Waltham Abbey Essex....69 K7
Waltham Chase Hants....35 H7

Waltham Cross Herts....69 K7
Waltham on the Wolds Leics....117 L6
Waltham St Lawrence W & M....49 K4
Waltham's Cross Essex....71 G1
Walthamstow Gt Lon....51 K1
Walton C Pete....102 D3
Walton Cumb....178 C6
Walton Derbys....133 G6
Walton Leeds....150 F6
Walton Leics....100 D6
Walton M Keyn....85 H7
Walton Powys....79 J3
Walton Shrops....95 L7
Walton Somset....31 G4
Walton Staffs....114 D5
Walton Staffs....114 D6
Walton Suffk....91 G8
Walton W Susx....20 D6
Walton Wakefd....142 A4
Walton Warwks....83 G4
Walton Wrekin....113 K7
Walton Cardiff Gloucs....64 C1
Walton East Pembks....55 H2
Walton Elm Dorset....32 C7
Walton Grounds W Nthn....83 L8
Walton Highway Norfk....103 K1
Walton-in-Gordano N Som....44 E4
Walton-le-Dale Lancs....139 H2
Walton-on-Thames Surrey....50 E5
Walton-on-the-Hill Staffs....114 F7
Walton-on-the-Hill Surrey....51 G7
Walton-on-the-Naze Essex....73 K3
Walton on the Wolds Leics....117 G7
Walton-on-Trent Derbys....115 L7
Walton Park N Som....44 E4
Walton West Pembks....54 D4
Walwen Flints....128 D4
Walwen Flints....128 E4
Walwen Flints....128 E5
Walwick Nthumb....179 L5
Walworth Darltn....169 G7
Walworth Gt Lon....51 J3
Walworth Gate Darltn....169 G6
Walwyn's Castle Pembks....54 E4
Wambrook Somset....15 G1
Wampool Cumb....177 H7
Wanborough Surrey....36 D1
Wanborough Swindn....47 J2
Wandon End Herts....68 E3
Wandsworth Gt Lon....51 H4
Wangford Suffk....107 J7
Wanlip Leics....100 D1
Wanlockhead D & G....186 C4
Wannock E Susx....23 K6
Wansford C Pete....102 B3
Wansford E R Yk....153 G2
Wanshurst Green Kent....39 J4
Wanstead Gt Lon....51 L1
Wanstrow Somset....32 B3
Wanswell Gloucs....63 K6
Wantage Oxon....48 B1
Wants Green Worcs....81 H4
Wapley S Glos....45 L3
Wappenbury Warwks....83 J2
Wappenham W Nthn....84 C6
Warbleton E Susx....23 K4
Warborough Oxon....66 F8
Warboys Cambs....102 F7
Warbreck Bpool....146 F8
Warbstow Cnwll....11 H4
Warburton Traffd....130 D2
Warcop W & F....167 H7
Warden Kent....53 M5
Warden Nthumb....179 L5
Ward End Birm....98 E5
Warden Street C Beds....86 C6
Ward Green Suffk....90 B2
Ward Green Cross Lancs....148 A8
Wardhedges C Beds....85 L8
Wardington Oxon....83 L6
Wardle Ches E....130 B8
Wardle Rochdl....140 D4
Wardley Gatesd....181 H6
Wardley Rutlnd....101 H3
Wardley Salfd....140 A7
Wardlow Derbys....132 D5
Wardsend Ches E....131 J3
Wardy Hill Cambs....103 K7
Ware Herts....69 K4
Wareham Dorset....17 H5
Warehorne Kent....25 J1
Warenford Nthumb....203 J7
Waren Mill Nthumb....203 J6
Warenton Nthumb....203 H7
Wareside Herts....69 K4
Waresley Cambs....86 E4
Waresley Worcs....81 J1
Ware Street Kent....39 K2
Warfield Br For....49 L4
Warfleet Devon....8 C5

Wargate Lincs....119 H5
Wargrave Wokham....49 J3
Warham Herefs....80 B7
Warham Norfk....121 L3
Wark Nthumb....179 K3
Wark Nthumb....202 E5
Warkleigh Devon....27 M6
Warkton N Nthn....101 K7
Warkworth Nthumb....191 K5
Warkworth N Nthn....83 L7
Warlaby N York....160 E4
Warland Calder....140 E4
Warleggan Cnwll....5 K1
Warleigh BaNES....46 A6
Warley Town Calder....141 G3
Warlingham Surrey....51 K7
Warmbrook Derbys....115 M1
Warmfield Wakefd....142 B4
Warmingham Ches E....130 D7
Warmington N Nthn....102 B5
Warmington Warwks....83 K5
Warminster Wilts....32 E2
Warmley S Glos....45 K4
Warmsworth Donc....142 E7
Warmwell Dorset....16 D7
Warndon Worcs....81 K4
Warnford Hants....35 J6
Warnham W Susx....37 J4
Warningcamp W Susx....21 H5
Warninglid W Susx....37 K5
Warren Ches E....131 H5
Warren Pembks....54 F7
Warrenby R & Cl....170 D5
Warrenhill S Lans....198 F5
Warren Row W & M....49 K3
Warren's Green Herts....69 H2
Warren Street Kent....40 E5
Warrington M Keyn....85 H4
Warrington Warrtn....130 B2
Warriston C Edin....211 H4
Warsash Hants....19 H2
Warslow Staffs....132 B7
Warsop Vale Notts....133 L6
Warter E R Yk....152 D5
Warthermaske N York....160 B6
Warthill N York....151 L5
Wartling E Susx....24 B5
Wartnaby Leics....117 J7
Warton Lancs....138 E2
Warton Lancs....147 K2
Warton Nthumb....190 E5
Warton Warwks....99 H3
Warwick Warwks....83 G2
Warwick Bridge Cumb....178 B7
Warwick-on-Eden Cumb....178 B7
Warwick Services Warwks....83 H4
Warwicksland Cumb....178 B3
Wasbister Ork....275 c3
Wasdale Head Cumb....156 B1
Wash Derbys....131 L3
Washall Green Herts....70 C1
Washaway Cnwll....5 H1
Washbourne Devon....8 B4
Washbrook Somset....30 F1
Washbrook Suffk....90 D6
Washfield Devon....29 G7
Washfold N York....159 J2
Washford Somset....29 J3
Washford Pyne Devon....28 E8
Washingborough Lincs....135 L5
Washington Sundld....181 H7
Washington W Susx....21 J4
Washington Services Gatesd....181 G7
Washwood Heath Birm....98 E5
Wasing W Berk....48 E6
Waskerley Dur....168 D2
Wasperton Warwks....83 G3
Wasps Nest Lincs....135 M6
Wass N York....161 J6
Wast Water Cumb....155 L2
Watchet Somset....29 K2
Watchfield Oxon....47 K1
Watchfield Somset....30 E2
Watchgate W & F....157 H3
Watchill Cumb....165 G2
Watcombe Torbay....8 D2
Watendlath Cumb....165 J7
Water Devon....13 H6
Water Lancs....140 C3
Waterbeach Cambs....87 K2
Waterbeach W Susx....20 E5
Waterbeck D & G....177 H3
Waterden Norfk....121 J3
Water Eaton Oxon....66 D5
Water Eaton Staffs....97 K1
Water End Bed....86 C5
Water End Bed....86 C5
Water End C Beds....85 L7
Waterend Cumb....164 F6
Water End E R Yk....152 B8

Water End Essex....88 B7
Water End Herts....68 D5
Water End Herts....69 G6
Waterfall Staffs....115 H1
Waterfoot Ag & B....194 C3
Waterfoot E Rens....208 F7
Waterfoot Lancs....140 C3
Waterford Herts....69 J4
Water Fryston Wakefd....142 D2
Watergate Cnwll....11 G6
Waterhead W & F....156 E2
Waterheads Border....200 B3
Waterhouses Dur....168 F3
Waterhouses Staffs....115 H2
Wateringbury Kent....39 H3
Waterlane Gloucs....64 D6
Waterloo Cnwll....10 F8
Waterloo Derbys....133 H4
Waterloo Herefs....79 L5
Waterloo Highld....247 K4
Waterloo N Lans....209 L6
Waterloo Norfk....122 C8
Waterloo P & K....223 G7
Waterloo Pembks....55 G6
Waterloo Sefton....138 C8
Waterloo Cross Devon....29 J8
Waterloo Port Gwynd....125 J6
Waterlooville Hants....19 M2
Watermead Bucks....67 K4
Watermillock W & F....166 B6
Water Newton Cambs....102 C4
Water Orton Warwks....98 F5
Waterperry Oxon....66 F6
Waterrow Somset....29 J6
Watersfield W Susx....21 G4
Waterside Bl w D....139 L3
Waterside Bucks....68 B7
Waterside Cumb....165 H2
Waterside Donc....143 H5
Waterside E Ayrs....184 C1
Waterside E Ayrs....196 F2
Waterside E Duns....209 H4
Water's Nook Bolton....139 K8
Waterstein Highld....258 A7
Waterstock Oxon....66 F6
Waterston Pembks....54 F3
Water Stratford Bucks....84 C8
Water Street Neath....42 B5
Waters Upton Wrekin....113 K7
Water Yeat W & F....156 D5
Watford Herts....68 E7
Watford W Nthn....84 B2
Watford Gap Services W Nthn....84 B2
Wath N York....149 L2
Wath N York....160 D7
Wath upon Dearne Rothm....142 C7
Watlington Norfk....104 C1
Watlington Oxon....67 G8
Watnall Notts....116 E2
Watten Highld....280 B5
Wattisfield Suffk....105 K8
Wattisham Suffk....89 K5
Watton Dorset....15 K4
Watton E R Yk....152 F6
Watton Norfk....105 J3
Watton-at-Stone Herts....69 J3
Watton Green Norfk....105 J3
Wattons Green Essex....70 D8
Wattston N Lans....209 K6
Wattstown Rhondd....42 F3
Wattsville Caerph....43 K3
Wauldby E R Yk....144 B2
Waulkmill Abers....244 K5
Waunarlwydd Swans....57 H6
Waun Fach Powys....61 J2
Waunfawr Cerdgn....92 D7
Waunfawr Gwynd....125 J7
Waungron Swans....57 G4
Waunlwyd Blae G....61 J5
Wavendon M Keyn....85 H7
Waverbridge Cumb....165 H1
Waverley Rothm....133 H2
Waverton Ches W....129 K7
Waverton Cumb....165 H1
Wawne E R Yk....153 H8
Waxham Norfk....123 J6
Waxholme E R Yk....145 J2
Way Kent....41 K2
Waye Devon....13 H8
Wayford Somset....15 J1
Waytown Dorset....15 L3
Way Village Devon....13 L1
Way Wick N Som....44 D6
Weacombe Somset....29 K3
Weald Oxon....65 L6
Wealdstone Gt Lon....50 F2
Weardley Leeds....150 D7
Weare Somset....44 E8
Weare Giffard Devon....27 H6
Wearhead Dur....167 K3

Wearne Somset....30 F5
Weasdale W & F....158 B2
Weasenham All Saints Norfk....121 J7
Weasenham St Peter Norfk....121 J7
Weaste Salfd....140 B8
Weatheroak Hill Worcs....98 D8
Weaverham Ches W....130 B5
Weaverslake Staffs....115 J7
Weaverthorpe N York....152 E2
Webbington Somset....44 D7
Webb's Heath S Glos....45 K4
Webheath Worcs....82 K2
Webton Herefs....80 A7
Wedderlairs Abers....256 F5
Wedding Hall Fold N York....149 G6
Weddington Kent....41 J3
Weddington Warwks....99 K5
Wedhampton Wilts....46 F7
Wedmore Somset....31 G1
Wednesbury Sandw....98 C4
Wednesfield Wolves....97 L3
Weecar Notts....135 G6
Weedon Bucks....67 K3
Weedon Bec W Nthn....84 C3
Weedon Lois W Nthn....84 B6
Weeford Staffs....98 F3
Week Devon....8 A2
Week Devon....27 K5
Week Devon....28 C7
Weeke Devon....13 H2
Weeke Hants....34 F5
Weekley N Nthn....101 J7
Week St Mary Cnwll....11 J3
Weel E R Yk....153 G7
Weeley Essex....73 H3
Weeley Heath Essex....73 H3
Weem P & K....232 C5
Weeping Cross Staffs....114 E7
Weethley Warwks....82 C4
Weeting Norfk....104 F5
Weeton E R Yk....145 K4
Weeton Lancs....138 D1
Weeton N York....150 C6
Weetwood Leeds....150 C8
Weir Lancs....140 C3
Weirbrook Shrops....112 F7
Weir Quay Devon....6 E2
Weisdale Shet....281 d5
Welborne Norfk....106 B2
Welbourn Lincs....118 C1
Welburn N York....151 M2
Welbury N York....160 F2
Welby Lincs....118 C4
Welches Dam Cambs....103 K6
Welcombe Devon....26 D7
Weldon N Nthn....101 K5
Weldon Bridge Nthumb....191 G6
Welford W Berk....48 B4
Welford W Nthn....100 E7
Welford-on-Avon Warwks....82 D5
Welham Leics....101 G5
Welham Notts....134 E3
Welham Bridge E R Yk....143 K1
Welham Green Herts....69 G6
Well Hants....36 A2
Well Lincs....137 H5
Well N York....160 C6
Welland Worcs....81 H7
Wellbank Angus....234 D7
Well End Bucks....49 L1
Well End Herts....69 G7
Wellesbourne Warwks....83 G4
Wellesbourne Mountford
    Warwks....83 G4
Well Head Herts....68 F2
Well Hill Kent....52 B6
Wellhouse W Berk....48 D4
Welling Gt Lon....51 M4
Wellingborough N Nthn....85 H2
Wellingham Norfk....121 J7
Wellingore Lincs....135 K8
Wellington Cumb....155 K2
Wellington Herefs....80 C5
Wellington Somset....29 L6
Wellington Wrekin....96 E1
Wellington Heath Herefs....81 G7
Wellington Marsh Herefs....80 C6
Wellow BaNES....45 L7
Wellow IoW....18 F6
Wellow Notts....134 D6
Wellpond Green Herts....69 L3
Wells Somset....31 J2
Wellsborough Leics....99 K3
Wells Green Ches E....113 M1
Wells Head C Brad....141 G1
Wells-next-the-Sea Norfk....121 K6
Wellstye Green Essex....70 F3
Well Town Devon....13 L1
Welltree P & K....221 G3
Wellwood Fife....210 E1

Welney Norfk....103 L4
Welshampton Shrops....113 G4
Welsh Bicknor Herefs....63 H4
Welsh End Shrops....113 H4
Welsh Frankton Shrops....112 E5
Welsh Hook Pembks....74 F6
Welsh Newton Herefs....63 G3
Welshpool Powys....94 F2
Welsh St Donats V Glam....42 F6
Welton Cumb....165 K2
Welton E R Yk....144 B2
Welton Lincs....135 K4
Welton W Nthn....84 B2
Welton le Marsh Lincs....137 J6
Welton le Wold Lincs....136 E2
Welwick E R Yk....145 J3
Welwyn Herts....69 G4
Welwyn Garden City Herts....69 G4
Wem Shrops....113 H5
Wembdon Somset....30 D3
Wembley Gt Lon....50 F2
Wembury Devon....7 G5
Wembworthy Devon....17 H1
Wemyss Bay Inver....207 K5
Wenallt Cerdgn....77 J1
Wendens Ambo Essex....87 K8
Wendlebury Oxon....66 E3
Wendling Norfk....105 J1
Wendover Bucks....67 L5
Wendron Cnwll....3 H5
Wendron Mining District Cnwll....3 H4
Wendy Cambs....87 G5
Wenfordbridge Cnwll....10 F7
Wenhaston Suffk....107 J8
Wennington Cambs....102 E7
Wennington Gt Lon....52 B3
Wennington Lancs....147 M2
Wensley Derbys....132 E7
Wensley N York....159 K5
Wentbridge Wakefd....142 D4
Wentnor Shrops....95 H5
Wentworth Cambs....103 K6
Wentworth Rothm....115 B8
Wenvoe V Glam....43 H7
Weobley Herefs....79 M5
Weobley Marsh Herefs....80 A5
Wepham W Susx....21 H5
Wereham Norfk....104 D3
Wergs Wolves....97 K3
Wern Gwynd....109 K4
Wern Powys....61 H3
Wern Powys....95 G1
Wern Shrops....112 D4
Werneth Low Tamesd....131 J1
Wernffrwd Swans....56 F6
Wern-Gifford Mons....62 C3
Wern-y-gaer Flints....128 F6
Werrington C Pete....102 D3
Werrington Cnwll....11 L5
Werrington Staffs....114 E2
Wervin Ches W....129 K5
Wesham Lancs....138 E1
Wessington Derbys....133 G8
West Aberthaw V Glam....42 F8
West Acre Norfk....121 G8
West Allerdean Nthumb....202 F4
West Alvington Devon....7 L6
West Amesbury Wilts....33 K3
West Anstey Devon....28 E5
West Appleton N York....160 B4
West Ashby Lincs....136 E5
West Ashling W Susx....20 D5
West Ashton Wilts....46 C7
West Auckland Dur....168 F5
West Ayton N York....163 H5
West Bagborough Somset....30 A4
West Bank Blae G....61 K6
West Bank Halton....129 L3
West Barkwith Lincs....136 C4
West Barnby N York....171 J8
West Barns E Loth....212 E3
West Barsham Norfk....121 K5
West Bay Dorset....15 K4
West Beckham Norfk....122 C4
West Bedfont Surrey....50 D4
Westbere Kent....41 G3
West Bergholt Essex....72 D2
West Bexington Dorset....15 M5
West Bilney Norfk....120 F8
West Blatchington Br & H....22 D6
West Boldon S Tyne....181 J6
Westborough Lincs....117 M3
Westbourne BCP....17 L4
Westbourne W Susx....20 B5
West Bourton Dorset....32 C5
West Bowling C Brad....141 J2
West Brabourne Kent....40 E6
West Bradenham Norfk....105 J2
West Bradford Lancs....148 C7
West Bradley Somset....31 J3

West Bretton Wakefd....141 L5
West Bridgford Notts....117 G4
West Briscoe Dur....168 B6
West Bromwich Sandw....98 C5
Westbrook Kent....41 K1
Westbrook W Berk....48 B4
Westbrook Wilts....46 D5
West Buckland Devon....28 B4
West Buckland Somset....30 B6
West Burrafirth Shet....281 c5
West Burton N York....159 H5
West Burton W Susx....21 G4
Westbury Bucks....84 B8
Westbury Shrops....95 H3
Westbury Wilts....46 C8
Westbury Leigh Wilts....32 E1
Westbury-on-Severn Gloucs....63 L4
Westbury-on-Trym Bristl....45 H3
Westbury-sub-Mendip Somset....31 H1
West Butsfield Dur....168 E2
West Butterwick N Linc....143 L6
Westby Lancs....138 D2
West Byfleet Surrey....50 D8
West Cairngaan D & G....172 E8
West Caister Norfk....107 K1
West Calder W Loth....210 D6
West Camel Somset....31 J6
West Chaldon Dorset....16 E6
West Challow Oxon....48 A1
West Charleton Devon....7 L6
West Chelborough Dorset....15 M2
West Chevington Nthumb....191 J6
West Chiltington W Susx....21 J3
West Chinnock Somset....31 G8
West Chisenbury Wilts....47 H8
West Clandon Surrey....50 D8
West Cliffe Kent....41 K6
Westcliff-on-Sea Sthend....53 J2
West Clyst Devon....13 M4
West Coker Somset....31 H8
West Combe Devon....7 L2
West Compton Somset....31 H2
West Compton Dorset....15 M4
West Compton Abbas Dorset....16 A4
Westcote Gloucs....65 J3
Westcote Barton Oxon....66 B7
Westcott Bucks....67 H4
Westcott Devon....14 D2
Westcott Surrey....37 H1
West Cottingwith N York....151 L7
Westcourt Wilts....47 J6
West Cowick E R Yk....143 G3
West Cross Swans....57 H7
West Curry Cnwll....11 K4
West Curthwaite Cumb....165 K1
Westdean E Susx....23 J7
West Dean W Susx....20 E4
West Dean Wilts....34 B5
West Deeping Lincs....102 C2
West Derby Lpool....129 J1
West Dereham Norfk....104 D3
West Ditchburn Nthumb....191 G2
West Down Devon....27 J3
Westdown Camp Wilts....33 H1
Westdowns Cnwll....10 F6
West Drayton Gt Lon....50 D3
West Drayton Notts....134 E5
West Dunnet Highld....280 B2
Wested Kent....52 B5
West Ella E R Yk....144 C2
West End Bed....85 J4
West End Br For....49 L5
West End Caerph....43 K3
West End Cumb....177 K7
West End E R Yk....144 A2
West End E R Yk....144 F2
West End E R Yk....145 H2
Westend Gloucs....64 A5
West End Hants....34 F7
West End Hants....35 K4
West End Herts....69 H5
West End Herts....69 J6
West End Lancs....139 L2
West End Leeds....150 B8
West End Lincs....145 K8
West End N Som....44 F5
West End N York....151 H7
West End Norfk....105 H2
West End Norfk....107 K1
West End Oxon....48 E2
West End S Glos....45 L1
West End Somset....31 L4
West End Surrey....50 B6
West End Surrey....50 E6
West End W & M....49 K4
West End W Susx....22 B4
West End Wilts....32 F6
West End Wilts....33 G6
West End Wilts....46 E3
West End Green Hants....49 G6

Place	County	Page	Grid
Westend Town	Nthumb	179	H6
Westenhanger	Kent	40	F7
Wester Aberchalder	Highld	250	F7
Wester Balblair	Highld	250	E3
Westerdale	Highld	279	K6
Westerdale	N York	161	L2
Westerfield	Suffk	90	E5
Westergate	W Susx	20	F6
Wester Hailes	C Edin	211	G5
Westerham	Kent	51	L8
Westerhope	N u Ty	180	F5
Westerland	Devon	8	C2
Westerleigh	S Glos	45	K3
Western Isles	W Isls	282	e6
Wester Ochiltree	W Loth	210	D4
Wester Pitkierie	Fife	223	K6
Wester Ross	Highld	260	F4
Westerton	W Susx	20	E5
Westerton of Rossie	Angus	235	G4
Westerwick	Shet	281	c6
West Ewell	Surrey	51	G6
West Farleigh	Kent	39	H3
West Farndon	W Nthn	83	M5
West Felton	Shrops	112	E6
Westfield	BaNES	45	K8
Westfield	Cumb	164	C5
Westfield	E Susx	24	E4
Westfield	Highld	279	J3
Westfield	N Lans	209	J4
Westfield	Norfk	105	K2
Westfield	Surrey	50	C7
Westfield	W Loth	210	B4
Westfields	Dorset	16	D2
Westfields	Herefs	80	C7
Westfields of Rattray	P & K	233	J6
Westfield Sole	Kent	53	G6
West Flotmanby	N York	163	K6
Westford	Somset	29	L6
Westgate	Dur	167	L3
Westgate	N Linc	143	K6
Westgate	Norfk	121	L3
Westgate Hill	C Brad	141	K2
Westgate-on-Sea	Kent	41	K1
Westgate Street	Norfk	122	D7
West Ginge	Oxon	48	C2
West Grafton	Wilts	47	K7
West Green	Hants	49	H7
West Grimstead	Wilts	33	L5
West Grinstead	W Susx	37	J6
West Haddlesey	N York	142	E2
West Haddon	W Nthn	84	C1
West Hagbourne	Oxon	48	D2
West Hagley	Worcs	97	K7
Westhall	Suffk	107	J7
West Hallam	Derbys	116	D3
West Hallam Common	Derbys	116	C3
West Halton	N Linc	144	A4
Westham	Dorset	16	C6
Westham	E Susx	23	L6
West Ham	Gt Lon	51	K2
Westham	Somset	30	F2
Westhampnett	W Susx	20	E5
West Handley	Derbys	133	H4
West Hanney	Oxon	66	B8
West Hanningfield	Essex	71	H7
West Harnham	Wilts	33	K5
West Harptree	BaNES	45	H7
West Harting	W Susx	20	C4
West Hatch	Somset	30	D6
West Hatch	Wilts	32	F5
West Haven	Angus	234	E8
Westhay	Somset	31	G2
Westhead	Lancs	138	F6
West Head	Norfk	104	B2
West Heath	Birm	98	C7
West Heath	Hants	48	E7
West Helmsdale	Highld	274	D5
West Hendred	Oxon	48	C1
West Heslerton	N York	163	G7
West Hewish	N Som	44	D6
Westhide	Herefs	80	D6
Westhill	Abers	245	J2
West Hill	Devon	14	C4
Westhill	Highld	252	D3
West Hoathly	W Susx	38	A6
West Holme	Dorset	17	G5
Westholme	Somset	31	J3
Westhope	Herefs	80	B5
Westhope	Shrops	95	L6
West Horndon	Essex	52	D1
Westhorp	W Nthn	83	L5
Westhorpe	Lincs	119	H5
Westhorpe	Suffk	90	B2
West Horrington	Somset	31	J2
West Horsley	Surrey	50	D7
West Horton	Nthumb	203	G7
West Hougham	Kent	41	H7
Westhoughton	Bolton	139	K6
Westhouse	N York	157	L7
Westhouses	Derbys	133	H8
West Howe	BCP	17	L3
West Howetown	Somset	29	G4
Westhumble	Surrey	50	F8
West Huntingtower	P & K	221	K2
West Huntspill	Somset	30	D2
West Hyde	C Beds	68	E4
West Hyde	Herts	50	C1
West Hythe	Kent	40	F8
West Ilkerton	Devon	28	C2
West Ilsley	W Berk	48	C3
West Itchenor	W Susx	20	C6
West Keal	Lincs	137	G7
West Kennett	Wilts	47	G5
West Kilbride	N Ayrs	195	K1
West Kingsdown	Kent	52	C6
West Kington	Wilts	46	A3
West Kirby	Wirral	128	F2
West Knapton	N York	162	F7
West Knighton	Dorset	16	D5
West Knoyle	Wilts	32	E4
Westlake	Devon	7	J4
West Lambrook	Somset	30	F7
Westland Green	Herts	70	B3
West Langdon	Kent	41	K6
West Lavington	W Susx	20	E3
West Lavington	Wilts	46	E8
West Layton	N York	168	F8
West Leake	Notts	116	E6
West Learmouth	Nthumb	202	C5
West Lees	N York	161	G2
West Leigh	Devon	13	G2
Westleigh	Devon	27	H5
Westleigh	Devon	29	J7
West Leigh	Somset	29	L5
Westleton	Suffk	91	K2
West Lexham	Norfk	121	J8
Westley	Shrops	95	J2
Westley	Suffk	89	G2
Westley Waterless	Cambs	88	C4
West Lilling	N York	151	K3
Westlington	Bucks	67	J5
West Linton	Border	199	K3
Westlinton	Cumb	177	L6
West Littleton	S Glos	45	M4
West Lockinge	Oxon	48	B2
West Lulworth	Dorset	16	F6
West Lutton	N York	152	E2
West Lydford	Somset	31	J4
West Lyn	Devon	28	C1
West Lyng	Somset	30	D5
West Lynn	Norfk	120	D7
West Malling	Kent	52	E7
West Malvern	Worcs	81	H6
West Marden	W Susx	20	C4
West Markham	Notts	134	E5
Westmarsh	Kent	41	J3
West Marsh	NE Lin	145	H5
West Marton	N York	148	F5
West Melbury	Dorset	32	E6
West Melton	Rothm	142	C7
West Meon	Hants	35	K6
West Meon Hut	Hants	35	K5
West Meon Woodlands	Hants	35	K5
West Mersea	Essex	72	E4
Westmeston	E Susx	22	E4
West Mickley	Nthumb	180	C6
Westmill	Herts	69	J4
Westmill	Herts	69	K2
West Milton	Dorset	15	L3
Westminster	Gt Lon	51	J3
Westminster Abbey & Palace	Gt Lon	51	J3
West Molesey	Surrey	50	E5
West Monkton	Somset	30	C5
West Moors	Dorset	17	L2
West Morden	Dorset	17	H3
West Morriston	Border	201	J5
West Morton	C Brad	149	K7
West Mudford	Somset	31	J6
Westmuir	Angus	234	A5
West Ness	N York	162	B6
West Newbiggin	Darltn	169	K7
Westnewton	Cumb	164	F2
West Newton	E R Yk	153	K8
West Newton	Norfk	120	F6
West Newton	Somset	30	D5
West Norwood	Gt Lon	51	J4
Westoe	S Tyne	181	J5
West Ogwell	Devon	13	J8
Weston	BaNES	45	L5
Weston	Ches E	114	A1
Weston	Devon	14	D3
Weston	Devon	14	E5
Weston	Dorset	16	D8
Weston	Halton	129	L3
Weston	Hants	35	M6
Weston	Herefs	79	L4
Weston	Herts	69	H1
Weston	Lincs	119	J6
Weston	N York	149	M6
Weston	Notts	134	D6
Weston	Shrops	95	H8
Weston	Shrops	96	D5
Weston	Shrops	112	D6
Weston	Staffs	114	H6
Weston	Suffk	107	J6
Weston	W Berk	48	B4
Weston	W Nthn	84	B6
Weston Beggard	Herefs	80	D7
Westonbirt	Gloucs	46	B1
Weston by Welland	N Nthn	101	G5
Weston Colley	Hants	35	G3
Weston Colville	Cambs	88	C4
Weston Corbett	Hants	35	L2
Weston Coyney	C Stke	114	E3
Weston Favell	W Nthn	84	F3
Weston Green	Cambs	88	C5
Weston Heath	Shrops	97	H1
Weston Hills	Lincs	119	J7
Weston in Arden	Warwks	99	K6
Westoning	C Beds	85	K8
Weston-in-Gordano	N Som	44	F4
Westoning Woodend	C Beds	68	C1
Weston Jones	Staffs	114	B6
Weston Longville	Norfk	122	C8
Weston Lullingfields	Shrops	112	F6
Weston-on-Avon	Warwks	82	E5
Weston-on-the-Green	Oxon	66	D3
Weston Patrick	Hants	35	L2
Weston Rhyn	Shrops	112	D4
Weston-sub-Edge	Gloucs	82	D7
Weston-super-Mare	N Som	44	C6
Weston Turville	Bucks	67	K5
Weston-under-Lizard	Staffs	97	H1
Weston under Penyard	Herefs	63	J3
Weston-under-Redcastle	Shrops	113	J5
Weston under Wetherley	Warwks	83	J1
Weston Underwood	Derbys	116	A3
Weston Underwood	M Keyn	85	G5
Weston-upon-Trent	Derbys	116	C6
Westonzoyland	Somset	30	E4
West Orchard	Dorset	32	D7
West Overton	Wilts	47	H5
Westow	N York	152	A3
West Panson	Devon	11	L4
West Park	Abers	245	H4
West Parley	Dorset	17	L3
West Peckham	Kent	39	G3
West Peeke	Devon	11	L4
West Pelton	Dur	180	F8
West Pennard	Somset	31	J3
West Pentire	Cnwll	4	C3
West Pinchbeck	Lincs	119	G6
West Porlock	Somset	28	F2
Westport	Somset	30	F6
West Pulham	Dorset	16	D1
West Putford	Devon	26	F7
West Quantoxhead	Somset	29	K3
Westquarter	Falk	210	B3
Westra	V Glam	43	J7
West Raddon	Devon	13	L2
West Rainton	Dur	169	J1
West Rasen	Lincs	135	L2
West Ravendale	NE Lin	145	G7
Westray	Ork	275	c2
Westray Airport	Ork	275	c1
West Raynham	Norfk	121	J6
West Retford	Notts	134	D3
Westridge Green	W Berk	48	E3
Westrigg	W Loth	210	B5
Westrop	Swindn	65	J8
West Rounton	N York	160	F2
West Row	Suffk	104	D8
West Rudham	Norfk	121	H6
West Runton	Norfk	122	D3
Westruther	Border	201	K3
Westry	Cambs	103	H4
West Saltoun	E Loth	212	A5
West Sandford	Devon	13	J2
West Sandwick	Shet	281	e3
West Scrafton	N York	159	K6
West Sleekburn	Nthumb	181	G2
West Somerton	Norfk	123	K7
West Stafford	Dorset	16	D5
West Stockwith	Notts	134	F1
West Stoke	W Susx	20	D5
West Stonesdale	N York	158	F2
West Stoughton	Somset	30	F1
West Stour	Dorset	32	C6
West Stourmouth	Kent	41	H3
West Stow	Suffk	89	G1
West Stowell	Wilts	47	H6
West Stratton	Hants	35	H3
West Street	Kent	40	A4
West Street	Kent	41	K4
West Street	Medway	52	F4
West Street	Suffk	89	K1
West Tanfield	N York	160	C7
West Taphouse	Cnwll	5	K2
West Tarbert	Ag & B	206	D2
West Tarring	W Susx	21	J6
West Thirston	Nthumb	191	H6
West Thorney	W Susx	20	C6
Westthorpe	Derbys	133	J4
West Thorpe	Notts	117	G6
West Thurrock	Thurr	52	C3
West Tilbury	Thurr	52	E3
West Tisted	Hants	35	K5
West Torrington	Lincs	136	B3
West Town	BaNES	45	G6
West Town	Hants	20	B3
West Town	Herefs	80	B3
West Town	N Som	44	F5
West Town	Somset	31	J4
West Town	Somset	32	B3
West Tytherley	Hants	34	C5
West Walton	Norfk	103	K1
Westward	Cumb	165	J2
Westward Ho!	Devon	27	G5
Westwell	Kent	40	C6
Westwell	Oxon	65	J5
Westwell Leacon	Kent	40	C5
West Wellow	Hants	34	C2
West Wembury	Devon	7	G5
West Wemyss	Fife	222	E8
Westwick	Cambs	87	J2
Westwick	Dur	168	D7
West Wick	N Som	44	D6
Westwick	Norfk	122	F6
West Wickham	Cambs	88	C5
West Wickham	Gt Lon	51	K5
West Williamston	Pembks	55	H5
West Winch	Norfk	120	E8
West Winterslow	Wilts	34	B4
West Wittering	W Susx	20	C7
West Witton	N York	159	J5
Westwood	Devon	14	B3
Westwood	Kent	41	K2
Westwood	Kent	52	D5
Westwood	Notts	116	D1
Westwood	Nthumb	179	H6
Westwood	Wilts	46	A7
West Woodburn	Nthumb	179	K2
West Woodhay	W Berk	48	B6
Westwood Heath	Covtry	99	H8
West Woodlands	Somset	32	C2
Westwoodside	N Linc	143	J7
West Worldham	Hants	35	M3
West Worthing	W Susx	21	K6
West Wratting	Cambs	88	C5
West Wycombe	Bucks	67	K8
West Wylam	Nthumb	180	D6
West Yatton	Wilts	46	B4
West Yoke	Kent	52	D5
West Youlstone	Cnwll	26	D7
Wetham Green	Kent	53	H5
Wetheral	Cumb	178	B7
Wetherby	Leeds	150	F6
Wetherby Services	N York	150	F6
Wetherden	Suffk	89	K3
Wetheringsett	Suffk	90	D2
Wethersfield	Essex	71	H1
Wetherup Street	Suffk	90	D2
Wetley Rocks	Staffs	114	F2
Wettenhall	Ches E	130	C7
Wetton	Staffs	132	B8
Wetwang	E R Yk	152	E4
Wetwood	Staffs	114	B5
Wexcombe	Wilts	47	K7
Wexham	Slough	50	C3
Wexham Street	Bucks	50	C2
Weybourne	Norfk	122	C3
Weybourne	Surrey	36	C1
Weybread	Suffk	106	E7
Weybread Street	Suffk	106	E7
Weybridge	Surrey	50	D6
Weycroft	Devon	15	G3
Weydale	Highld	279	L3
Weyhill	Hants	34	D2
Weymouth	Dorset	16	C6
Whaddon	Bucks	84	F8
Whaddon	Cambs	87	G6
Whaddon	Gloucs	64	B4
Whaddon	Wilts	33	L5
Whaddon	Wilts	46	C6
Whale	W & F	166	C6
Whaley	Derbys	133	K5
Whaley Bridge	Derbys	131	K3
Whaley Thorns	Derbys	133	K5
Whaligoe	Highld	280	D8
Whalley	Lancs	148	C8
Whalley Banks	Lancs	139	L1
Whalsay	Shet	281	f5
Whalton	Nthumb	180	D3
Whaplode	Lincs	119	K6
Whaplode Drove	Lincs	103	G1
Wharf	Warwks	83	K5

Wharfe N York 148 D2
Wharles Lancs 147 J8
Wharley End C Beds 85 J6
Wharncliffe Side Sheff 132 F1
Wharram-le-Street N York ..152 C3
Wharton Ches W 130 C6
Wharton Herefs 80 C4
Washton N York 159 L2
Whasset W & F 157 H6
Whatcote Warwks 83 G6
Whateley Warwks 99 G3
Whatfield Suffk 89 L6
Whatley Somset 15 H1
Whatley Somset 32 B2
Whatley's End S Glos 45 K3
Whatlington E Susx 24 D4
Whatsole Street Kent 40 F6
Whatstandwell Derbys 116 B1
Whatton-in-the-Vale Notts ..117 K4
Whauphill D & G 173 K5
Whaw N York 150 H2
Wheal Peevor Cnwll 4 A6
Wheal Rose Cnwll 4 B6
Wheatacre Norfk 107 J4
Wheatfield Oxon 67 G7
Wheathampstead Herts 68 F4
Wheathill Shrops 96 E7
Wheathill Somset 31 J5
Wheatley Hants 36 A3
Wheatley Oxon 66 E6
Wheatley Hill Dur 169 K3
Wheatley Hills Donc 142 F6
Wheatley Lane Lancs 148 L6
Wheaton Aston Staffs 97 J1
Wheddon Cross Somset 29 G3
Wheelbarrow Town Kent 40 F6
Wheeler End Bucks 67 K8
Wheeler's Green Wokham 49 J4
Wheelerstreet Surrey 36 E3
Wheelock Ches E 130 E2
Wheelock Heath Ches E 130 E8
Wheelton Lancs 139 J3
Wheldale Wakefd 142 C3
Wheldrake C York 151 L6
Whelford Gloucs 65 H7
Whelpley Hill Bucks 68 C6
Whelpo Cumb 165 J3
Whelston Flints 128 F4
Whempstead Herts 69 J3
Whenby N York 151 K2
Whepstead Suffk 89 G4
Wherstead Suffk 90 E2
Wherwell Hants 34 E3
Wheston Derbys 132 C4
Whetsted Kent 39 G4
Whetstone Gt Lon 69 H8
Whetstone Leics 100 C4
Wheyrigg Cumb 165 G1
Whicham Cumb 155 L6
Whichford Warwks 83 H8
Whickham Gatesd 180 F6
Whiddon Devon 12 B3
Whiddon Down Devon 13 G4
Whigstreet Angus 234 D6
Whilton W Nthn 84 C2
Whimble Devon 11 L2
Whimple Devon 14 B3
Whimpwell Green Norfk 123 H5
Whinburgh Norfk 105 K2
Whin Lane End Lancs 147 H7
Whinnieliggate D & G 175 H4
Whinnow Cumb 177 J8
Whinnyfold Abers 257 K5
Whinny Hill S on T 169 K7
Whippingham IoW 19 H5
Whipsnade C Beds 68 C2
Whipton Devon 13 M4
Whirlow Sheff 132 F3
Whisby Lincs 135 H6
Whissendine Rutlnd 117 L8
Whissonsett Norfk 121 K7
Whistlefield Ag & B 218 C8
Whistlefield Inn Ag & B 217 J6
Whistley Green Wokham 49 J4
Whiston Knows 129 L2
Whiston Rothm 133 J2
Whiston Staffs 114 D8
Whiston Staffs 115 G2
Whiston W Nthn 85 G3
Whiston Cross Shrops 97 H3
Whiston Eaves Staffs 115 G3
Whitacre Fields Warwks 99 H5
Whitbeck Cumb 155 K5
Whitbourne Herefs 81 G4
Whitburn S Tyne 181 J5
Whitburn W Loth 210 C6
Whitby Ches W 129 J4
Whitby N York 171 K8
Whitbyheath Ches W 129 J5
Whitchester Border 212 F7

Whitchurch BaNES 45 J5
Whitchurch Bucks 67 J3
Whitchurch Cardif 43 J5
Whitchurch Devon 12 C8
Whitchurch Hants 34 F1
Whitchurch Herefs 63 H4
Whitchurch Oxon 48 F3
Whitchurch Pembks 74 C7
Whitchurch Shrops 113 J3
Whitchurch Canonicorum
    Dorset 15 J3
Whitchurch Hill Oxon 48 F3
Whitcombe Dorset 16 D5
Whitcot Shrops 95 J5
Whitcott Keysett Shrops 95 G6
Whiteacre Kent 40 E5
Whiteacre Heath Warwks 99 G5
Whiteash Green Essex 71 J1
White Ball Somset 29 K7
Whitebridge Highld 250 E8
Whitebrook Mons 63 H6
Whitebushes Surrey 37 L1
Whitecairns Abers 257 G8
Whitechapel Gt Lon 51 J3
White Chapel Lancs 147 L7
Whitechurch Pembks 75 K5
Whitecliff Gloucs 63 H5
White Colne Essex 72 C1
White Coppice Lancs 139 J4
Whitecraig E Loth 211 K5
Whitecroft Gloucs 63 J6
Whitecrook D & G 172 F3
Whitecross Cnwll 2 E4
White Cross Cnwll 3 H6
Whitecross Cnwll 10 D8
Whitecross Falk 210 C4
White End Worcs 81 H8
Whiteface Highld 263 J2
Whitefarland N Ayrs 194 D3
Whitefaulds S Ayrs 183 H1
Whitefield Bury 140 B6
Whitefield Devon 28 C4
Whitefield Somset 29 K5
Whitefield Lane End Knows ..129 K2
Whiteford Abers 256 C6
Whitegate Ches W 130 C6
Whitehall Hants 49 H8
Whitehall Ork 275 e3
Whitehall W Susx 37 H6
Whitehaven Cumb 164 C7
Whitehill Hants 36 B4
Whitehill Kent 40 C3
Whitehill Leics 99 L1
Whitehills Abers 268 B3
Whitehouse Abers 256 A8
Whitehouse Ag & B 206 C6
Whitehouse Common Birm ...98 E4
Whitekirk E Loth 212 D3
White Kirkley Dur 168 C3
White Lackington Dorset 16 D3
Whitelackington Somset 30 F7
White Ladies Aston Worcs 81 L4
Whiteleaf Bucks 67 K6
White-le-Head Dur 180 E7
Whiteley Hants 19 J2
Whiteley Bank IoW 19 J7
Whiteley Green Ches E 131 H4
Whiteley Village Surrey 50 E6
Whitemans Green W Susx 22 D2
White Mill Carmth 58 E4
Whitemire Moray 253 J1
Whitemoor C Nott 116 F3
Whitemoor Cnwll 5 G3
Whitemoor Derbys 116 B2
Whitemoor Staffs 131 H7
Whiteness Shet 281 d6
White Notley Essex 71 J3
Whiteoak Green Oxon 65 M4
White Ox Mead BaNES 45 L7
Whiteparish Wilts 34 B6
White Pit Lincs 137 G4
Whiterashes Abers 256 F7
White Roding Essex 70 F4
Whiterow Highld 280 E6
Whiterow Moray 265 G8
Whiteshill Gloucs 64 B5
Whitesmith E Susx 23 J4
White Stake Lancs 139 G3
Whitestaunton Somset 30 D8
Whitestone Devon 13 K4
White Stone Herefs 80 D6
Whitestone Warwks 99 K5
Whitestone Cross Devon 13 L4
Whitestreet Green Suffk 89 K7
Whitewall Corner N York 152 B2
White Waltham W & M 49 K3
Whiteway BaNES 45 L6
Whiteway Gloucs 64 C5
Whitewell Lancs 148 B6
Whiteworks Devon 12 E8

Whitfield C Dund 234 C8
Whitfield Kent 41 J6
Whitfield Nthumb 179 H7
Whitfield S Glos 63 K8
Whitfield W Nthn 84 B7
Whitfield Hall Nthumb 179 H7
Whitford Devon 14 F3
Whitford Flints 128 D4
Whitgift E R Yk 143 K3
Whitgreave Staffs 114 D6
Whithorn D & G 174 C6
Whiting Bay N Ayrs 195 G6
Whitkirk Leeds 142 B1
Whitland Carmth 55 L3
Whitlaw Border 188 E4
Whitletts S Ayrs 196 D6
Whitley N York 142 E4
Whitley Readg 49 H5
Whitley Sheff 133 G1
Whitley Wilts 46 C5
Whitley Bay N Tyne 181 J4
Whitley Chapel Nthumb 179 L7
Whitley Heath Staffs 114 C6
Whitley Lower Kirk 141 K4
Whitley Row Kent 38 D3
Whitlock's End Solhll 98 E8
Whitminster Gloucs 63 M5
Whitmore Dorset 17 L1
Whitmore Staffs 114 C3
Whitnage Devon 29 J7
Whitnash Warwks 83 H3
Whitney-on-Wye Herefs 79 J5
Whitrigg Cumb 165 G3
Whitrigg Cumb 177 H7
Whitrigglees Cumb 177 H7
Whitsbury Hants 33 K7
Whitsome Border 202 D3
Whitson Newpt 44 D2
Whitstable Kent 40 E2
Whitstone Cnwll 11 K3
Whittingham Nthumb 190 F4
Whittingslow Shrops 95 K5
Whittington Derbys 133 H4
Whittington Gloucs 64 E3
Whittington Lancs 157 K7
Whittington Norfk 104 C2
Whittington Shrops 112 E5
Whittington Staffs 97 J6
Whittington Staffs 98 F2
Whittington Warwks 99 J4
Whittington Worcs 81 K4
Whittington Moor Derbys 133 G5
Whittlebury W Nthn 84 D6
Whittle-le-Woods Lancs 139 H3
Whittlesey Cambs 102 F4
Whittlesford Cambs 87 K5
Whittlestone Head Bl w D 139 L4
Whitton N Linc 143 M3
Whitton Nthumb 190 F6
Whitton Powys 79 J2
Whitton S on T 169 K6
Whitton Shrops 80 D1
Whitton Suffk 90 D5
Whittonditch Wilts 47 L4
Whittonstall Nthumb 180 C7
Whitway Hants 48 C7
Whitwell Derbys 133 K4
Whitwell Herts 68 F3
Whitwell IoW 19 J8
Whitwell N York 160 D3
Whitwell Rutlnd 101 K2
Whitwell-on-the-Hill N York ..151 M3
Whitwell Street Norfk 122 B7
Whitwick Leics 116 D8
Whitwood Wakefd 142 B3
Whitworth Lancs 140 D4
Whixall Shrops 113 H4
Whixley N York 150 F4
Whorlton Dur 168 F7
Whorlton N York 161 G2
Whyle Herefs 80 D3
Whyteleafe Surrey 51 J7
Wibdon Gloucs 63 H7
Wibsey C Brad 141 J2
Wibtoft Warwks 100 B6
Wichelstowe Swindn 47 H2
Wichenford Worcs 81 H3
Wichling Kent 40 B4
Wick BCP 18 B5
Wick Devon 14 E1
Wick Highld 280 E6
Wick S Glos 45 K4
Wick Somset 30 B2
Wick Somset 30 F5
Wick V Glam 42 D7
Wick W Susx 21 H6
Wick Wilts 33 L6
Wick Worcs 81 M6
Wicken Cambs 88 B1
Wicken W Nthn 84 E7

Wicken Bonhunt Essex 87 K8
Wickenby Lincs 136 A3
Wick End Bed 85 K5
Wicken Green Village Norfk ..121 J5
Wickersley Rothm 133 J2
Wicker Street Green Suffk 89 K6
Wickford Essex 71 H8
Wickham Hants 19 K2
Wickham W Berk 48 B5
Wickham Bishops Essex 71 K5
Wickhambreaux Kent 41 H3
Wickhambrook Suffk 88 E4
Wickhamford Worcs 82 C7
Wickham Green Suffk 90 C2
Wickham Green W Berk 48 B4
Wickham Heath W Berk 48 B5
Wickham Market Suffk 91 G4
Wickhampton Norfk 107 J2
Wickham St Paul Essex 89 G7
Wickham Skeith Suffk 90 C2
Wickham Street Suffk 88 E4
Wickham Street Suffk 90 C1
Wickhurst Green W Susx 37 H5
Wick John o' Groats Airport
    Highld 280 E5
Wicklewood Norfk 106 B3
Wickmere Norfk 122 D5
Wick St Lawrence N Som 44 D6
Wickstreet E Susx 23 J5
Wickwar S Glos 45 L1
Widdington Essex 70 D1
Widdop Calder 140 D1
Widdrington Nthumb 191 K7
Widdrington Station Nthumb ..191 J7
Widecombe in the Moor Devon ..13 G7
Widegates Cnwll 6 B3
Widemouth Bay Cnwll 11 H2
Wideopen N Tyne 181 G4
Widford Essex 71 G6
Widford Herts 70 B4
Widham Wilts 47 G1
Widley Hants 19 M2
Widmer End Bucks 67 L7
Widmerpool Notts 117 G6
Widmore Gt Lon 51 L5
Widnes Halton 129 L3
Widworthy Devon 14 F3
Wigan Wigan 139 H6
Wigborough Somset 31 G7
Wiggaton Devon 14 C4
Wiggenhall St Germans Norfk ..120 D8
Wiggenhall St Mary
    Magdalen Norfk 104 B1
Wiggenhall St Mary the Virgin
    Norfk 104 B1
Wiggenhall St Peter Norfk 104 C1
Wiggens Green Essex 88 D6
Wiggenstall Staffs 132 B7
Wiggington Shrops 112 E4
Wigginton C York 151 J4
Wigginton Herts 68 B5
Wigginton Oxon 83 J8
Wigginton Staffs 99 G2
Wigginton Bottom Herts 68 B5
Wigglesworth N York 148 E4
Wiggonby Cumb 177 J8
Wiggonholt W Susx 21 H3
Wighill N York 151 G6
Wighton Norfk 121 L3
Wightwick Wolves 97 K4
Wigley Derbys 132 F5
Wigley Hants 34 D7
Wigmore Herefs 80 A2
Wigmore Medway 53 G6
Wigsley Notts 135 G5
Wigsthorpe N Nthn 102 A6
Wigston Leics 100 D1
Wigston Fields Leics 100 D3
Wigston Parva Leics 100 A5
Wigthorpe Notts 134 B3
Wigtoft Lincs 119 J4
Wigton Cumb 165 H1
Wigtown D & G 174 C4
Wigtwizzle Sheff 141 L8
Wike Leeds 150 D7
Wilbarston N Nthn 101 H5
Wilberfoss E R Yk 151 M5
Wilburton Cambs 103 K8
Wilby N Nthn 85 G2
Wilby Norfk 105 L5
Wilby Suffk 90 F1
Wilcot Wilts 47 H6
Wilcott Shrops 112 F7
Wilcove Cnwll 6 E4
Wilcrick Newpt 44 E2
Wilday Green Derbys 132 F5
Wildboarclough Ches E 131 K6
Wilden Bed 86 B4
Wilden Worcs 81 J1
Wilde Street Suffk 104 D7

Wildhern Hants....34 D1
Wildhill Herts....69 H5
Wildmanbridge S Lans....209 L8
Wildmill Brdgnd....42 D5
Wildmoor Hants....49 G7
Wildmoor Worcs....98 B8
Wildsworth Lincs....143 K8
Wilford C Nott....116 F4
Wilkesley Ches E....113 K3
Wilkhaven Highld....264 E3
Wilkieston W Loth....210 F5
Wilkin's Green Herts....69 G5
Wilksby Lincs....136 E7
Willand Devon....29 J8
Willards Hill E Susx....24 C2
Willaston Ches E....113 L1
Willaston Ches W....129 H4
Willen M Keyn....85 G7
Willenhall Covtry....99 K8
Willenhall Wsall....98 B4
Willerby E R Yk....144 C2
Willerby N York....163 H6
Willersey Gloucs....82 D7
Willersley Herefs....79 K6
Willesborough Kent....40 D7
Willesborough Lees Kent....40 D6
Willesden Gt Lon....51 G2
Willesleigh Devon....27 L4
Willesley Wilts....46 B1
Willett Somset....29 K4
Willey Shrops....96 F3
Willey Warwks....100 B6
Willey Green Surrey....50 B8
Williamscot Oxon....83 L6
Williamstown Rhondd....42 F4
Willian Herts....69 G1
Willicote Warwks....82 E5
Willingale Essex....70 E5
Willingdon E Susx....23 K6
Willingham Cambs....87 H1
Willingham by Stow Lincs....135 H3
Willingham Green Cambs....88 C4
Willingham St Mary Suffk....107 J6
Willington Bed....86 C5
Willington Derbys....116 A6
Willington Dur....169 G4
Willington Kent....39 K3
Willington N Tyne....181 H5
Willington Warwks....83 G7
Willington Corner Ches W....129 M6
Willitoft E R Yk....143 J1
Williton Somset....29 K3
Willoughby Lincs....137 J5
Willoughby Warwks....83 M2
Willoughby Hills Lincs....119 K3
Willoughby-on-the-Wolds
    Notts....117 H6
Willoughby Waterleys Leics....100 C5
Willoughton Lincs....135 J1
Willow Green Ches W....130 B4
Willows Green Essex....71 H3
Willsbridge S Glos....45 K5
Willsworthy Devon....12 D6
Willtown Somset....30 F6
Wilmcote Warwks....82 E4
Wilmington BaNES....45 K6
Wilmington Devon....14 F3
Wilmington E Susx....23 J6
Wilmington Kent....52 B4
Wilmslow Ches E....131 G3
Wilnecote Staffs....99 G3
Wilpshire Lancs....139 K1
Wilsden C Brad....149 K8
Wilsford Lincs....118 D3
Wilsford Wilts....33 K3
Wilsford Wilts....47 G7
Wilsham Devon....28 D1
Wilshaw Kirk....141 H6
Wilsill N York....150 A3
Wilsley Green Kent....39 K6
Wilsley Pound Kent....39 K6
Wilson Herefs....63 H2
Wilson Leics....116 C6
Wilsontown S Lans....198 F2
Wilstead Bed....85 L6
Wilsthorpe Lincs....102 B2
Wilstone Herts....67 L4
Wilstone Green Herts....67 M4
Wilton Cumb....164 D8
Wilton Herefs....63 H2
Wilton N York....162 F6
Wilton R & Cl....170 D6
Wilton Wilts....33 J4
Wilton Wilts....47 K6
Wilton Dean Border....188 E3
Wimbish Essex....88 B7
Wimbish Green Essex....88 C8
Wimbledon Gt Lon....51 G5
Wimblington Cambs....103 J5
Wimboldsley Ches W....130 D7

Wimborne Minster Dorset....17 K3
Wimborne St Giles Dorset....33 H8
Wimbotsham Norfk....104 C2
Wimpole Cambs....87 G5
Wimpstone Warwks....82 F5
Wincanton Somset....32 B5
Winceby Lincs....136 F6
Wincham Ches W....130 C4
Winchburgh W Loth....210 E4
Winchcombe Gloucs....64 F2
Winchelsea E Susx....25 G4
Winchelsea Beach E Susx....25 G4
Winchester Hants....35 G5
Winchester Services Hants....35 H4
Winchet Hill Kent....39 J5
Winchfield Hants....49 J8
Winchmore Hill Bucks....68 B8
Winchmore Hill Gt Lon....69 J8
Wincle Ches E....131 J6
Wincobank Sheff....133 G1
Winder Cumb....164 D7
Windermere W & F....156 F3
Winderton Warwks....83 H7
Windhill Highld....250 F2
Windlehurst Stockp....131 J3
Windlesham Surrey....50 A6
Windmill Cnwll....10 B7
Windmill Derbys....132 C4
Windmill Hill E Susx....23 L5
Windmill Hill Somset....30 D7
Windrush Gloucs....65 J4
Windsole Abers....267 L4
Windsor W & M....50 B4
Windsoredge Gloucs....64 B7
Windsor Green Suffk....89 H4
Windygates Fife....222 F7
Windyharbour Ches E....131 G5
Windy Hill Wrexhm....129 G8
Wineham W Susx....22 C3
Winestead E R Yk....145 H3
Winewall Lancs....148 F7
Winfarthing Norfk....106 C6
Winford IoW....19 J6
Winford N Som....45 G6
Winforton Herefs....79 K6
Winfrith Newburgh Dorset....16 F5
Wing Bucks....67 L3
Wing Rutlnd....101 K3
Wingate Dur....169 L3
Wingates Bolton....139 K6
Wingates Nthumb....191 G7
Wingerworth Derbys....133 G6
Wingfield C Beds....68 C2
Wingfield Suffk....106 E7
Wingfield Wilts....46 B7
Wingfield Green Suffk....106 E7
Wingham Kent....41 H4
Wingland Lincs....120 B6
Wingmore Kent....41 G6
Wingrave Bucks....67 L3
Winkburn Notts....134 E7
Winkfield Br For....49 L4
Winkfield Row Br For....49 L5
Winkhill Staffs....115 H1
Winkhurst Green Kent....38 D3
Winkleigh Devon....12 F1
Winksley N York....150 C2
Winkton BCP....18 B4
Winlaton Gatesd....180 E6
Winlaton Mill Gatesd....180 E6
Winless Highld....280 D5
Winllan Powys....112 C7
Winmarleigh Lancs....147 J6
Winnall Hants....35 G5
Winnersh Wokham....49 J5
Winnington Ches W....130 C5
Winscales Cumb....164 D5
Winscombe N Som....44 E7
Winsford Ches W....130 C6
Winsford Somset....28 E4
Winsham Devon....27 J3
Winsham Somset....15 J2
Winshill Staffs....115 M7
Winshwen Swans....57 J5
Winskill W & F....166 D4
Winslade Hants....35 K1
Winsley Wilts....46 A6
Winslow Bucks....67 J2
Winson Gloucs....65 G5
Winsor Hants....34 D8
Winstanley Wigan....139 H7
Winster Derbys....132 E7
Winster W & F....156 F4
Winston Dur....168 F7
Winston Suffk....90 E3
Winstone Gloucs....64 D5
Winston Green Suffk....90 E3
Winswell Devon....27 J8
Winterborne Came Dorset....16 D5
Winterborne Clenston Dorset....17 G2

Winterborne Herringston
    Dorset....16 D5
Winterborne Houghton Dorset....16 F2
Winterborne Kingston Dorset....17 G3
Winterborne Monkton Dorset....16 C5
Winterborne Stickland Dorset....16 F2
Winterborne Tomson Dorset....17 G3
Winterborne Whitechurch
    Dorset....17 G3
Winterborne Zelston Dorset....17 H3
Winterbourne S Glos....45 J3
Winterbourne W Berk....48 C4
Winterbourne Abbas Dorset....16 B4
Winterbourne Bassett Wilts....47 G5
Winterbourne Dauntsey Wilts....33 L4
Winterbourne Earls Wilts....33 L4
Winterbourne Gunner Wilts....33 L4
Winterbourne Monkton Wilts....47 G4
Winterbourne Steepleton
    Dorset....16 B4
Winterbourne Stoke Wilts....33 J3
Winterbrook Oxon....48 F1
Winterburn N York....149 G4
Winteringham N Linc....144 A3
Winterley Ches E....130 E8
Wintersett Wakefd....142 B4
Winterslow Wilts....34 B4
Winterton N Linc....144 A4
Winterton-on-Sea Norfk....123 K7
Winthorpe Lincs....137 K6
Winthorpe Notts....135 G8
Winton BCP....17 L4
Winton E Susx....23 H6
Winton N York....160 F3
Winton W & F....167 H8
Wintringham Cambs....86 D3
Wintringham N York....162 F8
Winwick Cambs....102 B7
Winwick W Nthn....100 D8
Winwick Warrtn....130 B1
Wirksworth Derbys....115 M1
Wirral....129 G3
Wirswall Ches E....113 J3
Wisbech Cambs....103 J2
Wisbech St Mary Cambs....103 J2
Wisborough Green W Susx....37 G5
Wiseman's Bridge Pembks....55 K5
Wiseton Notts....134 E2
Wishanger Gloucs....64 D5
Wishaw N Lans....209 L7
Wishaw Warwks....98 F4
Wisley Surrey....50 D7
Wispington Lincs....136 D5
Wissenden Kent....40 B7
Wissett Suffk....107 H7
Wissington Norfk....104 D4
Wissington Suffk....89 J8
Wistanstow Shrops....95 K6
Wistanswick Shrops....113 L5
Wistaston Ches E....113 L1
Wistaston Green Ches E....130 D8
Wisterfield Ches E....131 G5
Wiston Pembks....55 H3
Wiston S Lans....198 F6
Wiston W Susx....21 K4
Wistow Cambs....102 F7
Wistow Leics....100 E4
Wistow N York....142 F1
Wiswell Lancs....148 C8
Witcham Cambs....103 J7
Witchampton Dorset....17 J2
Witchford Cambs....103 K7
Witcombe Somset....31 G6
Witham Essex....71 K4
Witham Friary Somset....32 B3
Witham on the Hill Lincs....118 D8
Witham St Hughs Lincs....135 H7
Withcall Lincs....136 E3
Withdean Br & H....22 D5
Witherenden Hill E Susx....23 L2
Witheridge Devon....28 D8
Witherley Leics....99 J4
Withern Lincs....137 H3
Withernsea E R Yk....145 J2
Withernwick E R Yk....153 K7
Withersdale Street Suffk....106 F7
Withersfield Suffk....88 D5
Witherslack W & F....156 F5
Withiel Cnwll....5 G2
Withiel Florey Somset....29 H4
Withielgoose Cnwll....5 G2
Withington Gloucs....64 F4
Withington Herefs....80 D6
Withington Manch....131 G1
Withington Shrops....96 D1
Withington Staffs....115 G4
Withington Green Ches E....130 F5
Withington Marsh Herefs....80 D6
Withleigh Devon....28 F8
Withnell Lancs....139 J3

Withnell Fold Lancs....139 J3
Withybed Green Worcs....82 B1
Withybrook Warwks....99 L6
Withycombe Somset....29 J3
Withyham E Susx....38 D6
Withy Mills BaNES....45 K7
Withypool Somset....28 E4
Withywood Bristl....45 H5
Witley Surrey....36 E3
Witnesham Suffk....90 E5
Witney Oxon....65 M5
Wittering C Pete....102 B3
Wittersham Kent....25 G2
Witton Birm....98 D5
Witton Norfk....107 G2
Witton Norfk....123 G5
Witton Gilbert Dur....169 G2
Witton Green Norfk....107 J3
Witton le Wear Dur....168 F4
Witton Park Dur....168 F4
Wiveliscombe Somset....29 K5
Wivelrod Hants....35 K3
Wivelsfield E Susx....22 E3
Wivelsfield Green E Susx....22 E3
Wivelsfield Station W Susx....22 E3
Wivenhoe Essex....72 F3
Wivenhoe Cross Essex....72 F2
Wiveton Norfk....122 A3
Wix Essex....73 H2
Wixams Bed....85 L6
Wixford Warwks....82 C4
Wix Green Essex....73 H2
Wixhill Shrops....113 J6
Wixoe Suffk....88 E6
Woburn C Beds....85 J8
Woburn Sands M Keyn....85 H8
Wokefield Park W Berk....49 G6
Woking Surrey....50 C7
Wokingham Wokham....49 K5
Wolborough Devon....13 K8
Woldingham Surrey....51 K7
Wold Newton E R Yk....163 J8
Wold Newton NE Lin....145 G8
Wolfclyde S Lans....199 H6
Wolferlow Herefs....80 F3
Wolferton Norfk....120 E6
Wolfhampcote Warwks....83 M2
Wolfhill P & K....233 H8
Wolf Hills Nthumb....179 G7
Wolf's Castle Pembks....74 F6
Wolfsdale Pembks....54 F3
Wollaston Dudley....97 K6
Wollaston N Nthn....85 H3
Wollaston Shrops....95 H1
Wollaton C Nott....116 E4
Wolleigh Devon....13 J6
Wollerton Shrops....113 K5
Wollescote Dudley....97 L6
Wolseley Bridge Staffs....115 G7
Wolsingham Dur....168 D3
Wolstanton Staffs....114 D2
Wolstenholme Rochdl....140 C5
Wolston Warwks....99 L8
Wolsty Cumb....176 E8
Wolvercote Oxon....66 C5
Wolverhampton Wolves....97 K4
Wolverhampton Halfpenny
    Green Airport Staffs....97 J5
Wolverley Shrops....113 G5
Wolverley Worcs....97 J7
Wolverton Hants....48 E7
Wolverton Kent....41 H6
Wolverton M Keyn....84 F7
Wolverton Warwks....82 F3
Wolverton Wilts....32 C4
Wolverton Common Hants....48 E7
Wolvesnewton Mons....62 F7
Wolvey Warwks....99 L6
Wolvey Heath Warwks....99 L5
Wolviston S on T....170 B5
Wombleton N York....161 L6
Wombourne Staffs....97 K5
Wombwell Barns....142 B7
Womenswold Kent....41 H5
Womersley N York....142 E4
Wonastow Mons....62 F5
Wonersh Surrey....36 F2
Wonford Devon....13 L4
Wonson Devon....12 F5
Wonston Dorset....16 E1
Wonston Hants....35 G3
Wooburn Bucks....49 M2
Wooburn Green Bucks....49 M1
Wooburn Moor Bucks....49 M1
Woodacott Devon....11 M1
Woodale N York....159 J6
Woodall Rothm....133 J3
Woodall Services Rothm....133 J4
Woodbank Ches W....129 H5
Woodbastwick Norfk....123 G8

Woodbeck Notts 134 F4
Wood Bevington Warwks 82 C4
Woodborough Notts 117 G2
Woodborough Wilts 47 G7
Woodbridge Devon 14 E4
Woodbridge Dorset 32 E7
Woodbridge Suffk 91 G5
Wood Burcote W Nthn 84 D6
Woodburn Mdloth 211 K5
Woodbury Devon 14 B5
Woodbury Salterton Devon 14 B5
Woodchester Gloucs 64 B6
Woodchurch Kent 40 B8
Woodchurch Wirral 129 G2
Woodcombe Somset 29 G2
Woodcote Gt Lon 51 J6
Woodcote Oxon 48 F3
Woodcote Wrekin 114 B8
Woodcote Green Worcs 81 L1
Woodcott Hants 48 B7
Woodcroft Gloucs 63 G7
Woodcutts Dorset 23 C7
Wood Dalling Norfk 122 B6
Woodditton Cambs 88 D3
Woodeaton Oxon 66 D5
Wood Eaton Staffs 114 C7
Wooden Pembks 55 J6
Wood End Bed 85 K6
Wood End Bed 86 B2
Wood End C Beds 85 J7
Wood End Cambs 103 H8
Wood End Gt Lon 50 E4
Wood End Herts 69 J2
Woodend Highld 228 B3
Woodend Staffs 115 K6
Woodend W Loth 210 H3
Woodend W Nthn 84 B5
Woodend W Susx 20 D5
Wood End Warwks 82 D1
Wood End Warwks 99 H4
Wood End Warwks 99 J6
Wood End Wolves 97 L3
Wood Enderby Lincs 136 E6
Woodend Green Essex 70 E2
Woodfalls Wilts 33 L6
Woodford Cnwll 26 C8
Woodford Devon 8 B5
Woodford Gloucs 63 K7
Woodford Gt Lon 69 L8
Woodford N Nthn 101 L8
Woodford Stockp 131 H3
Woodford Bridge Gt Lon 51 L8
Woodford Green Gt Lon 69 L8
Woodford Halse W Nthn 84 A5
Woodford Wells Gt Lon 69 L8
Woodgate Birm 98 C6
Woodgate Devon 29 K7
Woodgate Norfk 121 K8
Woodgate Norfk 121 M8
Woodgate W Susx 20 F6
Woodgate W Susx 37 L4
Woodgate Worcs 81 M2
Wood Green Gt Lon 51 J1
Woodgreen Hants 33 L7
Woodgreen Oxon 66 A5
Woodhall N York 159 H4
Woodhall Hill Leeds 141 M4
Woodhall Spa Lincs 136 C7
Woodham Bucks 67 H3
Woodham Dur 169 H5
Woodham Surrey 50 D6
Woodham Ferrers Essex 71 J7
Woodham Mortimer Essex 71 K6
Woodham Walter Essex 71 K5
Woodhaven Fife 223 G2
Wood Hayes Wolves 97 L3
Woodhead Abers 256 E4
Woodhill Shrops 97 G6
Woodhill Somset 30 C6
Woodhorn Nthumb 101 H1
Woodhorn Demesne Nthumb 181 H1
Woodhouse Leeds 141 L1
Woodhouse Leics 116 F8
Woodhouse Sheff 133 H3
Woodhouse Wakefd 142 B3
Woodhouse Eaves Leics 116 F8
Woodhouse Green Staffs 131 H4
Woodhouselee Mdloth 211 H6
Woodhouselees D & G 177 L4
Woodhouse Mill Sheff 133 H3
Woodhouses Cumb 177 K8
Woodhouses Oldham 140 D7
Woodhouses Staffs 98 D2
Woodhouses Staffs 115 J7
Woodhuish Devon 8 D4
Woodhurst Cambs 103 G8
Woodingdean Br & H 22 E6
Woodkirk Leeds 141 L3
Woodland Abers 256 F7
Woodland Devon 7 J4

Woodland Devon 8 B1
Woodland Dur 168 D5
Woodland Kent 40 F7
Woodland S Ayrs 182 F4
Woodland Head Devon 13 H3
Woodlands Donc 142 E6
Woodlands Dorset 17 L1
Woodlands Hants 18 E1
Woodlands Kent 52 C6
Woodlands N York 150 D5
Woodlands Somset 29 L3
Woodlands of Durris Abers 245 H4
Woodlands Park W & M 49 L3
Woodlands St Mary W Berk 47 M4
Woodland Street Somset 31 J3
Woodland View Sheff 132 F2
Wood Lane Shrops 112 F5
Wood Lane Staffs 114 C2
Woodleigh Devon 7 L5
Woodlesford Leeds 142 B2
Woodley Stockp 131 J1
Woodley Wokham 49 J4
Woodmancote Gloucs 63 M7
Woodmancote Gloucs 64 F2
Woodmancote Gloucs 64 E5
Woodmancote W Susx 20 C5
Woodmancote W Susx 22 C4
Woodmancote Worcs 81 L6
Woodmancott Hants 35 H2
Woodmansey E R Yk 153 G8
Woodmansgreen W Susx 36 C5
Woodmansterne Surrey 51 H7
Woodmanton Devon 14 B5
Woodmarsh Wilts 46 B7
Woodmill Staffs 115 J7
Woodminton Wilts 33 H6
Woodnesborough Kent 41 J4
Woodnewton N Nthn 102 A4
Woodnook Notts 116 D1
Wood Norton Norfk 121 M6
Woodplumpton Lancs 139 G1
Woodrising Norfk 105 K3
Wood Row Leeds 142 B2
Woodrow Worcs 97 K8
Wood's Corner E Susx 24 B3
Woods Eaves Herefs 79 K5
Woodseaves Shrops 113 M5
Woodseaves Staffs 114 B6
Woodsend Wilts 47 J4
Woodsetts Rothm 133 L3
Woodsford Dorset 16 E4
Wood's Green E Susx 39 G6
Woodside Br For 50 B5
Woodside Cumb 164 D4
Woodside Essex 70 C6
Woodside Fife 223 G5
Woodside Gt Lon 51 J5
Woodside Hants 18 E5
Woodside Herts 69 H5
Woodside P & K 233 J7
Woodside Green Kent 40 B4
Woodstock Oxon 66 C4
Woodstock Pembks 75 H7
Woodston C Pete 102 D4
Wood Street Norfk 123 H7
Wood Street Village Surrey 36 E1
Woodthorpe Derbys 133 J5
Woodthorpe Leics 116 F8
Woodthorpe Lincs 137 H4
Woodton Norfk 106 F4
Woodtown Devon 27 G6
Woodvale Sefton 138 C5
Woodville Derbys 116 A7
Woodwall Green Staffs 114 B5
Wood Walton Cambs 102 F7
Woodyates Dorset 33 H7
Woody Bay Devon 28 B1
Woofferton Shrops 80 C2
Wookey Somset 31 H2
Wookey Hole Somset 31 H2
Wool Dorset 17 G5
Woolacombe Devon 27 H2
Woolage Green Kent 41 H5
Woolage Village Kent 41 H5
Woolaston Gloucs 63 H7
Woolaston Common Gloucs 63 H6
Woolavington Somset 30 E3
Woolbeding W Susx 36 C6
Woolbrook Devon 14 D5
Woolcotts Somset 29 H4
Wooldale Kirk 141 J6
Wooler Nthumb 202 F7
Woolfardisworthy Devon 13 J1
Woolfardisworthy Devon 26 F6
Woolfold Bury 140 B5
Woolfords S Lans 199 G2
Woolhampton W Berk 48 E5
Woolhope Herefs 80 E8
Woolland Dorset 16 E1
Woollard BaNES 45 J6

Woollensbrook Herts 69 K5
Woolley BaNES 45 L5
Woolley Cambs 102 C8
Woolley Cnwll 26 D7
Woolley Derbys 133 G7
Woolley Wakefd 141 M5
Woolley Bridge Derbys 131 K1
Woolley Edge Services
Wakefd 141 M5
Woolley Green W & M 49 K3
Woolmere Green Worcs 81 M3
Woolmer Green Herts 69 H3
Woolmerston Somset 30 D4
Woolminstone Somset 15 J1
Woolpack Kent 39 L6
Woolpit Suffk 89 K3
Woolpit Green Suffk 89 K3
Woolscott Warwks 83 L2
Woolsgrove Devon 13 J2
Woolsington N u Ty 180 F5
Woolstaston Shrops 95 L4
Woolsthorpe by
Colsterworth Lincs 118 B6
Woolsthorpe by Belvoir Lincs 117 L5
Woolston C Sotn 19 G2
Woolston Devon 7 L5
Woolston Devon 7 L6
Woolston Shrops 95 K6
Woolston Shrops 112 D6
Woolston Somset 29 K3
Woolston Somset 31 L5
Woolston Warrtn 130 C2
Woolstone Gloucs 64 D1
Woolstone M Keyn 85 G7
Woolstone Oxon 47 L2
Woolston Green Devon 8 A2
Woolton Lpool 129 K2
Woolton Hill Hants 48 B6
Woolverstone Suffk 90 E7
Woolverton Somset 46 A8
Woolwich Gt Lon 51 L3
Woonton Herefs 79 L5
Woonton Herefs 80 D3
Wooperton Nthumb 190 F2
Woore Shrops 114 A3
Wootten Green Suffk 90 F1
Wootton Bed 85 K6
Wootton Hants 18 C4
Wootton Herefs 79 L5
Wootton IoW 19 J5
Wootton Kent 41 H6
Wootton N Linc 144 D4
Wootton Oxon 66 B3
Wootton Oxon 66 C6
Wootton Shrops 112 E6
Wootton Staffs 114 C6
Wootton Staffs 115 H3
Wootton W Nthn 84 E4
Wootton Bassett Wilts 46 F3
Wootton Bridge IoW 19 J5
Wootton Broadmead Bed 85 K6
Wootton Common IoW 19 J5
Wootton Courtenay Somset 29 G2
Wootton Fitzpaine Dorset 15 J3
Wootton Rivers Wilts 47 J6
Wootton St Lawrence Hants 48 E8
Wootton Wawen Warwks 82 K3
Worcester Worcs 81 K4
Worcester Park Gt Lon 51 G6
Wordsley Dudley 97 K6
Worfield Shrops 97 G4
Worgret Dorset 17 H5
Workhouse End Bed 86 B5
Workhouse Green Suffk 89 H7
Workington Cumb 164 D5
Worksop Notts 134 B4
Worlaby Lincs 136 E4
Worlaby N Linc 144 C5
Worlds End Bucks 67 L5
Worlds End Hants 19 L1
World's End W Berk 48 C3
Worlds End W Susx 22 E3
Worle N Som 44 D6
Worleston Ches E 130 C8
Worlingham Suffk 107 J5
Worlington Devon 28 D8
Worlington Suffk 104 D8
Worlingworth Suffk 90 F2
Wormald Green N York 150 D3
Wormbridge Herefs 62 E1
Wormegay Norfk 104 D1
Wormelow Tump Herefs 62 F1
Wormhill Derbys 132 C5
Wormhill Herefs 80 A7
Wormingford Essex 72 D1
Worminghall Bucks 66 F5
Wormington Gloucs 82 B7
Worminster Somset 31 J2
Wormit Fife 223 G2
Wormleighton Warwks 83 K4

Wormley Herts 69 K6
Wormley Surrey 36 E3
Wormleybury Herts 69 K6
Wormley Hill Donc 143 G4
Wormshill Kent 53 J7
Wormsley Herefs 80 A5
Worplesdon Surrey 50 B8
Worrall Sheff 132 F1
Worrall Hill Gloucs 63 J4
Worsbrough Barns 142 A7
Worsbrough Bridge Barns 142 A7
Worsbrough Dale Barns 142 B7
Worsley Salfd 139 M7
Worstead Norfk 122 F6
Worsthorne Lancs 140 C1
Worston Devon 7 H4
Worston Lancs 148 D7
Worth Kent 41 K4
Worth Somset 31 H2
Worth W Susx 37 L4
Wortham Suffk 106 B7
Worthen Shrops 95 H2
Worthenbury Wrexhm 112 F2
Worthing Norfk 121 M7
Worthing W Susx 21 K6
Worthington Leics 116 C7
Worth Matravers Dorset 17 J7
Worthybrook Mons 62 F5
Worting Hants 48 F8
Wortley Barns 141 M7
Wortley Gloucs 45 M1
Wortley Leeds 141 L1
Worton N York 159 G5
Worton Wilts 46 E7
Wortwell Norfk 106 F6
Wotherton Shrops 95 G3
Wothorpe C Pete 101 M2
Wotter Devon 7 H3
Wotton Surrey 37 H2
Wotton-under-Edge Gloucs 63 M8
Wotton Underwood Bucks 67 G4
Woughton on the Green
M Keyn 85 G7
Wouldham Kent 52 F6
Woundale Shrops 97 H5
Wrabness Essex 73 J1
Wrafton Devon 27 J4
Wragby Lincs 136 B4
Wragby Wakefd 142 C4
Wramplingham Norfk 106 C2
Wrangaton Devon 7 K3
Wrangbrook Wakefd 142 D5
Wrangle Lincs 119 M2
Wrangle Common Lincs 119 M1
Wrangle Lowgate Lincs 119 M1
Wrangway Somset 29 L7
Wrantage Somset 30 D6
Wrawby N Linc 144 C6
Wraxall N Som 44 F4
Wraxall Somset 31 K4
Wray Lancs 147 M2
Wraysbury W & M 50 C4
Wrayton Lancs 147 M2
Wrea Green Lancs 138 E2
Wreaks End W & F 156 B5
Wreay Cumb 166 B1
Wreay W & F 166 B6
Wrecclesham Surrey 36 B2
Wrekenton Gatesd 181 G7
Wrelton N York 162 D5
Wrenbury Ches E 113 K2
Wrench Green N York 163 H5
Wreningham Norfk 106 D4
Wrentham Suffk 107 K6
Wrenthorpe Wakefd 141 M3
Wrentnall Shrops 95 K3
Wressle E R Yk 143 H2
Wressle N Linc 144 B6
Wrestlingworth C Beds 86 E5
Wretton Norfk 104 D3
Wrexham Wrexhm 112 E2
Wrexham Industrial Estate
Wrexhm 112 F2
Wribbenhall Worcs 97 H8
Wrickton Shrops 96 E6
Wrightington Bar Lancs 139 G5
Wright's Green Essex 70 D4
Wrinehill Staffs 114 B2
Wrington N Som 44 F6
Writhlington BaNES 45 K8
Writtle Essex 71 G6
Wrockwardine Wrekin 96 E1
Wroot N Linc 143 H7
Wrose C Brad 149 L8
Wrotham Kent 52 D7
Wrotham Heath Kent 52 D7
Wrottesley Staffs 97 J3
Wroughton Swindn 47 H3
Wroxall IoW 19 J7
Wroxall Warwks 82 F1

Wroxeter Shrops............96 D2
Wroxham Norfk............122 F8
Wroxton Oxon...............83 K7
Wyaston Derbys............115 K3
Wyatt's Green Essex.......70 F7
Wyberton Lincs............119 K3
Wyboston Bed...............86 D4
Wybunbury Ches E.........113 M2
Wychbold Worcs............81 L2
Wych Cross E Susx.........38 C7
Wychnor Staffs............115 K8
Wychwood Ches E..........114 A1
Wyck Hants................35 M3
Wyck Rissington Gloucs....65 J3
Wycliffe Dur..............168 E7
Wycoller Lancs............149 G8
Wycomb Leics.............117 K6
Wycombe Marsh Bucks......67 L8
Wyddial Herts.............69 K1
Wye Kent..................40 D6
Wyesham Mons.............63 G4
Wyfordby Leics...........117 L7
Wyke C Brad..............141 J2
Wyke Devon................13 K3
Wyke Devon................15 G3
Wyke Dorset...............32 D5
Wyke Shrops...............96 E3
Wyke Surrey...............50 A8
Wyke Champflower
  Somset..................31 L4
Wykeham N York...........163 H6
Wyken Covtry..............99 K7
Wyken Shrops..............97 H4
Wyke Regis Dorset.........16 C7
Wykey Shrops.............112 F6
Wykin Leics...............99 L4
Wylam Nthumb.............180 D6
Wylde Green Birm..........98 E4
Wylye Wilts...............33 H3
Wymeswold Leics..........117 G6
Wymington Bed.............85 J2
Wymondham Leics.........117 M7
Wymondham Norfk.........106 C3
Wyndham Brdgnd...........42 E3
Wynford Eagle Dorset......16 B3
Wynyard Park S on T......169 L5
Wynyard Village S on T...169 L5
Wyre Piddle Worcs.........81 M5
Wysall Notts.............117 G6
Wyson Herefs..............80 C2
Wythall Worcs.............98 D8
Wythall Green Worcs.......98 D8
Wytham Oxon...............66 C5
Wythburn Cumb...........165 K7
Wythenshawe Manch.......131 G2
Wythop Mill Cumb.........165 G5
Wyton Cambs..............86 F1
Wyton E R Yk.............144 F1
Wyton on the Hill Cambs..102 F8
Wyverstone Suffk..........90 B2
Wyverstone Street Suffk...89 L2
Wyville Lincs............118 A5

Y

Yaddlethorpe N Linc......143 M6
Yafford IoW...............19 G7
Yafforth N York..........160 E4
Yalberton Torbay...........8 C3
Yalding Kent..............39 H3
Yanwath W & F...........166 C5
Yanworth Gloucs...........65 G4
Yapham E R Yk...........152 B5
Yapton W Susx............21 G6
Yarborough N Som.........44 D7
Yarbridge IoW............19 K6
Yarburgh Lincs...........136 F1
Yarcombe Devon...........14 F1
Yard Devon................28 D6
Yardley Birm..............98 E6
Yardley Gobion W Nthn....84 E6
Yardley Hastings W Nthn...85 G4
Yardley Wood Birm........98 E7
Yardro Powys..............79 J3
Yarford Somset............30 B5
Yarkhill Herefs...........80 E6
Yarley Somset.............31 H2
Yarlington Somset.........31 L5
Yarm S on T.............169 L8
Yarmouth IoW.............18 E5
Yarnacott Devon...........27 L5
Yarnbrook Wilts...........46 C7
Yarner Devon..............13 H7
Yarnfield Staffs.........114 D5
Yarnscombe Devon.........27 K6
Yarnton Oxon..............66 C5
Yarpole Herefs............80 B2
Yarrow Border............200 D7

Yarrow Somset.............30 E2
Yarrow Feus Border.......200 D7
Yarrowford Border........200 E7
Yarsop Herefs.............80 A6
Yarwell N Nthn...........102 B4
Yate S Glos...............45 L3
Yateley Hants.............49 K6
Yatesbury Wilts...........46 F4
Yattendon W Berk..........48 E4
Yatton Herefs.............80 A2
Yatton N Som..............44 E6
Yatton Keynell Wilts......46 C4
Yaverland IoW.............19 K6
Yawl Devon................15 H4
Yawthorpe Lincs..........135 H1
Yaxham Norfk.............105 K1
Yaxley Cambs............102 D5
Yaxley Suffk.............106 C8
Yazor Herefs..............79 M6
Yeading Gt Lon............50 E3
Yeadon Leeds............150 B7
Yealand Conyers Lancs....157 H7
Yealand Redmayne
  Lancs..................157 H7
Yealand Storrs Lancs.....157 H7
Yealmbridge Devon.........7 H4
Yealmpton Devon...........7 H4
Yearby R & Cl............170 E6
Yearngill Cumb...........164 F2
Yearsley N York..........161 J7
Yeaton Shrops............113 G7
Yeaveley Derbys..........115 K3
Yeavering Nthumb........202 E7
Yedingham N York.........162 F6
Yelford Oxon..............66 A6
Yell Shet................281 e3
Yelland Devon.............27 J4
Yelling Cambs.............86 F3
Yelvertoft W Nthn........100 D8
Yelverton Devon...........7 G1
Yelverton Norfk..........106 F3
Yenston Somset............32 B6
Yeoford Devon.............13 H3
Yeolmbridge Cnwll.........11 L5
Yeo Mill Devon............28 E5
Yeo Vale Devon............27 G6
Yeovil Somset.............31 J7
Yeovil Marsh Somset.......31 J7
Yeovilton Somset..........31 J6
Yerbeston Pembks..........55 H5
Yesnaby Ork.............275 b4
Yetlington Nthumb........190 E4
Yetminster Dorset.........16 B1
Yetson Devon...............8 B4
Yettington Devon..........14 B5
Yetts o'Muckhart
  Clacks.................221 H6
Yews Green C Brad........141 H2
Yew Tree Sandw............98 C4
Y Felinheli Gwynd........125 J6
Y Ferwig Cerdgn...........75 L2
Y Ffôr Gwynd............109 G4
Yielden Bed...............85 K2
Yieldingtree Worcs........97 K7
Yieldshields S Lans......198 E3
Yiewsley Gt Lon...........50 D3
Y Nant Wrexhm............112 D2
Ynys Gwynd..............109 L4
Ynysboeth Rhondd..........43 G3
Ynysddu Caerph............43 J3
Ynysforgan Swans..........57 J5
Ynyshir Rhondd............42 F3
Ynyslas Cerdgn............92 D5
Ynysmaerdy Rhondd.........42 F5
Ynysmeudwy Neath..........57 K4
Ynystawe Swans............57 J5
Ynyswen Powys.............60 C4
Ynyswen Rhondd............42 E2
Ynysybwl Rhondd...........43 G3
Ynysymaengwyn Gwynd......92 D3
Yockenthwaite N York....158 F6
Yockleton Shrops..........95 K2
Yokefleet E R Yk.........143 K3
Yoker C Glas.............208 E5
York C York..............151 J5
York Lancs..............139 L1
Yorkletts Kent............40 E3
Yorkley Gloucs............63 J5
Yorkshire Dales
  National Park........158 F7
York Town Surrey..........49 L7
Yorton Heath Shrops......113 H7
Youlgreave Derbys........132 D6
Youlthorpe E R Yk........152 B5
Youlton N York...........151 G3
Youngsbury Herts..........69 K3
Young's End Essex.........71 H3
Yoxall Staffs............115 J7
Yoxford Suffk.............91 J2
Y Rhiw Gwynd............108 D6

Yr Wyddfa Gwynd.........109 L1
Ysbyty Cynfyn
  Cerdgn..................93 G7
Ysbyty Ifan Conwy........110 F2
Ysbyty Ystwyth Cerdgn....77 K1
Ysceifiog Flints.........128 D5
Ysgubor-y-Coed
  Cerdgn..................92 E4
Ystalyfera Neath..........57 L3
Ystrad Rhondd.............42 F3
Ystrad Aeron Cerdgn.......76 F4
Ystradfellte Powys........60 D4
Ystrad Ffin Carmth........77 L6
Ystradgynlais Powys.......60 B5
Ystrad Meurig Cerdgn......77 K2
Ystrad Mynach Caerph......43 J3
Ystradowen Carmth.........59 L6
Ystradowen V Glam.........42 F6
Ystumtuen Cerdgn..........92 F7
Ythanbank Abers..........257 G5
Ythanwells Abers........256 B4
Ythsie Abers............256 F5

Z

Zeal Monachorum Devon....13 G2
Zeals Wilts...............32 C4
Zelah Cnwll................4 C4
Zennor Cnwll...............2 C3
Zoar Cnwll.................3 J7
Zouch Notts.............116 E6

Map pages north

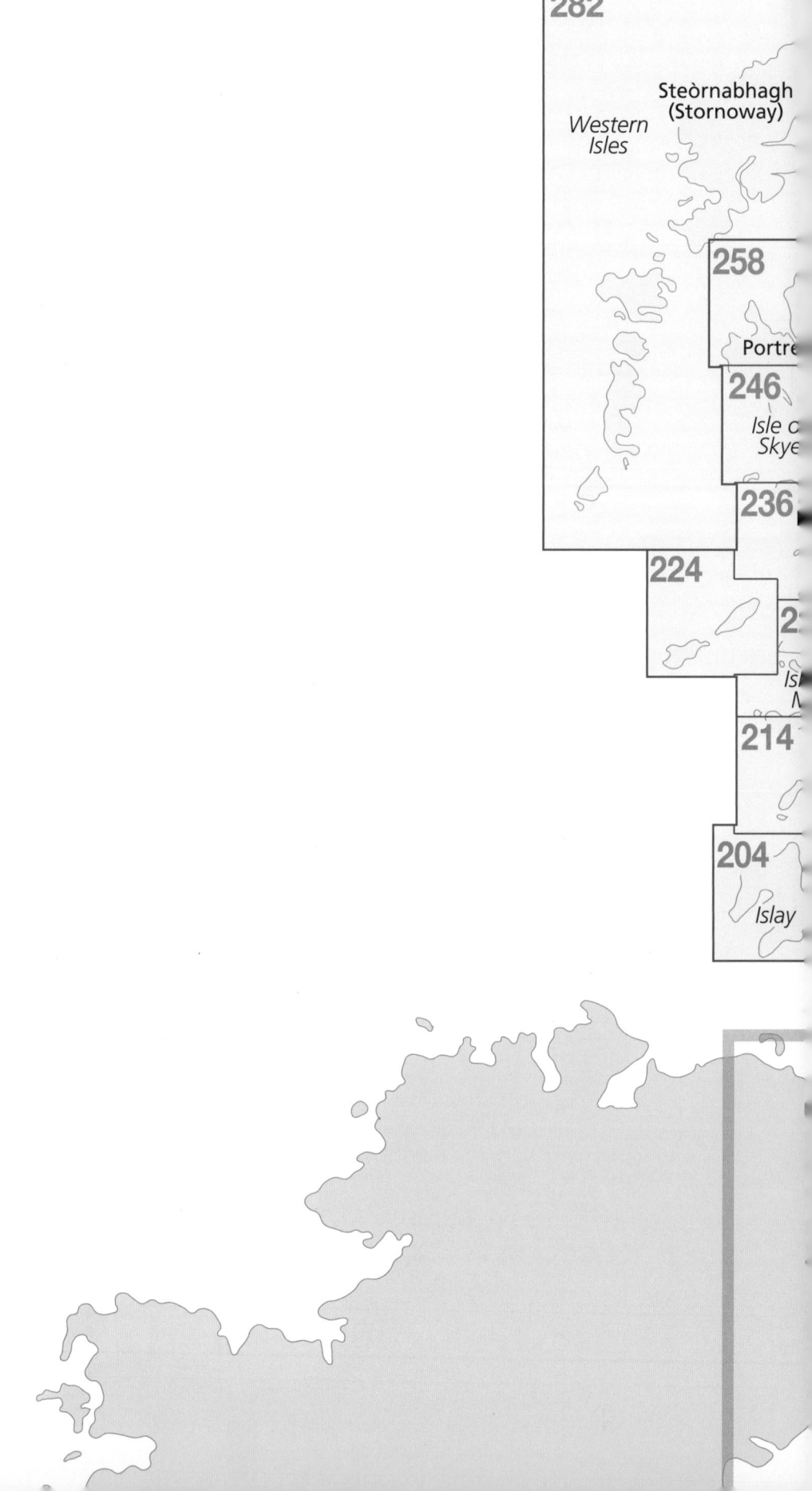

282

Steòrnabhagh
(Stornoway)

Western
Isles

258

Portre

246

Isle o
Skye

236

224

2

Is
M

214

204

Islay